Southern Africa

Alan Murphy

Kate Armstrong, James Bainbridge, Matthew D Firestone

Mary Fitzpatrick, Nana Luckham, Nicola Simmonds

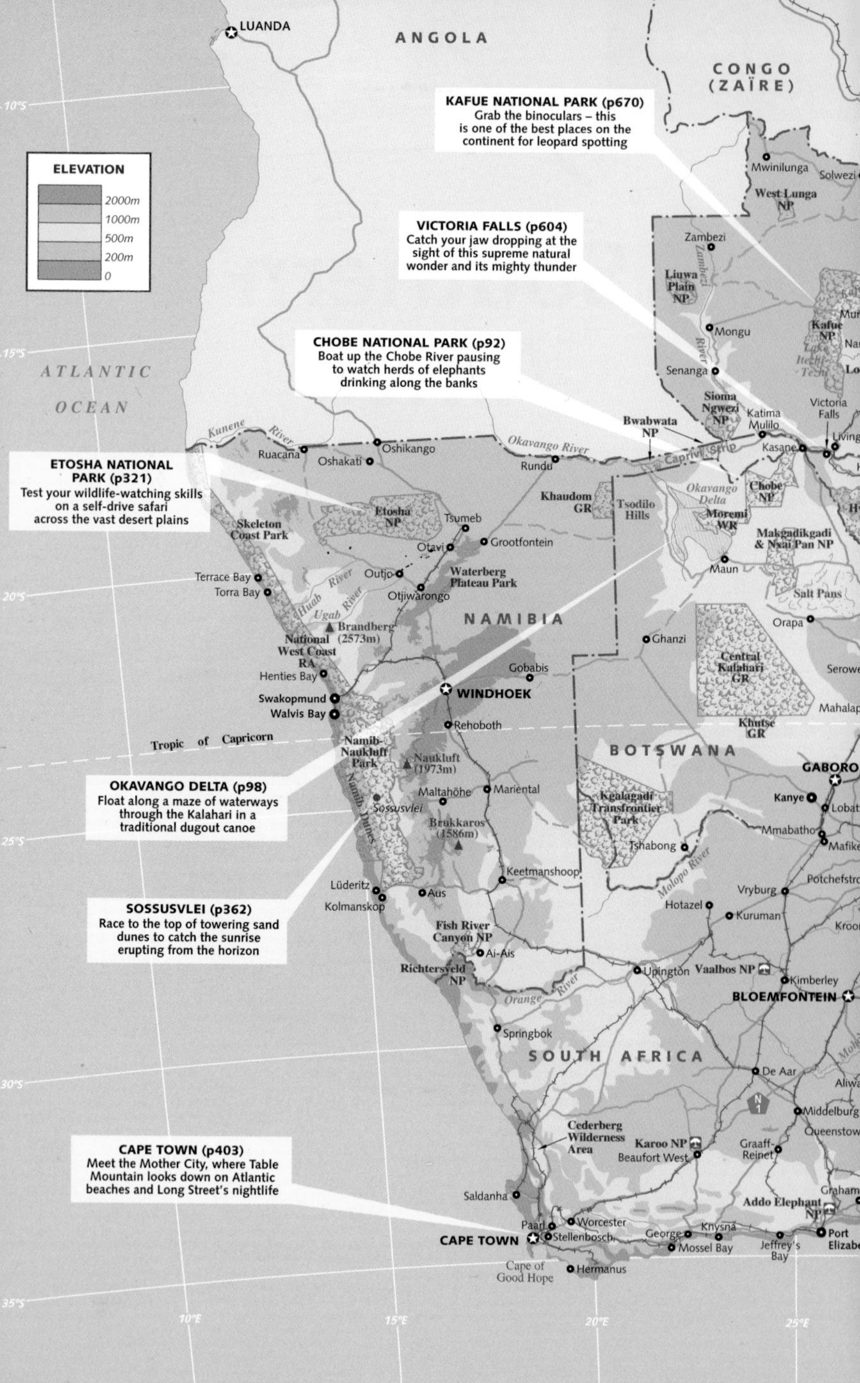

KAFUE NATIONAL PARK (p670)
Grab the binoculars – this is one of the best places on the continent for leopard spotting
VICTORIA FALLS (p604)
Catch your jaw dropping at the sight of this supreme natural wonder and its mighty thunder
CHOBE NATIONAL PARK (p92)
Boat up the Chobe River pausing to watch herds of elephants drinking along the banks
ETOSHA NATIONAL PARK (p321)
Test your wildlife-watching skills on a self-drive safari across the vast desert plains
OKAVANGO DELTA (p98)
Float along a maze of waterways through the Kalahari in a traditional dugout canoe
SOSSUSVLEI (p362)
Race to the top of towering sand dunes to catch the sunrise erupting from the horizon
CAPE TOWN (p403)
Meet the Mother City, where Table Mountain looks down on Atlantic beaches and Long Street's nightlife
ELEVATION
2000m
1000m
500m
200m
0
ANGOLA
CONGO (ZAÏRE)
NAMIBIA
BOTSWANA
SOUTH AFRICA
ATLANTIC OCEAN
LUANDA
WINDHOEK
CAPE TOWN
BLOEMFONTEIN
Tropic of Capricorn

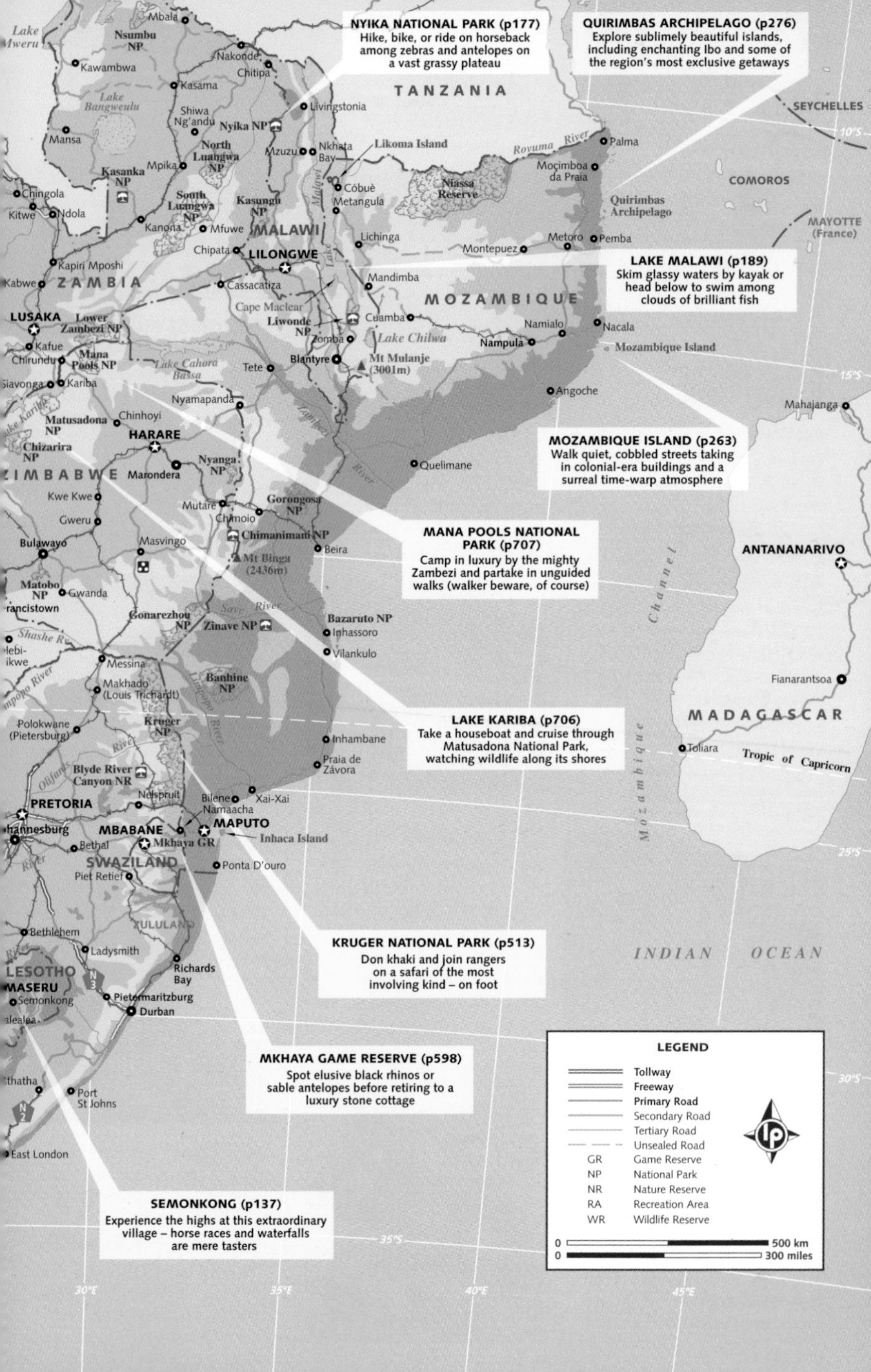
NYIKA NATIONAL PARK (p177)
Hike, bike, or ride on horseback among zebras and antelopes on a vast grassy plateau
QUIRIMBAS ARCHIPELAGO (p276)
Explore sublimely beautiful islands, including enchanting Ibo and some of the region's most exclusive getaways
LAKE MALAWI (p189)
Skim glassy waters by kayak or head below to swim among clouds of brilliant fish
MOZAMBIQUE ISLAND (p263)
Walk quiet, cobbled streets taking in colonial-era buildings and a surreal time-warp atmosphere
MANA POOLS NATIONAL PARK (p707)
Camp in luxury by the mighty Zambezi and partake in unguided walks (walker beware, of course)
LAKE KARIBA (p706)
Take a houseboat and cruise through Matusadona National Park, watching wildlife along its shores
KRUGER NATIONAL PARK (p513)
Don khaki and join rangers on a safari of the most involving kind – on foot
MKHAYA GAME RESERVE (p598)
Spot elusive black rhinos or sable antelopes before retiring to a luxury stone cottage
SEMONKONG (p137)
Experience the highs at this extraordinary village – horse races and waterfalls are mere tasters
TANZANIA
ZAMBIA
MALAWI
MOZAMBIQUE
ZIMBABWE
SWAZILAND
LESOTHO
MADAGASCAR
SEYCHELLES
COMOROS
MAYOTTE (France)
INDIAN OCEAN
Mozambique Channel
Tropic of Capricorn
LUSAKA
LILONGWE
HARARE
PRETORIA
MBABANE
MAPUTO
MASERU
ANTANANARIVO
LEGEND
Tollway
Freeway
Primary Road
Secondary Road
Tertiary Road
Unsealed Road
GR Game Reserve
NP National Park
NR Nature Reserve
RA Recreation Area
WR Wildlife Reserve
500 km
300 miles

On the Road

ALAN MURPHY Coordinating Author
I'm in my element here. Right in the midst of colossal Kafue National Park (p670) watching a bull elephant with huge tusks in the distance. (Yes, my foot hovers close to the accelerator.) In the foreground are pukus, impalas and some rather skittish baboons.

MARY FITZPATRICK This shot on Lake Niassa (p270) shows Mozambique's 'other' coast. Getting there – via boat or adventurous overland journey – is half the fun. It's a place where it's easy to stay for days, surrounded by the rhythms of traditional life, mesmerised by star-filled night skies and lapping waves.

KATE ARMSTRONG The highlands (p134) of Lesotho don't see many visitors. These women were more than happy to have their photos taken; their surprise and joy at seeing themselves on a digital screen was unforgettable. We couldn't communicate in each other's languages – laughter was our international language.

NANA LUCKHAM This picture was taken by the Lingadzi River in the Lilongwe Wildlife Centre (p170), a beautiful, peaceful sanctuary in the heart of the city. I'd just finished a tour during which I learnt about the centre's rehabilitation programs for rescued, orphaned and injured wild animals, and caught a glimpse of Bella, the one-eyed lion.

JAMES BAINBRIDGE This rocky scene may look like a remote wilderness, but it's actually Lion's Head (p418), overlooking Cape Town. The only sounds I could hear, hundreds of metres above the Mother City, were the wind whistling through the grass and the call to prayer rising from a mosque in Bo-Kaap.

MATTHEW D FIRESTONE This picture was taken just before a somewhat ungraceful landing on the edge of the Namib Desert just outside Swakopmund (p346). As I quickly learned, jumping out of the plane and pulling the cord is the easy part; landing on your legs – not sorely on your bum – takes a bit of practice.

NICOLA SIMMONDS It was a sublime African morning. The 'cubs' looked anything but cute and cuddly; more unfazed and unpredictable. Still, we walked through the long dry grass of the vleis, slightly running to keep up, hands gripping sticks, hearts in mouth...

For author biographies see p790.

Traveller Highlights

When you're watching elephants snorkel across a river, the rippling power of a stalking leopard as it bursts into a sprint or the unfeasibly colourful migration of carmine bee-eaters in a total wilderness setting, Southern Africa feels like another planet. And alongside this wildlife wonderland are ancient cultures, a craft scene that rivals anything on the continent, and classic African landscapes including vast twinkling lakes, thunderous waterfalls and rolling dunes. Welcome to Southern Africa.

ANDREW EAMES/GUARDIAN NEWS & MEDIA LTD 2009

1 TRANS-KAROO EXPRESS

Catch the trans-Karoo tourist-class train (p575) from Johannesburg to Cape Town to see South Africa in all its blotchy glory. Leaving Jo'burg's razor wire and biltong ads behind, the train passes through obscure North-West Province towns, where denim suits and peroxide-blond hair are de rigueur, and the train porters greet cohorts on empty platforms: 'Howzit! Izzit? Shame!' The 27-hour journey passes so easily that you only realise you're delayed when you notice you've been waving at some schoolchildren for an hour. In the morning, rub your eyes in the dining car and tell the waiter how you like your eggs done, as the train breezes through the Winelands towards Table Mountain.

James Bainbridge, Lonely Planet Author

VINCENT TALBOT

SKYDIVING OVER SWAKOPMUND

Some say that the plane ride is the scariest part of the skydive (p352), and it can be hard not to lose your cool if you hit a pocket of turbulence. But, once you've reached your cruising altitude of 3000m, just give into your adrenaline and take the plunge – when you're free-falling at 220km/h, the ground approaches mighty quickly!

Matt Firestone, Lonely Planet Author

3

MATTHEW FIRES

2

HARARE INTERNATIONAL FESTIVAL OF THE ARTS

Harare International Festival of the Arts (HIFA; p700), in the last week of April, is an extraordinary event, not just an extraordinary Zimbabwean event. International dance, music, opera, acrobatics and theatre acts are brought to Harare by foreign embassies. Alongside these in the jam-packed timetable are local acts from around Zimbabwe. So popular is this festival that the name HIFA has become a verb in local parlance: to 'HIFA' means sprinting from act to act, watching, dancing and drinking into the wee hours only to wake up and start all over again.

Nicola Simmonds, Lonely Planet Author

DAVI

4

WALKING SOUTH LUANGWA

A walking safari in South Luangwa National Park (p652), one of the best wilderness areas in Africa, is a unique and special way to experience the African bush. If you were ever under the misapprehension that the parks are like zoos, it will be blown away once you've trod the same ground as the animals. It's exhilarating and slightly intimidating wondering what's behind the next corner, up a tree or under the water…

Alan Murphy, Lonely Planet Author

THE MIGHTY SPRAY

When you stand before Victoria Falls (p604), the clichés abound, for this is the mighty Mosi-oa-Tunya or 'The Smoke that Thunders'. Unfortunately, visiting the falls during the peak of the heaviest rainy season in decades results in an entirely different experience. Wrapped in layers of plastic, clutching my water-logged camera with a kung-fu action grip, I am pelted by sheets of mist and gusts of spray that pay fitting tribute to the fury of the falls.

Matt Firestone, Lonely Planet Author

5

RICHARD I'ANSON

QUIRIMBAS ARCHIPELAGO

No matter how many beautiful beaches and islands you've seen, there are few coastal stretches that compare with the northern Mozambique coastline around the Quirimbas Archipelago (p276). The waters are the requisite turquoise, the sand is fine and white, and life seems to have changed little over the centuries. The dhow is the main (often only) means of transport and local communities live by the rhythms of the tides and the moon. We happened to arrive on sleepy, sunbaked Ibo Island on a holiday and were treated to a morning of dancing and singing under the shade of a huge, spreading mango tree. Afterwards, a young boy led us through the sandy lanes to a tiny house with a hand-painted 'café' sign tacked outside. Inside, a group of laughing women offered us plates of piping-hot rice and sauce.

Mary Fitzpatrick, Lonely Planet Author

6

JULIAN LOVE/PHOTOLIBRARY

SANI TOP

The drive up Sani Pass (p507) – the only link between KwaZulu-Natal and Lesotho – is a spectacular ride around hairpin bends up to the kingdom of Lesotho. At 2865m, this is the highest pass in South Africa. The vistas are magical: stunning views of looming cliffs, rivers, mountain peaks and flat lands. On a cloudy day (the weather can be unpredictable here) all is obscured, but if the fog lifts, a magical landscape may be gradually revealed from Sani Top.

Kate Armstrong, Lonely Planet Author

8

KATE ARMST

7

ARIADNE VAN ZANDBERGEN

LAKE MALAWI

Malawi's prime attraction is without a doubt the gleaming lake (p161) that slices straight through its heart. Blissfully uncrowded beaches skirt its shores, kayakers glide over translucent waters and snorkellers swim with clouds of colourful fish.

Nana Luckham, Lonely Planet Author

9

ARIADNE VAN ZANDE

SWAZILAND

Swaziland (p583) is a highlight in itself. Don't let the country's compact size fool you. This tiny place has the lot, all spread over extraordinary landscapes. Nowhere else in Africa can you so readily access such varied experiences: mountain wildernesses and African plains, superb handicrafts and fun outdoor adventures. For genuine cultural activities, the festivals here are top of the (ceremonial) pops.

Kate Armstrong, Lonely Planet Author

Contents

Mozambique 217

Namibia 294

Regional Map Contents

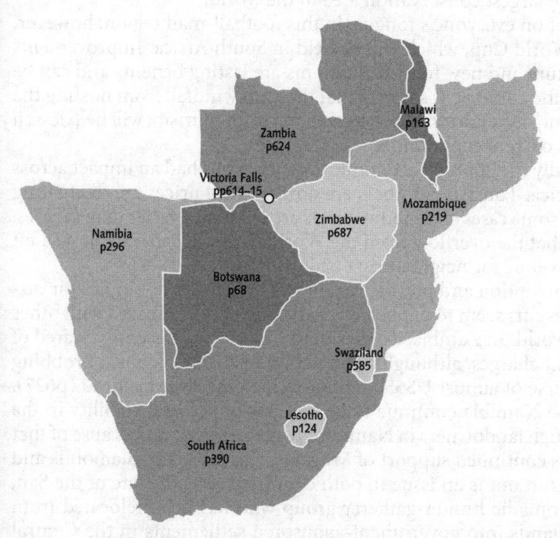

Destination Southern Africa

Southern Africa's ambient rhythm swoons visitors into a blissful stupor – change down a gear and immerse yourself in the region's enchanting, at times otherworldly, offerings. This corner of the continent is one of the last bastions of accessible wilderness on the planet – whether it's the astonishing variety and density of wildlife, dreamy African landscapes, or world-class natural features such as thundering Victoria Falls, a visit to Southern Africa will sear itself in your mind. Enmeshed in this wilderness is a multitude of ethnic groups, many known for their hospitality and some with direct links to our Stone Age ancestors. If you're serious about the family tree, this is where it *all* began.

Incredibly rich in cultural diversity, Southern Africa constitutes a loose grouping of nations, each with a distinct heritage, although the countries share many common attributes. Some of these attributes, such as poverty, food insecurity and the spread of HIV/AIDS (p38) affect all the countries in the region and are challenges that need coordination, commitment and a long-term approach, both from countries within the region and the international community. This commitment came to fruition recently when the world's richest nations agreed to write off the debt owed by the world's poorest countries, which include Zambia, Mozambique and Malawi.

The establishment of transfrontier parks (p63), linking wildlife migration routes across borders in pursuit of sustainable development, is a very positive development; such conservation work can assist in helping local peoples when they benefit from the associated extra income, employment and development projects. The Kavango–Zambezi Transfrontier Conservation Area, taking in areas of Botswana, Namibia, Zimbabwe and Zambia, is set to become the largest conservation area in the world.

The subject on everyone's tongue, in this football-mad region, however, is the 2010 World Cup, which will be held in South Africa. Improvements in infrastructure and new football stadiums are lasting benefits and can be seen all over the country. It's hoped that the cash windfall from hosting the event, especially the enormous boost expected from tourism, will help lessen the country's current economic woes.

Undoubtedly the 2008-09 economic downturn has had an impact across Southern Africa. Tourism numbers are down, petrol prices are fluctuating wildly and in some cases commodity prices are increasing faster than salaries. The hope is that the overflow from the World Cup will generate quite a bit of tourism revenue for neighbouring countries too.

Politics, corruption and presidential power are always hot topics for discussion and events seem to happen at a lightning pace compared with other parts of the world. In Zambia, ex-president Chiluba was recently cleared of embezzlement charges, although a conviction in a British court of robbing the public purse of almost US$50 million is hanging over his head (p627). Botswana and Namibia continue to be beacons of political stability in the region, although landowners in Namibia are getting nervous because of that government's continued support of Mugabe. The subject of diamonds and when they'll run out is an issue in both countries, as is the fate of the San, an ancient nomadic hunter-gatherer group who has been relocated from its ancestral lands into government-sponsored settlements in the Central Kalahari (p74). The issue remains highly contentious.

In South Africa, a controversial figure, Jacob Zuma (also known as JZ) was assured of victory in the 2009 elections when charges against him, relating to a US$4.8 billion arms deal, were dropped just weeks before the polls opened. He promised in his first state of the nation speech to create 500,000 new jobs by the end of 2009, although the *Sowetan* newspaper responded with a mocking headline: '2380 jobs a day for the rest of the year!' In July 2009, rubber bullets flew as union strikes sparked violent expressions of general discontent with continuing deprivation in the townships. Crime continues to grab headlines too and undermine South Africa's reputation as a tourism destination (p396), although these figures should be seen in perspective because as a tourist you'd be either foolhardy or extremely unlucky to become a victim of serious crime in this country.

In February 2009, the ruling party in Zimbabwe, Zanu-PF, formed a unity government with the opposition MDC, led by Morgan Tsvangirai (p690). Whether real change will follow remains to be seen. Everyone in that country talks about money – or prices. From the end of 2007 to the end of 2008, the real rate of inflation was seven sextillion percent! Then the economy finally collapsed. 'Dollarisation' happened at the beginning of 2009, which means the US$ is now legal tender and prices have stabilised (p691).

The political situation in Mozambique is fairly steady, with the government leading an anti-corruption campaign that is getting a lot of press. Arrests have been made, although these actions have not yet affected the lives of ordinary people – corruption is very ingrained in the culture as it is in many Southern African countries. The north of Mozambique is getting a much needed boost to its infrastructure with a slowly improving road network in the north (such as soon-to-open bridge links over the Rovuma and Zambezi rivers).

Unfortunately political infighting and corruption have tended to be the 'normal' state of affairs in Malawi. President Mutharika was returned to power in 2009 in a decisive victory, and although he has also led an anti-corruption campaign, fighting between himself and his predecessor, ex-president Muluzi, has curtailed the effectiveness of the government, especially in responding to food shortages in recent years.

The political situation is currently calm in Lesotho, following violence, intimidation and torture in the controversial 2007 elections, although the elections of 2012 may bring tensions to the fore once again. There have been allegations of corruption in relation to Lesotho's dam projects (p134); selling water to South Africa and, in the process, displacing villages and causing environmental concerns.

In September 2008 the king and government in Swaziland were criticised over the country's lavish 40:40 celebrations, which jointly marked the King's 40th birthday and the Swazi Nation's 40 years of Independence from Britain. However, it seems there are more people outside of, rather than inside, Swaziland who would like to see the pace of democratic reform increase.

If you're wondering where to start your Southern Africa journey, South Africa – one of the most inspiring and hope-filled places on the continent – makes a great launching pad for the region. A region that you could easily spend a lifetime exploring. You could tour Botswana's wildlife-rich savanna grasslands; trek around Namibia's quintessential African landscapes – rust-red desert and vast open horizons; put a toe into Zimbabwe, one of the region's most beautiful and untouristed countries; swim along the uncrowded beaches and romantic offshore islands of Mozambique; discover a piece of heaven on earth under the waters of sparkling Lake Malawi; romp around some of the continent's most majestic national parks in Zambia; explore mountains and big sky country in Lesotho; discover one of the continent's last remaining monarchies in gorgeous Swaziland; or just revel in the multitude of African pleasures and treasures at your fingertips in South Africa.

Wherever you decide to go, this is home for adventure seekers, but adventure comes in many forms. Want to bungee jump? Sure, no problem. Fly over mighty Victoria Falls? Absolutely. White-water raft raging rapids? Of course. But do you really want a rush? Then go step onto the streets, catch a local bus, duck into a village, have a drink at a *shebeen* (unlicensed bar), or track lions in the African wilderness. Southern Africa will fill that part of your heart that yearns for adventure. This is where humanity kicked off – it's about time you came home.

Getting Started

Southern Africa varies tremendously: it's suitable for backpackers getting by on packets of chewy biltong, right through to those who prefer crisp linen and cocktails in the bush. It all depends on the country you want to spend time in and the activities you pursue.

Anyone with limited time will want to plan their trip carefully, while those not watching the clock may prefer to just follow their whims and take life at a leisurely pace. Note though, travel in countries such as Zambia will always benefit from a bit of forward planning. The right attitude is what's most important – take precautions, but don't be paranoid, whether in Johannesburg or sunning yourself by Lake Malawi.

Don't run around trying to fit too much into your time – Africa needs to be approached with a sense of fun and patience. Before long you'll find yourself in tune with the rhythm of its friendly people, wild landscapes and majestic wildlife.

WHEN TO GO

High season is from April to August (winter), when most of Southern Africa is basking in temperate sunshine, with comfortable (but often very chilly) nights. The shoulder seasons of February to March and September to October are also usually quite comfortable in the central part of the region.

In the north, you can plan on inclement weather from November to March; the heat can be oppressive and travel can be more difficult due to flooded rivers and washed-out roads. Wildlife viewing is also less rewarding during these months than in the winter (and some parks close completely), but birdwatching is at its best, and you're likely to see the most dramatic skies and thunderstorms imaginable.

The Cape area, however, experiences a Mediterranean climate with winter rain, which means that the high season is the opposite of the rest of Southern Africa. The high season in Cape Town runs from October to March, while May to August is characterised by rains and blustery winds. April and September can go either way.

See Climate Charts (p745) for more information.

Keep in mind the South African school holidays, too, when vast numbers of people head for the coast and national parks of South Africa and neighbouring countries. Hotels and campsites can fill completely, and prices skyrocket.

Another factor to consider is large events in the region – such as the 2010 FIFA World Cup in South Africa – when accommodation is more difficult (and pricey) to find.

See the Climate and When to Go sections at the beginning of each chapter for country-specific details.

COSTS & MONEY

Generally speaking, prices in Southern Africa are around 50% to 75% of what they are in Europe, Australasia or North America. The rand has softened recently, meaning South Africa still remains very good value, and the crisis in Zimbabwe (see p687 for some background) brought about the dollarisation of the currency in 2009, bringing some much-needed stability to prices. Botswana is always considerably more expensive than these countries, while Malawi and Mozambique offer a wide range of options, from dirt cheap to exceptionally expensive. Tourism in Zambia is mainly locked into the top-end safari market, but there are options for budget and, especially, midrange travellers. In general, locally produced items will be good value wherever you

DON'T LEAVE HOME WITHOUT

- A sense of fun and a relaxed attitude towards African travel.
- Binoculars for wildlife viewing and a snazzy camera for taking great wildlife shots.
- An appetite for biltong, *boerewors* and *mielie pap* (see p45).
- Your yellow fever vaccination card, if you've been travelling in affected countries (see p773).
- A basic medical kit that includes ointment to relive itchy bites; and *anything* to repel pesky tsetse flies
- A GPS if you're going bush in your own vehicle.
- Reading a few books (see p22), or bringing one along for long, bumpy bus rides.
- A tent, sleeping bag and sheet liner (which may also come in handy at budget hotels) for camping. A camping stove is also essential for overnight hiking, as fires are not allowed in many areas – one that runs on petrol will be the least hassle.

go, while imported goods may be twice what they cost in the West (thanks to import duties).

Serious backpackers may get by on an average of US$15 per day, including accommodation, food and transport, although US$20 allows more flexibility. For a bit more comfort, US$25 to US$35 per day is a reasonable budget for day-to-day living expenses. To stay in midrange hotels, eat well and travel in comfort when possible, you're looking at around US$50 per day or more. Top-end travellers should expect to pay at least US$75 per day, but US$100 upward is more realistic (note that your budget will skyrocket if you're staying in private game reserves or even some national parks).

Along with these basic costs, you'll have to consider visa and national park fees, plus the cost of any tours or activities (such as wildlife safaris or white-water rafting). To hire a car, you'll find the cheapest deals in South Africa (p579), where some companies will allow you to take the vehicle into neighbouring countries for a minimal extra charge.

See the Transport sections of individual country chapters, and the Money sections in country-specific Directories, for more information on costs.

HOW MUCH?

2WD car hire US$50–100

Box of fruit at roadside US$1–3

Wildlife safari US$100 and up

Hourly internet access US$1–3

Traditional dance performance US$10–25

TRAVELLING RESPONSIBLY

Tourism has a substantial effect on the destinations most frequented by foreign visitors. While some of these effects are absolutely beneficial, providing local income and incentive for environmental conservation, other aspects of tourism can seriously disrupt local economies and ecologies. Seek out entities that promote sustainable, community-oriented tourism – the list on the website of **Fair Trade in Tourism South Africa** (www.fairtourismsa.org.za) is a good place to start. Please take note of the following guidelines and help minimise the negative aspects of tourism while reinforcing its benefits to local communities:

- Many businesses are run by Europeans and white South Africans: take note of how they treat their local staff, and channel your money accordingly.
- If you're travelling independently, be upfront about asking at the accommodation and other businesses you deal with about their 'green' credentials.
- Save water; it's a precious resource, especially in Namibia, where you should be extra careful about water conservation – particularly during the dry season.
- Support local enterprise. But when buying locally made souvenirs, avoid items made from natural material – wood, skin, ivory etc – un-

less they come from a sustainable source (admittedly, this is difficult to check).

- Ask for permission before you take any close-up photographs of people and, if payment is requested, either pay up or put the camera away.
- Don't give money or sweets as gifts for children. If you want to help them, find the village school and donate some pens or schoolbooks, or seek out the clinic and donate unwanted first-aid items. Don't allow schoolkids to guide you during school hours as this encourages them to play truant.
- Budget your trip, and devote 10% (or more) before you go to donate to charities that will directly help the areas you visit.

TOP 10

MUST-SEE MOVIES

These are some of the most insightful and revealing films about Southern Africa to have been produced in recent years.

1 *District 9* (Director Neill Blomkamp, 2009)
2 *Hansie* (Director Regardt van den Bergh, 2008)
3 *Tsotsi* (Director Gavin Hood, 2006)
4 *Yesterday* (Director Darrell James Roodt, 2005)
5 *Amandla! A Revolution in Four-Part Harmony* (Director Lee Hirsch, 2003)
6 *Drum* (Director Zola Maseko, 2005)
7 *Zulu Love Letter* (Director Ramadan Suleman, 2004)
8 *Wah-Wah* (Director Richard E Grant, 2005)
9 *In My Country* (Director John Boorman, 2005)
10 *Red Dust* (Director Tom Hooper, 2005)

FAVOURITE FESTIVALS & EVENTS

Seeing a local festival can be a highlight of your trip to Southern Africa and a window into the local culture. There are plenty of traditional celebrations throughout the year – here's a list of our favourites:

1 Harare International Festival of the Arts, Zimbabwe, late April (p700)
2 Incwala ceremony, Swaziland, late December/early January (p593)
3 Kuomboka ceremony, Zambia, late March/early April (p669)
4 Lake of Stars, Malawi, October (p211)
5 Maitisong Festival, Botswana, March or April (p113)
6 Morija Arts & Cultural Festival, Lesotho, early October (p137)
7 Afrika Burns, South Africa, November (p570)
8 Oktoberfest, Namibia, October (p310)
9 Timbilas Festival, Mozambique, around August (p285)
10 Umhlanga (Reed) Dance, Swaziland, August/September (p593)

CONDUCT IN SOUTHERN AFRICA

A few straightforward courtesies may greatly improve a foreigner's chances of acceptance by the local community, especially in rural areas. In Southern Africa, pleasantries are taken quite seriously, and it's essential to greet or say goodbye to someone entering or leaving a room. Learn the local words for hello and goodbye and use them unsparingly; it's also good form to enquire about someone's wellbeing. Emphasis is placed on handshakes all over the region. The Batswana (in Botswana) are particularly sensitive to proper greetings (always be polite) and handshakes (grab your right elbow with your left hand while shaking). The African handshake consists of three parts: the normal Western handshake, followed by the linking of bent fingers while touching the ends of upward-pointing thumbs, and then a repeat of the conventional handshake.

As in most traditional societies, the achievement of old age is an accomplishment worthy of respect, and elders are treated with deference – they should be accorded utmost courtesy. Teachers, doctors and other professionals often receive similar treatment.

When visiting rural settlements, it's a good idea to request to see the chief to announce your presence and ask permission before setting up camp or wandering through.

If you're offered a gift, don't feel guilty about accepting it, as refusal may bring shame on the giver. To receive a gift politely, accept it with both hands and perhaps bow slightly.

At beach resorts throughout the region it's fine to dress in shorts and sleeveless tops. Elsewhere, you'll have an easier time if you wear more conservative garb.

- Don't watch sacred dances staged solely for tourists, and don't go to sacred sites that offend local beliefs. Make an effort to learn about the culture that you are interacting with and respect the fragility and cultural importance of rock paintings throughout the region.
- Respect local protocol with regard to clothing – avoid very skimpy and ripped/dirty clothes as well as topless sunbathing.
- Don't drive 4WDs off road or on sand dunes and especially don't drive on beaches in Mozambique, where it's harmful to the environment – and illegal.
- Be aware of the source of your seafood. Overfishing and inappropriate fishing methods mean that, although Southern Africa's waters are bountiful, many species are over-exploited and some stocks are running dangerously low.

Organisations with information on responsible travel and sustainable environmental practices include **Tourism Concern** (☎ 020-7133 3800; www.tourismconcern.org.uk; Stapleton House, 277-281 Holloway Rd, London N7 8HN); and **Action for Southern Africa** (☎ 020-3263 2001; www.actsa.org; 231 Vauxhall Bridge Rd, London SW1V 1EH), which campaigns for (among other things) sustainable tourism throughout the region.

For further information on responsible tourism, see p64.

TRAVEL LITERATURE

The Ukimwi Road by Dervla Murphy recounts the adventures of the famously eccentric 60-year-old Irish grandmother as she cycles through Africa, from Kenya to Zimbabwe, along the way downing numerous beers and observing life at a human scale – most notably the harrowing effects of HIV/AIDS.

A fun and fascinating collection of stories about cars, bars, parties, rebellions, relationships and other diverse subjects in several African countries, *Mr Bigstuff & the Goddess of Charm* by Fiona Sax Ledger includes some insightful conversations with Zambian politicians.

Drawn from the Plains: Life in the Wilds of Namibia & Mozambique by Lynne Tinley has lovely descriptions of life in the bush in Etosha and Gorongosa National Parks.

No Place Like & Other Stories by Southern African Women Writers, edited by Robin Malan, is a compelling collection of short stories that focus on the women of Botswana, Zimbabwe, South Africa and Namibia. The tone varies between ironic, intimate and emotionally charged, with stories often set within the larger political landscape.

Mukiwa by Peter Goodwin is a book that grabs your heart and stays in your head. It is the story of a small Rhodesian boy who witnesses the murder by guerrillas of a neighbour…and then the tumultuous end of white rule. *Mukiwa* captures much of the beauty and mystery of Zimbabwe and Southern Africa.

Lost World of the Kalahari by Laurens van der Post is a captivating account of the author's rediscovery of the San at a time when Southern Africa was under colonial rule. The book details the author's arduous expedition deep into the wild Kalahari and reveals the unique indigenous culture of Africa's last Stone Age people.

Scribbling the Cat: Travels with an African Soldier by Alexandra Fuller winds its way through Zambia, Zimbabwe and Mozambique. Fuller travels into a war-scarred past with her companion, revealing a legacy of conflict and its effects on them and the region's indigenous peoples.

One of the most prominent contemporary South African authors is Zakes Mda, who – with the publication of *Ways of Dying* in 1995 – made a successful transition from poet and playwright to acclaimed novelist. *The Whale Caller* (2005) takes a somewhat sceptical look at the optimism surrounding the new South Africa.

INTERNET RESOURCES

African Encounter (www.africanencounter.com) This site is run by a travel agent who specialises in itineraries of Southern Africa. It's good for information on getting around Zimbabwe.

All Africa (http://allafrica.com) A gateway to all things African, this website posts around 1000 articles a day, collated from over 125 different news organisations.

iafrica.com (www.iafrica.com) This diverse South African–dominated site includes travel, news and lifestyle sections, plus links to sites on other Southern African countries.

Lonely Planet (www.lonelyplanet.com) Here you will find several pages of information on each country in Southern Africa and the Thorn Tree notice board, where you can ask questions before you go or dispense advice when you get back.

Open Africa (www.openafrica.org) This excellent site details off-the-beaten track tourism routes supporting job creation and conservation through Southern Africa.

Political Africa (www.politicalafrica.com) This website features the latest stories on Africa, from various news services around the world, and links to sport, economics and the UN in Africa, among many others.

Itineraries

CLASSIC ROUTES

NATURE & FUN IN THE SUN

Three Weeks to One Month/ Kruger to Southern Mozambique

Using **Johannesburg** (p527) as a gateway, head east via **Nelspruit** (p518) to world-renowned **Kruger National Park** (p513). The teeming wildlife will undoubtedly mesmerise you for several days.

If you've time, duck out of Orpen Gate for a look at **Blyde River Canyon** (p522). From Kruger, continue south into Swaziland, where you can spend a few days hiking through the grasslands and forests of **Malolotja Nature Reserve** (p596) before heading on via **Mbabane** (p589) to the tiny, but brilliant **Mkhaya Game Reserve** (p598), noted for its black rhinos.

Then head to culturally intriguing **Maputo** (p226) via the Mozambican border town of **Namaacha** (p239). Head north on the EN1 and, if you're getting desperate for a dip, stop at **Xai-Xai's** (p240) quiet beaches. Continue up the EN1 to **Inhambane** (p241), one of the country's oldest and most charming towns. Beaches close by include legendary **Tofo** (p243), with azure waters, and the more sedate **Barra** (p245). If you've more steam, trundle a bit further north to **Vilankulo** (p246), the gateway to the tropical paradise of Bazaruto Archipelago.

This 2000km-plus route serves up delightful variety, and with a month up your sleeve you can get a good sampling of wildlife and local culture and still have time to laze on the beach. Short on time? Whiz through Swaziland and stick to motorways where possible.

NATURAL WONDER & SENSATIONAL SAFARIS

One Week/Victoria Falls to the Okavango Delta

Start your trip at one of the great natural wonders of the world, **Victoria Falls** (p604), whose mighty spray can be seen from 50km away. For the best perspectives, visit from both **Livingstone** (Zambia; p608) and the town of **Victoria Falls** (Zimbabwe; p616). There's a plethora of activities on offer, including serene canoe trips on top of the falls and, for those after an adrenalin rush, rafting below the falls down the churning Zambezi. Also be sure to check out **Mosi-oa-Tunya Game Park** (p615) and the rainforests of Victoria Falls National Park.

From the Zambian side, cross the nearby border at Kazungula and head for **Kasane** (p92) in Botswana, the gateway town to the stunning, wildlife-rich **Chobe National Park** (p92). Here you can organise wildlife drives and river cruises along the Chobe riverfront, where nearly every Southern African mammal species is represented.

From Chobe it's an easy hop, skip and jump southwest to **Maun** (p98) and Botswana's tourist magnet, the vast **Okavango Delta** (p98), where one of the world's most impressive ecosystems breathes life into the Kalahari sands and attracts astonishing amounts of wildlife and incalculable numbers of birds.

Once in Maun, you can do a mokoro (dugout canoe) trip in the **Eastern Delta** (p103), take a safari in **Moremi Game Reserve** (p105), or splash out on a fly-in trip into the **Inner Delta** (p104). From Maun, take a minibus clockwise around the delta towards Namibia, perhaps stopping in Sepupa to take a boat to **Seronga** (p107) and do a mokoro trip in the **Okavango Panhandle** (p107).

This 700km itinerary will take you through some of Southern Africa's biggest draws. When viewing wildlife, try not to squeeze too much in – take a break here and there. You could whiz through in seven days, or have a more relaxed 10 days or two weeks.

A SOUTHERN AFRICAN SLICE **One Month/Cape Town to Windhoek**

A car is definitely your best bet for this mega road trip. After a few days in **Cape Town** (p403), including a stay at a township B&B, tear yourself away from this wonderful city and head to the fertile valleys of the Winelands, with a night or two in **Stellenbosch** (p429) or **Franschhoek** (p433).

From here, continue east to the artists' enclave of **Montagu** (p439), and then via the scenic Route 62 through the Little Karoo to **Oudtshoorn** (p440), South Africa's ostrich capital. Some possible detours along the way include a trip to **Hermanus** (p436) for whale watching if the season is right, or to **Cape Agulhas** (p437) for the thrill of standing at Africa's southernmost point.

From Oudtshoorn take the N12 north and then loop back towards Cape Town via the N1, link up with the N7 and head for **Namakwa** (p458) to see the fabulous wildflower displays, which are especially good in August and September.

Keep tracking up the N7, cross into Namibia at **Vioolsdrif** (p459) and head to **Hobas** (p375) to see the **Fish River Canyon National Park** (p374), a jaw-dropping natural sight that's also Namibia's premier walking destination.

Further north along the B1, **Keetmanshoop** (p366) has some colonial architecture; if this grabs you, head west along the B4 to the surreal **Lüderitz** (p368), a coastal colonial relic. Heading back to the B1, turn north at the C13 and make a beeline for the baroque **Duwisib Castle** (p366), which is well worth exploring. You can stay 300m from the castle on a rustic farm and visit the nearby historic blacksmith shop. From there head to **Mariental** back on the B1, and it's another couple of hours to **Windhoek** (p304), the small, colourful and cosmopolitan capital city with its bracing highland climate.

For road-trip lovers. Even if you can't squeeze in all of this 3000km-plus journey, you'll come away with an immense appreciation of this remarkable region. Looking to make cuts? Shave some kilometres off the Western Cape loop. To avoid white-line fever allow at least a month.

ROADS LESS TRAVELLED

DUSTY ROADS & SHIMMERING WATERS

Three Weeks to One Month/ Lusaka to Nkhata Bay

Start with a few days in Zambia's cosmopolitan capital, **Lusaka** (p631), with its genuine African feel and the country's best nightlife. Then head out on the highway to the stunning **Lower Zambezi National Park** (p663), with its beautiful flood plain that's dotted with acacias and other large trees. There's no public transport to the park, so you'll need your own car to get there, or go on an organised tour. Hook up with the Great East Rd and head to chaotic **Chipata** (p651). Here you can organise a trip to **South Luangwa National Park** (p652), one of the most majestic parks on the continent. Make sure that you do a walking safari when you're here. From Chipata you can drive to **Mfuwe Gate** (p652), or take one of the minibuses that make the trip to Mfuwe village. The really adventurous could try to reach the wild and spectacular **North Luangwa National Park** (p657), but it's important that you seek local advice before doing this.

Then it's on to Malawi and the town of **Lilongwe** (p167), which is worth a day or two to check out the old town and the local Nature Sanctuary. From Lilongwe strike out north along the M1 to **Nkhata Bay** (p181) on Lake Malawi, which is perfect for swimming, kayaking or just lazing about after some hard weeks on the road. Possible detours on the way to Nkhata include the gently rolling hills of **Kasungu National Park** (p186) and historic **Nkhotakota** (p186) from where you can organise a trip to the wild **Nkhotakota Wildlife Reserve** (p187), where you have a good chance of seeing elephants.

A 2000km route through the Southern African outback. Travelling in Zambia offers a taste of the real Africa, and the dusty roads will become a distant memory once you're lazing by the crystal-clear waters of Lake Malawi. Allow at least three weeks.

LAKESHORE TO SEASHORE

Three Weeks to One Month/ Nkhata Bay to Pemba

Drag yourself out of the crystal waters at **Nkhata Bay** (p181) and hop onto the *Ilala* ferry for the blissful **Likoma Island** (p183), where swimming, snorkelling and local cultures are the star attractions. Splash out for a night at Kaya Mawa if you've the pennies – it's one of Africa's finest paradise retreats. Take the ferry over to the Mediterranean-esque **Chizumulu Island** (p184), with its idyllic beaches, and return by dhow (if the waters are calm enough).

From Likoma hop back on the ferry to Metangula and from there take the Dangilila up towards **Cóbuè** (p271), on the other side of the lakeshore in Mozambique. (Or, take a dhow direct from Likoma to Cóbuè). Stay the night just south of Cóbuè at Nkwichi Lodge, a magnificent bush retreat that is part of an important development and conservation project; it's well worth a splurge. If your budget isn't up to Nkwichi, try one of several backpacker-friendly places in Cóbuè itself. After exploring the lake area, head south to cool **Lichinga** (p269); surrounded by scenic, rugged terrain, it is the capital of remote Niassa province. Carry on through to **Mandimba** (p269) and on to bustling **Cuamba** (p268), where you can pick up a train all the way through to **Nampula** (p261). Then jump on a bus to magnificent **Mozambique Island** (p263), with its intriguing architecture and time-warp atmosphere. If you need a beach break after exploring the island, hire a dhow to take you over to **Chocas** (p267) and the lovely nearby beach at **Cabaceira Pequena** (p267). The trip finishes up a bit further north at **Pemba** (p273), which is the gateway to the superb Quirimbas Archipelago.

This 1500km Mozambican bush adventure could be tacked onto 'Dusty Roads & Shimmering Waters', but it also stands well alone. Mozambique Island makes a wonderful contrast to the bush, and you can finish on the beach in the tropical island paradise of Quirimbas Archipelago.

MESMERISING WILDERNESS & CULTURE

Three Weeks/Skeleton Coast to the Kalahari

Starting on Namibia's Skeleton Coast, a treacherous coastline with rusting shipwrecks and desert wilderness, check out the **Cape Cross Seal Reserve** (p344). Track north along the coast to **Torra Bay** (p345), where you can camp, or head for **Terrace Bay** (p345) for more luxurious accommodation. Then travel west into the wonders of **Damaraland** (p336), with its wild, open spaces, and make a beeline for **Twyfelfontein** (p336), one of the most extensive galleries of rock art in Africa. Then journey further east to **Outjo** (p317), which is a staging post for visits to **Etosha National Park** (p321), teeming with animals and one of the continent's great wildlife-viewing sites.

Exit Etosha via von Linqequist Gate and proceed to **Tsumeb** (p320), one of the country's prettiest towns with its vivid jacarandas and flame trees. Track northeast along the B8 into Botswana at the border town of Mohembo. Drive down the west side of the **Okavango Delta** (p98), perhaps stopping in Sepupa to take a boat to **Seronga** (p107) to do a mokoro trip in the Okavango Panhandle.

The last leg of this ambitious trip is the gigantic **Central Kalahari Game Reserve** (p108) to the southeast, lying at the heart of Botswana. Enter at the Matswere Gate at the northeastern end of the reserve: wildlife includes lions and brown hyenas. You can finish your trip by exiting the same gate and travelling east to **Francistown** (p85).

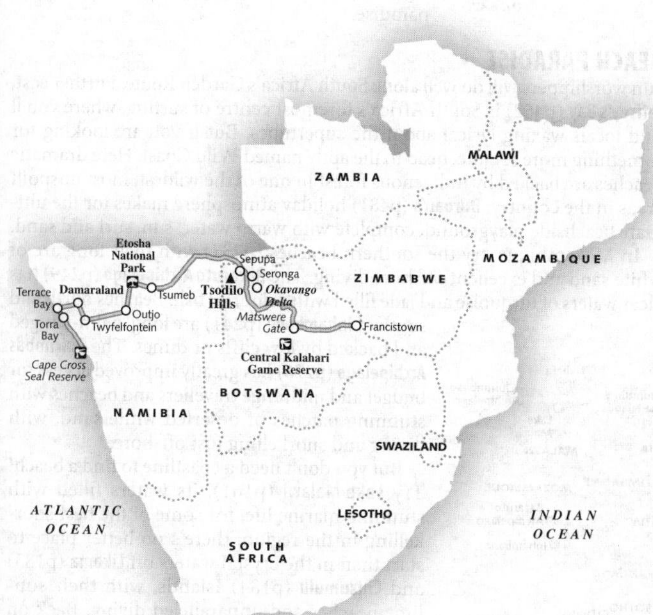

This 3000km-plus trip into some of Southern Africa's most inhospitable and magnificent terrain is challenging – much of it is 4WD territory and you'll need your own car. You could push through in three weeks, but take a month and spend time in the Kalahari.

TAILORED TRIPS

WORLD HERITAGE SITES

Southern Africa's Unesco-protected World Heritage Sites encapsulate some of the most valuable cultural icons, historic sites and natural landscapes on the continent. South Africa hosts fossil hominid sites including **Sterkfontein Caves** (p539), referred to as the Cradle of Humankind. Further north, **Mapungubwe National Park** (p561) incorporates wonderful historical sites from an ancient kingdom. **iSimangaliso Wetland Park** (p498) is a brilliant ecotourism destination, and the **Ukhahlamba-Drakensberg Park** (p502) is an otherworldly mountainous area splashed with San rock art. In the west, just offshore from Cape Town, **Robben Island** (p410) is a shrine to the struggle, with tours led by former inmates.

Zimbabwe boasts impressive cultural sites such as **Great Zimbabwe** (p718), once the greatest medieval city in sub-Saharan Africa. Close by, **Matobo National Park** (p724) has one of the world's best collections of San rock art. In the north, **Mana Pools National Park** (p707) is known for its walking safaris. **Victoria Falls** (p604), to the west, is one of the world's seven natural wonders.

Mozambique Island (p263) in Mozambique is a portal to the past with its intriguing architectural legacy and **Lake Malawi** (p190) is a snorkelling paradise.

BEACH PARADISE

Sun worshippers will do well along South Africa's Garden Route. Further east, **Jeffrey's Bay** (p462) is South Africa's foremost centre of surfing, where you'll find locals waxing lyrical about the supertubes. But if you are looking for something more remote, head to the aptly named Wild Coast. Here dramatic beaches are backed by indigenous forest in one of the wildest, most unspoilt areas in the country. **Durban's** (p481) holiday atmosphere makes for the ultimate beachside playground, complete with warm water, sun, surf and sand.

In Mozambique, try the southern beaches (p237) with their long arc of white sand and excellent offshore diving. The **Bazaruto Archipelago** (p249) has clear waters of turquoise and jade filled with colourful fish. Beaches north and south of **Inhambane** (p241) are long, palm-fringed and backed by low cliffs or dunes. The **Quirimbas Archipelago** (p276) has greatly improved access for budget and midrange travellers and beaches with stunning patches of deserted white sand, with diving and snorkelling just offshore.

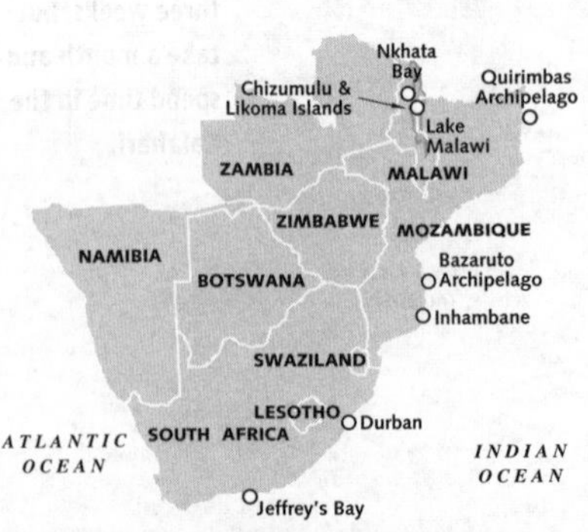

But you don't need a coastline to find a beach! Try **Lake Malawi** (p161), its waters filled with stunning marine life, for some of the best snorkelling in the region; there's no better place to start than in the crystal waters off **Likoma** (p183) and **Chizumulu** (p184) Islands, with their sublime beaches and unparalleled diving. Back on the lakeshore, get seduced into lazing at **Nkhata Bay** (p181).

MAJESTIC WILDLIFE & AFRICAN LANDSCAPES

Africa and its wildlife have a mystique that's simply awe-inspiring. In South Africa, world-class **Kruger National Park** (p513) has an astonishing variety and number of animals, while accessible **Pilanesberg National Park** (p555) with its extinct volcanic crater is good for spotting wild dogs. At **uMkhuze Game Reserve** (p500) sit by a pan at dawn listening to the sounds of the bush, watching the wildlife parade before you. For unforgettable sunsets and wild storms, head to the hauntingly beautiful **Kgalagadi Transfrontier Park** (p456), with its shifting red and white sands. If you're after separation from the world, try **Sehlabathebe National Park** (p136) in Lesotho.

In Malawi, hippos, elephants and kingfishers dominate the lush surrounds and tranquil Shire River at **Liwonde National Park** (p192), while **Nyika National Park** (p177) has antelopes, endless views and clean, crisp air. Monstrous **Kafue National Park** (p670) is Zambia's foremost park for spotting leopard, while **South Luangwa** (p652) is Africa at its most stunning.

In Zimbabwe the breathtaking **Eastern Highlands** (p709) are a wilderness wonderland of formidable peaks, savanna valleys and hiking trails.

The dramatic rehabilitation of **Gorongosa National Park** (p253) in Mozambique has put it firmly on the wilderness map and **Niassa Reserve** (p271) offers the ultimate in Southern African bush experiences.

Namibia's **Etosha National Park** (p321) is one of the continent's great wildlife-viewing destinations, while the **Okavango Delta** (p98) in Botswana contains water-soaked Kalahari sands, a staggering animal population and magnificent desert vistas.

A LITTLE BIT OF HISTORY

Southern Africa's historical roots are firmly planted in the extraordinary San rock art sprinkled around the region. Some of the best examples are in **Matobo National Park** (p724) in Zimbabwe and **Twyfelfontein** (p336) in Namibia.

The stone ruins of **Great Zimbabwe** (p718), a rare example of medieval African architecture, are well worth a ramble.

In Mozambique, European extravagance is evident in the **Palace of São Paulo** (p265) and the oldest European building in the southern hemisphere, the **Chapel of Nossa Senhora de Baluarte** (p265); both are found on timeless Mozambique Island, which has a diverse cultural heritage.

A unique pocket of colonial Africa can be found at unspoilt **Livingstonia** (p176) in Malawi, where the fascinating museum details European missionary work. At **Nkhotakota** (p186) you can sit under the tree where explorer David Livingstone persuaded a local chief to end the slave trade.

Reminiscent of a medieval castle with its maze of dusty corridors and stairways, bizarre **Shiwa House** (p647) in Zambia is a rambling English-style edifice in the middle of the African bush.

In Jo'burg the **Apartheid Museum** (p530) tells the chilling apartheid story with sensory verve, while **Cape Town** (p403) is awash with European history.

History

The precolonial history of Southern Africa is a compelling, interwoven web of peoples on the move throughout this vast region – the original travellers on our planet. It's also a story of technology and its impact on our early ancestors. Although Southern Africa's history stretches far back into the mists of time, the only records today are intriguing fossil remains and an extraordinary human diary of Stone Age rock art.

The region has revealed many archaeological records of the world's earliest human inhabitants. It's generally agreed among scientists that the first 'hominids' (upright-walking humanlike creatures) became established in the savannas of East and Southern Africa nearly four million years ago, although hominid remains dating to between six and seven million years old have been found further north in Chad.

Sterkfontein in South Africa is regarded as one of the richest places on the planet for early human remains and is a World Heritage Site. In Malawi, archaeologists have found remains thought to date back as far as 2.5 million years.

The Scramble for Africa: White Man's Conquest of the Dark Continent from 1876 to 1912 by Thomas Pakenham details the colonial history of Southern Africa and the continent in well-written and entertaining prose.

It is surmised that about two million years ago several hominid species evolved, with *Homo erectus* developing basic tool-making abilities and eventually becoming dominant. Later evolving into *Homo sapiens* (modern humans), these early Africans are believed to have backpacked to other parts of the world, where local factors determined the racial characteristics of each group.

Today, remains of temporary camps and stone tools are found throughout Southern Africa, and one site in Namibia suggests that 750,000 years ago, these early people were hunting elephants and cutting up carcasses with large stone axes. By 150,000 years ago, people were using lighter spear heads, knives, saws and other tools. (Archaeologists classify this period of tool making as the Stone Age, subdivided into the Early, Middle and Late stages, although the term applies to the people's level of technological development, rather than to a specific period.) See Matobo in Zimbabwe, p724, and Morija in Lesotho, p137, for details of where to see early Stone Age artefacts.

An Introduction to the History of Central Africa – Zambia, Malawi and Zimbabwe by AJ Wills provides a comprehensive work on the region and is considered one of the best around.

EARLY KHOISAN INHABITANTS

Thousands of years ago, humans in Southern Africa developed an organised hunting and gathering society. Use of fire was universal, tools became more sophisticated (made from wood and animal products as well as stone), and make-up (natural pigments used for personal adornment) was in fashion. These Boskop people (named after the site in South Africa where their remains were discovered) are believed to be the ancestors of the San people, who still exist in isolated pockets today.

TIMELINE

c 3.5 million BC

In Southern Africa, evidence of early hominid fossils dating back millions of years has been discovered at the Sterkfontein Caves in Gauteng, northwest of Johannesburg in South Africa.

c 2 million BC

Homo erectus becomes the dominant hominid species, later evolving into what we now define as modern humans; sub-Saharan Africa really was the birthplace of humanity.

c 100,000 BC

Zambia's most celebrated early inhabitant, Broken Hill Man, lives and dies. Evidence unearthed by archaeologists in Malawi suggests that Early Stone Age settlements existed along the shore of Lake Malawi at this time.

Eventually, tools became smaller and better designed, which increased hunting efficiency and allowed time for further innovation, artistic pursuits and admiring the fiery African sunsets. This stage is called the Microlithic Revolution because it was characterised by the working of small stones. The remains of microliths are often found alongside clear evidence of food gathering, shellfish remains and the working of wood, bone and ostrich eggshell.

The artistic traditions of the San are evidenced by pottery and especially by the wonderful paintings that can be seen today in rock shelters and caves all over Southern Africa (see the boxed text, p34). The better examples capture the elegance and movement of African wildlife with astonishing clarity. More recent paintings even depict white farmers.

Despite these artistic and technical developments, the San had no knowledge of metal working, and thus remain classified as Stone Age people.

The San and another group called the Khoikhoi are thought to share a common ancestry: differences between the peoples were slight, based more on habitat and lifestyle than on significant physiological features. (The Khoikhoi kept cattle, which were a source of food and transport, and were even trained to charge the enemy in warfare.) They also shared a language group, characterised by distinctive 'click' sounds. Today these two peoples are regarded as one, termed Khoisan or Khoi-San, and are mostly found in remote parts of Namibia and Botswana.

In recent times the San have been controversially relocated from their ancestral lands to new government settlements such as New Xade in the central Kalahari in Botswana. For more information see the boxed text, p74.

To learn more about the San, including current issues for survival, see www.kalaharipeoples.org, created by a nonprofit organisation involved with the people of the Kalahari.

THE BANTU MIGRATION

While the Khoisan were developing, in West Africa another group with larger body types and darker skin was emerging: the Bantu.

Their advanced skills led to improved farming methods and the ability to make unwanted guests of themselves on their neighbours' lands. Over 2000 years ago the Bantu moved into the Congo basin and, over the next thousand years, spread across present-day Uganda, Kenya and Tanzania and migrated south into Zambia, Malawi, Mozambique and other parts of Southern Africa. The term 'migration' here refers to a sporadic spread over many hundreds of years. Typically, a group would move from valley to valley or from one water source to the next. This process inevitably had a knock-on effect, as weaker ethnic groups were constantly being 'moved on' by invaders from other areas.

At first, the Bantu in Southern Africa apparently lived in relative harmony with the original Khoisan inhabitants, trading goods, language and culture. However, as Bantu numbers increased, some Khoisan were conquered or absorbed by this more advanced group of peoples, while the remainder were pushed further and further into inhospitable lands.

c 30,000 BC

Evidence suggests that the peoples of Southern Africa had developed an organised hunting and gathering lifestyle, made possible by more sophisticated tools and weapons.

c 20,000 BC

The San had made significant technological progress by this time although it was restricted to stone. This meant increased time for leisure and artistic pursuits, which included rock art.

c 8000 BC

There is evidence that the San began producing pottery around this time, supporting the notion that their progress allowed them increased time away from hunting and gathering food.

ANCIENT ROCK ART

Discovering some of the magnificent rock art sprinkled around Southern Africa, a remarkable human diary left by an ancient people, is a major highlight for many visitors. There's a lot of speculation about the origins of the ancient rock paintings and engravings. Due to the tools and animal remains left around major sites, and the scenes depicted, it's believed the artists were the early San people.

A tantalising sliver of mankind's Stone Age existence, these sites provide a snapshot of the way the San lived and hunted, and their spirituality. The most poignant thing about rock art is that it remains in the spot where it was created. Unlike works seen in a museum, you may catch a glimpse of the inspiration that actually went into these paintings. Although rock art is found all over Southern Africa, the best examples are probably in Matobo National Park (p724), and in Domboshawa and Ngomakurira (p703), all in Zimbabwe; the Tsodilo Hills in Botswana; Twyfelfontein (p336) in Namibia; and Giant's Castle (p506) in South Africa.

Most rock paintings reflected people's relationship with nature. Some rock paintings are stylised representations of the region's people and animals, but the majority are realistic portrayals of hunters, giraffes, elephants, rhinos, lions, antelopes and so on in rich red, yellow, brown and ochre.

Common themes include the roles of men and women, hunting scenes and natural medicine. Examples of the last include trance dancing and spiritual healing using the San life force, known as *nxum,* which was invoked to control aspects of the natural world, including climate and disease. All these elements still feature in San tradition.

Although climatic onslaught means the earliest works have long faded, flaked and eroded into oblivion, the dry climate and sheltered granite overhangs have preserved many of the more recent paintings. Three distinct periods have been identified: the earliest paintings seem to reflect a period of gentle nomadism, during which people were occupied primarily with the hunt; later works, which revealed great artistic improvement, suggest peaceful arrivals by outside groups, perhaps Bantu or Khoikhoi; the final stage indicates a decline in the standard of the paintings – or they may be imitations of earlier works by more recently arrived peoples.

Red pigments were ground mainly from iron oxides, which were powdered and mixed with animal fat to form an adhesive paste. The whites came from silica, powdered quartz and white clays, and were by nature less adhesive than the red pigments. For this reason white paintings survive only in sheltered locations, such as well-protected caves. Both pigments were applied to the rock using sticks, the artists' fingers and brushes made from animal hair.

While admiring the rock art of Southern Africa, please keep in mind the fragility of the paintings (p20).

BANTU CULTURE & EARLY KINGDOMS

A feature of Bantu culture was its strong social system, based on extended family or clan loyalties and dependencies, and generally centred on the rule of a chief. Some chiefdoms developed into powerful kingdoms, uniting many disparate ethnic groups and covering large geographical areas.

c 8000 BC

The San come under pressure from another group called the Khoikhoi (or Khoi-Khoi), known in more recent times as Hottentots. These two peoples are thought to share a common ancestry.

c 2000–500 BC

Iron-skilled Bantu migrate from West Africa through the Congo basin into present-day Zambia and Malawi, and over the centuries spread into other parts of East and Southern Africa.

500–1000 AD

The Gokomere people and subsequent groups around the area now known as Zimbabwe develop gold-mining techniques and produce progressively finer-quality ceramics, jewellery, textiles and soapstone carvings.

Cattle played an essential role in the lives of Southern Africa's Bantu population. Apart from providing food, skins and a form of capital, cattle were also most essential when it came to bride wealth. Marriage involved the transfer of a woman to the household of her husband. In turn, the cattle from the husband's family were reassigned to the family of the bride's father. A man who had many daughters would one day end up with many cattle.

One of the earliest Bantu kingdoms was Gokomere, in the uplands of Zimbabwe. The Gokomere people are thought to be the first occupants of the Great Zimbabwe site (p718), near present-day Masvingo.

History of Southern Africa by JD Omer-Cooper provides an excellent, highly readable account of the early peoples of Southern Africa, including fascinating cultural detail that differentiates the many Bantu-speaking groups.

EARLY TRADERS

Meanwhile, from the latter half of the 1st millennium, Arabs from the lands around the Red Sea were sailing southwards along the eastern seaboard of Africa. They traded with the local Bantu inhabitants, who by this time had reached the coast, and bought ivory, gold and slaves to take back to Arabia.

Between AD 1000 and 1500 the Arab-influenced Bantu founded several major settlements along the coast, from Mogadishu (in present-day Somalia) to Kilwa (in southern Tanzania), including Lamu (Kenya) and Zanzibar (Tanzania). In Kenya and Tanzania particularly, the Bantu people were influenced by the Arabs, and a certain degree of intermarriage occurred, so that gradually a mixed language and culture was created, called Swahili, which remains intact today.

From southern Tanzania the Swahili-Arabs traded along the coast of present-day Mozambique, establishing bases at Quelimane (p257) and Mozambique Island (p263).

From the coast the Swahili-Arabs pushed into the interior, and developed a network of trade routes across much of East and Southern Africa. Ivory and gold continued to be sought after, but the demand for slaves grew considerably, and reached its zenith in the early-19th century when the Swahili-Arabs and dominant local ethnic groups are reckoned to have either killed or sold into slavery 80,000 to 100,000 Africans per year.

Click onto www.h-net.org/~safrica, and join in with this electronic discussion group on all things pertaining to the history and culture of Southern Africa.

LATER BANTU KINGDOMS & PEOPLE

As early as the 11th century, the inhabitants of Great Zimbabwe had come into contact with Arab-Swahili traders from the coast. Great Zimbabwe became the capital of the wealthiest and most powerful society in Southern Africa – its people the ancestors of today's Shona people – and reached the zenith of its powers around the 14th century (see p687), becoming the greatest medieval city in sub-Saharan Africa.

From around the 11th century it appears that more advanced Bantu-speaking Iron Age people migrated to the area, absorbing the earlier immigrants. As they settled they branched out into a number of cultural groups. One of these groups, the Nguni, was distinguished from its neighbours by strict matrimony rules – marriage was forbidden to a partner that could be

13th Century

Construction of Great Zimbabwe commences – the city grows into a powerful religious and political capital, becoming the heart of Rozwi culture and the greatest medieval city in sub-Saharan Africa.

1498

Portuguese explorer Vasco da Gama lands at Mozambique Island. Over the next 200 years, the Portuguese establish trading enclaves along the coast and several settlements in the interior along the Zambezi Valley.

1616

Portuguese explorer Gaspar Bocarro journeys from Tete (on the Zambezi River) through the Shire Valley to Lake Chilwa (to the south of Lake Malawi), then through the south of Tanzania and back into Mozambique.

THE BANTU

The Bantu peoples could more accurately be called 'Bantu-speaking peoples' since the word 'Bantu' actually refers to a language group rather than a specific race. However, it has become a convenient term of reference for the black African peoples of Southern and Eastern Africa, even though the grouping is as ill-defined as 'American' or 'Asian'. The Bantu ethnic group comprises many subgroups, each with their own language, customs and traditions.

Estimates vary, but it's reckoned that of all the slaves captured in the interior of Africa, two in every three died before reaching their final destination.

traced to a common ancestor. The Xhosa (p461) were the southernmost of these people. Covering large areas of present-day South Africa, Botswana and Lesotho were the Sotho-Setswana, who encouraged intercousin marriage. The Venda, who have a matriarchal culture and are thought to be related to the Shona people (p561) of Zimbabwe, occupied the north of Limpopo province in South Africa.

Further north, between the 14th and 16th centuries, another Bantu group called the Maravi (of whom the Chewa became the dominant ethnic group) arrived in Southern Africa from the Congo Basin and founded a powerful kingdom covering southern Malawi and parts of present-day Mozambique and Zambia. Masks made by a men's secret society called Nyau were an integral part of ceremonies for this group. As well as representing cultural ideals with themes such as wisdom, sickness, death and ancestors, masks also caricatured undesirables such as slave-traders, invaders and colonial figures.

In 1660 Jan van Riebeeck planted a bitter-almond hedge separating the Dutch from the Khoikhoi. Parts of the hedge can still be seen today (p415).

At about the same time the Tumbuka and the Phoka groups migrated into the north of Malawi (see p162). The Tumbuka are known for their healing practices, which combine traditional medicine and music.

During the 16th and 17th centuries, another Bantu group called the Herero migrated from the Zambezi Valley into present-day Namibia, where they came into conflict with the San and competed with the Khoikhoi for the best grazing lands. Eventually, most indigenous groups submitted to the Herero. Only the Nama people, thought to be descended from early Khoikhoi groups, held out. One of Africa's most traditional cultures, the Himba people (see the boxed text, p342) in Namibia, are descended from the Herero.

Today's Herero women are distinguished by their extravagant neck to ankle Victorian dresses, petticoats and large hats – a by-product of contact with German missionaries.

The power of the Bantu kingdoms started to falter in the late 18th and early 19th centuries due to a major dispersal of indigenous ethnic groups called the *difaqane*, and a rapid increase in the number of European settlers.

THE DIFAQANE

The *difaqane* (meaning 'forced migration' in Sotho, or *mfeqane*, 'the crushing', in Zulu) was a period of immense upheaval and suffering for the indigenous peoples of Southern Africa. It originated in the early 19th century when the Nguni ethnic groups in modern KwaZulu-Natal (South

17th century

Competing European powers begin settling in South Africa in small numbers, mostly in the Cape. This signals the eventual change of life for the peoples of Southern Africa that European colonialism brought.

mid-17th century

European colonists come into conflict with the San. The early Boers' campaign of land seizures and forced migrations lasts for 200 years and results in the deaths of as many as 200,000 indigenous people.

19th century

The *difaqane* (forced migration) sees waves of Southern Africa's peoples displaced as the powerful warrior army of Shaka Zulu uproots ethnic groups in their path, forcing them to flee to new territory.

Africa) changed rapidly from loosely organised collections of chiefdoms to the more centralised Zulu Nation. Based on its highly disciplined and powerful warrior army, the process began under Chief Dingiswayo, and reached its peak under the military commander Shaka Zulu.

Shaka was a ruthless conqueror and his reputation preceded him. Not surprisingly, ethnic groups living in his path chose to flee, in turn displacing neighbours and causing disruption and terror across Southern Africa. Ethnic groups displaced from Zululand include the Matabele, who settled in present-day Zimbabwe, while the Ngoni fled to Malawi and Zambia. Notable survivors were the Swazi (p584) and Basotho (p124), who forged powerful kingdoms that became Swaziland and Lesotho.

The Makololo were uprooted from Zululand during the *difaqane* and moved into southwest Zambia, where they displaced the Tonga people. To this day the dominant language of much of western Zambia remains Makololo.

EUROPEAN COLONISATION & SETTLEMENT

Although there had been a European presence in Southern Africa for several hundred years, in 1820 the British Cape Colony saw a major influx of settlers. Around 5000 were brought from Britain on the promise of fertile farmland around the Great Fish River, near the Shipwreck Coast, Eastern Cape. In reality, the settlers were brought in to form a buffer between the Boers (to the west of the river) and the Xhosa (amaXhosa; to the east), who competed for territory.

From this point, European settlement rapidly spread from the Cape Colony to Natal and later to the Transvaal – especially after the discovery of gold and diamonds. In many cases Europeans were able to occupy land abandoned by African people following the *difaqane* (see p391).

Over the next 100 to 150 years an ever-increasing number of Europeans from South Africa settled in areas that became the colonies of Swaziland, Nyasaland (Malawi), Northern and Southern Rhodesia (Zambia and Zimbabwe), Bechuanaland (Botswana), Basotholand (Lesotho), German South West Africa (Namibia) and Portuguese East Africa (Mozambique). With this change, Southern Africans would never again be permitted to follow entirely traditional ways.

For the colonial and modern history of the individual countries, see the relevant country chapters.

In Quest of Livingstone by Colum Wilson & Aisling Irwin is the story of two British travellers who followed the footsteps of David Livingstone, the great explorer, through Southern Africa.

1836

Groups of Boers, dissatisfied with British rule in the Cape Colony, begin a decade of migration known as the Great Trek; increasing numbers of Voortrekkers abandon their farms and cross the Senqu (Orange) River.

19th century

The face of Southern Africa changes significantly as the earlier trickle of European settlers to South Africa becomes widespread colonial settlement, filtering through to many parts of the region.

2006

A resettlement program relocating nearly all of Botswana's and Namibia's San from their ancestral lands earns the Botswana government a reprimand from the UN's Committee on the Elimination of Racial Discrimination.

The Culture

DAILY LIFE

Southern Africa covers an enormous geographical area with an incredibly diverse population that has stark wealth differentiation between and within the countries of the region. Therefore, giving a precise impression of daily life for Southern Africans is virtually impossible. However, there are some generalisations we can make that represent very real (and in some cases terrifying) trends afflicting everyday life in the region. For more country-specific detail, please see this section near the beginning of each country chapter.

The Southern African People's Solidarity Network (SAPSN; www.sapsn.org), is a network of civil society organisations that promote socioeconomic policies sympathetic to the rights of people in the region.

In this southernmost region of the continent, life varies considerably between the 'haves' and the 'have nots'. Middle-class and wealthy families live in homes reflecting that wealth, and many leafy, richer neighbourhoods could be just about anywhere in the Western world. Leisure time is often defined by time spent at upmarket (and in the case of South Africa, heavily guarded) shopping centres, which provide alfresco dining, plenty of retail therapy and certainly a place 'to be seen'.

However, for the millions of Southern Africans (the vast majority of the population) who still live in great poverty, life is about survival. Simple huts or enclosures contain large extended families, and obtaining and preparing food is the focus of daily life.

There are two major plights affecting the households of the majority of Southern Africa's population. Firstly, the food insecurity that afflicts the region is a distressing problem that devastates households and seems to have no end in sight. Dependent on the rains, the region is caught up in a merciless cycle of drought (and in some cases floods) that, when combined with other factors (see the boxed text, opposite), leads to regular food shortages.

The largest problem facing the people of Southern Africa, though, is HIV/AIDS. The sub-Saharan region is the worst-affected region in Africa and, while the statistics are simply dreadful, the socioeconomic effects are overwhelming. Two thirds (about 22 million people) of the global total of people with HIV live in sub-Saharan Africa. South Africa has the world's largest HIV-positive population (5.7 million people), and national adult HIV prevalence is above 15% in that country as well as in Botswana, Lesotho, Namibia, Zambia and Zimbabwe. Swaziland has an HIV prevalence rate of around 26% – the highest ever documented in a country anywhere in the world. Lesotho and Mozambique are suffering from an increase in the epidemic, particularly among pregnant women and young people. However, in more positive recent developments, Botswana and Zimbabwe have both recently recorded drops in HIV infections, proving that through education, change is possible.

Have a look at www.safaids.org.zw for the latest news on the battle against HIV/AIDS in Southern Africa.

Unlike diseases that attack the weak, HIV/AIDS predominantly hits the productive members of a household – young adults. It's particularly rife among those who are highly educated, and have relatively high earnings and mobility. This has an enormous impact on household incomes, with the region facing the loss of a large proportion of a generation in the prime of its life. This has also meant a sharp increase in the number of orphans, of grandparents being pressured into assuming parenting roles of young children, and of children pulled out of school to care for the sick, grow food or earn money. There's still a lot of stigma attached to HIV/AIDS too, and many locals won't admit to the cause of a loved one's death.

HIV/AIDS has led to a sharp decrease in life expectancy in Southern Africa. Recent projections have put life expectancy at just under 50 years

FAMINE & FLOOD

Food shortages and hunger remain critically serious problems in Southern Africa. At one stage in 2005, it was feared that between 10 and 12 million people faced potential starvation. Heard it all before? Well, that's probably because the region suffers from a seemingly endless cycle of food insecurity – but that doesn't make it any less real or less horrifying.

The simple reason for the food shortage is prolonged dry spells, which lead to crop failure. The reasons behind the region's continued problems in feeding itself, however, are more complex and deeply rooted. There is a multitude of causes including inadequate agricultural policies, the ripping away of a generation of workers through the HIV/AIDS epidemic, a lack of employment opportunities, bad governance and environmental degradation.

In addition to these problems, floods also wreak havoc, especially in western Zambia, and northern Namibia and Botswana. In 2009, the Zambezi River was at its highest level in 60 years and severe flooding in Zambia and Namibia displaced thousands of people and destroyed crops and infrastructure

If you're looking to make a financial donation to assist in alleviating food shortages or would like information, you can get in touch with the following organisations (most accept donations online):

Christian Charity Tearfund (www.tearfund.org) Local Christian organisations work in conjunction with Tearfund running food-for-work programs and supporting agricultural projects.

Oxfam (www.oxfam.org.uk) Plenty of up-to-date information about food shortages, as well as on its work in Malawi, Mozambique, Zambia and Zimbabwe.

Red Cross (www.redcross.org.uk) Provides emergency food aid when required throughout the region, especially in Lesotho, South Africa, Zambia and Zimbabwe.

UN World Food Programme (www.wfp.org) Make a direct donation to help feed people in the region, specifying that you want your money to go towards the effort in Southern Africa.

World Vision (www.worldvision.org) As one of the largest long-term development and relief NGOs operating in the region, World Vision provides emergency food distribution and helps to recover lost livelihoods.

across the region – between 1990 and 1995 it peaked at just over 60 years. With hundreds of thousands dying every year in Southern Africa from AIDS alone, population growth is estimated to be near zero in most countries and even falling into the negative.

All the countries in Southern Africa are conservative in their attitudes towards gay men and lesbians (see p748). In traditional African societies gay sexual relationships are a cultural taboo. In practice, rights for gay citizens contrast strongly between countries. South Africa's progressive constitution, for example, outlaws discrimination on the basis of sexual orientation, and gay couples have won many rights. On the other hand Namibia and Zimbabwe have strongly condemned homosexuality, with President Mugabe describing homosexuals as 'worse than pigs and dogs'.

South Africa has one of the highest incidences of rape in the world (p396) and, as many are too afraid to report the crime, the true extent of the problem is probably much worse than official figures would suggest. Another tragic issue in the region is sexual abuse in schools; the sexual abuse of girls by teachers is an enormous problem, and as a result, many girls are reluctant to attend school. The perpetrators often cite low wages and poor working conditions as justification for partaking in this perceived 'fringe benefit'. Sadly, national and local governments and individuals have so far done little to express their intolerance for such unacceptable behaviour.

Working to end violence against women and supporting victims of rape, Rape Crisis is based in Cape Town South Africa. Click onto www.rapecrisis.org.za if you'd like to learn more about its work.

SPORT

Football (soccer) is without doubt the most popular sport across Southern Africa, especially for black Africans. You'll see dusty fields everywhere

2010 FIFA WORLD CUP

At the time of research, excitement in Southern Africa was growing over the kick-off of the **2010 FIFA World Cup** (www.fifa.com/worldcup), which is being hosted in South Africa. Beginning on 11 June and running for a month, matches will be held at 10 venues from Cape Town to Polokwane (Pietersburg), and the country is spending more than US$1 billion on building new stadiums and renovating existing structures. The event is causing a groundswell of expectation in the entire region, which is expected to benefit from the international spotlight and a flood of visitors during the competition (around 350,000 visitors). For this football-mad region, it's the biggest sporting event in its history.

with ragtag balls used for informal matches – training grounds for the big leagues.

Essentially the national leagues work in a similar way to European football. Unsurprisingly, South Africa has the major league (www.psl.co.za), which runs from August to May. The winners of each league qualify for the African Champions League, in which the champions of countries from all over the continent compete. The best countries compete in the African Cup of Nations, held every two years: the next one is in Angola in 2010.

For all your Southern African football news, including the regional competition, see www.cosafa.com.

The Cosafa Castle Cup, run by the Council of Southern Africa Football Associations, is the annual regional competition, with participation by 14 countries, including all nine Southern African countries. Angola, South Africa, Zambia and Zimbabwe are the most successful, having won the Cup three times each.

Although cricket, rugby and golf have traditionally been the domain of the white population, they have grown in stature and popularity, especially in South Africa, with that country's return to the international scene. The South African cricket team in particular has been experiencing a lot of on-field success in recent times. They head the official International Cricket Council (ICC) rankings as both the best international Test cricket and One Day international team. They beat England (in England) and drew against India (in India) in 2008, but perhaps their greatest feat in recent times was their defeat of Australia in a three Test Match series in 2008/09 in Australia (although the Aussies soon had revenge trouncing the Proteas in South Africa in early 2009).

For all your cricket news click onto www.cricinfo.com, including the latest ICC rankings by country, match reports, articles by leading commentators and the results of recent games.

Zimbabwe also fields an international cricket side in One Day cricket (though it no longer competes in Test Match cricket). The current team is not very competitive.

MULTICULTURALISM

Southern Africa's population is made up of Bantu-speaking people (the majority) who migrated from the north and west of the African continent (p33), later-arriving Europeans (including Dutch, British, Portuguese and Germans), Indians and pockets of the Khoisan (an ancient Stone Age people who survive in small numbers, mainly in Botswana and Namibia; see p32). 'Bantu' refers to a convenient language-grouping, not a race, and in reality the Bantu ethnic group comprises many subgroups or tribes, each with its own language, customs and traditions, living all over the region.

Broadly speaking, two societies and cultures (Western and African) run in parallel, and they rarely cross. As you might expect, in a Western situation social customs are similar to those in Europe, although often a touch more formal – but at the same time more friendly – than in other parts of the Western world. For example, Afrikaners will often shake hands and say their name, even if you're only meeting them briefly. While you'll meet locals of European origin and 'Europeanised' black Africans all over the region, the societies and cultures are predominantly African.

Southern Africa is very multicultural and surprisingly peaceful given the extraordinary number of ethnic groups. While much of the focus in South Africa has been on black and white relations, there is also friction and distrust between blacks, coloureds and South Africans of Indian descent. However, in the case of South Africa, the relatively peaceful transition to democracy from the last remaining white minority government in the region in 1994 (p394) was a true miracle of multiculturalism, despite ongoing racial friction.

Many countries within Southern Africa are incredibly ethnically diverse. This is exemplified in South Africa, which has 11 official languages!

Integrating European and African populations has been a source of tension for many years in the region, exacerbated by colonial rule, apartheid governments and, in Zimbabwe, a policy of reclaiming white-owned farms in recent years. However, disharmony stretches much further back with the destruction and dispersal of the *difaqane* (p36), which led to tribal affiliations being disrupted among various Bantu groups in the region. This was exacerbated in South Africa by the Great Trek and the Voortrekkers, who settled into areas they believed were 'vacant' (see p391).

Migration from the poorer countries to the wealthier countries in the region has also brought about tensions and hostility. South Africa for example has far more job opportunities than other countries in the region, and this has led to a great number of migrant workers (many illegal) drifting there. Africans who look different or don't speak the local language are often harassed by officialdom and the police. Locals are often suspicious of such people too as they think they are stealing their jobs and are responsible for crime.

Likewise, there has been a drift (some say avalanche) of Zimbabweans looking for work illegally in Botswana. The reason is simple – Botswana has a booming economy while Zimbabwe's economy has taken a severe downturn since the turn of the century; hopefully recent political changes in that country along with the dollarisation of the economy (p691) will help make things more stable.

Masters of Illusion: The World Bank and the Poverty of Nations by Catherine Caufield discusses the influence that the global development lending agency has had on poor countries around the world.

Back home, a migrant's money makes a big difference to the local economy – Lesotho is a good example, with many travelling to South Africa until the late 1990s to work in mines and sending money back home to their families. It is widely agreed, however, that this type of migration has also contributed to the spread of HIV/AIDS.

RELIGION

Christianity

Most people in Southern Africa follow Christianity or traditional religion, often combining aspects of both. South Africa, Malawi, Botswana and Namibia have very high Christian populations (between 70% and 80% of the general population), while Mozambique has the lowest (around 35%). All the Western-style Christian churches are represented (Catholics, Protestants, Baptists, Adventists etc), most of which were introduced in colonial times by

MOVERS & SHAKERS

For most country chapters in this book we've included a boxed text called 'Movers & Shakers', which profiles an influential African from that country, including Oliver Mtukudzi (Zimbabwe; p715), Nelson Mandela (South Africa; p395), Sir Seretse Khama (Botswana; p70), Samuel Nujoma (Namibia; p300), John Chilembwe (Malawi; p164), Malangatana Valente Ngwenya (Mozambique; p224), King Mswati III (Swaziland; p587) and Kenneth Kaunda (Zambia; p626). If you want an insight into some of the extraordinary people who have influenced life in Southern Africa, keep an eye out for these boxes.

Christianity in Southern Africa is known for its conservatism. Roman Catholic bishops in the region have controversially condemned the use of condoms in the fight against HIV/AIDS.

European missionaries. Their spread across the region reflects their colonial roots – the dominant Christian sect in Namibia is German Lutheranism, while Malawi is dominated by Protestant churches, founded by British missionaries. Mozambique's Portuguese heritage means Roman Catholicism is favoured among that country's Christians.

The influence of missionaries has been beneficial in education, campaigning against the slave trade, and in trying to raise the standard of living in Southern Africa; however, this was tempered by their search for ideological control and disruption to traditional cultures. They were certainly influential in Malawi (see p163) where the country's history and existence was shaped by missionaries such as Dr Livingstone.

Although Christian denominations in Southern Africa are generally conservative, many churches actively participate in the fight against HIV/AIDS. Organisations such as **CUAHA** (Churches against HIV/AIDS; www.cuaha.info) and **CRWRC** (Christian Reformed World Relief Committee; www.crwrc.org/pages/crwrc_aids.cfm) work with local churches to support families, care for those afflicted by the disease and reduce the stigma associated with HIV/AIDS.

South Africa's Archbishop Desmond Tutu said, 'When the missionaries came to Africa they had the Bible and we had the land. They said, "Let us pray." We closed our eyes. When we opened them we had the Bible and they had the land.'

Many indigenous Christian faiths have also been established, ranging from a small congregation meeting in a simple hut to vast organisations with millions of followers, such as the Zion and Apostolic churches in Zimbabwe and South Africa. In South Africa alone the Zion Church claims four million followers (the largest in the country).

Islam, Hinduism & Judaism

Islam is also followed in some areas, predominantly in the north of Malawi and along its lakeshore, and in the northern provinces of Mozambique, where 35% of the population attest to the Islamic faith, the highest percentage in Southern Africa. There are also Hindus and Jews, particularly in South Africa, but their numbers are small.

Traditional

There are many traditional religions in Southern Africa, but no great temples or written scriptures. For outsiders, beliefs can be complex (and to the Western mind, illogical), as can the rituals and ceremonies that surround them. Most traditional religions are animist – based on the attribution of life or consciousness to natural objects or phenomena – and many accept the existence of a Supreme Being, with whom communication is possible through the intercession of ancestors. Thus, ancestors play a particularly strong role. Their principal function is to protect the tribe or family, and they may on occasion show their pleasure (such as a good harvest) or displeasure (such as a member of the family becoming sick).

WITCHCRAFT

Within many traditional African religions, there is a belief in spells and magic (usually called witchcraft or, in some places, *mutu*). In brief simplistic terms it goes like this: physical or mental illnesses are often ascribed to a spell or curse having been put on the sufferer. Often, a relative or villager is suspected of being the 'witch' who placed the curse, often for reasons of spite or jealousy. A traditional doctor, also called a diviner or witchdoctor, is then required to hunt out the witch and cure the victim. This is done in different ways in various parts of the region, and may involve the use of herbs, divining implements, prayers, chanting, dance or placing the spell in a bottle and casting it into a remote spot (if you find such a bottle in the bush, don't touch it).

However, services do not come free of charge, and many witchdoctors demand high payments – up to US$20, in countries where an average month's earnings may be little more than this. The 'witches' who are unearthed are frequently those who cannot defend themselves – the sick, the old or the very poorest members of society. There are even reports of very young children being accused by witchdoctors of harbouring evil spirits.

ARTS

Rock art created by the San people since time immemorial is the one artistic tradition that unifies the region, and can still be seen today in many Southern African countries (see the boxed text, p34).

The countries and indigenous peoples of Southern Africa all have their own artistic traditions, often interwoven with culture and beliefs. See the individual country chapters for country-specific information.

When travelling around the region, the more popular handicrafts you're likely to see (and be able to purchase) include San crafts (particularly in Namibia and Botswana) such as jewellery and leatherwork, bows and arrows and ostrich shell beads; mohair products such as tapestries and ponchos, especially in Lesotho and South Africa; wooden carvings, particularly in places where tourists are likely to wander – wildlife carvings such as huge giraffes are popular, and you'll even find earthmovers, aeroplanes and helicopters; exquisite palm-woven and African-themed baskets, particularly renowned in Botswana and Zambia; pottery, often highly decorative and of course very practical; Shona sculpture (Zimbabwean), renowned worldwide, with recurring themes such as the metamorphosis of man into beast, and Makonde sculpture (Mozambican); glassware and candles (Swazi) in the shape of regional wildlife and in the case of the former often made from recyclable material; and township art, which has developed sober themes in an expressive, colourful and usually light-hearted manner. Ranging from complex wirework toys to prints and paintings, deceptively naive images in township art can embody messages far from simple. It developed through the political trauma in South Africa, and this is often reflected in the violent themes of the work. It has also spread to other countries in the region.

In South Africa the woodcarvers of Limpopo's Venda region have started to gain international recognition.

Galleries in the region display works from Southern African artists and include more traditional sculpture and paintings. Painters often interpret the landscape, wildlife and the diverse peoples of the region – Namibia, South Africa, Mozambique and Zambia in particular have galleries that display work from local artists.

> If you've developed a taste for wonderful Shona sculpture, but had no room in your bag to bring some home, see www.shonaart.co.za to order online.

> *Images of Power* by D Lewis-Williams and T Dowson is a fascinating study of the art of the San people, utilising modern scientific techniques and rediscovered records of discussions between the San and early European settlers.

Literature

Southern Africa has a strong tradition of oral literature among the various Bantu groups. Traditions and stories were preserved and passed on from generation to generation. In many parts of the region written language was introduced only by Christian missionaries and assumed more importance in the 20th century. Common forms of literature that have developed include short stories, novels and poetry.

Although writers have focused on themes usually concerning their own country, there are common threads. Nationalism, white minority rule, the struggle for independence and life after colonialism are all themes explored by Southern African writers. In Malawi (p166) oppression and abuse of power were common themes through the Banda years, after independence. Samson Kambalu is a contemporary author who writes about growing up in '70s and '80s Malawi. Guerrilla poets such as Marcelino dos Santos from Mozambique (p223) make fascinating reading. In many countries the growth of literature has paralleled the struggle for independence and freedom.

Works by authors such as Bessie Head from Botswana (p72) address African village life and landscape, and Zimbabwean writers (p692) include precolonial traditions, myths and folk tales in their writings.

Stephen Gill has written several historical books on Lesotho (p140) and, thanks to him, archives were established and much local history saved.

The Penguin Book of Southern African Stories, edited by Stephen Gray, features stories (some of which are thousands of years old) from around the region. The stories show the similarities and common threads in various literary traditions.

White South African writers have had much overseas success, with literary giants such as Nadine Gordimer and JM Coetzee both awarded Nobel prizes for literature. If you want to get a sense of where South Africa has come from and where it's going, delving into its literary roots is a good place to start (p398). Local literature takes you back into the days of apartheid (from both a black and a white perspective) and the realities of building the rainbow nation.

Architecture

The greatest indigenous architectural legacy is in the past – in Zimbabwe the ruins of great stone cities such as Great Zimbabwe (p718) and Khami are rare examples of medieval African architecture in the region. Mapungubwe (p561) in South Africa also contains excellent examples of ancient historical buildings from a forgotten kingdom.

Architecturally, the colonial legacy in Southern Africa is dominated by European designs, with South Africa containing by far the best examples. Pretoria's stately Union Building has won much acclaim, while art deco design sprang up in Durban and Cape Town after building booms in the early 20th century. Unique Cape Dutch buildings, especially townhouses, can be seen throughout Cape Town. Examples of 19th- and 20th-century English architecture (especially Victorian) can be seen in many parts of the region and at times in the most unlikely of places (such as Livingstonia in Malawi, p176, and Shiwa Ng'andu in Zambia, p647), while in Namibia, Germany has left a colonial legacy of late 19th century–designed places, including art nouveau design. In Mozambique, Mozambique Island is an architectural treasure trove and includes the oldest European building in the southern hemisphere (p263). Maputo's very fine train station, dating from 1910, was selected by *Newsweek* magazine recently as one of the 10 best in the world.

Safari lodges, such as those in Zimbabwe, can be architecturally exceptional – a mix of an English sensibility with African pieces and environment.

Dance

In Southern Africa, dance, along with music, is often closely linked with, and plays an important role in, social function rather than being mere entertainment. Movement is regarded as an important type of communication in traditional African societies, and dance can be associated with contact between spirits and the living; traditional healers often performed curative dances to rid patients of sickness. Symbolic gestures, mime, props, masks, costumes and body painting can all play a part. If you have the chance to see traditional song and dance while you're in Southern Africa, try not to miss out; places where it's possible to do this are listed throughout the country chapters.

Dance also helps to define culture, and in Swaziland, for example, the Umhlanga (reed) dance (see the boxed text, p593) plays a very important role in society, drawing the nation together and reinforcing Swazi culture. Mozambicans are excellent dancers, and Arabic influence is evident in their slow, swaying rhythms – check out the Mozambique National Company of Song & Dance (p234).

FOOD & DRINK

The business of eating tends to be all about survival for most of the population, and much of the day's activity is associated with the preparation of meals. In a region racked by famine, with many countries not able to consistently produce enough food to feed their own population, food is about functionality, not creativity.

Although food is not a real highlight of Southern Africa, the variety and quality of food for visitors and well-to-do locals is improving all the time. Certainly an urban setting will usually mean more variety for visitors, and the colonial legacy in some countries does mean some intriguing culinary combinations.

South Africa is the best place to eat and certainly has the most variety, an inheritance of its varied African, European and Asian population. Here you'll find a fusion of influences from the curry and coriander that wafted over the Indian Ocean, to Afrikaner favourites such as steaks the size of half a cow and *boerewors* (a tasty Afrikaner sausage), and Cape Malay cuisine, an exotic mix of spices and local produce.

Seafood is popular in places that have a coastline (be it lake or ocean), both with locals and travellers. In Swaziland you'll readily find prawns on menus, courtesy of Mozambique, which itself blends a variety of influences (African, Indian and Portuguese) into its delectable seafood offerings. In Malawi eating *chambo* (fried fish) by the lake is a highlight. Around the Cape and Winelands of South Africa, look for lightly spiced fish stews, *snoekbraai* (grilled snoek), mussels, oysters and even lobster.

A favourite for many visitors to Southern Africa is the fruit, and depending on the season you'll find bananas, pineapples, pawpaws (papayas), mangoes and avocados in plentiful supply.

The San eat *hoodia*, a prickly, cucumber-like plant, to suppress their appetite on long hunting treks – in the West *hoodia* is used in one of the most popular weight-loss drugs on the market.

Staples & Specialities

In parts of Southern Africa, especially in South Africa, Namibia and Botswana, meat features as a staple, and anything that can be grilled, is – including ostrich, crocodile, warthog and kudu. Meat also features in local celebrations.

Takeaway snack food found on the street may include bits of grilled meat, deep-fried potato or cassava chips, roasted corn cobs, boiled eggs, peanuts (called ground nuts locally), biscuits, cakes, fried dough balls (which approximate doughnuts) and miniature green bananas. Prices are always dirt cheap (unfortunately, often with the emphasis on dirt).

For something more substantial, but still inexpensive, the most common meal is the regional staple, boiled maize meal, which is called mielie pap in South Africa and Namibia, *sadza* in Zimbabwe, and *nshima* or *nsima* in countries further north. In Botswana, the staple is known as *bogobe*, in which sorghum replaces the maize. When fresh and well cooked, all varieties

TRAVEL YOUR TASTEBUDS

If you're not squeamish about watching wildlife during the day and then sampling it in the evening, meat lovers can try some (nonendangered) local produce: such dishes as warthog stew, buffalo steak and impala sausages go down a treat. They can be hard to find, but wildlife lodges and upmarket restaurants are usually the best bet.

Bunny chow is a South African favourite, also popular in Swaziland. It's basically curry inside a hollowed-out loaf, messy to eat but quite delicious.

African bush tucker varies across the region among Southern Africa's indigenous groups – for example, the San still eat many desert creatures including caterpillarlike mopane worms, prepared in many different ways, such as deep-fried, or just eaten raw.

FOOD ETIQUETTE

Most travellers will have the opportunity to share an African meal sometime during their stay and will normally be given royal treatment and a seat of honour. Although concessions are sometimes made for foreigners, to avoid offence be aware that table manners are probably different to those you're accustomed to. The African staple, maize or sorghum meal, is the centre of nearly every meal. It is normally taken with the right hand from a communal pot, rolled into balls, dipped in some sort of *relish* – meat, beans or vegetables – and eaten. As in most societies, it is considered impolite to scoff food, or to hoard it or be stingy with it. If you do, your host may feel that he or she hasn't provided enough. Similarly, if you can't finish your food, don't worry; the host will be pleased that you have been satisfied. Often, containers of water or home-brew beer may be passed around from person to person. However, it is not customary to share coffee, tea or bottled soft drinks.

are both tasty and filling, and are usually eaten with a *relish* (sauce or stew), which is either very simple (eg boiled vegetable leaves) or something more substantial, such as a stew of beef, fish, beans or chicken.

The main meal is at noon, so most cheap eateries are closed in the evening. In the morning you can buy coffee or tea (with or without milk – the latter is cheaper) and bread, sometimes with margarine, or maybe a slightly sweetened breadlike cake.

Up a notch, and popular with tourists, are traditional meals of mielies (cobs of maize) and *relish*, or Western dishes, such as beef or chicken served with rice or chips (fries). More elaborate options, such as steaks, pies, fish dishes, pasta and something that resembles curry over rice, are worth trying for a change.

Most cities also have speciality restaurants serving genuine (or at least pretty close to it) Indian, Thai, Chinese, Lebanese, Mexican or ethnic African (such as Ethiopian or West African) cuisine.

Drinks

You can buy tea and coffee in many places, from top-end hotels and restaurants to humble local eating houses.

In bars, hotels and bottle stores you can buy beer and spirits, either imported international brands or locally brewed drinks. South African and Namibian beers (Windhoek is excellent) are available throughout the region, and in many areas they dominate local markets. Wonderful South African wines are widely available, as is a growing range of extremely popular spirit coolers.

Traditional beer of the region is made from maize, brewed in the villages and drunk from communal pots with great ceremony on special occasions, and with less ado in everyday situations. This product, known as *chibuku* (or *shake-shake*), is commercially brewed in many countries and sold in large blue paper cartons, or by the bucketful. It's definitely an acquired taste, and it does pack a punch.

Where to Eat & Drink

Street food is sold at roadsides, bus stations (and sometimes through windows of moving buses), and markets all over Africa; cleanliness is not a top priority, but it's cheap and convenient.

A food stall (also called a tea stall or a *barraca* in Mozambique), which is a basic eatery selling inexpensive African food housed in a shack or hut, can typically be found in markets, bus stations and around industrial areas, or any part of town with low rent and a good passing trade. Chowing down at one of these places can be a good way to meet locals. Meals at food stalls are served in a bowl, and while some locals prefer to eat with their hands, spoons are normally available. You may eat standing up, or at a simple table with chairs.

A grade above the food stalls are the takeaways and cheap restaurants in cities, large towns, and areas frequented by tourists. These tend to be slightly larger and cleaner and have better facilities.

Up another level are cheap to midrange restaurants (called a *salã de cha* in Mozambique), with tablecloths, menus and waiters, where meals cost from US$3 to US$5. Moving up the scale to the midrange, you'll typically pay US$5 to US$10 per person for the standard beef, chicken, fish, lamb and other dishes, but the price is justified by better quality, presentation, location and cleanliness.

You'll find straightforward international standards at top-end hotels and restaurants in cities and tourist areas, including plenty of steak places as well as French, British and Italian options.

South Africa, Namibia and Botswana have plenty of Western-style fast-food options – particularly popular are places specialising in fried or peri-peri (hot chilli) chicken. Chains are becoming common, and in new shopping malls you'll even find fast-food Thai, seafood and Middle Eastern outlets.

Want to cook it yourself? Pick up a copy of *Cooking the Southern African Way* by Kari Cornell. It includes authentic ethnic foods (even vegetarian recipes) from across the region; there's even a section on holiday and festival food.

Vegetarians & Vegans

Vegetarianism isn't widely understood in Africa, and many locals think a meal is incomplete unless at least half of it once lived and breathed. That said, if you're not worried about variety or taste, finding inexpensive vegetarian options isn't that difficult. In the cheapest places, you may have to stick to the mielies and greens. A step above that would be eggs and chips (which may be fried in animal fat) with whatever vegetables may be available. Those who eat fish should have even more luck, but note that many places will even serve chicken as a vegetarian dish, on the notion that it's not really meat. Nearly all midrange and upmarket restaurants offer some sort of genuine vegetarian dish, even if it's just a vegetable omelette or pasta and sauce. In larger cities and towns, a growing number of places specialise in light vegetarian cuisine – especially at lunchtime – and of course, Lebanese, Indian and Italian restaurants usually offer various interesting meat-free choices.

Music in Southern Africa

Jane Cornwell

Long before there were borders, there was music. Thousands of years ago, right across the handful of countries we now loosely term Southern Africa, a host of cultures were singing, dancing and creating rhythms to accompany their lives. And arguably it is music, more than any other aspect of culture, that has best survived the onslaught of Western influences. Not always untarnished, though: while some traditions persist, others have merged, shape-shifted, formed new genres. South Africa alone has the greatest range of musical styles on the African continent, helped along by its gargantuan recording industry. Some of these styles have spilled over into neighbouring countries, all of which have styles of their own.

The Drumcafe's Traditional Music of Black South Africa (2005), by Laurie Levine, is an exploration of the traditional music of black South Africa in ceremonies and rituals. The book includes musical scores, a look at some well-known artists and a handy CD. See also *www.drumcafe.org*

Music still marks the important stages of a Southern African person's life. It still enlightens, heals, invokes spirits. It still makes people dance, sing, holler. It does all this whatever the instrument – whose form can change according to ethnicity, geography, gender of the player and, sometimes, whatever objects are lying around. Expressing oneself through music isn't always easy: think long-suffering, government-censored Zimbabwe; or Namibia, whose music industry lacks distribution networks and major record labels and is only now slowly addressing the fact; or Mozambique, where most artists don't receive royalties, and promoters frequently don't pay. Regardless, music still pulses in Southern Africa like a heartbeat. So remember: just because you can't buy it – or even see or hear it – doesn't mean that it isn't there.

Held in May and December respectively, the Namibian Music Awards and the Sanlam-NBC Music Awards are two separate events intended to highlight and promote Namibian musicians and music producers.

A POTTED HISTORY

It's better, initially, to think ethnicity rather than country. Southern Africa is one of the world's oldest inhabited regions, after all. So old, in fact, that its earliest music can be traced back some 4000 years to the Stone Age, when groups of hunter-gatherer San played basic flutes and rattles and sang in their unique click language. Today's San still sound wonderfully ethereal, their singing, clapping trance dance the stuff of ritual, tourist haunts and left-field record labels. But it's the glorious vocal polyphony of the Bantu-speaking people – the Zulu, Xhosa and Sotho of the present day – that has come to characterise the region; this is the music that attracted Paul Simon before he recorded his seminal 1988 album *Graceland*.

Rage (www.rage.co.za) is *the* online South African magazine for black urban music news, features and reviews; also contains excellent articles on SA music history.

Long before the Christian missionaries and colonialists arrived in the 19th century, there were kingdoms. In Zambia, each king had his own royal musician, just as each kingdom had its own music. Singing often accompanied instrumental music played on horns, percussion, drums and the stringed *babatone* – the inspiration for the contemporary Zambian style, *kalindula* (see p53). Elsewhere, herders used flutes and other instruments to help control the movement of cattle. (Oh, and the first major style of South African popular music? None other than pennywhistle jive, later known as *kwela*.) The Bantu of Namibia played gourds, horn trumpets and marimbas, while the various ethnic groups of Malawi travelled widely, spreading musical influences from the Zulu of South Africa and the Islamic Yao people of Tanzania.

Colonial rule altered everything. The folk forms of Mozambique, a former Portuguese colony, bear hallmarks of colonial rule – though its main style, *marrabenta* (see p54), flourished after independence. Mozambican bands played a roots style similar to that heard in Tanzania and Zambia, while musicians in the heart of the country played a style like that of Zimbabwe. The music of southern Mozambique was altered by the influx of workers returning from the South African mines (revolutionary lyrics were delivered over regional melodies), just as the workers who have migrated from Lesotho to the mines and cities of neighbouring South Africa have developed a rich genre of sung oral poetry – or word music – that focuses on the experiences of migrant life. African folk music also became popular in Zambia, as troubadours entertained exhausted miners. In South Africa, Dutch farmers brought a European folk music that became what is known today as *boeremusiek*.

It's no wonder, then, that the banjo, violin, concertina and electric guitar have all had a profound influence on Southern African music. Malawian banjo-and-guitar duos were huge in the 1950s and '60s, after which South African *kwela* (see below) took over. The influence of guitar-based rumba from Zaire (now the Congo) was felt right across the region (political upheaval saw many Congolese musicians relocate to Southern Africa); its upstart cousin, soukous, has made its presence felt in everything from Zambian *kalindula* to Malawian *kwasa kwasa* (see p54). The gospel mega-genre has evolved from the teachings of 19th-century Christian missionaries, which were customised accordingly. Reckon those chord sequences in South African songs are familiar? Blame the Church.

Numerous musical styles have been born out of oppression, too. Ladysmith Black Mambazo's 'tiptoe' *isicathimiya* music, with its high-kicking, soft-stepping dance, has its origins in the all-male miners' hostels in South Africa's Natal Province (now KwaZulu-Natal) in the 1930s, with workers at pains not to wake their bosses. *Kwela* music, like most modern South African styles, came out of the townships; *kwela*, meaning 'jump up', was the instruction given to those about to be thrown into police vans during raids. Thomas Mapfumo's *chimurenga* (see p53) is once again the music of resistance in Zimbabwe, even if – for the majority of Zimbabwean musicians – outspokenness is just not the Zimbabwean way (see the boxed text, p50). Even the prolific Oliver 'Tuku' Mtukudzi (whose infectious dance pop, informed by the country's *jit*-jive and *tsava* rhythms, is known simply as 'Tuku music') has never done more than express his 'great disappointment' – though he did write Zimbabwe's first song about HIV/AIDs. (For more on Mtukudzi, see the boxed text, p715.)

Zimbabwe's first feature film, *Jit* (director Michael Raeburn, 1993), is an endearing romantic comedy, lifted by its exotic setting and irresistible *jit*-jive soundtrack. Boy, who has a pesky, beer-obsessed ancestral spirit, decides to get girl – who happens to have a gangster boyfriend. Fun, uplifting stuff.

In Malawi the intentionally controversial songs of politician and reggae giant Lucius 'The Soldier' Banda has spawned a slew of similarly antsy reggae outfits; there is also a softer reggae led by Black Missionaries and other Malawian Rastafarians. In postapartheid South Africa, freedom of expression is pretty much expected: rap, hip-hop and their indigenous sibling *kwaito* are as socially concerned as they are un-PC, depending on who you're listening to. South African jazz remains some of the best in the world; the international success of the likes of Afro-jazz chanteuse Simphiwe Dana and Afropop outfit Freshlyground has new audiences in new countries taking notice.

The popular music of Southern Africa has created itself by mingling local ideas and forms with those from outside the region. And while every country has its own distinctive and constantly evolving array of styles supported by local audiences, that doesn't mean you won't be in one place and hear something from somewhere else.

Launched in January 2009, Zimwaves (www.zimwavesradio.net) is a South Africa–based internet radio station that embraces banned protest music and airs Zimbabwe news feeds from the voice of America.

MUSICAL INSTRUMENTS

As with most traditional African instruments, the membranophones, chordophones, aerophones and idiophones of Southern Africa (OK, it's drums and string, wind and percussion instruments) tend to be found in rural areas. Local materials and found objects are often used to musical effect.

THE LION OF ZIMBABWE: THOMAS MAPFUMO

The Lion of Zimbabwe isn't exactly roaring, but he's pretty furious. Over 25 years of misrule by Robert Mugabe's government has seen his country's economy collapse. Crime, unemployment and food prices have soared; corruption and censorship are rife. Human rights abuses abound. 'These are not good circumstances,' says Thomas Mapfumo, who left Harare for the USA after the April 2000 elections, when his life was threatened. What makes things worse for the Zimbabwean musician is that this is a government he helped to bring about.

The politicisation of TM, as he is known, began in the mid-1970s in what was then Rhodesia. With the traditions and customs of his country subjugated by the ruling white minority, he began his career playing covers of American hits. But as the country lurched towards civil war, Mapfumo adopted a more revolutionary stance. He was banned from the airwaves. Decades later, his 2005 album, *Rise Up* (Real World Records), was similarly censored, though it still pulses from Harare's short-wave underground outfits. Its songs exhort the poor of Zimbabwe to fight for their rights; the youthful fire is also there on 2007's *The Long Walk* (High Times Records), originally released as *Ndangariro* in 1984.

As a boy from the countryside Mapfumo had learned Shona music from his grandparents, members – like 70% of the country's population – of an old culture with its own language and traditions. The Shona's signature instrument was the *mbira* – the so-called 'thumb piano' – an instrument with a sound known to invite ancestor spirits to possess the living during Shona religious ceremonies. Mapfumo began to arrange its splattering rhythms for the guitars of his band, Blacks Unlimited. The Shona-language lyrics of Blacks Unlimited sustained guerrilla fighters in the bush.

'We were an oppressed people in our own land,' Mapfumo says. 'When civil war came I found a focus.' He called the music *chimurenga,* which is Shona for 'struggle'. The white population was unable to understand the Shona language, but there was no ignoring Mapfumo's popularity in the wake of his album, *Hokoyo* (Watch Out; 1978), his first full-length release. The Ian Smith regime arrested Mapfumo in 1979, detaining him without trial for 90 days.

'They thought my music was encouraging youngsters to leave the country to train and come back fighting the government,' says Mapfumo, who cites Malcolm X and Martin Luther King as inspirations. 'I kept telling them it was just the traditional music of the people of Zimbabwe. There was no way I wasn't going to sing it.'

He remained prolific until Zimbabwean independence in 1980, releasing album after socially aware album and influencing other home-grown stars such as Oliver 'Tuku' Mtukudzi. With over 30 years of touring to his credit, his Blacks Unlimited *pungwes* – dance marathons featuring songs decrying HIV/AIDS, alcoholism and domestic violence – are the stuff of legend. He was unofficially bestowed with Zimbabwe's national symbol, the lion, as an alias, and exile has only increased his ire.

The year 2003 was the first time since 1962 that Mapfumo did not perform his traditional year-end shows in his homeland. Wisely, it seems: a bootleg release of a concert in England – featuring 'Masoja Nemapurisa', a song that told of police brutality – had youths loyal to Mugabe's Zanu-PF party destroying any copies they found.

Mapfumo and Blacks Unlimited continue to perform internationally; in 2005 Mapfumo opened the Live8 Africa concert in Cornwall, England. In 2009 he and his band played a free show on Santa Monica Pier in Los Angeles and an African music festival in Leeds, England. 'Down with dictatorships!' Mapfumo is wont to say between songs.

It took Mapfumo a while to admit that Mugabe's government was failing to deliver. 'We supported them when they were fighting in the bush. When they came to power they promised us many things, but the people are still suffering and the country is a mess. So what did we fight for?' He sighs. 'I see myself as a representative,' he adds. 'If anyone points a finger at me, they're pointing it at the people.'

For more from Mapfumo, see www.thomasmapfumo.blogspot.com.

In Namibia and Zimbabwe they tie dry cocoons together and strap them to dancers' ankles and waists; in Swaziland and South Africa, ankles rattle with dried fruit. Right across the region, everything from seeds, sticks and stalks to horsehair, oryx horns and goatskins are being shaken and blown, plucked and beaten. Some people in Namibia customise their drums by carving human faces into them.

The MaNyungwe people of northeastern Zimbabwe and northwestern Mozambique play *nyanga* music on panpipes, using different interlocking parts and quick bursts of singing in a sort of highly melodic musical round called *hocketting*. The Tonga people of Zambia do a similar thing with the animal horns called *nyele*. Variations on musical themes abound. The people of Sesfontein, Namibia, play reed pipes made from papaya stems. Basotho herding boys fashion their *lekolulo* flutes from sticks, cords and reeds. Everywhere, too, there is men's music and women's music, just as there are men's dances and women's dances. In Lesotho men use their mouths to play the stringed *setolo-tolo*. Namibian women play the scraped mouth-resonated bow.

Radio Chikuni (www.chikuniradio.org) is a community radio station broadcasting from Zambia's Chikuni Mission Station. It is dedicated to preserving the music and culture of the Batonga people – for whom music is a means of personal expression and communication – and, of course, to spreading the word.

There is a huge variety of drums (*ngoma* is the general term in the Bantu language). Stick-struck and hand-struck. Square, round and goblet-shaped. Small cowhide-covered ones for Zulu children. *Khetebu* 'bush-tom' drums beloved by the South African Tsonga. *Namalwa* 'lion-drums' of Zambia, played by inserting a stick through the drum head and rubbing. High-pitched talking drums (which are more commonly found in West Africa), held tight under the armpit and beaten with hook-shaped sticks; the Chewa people of Zambia call theirs the *vimbuza*. Drum families – mother, father, son, played in sets of three – like the conical drums of the northeast of Namibia. Drums to accompany reed ensembles, a cappella groups and, more often than not, ankle-rattling dances.

U-Carmen eKhayelitsha (2005) is an award-winning movie version of George Bizet's *Carmen*, set in a modern-day Cape Town township and combining music from the original opera with traditional African music.

If drums are the region's collective heartbeat, then the bow is its lonely soul. Southern Africa has several kinds of musical bow, many resembling the Brazilian *berimbau:* braced, mouth and/or gourd-resonated bows. Large hunting bows used as mouth bows. Two-stringed bows, played while simultaneously singing and resonating. Multiple bows with multiple strings. Mouth bows that use palm leaves instead of strings. String instruments abound: the lute (both strummed and bowed) is present in several forms. The Setswana of Botswana sing and strum the violinlike *segaba* (that's one string attached to a tin). The dances of the Nama of Namibia use flutes, drums and strings to emulate animal sounds.

The xylophone is also prevalent: the xylophone music of southern Malawi has influenced contemporary music in both East and Southern Africa. Mallet instruments with wooden keys are the main instrument of the Lozi and Nkoya of western Zambia, who place slats of wood over a long platform and gourds in descending size; up to four people play simultaneously. The marimbas of South Africa feed into the *mbaqanga* (township jive) style. It's an entirely different sound from that of the *mbila* (plural *timbila*) as played by the Chopi people of coastal Mozambique, which features resonators made from gourds and a buzzing tone created via a sheet of plastic (formerly an animal skin) over a hole in the ground. The master of *timbila* is the great Venancio Mbande, who still rehearses regularly with his large orchestra at his homestead in Chopiland.

Featuring big-name UK and African live acts and DJs, the award-winning three-day Lake of Stars Malawi Music Festival is held on the palm-fringed shores of Lake Malawi each October. It attracts around 1500 locals and travellers; proceeds go to charity.

But perhaps no instrument is as distinctively Southern African as the *mbira*, a hand-held instrument with small metal keys attached to an amplifying wooden box or calabash; attached shells and/or bottle tops distort and fuzz its sound. There are many traditions of so-called 'thumb pianos', each with a different name according to size and origin – it's the *kankobela* for the Tonga of Zambia. But it is Zimbabwe with which the *mbira* is generally identified: central to the Shona's marathon religious trance ceremonies known as *bira*, interlocking *mbira* patterns are considered both healing and spiritual. Since independence the *mbira* has been adapted to modern styles, such as the *chimurenga* guitars' bands.

Featuring music and interviews by Abdullah Ibrahim, Hugh Masekela and Miriam Makeba among others, Lee Hirsch's documentary *Amandla!! A Revolution in Four Part Harmony* (2002) explores the role of music in the fight against apartheid. Made over nine years, this is a deeply affecting film.

Oh, and then there's the voice. Be they roaring Zulu choirs or clicking San, four-part Nama harmonies or ululating Zambian churchgoers, the people of Southern Africa really do sing up some glorious polyphonic storms. Keep an ear out.

MUSICAL STYLES

A rich network of musical styles has developed in Southern Africa. And although those of South Africa are probably the best known, the entire region is humming with musical traditions, expressions and textures. In most countries there are polyphonic, repetitive patterns and call-and-response singing. There are styles that reflect ethnic diversity and geography. Cities are dominated by pop, rock, jazz and urban music, much of which combines core African principles with Western influences. Electric guitars fuel genres such as *afroma* in Malawi, *jit*-jive in South Africa, Zam-rock in

ANCIENT RHYTHMS: STELLA CHIWESHE

The majestic Stella Chiweshe has been performing with the *mbira* – the classic Zimbabwean thumb piano – for over 40 years. She is the first Southern African female *mbira* player to gain international recognition; her recordings capture the power and enchantment of this ancient instrument, traditionally revered as a medium of healing and of contact with ancestral spirits. Though based in Germany, Chiweshe recorded her 2006 double album *Double Check* (Piranha) in Zimbabwe, though she was plagued by a range of distractions, from petrol shortages to computer breakdowns. It features drums, guitars, marimbas – and the trancey, shimmering *mbira* sound.

'I first heard *mbira* from an old man when I was eight years old,' says Chiweshe, who was born in 1946 in Mujumhi, a village in Mhondoro, Zimbabwe. 'The people were listening to the drums, whose rhythm stayed so loud inside me I thought people could hear it.' She liked to accompany her grandfather on cattle-herding duty, insisting they go as far away as possible so she could sing loud and hard. Throughout her childhood – before independence and the success of the Second Chimurenga (Civil War; 1972–80) – *mbiras* were kept hidden, because the colonial government and the church had banned the instrument, fearing its power over the Shona.

Playing *mbira* was punished with prison and the ceremonies were secret: 'They told us when we were children to run away from people who played those instruments and to run towards the mission to tell the priest that we had seen the people of Diabore [Satan's people].' Chiweshe, the great-granddaughter of Munaka, a resistance fighter hanged by the British in days of the First Chimurenga (Civil War; 1896–97), was undeterred. She wasn't prepared to be limited by her sex, either. Her nonstop rhythm-making on any object she could find saw her creeping into ceremonies to watch. Only once did a man try to eject her: 'I screamed so much that I filled the house and they let me stay.'

By the time Chiweshe was 17 her passion to play *mbira* was like 'a ball of fire' and over the next decade, with the guidance of her uncle, she became a gifted *maridzambira* (*mbira* player), playing at healing ceremonies, weddings, funerals, concerts and parties, and even releasing a single, *Kasahwa,* in 1975, which went gold. After independence in 1980 she was invited to join the National Dance Company, newly formed to familiarise the liberated Zimbabweans with the richness of their cultural heritage. They toured throughout Zimbabwe, Mozambique and then Australia, India, North Korea and Europe. Chiweshe returned on solo tours.

Following the counsel of her spirit guide, she took the *mbira* to the denizens of Harare and to new generations in Zimbabwe and across the globe. In the process she's healed countless troubled souls. Known at home as Her Majesty, Chiweshe has recorded countless local singles and seven international albums; catch a gig to get a copy of 2009's self-released *Ndondopetera.*

Zambia. Local sounds keep migrating, metamorphosing. New genres keep forming. The following is a by-no-means-definitive round-up of what is being listened to.

Chimurenga

In Zimbabwe in the late 1970s the musician Thomas Mapfumo and the Blacks Unlimited transferred traditional Shona *mbira* patterns to the electric guitar. They sang songs of resistance, using bright, harmonised vocals, against the white-controlled Rhodesian government. *Chimurenga,* meaning 'struggle', became a tool of social activism and, with lyrics in Shona, a secret means of communication. Banned by Zimbabwean state radio then, much of today's *chimurenga* bubbles away underground, though artists such as Raymond Majongwe have started eschewing political lyrics to gain airplay. Apolitical, good-time *sungura* guitar music (the current industry's favoured genre) and bland Shona impersonations of hip-hop and *ragga* (a dance-oriented style of reggae) abound.

Zimbabwe contemporary vibes (www.zimvibes.com) is a music, fashion arts and culture website with links to internet radio and beyond.

Gospel

Gospel music is huge everywhere. In Malawi spiritual songs are sung in church, at school assemblies and political functions, and during everyday tasks. Many of Zambia's Christian churches boast US-style gospel synthesisers and guitars. The effects of popular influences on the realm of the church can be heard in the music of top-sellers Adonai Pentecostal Singers and Emphraim. Traditional Botswanan music is present in their church singing. Zimbabwe's lucrative gospel market is dominated by Pastor Charles Charamba and his *sungura*-based songs (gospel singers in Zimbabwe are as big as the biggest popular music stars). South Africa is the really commercial holy roller: a mega-selling amalgam of European, American, Zulu and other African traditions, neatly divided into traditional and modern styles. Look out for Rebecca Malope, South African Gospel Singers and the 2009 Grammy-winning Soweto Gospel Choir.

Held each July in Selebi-Phikwe, between Gaborone and Francistown, Botswana's National Music Eisteddfod showcases traditional dances and music from around the country, courtesy of its schools, colleges and choirs.

Jazz

What Malawi calls 'jazz' began in the late 1960s when, inspired by South African *kwela* music, bands such as Chimvu Jazz featured semirural musicians on acoustic instruments – a tradition that continues today. In Botswana most popular music tends to be labelled 'jazz', but it is probably *gumba-gumba* ('party-party') music – modernised Zulu and Setswana music mixed with traditional jazz – that comes closest to it. Zambia's Zam-rock has its jazzy elements. But if you're after jazz that is structurally, harmonically and melodically distinctive – and is, unequivocally, jazz – then head to South Africa. What was famously an expatriate music representing the suffering of a people is now a thriving, progressive force. Moses Khumalo, Judith Sephumo, Andile Yenana and the legendary Abdullah Ibrahim and his reformed ensemble Ekaya are at the vanguard.

Filmmaker and musician Kenny Gilmore is on a mission to raise the profile of Malawian music. His documentary *Deep Roots Malawi* (due for release January 2010) showcases the country's musical traditions; his band Sangalala fuses pop, reggae, jazz and blues with Malawian rhythms. For more, see www.myspace.com/sangalala.

Kalindula

The urban dance style known as *kalindula* has its roots in the Bemba traditions of northern Zambia's Luapula Province – where a stringed instrument called the *babatone* swings like a double bass. Inspired (like many Southern African genres) by Congolese rumba, *kalindula* took hold in the mid-1970s in the wake of the presidential decree that 95% of broadcast music should be Zambian. Most *kalindula* bands broke up following the country's economic collapse in the 1990s. But with the likes of dreadlocked

TOP 10 SOUTHERN AFRICAN ALBUMS

- *Rise Up* (Real World), Thomas Mapfumo
- *Senzo* (Sunny Side Records), Abdullah Ibrahim
- *Double Check* (Piranha), Stella Chiweshe
- *Best of Miriam Makeba and the Skylarks* (BMG), Miriam Makeba
- *Soul Marrabenta* (Riverboat), Mabula
- *Shaka Zulu* (Warner), Ladysmith Black Mambazo
- *Rebel Woman* (Cumbancha), Chiwoniso
- *Indestructible Beat of Soweto Volume One* (Earthworks), various artists
- *Zambia Roadside* (Sharp Wood Productions), various artists
- *A Handful of Namibians* (On the Corner), various artists

Brian Chilala fusing rock, reggae and *kalindula* beats, and the popularity of Black Muntu's 'kalifunku' sound, *kalindula* is enjoying a renaissance.

Kwaito

Post 1994, *kwaito* (*kway*-to, meaning hot or angry) exploded onto South Africa's dance floors. A rowdy mix of bubblegum, hip-hop, R&B, *ragga*, *mbaqanga*, traditional, jazz, British and American house music – *kwaito* is nothing short of a lifestyle. Chanted or sung in township slang (usually over programmed beats), *kwaito*'s lyrics range from the anodyne to the fiercely political. Given an international lease of life as the soundtrack for the feature film *Tsotsi* (which bagged the 2006 Oscar for Best Foreign Film, and saw *kwaito* star Zola playing a gangster), *kwaito* is similarly huge across the Southern African region. It's Lesotho's favourite music style. If you're in Namibia, look out for The Dogg and Gazza. In Zambia, try the *kwaito*-house of Ma Africa. If you're in South Africa, take your pick.

Yfm (www.yfm.co.za) is South Africa's most popular youth station, with an emphasis on live podcasting and blogging and a 50% self-imposed local music quota.

Kwasa Kwasa

Beginning in Zaire in the mid-1980s and spreading quickly to surrounding areas, *kwasa kwasa* (from the French street slang, *quoi ca?* – what's this?) took its cue from Congolese rumba and soukous. Characterised by an all-important lead guitar and lighter background drumming, *kwasa kwasa* songs typically let guitar and drums set the pace before the vocals enter, with an intricate guitar solo somewhere in the middle. Arguments rage over whether *kwasa kwasa* is actually just rumba; for others it's simply a dance style. Everyone from politicians to street vendors knows how to do the *kwasa kwasa*, booties wildly gyrating – à la American hip-hop – while legs and torsos are kept still.

Marrabenta

Want the latest music news from Mozambique? Find daily updates of goings on at www.einnews.com/mozambique/newsfeed-mozambique-music.

Sounding a little like salsa or merengue, *marrabenta* is the best-known urban dance music in Mozambique, and one created from a fusion of imported European music played on improvised materials: oil cans, wooden stakes and fishing lines. Taking its name from the Portuguese word 'to break' (hard-playing musos frequently snapped their guitar strings), *marrabenta*'s local-language songs of love and social criticism were banned by Portuguese colonialists – ensuring its popularity post-independence. Stalwart *marrabenta* band Ghorwane uses horns, guitars, percussion and strong vocal harmonies; *marrabenta*-meets-dance-music diva Mingas is a mega-celebrity.

Rap & Hip-Hop

The genre that was born in New York over three decades ago now has another home in (or has come back to) Africa – with some fascinating hybrids as a result. Young Swaziland rap groups – and indeed, rap groups across Southern Africa – are using the medium to educate listeners about HIV/AIDS. South Africa's rappers are exploring uncharted territory: founder member of cult crews Groundworks and Audio Visual, Ben Sharpa fuses hip-hop, dubstep and electronica with sparkling lyrics. In Namibia, ex-con and one-time street kid Jericho, aka J-Twizzle, is one of the country's most successful MCs. In Botswana, Game Zeus Bantsi is flying the flag for homegrown rap: 'We need to set goals, organise systems of distribution, proper management and strategic marketing. We need to work together,' he says.

Environment

Southern Africa's environment is as fragile as elsewhere on the continent, with exploitation and mismanagement the cause of many long-term problems. In order to ensure you have a minimal impact on this unique place, please keep in mind every visitor's shared responsibility (p20).

THE LAND

Southern Africa consists of a plateau rising from 1000m to 2000m, with escarpments on either side. Below the escarpments lies a coastal plain, which is narrowest in Namibia and widest in southern Mozambique.

Good safari companions: Chris and Tilde Stuart's *Field Guide to Mammals of Southern Africa* and *A Field Guide to the Tracks and Signs of Southern and East African Wildlife,* and *The Safari Companion: A Guide to Watching African Mammals,* by Richard Estes.

The most prominent break in the Southern African plateau is the Great Rift Valley – a 6500km-long fissure where tectonic forces have attempted to rip the continent of Africa in two. This enormous fault in the earth's crust runs from the Jordan Valley (between Israel and Jordan) in the north, southward through the Red Sea, where it enters Ethiopia's Danakil Depression. At this point, it heads south across Kenya, Tanzania and Malawi, dividing in two at one stage, to form the great lakes of East Africa. Lake Malawi is the third-largest lake in Africa and lies in a trough formed by the valley. This feature has created unique fish life. The lake has more fish species than any inland body of water in the world – there are over 500, and 350 of these are endemic to the lake. This spreading zone ends at the present site of Lake Kariba (p660), between Zimbabwe and Zambia.

The highest part of the region is Lesotho (often called the Kingdom in the Sky) and the neighbouring Drakensberg area, where many peaks rise above 3000m, including Thabana-Ntlenyana (p136; 3482m), which is the highest point in Southern Africa. Other highland areas include the Nyika Plateau (in northern Malawi and northeastern Zambia; p177), Mt Mulanje (in southern Malawi; p205), the Eastern Highlands (between Zimbabwe and Mozambique; p709) and the Khomas Hochland (Central Namibia; p310).

These highlands provide jaw-dropping scenery, as well as some of the best-preserved and most distinctive plants, wildlife and ancient rock art (see the boxed text, p34) in the region. Hiking, climbing and mountain biking are just some of the myriad activities on offer in these often wonderfully preserved patches of African wilderness.

Lower and more isolated hills include the characteristic inselbergs of Namibia (see Spitzkoppe, p336) and South Africa's Karoo (p475), and the lush Zomba Plateau (p196) in central Malawi.

WILDLIFE

Click onto www.conservation-southernafrica.org for information about conservation work in Southern Africa's transfrontier conservation areas, and continuing work to create wildlife and habitat corridors.

Southern Africa contains some of the most accessible and varied wildlife watching found anywhere on the continent, and it's the major attraction of the area. Countries all over the region provide opportunities, and each has its highlights (even smaller countries such as Swaziland have magnificent wildlife viewing, which can offer great alternatives to better-known parks), but for sheer variety and numbers, South Africa and Botswana top the list.

The best times of day for wildlife viewing are early in the morning and in the late afternoon/evening, when many animals are looking for their next meal. Planting yourself at a water hole at these times can be very rewarding. Night safaris provide wonderful wildlife-viewing opportunities, especially to see many nocturnal animals such as genets and bushbabies (look in the trees, not just on the ground).

Happily, Southern African parks are some of the best managed in Africa, and the development of the massive transfrontier parks (see the boxed text, p63) in the region, which link national parks and wildlife migration routes in different countries, should open up even more opportunities for wildlife viewing.

Rhinos aren't named for their colour, but for their lip shape: 'white' comes from *wijde* (wide) – the Boers' term for the fatter-lipped white rhino.

Animals

Nowhere else on the planet is there such a variety and quantity of large mammal species. Southern Africa boasts the world's largest land mammal (the African elephant), as well as the second largest (white rhino) and the third largest (hippopotamus). It's also home to the tallest (giraffe), fastest (cheetah) and smallest (pygmy shrew). You stand a great chance of seeing the Big Five – black rhinos, Cape buffalo, elephants, leopards and lions – but the region also supports a wonderful array of birds, reptiles, amphibians and even insects (often in less-appreciated quantities). The longer you spend in Southern Africa the more you'll appreciate the subtleties of the region, including the delight of spotting some of the less-famous species. If you're up for a challenge, the lesser-known 'Little Five' are the rhinoceros beetle, buffalo weaver, elephant shrew, leopard tortoise and ant lion. See the colour Wildlife Guide (p145) for a glimpse of the region's spectacular wildlife.

ENDANGERED SPECIES

After years of poaching, the black rhino is the highest-profile entry on Southern Africa's endangered species list (good places to spot these include Hluhluwe-Imfolozi Park, in South Africa, p498; Etosha National Park, in Namibia, p321; and Mkhaya Game Reserve, in Swaziland, p598); see p65 for more on these animals. The beautiful African wild dog (seen, with luck, in Hluhluwe-Imfolozi Park, Kruger National Park, p513, and South Luangwa National Park, p652), with its matriarchal system, is also listed as endangered. The riverine rabbit is one of Southern Africa's most endangered mammals, and the mountain zebra, hippopotamus and African lion are considered vulnerable in the wider region.

The lure of riches to be made from ivory is staggering. By the late 1980s the price of 1kg of ivory (US$300) was three times the *annual* income of over 60% of Africa's population.

Turtles don't fare well, with the loggerhead and green turtle listed as endangered, while the hawksbill turtle is critically endangered.

BIRDS

Birds rate highly among the many attractions of Southern Africa. For sheer abundance and variety, few parts of the world offer as much for the bird-watcher, whether expert or beginner. Southern Africa is host to nearly 10% of the world's bird species – over 900 species have been recorded in the region. More than 130 are endemic to Southern Africa or are near-endemic, being found also only in adjoining territories to the north.

Ian Sinclair's *Field Guide to the Birds of Southern Africa* is a comprehensive work with colour plates of all avian species in the region. The abridged *Illustrated Guide to the Birds of Southern Africa* concentrates on commonly observed species.

This astonishing variety can be attributed to the number of habitats. These habitats are well defined and can be separated into eight main categories: forest; savanna-woodland; fynbos; grassland-semidesert; Karoo (South Africa's desertlike interior); the Namib Desert; freshwater areas (rivers, marshes, lakes, pans and their adjoining shores); and seashore areas (including areas of brackish water where fresh water meets salt water in lagoons and estuaries).

All the national parks and reserves are home to a great range of bird life, especially Mana Pools (p707), Victoria Falls (p620) and Hwange (p725) National Parks in Zimbabwe; Etosha (p321), Mudumu (p333) and Mamili (p333) National Parks in Namibia; and Chobe National Park (p92) and virtually any part of the Okavango Delta (p98) in Botswana. Mozambique has more than half of all bird species identified in Southern Africa; on Inhaca Island (p236) alone, about 300 bird species have been recorded.

CLOSE ENCOUNTERS OF THE WILD KIND

Although you'll hear plenty of horror stories, the threat of attack by wild animals in Africa is largely exaggerated and problems are extremely rare. However, it is important to remember that most African animals are *wild* and that wherever you go on safari, particularly on foot, there is always an element of danger.

The tips below will further diminish your chances of a close encounter of the unpleasant kind, and on organised safaris you should always get advice from your guide.

- Buffalo are usually docile in a herd, but lone individuals can be unpredictable, making them particularly dangerous. If you encounter a buffalo while walking in the bush, back away quietly and slowly. If it charges, climb the nearest tree or dive into the bush and 'run like a rat'.
- Elephants are not bloodthirsty creatures, but those who have had trouble from humans previously may feel the need to go on the offensive. Lone males can be skittish, and a herd of females with baby elephants will almost always be protective and wary of an approach. Keep your distance – if an elephant holds its trunk erect and sniffs the air, it probably detects your presence and may charge rather than retreat. In this case you should be the one who retreats – but move away slowly.
- Hippos aren't normally vicious, but they may attack if you get too close or come between them and the water, or between adults and young. It's true that hippos kill more humans in Africa than any other animal. When boating or canoeing, paddle well away from them, and never pitch a tent in an open area along vegetated riverbanks, as it's probably a hippo run.
- Crocodiles also present risks, and when they're snoozing in the sun they look more like logs or branches. Never swim, paddle or even collect water without first making a careful assessment of what's occupying the water. Local advice is best but, if it's not available, assume the worst.
- Hyenas are potentially dangerous, although they're normally just after your food. They aren't particularly fussy either: they'll eat boots and equipment left outside a tent and have been known to gnaw right through vehicle tyres!
- Lions have also been known to investigate lodges and camp sites. If you're camping in the bush, zip your tent up completely. If you hear a large animal outside, lie still and don't try to leave your tent. While walking in the bush, if you encounter a lion try to avoid an adrenalin rush (easier said than done), and don't turn and run. If you act like prey, the lion could respond accordingly.
- Rhinos tend to be wary of humans, although they may charge vehicles that get too close. Remember, too, that black rhinos are far more aggressive than white rhinos – unsurprising, as they were hunted almost to extinction. If you are caught out on foot and can't immediately climb a tree, face the charge and step to one side at the last moment in bullfight style (again, easier said than done).
- Most importantly, don't let the above scare you! Wildlife viewing just requires a bit of common sense, and by following a few simple guidelines you're sure to have a trouble-free experience. Remember that viewing wildlife in its natural habitat may present dangers not found in a zoo, but it's a large part of what makes a visit to Southern Africa so special, and is incomparable to seeing an animal in a cage.

Highlights in the region include the world's largest bird (the ostrich) and heaviest flying bird (the Kori bustard). Also in abundance are weavers, which share their huge citylike nests (often attached to telephone poles) with pygmy falcons, the world's smallest raptors. Also keep an eye out for majestic birds of prey such as the African fish eagle, bateleur (a serpent-eagle), martial eagle, red-necked falcon and chanting goshawk, as well as secretary birds, rollers, vividly coloured bee-eaters, sunbirds and rainbow-flecked kingfishers.

Birdwatching is good all year round, with spring (August to November) and summer the best.

REPTILES

Southern Africa's most notable reptile is the Nile crocodile. Once abundant in lakes and rivers across the region, its numbers have been greatly reduced by hunting and habitat destruction. Female crocs lay up to 80 eggs at a time, depositing them in sandy areas above the high-water line. After three months' incubation in the hot sand, the young emerge. Many live up to 70 years.

For information on campaigns to save elephants, and the fight against the illegal international trade in wildlife, visit the website of the International Fund for Animal Welfare (www.ifaw.org).

Southern Africa has a complement of both venomous and harmless snakes, but most fear humans and you'll be lucky to even see one. The largest snake – generally harmless to humans – is the python, which grows to over 5m in length. The puff adder, which inhabits mainly mountain and desert areas, grows to about 1m long. Like all reptiles it enjoys sunning itself, but it is very slow and sometimes trodden on by unwary hikers – with very unpleasant results.

Other seriously dangerous snakes include the fat and lazy gaboon viper; the black mamba; the boomslang, which lives in trees; the spitting cobra, which needs no introduction; and the zebra snake, which is one of the world's most aggressive serpentine sorts. If you're tramping in snake country, be sure to watch your step.

Lizards are ubiquitous from the hot and dusty Kaokoveld in Namibia to the cool highlands of the Nyika Plateau in Malawi, and from the bathroom ceiling to the kitchen sink. The largest of these is the water monitor, a docile creature that reaches over 2m in length and is often seen lying around water holes, perhaps dreaming of being a crocodile. Two others frequently seen are chameleons and geckos – the latter often in hotel rooms; they are quite harmless and help to control the bug population.

The Johannesburg-based Endangered Wildlife Trust (www.ewt.org.za) is a good source of information on South Africa's endangered species and has links to broader Southern African conservation projects.

Plants

The following rundown of major vegetation zones (arranged roughly south to north, and from the coasts to the inland areas) is greatly simplified, but provides a useful overview.

Southern Africa's distinctive fynbos zone occurs around the Cape Peninsula and along the south coast of South Africa, interspersed with pockets of temperate forest, where you'll find trees such as the large yellowwood, with its characteristic 'peeling' bark.

The west coast of Southern Africa consists largely of desert, which receives less than 100mm of precipitation per year. Vegetation consists of tough grasses, shrubs and euphorbias, plus local specialities, including the bizarre welwitschia (a miniature conifer) and kokerboom (a type of aloe).

Along the east coast of Southern Africa, the natural vegetation is coastal bush, a mixture of light woodland and dune forest; high rainfall has also created pockets of subtropical forest.

Trees of Southern Africa, by Keith Coates Palgrave, provides the most thorough coverage of the subcontinent's arboreal richness, illustrated with colour photos and paintings.

In South Africa's Karoo, typical vegetation includes grasses, bushes and succulents that bloom colourfully after the rains. Much original Karoo vegetation has been destroyed since the introduction of grazing animals and alien plants (see p60).

To the east lie the temperate grasslands of the 'highveld' and to the north, a vast arid savanna, characterised by acacia scrub, which takes in most of central Namibia, much of Botswana and the northern parts of South Africa.

To the north and east is the woodland savanna, consisting of mainly broadleaf deciduous trees. Dry woodland, dominated by mopane trees, covers northern Namibia, northern Botswana, the Zimbabwean lowveld and the Zambezi Valley. In wetter areas – central Zimbabwe, northern Mozambique

IVORY & ELEPHANT CULLING CONTROVERSY

A major issue all over Southern Africa concerns the emotive issue of elephant conservation. In the West people generally hold a preservationist viewpoint, that elephant herds should be conserved for their own sake or for aesthetic reasons; however, the local sentiment maintains that the elephant must justify its existence on long-term economic grounds for the benefit of local people, or for the country as a whole (a conservationist view). In fact, the same arguments can be applied to most other wildlife.

Since the 1970s various factors (especially the value of ivory) led to an increase in elephant poaching in many parts of Africa. The temptation to poach was great, although the real money was made not by poachers – often villagers who were paid a pittance for the valuable tusks – but by dealers. The number of elephants in Africa went from 1.3 million to 625,000 between 1979 and 1989, and in East Africa and some Southern African countries – notably Zambia – elephant populations were reduced by up to 90% in about 15 years. But in other Southern African countries where parks and reserves are well managed, in particular South Africa, Botswana and Namibia, elephant populations were relatively unaffected.

In 1989, in response to the illegal trade and diminishing numbers of elephants, a world body called the Convention on International Trade in Endangered Species (CITES) internationally banned the import and export of ivory. It also increased funding for antipoaching measures. When the ban was established, world raw ivory prices plummeted by 90%, and the market for poaching and smuggling was radically reduced.

Although elephant populations recovered in some ravaged areas, Southern African human populations continued to grow, and another problem surfaced. Elephants eat huge quantities of foliage but, in the past, herds would eat their fill then migrate to another area, allowing time for the vegetation to regenerate. However, an increasing human population pressed the elephants into smaller and smaller areas – mostly around national parks – and the herds were forced to eat everything available. In many places, the bush began to look as if an atom bomb had hit. This increase in people also leads to human–elephant conflict: in far-north Mozambique, for example, elephants are eating and destroying crops, while drought in Zimbabwe has led to conflict between humans and elephants competing for water resources.

Increasingly across the region, park authorities are facing elephant overpopulation. Botswana, parts of Namibia's Caprivi region, Zimbabwe and South Africa's Kruger National Park are particularly affected. In Zimbabwe there is raging controversy over whether elephants are in plague proportions or not. Proposed solutions include relocation (whereby herds are permanently transplanted to other areas) and contraception. In Kruger in 2005, park authorities recom-

and most of Zambia and Malawi – the dominant vegetation is moist woodland, or miombo. A mix of the two, which occurs in northeastern South Africa and central Mozambique, is known as mixed woodland, or 'bushveld'.

Small pockets of high ground all over the region have a vegetation zone termed afro-montane, which occurs in highland areas where open grasslands are interspersed with heathland and isolated forests.

There are more than 700 alien plant species in the region, and about 10% of these are classed as invasive aliens – that is, they thrive to the detriment of endemic species.

INTRODUCED SPECIES

Introduced plant species present a real threat to Southern African ecosystems. For example, Australian wattle trees and Mexico mesquite flourish by sinking their roots deeper into the soil than indigenous trees, causing the latter to suffer from lack of nourishment. The Australian hakea shrub was introduced to serve as a hedge, and is now rampant, displacing native trees and killing off smaller plants. Areas such as South Africa's unique Cape fynbos floral kingdom are threatened by Australian acacias, which were introduced for their timber products, or to stabilise sand dunes.

Many rivers and dams are also clogged with invasive species, and introduced European grasses, especially on sand dunes, are also a threat.

mended culling to return the elephant population to a manageable 7500 (down from 12,500). South Africa's announcement to reverse a ban on elephant culling from 1 May 2008 – although culling would only happen as a last resort once other options had been exhausted – caused outrage among many conservation groups, as culling has been banned for 15 years in South African parks.

This is an issue that generates much debate: proponents cite the health of the parks, including other wildlife and the elephants themselves; while organisations such as International Fund for Animal Welfare (IFAW) are appalled at such a solution, which they claim is cruel, unethical and scientifically unsound. IFAW believes aerial surveys of elephant numbers are inaccurate, that population growth has not been accurately surveyed and, further, that other solutions have not been looked at carefully enough, including more transfrontier parks crossing national borders.

Southern African countries such as South Africa and Botswana currently have large ivory stockpiles due to natural attrition and through the seizure of illegal ivory hauls. Culling obviously provides large quantities of legal ivory too. In the past this could have been sold to raise funds for elephant management; however, the CITES ban complicates this process.

In March 1999, however, Botswana, Namibia, South Africa and Zimbabwe were permitted by CITES to resume strictly controlled ivory exports. Despite these measures, opponents of the trade warned that elephant poaching would increase in other parts of Africa, as poached ivory could now be laundered through the legal trade. Sure enough, 1999 saw an increase in poaching all over Africa, from Kenya to Gabon, and in late 1999 a Zimbabwean newspaper reported that 84 elephants had been poached in Zimbabwe that year.

In late 2008 CITES approved instead a one-off sale of ivory from South Africa, Botswana, Namibia and Zimbabwe. Approval came when the organisation was satisfied that the countries concerned had established up-to-date and comprehensive data on elephant poaching and population levels, including an assessment of the future impact of ivory sales. This time 101 tonnes was auctioned to buyers from China and Japan for about US$15 million. These countries are now in a 'resting period' and CITES will not consider any further ivory sales for the following nine years. However there is still much dispute about whether controlled ivory sales, such as an annual export allowance, should be permitted, with Southern African countries with excessive elephant populations and large ivory stockpiles pushing hard for a further relaxation of the ban. Some argue that Southern Africa is paying for the inability of other African countries to manage and protect their wildlife, and that the ban on the ivory trade is an unfair punishment.

It remains to be seen whether the ban will be lifted. Meanwhile debate about the ivory trade, and the culling solution to overpopulation, rages on.

Recognition of these problems means that alien plants, originally introduced as commercial plants or as ornamental garden plants, may often not be grown on public or private property.

NATIONAL PARKS

The term 'national park' is often used in Southern Africa as a catch-all term to include wildlife reserves, forest parks, or any government conservation area; there are also several privately owned reserves.

See www.peaceparks.org for all the latest news on the transfrontier parks in the region, including progress reports and maps of all the parks.

The beauty of the parks and reserves is that they all have an individual identity – a unique character born from the varied landscapes, wildlife and vistas. Happily, this means you can spend a lot of time visiting parks and never get bored!

Most parks in Southern Africa conserve habitats and wildlife species and provide recreational facilities for visitors. South African parks are among the best managed in the world, and most of the rest are very good, although Zimbabwean parks have declined, some of Zambia's parks are still recovering from years of neglect, and those in Mozambique are still being developed, with those such as Gorongosa leading the way.

NATIONAL PARKS IN SOUTHERN AFRICA

Southern Africa's national parks are simply outstanding. However facilities, geography and wildlife-viewing opportunities vary considerably across the region. World-famous national parks such as Kruger, Etosha, South Luangwa and Chobe offer excellent wildlife viewing, and usually a dazzling array of accommodation options, while lesser-known gems such as Hlane Royal National Park (p598) or Mkhaya Game Reserve (p598) are usually smaller and quieter than their famous counterparts.

Botswana

- Makgadikgadi & Nxai Pan (p90) – vast and remote, this is the site of Southern Africa's last great wildlife migrations.
- Chobe (p92) – a large and varied park with both a wildlife-rich riverfront and broad savanna plains. It's particularly known for its large elephant herds.
- Moremi (p105) – this beautiful park takes in a portion of the stunning Okavango Delta.
- Central Kalahari (p108) – Botswana's largest park, with the widest horizons you'll ever see.

Malawi

- Liwonde (p192) – a magical lowland park with wonderful, varied bird life, including a stunning rainbow-flecked kingfisher population, and excellent elephant and hippo viewing.
- Mt Mulanje (p205) – the 'island in the sky', with sheer peaks and excellent hiking.
- Nyika (p177) – unique montane grassland area, with endless views and splendid horse riding.
- Lengwe (p207) – this lovely park in southern Malawi protects a range of antelopes (including the rare nyala), as well as diverse bird species.

Mozambique

- Gorongosa National Park (p253) – this park is being rehabilitated with international backing and the wildlife is making a real comeback. The community development element is a highlight.

Namibia

- Waterberg Plateau Park (p317) – this sky island features walking tracks and a repository for endangered wildlife.
- Fish River Canyon (p374) – Africa's grand canyon presents one of the most spectacular scenes on the continent and Namibia's most popular hiking track.
- Etosha (p321) – this vast park is one of Africa's most renowned wildlife-viewing venues – and deservedly so. It features an enormous pan and numerous water holes, and is one of the best places in the region to see black rhinos.
- Namib-Naukluft (p358) – one of the world's largest national parks, this stunning and magical wilderness takes in world-famous sand dunes and wild desert mountains, with excellent hiking.
- Sperrgebiet National Park (p372) – in this country's famous diamond fields, the country's newest (2008) national park is set to become the gem of Namibia's protected spaces.

South Africa

- Drakensberg (p502) – this mountain region may be low on the Big Five, but it's high on awe-inspiring mountain scenery, rock art and extensive hiking opportunities.
- iSimangaliso Wetland Park (p498) – this coastal wetland in a remote part of the country presents a unique ecosystem of global significance.
- Tsitsikamma (p461) – a lovely coastal park with forests, fynbos, beaches, rocky headlands and a world-renowned hiking trail.
- Hluhluwe-Imfolozi (p498) – near the Zulu heartland, this bushland park is best known for its rhino populations.

- Kruger (p513) – South Africa's most popular national park covers an enormous area and offers the classic wildlife experience, while boasting top-notch facilities.
- Pilanesberg (p555) – this park protects an unusual complex of extinct volcanoes with towering rocky outcrops and an impressive variety and number of wildlife, including wild dogs.

Zambia

- Kafue (p670) – massive and genuinely wild, with an impressive range of habitats and wildlife.
- Kasanka (p645) – a pioneering, privately managed park, noted for sightings of the rare sitatunga antelope.
- Lower Zambezi (p663) – spectacular setting, escarpments and plains, plus the great river itself. It's best appreciated on multiday canoe trips.
- South Luangwa (p652) – this wild and pristine wildlife park is growing more popular, but many still consider it 'Africa's best-kept secret'.

Zimbabwe

- Matusadona (p706) – with both lakefront and mountain habitats south of Lake Kariba, this rewarding wildlife park is known for its enormous buffalo herds and lion populations.
- Nyanga (p713), Bvumba (p711), Chimanimani (p715) – these three parks in the misty Eastern Highlands offer mountain retreats and excellent hiking opportunities.
- Hwange (p725) – Zimbabwe's best-known wildlife park holds one of the most dense wildlife populations in Africa. It's conveniently close to Victoria Falls.
- Mana Pools (p707) – combines the Zambezi Escarpment, a swath of bushland and beautiful riverine scenery to create a varied wildlife experience. Canoe safaris are popular.

Transfrontier Peace Parks

In addition to national parks there are several transfrontier conservation areas at various stages of completion. These mammoth ventures cross national borders and are flagship conservation projects designed to re-establish age-old migration routes.

- Kgalagadi Transfrontier Park (p456) – this park combines Northern Cape's old Kalahari Gemsbok National Park with Botswana's Gemsbok National Park.
- Great Limpopo Transfrontier Park – this spreads nearly 100,000 sq km (larger than Portugal) across the borders of South Africa (Kruger National Park; p513), Mozambique (Limpopo National Park; p240) and Zimbabwe (Gonarezhou National Park; p720).
- |Ai-|Ais/Richtersveld Transfrontier Park – incorporates the spectacular desert mountain scenery of Ai-Ais Hot Springs Game Park (p375), in Namibia, and the Richtersveld National Park (see the boxed text, p461), in South Africa.
- Greater Mapungubwe Transfrontier Conservation Area – a conservation area in progress straddling the borders of South Africa, Botswana and Zimbabwe.
- Maloti/Drakensberg Transfrontier Project – a project that protects the natural and cultural heritage of the Maloti-Drakensberg Mountains.
- Kavango-Zambezi Transfrontier Conservation Area – a work in progress situated around the border convergence of Angola, Botswana, Namibia, Zambia and Zimbabwe, and set to become the world's biggest conservation area, taking in the Caprivi Strip (p326), in Namibia, Chobe National Park (p92) and the Okavango Delta (p98), in Botswana, and Victoria Falls (p604), in Zambia.

Malawi and Zambia are setting up the first transfrontier park outside South Africa. The area combines the Nyika Plateau on both sides of the border, Malawi's Vwaza Marsh Wildlife Reserve and Kasungu National Park, with Zambian forest reserves, Musalangu Game Management Area and Lukusuzi National Park.

In most parks and reserves harbouring large (and potentially dangerous) animals, visitors must travel in vehicles or on an organised safari, but several do allow hiking or walking with a ranger or safari guide.

Nearly all parks charge an entrance fee, and in almost all cases foreigners pay substantially more than local residents or citizens. This may rankle some visitors – and some parks are seriously overpriced – but the idea is that residents and citizens pay taxes to the governments that support the parks, and therefore are entitled to discounts.

Park Accommodation

Most parks and reserves contain accommodation, so you can stay overnight and take wildlife drives in the early morning and evening. Accommodation ranges from simple campsites to luxury lodges run by companies that have concessions inside the parks. Prices vary to match the quality of facilities. In some countries you can just turn up and find a place to camp or stay; in other countries reservations are advised (or are essential at busy times). For details, see individual country chapters.

ENVIRONMENTAL ISSUES

Some national parks and protected areas are rehabilitated by funding from overseas. In some cases the funder is in partnership with the local wildlife authority – examples include Gile Reserve in Mozambique and Liuwa Plains National Park in Zambia.

All over Southern Africa, an ever-growing human population places demands on the land and other natural resources. To conserve these resources – and the region's wild areas and ecosystems – most experts agree that population growth must be contained by improving education (especially for women) and raising living standards by fostering economic growth. Human–elephant conflict, for example, is becoming a problem in areas such as northern Mozambique (p225).

Land degradation is a serious regional problem; about one quarter of South Africa's land is considered to be severely degraded (see p402). In former homeland areas, years of overgrazing and overcropping have resulted in massive soil depletion. This, plus poor overall conditions, is pushing people to the cities, further increasing urban pressures. Lesotho has severe land erosion (see p128) due to large-scale ploughing and introduced merino sheep and mohair goats.

Water is another issue and droughts are common in the region (see the boxed text, p39). To meet demand rivers have often been dammed or modified. While this has improved water supplies to some areas, it has also disrupted local ecosystems and caused increased silting.

Deforestation wreaks havoc across Southern Africa, especially when indigenous trees are replaced by more aggressive introduced species. In Malawi the use of wood for fuel is very high and, because of food insecurity, people increasingly rely on woodlands to serve their needs. Illegal timber practices are more difficult to combat, with entrenched interests at every level. An illustration of the challenges is seen in northern and central Mozambique, where tropical hardwoods are felled with little or no regulation. Zambia also has a serious illegal logging predicament.

The implications of climate change on Southern African countries are studied in a report at www.cru.uea.ac.uk/~mikeh/research/cc_safr.htm.

Poaching is still a problem in countries such as Malawi and Zambia and has increased dramatically in Zimbabwe since the land seizures, and world-class parks and antipoaching policies are under threat.

Many Africans believe conservation for its own sake is a luxurious Western notion that the people of Southern Africa simply cannot afford. To concede the benefits of conservation, locals need to see some of these benefits, and that's where tourism comes in. If the money earned from visitors coming to enjoy the animals and environment stays in the pockets of locals (or in the country as a whole), then this will encourage wildlife and environmental protection.

HUNTING – ANIMAL WELFARE VS ECONOMICS

In some parts of Southern Africa, areas of land are set aside for hunting, and hunters are charged 'trophy fees' to shoot animals. This is abhorrent to many people – especially in Western countries.

On the one hand it is argued that trophy or sport hunting is a form of tourism that stimulates local economies and thereby fosters 'conservation-minded' attitudes. For people who lack other resources the trophy fees are large (thousands of US dollars for animals such as elephants or lions) and an invaluable source of income. Paradoxically, the financial benefit of hunting tourism encourages the management and protection of these animals and their environment. Hunting, it is argued, provides an enticement to landowners to maintain the natural habitats that provide a home for the hunted animals.

On the other hand, killing an animal for fun is simply morally and ethically wrong to many people, and this is accentuated once the beauty, grace and intelligence of many African animals is witnessed in the wild. Can killing for fun ever be justified in a modern society? Hunters claim that killing is not the purpose of hunting; instead, it's all about outwitting and learning behavioural patterns of their prey. Their respondents' answer: then why not take a camera instead of a rifle? It is also argued that slaughtering wildlife in order to raise conservation funds to save it is a twisted way of thinking. Further, improperly managed, trophy hunting can have seriously detrimental effects on wildlife, especially threatened and endangered species.

Although conservation organisations do not agree on policy towards hunting, the World Wildlife Fund (WWF) has a pragmatic attitude, stating that 'for endangered species, trophy hunting should only be considered when all other options have been explored...and that trophy hunting, where it is scientifically based and properly managed, has proven to be an effective conservation and management method in some countries and for certain species'.

In 2004, CITES lifted a ban on hunting the black rhino, once a potent symbol of endangered African animals, allowing an annual hunt quota of five each for South Africa and Namibia. Conservationists opposed to the move say that the rhino is still a target for poachers, with its horn being highly valued in Asia and the Middle East. It is claimed that hunting quotas would make it far easier to cover up the illegal trade of rhino horns from poached animals. Also, the black rhino remains critically endangered in most countries outside Southern Africa. Namibia and South Africa have pledged to spend the substantial revenues from the allowed quota to improve conservation in their countries.

In 2007 South Africa enacted a new law to end the practice of 'canned hunting', in which wildlife bred in captivity are killed by tourists in sealed reserves. The law makes breeding predators such as cheetahs, lions or leopards, specifically for hunting, illegal. In 2009 a test case brought before the courts by lion breeders found in favour of the ban, which might end this practice for good in the country.

Income is also generated by the jobs that hunting and wildlife tourism create, such as game rangers, tour guides and various posts in the associated hotels, lodges and camps. Further spin-offs include the sale of crafts and curios.

In the global fight against climate change, alternative energy sources are a new challenge for all countries in the region as they become more developed. South Africa is ranked in the top 15 worldwide contributors to global warming, with about 90% of the country's electricity coming from coal-firing plants. Dams and hydroelectric plants can have very detrimental effects on local and regional ecosystems – Namibia's energy crisis (p303) has put on the table several plans for power generation, which were under review at the time of research.

For community initiatives and projects designed to combat local issues, as well as examples of ecotourism, see the Environment section in individual country chapters.

Earthlife Africa (www.earthlife.org.za) is an active environmental group operating in South Africa and Namibia. It's a good contact for anyone wanting to get involved.

Botswana

Landlocked Botswana offers extremes of environment and diversity of landscape, the total sum of which is like nothing else in Africa. Roughly the same size as Kenya, France or Texas, Botswana is almost covered with scrub brush and savanna grasslands, which together facilitate vast migrations of wildlife that have become a rare occurrence elsewhere on the continent. The country is also interspersed with pockets of ecological wonderment, from the sunbaked salt pans of the Makgadikgadi superlake, to the emerald-green waterways of the Okavango Delta.

Of course, this is only half the picture, for Botswana is truly an African political and economic success story. After achieving democratic rule in 1966, Botswana was discovered to have three of the world's richest diamond-bearing formations within its borders. Today, the country enjoys economic stability and a high standard of education and health care, which, with the exception of South Africa, is unequalled elsewhere in sub-Saharan Africa. Botswana is also one of the most predominantly urban societies in the world, and providing vocational and professional jobs has become one of the highest priorities on the government's agenda.

However, this modern veneer belies the fact that much of Botswana remains a country for the intrepid – not to mention relatively wealthy – traveller. A largely roadless wilderness of seemingly endless spaces, Botswana demands time, effort and, above all else, lots of cash to enjoy it to its full. But, Botswana is truly the Africa of your dreams, and with the full complement of predators and prey on display, it never ceases to amaze first-timers and seasoned safari vets alike.

FAST FACTS

- **Area** 582,000 sq km
- **Capital** Gaborone
- **Country code** ☎ 267
- **Famous for** Okavango Delta, Chobe National Park, the Kalahari
- **Languages** English, Setswana
- **Money** Pula (P)
- **Phrases** *Dumela?* (How are you?); *dankie* (thank you)
- **Population** 1.64 million

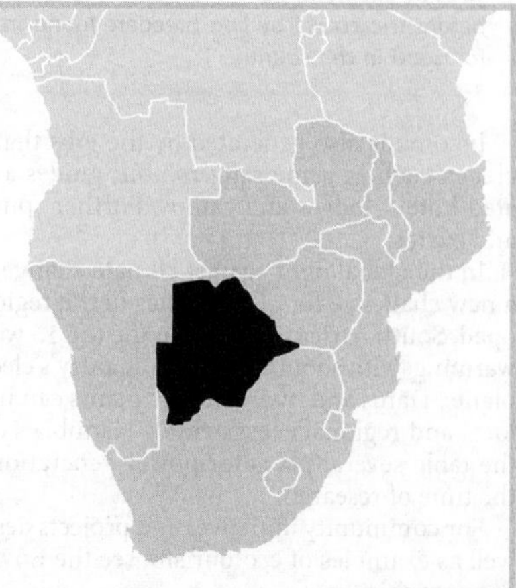

HIGHLIGHTS

- **Okavango Delta** (p98) Glide through the watery expanses in a mokoro, a traditional dugout canoe.
- **Chobe National Park** (p92) Spot the Big Five (lions, leopards, buffalos, elephants, rhinos) at Botswana's premier safari park.
- **Central Kalahari Game Reserve** (p108) Test the limits of your survival instincts on a 4WD camping expedition.
- **Makgadikgadi Pans & Nxai Pan National Park** (p90) Follow the herds of migrating zebras and wildebeests over this baobab-dotted salt-pan complex.
- **Off the beaten track** (p105) Have a rugged and remote safari experience in the Moremi Game Reserve.

ITINERARIES

- **Three Days** Botswana's tourist highlight is the Okavango Delta (p98), and if you have only a few days, this is where you'll want to focus. Choose Maun (p98) or the Okavango Panhandle (p107) as your base and organise a mokoro trip through the wetlands, followed with a wildlife-viewing trip through Moremi Game Reserve (p105).
- **One Week** Combine your visit to the delta with a safari through Chobe National Park (p92), one of the world's top safari experiences. Either go overland through the rugged interior of the park, or cruise (or boat) along the wildlife-rich riverfront.
- **One Month** With a month (and lots of money), you can hire a 4WD or link in with a reputable safari company and see the best of the country: do a mokoro trip in the delta (see the boxed text, p104), safari in Moremi and Chobe, cruise on the Okavango Panhandle and explore the furthest reaches of the Kalahari (p108).

CLIMATE & WHEN TO GO

Although it straddles the Tropic of Capricorn, Botswana experiences extremes in both temperature and weather. In the winter (late May to August), days are normally clear, warm and sunny, and nights are cool to cold. Wildlife never wanders far from water sources so sightings are more predictable than in the wetter summer season. This is also the time of European, North American and – most importantly – South African school holidays, so some areas can be busy, especially between mid-July and mid-September. In summer (October to April), wildlife is harder to spot and rains can render sandy roads impassable. This is also the time of the highest humidity and the most stifling heat; daytime temperatures of over 40°C are common. See p745 for more information on the climate in Southern Africa.

> **HOW MUCH?**
>
> - **One-day mokoro trip** P500
> - **Ostrich-eggshell bracelet** P35
> - **Stalk of sugar cane** P3-5
> - **Foreign newspaper** P10-15
> - **Night in a budget hotel** P175
>
> **LONELY PLANET INDEX**
>
> - **1L of petrol** P10
> - **1L of bottled water** P5
> - **Bottle of beer** P7
> - **Souvenir T-shirt** P55
> - **Snack** P9

HISTORY

For a detailed account of the precolonial history of the whole Southern African region, including Botswana's precolonial history, see p32.

The Boers & the British

In 1836, feeling pressured by the British in the British Cape Colony, about 20,000 Boers set out on the Great Trek across the Vaal River into Batswana and Zulu territory, staking out new farms for themselves and displacing local villagers.

Bent on establishing trade links with the Dutch and Portuguese, the Boers set up their own free state, ruling the Transvaal Republic – a move ratified by the British in the Sand River Convention of 1852. This effectively placed the Batswana under the rule of the so-called new South African Republic and a period of rebellion and heavy-handed oppression ensued. Following heavy human and territorial losses, the Batswana chiefs petitioned the British government for protection from the Boers.

Britain, though, already had its hands full in Southern Africa and was in no hurry to take on and support a country of dubious profitability. Instead, it offered to act as arbitrator in the dispute. By 1877, however, animosity against the Boers had escalated to such a dangerous level that the British conceded and annexed the Transvaal – thereby starting the first Anglo-Boer War. The war continued until the Pretoria Convention of 1881, when the British withdrew from the Transvaal in exchange for Boer allegiance to the British Crown.

With the British out of their way, the Boers once again looked northwards into Batswana territory and pushed westwards into the Molopo Basin. In 1882, the Boers managed to subdue the towns of Taung and Mafikeng and proclaimed them the republics of Stellaland and Goshen. They may have gone much further if it wasn't for a significant event that was to change regional politics radically. This was the annexation of German South-West Africa (modern-day Namibia) by the Germans in the 1890s.

With the potential threat of a German–Boer alliance across the Kalahari cutting them off from their dreams of expanding their interests into mineral-rich Rhodesia (Zimbabwe), the British started to look seriously at the Batswana petitions for protection. And in 1885 they proclaimed a protectorate over their Setswana allies, known as the British Crown Colony of Bechuanaland.

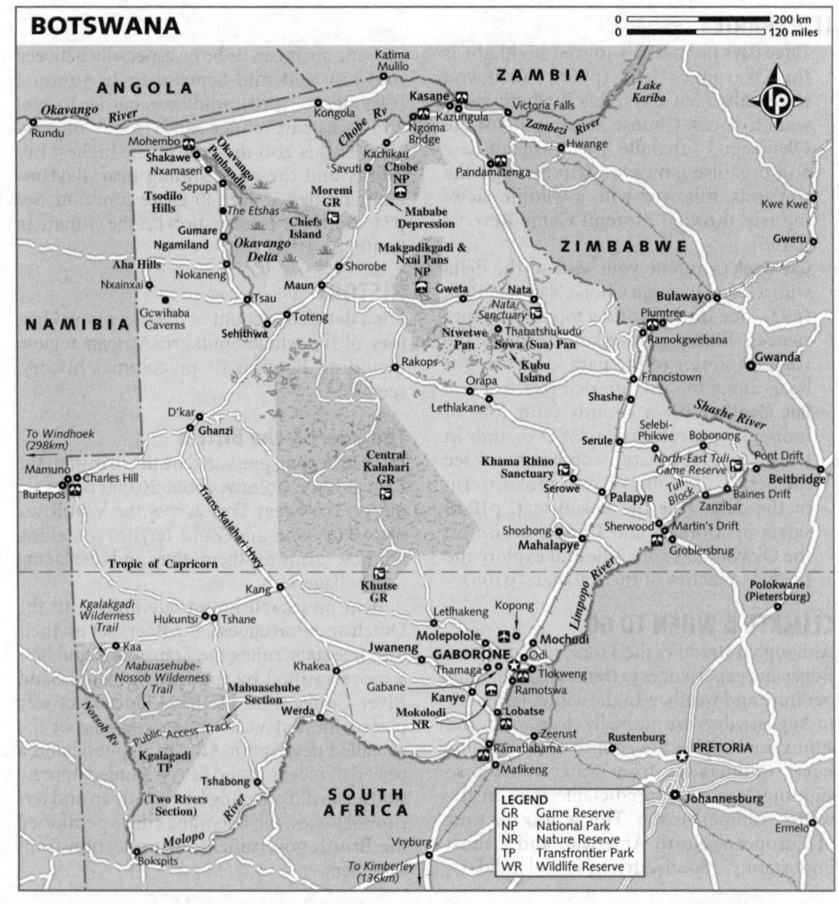

TRAVEL TIPS

Travelling cheaply in Botswana isn't impossible, but if you can't afford a flight into the Okavango, a day or two at Moremi Game Reserve or Chobe National Park, or a 4WD trip through the Kalahari, you may want to think twice before visiting. Safari lodges – especially those in the Okavango Delta and Chobe National Park – are for the most part exclusive haunts of the wealthy, and you'll rarely find anything for less than US$300 for a double. Hotels, camping, car hire, domestic air flights, meals, alcohol and self-catering prices are comparable to those in Europe, North America, Australia and New Zealand, and although buses and trains are quite economical (US$1 per hour of journey time), they won't take you to the most interesting parts of the country.

Cecil John Rhodes

British expansion in Southern Africa came in the form of a private venture under the auspices of the British South Africa Company (BSAC), owned by millionaire businessman Cecil John Rhodes.

By 1889 Rhodes already had a hand in the diamond-mining industry in Kimberley, South Africa, and he was convinced that other African countries had similar mineral deposits just waiting to be exploited. He aimed to do this through a system of land concessions that offered cheap land to private companies in order to colonise new land for the Crown. The system was easily exploited by Rhodes, who fraudulently obtained large tracts of land from local chiefs by passing off contracts as treaties. For their part, the British turned a blind eye as they eventually hoped to transfer the entire Bechuanaland protectorate to the BSAC and relieve themselves of the expense of colonial administration.

Realising the implications of Rhodes' aspirations, three Batswana chiefs, Bathoen, Khama III and Sebele, accompanied by a sympathetic missionary, WC Willoughby, sailed to England to appeal directly to the British parliament for continued government control of Bechuanaland. Instead of taking action, Colonial Minister Joseph Chamberlain advised them to contact Rhodes directly and work things out among themselves. Chamberlain then conveniently forgot the matter and went on holiday.

Naturally, Rhodes was immovable, so the delegation turned to the London Missionary Society (LMS) who, through a campaign, took the matter to the British public. Fearing that the BSAC would allow alcohol in Bechuanaland, the LMS and other Christian groups backed the devoutly Christian Khama and his entourage. The British public in general felt that the Crown should be administering the empire, rather than the controversial Cecil Rhodes. When Chamberlain returned from holiday, public pressure had mounted to such a level that the government was forced to concede to the chiefs. Chamberlain agreed to continue British administration of Bechuanaland, ceding only a small strip of the southeast (now known as the Tuli Block) to the BSAC for the construction of a railway line to Rhodesia.

Colonial Years

By 1899, Britain had decided it was time to consolidate the Southern African states and declared war on the Transvaal. The Boers were overcome in 1902, and in 1910 the Union of South Africa was created, comprising Natal, the Cape Colony, Transvaal and the Free State – with provisions for the future incorporation of Bechuanaland and Rhodesia.

By selling cattle, draught oxen and grain to the Europeans streaming north in search of farming land and minerals, Bechuanaland had enjoyed an initial degree of economic independence. However, the construction of a railway through Bechuanaland to Rhodesia, and a serious outbreak of foot-and-mouth disease in the 1890s, destroyed the transit trade. This new economic vulnerability, combined with a series of droughts and the need to raise cash to pay British taxes, sent many Batswana to South Africa to look for work on farms and in mines; as much as 25% of Botswana's male population was abroad at any one time. This accelerated the breakdown of traditional land-use patterns and eroded the chiefs' powers.

The British government continued to regard the protectorate as a temporary entity, until it could be handed over to Rhodesia or the new Union of South Africa. Hence investment and administrative development within the territory were kept to a bare minimum. Even when there were moves in the 1930s to reform administration or initiate agricultural and mining development, these were hotly disputed by leading Setswana chiefs, on the grounds that they would only enhance colonial control. So the territory remained divided into eight largely self-administering 'tribal' reserves and five white-settler farm blocks with the remainder classified as 'crown' (ie state) lands. Similarly, the administrative capital, Mafikeng, which was actually situated outside the protectorate's border in South Africa, remained where it was until 1964.

Independence

The extent of Botswana's subordination to the interests of South Africa during this period became clear in 1950. In a case that caused political controversy in Britain and across the Empire, the British government banned Seretse Khama from the chieftainship of the Ngwato and exiled him for six years. This, as secret documents have since revealed, was in order to appease the South African government which objected to Seretse's marriage to a British woman at a time when racial segregation was enforced in South Africa.

Such meddling only increased growing political agitation and throughout the 1950s and '60s Batswana political parties started to surface and promote the idea of independence. Following the Sharpeville Massacre in 1960, South African refugees Motsamai Mpho of the African National Congress (ANC), and Philip Matante, a Johannesburg preacher affiliated with the Pan-Africanist Congress, joined with KT Motsete, a teacher from Malawi, to form the Bechuanaland People's Party (BPP). Its immediate goal was independence.

In 1962, Seretse Khama and Kanye farmer Ketumile 'Quett' Masire formed the moderate Bechuanaland Democratic Party (BDP). The BDP formulated a schedule for independence, drawing on support from local chiefs such as Bathoen II of the Bangwaketse, and traditional Batswana. The BDP also called for the transfer of the capital into Botswana (from Mafikeng to Gaborone) and a new nonracial constitution.

The British accepted the BDP's peaceful plan for a transfer of power, and Khama was elected president when general elections were held in 1965. On 30 September 1966, the country – now called the Republic of Botswana – was granted full independence.

With a steady hand, Seretse Khama steered Botswana through its first 14 years of independence. He guaranteed continued freehold over land held by white ranchers and adopted a strictly neutral stance (at least until near the end of his presidency) towards South Africa and Rhodesia. The reason, of course, was Botswana's economic dependence on the giant to the south,

MOVERS & SHAKERS: SERETSE KHAMA

When Bangwato chief (*kgosi* in Setswana) Khama III died in 1923, he was succeeded by his son, Sekgoma, who died only two years later. Because the next heir to the throne, Seretse Khama, was only four years old, the job of regent went to his 21-year-old uncle, Tshekedi Khama, who left his studies in South Africa to return to Serowe.

Uproar in the Khama dynasty occurred in 1948 when Seretse married an Englishwoman, Ruth Williams, while studying law in London. As a royal, Seretse was expected – in fact required – to take a wife from a Batswana royal family. Indignant at such a breach of tribal custom, Tshekedi stripped his nephew of his inheritance. Seretse was exiled from Serowe by Bangwato leaders, and from the protectorate by the British, who assured him that he'd be better off in London.

However, Tshekedi lost his regency when an overwhelming majority of the Bangwato backed Seretse over his uncle, forcing Tshekedi to gather his followers and settle elsewhere. Subsequent breakdowns in Bangwato tribal structure prompted Tshekedi to return to Serowe in 1952 with a change of heart. Seretse was still being detained in Britain though, and it wasn't until 1956, when he renounced his claim to the Bangwato throne, that he was permitted to return to Serowe with his English wife.

While in Serowe, Seretse and his wife began campaigning for Botswana's independence. Eventually, Seretse was knighted for his efforts, and became the country's first president, a post he held until his death 14 years later. In a final act of reconciliation, Sir Seretse Khama was buried in the Royal Cemetery in Serowe. His son, Ian, is still chief of the Bangwato and currently president of Botswana.

from where they imported the majority of their foodstuffs and where many Batswana worked in the diamond mines. Nevertheless, Khama refused to exchange ambassadors with South Africa and officially disapproved of apartheid in international circles.

Modern Politics

Sir Seretse Khama died in 1980 but his Botswana Democratic Party (BDP), formerly the Bechuanaland Democratic Party, continues to command a substantial majority in the Botswana parliament. Sir Ketumile 'Quett' Masire, who succeeded Khama as president from 1980 to 1998, followed the path laid down by his predecessor and continued to cautiously pursue pro-Western policies. Festus Mogae largely continued this trend from 1998 to 2008.

Over the course of the last 40 years the BDP has managed the country's diamond windfall wisely. Diamond dollars have been ploughed into infrastructure, education and health. Private business has been allowed to grow and foreign investment has been welcomed. From 1966 to 2005, Botswana's economy grew faster than any other in the world.

Festus Mogae handed over the presidency to Vice President Ian Khama (son of Sir Seretse Khama) on 1 April 2008, a move that generated some grumbles as Khama was never elected as president. Since assuming power Khama has cracked down on drinking, demanding earlier curfews at bars (sometimes enforced, sometimes not). In addition, Khama, former commander of the Botswana Defence Force, has appointed military and law-enforcement colleagues to government posts traditionally held by civilians. For example, a former police commandant was made director of BTV, the national TV channel, in 2009, which provoked some uproar from local journalists who said they were worried about government interference in news gathering.

On 16 October 2009, Ian Khama was sworn in after his BDP party dominated the election as predicted. The party won 45 out of 57 seats in Parliament, but the election was noteworthy in that there was a shake up in the third parties (see p72).

THE CULTURE

The National Psyche

Proud, conservative, resourceful and respectful, the Batswana have an ingrained feeling of their national identity and an impressive belief in their government and their country. Their history – a series of clever manoeuvres that meant they were able to avoid the worst aspects of colonisation – does them proud and lends them a confidence in themselves, their government and the future that is rare in postcolonial Africa. Admittedly this faith in government and progress has been facilitated by Botswana's incredible diamond wealth, which has allowed significant investment in education, health and infrastructure.

Daily Life

Traditional culture also acts as a sort of societal glue. Respect for one's elders, firmly held religious beliefs, traditional gender roles and the customary *kgotla* (a specially designated meeting place in each village where grievances can be aired in an atmosphere of mutual respect) create a well-defined social structure with some stiff mores at its core. But despite some heavyweight social responsibilities the Batswana have an easygoing and unhurried approach to life, and the emotional framework of the extended family generally makes for an inclusive network. As the pace and demands of modern life increase this support is becoming ever more vital as men and women migrate to cities to work in more lucrative jobs, usually leaving children behind to be cared for by other family members.

Population

Botswana's population in 2009 was estimated at almost two million. The country has one of the highest rates of HIV infection in the world. Since the early 1990s the annual birth rate has dropped from 3.5% to about 2.3%. The annual population-growth rate was estimated at a negative: minus 0.04% in 2006. This figure has since been replaced by a growth rate of 1.9%. Officially, life expectancy soared from 49 years at the time of independence (1966) to about 70 years by the mid-1990s. It's thought that without the scourge of AIDS, life expectancy in Botswana would now be around 74 years, on a par with the USA. Instead, today's figure is about 62 years, which is still a marked improvement of 33 years, the expected life span around 2006. That increase is a testament to the government's generally sound handling of antiretroviral-drug distribution and commitment to condom distribution and sex education.

WHAT NEXT?

In 1970, Botswana ranked as one of the world's poorest countries, with a shocking GDP per capita per annum below US$200. Educational facilities were minimal, with less than 2% of the population having completed primary school and fewer than 100 students enrolled in university. In the entire country there was only one, 12km-long, paved road. It's hardly surprising, then, that the country played no role in regional or continental politics.

Then, in 1967, Botswana effectively won the jackpot with the discovery of diamonds at Orapa. Two other major mines followed, at Letlhakane in 1977, and Jwaneng in 1982, making Botswana the world's leading producer of gem-quality stones. This catapulted the country from a poor, provincial backwater to a regional player of some substance able to form the Southern African Development Community (SADC), whose function is to coordinate the disparate economies of the region.

However, as its life span is estimated at only 35 years, the diamond boon has its dark side. Botswana faces a bleak future if its people can't find alternative revenue streams. It's a difficult dilemma for a government that is desperately trying to diversify a precarious economy into manufacturing, light engineering, food processing and textiles. Tourism, too, is set to play a major role in the country's future, although the challenge will be to increase revenue without adversely impacting on the environment and local communities.

With nearly 30% of the population still living below the poverty line and the growing popularity of the socialist Botswana National Front (BNF) and the social democratic Botswana Congress Party (BCP), now in alliance with each other to create opposition to the dominant BDP, Botswana's future is less assured now than it has been at any time in the last 40 years.

Immigration & Emigration

Due to the political and economic instability that swept through Zimbabwe in recent years, the volume of illegal immigrants crossing into Botswana in search of work is on the rise. According to Botswana's Department of Immigration, on average over 25,000 Zimbabwean illegal immigrants are apprehended and repatriated each year. When interviewed, immigrants claimed that their motivation for fleeing Zimbabwe was the lack of opportunities for stable employment. Many Zimbabwean families survive on remittances from family members working abroad.

ARTS & CRAFTS

Handicrafts

The original Batswana artists managed to convey individuality, aesthetic value and aspects of Batswana life through their utilitarian implements. Baskets, pottery, fabrics and tools were decorated with meaningful designs derived from tradition. Europeans introduced new forms of art, aspects of which were integrated and adapted to local interpretation, particularly in weavings and tapestries. The result is some of the finest and most meticulously executed work in Southern Africa.

Literature

As indigenous languages have existed in written form only since the coming of the Christian missionaries, Botswana lacks an extensive literary tradition. What survives of the ancient myths and poetry of the San, Setswana, Herero and other groups has been handed down orally.

Botswana's most famous modern literary figure was Bessie Head, who settled in Sir Seretse Khama's village of Serowe and wrote works that reflected the harshness and beauty of African village life and the Botswanan landscape. Her most widely read works include *Serowe – Village of the Rain Wind, When Rain Clouds Gather, Maru, A Question of Power, The Cardinals, A Bewitched Crossroad* and *The Collector of Treasures;* the last is an anthology of short stories. Head died in 1988.

Recent additions to Botswana's national literature are the works of Norman Rush, which include the novel *Mating,* set in a remote village, and *Whites,* which deals with the country's growing number of expatriates and apologists from South Africa and elsewhere.

ENVIRONMENT

The Land

With an area of 582,000 sq km, landlocked Botswana extends 1100km from north to south and 960km from east to west, making it about the same size as Kenya or France.

Most of the country lies at an average elevation of 1000m and consists of a vast and nearly level sand-filled basin covered with scrub-covered savanna. The Kalahari (Kgalagadi), a semi-arid expanse of wind-blown sand deposits and long, sandy valleys, covers nearly 85% of Botswana, including the entire central and southwestern regions. In the northwest the Okavango River flows in from Namibia and soaks into the sands, forming the Okavango Delta, which covers an area of 15,000 sq km. In the northeast are the great salty clay deserts of the Makgadikgadi Pans.

Wildlife

Most of the country is covered with scrub brush and savanna grassland, although small areas of deciduous forest (mopane, msasa and Zambezi teak) thrive on the Zimbabwean border. The Okavango and Linyanti wetlands of the northwest are characterised by riverbank and swamp vegetation, which includes reeds, papyrus and water lilies as well as larger trees such as acacia, jackalberry, leadwood and sausage trees.

Because the Okavango Delta and the Chobe River provide an incongruous water supply in the otherwise dry savanna, nearly all Southern African mammal species, including such rarities as pukus, red lechwes, sitatungas and wild dogs, are present in Moremi Game Reserve, parts of Chobe National Park and the Linyanti Marshes. In the Makgadikgadi & Nxai Pan National Park, herds of wildebeests, zebras and other hoofed mammals migrate between their winter range on the Makgadikgadi plains and the summer lushness of the Nxai Pan region.

National Parks

Botswana's national parks are among Africa's wildest, characterised by open spaces where nature still reigns supreme, and although they do support a few private safari reserves, there's next to no infrastructure and few amenities.

The major parks include the Central Kalahari Game Reserve, Chobe National Park, Khutse Game Reserve, Kgalagadi Transfrontier Park (an amalgamation of Botswana's former Mabuasehube-Gemsbok National Park and South Africa's Kalahari-Gemsbok National Park), Makgadikgadi & Nxai Pan National Park and Moremi Game Reserve. The northeast Tuli Game Reserve is not a national park, but rather is cobbled together from several private reserves.

All public national parks and reserves in Botswana are run by the **DWNP** (☎ 318 0774; dwnp@gov.bw; Government Enclave, Khama Cres, Gaborone; 🕑 7.30am-12.45pm & 1.45-4.30pm Mon-Fri), which is responsible for maintaining the Botswanan section of the **Kgalagadi Transfrontier Park** (www.botswana-tourism.gov.bw/transfrontier). Because this park is jointly run by the DWNP and its South African counterpart, opening hours, camping costs and entry fees are different from the rest of the DWNP parks (see p110).

The gates for each DWNP park are open from 6am to 6.30pm (1 April to 30 September) or from 5.30am to 7pm (1 October to 31 March). It is vital that all visitors are out of the park, or settled into their campsite, outside these hours. Driving after dark is strictly forbidden.

BOOKING

Reservations for any DWNP campsite can be made up to 12 months in advance at the DWNP office in Gaborone. You can also book through the **Maun Office** (☎ 686 1265; Boseja, Maun), beside the police station. Chobe National Park bookings are also available from the **Kasane Office** (☎ 625 2486).

Be advised that you can no longer pay for your permits at park gates anymore. Also, all reservations, cancellations and extensions must be made at the Gaborone or Maun

NATIONAL PARK FEES PER DAY

Infants and children up to the age of seven are entitled to free entry into the national parks.

	Citizens	Residents	Foreigners	Safari Participants
adult	P10	P30	P120	P70
child (8-17)	P5	P15	P60	P35
camping	P5	P20	P30	
vehicles <3500kg		P10		P50

THE SAN

Once the San roamed over most of the African continent. Certainly they were living around the Kalahari and Tsodilo Hills as far back as 30,000 years ago, as archaeological finds in the Kalahari have demonstrated. Some linguists even credit them with the invention of human language. Unlike most other African countries, where the San have perished or disappeared through war and interbreeding, Botswana and Namibia retain the remnants of their San communities – barely 100,000 individuals in total, which may include many San of mixed descent. Of these, around 60% live in Botswana (the !Kung, G//ana, G/wi and !xo being the largest groups) and 35% in Namibia (the Naro, !Xukwe, Hei//kom and Ju/hoansi), with the remainder scattered throughout South Africa, Angola, Zimbabwe and Zambia.

The Past

Traditionally the San were nomadic hunter-gatherers who travelled in small family bands (usually between around 25 and 35 people) within well-defined territories. They had no chiefs or hierarchy of leadership and decisions were reached by group consensus. With no animals, crops or possessions, the San were highly mobile. Everything that they needed for their daily existence they carried with them.

Initially the San's social flexibility enabled them to evade conquest and control. But as other powerful tribes with big herds of livestock and farming ambitions moved into the area, inevitable disputes arose over the land. The San's wide-ranging, nomadic lifestyle (some territories extended over 1000 sq km) was utterly at odds with the settled world of the farmers and soon became a source of bitter conflict. This situation was rapidly accelerated by European colonists, who arrived in the area during the mid-17th century. The early Boers' campaign of land seizures and forced population migrations lasted for 200 years and it is estimated that around 200,000 indigenous people died as a result of these events. Such territorial disputes, combined with modern policies on game conservation, have seen the San increasingly disenfranchised and dispossessed. What's more, in the modern world their disparate social structure has made it exceedingly difficult for them to organise pressure groups to defend their rights and land as other groups have done.

The Present

Today the San are largely impoverished. Many work on farms and cattle posts or live in resource-poor settlements centred on boreholes in western Botswana and northeastern Namibia as debate rages around them as to their 'place' in modern African society.

DWNP offices in person, or by email or letter – not over the telephone.

Payment in either Botswanan pula or by credit card must be received within one month or you forfeit the booking. In either case, the DWNP will send you, by fax, letter or email, a receipt with a reference number on it that you must keep and quote if you need to change your reservation.

Once you have booked it is difficult to change anything, so make sure to plan your trip well and allow enough time to get there and look around. A refund (less a 10% administration charge) is only possible with more than 30 days' notice.

Environmental Issues

While much of Botswana is largely wide open and pristine, it does face several ecological challenges. The main one revolves around its 3000km of 1.5m-high 'buffalo fence', officially called the 'veterinary cordon fence' – a series of high-tensile-steel wire barriers that cross some of the country's wildest terrain. The fences were first erected in 1954 to segregate wild buffalo herds from domestic free-range cattle and thwart the spread of foot-and-mouth disease. However, it hasn't been proven that the disease is passed from species to species and the fences not only prevent contact between wild and domestic bovine species, but also prevent other wild animals from migrating to water sources along age-old seasonal routes.

While Botswana has set aside large areas for wildlife protection, they don't constitute independent ecosystems, and migratory

Nearly all of Botswana's and Namibia's San were relocated from their ancestral lands to new government settlements such as New Xade in the central Kalahari. It's one of the biggest political hot potatoes for the current Botswanan government. In 2006 this resettlement program earned the government a reprimand from the UN's Committee on the Elimination of Racial Discrimination. The Botswanan government maintains that its relocation policies have the San's best interests at heart (see the section 'Relocation of Basarwa' on the government website, www.gov.bw). Development, education and modernisation are its buzzwords. However, many San actively rejected the government's version of modernisation if it meant giving up their ancestral lands and traditions.

A significant landmark for the San was the ruling of South Africa's highest court in favour of the Richtersveld people (relatives of the San) of Northern Cape Province in 2003. For the first time, the court recognised that indigenous people have both communal land ownership and mineral rights over their territory. Such a ruling had important implications for countries such as Botswana, which operates under the same Roman-Dutch legal system.

The court case brought by the First People of the Kalahari (FPK) against the government's relocation policies was concluded in May 2006, and roughly 1000 San attached their names to the effort. During the proceedings many San tried to return home to the Central Kalahari Game Reserve (CKGR), but most were forced off the grounds of the reserve. In December 2006 the high court ruled that the eviction of the San was 'unlawful and unconstitutional'. One justice went so far as to say that not allowing the San to hunt in their homeland 'was tantamount to condemning the residents of the CKGR to death by starvation'.

The Future

The outlook for the San is uncertain. One of Africa's greatest dilemmas in the 21st century is how to preserve old cultures and traditions while accepting and adapting to the new.

Historical precedents, like those of the fates of the Native Americans, the Innu of Canada and the Australian Aborigines, certainly don't encourage optimism. But the groundswell of protest generated by grassroots bodies such as the Southern African minorities organisation WIMSA (Working Group for Indigenous Minorities of Southern Africa; www.san.org.za) is gaining ever more international attention.

Tourism provides some measure of economic opportunity for the San, who are often employed in Ghanzi- and Kalahari-based lodges as game guides and trackers. But supporters of the San argue that for this race to survive into the 21st century, they require not only self-sufficiency and international support but institutional support and recognition from within the government.

wildlife numbers (particularly wildebeests, giraffes and zebras) continue to decline. Cattle ranching is a source of wealth and a major export industry, but all exported beef must be disease-free, so understandably ranchers have reacted positively to the fences, and the government tends to side with the ranchers.

Botswana also has water issues. From the time of the first European colonists, both settlers and developers have been eyeing the Okavango Delta as a source of water to transform northwestern Botswana into lush, green farmland. Nowadays, pressure from population growth, mining interests and increased tourism – particularly around Maun – are straining resources and placing the delta at the crux of a debate between the government, ranchers, engineers, developers, tour operators, rural people and conservationists.

See p20 for information on what you can do to travel responsibly in Botswana.

FOOD & DRINK

Food

Although eating out isn't particularly exciting – Botswana has no great national cuisine to knock your socks off – self-caterers will find the pickings among the best in Africa. Restaurants normally serve up decent, if unimaginative, fare. Vegetarian and international cuisines haven't really caught on, but in Gaborone, Francistown and Maun, you'll find Chinese, Indian, French and Italian options. In smaller towns, expect little menu variation: chicken, chips, beef and greasy fried snacks are the norm.

Forming the basis of most traditional Batswana meals are *mabele* (sorghum) or *bo-*

gobe (sorghum porridge), or the increasingly popular imported *mielies* (cobs of maize) and mielie pap (maize porridge). All of these are typically served with some sort of meat relish and eaten with the fingers.

Open markets aren't as prevalent here as in neighbouring countries, but Gaborone, Francistown and Maun do have growing informal markets where you'll find inexpensive produce and other staples.

Drinks

A range of 100%-natural fruit juices from South Africa are sold in casks in supermarkets in the major cities and towns. You'll also find a variety of teas, coffee and soft drinks.

Botswana's main domestic drop is the very light St Louis Special Light lager (you can't drink it fast enough to feel it). You'll also find Castle, Lion and Windhoek Lager (from Namibia), as well as a growing range of spirit coolers. Some of the more popular traditional alcoholic drinks are illegal, including *mokolane* wine, a potent swill made from distilled palm sap. Another is *kgadi,* made from a distilled brew of brown sugar and berries or fungus. Other home brews include the common *bojalwa,* an inexpensive, sprouted sorghum beer that is also brewed commercially; a wine made from fermented marula fruit; light and nonintoxicating *mageu,* made from mielies or sorghum mash; and *madila,* a thickened sour milk.

GABORONE

pop 185,000

Botswana's small capital often doesn't get a lot of love from its own residents, let alone tourists. And let's be fair: you probably came to Botswana for the wildlife, not the nightlife. But nightlife is here in Gaborone, as well as the pulse of the Botswanan nation. The capital may be a village that has grown too large, but it is the place – and this place exists everywhere in Africa – where a farmer moves to make his fortune, or students train to lead their nation and the official course of the country is determined.

HISTORY

In 1964, when the village of Gaborone (named for an early Tlokwa chief) was designated as the future capital of independent Botswana, the task of designing the new city was assigned to the Department of Public Works, which never envisaged a population of more than 20,000. By 1990, however, the population was six times that, and Gaborone is now among the fastest-growing cities in Southern Africa.

ORIENTATION

Gaborone sprawls to such an extent that outer neighbourhoods are called 'Phases' and 'Extensions' (poetic, eh?). It lacks a definitive town centre, so many shops, restaurants and offices are located in or near suburban malls and shopping centres, which form their own pulsing nodes throughout town. The Mall – also called the Main Mall – is the business heart of Gaborone and has a handful of shops, restaurants, banks and internet centres. Almost all government offices, and several embassies, are situated to the west of the Mall, in and around State and Embassy Drs. There are also a number of shopping malls that are located outside the city centre, which are easily accessible by combi (minibus).

INFORMATION

Bookshops

Exclusive Books (Riverwalk Mall) This reader-recommended bookshop has a wide range of literature, nonfiction and travel books.

Kingston's Bookshop (Broadhurst Mall) Has a huge array of novels, postcards and books and maps about Botswana and the region.

Emergency

Ambulance (☎ 997)
Central Police Station (☎ 355 1161; Botswana Rd)
Fire department (☎ 998)
Police (☎ 999)

Internet Access

Many hotels are increasingly offering internet access, via either wi-fi or network cables.

Aim Internet (Botswana Rd; per hr P15) Next to the Cresta President Hotel.

Sakeng Internet Access Point (The Mall; per hr P15) In the Gaborone Hardware Building.

Medical Services

Gaborone Hospital Dental Clinic (☎ 395 3777; Segoditshane Way) Part of the Gaborone Private Hospital.

Gaborone Private Hospital (☎ 300 1999; Segoditshane Way) For anything serious, head to this reasonably modern, but expensive hospital, opposite Broadhurst Mall. The best facility in town.

Princess Marina Hospital (☎ 355 3221; Notwane Rd) Equipped to handle standard medical treatments and emergencies, but shouldn't be your first choice for treatment.

Money

Major branches of Standard Chartered and Barclays Banks have foreign-exchange facilities and ATMs, and offer cash advances. The few bureaux de change around the city offer quick service at better rates than the banks, but charge up to 2.75% commission.

Barclays Bank (☎ 355 3411; Khama Cres)

Edcom Bureau de Change (☎ 361 1123) Near the train station.

Prosper Bureau de Change African Mall (☎ 360 0478) Broadhurst Mall (☎ 390 5358)

SAA City Center (☎ 355 2021; Gaborone Hardware Bldg, The Mall) The American Express representative.

Standard Chartered Bank (☎ 355 2911; The Mall)

Western Union (☎ 367 1490; Gaborone Hardware Bldg, The Mall)

Post

In addition to the **Central Post Office** (The Mall), there is also a post office located across the road from Broadhurst Mall.

Tourist Information

Department of Tourism (☎ 355 3024; www.gov.bw/tourism; 2nd fl, Standard Chartered Bank Bldg, The Mall; 🕑 7.30am-12.30pm & 1.45-4.30pm Mon-Fri) The tourism department has modernised and runs a very helpful operation these days.

Department of Wildlife & National Parks (DWNP; ☎ 318 0774; dwnp@gov.bw; Government Enclave, Khama Cres, Gaborone; 🕑 reservations 7.30am-12.45pm & 1.45-4.30pm Mon-Fri) One of the two accommodation-booking offices (the other is in Maun; see p98) for all national parks and reserves run by the DWNP.

SIGHTS

The **National Museum & Art Gallery** (☎ 397 4616; 331 Independence Ave; admission free; 🕑 9am-6pm Tue-Fri, 9am-5pm Sat & Sun) is a repository of stuffed wildlife and cultural artefacts, including displays on San crafts, culture and hunting techniques, traditional and modern African and European art, and ethnographic and cultural exhibits.

The **Gaborone Game Reserve** (☎ 318 4492; per person P120, per vehicle P50; 🕑 6.30am-6.30pm), 1km east of Broadhurst, is accessible only by private vehicle (no bikes or motorcycles), and is home to a variety of grazers and browsers. Access is from Limpopo Dr; turn east immediately south of the Segoditshane River.

Diamond Trading Company (☎ 395 1131; cnr Nelson Mandela Dr & Khama Cres) is designed to make use of natural daylight – without direct sunlight – for the purpose of sorting and grading diamonds from the world's largest diamond mine at Jwaneng. If you have time and aren't put off by red tape, you can muster a group and arrange a tour.

ACTIVITIES

The best golf in the city is a little outside of it, about 14km north in **Phakalane Golf Estate** (☎ 360 4000; Golf Dr, Phakalane), tucked away into a kind of out-of-place, woodland-and-fancy-housing setting. Green fees for 18 holes are P140. **Gaborone Golf Course** is about 2km south of Broadhurst; temporary membership, which includes use of the swimming pool, bars and restaurants, costs P75 per day. Green fees for 9/18 holes are an extra P20/40, and equipment is available for rental at the pro shop.

TOURS

If you've got a day or two to kill in Gabs, do yourself a favour: get in touch with local resident and Gaborone expert Marilyn Garcin, who runs **Garcin Safaris** (☎ 393 8190; www.garcinsafaris.com). She does great tours of the city, including a *No. 1 Ladies Detective Agency*–focused jaunt, and is a good contact for arranging onward travel into the rest of the country.

FESTIVALS & EVENTS

The national holidays of **Sir Seretse Khama Day**, **President's Day** and **Botswana/Independence Day** (see p113) are always cause for celebration in the capital. Details about these events are advertised in local English-language newspapers and in the 'What's On' column of the *Botswana Advertiser*. Gaborone also plays host to a number of local festivals and events:

Maitisong Festival Established in 1987, the Maitisong Festival is the largest performing-arts festival in Botswana, and is held annually for seven days during the last week of March or the first week of April.

Traditional Dance Competition Late March.

Industry & Technology Fair Held at the Gaborone Show Grounds in May.

International Trade Fair Also held at the Gaborone Show Grounds, in August.

GABORONE

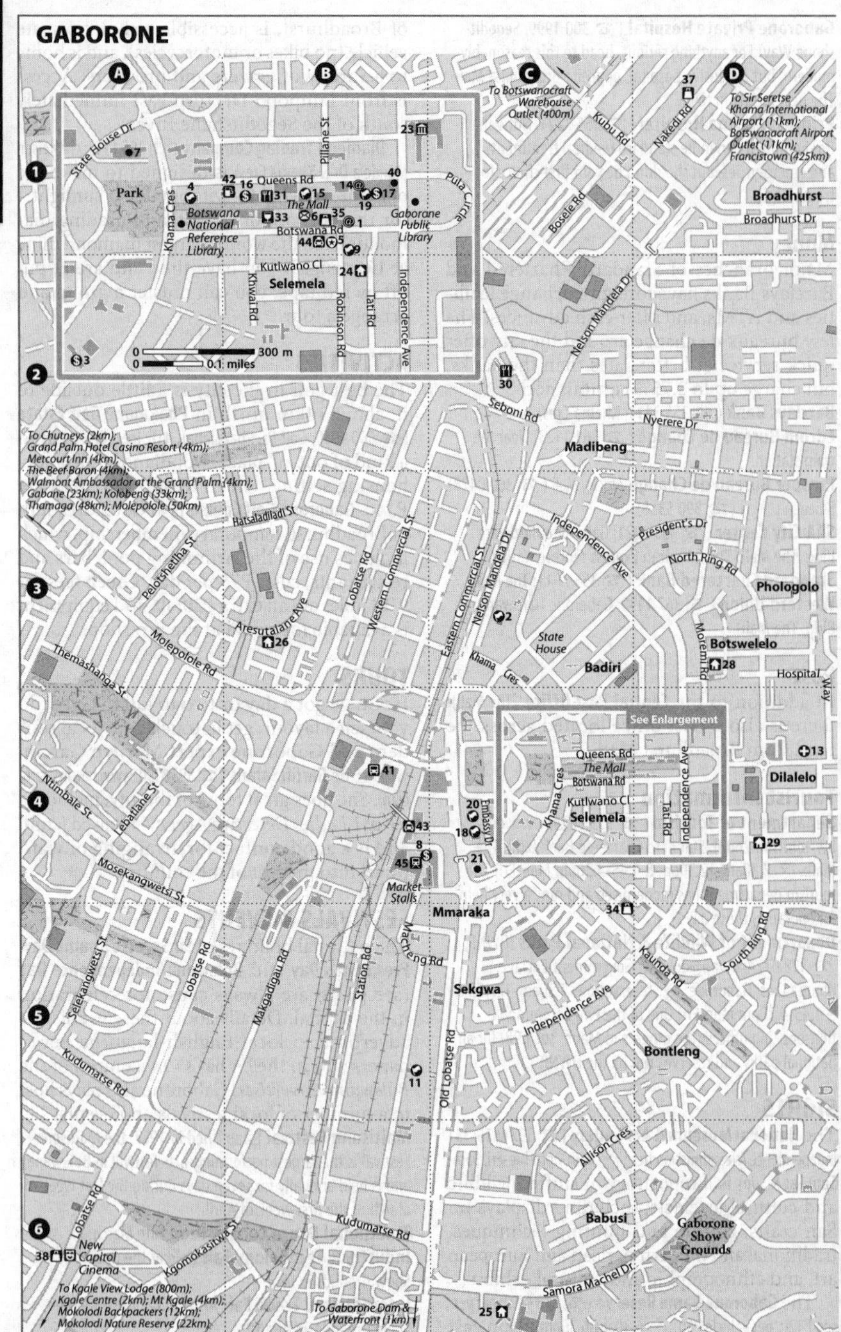
To Botswanacraft Warehouse Outlet (400m)
To Sir Seretse Khama International Airport (11km); Botswanacraft Airport Outlet (11km); Francistown (425km)
State House Dr
Park
Khama Cres
Botswana National Reference Library
Queens Rd
The Mall
Botswana Rd
Kutlwano Cl
Selemela
Khwai Rd
Robinson Rd
Tati Rd
Independence Ave
Pillane St
Pula Circle
Gaborone Public Library
300 m
0.1 miles
Kubu Rd
Nakedi Rd
Bosele Rd
Broadhurst
Broadhurst Dr
Nelson Mandela Dr
Seboni Rd
Nyerere Dr
Madibeng
To Chutneys (2km); Grand Palm Hotel Casino Resort (4km); Metcourt Inn (4km); The Beef Baron (4km); Walmont Ambassador at the Grand Palm (4km); Gabane (23km); Kolobeng (33km); Thamaga (48km); Molepolole (50km)
Hatsaladiladi St
Pelotshetlha St
Aresutalane Ave
Lobatse Rd
Western Commercial St
Eastern Commercial St
Independence Ave
President's Dr
North Ring Rd
Phologolo
Molepolole Rd
State House
Khama Cres
Badiri
Botswelelo
Moremi Rd
Hospital Way
Themashanga St
See Enlargement
Dilalelo
Ntimbale St
Lebatlane St
Embassy Dr
Mosekangwetsi St
Market Stalls
Mmaraka
Selekangwetsi St
Makgadigau Rd
Station Rd
Macheng Rd
Sekgwa
Kaunda Rd
South Ring Rd
Kudumatse Rd
Old Lobatse Rd
Bontleng
Allison Cres
Babusi
Gaborone Show Grounds
Kgomokasitwa St
Samora Machel Dr
New Capitol Cinema
To Kgale View Lodge (800m); Kgale Centre (2km); Mt Kgale (4km); Mokolodi Backpackers (12km); Mokolodi Nature Reserve (22km)
To Gaborone Dam & Waterfront (1km)

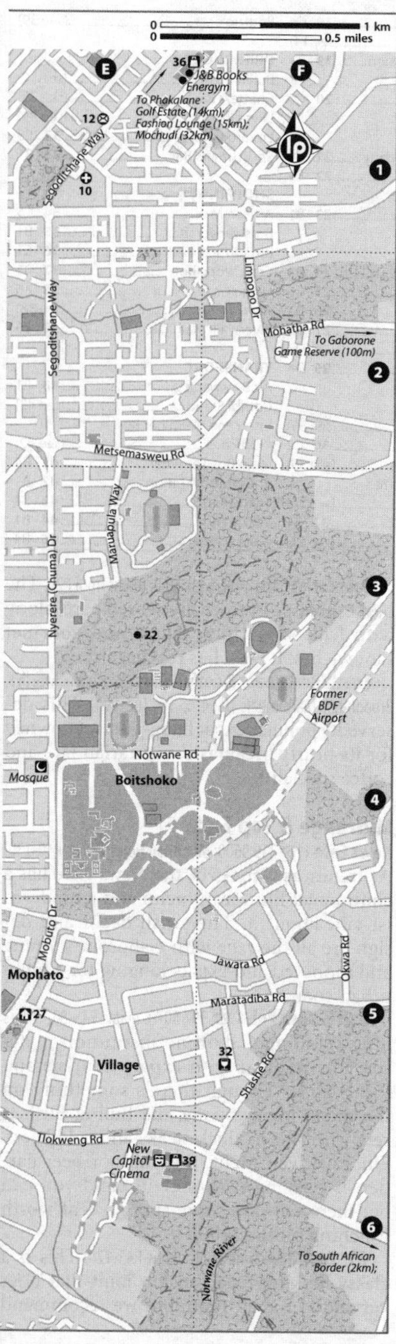

SLEEPING

Budget

Mokolodi Backpackers (☎ 411 1165; campsite/dm/chalet P75/120/325; 💻) If you're doing the budget thing, the self-drive thing or the overland thing, this is a good option, and the only real backpacker vibe around Gaborone. About 10km southwest of the city, it offers attractive chalets and good campsites, and the dorms aren't a bad deal either.

Tindi Lodge (☎ 395 3648; 487 South Ring Rd; r without/with bathroom P230/240) This friendly, family-run lodge is a little worn, but rooms are comfortable enough if you're looking to just crash at night.

Brackendene Lodge (☎ 391 2886; Tati Rd; r from P290; ❄ 💻) The Brackendene is one of the better-value hotels in town. Rooms are simple but large, and kitted out with TVs and air-con; there's reliable internet in the lobby (supposedly moving into rooms, fingers crossed) and you're within easy walking distance of the mall.

Ditshane Lodge (☎ 316 3737; 18576 Aresutalane Ave; s/d P300/350; ❄ 🅿) It may not be the most memorable stay of your trip, but Ditshane is an economical option for anyone in need of a good night's rest with basic fixtures like TV, secure parking and a little bit of thatch-chic.

Kgale View Lodge (☎ 321 7555; Phase 4, Plot 222258; r from P400) This locally recommended B&B has friendly service, cosy rooms and a generally welcoming atmosphere. You'll find it just southwest of town. It's the sort of place that books up fast with return customers, so call ahead.

Midrange & Top End

All places listed below offer rooms with a private bathroom, cable TV and air-con. Breakfast is not included in the prices.

Metcourt Inn (☎ 391 2999, 363 7777; www.metcourt.com; Molepolole Rd; s/d P465/535; ❄) Located within the Grand Palm Hotel complex, this lovely little three-star option will likely put you in mind of every business hotel you've ever stayed in, which can be a good thing after the bush.

Motheo Apartments (☎ 318 1587; motheo@info.bw; Moremi Rd; apt P396-786; ❄ 💻 🅿) Has a good range of self-catering apartments that are a nice alternative to the big concrete blocks that characterise so many other Gaborone hotels. The apartments come with internet, DSTV

BOTSWANA

INFORMATION
Aim Internet......1 B1
Angolan Embassy......2 C3
Barclays Bank......3 A2
British High Commission......4 A1
Central Police Station......5 B1
Central Post Office......6 B1
Department of Tourism......(see 17)
Department of Wildlife & National Parks......7 A1
Edcom Bureau de Change......8 B4
Exclusive Books......(see 39)
French Embassy......9 B1
Gaborone Hospital Dental Clinic......(see 10)
Gaborone Private Hospital......10 E1
German Embassy......(see 36)
Kingston's Bookshop......(see 36)
Namibian High Commission......11 B5
Post Office......12 E1
Princess Marina Hospital......13 D4
Prosper Bureau de Change......(see 34)
Prosper Bureau de Change......(see 36)
SAA City Center......(see 14)
Sakeng Internet Access Point......14 B1
South African Embassy......15 B1
Standard Chartered ATM......16 B1
Standard Chartered Bank......17 B1
US Embassy......18 C4
Western Union......(see 14)
Zambian High Commission......19 B1
Zimbabwean High Commission......20 C4

SIGHTS & ACTIVITIES
Diamond Trading Company......21 C4
Gaborone Golf Course......22 E3
National Museum & Art Gallery......23 B1

SLEEPING
Brackendene Lodge......24 B2
Cresta Lodge......25 C6
Ditshane Lodge......26 B3
Mondior Summit......27 E5
Motheo Apartments......28 D3
Tindi Lodge......29 D4

EATING
25° East......(see 39)
Bull & Bush Pub......30 C2
Equatorial Cafe......(see 39)
Kgotla Restaurant & Coffee Shop......(see 36)
King's Takeaway......31 B1
News Cafe......(see 27)
Rodizio's......(see 39)

DRINKING
Bull & Bush Pub......(see 30)
Chatters Bar......(see 25)
Linga Langa......(see 39)
Lizzard Lounge......32 F5
Sportsmans Bar......33 B1

SHOPPING
African Mall......34 C5
Botswanacraft......35 B1
Broadhurst Mall......36 E1
Craft Workshop......37 D1
Game City Mall......38 A6
Jewel of Africa......(see 38)
Riverwalk Mall......39 E6

TRANSPORT
Air Botswana......40 B1
Combi Stand......(see 43)
Intercape Mainliner Bus Office......(see 42)
Main Bus Terminal......41 B4
Shell Petrol Station......42 B1
Taxi Stand......43 B4
Taxi Stand......44 B1
Train Station......45 B4

(Digital Satellite TV) and various other mod-cons and are all self-catering.

Cresta Lodge (☎ 397 5375; www.cresta-hospitality.com; Samora Machel Dr; r from P900;) Located 2km outside the city centre, the attractively landscaped Cresta Lodge is a good choice if you're looking for a quiet night's rest in a three-star setting outside the urban sprawl.

Walmont Ambassador at the Grand Palm (☎ 363 7777; www.walmont.com; Molepolole Rd; d from P1267;) Located 4km west of the city centre, this resolutely modern and polished hotel is situated in a Las Vegas–inspired minicity complete with restaurants, bars, a casino, cinema and spa. You'll pay to stay, but it's worth it for the pampering.

Mondior Summit (☎ 319 0600; www.mondior.com; Corner Mobuto Dr & Maratadiba Rd; s/d from P1312/1922;) Probably the best hotel in town, the Mondior is chock-a-block with all the mod-cons you need and boasts Africa chic – think big plush rooms bathed in warm, rich, monochrome-colour schemes. There's every imaginable service available and a general sense of contemporary poshness throughout.

EATING

Budget

King's Takeaway (The Mall; meals P20-40) This local favourite serves up inexpensive burgers, chips and snacks to hungry office workers.

Equatorial Cafe (Riverwalk Mall; mains from P20) The best espressos in town are served here, along with fruit smoothies, falafel and gourmet sandwiches. It even has real bagels!

Kgotla Restaurant & Coffee Shop (above Woolworth's, Broadhurst Mall; meals US$4-6; Tue-Sun) This deservedly popular expat hang-out is renowned for its hearty breakfasts, vegetarian fare and coffee specialities.

Midrange & Top End

News Cafe (☎ 319 0600; Mondrian Hotel; mains P40-130) As trendy as Gabs gets, the News Cafe has a continental European menu and a modernist vibe about it. The swish decor and design are all the rage with Gaborone's young and moneyed and expats longing for a bit of urban cool.

Bull & Bush Pub (☎ 397 5070; mains P45-80) This long-standing Gaborone institution is deservedly popular with expats, tourists and locals alike. Though there's something on the menu for everyone, the Bull & Bush is renowned for its thick steaks and cold beers. On any given night, the outdoor beer garden is buzzing with activity, and you can bet there's always some sports event worth watching on the tube.

25º East (Riverwalk Mall; mains P45-120) This is a classy-looking Asian-fusion joint that does very good Indian food, but we recommend passing on the Thai dishes. We know, we know – you see Thai food in Gaborone and get sorely tempted, but it's just not up to scratch here.

Chutneys (☎ 319 0545; mains P50-90; West Ring Rd) This gorgeous spot northwest of the town centre serves the best Indian food in Botswana – a good and varied collection of curries that are a brilliant break from *pap* and meat and more *pap*. The focus is on South Indian specialities, but there are all sorts of delicious dishes on the menu pulled from all around the subcontinent.

Beef Baron (☎ 363 7777; mains from P90; Grand Palm Resort) With a subtle name like 'Beef Baron,' is there any wonder what's on offer? And yet there are surprises here, and generally pleasant ones at that. Steak this may be, but it's widely recognised as the best steak in the city; saw into one of those fat boys and thank us later.

Rodizio's (Riverwalk Mall; set menu from P130) Part of a chain of Brazilian super meat houses/samba parties, this place offers a drill that may be familiar to you: guys walk around with skewers of meat. You hold up little flags indicating if you want more or less. Gastrointestinal overload eventually occurs, but at least you die with a smile on your face and meat juice on your lips.

DRINKING & ENTERTAINMENT

Bull & Bush Pub (☎ 397 5070) This popular restaurant (see opposite) is also the centre for expat nightlife, where young Gaborone-ites go to behave badly and party to excess. That said, the dance floor gets hot, the beer is cold and all in all this can be a hell of a fun place.

Chatters Bar (Cresta Lodge, Samora Machel Dr) This classy bar is located in the Cresta Lodge (opposite), and features smooth, easy-listening live music most nights of the week. The bar is well stocked, though it's a bit pricey.

Fashion Lounge (Phakalane) About 15km north of the city (all taxi drivers know where it is), this is Gabs' attempt at a sophisticated Manhattan martini bar. The bar actually pulls it off, but it does feel weird to be among all the *Sex in the City* wannabees in Botswana.

Lizzard Lounge (The Village) Very popular with local Batswana, those who play at being gangstas and, we've heard, real gangsters. Great for dancing, but it does get a little rough some nights.

Linga Langa (Riverwalk Mall) A vague cross between an American sports bar and a British pub, which gets pretty packed on weekend nights – it's a good place to start the evening.

Sportmans Bar (Botswana Rd) This friendly local watering hole is conveniently located on The Mall, and has a couple of pool tables in case you're looking to do something other than drink.

SHOPPING

For shoppers, Gaborone boasts a series of shopping malls that are headed up by the lovely Riverwalk Mall and the enormous Kgale Centre. Lesser options include Broadhurst Mall, The Mall and African Mall.

Botswanacraft (www.botswanacraft.bw; Warehouse ☎ 362 4471; The Mall ☎ 355 3577; Airport ☎ 361 2209) Botswana's largest craft emporium sells traditional souvenirs from all over the country, including weavings from Odi and pottery from Gabane and Thamaga. If you're deficient at bargaining, fear not – prices are fixed.

Jewel of Africa (☎ 361 4359; jewel@global.bw; Game City Mall) This attractive shop offers an eclectic range of carvings, sketches, shawls and other assorted African knick-knacks. Although not everything is made in Botswana, prices here are reasonable (and fixed).

Craft Workshop (☎ 355 6364; 5648 Nakedi Rd, Broadhurst Industrial Estate) This small complex of shops sells crafts and souvenirs, and also plays host to a flea market on the morning of the last Sunday of each month. To get there take the 'Broadhurst Route 3' combi.

GETTING THERE & AWAY

Air

From Sir Seretse Khama International Airport, 14km north of the centre, **Air Botswana** (☎ 395 2812; Botswana Insurance Company House, The Mall) operates scheduled domestic flights to and from Francistown (US$100), Maun (US$155) and Kasane (US$155). The office also serves as an agent for other regional airlines.

Bus

Intercity buses and minibuses to Johannesburg (P80, seven hours), Francistown (P35, six hours), Selebi-Phikwe (P42, six hours), Ghanzi (P70, 11 hours), Lobatse (P10, 1½ hours), Mahalapye (P17, three hours), Palapye (P30, four hours) and Serowe (P32, five hours) depart from the main bus terminal. The main bus terminal also offers local services to Kanye (P10, two hours), Jwaneng (P28, three hours), Manyana (P6, 1½ hours), Mochudi

(P7, one hour), Thamaga (P5, one hour) and Molepolole (P9, one hour).

To reach Maun or Kasane, change in Francistown. Buses operate according to roughly fixed schedules and minibuses leave when full.

The Intercape Mainliner to Johannesburg (US$25, 6½ hours) runs from the Shell petrol station beside the Mall. Tickets can be booked either through your accommodation or at the Intercape Mainliner Office.

Train

The day train departs for Francistown daily at 10am (club/economy class US$4/8, 6½ hours). The night train departs nightly at 9pm (1st-class sleeper/2nd-class sleeper/economy US$25/20/5, 8¼ hours). Coming from Francistown, the overnight service continues to Lobatse (US$1, 1½ hours) early in the morning, with only economy-class seats available from Gaborone. For current information, contact **Botswana Railways** (☎ 471 1375; www.botswanarailways.co.bw).

GETTING AROUND

To/From the Airport

Taxis rarely turn up at the airport; if you do find one, you'll pay around P70 to travel to the centre of town. The only reliable transport between the airport and town is the courtesy minibuses operated by the top-end hotels for their guests. If there's space, nonguests may talk the driver into a lift.

Car

The following international car-rental companies have agencies (which may not be staffed after 5pm) at the airport:

Avis (☎ 391 3093)
Budget (☎ 390 2030)
Imperial (☎ 390 6676)

Combi

Packed white combis, recognisable by their blue number plates, circulate according to set routes and cost P2.70 per ride. They pick up and drop off only at designated combi stops marked 'bus/taxi stop'. The main city loop passes all the main shopping centres except the Riverwalk Mall and the Kgale Centre, which are on the Tlokweng and Kgale routes, respectively. Combis can be hailed either along major roads or from the combi stand.

Taxi

Taxis, which can also be easily identified by their blue number plates, are surprisingly difficult to come by in Gabs. Very few cruise the streets looking for fares, and most are parked either in front of the train station or on Botswana Rd. If you manage to get hold of one, fares (negotiable) are generally P25 to P40 per trip around the city.

Contact the following companies if you want to book a taxi.

Final Bravo Cabs (☎ 312 1785)
Speedy Cabs (☎ 390 0070)

AROUND GABORONE

KOPONG

Arne's Country Retreat (☎ 712 34567; arnes.retreat@gmail.com; Lentsweletau Rd) is a friendly, Swedish-run ranch specialising in horse riding, though it also offers cheap and tranquil accommodation. Camping costs US$5 per person, while double rooms with private bathrooms in the rustic guesthouse cost US$20. Take the road from Gaborone towards Molepolole, then head to Kopong and follow the signs.

ODI

This small village (pronounced *oo*-dee) is best known for its internationally acclaimed **Odi Weavers** (☎ 339 2268; 🕑 8am-4.30pm Mon-Fri, 10am-4.30pm Sat & Sun), who produce and sells a range of locally made weavings, tapestries, bedspreads and cushions. Take a northbound minibus from Gaborone and get off at Odi Junction; from here, you'll probably have to hitch the final 7km to the workshop.

MOCHUDI

Mochudi, one of Botswana's most fascinating villages, was first settled by the Kwena in the mid-1500s, as evidenced by ruined stone walls in the hills. In 1871 came the Kgatla people, who had been forced from their lands by northward-trekking Boers. The Cape Dutch–style **Phuthadikobo Museum** (☎ 577 7238; fax 574 8920; admission free, donation suggested; 🕑 8am-5pm Mon-Fri, 2-5pm Sat & Sun), established in 1976, is one of Botswana's best, with displays on the village and its Kgatla history. After visiting the museum, it's worth spending an hour appreciating the variety of designs in the town's mud-walled architecture.

Buses to Mochudi depart from Gaborone when full. By car, head north to Pilane and turn east; after 6km, turn left at the T-junction and then right just before the hospital, into the historic village centre.

THAMAGA

The rural village of Thamaga is home to the **Botswelelo Centre** (☎ 599 9220; Molepolole Rd; tours P3; ⌚ 8am-5pm), which is also known as Thamaga Pottery. This nonprofit community project was started by missionaries in the 1970s and now sells a wide range of creations for good prices. Tours must be booked in advance. Buses run frequently from the main bus terminal in Gaborone (P7, one hour).

About 5km east of here, in Mmankgodi, is **Bahurutshe Cultural Lodge** (☎ 316 3737; www.bahurutsheculturallodge.com; campsite/chalets P50/350), an innovative cultural village/chalet complex/campground where visitors can very easily access the traditional elements of Setswana music, dance and cuisine. The comfy chalets really play up the African-hut thing, with cool stone-and-mud walls and rustic-smelling thatch enclosing you come evening.

MOKOLODI NATURE RESERVE

This 3000-hectare private **reserve** (☎ 316 1955; www.mokolodi.com; ⌚ 7.30am-6pm) was established in 1991 and is home to giraffes, elephants, zebras, baboons, warthogs, hippos, kudu, impala, waterbucks and klipspringers. The reserve also protects some retired cheetahs, leopards, honey badgers, jackals and hyenas, as well as over 300 species of birds.

Mokolodi also operates a research facility, a breeding centre for rare and endangered species, a community education centre and a sanctuary for orphaned, injured or confiscated birds and animals. It also accepts volunteers, though an application must be submitted prior to arrival, and a maintenance fee is levied according to the length of the program. See the website for more information.

It is important to note that the entire reserve often closes during the rainy season (December to March) – phone ahead before you visit at this time. Visitors are permitted to drive their own vehicles around the reserve (you will need a 4WD in the rainy season), though guided tours by jeep or on foot are available. If you're self-driving, don't forget to pick up a map from the reception office so you don't get lost.

Park entry fees cost P65 per person per day. If you're not self-driving, two-hour day or night wildlife drives cost P120 per person. There are a number of other activities on offer like cheetah petting (P290), rhino tracking (P485) and horse safaris (P145).

Spending the night in the reserve is a refreshing alternative to staying in Gaborone. Though pricey, the **campsites** (per person P80) at Mokolodi are secluded and well groomed, and also feature braai (barbecue) pits and thatched bush showers (with steaming-hot water) and toilets. If you want to safari in style, there are three-person **chalets** (weekdays/weekend per day P420/560) and six- to eight-person **chalets** (weekdays/weekend per day P560/765) situated in the middle of the reserve. Advance bookings are necessary. If you don't have a vehicle, staff can drive you to the campsite and accommodation areas for P10.

The entrance to the reserve is located 12km south of Gaborone. To travel by public transport, take a bus to Lobatse and get off at the signed turn-off. From there, it's a 1.5km walk to the entrance.

EASTERN BOTSWANA

Eastern Botswana is, in many ways, the Batswana heartland, a land of scrub and seasonal rains that is interspersed with agricultural ranches, fields and stone-strewn tracts. In between cattle posts and farms are settlements that serve as population nodes for the Batswana people But you shouldn't think of Eastern Botswana as just a depot for catching the next bus or the location of the garage for servicing your 4WD. Besides interacting with Setswana culture at arguably its most accessible, you'll find a fair few private farms and reserves here that are good camping options for independent-minded travellers.

SEROWE

In 1902, Chief Khama III abandoned the Bangwato capital in Phalatswe, and built Serowe on the ruins of an 11th-century village at the base of Thathaganyana Hill. Serowe was later immortalised by South African writer Bessie Head, who included the village in several of her works, including the renowned *Serowe – Village of the Rain Wind*.

Although the modern town centre is drab and of little interest to travellers, it's worth

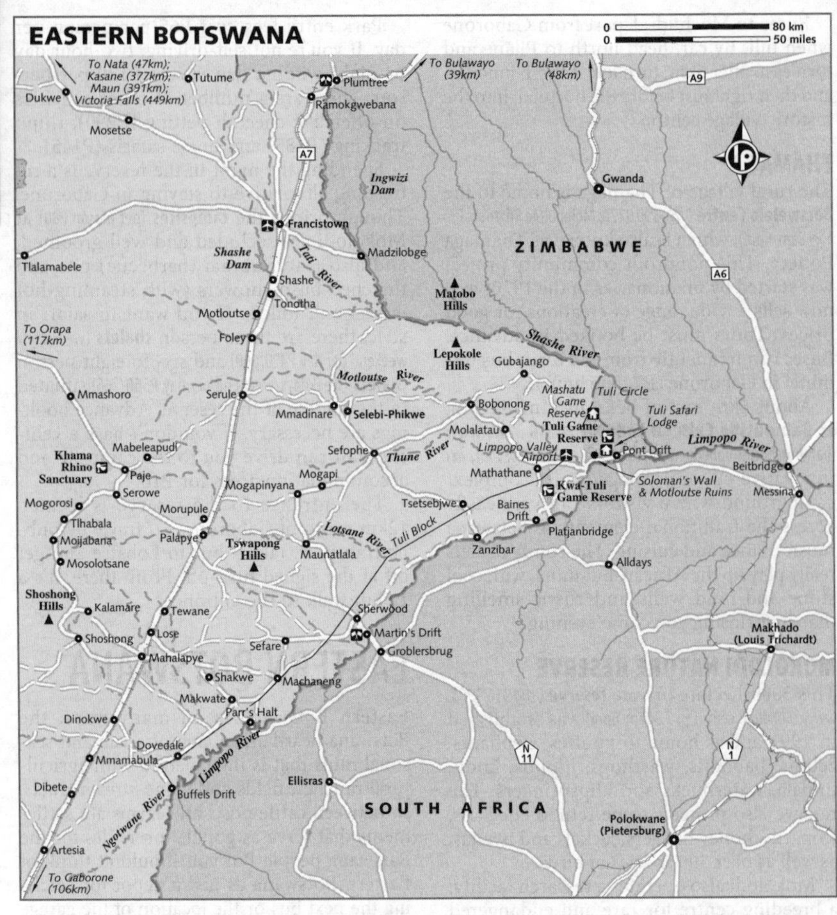

visiting the **Khama III Memorial Museum** (☎ 463 0519; admission free, donation welcome; 🕒 8am-5pm Tue-Fri, 10am-4.30pm Sat), which was opened in 1985 and outlines the history of the Khama family. The museum includes the personal effects of Chief Khama III and his descendants as well as various artefacts illustrating Serowe's history. The museum is about 800m from the central shopping area on the road towards Orapa.

Before leaving town, hike up to the top of Thathaganyana Hill where you'll find the **Royal Cemetery**, which contains the graves of Sir Seretse Khama (see the boxed text, p70) and Khama III; the latter is marked by a bronze duiker (a small antelope), which is the Bangwato totem. Be advised that police consider this area to be sensitive, so visitors need to seek permission (and possibly obtain a guide) from the police station in the barracks house. To reach the station, follow the road opposite the Dennis petrol station until you reach the *kgotla* and the surrounding barracks; one of the buildings houses the police station.

The small but quaint **Tshwaragano Hotel** (☎ 463 0377; s/d P180/210) is built on the slopes of Thathaganyana Hill, and boasts great views of the town. The attached bar–restaurant is usually the most hopping place in town (this assessment, believe us, is relative). Tshwaragano is located above the shopping area on the road to Orapa.

Buses travel between Serowe and Gaborone (P25, four hours) about every hour. Alternatively, from Gabs catch a Francistown-bound bus, disembark at the turn-off to Serowe just north of Palapye, and catch a shared taxi or combi to Serowe. Combis and shared taxis also depart for Orapa (P50, four hours) when full; these combis pass by the entrance to the Khama Rhino Sanctuary. Most buses, combis and taxis leave from a spot near Ellerines furniture shop in the central shopping area, while the mammoth bus station nearby remains empty.

KHAMA RHINO SANCTUARY

In response to declining rhinoceros populations in Botswana, the residents of Serowe banded together in 1989 to establish this 4300-hectare **sanctuary** (☎ 463 0713; www.khamarhinosanctuary.com; per person/vehicle under 5 tons/over 5 tons P33/41/133; ⏰ 8am-7pm). Today, the sanctuary protects the country's last remaining population of rhinos – 34 white and two black rhinos currently reside in Khama (with a baby black on the way as of this writing). The sanctuary is also home to wildebeests, impalas, ostriches, hyenas, leopards and over 230 species of birds.

The main roads within the sanctuary are normally accessible by 2WD in the dry season, though 4WD vehicles are necessary in the rainy season. However, all vehicles can reach the campsite and accommodation areas in any weather. The office at the entrance sells useful maps of the sanctuary as well as basic nonperishable foods, cold drinks and firewood.

No vehicle? Two-hour day/night wildlife drives cost P333 and can take up to four people. Nature walks (P133) and rhino-tracking excursions (P200), both one to two hours long, can also be arranged. You can also hire a guide to accompany your vehicle for P115.

Shady campsites (per person P53) with braai (barbecue) pits are situated adjacent to clean toilets and (wonderfully hot) showers, while six-person student dorms go for P293. If you're looking to splurge for a night or two, rustic four-person chalets (P366 to P399) and six-person A-frames (P512 to P800) have basic kitchen facilities and private bathrooms. If you don't have a vehicle, staff can drive you to the campsite and accommodation areas for a nominal charge.

The entrance gate to the sanctuary is about 26km northwest of Serowe along the road to Orapa (turn left at the unsigned T-junction about 5km northwest of Serowe). Khama is accessible by any bus or combi heading towards Orapa, and is not hard to reach by hitching.

FRANCISTOWN

pop 115,000

In 1867 Southern Africa's first gold rush was ignited when German Karl Mauch discovered gold along the Tati River in Botswana. Two years later, a group of Australian miners along with Englishman Daniel Francis arrived on the scene in search of their fortune. Although Francis headed for the newly discovered Kimberley diamond fields in 1870, he returned 10 years later to negotiate local mining rights with the Ndebele king, Lobengula, and laid out the town that now bears his name.

Today, the second-largest city in Botswana is known more for its wholesale shopping than its mining history. Although there's nothing of much interest in Francistown to travellers, it's a useful (and often necessary) stopover on the way to/from Kasane, Nata, Maun or Victoria Falls.

Information

If you're staying for more than a little bit, it's worth picking up a copy of the *Northern Advertiser* (P3) or *Metro* (P2), both published weekly. For a list of local attractions, pick up a copy of *Exploring Tati: Places of Historic and Other Interest in and Around Francistown* by Catrien van Waarden for P35 (available at the museum).

The Barclays and First National Banks along Blue Jacket St, among other banks, have ATMs and foreign-exchange facilities.

Ebrahim Store (☎ 241 4762; Tainton Ave) The place to buy camping gear.
Nyangabgwe Hospital (☎ 211 1000, emergency 997)
Police station (☎ 241 2221, emergency 999; Haskins St)
Polina Laundromat (Blue Jacket St)
Post Office (Blue Jacket St)

Sights

SUPA-NGWAO MUSEUM

Housed in the 100-year-old Government Camp, this **museum** (☎/fax 240 3088; snm@info.bw; off New Maun Rd; admission free; ⏰ 8am-5pm Mon-Fri, 9am-5pm Sat) includes a prison and a police canteen. The museum contains small, interesting displays about local and regional culture and history (*supa-ngwao* appropriately means 'to show culture' in the Setswana language).

Sleeping

Tati River Lodge (☎ 240 6000; www.trl.co.bw; campsite per person P40, s/d from P540/629; ❄ 🏊) Located on the other side of the Tati River from the Marang

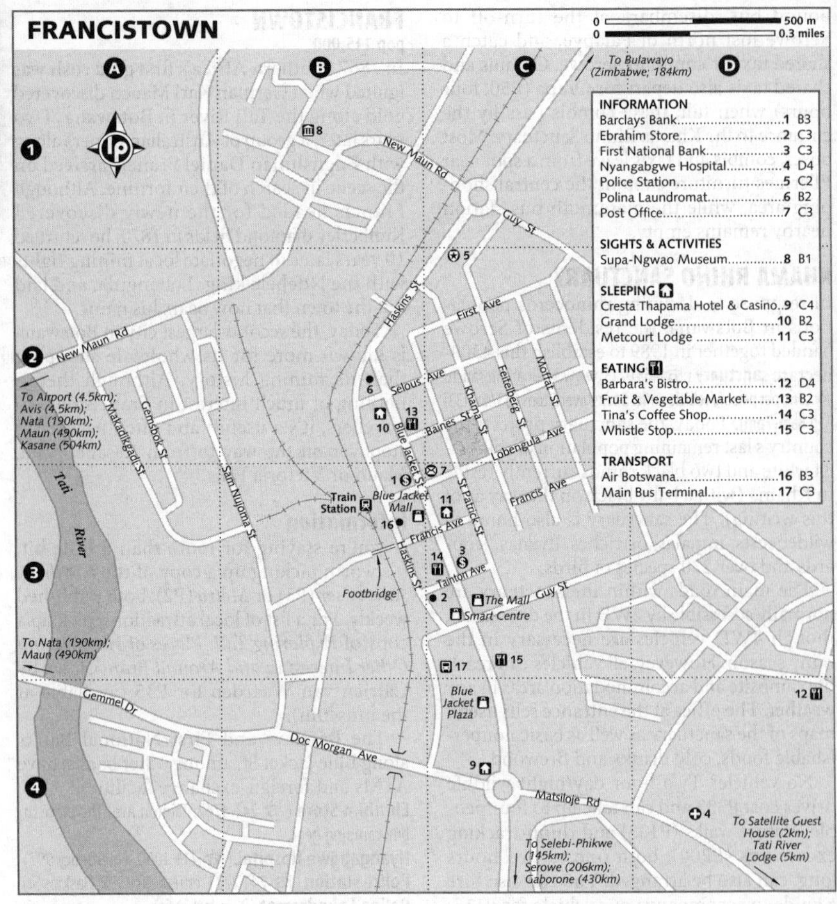

Hotel, this is a pretty pleasant midmarket option that feels like an old-school country motel. It's popular with locals and strikes a decent balance between rustic and roadside.

Satellite Guest House (☎ 241 4665; s/d P200/250) This walled compound of motel-style units is uninspiring, though it's certainly cheap if you're counting every pula. It's out in the suburbs (3.5km southeast from the city centre), and can get noisy if there are a lot of guests.

Grand Lodge (☎ 241 2300; Blue Jacket St; s/d P250/300; ❄) This is an excellent choice if you want to stay in the city centre. Standard rooms become something special when you add air-con, cable TV, a fridge and a hotplate.

Metcourt Lodge (☎ 241 1100; Blue Jacket St; d P540; ❄) The Metcourt chain offers reliably comfy, solidly three-star accommodation across Botswana, and it doesn't disappoint in Francistown. The attached restaurant is good for a steak and a beer after long dusty days.

Cresta Thapama Lodge (☎ 241 3872; www.cresta-hospitality.com; cnr Blue Jacket St & Doc Morgan Ave; s/d incl breakfast from P750; ❄ 🏊) Francistown's most upmarket hotel boasts a four-star rating, though the overall ambience is bit stuffy. But if you're a fan of luxury and formality, you'll revel in the colonial-inspired rooms and can unwind in the casino or on the squash and tennis courts.

Eating

Self-caterers have a choice of several well-stocked supermarkets, as well as the fruit and vegetable market on the corner of Blue Jacket and Baines Sts.

Barbara's Bistro (Francistown Sports Club; meals from P30) Located in the eastern outskirts of town, this quaint, leafy spot is a good choice for inexpensive local specialities such as beef stew and pap.

Tina's Coffee Shop (Blue Jacket St; meals P25-50) Whether you're here for a cuppa and cake or a heavy plate of chicken and rice, you'll enjoy the cosy atmosphere of this popular local shop.

Whistle Stop (Blue Jacket St; mains P25-50) Start your day right with a hearty breakfast from the Whistle Stop. Otherwise, if you are not an early riser, it also serves a good variety of grilled meats, fish, burgers and desserts.

Getting There & Away

AIR

You can fly between Francistown and Gaborone with **Air Botswana** (☎ 241 2393; Francis Ave) for around US$100.

BUS & COMBI

From the main bus terminal, located between the train line and Blue Jacket Plaza, buses and combis connect Francistown with Gaborone (P40, six hours), Maun (P60 five hours), Kasane (P65, seven hours), Nata (P25, two hours), Serowe (P23, 2½ hours), Selebi-Phikwe (P15, two hours) and Bulawayo, Zimbabwe (P30, two hours). Buses run according to rough schedules; combis leave when full.

TRAIN

The overnight train to Gaborone (1st-/2nd-class sleeper US$25/20, economy US$5, 8¼ hours) leaves at 9pm; the day train (club/economy class US$4/8, 6½ hours) leaves at 10am. The overnight service continues to Lobatse (US$1, 1½ hours) in the morning.

Getting Around

As well as the ubiquitous combis, taxis cruise the streets and park at the bus station. A combi or shared taxi around town costs US$0.50.

Avis (☎ 241 3901) has an office at the airport, which is about 5.5km west of the town centre.

TULI GAME RESERVE

Tucked into the nation's right-side pocket, the Tuli Block is a 10km- to 20km-wide swath of freehold farmland extending over 300km along the northern bank of the Limpopo River. The main attraction is the Tuli Game Reserve, a vast moonscape of muddy oranges and browns overlooked by deep-blue sky. It's the sort of Dali-esque desert environment that puts one in mind of Arizona or Australia, yet the barren beauty belies a land rich in life. Elephants, hippos, kudu, wildebeests and impalas as well as small numbers of lions, cheetahs and leopards circle each other among rocks and *kopjes* scattered with artefacts from the Stone Age onwards; a well-supplied archaeologist would be in dusty heaven up here. More than 350 species of birds have also been recorded in the reserve.

Information

One advantage of visiting the Tuli Game Reserve is that entrance is free. Night drives (not permitted in government-controlled parks and reserves) are also allowed, so visitors can often see nocturnal creatures, such as aardwolves, aardvarks and leopards. The disadvantage is that the Tuli Block is private land, so visitors are not allowed to venture off the main roads or camp outside the official campsites and lodges. Also, exploring this region without a private vehicle is virtually impossible. The best time to visit is from May to September when animals are forced to congregate around permanent water sources.

Sights

The landscape in Tuli Block is defined by its unusual rock formations. The most famous feature is **Solomon's Wall**, a 30m-high natural dolerite dyke cut through the landscape on either side of the riverbed. Nearby are the **Motloutse Ruins**, remnants of a Great Zimbabwe–era stone village that belonged to the kingdom of Mwene Mutapa. Both sights can be explored on foot, and are accessible from the road between Zanzibar and Pont Drift.

Sleeping

Kwa-Tuli Game Reserve (Map p84; ☎ South Africa 27-15-964 3895; www.kwatuli.co.za; campsite per person (in Rand) R395) Set deep inside the block, Kwa-Tuli consists of two camps, Island and Koro. The former holds a series of luxury safari tents (for a middle-income price) perched on an island in the midst of the Limpopo River. Koro

Camp is the headquarters of the nonprofit Tuli Conservation Project.

Tuli Safari Lodge (Map p84; ☎ 264 5303; www.tulilodge.com; regular campsite from P55, tent camp with full board & wildlife drives per person from P385, r with full board & wildlife drives per person low/high season from P1135/1500;) This lodge is set in a riverine oasis and is surrounded by red-rock country that teems with wildlife. Because it offers a range of accommodation to suit most budgets, it often feels more relaxed and less formal than many of the other exclusive private reserves in the country.

Mashatu Game Reserve (Map p84; ☎ 27-11-442 2267; www.mashatu.com; luxury tent/chalet with full board & wildlife drives per person US$250/375;) One of the largest private wildlife reserves in Southern Africa, this place is renowned for its big cats and frighteningly large elephant population (current estimates are well over 1000). The main camp is one of Botswana's most exclusive resorts and is home to the Gin Trap, a dugout bar that overlooks a floodlit watering hole.

Getting There & Away

Mashatu and Tuli support a scheduled flight between Johannesburg, Kasane and the Limpopo Valley Airport (Map p84), which is usually booked as part of a package with either of the reserves.

Most roads in Tuli Block are negotiable by 2WD, though they can get rough in places over creek beds, which occasionally flood during the rainy season. From Sherwood, a graded gravel road runs parallel to the South African border and provides access to the various lodges. The lodges can also be accessed from the west via the paved road from Bobonong.

If you're coming from South Africa, note that the border crossing at Pont Drift usually requires a 4WD, and can be closed when the river is too high. If you've prebooked your accommodation, you can leave your vehicle with the border police and then get a transfer by vehicle (if dry) or by cableway (if the river is flooded) to your lodge.

MAKGADIKGADI PANS

The Sowa (Sua), Nxai and Ntwetwe Pans collectively comprise the 12,000-sq-km Makgadikgadi Pans. While Salar de Uyuni in Bolivia is the biggest single pan in the world, the Makgadikgadi network of parched-white dry lakes is larger. During the sizzling heat of the late winter (August), the stark pans take on a disorienting and ethereal austerity. Heat mirages destroy the senses as imaginary lakes shimmer and disappear, ostriches take flight and stones turn to mountains and float in mid-air. But, as the annual rains begin to fall in the late spring, depressions in the pans form temporary lakes and fringing grasses turn green with life. Herd animals arrive to partake of the bounty, while water birds flock to feed on algae and tiny crustaceans.

NATA

The dust-bowl town of Nata serves as the gateway to the Makgadikgadi Pans, as well as an obligatory fuel stop if you're heading to either Kasane or Maun. Be aware that elephants graze alongside the highway in this region, so take care during the day and avoid driving at night.

The best lodging in this area used to be **Nata Lodge** (☎ 621 1260; www.natalodge.com; campsite per person P55, d luxury tent P478, chalet from P572;), which burnt down in 2008. Owners say that a new and better hotel is literally rising from the ashes, and the renovated Nata Lodge should be open by the time you read this guide. Like its predecessor, it will consist of a good mix of luxury chalets and cheap campsites, all set amid a verdant oasis of monkey-thorn trees, marula and mokolane palms.

Hourly combis travel between Kasane (P50, five hours) and Francistown (P20, two hours), and Maun (P40, five hours) and Francistown (P15, two hours), pass by the North Gate Restaurant.

SOWA (SUA) PAN

Sowa (also spelt Sua) Pan is mostly a single sheet of salt-encrusted mud stretching across the lowest basin in northeastern Botswana. Sowa means 'salt' in the language of the San, who once mined the pan to sell salt to the Bakalanga. Today, it is mined by the Sua Pan Soda Ash Company, which sells sodium carbonate for industrial manufacturing.

Nata Delta

During the rainy season, huge flocks of waterbirds congregate at the Nata Delta, which is formed when the Nata River flows into the northern end of the Sowa Pan. When the

EXPLORING THE MAKGADIKGADI PANS

It is important to stress that to explore the pans properly and independently requires more of a 4WD expedition than a casual drive. Lost travellers are frequently rescued from the pans, and there have been a number of fatalities over the years. Prospective drivers should keep in mind that salt pans can have a mesmerising effect, and even create a sense of unfettered freedom. Once you drive out onto the salt, remember that direction, connection, reason and common sense can seem to dissolve. You should be aware of where you are at all times by using a map and compass (remember, GPS units are not foolproof).

It's often safer (and sometimes cheaper in the long run) to explore the pans on an organised tour with a knowledgeable guide. The pans can be visited on day trips or overnight trips offered by the lodges listed in this region, or on an overnight trip from lodges in Maun (p98).

rains are at their heaviest from December to February, the pan is covered with a thin film of water that reflects the sky and obliterates the horizon. Access is via a 4WD track from the village of Nata.

Nata Bird Sanctuary

This 230-sq-km community-run **wildlife sanctuary** (Map p91; ☎ 7165 6969, 7154 4342; admission per person/vehicle per day US$4/2; 🕑 7am-7pm) was proposed in 1988 by the Nata Conservation Committee and established four years later with the help of several local and international nongovernmental organisations (NGOs). Local people voluntarily relocated 3500 cattle and established a network of tracks throughout the northeastern end of Sowa Pan.

In the dry season (May to October), it's possible to drive around the sanctuary in a 2WD with high clearance, though it's best to inquire about the condition of the tracks in the sanctuary prior to entering. During the rainy season, however, a 4WD is essential.

Nata Bird Sanctuary offers several serene and isolated campsites (Map p91) with clean pit toilets, braai (barbecue) pits and cold showers. Camping here costs P30 per person, and all sites are accessible by 2WD if it hasn't been raining heavily. From the campsites, it's possible to access the pan on foot (7km), though you should bring a compass with you, even if you're only walking a few hundred metres into the pan.

The entrance to the sanctuary is 15km southeast of Nata.

Sowa (Sua) Spit

This long, slender protrusion extends into the heart of the pan, and is the nexus of Botswana's lucrative soda ash industry. Although security measures prevent public access to the plant, private vehicles can proceed as far as Sowa (Sua) village on the pan's edge. Views of the pan from the village are limited, though it's easily accessible if you're travelling through the area in a 2WD.

Kubu Island

Along the southwestern edge of Sowa Pan is this ghostly, baobab-laden rock, which is entirely surrounded by a sea of salt. In Setswana, *kubu* means 'hippopotamus', and as unlikely as it may seem given the current environment and climate, this desolate area may have been inhabited by people as recently as 500 years ago. On one shore lies an ancient crescent-shaped stone wall of unknown origin, which has yielded numerous artefacts. Kubu Island is now protected as a national **monument** (admission per person/vehicle US$4.50/5.50) with proceeds going to the local community. There is also a small **campsite** (Map p91; ☎ 297 9612; per person US$5.50) with pit toilets, though you will have to carry in your own water.

Access to Kubu Island (S 20°53.740', E 25°49.426') involves negotiating a maze of grassy islets and salty bays. Increased traffic has now made the route considerably more obvious, but drivers still need a 4WD and a compass or GPS equipment

GWETA

Gweta is an obligatory fuel stop if you are heading to either Kasane or Maun, a dusty crossroads on the edge of the pans framed by bushveld and big skies. The name of the village is derived from the croaking sound made by large bullfrogs, which, incredibly, bury themselves in the sand until the rains provide sufficient water for them to emerge and mate.

There are two good hotels in Gweta. In the centre of town, **Gweta Lodge** (Map p91; ☎ 621

2220; www.gwetalodge.com; campsite per person P40, luxury tent P350, rondavel P350, r s/d from P650/800;) is a supremely friendly place that manages to pull off a balance between a sense of Southern African colonial outpost (note the lithographs in the kitchen) and funky, end-of-the-world party place.

About 4km east of Gweta, you'll see a huge concrete aardvark (no, you're not hallucinating) that marks the turn-off for **Planet Baobab** (Map p91; ☎ 7283 8334; www.unchartedafrica.com; campsites per person US$13, 2-/4-person huts from US$139/227;). Here you get a great open-air bar filled with vintage travel posters, metal seats covered in cowhide, beer-bottle chandeliers and the like. Outside, rondavels and chalets are scattered over the gravel, and staff contribute to a vibe as funky as it is friendly.

Hourly combis travelling between Kasane (P35, four hours) and Francistown (P30, three hours), and Maun (P25, four hours) and Francistown (US$3, three hours) pass by the Maano Restaurant.

NTWETWE PAN

Although the Ntwetwe Pan was once fed by the Boteti River, it was left permanently dry following the construction of the Mopipi Dam, which provides water for the diamond mines in Orapa. Ironically, Ntwetwe is now famous for its extraordinary lunar landscape, particularly the rocky outcrops, dunes, islets, channels and spits found along the western shore.

On the Gweta–Orapa track, 27km south of Gweta, is **Green's Baobab** (Map p91; S 20°25.543', E 25°13.859'), which was inscribed by the 19th-century hunters and traders Joseph Green and Hendrik Matthys van Zyl as well as other ruthless characters.

About 11km further south is the turn-off to the far more impressive **Chapman's Baobab** (Map p91; S 20°29.392', E 25°14.979'), which has a circumference of 25m and was historically used as a navigation beacon. It also may have been used as an early post office by passing explorers, traders and travellers, many of whom left inscriptions on its trunk.

The enormous crescent-shaped dune known as **Gabatsadi Island** (Map p91) has an expansive view from the crest that has managed to attract the likes of Prince Charles. (He went there to capture the indescribably lonely scene in watercolour, but the paints ran because it was so hot!) The island lies just west of the Gweta–Orapa track, about 48km south of Gweta.

MAKGADIKGADI & NXAI PAN NATIONAL PARK

West of Gweta, the main road between Nata and Maun slices through Makgadikgadi Reserve and Nxai Pan National Park, which protects large tracts of salt pans, palm forests, grasslands and savannas. Since both parks complement one another in enabling wildlife migrations, Makgadikgadi Pans Game Reserve and Nxai Pan National Park were established concurrently in the early 1970s, and combined into a single park in the mid-1990s.

Makgadikgadi Pans Game Reserve

This 3900-sq-km park extends from the Boteti River in the west to the Ntwetwe Pan in the east. Although the Boteti River only flows after good rains, wildlife congregates along the river during the dry season when the flow is reduced to a series of shallow pools, the only source of permanent water in the reserve. During years of average to low rainfall, between May and October, the Boteti experiences one of Southern Africa's most spectacular wildebeest and zebra migrations.

The DWNP runs two campsites in the reserve. The **Khumaga Camp Site** (Map p91; S 20°27.350', E 24°46.136') is well developed with sit-down flush toilets, cold showers and running water (nondrinkable). The **Njuca Hills Camp Site** (Map p91; S 20°25.807', E 24°52.395') is less developed, with pit latrines and no running water, but the surrounding hills boast staggering views of migrating wildlife.

Leroo-La-Tau (Map p91; ☎ 686 0300; www.africansecrets.net/llt_home.html; s/d US$200/275;) is a recommended safari lodge made up of several East African–style canvas tents with private verandahs that overlook the Boteti riverbed. Wildlife viewing in the surrounding reserve is awesome, and readers consistently rave about the spotless rooms, wonderful facilities and professional service. Rates include full board, wildlife drives, bush walks and a range of activities. Transfers from Maun cost US$100 per vehicle (with six passengers).

The main entrance to the national park is 141km west of Nata and 164km east of Maun. Another gate is located at Khumaga to the west. A 4WD is needed to drive around the park, though the campsites and lodge are accessible by 2WD.

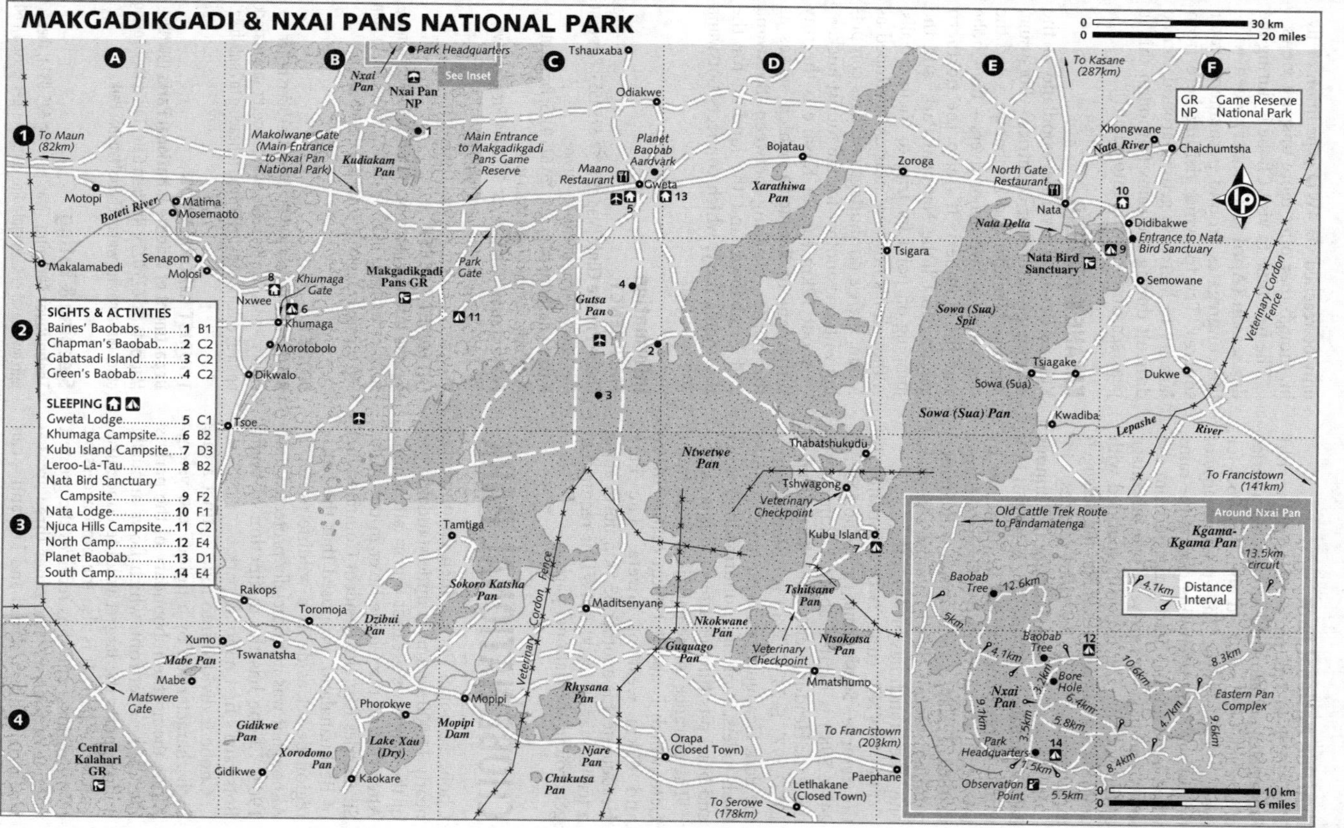
MAKGADIKGADI & NXAI PANS NATIONAL PARK
SIGHTS & ACTIVITIES
Baines' Baobabs.....1 B1
Chapman's Baobab.....2 C2
Gabatsadi Island.....3 C2
Green's Baobab.....4 C2
SLEEPING
Gweta Lodge.....5 C1
Khumaga Campsite.....6 B2
Kubu Island Campsite.....7 D3
Leroo-La-Tau.....8 B2
Nata Bird Sanctuary Campsite.....9 F2
Nata Lodge.....10 F1
Njuca Hills Campsite.....11 C2
North Camp.....12 E4
Planet Baobab.....13 D1
South Camp.....14 E4
GR Game Reserve
NP National Park
30 km
20 miles
To Maun (82km)
To Kasane (287km)
To Francistown (141km)
To Francistown (203km)
To Serowe (178km)
Veterinary Cordon Fence
Veterinary Checkpoint
Makalamabedi
Motopi
Boteti River
Matima
Mosemaoto
Senagom
Molosi
Makolwane Gate (Main Entrance to Nxai Pan National Park)
Nxai Pan
Nxai Pan NP
Park Headquarters
See Inset
Kudiakam Pan
Main Entrance to Makgadikgadi Pans Game Reserve
Park Gate
Makgadikgadi Pans GR
Khumaga Gate
Khumaga
Nxwee
Morotobolo
Dikwalo
Tsoe
Tshauxaba
Odiakwe
Maano Restaurant
Planet Baobab Aardvark
Gweta
Gutsa Pan
Ntwetwe Pan
Bojatau
Xarathiwa Pan
Zoroga
Tsigara
Thabatshukudu
Tshwagong
Kubu Island
North Gate Restaurant
Nata
Nata Delta
Nata Bird Sanctuary
Sowa (Sua) Spit
Sowa (Sua) Pan
Sowa (Sua)
Tsiagake
Kwadiba
Xhongwane
Nata River
Chaichumtsha
Didibakwe
Entrance to Nata Bird Sanctuary
Semowane
Dukwe
Lepashe River
Tamtiga
Sokoro Katsha Pan
Maditsenyane
Nkokwane Pan
Guquago Pan
Tshitsane Pan
Ntsokotsa Pan
Mmatshumo
Letlhakane (Closed Town)
Paephane
Orapa (Closed Town)
Rhysana Pan
Njare Pan
Chukutsa Pan
Mopipi
Mopipi Dam
Phorokwe
Lake Xau (Dry)
Kaokare
Dzibui Pan
Toromoja
Rakops
Tswanatsha
Xumo
Mabe Pan
Mabe
Matswere Gate
Gidikwe Pan
Gidikwe
Xorodomo Pan
Central Kalahari GR
Around Nxai Pan
Old Cattle Trek Route to Pandamatenga
Kgama-Kgama Pan
13.5km circuit
Distance Interval
Eastern Pan Complex
Baobab Tree
Bore Hole
Nxai Pan
Park Headquarters
Observation Point
10 km
6 miles

Nxai Pan National Park

This 2578-sq-km park lies on the old **Pandamatenga Trail**, which connected a series of boreholes and was used until the 1960s for overland cattle drives. The grassy expanse of the park is most interesting during the rains when large animal herds migrate from the south, and predators arrive to take advantage of the bounty. The region is speckled with umbrella acacias, and resembles the Serengeti in Tanzania (without the safari vehicles).

In the south of the park are the famous **Baines' Baobabs** (S 20°06.726', E 24°46.136'), which were immortalised in paintings by the artist and adventurer Thomas Baines in 1862. Today, a comparison with Baines' paintings reveals that in almost 150 years, only one branch has broken off.

The DWNP runs two campsites in the reserve. **South Camp** (S 19°56.159', E 24°46.598') is located about 1.5km east of the Park Headquarters, while **North Camp** (S 19°52.797', E 24°47.358') is 6.5km north of the Park Headquarters. Both have sit-down flush toilets, running (nondrinkable) water and braai pits (though firewood is scarce).

The entrance to the park is at Makolwane Gate, which is about 140km east of Maun and 60km west of Gweta. The Park Headquarters is another 35.5km north along a terrible sandy track. A 4WD is required to get around the national park.

CHOBE NATIONAL PARK

Chobe National Park, which encompasses nearly 11,000 sq km, is understandably one of the country's greatest tourist attractions. After visiting the Chobe River in the 1930s, Sir Charles Rey, the Resident Commissioner of Bechuanaland, proposed that the entire region be set aside as a wildlife preserve. Although it was not officially protected until 1968, Chobe has the distinction of being Botswana's first national park.

Chobe is divided into four distinct areas, each characterised by a unique ecosystem. Along the northern boundary of the park is the Chobe riverfront, which flows annually and supports the largest wildlife concentration in the park. It is also the most accessible of the regions, and thus receives the greatest volume of tourists. The other three areas – Nogatsaa/Tchinga, Savuti and Linyanti – can only be reached via 4WD expedition or fly-in, though they offer more unspoilt views.

The best time to visit Chobe is during the dry season (April to October) when wildlife congregates around permanent water sources. Try to avoid visiting here from January to March as getting around can be difficult during the rains (although this is peak season for flying into Savuti).

KASANE & AROUND

Kasane lies in a riverine woodland at the meeting point of four countries – Botswana, Zambia, Namibia and Zimbabwe – and the confluence of two major rivers – the Chobe and the Zambezi. It's also the northern gateway to Chobe National Park, and the jumping-off point for trips to Victoria Falls. Although it's nowhere near as developed as Maun, there's no shortage of lodges competing with one another for the tourist buck.

About 12km east of Kasane is the tiny settlement of **Kazungula**, which serves as the border crossing between Botswana and Zimbabwe, and the landing for the Kazungula ferry, which connects Botswana and Zambia.

Information

EMERGENCY

Chobe Private Clinic (Map p94; ☎ 625 1555; President Ave) Offers 24-hour emergency service.

Kasane Hospital (Map p94; ☎ 625 0333; President Ave) Public hospital on the main road.

Police station (Map p94; ☎ 625 2444; President Ave; 24hr) Also along the main road.

INTERNET ACCESS

Kasane Internet (Map p94; ☎ 625 0736; Audi Centre, President Ave; per hr US$5; 8am-5pm Mon-Fri, to 1pm Sat) Internet in Kasane is dead-slow and unreliable.

MONEY

Barclays Bank (Map p94; President Ave) Offers better exchange rates than the bureaux de change. Be sure to stock up on US dollars (post-1996) if you're heading to Zimbabwe.

TOURIST INFORMATION

Department of Wildlife & National Parks (DWNP; Map p94; ☎ 625 0235; Northern Gate) This is the booking office for campsites within Chobe National Park.

Sleeping & Eating

Thebe River Camping (Map p94; ☎ 625 0314; thebe@info.bw; Kasane-Kazungula Rd; campsite per person P60;

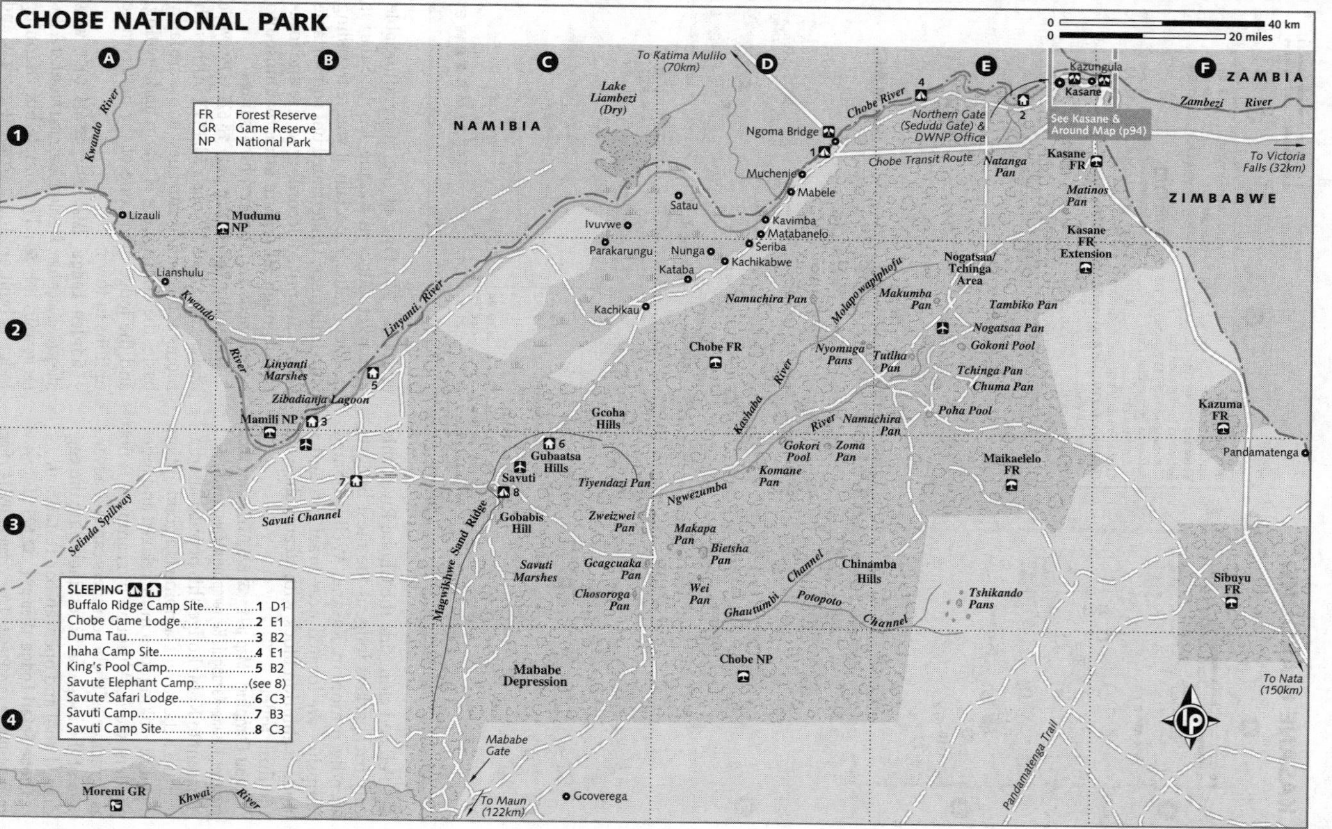
CHOBE NATIONAL PARK
0 40 km
0 20 miles
FR Forest Reserve
GR Game Reserve
NP National Park
SLEEPING
Buffalo Ridge Camp Site 1 D1
Chobe Game Lodge 2 E1
Duma Tau 3 B2
Ihaha Camp Site 4 E1
King's Pool Camp 5 B2
Savute Elephant Camp (see 8)
Savute Safari Lodge 6 C3
Savuti Camp 7 B3
Savuti Camp Site 8 C3
NAMIBIA
ZAMBIA
ZIMBABWE
Zambezi River
To Victoria Falls (32km)
To Ratima Mulilo (70km)
To Nata (150km)
To Maun (122km)
See Kasane & Around Map (p94)
Kazungula
Kasane
Kasane FR
Kasane FR Extension
Matinos Pan
Northern Gate (Sedudu Gate) & DWNP Office
Chobe Transit Route
Natanga Pan
Chobe River
Ngoma Bridge
Muchenje
Mabele
Kavimba
Matabanelo
Seriba
Kachikabwe
Nunga
Kataba
Satau
Lake Liambezi (Dry)
Ivuvwe
Parakarungu
Kachikau
Linyanti River
Lizauli
Lianshulu
Mudumu NP
Kwando River
Linyanti Marshes
Zibadianja Lagoon
Mamili NP
Savuti Channel
Selinda Spillway
Moremi GR
Khwai River
Mababe Gate
Gcoverega
Mababe Depression
Magwikhwe Sand Ridge
Savuti
Gubaatsa Hills
Gobabis Hill
Savuti Marshes
Gcoha Hills
Tiyendazi Pan
Zweizwei Pan
Gcagcuaka Pan
Chosoroga Pan
Makapa Pan
Bietsha Pan
Wei Pan
Ngwezumba
Chobe FR
Chobe NP
Namuchira Pan
Kashaba River
Nogatsaa/Tchinga Area
Makumba Pan
Tutlha Pan
Nyomuga Pans
Namuchira Pan
Gokori Pool
Komane Pan
Zoma Pan
Ghaumbi Channel
Potopoto Channel
Chinamba Hills
Tambiko Pan
Nogatsaa Pan
Gokoni Pool
Tchinga Pan
Chuma Pan
Paha Pool
Maikaelelo FR
Tshikando Pans
Pandamatenga Trail
Kazuma FR
Pandamatenga
Sibuyu FR

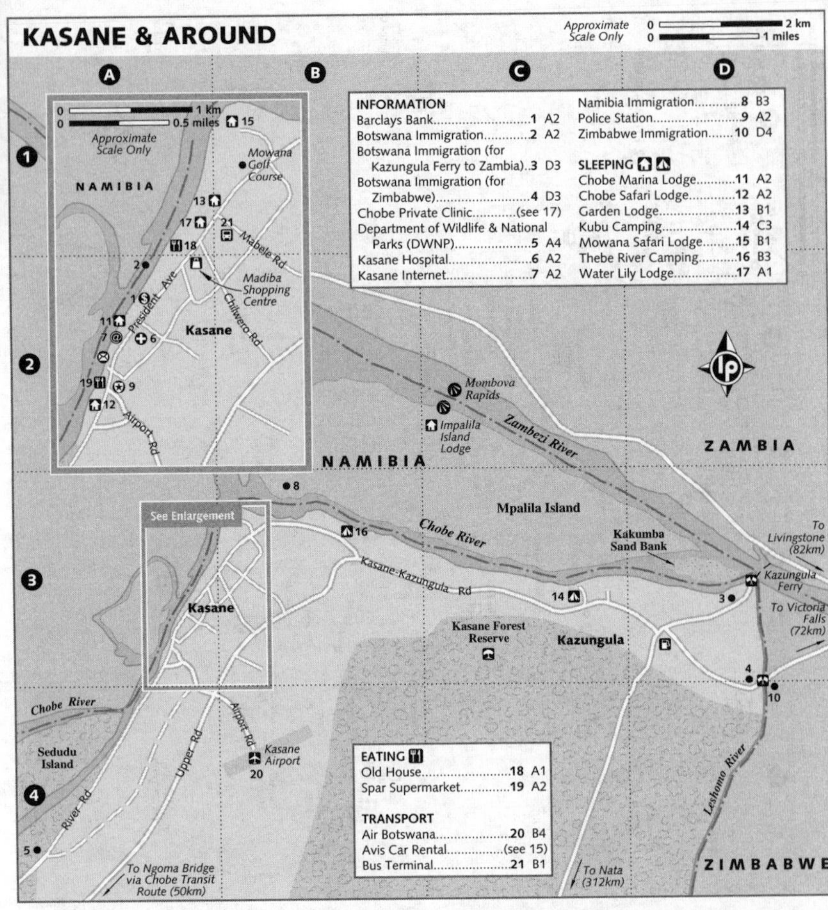

) Perched alongside the Chobe River, this leafy backpackers lodge is the most budget-friendly option in Kasane. Well-groomed campsites are located near braai pits and a modern ablution block with steamy showers and flush toilets.

Kubu Camping (Map p94; ☎ 625 0312; www.kubulodge.net; Kasane-Kazungula Rd; campsite per person P60;) Adjacent to Kubu Lodge, this popular alternative to Thebe River Camping is a good option if you're looking for a more relaxed and independent scene. Although the campsite is not as attractive as Thebe, campers can take advantage of the lodge facilities, including the egg-shaped pool and open-air bar-restaurant.

Chobe Safari Lodge (Map p94; ☎ 625 0336; www.chobesafarilodge.com; President Ave; campsite US$14, r from US$134;) One of the more affordable upmarket lodges in Kasane, Chobe Safari is excellent value, especially if you're travelling with little ones. Understated but comfortable rooms are priced according to size and location, though all feature attractive mosquito netted beds and modern furnishings.

Water Lily Lodge (Map p94; ☎ 625 1775; liyaglo@botsnet.bw; Kasane-Kazungula Rd; P550) Although rooms at this family-run guest house are fairly basic, the atmosphere is warm and inviting, and the lodge offers one of the better-value options in town.

Garden Lodge (Map p94; ☎ 625 0051; www.thegardenlodge.com; President Ave; r incl breakfast & dinner from $US 180;) The simple but charming lodge is built around a tropical garden, and features a number of well-furnished rooms that exude a homey atmosphere. It's a little more quirky than the average lodge in these parts, with hints of eccentricity that put it in front of the pack.

Chobe Marina Lodge (Map p94; ☎ 625 2221; www.chobemarinalodge.com; President Ave; s/d US$408/544;) This place occupies an attractive spot along the river and is conveniently located in the centre of Kasane. The rooms, like that of the Safari Lodge, are much of a muchness in terms of their blending of the African aesthetic with mod cons, but they're still pretty lovely. Prices include all meals, activities, park fees and airport transfers.

All of the above hotels have good attached restaurants, and there is a Spar supermarket just near Chobe Safari Lodge if you're self-catering. While closed as of research, the Old House, Kasane's only stand-alone restaurant, should be open by the time you read this.

Getting There & Away

AIR

Air Botswana connects Kasane to Maun (US$100) and also Gaborone (US$155). **Air Botswana** (Map p94; ☎ 625 0161) has an office at Kasane airport, which is near the centre of town.

BUS & COMBI

Combis heading to Francistown (P65, seven hours), Maun (P60, six hours), Nata (P55, five hours) and Gweta (P45, four hours) run when full from the Shell petrol station bus terminal (Map p94) on Mabele Rd. Thebe River Camping and Chobe Safari Lodge also run private shuttle buses to Livingstone/Victoria Falls (US$45, two hours). All these operations will usually pick up booked passengers at their hotels around 10am.

CAR & MOTORCYCLE

The direct route between Kasane and Maun is only accessible by 4WD in the dry season, and sometimes during heavy rains becomes impossible to navigate by anything but huge, state-of-the-art 4WDs. Also remember that there is nowhere along the Kasane–Maun road to buy fuel, food or dinks, or get vehicle repairs.

All other traffic between Kasane and Maun travels via Nata, but this road is also, unfortunately, a nightmare. While a 2WD can make it, be prepared for a stunningly awful series of potholes and the like on your way up.

MOBILE SAFARIS

Other than motoring through Chobe National Park in a private or rented 4WD, the only way to travel overland directly between Maun and Kasane is on a 4WD 'mobile safari'. This is a glorious way to travel through Botswana's two major attractions, but safaris are expensive and can be tough going in the middle of the wet season (January to March). For more information, contact one of the tour operators in Maun (see p98).

Getting Around

Combis travel regularly between Kasane and Kazungula, and continue to the immigration posts for Zambia and Zimbabwe if requested. The standard fare for anywhere around Kasane and Kazungula is about P20.

If you're looking to rent a car for the day, **Avis** (☎ 625 0144) has an office in the Mowana Safari Lodge.

CHOBE RIVERFRONT

The Chobe riverfront rarely disappoints. Whether you cruise along the river in a motor boat, or drive along the banks in a Land Rover, you're almost guaranteed an up-close encounter with some of the largest elephant herds on the continent. The elephant population at Chobe numbers in the thousands and, although they're fairly used to being gawked at by camera-wielding tourists, being surrounded by a large herd is an awe-inspiring (and somewhat terrifying) experience.

Sleeping

Ihaha Camp Site (Map p93) is the closest DWNP campsite to Kasane, located along the riverfront about 27km from the Northern (Sedudu) Gate. This well-developed campsite has sit-down flush toilets, (cold) showers and a braai area. Unfortunately, it has become a target for thieves from across the rivers, so campers must remain vigilant.

Buffalo Ridge Camp Site (Map p93; ☎ 625 0430; campsite per person US$5.50) This basic camping area is immediately uphill from the Ngoma Bridge border crossing near the western end of the Chobe transit route. Unlike Ihaha, Buffalo Ridge is privately owned, so you do not need a reservation with the DWNP to camp here.

Chobe Game Lodge (Map p93; ☎ 625 0340/1761; www.chobegamelodge.com; low/high season per person US$500/720;) This highly praised safari lodge is one of Botswana's pinnacles of luxury. The

DIANE MOSWEU, WILDLIFE GUIDE, KASANE

How did you become a game guide? I started in 2005, after moving here from my home place in Shakewe. We grew up in areas with a high concentration of wildlife. I used to herd cattle in the bush before I went to school. When I left that place I didn't intend to work as a guide – I worked at the airport for three years. The people who employed me encouraged me to do this as a career.

So for you the learning part was mastering the driving I found it very difficult. But I knew spotting wildlife from my childhood.

How do you like the work? Really. I am enjoying the work. I like meeting people from different places and telling them more about our life in Africa, especially people who are from outside Africa.

Is it funny to see us foreigners shocked at animals? It's not a surprise because I know where you come from is more urban. I don't like staying in urban areas. I came to Kasane because it is quieter than Maun.

Isn't enough of Botswana's wildlife protected? Shouldn't land be opened for development? I think it is very important throughout the world to conserve these resources for future generations. They have been threatened all along, until we realised they are nearly wiped out. Some of the people I guide are very educated, and they can sensitise other people in their home places. Local people support the parks. I knew these were here from school. We learn in school it's very important to protect these lands. And even now we are teaching our parents about the financial benefits of these natural resources.

How would you improve the park system? A lot of government guys [park service rangers and workers] get rotated out quickly. It would be better if they were here for a long time, so they know where the wildlife is and where the poachers are.

lodge itself is constructed in the Moorish style and flaunts high arches, barrel-vaulted ceilings and tiled floors. The individually decorated rooms are elegant yet soothing, and some have views of the Chobe River and Namibian flood plains.

Getting There & Away

From central Kasane, the Northern (Sedudu) Gate is about 6km to the southwest. Unlike for all other national parks operated by the DWNP, you do not need a campsite reservation to enter, though you will be expected to leave the park prior to closing if you do not have one. All tracks along the riverfront require a 4WD vehicle, and you will not be admitted to the park without one.

You can exit the park either through the Sedudu Gate by backtracking along the river or via the Ngoma Bridge Gate near to the Namibian border. If you exit via Ngoma, you can return to Kasane via the Chobe Transit Route. (If you're simply bypassing Chobe en route to/from Namibia, you do not have to pay any park fees to travel on this road.) Be advised that elephants frequently cross this road, so keep your speed down and do not drive at night.

SAVUTI

Savuti's flat, wildlife-packed expanses are awash with distinctly African colours and vistas. The area contains the remnants of a large 'superlake' that once stretched across northern Botswana, although the modern landscape has a distinctive harsh and empty feel to it. Because of the roughness of the terrain and the difficulty in reaching the area, Savuti is an obligatory stop for all 4WD enthusiasts en route between Kasane and Maun. It is also the domain of the rich and powerful – Savuti has the dubious distinction of being one of the most elite tourist destinations in Botswana.

Sleeping

CAMPING

Savuti Camp Site (Map p93) has sit-down flush toilets, braai pits, (hot!) showers and plenty of shade. Baboons are a real nuisance though, and unwary campers have been cleaned out the second their backs have been turned.

LODGES

The two lodges listed here must be booked in advance; all rates include meals, drinks, excursions and park fees. Return air fares from Maun cost between US$150 to US$200 per person (slightly less from Kasane).

Savute Safari Lodge (Map p93; ☎ Bookings through Desert & Delta Safaris, Maun, 686 1243; www.desertdelta.com; low/high season per person US$476/686) Next to the former site of the legendary Lloyd's Camp, this relatively new upmarket retreat consists of 12 contemporary thatched chalets that are simple yet functional in design. The main safari lodge is home to a sitting lounge, an elegant dining room, a small library and a cocktail bar.

Savute Elephant Camp (Map p93; ☎ bookings through Orient-Express Safaris, Maun, 686 0302; www.orient-express.com; low/high season per person US$615/1205;) The premier camp in Savuti is made up of 12 lavishly appointed East African–style lodges complete with antique-replica furniture. The main tent houses a dining room, lounge and bar, and is next to a swimming pool that overlooks a pumped waterhole.

Getting There & Away

Chartered flights use the airstrip several kilometres north of the lodges in Savuti.

Under optimum conditions, it's a four-hour slog from Northern (Sedudu) Gate to Savuti, though be advised that this route is often unnavigable from January to March. Access is also possible from Maun or the Moremi Game Reserve (p105) via Mababe Gate, though the track is primarily clay and very tough going when wet. All of these routes require a state-of-the-art 4WD vehicle (see p118 for information on hiring vehicles) and some serious off-road experience.

LINYANTI MARSHES

In the northwest corner of Chobe National Park, the Linyanti River spreads into a 900-sq-km flooded plain that attracts stunning concentrations of wildlife during the dry season. The marshes are home to stable populations of elephants, lions, wild dogs, cheetahs and leopards – this is some of the best predator viewing in Southern Africa. But one of Linyanti's main attractions is its isolation. Since the marshes are technically not part of Chobe National Park, the lodges are not governed by the DWNP regulations, which means that night drives and wildlife walks (with armed guards) are permitted.

Sleeping

CAMPING

Linyanti camp site (Map p93) is operated by the DWNP and has braai pits, hot showers, sit-down flush toilets and, in the dry season, lots of elephants.

LODGES

The camps listed here are run by **Wilderness Safaris** (☎ Johannesburg 27-11-807 1800 in South Africa; www.wilderness-safaris.com), and with the exception of King's Pool, feature luxury tents with en-suite bathrooms and hot-water showers. All the camps here must be booked in advance, and all rates include meals, drinks, excursions and airport transfers. Return air fares from Maun cost between US$150 to US$200 per person, or slightly less from Kasane.

Savuti Camp (Map p93; low/high season US$550-700) Slightly more exclusive than Linyanti, this six-person camp is located next to a perennial waterhole in the Savuti Channel, which attracts large concentrations of elephants and lions during the dry season.

Duma Tau (Map p93; low/high season US$620/850) Slightly larger than Savuti, this 10-person camp overlooks the hippo-filled Zibadianja Lagoon from a mangosteen grove. The lagoon can be explored by boat when the water levels are high, or you can kick back in a luxury tent under thatch.

King's Pool Camp (Map p93; low/high season US$750/1075) Occupying a magical setting on a Linyanti River oxbow overlooking a lagoon, this 10-person camp is the most luxurious of the four properties. Accommodation at King's Pool is in private thatched chalets featuring indoor and outdoor showers.

Getting There & Away

The only proper track to Linyanti Marshes starts in Savuti, but it's extremely sandy and difficult to negotiate year-round. Most guests choose to fly in to their camp on a chartered flight from Maun or Kasane (see p98 for tour operators).

OKAVANGO DELTA

The 1430km Okavango River rises in central Angola, then flows southeast across Namibia's Caprivi Strip before entering Botswana east of Shakawe. There, 18.5 billion cubic metres of water spread annually like an open palm across the flat landscape, consumed as it spreads by the thirsty air and swallowed by the Kalahari sands. Eventually, the river loses itself in a 16,000-sq-km maze of lagoons, channels and islands. In this desert country, the incongruous waters of the resulting wetland – known as the Okavango Delta – attract myriad birds and other wildlife, as well as most of Botswana's tourists.

MAUN

Maun (pronounced 'mau-*uu*nn') is Botswana's primary tourism hub and the self-proclaimed gateway to the Okavango Delta. Essentially consisting of a few intersections surrounded by long stretches of block housing, this is nonetheless one of the more interesting towns in Botswana, attracting a reliably mad crew of bush pilots, tourists, campers, volunteers and luxury-safari buffs. It's a decent-enough base for a day or two, which is the amount of time most people spend here, and serves as a natural centre point between Kasane, the Magkadikgadi and the Kalahari.

Orientation

Central Maun contains most of the restaurants, shops and travel agencies, while the village of Matlapaneng, 10km northeast of the centre, has most of the budget lodges and campsites. In between are the Sedia Hotel and several other tourist-oriented businesses.

Information

EMERGENCY

Delta Medical Centre (☎ 686 1411; Tsheke Tsheko Rd) Near the tourist office along the main road; this is the best medical facility in Maun. It offers a 24-hour emergency service.

Maun General Hospital (☎ 686 0661; Shorobe Rd) About 1km southwest of the town centre.

MedRescue (☎ 680 0598, 686 0991, 686 1831) For evacuations in the bush.

Police station (☎ 686 0223; Sir Seretse Khama Rd)

INTERNET ACCESS

Many hotels now offer internet access.

Afro-Trek I-Café (Map p100; ☎ 686 2574; Shorobe Rd; per hr P50) In the Sedia Hotel.

PostNet (Map p100; ☎ 686 5612; Maun Shopping Centre; per hr P50; 🕑 9am-6pm Mon-Fri, 9.30am-3pm Sat)

MONEY

The Mall has branches of Barclays Bank (Map p100) and Standard Chartered Bank (Map p100), which have foreign-exchange facilities and offer better rates than the bureaux de change.

POST

Post office (Map p100; 🕑 8.15am-1pm & 2.15-4pm Mon-Fri, 8.30-11.30am Sat) Near The Mall.

TOURIST INFORMATION

Department of Wildlife & National Parks (DWNP; Map p100; ☎ 686 1265; Kudu St; 🕑 7.30am-12.30pm & 1.45-4.30pm Mon-Sat, 7.30am-noon Sun) To book national parks campsites, go to the reservations office, which is housed in a caravan behind the main building.

Tourist office (Map p100; ☎ 686 0492; Tsheke Tsheko Rd; 🕑 7.30am-12.30pm & 1.45-4.30pm Mon-Fri) Provides information on the town's many tour companies and lodges.

Sights

The **Maun Environmental Education Centre** (Map p100; ☎ 686 1390; admission free; 🕑 7.30am-12.30pm & 1.45-4.40pm), on the eastern bank of the Thamalakane River, aims to provide school children with an appreciation of nature. If you're in town, it's worth an hour or so rambling around the bush here.

The **Nhabe Museum** (Map p100; ☎ 686 1346; admission free, donation welcome; 🕑 9am-5pm Mon-Fri, 9am-4pm Sat), housed in a historic building, features art exhibitions and outlines the natural history and cultures of the Okavango. Peripheral activities include local theatre presentations and sales of locally produced arts and crafts.

The community-run **Okavango Swamps Crocodile Farm** (admission US$2; 🕑 9am-4.30pm Mon-Sat) is basically all the encouragement you need to keep your hands and feet inside the mokoro while cruising through the delta.

Tours

Most delta lodges are affiliated with specific agencies and lots of safari companies run mokoro trips and 4WD safaris, so it's wise to check around before choosing one (see p120 for some recommended listings).

Travel Wild (Map p100; ☎ 686 0822; www.travelwildbotswana.com; Mathiba I St), opposite the airport,

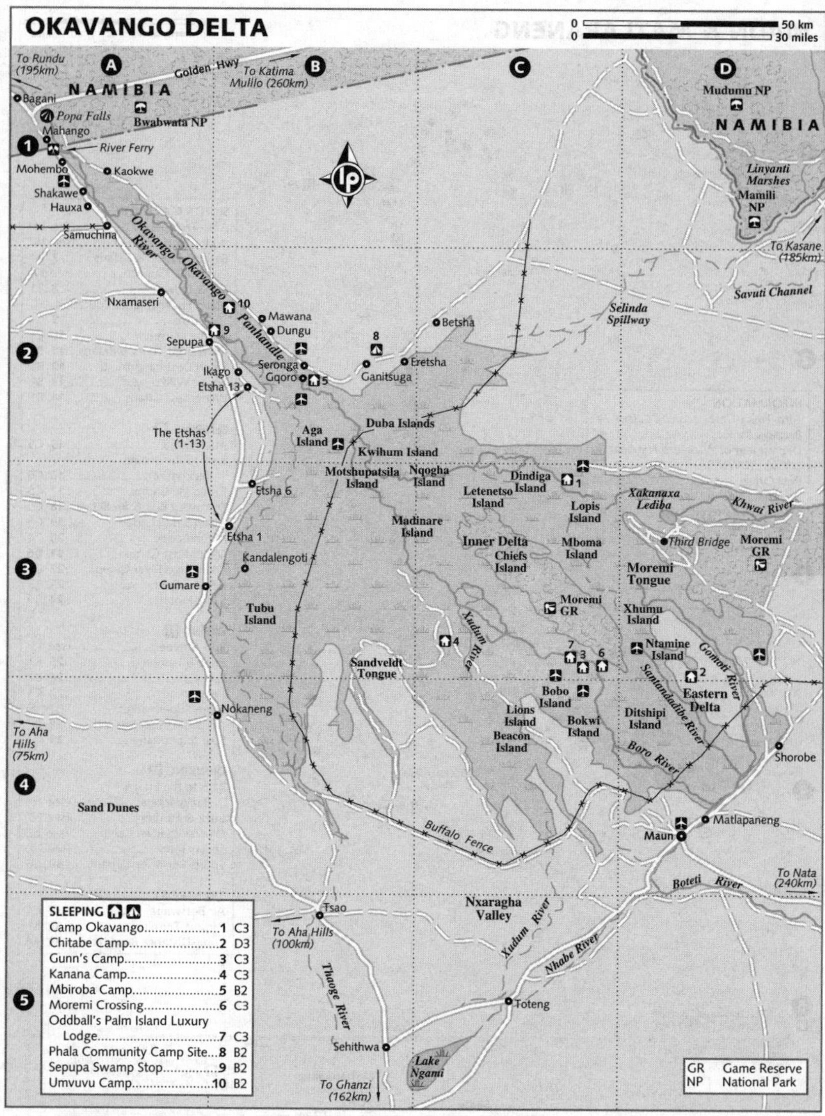

serves as a central booking and information office for lodges, safaris and other adventures.

Safari Destinations (Map p100; ☎ 686 0822/3; travelwild@dynabyte.bw; Mathiba I St) serves as a good clearing house for information on booking agencies. The staff can't provide you with direct bookings, but they've got great contacts with all local safari providers.

Sleeping

Back to the Bridge Backpackers (Map p100; ☎ 686 2037; hellish@info.bw; Hippo Pools, Old Matlapaneng Bridge; campsites per person P30, s rooms P80, s/d tents per person P120/90; 💻 🍽) 'The Bridge', as it's known, has a great bar-at-the-end-of-the-world kind of vibe. Bush pilots and backpackers chat each other up, dogs play with kids and a regular

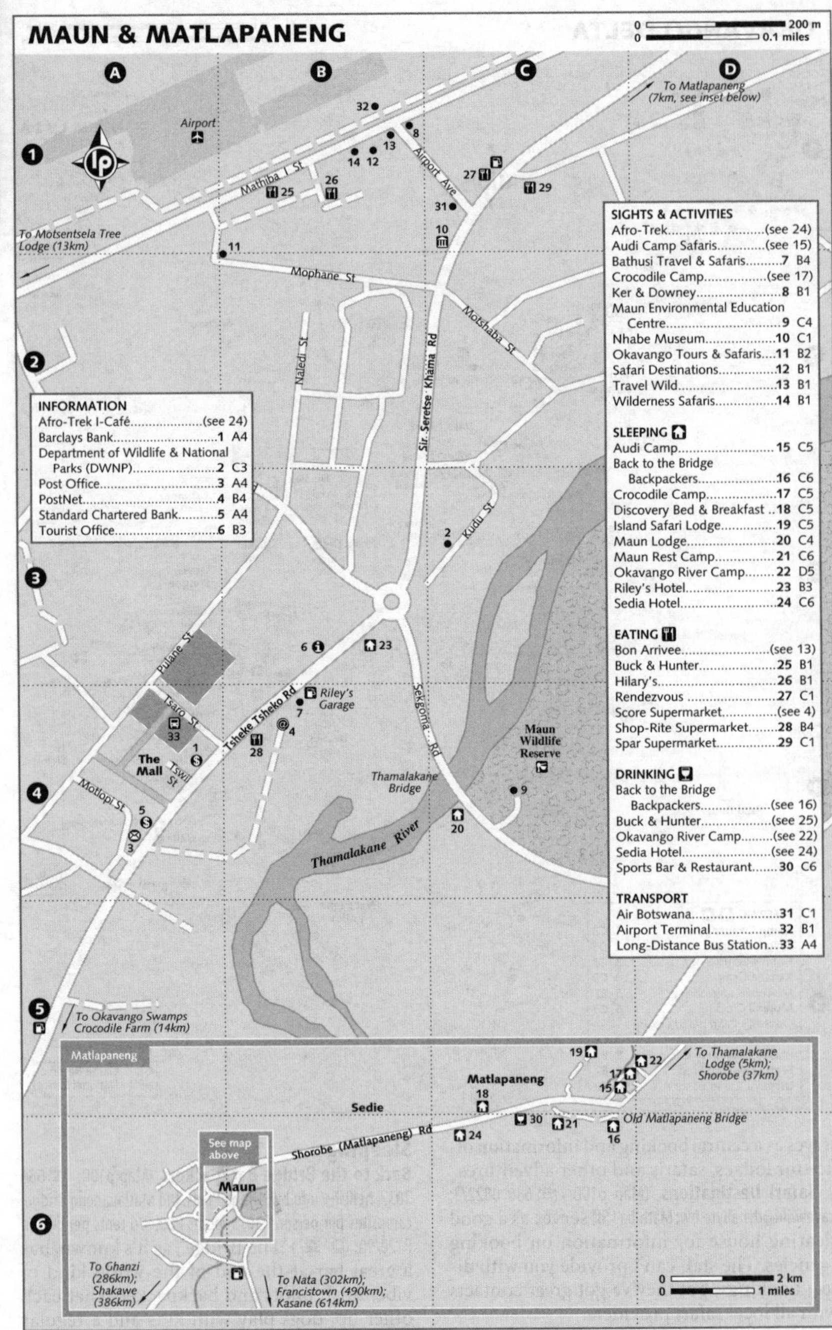
MAUN & MATLAPANENG
0 200 m
0 0.1 miles
A
B
C
D
1
2
3
4
5
6
To Matlapaneng (7km, see inset below)
Airport
To Motsentsela Tree Lodge (13km)
Mathiba I St
Airport Ave
Mophane St
Motshaba St
Naledi St
Sir Seretse Khama Rd
Kudu St
Pulane St
Tsaro St
Tshekes Tsheko Rd
Riley's Garage
The Mall
Tswii St
Motlopi St
Sekgoma Rd
Thamalakane Bridge
Thamalakane River
Maun Wildlife Reserve
To Okavango Swamps Crocodile Farm (14km)
INFORMATION
Afro-Trek I-Café (see 24)
Barclays Bank 1 A4
Department of Wildlife & National Parks (DWNP) 2 C3
Post Office 3 A4
PostNet 4 B4
Standard Chartered Bank 5 A4
Tourist Office 6 B3
SIGHTS & ACTIVITIES
Afro-Trek (see 24)
Audi Camp Safaris (see 15)
Bathusi Travel & Safaris 7 B4
Crocodile Camp (see 17)
Ker & Downey 8 B1
Maun Environmental Education Centre 9 C4
Nhabe Museum 10 C1
Okavango Tours & Safaris 11 B2
Safari Destinations 12 B1
Travel Wild 13 B1
Wilderness Safaris 14 B1
SLEEPING
Audi Camp 15 C5
Back to the Bridge Backpackers 16 C6
Crocodile Camp 17 C5
Discovery Bed & Breakfast 18 C5
Island Safari Lodge 19 C5
Maun Lodge 20 C4
Maun Rest Camp 21 C6
Okavango River Camp 22 D5
Riley's Hotel 23 B3
Sedia Hotel 24 C6
EATING
Bon Arrivee (see 13)
Buck & Hunter 25 B1
Hilary's 26 B1
Rendezvous 27 C1
Score Supermarket (see 4)
Shop-Rite Supermarket 28 B4
Spar Supermarket 29 C1
DRINKING
Back to the Bridge Backpackers (see 16)
Buck & Hunter (see 25)
Okavango River Camp (see 22)
Sedia Hotel (see 24)
Sports Bar & Restaurant 30 C6
TRANSPORT
Air Botswana 31 C1
Airport Terminal 32 B1
Long-Distance Bus Station 33 A4
Matlapaneng
To Thamalakane Lodge (5km); Shorobe (37km)
Matlapaneng
Sedie
Old Matlapaneng Bridge
Shorobe (Matlapaneng) Rd
See map above
Maun
To Ghanzi (286km); Shakawe (386km)
To Nata (302km); Francistown (490km); Kasane (614km)
0 2 km
0 1 miles

EXPLORING THE OKAVANGO DELTA

Stretching across northwestern Botswana, the Okavango Delta is a complex and unique ecosystem as well as Botswana's premier tourist attraction. Although the size and scope of the region is often a deterrent for independent travellers, it's easier to plan a trip through the region than you'd imagine, especially if you think of the delta as having four distinct areas:

- **Eastern Delta** (p103) This part of the delta is far-more accessible, and therefore cheaper to reach, from Maun than the Inner Delta and Moremi. You can easily base yourself in Maun and arrange a day trip by mokoro or an overnight bush-camping trip for far less than the cost of staying in (and getting to) a lodge in the Inner Delta or Moremi.
- **Inner Delta** (p104) The area that spreads west, north and south of Moremi is classic delta scenery where you can truly be seduced by the calming spell of the region. Accommodation is in top-end luxury lodges, almost all of which are only accessible by expensive chartered flights.
- **Moremi Game Reserve** (p105) This region includes Chiefs Island and the Moremi Tongue, and is the most popular destination within the delta. The Moremi Game Reserve is the only protected area within the delta, so wildlife is plentiful, but you will have to pay daily park-entry fees. Moremi has a few campsites run by the DWNP as well as several truly decadent lodges with jaw-dropping prices. The Moremi Game Reserve is accessible by 4WD from Maun or Chobe as well as by charter flight.
- **Okavango Panhandle** (p107) This swampy extension of the Inner Delta stretches northwest towards the Namibian border, and is the main population centre in the region. Although this area does not offer the classic delta experience, it is growing in popularity due to its ease of accessibility via public transport or 2WD. Since the area is not controlled by a lodge or by the DWNP, a number of villages in the panhandle have established accessible campsites, and also offer affordable mokoro trips and fishing expeditions.

If you're planning a 4WD expedition through the park, you will have to be completely self-sufficient as petrol and supplies are only available in Kasane and Maun. If the prospect of driving yourself through the wilds of Botswana is a little too much to handle, the hotels and lodges in Maun can help you organise a trip through the delta. For more information, see p98.

cast of drunks keeps the bar propped up (or is that the other way 'round?).

Island Safari Lodge (Map p100; ☎ 686 0300; www.africansecrets.net; Matlapaneng; campsite per person P40, s/d chalet P350/500) One of the original lodges in Maun, Island Safari Lodge is also still one of its best. The lodge runs a professional, well-established series of safaris, the African-style rondavel housing is charming and comfy, and the verandah is a great spot for watching the river flow by on lazy Okavango afternoons.

Crocodile Camp (Map p100; ☎ 686 0265; www.crocodilecamp.com; Matlapaneng; campsite per person P40, tent from P140, s/d chalet from P300; 🅟) 'Croc Camp' occupies a superb spot right on the river, and the campsite has such Maun rarities as grass, and the pre-erected linen tents are a good option if you're looking for a little safari chic. There's also a number of thatched riverside chalets with bathroom.

Okavango River Camp (Map p100; ☎ 686 3707/0298; www.okavango-river-lodge.com; Matlapaneng; campsite per person US$3, s/d chalet US$35/40) This down-to-earth spot off Shorobe Rd has a lovely setting on the riverbank. The owners are friendly and unpretentious and pride themselves on giving travellers useful (and independent) information on trips through the delta.

Maun Rest Camp (Map p100; ☎ 686 2623; simonjoyce@info.bw; Shorobe Rd, Matlapaneng; campsite per person from P45, tents from P300) This no-frills rest camp off Shorobe Rd is spotless and boasts what justifiably may be called 'the cleanest ablution blocks in Maun'. The owners also pride themselves on turning away the overland truck-and-party crowd, so you can be assured of a quiet and undisturbed night's rest here.

Audi Camp (Map p100; ☎ 686 0599; www.okavangocamp.com; Matlapaneng; campsite per person from P45, s/d tents from P240/300; 🖳 🅟) Off Shorobe Rd, Audi Camp is a fantastic campsite that's become increasingly popular with families, although independent overlanders will feel utterly welcome as well. Management is friendly and very helpful, and there's a wide range of safari activities to book.

Discovery Bed & Breakfast (Map p100; ☎ 680 0627; www.discoverybedandbreakfast.com; Matlapaneng: s/d from P200/300;) Discovery does a cool job of creating a traditional-for-tourists African village-vibe in the midst of Maun. The thatched, rondavel-style housing looks pretty bush from the outside and feels as posh as a nice hotel on the inside. A pretty garden connects the dusty grounds, and there's a good communal fire pit for safari stories with fellow travellers.

MIDRANGE & TOP END

Riley's Hotel (Map p100; ☎ 686 0204; Tsheke Tsheko Rd; chalet/s/d P570/675/760;) Riley's is the only hotel or lodge in central Maun. It offers comfortable rooms in a convenient and quiet setting, and a remodelling of the grounds is giving the place a little more character and value for money. Popular with Batswana businessmen and government workers, but don't come here for a lodge/wilderness experience.

Sedia Hotel (Map p100; ☎ 686 0177; www.sedia-hotel.com; Shorobe Rd, Sedie; campsite per person P20, s/d/chalet P600/675/850;) If you're in need of modern comforts, the Sedia Hotel is a good option. This resortlike complex features an outdoor bar, a continental-inspired restaurant and a huge swimming pool. You can choose from a number of rooms and self-contained chalets, or simply pitch a tent and take advantage of all the hotel facilities.

Thamalakane Lodge (Map p100; ☎ 686 4313; thamalakanelodge@ngami.net; Shorobe Rd; P950;) With a beautiful setting on a sun-drenched curve of the Thamalakane River, overlooking wading hippos and waving reeds, Thamalakane wins in the location, location, location stakes. But it has also got beautiful little chalets, stuffed with modern amenities and dressed up in safari-chic tones, and a kitchen cranking out arguably the best food in Maun.

Maun Lodge (Map p100; ☎ 686 3939; www.maunlodge.com; Sekgoma Rd; chalet/r from US$86/99;) This upmarket option is just south of the town centre and boasts all the luxuries you'd expect at this price. It's certainly a comfortable option, though it's lacking in personality and atmosphere, especially if you're coming from (or going to) any of the luxury lodges in the delta.

Motsentsela Tree Lodge (Map p100; ☎ 680 0757; treelodge@netspread.co.bw; r from US$220;) This private farm/reserve, about 13km west of the airport, is a lovely luxury option that maintains a good crew of regular visitors. These returnees are probably impressed by the on-site wandering giraffe, kudu and ostrich, the large, beautifully decked-out private cabins or the utter sense of calm and quiet here far away from Maun's bustle (as it were). Contact the lodge to book ahead and arrange transfers or get directions.

Eating

Besides the restaurants listed below, Maun has versions of every peri-peri-obsessed fast-food chain in southern Africa and well-stocked supermarkets, including the Score Supermarket in the Maun Shopping Centre; Spar Supermarket in both the Mokoro Shopping and Ngami Centres; and the Shop-Rite on Tsheke Tsheko Rd (all on Map p100).

Rendezvous (Map p100; ☎ 287 6183; Engen Complex; cafe P35-65, restaurant P50-100) Rendezvous is split into two very excellent halves. The cafe does pretty good pizzas, sandwiches and the like, and thank the tech gods, actually has reliable wireless internet access. The attached restaurant does more upmarket, candlelit fare, all of which is very fine for those needing a bit of white-linen civilisation.

Bon Arrivee (Map p100; ☎ 680 0330; Mathiba I St; meals P35-80) They lay on the pilot puns and flight-deck jokes very thick at this airport-themed place, which sits, of course, right across from the airport. The food is good – lots of pasta, steak and seafood stuff – but don't come here an hour before your flight expecting quick turnaround.

Hilary's (Map p100; ☎ 686 1610; meals from P40; 8am-4pm Mon-Fri, 8.30am-noon Sat) Just off Mathiba I St, this homey place offers a choice of wonderfully earthy meals, including home-made bread, baked potatoes, soups and sandwiches. It's ideal for vegetarians and anyone sick of greasy sausages and soggy chips.

Buck & Hunter (Map p100; ☎ 680 1001; Mathiba I St; meals P40-80) This used to be a pretty wild pub, the northern outpost of Gaborone's own Bull & Bush. Today, thanks to stricter alcohol enforcement, the Buck is a bit more sedate, although it's still reasonably popular with expats and locals. In any case, the beer is cold and the steak is thick, so get over here already.

Drinking

Every one of the lodges listed above has its own bar, but at the time of research the only places that really kicked off if you were in need of a party were Back to the Bridge Backpackers (p99) and Okavango River Camp (p101). The Sedia Hotel (opposite) has a poolside English-style pub that's regularly packed with Germans. Of course, there are a fair few *shebeen* shacks serving home-brewed sorghum beer to a local crowd; the staff at your hotel or lodge can point you in the right direction for this sort of off-license fun. Buck & Hunter (opposite) and the **Sports Bar & Restaurant** (Shorobe Rd, Sedie), near Maun Rest Camp, are also good for a beer or 10. See Map p100 for the location of these places.

Getting There & Away

AIR

You can fly to Gaborone (US$155) or Kasane (US$100) daily with **Air Botswana** (Map p100; ☎ 686 0391; Airport Ave).

BUS & COMBI

The station for long-distance buses and combis is along Tsaro St. One bus leaves at least every hour between 6.30am and 4.30pm for Francistown (P55 to P60, five hours), via Gweta (P35, four hours) and Nata (P45, five hours). Combis leave for Kasane (P60, six hours) when full. For Gaborone, change in either Ghanzi or Francistown.

To Ghanzi (P35 to P40, five hours), via D'kar (P28 to P32, 3½ hours), buses leave at about 7.30am and 10.30am, but it's best to check at the station or tourist office for current schedules. To Shakawe (P70, seven hours), five or six buses leave between 7.30am and 3.30pm, and stop at Gumare and Etsha 6. Combis to Shorobe (P3, one hour) leave when full from just north of the bus station.

For more information about public buses and shuttle minibuses between Maun and Namibia, Zambia and Zimbabwe, see p115.

CAR & MOTORCYCLE

The direct route between Kasane and Maun is accessible by 4WD only in the dry season, and during heavy rains is sometimes impossible to travel by any means other than huge, state-of-the-art 4WDs. Also remember that there is nowhere along this direct route to buy fuel, food or drinks, or get vehicle repairs. All other traffic between Maun and Kasane travels via Nata.

MOBILE SAFARIS

Other than touring through Chobe National Park in a private or rented 4WD, the only way to travel overland directly between Maun and Kasane is on a 4WD 'mobile safari'. This is a glorious way to travel though Botswana's two major attractions as you'll see a plethora of wildlife while exploring some of the country's most rugged corners, though safaris are expensive, and can be tough-going in the middle of the wet season (January to March). For more information, contact one of the tour operators listed in this chapter (p98).

Getting Around

TO/FROM THE AIRPORT

Maun airport is close to the town centre, so taxis rarely bother hanging around the terminal when planes arrive. If you have prebooked accommodation at an upmarket hotel or lodge in Maun or the Okavango Delta, make sure it provides a (free) courtesy combi. Others will have to ask the courtesy-combi driver for a lift (P10), or walk about 300m down Airport Ave to Sir Seretse Khama Rd and catch a combi.

COMBIS & TAXIS

Combis marked 'Maun Route 1' or 'Sedie Route 1' travel every few minutes during daylight hours between the station in town and a stop near Crocodile Camp in Matlapaneng. The standard fare for all local trips is P2.70.

Taxis also ply the main road and in the evening are the only form of transport other than private vehicle. They also hang around a stand along Pulane St in the town centre. A typical fare from central Maun to Matlapaneng costs about P10/30 in a shared/private taxi. To preorder a taxi, try **Atol Taxi Cabs** (☎ 686 4770/1).

EASTERN DELTA

The Eastern Delta includes the wetlands between the southern boundary of Moremi Game Reserve and the buffalo fence that crosses the Boro and Santandadibe Rivers, north of Matlapaneng. If you're short of time and/or money, this part of the delta remains

TRAVELLING BY MOKORO

Most visitors to the Okavango spend at least some time travelling by mokoro (plural, mekoro), a shallow-draught dugout canoe hewn from ebony or sausage-tree log (or, more recently, moulded from fibreglass). The mekoro are poled from a standing position and their precarious appearance belies their amazing stability. A mokoro normally accommodates the poler, two passengers and their food and camping equipment.

While one-day trips (with a return drive lasting several hours from Maun) or more expensive fly-in (one-day or multiday) trips are possible in the Eastern Delta, most people prefer a multiday trip where travellers ride for several days with the same poler, breaking their journey with walks on palm islands and moving between established camps or wild-camping along the way. In this case, the quality of the experience depends largely upon the skill of the poler, the meshing of personalities and the passengers' enthusiasm.

The importance of finding a competent poler cannot be overstated, especially when you're expecting them to negotiate labyrinthine waterways or lead you on bushwalks through wildlife country. The keenest polers can speak at least some English; warn you about dangers (never swim without first asking the poler!); recognise and identify plants, birds and animals along the way; explain the delta cultures; and perhaps even teach clients how to fish using traditional methods.

If you're organising a budget mokoro trip, inquire in advance as to whether you're expected to provide food for your poler. Even if the polers do bring their own supplies, many travellers prefer to share meals. The polers may, for example, provide a sack of mealie meal (ground maize) and cooking implements while travellers supply the relishes: tins of curries, stews and vegetables. If you have arranged to provide your poler's meals, the standard daily rations are 500g of mealie meal, 250g of white sugar, six tea bags and sufficient salt and powdered milk.

Although it's still possible to negotiate with independent polers (ask around in town for how to contact them), most visitors organise mokoro trips through delta lodges or Maun safari companies, or through the Okavango Polers Trust in Seronga (see p107).

an affordable and accessible option. Mokoro trips in the Eastern Delta are mainly organised by Maun lodges and tour companies (see p120).

Sleeping

Chitabe Camp (Map p99; ☎ Johannesburg 27-11-807 1800; www.wilderness-safaris.com; low/high season per person US$365/700;) Near the Santandadibe River, along the southern edges of Moremi Game Reserve, Chitabe is an island oasis (only accessible by boat or plane) renowned for the presence of Cape hunting dogs and other less common wildlife. Accommodation is in East African–style luxury tents with bathroom, which are built on wooden decks and sheltered beneath the shade of a lush canopy.

INNER DELTA

Roughly defined, the Inner Delta occupies the areas west of Chiefs Island and between Chiefs Island and the base of the Okavango Panhandle. Mokoro trips through the Inner Delta are almost invariably arranged with licensed polers affiliated with specific lodges, and operate roughly between June and December, depending on the water level.

Sleeping

Oddball's Palm Island Luxury Lodge (Map p99; ☎ 686 1154; www.oddballs-camp.com; tents low/shoulder/high season from US$200/275/325) Although it occupies a less-than-exciting woodland beside an airstrip, Oddball's is within walking distance of some classic delta scenery. For years, this lodge catered primarily to backpackers and was by far the most affordable option in the delta. Although it's still one of the cheapest lodges in the region, Oddball's has gone upmarket in recent years, improving its facilities; its new price tag is a little high considering you're still staying in budget dome tents.

Gunn's Camp (Map p99; ☎ 686 0023; www.gunnscamp.com; s/d US$375/470) Gunn's is a beautiful option for those wanting the amenities of a high-end safari – expertly cooked meals, attentive service and wonderful views over its island location in the delta. The elegant tented rooms are as comfy and soft as you please, but there is more of a feeling of being engaged with the wilderness, what with the hippos, warthogs and even elephants that occasionally wander through the grounds.

Kanana Camp (Map p99; ☎ 686 0375; www.kerdowneybotswana.com; low/high season US$425/500) This classy retreat occupies a watery site in a maze of grass and palm-covered islands. It's an excellent base for wildlife-viewing by mokoro around Chiefs Island or fishing in the surrounding waterways. Accommodation is in eight well-furnished linen tents that are shaded by towering riverine forest.

Moremi Crossing (Map p99; ☎ 686 0023; www.gunns-camp.com/moremi_crossing.php; s/d US$425/650) A collection of lovely chalets flank a gorgeous (and enormous) thatched dining-and-bar area that overlooks a long flood plain where you can often see giraffes and elephants wandering around. The management is friendly, and the camp is to be commended for pioneering a water/plumbing system that minimises its environmental impact (it is also quite a feat of engineering – you should ask to see how it all works).

Getting There & Away

The only way in and out of the Inner Delta is by air. This is an expensive extra, but the pain is alleviated if you look at it as two scenic flights. Chartered flights to the lodges listed above typically cost about US$150 to US$200 return to/from Mekoro, or 4WD vehicles will meet your plane and take you to your lodge.

MOREMI GAME RESERVE

Moremi Game Reserve (sometimes also called the Moremi Wildlife Reserve) is the only part of the Okavango Delta that is officially cordoned off for the preservation of wildlife. It was set aside as a reserve in 1963 when it became apparent that poaching was decimating wildlife populations. Named after the Batswana chief Moremi III, the reserve has been extended over the years and now encompasses almost 5000 sq km – over one-third of the entire delta.

Information

The Moremi Game Reserve is administered by the DWNP, and entry and camping fees must be paid for *in advance* at the DWNP office in Maun (p98). You *cannot* pay the entrance fee at the gate. DWNP campsites are often booked well in advance, especially during South African school holidays (mid-April, July, September and December to January), so try to book as early as possible.

Visitors must pay entry fees and camp at either of the two main gates. From Maun, the entrance is South (Maqwee) Gate, about 99km north of Maun along a sandy 4WD track, via Shorobe. From the east, a track links Chobe National Park with Moremi across a shaky wooden bridge over the Khwai River. The other gate – and the park headquarters – is at North (Khwai) Gate.

Sights

THIRD BRIDGE

This is literally the third log bridge you will see after you enter the reserve at South Gate (Map p99). It's a rustic and beautiful bridge spanning a sandy, tannin-coloured pool on the Sekiri River, which is an idyllic spot to camp and enjoy a picnic. Contrary to official advice, and despite DWNP regulations, many ignorant visitors swim here, but it's a *very* bad idea – and foolhardy because of the presence of hippos and crocs among the reeds.

MBOMA ISLAND

The grassy savanna of this 100-sq-km island (Map p106), which is actually just a long extension of the Moremi Tongue, contrasts sharply with surrounding landscapes. The 25km sandy Mboma Loop starts about 2km west of Third Bridge and is a pleasant side trip.

XAKANAXA LEDIBA

With one of Africa's largest heronries, Xakanaxa Lediba (Xakanaxa Lagoon; Map p106) is renowned as a birdwatchers' paradise. Potential sightings here include herons, marabous, saddle-bill storks, egrets and ibises (wood, sacred and glossy). The area also supports an array of other wildlife and large numbers of fish.

Sleeping

CAMPING

The DWNP operates each of the four campsites in the Moremi Game Reserve. Each site has an ablutions block with cold showers (or hot showers if you have firewood to crank up the boilers), sit-down flush toilets, running water (which needs to be boiled or purified for drinking) and picnic tables.

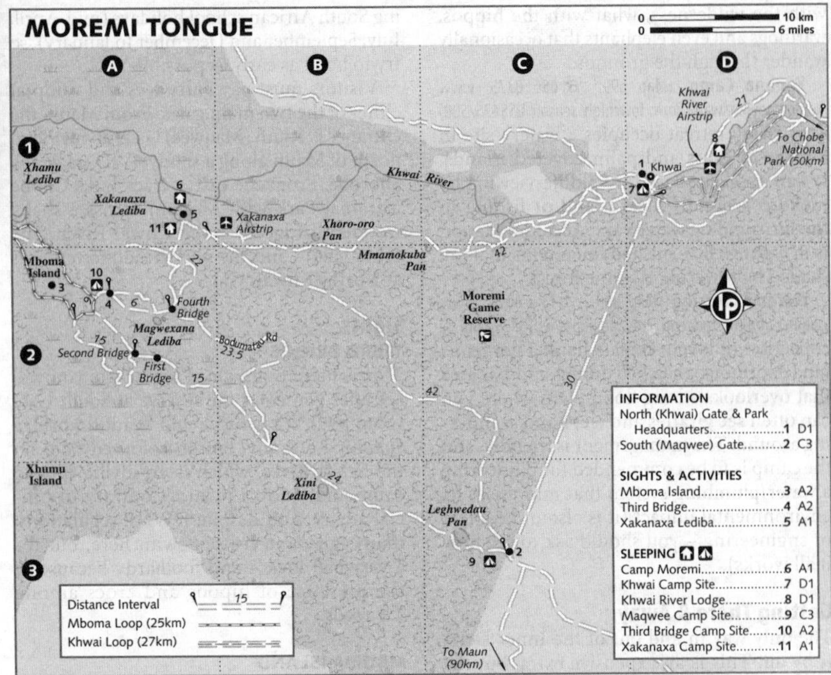

Khwai Camp Site (Map p106; North Gate) The campsite here is shady and well developed. There are a couple of small shops in Khwai village on the other side of the river, selling food and other supplies.

Maqwee Camp Site (Map p106; South Gate) The campsite here is reasonably developed though the ablution blocks are a bit run down. Be careful not to leave any food lying about as the baboons here are aggressive and ill-tempered.

Third Bridge Camp Site (Map p106; Third Bridge) On the edge of a lagoon (so watch out for hippos and crocs), the most popular campsite in Moremi is starting to show its age, though it's still a beautiful place to pitch for the night. However, the Third Bridge area is overrun with baboons, so again, be careful not to leave any food lying about. Also, avoid camping on the bridge or sleeping in the open because wildlife – especially lions – use the bridge as a thoroughfare.

Xakanaxa Camp Site (Map p106; Xakanaxa Lediba) This campsite occupies a narrow strip of land surrounded by marshes and lagoons. But watch out for wildlife – campers are frequently woken during the night by elephants, and a young boy was tragically killed by hyenas here in 2000.

LODGES

Camp Moremi (Map p106; ☎ 686 1244; www.desertdelta.com; low/shoulder/high season per person US$396/476/686) This long-standing wilderness retreat sits amid giant ebony trees next to Xakanaxa Lediba and is surrounded by wildlife-rich grasslands. The most famous attraction in Moremi is Pavarotti, a retired hippo who has adopted the camp as his home. Accommodation is in East African–style linen tents that are attractively furnished with wood fixtures.

Camp Okavango (Map p99; ☎ 686 1243; www.desertdelta.com; low/shoulder/high season per person US$396/476/686, ste US$616/726/915) Set amid sausage and jackalberry trees just outside of Moremi, this charming lodge is very elegant, and the staff are famous for their meticulous attention to detail. If you want Okavango served up with silver tea service, candelabras and fine china, this is the place for you.

Khwai River Lodge (Map p106; ☎ 686 1244; www.desertdelta.com; low/shoulder/high season per person

US$396/476/686) Perched on the northern shores of the Khwai River, this opulent lodge overlooks the Moremi Game Reserve, and is frequently visited by large numbers of hippos and elephants. Accommodation is in 15 luxury en suite tents that are larger and more extravagant than most upmarket hotel rooms.

Getting There & Away

There's no public transport to Moremi, so you'll need to organise a 4WD vehicle or a drive-in or fly-in safari. If you're booked into one of the delta camps, air, road or boat transport is normally arranged by the camp, but usually for an additional charge.

THE OKAVANGO PANHANDLE

In northwestern Botswana, the Kalahari sands meet the Okavango Delta. In the Okavango Panhandle, the river's waters spread across the valley on either side to form vast reed beds and papyrus-choked lagoons. Here a cosmopolitan mix of people (Mbukushu, Yei, Setswana, Herero, European, San and refugee Angolans) occupy clusters of fishing villages and extract their livelihoods from the rich waters. They're also increasingly catering to the growing numbers of visitors to the region, where mokoro trips and accommodation are more affordable than in other parts of the Okavango Delta.

Sleeping

CAMPING

Camping is also available at most of the lodges listed here.

Phala Community Camp Site (Map p99; Ganitsuga; campsite per person US$4) This rustic campsite is friendly, welcoming and far from the tourist crowd. Phala is near Ganitsuga village, about 23km east of Seronga and is accessible by a sturdy 2WD or by hitching from Seronga. A basic shop sells provisions and drinks.

LODGES

Mbiroba Camp (Map p99; ☎ 687 6861; www.okavangodelta.co.bw; campsite per person P55, rondavels P110, chalets from P250) This impressive camp is run by the Okavango Polers Trust and is the usual launch point for mokoro trips into the delta. The camp features a well-groomed and shady campsite, as well as an outdoor bar, traditional restaurant and rustic two-storey chalets. Mbiroba is 3km from Seronga village.

Sepupa Swamp Stop (Map p99; ☎ 687 7073; www.swampstop.co.bw; Sepupa; campsite per person P40, tents from P120) This laid-back riverside campsite is secluded, handy to Sepupa village, very affordable and accessible (3km) from the road between Maun and Shakawe. The lodge can arrange mokoro trips through the Okavango Polers Trust and transfers to Sepupa, as well as boat trips for US$14/91 per hour/day.

Umvuvu Camp (Map p99; ☎ 7153 4340; www.okavangopanhandle.com; campsite per person P40, s/d tents P150/200) Umvuvu is superfriendly and a good spot to enjoy the slow pace of river life minus the amenities of the safari package tour. The location is beautiful and the lodge well managed, so you're never far from an excursion or the wet wilderness itself.

THE OKAVANGO POLERS TRUST

Established in 1998 by the people of Seronga, the **Okavango Polers Trust** (☎ 687 6861; www.okavangodelta.co.bw) provides cheap, accessible mokoro trips and accommodation for visitors. Since the collective is run entirely by the village, all profits are shared by the workers, invested into the trust and used to provide the community with better facilities. The trust directly employs nearly 100 people, including polers, dancers, cooks, managers and drivers. Since there aren't any travel agencies or safari operators sharing in the profits, the cooperative can afford to charge less for mokoro trips. Although it's not uncommon to pay upwards of US$200 per person per day for a mokoro trip out of Maun, the trust charges around P500 (US$75) per day for two people. Keep in mind however that you must self-cater (ie bring your own food, water and, if necessary, camping and cooking equipment).

There's no longer a daily bus from Mohembo to Seronga, but it's almost always possible to hitch from the free Okavango River ferry in Mohembo. Plan on paying about P5 for a lift. When they're operating, water taxis run along the Okavango between Sepupa Swamp Stop (above) and Seronga (P30, two hours); transfers from the Seronga dock to Mbiroba Camp, 3km away, cost P70. Otherwise, Sepupa Swamp Stop charters 18-passenger boats for P700.

THE KALAHARI

The Kalahari sands stretch across parts of seven countries: Democratic Republic of Congo (formerly Zaïre), Angola, Zambia, Namibia, Botswana, Zimbabwe and South Africa, and form one of Africa's most prominent geographical features. While a small portion is classic desert, most of the Kalahari is a vast deposit of sandy sediments that receive too much rainfall to be officially classified as an arid zone.

In Botswana, the Kalahari (*Kgalakgadi* in Setswana) offers a solitude all its own. Distances are vast, transport is rare and facilities are few and far between; off main routes, the scant villages huddle around feeble boreholes.

KHUTSE GAME RESERVE

The 2600-sq-km Khutse Game Reserve makes a popular weekend excursion for adventurous Gaborone dwellers. Expect to see a variety of antelopes, as well as such predators as lions, leopards, brown and spotted hyenas, jackals, caracals (which the San people believe to be the incarnation of the morning star) and even hunting dogs.

Khutse has eight DWNP-operated campsites, but only Wildlife Camp, near the entry gate, has (brackish) running water and showers. Khutse Campsite, with rudimentary camping facilities, is 14km west of the entry gate. The most distant site is the very pleasant Moreswa Pan, 67km from the gate, which has a natural water source that attracts wildlife.

Khutse is administered by the DWNP, so camping is only allowed at designated campsites, which must be booked in advance at the DWNP office in Gaborone (p77) or Maun (p98). You will not be permitted into the park without a campsite reservation. Visitors must be self-sufficient in food, water and fuel.

The entrance gate is 226km from Gaborone; at Letlhakeng the sealed road becomes a rough 103km sandy 4WD track.

CENTRAL KALAHARI GAME RESERVE

The Central Kalahari Game Reserve covers 52,000 sq km and is Africa's largest protected area, sprawling across the nearly featureless heart of Botswana. It's perhaps best known for Deception (or Letiahau) Valley, the site of Mark and Delia Owens' 1974 to 1981 brown-hyena study, which is described in their book *Cry of the Kalahari*. At Deception Pan brown hyenas emerge just after dark and you may also see lions. Three similar fossil valleys – the Okwa, the Quoxo (or Meratswe) and the Passarge – also bring topographical relief to the virtually featureless expanses, although the rivers ceased flowing more than 16,000 years ago. Other pans in the northern area of the reserve – Letiahau, Piper's, Sunday and Passarge – are artificially pumped to provide water for wildlife.

The only reasonably convenient public access is via the Matswere gate in the northeastern corner of the reserve.

Sleeping

There are basic DWNP campsites at Deception Pan, Leopard Pan, Kori, Lekhubu, Letiahau Pan, Sunday Pan and Piper's Pan, but all lack facilities. The well-known Deception Pan enjoys a few rare, shady acacia trees, while Piper's Pan is known for its bizarre ghost trees. Other remote campsites include Xaka, Molapo, Gope and Xade in the southern part of the reserve. Marginally drinkable water is available only at the Matswere Game Scout Camp, near the northeastern gates of the reserve.

Deception Valley Lodge (☎ South Africa 27-12 665 8554; www.deceptionvalley.co.za; low/high season per person US$305/550;) is an exclusive bush retreat on the edge of the reserve. Designed to blend into surrounding landscape, it offers a luxurious ambience. The soothing rooms combine Victorian and African design elements, and feature a private lounge and outdoor hot shower. The lodge is approximately 120km from Maun; the route is accessible to 2WD vehicles during the dry season.

Getting There & Away

Xade, Okwa and Deception Pan have airstrips that attract upmarket fly-in safaris from Maun.

Most Maun-based safari operators can organise custom drive-in tours, but independent access requires a high-clearance 4WD vehicle, a compass or GPS, and reserve petrol (the nearest supplies are at Ghanzi, Kang and Rakops). From Matswere Game Scout Camp, it's 70km to Deception Pan. The al-

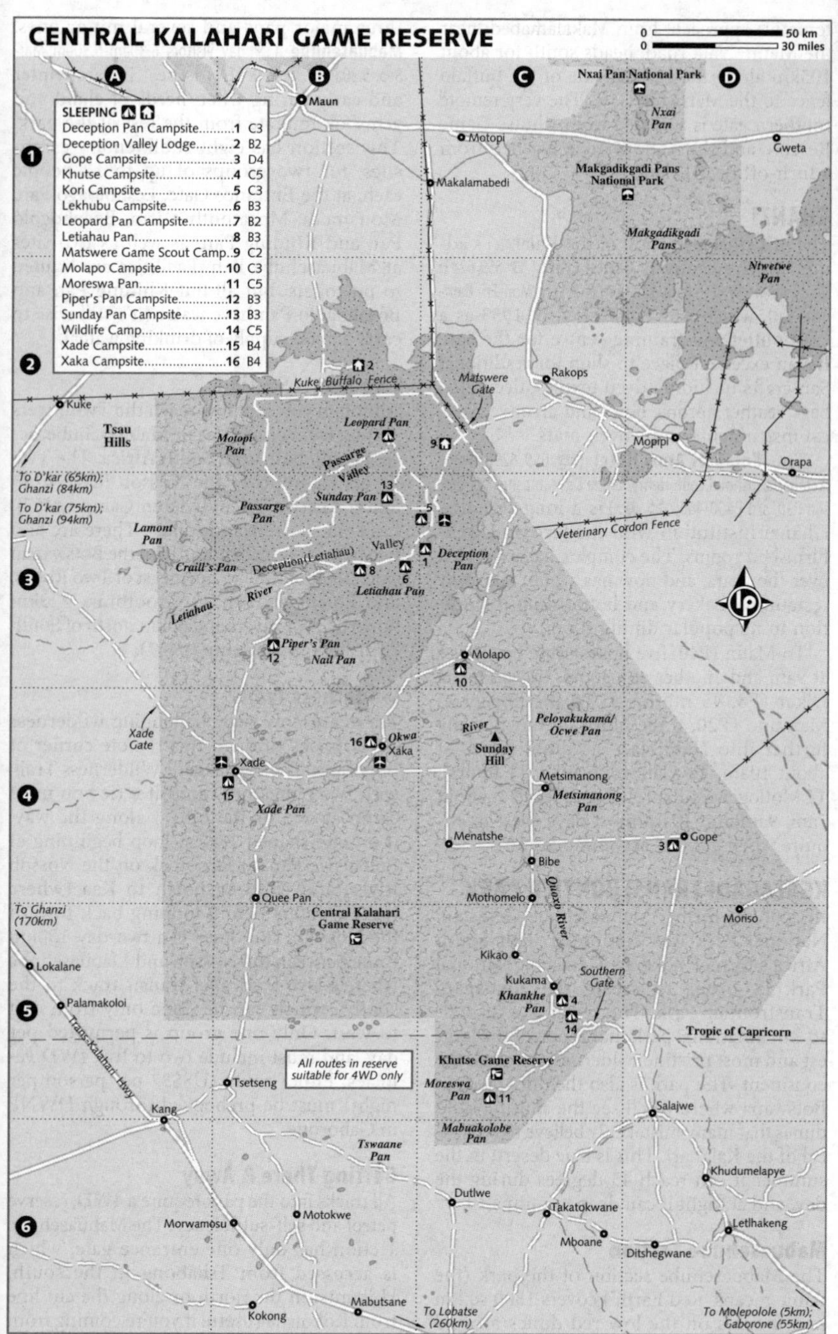

CENTRAL KALAHARI GAME RESERVE
0 50 km
0 30 miles
SLEEPING
Deception Pan Campsite..........1 C3
Deception Valley Lodge..........2 B2
Gope Campsite..........3 D4
Khutse Campsite..........4 C5
Kori Campsite..........5 C3
Lekhubu Campsite..........6 B3
Leopard Pan Campsite..........7 B2
Letiahau Pan..........8 B3
Matswere Game Scout Camp..9 C2
Molapo Campsite..........10 C3
Moreswa Pan..........11 C5
Piper's Pan Campsite..........12 B3
Sunday Pan Campsite..........13 B3
Wildlife Camp..........14 C5
Xade Campsite..........15 B4
Xaka Campsite..........16 B4
Maun
Nxai Pan National Park
Nxai Pan
Motopi
Gweta
Makalamabedi
Makgadikgadi Pans National Park
Makgadikgadi Pans
Ntwetwe Pan
Kuke Buffalo Fence
Matswere Gate
Rakops
Kuke
Tsau Hills
Motopi Pan
Leopard Pan
Passarge Valley
Sunday Pan
Mopipi
Orapa
To D'kar (65km); Ghanzi (84km)
To D'kar (75km); Ghanzi (94km)
Passarge Pan
Lamont Pan
Veterinary Cordon Fence
Deception (Letiahau) Valley
Deception Pan
Craill's Pan
Letiahau Pan
Letiahau River
Piper's Pan
Nail Pan
Molapo
Xade Gate
Okwa River
Xaka
Sunday Hill
Peloyakukama/ Ocwe Pan
Xade
Metsimanong
Metsimanong Pan
Xade Pan
Menatshe
Gope
Bibe
Quoxo River
Mothomelo
Quee Pan
To Ghanzi (170km)
Central Kalahari Game Reserve
Moriso
Kikao
Lokalane
Kukama
Khankhe Pan
Southern Gate
Palamakoloi
Tropic of Capricorn
Trans-Kalahari Hwy
All routes in reserve suitable for 4WD only
Khutse Game Reserve
Moreswa Pan
Tsetseng
Kang
Salajwe
Mabuakolobe Pan
Tswaane Pan
Khudumelapye
Dutlwe
Motokwe
Takatokwane
Morwamosu
Letlhakeng
Mboane
Ditshegwane
Mabutsane
Kokong
To Lobatse (260km)
To Molepolole (5km); Gaborone (55km)

ternative approach, from Makalamabedi near the Maun–Nata road, heads south for about 105km along the eastern side of the buffalo fence to the Matswere Gate. The very remote southern gate is accessed from Khutse Game Reserve and the Xade Gate is reached from a turn-off near D'kar.

GHANZI

The principal attraction of the Kalahari's administrative centre is **Gantsi Craft** (☎ 659 6241; Henry Jankie Dr; 🕑 8am-12.30pm & 2-5pm Mon-Fri, 8am-noon Sat), which was established in 1953 as a craft outlet and training centre for the San. It's an excellent place to shop for traditional San crafts including dyed textiles, decorated bags, leather aprons, bows and arrows, musical instruments and woven mats.

The **Kalahari Arms Hotel** (☎ 659 6298; www.kalahariarmshotel.com; Henry Jankie Dr; campsites per person P30, s/d P400/460;) is a long-standing Ghanzi institution with modern and well-furnished rooms. The complex has expanded over the years, and now has a pub, takeaway restaurant, bakery and bottle shop in addition to its popular dining room.

To Maun (P40, five hours), one bus leaves at 9am and another at 3.30pm, travelling via D'kar (P8, 45 minutes). To the border at Mamuno (P20, three hours) – but not any further into Namibia – a combi leaves at about 10am. To Gaborone (P80, 11 hours), TJ Motlogewa's Express buses leave at about 7am, 9am and 10am most days (best to enquire when at your accommodation).

KGALAGADI TRANSFRONTIER PARK

In 2000 the former Mabuasehube-Gemsbok National Park was combined with South Africa's former Kalahari-Gemsbok National Park in order to create the Kgalagadi Transfrontier Park. The result is a 28,400-sq-km binational park that is one of the largest and most pristine wilderness areas on the continent. The park is also the only place in Botswana where you'll see the shifting sand dunes that many mistakenly believe to be typical of the Kalahari. This is true desert; in the summer it can reach 45 degrees during the day, and at night it can drop to minus 10.

Mabuasehube Section

The Mabuasehube section of the park (the name means 'Red Earth') covers 1800 sq km and focuses on the low red dunes around three major pans and several minor ones. **Mabuasehube** (🕑 day visitors 6.30am-6.30pm Mar-Sep, 5.30am-7.30pm Oct-Feb) is best in late winter and early spring when herds of eland and gemsbok migrate from the rest of the park. This section has eight rudimentary campsites, for two groups of up to 12 people each, at the Entrance Gate, Lesholoago Pan, Monamodi, Mpaathutlwa Pan, Bosobogolo Pan and Khiding Pan, as well as two sites at Mabuasehube Pan. Facilities are limited to pit toilets, but all but Khiding Pan and Bosobogolo Pan have water (it's still wise to carry a good supply of drinking water).

Two Rivers Section

Although you can now reach the Two Rivers section from either Kaa or Mabuasehube, access is still best from South Africa. The Two Rivers Camp, over the Nossob River from South Africa's Twee Rivieren Camp (p457), has cold showers and toilets. There are also two basic sites further north on the Botswanan side: Rooiputs, 30km northeast of Two Rivers, and Polentswe Pan, at Grootbrak, 223km north of Two Rivers and 60km north of South Africa's Nossob Camp (p457).

Wilderness Trails

There are now two challenging wilderness 4WD tracks through this remote corner of Botswana. The Kgalakgadi Wilderness Trail, with two obligatory campsites (ie you must camp at one or the other) along the way, is a bone-shaped 285km loop beginning at Polentswe Pan, at Grootbak on the Nossob River, and winding north to Kaa (where there's water) before looping back toward the Nossob. The other is a two-day 150km route between the Nossob and Mabuasehube (there's also a parallel transit track to the south), which can be done only from east to west. Only one group is permitted per day, and must include two to five 4WD vehicles. Either route (US$37 per person per night) must be prebooked through DWNP in Gaborone.

Getting There & Away

All tracks into the park require a 4WD, reserve petrol and self-sufficiency. The Mabuasehube section has only one entrance gate, which is accessed from Tshabong in the south, Hukuntsi in the north or along the cut line from Kokotsha (useful if you're coming from

Gaborone). For the Two Rivers section, you can enter only at Kaa, which is accessed via Kang, Hukuntsi and Tshatswa (Zutshwa), or via South Africa.

BOTSWANA DIRECTORY

ACCOMMODATION

Botswana has a number of comfortable campsites and an array of upper-midrange hotels and top-end lodges – but there is little in between. Budget travellers who do not want to camp may have to, so it is recommended to take a tent anyway.

Where appropriate, accommodation options are split into budget, midrange and top-end categories for ease of reference. Upmarket places tend to price in US dollars as opposed to pula, and we have listed prices using both currencies. In general, a budget double room is anything under P350 per night. Midrange accommodation is priced anywhere from P350 to P800. Note that there's a real dearth of midrange places in the Okavango Delta, which is largely given over to luxury camps and top-end lodges that can set you back around US$500, although this can rise stratospherically to around US$1000 in the delta. Discounted rates for children are rare, although a number of lodges do offer special family rooms.

While most budget and lower-midrange options tend to have a standard room price, many top-end places change their prices according to low/shoulder/high season. High season is from June to November, low season corresponds with the rains (December to March or April) and the shoulder is a short April-and-May window. A 10% government tax is levied on hotels and lodges (but not all campsites) and is included in prices listed in this book.

Camping

Quite a few hotels and lodges along the road system have campsites with varying amenities for around P30 to P60 per night, which normally includes access to the lodge bar and swimming pool. Wild-camping is permitted only outside national parks, private land and government freehold lands. If you can't escape local scrutiny, visit the local *kgosi* or police station to request permission to camp and get directions to a suitable site.

In national parks, the typically rudimentary camps have little more than braai pits and flush toilets; many are simply dusty clearing in the scrub. However, you can't just turn up at the park gates and get a campsite; they must be prebooked through Department of Wildlife & National Parks (DWNP) offices (see p77).

Hotels

Every town has at least one hotel, and larger towns and tourist areas offer several in different price ranges. However, you won't find anything as cheap as in most other African countries, and the less expensive hotels in Botswana sometimes double as brothels.

Safari Camps & Lodges

Most safari camps and lodges are found around Chobe National Park, the Tuli Block, the Linyanti Marshes, the Moremi Game Reserve

PRACTICALITIES

- Botswana generates electricity at 220 volts AC, 50Hz, though confusingly they use two types of plugs: the South African type with its three round prongs, and the UK type with the three square prongs.
- *Daily News,* published by the Department of Information & Broadcasting, is distributed free in Gaborone and includes government news, plus major national and international news.
- Print and slide film, batteries and accessories as well as video cartridges are available in Gaborone, Francistown and Maun, though they're not cheap, and you might not find your desired brand.
- Nationwide programming is provided by Radio Botswana, broadcasting in both English and Setswana, while most of the country has access to Botswana TV (BTV), which broadcasts local, African and international news.
- Botswana uses the metric system for everything.

and all over the Okavango Delta. They range from tiny tented camps to large complexes of brick or reed chalets. While a few lodges are accessible by car or 4WD, most Okavango Delta camps are accessed only by air, which will add around US$150 to US$200 to your bill. All remote camps and lodges require prebooking, but some road-accessible options around Kasane and Maun may accept walk-ins.

ACTIVITIES

Since Botswana is largely a high-budget, low-volume tourist destination, activity tourism focuses on the more expensive options: wildlife viewing, 4WD safaris etc. If you're really flush with cash, the sky is the limit, and you can choose between elephant or horseback safaris in the Okavango, learning to fly in Maun, quadbiking on the Makgadikgadi Pans, or hiring a 4WD and heading out into the Kalahari. Hiking opportunities are limited to the Tsodilo Hills in the northwest and several small ranges in the eastern and southeastern parts of the country. Wildlife hikes can also be arranged for guests of Okavango Delta lodges or participants on mokoro safaris.

BOOKS

General

Kalahari – Life's Variety in Dune and Delta by Michael Main and *Okavango – Jewel of the Kalahari* by Karen Ross chart the phases of the Kalahari and the Okavango Delta, respectively, with particular attention to their vegetation, wildlife and geological and cultural histories. They're full of personality and good colour photos.

A Story Like the Wind by Laurens van der Post is an entertaining, fictional treatment of a meeting between European and San cultures. Its sequel is *A Far Off Place*.

The Sunbird by Wilbur Smith is a light read telling two fanciful and highly entertaining tales about the mythical 'lost city of the Kalahari'.

Guidebooks

African Adventurer's Guide to Botswana by Mike Main concentrates on off-road information, including GPS coordinates, for those venturing into the great unknown with their own vehicles. It's available in better bookshops around Southern Africa. Botswana is covered in more detail in Lonely Planet's *Botswana & Namibia* guidebook.

History & Culture

Ditswammung – The Archaeology of Botswana by P Lane, A Redi and A Segobye is a weighty tome, compiled by the Botswana Society, and is the definitive work for archaeology buffs.

History of Botswana by T Tlou & Alec Campbell is the most readable account of Botswana's history from the Stone Age to modern times.

A Marriage of Inconvenience: The Persecution of Seretse and Ruth Khama by Michael Dutfield details the negative responses to the marriage of Ngwato heir and Botswana's first president, Sir Seretse Khama, and Englishwoman Ruth Williams in the 1950s.

Travel Literature

Lost World of the Kalahari by Laurens van der Post is a classic work dealing with the San people and contains some wonderful background on the Tsodilo Hills. The author's quest for an understanding of San religion and folklore is continued in *Heart of the Hunter* and *The Voice of the Thunder*.

Starlings Laughing by June Vendall-Clark is a memoir describing the end of the colonial era in Southern Africa. The author spent many years in the Maun area.

Cry of the Kalahari by Mark & Delia Owens is an entertaining and readable account of an American couple's seven years studying brown hyenas in the Central Kalahari.

With My Soul Amongst Lions and *Last of the Free* by Gareth Patterson carry Joy and George Adamson's *Born Free* legacy from Kenya to Mashatu, in Botswana's Tuli Block. These rather tragic tales may make depressing reading for anyone inspired by Adamson's early efforts and visions.

BUSINESS HOURS

Normal business hours are 8am to 5pm (often with a one- or two-hour closure for lunch). On Saturday shops open around 8am and close at noon or 1pm; on Sunday there's scarcely any activity anywhere. In larger towns, banking hours are from 9am to 3.30pm Monday to Friday and 8.30am to 11am Saturday. Post offices are open from 8.15am to 4pm (closing for lunch between 12.45am and 2pm). Government offices are open from 7.30am to 12.30pm and 1.45pm to 4.30pm Monday to Friday.

Restaurant opening hours vary according to the type of establishment – as a rule cafes and cheap eats will be open all day, closing in early evening. More expensive restaurants will be open from around 10.30am to 11pm Monday to Saturday, usually with a break between lunch and dinner. Run-of-the-mill bars open around 5pm until late, while nightclubs and late-night drinking spots open their doors around 9pm (or 10pm) and keep going until 5am.

In this chapter we have only listed opening hours where they differ significantly from these broad guidelines.

CHILDREN

Although Botswana is a safe country for children to travel in, be advised that child-related goods and services are extremely limited, particularly in the far fringes of the Kalahari and the Okavango Delta.

CUSTOMS REGULATIONS

Botswana is a member of the Southern African Customs Union, which allows unrestricted carriage of certain items between member countries duty free. From outside the union, you can import up to 400 cigarettes, 50 cigars and 250g of tobacco duty-free. Edible animal products such as untinned meat, milk and eggs are confiscated at the border.

DANGERS & ANNOYANCES

The greatest dangers in Botswana are posed by natural elements, combined with a lack of preparedness. While police and veterinary roadblocks, bureaucracy and bored officials may become tiresome, they're mostly just a harmless inconvenience. Although theft occurs, Botswana enjoys a very low crime rate compared with other African (and many Western) countries.

EMBASSIES & HIGH COMMISSIONS

All the diplomatic missions listed below are located in Gaborone. Many more countries have embassies or consulates that are located in South Africa.

Angola (☎ 390 0204; fax 397 5089; Plot 13232 Khama Crescent, Nelson Mandela Dr, PO Box 111)

France (☎ 397 3863; www.ambafrance-bw.org; 761 Robinson Rd, PO Box 1424; 🕑 8am-4pm Mon-Fri)

Germany (☎ 395 3143; www.gaborone.diplo.de; 3rd fl, Professional House, Broadhurst Mall, Segodithsane Way)

Namibia (☎ 390 2181; fax 390 2248; 2nd fl, Debswana House, PO Box 987; 🕑 7.30am-1pm & 2-4.30pm Mon-Fri)

South Africa (☎ 390 4800/1/2/3; sahcgabs@botsnet.bw; 29 Queens Rd, PO Box 00402; 🕑 8am-12.45pm & 1.30-4.30pm Mon-Fri)

UK (☎ 395 2841; www.britishhighcommission.gov.uk/botswana; Plot 1079-1084 Main Mall, Queens Rd, PO Box 0023; 🕑 8am-12.30pm & 1.30-4.30pm Mon-Thu, 8am-1pm Fri)

USA (☎ 395 3982; http://gaborone.usembassy.gov/; Embassy Dr, PO Box 90; 🕑 9am-4pm Mon-Fri)

Zambia (☎ 395 1951; fax 395 3952; Plot No 1118 Queens Rd, The Mall, PO Box 362; 🕑 8.30am-12.30pm & 2-4.30pm Mon-Fri)

Zimbabwe (☎ 391 4495; fax 390 5863; Government Enclave, Plot 8850, PO Box 1232; 🕑 8am-1pm & 2-4.30pm Mon-Fri)

FESTIVALS & EVENTS

Botswana stages few major celebratory events. Gaborone's **Maitisong Cultural Centre** (☎ 367 1809; fax 358 4946; www.info.bw/~maitisong), in March or April, features local and regional music, dance and drama. Celebrations are held all over the country on Sir Seretse Khama Day, President's Day and Botswana/Independence Day.

HOLIDAYS

Public holidays in Botswana include the following:

New Year's Day 1 January
Day after New Year's Day 2 January
Easter March/April – Good Friday, Holy Saturday and Easter Monday
Labour Day 1 May
Ascension Day April/May
Sir Seretse Khama Day 1 July
President's Day July
Botswana/Independence Day 30 September
Day after Independence Day 1 October
Christmas 25 December
Boxing Day 26 December

INTERNET ACCESS

Despite the fact that Botswana has one of the most well-developed telecommunications networks on the continent, internet access is surprisingly poor and connection is unreliable and slow.

Main towns like Gaborone, Francistown, Kasane and Maun all have cybercafes. Plan on spending between P20 and P50 per hour online. Some hotels and lodges offer internet access, especially those at the top of the range in main urban centres.

INTERNET RESOURCES

Following is a list of helpful websites:

Botswana Government (www.gov.bw) Contains current news and links to business and government departments.

Info Botswana (www.info.bw) Includes links to tourism operators, plus the latest news and weather.

On Safari (www.onsafari.com) Gives details on tour companies and lodges in Botswana and Southern Africa.

University of Botswana (www.ub.bw) Provides information on history, archaeology, politics, society and tourism.

LANGUAGE

English is the official language of Botswana and the medium of instruction from the fifth year of primary school. The most widely spoken language, however, is Setswana, which is the first language of over 90% of people. For more on language, see p775.

MAPS

The most accurate country map is the *Shell Tourist Map of Botswana,* which shows major roads and includes insets of tourist areas and central Gaborone. Almost as good is Rainbird Publishers' 1:2,500,000 *Explorer Map Botswana*. The 1:1,750,000 *Republic of Botswana*, published by Macmillan, also contains insets of Gaborone and the tourist areas. The detailed *ContiMap* is a decent road map that sells for US$10.

MONEY

Botswana's unit of currency is the pula (meaning 'rain'), which is divided into 100 thebe (meaning 'raindrops'). Bank notes come in denominations of P5, P10, P20, P50 and P100, and coins in denominations of 5t, 10t, 25t, 50t, P1, P2 and P5.

ATMs

ATMs are common in major cities and towns, and accept most major Western cards.

Credit Cards

Most major credit cards (especially Visa and MasterCard) are accepted at the tourist hotels and restaurants in the larger cities and towns.

Moneychangers

To change cash, both Barclays and Standard Chartered banks charge 3% commission, while the former charges 3% to change travellers cheques.

Tipping

In most places a service charge is added as a matter of course, but the official policy of courting upmarket tourists only has increased expectations. If you're minded to give a tip for good service, an amount of about 10% of the total bill would be reasonable..

Travellers Cheques

Travellers cheques are falling into disuse in Botswana, though they can still be changed in tourist centres such as Maun and Kasane.

POST

Botswana Post (www.botspost.co.bw) is generally reliable although it can be slow, so allow at least two weeks for delivery to or from any overseas address. Postcards and standard letters (weighing up to 10g) cost P3.30 to other African countries, P4.10 to Europe and P4.90 to the rest of the world.

TELEPHONE & FAX

Botswana's country code is ☎ 267; there are no internal area codes, so when phoning from outside Botswana, dial ☎ 267 followed by the phone number. From Botswana, the international access code is ☎ 00, which should be followed by the country code, area code (if applicable) and telephone number.

Reliable coin and card telephone boxes are found in post offices and in shopping centres in all major towns. Phonecards in varying denominations are sold at shops, post offices and some petrol stations.

Botswana has two global mobile (cell) phone networks, **Mascom Wireless** (www.mascom.bw) and **Orange Botswana** (www.orange.co.bw), of which Mascom is by far the largest provider. Still, even Mascom's coverage is patchy, and is confined to the eastern corridor, from Gaborone in the southeast to Francistown in the east. Outside of these areas you'll find reception is minimal, with little areas of coverage over Maun, Ghanzi and Mamuno. This is set to change as the market is moving forward steadily, and it is worth contacting your mobile operator for up-to-date information.

TOURIST INFORMATION

The main tourist office in the capital is the actual office of the **Department of Tourism** (☎ 391 3111; www.botswanatourism.co.bw; 2nd fl, Standard Chartered Bank Bldg, The Mall). The department also has information offices in Maun, Kasane and Selebi-Phikwe.

VISAS

Visas are not required by citizens of most Commonwealth countries, most European countries or the USA; however, Israelis do need visas. On entry, everyone is granted a 30-day stay. For further information, see right.

VISA EXTENSIONS

Extensions are available for up to three months. You may be asked to show an onward air ticket or proof of sufficient funds for your intended stay. For more than a three-month extension, apply to the Immigration & Passport Control Officer at the **Department of Immigration Head Office** (☎ 361 1300; cnr State House Dr & Khama Cres, PO Box 942, Gaborone) before your trip.

Working visas are also available for non-residents – see following.

WORK

Botswana is developing rapidly and the education system cannot produce enough skilled professionals in several fields. Those with training and experience as medical doctors, secondary-school teachers, professors, engineers and computer professionals will find the warmest welcome. Most foreigners choose to remain in or around Gaborone, Francistown or Maun, but if you're willing to work in the bush, your chances of employment will increase. Foreigners are normally granted a three-year renewable residency permit. Applications must be submitted from outside the country to the **Department of Immigration** (☎ 361 1300; PO Box 942, Gaborone).

Numerous NGOs and international volunteer organisations – the Peace Corps, VSO (Voluntary Service Overseas) and similar – are also active in Botswana, and accept volunteer placements.

TRANSPORT IN BOTSWANA

GETTING THERE & AWAY

This section covers travel between Botswana and its neighbouring countries only. Information on travel to Southern Africa from elsewhere in Africa or from other continents is outlined in the Transport in Southern Africa chapter (p755).

Entering the Country

PASSPORT

All visitors entering Botswana must hold a passport that is valid for at least six months. Also, allow a few empty pages for stamp-happy immigration officials, especially if you're crossing over to Zimbabwe and/or Zambia to see Victoria Falls.

Members of the EU, the USA, South Africa, Scandinavia, Balkan countries and all members of the Commonwealth (with the exception of Ghana, India, Sri Lanka, Nigeria and Mauritius) will be granted a one-month entry permit on arrival (passport photos required). Other nationalities will need to obtain a visa before they arrive in the country.

Air

AIRPORTS & AIRLINES

Botswana's main airport is **Sir Seretse Khama International Airport** (GBE; Map pp78-9; ☎ 35 11 91), located 11km north of the capital Gaborone. Although this is well served with flights from Jo'burg and Harare it is seldom used by tourists as an entry point into the country. Far more popular are **Maun Airport** (MUB; Map p100; ☎ 66 02 38) and **Kasane Airport** (BBK; Map p94; ☎ 65 01 36). There is also an airstrip near Pont Drift (in the Tuli Block) for chartered flights from South Africa.

The national carrier is Air Botswana, which flies routes within Southern Africa. Air Botswana has offices in located in Gaborone, Francistown, Maun, Kasane and Victoria Falls (Zimbabwe). It's worth noting that at present you cannot reserve tickets via its website.

Airlines Flying To/From Botswana

No European or North American airline flies directly into Botswana. The country is only served by two airlines and a number of special-charter flights. Most travellers fly into either Jo'burg or Cape Town in South Africa (both of which are served by an array of international and domestic carriers) and hop on a connecting flight.

Air Botswana (BP; ☎ 390 5500; www.airbotswana.co.bw)

South African Airways (☎ Gaborone airport 390 5740, international 27-11 978 5313; www.flysaa.com)

Border Crossings

Botswana has a well-developed road network with easy access from neighbouring countries. All borders are open daily. It is advisable to try to reach the crossings as early in the day as possible to allow time for any potential delays. Immigration posts at some smaller border crossings close for lunch between 12.30pm and 1.45pm. To cross remote borders on the Botswana side you may need to get your visa at the nearest police station in lieu of an immigration post.

NAMIBIA

The most common – and safest – crossing is at Mamuno, between Ghanzi and Windhoek, although the border post at Mohembo is also popular. The only other real option is the crossing at Ngoma Bridge across the Chobe River. The Kasane/Mpalila Island border is only available to guests who have prebooked accommodation at upmarket lodges on the island.

Drivers crossing the border at Mohembo must secure an entry permit for Mahango Game Reserve at Popa Falls. This is free if you're transiting, or US$3 per person per day plus US$3 per vehicle per day if you want to drive around the reserve (which is possible in a 2WD). From Divundu turn northwest towards Rundu and Windhoek, or east towards Katima Mulilo (Namibia), Kasane (Botswana) and Victoria Falls (Zimbabwe), or take the ferry to Zambia.

By Bus

On Monday and Friday you can catch the shuttle-bus service from Maun to Windhoek, via Ghanzi, with Audi Camp (see p101). The fare is US$55 per person one way (10 hours). Shuttles leave Maun on Wednesday and return from Windhoek on Monday. Prebooking is essential. Contact Audi Camp to arrange a pick-up or drop-off in Ghanzi for a negotiable fare. This may also be done as a return trip, including an inexpensive Audi Camp safari in Botswana's Okavango Delta.

SOUTH AFRICA

Most people travelling overland between Botswana and South Africa use the borders at Ramatlabama (between Lobatse and Mafikeng), Tlokweng Gate (between Gaborone and Zeerust) or Pioneer Gate (between Lobatse and Zeerust). The other border crossings serve back roads across the Limpopo River in the Tuli Block region and the Molopo River in southern Botswana.

It is vital to note that some crossings over the Limpopo and Molopo Rivers are drifts (river fords) that cannot be crossed by 2WD in wet weather. In times of very high water, these crossings may be closed to all traffic.

By Bus

Intercape Mainliner (☎ South Africa 086-128 7287, in Botswana 397 4294; www.intercape.co.za) runs a service from Jo'burg to Gaborone (from SAR180, 6½ hours, one daily); while you need to get off the bus to sort out any necessary visa formalities, you'll rarely be held up for too long at the border. That said, arranging your visa in advance will save time.

You can also travel between South Africa and Botswana by combi. From the far (back) end of the bus station in Gaborone, combis leave when full, to a number of South African destinations including Jo'burg (P140/SAR160, five to seven hours). Payment is possible in Botswanan pula or South African rand. Be warned that you'll be dropped in Jo'burg's Park Station, which is *not* a safe place to linger.

ZAMBIA

Botswana and Zambia share what is probably the world's shortest international border: about 750m across the Zambezi River. The only way across the river is by ferry from Kazungula, which normally operates from 6am to 6pm daily. We weren't able to reach Kazungula on this research trip, but expect the ferry to cost around US$0.75 per person, US$10 for a motorbike, US$15 for a car and US$25 for a 4WD.

There is no regular public transport from the Zambian side of the river, although there is one combi that goes to Dambwa (P30, one hour), 3km west of Livingstone. If you don't have a vehicle, ask for a lift to Livingstone, Lusaka or points beyond at the ferry terminal or on the ferry itself. See also p667 for information.

ZIMBABWE

The two most commonly used borders are at Ramokgwebana/Plumtree and Kazungula. There's also a lesser-used back-road crossing at Pandamatenga. Given the current state of the country you can expect to pay certain unofficial 'taxes' at the border. Our favourite at the time of research was a carbon-emissions tax!

By Bus

Incredibly, there is *no* public transport between Kasane, the gateway to one of

Botswana's major attractions (ie Chobe National Park), and Victoria Falls. Other than hitching, the only method of transport is the tourist 'shuttle minibus' (about one hour). Most combis won't leave unless they have at least two passengers.

From Kasane, Thebe River Camping (p92) offers private transfers to Livingston/Victoria Falls (US$50, two hours). This operation usually picks up booked passengers at their hotels around 10am.

Audi Camp (see p101) in Maun offers a shuttle bus from Maun to Victoria Falls (US$60, seven hours), via Nata and Kasane, on Sunday, which returns from Victoria Falls on Monday.

Between Francistown and Bulawayo, several combis (P30, two hours) leave daily in both directions. For anywhere else in western Zimbabwe, get a connection in Bulawayo.

Bus

Trying to enter and travel around Botswana on public transport is a big headache. Public transport is aimed at moving people between population centres and will rarely deliver you to the more exciting tourist spots.

Car & Motorcycle

Crossing land borders with your own vehicle or a hire car is generally straightforward as long as you have the necessary paperwork – the vehicle-registration documents if you own the car, or a letter from the hire company stating that you have permission to take the car over the border, and proof of insurance.

A vehicle registered outside Botswana can be driven around the country for six months, and an insurance policy purchased in a SACU (South African Customs Union) country (South Africa, Botswana, Namibia, Lesotho, Swaziland), is valid in Botswana for six months. If you don't have third-party insurance from another SACU country, you must buy it at a Botswanan border. Everyone driving into Botswana must pay road tax (officially called a 'National Road Safety Fund Levy'), which costs around P100 per vehicle and is valid until the end of the current year.

GETTING AROUND

Botswana's public-transport network is limited and, at times, expensive. Although domestic air services are fairly frequent and usually reliable, Air Botswana (and charter flights) are not cheap and only a handful of towns are regularly served. The railway service is inexpensive and dependable, but it is terribly slow and is restricted to one line along the thin, populated strip of eastern Botswana. Public buses and combis are also cheap and reasonably frequent, but are confined to the limited number of paved roads so the more interesting places are not accessible. All in all, hiring a vehicle is the best and most practical option.

Air

The national carrier, Air Botswana, operates a limited number of domestic flights between larger towns around the country, namely Gaborone, Francistown, Maun and Kasane. It also offers occasional packages between Gaborone and Maun, including hotels and sightseeing tours – check with the airline, or look for advertisements in the local English-language newspapers.

One-way fares are more expensive than return fares, so plan your itinerary accordingly; children aged under two sitting on the lap of an adult cost 10% of the fare and children aged between two and 12 cost 50% of the fare. Passengers are allowed 20kg of luggage (unofficially, a little more is often permitted if the flight is not full).

CHARTER FLIGHTS

Charter flights are often the best and, sometimes, the only way to reach remote lodges and isolated villages, but they are an expensive extra cost.

On average a one-way fare between Maun and a remote lodge in the Okavango Delta will set you back around US$150 to US$200. These services are now highly regulated and flights must be booked as part of a safari package, with a mandatory reservation at one of the lodges. This is essential; you can't simply turn up in these remote locations and expect to find a bed for the night, as many lodges are very small. Likewise, you are not permitted to book accommodation at a remote lodge in the delta without also booking a return air fare at the same time. Packages can be booked through agencies in Maun.

It is very important to note that passengers on charter flights are only allowed 10kg to 12kg of luggage each (check the exact amount when booking). However, if you have an extra 2kg to 3kg the pilot will usually only mind if the plane is full of passengers.

Bicycle

Botswana is largely flat – and that's about the only concession it makes to cyclists. Some travellers still take a bicycle in the hope of avoiding the uncertainties of hitching and public transport, but unless you're an experienced cyclist and equipped for the extreme conditions, abandon any ideas you may have about a Botswana bicycle adventure. Also bear in mind that bicycles are not permitted in Botswana's national parks and reserves, and cyclists may encounter potentially dangerous wildlife while travelling along any highway or road.

Bus

Buses and combis travel regularly along all major highway routes in Botswana, but services are less frequent in the western part of the country than along the eastern corridor. With few exceptions, small villages are served only if they lie along major highways. On the most popular runs, combi services operate according to demand and depart when full, while buses follow a fixed schedule. Botswana's small population means that its public-transport service is quite limited. In all cases, there are no advance bookings; tickets are sold only on board.

Car & Motorcycle

The best way to travel around Botswana is to hire (or buy) a vehicle. With your own car or motorbike, you can avoid public transport (which is limited to routes between major towns) and organised tours. The downside is that distances are long and the cost of hiring a vehicle in Botswana is high – though it's probably cheaper in South Africa (see p579).

You cannot hire a motorbike in Botswana and although it can be great fun to ride dirt bikes along desert tracks, in between are roads and tracks where clouds of dust and sand kicked up by other vehicles could make for a miserable experience on a motorbike. It's also important to note that motorbikes are *not* permitted in national parks and reserves for safety reasons.

DRIVING LICENCE

Your home driving licence is valid for six months in Botswana, but if it isn't written in English you must provide a certified translation. In any case, it is advisable to obtain an International Driving Permit (IDP). Your national automobile association can issue this and it is valid for 12 months.

FUEL & SPARE PARTS

The cost of fuel (petrol) is relatively expensive in Botswana, around US$0.75 per litre, but prices vary according to the remoteness of the petrol station. Petrol stations are open 24 hours in Gaborone, Francistown, Maun, Mahalapye and Palapye; elsewhere, they open from about 7am to 7pm daily.

As a general rule you should never pass a service station without filling up and it's advisable to carry an additional 100L of fuel (either in long-range tanks or jerry cans) if you're planning on driving in more remote areas.

Spare parts are readily available in most major centres, but not elsewhere. If you are planning on some 4WD driving it is advisable to carry the following: two spare tyres, jump leads, tow rope and cable, a few litres of oil, wheel spanner and a complete tool kit.

If you're renting a hire car make sure to check you have a working jack (and know how to use it!) and a spare tyre.

HIRE

In order to rent a car you must be aged at least 21 (some companies require drivers to be over 25) and have been a licensed driver in your home country for at least two years (sometimes five).

Most major international car-rental companies will allow you to take a vehicle to South Africa, Lesotho, Swaziland, Namibia and Zimbabwe, but only if you have cleared it with the company beforehand so staff can sort out the paperwork. Rental companies are less happy about drivers going to Zambia and will not allow you to go anywhere else in Africa. It is possible to hire a car, for example, in Gaborone and return it to Johannesburg (South Africa) or Windhoek (Namibia), but this will cost extra.

Naturally, always check the paperwork carefully and thoroughly examine the vehicle before accepting it; make sure the 4WD engages properly and that you understand how it works. Also check the vehicle fluids, brakes, battery and so on – the Kalahari is a harsh place to find out that the company (or you) has overlooked something important.

It is probably best to deal with one of the major car-rental companies listed below. For information about hiring a car in South Africa, see p579.

Avis (www.avis.com) Offices in Gaborone, Francistown, Maun, Kasane and all over Southern Africa.
Budget (www.budget.co.za) Offices in Gaborone, as well as in South Africa, Zimbabwe and Namibia.
Imperial (www.imperialcarrental.co.za) Offices in Gaborone and Francistown, and in the major cities of South Africa, Namibia and Zambia.
Tempest (www.tempestcarhire.co.za) This large South African–based company has offices in Gaborone and throughout South Africa, and in Namibia.

INSURANCE

Although insurance is not compulsory, it is *strongly* recommended. No matter who you hire your car from make sure you understand what is included in the price (unlimited kilometres, tax, insurance, collision-waiver and so on) and what your liabilities are. Most local insurance policies do not include cover for damage to windshields and tyres.

Third-party motor insurance is a minimum requirement in Botswana. However, it is also advisable to take out a Damage (Collision) Waiver, which costs around US$20 extra per day for a 2WD, and about US$40 extra per day for a 4WD. Loss (Theft) Waiver is also an extra worth having. For both types of insurance, the excess liability is about US$1500 for a 2WD and US$3000 for a 4WD. If you're only going for a short period of time it may be worth taking out the Super Collision Waiver, which covers absolutely everything, albeit at a price.

PURCHASE

Unless you're going to be staying in Botswana for several years, it's not worth purchasing a vehicle in-country. The best place to buy a vehicle is across the border in South Africa. For more information on purchasing a vehicle in South Africa see p764.

ROAD CONDITIONS

At the time of independence in 1966, Botswana's only paved road extended for 5km from the Lobatse train station to the High Court building. (The road was completed in 1947 in preparation for the visit by King George VI.)

These days good paved roads link all the major population centres. Tracks with sand, mud, gravel and rocks (and sometimes all four) – normally accessible by 2WD except during exceptional rains – connect most villages and cross a few national parks.

Most other 'roads' are poorly defined and badly mapped tracks that should only be attempted by 4WD. In the worst of the wet season (December to February), 4WDs should carry a winch on some tracks (eg through Chobe National Park); and a compass or, better, global positioning system (GPS) equipment. A GPS is essential equipment for driving by 4WD around the salt pans of the Kalahari or northeastern Botswana at any time.

ROAD RULES

To drive a car in Botswana, you must be at least 18 years old. Like in most other Southern African countries, traffic keeps to the left side of the road. The national speed limit is 120km/h on paved roads, 80km/h on gravel roads and 40km/h in all national parks and reserves. When passing through towns and villages, assume a speed limit of 60km/h, even in the absence of any signs.

Highway police use radar and love to fine motorists (about US$10, plus an additional US$1 for every 10km by which you exceed the limit) for speeding. Sitting on the roof of a moving vehicle is illegal, and wearing seatbelts (where installed) is compulsory in the front (but not back) seats. To drink-drive is against the law, and your insurance policy will be invalid if you have an accident while drunk. Driving without a licence is also a serious offence.

If you have an accident causing injury, it must be reported to the authorities within 48 hours. If vehicles have sustained only minor damage and there are no injuries – and all parties agree – you can exchange names and addresses and sort it out later through your insurance companies.

Wild animals, including elephants and the estimated three million wild donkeys in Botswana, can also be a hazard, even along the highways. The Maun–Nata and Nata–Kasane roads are frequented by elephants and should be driven with caution. The chances of hitting a wild or domestic animal are far, far greater after dark, so driving at night is definitely not recommended.

One common but minor annoyance is the so-called 'buffalo fences' (officially called Veterinary Cordon Fences; see p74). These are set up to stop the spread of disease from wild animals to livestock. Simply slow down while the gate is opened and make an effort to offer a friendly wave to the bored gate attendant.

Hitching

Hitching in Botswana is an accepted way to get around given that public transport is sometimes erratic in remote areas. There are even established rates for main routes. Travellers who decide to hitch, however, should understand that they are taking a small but potentially serious risk. People who do choose to hitch will be safer if they travel in pairs and let someone know where they are planning to go.

The equivalent of a bus fare will frequently be requested in exchange for a lift, but to prevent uncomfortable situations at the end of the ride determine a price before climbing in.

Local Transport

Public transport in Botswana is geared towards the needs of the local populace and is confined to main roads between major population hubs. Although cheap and reliable, it is of little use to the traveller as most of Botswana's tourist attractions are off the beaten track.

COMBI (MINIBUS)

Combis, recognisable by their blue number plates, circulate according to set routes around major towns such as Gaborone, Kasane, Ghanzi, Molepolole, Mahalapye, Palapye, Francistown, Selebi-Phikwe, Lobatse and Kanye.

TAXI

Licensed taxis are also recognisable by their blue number plates. They rarely bother hanging around the airports at Gaborone, Francistown, Kasane and Maun, so usually the only reliable transport from those airports is a courtesy bus operated by a top-end hotel or lodge. These are free for guests but normally anyone else can negotiate a fare with the bus driver. Taxis are always available *to* the airports.

It is not normal for taxis to cruise the streets for fares – even in Gaborone. If you need one, telephone a taxi company to arrange a pick-up or go to a taxi stand (usually near the bus or train stations). Fares for taxis are negotiable but fares for occasional shared taxis are fixed. Taxis can be chartered – about US$45 to US$60 per day, although this is negotiable depending on how far you want to go.

Tours

From Maun (p98), which is the traditional jumping-off point for the Okavango Delta, it's also easy to book tours to other parts of Botswana, most notably to Chobe National Park and the Central Kalahari Game Reserve. These excursions are often added to the end of delta tours. Maun is also the base for overland safaris to Kasane via Chobe National Park.

A good place to start is at **Travel Wild** (☎ 686 0822; fax 686 0493; travelwild@dynabyte.bw), opposite the airport, which serves as a central booking and information office for lodges, safaris and other adventures.

The following Botswana tour operators are recommended:

Afro-Trek (☎ 686 0177; www.afrotrek.com) This company (p98) specialises in midmarket safaris around the country.

Audi Camp Safaris (Map p100; ☎ 686 0500; www.okavangocamp.com) This budget operator is run out of the popular Audi Camp in Maun and is an excellent place to book trips around the delta area.

Bathusi Travel & Safaris (Map p100; ☎ 686 0647; www.info.bw/~bathus) Also in Maun, this company specialises in upmarket safaris around the Delta, particularly high fly-ins and luxury tented camps.

Crocodile Camp Safaris (Map p100; ☎ 686 0265; www.botswana.com) This budget operator is located at the Crocodile Camp in Maun, and is a budget backpackers' favourite.

Island Safari Lodge (Map p100; ☎ 686 0300; www.africansecrets.net/isl_home.html) Another popular budget operator in Maun, this establishment is run out of a lodge of the same name.

Maun Rest Camp (Map p100; ☎ 686 3472; simonjoyce@info.bw) This budget operator specialises in mobile camping safaris, and is run out of the Maun Rest Camp.

Ker & Downey (Map p100; ☎ 686 0375; www.kerdowney.com) One of Botswana's – indeed perhaps the world's – most exclusive tour operators, Ker & Downey has an enviable reputation spanning decades, of committed service to high-end customers.

Okavango River Lodge (Map p100; ☎ 686 3707; freewind@info.bw; Shorobe Rd, Maun) Yet another popular budget operator run out of the Okavango River Lodge in Maun.

Okavango Tours & Safaris (Map p100; ☎ 686 1154; www.okavango.bw) This well-established operator specialises in upmarket lodge-based tours, and provides good competition for some of the more famous players.

Wilderness Safaris (Map p100; ☎ Johannesburg 27-11-807 1800; www.wilderness-safaris.com) This Southern Africa–wide operator specialises in upmarket safaris of tremendous quality and service.

Train

The Botswana railway system is limited to one line running along eastern Botswana. It stretches from Ramokgwebana on the Zimbabwean border to Ramatlabama on the South African border, and was once part of the glorious Johannesburg–Bulawayo train service, which is sadly now defunct. Although cheap and reliable, the railway is painfully slow and serves places of little or no interest to the tourist.

There are two different types of train – there is the quicker and more expensive 'day train', and the slower and cheaper 'night train'. Both travel the route between Lobatse and Francistown, via Gaborone, Pilane, Mahalapye, Palapye, Serule and other villages.

Schedules and tickets are available at all train stations, but reservations are only possible at Gaborone, Francistown and Lobatse (for trips beyond Gaborone). For 1st- and 2nd-class fares, advance bookings are essential; economy-class passengers can buy a ticket in advance or on the train.

Lesotho

Lesotho (le-*soo*-too) is called Southern Africa's 'kingdom in the sky' for good reason. This small but stunningly beautiful, mountainous nation is nestled islandlike in the middle of South Africa. It's an intriguing anomaly in a region of modernity, and makes a fascinating travel detour from its larger neighbour.

The country offers not only superb mountain scenery, but a proud traditional people, endless hiking trails, and the chance to explore remote areas on Basotho ponies.

The 'lowland' areas (all of which are still above 1000m) have craft shopping and dinosaur footsteps, while the highlands in the northeast and centre feature towering peaks (over 3000m), and verdant valleys.

Lesotho came into being during the early 19th century, when both the *difaqane* (forced migration) and Boer incursions into the hinterlands were at their height. Under the leadership of the legendary king Moshoeshoe the Great, the Basotho people sought sanctuary and strategic advantage amid the forbidding terrain of the Drakensberg and Maluti Mountains.

Getting around is reasonably easy – ordinary hire cars will get you to most places; public transport is extensive, albeit slow. Hiking and pony trekking from village to village are the best ways of exploring.

FAST FACTS

- **Area** 30,355 sq km
- **Capital** Maseru
- **Country code** ☎ 266
- **Famous for** Ponies, royalty, dams, Basotho hats and blankets
- **Languages** South Sotho, English
- **Money** Loti (plural maloti)
- **Phrases** *Khotso* (hello, or literally 'peace'); *kea legoha* (thank you)
- **Population** 1.8 million

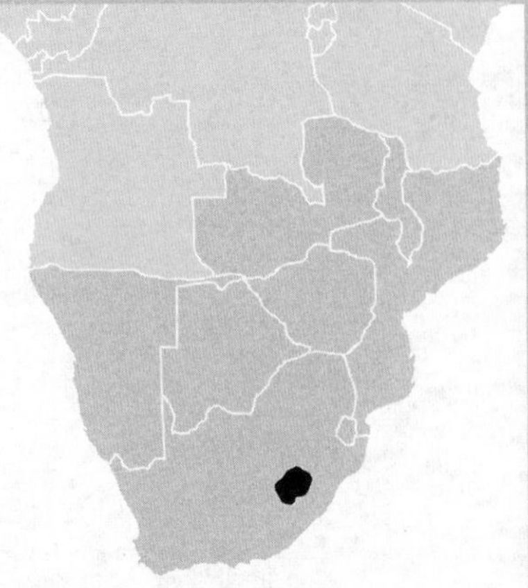

HIGHLIGHTS

- **Lodge living** (p137, p138, p132 and p132) Experiencing a unique lodge-village experience at Semonkong, Malealea, Roma or Ramabanta.
- **Sani Top** (p135) Absorbing the awesome vistas from Sani Pass and hiking the challenging wilderness hikes of the northern highlands.
- **Ts'ehlanyane National Park** (p135) Revelling in the nature and hikes (and even the luxury lodge) of this under-rated wilderness.
- **Off the beaten track** (p137) Hiking from Semonkong in the beautiful Thaba Putsoa mountains to the Ketane Falls.

ITINERARIES

- **One week** From **Maseru** (p128), head south to **Morija** (p137) where you'll find Morija Museum & Archives, a great museum with Basotho culture displays. Continue to **Malealea** (p138) or **Semonkong** (p137) – the 'gems' of Lesotho – to go pony trekking and hiking. You may be able to squeeze in a trip to **Quthing** (Moyeni; p139) to check out the 180-million-year-old dinosaur footprints.
- **Two weeks** Visit **Teyateyaneng** (p133), north of Maseru, the craft centre of Lesotho, or slightly further north, **Bokong Nature Reserve** (p135). Get a taste of the mountainous 'lowlands' by heading to **Morija** (p137), **Malealea** (p138) or **Semonkong** (p137), **Roma** (p132) and **Quthing** (p139). Continue northeast via **Qacha's Nek** (p137) to the remote **Sehlabathebe National Park** (p136) or **Mt Moorosi** (p139).
- **One month** Head northeast to **Teyateyaneng** (p133) and **Butha-Buthe** (p134), with a side trip to the beautiful **Bokong Nature Reserve** (p135) or **Ts'ehlanyane National Park** (p135). Then take in some of the country's most impressive scenery on a circuit to **Mokhotlong** (p135) and up to the magnificent **Sani Top** (p135). Return to Maseru via **Thaba-Tseka** (p134) and the **Katse Dam** (p133), or via the **Mohale Dam** (p132) and **Roma** (p132), before heading east to **Morija** (p137) and following the two-week itinerary. Note: unfortunately it's difficult to circumnavigate the country – the road between Sehlabathebe in the east and Sehonghong in the northeast requires a 4WD.

HOW MUCH?

- **Traditional dance/cultural group** M30-60
- **Internet** M10 per hour
- **Coffee** M10
- **Banana** M3
- **Genuine (wool) Basotho blanket** M650

LONELY PLANET INDEX

- **1L petrol** M6.50 (but fluctuates)
- **1L bottled water** M8-10
- **Bottle of beer** M10
- **Souvenir T-shirt** M100-150
- **Bag of fat cakes (fried savoury doughnuts)** M1-3

CLIMATE & WHEN TO GO

Clear, cold winters, with frosts and snow (and unpredictable changes) in the highlands, await you in Lesotho, so pack warm clothing. During summertime (late November to March), dramatic thunderstorms are common, as are all-enveloping clouds of thick mist, and roads can be affected by flooding rivers. Temperatures at this time can rise to over 30°C in the valleys, though it's usually much cooler in the mountains, even dropping below freezing. Most of Lesotho's rain falls between October and April. Throughout the year, the weather is notoriously changeable.

Visits are possible at any time, with spring and autumn optimal.

HISTORY

Lesotho was settled by Sotho peoples as late as the 16th century. The Khoisan, and possibly some Nguni people, lived among them, intermarrying and mingling their languages.

The early society was made up of small chiefdoms. Cattle and cultivation were the economy's mainstays. Their products were traded for iron from the northeast of South Africa.

By the early 19th century white traders were on the scene, exchanging beads for cattle. They were soon followed by the Voortrekkers (Boer pioneers) and pressure on Sotho grazing lands grew. Even without white encroachment, Sotho society had to accept that it had

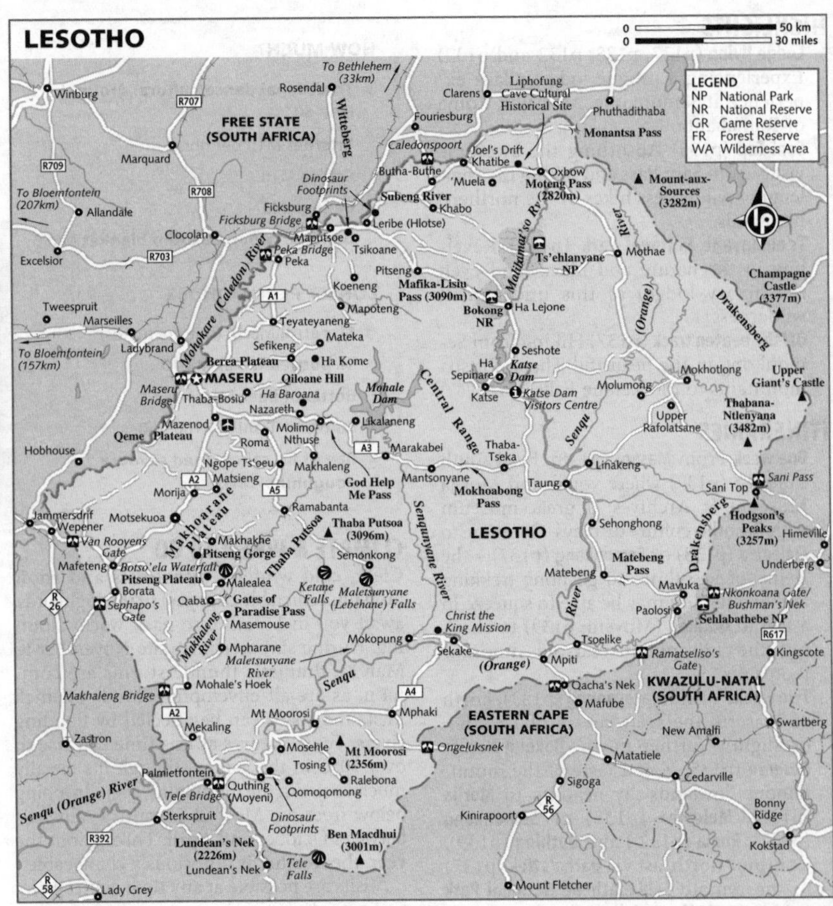

expanded as far as it could and would have to adapt to living in a finite territory. On top of this came the disaster of the *difaqane* (see p36).

The rapid consolidation and expansion of the Zulu state under the leadership of Shaka (see p36), and later Dingaan, resulted in a chain reaction of turmoil throughout the whole of Southern Africa. That the loosely organised Southern Sotho society survived this period was largely due to the abilities of Moshoeshoe (pronounced mo-*shesh*) the Great.

Moshoeshoe the Great

Moshoeshoe began as a leader of a small village and in around 1820 he led his villagers to Butha-Buthe (Place of Lying Down). From this mountain stronghold his people survived the first battles of the *difaqane* and in 1824 Moshoeshoe began his policy of assisting refugees who helped in his defence. Later in the same year he moved his people to Thaba-Bosiu (Mountain at Night), a more easily defendable mountain top.

From Thaba-Bosiu, Moshoeshoe played a patient game of placating the stronger local rulers and granting protection, land and cattle to refugees. These people were to form Basotholand. At the time of Moshoeshoe's death in 1870, the population was more than 150,000.

The welcome Moshoeshoe gave to missionaries, and his ability to take their advice without being dominated by them, was another factor in Basotholand's emergence and survival. The first missionaries arrived in 1833 from the Paris Evangelical Missionary Society. In return for a degree of Christianisation of Sotho customs, the missionaries were disposed to defend the rights of 'their' Basotho against the new threat – British and Boer expansion.

The Boers had crossed the Orange River in the 1830s, and by 1843 Moshoeshoe was sufficiently concerned by their numbers to ally himself with the British Cape government. The British Resident, installed in Basotholand as a condition of the treaties, decided Moshoeshoe was too powerful and engineered an unsuccessful attack on his kingdom.

In 1854 the British withdrew from the area, having fixed the boundaries of Basotholand. The Boers pressed their claims on the land, and increasing tension led to the Free State–Basotho Wars of 1858 and 1865. After success in the first war, Moshoeshoe was forced in the second to sign away much of his western lowlands.

Moshoeshoe again called on British assistance in 1868, this time on the imperial government in London. A high commission adjudicated the dispute and the result was the loss of more Basotho land. It was obvious that no treaty between Boers and Basotho would hold for long. Continual war between the Free State and Basotholand was not good for British interests, so the British annexed Basotholand and handed it to the Cape Colony to run in 1871.

After Moshoeshoe the Great

The year after Moshoeshoe the Great's death, squabbles over succession divided the country. The Cape government exploited this and reduced the powers of chiefs, limiting them to their individual areas.

The Gun War of 1880 began as a protest against the Cape government's refusal to allow the Basotho to own firearms, but it quickly became a battle between the rebel chiefs on one side and the government and collaborating chiefs on the other. The war ended in a stalemate with the Cape government being discredited.

A shaky peace followed; in 1884 the British government again took control of Basotholand. Its decision to back strong local leaders helped to stabilise the country. One unexpected benefit of direct British rule was that when the Union of South Africa was created, Basotholand was classified as a British Protectorate and was not included in the Union.

Home Rule & Independence

In 1910 the advisory Basotholand National Council was formed from members nominated by the chiefs. After decades of allegations of corruption and favouritism, reforms in the 1940s introduced some democratic processes into council appointments.

In the mid-1950s the council requested internal self-government from the British. In 1960 a new constitution was in place and elections were held for a Legislative Council.

Meanwhile, political parties had formed, including the Basotholand Congress Party (BCP), similar to South Africa's African National Congress (ANC), and the Basotholand National Party (BNP), a conservative party headed by Chief Leabua Jonathan.

The BCP won the 1960 elections, then demanded, and won, a new constitution that paved the way to full independence from Britain in 1966. However, after the 1965 elections the BCP lost power to the BNP, and Chief Jonathan became the first prime minister of the new Kingdom of Lesotho. During the election campaign the BNP promised cooperation with the South African apartheid regime and in turn received massive support from it.

As most of the civil service was still loyal to the BCP, Jonathan did not have an easy time. Stripping King Moshoeshoe II of the few powers that the new constitution had left him did not endear Jonathan's government to the people, and the BCP won the 1970 election.

Jonathan responded to the election results by suspending the constitution, arresting and expelling the king, and banning opposition parties. The king was eventually allowed to return from exile in Holland, and Jonathan attempted to form a government of national reconciliation. This ploy was partly successful, but some BCP members, including the leader Ntsu Mokhehle, resisted and attempted to stage a coup in 1974. The coup failed miserably and resulted in the death of many BCP supporters and the jailing or exile of the BCP leadership.

Jonathan changed tack in his attitude to South Africa, calling for the return of land in the Orange Free State that had been stolen from the original Basotholand, and criticising apartheid, allegedly offering refuge to ANC guerrillas, and flirting with Cuba. Relations soured; South Africa closed Lesotho's borders, strangling the country.

The Lesotho military took action. Jonathan was deposed in 1986 and the king was restored as head of state. This was a popular move, but eventually agitation for democratic reform rose again. In 1990 King Moshoeshoe II was deposed by the army in favour of his son, Prince Mohato Bereng Seeisa (Letsie III). Elections in 1993 resulted in the return of the BCP.

The BCP was split between those who wanted Prime Minister Ntsu Mokhehle to remain as leader and those who didn't. Mokhehle formed the breakaway Lesotho Congress for Democracy (LCD) party and continued to govern.

In 1995 Letsie III abdicated in favour of his father and, five years after being deposed, Moshoeshoe II was reinstated. He restored calm to Lesotho after a year of unrest. Tragically, less than a year later he was killed when his 4WD plunged over a cliff in the Maluti Mountains. Letsie III was again made the king.

Elections & Invasion

Elections were held in 1998 amid accusations of widespread cheating by the LCD, which won with a landslide. Tensions arose and meanwhile, Mokhehle handed over to his successor Pakalitha Mosisili.

In September 1998, following months of protests, the government called on the Southern African Development Community (SADC) treaty partners, Botswana, South Africa and Zimbabwe, to help restore order. Troops invaded the kingdom and fighting ensued in Maseru.

In May 2002, Mosisili's LCD party won again and he began a second five-year term.

The 2007 elections were highly controversial, with the newly formed All Basotho Convention (ABC) party accusing the LCD party of manipulating the allocation of seats. National strikes ensued and several ministers were allegedly attacked by gunmen. There was an assassination attempt on ABC's leader, Tom Thabane, and many people were detained and tortured.

Lesotho Today

The political situation is currently calm, although the elections of 2012 may bring tensions to the fore once again.

Lesotho ranks among the region's poorer countries, and has few natural resources. During the last century, Lesotho's main export was labour – approximately 60% of males worked mainly in mining in South Africa. In the late 1990s, the restructuring of the South African gold-mining industry, mechanisation and the closure of mines resulted in massive job losses. Meanwhile, the Lesotho economy – under transformation due to a rapid growth of the textile industry – collapsed.

It is hoped that economic initiatives, such as the Economic Partnership Agreement (EPA), signed with the EU in 2007 to create free trade zones, will help revive the local business sector.

THE CULTURE

The National Psyche

Pride is at the core of the Basotho people, not surprisingly given the incredible history of their nation. The Basotho are remarkably free

FAMINE IN LESOTHO

Lesotho, particularly rural Lesotho, is extremely vulnerable to food shortages; the mountain kingdom's annual cereal production is declining because of unpredictable weather, long-term soil erosion and the impact of HIV/AIDS. On top of this, the country faces trade constraints and declining employment opportunities, leaving many vulnerable to food insecurity. Subsistence farming used to be the main food source for most people, but today many rent out their land for others to cultivate, thereby losing their ability to grow their own food. Per capita agricultural production in real terms has been falling for decades, and today, tens of thousands of the most vulnerable people are relying on external food aid. Many people in the country's lowlands do not have access to water for domestic use, and travel long distances each day to fetch it – an irony given that the Lesotho Highlands Water Project supplies South Africa with millions of cubic metres of water each year (see the boxed text, p134).

of the effects of apartheid and warmly welcome travellers to their kingdom. Like their African neighbours, they have a wonderfully carefree attitude to time. The traditional class system has altered – herding, once a revered position, is done by the poorest boys (many families are said to sell their sons to wealthy families to be herders), although the population continues to rely on and respect its community chiefs. The Basotho blanket, worn proudly by many in the rural areas, reflects one's status in the community, according to the quality, material and design of the blanket itself.

Daily Life

Traditional culture, which is still strong, consists largely of the customs, rites and superstitions with which the Basotho explain and enrich their lives. Music also plays an important part in their lives (see right).

Traditional medicine mixes rites and customs with a *sangoma* (witchdoctor), who develop their own charms and rituals. The Basotho are traditionally buried in a sitting position, facing the rising sun – ready to leap up when called.

Poverty and death is ever-present in Lesotho. Life for most people is harsh, with the majority trying to eke out a living through subsistence agriculture, especially livestock; unemployment currently stands at about 45%. The spectre of AIDS is high – the infection rate (adult prevalence) is estimated at 24%.

Most Lesotho in rural communities live in rondavels, round huts with mud walls (often decorated) and thatched roofs.

Population

The citizens of Lesotho are known as the Basotho people. Most are Southern Sotho and most speak South Sotho. The melding of the Basotho nation was largely the result of Moshoeshoe the Great's 19th-century military and diplomatic triumphs (see p124); many diverse subgroups and peoples have somehow merged into a homogeneous society.

RELIGION

Around 80% of the population is believed to be Christian (mainly Roman Catholic, Anglican and Episcopalian). The remaining 20% live by traditional Basotho beliefs. There are many churches throughout the country, many of which were (or continue to be) built by missionaries (see p124).

ARTS & CRAFTS

Architecture

Traditional Basotho huts – rondavels – are one-room huts of stone and mud with thatched roofs, that serve as the living area, kitchen and bedroom. Many are exquisitely decorated with murals, often imbued with symbols and meaning, such as visual prayers for rain. For further information, see *African Painted Houses* by Gary N Van Wyk (1998).

Music

Music and dance are important components of ceremony and everyday life. There are various musical instruments, from the *lekolulo* (a flutelike instrument played by herd boys), to the *thomo* (a stringed instrument played by women) and the *setolo-tolo* (a stringed instrument played with the mouth, by men). For more information see p48.

Tapestry Weavings

Tapestry and rug weaving is practised in many regions of Lesotho and good-quality items can be found around Teyateyaneng and the fringes of Maseru. Often, the woven pieces convey typical life in the villages, with bright figures undertaking daily activities or celebrations. Most handwoven goods are from pure wool and mohair. Other handicrafts specific to the area include Basotho hat baskets, and grass and clay products.

ENVIRONMENT

The Land

From Lesotho's northern tip to its western side, where it juts out almost to the town of Wepener in South Africa, the border is formed by the Mohokare (Caledon) River. The eastern border is defined by the rugged escarpment of the Drakensberg Mountains, and high country forms much of the southern border.

All of Lesotho exceeds 1000m in altitude, with peaks in the central ranges and near the Drakensberg reaching to more than 3000m. Lesotho has the highest lowest point of any country. The tallest mountain in Southern Africa (the highest point south of Mt Kilimanjaro) is the 3482m Thabana-Ntlenyana, near Sani Pass in eastern Lesotho.

LESOTHO

Wildlife

ANIMALS

Due mainly to its altitude, Lesotho is home to fewer animals than many Southern African countries. You may come across rheboks and reedbucks, and in the Drakensberg, elands are still present. Baboons and jackals are reasonably common and there are also mongooses and meerkats.

The bird life is rich, with just under 300 species recorded. The Drakensberg is an excellent place for birdwatching, and bearded vultures and black eagles are both found here. Lesotho is one of the few places you may spot the extremely rare bald ibis.

PLANTS

The high plains and mountains are home to Cape alpine flowers. The national flower, spiral aloe, is a strange plant unique to Lesotho. Its leaves form rows of striking, spiral patterns and you'll see it in left- and right-handed varieties on the slopes of the Maluti Mountains.

National Parks

Sehlabathebe is Lesotho's most famous national park. Its high-altitude grasslands, lakes, bogs and otherworldly rock formations offer a wonderful wilderness experience and are ideal for hiking. Sehlabathebe is under the jurisdiction of the **Ministry of Tourism, Environment & Culture** (Map p129; ☎ 2231 1767, 2232 6075; New Postal Office Bldg, 6th fl, Kingsway, Maseru).

The country's other main conservation areas – Ts'ehlanyane National Park, Bokong Nature Reserve and the Liphofung Cave Cultural Historical Site (see p135) – are under the jurisdiction of **Lesotho Northern Parks** (☎ 2246 0723), which handles all accommodation bookings. All have simple accommodation (Except Bokong, which has camping only), established trails and helpful staff, and are relatively easy to access, making them well worth visiting.

Environmental Issues

This high, corrugated and often freezing kingdom is a tough environment at the best of times. Serious erosion exists in Lesotho due to the pressures of modern farming techniques and overgrazing. Heavy summer rains wash away unacceptably large amounts of topsoil, as well as create dongas (eroded gullies). Action is being taken to tackle erosion, including the reclamation of dongas through the building of rock dams-cum-terraces to capture silt and detritus, but in the future, large tracts of land will become uncultivatable.

There are also serious environmental concerns about the controversial Lesotho Highlands Water Project, which provides water and electricity to South Africa (see the boxed text, p134).

In order to protect and develop the eastern-alpine ecosystem of the Maluti-Drakensberg Mountains, the multimillion-dollar Maluti-Drakensberg Transfrontier Conservation & Development Project between South Africa and Lesotho was established in 2001.

FOOD & DRINK

You won't be writing home about the food in Lesotho. It's not notably bad, but it's nothing special either. The staples here are much the same as in South Africa. Maseru now boasts a decent selection of restaurants serving a range of local and foreign foods, but outside the capital you'll usually have to take what you're given.

MASERU

pop Maseru District 430,000 / elevation 1600m

Maseru is the kind of place that grows on you. It sprawls across Lesotho's lower-lying western edge, rimmed by the Berea and Qeme Plateaus. This previously quiet backwater has rapidly expanded over the past few decades, and has a modest array of modern amenities. While the city has few sights, Maseru is where you can get your bearings and stock up on supplies before heading into the highlands and beyond.

ORIENTATION

Maseru's main street is Kingsway (paved in 1947 for a visit by the British royals). Kingsway runs from the border crossing at Maseru Bridge right through town to the Circle, a traffic roundabout and landmark. At the Circle the street splits to become two important traffic arteries: Main North Rd (for Teyateyaneng and points north) and Main South Rd (for Mohale's Hoek and points south). A bypass road rims the city to the south.

Maps

The **Department of Land, Surveys & Physical Planning** (☎ 2232 2376; Lerotholi Rd; 🕒 9am-3pm

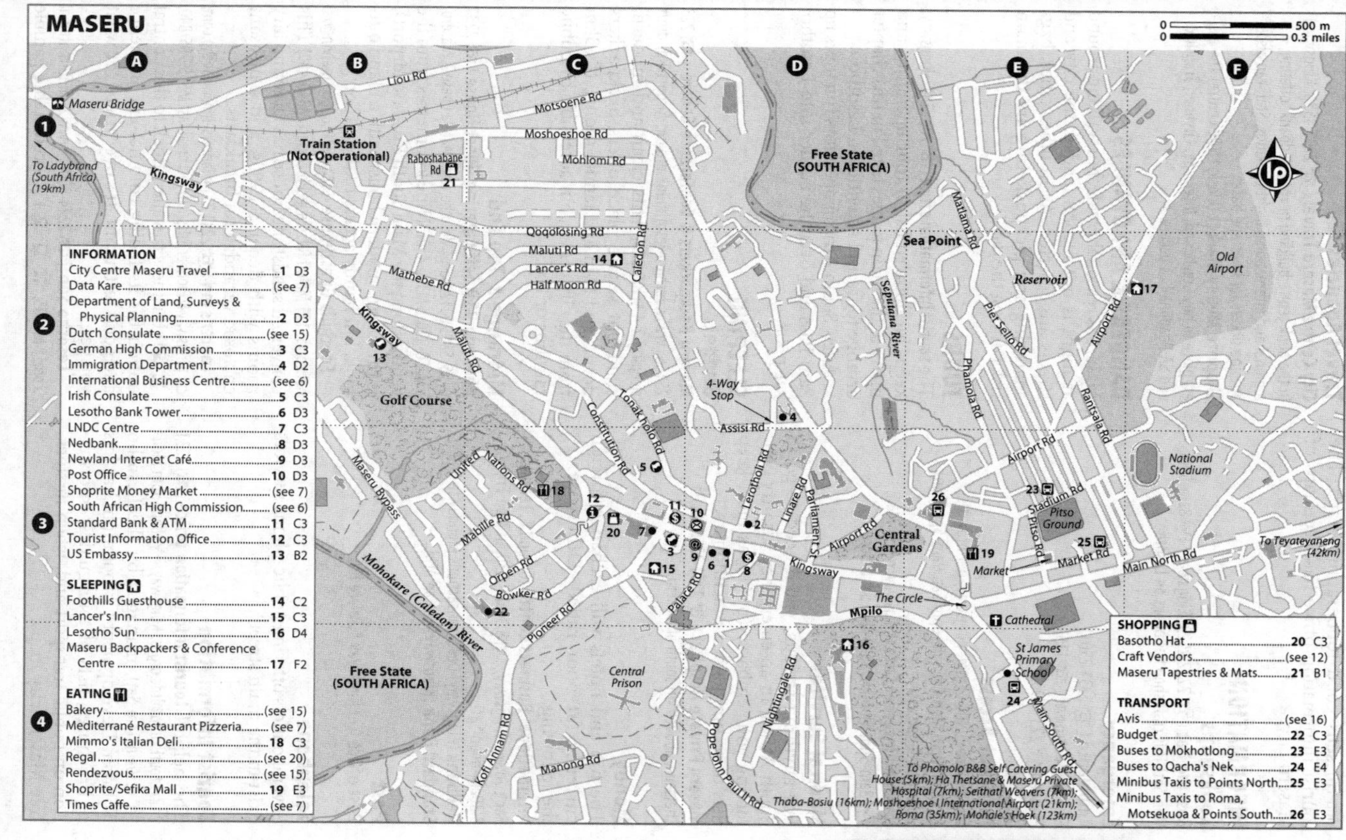
MASERU
INFORMATION
City Centre Maseru Travel....1 D3
Data Kare....(see 7)
Department of Land, Surveys & Physical Planning....2 D3
Dutch Consulate....(see 15)
German High Commission....3 C3
Immigration Department....4 D2
International Business Centre....(see 6)
Irish Consulate....5 C3
Lesotho Bank Tower....6 D3
LNDC Centre....7 C3
Nedbank....8 D3
Newland Internet Café....9 D3
Post Office....10 D3
Shoprite Money Market....(see 7)
South African High Commission....(see 6)
Standard Bank & ATM....11 C3
Tourist Information Office....12 C3
US Embassy....13 B2
SLEEPING
Foothills Guesthouse....14 C2
Lancer's Inn....15 C3
Lesotho Sun....16 D4
Maseru Backpackers & Conference Centre....17 F2
EATING
Bakery....(see 15)
Mediterrané Restaurant Pizzeria....(see 7)
Mimmo's Italian Deli....18 C3
Regal....(see 20)
Rendezvous....(see 15)
Shoprite/Sefika Mall....19 E3
Times Caffe....(see 7)
SHOPPING
Basotho Hat....20 C3
Craft Vendors....(see 12)
Maseru Tapestries & Mats....21 B1
TRANSPORT
Avis....(see 16)
Budget....22 C3
Buses to Mokhotlong....23 E3
Buses to Qacha's Nek....24 E4
Minibus Taxis to Points North....25 E3
Minibus Taxis to Roma, Motsekuoa & Points South....26 E3
Maseru Bridge
To Ladybrand (South Africa) (19km)
Train Station (Not Operational)
Free State (SOUTH AFRICA)
Sea Point
Reservoir
Old Airport
National Stadium
Golf Course
Central Gardens
Pitso Ground
Central Prison
Cathedral
St James Primary School
The Circle
Mpilo
4-Way Stop
Mohokare (Caledon) River
Seputana River
To Teyateyaneng (42km)
To Phomolo B&B Self Catering Guest House (5km); Ha Thetsane & Maseru Private Hospital (7km); Seithati Weavers (7km); Thaba-Bosiu (16km); Moshoeshoe I International Airport (21km); Roma (35km); Mohale's Hoek (123km)
500 m
0.3 miles

LESOTHO

Mon-Fri) sells good topographic maps. The tourist information office has free maps of Maseru city.

INFORMATION

Bookshops

Basotho Hat (☎ 2232 2523; Kingsway; 8am-5pm Mon-Sat) This craft shop has books on Lesotho.

Emergency

Ambulance (☎ 2231 2501)
Fire Department (☎ 115)
Police (☎ 2231 9900)

Internet Access

Data Kare (LNDC Centre, Kingsway; per hr M10; 8am-8pm Mon-Fri, 8am-6pm Sat, 9am-5pm Sun) Slow internet access.
Newland Internet Cafe (Kingsway; per hr M10; 8am-5pm Mon-Fri, 8am-4pm Sat & Sun)

Medical Services

For anything serious, you'll need to go to South Africa. In an emergency, also try contacting your embassy (p141), as most keep lists of recommended practitioners.

Maseru Private Hospital (☎ 2231 3260) In Ha Thetsane, about 7km south of Maseru.

Money

The top-end hotels will exchange foreign currency (at poor rates). Otherwise try the following.

International Business Centre (Ground fl, Lesotho Bank Tower, Kingsway; 8.30am-3.30pm Mon-Fri, 8.30am-noon Sat)
Nedbank (Kingsway) Does transactions Monday to Friday.
Standard Bank (Kingsway) Has an ATM.

Post

Post office (cnr Kingsway & Palace Rd)

Telephone

Several outlets offering public-phone services exist in the main street.

Tourist Information

The helpful **tourist information office** (☎ 2231 2427; touristinfo@ltdc.org.ls; Kingsway; 8am-5pm Mon-Fri, 8.30am-1pm Sat), managed by the Lesotho Tourism Development Corporation, has lots of brochures, lists of tour guides, information on public transport and, when in stock, free Maseru city maps.

Travel Agencies

City Centre Maseru Travel (☎ 2231 4536; Kingsway) In the book centre building next to Nedbank, offering regional and international flight bookings. Staff can also arrange tickets for Intercape buses.
Shoprite Money Market (kiosk, LNDC Centre) The easiest place to buy Greyhound, Intercape, Cityliner, Translux and SA Roadlink bus tickets.

DANGERS & ANNOYANCES

Maseru is reasonably safe, but walking around at night is not recommended; the city and streets are deserted. As in other cities, bag-snatching and pickpocketing are the main risks during the day.

TOURS

The **tourist information office** (☎ 2231 2427; Kingsway) keeps an updated list of tour operators, and many of the main lodges listed in this chapter arrange tours and activities in Lesotho.

A few South African operators run tours up Sani Pass and over the border into Lesotho; see p508.

SLEEPING

Budget

Maseru Backpackers & Conference Centre (☎ 223 25166; www.durham-lesotholink.org.uk; Airport Rd; dm/r sleeping 2-4 M100/320) This clean and modern, staid but secure place offers backpackers dorms and twin and family rooms. It's 3km from the city centre, but accessible by public minibus or taxi.

Midrange & Top End

Phomolo B&B Self Catering Guest House (☎ 2231 0755, 5805 0012; baso@ilesotho.com; Matala Phase 2, Maseru, s M250-320, d M350-450). Nine kilometres from the centre along the Main South Road (to airport), is this clean, modern house with a bland outlook, but handy access to the airport.

Foothills Guesthouse (☎ 5870 6566; melvin@xsinet.co.za; 121 Maluti Rd; s/d incl breakfast M340/480) This converted sandstone house has large and airy rooms with decor c 1960s, and a pleasant enclosed verandah for breakfasts.

Lancer's Inn (☎ 2231 2114; lancers-inn@ilesotho.com; cnr Kingsway & Pioneer Rd; s/d/tr incl breakfast M655/795/840;) Business travellers flock to this central option for its fading colonial-era ambience and good restaurant. It's overpriced for what you get.

Lesotho Sun (☎ 2224 3000; www.suninternational.com; r M1105;) A predictable gamble (ask about specials). Perched on a quiet hillside with a great setting overlooking town, it boasts a casino and two restaurants.

EATING

Times Caffe (Level 1, LNDC Centre; mains M18-50; breakfast, lunch & dinner) While the setting is funky, travellers say it's unreliable – the menu features many things which are never available. It might be better to stick to coffee.

Mediterrané Restaurant Pizzeria (2231 2960; LNDC Centre; mains M35-50; lunch & dinner) This casual diner draws the crowds for good oven-baked pizzas, burgers and grills. There's outdoor seating, popular for coffees.

Mimmo's Italian Deli (2232 4979; Maseru Club, United Nations Rd; mains M30-80; lunch & dinner) A pleasant place housed in an old building with an outdoor terrace; the wood-oven pizzas are great, pasta less so.

Regal (2231 3930; Level 1, Basotho Hat; mains M35-80; lunch & dinner; V) This smart place has tasteful decor, a relaxed ambience and dishes up everything from Indian curries to Chinese noodles, as well as excellent vegetarian options.

Rendezvous (2231 2114; Lancer's Inn, Kingsway; mains M37-85; breakfast, lunch & dinner) A fave among the expats and locals who goss in the garden cafe or have a tipple in the traditional chandeliered restaurant.

Self-caterers should head to the well-stocked supermarket Shoprite, with outlets in the LNCD Centre and the Sefika Mall, or the **bakery** (7am-8.30pm) next to Lancer's Inn, with good pies, cakes and other delicacies.

LESOTHO PRICES

At the time of research, a thriving commercial activity had affected both the economy and tourist experience – the conference industry. In response to conferences (particularly those in the government sector), many B&Bs had been constructed with 'conference facilities' attached. Accommodation rates of many local establishments seem high for what you get; this does not affect many established lodges and some bed and breakfasts. Transport costs rise regularly, often in line with inflation. Please note, therefore, while all rates were accurate at the time of research, this chapter is particularly susceptible to price fluctuations.

SHOPPING

Basotho Hat (2232 2523; Kingsway; 8am-5pm Mon-Fri, 8am-4.30pm Sat) This government-run craft shop is the best place to start, although prices are generally higher than elsewhere in the country. The horsehair fly whisks sold here make good investments for hikers and horse riders.

The craft vendors in front of the tourist information office have a supply of woven Basotho hats and other souvenirs. For tapestries try **Maseru Tapestries & Mats** (2231 1773; Raboshabane Rd) or **Seithati Weavers** (2231 3975; www.villageweavers.co.ls; Main South 1 Rd), about 7km from town.

GETTING THERE & AWAY

Bus & Minibus Taxi

The hectic bus and minibus taxi departure points are in or around the Pitso Ground (and nearby streets) to the northeast of the circle. To avoid feeling overwhelmed by the throngs of people and buses, check first with the tourist office for specific departure points.

Shoprite's 'Money Market' kiosk in the LNDC Centre sells Greyhound and Intercape bus tickets.

From Maseru, buses depart to many destinations. Sample fares include Mafeteng (M25), Roma (M12) and Mokhotlong (M80).

Car

Avis (2235 0328) is at Lesotho Sun and the airport, **Imperial** (58720215) is at the airport and **Budget** (2231 6344) at Maseru Sun, southwest of junction of Kingsway and Pioneer Rd.

GETTING AROUND

To/From the Airport

Moshoeshoe I International Airport is 21km from town, off Main South Rd. Minibus taxis to the airport depart from the transport stand at Sefika Mall (also referred to by locals as new taxi rank). A private taxi will charge around M80.

Taxi & Minibus Taxi

The standard minibus taxi fare around town is M4. Taxi companies include **Planet** (2231 7777), **Luxury** (2232 6211) and **Executive Car Hire & Travel** (2231 4460). These can also be chartered for long-distance transport elsewhere in the country.

AROUND MASERU

Most towns in Lesotho have risen around trading posts or protectorate-era administration centres, but none of these towns approach Maseru in size or facilities.

THABA-BOSIU

Moshoeshoe the Great's mountain stronghold, first occupied in July 1824, is about 16km east of Maseru. Thaba-Bosiu (Mountain at Night) played a pivotal role in the consolidation of the Basotho nation. The name may be a legacy of the site being first occupied at night, but many legends exist.

At the mountain's base is a **visitors information centre** (admission M10; 8am-5pm Mon-Fri, 9am-1pm Sat) where you can organise an official guide to accompany you on the short walk to the top of the mountain.

Good views from here include those of the **Qiloane Hill** (inspiration for the Basotho hat), along with the remains of fortifications, Moshoeshoe's grave and parts of the original settlement.

Sleeping & Eating

A smart new complex – with accommodation – was being constructed near the visitors centre at the time of research.

Mmelesi Lodge (5886 1116; s/d/tr M360/400/500) offers well-organised rondavels, about 2km before the visitors centre.

Getting There & Away

Minibuses to Thaba-Bosiu (M10, 30 minutes) depart from Maseru at the Sefika Mall transport stand. If you're driving, take the Mafeteng Rd for about 13km and turn left at the Roma turn-off; after about 6km take the signposted road left. Thaba-Bosiu is 10km further along.

ROMA

Roma, 35km from Maseru, is Lesotho's centre of learning, with the country's only university. Several attractive sandstone buildings are dotted around the town, and the entry to town by the southern gorge is spectacular.

Just north of Roma are the **Ha Baroana** rock paintings. They are one of Lesotho's more publicised rock-art sites (there are many being discovered and not publicised), and are worth a visit if you have extra time, although neglect and vandalism have taken their toll.

To reach the paintings from Roma head back to the Maseru road and turn right in the direction of Thaba-Tseka for about 12km to Nazareth. Just before Nazareth follow the signposted gravel track to the paintings for 3km to Ha Khotso. Turn right at a football field and continue 2.5km to a hilltop. A footpath zigzags down the hillside to the rock shelter with the paintings. Minibus taxis go as far as Nazareth.

Sleeping & Eating

Trading Post Guest House (082-7732180; www.tradingpost.co.za; campsites per person M75, dm M125, r per person M175-200, with half board M375;) is in a trading post that has been operated since 1903 by the Thorn family, which runs the guesthouse. Accommodation includes garden rooms, rondavels and the original sandstone homestead, with shared kitchen, set in a lush garden. A self-contained cottage sleeps six for M400. Breakfasts (M55) and dinners (M95) are available. Pony trekking, hiking, 4WD trails and other action adventures can be arranged. There are even *minwane* (dinosaur footprints) nearby.

The same owners run the delightful **Trading Post Adventures Guest House** (campsites per person M75, rondavels with half board per person M400, dm/r per person M125/200; stables per person self cater/with half board M250/375), 40km southeast along the same road at Ramabanta village. A range of luxury ron-

WORTH A VISIT – MOHALE DAM

The Mohale Dam is worth seeing only if you haven't visited Katse Dam (see opposite) or if you're passing by. Built across the Senqunyane River, the impressive 145m-high rock-fill dam was completed in 2004 as the second phase of the Lesotho Highlands Water Project. There are commanding views of the lake and massive mountains beyond. This is easiest done with your own wheels if you're passing Likalaneng on the way to Roma or Thaba-Tseka. You can drive as far as the Mohale Tunnel, through which water can flow 32km to the Katse Dam and vice versa. Alternatively, the Thaba-Tseka–Maseru bus stops at Likalaneng, from where it's a short walk to the visitors centre (tours available).

LESOTHO

davels and a basic backpackers lodge are set on lush lawns overlooking the mountains. Staying here provides the chance to link up Roma, Ramabanta and other places in the area on overnight hikes and pony treks.

Getting There & Away

Minibus taxis run throughout the day to/from Maseru (M18, 30 minutes).

NORTHERN LESOTHO

Northern Lesotho – the area from Maseru up to Butha-Buthe and the main gateway to the spectacular northeastern highlands – is relatively densely populated, and dotted with a series of bustling lowland towns. While there are few formal tourist sights, the region's local flavours – markets, welcoming locals and the unique geographical backdrop – provide a genuine experience.

Regular minibus taxis run between Maseru and the towns. Maputsoe is a major transport junction, and for northbound transport from Maseru, you'll usually need to change vehicles there. Minibus taxis to Maseru (M17, one hour), Butha-Buthe (M13, 45 minutes) and Leribe (M7, 30 minutes) run throughout the day from the Total petrol station.

TEYATEYANENG

Referred to as 'TY', Teyateyaneng (Place of Quick Sands) has been developed as the craft centre of Lesotho. Some of the best come from: Helang Basali Crafts at St Agnes Mission, about 2km before Teyateyaneng; Setsoto Design, near Blue Mountain Inn; Hatooa Mose Mosali; and Elelloang Basali Weavers about 4km to the north of TY. At most places you can watch the weavers at work.

Blue Mountain Inn (☎ 2250 0362; s/d M560/675;) offers clean rooms set in a pretty compound, and a restaurant.

Minibus taxis run between Teyateyaneng and Maseru (M14, 45 minutes, 35km). Chartering a taxi from Maseru costs around M150 one way.

HA KOME CAVE HOUSES

The **Ha Kome cave houses** are an anomaly in this area, 21km from TY and several kilometres from the village of Mateka. These extraordinary inhabited mud dwellings are nestled under a rock overhang, hidden within the pink and orange cliffs. Why the houses exist is a little vague. At the time of research a new owner was taking over management; see the tourist office for details and hours.

To get there, follow the signs from Mateka. Due to one unpaved section, plus the last steep, rocky 1.5km to the visitors centre, a 4WD is required.

LERIBE

Leribe (also known as Hlotse) is a busy regional market hub. It served as an administrative centre under the British, as witnessed by a few old buildings slowly decaying in the leafy streets. The main sight is the crumbling **Major Bell's Tower** near the market, a government storehouse (1879).

The **Leribe Craft Centre** (☎ 2240 0323; 8am-4.30pm Mon-Fri, 9.30am-1pm Sat) sells a range of high-quality mohair goods. There is a set of **dinosaur footprints** a few kilometres south of Leribe at Tsikoane village. Take the small dirt road to the right at the Tsikoane Primary School, towards some rocky outcrops. At the church, ask the way to the *minwane*, 1km up the mountainside.

Leribe Hotel (☎ 2240 0559; Main St; s/d M395/510) is somewhere to stay only if you're desperate; this colonial relic, with modern entrance, has seen better days. Meals are M85.

HIGHLANDS WATER PROJECT

Katse

Tiny Katse is the purpose-built former base for the Lesotho Highlands Water Project and the site of Africa's highest dam wall (185m). The green hilly area makes for a relaxing pause – even if you don't give a damn about engineering feats.

There's a **visitors centre** (8am-5pm Mon-Fri, 9am-2pm Sat & Sun), just east of the Katse village junction along the main road. Guided tours depart at 9am and 2pm (weekdays) and 9am and 11am (weekends). Exposed and windy camping is on offer nearby (M20).

It's well worth visiting the small but interesting **Katse Botanical Garden** (☎ 2291 0311; M5; 8am-5pm Mon-Fri, 9am-6pm Sat & Sun), established to protect the spiral aloes displaced by the dam's construction.

Orion Katse Lodge (☎ 2291 0202, 2291 0813; www.oriongroup.co.za; s/d incl breakfast M590/1000, guesthouse M690-1060) at the far end of the suburb-like

Katse village beyond the barrier gate, resembles a hospital in so many ways.

The spectacular road from Leribe to Katse passes the lowland village of Pitseng before climbing over the Maluti Mountains. Be careful in the rain – the roads are slick. An alternative sleeping accommodation option, based in Pitseng, is **Aloes Guest House** (☎ 2700 5626; s/d M250/730).

Minibus taxis go daily from Leribe to Katse (M66, three to five hours), with some continuing on to Thaba-Tseka (M101).

BUTHA-BUTHE

Moshoeshoe the Great named this frontier town Butha-Buthe (Place of Lying Down); it was here that his people first retreated during the *difaqane*. The Maluti Mountains form a beautiful backdrop.

Ask for directions to **Ha Thabo Ramakatane Youth Hostel** (dm M100). It's about 4km from the village and accessible only via 4WD or walking. We're talking basic – part of the house has no electricity, there's gas cooking, and water comes from the well – but it's as authentic as it comes.

Crocodile Inn (☎ 2246 0223; Reserve Rd; s/d/tr from M250/312/455, s/d rondavel M300/758) Price/quality ratios here are a bit of a croc – that said, the rooms and rondavels are simple but clean and there's a restaurant, the town's main dining establishment.

A minibus taxi from Maputsoe to Butha-Buthe costs M18 (20 minutes).

OXBOW

Over the dramatic 2820m Moteng Pass, Oxbow consists of several lodges and huts nestled amid some wonderful mountain scenery. (Beware the treacherous hairpin bends in winter.) Skiing is available through **Afri-Ski** (www.afriski.co.za), 11km past Oxbow.

New Oxbow Lodge (☎ in South Africa 051-933 2247; www.oxbow.co.za; s/d incl breakfast M462/759) is an incongruous Austrian-style chalet on the banks of the Malibamat'so River, with accommodation and a cosy restaurant-bar.

A bus between Maseru and Mokhotlong goes via Oxbow (M70, 4½ hours). Several minibus taxis run daily between Butha-Buthe and Oxbow (M35, 1½ hours).

EASTERN LESOTHO

The awesome eastern highlands area is defined by the rugged escarpment of the Drakensberg. It's best known for Sani Pass, but it also boasts the highest mountain in Southern Africa, the 3482m Thabana-Ntlenyana. This stunning mountain region features highland villages, rondavels, shepherds and sandstone rock shelters. It's *the* place for serious hikers.

THABA-TSEKA

This remote scrappy town is on the eastern edge of the Central Range, over the sometimes-tricky Mokhoabong Pass. It was established in 1980 as a centre for the mountain district.

You can bunk down at the **Farmer Training Centre** (☎ 2290 0294; r M50), on the street behind the tower, or at the **Buffalo Hotel** (☎ 2700 7339; s/d M350/500), 4km from the centre.

The Lilala Butchery & General Cafe serves sandwiches and drinks.

Three buses run daily between Maseru and Thaba-Tseka (M55, seven hours). Minibuses and buses also go to Sehonghong

LESOTHO'S WHITE GOLD

For Lesotho, water is a big money spinner. The Lesotho Highlands Water Project (LHWP) is an ambitious scheme developed jointly by Lesotho and South Africa to harness Lesotho's abundant water resources to provide water to a large tract of Southern Africa and hydropower to Lesotho. The project, being implemented in stages until 2020, will result in several major dams, two of which are completed – the Katse Dam (see p133) and Mohale Dam (Likalaneng; see the boxed text, p132), and about 200km of tunnels.

In many ways the project has been a positive for the country – roads and telecommunications have vastly improved – but it has not been without controversy. Detrimental effects include flooding of significant portions of Lesotho's already scarce arable land; relocation difficulties for affected villagers; and corruption prosecutions of international companies involved in the project.

For further information see www.lhwp.org.ls.

HIGHLAND PARKS & RESERVES

While the building of a series of dams on the Senqu (Orange) River has created controversy, not least over environmental concerns, it has also led to the creation of the following nature reserves. For bookings and inquiries contact **Lesotho Northern Parks** (☎ 2246 0723), which handles all accommodation bookings.

Bokong Nature Reserve

The bearded vulture, the ice rat and the Vaal rhebok are just some of the denizens of this **reserve** (adult/child M10/5; campsites M40, basic 4-person huts M250; 8am-5pm), at the top of the 3090m Mafika-Lisiu Pass, near the Bokong River. The park is also home to Afro-alpine wetland sponges and an impressive waterfall. There are a number of day walks, a visitors centre and an overnight camping ground. Guides (per person M20) and pony trekking (from M100) can be arranged.

Ts'ehlanyane National Park

Deep in the rugged Maluti Mountains this 5600-hectare **national park** (admission per person/vehicle M40/10; campsites from M50) protects a beautiful, high-altitude patch of rugged wilderness, including one of Lesotho's only stands of indigenous forest. This underrated and underused place is about as far away from it all as you can get and is perfect for hiking.

In addition to day walks, there's a challenging 39km hiking trail from Ts'ehlanyane southwest to Bokong Nature Reserve through some of Lesotho's most dramatic terrain. Guides can be arranged. Pony trekking (per half/full day M300/350) can be arranged through Lesotho Northern Parks with advance notice or through Maliba Mountain Lodge.

The country's newest lodge, **Maliba Mountain Lodge** (☎ 031-266 1344 in Durban; d full board per person R2740), is Lesotho's smartest accommodation, along the lines of luxury lodges in neighbouring South Africa.

Liphofung Cave Cultural Historical Site

San rock art and historical links that go back as far as the Stone Age are the attractions of this small 4-hectare **reserve** (adult/child M25/10; campsites M40, r per person M250, minimum 2), just off the main Butha-Buthe–Oxbow road. There are also horse trails (M50 per hour), a cultural centre (8am-5pm Mon-Fri) and a small craft shop.

(M28/M45, 2½/four hours); from here you'd need to try your luck for a lift. For Mokhotlong (M30, two hours) change at Linakaneng (M28, three hours). Several minibus taxis travel daily to Leribe (M60) via Katse (M25).

MOKHOTLONG

Mokhotlong (Place of the Bald Ibis) is situated 270km from Maseru and is the first major town north of Sani Pass. It has an appealing Wild West feel to it, with locals – sporting Basotho blankets – on their horses, and basic shops.

Molumong Guesthouse & Backpackers (☎ in South Africa 033-394 3072; molumong@worldonline.co.za; campsites per person M60, dm/d M100/220) is a rustic lodge and former colonial trading post, about 15km southwest of Mokhotlong. It's a basic (electricity-free) self-catering stay so bring your own food. Pony trekking is available.

St James Lodge (☎ in South Africa 033-326 1601; stjamesguestlodge@yahoo.com; dm/d per person M125/175) is housed in an old stone building on a working mission. Bring your own stuff as it's self-catering, and offers pony trekking and scenic walks. It's 12km south of Mokhotlong on the road to Thaba-Tseka.

The **Senqu Hotel** (☎ 2292 0330; s M260-320, d M320-380) is 2.5km from the buses on the western end of town. Nearby **Grow** (☎ 2292 0205; dm M70), a Lesotho-registered development office, has basic dorms and a simple kitchen.

Regular public transport runs to/from Butha-Buthe (M55, six hours), Maseru (M80, eight hours), Linakaneng (for Molumong Lodge) and Sani Top.

SANI TOP

Sani Top sits atop the steep Sani Pass, the only dependable (albeit winding) road into Lesotho through the uKhahlamba-Drakensberg mountain range in KwaZulu-Natal. It offers stupendous views on clear days and unlimited hiking possibilities.

From the Sani Top Chalet (see below) at the top of the pass there are several day walks, including a long and strenuous trek to **Thabana-Ntlenyana** (3482m), the highest peak in Southern Africa. A guide is a good idea.

Hodgson's Peaks (3257m) is a much easier hike 6km south, from where you can see into Sehlabathebe National Park and KwaZulu-Natal.

There is a rugged three-day hike from Sani Top Chalet south along the remote escarpment edge to Sehlabathebe National Park (see right). The altitude of much of this remote area is more than 3000m; try this only if you're well prepared, experienced and in a group of at least three people with a guide.

Other hikes in this area are outlined in the excellent *A Backpackers' Guide to Lesotho* by Russell Suchet, available through the **Morija Museum** (☎ 2236 0308; www.morijafest.com) or **Sani Lodge** (☎ in South Africa 033-702 0330; www.sanilodge.co.za) at Sani Pass.

Sleeping & Eating

Sani Top Chalet (☎ in South Africa 033-702 1158; www.sanitopchalet.co.za; campsites per person M80, dm M150, rondavels s/d M650/1000) On the edge of the escarpment at a lofty 2874m, this popular place resembles an old-fashioned ski chalet and boasts the highest pub in Africa, plus cosy rondavels and excellent meals. The backpackers' dorms recently moved to new premises several hundred metres from the pub. In winter, the snow is sometimes deep enough for skiing; pony trekking can be arranged with advance notice.

On the KwaZulu-Natal side of the pass, Sani Lodge is a convenient and pleasant sleeping option; see p507.

Getting There & Away

A minibus taxi runs daily from Mokhotlong via Sani Top down to Underberg (South Africa) and back (five hours).

If you're driving, you'll need a 4WD to go up the pass. The border crossings are open 6am to 6pm daily. Note: allow enough time at either end and check the border times – they do change.

Hostels on the KwaZulu-Natal side arrange transport up the pass, and various agencies in Underberg and Himeville (the nearest South African towns) arrange tours; see p508 and p508.

SEHLABATHEBE NATIONAL PARK

Lesotho's first national park, proclaimed in 1970, is remote, rugged and beautiful. Getting there is a worthwhile adventure, especially for wilderness, seclusion and fishing. The rolling grasslands, wildflowers and silence provide a sense of isolation, which is indeed the case, apart from the prolific bird life (including the bearded vulture) and the odd rhebok. Hiking (and horse riding from Sani Top or the Drakensberg) is the main way to explore the waterfalls and surrounds.

You'll need to bring all your food, and be well prepared for the elements. This summer rainfall area has frequent thick mists, potentially hazardous to hikers. Winters are clear but cold at night, with occasional light snowfalls.

Sleeping & Eating

Buses reach Sehlabathebe in the evening, which means you'll need to stay overnight in Mavuka village near the park gate.

Camping is permitted throughout the park, though there are no facilities besides plenty of water.

Sehlabathebe Park Lodge (☎ 2231 1767 or 2232 6075; campsites per person M30, r per person M80) This time-warped lodge, on a remote flat grassland and looking onto hills and ponds, was built in the 1970s for the then prime minister. Bring all your own food, plus extra fuel – there's none available at the park. Coal is available for purchase from the caretaker. The lodge sleeps 12 people, and has bedding and a fully equipped kitchen. Due to its isolation, it's not recommended for lone travellers. Bookings are made through the Ministry of Tourism, Environment & Culture (p128) in Maseru, which currently has jurisdiction over the whole of the park.

A basic sleeping option is Mabotle Hotel in Mavuka itself. Despite the dusty and shabby setting, the rondavels have clean linoleum floors and bathrooms. There is a reason: there is no water (but helpful staff will bring you a bucket).

Getting There & Away

A daily bus connects Qacha's Nek and Sehlabathebe, departing from Qacha's Nek at around noon and Sehlabathebe at 5.30am (M40, five hours). The bus terminates in Mavuka village, near the park gate. From here, it's about 12km further on foot to the lodge. If you're driving, the main route into the park is via Quthing and Qacha's Nek. The road from Qacha's Nek is unpaved but in reasonable condition, and negotiable at most times of the year in 2WD. You can arrange to leave your vehicle at the police station in Paolosi village while you're in the park.

Keen walkers can hike the 10km up the escarpment from Bushman's Nek in KwaZulu-Natal. From Bushman's Nek to the Nkonkoana Gate border crossing takes about six hours. Horses can also be arranged through **Khotso Trails** (☎ in South Africa 033-701 1502; www.khotsotrails.co.za) in Underberg.

QACHA'S NEK

This pleasant town was founded in 1888 as a mission station near the pass (1980m) of the same name. It has an attractive church, colonial-era sandstone buildings and California redwood trees.

The modest **Anna's B&B** (☎ 2295 0374; annasb&b@leo.col.ls; s M100-150, d M180-280) offers a variety of rooms.

Letloepe Lodge (☎ 2295 0383; www.letloepelodge.co.ls; dm/s incl breakfast M140/285/ d incl breakfast M420-520), a 'palace just below the clouds' has a restaurant, a serene outlook and lofty prices for what you get.

Minibus taxis go from Qacha's Nek and Maseru via Quthing (M100, six hours). A daily bus runs between Maseru and Qacha's Nek (M100, nine hours), and another between Qacha's Nek and Sehlabathebe National Park, departing around noon (M30, five hours).

SOUTHERN LESOTHO

Southern Lesotho – from Semonkong to Morija and southeast to Quthing – is less developed than the northwest between Maseru and Butha-Buthe, with massive mountain ranges, awesome valleys, and villages that have an enticing off-the-beaten-track feel.

SEMONKONG

Semonkong (Place of Smoke) is a one-horse town in the serene and lofty Thaba Putsoa range. **Maletsunyane Falls** (Lebahane Falls; 204m) are a 1½-hour walk away and are at their most awesome in summer – especially from the bottom of the gorge. **Ketane Falls** (122m) are an exciting day's ride (30km) from Semonkong.

our pick Semonkong Lodge (☎ 266-2700 6037, 62021021; www.placeofsmoke.co.ls; campsites per person M70, dm/s/d M110/330/560, rondavels s/d M385/600), near the Maletsunyane River, is tops in every sense and, although it's a three- to eight-hour trawl up the mountain (depending on what form of transport you take), it's worth the effort. Those in private rooms are served a cuppa in bed in the morning. There's a kitchen for those who want to self cater, but the bar-restaurant serves possibly the best (Westernised) food in Lesotho. You can also organise a smorgasbord of activities from the lodge, including day and overnight hikes (per person from M250), pony treks (per person from M250) and – as you'll hear – the world's longest commercially operated single-drop abseil (204m) down the Maletsunyane Falls. Trout fishing is also an option. Even quirkier is the pub crawl on the back of a donkey.

Buses between Maseru and Semonkong (M100) leave from either town in the morning, arriving in late afternoon.

MORIJA

Morija, 40km from Maseru, is a tiny town with a big history, and the site of the first European mission in Lesotho. It's a must for anyone interested in Lesotho's history and culture. **Morija Museum & Archives** (☎ 2236 0308; www.morijafest.com; admission M10; 🕒 8am-5pm Mon-Sat, noon-5pm Sun), the best museum in Lesotho, holds well-presented Basotho ethnographical exhibits, archives and artefacts.

The annual **Morija Arts & Cultural Festival** (www.morijafest.com) is organised by the museum. This popular, annual event is held in early October and showcases the diversity of Sotho culture through dance, music and theatre, and includes horse racing and *moraba-raba* (similar to chess) competitions. The festival began in 1999 as a means of reuniting the people of Lesotho after the turmoil created by the 1998 political upheaval, and to revive aspects of culture and boost tourism.

Mophato Oa Morija (☎ 2236 0219; mophato@leo.co.ls; dm M60) is an ecumenical conference centre that is sometimes willing to accommodate travellers.

Morija Guest House (☎ 6306 5093; www.morija guesthouses; r per person with shared bathroom M170-200) is a comfortable and attractive stone-and-thatch house with great views, a kitchen, and selection of sleeping options.

Minibus taxis run throughout the day between Maseru and Morija (M13, 45 minutes).

LESOTHO

MALEALEA

Shortly before Malealea is the Gates of Paradise Pass. A plaque announces 'Wayfarer – pause and look upon a Gateway of Paradise'. This says it all – about the region, village and the lodge. The breathtaking mountains feature caves with **San rock art**, and you can enjoy a well-organised pony trek from here or wander on foot through the region.

Today, the heart of the village is Malealea Lodge, which offers a smorgasbord of cultural and outdoor activities.

Activities

This is one of the best places in Lesotho to arrange **pony trekking** (per day M160-200, overnight rides M330, minimum 2 people, r in local hut per person extra M60). This offers a good chance to meet Basotho villagers and experience the awesome scenery of **Botso'ela Waterfall** (two hours return); **Pitseng Gorge** (six hours return, bring swimwear); **Pitseng Plateau** (one hour return); and along the Makhaleng River. The villagers provide the ponies and guide; this provides a significant contribution to the local village economy.

For walkers, Malealea Lodge has route maps for short **walks** (two hours) to overnight and longer **hikes** and can arrange pack ponies for your gear. The walks incorporate waterfalls, gorges, plateaus and surrounding villages and **San rock art sites**.

Village visits provide a stimulating insight into the local people and their customs. You can visit the tiny **museum**, housed in a traditional Basotho hut, a **sangoma** (witchdoctor) and a **reclaimed donga**.

Sleeping

our pick **Malealea Lodge** (☎ in South Africa 082-5524215; www.malealea.co.ls, www.malealea.com; campsites per person M50, backpacker huts with shared bathroom per person M120-140, r per person M200-250) The hub of local life, award-winning Malealea Lodge – a former trading post established by Mervyn Smith (1905) – provides an extraordinary entrée into the 'Kingdom in the Sky'. The lodge works closely with community – its foundation (from tourist revenue and donations) supports projects in the area. Almost every night the local choir performs at the lodge.

The wealth of accommodation options ranges from campsites and two-person 'forest', or backpacker, huts in a pretty wooded setting away from the lodge, to simple, cosy rooms and rondavels with bathrooms.

Hungry hikers love the bar, hearty meals (breakfast/lunch/dinner M60/70/100) and self-catering facilities. A village shop stocks basic goods. Bookings must be made through South Africa. September to November are the busy months.

Getting There & Away

Regular minibus taxis connect Maseru and Malealea (M30, 2½ hours, 83km). Otherwise, catch a minibus taxi from Maseru or Mafeteng to the junction town of Motsekuoa (M13, two hours), from where there are frequent connections to Malealea (M18, 30 minutes).

If you're driving, head south from Maseru on Mafeteng Rd (Main Rd South) for 52km to Motsekuoa. Here, look for the Malealea Lodge sign and the collection of minibus taxis. Turn left (east) onto a sealed road. Ten kilometres further on take the right fork and continue another 15km. At the Malealea sign it's another 7km along an unsealed road to the lodge.

It's also possible to approach Malealea from the south, via Mpharane and Masemouse, but the road is rough and most drivers travel via Motsekuoa.

MAFETENG

Mafeteng (Place of Lefeta's People) is named after an early magistrate Emile Rolland, who was known to the local Basotho as Lefeta (One who Passes By). Little has changed; you'd do best to move on. That said, the town is an important transport interchange, a border junction (it's 22km to Wepener in Free State) and a possible stocking-up point.

Straight out of the '60s TV sitcom *Lost in Space*, polygon-shaped **Mafeteng Hotel** (☎ 2270 0236; s/d/tr from M220/280/360; 🅿) is a blast from the past. There's a restaurant, plus rondavels in the garden.

Frequent minibus taxis connect Mafeteng with Maseru (M25, 1½ hours) and Mohale's

Hoek (M16, 30 minutes). For Quthing, change at Mohale's Hoek.

MOHALE'S HOEK

More agreeable than Mafeteng, this comfortable town is 125km from Maseru. The younger brother of Moshoeshoe the Great, Mohale, gave this land to the British for administrative purposes in 1884.

The best bet of a motley lot is **Hotel Mount Maluti** (☎ 2278 5224; mmh@leo.co.ls; s/d incl breakfast M257/380) with motel-style (and overpriced) rooms plus a restaurant.

QUTHING

Quthing, the southernmost major town in Lesotho, is also known as Moyeni (Place of the Wind). It was established in 1877, abandoned during the Gun War of 1880 and then rebuilt at the present site.

The town comprises Lower Quthing and Upper Quthing, the former colonial administrative centre, with good facilities and even better views overlooking the dramatic Senqu (Orange) River Gorge. There are minibus taxis between Lower and Upper Quthing.

About 1.5km off the highway, 5km west of Quthing, is the intriguing **Masitise Cave House Museum** (☎ 5879 4167; entry by donation), now a museum, built into a San rock shelter in 1866 by Reverend Ellenberger. Ask for the key from the local pastor in the house next to the church. Accommodation is available on a B&B basis and in the unrenovated rondavels. There are **San rock art** paintings nearby.

Quthing's other claim to fame is a proliferation of **dinosaur footprints**. The most easily accessible are just off the main road to Mt Moorosi; watch for the small, pink building to your left. These footprints are believed to be 180 million years old.

Between Quthing and Masitise, and visible from the main road, is **Villa Maria Mission**, with a striking, twin-spired sandstone church.

At Qomoqomong, 10km from Quthing, there's a collection of **San rock art** paintings; ask at the General Dealers store about a guide for the 20-minute walk to the paintings.

The road from Quthing to Qacha's Nek, along the winding Senqu (Orange) River Gorge, is one of Lesotho's most stunning drives. If you're equipped, the whole area is ideal for hiking.

En route is the village of **Mt Moorosi**, named after a Basotho chieftain who in 1879 stuck it out for eight months against the British on his fortified mountain until he was killed; the pretty **Mphaki** village, a possible base for hiking; and **Christ the King Mission**, with wide views over the Senqu River valley. It's a good two- to three-day hike from the mission, north to Semonkong (p137).

Sleeping & Eating

Fuleng Guest House (☎ 2275 0260; r per person M250-300) Perched in Upper Quthing, this is the place for excellent-value rooms and rondavels with a view, plus a friendly local experience.

Moorosi Chalets (☎ in South Africa 082-5524215; www.malealeatours.com/destinations/lesotho/mount-moorosi.html; campsites M70, huts with shared bathroom per person M120, self-catering house per person M120, rondavel per person M200) The chalets are part of a community program and are secondary to the amazing activities on offer – from village stays to fishing, best organised in advance. The chalets are 6km from Mt Moorosi village; take the turn-off to Ha Moqalo 2km out of the village in the direction of Qacha's Nek.

Getting There & Away

Minibus taxis run daily between Quthing and Maseru (M60, 3½ hours) and Qacha's Nek (M70, three hours). The Quthing–Qacha's Nek road is sealed the entire way despite what many maps indicate.

LESOTHO DIRECTORY

ACCOMMODATION

Maseru has a reasonable range of accommodation. Most towns have small hotels that have survived from protectorate days, although many are run-down bars and liquor stores that also provide accommodation. New lodges and B&Bs have sprung up over recent years.

Camping is most viable away from population centres. Always ask permission of the local landowners and chief, and expect to pay a small fee. Camping is also possible in national parks.

For a small fee, you can sometimes score a bed at the missions or Farmer Training Centres; the latter are at Thaba-Tseka and Qacha's Nek.

Prices for accommodation in this chapter are budget M300 and below, midrange M300 to M800, top end M800 and above.

PRACTICALITIES

- Several newspapers such as *Southern Star* are available in Maseru and other towns. Day-old South African newspapers are also available in Maseru.
- Thanks to a transmitter, you can pick up the BBC's World Service on short wave, medium wave (1197kHz) and FM.
- Lesotho's electricity is generated at 220V. Appliances have three round prongs as used in South Africa.
- Lesotho uses the metric system.

ACTIVITIES

Abseiling

Hit the heights at Semonkong Lodge for the longest commercially operated single-drop abseil (204m) down the Maletsunyane Falls (see p137).

Birdwatching

About 280 species of bird have been recorded in Lesotho – a surprising number for a landlocked country. The mountainous terrain provides habitats for many species of raptor (birds of prey). You might see the Cape vulture or the rare bearded vulture or lammergeyer.

Good birdwatching places include eyries in the Maluti Mountains and near the eastern Drakensberg escarpment.

Fishing

Trout fishing is very popular in Lesotho; the season runs from September to the end of May. There is a minimal licence fee, a bag limit of 12 fish and a minimum size limit of 25cm; only rod and line and artificial nonspinning flies may be used. For more information contact the **Livestock Division of the Ministry of Agriculture** (☎ 2232 3986; Private Bag A82, Maseru 100).

The closest fishing area to Maseru is the Makhalaneng River (a two-hour drive from Maseru). Other places where you can cast a line include Malibamat'so River near Butha-Buthe, 2km below Oxbow Lodge; Khubelu and Mokhotlong Rivers near Mokhotlong; Tsoelikana River, Park Ponds and Leqooa River near Qacha's Nek; Thaba-Tseka main dam, Semonkong, and Katse and Mohale Dams.

Indigenous fish include barbel in lowland rivers, yellowfish in the mountains and the Maloti minnow in the upper Tsoelikana.

Hiking

Lesotho offers great remote-area trekking in a landscape reminiscent of the Tibetan plateau. The eastern highlands and the Drakensberg crown attract serious hikers, with the walk between Qacha's Nek and Butha-Buthe offering the best challenge.

As well as the appropriate hiking gear, you will need a compass and the relevant 1:50,000 or 1:250,000 maps from the **Department of Land, Surveys & Physical Planning** (Map p129; ☎ 2232 2376; Lerotholi Rd, Maseru; 🕑 9am-3pm Mon-Fri).

Be prepared – walking can be dangerous – zero temperatures (even in summer), thunderstorms and thick fog are common. In summer many of the rivers flood, and fords can become dangerous: route changes might be necessary. By the end of the dry season clean water can be scarce.

Bring all your own supplies, especially specialist hiking supplies.

Hikers should respect the mounds of stones (cairns) marking graves. However, a cairn near a path, especially between two hills, can be added to by passing travellers; ensure your good luck by spitting on a stone and throwing it onto the pile.

Note that a white flag waving from a village means that *joala* (sorghum beer) has just been brewed; a yellow flag indicates maize beer; red is for fresh meat; and green is for vegetables.

Pony Trekking

This is an excellent and popular way of seeing the Lesotho highlands, and is offered by Malealea Lodge (p138), Trading Post Guest House (p132) and Semonkong Lodge (p137).

You will usually need to bring food, a sleeping bag, rainwear, sunscreen, warm clothing, a torch (flashlight) and water purification tablets.

BOOKS

A Backpacker's Guide to Lesotho by Russell Suchet features walks around Lesotho and is a must for hikers. Poignant personal accounts by Basotho include *Singing Away the Hunger* by Mpho Matsepo Nthunya et al, and *Shepherd Boy of the Maloti* by Thabo

Makoa. For history, read *A Short History of Lesotho* by Stephen Gill.

BUSINESS HOURS

Most businesses are open from 8am to 5pm weekdays (8.30am to 1pm Wednesdays) and 8am to 1pm Saturdays. The civil service works between 8am and 4.30pm weekdays with a break for lunch from 12.45pm to 2pm.

CUSTOMS REGULATIONS

Customs regulations are broadly the same as those for South Africa (see p569). Visitors from the South African customs union – Botswana, Swaziland and South Africa – cannot bring in alcohol.

DANGERS & ANNOYANCES

You may receive unmenacing requests for money, especially if hiking somewhere without a guide. In the highlands, you'll receive incessant requests for 'sweets! sweets!' from school children and herd boys. Tourists throwing out sweets has become an increasing problem; it causes begging so please refrain. Children throwing stones at cars sometimes occurs in the highlands.

Several lives (mainly those of herd boys) are lost each year from lightning strikes. Keep off high ground during electrical storms and avoid camping in the open.

Never go out into the mountains, even in summer or for an afternoon, without a sleeping bag, tent and sufficient food for a couple of days in case you get fogged in.

On the last Friday of the month, many people are paid and some get drunk; things can get boisterous.

There's a slight risk of being robbed in Lesotho; muggings are common in Maseru.

EMBASSIES & CONSULATES

A number of countries have representation in Maseru.

China (☎ 2231 6521; http://ls.china-embassy.org/eng; United Nations Rd, Maseru)
France (Map p129; ☎ 2232 5722; www.alliance.org.za; Alliance Française Bldg, cnr Kingsway & Pioneer Rd, Maseru)
Germany (Map p129; ☎ 2233 2292; c/o Alliance Française Bldg, cnr Kingsway & Pioneer Rd, Maseru)
Ireland (Map p129; ☎ 2231 4068; Tonakholo Rd, Maseru)
Netherlands (Map p129; ☎ 2231 2114; Lancer's Inn, Kingsway, Maseru)
South Africa (Map p129; ☎ 2231 5758; 10th fl, Lesotho Bank Tower, Kingsway, Maseru)
USA (Map p129; ☎ 2231 2666; http://maseru.usembassy.gov; 254 Kingsway, Maseru)

FESTIVALS & EVENTS

Morija Arts & Cultural Festival (www.morijafest.com) is held in Morija in early October (see p137).

HOLIDAYS

Lesotho's public holidays:

New Year's Day 1 January
Moshoeshoe Day 11 March
Good Friday March/April
Easter Monday March/April
Hero's Day 25 May
Workers' Day 1 May
Ascension Day May
King's Birthday 17 July
Independence Day 4 October
Christmas Day 25 December
Boxing Day 26 December

INTERNET RESOURCES

African Studies – Lesotho Page (www.sas.upenn.edu/African_Studies/Country_Specific/Lesotho.html) Reliable links to a number of other Lesotho websites.
Kingdom in the Sky (www.seelesotho.com) An excellent resource run by a private lodge, with all kinds of information for planning a trip to Lesotho.
Lesotho Government (www.lesotho.gov.ls) Useful, although sometimes outdated, information.

LANGUAGE

The official languages are South Sotho and English. For some useful words and phrases in South Sotho, see p783.

MAPS

The **Department of Land, Surveys & Physical Planning** (Map p129; ☎ 2232 2376; Lerotholi Rd, Maseru; 9am-3pm Mon-Fri) sells a good 1:50,000 map of Maseru (M35), a 1:250,000 map of Lesotho (M50), plus 1:50,000 hiking maps covering the country (M35). Look for the brown building marked 'LSPP'. Maseru's **tourist information office** (Map p129; ☎ 2231 2427; touristinfo@ltdc.org.ls; Kingsway; 8am-5pm Mon-Fri, 8.30am-1pm Sat) also sells a Lesotho map (M10).

MONEY

The unit of currency is the loti (plural maloti; M), which is divided into 100 liesente. The loti is fixed at a value equal to the South African rand, and rands are accepted everywhere (however, maloti are not accepted outside Lesotho).

ATMs & Cash

If changing foreign currency, do it in South Africa before you come – rates are better. There are a few ATMs in Maseru, but not all take international cards.

The only banks where you can reliably change foreign currency, including travellers cheques, are in Maseru (see p130).

Credit Cards

Most hotels, restaurants and travel agencies will accept credit cards. As a last resort, you can change money for low rates at larger hotels.

Tipping

Wages are low in Lesotho. In rural parts of Lesotho it's normal to round up the bill, and in tourist areas it's usual to tip around 10%.

POST

Post offices are open from 8am to 4.30pm weekdays and 8am to noon Saturday.

TELEPHONE

Lesotho's telephone system works reasonably well, but only where there is access – it is limited in the highlands. International phone calls are expensive; if possible, wait until you are in South Africa. Note: no telephone networks function in the highlands. Mobile-phone signals are extremely rare and can be picked up on a few mountain passes only. They should not be relied upon. The main mobile-phone service is **Vodacom Lesotho** (www.vodac om.co.ls).

TOURIST INFORMATION

The only **tourist information office** (Map p129; ☎ 2231 2427; touristinfo@ltdc.org.ls; Kingsway; 8am-5pm Mon-Fri, 8.30am-1pm Sat) is in Maseru and is managed by the Lesotho Tourism Development Corporation. It provides brochures, lists of tour guides, information on public transport and basic maps.

VISAS

Citizens of most Western European countries, the USA and most Commonwealth countries are granted an entry permit (free) at the border or airport. The standard stay permitted is between 14 and 28 days and is renewable by leaving and re-entering the country or by application to the **Director of Immigration & Passport Services** (☎ 2232 3771, 2232 1110; PO Box 363, Maseru 100).

For citizens of other countries, if you arrive at the Maseru Bridge border without a visa you might be given a temporary entry permit, which allows you to apply for a visa in Maseru at the Ministry of Immigration. Don't count on this, though, as it depends on the whim of the border officials.

Visa requirements change, so first check with your embassy or consulate. No vaccination certificates are required unless you have recently been in a yellow-fever area.

TRANSPORT IN LESOTHO

GETTING THERE & AWAY

This section covers travel between Lesotho and its neighbour, South Africa. (For information on reaching Lesotho from elsewhere on the African continent and from other continents, see p755.)

Entering Lesotho

Most travellers enter Lesotho overland from South Africa, although it's also possible to fly in from Johannesburg. A passport is required for entering Swaziland.

Entry permits are easy to get at any of Lesotho's borders and at the airport. See Visas (see left and p752). Vaccination certificate requirements are the same as for South Africa.

Air

Lesotho's Moshoeshoe I International Airport is 21km from Maseru.

South African Airways (SAA; ☎ 27-11-978 5313) flies daily between Moshoeshoe I International Airport and Johannesburg for around R1300, one way.

Border Crossings

All Lesotho's borders are with South Africa. Most people enter via Maseru Bridge (open 24 hours). Other main border crossings include Ficksburg Bridge (open 24 hours), Makhaleng Bridge (open 8am to 4pm), and Sani Pass (6am to 6pm, but check, as times alter), but these often have long queues.

DEPARTURE TAX

A M50 departure tax is payable on leaving the airport.

Most of the other entry points in the south and the east of the country involve very difficult, rough roads.

Bus

Intercape (www.intercape.co.za) offers bus services to a changing timetable between Bloemfontein and Maseru (from M240, 1¾ hours). After your passport is stamped you need to catch a car taxi (called a four-by-one) from the Lesotho border to the Maseru taxi rank.

Via minibus taxi, daily minibuses run between Bloemfontein and Maseru (R50, two hours). Another option is to head from Bloemfontein to Botshabelo (R35, one hour) from where you can catch a connection to Maseru (R20, 1½ hours), though direct services may be available. Other useful connections include a daily minibus taxi between Mokhotlong (Lesotho) and Underberg (South Africa) via Sani Pass; and several minibus taxis daily between Qacha's Nek (Lesotho) and Matatiele (South Africa).

There are at least three buses weekly between Johannesburg and Maseru (six to seven hours), as well as daily minibus taxis between both Johannesburg and Ladybrand (16km from the Maseru Bridge border crossing) and Maseru. All these services will bring you into Maseru coming from South Africa; if you are leaving Maseru, you'll need to go to the South Africa side of Maseru Bridge.

Car

You can't enter Lesotho via Sani Pass unless your vehicle is 4WD. The border crossings are open 6am to 6pm daily. Note: allow enough time at either end, plus always check the times – they do change. Check details with border staff.

GETTING AROUND

Bicycle

Extremely mountainous Lesotho is an excellent mountain-bike cycling destination – for the seriously fit only. Dangers include icy roads, thunderstorms and flooding. The classic mountain-bike route in Lesotho is over the Sani Pass. The odd lodge rents out bicycles (most on the South African side of the Sani Pass).

Bus & Minibus Taxi

A good network of slow, no-frills buses and faster minibus taxis access many towns. Minibuses leave when full; no reservations are necessary. You'll be quoted long-distance fares on the buses but it's best to just buy a ticket to the next major town, as most of the passengers will get off there and you might be stuck waiting for the bus to fill up again, while other buses leave before yours. Buying tickets in stages is only slightly more expensive than buying a direct ticket.

Car & Motorcycle

DRIVING LICENCE

An international or domestic driving licence is necessary.

FUEL & SPARE PARTS

Fuel – including unleaded fuel and diesel – is available in the major towns, but diesel and unleaded is not always available in the highlands; fill up whenever possible and carry a jerry can with extra fuel. Spare parts are limited; carry tools and spare tyres. Tyre repairers are as common as mountains in 'them-thar parts'.

HIRE

In Lesotho it is far more economical to use a car hired in South Africa; ensure that you have written agreement from the hirer. There is a road tax of around M5, payable on entering Lesotho.

Avis (☎ 2235 0328), **Budget** (☎ 2231 6344) and **Imperial** (☎ 5872 0215) have offices in Maseru (see p131).

INSURANCE

Insurance is strongly recommended (and in many cases incorporated in the rental price), including for third-party damage and damage to or loss of your vehicle. Check carefully what you are covered for – hail damage is a possibility in Lesotho.

ROAD CONDITIONS & HAZARDS

Driving in Lesotho is getting easier with new sealed roads in the country's north, but a 4WD is obligatory for the country's rough unsealed roads. Main routes are numbered with the letter 'A'; secondary roads take a 'B'. Motorcycles are fine on the sealed roads. Beware of treacherously slippery roads in winter.

Unsealed roads can be rough. Before attempting a difficult drive, try to get local info on current conditions: ask at a police station as no warning signs are displayed. Major hazards are steep hairpin bends, flooding rivers (after summer storms), ice and snow in winter, people and animals. Police roadblocks do random checks, usually for stolen cars.

ROAD RULES

In Lesotho, vehicles are driven on the left-hand side. The national speed limit is 80km/h and the speed limit in villages is 50km/h. Seat belts must be worn at all times. It's obligatory to carry your licence, a vehicle registration booklet and safety triangle.

Tours

Tour operators in Lesotho are hard to find. The tourist information office in Maseru publishes a list of local operators.

Malealea Lodge (p138) and Semonkong Lodge (p137) probably offer the best range of tours, ranging from cross-country horse treks to 4WD excursions and walks between the two lodges. However, they don't offer a comprehensive overland tour of the entire country.

WILDLIFE & HABITAT

David Lukas

Southern Africa encompasses some of the most diverse landscapes on the continent, with habitats ranging from verdant forests to stony deserts and soaring mountains, lush grasslands and classic African savannas. It is home to penguins and hippos, great white sharks and elephants, and many more animals that will surprise and amaze visitors. Approximately 15% of the region receives some sort of formal protection – though this figure includes hunting concessions, and nearly all areas face some form of pressure from human encroachment. Kruger National Park and Kgalagadi Transfrontier Park include some of the region's largest and most significant protected areas.

DAVE HAMMAN

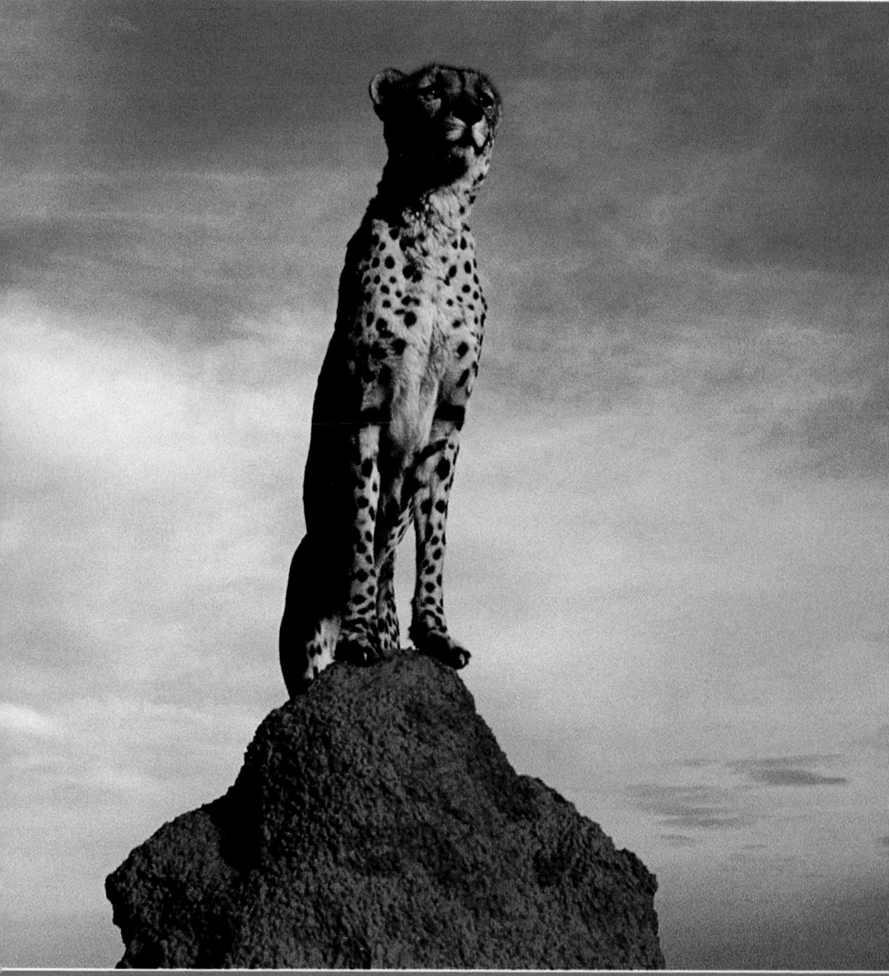

Cats

In terms of behaviour, the seven cats found in Southern Africa are little more than souped-up housecats; it's just that they might weigh half as much as a horse or move as fast as a speeding car. With their excellent vision and keen hearing, cats are superb hunters. And some of the most stunning scenes in Africa are the images of big cats making their kills. If you happen across one of these events, you won't easily forget the energy and ferocity of these life-and-death struggles.

1

❶ Cheetah

Weight 40–60kg; length 200–220cm

Less cat than greyhound, the cheetah is a world-class sprinter. Although it reaches 112km/h, the cheetah runs out of steam after 300m and must cool down for 30 minutes before hunting again. This speed comes at another cost – the cheetah is so well adapted for running that it lacks the strength and teeth to defend its food or cubs from attack by other large predators.

❷ Caracal

Weight 8–19kg; length 80–120cm

The caracal is a gorgeous tawny cat with extremely long, pointy ears. This African version of the northern lynx has jacked-up hind legs like a feline dragster. These beanpole kickers enable the slender animal to make vertical leaps of 3m and swat birds out of the air.

❸ Black-Footed Cat

Weight 1–2kg; length 40–60cm

More kitten than cat, this pint-sized predator is one of the smallest cats in the world. Though only 25cm high, this nocturnal animal is a fearsome hunter that can leap six times its height and must eat a prey item every hour.

❹ Lion

Weight 120–150kg (female), 150–225kg (male); length 210–275cm (female), 240–350cm (male)

Those lions sprawled out lazily in the shade are actually Africa's most feared predators. Equipped with teeth that tear effortlessly through bone and tendon, they can take down an animal as large as a bull giraffe. Each group of adults (a pride) is based around generations of females that do all the hunting; swaggering males fight among themselves and eat what the females catch.

❺ Leopard

Weight 30–60kg (female), 40–90kg (male); length 170–300cm

More common than you realise, the leopard relies on expert camouflage to stay hidden. During the day you might only spot one reclining in a tree after it twitches its tail, but at night there is no mistaking the bone-chilling groans of these animals, which sound like wood being sawn at high volume.

❻ Wildcat

Weight 3–6.5kg; length 65–100cm

If you see what looks like a tabby wandering along fields and forest edges, you might be seeing a wildcat, the direct ancestor of our domesticated housecats. Occurring wherever there are abundant mice and rats, the wildcat is readily found on the outskirts of villages, where it can be best identified by its unmarked rufous ears and longish legs.

Primates

While East Africa is the evolutionary cradle of primate diversity, giving rise to over 30 species of monkeys, apes, and prosimians (the 'primitive' ancestors of modern primates), Southern Africa is a relative newcomer on the scene and only home to a half-dozen or so species. However, these versatile, intelligent animals have many fascinating behaviours and complex social systems that can provide hours of entertainment.

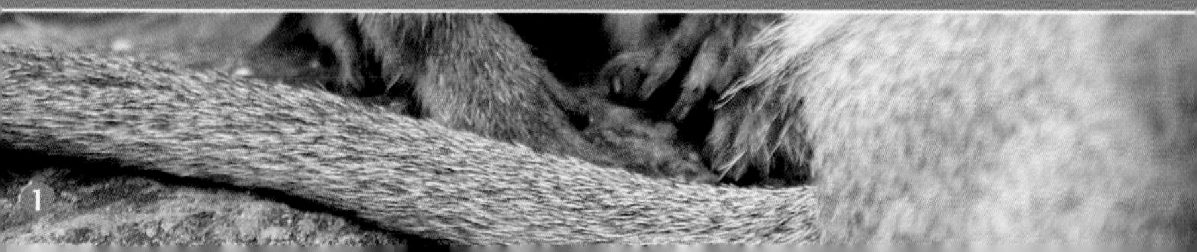

❶ Vervet Monkey

Weight 4–8kg; length 90–140cm

These locally common monkeys spend a lot of time on the ground, but always in close proximity to trees, where they can escape from their many predators. For this reason they are largely restricted to well-wooded areas. Each troop of vervets is composed of females that defend a home range passed down from generation to generation, while males fight each other for bragging rights and access to females. If you think their appearance too drab, check out the extraordinary blue and scarlet colours of their sexual organs when they get excited.

❷ Chacma Baboon

Weight 12–30kg (female), 25–45kg (male); length 100–200cm

Common enough to be overlooked once you've seen a few, chacma baboons are worth watching because they have exceedingly complex social dynamics. See if you can spot signs of friendship, deception or deal-making within a troop. Their very long muzzles and bare faces are an adaptation for making emphatic facial signals at each other, and you're likely to see a lot of exaggerated expressions if you spend any time watching these baboons.

❸ Greater Galago

Weight 550–2000g; length 55–100cm

A cat-sized nocturnal creature with doglike face, the greater galago belongs to a group of prosimians that have changed little in 60 million years. Best known for its frequent bawling cries (hence the common name 'bushbaby'), the galago would be rarely seen except that it readily visits feeding stations at some safari lodges. Living in a world of darkness, galagos communicate with each other through scent and sound.

❹ Samango Monkey

Weight 3.5–5.5kg (female), 5.5–12kg (male); length 100–160cm

Samango monkeys are part of a large group of highly variable African primates collectively called gentle or blue monkeys. Unlike savanna-dwelling vervet monkeys, these monkeys are found exclusively in forests, where they live in peaceful female-based social groups.

1

Cud-Chewing Mammals

Africa is arguably most famous for its astounding variety of ungulates – hoofed mammals, including buffaloes, giraffes and rhinos. Many of these animals live in groups to protect themselves from the continent's formidable predators, with herds once numbering in the hundreds of thousands. The ruminant (cud-chewing) subgroup of ungulates that have horns are called bovines. Among this family, the antelopes are particularly numerous, with more than 20 species in Southern Africa.

2

3

4

❶ Wildebeest

Weight 140–290kg; length 230–340cm

Unlike the famous herds that traverse the Serengeti, most wildebeest of Southern Africa are rather sedentary creatures, moving only as the seasons fluctuate. Because they favour expansive views, wildebeests are in turn easily viewed themselves.

❷ Impala

Weight 40–80kg; length 150–200cm

Gregarious and having a prodigious capacity to reproduce, impalas can reach great numbers very quickly, effectively outstripping predators' ability to eat them all. Females gather in huge clans while roaring males compete furiously for rights to mate. If they get scattered they use high kicks to disperse odours that help them find each other. Visit Namibia's Etosha National Park to see the unique black-faced impala.

❸ Sitatunga

Weight 40–80kg (female), 80–120kg (male); length 150cm

One of Southern Africa's most fascinating antelopes is the aquatic sitatunga that lives solely among the dense reeds of permanently inundated swamps and marshes. These capable swimmers will readily submerge themselves in the face of danger, making these tiny, shy creatures hard to find and highly sought after by visitors. Listen for their loud barking at night.

❹ Gemsbok

Weight 180–240kg; length 230cm

With towering 1m-long horns and boldly patterned face, this elegant desert antelope can survive for months on the scant water it derives from the plants it eats. Other adaptations include surviving temperatures that would kill other animals and having a lowered metabolism so it doesn't have to eat much food.

❺ Klipspringer

Weight 8–18kg; length 80–125cm

Bug-eyed and perpetually walking on its tippy-toes, the tiny klipspringer finds safety on steep rocky outcrops throughout the region. Here, pairs establish permanent territories and communicate with each other by whistling and leaving scents produced by a dark gland in front of their eye.

❻ Hartebeest

Weight 120–220kg; length 190–285cm

Yes the long face of the hartebeest is an odd sight, but it allows this short-necked antelope to reach down and graze while still looking up for predators. Commonly seen on open plains, the red-tinged hartebeest is easily recognised by its set of strangely twisted horns.

❼ African Buffalo

Weight 250–850kg; length 220-420cm

Imagine a cow on steroids, then add a particularly fearsome set of curling horns, and you get the massive African buffalo. Thank goodness they're usually docile, because an angry or injured buffalo is an extremely dangerous animal.

1

Hoofed Mammals

A full stable of Africa's mega-charismatic animals can be found in this group of ungulates. Other than the giraffe, these are not ruminants and can be seen over a much broader range of habitats than bovines. They have been at home in Africa for millions of years and are among the most successful mammals to have ever wandered the continent. Without human intervention, Africa would be ruled by elephants, zebras, hippos and warthogs.

2

❶ Warthog

Weight 45–75kg (female), 60–150kg (male); length 140–200cm

Despite their fearsome appearance and sinister tusks, only big male warthogs are safe from lions, cheetahs and hyenas. To protect themselves when attacked, warthogs run for burrows and back in while slashing wildly with their tusks.

❷ Giraffe

Weight 450–1200kg (female), 1800–2000kg (male); height 3.5–5.2m

The giraffe does a great job with upward activity – reaching up to grab high branches, towering above the competition – but stretching down to get a simple drink of water is difficult. Though they stroll along casually, they can outrun any predator.

❸ Mountain Zebra

Weight 230–380kg; length 260–300cm

The unique mountain zebras of central Namibia and South Africa differ from their savanna relatives in having unstriped bellies and rusty muzzles. Although each zebra is as distinctly marked as a fingerprint, scientists still aren't sure what function these patterns serve. Do they help zebras recognise each other?

❹ Rock Dassie

Weight 1.8–5.5kg; length 40–60cm

It doesn't seem like it, but those funny tailless squirrels you see lounging on rocky outcrops in central Namibia are an ancient cousin to the elephant. You won't see some of the features that dassies (known elsewhere in Africa as hyraxes) share with their larger kin, but look for tiny tusks when one yawns.

❺ African Elephant

Weight 2200–3500kg (female), 4000–6300kg (male); height 2.4–3.4m (female), 3–4m (male)

Widespread throughout Southern Africa, up to 55,000 elephants congregate in the lush wetlands of Chobe National Park (p92). There are also the unique desert-loving elephants of Namibia. Referred to as 'king of beasts', elephants are ruled by a lineage of elder females

❻ Black Rhinoceros

Weight 700–1400kg; length 350–450cm

Pity the rhinoceros for having a horn worth more than gold. Once abundant south of the Sahara, the rhino has been poached to the brink of extinction and females might give birth only every five years. The best viewing site in Africa is probably Etosha National Park's Okakuejo water hole (see p321).

❼ Hippopotamus

Weight 510–3200kg; length 320–400cm

The hippopotamus is one strange creature. Designed like a floating beanbag with tiny legs, the hippo spends its time in or very near water, chowing down on aquatic plants. Placid? No way! Hippos have tremendous ferocity and strength when provoked.

Other Carnivores

It is a sign of Africa's ecological richness that the continent supports a remarkable variety of predators. In addition to seven types of cats, Southern Africa is home to several dozen other carnivores ranging from slinky mongooses to highly social hunting dogs. All are linked in having 'carnassial' (shearing) teeth, but visitors may be more interested in witnessing the superb hunting prowess of these highly efficient hunters. When it comes to predators, expect the unexpected and you'll return home with a lifetime of memories!

1 Spotted Hyena

Weight 40–90kg; length 125–215cm

The spotted hyena is one of Southern Africa's most unusual animals. Living in packs ruled by females that grow penislike sexual organs, these savage fighters use their bone-crushing jaws to disembowel terrified prey on the run or to do battle with lions. The sight of maniacally giggling hyenas at a kill, piling on top of each other in their eagerness to devour hide, bone and internal organs, is unsettling.

2 Bat-Eared Fox

Weight 3–5kg; length 70–100cm

This delightful tawny animal has huge ears that it swivels in all directions to pick up the sounds of subterranean food items, such as termites, which it unearths with bursts of frantic digging. Monogamous pairs of these highly social foxes will often mingle with other pairs and families when hunting for food.

3 Meerkat

Weight 0.5–1kg; length 50cm

The region's several species of mongoose is best represented by the delightfully named meerkat. When not wrestling and playing, energetic and highly social meerkats spend much of their time standing up with looks of perpetual surprise. If threatened, they all spit and jump up and down together.

4 Hunting Dog

Weight 20–35kg; length 100–150cm

Fabulously and uniquely patterned so that individuals recognise each other, hunting dogs run in packs of 20 to 60 that ruthlessly chase down antelopes and other animals. Organised in complex hierarchies maintained by rules of conduct, these highly social canids are incredibly efficient hunters. At the same time, disease and persecution has pushed them into near extinction and they now rank as one of Africa's foremost must-see animals.

5 Cape Fur Seal

Weight 350kg (males), 80kg (females); length 120–200cm

Over two million fur seals can be found along the coastlines of Southern Africa, with most of them occurring at one of several dozen giant breeding colonies. Not a particularly social creature, but forced to gather in dense numbers as protection against marauding brown hyenas or great white sharks, these colonies are turbulent, noisy and exciting to watch.

1

Birds of Prey

Southern Africa is home to about 70 species of hawks, eagles, vultures and owls, meaning that you are likely to see an incredible variety of birds of prey here. Look for them perching on trees, soaring high overhead, or gathered around a carcass; though the scolding cries of small birds harassing one of these feared hunters may be your first clue to their presence.

2

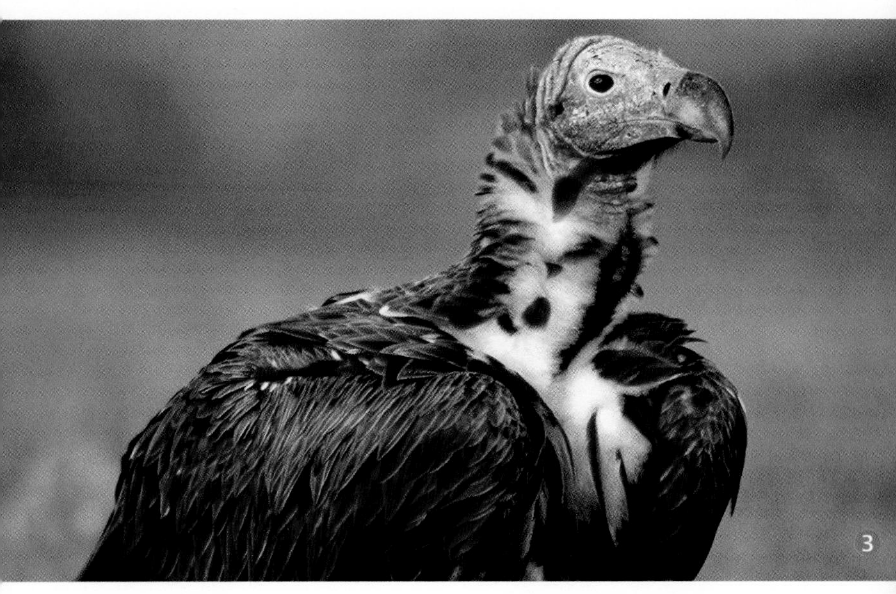

❶ African Fish Eagle

Length 75cm

Given its name, it's not surprising that you'll see the African fish eagle hunting for fish. With a wingspan of more than 2m this cousin of the American bald eagle presents an imposing appearance, but it is most familiar for its loud ringing cries that have become known as 'the voice of Africa'.

❷ Bateleur

Length 60cm

The bateleur is an attractive serpent-eagle with a funny name. French for 'tightrope-walker', the name refers to its distinctive low-flying aerial acrobatics. Look for this eagle's white wings and odd tailless appearance; If close up observe the bold colour pattern and scarlet face.

❸ Lappet-Faced Vulture

Length 115cm

Seven of Southern Africa's eight vultures can be seen mingling with lions, hyenas and jackals around carcasses. Here, through sheer numbers, they compete, often successfully, for scraps of flesh and bone. It's not a pretty sight when gore-encrusted vultures take over a carcass that no other scavenger wants, but it is the way nature works. The monstrous lappet-faced vulture, a giant among vultures, gets its fill before other vultures move in.

❹ Bearded Vulture

Length 110cm

Around the soaring cliffs of the Drakensberg you may be lucky to spot one of the world's most eagerly sought-after birds of prey – the massive bearded vulture, also known as the lammergeyer – best known for its remarkable habit of dropping bones onto rocks from great heights to get at their succulent marrow.

❺ Pale Chanting Goshawk

Length 55cm

Clusters of these slim grey raptors with stunning red beaks and legs are often seen perched low on bushes or fallen trees. Look closely because they are probably following another small hunter like a honey badger, to snap up anything escaping the badger's notice.

❻ Secretary Bird

Length 100cm

In a region flush with unique birds, the secretary bird literally stands head and shoulders above the masses. With the body of an eagle and the legs of a crane, the secretary bird walks up to 20km a day in search of vipers, cobras and other snakes that it kills with lightning speed and agility. This idiosyncratic, grey-bodied raptor is commonly seen striding across the savanna.

Other Birds

Come to Southern Africa prepared to see an astounding number of birds in every shape and colour imaginable. If you're not already paying attention to all the birds you see, you may come to find them an energising and pleasant diversion after a couple of days of staring at sleeping lions.

1

❶ Lesser Flamingo
Length 100cm
Coloured deep rose-pink and gathering by the hundreds of thousands on shimmering salt lakes, lesser flamingos create some of the most dramatic wildlife spectacles found in Africa, especially when they all fly at once or perform synchronised courtship displays.

❷ Cape Gannet
Length 85cm
It's hard to beat the spectacular mayhem at a gannet breeding colony. When not gathering in vast numbers to nest on offshore islands, these crisply marked seabirds congregate by the thousands to catch fish with high-speed dives into the waves.

❸ Ostrich
Length 200–270cm
If you think the ostrich looks prehistoric, you aren't far off. These ancient flightless birds escape predators by running away at 70km/h or lying flat on the ground to resemble a pile of dirt. Most that you see in Southern Africa are from feral stock, but genuinely wild ostriches are still found in the Kalahari.

❹ Jackass Penguin
Length 60cm
Yes, they are silly looking, but jackass penguins are actually named for their donkey-like calls, part of the ecstatic courtship displays given by the males. Found along the coast and on offshore islands, some penguin colonies are ridiculously tame.

❺ Hamerkop
Length 60cm
The hamerkop is a stork relative with an oddly crested, cartoonish, woodpeckerlike head. Nicknamed the 'hammerhead', it is frequently observed hunting frogs and fish at the water's edge. Look for its massive 2m-wide nests in nearby trees.

❻ Ground Hornbill
Length 90cm
Looking somewhat like a turkey, the ground hornbill spends its time on the ground stalking in search of insects, frogs, reptiles and small mammals that it kills with fierce stabs with its large powerful bill. Check out the bare, bright-red skin on its head.

❼ Lilac-Breasted Roller
Length 40cm
Nearly everyone on safari gets to know the gorgeously coloured lilac-breasted roller. Related to kingfishers, rollers get their name from the tendency to 'roll' from side to side in flight as a way of showing off their iridescent blues, purples and greens.

❽ Namaqua Sandgrouse
Length 25cm
Resembling stocky painted pigeons, these hardy desert birds fly up to 20km a day to reach water holes, where they line up in great numbers to drink at the water's edge. Males soak their breast feathers and fly back to the nest so their chicks can drink too.

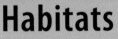

LUKE HUNT

Habitats

Your wildlife-viewing experience will be greatly enhanced if you are able to recognise some of Southern Africa's primary habitats and learn which animals you can expect in each one.

① Semi-Arid & Arid Desert

Large swathes of Southern Africa are covered by some type of sandy or rocky desert ecosystem. Deserts are distinguished by their levels of rainfall, with arid deserts rarely seeing more than 50mm of rain a year and semi-arid deserts averaging 125 to 250mm of rain. Lack of water limits larger animals, such as zebras, lions and elephants, to water holes, but when it rains this habitat explodes with plant and animal life. During the dry season many plants shed their leaves to conserve water and grazing animals move on in search of food and water.

② Savanna & Grassland

Savanna is *the* classic African landscape – broad rolling grasslands dotted with acacia trees and filled with abundant animals. This habitat is home to herds of zebras, giraffes and antelopes, in addition to fast-sprinting predators such as cheetahs.

③ Wetlands

Because so much of Southern Africa is dry desert or woodland, animals of all types congregate in huge numbers wherever water can be found in abundance. This is especially true when the mighty Okavango River floods some 16,000 sq km of the Kalahari Desert each year, creating one of the grandest explosions of life on the planet, with everything from elephants to hippos to red lechwes (a unique aquatic antelope) occurring by the thousands. But on a smaller scale this same profusion of life can be found along many other rivers and wetlands throughout Southern Africa.

④ High Mountains

Don't expect snowy crags and glaciers; the mountains of Southern Africa are islands of critical habitat amid vast plains of desert and savanna. Many unique animals, such as klipspringers and mountain zebras, either live year-round on the high rocky crags of these mountains, or else retreat there seasonally to escape the searing heat of the lowlands.

Malawi

With Tanzania's and Zambia's big-name national parks and Mozambique's glorious beaches on the doorstep, Malawi has often been left on the sidelines while her neighbours bask in the limelight. And when she *has* made a splash on the international scene it's usually for the HIV/Aids rate or poverty statistics, not for the beauty and diversity of her environment or the locals' friendliness – a shame, because this small strip of land has serious crowd-pleasing potential.

Slicing through the landscape in a trough formed by the Great Rift Valley is the third-largest lake in Africa – Lake Malawi. A shimmering mass of crystal water, its depths swarm with clouds of vivid cichlid fish, and its shores are lined with secret coves, pristine beaches, lively fishing villages and dark, forested hills. Diving, snorkelling and kayaking can all be had here, and when you're done there's everything from backpacker-friendly beach huts to glamorous five-star resorts in which to lay your head.

It's not all about the lake, though. Suspended in the clouds in Malawi's deep south are the dramatic peaks of Mt Mulanje, criss-crossed with streams, waterfalls and walking trails. Head north and you'll find the wild wilderness of the Nyika Plateau, where you can hike through rolling grasslands to reach a colonial hilltop town. And while a safari in one of Malawi's many national parks and reserves can't match her neighbours for sheer 'Big Five' excitement, you can get up close to some pretty impressive beasts without having to fight with other cars.

Malawi is often described as 'Africa for beginners' and true to form its compact size, decent transport links and relative safety make it easy to get around. What's more, the legendarily helpful locals and stunning backdrops will make sure that you'll have a fantastic time doing so.

FAST FACTS

- **Area** 118,484 sq km
- **Capital** Lilongwe
- **Country code** ☎ 265
- **Famous for** Lake Malawi, friendly locals, Madonna's adoptive babies
- **Languages** English, Chichewa
- **Money** Malawi kwacha (MK)
- **Phrase** *Muli bwanji?* (How are you?)
- **Population** 13.1 million
- **Number of endangered species** 154

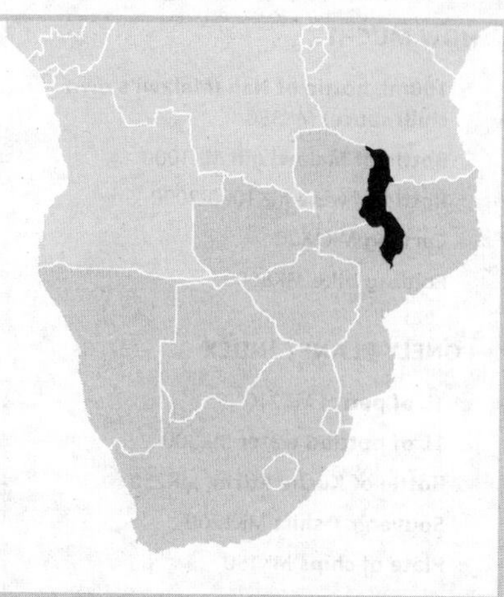

HIGHLIGHTS

- **Lake Malawi** (p189) Soak up the sun in private coves, glide over glassy waters by kayak, or head beneath the surface and discover a world of impossibly brilliant fish.
- **Viphya Plateau** (p184) Wander past vast granite boulders and hike through sweeping valleys in this gorgeous highland area.
- **Mt Mulanje** (p205) Scramble up twisted peaks, sleep in mountain huts and soak up the astounding views.
- **Liwonde National Park** (p192) Spot hippos, crocs and kingfishers on the Shire River, or get up close to elephants on foot.
- **Likoma Island** (p183) Escape to dreamy beaches and explore traditional villages, panoramic walks and the magnificent cathedral.

ITINERARIES

- **Three days** Spend a day getting acclimatised in Lilongwe (p167) before going down to Liwonde National Park (p192) for two days of elephant and hippo spotting.
- **One week** Head down from Blantyre (p197) to the woodland and streams of the Zomba Plateau (p196), then make for Mulanje (p204) for three or four days' hiking across the mountain's twisted peaks.
- **Two weeks** Head north from Lilongwe (p167) to hike, bike or simply soak up the cool, highland atmosphere of the Viphya Plateau (p184). Further north and you can choose between the wild spaces of Vwaza Marsh (p179) or Nyika Plateau (p177) and the colonial hilltop town of Livingstonia (p176). Then head for Nkhata Bay (p181) for some beachside frolics, before catching the *Ilala* ferry (p214) over to Likoma (p183) or Chizumulu Island (p184). Charter a flight or wait for the *Ilala* to take you back to the mainland.
- **One month** With more time on your hands you can take in all of the highlights above and add a few more: perhaps the southern beach resorts of Cape Maclear (p189) or Senga Bay (p187); or head to the little-visited but beautiful wilderness spots of the Majete Wildlife Reserve (p207) and Mwabvi Wildlife Reserve (p208).

HOW MUCH?

- **100mL bottle of Nali (Malawi's own chilli sauce)** MK350
- **Bottle of Malawi gin** MK1000
- **Bottle of wine** MK1000-2000
- **Carving** MK1500
- **Folding bike** MK8000

LONELY PLANET INDEX

- **1L of petrol** MK210
- **1L of bottled water** MK300
- **Bottle of Kuche Kuche** MK250
- **Souvenir T-shirt** MK1200
- **Plate of chips** MK150

CLIMATE & WHEN TO GO

Malawi has a single wet season, from November to April, when daytime temperatures are warm and conditions humid. The best time to visit Malawi is during the dry season from April or May to October. The months of October and November, at the end of the dry season, are the best time for wildlife viewing; however, the temperatures can be uncomfortably hot. Average daytime maximums in the lower areas are about 21°C in July and 26°C in January. In highland areas, average daytime temperatures in July are between 10°C and 15°C, while in September they reach 20°C and above. See p745 for climate charts.

HISTORY

The precolonial history of Malawi is linked to the history of Southern Africa as a whole. For more detail, see p32.

Early Migrations

Since the first millennium the Bantu people migrated from Central Africa into the area now occupied by Malawi. Migration to the area stepped up with the arrival of the Tumbuka and Phoka groups, who settled around the highlands of Nyika and Viphya during the 17th century, and the Maravi people (from whom the modern-day Chewa are descended), who established a large and powerful kingdom in the south.

The early 19th century brought with it two more significant migrations. The Yao invaded southern Malawi from western Mozambique, displacing the Maravi, while groups of Zulu migrated northward to settle in central and northern Malawi (where they became known as the Ngoni).

The Rise of Slavery

Slavery, and a slave trade, had existed in Africa for many centuries, but in the early 19th century demand from outside Africa increased considerably. Swahili-Arabs, who dominated the trade on the east coast of Africa, pushed into the interior, often using the services of powerful local tribes such as the Yao to raid and capture their unfortunate neighbours. Several trading centres were established in Malawi, including Karonga and Nkhotakota – towns that still bear a strong Swahili-Arab influence today.

Livingstone & the First Missionaries

The first Europeans to arrive in Malawi were Portuguese explorers who reached the interior from Mozambique in the early 1600s. The most famous explorer to reach this area, though, was David Livingstone from Scotland, whose exploration heralded the arrival of Europeans in a way that was to change the nature of the region forever.

Livingstone's first foray into Malawi was unplanned. In 1858 he found his route up the Zambezi was blocked at Cahora Bassa, so he followed a major Zambezi tributary called the Shire into southern Malawi. He reached Lake Malawi in September 1859 and provided fodder for thousands of tourist brochures to come by reportedly dubbing it the 'lake of stars'.

Livingstone died near the village of Chief Chitambo, southeast of Lake Bangweulu in Zambia, in 1873. His death inspired a legion of wannabes to come to Africa. In 1875 a group from the Free Church of Scotland built a new mission at Cape Maclear, which they named Livingstonia, and in 1876 the Established Church of Scotland built a mission in the Shire Highlands, which they called Blantyre. Cape Maclear proved to be malarial, so the mission moved to Bandawe, then finally in 1894 to the high ground of the eastern escarpment. This site was successful; the Livingstonia mission flourished and is still there today (see p176).

The Colonial Period

By the 1880s the competition among European powers in the area was fierce. In 1889 Britain allowed Cecil Rhodes' British South Africa

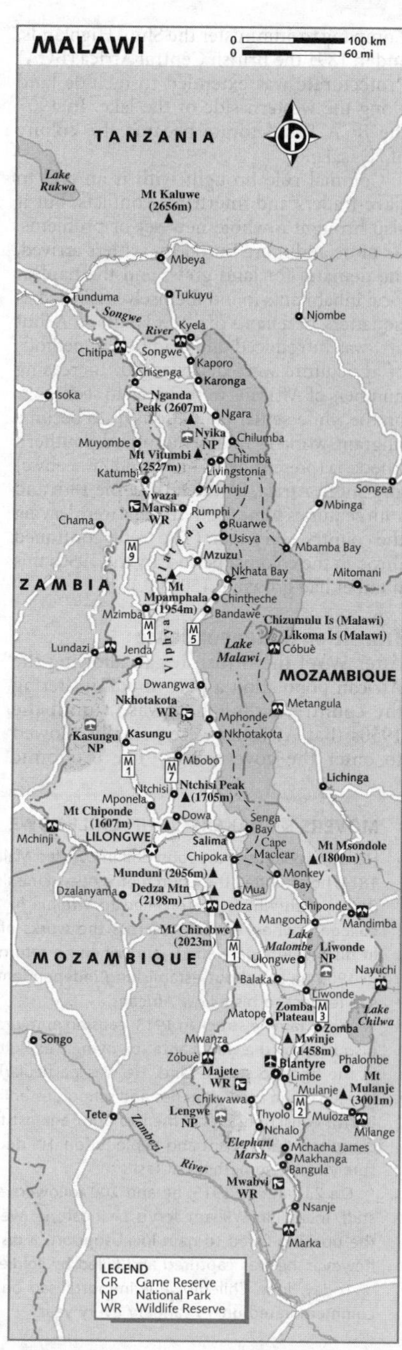

Company to administer the Shire Highlands, and in 1891 the British Central Africa (BCA) Protectorate was extended to include land along the western side of the lake. In 1907 the BCA Protectorate became the colony of Nyasaland.

Colonial rule brought with it an end to slave-traders and intertribal conflicts, but it also brought a whole new set of problems. As more and more European settlers arrived, the demand for land grew, and the hapless local inhabitants found themselves labelled as 'squatters' or tenants of a new landlord. A 'hut tax' was introduced and traditional methods of agriculture were discouraged. Increasing numbers of Africans were forced to seek work on the white-settler plantations or to become migrant workers in Northern and Southern Rhodesia (present-day Zambia and Zimbabwe) and South Africa. By the turn of the 18th and 19th centuries some 6000 Africans were leaving the country every year. (The trend continued through the colonial period: by the 1950s this number had grown to 150,000.)

Transition & Independence

After WWI the British began allowing the African population a part in administering the country, although it wasn't until the 1950s that Africans were actually allowed to enter the government. The economic front was similarly sluggish; Nyasaland proved to be a relatively unproductive colony with no mineral wealth and only limited plantations.

In 1953, in an attempt to boost development, Nyasaland was linked with Northern and Southern Rhodesia in the Federation of Rhodesia and Nyasaland. But the federation was opposed by the pro-independence Nyasaland African Congress (NAC) party, led by Dr Hastings Kamuzu Banda. The colonial authorities declared a state of emergency and Banda was jailed.

By mid-1960 Britain was losing interest in its African colonies. Banda was released, and returned to head the now renamed Malawi Congress Party (MCP), which won elections held in 1962. The federation was dissolved, and Nyasaland became the independent country of Malawi in 1964. Two years later, Malawi became a republic and Banda was made president.

The Banda Years

President Banda soon began consolidating his position by forcing members of the opposition into exile, banning political parties, declaring himself 'president for life', and banning the foreign press. Miniskirts, women in trousers, long hair for men and other such signs of Western debauchery were outlawed.

MOVERS & SHAKERS: JOHN CHILEMBWE

Hero and revolutionary John Chilembwe led Malawi's first serious fight against colonial rule. Born in 1871, he attended the Church of Scotland mission and later worked for Baptist missionary Joseph Booth, with whom he travelled to Virginia in 1897. A spell at an African American theological college – where he came across the works of Booker T Washington and other abolitionists – lit his revolutionary spark, and when he returned to Nyasaland as an ordained Baptist minister in 1900 he set about establishing independent African schools and preaching self-reliance and self-respect to his fellow Africans.

When famine struck in 1913, causing immigrants to pour in from Mozambique, Chilembwe was disgusted by the way plantation owners exploited not only his parishioners but also the refugees in the fight to secure land. He was particularly galled by one William Jervis Livingstone, who burned down rural churches and schools established by Chilembwe. When, shortly afterwards, the British conscripted local men to fight against the Germans in Tanzania during WWI, Chilembwe complained of racism and exploitation. He decided to 'strike a blow and die, for our blood will surely mean something at last'.

On 23 January 1915, he and 200 followers attacked local plantations. Three white plantation staff, including William Jervis Livingstone, were killed, as were several African workers. When the uprising failed to gain local support, a distraught Chilembwe tried to flee to Mozambique; however, he was captured and killed by soldiers 10 days later.

Today, John Chilembwe is immortalised on Malawi's banknotes and John Chilembwe Day is commemorated on 15 January every year.

Alongside this move towards dictatorship, Banda remained politically conservative, giving political support to apartheid South Africa, which, in turn, rewarded Malawi with aid and trade.

With the end of the East–West 'cold war' in the 1990s, things began to get dicey for Banda. South Africa and the West no longer needed to support him, and inside the country opposition was swelling. In 1992 the Catholic bishops of Malawi condemned the regime and called for change, and demonstrations, both peaceful and violent, added their weight to the bishops' move. As a final blow, donor countries restricted aid until Banda agreed to relinquish total control.

In June 1993 a referendum was held for the people to choose between a multiparty political system and Banda's autocratic rule. Over 80% of eligible voters took part; those voting for a new system won easily, and Banda accepted the result.

Multiparty Democracy

At Malawi's first full multiparty election in May 1994, the victor was the United Democratic Front (UDF), led by Bakili Muluzi. On becoming president, Muluzi moved quickly – political prisons were closed, freedom of speech and print was permitted, and free primary school education was to be provided. The Muluzi Government also made several economic reforms with the help of the World Bank and the IMF; these included the withdrawal of state subsidies and the liberalisation of foreign exchange laws.

In November 1997 Dr Banda finally died. His age was unknown, but he was certainly over 90.

In 2002, after failing to pass a bill that would have given him life presidency, Muluzi chose Bingu wa Mutharika as his successor, and in 2004 he duly won the election. Many thought he would simply follow in Muluzi's footsteps, but he soon declared his independence by quitting the UDF and setting up his own party, the Democratic Progressive Party (DPP). He set about stemming corruption, stepping up the fight against HIV/Aids, attempting to attract greater foreign investment, and introducing a hugely popular fertiliser subsidy program – all of which led to slow and steady economic growth. In 2009 Mutharika was re-elected with a two-thirds majority in parliament.

THE CULTURE

The National Psyche

Malawians have a reputation as being among the friendliest people in Africa – most of them live up to the hype and are proud of it. Humour is prevalent in the Malawian way of life and is often used as a way of diffusing tension or greeting a misunderstanding. Malawians are also laid-back and lacking in Western impatience. They don't see the point of sweating over or complaining about the small things in life.

Malawians are also pretty conservative. Women tend to dress modestly and respectable ladies are not seen in bars unaccompanied. Public drunkenness is frowned upon, as are open displays of affection between men and women.

Daily Life

Malawi remains one of the world's poorest countries, with a per capita gross national product (GNP) of less than US$250. Nearly half the population is chronically malnourished and life expectancy is only 43 years, due in large part to the HIV/Aids infection rate in Malawi, which runs at almost 12%.

Over 80% of the population live in rural areas. Yet Malawi is urbanising rapidly, and the rate of population growth in the cities is far higher than that in rural areas.

Population

According to the 2008 census, Malawi's total population is around 13.1 million. This is growing by around 2.4% a year. Because the country is small, this creates one of the highest population densities in Africa. People living in rural areas are engaged in subsistence farming or fishing, or working on commercial farms and plantations. Around half the population is under 15 years of age.

Multiculturalism

Malawi's main ethnic groups are Chewa, dominant in the centre and south; Yao in the south; and Tumbuka in the north. Other groups include the Ngoni (also spelt Angoni), inhabiting parts of the central and northern provinces; the Chipoka (or Phoka) in the central area; the Lambya; the Ngonde (also called the Nyakyusa) in the northern region; and the Tonga, mostly along the lakeshore.

There are small populations of Asian and European people living mainly in the cities and involved in commerce, farming (mainly tea plantations) or tourism.

SPORT

The most popular sport in Malawi is football (soccer), which is played throughout the country at all levels, from young boys on makeshift pitches to the national team. Malawi's national team is nicknamed the Flames.

RELIGION

Around 75% of Malawians are Christians. Some are Catholic, while many Malawians follow indigenous Christian faiths that have been established locally.

Malawi has a significant Muslim population of around 20%. Alongside the established churches, many Malawians also follow traditional animist religions.

ARTS & CRAFTS

Dance

Across Malawi dance is an important social element, and most dances are rooted in traditional beliefs and customs. The most notable traditional dance in Malawi is the *Gule Wamkulu*, indigenous to the Chewa people, but also enjoyed by some other tribes. The dance reflects traditional religious beliefs in spirits and is connected to the activities of secret societies. Leading dancers are dressed in ragged costumes of cloth and animal skins, usually wearing a mask, and occasionally on stilts.

Literature

Like most countries in Africa, Malawi has a rich tradition of oral literature.

Poetry is very popular. Steve Chimombo is a leading poet whose collections include *Napolo Poems*. Jack Mapanje's first poetry collection, *Of Chameleons and Gods,* was published in 1981. Much of its symbolism was obscure for outsiders, but not for President Banda – in 1987 Mapanje was arrested and imprisoned without charge; he was eventually released in 1991.

Legson Kayira's semiautobiographical *I Will Try* and *The Looming Shadow* earned him acclaim in the 1970s. A later work is *The Detainee*.

Another notable novelist is Sam Mpasu. His *Nobody's Friend* was a comment on the secrecy of Malawian politics – it earned him a 2½-year prison sentence. After his release he wrote *Prisoner 3/75* and later became minister for education in the new UDF government.

Samson Kambalu's recent autobiography *The Jive Talker: Or, how to get a British Passport* tells of his transition from schoolboy at the Kamuzu Academy to conceptual artist in London.

Music

Traditional music and dance in Malawi are closely linked, as elsewhere in Africa, and often form an important social function beyond entertainment. In Malawi there are some countrywide traditions, and also some regional specialities where local tribes have their own tunes and dances.

Home-grown contemporary music has become increasingly popular in Malawi, due largely to influential and popular musicians such as Lucius Banda, who performs soft 'Malawian-style' reggae, and the late Evison Matafale. Other reggae names to look out for are the Black Missionaries and Billy Kaunda.

ENVIRONMENT

The Land

Pint-sized, landlocked Malawi is no larger than the US state of Pennsylvania. It's wedged between Zambia, Tanzania and Mozambique, measuring roughly 900km long and between 80km and 150km wide, with an area of 118,484 sq km.

Lying in a trough formed by the Rift Valley, Lake Malawi makes up over 75% of Malawi's eastern boundary. Beyond the lake, escarpments rise to high rolling plateaus covering much of the country.

Wildlife

If you're not concerned with simply ticking off the 'Big Five', Malawi has plenty to offer. Liwonde National Park is noted for its herds of elephants and antelopes and is a good place to see hippos and crocodiles. Nyika National Park is renowned for roan antelopes and reedbucks; and you'll also see zebras, warthogs, jackals and possibly leopards. Nearby Vwaza Marsh is known for its hippos as well as elephants, buffalo, waterbucks and other antelope. In southern Malawi, Lengwe National Park supports a population of nyalas – at the northern limit of their distribution in Africa.

Lake Malawi has more fish species than any other inland body of water in the world, with a total of over 600. Most of these are of the family *Cichlidae* – the largest family of fish in Africa – and 99% of these cichlids are endemic to the lake.

For birdwatchers, Malawi is rewarding: over 600 species have been recorded. Birds rare elsewhere in southern Africa but more easily seen here include the African skimmer, Boehm's bee-eater and the wattled crane.

National Parks

Malawi has five national parks. These are (from north to south) Nyika, Kasungu, Lake Malawi (around Cape Maclear), Liwonde and Lengwe. There are also four wildlife reserves – Vwaza Marsh, Nkhotakota, Mwabvi and Majete – making 16.4% of Malawi's land protected.

FOOD & DRINK

The staple diet for most Malawians is *nsima*, a thick, doughy maize porridge that's bland but very filling. It's eaten with the hands and always accompanied by beans or vegetables and a hot relish, and sometimes meat or fish.

Fish is particularly good in Malawi, and *chambo*, the popular breamlike variety, can be found on every menu. *Kampango*, a lake fish similar to catfish, is also often served.

If you like lagers, the local Kuche Kuche is good, though many travellers to Malawi prefer the beer produced by Carlsberg at its Blantyre brewery. There are three main types of beer: 'greens' (lager), 'browns' (like a British ale) and 'golds' (a stronger brew).

LILONGWE

Lilongwe might be Malawi's capital but don't come expecting major attractions, great shopping or a happening music scene – compared to many other African capitals the city is a sleepy backwater. That said, it has a quiet charm that makes it an enjoyable place to hang out for a day or two. The modern city centre and business hub is a dead loss in terms of atmosphere and activities, but the Old Town, where most tourists end up spending their time, has a friendly vibe. There are craft stalls, cafes and restaurants, as well as good bookshops and internet cafes in which to do your onward planning. If you crave action, head for Lilongwe's main market and bus stations for lively streets filled with music, blaring horns and hawkers.

MAD ABOUT MILK?

No, those aren't milk cartons lying on the ground the night after a party. Chibuku – traditional 'opaque' beer made from maize – is sold commercially in cardboard containers. It's thick and sour and tastes pretty nasty. Make sure to shake the carton before drinking.

ORIENTATION

Lilongwe has two centres. City Centre has ministries, embassies, some smart hotels, airline offices, travel agents and several restaurants and cafes. Old Town has a good range of places to stay, the bus station, the main market, some more tour and travel companies, and shops. More importantly, City Centre is a quiet and sterile place, whereas Old Town is livelier. The two centres are 3km apart and frequent minibuses run between them.

Maps

Survey maps of Malawi and some of its cities are available from the **Department of Surveys Map Sales Office** (Map p170), about 500m south of the roundabout where Glyn Jones Rd meets Kamuzu Procession Rd. Regional and city maps cost MK650, survey maps covering the whole of Malawi cost MK3500.

INFORMATION

Bookshops

Bookmart (Map p170; Uplands House, Kamuzu Procession Rd; 🕓 8.30am-4.30pm Mon-Fri, to 1pm Sun) Excellent secondhand bookshop with a wide range of recent bestsellers, classics and travel books. Books cost between MK150 and MK700, depending on their condition.

Central Africana (Map p170; ☎ 01-756317; www.centralafricana.com; Old Town Mall) Has a diverse selection of travel, history and nature books, both new and secondhand. It's a good place to find out-of-print or hard-to-find Malawi guidebooks.

Emergency

Ambulance (☎ 998)
Fire ☎ 01-757999
Police (☎ 01-753333)
Rapid Response Unit (☎ 997)

MALAWI

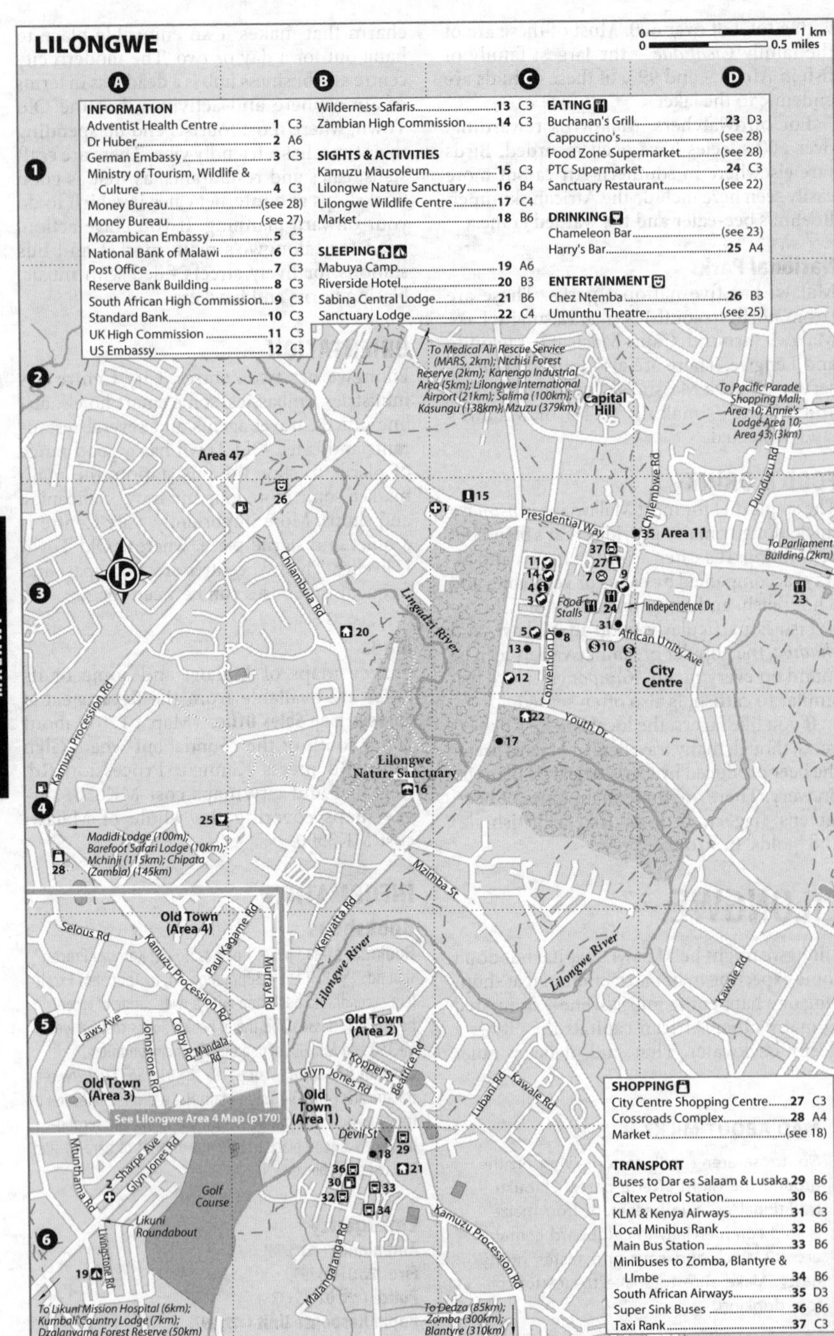
LILONGWE
0 1 km
0 0.5 miles
A
B
C
D
1
2
3
4
5
6
INFORMATION
Adventist Health Centre 1 C3
Dr Huber 2 A6
German Embassy 3 C3
Ministry of Tourism, Wildlife & Culture 4 C3
Money Bureau (see 28)
Money Bureau (see 27)
Mozambican Embassy 5 C3
National Bank of Malawi 6 C3
Post Office 7 C3
Reserve Bank Building 8 C3
South African High Commission 9 C3
Standard Bank 10 C3
UK High Commission 11 C3
US Embassy 12 C3
Wilderness Safaris 13 C3
Zambian High Commission 14 C3
SIGHTS & ACTIVITIES
Kamuzu Mausoleum 15 C3
Lilongwe Nature Sanctuary 16 B4
Lilongwe Wildlife Centre 17 C4
Market 18 B6
SLEEPING
Mabuya Camp 19 A6
Riverside Hotel 20 B3
Sabina Central Lodge 21 B6
Sanctuary Lodge 22 C4
EATING
Buchanan's Grill 23 D3
Cappuccino's (see 28)
Food Zone Supermarket (see 28)
PTC Supermarket 24 C3
Sanctuary Restaurant (see 22)
DRINKING
Chameleon Bar (see 23)
Harry's Bar 25 A4
ENTERTAINMENT
Chez Ntemba 26 B3
Umunthu Theatre (see 25)
To Medical Air Rescue Service (MARS, 2km); Ntchisi Forest Reserve (2km); Kanengo Industrial Area (5km); Lilongwe International Airport (21km); Salima (100km); Kasungu (138km); Mzuzu (379km)
Capital Hill
To Pacific Parade Shopping Mall; Area 10; Annie's Lodge Area 10; Area 43; (3km)
Area 47
Presidential Way
Chilembwe Rd
Dunduzu Rd
Area 11
To Parliament Building (2km)
Chilambula Rd
Lingadzi River
Food Stalls
Independence Dr
African Unity Ave
Convention Dr
City Centre
Youth Dr
Kamuzu Procession Rd
Lilongwe Nature Sanctuary
Madidi Lodge (100m); Barefoot Safari Lodge (10km); Mchinji (115km); Chipata (Zambia) (145km)
Mzimba St
Kenyatta Rd
Lilongwe River
Old Town (Area 4)
Selous Rd
Kamuzu Procession Rd
Paul Kagame Rd
Murray Rd
Laws Ave
Johnstone Rd
Colby Rd
Mandala Rd
Old Town (Area 3)
See Lilongwe Area 4 Map (p170)
Old Town (Area 2)
Koppel St
Beatrice Rd
Glyn Jones Rd
Old Town (Area 1)
Lubani Rd
Kawale Rd
Devil St
Mtunthama Rd
Sharpe Ave
Glyn Jones Rd
Golf Course
Likuni Roundabout
Livingstone Rd
Malangalanga Rd
Kamuzu Procession Rd
To Likuni Mission Hospital (6km); Kumbali Country Lodge (7km); Dzalanyama Forest Reserve (50km)
To Dedza (85km); Zomba (300km); Blantyre (310km)
SHOPPING
City Centre Shopping Centre 27 C3
Crossroads Complex 28 A4
Market (see 18)
TRANSPORT
Buses to Dar es Salaam & Lusaka 29 B6
Caltex Petrol Station 30 B6
KLM & Kenya Airways 31 C3
Local Minibus Rank 32 B6
Main Bus Station 33 B6
Minibuses to Zomba, Blantyre & Llmbe 34 B6
South African Airways 35 D3
Super Sink Buses 36 B6
Taxi Rank 37 C3
MALAWI

Internet Access

Internet is readily available in Lilongwe and there are several cheap options, both in the Old Town and City Centre.

Comptech Cyber Café (Map p170; Mandala Rd; per min MK5) Fast internet connection, printing and photocopying as well as Skype telephone service.

Licom Internet Café (Map p170; Mandala Rd; per min MK5; 7.30am-8pm)

RSS Internet Cafe (Map p170; Kamuzu Procession Rd; per min MK4.50) Offers quick access.

Medical Services

Adventist Health Centre (Map p168; 01-775456/680; Presidential Way) Good for consultations, plus eye and dental problems.

Capital Pharmacy (Map p170; 01-754294; Nico Centre; 8am-5pm Mon-Fri, to 1pm Sat & Sun)

Dr Huber (Map p168; 01-750404, 099 969548; Glyn Jones Rd) A good option for private consultations.

Likuni Mission Hospital (off Map p168; 01-766602/574; Glyn Jones Rd) A better option than Lilongwe Central Hospital, 7km southwest of Old Town, with public wards, private rooms, and some expat European doctors on staff.

Medical Air Rescue Service Clinic (MARS; off Map p168; 01-795018/794967; emergency line 794242; www.marsmalawi.com; Ufulu Rd, Area 43) Has an intensive care unit, a dental surgery and offers laboratory tests for malaria, bilharzia and HIV among others. MARS also has road and air ambulances with staff highly trained in emergency treatment. MARS is linked to Health International and can arrange evacuation to Harare or Jo'burg if things get serious.

Money

Money Bureau City Centre (Map p168; 01-772239; Centre House Arcade, City Centre Shopping Centre); Crossroads (Map p168; 01-750789; Crossroads Complex); Old Town (Map p170; 01-750659; Nico Shopping Centre, Kamuzu Procession Rd) has good rates, doesn't charge commission and does cash advances on credit cards.

National Bank of Malawi City Centre (Map p168; African Unity Ave); Old Town (Map p170; Kamuzu Procession Rd) You can change money here and get a cash advance on your Visa card. There's a 24-hour ATM that accepts Visa.

Standard Bank City Centre (Map p168; African Unity Ave); Old Town (Map p170; Kamuzu Procession Rd) Offers the same facilities as National Bank of Malawi but the ATM also accepts MasterCard and Maestro.

Victoria Forex (Map p170; 08-825545; Nico Shopping Centre, Old Town) Offers a similar service to Money Bureau.

Photography

Lee Photo Studio (Map p170; Nico Shopping Centre; 7.30am-5pm) Digital printing costs MK80 per photo. A set of passport photos costs MK700. They also sell and print rolls of film.

Post

Post office (7.30am-noon & 1-5pm Mon-Fri) City Centre (Map p168; next to City Centre Shopping Centre); Old Town (Map p170; Kamuzu Procession Rd)

Tourist Information

Ministry of Tourism, Wildlife & Culture (Map p168; 01-755499; Tourism House; 7.30am-5pm Mon-Fri, 8-10am Sat) The tourist office is located here, off Convention Dr, but information and advice is minimal. For details on tours, flights and hotels you're better off at a travel agency.

Travel Agencies

Kiboko Safaris (Map p168; 01-751226; www.kiboko-safaris.com; Mandala Rd) Specialises in budget camping safaris throughout Malawi and Zambia, although it also has 'luxury' options.

Land & Lake Safaris (Map p170; 01-757120; www.landlake.net; Mandala Rd) Well-established and knowledgeable company organising tours for all budgets in both Malawi and Zambia.

Wilderness Safaris (Map p168; 01-771393/153; www.wilderness-safaris.com; Bisnowaty Complex, Kenyatta Dr) Excellent operator providing top-end safaris and lodge bookings throughout Southern Africa.

DANGERS & ANNOYANCES

For years muggings were a serious problem around the Nature Sanctuary. Though the situation has improved in recent years, it's still not wise to walk around the area. If you're visiting the Wildlife Centre, take a taxi or a minibus.

During the day, it's fine to walk everywhere around the Old Town and City Centre, although it's much quieter in the City Centre at the weekend so you should be on your guard. At night, Malangalanga Rd can be dangerous, and walking to Area 3 of the Old Town is not recommended. The bridge between the Old Town's Areas 2 and 3 is a favourite haunt for muggers. If you arrive on a bus after dark, take a minibus or taxi to your accommodation.

SIGHTS & ACTIVITIES

The main **market** (Map p168; Malangalanga Rd) near the bus station in Old Town is a pocket of frenetic activity, and worth a visit even if you don't want to buy anything. You'll find all manner of things on sale here – bicycle parts, live chickens, vegetables, dustbins,

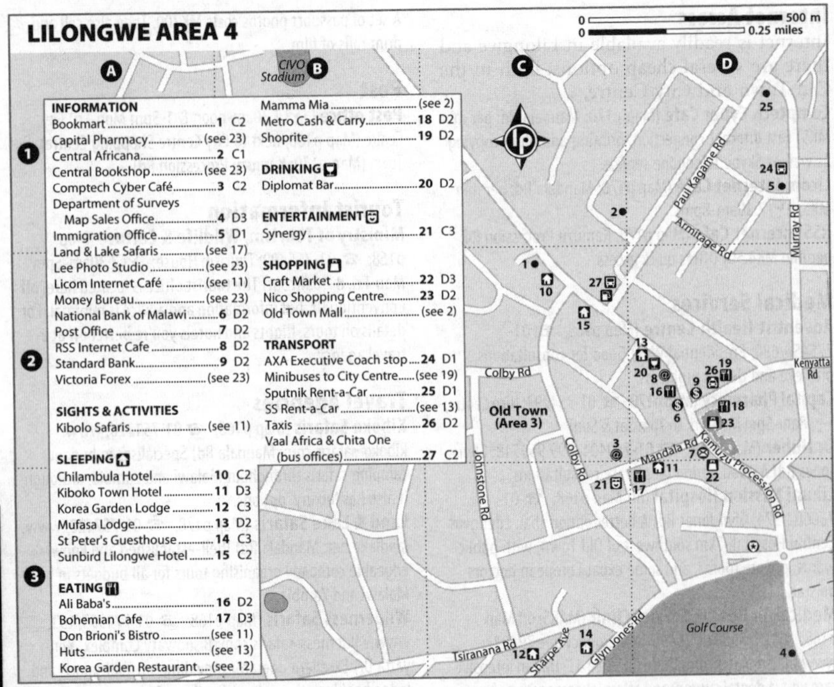

underwear…the list goes on. Be aware, however, that pickpockets operate in the crowds.

To get an in-depth look at Malawi's most important cash crop, go to the public gallery overlooking the **tobacco auction floors** (off Map p168; ☎ 01-710377; Kenango Industrial Area; admission free) at the Auction Holdings warehouse about 7km north of the city centre, east of the main road towards Kasungu and Mzuzu. This is best reached by taxi, but local minibuses serve the industrial area. Alternatively, you can arrange visits with a car and driver/guide through the companies listed under Travel Agencies p169). The auction season is April or May to September.

In between City Centre and Old Town and alongside the Lingadzi River is the 180-hectare **Lilongwe Nature Sanctuary**. Once one of the city's most popular attractions, the area became neglected and run down. Luckily, a joint agreement between the Lilongwe Wildlife Trust and the Department of National Parks & Wildlife is restoring the area to its former glory. Taking pride of place is the new **Lilongwe Wildlife Centre** (Map p168; ☎ 01 757120; www.lilongwewildlife.org; Kenyatta Dr; 8am-4pm Mon-Fri, to noon Sat; adult/child MK840/420), an animal rescue and educational facility. The centre's ultimate aim is to rehabilitate the animals for a life back in the wild and it has a strict no-breeding, no-trade and no-unessential contact policy. The entrance fee includes an informative tour.

To get up close to the country's movers and shakers, head to the **Parliament Building** (Map p168; Presidential Way), which moved from Zomba in the mid-1990s to the ostentatious palace of former president Banda on the outskirts of Lilongwe. At the time of writing, work was underway on a shiny new parliament building near Capital Hill, which should be completed by 2011.

If you're interested in seeing the final resting place of Malawi's first president, Dr Hastings Kamuzu Banda, head for the marble-and-granite **Kamuzu Mausoleum** (Map p168; Presidential Way) in Heroes Acre. Construction finished in 2006 at a whopping cost of US$600,000.

SLEEPING

Old Town is the most convenient area of the city to stay due to its eating, drinking and transport facilities.

Budget

Mabuya Camp (Map p168; ☎ 01-754978; www.mabuyacamp.com; Livingstone Rd; campsites per person US$4, dm US$6, d & tw US$18; P) If you're looking for Lilongwe's liveliest backpacker spot, you've found it. This place buzzes with a happy mixture of solo travellers, overlanders and volunteers relaxing by the pool and in the large shady gardens. There are dorms and a double in the main house as well as chalets and plenty of camping pitches in the garden.

St Peter's Guesthouse (Map p170; ☎ 01-752812, 08-317769; Glyn Jones Rd; r without bathroom MK1800) Offers excellent, clean and safe rooms with nets, all of which open onto a peaceful courtyard garden. It's quiet and part of the parish so guests should be respectful.

Sabina Central Lodge (Map p168; ☎ 0888-373172; r MK2700) The main advantage of staying here is that it's close to the bus and minibus stations if you've got an early morning start. Rooms are large with TV and fan, and not too noisy considering their location.

Mufasa Lodge (Map p170; ☎ 0999-071665; Kamuzu Procession Rd, Area 4; dm from US$10, tw without bathroom US$28, tw & d US$35) This is a fantastic new addition to Lilongwe's budget scene. It may not have a pool or large gardens but who needs them when you have a balcony with city views, top-notch bathrooms and a home-away-from-home atmosphere? You can choose from doubles, singles or dorms and there's an excellent self-catering kitchen.

Midrange

Korea Garden Lodge (Map p170; ☎ 01-753467, 757854, 759700; www.kglodge.net; Tsiranana Rd; s/d shared bathroom US$26/28, s/d from US$41/52, s/d executive room with air-con from US$73/78) This rambling hotel has rooms to suit every budget, from tiny but wallet-friendly 'bronze' rooms that share a bathroom to executive rooms with all the mod cons. You also get the advantage of a bar, and the chance to sample Korean food at the in-house restaurant.

Kiboko Town Hotel (Map p170; ☎ 01-751226; www.kiboko-safaris.com; Mandala Rd; s/d incl breakfast from US$48/58) Locationwise, Kiboko can't be beat. It's in the heart of Mandala Rd, a mere skip away from Old Town's banks, shops and internet cafes. The rooms aren't bad either – four-poster beds and comfy bed linen are complemented with jazzy African prints, and they all have scrupulously clean bathrooms. Downstairs is a cafe (open for breakfast and lunch) serving burgers, sandwiches and Dutch apple pancakes.

Riverside Hotel (Map p168; ☎ 01-750511; Chilambula Rd; riverside@malawi.netlarge; s/d MK8000/9000) A gleaming white lobby full of plush leather chairs leads to comfortable tiled rooms with fan, DSTV (satellite TV) and tea and coffee facilities. Should you get a hunger on, there's a restaurant serving Malawian and Indian curries and grills.

Chilambula Hotel (Map p170; ☎ 01-751560; Kamuzu Procession Rd; r from MK9350) Most rooms here open out onto a balcony overlooking the hub of Old Town and have sweeping views over the city. All are large with canopied beds, air-con and fridges, and the executive rooms in particular are massive and come with sofas, chairs, coffee tables, coffee makers and faux-marble bathrooms.

Madidi Lodge (off Map p168; ☎ 01-752661; www.madidilodge.com; Area 9; s/d standard US$85/110, ste US$110/128) An oasis of calm just a short walk from Crossroads Complex. Wood-and-brick rooms are decorated with African artefacts and come with fridges, DSTV and safes. The restaurant specialises in producing three-course menus from around the continent.

Top End

Sunbird Lilongwe Hotel (Map p170; ☎ 01-756333; Kamuzu Procession Rd; s/d from US$113/134; P) Set amid sprawling, manicured gardens, this hotel is well appointed (there's a business centre, car hire and an Air Malawi desk) but rather uninspiring. On the plus side, several of the previously tired rooms have been renovated and have a more modern, boutique hotel feel.

Sanctuary Lodge (Map p168; ☎ 01-775200/201/202; www.thesanctuarylodge.net; campsites per adult/child US$9/6, s/d incl breakfast from US$125/175) Just outside the city's nature sanctuary, this peaceful ecolodge is encased in 8 hectares of woodland along the Lingadzi River. Made from environmentally friendly building materials, it has cool and quiet stone chalets, and a campsite with plenty of braai (barbecue) sites and good hot showers (there are also plans to build a pool, bar and restaurant just for campers).

EATING

Restaurants

Korea Garden Restaurant (Map p170; ☎ 01-753467; starters MK500-700, mains MK1000-2200; breakfast, lunch & dinner) Within the Korea Garden Lodge, this

MALAWI

place serves a small selection of flavoursome Korean favourites such as *bulgogi* and *kimchi* alongside the usual Malawian chicken, chips and *chambo*.

Huts (Map p170; ☎ 01-752912; off Kamuzu Procession Rd; mains from MK750; ⏰ noon-1.30pm & 6.15pm-9.30pm Mon-Sat) Come here for your fix of tandoori and madras. The food is filling, tasty and good value.

Don Brioni's Bistro (Map p170; ☎ 01-756998; Mandala Rd; mains from MK800; ⏰ lunch & dinner) Long-time favourite Don Brioni's is a laid-back Italian-style bistro that fills up with an energetic mix of tourists and locals each evening. Food is excellent and comes in generous portions – you can choose from the main menu or from an always interesting blackboard of daily specials.

Buchanan's Grill (Map p168; ☎ 01-772846/59; Four Seasons Centre, Presidential Way; mains MK1000-2300; ⏰ lunch & dinner Mon-Sat). Sit in the old-fashioned dining room or on a verandah next to a tinkling waterfall and frog ponds at this stylish restaurant within a garden centre. What's on the menu? Great hunks of beef, ribs, schnitzels and juicy burgers. If you've less of a bloodlust there are fish, pasta and salad dishes to keep you happy.

Mamma Mia (Map p170; ☎ 01-758362; Old Town Mall; mains from MK1400; ⏰ lunch & dinner) The spaghetti and massive pizzas are the main event here but it also does a good selection of seafood and hearty plates of red meat. Food is served in a dark dining room or on a large covered terrace overlooking the Old Town Mall.

Sanctuary Restaurant (Map p168; ☎ 01-754560; www.thesanctuarylodge.net, meals from MK1300; ⏰ lunch & dinner) Based at the Sanctuary Lodge, this is a very elegant restaurant with a safari-lodge vibe and a large terrace overlooking the lodge swimming pool. Food here is good – from baguettes to chicken or T-bone steaks – and the restaurant is romantically candlelit at night. You can also pop in for a coffee and cake on a grassy lawn underneath the shady trees.

Cafes & Quick Eats

Ali Baba's (Map p170; ☎ 01-755224; Kamuzu Procession Rd; dishes MK500-900; ⏰ 8am-9pm Mon-Fri, 10am-8pm Sun) This popular fast-food place dishes up burgers and wraps as well as sturdier plates of curries and stews.

Bohemian Cafe (Map p170; ☎ 01-757120; Mandala Rd, Old Town; snacks from MK450; ⏰ 8am-4.30pm Mon-Fri, 9am-2pm Sat) Order at the counter at the back of Land & Lake Safaris and then sit out in a cheery vine-covered courtyard with a view of the busy street. On offer are big breakfasts, milkshakes and toasties as well as treats for the sweet-toothed, such as apple pie and ice cream.

Cappuccino's (Map p168; Crossroads Complex; dishes MK1200-1600, cappuccino MK280; ⏰ 7.30am-6pm Mon-Fri, 8am-6pm Sat) There's a small terrace overlooking the mall, a collection of magazines for browsing and a small menu of English breakfasts, salads, wraps and sandwiches.

Self-Catering

There are decent supermarkets all over the city. **Shoprite** (Map p170; Kenyatta Rd) in Old Town has the best range and you can buy all sorts of food and even camping supplies. **Metro Cash & Carry** (Map p170; Kamuzu Procession Rd) has more limited and cheaper stock. Near the City Centre Shopping Centre there's a **PTC** (Map p168; City Centre) and a **Food Zone Supermarket** (Map p168; Crossroads Complex), which has a selection of imported treats.

DRINKING & ENTERTAINMENT

Bars & Nightclubs

Synergy (Map p170; Malangalanga Rd) A lively new club that plays everything from house and Western pop to Congolese rumba and is frequented by a mix of locals, volunteers and backpackers.

Chameleon Bar (Map p168; Four Seasons Centre, Presidential Way; ⏰ 11am-midnight Mon-Sat, to 10pm Sun) This place is popular with Malawians and expats and puts on regular live music and DJ nights. Sundays are for laid-back afternoon jazz. It has a menu of enticing cocktails and tables outside at which to enjoy them.

Harry's Bar (Map p168; ☎ 01-757979; ⏰ 6pm-late) Harry's is an institution. The owner is a mine of information on the Malawian music scene and the bar is the place to come if you want to get the low-down on local bands and DJs.

Chez Ntemba (Map p168; Area 47; ⏰ 6pm-late) Part of the Congolese nightclub chain that has branches across Southern Africa, this is Lilongwe's most fun night out. Hoards of sweaty bodies pack the place out to dance to DJs and live bands with a totally African flavour.

Diplomat Bar (Map p170; Kamuzu Procession Rd; ⏰ noon-late) Small in stature but big on atmosphere, this pint-sized Old Town bar buzzes with a mixed crowd of expats, travellers and locals at the weekend, when the action often spills out onto the street.

Theatre

Umunthu Theatre (☎ 01-757979; www.umunthu.com) The highlight of Lilongwe's cultural scene, Umunthu puts on regular live music, films, club nights, and variety shows, showcasing the best of Malawian talent.

SHOPPING

Malls

At the time of writing a new shopping centre was being constructed behind the Nico Shopping Centre and opposite Shoprite. It is due to open in late 2010 and will include a Game supermarket and a Woolworths.

Nico Shopping Centre (Map p170; Kamuzu Procession Rd) Has a bookshop, travel agency, pharmacy and several other shops.

Crossroads Complex (Map p168; Kamuzu Procession Rd) Houses banks, a hotel, minigolf and a variety of upscale shops.

City Centre Shopping Centre (Map p168; off Independence Dr) A collection of buildings containing shops, travel agents, restaurants, a bank and a post office.

Old Town Mall (Map p170; off Chilambula Rd) This small mall has a couple of bookshops and craft stores.

Markets

The city's main market (Map p168) is by the bus station. There's also a craft market (Map p170) outside the Old Town post office, where vendors sell everything from woodcarvings to basketware and jewellery.

GETTING THERE & AWAY

Air

For details of flights, see p212 and p214. Airlines with offices in Lilongwe include the following:

Air Malawi (off Map p168; ☎ 01-700811; Lilongwe International Airport)

KLM & Kenya Airways (Map p168; ☎ 01-774227; City Centre)

South African Airways (Map p168; ☎ 01-772242, 770307; Capital Hotel, City Centre)

Bus

AXA City Trouper and commuter buses leave from the main bus station where you'll find their ticket office (Map p168), though you can also buy tickets at Postdotnet inside the City Centre PTC, at Nico Shopping Centre and at Crossroads Complex.

AXA executive coaches depart from outside the City Centre PTC before stopping at the immigration office on Murray Rd and making their way to Blantyre. An executive ticket between the two cities costs MK3100.

Destinations from the main bus station include Mzuzu (MK1200, five hours, two or three daily), Blantyre (MK700 to MK1400, four hours, three daily), Kasungu (MK480, two hours, two daily), Nkhotakota (MK610, three hours, two daily), Nkhata Bay (MK900, five hours, one daily), Salima (MK390, one hour, two daily), Dedza (MK310, one hour), and Monkey Bay (MK1000, six hours, one daily).

A number of other bus companies, including Coachline and Zimatha, also leave from the main bus station at similar rates and times. Super Sink buses depart for Mzuzu from the Caltex petrol station next to the main bus station between 7am and 8am (MK1000; six hours).

Long-distance minibuses depart from behind the bus station to nearby destinations such as Zomba (MK1200, four to five hours), Dedza (MK500, 45 to 60 minutes), Mchinji (MK450, 90 minutes), and the Zambian border (MK700, two hours), Nchitsi (MK500, 2½ hours), Kasungu (MK600, two hours), Limbe (MK1000; three to four hours) and Nkhotakota (MK1100, three hours).

Vaal Africa (Map p170; ☎ 0999-200086) leaves from the Total petrol station in Old Town on Tuesday and Saturday at 6am, arriving in Johannesburg at 11am the following day (one way MK14,500). **Chita One** (Map p170; ☎ 0999-545453/0999 022221) leaves on Wednesday and Sunday at 6am from near the Old Town Mall (one way MK15,500).

From Devil St, **Zambia–Botswana Coach** (☎ 0999-405340) leaves Tuesday and Friday at 6am arriving in Lusaka at 5pm (MK6000). Kob's Coach leaves the same day, for the same price, at 5.30 am. The Taqwa Coach departs (Map p168) at 7pm on Saturday, Sunday and Tuesday for the 27-hour journey to Dar es Salaam (MK8000), continuing on to Nairobi (MK14,000).

GETTING AROUND

To/From the Airport

Lilongwe international airport (off Map p168) is 21km north of the city. A taxi from the airport into town costs MK2000.

The Airport Bus collects passengers from most of the hotels and lodges in town around three hours before a flight departure. The cost is MK1000. You can also pick it up at the airport after arriving.

Bus

The most useful local minibus service for visitors is between Old Town and City Centre. From Old Town, local minibuses (marked Area 12) leave from either the bus rank near the market or next to Shoprite. They then head north up Kenyatta Rd, via Youth and Convention Drs or via Independence Dr, to reach City Centre. From City Centre back to Old Town, the bus stop for the return journey is at the northern end of Independence Dr. The fare between the two centres is MK80.

Taxi

The best places to find taxis are the main hotels. There's also a rank on Presidential Way, just north of City Centre Shopping Centre (Map p168). Taxis also congregate outside Shoprite in Old Town (Map p170). The fare between Old Town and City Centre is about MK1000. Short journeys within either City Centre or Old Town cost around MK600. It's always best to negotiate a price with the driver first.

NORTHERN MALAWI

Out of the way and sometimes forgotten, northern Malawi is where ravishing highlands meet hippo-filled swamps, vast mountains loom over empty beaches, and colonial relics litter pristine islands and hilltop villages. It is Malawi's most sparsely populated region, and the first taste many travellers get of this tiny country after making the journey down from East Africa.

This section covers most parts of the Northern Province, from the northern tip of the country down to Mzuzu and Nkhata Bay. Places are described roughly from north to south.

KARONGA

In the surrounding dry and dusty country, Karonga is a relaxed little town with wide streets, wandering cattle and shopfronts straight out of a western; you can almost see the tumbleweed rolling down the street.

The town is strung out for about 2km along the main street between a roundabout on the north–south road and the lakeshore, but there are plenty of bicycle taxis that will take you anywhere you want to go in town for around MK80.

Information

Karonga has both Standard and National Banks. There's also an **internet cafe** (Cultural & Museum Centre Karonga; per min MK10; 8am-5pm Mon-Sat, 2pm-5pm Sun).

Sights & Activities

Culture & Museum Centre Karonga (CMCK; www.palaeo.net/cmck; ☎ 01-362579; 8am-5pm Mon-Sat, 2-5pm Sun) celebrates the numerous fossil discoveries made in these parts, and the skeleton of the Malawisaurus (or a copy of it anyway) takes pride of place. Visits are in the form of a guided tour. Following the path of a giant snake along the museum floor, you're taken on a whistle-stop journey of the life of the planet and the Karonga district in particular.

Sleeping

Mufwa Lakeshore Lodge & Camping (☎ 01-362390, 0999-778451; s/d with shared bathroom MK1200/2100 self-contained s/d MK2500/3800, campsite per person MK700) A lodge overlooking the lake with a large, green lawn might sound like a good thing but in reality the owners don't make much of it. Bland and basic are the watchwords for the rooms here. The property can be difficult to find – there is no identifying sign and it's set back from the road; the turn-off is located after the National Bank of Malawi.

Safari Lodge (☎ 01-362340; s/d MK3000/3750;) On the road to the lake, this place has spacious rooms but as with many places in this town they area bit run down. Room 12 (MK4000) costs extra because you're paying for the privilege of air-conditioning, but as there's no other difference it's not really worth it.

Safari Lodge Annex (☎ 01-362340; standard/executive/chalet MK4500/4800/6500) Just around the corner from Safari Lodge is its much more attractive and better-endowed sister. There are solid brick chalets here with large bathrooms and separate sitting areas, as well as a pretty garden. Food is available here too, with snacks/mains from MK450/700.

Getting There & Away

AXA City Trouper buses leave for Lilongwe at 12.30pm daily (MK2000, 10 hours) before

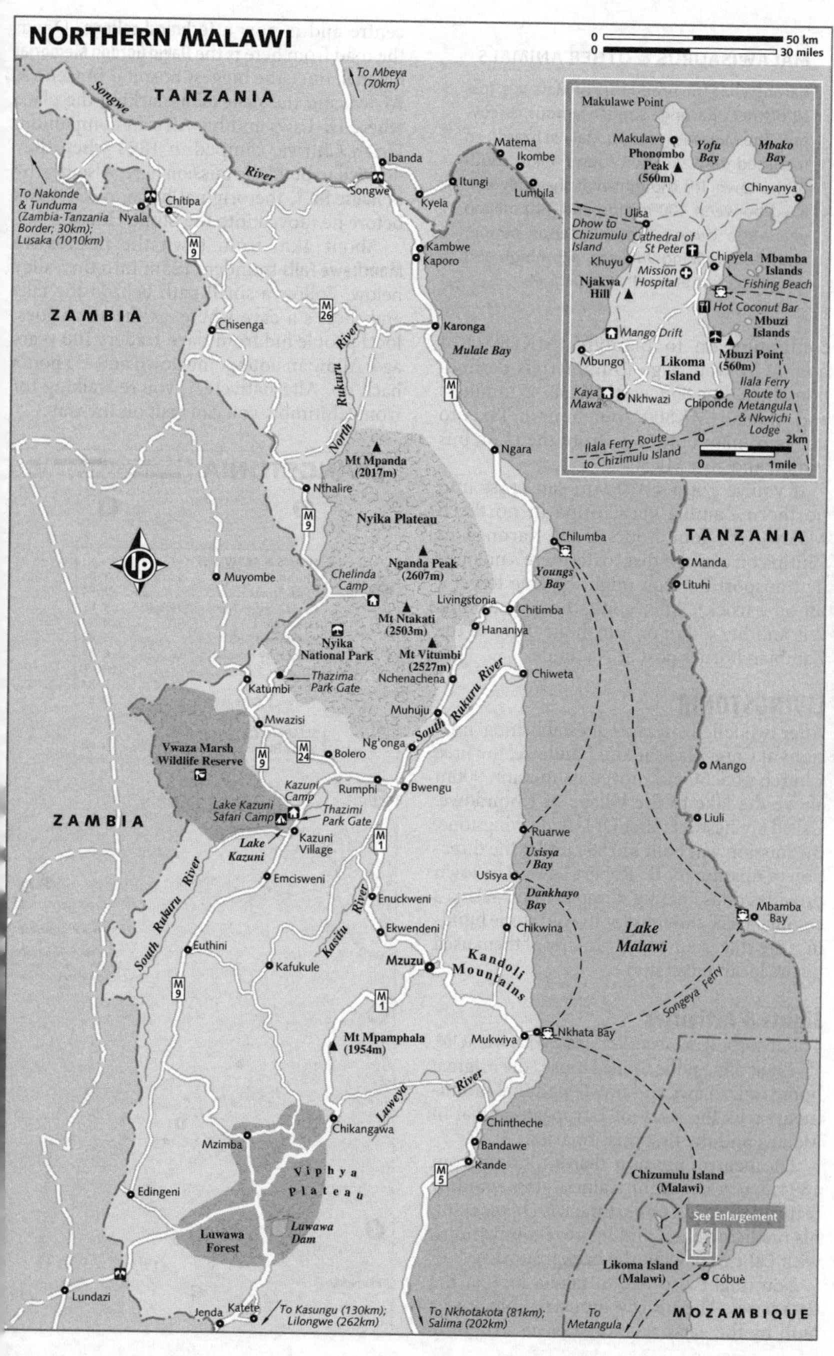
NORTHERN MALAWI
0 50 km
0 30 miles
TANZANIA
ZAMBIA
ZAMBIA
TANZANIA
MOZAMBIQUE
Songwe River
To Mbeya (70km)
To Nakonde & Tunduma (Zambia-Tanzania Border; 30km); Lusaka (1010km)
Nyala
Chitipa
Ibanda
Songwe
Kyela
Itungi
Matema
Ikombe
Lumbila
Kambwe
Kaporo
Chisenga
Karonga
Mulale Bay
North Rukuru River
Mt Mpanda (2017m)
Ngara
Nthalire
Nyika Plateau
Nganda Peak (2607m)
Muyombe
Chelinda Camp
Mt Ntakati (2503m)
Nyika National Park
Mt Vitumbi (2527m)
Livingstonia
Chitimba
Hananiya
Chilumba
Youngs Bay
Thazima Park Gate
Katumbi
Nchenachena
Chiweta
Mwazisi
Muhuju
South Rukuru River
Vwaza Marsh Wildlife Reserve
Ng'onga
Bolero
Kazuni Camp
Rumphi
Bwengu
Lake Kazuni Safari Camp
Thazimi Park Gate
Lake Kazuni
Kazuni Village
Emcisweni
Ruarwe
Usisya Bay
Usisya
Dankhayo Bay
Enuckweni
Kasitu River
Ekwendeni
Chikwina
Lake Malawi
Euthini
Kafukule
Mzuzu
Kandoli Mountains
Mt Mpamphala (1954m)
Mukwiya
Nkhata Bay
Songeya Ferry
Luweya River
Chikangawa
Chintheche
Bandawe
Kande
Mzimba
Viphya Plateau
Edingeni
Luwawa Forest
Luwawa Dam
Lundazi
Jenda
Katete
To Kasungu (130km); Lilongwe (262km)
To Nkhotakota (81km); Salima (202km)
To Metangula
Chizumulu Island (Malawi)
See Enlargement
Likoma Island (Malawi)
Cóbuè
Manda
Lituhi
Mango
Liuli
Mbamba Bay
M9
M26
M1
M24
M5
Makulawe Point
Makulawe
Phonombo Peak (560m)
Yofu Bay
Mbako Bay
Chinyanya
Ulisa
Dhow to Chizumulu Island
Cathedral of St Peter
Khuyu
Chipyela
Mbamba Islands
Mission Hospital
Fishing Beach
Njakwa Hill
Hot Coconut Bar
Mango Drift
Mbuzi Islands
Mbungo
Likoma Island
Mbuzi Point (560m)
Kaya Mawa
Nkhwazi
Chiponde
Ilala Ferry Route to Metangula & Nkwichi Lodge
Ilala Ferry Route to Chizimulu Island
0 2km
0 1mile

> **MALAWISAURUS & OTHER ANIMALS**
>
> Karonga has the proud title of Malawi's 'fossil district'. Karonga's most famous discovery? The Malawisaurus (or Malawi lizard) – a fossilised dino skeleton found 45km south of the town. It's thought that the scaly one lived between 100 million and 140 million years ago during the cretaceous period, and was a hulking 9m long, 4.3m high and weighed in at around 11,000kg.

continuing on to Blantyre (MK2800, 14 hours). Minibuses go to numerous destinations, including Songwe (MK230, 45 minutes) and Mzuzu (MK800, four hours). Taxis to the Tanzanian border go from the main bus station and cost MK500.

If you've got a 4WD you can cross into northern Zambia via Chitipa in northern Malawi. It's four hours from Karonga to Chitipa on a rough dirt road (there's no public transport but you might be able to get a lift on a truck). After going though customs it is another 80km or four-hour drive to the Zambian border post at Nakonde.

LIVINGSTONIA

After two failed attempts at establishing missions at Cape Maclear and Bandawe, the Free Church of Scotland moved its mission 900m above the lake to the village of Khondowe. Called Livingstonia after Dr David Livingstone, the mission was built in 1884 under the direction of missionary Dr Robert Laws. The town provides a fascinating glimpse into Malawi's colonial past, and most of the old stone buildings are still around today (many of them used by the local university).

Sights & Activities

The absorbing **museum** (admission/photos MK250/100, 7.30am-5pm) in the Stone House (the original home of Dr Laws and now a national monument) tells the story of European arrival in Malawi and the first missionaries.

The nearby mission **church**, dating from 1894, has a beautiful stained-glass window featuring David Livingstone with his sextant, his medicine chest and his two companions, with Lake Malawi in the background.

You might also like to take a look at the **clock tower**. The nearby industrial block was built by the early missionaries as a training centre and is now a **technical college**. Down the road from here is the **David Gordon Memorial Hospital**, once the biggest hospital in Central Africa, and the **stone cairn** marking the place where Dr Laws and his African companion, Uriah Chirwa, camped in 1894 when they decided to build the mission here. Also nearby is **House No 1**, the original home of Dr Laws before he moved into the Stone House.

About 4km from town the impressive **Manchewe Falls** thunders 125m into the valley below. Follow a small path behind the falls and there's a cave where, as the story goes, local people hid from slave-traders 100 years ago. Allow an hour going down and 1½ hours back up. Alternatively, if you're walking to/from Chitimba, you can visit on the way.

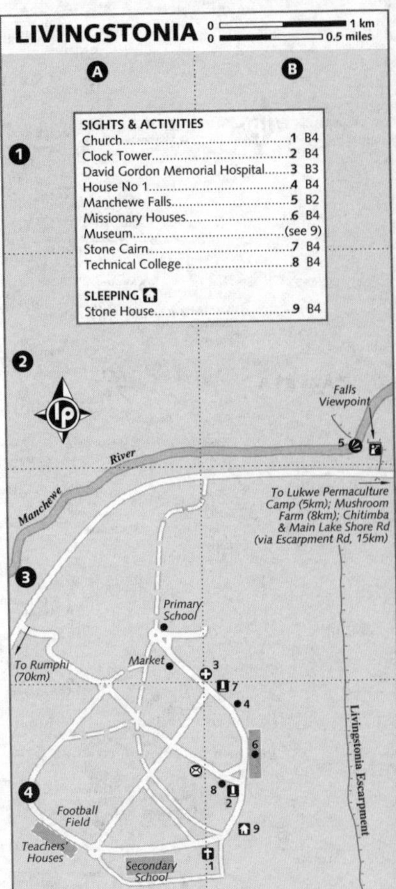

The more adventurous can go abseiling or try out a gorge swing. For more details contact Mushroom Farm (below).

Sleeping & Eating

our pick **Mushroom Farm** (☎ 0999-652485; www.themushroomfarmmalawi.com; campsites per person MK640, tent hire MK800, s/d from MK4000) Drive in to this sustainable bush retreat from the Livingstonia road and the views will hit you smack in the face. Camping spots with their own little fire pit sit right at the cliff edge and there are some gorgeous rooms here, including a wood-and-thatch double completely open at the front to take in the views to the max, and a room with traditional cob walls that looks like it could house a hobbit. It's roughly 10km up the escarpment road and is signposted on the left. Pick-ups can be arranged from the Livingstonia turn-off for US$30.

Lukwe Permaculture Camp (☎ 0999-434985/792311, campsites/dm US$5/10, s/d cabin US$15/20) On the northern side of the escarpment road, above the steep zigzags, an hour's walk east (downhill) from Livingstonia, or about 10km from Chitimba if you're coming up. Thatch cabins sit along the edge of the escarpment with dramatic views over Lake Malawi, and there's a chilled lounge with fire pit, comfy chairs and a friendly atmosphere. The food here is mostly European, such as lasagne and pasta, and they grow all their own salad ingredients (food should be ordered in advance; meals MK500 to MK1200). Rooftop campers can also be catered for.

Stone House (☎ 01-368223; campsites per person MK600, r per person MK1400, laundry MK200) Sleeping in Dr Laws' old house – complete with creaky wooden floorboards and pieces of original furniture – is probably the most atmospheric way to spend the night in Livingstonia. There's a verandah with outrageous views over the escarpment and wholesome meals are available (English breakfast MK250, *nsima* and beef stew MK350).

Getting There & Away

From the main north–south road between Karonga and Mzuzu, the road to Livingstonia turns off at Chitimba, forcing its way up the escarpment in a series of acute hairpin bends. Drivers should attempt this only in a 4WD, and only if there's been no rain. There's no bus, and you'll wait a very long time if you're hitching.

The alternative is to walk up – it's about 15km and steep, so it takes four hours from Chitimba if you follow the road. There are shortcuts that can cut it to three hours, but these are even steeper.

The other way to reach Livingstonia, especially if you're coming from the south, is to drive up the dirt road from Rumphi, for which you'll also need a 4WD. If you don't have wheels, it's also possible to get a truck up this route. It leaves at 2pm on Tuesday and Thursday from outside the PTC supermarket in Rumphi and takes about five hours.

A third option is to walk to Livingstonia from the Nyika Plateau. See the boxed text, p179, for details.

NYIKA NATIONAL PARK

No, someone hasn't just airlifted some zebras and dropped them in Europe; you're still in southern Africa. But at 1800m above sea level the Nyika Plateau – the main attraction of Malawi's **Nyika National Park** (entry fees per person US$5 & per car US$2; 🕒 6am-6pm) – is decidedly different from the rest of Malawi: think Yorkshire moors meets the Black Forest. Gently sloping hills, broad valleys, and grasslands are met by sporadic pockets of thick pine trees and gin-clear streams; most mornings the air is cold and a fine blue mist cloaks the landscape.

With a 3200-sq-km expanse you can quite easily spend the day hiking in the hills without happening upon another soul – except for the animals, that is. Plenty of zebras, bushbucks, reedbucks and roan antelopes (rare elsewhere) roam this domain and you may also spot elands, warthogs, klipspringers, jackals, duikers and possibly hyenas and leopards. If you're a twitcher, more than 400 species of bird have been recorded here. After the wet season the landscape bursts into life in a blaze of wildflowers. There are around 200 species of orchid alone growing on the plateau.

It can get surprisingly cold on the Nyika Plateau, especially at night from June to August, when frost is not uncommon. Log fires are provided in the chalets and rooms, but bring a warm sleeping bag if you're camping.

Activities

Wilderness Safaris (www.wilderness-safaris.com), which also runs the excellent Mvuu Lodge and Camp in Liwonde National Park, has won the tender to run the park's tourist concessions. It has renovated the existing accommodation, and resumed horse-riding and mountain-biking safaris.

Sleeping

Camping ground (campsites per person US$10) About 2km west of the main Chelinda Camp, this camp is set in a secluded site with vistas of the plateau's rolling hills. The site has permanent security, clean toilets, hot showers, endless firewood and shelters for cooking and eating.

Chelinda Camp (contact ☎ 01-771393; www.wilderness-safaris.com) Chelinda Camp is a series of self-catering stone bungalows tucked into the forest. All of them have huge stone fireplaces, sitting rooms and fully equipped kitchens for self-caterers. The camp has recently been renovated by Wilderness Safaris.

Chelinda Lodge (contact ☎ 01-771393; www.wilderness-safaris.com) This is a luxury catered lodge, 1km from Chelinda Camp. A cluster of log cabins sitting in a clearing of pine trees on the side of a hill, it looks like something out of the pages of a children's story book. The lodge was being renovated at the time of research and scheduled to reopen in mid-2010. Roaring fires, luxury bathrooms and gourmet dinners should be the order of the day.

All self-caterers should stock up in either Mzuzu or Rumphi. There's a small shop at Chelinda for National Parks staff but provisions are often basic and supplies sporadic.

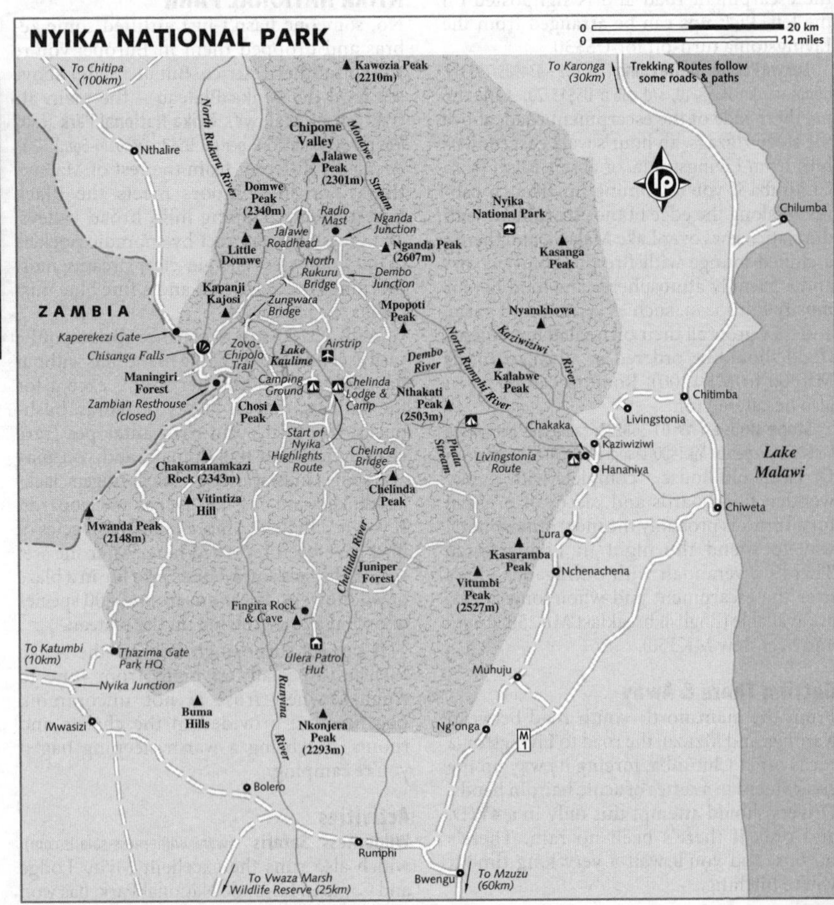

TREKKING ON THE NYIKA PLATEAU

The only set route on Nyika – and by far the most popular – goes from Chelinda to Livingstonia. It's a hugely rewarding and spectacular walk, crossing east through high grassland, then dropping steeply through the wooded escarpment and passing through villages and farmland to reach the old mission station at Livingstonia. This route takes three days. The third night is spent in Livingstonia, and you can walk down to Chitimba at the lakeshore on the fourth day. For advice, contact **Wilderness Safaris** (www.wilderness-safaris.com), in charge of tourist concessions in the park as of 2009. It should be able to help you with guides and porters.

Getting There & Away

Getting to the park by public transport can be a bit of an ordeal. There are no public buses into the park; the nearest you can get is the service from Mzuzu to the small town of Rumphi (MK250). There you might be able to find a truck going to the border town of Chitipa to drop you off at the turn-off to Chelinda Camp, but then you'd have a good 20km to walk.

Charter flights to Nyika weren't operating at the time of research but might start up again now that Wilderness Safaris has won the park's tourism concession.

The main Thazima gate is in the southwest of the park, 54km from Rumphi; to Chelinda Camp it's another 55km. It's a dirt road after Rumphi and in fair condition as far as Thazima gate. In the park the tracks are rough and really only suitable for 4WD vehicles or 2WD vehicles with high clearance. Fuel is available at Chelinda but in limited supply, so it's best to fill up before you enter the park.

VWAZA MARSH WILDLIFE RESERVE

This 1000-sq-km reserve is not on the mainstream tourist track, but with its compact size and plentiful buffalo, elephant and hippo population it shouldn't be overlooked.

As with many of Malawi's parks, poachers have hit Vwaza in the past but the animal numbers are still reasonably healthy. As well as a plethora of antelope – puku, impala, roan and kudu, to name a few – there are around 2000 buffalo and 300 elephants, as well as some 500 hippos in Lake Kazuni. Vwaza's birdwatching is also excellent. There are 300 species here and this is one of the best places in Malawi to see waders, including storks and herons. There are few predators, but occasionally a lion or leopard is spotted.

The best time of year to visit is in the dry season; just after the rainy season, the grass is high and you might go away without seeing anything.

Sleeping

At the time of writing the government was running park accommodation, but had chosen an (as yet) unnamed private company to take over the tourism concession.

Kazuni Camp (campsite per person US$6, s/d chalet with shared bathroom US$10/20) Has simple, rustic chalets with clean sheets and mosquito nets. They are separated by a decent stretch of bush, so you still get a sense of privacy and wilderness, and they're close to the water so that elephants and hippos are frequent nighttime visitors. You must bring food, and there are cooking stations with barbecues.

Lake Kazuni Safari Camp (huts US$30) Consists of low-key grass and brick chalets with bathroom, in a fantastic position overlooking the floodplains. There's a restaurant sitting underneath the acacia trees. As with Kazuni Camp, this place was in limbo at the time of writing, waiting for the private company to take over the tender.

Getting There & Away

If you're travelling by public transport, first get to Rumphi, reached from Mzuzu by minibus for MK400 (1½ hours), or public bus for MK250 (one hour). From Rumphi there are plenty of *matola* (pick-ups) travelling to and from the Kazuni area and you should be able to get a lift to the main gate for around MK500 to MK700. Otherwise, buses and minibuses to Mzimba might drop you at Kazuni village, which is about 1km from the park gate.

By car, head west from Rumphi. Turn left after 10km (Vwaza Marsh Wildlife Reserve is signposted), and continue for about 20km. Where the road swings left over a bridge, go straight on to reach the park gate and camp after 1km.

MZUZU

Mzuzu is the largest town in northern Malawi and serves as the transport hub for the region.

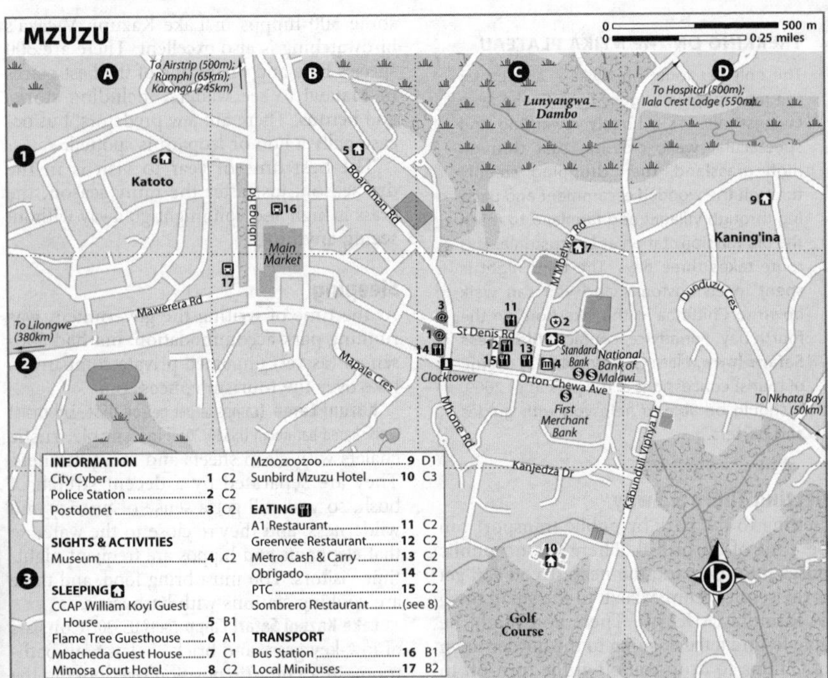

Travellers heading to Nkhata Bay, Nyika, Viphya or to and from Tanzania are likely to spend a pleasant night or two here on the way. Mzuzu feels compact and friendly, the climate is cool and it centres on a long tree-lined avenue. It has banks, shops, a post office, supermarkets, pharmacies, petrol stations and other facilities, which are especially useful if you've come into Malawi from the north.

Internet access is available at **City Cyber** (per 10min MK100; 8am-5pm Mon-Fri, to 4pm Sat) or at **Postdotnet** (per 30min MK200; 8am-5pm Mon-Fri, to 12.30pm Sat), both on Boardman Rd.

Sights & Activities

The **museum** (☎ 01-332071; M'Mbelwa Rd; admission MK100; 7.30am-noon & 1-5pm, tours 9am, 11am, 1.30pm & 2pm) has displays on the people and the land of northern Malawi including the Tumbuka, the Tonga and the Ngoni. If you're planning to go to Livingstonia, there's an interesting exhibition telling the story of the missionaries' journey.

Sleeping

Mzoozoozoo (☎ 0888-864493; campsites MK300, dm MK800, d MK1400) The town's most popular backpacker haunt has a selection of dorms and rooms in timber bungalows and a very lively bar that attracts people who are not even staying there. Good meals are available from around MK700, and it's an excellent place to collect up-to-date information for your onward journey.

CCAP William Koyi Guest House (☎ 01-931961; Boardman Rd; campsites/dm per person MK350/500, r with/without bathroom MK2500/950) Quiet and good value for budget travellers. It's owned by the church so it's generally safe and secure, although there's no booze and you'll have to act in a respectful fashion. Cheap meals are available from MK400 to MK500 and a full English breakfast costs MK250.

Flame Tree Guesthouse (☎ 01-310056, 0999-511423; campsite per person MK500, s/d incl breakfast MK3000/3800) Spotless units are centred around a shady garden and all of them have a little piece of verandah to call their own. The neat lounge has DSTV and a book exchange. If ordered in advance, dinner (meals start at around MK800 and include curries, steak and chips and chicken) can be served on the verandah.

Mbacheda Guest House (M'Mbelwa Rd, s/d with shared bathroom MK750/1500, r MK2500) Basic, cheap and friendly, this place has the added advantage of having a bus station in its grounds. If you're planning a trip to Jo'burg or Harare the Danorarea bus goes from here.

Mimosa Court Hotel (☎ 01-312833/609; s/d MK8000) This is an excellent midrange choice – large bright corridors open up into scrupulously clean bedrooms, with plenty of wardrobe space, funky art on the walls and cheesy lion-print rugs. It's in a great location right in the centre of town, and the welcome is warm.

Sunbird Mzuzu Hotel (☎ 01-332622; www.sunbirdmalawi.com; s/d from US$96/117;) Mzuzu's plushest hotel has rooms with all the trimmings – deep-pile carpets, DSTV, room service. Most are quiet with a view of the town's golf course and the service is friendly and efficient.

Eating

Obrigado (Boardman Rd; snacks/meals from MK50/300; 6am-9pm) Soak up your beer with a mixed plate of samosas and gizzards, or tuck into a plate of offal and chips in this large outdoor cafe and beer garden. Fountains, trees and an enormous zebra statue accompany your meals, and at the weekend it puts on live music.

Greenvee Restaurant (☎ 0888-899666; St Denis St; mains from MK600; 6am-10pm) There's a big verandah from where to watch the street action and a small menu of *nsima*, stews and offal at this friendly little restaurant.

A1 Restaurant (St Denis St; mains around MK900; 11.45am-2pm & 6-10pm; V) A large selection of vegetarian dishes as well as chicken tikka masala and other Indian restaurant standbys are served within these bright purple, red and blue walls.

Sombrero Restaurant (☎ 01-312833/608; meals MK500-900; breakfast, lunch & dinner) The food here has a reputation as some of the best in town and the small sunny terrace and congenial atmosphere make it a fun place for a meal. Steaks, fish and curries are on the menu.

Self-caterers can stock up at the **PTC** (Orton Chewa Ave) or the **Metro Cash & Carry** (M'Mbelwa Rd)

Getting There & Away

AXA City Trouper buses go to Lilongwe daily (MK1200, five hours, 6.30am and 5pm), as do local buses (MK1000, six to seven hours, 7.30am and 6pm). City Trouper buses also go to Karonga, (MK800, four hours, 6.30am and 10am) and local buses leave to Karonga (MK600, five hours, noon) via Rumphi (MK250) and Chitimba (MK540).

Minibuses go to Lilongwe (MK1300, five hours) Nkhata Bay (MK350; one to two hours), Karonga (MK800, three to four hours), Chitimba (MK700, two hours), Rumphi (MK400, one hour), and the Tanzanian border (MK1200, four hours).

National Bus Company has daily departures to Lilongwe (MK1000), Blantyre (MK2000), and Salima (MK1100).

The **Taqwa bus** (☎ 0999-670468), originating in Lilongwe, travels between Mzuzu and Nairobi on Tuesday and Sunday (MK15,000), calling at Songwe for the border (MK1500), Mbeya (MK3500) and Dar es Salaam (MK8000). You should report to the bus station at 11.30pm for a midnight departure. The bus crosses the border at first light, goes through Mbeya in the morning, gets to Dar es Salaam late in the afternoon and leaves for Nairobi the next morning.

Danorarea Tours (☎ 0888-639363) leaves from the forecourt of the Mbacheda Guest House at 7pm on Friday, going to Harare (MK7500) and Jo'burg (MK15,000)

NKHATA BAY

Nkhata Bay has a different feel from its beachside rivals. Get out of town, look back at the houses and lodges crawling up the lush hillside and you could almost be in St Lucia. The centre of gravity is a small town centre, nestled into a gully with the bay to the east and a gentle rise of dense forest to the west. It's a busy clutch of markets, craft stalls, local activity and wandering visitors.

Strung along the coast from the town centre is a collection of lodges, most secreted in small bays, ranging from backpacker party magnets to laid-back clusters of reed huts on the beach.

Information

There's nowhere to change money so make sure you cash up in Mzuzu or Lilongwe. Some of the lodges accept credit cards, US currency and travellers cheques. Internet access is available at **Aqua Africa** (per min MK12; 10am-4pm Mon-Sat) and the **L-Net Internet Cafe** (per min MK8; 7am-5pm Mon-Fri, 8am-12.30pm Sat & Sun).

Dangers & Annoyances

Travellers have been attacked and robbed when walking outside the town centre (especially

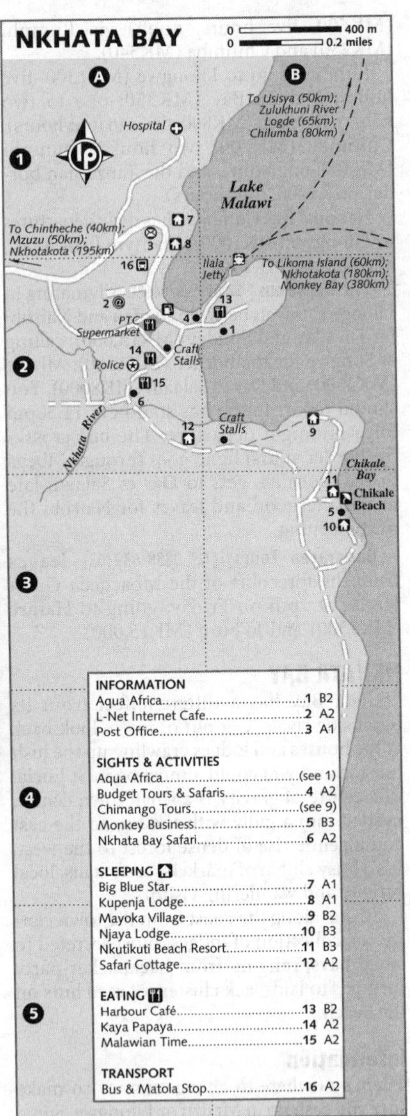

to/from Chikale Beach), so take extra care when walking this route as it can be quite deserted.

Activities

SWIMMING

On the southern side of Nkhata Bay, **Chikale Beach** is a popular spot for swimming and lazing on the sand, especially at weekends. Snorkelling equipment is free for guests at most of the lodges.

KAYAKING

For something more active, both **Monkey Business** (☎ 01-252365) on Chikale Beach, just next to Njaya Lodge, and **Chimango Tours** (☎ 0999-268595) based at Mayoka Village, can organise fully inclusive (meals, kayaks, guides and tents) paddling excursions personally tailored to your needs, anything from a half-day to a few days down the coast.

DIVING

Aqua Africa (☎ 01-352284; www.aquaafrica.co.uk) offers a number of different diving options from five-day PADI Open Water courses for US$310 and casual day dives for US$40 to full-on Dive Master courses for US$500.

Tours

Budget Tours & Safaris (☎ 0999-278903; www.budget-safaris.com) Based at Safari Resthouse; organises well-run and interesting safaris around northern Malawi. A five-day safari to Vwaza Marsh Reserve, Nyika National Park and Livingstonia costs around US$360, including all meals and camping. It can also arrange a 4WD car with driver from US$120 per day.

Nkhata Bay Safari (☎ 0999-265064; daviemzungu@yahoo.co.uk; office 🕒 7am-5pm) Offers tours to Vwaza, Nyika and Livingstonia as well as further afield to Liwonde National Park and the Zomba Plateau. The average cost is US$80 per person per day all-inclusive. They can arrange bus bookings for Tanzania, cabins for the *Ilala* ferry, flights and lodges. If the office in closed, you can also get information about their tours from Njaya Lodge.

Sleeping

Big Blue Star (☎ 01-352316; s.mccombe@googlemail.com; campsite per person US$3, dm/s/d with shared bathroom US$5/10/20) A large, busy and friendly place near the centre of town with a touch of the Caribbean. You can either camp or stay in colourful red, yellow and green striped dorms and reed huts. Social life comes courtesy of the lively bar (yes, they play a lot of reggae), where you can get chatting with one of the many locals who hang out here.

Kupenja Lodge (☎ 0999-284153; campsite per person US$3, s/d US$8/15) This place is quiet and relaxed with less of a party vibe than some of the other lodges but friendly just the same. The stone huts here are pretty basic and not that well soundproofed (you can hear a lot of noise from the town) but they are clean with excellent views and there's a lovely stretch of beach here. The homemade meals are delicious.

Mayoka Village (☎ 01-352421; www.mayokavillage.com; per person campsites/dm/huts US$3/4/5, chalets s/d with shared bathroom US$8/16, chalets s/d US$25/50) Probably the most popular lodge in Nkhata Bay and it's easy to see why. There's a rambling collection of chalets and beach huts, including bathrooms with huge stone baths, and back-to-basics traditional mud-and-reed huts near the water with spotless shared facilities. There isn't a stretch of sand to sunbathe on here, but there are plenty of strategically placed sunbathing spots. Life revolves around the buzzing waterfront bar, which serves excellent food and has been the scene of many a raucous party.

Njaya Lodge (☎ 01-352342; www.njayalodge.com; campsites per person US$7, bandas per person US$12, chalets US$20, family cottages with bathroom per person from US$28) This is the furthest lodge from town and often one of the quietest, but that's no bad thing. A selection of huts and chalets is hidden in lush hillside grounds; best are the beautiful stone rooms right above the waves with a set of stone steps going directly into the water. There's an open restaurant and bar area with Moroccan-style arches, and a terrace overlooking the lake. If you've run out of cash it also accepts credit cards.

Nkutikuti Beach Resort (☎ 01-352286; s/d/tw MK4500/6000/7500) You'll definitely get away from backpackers if you come and stay here. Most of the clientele are on conferences or are Malawians or Tanzanians on holiday. The rooms look like they haven't seen a lick of paint in quite a while, but on the plus side some of them are well located, along a little ridge right above the water.

Safari Cottage (☎ 0999-278903; www.safari-cottage.com; cottage per day US$65) If you can get a group together (or if you want a whole house to yourself) this is a fantastic self-catering option. The cottage sleeps five in three bedrooms, and there's a lounge with TV and stereo, a self-catering kitchen and a big wide verandah with views out over the lake. There's a daily cleaning service, 24-hour security and you can get your laundry done.

Eating & Drinking

Kaya Papaya (mains from MK600; ⏰ 7am-late) It's hard to miss this bright purple place. Downstairs is a little garden with brightly patterned deck chairs to chill out in and upstairs is an expansive open deck where you can order food (served until 9pm) and look down on the day-to-day business of the town. The Thai dishes here make a good alternative to the norm and there's a bar that stays open until the last person leaves.

Harbour Café (light meals from MK600, mains MK900; ⏰ 10am-9pm) Opposite Aqua Africa is this open-air eatery with views of the lake as well as the village streets. It serves tasty breakfasts, burgers and baguettes for lunch and at dinnertime there are daily specials such as lasagne. If you just fancy a snack there are homemade cakes, ice cream and milkshakes.

Malawian Time (plate MK350, set meal incl soup & dessert MK750; ⏰ 8am-6pm) This one is different. You can order plates (a small selection of different dishes on one platter) or larger set meals of beautifully presented Malawian-Japanese food, including croquettes, meatballs with peanuts, and sandwiches. There's an open kitchen at the front of the cafe with a couple of outdoor tables, and the dining room at the back is half restaurant, half cool craft shop.

Getting There & Away

All buses and minibuses depart from the bus stop on the main road. AXA buses run to Mzuzu (MK300, two hours) and minibuses run to Nkhotakota (MK700, five hours), Chintheche (MK300, one hour) and Mzuzu (MK350, one to two hours). To reach Lilongwe, the quickest option is usually to go to Mzuzu and transfer. Many travellers also come or go on the *Ilala* ferry (see p214).

LIKOMA ISLAND

Bobbing in crystalline waters, 17-sq-km Likoma makes an idyllic escape from the 'mainland'. The island is peppered with sublime crescent bays and there are outstanding views out over to the mountain ranges of her nearest neighbour, Mozambique. About 6000 people make their home here, and the island's relative isolation from the rest of Malawi has allowed the locals to maintain their reserved culture, shaped partly by the religious legacy of missionaries, but also by the lack of any transient population. Walk around the island and you might agree that these are the friendliest people in Malawi.

Sights

In Chipyela, the huge Anglican **Cathedral of St Peter**, built by missionaries between 1903 and

1905, should not be missed. You can climb the tower for spectacular views. Nearby, the neat **marketplace** contains a few shops and stalls. Down on the lakeshore is a beach where local boats come and go, and the people wash and sell fish. The *Ilala* stops at another beach about 1km to the south.

Sleeping & Eating

Mango Drift (☎ 0999-746122; mailmangodrift@gmail.com; campsites per person US$3, dm US$5, s/d chalet with shared bathroom US$10/15) Stone, reed and thatched chalets are basic but have nets, power points and lock boxes to stash your valuables. They are spread across a beautiful beach on the western side of the island. There's a bar under a mango tree and clean hot showers.

Kaya Mawa (www.kayamawa.com; full-board chalet per person MK350, single supplement MK150) Chalets are carefully constructed around a rocky bay – there are stone baths, walls made from slabs of existing granite, and rock faces used as shower screens. The lodge was due to close for remodelling at the time of research, to reopen in spring 2010, with refurbished rooms and bathrooms and a watersports centre.

Hot Coconut Bar (mains MK200) A popular spot with locals and they're always happy to chat to tourists when they pop in for a drink.

Getting There & Away

Nyassa Air Taxi (☎ 01-761443; www.nyassa.mw) provides charter flights to Likoma. The more of you there are, the cheaper it is per person. For example, a one-way flight from Lilongwe to Likoma Island ranges from US$320 to US$210 per person depending on how many of you there are.

The *Ilala* ferry (p214) stops at Likoma Island twice a week, usually for three to four hours, so even if you're heading elsewhere you might be able to nip ashore to have a quick look at the cathedral. Check with the captain before you leave the boat.

Heading south, the *Ilala* then sails to Metangula on the Mozambican mainland. Local dhows also sail to Cóbuè for MK250.

CHIZUMULU ISLAND

'Chizzie' is smaller than Likoma (and just a few kilometres away) and even more detached from the mainland. Stretches of lucid azure water and white rocky outcrops give this island a Mediterranean flavour, while the backdrop of dry scrub is positively antipodean. The slow and friendly village activity on the perimeter of idyllic beaches is, however, unmistakably Malawian. If you want to visit both islands, transport links make it best to go to Chizumulu first.

Wakwenda Retreat (campsites/dm US$3/5, r from US$10), smack bang on a postcard-perfect beach, is utter chill-out material. The sizeable bar is constructed around a massive, hollow baobab tree, and the shaded lounge area is often the focus of lazy activity, such as snorkelling (free gear), card games and goat barbecues. The restaurant (meals from MK600) serves food communal-style so it's easy to get to know the other guests.

The *Ilala* ferry (p214) stops right outside Wakwenda Retreat, so even if you're not staying on the island you can pop over for a drink. There are daily dhow ferries between Likoma and Chizumulu costing around MK200 per person. The trip can take anything from one to three hours, depending on the weather.

CENTRAL MALAWI

This small corner of Malawi packs a lot into a small space. Backpacker beach huts, family-friendly resorts and luxury hotels dot the coastline, and just a short drive up from the lake is the Viphya Plateau, a haunting wilderness of mountains, grasslands and mist-shrouded pines. Nkhotakota Wildlife Reserve and Kasungu National Park, both neglected for many years, now have fine lodges and improved access.

This section covers most parts of Malawi's Central Province, with the addition of the Viphya Plateau. Places are described north to south.

VIPHYA PLATEAU

The Viphya Plateau forms the spine of central and northern Malawi, snaking a cool path past flat scrubland, dusty towns and sunny beaches. Tightly knit forests give way to gentle valleys and rivers, and huge granite domes rise softly from the earth like sleeping beasts. Indigenous woodland bristles with birds and wildflowers, and antelope and monkeys are often spotted darting through the trees.

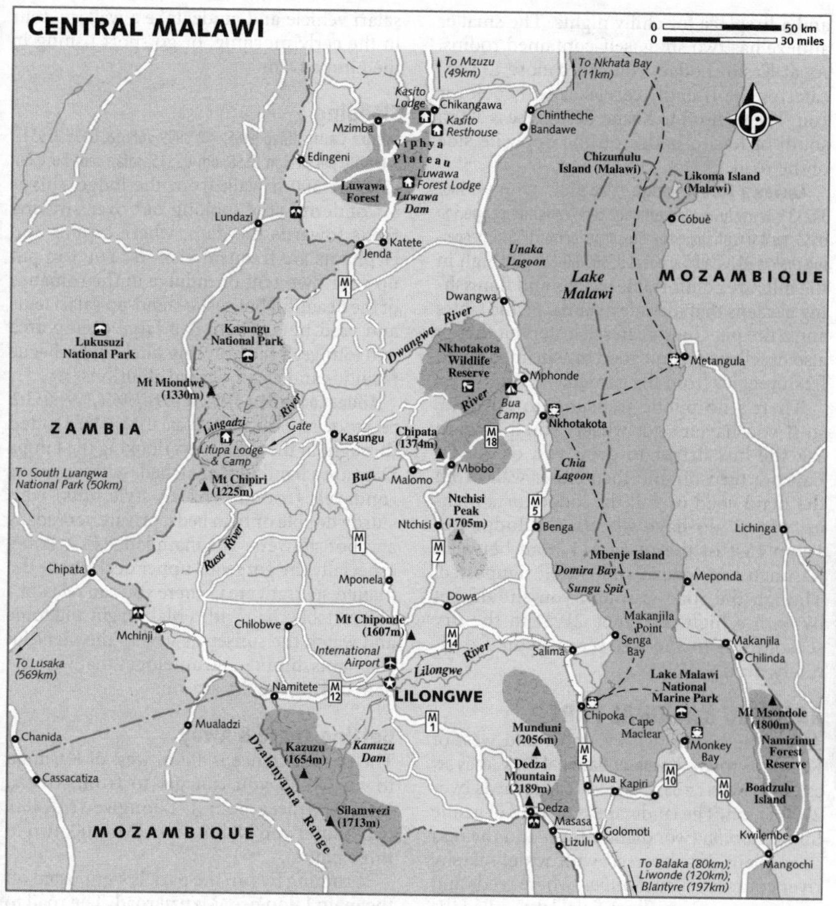

If you want to stay for a few days there are a few peaceful forest lodges. Activity junkies should head for Luwawa Forest Lodge (p186), where activities organised on the plateau include rock climbing/mountain biking (half-day US40/18 per person).

Sleeping

Kasito Lodge (Map p185; ☎ 0888-757342; per bed MK800) There's a cosy communal lounge here and a number of sleeping options – you can hire a bed in a room dormitory-style, rent a room in its entirety or even rent out the whole lodge. You'll have to bring all your provisions as there is no food available, but there's a resident housekeeper who can cook for you if you choose. The main asset here is the terraced garden where you can picnic or barbecue while taking in stunning views.

To reach Kasito by car from the south, you continue 27km beyond the Mzimba junction on the main sealed road towards Mzuzu; the lodge is signposted on your left. Coming from the north, you pass a large wood factory at Chikangawa village, and the turn-off to the lodge is a few kilometres beyond here on the right. If you're travelling by bus, ask the driver to drop you at the junction. Kasito Lodge is less than 1km from here.

Kasito Resthouse (Map p185; ☎ 0888-757342; s/d MK700/1400, whole house MK4200) There are two charming bungalows here, 50m off the main road. The largest has very clean, well-kept rooms, a kitchen with a wood-burning stove and a fireplace for chilly nights. The smaller annexe has two snug, self-contained rooms. As at Kasito Lodge, you can choose to self-cater or the friendly caretaker will cook for you. The turn-off to Kasito Resthouse is 200m south of Kasito Lodge on the opposite side of the road.

Luwawa Forest Lodge (Map p185; ☎ 01-991106/342333; www.luwawaforestlodge.com; campsite per person US$5, tw & tr with shared bathroom per person US$35, per person chalets B&B/half/full board US$60/80/85) Set high in the hills are comfortable chalets and flourishing gardens that include a sauna, picnic tables and a fire pit. Guests can self-cater but there's also excellent organic food on-site made with fresh veggies from the garden.

There's no public transport to Luwawa, so if you haven't got wheels you'll have to ask the bus driver to drop you off at the Luwawa turn-off and then either walk from the main road or call the lodge for a pick-up. If you do have wheels, the lodge lies 10km east of the main M1 road between Kasungu and Mzuzu and is well signposted. Though the road is rough you should get by with a high-clearance 2WD in the dry season, but in the wet season you'll definitely need a 4WD.

KASUNGU NATIONAL PARK

Along the border with Zambia and west of Kasungu town, **Kasungu National Park** (entry per person US$5 & per car US$2; 🕑 6am-6pm) sprawls over 2100 sq km. The landscape is formed of gentle hills, *miombo* (woodland), bush and the odd open plain, interspersed with wide, marshy river courses called *dambos*, where reeds and grasses grow. A small artificial lake, called the Lifupa Dam, sits at the park's centre.

Poachers have hit the part severely over the past few decades, particularly during the 1980s and '90s, reducing the once-prolific wildlife to a trickle. Only 150 or so elephants remain in the park, once famous for its elephants. Predators are present in the park but you've a better chance of seeing hyenas, leopards or servals than lions. If you're staying overnight at the lodge or camp you may well see hippos in the lake and you'll certainly hear them at night. Birdwatchers will be well rewarded – over 300 species include water, woodland and grassland species.

All activities in the park revolve around Lifupa Lodge and Camp. You can arrange for a guide to accompany you in your car, rent a safari vehicle and guide, take a walking tour in the early morning, or go sport fishing in the Lifupa Dam.

Sleeping

Lifupa Camp (Map p185; ☎ 0999-768658, 0999 925512; campsite per person US$8, dm US$15, safari tent/bush hut US$25) A 500m walk from the lodge, this is a wonderful spot looking out over swaying reeds towards the dam, where hippos and elephants are frequent visitors. You can put up your own tent or indulge in the romance of the beautiful but rustic stand-up safari tents and reed huts. There is a large dining area and lounge, a self-catering kitchen, barbecue facilities and clean, shared ablutions.

Lifupa Lodge (Map p185; ☎ 0999-768658, 0999 925512; per person incl breakfast/full board US$80/110) Dotted throughout the grasses overlooking the Lifupa Dam are a handful of thatched, self-contained rondavels (round, African-style huts) with sturdy double or twin beds, private verandahs and hot showers. The main lodge is striking, especially the gorgeous upper deck above the main restaurant area, where you can relax in a comfortable chair with a Malawi gin and tonic and watch the sunset, as well as the plentiful elephants, hippos and antelopes that visit the dam during the dry season.

Getting There & Away

The park entrance is 40km west of Kasungu town, which you can get to from Mzuzu (MK550, three hours), Lilongwe (MK480, two hours) and Nkhotakota (MK500, two to three hours).

If coming by car, the park is signposted off the main Lilongwe–Mzuzu road. The road to the entrance is mostly good-quality dirt road. From the entrance, it's 21km by the shortest route to Lifupa Lodge, for which you'll need a high-clearance car. There's no public transport to the park, so without a car you'd have to hitch from Kasungu – the best place to wait is the turn-off to the park (signposted) near the petrol station on the main road.

NKHOTAKOTA

Though it may seem dull and unassuming, Nkhotakota has a significant and sinister place in Malawi's history. In the 1800s the town was home to a huge slave market, from where thousands of unfortunate captives were shipped annually across the lake to Tanzania, before being forced to march to the coast.

Buses and minibuses stop and pick up from the fuel station on the main north–south road. You can get online at the **Nkhotakota Internet Café** (☎ 01-292284; per min MK8; 7.30am-4.30pm Mon-Fri, 8am-6pm Sat, 2pm-6pm Sun).

our pick **Stima Inn** (☎ 0999-260005; www.sanibeachresort.com, mwstars@absamail.co.za; dm per person MK1000, s MK1000-4200, d MK3500-8400), within convenient staggering distance of the *Ilala* ferry, is the best place to stay in town. From the outside the building looks like part of an old ocean liner, with a couple of old car parts thrown in for good measure. The beautiful interior – with its central courtyard lounge open to the lake breezes and quirky nautical touches – is like a cross between a Moroccan *riad* and an old tugboat. Gorgeous rooms are brightened up with warm patterned rugs and sequinned cushions.

Getting There & Away

You can get to Nkhotakota by the *Ilala* ferry (p214). AXA buses go to and from Lilongwe (MK610, three hours). The bus will drop you off roughly outside Nkhotakota's Shell petrol station, which is on the highway. Minibuses also leave from here and go to Salima (MK350, two hours) and Nkhata Bay (MK700, four to five hours).

NKHOTAKOTA WILDLIFE RESERVE

Nkhotakota Wildlife Reserve (entry fees US$5 per person & per car US$2; 6am-6pm) lies west of the main lakeshore road. It's 1800 sq km of rough, somewhat inhospitable terrain and few navigable roads. There's a healthy elephant population, though, as well as roan and sable antelope, buffalo, baboons, waterbucks and even a few lions and leopards – it's just that wildlife can be difficult to spot because of the dense vegetation. More than 200 species of bird include palm-nut vultures, kingfishers and ground hornbills. The Bua River is excellent for salmon fishing.

The Department of National Parks & Wildlife is doing a lot to improve the park's infrastructure and discourage poaching. It has acquired new vehicles for its antipoaching scouts and in 2009 put forward four concessions for ecotourism development, the first of which has been awarded. There are also long-term plans to reintroduce wildlife species that have disappeared over the years, such as black rhino, and to boost existing populations of elephants, buffalo and zebras.

Sleeping

At the time of research there were two basic campsites in the park, the best of which was Bua Camp in a clearing on the banks of the stunning, rocky Bua River. All the facilities at Nkhotakota Wildlife Reserve are being upgraded, however. The first of the park's ecoconcessions was awarded in an area known as Tongole in early 2009, and an upmarket ecolodge – to be called the **Tongole Wilderness Lodge** (www.tongole.com) – was set to open early in 2010.

Getting there & Away

The turn-off to Bua is 10km north of Nkhotakota town, followed by a rough dirt track. You will need your own wheels to get here. You could also enter the park from the south via the very potholed Nkhotakota–Kasungu road.

SENGA BAY

Sitting at the eastern end of a broad peninsula that juts into the lake from Salima, Senga Bay is the closest beach resort to the capital, filling up with city types on balmy weekends. It has pretty beaches and a range of accommodation to suit all budgets. However, the town is lacking a real heart and resorts are spread over a distance of about 10km, so without wheels you'll need to make use of local bicycle taxis.

Dangers & Annoyances

Some of the beaches here are flat and reedy – perfect conditions for bilharzia (see p773), so get advice from your hotel or lodge to see if it's safe.

Many travellers have complained about persistent hassling from local youths, all wanting to sell souvenirs or arrange boat rides. Be polite and firm in your dealings and you should be OK.

Sights & Activities

Trips to nearby **Lizard Island** to see its population of giant monitor lizards and its cormorant colony are popular. Many lodges and local guides can arrange this and it should cost about US$30. Alternatively, from Senga Bay town, you can go hiking in the nearby Senga Hills. There are a few trails but nothing well established, so they can be hard to follow if the grass is long – it's best to hire a local guide from your hotel to show you the way.

About 10km south of Senga Bay is **Stewart Grant's Tropical Fish Farm** (☎ /fax 01-263165), which breeds and exports cichlids. If you're genuinely interested you can take a half-hour tour of the farm.

Sleeping

Tom's (☎ 01-263017; campsites per person MK500; r MK2000) A vast, shady campsite with spotless showers and toilets, hot water and a barbecue pit. For those who don't fancy being under canvas it also has a few cheap backpacker rooms. On site is Tom's Bar and a small boutique–workshop where you can get your hands on clothes made from traditional Malawian fabric.

Wamwai Beach Lodge (☎ 0888-709999; campsite per person MK300; dm per person MK1500, d & tw MK4500) The wide verandah that wraps around this charming bungalow is a fantastic spot to chill and look out at the fishing boats from the local village. Inside are several homely rooms, a fantastic, airy dorm and a dining room – all decked out in plenty of wood and bright local fabrics. Food here is a treat. As well as substantial mains such as chicken curry (MK1300), the baking-enthusiast owner whips up fresh goodies daily. A PADI school was being set up at the time of research.

Steps Campsite (campsite per person MK1000) This fantastic spot combines beautiful views and a clean white sandy beach with excellent facilities – there's a volleyball pitch, very clean, hot showers, individual power points and round the clock security. A raised, circular bar provides the focal point for the campsite and makes a lovely spot for sundowners. Should you get hungry, you can order meals from the Livingstonia Beach Hotel next door.

our pick **Safari Beach Lodge** (☎ 01-263143, 0999-365494; www.safaribeachlodge.net; s/d MK11,900/16,100;) . It all starts off well – there are large modern rooms with TV and air-con in the main building, as well as a great restaurant and a large verandah with comfy cane chairs – but the best is yet to come. A quick scramble up the hill reveals a row of gorgeous stone huts perching cliffside. They all have wide balconies overlooking the lake, simple interiors and separate, open-air bamboo-and-rock showers (watch out for the soap-stealing baboons). Follow a path down to a private beach where you'll find kayaks and snorkels and a swing for two – it's a perfect spot for the regular Saturday barbecues. The lodge is 1km off the main road; turn off just before the gates to the Sunbird Livingstonia Beach Hotel.

Sunbird Livingstonia Beach Hotel (☎ 01-263222/444; www.sunbirdmalawi.com; s/d from US$107/129;) Built back in the 1920s, this was once a favourite haunt for fancy colonial balls and banquets before falling into disrepair and disrepute. These days it's pristine and gorgeous, and once again injects a touch of glamour into Senga Bay. A vast selection of rooms and chalets sits along a perfect stretch of beach that is only broken up by the occasional perfectly coordinated beach lounge.

Eating & Drinking

Tom's Bar (🕒 8am-late) A popular little spot with both locals and visitors for a cold beer. It closes when the last person leaves.

Red Zebra Cafe (mains MK850-1200, waffles MK450; 🕒 7am-10.30pm) Black-and-white pictures of rock legends and an eclectic soundtrack of chilled summer tunes set the scene here, and if you tire of lounging on the beach, a table on the verandah of this vibey cafe is a good alternative. Daily offerings are scribbled on the blackboard and include grills, stews, curries and waffles. Things kick off on weekend evenings and live bands occasionally put in an appearance.

Getting There & Away

First get to Salima. To reach Salima from Lilongwe, it's easiest to take a minibus (MK450, one hour). There are also minibuses to Nkhata Bay (MK900, six to seven hours) and Mzuzu (MK1000, seven to eight hours). From Salima, local pick-ups run to Senga Bay (MK200), dropping you in the main street. If you're travelling to/from Cape Maclear, consider chartering a boat; it's not too expensive (around US$180) if you get a group together, it's good fun and it saves one hell of a trip on the bus.

MONKEY BAY

This small town is a port and ship-repair centre hidden behind the Cape Maclear headland. The town itself isn't particularly interesting but there are a couple of good places to stay should you end up here for a night or two. And you might well do if travelling by the *Ilala* ferry. Monkey Bay also has a market and a PTC supermarket but no ATM or money exchange.

MUA MISSION

Midway between Salima and Balaka, Mua is a small town that's famous for a not-so-small mission. Built at the beginning of the 20th century by Catholic 'White Fathers', Mua Mission houses a school, a hospital and the fascinating **Kungoni Centre** (☎ 01-262706; www.kungoni.org; 7.30am-4pm Mon-Sat), an important focal point for cultural information and training.

The main attraction is the **Chamare Museum**, which has three exhibition rooms concentrating on the region's three main cultural groups (Chewa, Ngoni and Yao) and their approach to traditional beliefs. A guide is included in the entrance fee of MK900; the tour takes at least an hour.

For overnight stays there's a selection of themed chalets a short walk up the hill from the mission itself.

Sleeping

Mufasa Rustic Camp (☎ 0999 258959; campsite per person MK450) At just 400m from the harbour, this newly opened beautiful beach spot is sure to be popular with backpackers. It is basic, hence the name, but offers hot showers, camping and rooms, though it is electricity-free. The owners will arrange pick-ups from the *Ilala* ferry by *túk-túk* and they also plan to do boat transfers to Cape Maclear.

Venice Beach Backpackers (campsite per person MK500, dm MK1120, s/d with shared bathroom MK2400/3200, r MK4000) This place, about 1.5km from the main road, is a worthy alternative to the lodges at Cape Maclear. There's a very clean stretch of beach, a chilled beach bar and a two-storey thatched building housing a selection of dorms and doubles as well as a top-floor viewing deck with plenty of hammocks.

Getting There & Away

From Lilongwe, AXA buses go to Monkey Bay, usually via Mua and the southern lakeshore (MK1000, four hours, one daily). From Lilongwe you're probably better off going by minibus to Salima (MK450, one hour), from where you might find a minibus or *matola* going direct to Monkey Bay.

It's much easier to reach Monkey Bay from Blantyre on the ordinary bus that travels via Liwonde and Mangochi (MK890, five to six hours, one daily). A quicker option is to go by minibus (MK1000, four to five hours), but you'll need to leave early in the morning and you might have to change at Mangochi.

Many travellers also use the *Ilala* ferry (p214) to travel up and down the country to or from Monkey Bay.

From Monkey Bay a *matola* ride to Cape Maclear should cost MK300. Although not far away, it can forever to get there and you could have to wait hours for a *matola* departure.

CAPE MACLEAR

A long piece of golden beach shielded by granite hills and thick green bush, Cape Maclear sits on a finger of land at the southern end of Lake Malawi, with the alluring Domwe and Thumbi Islands bobbing offshore in a glassy blue bay. It's one of Southern Africa's legendary backpacker hang-outs and the kind of place where plans are forgotten as you sink into a daily rhythm of sunbathing, snorkelling and hanging out in the local village. There are plenty of options here to keep all sorts happy – from reed huts and tents on the beach to upmarket lodges serving fine French cuisine.

Information

The **Billy Riordan Clinic** (regular fee MK8500; minor complaints 8am-noon & 2-4pm Mon-Fri, emergency 10am-noon & 3-4pm Sat & Sun) dispenses bilharzia medicine daily at 4.30pm for MK3000.

Skyband has come to Cape Maclear so most of the lodges have wi-fi and many will lend you a laptop to check your mail.

Dangers & Annoyances

Scams to watch out for at Cape Maclear include the boys who take money in advance for a boat ride or barbecue and then disappear, or who take you on a boat then go through your day pack while you're snorkelling. More serious robberies do occasionally happen on the beach or surrounding hills; violence is very unlikely, but don't carry anything valuable.

Sights

Much of the area around Cape Maclear, including several offshore islands, is part of **Lake Malawi National Park** (entry per person US$5 & per car US$1), one

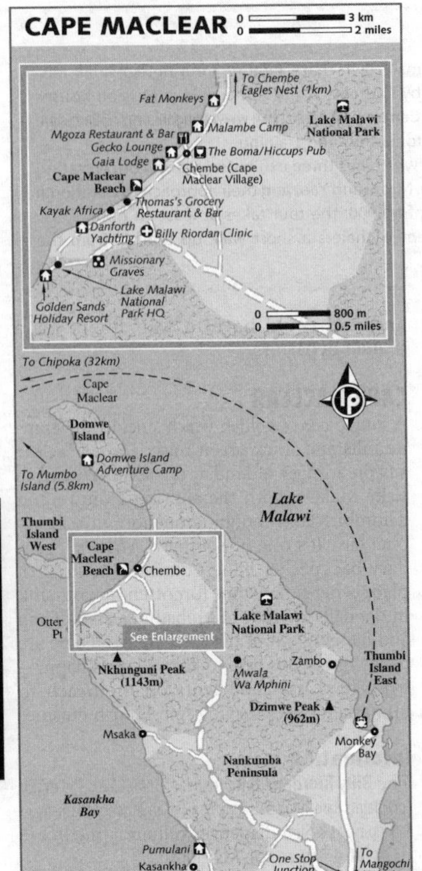

of the few freshwater aquatic parks in Africa, and designated a Unesco World Heritage Site in 1986. The park headquarters are just inside the gate along with a **visitors centre** that doubles up as a small **museum and aquarium** (🕒 7.30am-noon & 1pm-5pm Mon-Sat, 10am-noon & 1-4pm Sun).

Just before the entrance gate to the national park is a sign pointing to a path that leads towards the hills overlooking the bay. A few hundred metres up here is a small group of **missionary graves**, marking the last resting place of the missionaries who attempted to establish the first Livingstonia Mission here in 1875.

Activities

The **Cape Maclear Tour Guides Association** is a membership organisation for the area's guides. Its aim is to make sure that business is fairly distributed among registered guides and that tourists are not hassled by touts. All registered guides work to a set price list, and your accommodation should be able to arrange a guide for any activities you wish to do.

WATER SPORTS

Guides registered with the Cape Maclear Tour Guides Association can organise a number of half- and full-day trips involving snorkelling. For example, trips to Thumbi Island will cost around US$30 per person including food, snorkel hire, park fees and fish-eagle feeding.

If you prefer to go snorkelling on your own, many places rent gear (rates start at about US$5). Otter Point, less than 1km beyond Golden Sands, is a small rocky peninsula and nearby islet that is popular with snorkellers and even more so with fish.

For diving, go to **Kayak Africa** (☎ 0999-942661; www.kayakafrica.net) or Danforth Yachting (opposite). Both offer PADI Open Water courses for around US$300, as well as casual dives for experienced divers.

Guides registered with the Cape Maclear Tour Guides Association can arrange a number of boat trips, including Thumbi Island and Otter Point from US$25 per person. Several of the lodges rent out kayaks.

HIKING

There's a good range of hikes and walks in the hills that form a horseshoe around the plain behind the village and the beach. You can go alone (see p189) or arrange a guide, either from the village, your lodge or at the national park headquarters. The park's rate for a guide is US$10 to US$15 per person for a full-day trip. A popular option is to head through woodland to a col below **Nkhunguni Peak**, the highest on the Nankumba Peninsula, with great views over Cape Maclear, the lake and surrounding islands. The path starts by the missionary graves. It's six hours return to the summit; plenty of water and a good sun hat are essential.

Sleeping

Golden Sands Holiday Resort (campsite per person MK500, 1-/2-/3-person rondavels MK800/900/1000) Built at the turn of the 20th century, Golden Sands was subsequently given to Queen Elizabeth as a gift and remained regularly in use until it was left to rot after independence. Now accommodation consists of camping or run-down rondavels in the grounds. The main advantage of staying here is that it's quiet and away from the bustle of the village, but you have to be prepared to rough it. Golden Sands sits at the far western end of the beach, a little past Lake Malawi National Park Headquarters. You will have to pay park fees to stay here because it is inside the park.

Malambe Camp (☎ 0999-258959; campsite per person MK450, dm MK700, standing tent MK800, hut MK1000). Choose from simple huts constructed from reed mats, permanent tents (with proper beds inside) or a large, light reed dorm. There's also space for camping, spotless showers and toilets, a self-catering kitchen, barbecues and a bar.

Fat Monkeys (d MK3500, dm MK1000, campsite per person MK500; 💻 📶) This is a rambling spot about 1km east of the village centre. There's a dorm, spacious and airy double rooms, a massive camping area with plenty of parking and a large bar right by the water. It's a lively place and popular with car campers.

Gaia House (☎ 0999-374631; www.gaia-house.com; campsites US$3.50, dm US$10, r US$23, f US$40; 💻 📶) Another top budget choice, with neat twins, doubles and dorms grouped around a cosy courtyard restaurant. The restaurant serves burgers, pancakes, breakfasts and toasties (meals around MK800), and there are hammocks to swing in and a thatched chill-out area right on the water. You can hire bikes for US$10 a day.

our pick **Gecko Lounge** (☎ 01-599188, 0999-787322; www.geckolounge.net; dm US$10, d US$55, self-catering chalet US$80; 💻 📶) Gecko is one of the best places to stay in Cape Maclear and has grown considerably over the past couple of years. Jaunty orange thatched huts contain a dorm, double rooms and self-catering units, all with solid beds, fans, nets and wooden lock boxes that are large enough to stash all your valuables and more. Hammocks and cane pods swing from the trees, and there's an attractive bar–lounge right on the water that hosts regular parties and live music. You can hire a laptop to check your emails (MK200 for 30 minutes), rent kayaks and snorkelling gear or hire DVD players and DVDs to watch in the comfort of your own room.

Danforth Yachting (☎ 0999-960077/960770; www.danforthyachting.com; full board per person US$125; 💻 📶). Come here for glamour, nautical-style. Nights are spent in seriously sexy rooms decked out in maritime shades of blue and green, and days can be spent making like a millionaire on the swanky yacht *Mufasa*, or perhaps enjoying a spot of champagne in the infinity pool. There's also a bar, restaurant and outdoor lounge area in front of a stretch of rich grass with prime views of the lake.

our pick **Kayak Africa** (☎ in South Africa 021-783 1955; www.kayakafrica.net) owns two incredibly romantic lodges just offshore from Cape Maclear on deserted Domwe and Mumbo Islands. **Domwe Island Adventure Camp** (per person incl kayak & snorkelling gear US$50) is the smaller and most rustic of the two. It's self-catering with furnished safari tents sharing eco-showers and toilets, as well as a bar and a beautiful staggered dining area, open to the elements and set among boulders. **Mumbo Camp** (per person incl meals, kayak & snorkelling gear US$180) has walk-in tents with bathrooms on wooden platforms, tucked beneath trees and above rocks, with spacious decks and astounding views.

Eating & Drinking

Beach barbecues arranged by local guides are popular with travellers. A chicken or fish barbecue accompanied by drummers costs around US$10 per person and can be arranged by your lodge or just asking around the village.

Thomas's Grocery Restaurant & Bar (dishes from MK400) The place to come for local food. Meals are the usual fish or chicken and chips or *nsima* with the odd nod to backpackers in the way of pasta and burgers. Seating is outdoors and a suitable place to watch the village go by.

Mgoza Restaurant & Bar (dishes MK700-1000; 🕑 10am-late) Come here for a relaxed beer or a cocktail. The inside bar has slinky, low, Moroccan-style seating and a picture window looking out towards the lake. Outside are a number of cosy seats in the grass and upstairs there's a viewing deck perfect for sundowners. It also serves bar meals.

Boma/Hiccups Pub (dishes MK700-1000; 🕑 noon-late). Sit in a window seat or at tables out on the street to watch the village action, enjoy tasty food in the courtyard restaurant at the back, or pull up a bar stool at the English-style bar (look out for the pirate-themed quotations). There's also a DJ booth up in the eaves and a 1st-floor dance floor that gets packed at the weekends.

Getting There & Away

By public transport, first get to Monkey Bay, from where a *matola* should cost MK300. If you're driving from Mangochi, the dirt road to Cape Maclear (signposted) turns west off the main road, about 5km before Monkey Bay. Be warned, however: it's a bumpy ride and, unless you're in a 4WD or high-clearance vehicle, it'll be slow going.

From Cape Maclear, if you're heading for Senga Bay ask around about chartering a boat. It will cost around US$180, but it's not bad when split between four to six people and much better than the long, hard bus ride. *Matola* leave for Monkey Bay from around 6am in the morning on a fill-up-and-go basis and take about an hour (MK300). From there you can get onward transport.

SOUTHERN MALAWI

This is the most developed and densely populated part of Malawi, home to the country's commercial capital and two of its major industries – sugar and tea. Southern Malawi also receives the highest proportion of foreign visitors, drawn by the chance to scale mountains and watch wildlife in an incredibly beautiful and diverse landscape. Places in this section are described roughly north to south.

LIWONDE

Straddling the Shire River, the small town of Liwonde is one of the gateways to Liwonde National Park. The river divides the town in two; to the east you'll find the main bus stations, the market, supermarkets and the train station. West of the river are several tourist lodges.

Sleeping

Shire Camp (☎ 0884-327794; campsite per person MK1000, chalet incl breakfast MK3500) An excellent budget choice with a fabulous setting bang on the river. You can either pitch a tent on the campsite or bed down in one of the kooky thatched chalets. There's an open-air restaurant (meals from MK300), with tables lined up mere feet from the river. Shire Camp is on the river's north bank. Take the dirt road on the right just before the National Bank.

Hippo View Lodge (☎ 01-542822/255; www.hippoviewlodge.com; superior s/d MK8900/13,800, VIP s/d MK11,400/17,300, f chalet MK35,000; (P) (✈) (💻) (📶)) Turn right down the dirt road just before the National Bank and look out for the two hippos flanking the road just before the entrance. Set in sprawling grounds next to the river, this is the classiest and best-equipped joint in town. All of the rooms are large, with air-con, DSTV, tea and coffee facilities and small seating areas. Should you wish to get out on the water, a wide range of boat trips is available.

Getting There & Away

Lakeshore AXA buses pass by Liwonde on their way up to Mangochi, but most drop off passengers at the turn-off and not in the town itself, so you're better off using a minibus; they run regularly from Zomba (MK250, 45 minutes), Limbe (MK500, three hours) and Mangochi (MK450, two hours). You can also get a minibus to the Mozambique border at Nayuchi (MK850).

LIWONDE NATIONAL PARK

Though small in stature, **Liwonde National Park** (entry US$5 & cars US$2) tops the list in visitor numbers and is Malawi's number-one wildlife destination. It can't rival the parks of neighbouring Zambia for big-game excitement, but Liwonde is still a beautiful and exciting place to visit.

The Shire River dominates the 548-sq-km park – a wide, meandering stretch lined by thick undergrowth and tall, statuesque palms. Surrounding it are floodplains, woodland and parched scrub. Unsurprising then, that the park is prime hippo- and croc-spotting territory, and you shouldn't let a trip here pass you by without canoeing on the river. Waterbucks are also common near the water, while beautiful sable and roan antelopes, zebras and elands populate the surreal flood plains in the east. Night drives can reveal spotted genets, bushbabies, scrub hares, side-striped jackals and even spotted hyenas. The main event here though is elephants – there are over 600 in Liwonde.

The combination of rich riverine, mopane and grassland habitats means that bird life here is varied, with more than 400 of Malawi's 650 species here including Pel's fishing owl, African skimmer and brown-breasted barbet.

Activities

If you have your own 4WD or high-clearance vehicle you can tour the park's

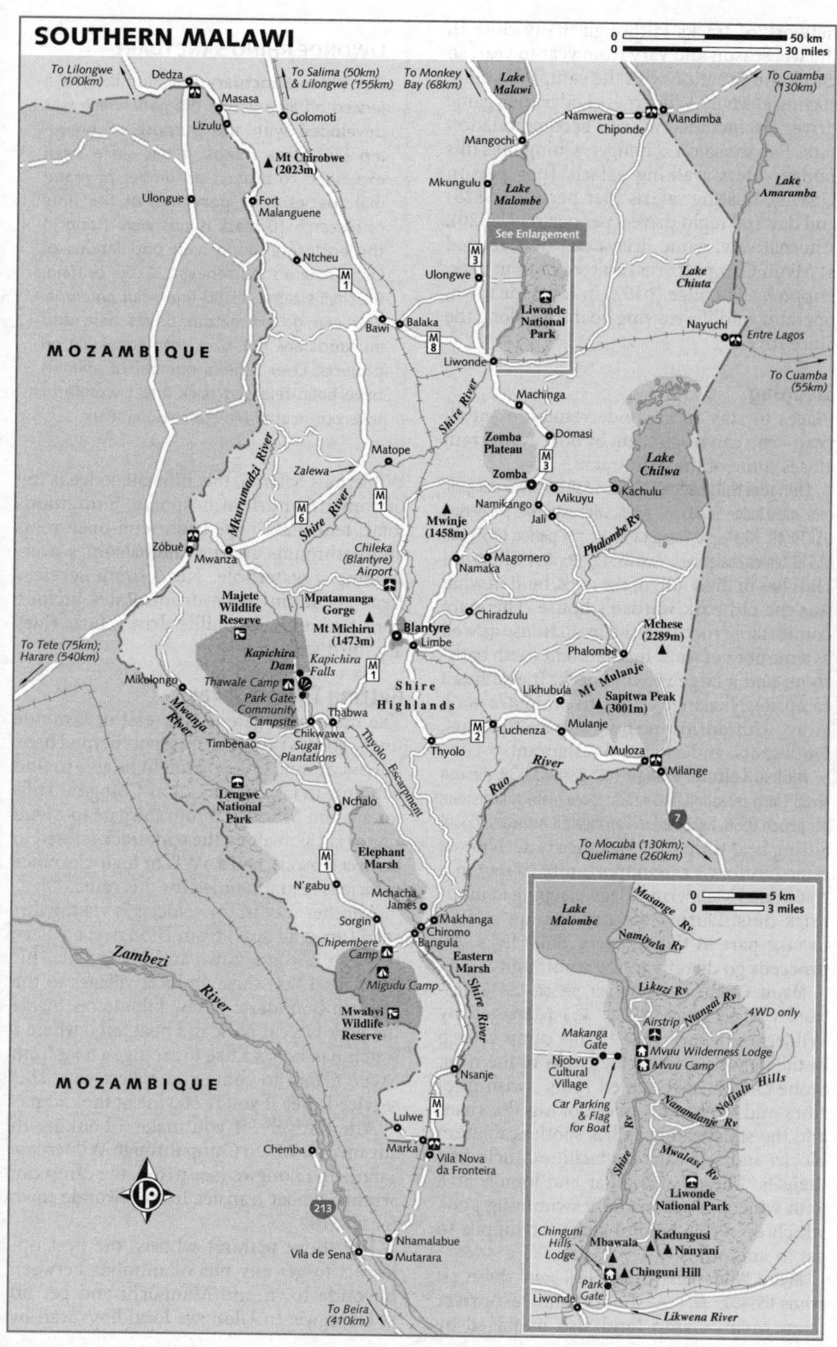
SOUTHERN MALAWI
0 50 km
0 30 miles
To Lilongwe (100km)
Dedza
Masasa
Lizulu
Golomoti
To Salima (50km) & Lilongwe (155km)
To Monkey Bay (68km)
Lake Malawi
To Cuamba (130km)
Namwera
Chiponde
Mandimba
Mangochi
Mt Chirobwe (2023m)
Mkungulu
Lake Malombe
Lake Amaramba
Ulongue
Fort Malanguene
See Enlargement
Ntcheu
Ulongwe
Liwonde National Park
Lake Chiuta
Bawi
Balaka
Nayuchi
Entre Lagos
MOZAMBIQUE
Liwonde
To Cuamba (55km)
Machinga
Shire River
Domasi
Zomba Plateau
Mkurumadzi River
Matope
Lake Chilwa
Zalewa
Zomba
Kachulu
Mikuyu
Namikango
Jali
Shire River
Mwinje (1458m)
Phalombe Rv
Zóbuè
Mwanza
Chileka (Blantyre) Airport
Magornero
Namaka
Majete Wildlife Reserve
Mpatamanga Gorge
Mt Michiru (1473m)
Chiradzulu
Mchese (2289m)
Blantyre
Limbe
To Tete (75km); Harare (540km)
Kapichira Dam
Kapichira Falls
Phalombe
Mikolongo
Thawale Camp
Park Gate; Community Campsite
Shire Highlands
Likhubula
Mt Mulanje
Sapitwa Peak (3001m)
Mwanja River
Thabwa
Chikwawa
Mulanje
Timbenao
Luchenza
Thyolo
Sugar Plantations
Thyolo Escarpment
River
Muloza
Milange
Ruo
Lengwe National Park
Nchalo
Elephant Marsh
To Mocuba (130km); Quelimane (260km)
N'gabu
Mchacha James
Sorgin
Makhanga
Chiromo
Bangula
Chipembere Camp
Eastern Marsh
Zambezi
River
Migudu Camp
Mwabvi Wildlife Reserve
Shire River
Nsanje
MOZAMBIQUE
Lulwe
Marka
Chemba
Vila Nova da Fronteira
Nhamalabue
Vila de Sena
Mutarara
To Beira (410km)
0 5 km
0 3 miles
Lake Malombe
Masange Rv
Namivala Rv
Likuzi Rv
Ntangai Rv
4WD only
Airstrip
Makanga Gate
Njobvu Cultural Village
Mvuu Wilderness Lodge
Mvuu Camp
Car Parking & Flag for Boat
Nafiulu Hills
Nanandanje Rv
Shire Rv
Mwalasi Rv
Liwonde National Park
Chinguni Hills Lodge
Mbawala
Kadungusi
Nanyani
Chinguni Hill
Park Gate
Liwonde
Likwena River
MALAWI

network of tracks (although many close in the wet season and vary from year to year, so check the situation with the camp). If you're staying at Mvuu Wilderness Lodge then game drives are included in your accommodation rate. For those on a budget, Chinguni Hills Lodge offers walking safaris (per person US$15), boating safaris (per person US$25) and day and night drives (per person US$20). Alternatively, game drives can be arranged at Mvuu Camp. If you can't stay in the park, Hippo View Lodge (p192) in Liwonde town, operates wildlife-viewing boat trips along the Shire River.

Sleeping

Places to stay in Liwonde remain open all year – you can reach them by boat even if rain closes some of the park tracks.

Chinguni Hills Lodge (☎ 0888-838159; www.chinguni.com; main lodge dm US$20, r/tent with bathroom per person US$30/40; Nkalango Camp campsite per person US$5, dm US$10, tented chalet per person US$15; Ⓟ) Chinguni Hills lies in the south of the park, built in what was the old park warden's house. There are comfortable rooms in the main house as well as a number of walk-in safari tents with bathroom and a large viewing deck. It also has a campsite, Nkalango Camp, five minutes' walk away, with dorms, plenty of space for tents, *braai* spots, and a bar and restaurant.

Njobvu Cultural Village (☎ 0888-623530, through Mvuu Camp reception 01-542135; www.njobvuvillage.com; per person US$6, full board incl all meals & activities US$30) Sitting near the park's Makanga Gate, Njobvu offers visitors a rare opportunity to stay in a traditional Malawian village, sleeping in mud-brick huts. During the day you are invited to take part in the villagers' daily lives. All proceeds go directly to the community.

Mvuu Camp (campsite per person US$10, full-board chalet per person US$250;) Managed by Wilderness Safaris (p169), this camp is deep in the park's north on the banks of the river. Stone chalets have tented roofs, swish interiors and verandahs overlooking the river, and the small campsite has spotless ablution blocks and self-catering facilities, including utensils. There's also a bar and lounge area with wide lake views and a swimming pool, which even has helpful steps for hippos to get in and out.

Mvuu Wilderness Lodge (full-board chalets per person US$400;) A short distance upriver from Mvuu Camp (and also managed by Wilderness Safaris), this intimate lodge is full of romantic bush atmosphere. Sumptuous safari tents have huge beds, semi-open roofs and bathrooms and private balconies overlooking a waterhole. Need room service? Beat on the in-room drum. Rates include park fees and all wildlife drives, boat rides and bird walks.

LIWONDE RHINO SANCTUARY

The **Rhino Sanctuary** (admission US$3) is a fenced-off area within the park which was developed with the purpose of breeding rare black rhinos. It has since been expanded to protect a number of mammal species from poaching. At the time of research 10 black rhinos were living in the enclosure along with populations of Lichtenstein's hartebeest, Cape buffalo, Burchell's zebra, eland and roan antelope. You can go on nature drives here and all funds are put back into conservation projects. Over time, a number of animals have been released back into Liwonde or taken to nearby Majete National Park.

Getting There & Away

The main park gate is 6km east of Liwonde town. There's no public transport beyond here, but ask around and you might be able to find a *matola* to take you as far as Chinguni Hills for around MK3000. From the gate to Mvuu Camp is 28km along the park track (closed in the wet season), and a 4WD or high-clearance vehicle is recommended for this route.

Another way in for vehicles is via the dirt road (open all year) from Ulongwe, a village between Liwonde town and Mangochi. This leads for 14km through local villages to the western boundary. A few kilometres inside the park is a car park and boat jetty, where a watchman hoists a flag to arrange a boat from Mvuu Camp to come and collect you. This service is free if you're staying at the camp.

Alternatively, if you make a booking in advance for Mvuu Camp through Wilderness Safaris in Lilongwe (see p169), the camp can arrange a boat transfer from Liwonde town for US$100.

For those without wheels, the best option is to get any bus or minibus between Liwonde town and Mangochi and get off at Ulongwe. In Ulongwe local boys wait by

MALAWI

the bus stop and will sometimes take you by bicycle to the park gates or to the banks of the river just outside it from where you can arrange to be picked up (MK600). They usually won't take you into the park itself (they don't want to risk coming across any elephants!). If you've got a lot of luggage there may be an extra charge or you may need two bikes. The ride takes about an hour, and you should leave with plenty of time before dusk.

ZOMBA

The capital of Malawi from 1891 until the mid-1970s, Zomba's colonial heritage is still much in evidence. It is home to wide, tree-lined streets, and, clambering up the town's gently sloping hills are a number of faded old colonial beauties, including the impressive State House. East of the main road is the town's friendly commercial centre. There's a lively market, banks, foreign-exchange bureaus and a couple of decent eateries.

Internet access is available at **Global Links Suppliers** (Map p195; per min MK5; 7.30am-5pm Mon-Sat), opposite the market.

Sleeping

Ndindeya Motel (Map p195; ☎ 01-525558; s/d/executive incl breakfast MK1850/2350/2950; P) A good budget option right in the heart of the action and a short walk from the bus station. Rooms are large and spread out across two rambling bright buildings. The executive rooms are the most spacious and have small lounge areas, but are also closest to the bar so noise can be a factor.

Annie's Lodge (Map p197; ☎ 01-527002; Livingstone Rd; standard/superior/executive/flats MK6995/8995/1195/16,995; P) The most gracious of Zomba's hotels. Scattered along a hillside is a jumble of white colonial buildings with green corrugated iron roofs and wide verandahs. Faded colonial glamour may be the name of the game outside, but inside the rooms are perfectly modern, with DSTV, air-con and large bathrooms.

Eating & Drinking

There are plenty of cheap hole-in-the-wall places around the bus station where you can pick up plates of chicken and *nsima* or chips for around MK200.

Uncle Dan's Café (Map p195; ☎ 01-527114; dishes from MK400; 7.30am-6pm Mon-Fri, to 7pm Sat, 8.30am-4.30pm

MALAWI

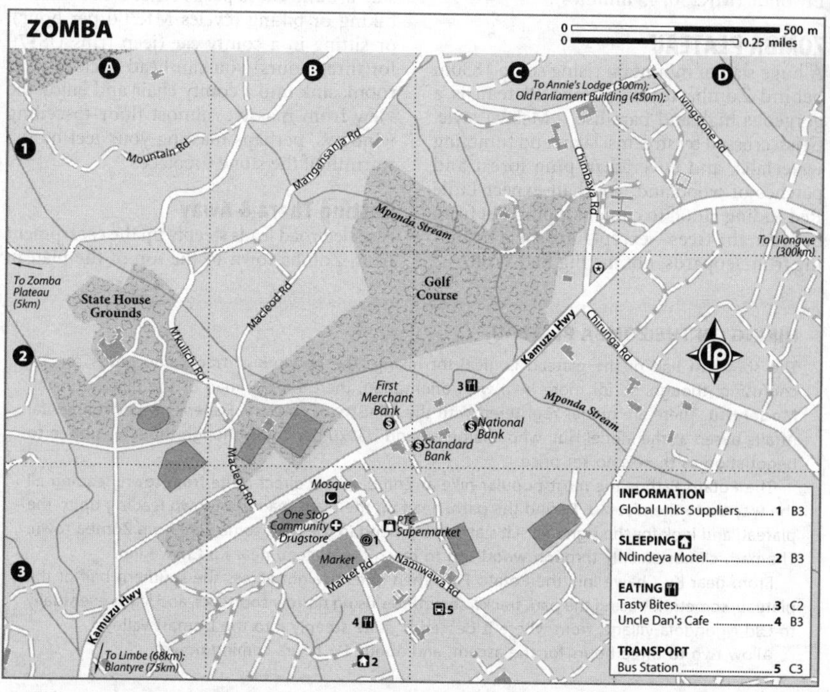

Sun). Good value and deservedly popular with travellers, this little cafe serves up fantastic homemade burgers and pasta dishes. It's also worth popping in at teatime – tea and cocoa with fresh-baked cookies and cakes costs MK500. Look for the sign saying 'Aaron & Lisa Pizzeria' – Uncle Dan's is inside.

Tasty Bites (Map p195; Kamuzu Hwy; dishes from MK500; 8am-8pm Wed-Mon) Flavoursome Pakistani curries, *shawarmas,* samosas and Indian tea are all on the menu along with Western meals such as burgers and steaks. The large dining room has a noticeboard with information about the local area and beyond, and there are a couple of tables for outside dining (though the view is of the car park and a main road).

Getting There & Away

Zomba is on a main Lilongwe–Blantyre route. AXA buses run to/from Zomba and Lilongwe (MK1000, five to six hours), Blantyre (MK350, 1½ to two hours), Liwonde (MK200, one hour) and Nkhata Bay (MK1720) via Mangochi (MK700). Minibuses go every hour or so to Limbe (MK390, one hour) and also leave for Lilongwe (MK1200, four to five hours) and Liwonde (MK250, 45 minutes).

MALAWI

ZOMBA PLATEAU

A huge slab of mountain rising some 1830m behind Zomba town, Zomba Plateau is a gorgeous highland paradise – Malawi style. Criss-crossed by streams, lakes and tumbling waterfalls, and covered in pine forest and patches of woodland, you half expect Little Red Riding Hood to come skipping out from between the trees – except here she'd be hiding from leopards, not the Big Bad Wolf.

The plateau can be explored on driveable tracks by car or on foot on the numerous winding paths and trails that ring and cross the mountain.

Sleeping

Forest Campsite (campsite per person MK400) An aptly named spot with toilets and wood-fired hot showers, all among large pine trees. It's fantastic in the sunshine but feels a bit spooky on misty days – and of those there are plenty.

Kuchawe Trout Farm (☎ 01-525271, 0888-638524; campsite per person MK600, r with shared bathroom MK1600, r MK2000, 4-bed self-contained chalets MK5000; P) The most convenient self-catering spot on the mountain has basic rooms in small stone cottages, or, better still, wooden hillbilly cabins with basic bathrooms, little kitchenettes and balconies. There's also a large, grassy campsite with sheltered dining spots and barbecue facilities.

our pick **Ku Chawe Inn** (☎ 01-514237; superior/deluxe r US$80/110; P) Perched on the hillside like a mist-cloaked Tuscan palace, surrounded by lively terraced gardens, and blessed with marvellous views over the plateau, red-brick Ku Chawe Inn is by far the nicest place to stay around these parts. After a hard day of hiking or biking (cycles MK300 per hour), or sitting in a comfy car (jeep trips US$70 for three hours) you can head back to your room, sink into a comfy chair and enjoy the view from massive, almost-floor-to-ceiling windows, perhaps toasting your feet by the warmth of the stone fireplace.

Getting There & Away

A sealed road leads steeply up the escarpment from Zomba town to the top of the plateau

HIKING ON THE ZOMBA PLATEAU

The southern half of the plateau is ideal for hiking. The network of tracks and paths can be confusing, though, so for more help with orientation, there's a 3-D map of the plateau in the **Model Hut**. There are guides registered with the Ministry of Forestry, Fisheries & Environmental Affairs based at the Model Hut, who charge around US$20 per day, although the rate is open to negotiation as there's no set price.

The Potato Path is the most popular hike at Zomba. It's a direct route from town, leading all the way up to the plateau. To find the path, head up the main road from town leading up to the plateau and look for the signpost – it's at a sharp bend in the road some 2km from Zomba town. The path climbs steeply through woodland to reach the plateau near Ku Chawe Inn.

From near Ku Chawe Inn, the Potato Path then goes straight across the southern half of the plateau, sometimes using the park tracks, sometimes using narrow shortcuts, and leads eventually to Old Ngondola village, from where it descends quite steeply into the Domasi Valley.

Allow two to three hours for the ascent, and about 1½ hours coming down.

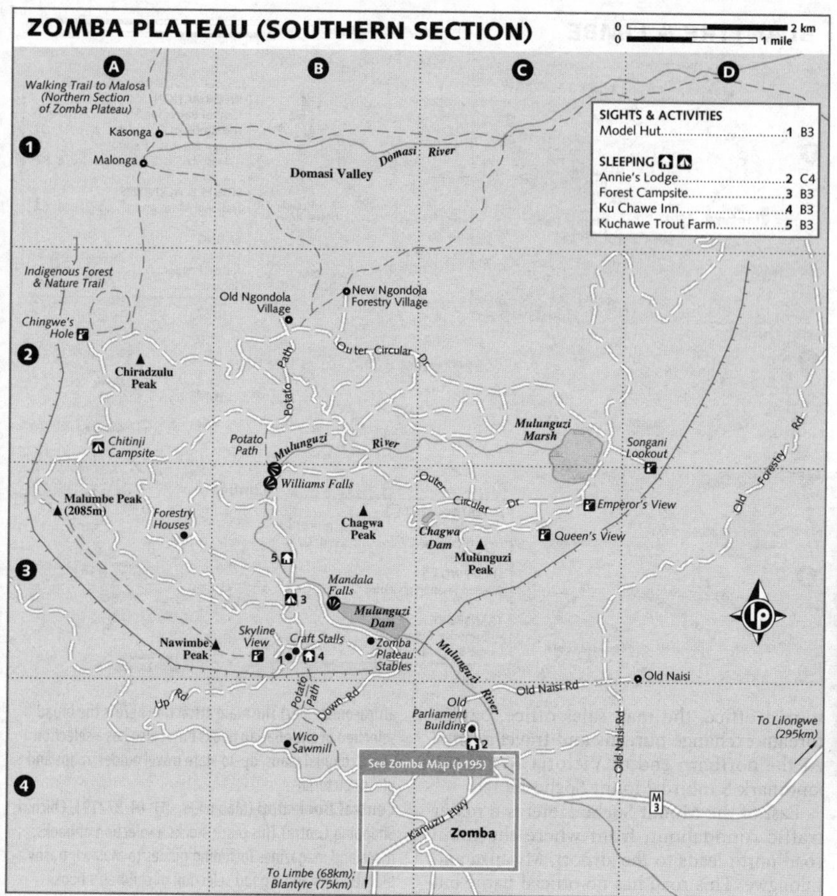

(about 5km). After the entrance gate, a two-way sealed road, known as Down Rd, veers east and continues for another 2km before turning to a dirt track. There is also an Up Rd, but this is now open only to walkers.

There's no bus up to the plateau, but local people hitch by the junction on the main street in Zomba town near the PTC supermarket. Alternatively, you can take a taxi (negotiable from around MK1500). Alternatively, you can walk all the way from Zomba town to the plateau via the road or on the Potato Path (see opposite).

BLANTYRE & LIMBE

Welcome to Malawi's most populous city, the oldest settlement in Malawi and the country's commercial and industrial hub. During the week Blantyre's city streets are alive with office workers, hawkers and shopkeepers. It has the best and most diverse choice of restaurants in the country, a charming national museum and a fascinating library and archives where you can get to grips with the country's history.

To the east Blantyre joins its more sedate sister city of Limbe, which is only of interest to travellers for its minibus station and grand old mission church. Unless stated otherwise, every address in this section is in Blantyre, rather than Limbe.

Orientation

Central Blantyre's main street is Victoria Ave; along here are several large shops, the

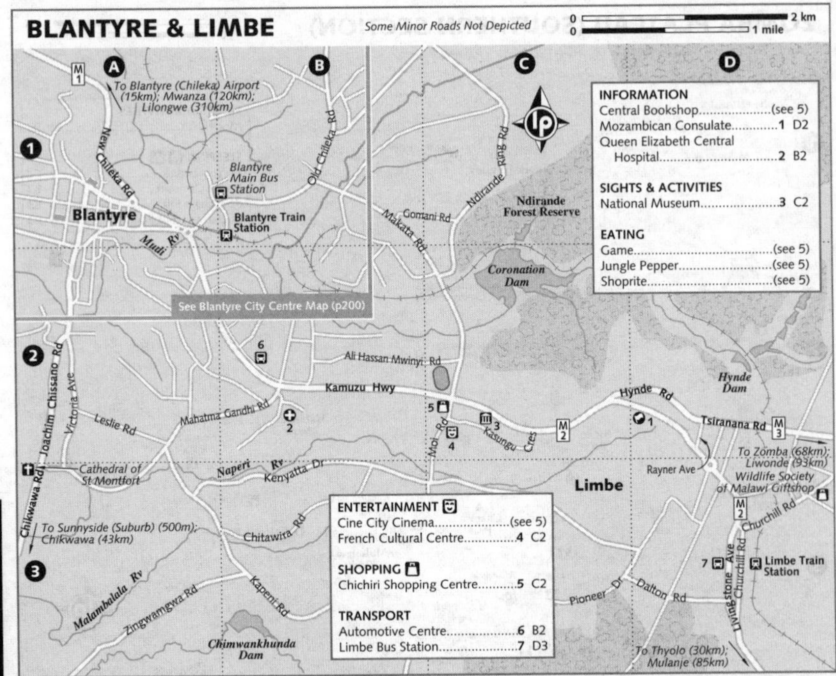

tourist office, the map sales office, banks, foreign exchange bureaus and travel agents. At the northern end of Victoria Ave is the landmark Sunbird Mount Soche Hotel.

East of the Mount Soche Hotel is a major traffic roundabout, from where the main road north leads to the airport, Mwanza and Lilongwe. This road has no official name but is known as New Chileka Rd. Approximately 500m further east is another roundabout, with a small clock on a concrete pedestal in the middle: from here Chileka Rd leads north to the bus station and outer suburbs.

MAPS

Survey maps of Blantyre and the surrounding area are available from the **Department of Surveys Map Sales Office** (Map p200; Victoria Ave). Regional and city maps cost MK650, survey maps covering the whole of Malawi cost MK3500.

Information

BOOKSHOPS

Central Africana Bookshop (Map p200; ☎ 01-876110; Uta Waleza Centre, Kidney Cres; centralafricana@africa-online.net) The main attraction here is the broad selection of antiquarian books but it also has a selection of old colonial maps, up-to-date travel guides, maps and glossy pictorials.

Central Bookshop (Map p198; ☎ 01-872191; Chichiri Shopping Centre) This place stocks a selection of books, maps and magazines including guides to Malawi, trashy blockbusters and a good selection of children's books.

EMERGENCY

Emergency numbers are as follows:

Ambulance ☎ 998
Fire ☎ 01-971999
Police ☎ 01-823333
Rapid Response Unit ☎ 997

INTERNET ACCESS

You will find plenty of internet bureaus in Blantyre.

E Centre Internet Café (Map p200; cnr Victoria Ave & Independence Dr; per min MK4.50; 8am-5pm Mon-Sat, 9am-4pm Sun) Reasonable-speed internet access. You can munch on homemade banana muffins (MK50) while you surf.

Icon Internet Café (Map p200; off Livingstone Ave; per min MK5) High-speed internet access.

MEDICAL SERVICES

Mwaiwathu Private Hospital (Map p200; ☎ 01-822999; Chileka Rd; 24hr) For private medical consultations or blood tests, this hospital, east of the city centre, is good. A consultation is US$10; all drugs and treatment are extra.

One Stop Pharmacy (Map p200; Chilembwe Rd; 8am-6pm Mon-Fri, 9am-2pm Sat) Well-stocked pharmacy that's a member of the national chain.

Queen Elizabeth Central Hospital (Map p198; ☎ 01-874333; 24hr) The Malaria Test Centre at this government-run hospital, off Chipembere Hwy, charges US$10 for a malaria test. Ask for directions as the test centre is hard to find.

Seventh Day Adventist Clinic (Map p200; ☎ 01-820006; Robins Rd) For medical or dental problems, this clinic charges US$10 for a doctor's consultation and US$10 for a malaria test.

MONEY

There are branches of the National Bank of Malawi and Standard Bank on Victoria Ave, both of which can change cash and travellers cheques and have 24-hour ATMs. **Victoria Forex Bureau** (Map p200; ☎ 01-821026; www.victoriaforex.com) usually has more competitive rates and charges no commission. You can get a speedy cash advance on your credit card here for a fee of MK500.

PHOTOGRAPHY

CES Photo Express (Map p200; Glyn Jones Rd; 7.30am-5pm Mon-Fri, 8am-1pm Sat) CES sells print film, develops digital photos and can provide passport photos.

POST

Post office (Map p200; Glyn Jones Rd; 7.30am-4.30pm Mon-Fri, 8am-10am Sat) Has poste restante and EMS express mail.

TOURIST INFORMATION

Tourist office (Map p200; ☎ Regional Tourism officer 0888-304362; 2nd fl, Government Complex, Victoria Ave; 7.30am-5pm Mon-Fri) This small office in the Department of Tourism stocks a few leaflets, sells maps of Malawi (MK500) and can offer enthusiastic, though not always that helpful, advice.

TRAVEL AGENCIES

Jambo Africa (Map p200; ☎ 01-823709/835356; www.jambo-africa.com; Sunbird Mount Soche Hotel, Glyn Jones Rd) Offers a wide range of tours and services including day tours in and around Blantyre. It can also arrange accommodation bookings around the country, car hire, and air and road transfers.

Soche Tours & Travel (Map p200; ☎ 01-820777; www.sochetours.mw; Chayamba Bldg, Victoria Ave) Offers car hire, transfers, local and international flight bookings, as well as tours of Blantyre and the region.

Ulendo Safaris (Map p200; ☎ 01-820752; www.ulendo.net; 3rd fl, Livingstone Towers, Glyn Jones Rd) Serves as booking agent for Kenya Airways and South African Airways and offers car hire, transfers and tours. It also owns a couple of luxury lodges in Lilongwe and the Satemwa Tea Estate.

Dangers & Annoyances

It's not safe to walk around the city alone at night – in particular, there have been reports of muggings on travellers walking in between Doogles lodge and the city after dark. Always use a taxi after dark. You should also watch out for your valuables when using the busy bus and minibus stations at Blantyre and Limbe.

Sights & Activities

Blantyre's most magnificent building is the red-brick **CCAP Church** (Map p200), officially called St Michael & All Angels Church. Built in the late 19th century, it's an impressive feat of elaborate brickwork moulded into arches, buttresses, columns and towers, topped with a grand basilica dome. Inside the church you'll find a number of memorials to people who died during the Mission's early years.

Set up in the 1990s, **Paper Making Education Trust (PAMET)** (Map p200; ☎ 01-823895; www.pamet.org.mw; 10 Chilembwe Rd) started out by training schools to recycle paper to make their own teaching materials. Today, it has a workshop and shop selling stationery, books and greeting cards made from a range of different materials, including banana bark, recycled paper and even elephant dung. For MK200 you can take a tour of the workshop to see how it's all done.

Malawi's **National Museum** (Map p198; Kasungu Cres; admission MK200; 7.30am-5pm) is of the small and dusty variety, with a number of not particularly well laid-out exhibits documenting the country's wildlife, human evolution and involvement in the slave trade. There are some gems here though, including a fascinating display on *Gule Wamkulu* – an important traditional dance for the Chewa. The museum is midway between Blantyre and Limbe, some 500m from the Chichiri Shopping Centre.

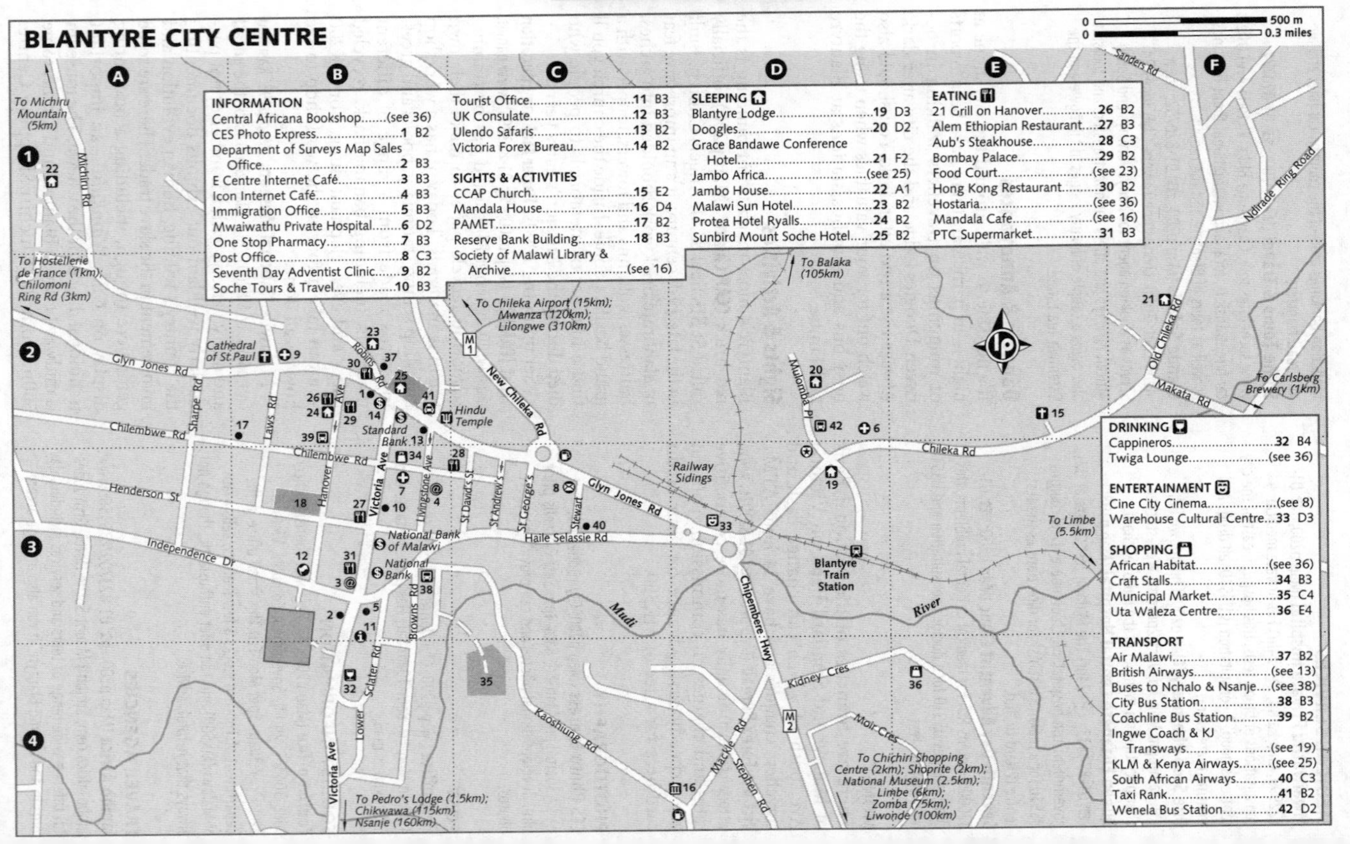

BLANTYRE CITY CENTRE
0 500 m
0 0.3 miles
INFORMATION
Central Africana Bookshop.......(see 36)
CES Photo Express.......1 B2
Department of Surveys Map Sales Office.......2 B3
E Centre Internet Café.......3 B3
Icon Internet Café.......4 B3
Immigration Office.......5 B3
Mwaiwathu Private Hospital.......6 D2
One Stop Pharmacy.......7 B3
Post Office.......8 C3
Seventh Day Adventist Clinic.......9 B2
Soche Tours & Travel.......10 B3
Tourist Office.......11 B3
UK Consulate.......12 B3
Ulendo Safaris.......13 B2
Victoria Forex Bureau.......14 B2
SIGHTS & ACTIVITIES
CCAP Church.......15 E2
Mandala House.......16 D4
PAMET.......17 B2
Reserve Bank Building.......18 B3
Society of Malawi Library & Archive.......(see 16)
SLEEPING
Blantyre Lodge.......19 D3
Doogles.......20 D2
Grace Bandawe Conference Hotel.......21 F2
Jambo Africa.......(see 25)
Jambo House.......22 A1
Malawi Sun Hotel.......23 B2
Protea Hotel Ryalls.......24 B2
Sunbird Mount Soche Hotel.......25 B2
EATING
21 Grill on Hanover.......26 B2
Alem Ethiopian Restaurant.......27 B3
Aub's Steakhouse.......28 C3
Bombay Palace.......29 B2
Food Court.......(see 23)
Hong Kong Restaurant.......30 B2
Hostaria.......(see 36)
Mandala Cafe.......(see 16)
PTC Supermarket.......31 B3
DRINKING
Cappineros.......32 B4
Twiga Lounge.......(see 36)
ENTERTAINMENT
Cine City Cinema.......(see 8)
Warehouse Cultural Centre.......33 D3
SHOPPING
African Habitat.......(see 36)
Craft Stalls.......34 B3
Municipal Market.......35 C4
Uta Waleza Centre.......36 E4
TRANSPORT
Air Malawi.......37 B2
British Airways.......(see 13)
Buses to Nchalo & Nsanje.......(see 38)
City Bus Station.......38 B3
Coachline Bus Station.......39 B2
Ingwe Coach & KJ Transways.......(see 19)
KLM & Kenya Airways.......(see 25)
South African Airways.......40 C3
Taxi Rank.......41 B2
Wenela Bus Station.......42 D2
To Michiru Mountain (5km)
To Hostellerie de France (1km); Chilomoni Ring Rd (3km)
To Chileka Airport (15km); Mwanza (120km); Lilongwe (310km)
To Balaka (105km)
To Carlsberg Brewery (1km)
To Limbe (5.5km)
To Chichiri Shopping Centre (2km); Shoprite (2km); National Museum (2.5km); Limbe (6km); Zomba (75km); Liwonde (100km)
To Pedro's Lodge (1.5km); Chikwawa (115km); Nsanje (160km)
Michiru Rd
Glyn Jones Rd
Chilembwe Rd
Henderson St
Independence Dr
Sharpe Rd
Laws Rd
Hanover
Victoria Ave
Livingstone Ave
St David's St
St Andrew's
St George's
Stewart
Haile Selassie Rd
Robins Rd
New Chileka Rd
Chileka Rd
Old Chileka Rd
Makata Rd
Sanders Rd
Ndirande Ring Road
Mulomba Pl
Chipembere Hwy
Kidney Cres
Moir Cres
Mackie Rd
Stephen Rd
Kaoshiung Rd
Browns Rd
Sclater Rd
Lower
Cathedral of St Paul
Hindu Temple
Standard Bank
National Bank of Malawi
National Bank
Railway Sidings
Blantyre Train Station
Mudi
River

Take a minibus headed for Limbe and ask to be let off at the museum. Otherwise, a taxi will cost around MK1000.

Mandala House (Map p200; ☎ 01-871932; Mackie Rd; 8.30am-4.30pm Mon-Fri, to 1pm Sat) is the oldest building standing in Malawi and was built back in 1882 as a home for the managers of the Mandala Trading Company. Inside the house is a cafe (p202), an art gallery and the **Society of Malawi Library & Archive** (9am-noon Mon-Fri, 6-7.30pm Thu), which contains a vast number of journals, books and photographs, some dating as far back as the 19th century.

Sleeping

BUDGET

Doogles (Map p200; ☎ 01-821128; Mulomba Pl; campsites US$3, dm US$5.50, chalets with shared bathroom US$16, d US$21;) A popular backpacker spot with dorms in the main house as well as a few self-contained chalets in the garden. There's also plenty of space for pitching tents and a lively bar that's also open to the general public. Be warned that the dorms in the main house are right behind the bar so can get pretty noisy.

Blantyre Lodge (Map p200; ☎ 01-834460; Chileka Rd; s/d from MK3500/5000;) This large hotel near the bus station has secure, bright rooms with TV, air-con and spick-and-span bathrooms. It usually has space so it's a good option for early-morning bus takers.

Grace Bandawe Conference Hotel (Map p200; ☎ 01-834267; s/d/ste MK4200/5400/6000;) Set in large gardens away from the noise of the city, this is a popular place for conferences and is more Malawian in flavour than some of other budget places in town. Rooms are very clean and brightened up by shiny bedspreads and lace curtains. There's a lounge where you can watch DSTV and meals are available (three-course meals MK1550).

MIDRANGE

Hostellerie de France (off Map p200; ☎ 01-869626; www.hostellerie-de-france.com; cnr Cilomoni Ring Rd & Kazuni Close; r/studio/apt from US$50/40100;) You'll find everything you need here, from dorms and executive doubles to apartments and studios, and there are discounts for long stayers. The swimming pool (and attached Jacuzzi!) looks out across the valley to Mt Ndirande (Map p204) and there's a restaurant with a pretty sophisticated menu (garlic mussels, goose-liver pâté, rabbit in white wine and mustard) and excellent French wines.

Jambo House (Map p200; ☎ 01-823709; www.jambo-africa.com; Kabula Hill; s/d with shared bathroom US$50/80, s/d US$55/90;) Owned by Jambo Africa and popular with long stayers, this little house has a large, comfortable lounge and top views of Mt Ndirande. The rooms are a bit of a let-down, though, and the bathrooms in particular are showing signs of wear – it's pretty overpriced for what you get. You can help yourself to drinks from the honesty bar, and if you order in advance the staff will cook you a meal and serve it in the dining area or in your room.

Pedro's Lodge (off Map p200; ☎ 01-833430; www.pedroslodge.com; 9 Smythe Rd, Sunnyside; s/d US$70/100;) Book in advance to stay at this small, family-run guesthouse where you'll immediately feel welcome. Eight clean, comfortable rooms with DSTV look out onto a small swimming pool and lush green lawn. The cosy restaurant is reminiscent of a Parisian neighbourhood bistro and serves delicious meals.

TOP END

Malawi Sun Hotel (Map p200; ☎ 01-824808; Robins Rd; s/d from US$100/120;) Self-confessed 'safari-style' joint that houses its rooms in two-storey blocks or small chalets and decks them out with solid wooden beds, animal-print chairs and curtains. It makes use of beautiful views over the surrounding hills with several strategically placed benches and an open lounge complete with balcony.

Sunbird Mount Soche Hotel (Map p200; ☎ 01-620588; mount soche@sunbirdmalawi.com; Glyn Jones Rd; s/d US$140/170;) This is a popular business hotel and is bursting with the requisite facilities. It's perhaps not such a good deal for tourists, though; the rooms are looking rather tired and aren't great value. If you do stay, plump for a room at a back; they have balconies with grand views over the hills.

Protea Hotel Ryalls (Map p200; ☎ 01-820955; ryalls@proteamalawi.com; 2 Hanover Ave; s/d US$215/245;) Ryalls is the oldest-established hotel in Malawi. It opened in 1922 and was a legendary stop for travellers on the route from the Cape to Cairo. The hotel has since grown and there's a less atmospheric new wing, but the original building has been renovated with old-fashioned flair and the plush rooms and communal areas are full of black-and-white photographs telling tales of old.

Eating

RESTAURANTS

Alem Ethiopian Restaurant (Map p200; ☎ 01-822529; Victoria Ave; dishes MK300-800; 8am-5pm Mon-Sat) Delicious *injera* (sour millet pancake) and *doro wot* (chicken with hot-pepper sauce) are on the menu here, but you can also have a plate of bland old chicken-and-chips or beef stew if you so desire.

Hong Kong Restaurant (Map p200; ☎ 01-820859; Robins Rd; mains MK700-1200; noon-2pm & 6-10pm Tue-Sun) This popular restaurant sits in a large red-and-white pagoda-style building. It makes a fine effort with the food, which comes in generous portions. Alongside the usual sweet-and-sour and spring rolls you'll find chicken with peanuts and whole chillies, and fried chicken gizzards.

Bombay Palace (Map p200; ☎ 0888-400400, 600600; Hanover Ave; starters MK650-1000, mains MK1200-2000; noon-1.45pm & 6.30-10pm, closed lunch Mon; wi-fi) Head here for fresh, delicately spiced Indian food – the best in town. Dishes such as sizzling mutton and chicken lollipops (deep-fried chicken with chilli and garlic) are served in a chic dining room lined with Indian paintings.

21 Grill on Hanover (Map p200; ☎ 01-820955; Protea Hotel Ryalls; starters MK1200, mains around MK2900; noon-2pm & 6.30-10pm) Folk say this is the poshest restaurant in Blantyre (or as the staff likes to boast, in the whole of Malawi) and it's hard to disagree. The restaurant is all soft upholstered chairs, book-lined walls and leather armchairs; and gentle piano music accompanies your excellent grilled meats and seafood. It feels a little as if you're secreted away in the annals of an exclusive gentleman's club.

Aub's Steakhouse (Map p200; ☎ 0999-960628/966507; Livingstonia Bldg, Chilembwe Rd; starters MK650-1000, mains MK1750-2300; noon-2pm & 7-10pm Mon-Sat; internet; wi-fi) Hankering after a huge hunk of dead cow or some finger-lickin' ribs? Mosey on down here and you'll be rewarded with a meat-, cheese- and carb-laden menu, all served up in the shadow of cowboy hat-, saddle- and horseshoe-adorned walls. For the faint-hearted there are 'ladies' or 'low-carb' portions.

Hostaria (Map p200; ☎ 0888-282828; Uta Waleza Centre, Kidney Cres; starters from MK500, mains from MK1200; noon-2pm & 7pm-9.30pm Mon-Sat) Yummy homemade pastas and pizzas are on the menu at this well-loved Italian restaurant as well as daily chalkboard meat and fish specials. The decor is pretty sweet too, with high ceilings, a mezzanine floor and funky chandeliers made out of Coke bottles.

FOOD STALLS & CAFES

Jungle Pepper (Map p198; ☎ 0888-826229, 0999-826229; www.junglepepperpizza.com; Chichiri Shopping Centre; pizzas MK1100-1400; 10.30am-2.30pm & 4.30-8.30pm) This popular takeaway pizza shop shares a big shaded courtyard with a number of other fast-food joints. Toppings veer towards the exotic, such as peri peri (also spelt piri piri) and mango chicken. You can also buy pizza by the slice for MK400.

our pick Mandala Cafe (Map p200; Mandala House, Mackie Rd; light meals MK1200; 8.30am-4.30pm Mon-Fri, to 12.30pm Sat; wi-fi) Sit on a breezy stone terrace or in the garden at a table fashioned from a tree trunk in the grounds of Mandala House (p201) at this chilled cafe. There are swings and a seesaw to keep the kids happy, a selection of tourist leaflets and magazines to browse and a speedy wi-fi hot spot. Regulars love the freshly brewed coffee, iced tea and homemade 'cakes of the day' (MK500), but you can also get savoury snacks and main meals.

Food Court (Map p200; Malawi Sun Hotel, Robins Rd; 10am-10pm) A popular collection of fast-food outlets grouped around a raised patio with fabulous views over the hills. Choices include Blue Savannah, which serves fried chicken, *shawarmas*, burgers and salads for around MK500, or ice-cream parlour Scoops & Shakes, where you can get your favourite chocolate bar whizzed into a milkshake for MK550.

SELF-CATERING

The main **PTC Supermarket** (Map p200; Independence Dr) sells food and other goods, much of it imported from South Africa or Europe and sold at similar prices. There are also huge Shoprite and Game supermarkets a few kilometres out of town at the **Chichiri Shopping Centre** (Map p198; Kamuzu Hwy).

Drinking & Entertainment

Warehouse Cultural Centre (Map p200; www.thewarehouse-malawi.net) Wedged between the railway line and a major roundabout, this former depot now consists of a soundproof theatre, a cafe and a bar. It's one of the country's most exciting venues and a staunch supporter of Malawian music, art, dance, theatre and literature.

MALAWI

French Cultural Centre (Map p198; ☎ 01-871250; direction@ccfmw.org; cnr Moi Rd & Kasungu Cres; ⏲ 8am-noon & 2pm-5.30pm Mon-Fri, 8am-noon Sat) The centre has an excellent and varied program of concerts, plays and readings.

Cappineros (Map p200; ☎ 0999-939260; Victoria Ave) A lively, friendly pub with a large beer garden that puts on regular music and theme events. You can play pool here or watch big-name sports, and solid grub is available. It's next to the Kairo International Casino. Look for the sign – it's down the drive.

Twiga Lounge (Map p200; ☎ 0999-966507) Uta Waleza Centre, Kidney Cres) This bar and nightclub is popular with young expats and Malawian professionals who come here to down cocktails and dance to the country's top DJs. Regular theme nights include School Disco.

Cine City Cinema (Map p198; ☎ 01-912873; Chichiri Shopping Centre; Mon-Thu MK1000, Fri-Sun MK1200; ⏲ closed Tue) Big-name films are shown at 5.30pm and 8pm daily with an extra 2.30pm showing at the weekend. It's in the basement of the Chichiri Shopping Centre, underneath Game Supermarket.

Shopping

Two kilometres out of town is the Chichiri Shopping Centre (Map p198), which has bookshops, pharmacies, boutiques and supermarkets.

African Habitat (Map p200; ☎ 01-873642; Uta Waleza Shopping Centre, Kidney Cres; 7.30am-4.30pm Mon-Fri, 8am-noon Sat) For high-end craft hunters, this is a good bet – it's a cavernous boutique crammed full of furniture, jewellery sculpture, art, textiles and books.

At a number of **craft stalls** (Map p200; Chilembwe Rd), the work on sale is excellent and browsing is refreshingly hassle-free. The more chaotic **Municipal Market** (Map p200; Kaoshiung Rd) is also worth a visit.

Getting There & Away

AIR

Blantyre's Chileka airport (Map p204) is about 15km north of the city centre.

Airline offices in Blantyre include the following:

Air Malawi (Map p200; ☎ 01-820811; Robins Rd; 7.30am-4.30pm Mon-Fri, 8am-noon Sat)
British Airways (Map p200; ☎ 01-824333/519; Livingstone Towers, Glyn Jones Rd)
KLM & Kenya Airways (Map p200; ☎ 01-824524; Sunbird Mount Soche Hotel)
South African Airways (Map p200; ☎ 01-820627; Nico House, Stewart St)

BUS & MINIBUS

Blantyre's main bus station (Wenela) for long-distance buses is east of the centre on Mulomba Pl. National Bus Company and AXA City Trouper buses run from here to Lilongwe (MK1200, four hours), Mzuzu (MK2000, nine to 10 hours), Monkey Bay (MK890, five to six hours) via Zomba (MK350, 1½ to two hours), Mulanje (MK400, 90 minutes) and Karonga (MK2800, 14 hours). AXA Executive coaches depart from the Automotive Centre (Map p198) at Ginnery Corner – where you'll also find the ticket office – and call at the Chichiri Shopping Centre and the Blantyre Lodge car park before departing the city. They leave twice daily to Lilongwe (MK3100, four hours).

Long-distance minibuses go from the bus station in Limbe (Map p198); most leave on a fill-up-and-go basis. It's often quicker to get a local minibus to Limbe bus station, and then a long-distance bus or 'half-bus' from there, rather than wait for AXA or other bus services in Blantyre. Routes include Zomba (MK390, one hour), Mulanje (MK450, 70 minutes) and the border at Muloza (MK750, 90 minutes).

Long-distance minibuses to the Lower Shire including Nchalo (MK400, two hours) and Nsanje (MK850, four hours) leave from the City Bus Station near Victoria Ave in Blantyre.

The car park next to Blantyre Lodge is the pick-up and drop-off point for long-distance bus companies headed for Jo'burg. **Ingwe Coach** (☎ 01-822313) goes to Jo'burg at 8.30am on Tuesday and Sunday (MK15,000, 25 hours). **KJ Transways** (☎ 01-914017) leaves for Jo'burg on Tuesday and Saturday at 7am (MK13,500, 25 hours). **Munomurama** buses leave Blantyre for Jo'burg from the Total petrol station on Chileka Rd on Wednesday and Saturday at 6am (MK16,500, 25 hours).

TRAIN

For information on trains that stop at Blantyre and Limbe, see p213 and p216.

Getting Around

TO/FROM THE AIRPORT

A taxi from the airport to the city costs around MK2000, but agree on a price with the driver first. The price can be negotiated down a bit if you're going from the city to the airport. If your budget doesn't include taxis, frequent local buses between Wanela bus station and Chileka township pass the airport gate. The fare is MK100.

BUS

Blantyre is a compact city, so it's unlikely you'll need to use public transport to get around, apart from the minibuses that shuttle along Chipembere Hwy between Wanela bus station and Limbe bus station. The one-way fare is MK80.

TAXI

You can find private hire taxis at the Mount Soche Hotel or at the bus stations. A taxi across the city centre is around MK500; between the centre and Wanela bus station costs from MK600; and from Blantyre to Limbe costs around MK1200.

AROUND BLANTYRE

Blantyre is surrounded by three 'mountains', Michiru, Soche and Ndirande, all actually large hills that can all be hiked to the summit. The most rewarding excursion is to Mt Michiru, 8km northwest of the city, a conservation area with nature trails. Animals that can be found here include monkeys, klipspringers and even leopards, but you're unlikely to see very much of them. Birdwatching is a much more rewarding activity – more than 400 species have been recorded in the area.

MULANJE

This lively small town sits in the shadow of Mt Mulanje and at the centre of Malawi's tea industry – the surrounding hills are covered in vibrant green tea plantations. If coming from the direction of Blantyre, you'll first hit the Chitakale Trading Centre (where the dirt road to Likhubula turns off the main sealed Blantyre–Mulanje road). Here you'll find the Mulanje Infocentre, a PTC supermarket and two petrol stations. Continue on for 2km and there's the main Mulanje town where you'll find the main bus station, hotels and banks.

Close to Likhubula on the main road, **Mulanje Motel** (☎ 01-466245; r with/without bathroom MK800/550) is a decent budget option.

Limbani Lodge (☎ 01-466390; r MK1000, VIP with fan s/d MK3000/3500; Ⓟ) has poky, miserable standard rooms down a long, dark corridor, but the VIP rooms are light, with plenty of room and small kitchenettes. Take the turning opposite the bus station near the school for the blind.

Hidden up a dirt road at the foot of the mountain, **Kara O' Mula** (☎ 01-466515; www.karaomula.com; s/d MK5850/7600, executive s/d MK7050/8800; Ⓟ), with its leafy grounds and wide terrace restaurant, is a perfect place to relax after a hard day's hiking.

Getting There & Away

AXA buses go to/from Blantyre (MK400, 1½ hours), as do minibuses (MK450, 70 minutes). If you're heading for the border with Mozambique, minibuses and *matola* run to

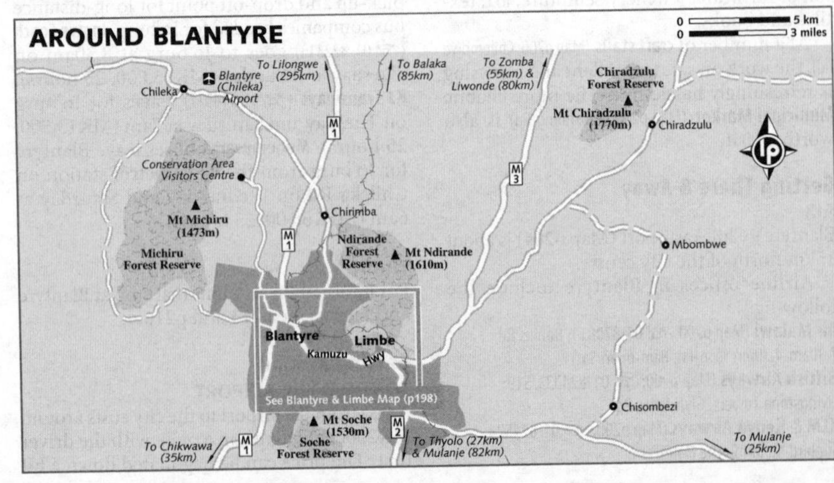

Muloza (MK300, 30 minutes). For more border crossing information, see p213.

MOUNT MULANJE

A huge hulk of twisted granite rising from the surrounding plains, Mt Mulanje towers over 3000m high. All over the mountain are dense green valleys, and rivers drop from sheer cliffs to form dazzling waterfalls. The locals call it the 'Island in the Sky' and on misty days (of which there are many) it's easy to see why – the mountain is shrouded in a cotton-wool haze, and its highest peaks burst through the cloud to touch the heavens.

Mulanje measures about 30km from west to east and 25km from north to south, with an area of at least 600 sq km. The highest peak is Sapitwa (3002m), the highest point in Malawi and in all Southern Africa north of the Drakensberg. There are other peaks on the massif above 2500m, and you can reach most of the summits without technical climbing.

Information

Hiking on Mt Mulanje is controlled by the **Likhubula Forestry Office** (PO Box 50, Mulanje; 7.30am-noon & 1-5pm), at the small village of Likhubula, about 15km from Mulanje town. Entry fees are MK100 per person, vehicle entry fee costs MK200 and the forestry office car park is MK100 a day. The friendly and helpful staff can arrange guides and porters from an official list. You must register here and make reservations for the mountain huts. Camping is permitted only near huts and only when they're full.

Also good for information is the **Mulanje Infocentre** (☎ 01-466466/506, infomulanje@malawi.net; Chitakale Trading Centre, cnr Phalombe Rd). It carries a good selection of books and maps and also rents out sleeping bags (per day MK500), thermal sleeping pads (per day MK250) and tents (per day MK700). It can also arrange mountain guides and porters.

As you arrive in Likhubula (or Mulanje town) you'll probably be approached by hopeful locals looking for work, but it's best to arrange guides and porters only at Likhubula Forestry Office, which keeps a registered list. There is a standard charge of around MK1000 per day per porter and MK1300 per guide (regardless of group size). The total fee for the whole trip should be agreed before departure and put in writing.

Dangers & Annoyances

Hikers should remember that Mulanje is a big mountain with notoriously unpredictable weather. After periods of heavy rain, streams can become swollen and impassable. Also, beware: much of the mountain's granite surface can become very slippery and dangerous when wet. Even during the dry season, it's not uncommon to get rain, cold winds and thick mists, which make it easy to get lost. Between May and August, periods of low cloud and drizzle (called *chiperone*) can last several days, and temperatures drop below freezing. Always carry a map, a compass and warm and waterproof clothing should the weather change, or you risk suffering from severe exposure.

Sleeping

BELOW THE MOUNTAIN

CCAP Guesthouse (campsites MK800, chalets per person MK2000) At the CCAP Mission, after the reserve gates, with cosy rooms, self-catering chalets and camping.

Likhubula Forest Lodge (☎ 01-467737; campsites per person MK900; s/d with shared bathroom & breakfast MK5000/7300, half board MK6800/10,800; s/d incl breakfast MK5800/8200, half board MK7700/11,800; whole lodge MK36,000) Also after the reserve gates, this lodge

HIKING ON MULANJE

There are about six main routes up and down Mulanje. The three main ascent routes go from Likhubula: the Chambe Plateau Path (also called the Skyline Path), the Chapaluka Path and the Lichenya Path. Other routes, more often used for the descent, are Thuchila Hut to Lukulezi Mission, Sombani Hut to Fort Lister Gap, and Minunu Hut to the Lujeri Tea Estate.

Once you're on the massif, a network of paths links the huts and peaks, and many different permutations are possible. Be warned that some of the routes are impassable or otherwise dangerous. The route from Madzeka Hut to Lujeri is very steep, for example, as are the Boma Path and the path from Lichenya to Nessa on the southwestern side of Mulanje. It takes anything from two to six hours to hike between one hut and the next.

in Likhubula has simple clean rooms including two with bathroom, a terrace with pretty views and a cosy lounge with a fireplace and rocking chairs – perfect for a few hours playing the lodge copy of Scrabble or browsing the shelf of old books and magazines. There's a separate annexe with its own small verandah.

ON THE MOUNTAIN

Forestry huts (campsites per adult/child MK400/200, huts per adult/child MK700/350) On Mulanje are eight forestry huts: Chambe, Chisepo, Lichenya, Thuchila (*chu*-chila), Chinzama, Minunu, Madzeka and Sombani. Each is equipped with benches, tables and open fires with plenty of wood. Some have sleeping platforms (no mattresses); in others you just sleep on the floor. You provide your own food, cooking gear, candles, sleeping bag and stove (although you can cook on the fire). A caretaker chops wood, lights fires and brings water, for which a small tip should be paid. Payments must be made at Likhubula Forestry Office – show your receipt to the hut caretaker. Camping is permitted near the huts when there are no more beds.

CCAP Cottage (beds MK700) On the Lichenya Plateau, this is similar to the forestry huts, but there are utensils in the kitchen, plus mattresses and blankets. You can make reservations at the CCAP Mission in Likhubula (see p205).

France's Cottage (beds MK700) A more comfortable option than the huts, this small two-bedroom cottage sleeps six and comes with a living room complete with cooking

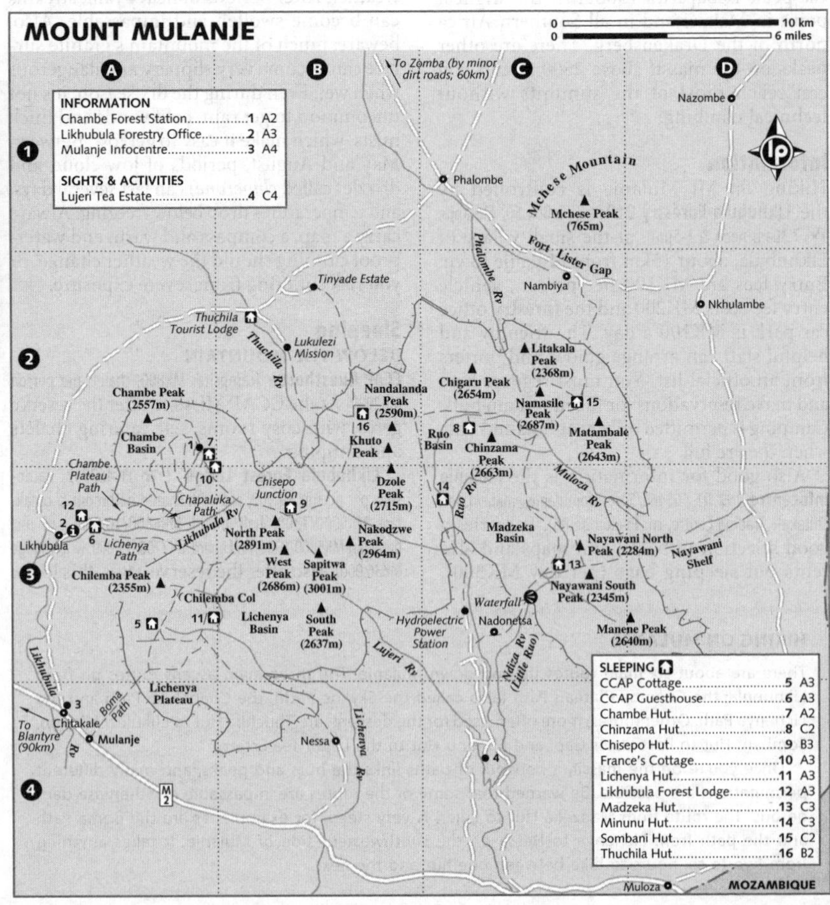

fireplace. There are two single beds and two bunk beds. It's in the Chambe basin near the Chambe hut.

Getting There & Away

See p203 for information on buses between Blantyre and Mulanje town. The dirt road to Likhubula turns off the main sealed Blantyre–Mulanje road at Chitikale, about 2km west of the centre of Mulanje town – follow the signpost to Phalombe. If you're coming from Blantyre on the bus, ask to be dropped at Chitikale. From here, irregular *matola* run to Likhubula (MK150). If you're in a group, you can hire the whole *matola* to Likhubula for around MK1000. Alternatively, you can walk (10km, two to three hours); it's a pleasant hike, with good views of the southwestern face of Mulanje on your right.

LOWER SHIRE

This is one of the least-visited areas of the country – a baking stretch of flat plains, swampland, sugar cane and maize fields, where the Shire River makes its final journey before plunging into the great Zambezi.

Majete Wildlife Reserve

Majete Wildlife Reserve (www.majete.org; adult/child/vehicle MK2000/1000/200, maps MK100) is a beautiful wilderness area of hilly *miombo* woodland and savannah, along the west bank of the Shire River. Years of poaching left the park depleted and dilapidated, but since **African Parks** (www.africanparks-conservation.com) took over in 2003 things have been looking up. A perimeter fence has been erected around the whole reserve and accommodation and roads have been upgraded.

There are now over 4000 animals in Majete, most translocated from other parks in Malawi and elsewhere in Southern Africa, including zebras, antelope, black rhinos, buffalo and over 140 elephants. There are plenty of hippos in the river and the park is also known for its rich bird life. In the long term it's hoped that Majete will become a 'Big Five' park. Come now and you'll be able to enjoy it all in peace.

SIGHTS & ACTIVITIES

There are 250km of tracks in the park, and you'll need a high-clearance car to get around – a 4WD is strongly recommended, especially during the wet season.

If you would rather partake in organised activities, there are bush walks (per person MK1500) game drives (per person MK3500), and for the brave, elephant tracking on foot (per person MK3500). You also can opt to have a scout join you in your own car (MK2000).

At the entrance to the park is a small open-air **heritage centre** and **gift shop** featuring a display of art and craftwork made in and around Majete by local people.

SLEEPING

Community Campsite (Map p193; campsite per person MK700, s/d shelters MK500/700) had just been built at the time of writing. To get there turn left just before the heritage centre. It's a peaceful spot, with spotless kitchen and barbecue facilities, ample firewood and a small bar with cold drinks, toilet paper, matches, and other essentials for sale. There are also a couple of raised thatched camping platforms reached by ladder, with dynamite views out over the park.

Thawale Camp (Map p193; bush tent half/full board per person from MK8750/9850, s supplement MK1650) is a beautiful upscale bush camp about 3km inside the reserve's main entrance. Each safari tent is set on a raised wooden platform in the bush, with a small verandah and gorgeous bathroom at the back. There's a central lodge for meals (the food is excellent). The camp isn't fenced so expect regular visits from elephants, buffalo and other creatures.

GETTING THERE & AWAY

Majete lies west of the Shire River, some 70km south of Blantyre. Follow the road to Chikwawa from where signs will direct you to the reserve. By public transport, the nearest you can get is Chikwawa.

Lengwe National Park

Lengwe is Malawi's southernmost **park** (entry fees per person US$5 & per car US$2). It's flat and arid with plenty of driveable tracks (yes, some even with a 2WD!) among mixed woodland and grassy *dambo* (wetlands). The sparse vegetation means that animal viewing is good here, and in the dry season animals congregate around the park's few permanent watering holes. Mammals include nyalas (at the northern limit of their distribution in Africa), bushbucks, impalas, duikers, kudus, warthogs and buffalo. There's also a large and varied bird population. The park has several walking trails and 'hides' overlooking the park's watering holes, where you can watch the animals come and graze. There's one within five minutes' walk of the lodge.

ACTIVITIES

The lodge can organise a wide range of activities in the park, such as game drives (per person US$25), walking safaris (per person US$12) and evening tours to Ndankwera Cultural Village, where you'll be fed and entertained for US$35 per person (minimum four people).

At the park entrance is a small gift shop selling woven rugs and bags as well as locally made produce such as *lengwe* peanut butter and baobab jam. At the time of research, construction was underway on a heritage centre and museum next door to the gift shop.

SLEEPING

Nyala Lodge (bookings through Jambo Africa ☎ 01-823709; www.jambo-africa.com; s/d chalets per person incl breakfast US$80/70, half board US$90/80, full-board US$125/115) A fully functioning lodge in a clearing in the bush, but there isn't a particularly great view from here and it lacks some of that romantic safari atmosphere. Very large thatched chalets have verandahs and spacious bathrooms; there's a central lounge and bar, and hammocks and chairs dotted throughout the grounds. For those on a budget there are a separate campsite and budget chalets for self-caterers (chalets per person US$30, camping per person US$6).

GETTING THERE & AWAY

By car, take the main road (M1) from Blantyre south towards Nsanje. Just before the town of Chikwawa a signpost indicates Lengwe National Park to the right. The park entrance is another 10km to the west through sugar-cane plantations.

Mwabvi Wildlife Reserve

Sitting at the country's southernmost tip, this **reserve** (entry per person MK750, per car MK300) is the smallest, most remote and least accessible in Malawi. Much of the wildlife has been wiped out by poachers though there are still buffalo, kudus, sable antelope, bushpigs, bushbucks and a handful of leopards.

Project African Wilderness (www.projectafricanwilderness.com) has taken over management of the reserve with the aim of protecting and restoring it. New camps have been built, there are plans to start fencing Mwabvi's borders in 2010, and new wildlife species will be introduced.

ACTIVITIES

At the main gates you can pay for a guide to accompany you in your car (US$2), organise a walking safari (per person US$10) or a game drive (per person US$15), or visit a local village on a cultural tour (per person US$5).

SLEEPING

There are two places to stay in Mwabvi, one inside and one outside the park. To make a booking at either one, contact **Project African Wilderness** (☎ 01-707346; barefoot@projectafricanwilderness.com).

Chipembere Camp (dm per person US$15, campsite per person US$5) With its main gate about 500m down the righthand fork (signposted to the camp) of a crossroads, this is a shady campsite with spotless ablutions and an airy dorm with large, mosquito-screened windows and a small library. There are barbecue and kitchen facilities.

our pick **Migudu Camp** (campsite per person US$15) This beautiful area inside the reserve has six camping spots well spread out among the bush, each with its own barbecue and viewing point. Site 3, hugged by a large grey and purple boulder, is the most picturesque. There's a walking trail from the campsite as well as a two-storey game-viewing deck with awe-inspiring views all the way over to the mountains that border the reserve and into Mozambique. At the time of writing you could only self-cater by barbecue, but they are building a kitchen and reception area and you will be able to buy cold drinks.

GETTING THERE & AWAY

Access is possible only with a 4WD. The reserve office is reached from the main road between Chikwawa and Nsanje, 8km off the main road just east of the village of Sorgin, and about 10km west of Bangula. It's a pleasant drive through millet fields and past villages, and well signposted. It's not possible to get here by public transport.

MALAWI DIRECTORY

ACCOMMODATION

Budget

In almost every town there is a council or government rest house. Prices vary from as little as US$2 up to around US$8 a double, but conditions vary from bare and basic to disgusting. In national parks and along the lakeshore, many places offer camping as well as self-catering chalets or cabins. Camping costs from around US$3 to US$10 dollars.

You'll find backpacker hostels all over the country, in the major cities as well as popular lakeshore destinations such as Cape Maclear and Nkhata Bay. Prices range from US$5 to US$10 for a dorm, about US$10 to US$15 per person for a double or triple with shared bathroom, up to around US$35 with bathroom. Camping is usually about US$3 to US$5.

Midrange

Midrange hotels and lodges range from about US$35 to US$95 per double, including taxes, usually with private bathroom and breakfast, sometimes with air-con.

Top End

Standard top-end hotels in the big cities and at beach resorts range from US$95 to US$250 for a double room, with in-room facilities such as bathroom, TV, air-con and phone. The price normally includes taxes and breakfast. Then there are the exclusive beach hotels and safari lodges, at which you'll pay anything from US$100 to US$450 per person, per night, though this price usually includes all meals and some activities.

ACTIVITIES

This section only provides a brief overview of what's available in Malawi: for more information see the relevant destination sections.

Lake Malawi is reckoned to be among the best freshwater diving areas in the world – and one of the cheapest places to learn how to dive. Places where you can hire scuba gear and take a PADI Open Water course include Nkhata Bay, Cape Maclear, Likoma Island and Senga Bay.

If you don't want to dive you can still have fun with the fish. Snorkelling gear can be hired from dive centres and most lakeside hotels.

Many of the more upmarket places along the lake have facilities for water-skiing or windsurfing. Kayaking is available at Cape Maclear and Nkhata Bay and at many of the lodges that dot the lakeshore.

You can go fishing in Lake Malawi for *mpasa* (also called lake salmon), *ncheni* (lake tiger), *sungwa* (a type of perch), *kampango* or *vundu* (both catfish). There are trout in streams on Nyika, Zomba and Mulanje Plateaus, and tigerfish can be hooked in the Lower Shire River. Anglers can contact the **Angling Society of Malawi** (www.anglingmalawi.com) for further details.

The main areas for hiking are Nyika and Mulanje. Other areas include Zomba and various smaller peaks around Blantyre. Mulanje is Malawi's main rock-climbing area, with some spectacular routes, although local climbers also visit smaller crags and outcrops. Rock climbing can also be arranged in Livingstonia and in the Viphya Plateau.

The **Mountain Club of Malawi** (www.mcm.org) provides a wealth of information about hiking on Mt Mulanje.

BOOKS

This section covers books specific to Malawi; titles on the whole Southern Africa region are covered on p22. Literature by Malawian writers is covered on p166.

Field Guides

Birds of Malawi: A Supplement to Newman's Birds of Southern Africa, by KB Newman, 'bridges the bird gap' between species covered in Southern and East Africa guides.

Guide to the Fishes of Lake Malawi National Park, by L Digby, is sometimes called the 'WWF guide' as this organisation was the publisher. In contrast to Koning's tome, this guide is small, portable and perfect for amateurs, although not easy to find as it was published in 1986.

Guidebooks

Day Outings from Lilongwe and *Day Outings from Blantyre*, both published by

PRACTICALITIES

- Malawi's main **newspapers** are *the Daily Times, the Malawi News* and the *Nation*. The *Chronicle* is a smaller publication but with a strong independent voice
- Malawi's national **radio station** is the Malawi Broadcasting Corporation. Commercial stations include Capital FM.
- **Television Malawi** was launched in 1999 and consists mostly of imported programs, news, regional music videos and religious programs. International satellite channels (through DSTV) are available in most midrange and top-end hotels.

the Wildlife Society of Malawi, are highly recommended.

Lonely Planet's *Zambia & Malawi* guide, gives more in-depth coverage of Malawi. *Trekking in East Africa* includes a good section on Malawi and is recommended for trekkers and hikers.

History

A Lady's Letters from Central Africa, by Jane Moir, was written in the 1890s by 'the first woman traveller in Central Africa'.

Nyasa – A Journal of Adventures, by ED Young is a local history book written in the 1870s (reprinted in 1984); it's a missionary's account of the original Livingstonia mission at Cape Maclear.

Travel

Venture to the Interior, by Laurens van der Post, describes the author's 'exploration' of Mt Mulanje and the Nyika Plateau in the 1940s, although in reality this was hardly trailblazing stuff.

BUSINESS HOURS

Offices and shops in the main towns usually open 8am to 5pm weekdays, with an hour for lunch from noon to 1pm. Many shops are also open Saturday morning. In smaller towns, shops and stalls are open most days, but keep informal hours. Bank hours are usually 8am to 3.30pm weekdays. Post and telephone offices usually open 7.30am to 5pm weekdays, sometimes with a break for lunch. In Blantyre and Lilongwe, they also open Saturday morning. Restaurants are usually open from noon to 2pm and 6pm to 9.30pm.

CHILDREN

There are few formal facilities for children in Malawi, but it is generally a safe and friendly place for children to visit. Most of the big international hotels in Blantyre and Lilongwe can provide babysitting services, family rooms and cots for babies, as can several of the tourist lodges up and down the coast. Similarly, many of the big city restaurants frequented by expats and tourists will be able to provide high chairs. Disposable nappies and formula are widely available in supermarkets and speciality shops in Lilongwe, Blantyre and Mzuzu but can be difficult to find elsewhere.

CUSTOMS REGULATIONS

Like any country, Malawi doesn't allow travellers to import weapons, explosives or narcotics. Plants and seeds, livestock and live insects or snails are also prohibited. It is illegal to take products made from endangered animals or plants out of the country. A yellow-fever certificate is required from people arriving from an infected area.

DANGERS & ANNOYANCES

Crime

Malawi was once one of the safest countries in the world for independent travellers, but in recent years incidences of robberies or muggings have increased. However, incidents are still rare compared with other countries, and violence is not the norm. Some safety advice is given on p169 and p199.

Wildlife

Potential dangers at Lake Malawi include encountering a hippo or crocodile, but for travellers the chances of being attacked are extremely remote. Crocodiles tend to be very wary of humans and are generally only found in quiet vegetated areas around river mouths (although they may sometimes be washed into the lake by floodwater). Therefore, you should be careful if you're walking along the lakeshore or have to wade through a river. Popular tourist beaches are safe, but, to be sure, you should seek local advice before diving in.

EMBASSIES & CONSULATES

Embassies & Consulates in Malawi

The following countries have diplomatic representation in Malawi:

> **GOVERNMENT TRAVEL ADVICE**
>
> The following government websites offer travel advisories and information on current hot spots.
>
> **Australia – Department of Foreign Affairs** (☎ 1300 139281; www.smarttraveller.gov.au)
>
> **Britain – Foreign Office** (☎ 0845 850 2829; www.fco.gov.uk)
>
> **Canada – Department of Foreign Affairs** (☎ 800 2676788; www.voyages.gc.ca)
>
> **US State Department** (☎ 888 4074747; http://travel.state.gov)

Germany (Map p168; ☎ 01-772555; Convention Dr, City Centre, Lilongwe)
Mozambique Embassy (Map p168; ☎ 01-774100; Convention Dr, City Centre, Lilongwe); Consulate (Map p198; ☎ 01-843189; 1st fl, Celtel Bldg, Rayner Ave, Limbe)
South Africa (Map p168; ☎ 01-773722, sahe@malawi.net; Kang'ombe Bldg, City Centre, Lilongwe)
UK High Commission (Map p168; ☎ 01-772400; off Kenyatta Rd, City Centre, Lilongwe); Consulate (Map p200; Hanover Ave, Blantyre)
USA (Map p168; ☎ 01-773166; Convention Dr, City Centre, Lilongwe)
Zambia (Map p168; ☎ 01-772590; Convention Dr, City Centre, Lilongwe)

FESTIVALS & EVENTS

The Malawi **Lake of Stars Music Festival** (www.lakeofstarsfestival.co.uk) takes place each October at various locations around the lake and attracts live-music acts from around Africa and the UK. It last for three days and proceeds go to charity.

HOLIDAYS

Public holidays in Malawi:
New Year's Day 1 January
John Chilembwe Day 15 January
Martyrs' Day 3 March
Easter March/April – Good Friday, Holy Saturday and Easter Monday
Labour Day 1 May
Freedom Day 14 June
Republic Day 6 July
Mother's Day October – second Monday
National Tree Planting Day December – second Monday
Christmas Day 25 December
Boxing Day 26 December

INTERNET ACCESS

You'll find several internet cafes in Lilongwe (p169), Blantyre (p198) and Mzuzu (p180) and most towns will usually have somewhere to check your email. The introduction of wireless broadband services by Skyband and Globe has made a huge difference. Many hotels and restaurants in Lilongwe, Blantyre and Mzuzu now have wi-fi connections, as do quite a few tourist hotels around the country. To get online, you must buy a prepaid voucher, which you can usually buy from wi-fi hot spots.

MONEY

Malawi's unit of currency is the Malawi kwacha (MK). This is divided into 100 tambala (t).

Banknotes include MK200, MK100, MK50, MK20, MK10 and MK5. Coins include MK1, 50t, 20t, 10t, 5t and 1t, although the small tambala coins are virtually worthless.

When top-end hotels, backpacker hostels, tourist lodges and travel agencies quote their rates in US dollars, we have done the same in this chapter. Note, however, that you can pay in hard currency or kwacha at the prevailing exchange rate.

ATMs

Standard and National Banks are the best bet for foreigners wishing to draw money out of their home account. Standard Bank accepts foreign Visa, MasterCard, Cirrus and Maestro cards at their ATMs. National Bank ATMs only take foreign Visa cards at present. ATMs accept foreign cards and are found in most cities and towns, including Lilongwe, Blantyre, Mzuzu, Karonga, Liwonde, Salima, Mangochi, Kasungu and Zomba.

Credit Cards

You can get cash with a Visa card at Standard Bank and the National Bank of Malawi in Blantyre and Lilongwe but it can take several hours. You're best off going to a foreign exchange bureau where transactions are completed on the spot.

You can use Visa cards at many large hotels and top-end restaurants, though there may be a surcharge of around 5%.

Tipping

In Malawi tipping is not generally expected, as many restaurants and services will add a service charge to your bill.

Travellers Cheques

You can change travellers cheques at most major banks and foreign exchange bureaus, although you will need to show them the original purchase receipt. You can sometimes use travellers cheques to pay at large hotels and lodges.

POST

To African destinations, letters less than 10g and postcards cost MK80. To Europe, India, Pakistan and the Middle East it's MK150 and to the Americas, Japan or Australasia postage is MK200. It's quicker to use the EMS

Speedpost service at post offices. Letters up to 500g cost MK750 to Europe and MK1000 to Australia and the USA.

Airmail parcels cost about MK2000 plus MK500 per kilogram to send items outside Africa. Surface mail is cheaper.

TELEPHONE

International calls (to destinations outside Africa) from public phone offices cost around MK500 per minute. The international code for Malawi if you're dialling from abroad is ☎ 265.

Telephone calls within Malawi are inexpensive – around MK50 per minute depending on the distance. Calls to mobiles within Malawi cost around MK70 per minute.

Mobile Phones

Mobile phone prefixes are ☎ 0888 or ☎ 0999 and the two major networks are TNM and Zain. SIM cards are readily available and the most convenient way to buy them is from one of the many street vendors. They cost around MK700 and include a small amount of airtime. You can buy top-up cards from street vendors, at supermarkets and petrol stations and they cost anything from MK35 to MK2800 depending on how much airtime you need.

Phone Codes

Malawi does not have area codes, but all landline numbers begin with ☎ 01, so whatever number you dial within the country will have eight digits. Numbers starting with 7 are on the Lilongwe exchange, those starting with 8 are in Blantyre, 5 is around Zomba, 4 is the south, 3 is the north and 2 is the Salima area.

TOURIST INFORMATION

There are tourist information offices in Blantyre and Lilongwe but you're much better off asking advice from your hostel or hotel, or from a travel agency. Outside Malawi, tourism promotion is handled by UK-based **Malawi Tourism** (☎ 0115-982 1903; fax 0115-981 9418; www.malawitourism.com).

VISAS

Visas are not required by citizens of Commonwealth countries, the USA and most European nations. On entering the country you'll be granted 30-day entry, which can then easily be extended at immigration offices in Blantyre (Map p200; Government Complex, Victoria Ave) or Lilongwe (Map p170; ☎ 01-754297; Murray Rd). The process is straightforward and free.

TRANSPORT IN MALAWI

GETTING THERE & AWAY

The main way to get to Malawi is by land or air. Overland, travellers might enter Malawi from Zambia, Mozambique or Tanzania. Boats also bring travellers over Lake Malawi from Mozambique. There are no direct flights to Malawi from Europe or the United States. The easiest way to reach the country by air is via Kenya, Ethiopia or South Africa. Flights, tours and rail tickets can be booked online at www.lonelyplanet.c om/travel_services.

Air

AIRPORTS & AIRLINES

Kamuzu International Airport (LLW; ☎ 01-700766), 12 miles north of Lilongwe city centre, handles the majority of international flights. Flights from South Africa, Kenya, Zambia and Tanzania also land in Blantyre at **Chileka International Airport** (BLZ; ☎ 01-694244). The country's national carrier is Air Malawi, which operates a number of internal and regional flights.

Airlines Flying to/from Malawi

Air Malawi (airline code QM; ☎ 01-265 820811/773680; www.airmalawi.com) has a decent regional network, with flights heading to Dar es Salaam, Johannesburg, Nairobi, Lusaka and Harare from Blantyre and Lilongwe.

South African Airways (airline code SA; ☎ 01-265 1 620617/772242; www.flysaa.com) flies twice weekly between Blantyre and Jo'burg, and five times weekly between Lilongwe and Jo'burg (with connections to Durban, Cape Town etc).

Kenya Airways (airline code KQ; ☎ 01-774227/624/524; www.kenya-airways.com) flies four times per week to/from Nairobi and six times per week to/from Lusaka

Ethiopian Airways (airline code ET; ☎ 01-771002/308; www.flyethiopian.com) flies four times a week from Addis Ababa.

Departure Tax

The US$30 departure tax is now included in the price of your ticket.

Border Crossings

MOZAMBIQUE

North

There are three border crossings from Malawi into northern Mozambique: Muloza, from where you can reach Mocuba in Mozambique, and Nayuchi and Chiponde, both of which lead to Cuamba in Mozambique.

Regular buses run from Blantyre, via Mulanje, to Muloza (MK750). From here, you walk 1km to the Mozambique border crossing at Milange, from where it's another few kilometres into Milange *vila* (town) itself. From Milange there's usually a chapa (pick-up or converted minibus) or truck about every other day in the dry season to Mocuba, where you can find transport on to Quelimane or Nampula.

Further north, minibuses and *matola* run a few times per day between Mangochi and the border crossing at Chiponde (MK800). It's then 7km to the Mozambique border crossing at Mandimba and the best way to get there is by bicycle taxi (US$2). Mandimba has a couple of *pensãos* (inexpensive hotels) and there's at least one vehicle daily, usually a truck, between here and Cuamba (US$4).

The third option is to go by minibus or passenger train from Liwonde to the border at Nayuchi (MK850). You can then take a chapa from the Mozambique side of the border to Cuamba.

Boat

The Lake Malawi steamboat *Ilala* (p214) stops at Metangula on the Mozambican mainland. If you're planning a visit you must get a visa in advance and make sure to get your passport stamped at Malawian immigration on Likoma Island or in Nkhata Bay.

Train

If you're heading to northern Mozambique, a passenger train departs Limbe on Wednesday at 7am, travelling via Balaka and Liwonde to the border at Nayuchi. The fare from Limbe to Nayuchi is US$3.30, but it's more popular to get on at Liwonde, from where it costs US$2. From Nayuchi (where there are money-changers) you can walk to Entre Lagos, and then get a chapa to Cuamba.

Central

If you are heading for central Mozambique, there are several buses per day from Blantyre to Nsanje (MK850), or all the way to the Malawi border at Marka (*ma*-ra-ka; MK900). It's a few kilometres between the border crossings – you can walk or take a bicycle taxi – and you can change money on the Mozambique side. From here pick-ups go to Mutarara, Nhamilabue and Vila de Sena. There's a twice-weekly train (Tuesday and Saturday, MK800) between Limbe and the Mozambique border at Nsanje.

South

The quickest way to reach Mozambique south of the Zambezi is to take a minibus to the Mozambique border crossing at Zóbuè (*zob*-way; MK500) and then a minibus to Tete (US$2), from where buses go to Beira and Maputo. You could also get a Blantyre–Harare bus to drop you at Tete and then get a bus to Beira or Maputo.

SOUTH AFRICA

There are a number of bus companies running services from Lilongwe and Blantyre to Jo'burg. **Vaal Africa** (☎ 0999-200086) operates a service between Lilongwe and Jo'burg on Tuesday and Saturday for MK14,500. **Chita One** (☎ 01-622313/829879) runs services to Jo'burg on Wednesday and Sunday for MK15,000. From Blantyre, try **Ingwe Coach** (☎ 01-822313). Buses from Lilongwe (MK15,000, Tuesday and Sunday) leave from outside the Total petrol station on Paul Kagame Rd in Old Town (Map p170). In Blantyre, most Jo'burg bound buses depart from the car park outside Blantyre Lodge.

TANZANIA

If you want to go the whole way between Lilongwe and Dar es Salaam, three buses a week (Tuesday, Saturday and Sunday) depart from Devil St in Lilongwe. There's a ticket office where you can book; fares are MK8000 to Dr es Salaam or MK14,000 if you continue on to Nairobi. These buses also pick up and drop off in Mzuzu and Mbeya (Tanzania) and are handy for going between northern Malawi and southern Tanzania.

If you're going in stages, buses and minibuses run between Mzuzu and Karonga (MK800, three to four hours), from where you can get a taxi to the Songwe border crossing (MK500). It's 200m across the bridge to the Tanzanian border crossing.

Once you're on the Tanzanian side of the border, minibuses and bicycle taxis travel the

5km distance to Kyela, from where you can get a bus to Dar es Salaam. You can change money with the bicycle-taxi boys but beware of scams.

ZAMBIA

There are four direct buses per week (two on Tuesday and two on Friday) between Lilongwe and Lusaka (MK6000), also departing from Devil St – the journey takes at least 12 hours. Regular minibuses run between Lilongwe and Mchinji (MK400). From here, it's 12km to the border. Local shared taxis shuttle between Mchinji and the border post for around MK200/1000 per person/whole car.

From the Zambian side of the border crossing, shared taxis run to Chipata (US$2), which is about 30km west of the border, from where you can reach Lusaka or South Luangwa National Park (for more details see p657).

If you've got a 4WD you can cross into northern Zambia via Chitipa in northern Malawi. It's four hours from Karonga to Chitipa on a rough dirt road, and then the Malawian border post is 5km out of town. After going though customs it is another 80km or four hours' drive to the Zambian border post at Nakonde.

GETTING AROUND

You can travel round Malawi by air, road, rail or boat. Compared to other countries in the region, distances between major centres are quite short, and generally roads and public-transport systems are good, making independent travel fairly straightforward.

Air

For domestic flights, departure tax is US$5.

AIRLINES IN MALAWI

Air Malawi (☎ 01-772123/753181/788415; www.airmalawi.com) Air Malawi's domestic schedule has diminished somewhat and the airline currently only operates regular flights between Lilongwe and Blantyre (MK12,000 one way). Air Malawi's booking system is not always reliable, so be prepared for lost reservations or double bookings.

Nyassa Air Taxi (☎ 01-761443; www.nyassa.mw) Provides charter flights to airstrips around the country, and to Mfuwe in Zambia in five- and seven-seater aircraft. The more of you there are, the cheaper it is per person. For example, a one-way flight from Lilongwe to Likoma Island ranges between US$320 and US$210 per person.

Boat

The **Ilala ferry** (☎ 01-587311; ilala@malawi.net) chugs passengers and cargo up and down Lake Malawi once per week in each direction. Travelling between Monkey Bay in the south and Chilumba in the north, it makes 12 stops at lakeside villages and towns in between. (You can get to the Mozambique mainland via the *Ilala;* see p213.)

The whole trip, from one end of the line to the other, takes about three days. The official schedules are detailed in the table (only selected ports are shown).

Northbound port	Arrival	Departure
Monkey Bay	-	10am (Fri)
Chipoka	1pm	4pm (Fri)
Nkhotakota	midnight	2am (Sat)
Metangula	6am	8am (Sat)
Likoma Island	1.30pm	6pm (Sat)
Nkhata Bay	1am	5am (Sun)
Ruarwe	10.15am	11.15am (Sun)
Chilumba	5pm (Sun)	-

Southbound port	Arrival	Departure
Chilumba	-	1am (Mon)
Ruarwe	6.45am	8am (Mon)
Nkhata Bay	12.45pm	8pm (Mon)
Likoma Island	3.15am	6.15am (Tue)
Metangula	noon	2pm (Tue)
Nkhotakota	5.30pm	7.30pm (Tue)
Chipoka	3.30am	7.30am (Wed)
Monkey Bay	10.30am (Wed)	-

The *Ilala* has three classes. Cabin class was once luxurious and the cabins are still in reasonable condition. The spacious first-class deck is most popular with travellers, due largely to the sociable bar. Economy covers the entire lower deck and is dark and crowded, and engine fumes permeate from below.

Reservations are usually required for cabin class. For other classes, tickets are sold only when the boat is sighted.

Sample Routes & Fares

All of the following sample fares are from Nkhata Bay.

Destination	Cabin (US$)	1st class (US$)	Economy (US$)
Likoma Island	52	20	7
Metangula	92	50	2
Ruarwe	46	19	6
Monkey Bay	141	82	18

MALAWI

Bus & Minibus

BUS

Malawi's main bus company is **AXA Coach Services** (☎ 01-876000; agma@agmaholdings.net). AXA operates three different classes. Executive coaches are the best and the most expensive. It's a luxury nonstop service with air-con, toilet, comfortable reclining seats, snacks and fresh coffee, good drivers and even an onboard magazine. Services operate between Blantyre and Lilongwe twice a day (see p173 and p203 for details) from special departure points in each city (not the main bus stations).

AXA Luxury Coach and City Trouper services are the next in line. These buses have air-con and reclining seats as well as TVs, but don't have toilets. These coaches ply the route between Blantyre and Karonga, stopping at all the main towns with limited stops elsewhere.

Lastly there are the country commuter buses. These buses have the most extensive network but they are also the slowest as they stop all over the place. Commuter buses are handy for backpackers as they cover the lakeshore route.

There are several other private bus companies that operate around Malawi, including Coachline and Zimatha. Most of these operate on a fill-up-and-go basis. Fares are about the same as AXA City Trouper services. If you're headed for Mzuzu, another alternative is the comfortable Super Sink Bus between Lilongwe and Mzuzu. There's one daily service in the early morning.

There are also local minibus services around towns and to outlying villages, or along the roads that the big buses can't manage. (In Malawi vehicles with about 30 seats are called 'half-buses' to distinguish them from big buses and minibuses.) All of these operate on a fill-up-and-go basis.

In rural areas, the frequency of buses and minibuses drops dramatically – sometimes to nothing. In cases like this, the 'bus' is often a truck or pick-up, with people just piled in the back. In Malawi this is called a *matola*.

RESERVATIONS

You can buy a ticket in advance for AXA Executive, Luxury Coach and City Trouper services, all of which have set departure times. They have offices at the main bus stations and departure points or you can also buy tickets at branches of **Postdotnet** (postdotnetmw.com), post-internet-business centres found in Malawi's major towns. A week's notice is sometimes needed for the Executive Coach, particularly for Friday and Sunday services.

Car & Motorcycle

The majority of main routes are mostly good-quality sealed roads, though the roads along less major routes are sometimes potholed, making driving slow, difficult and dangerous. Secondary roads are usually graded dirt and also vary in condition. Rural routes are not so good, and after heavy rain they are often impassable, sometimes for weeks. Several of the lodges along the lakeshore have poor access roads that need a 4WD. The same goes for the country's national parks and wildlife reserves.

BRING YOUR OWN VEHICLE

If you're bringing a car into Malawi from any other country without a carnet, a temporary import permit costs US$3 (payable in kwacha) and compulsory third-party insurance is US$25 for one month. There's also a US$20 road tax fee – you must produce the documentation for this if you are driving the car out. When you leave Malawi, a permit handling fee of US$5 is payable. Receipts are issued.

DRIVING LICENCE

You need a full driver's licence (international diving licence is not necessary), which normally requires a minimum age of 23 and two years' driving experience.

FUEL & SPARE PARTS

Fuel costs around MK210/199 per litre for petrol/diesel. Supplies are usually reliable and distances between towns with filling stations are not long in Malawi, so you rarely need to worry about running dry. Spare parts are available in Lilongwe, Blantyre and Mzuzu.

HIRE

Self-drive rates for a small car with unlimited mileage start at around US$50 per day. For a 4WD you're looking at around US$150 per day. To this add 17.5% government tax, plus another US$3 to US$7 a day for insurance. There will usually be a fee of about 5% for using a credit card. Also, most companies will quote you in dollars but if you pay by card they'll have to exchange this into kwacha first – usually at a hugely unfavourable rate.

If you'd rather not drive yourself, most companies will arrange a driver for you at a cost of around US$45 a day.

Rental companies in Malawi include the following:

Avis (☎ in Lilongwe 01-756103, 756105, in Blantyre 01-692368) Also has offices at Lilongwe and Blantyre airports and at some large hotels.

Sputnik Rent-a-car (☎ 01-761563; www.sputnik-car-hire.mw; Lilongwe)

SS Rent-a-car (☎ in Lilongwe 01-751478, in Blantyre 01-822836; www.ssrentacar.com)

INSURANCE

Third-party insurance is a requirement for all drivers, but this can be arranged through car-rental companies or purchased at border posts.

ROAD RULES

Malawians drive on the left, and seat belts are compulsory. Speed limits are 80km/h (main roads) and 60km/h (built-up areas).

Tours

Several companies organise tours around the country, ranging from a few days to three weeks. The following is a list of major tour operators in Malawi, with a variety of budgets to suit most pockets.

Budget Safaris (☎ 0999-278903; www.budget-safari.com; Nkhata Bay) Organises a wide range of individually tailored tours all around Malawi and Zambia (you can choose whether to camp or stay in comfortable lodges). Prices start at around US$360 per person for a five-day tour of Vwaza Marsh and Nyika. It also offers birding tours and car rental.

Kiboko Safaris (☎ 01-751226; www.kiboko-safaris.com) These guys are the best option for budget trips, with a range of wallet-friendly camping tours on offer, including week-long tours of southern or northern Malawi, trips to South Luangwa and Vic Falls, and a 15-day East Africa Odyssey. Prices start at around US$70 for budget camping tours and US$120 for a more comfortable tour staying in chalets.

Land & Lake Safaris (☎ 01-757120; www.landlake.net) An excellent company running tours to suit all budgets, from three-day camping safaris in South Luangwa (per person US$375) to a luxury 11-day extravaganza combining South Luangwa with sailing on Lake Malawi (per person US$2500). It also runs specialised birding and hiking tours.

Train

Trains run every Wednesday between Blantyre and Balaka (MK500), but passengers rarely use them as road transport on this route is quicker and cheaper. The service of most use to travellers is the twice-weekly train service (Tuesday and Saturday) between Limbe and the Mozambique border at Nsanje (MK800).

Central East African Railways took over the running of the railway in 2008. A US$7 million investment hopes to revitalise the railway and extend it to link up with Chipata in Zambia.

Mozambique

Mozambique is southern Africa's insider's tip. It offers beautiful, uncrowded beaches, romantic islands, diving and snorkelling, an intriguing history, and a fascinating melange of cultures. Choose between a comfortable, pampered beach holiday or a rugged bush adventure that lets you experience Africa wild and untamed.

Along the coast, the attractions are countless. Mozambique is renowned throughout the region for its fantastic beaches, where you can laze on white sands under swaying palms or slip through turquoise waters on a dhow in remote island archipelagos. Other highlights include Mozambique Island, with its cobbled streets and stately colonial-era churches, and Ibo Island, with its crumbling ruins and time-warp atmosphere. Inland are Gorongosa National Park and the Niassa Reserve, both of which abound in stunning vistas and wildlife – although it can take luck and persistence to spot the animals. Maputo, the country's lively capital, is unlike any other city in the region, with its Mediterranean vibe, sidewalk cafes, art galleries and renowned nightlife. Throughout – and in contrast to the more strait-laced neighbours, all former British colonies or protectorates – Mozambique's modern face reflects a unique fusion of African, Arabic, Indian and Portuguese influences. Its cuisine is spicier, its rhythms more tropical and its pace more laid-back.

If you're inclined to something tamer, stick to the south, where roads are good and accommodation options abound. Further north, allow plenty of time for getting around and be prepared to rough it – although there are some delightful surprises, especially on the islands.

FAST FACTS

- **Area** 801,590 sq km
- **Capital** Maputo
- **Country code** ☎ 258
- **Famous for** Mozambique Island, *marrabenta* music, Makonde woodcarvings
- **Languages** Portuguese, various African languages
- **Money** Metical (Mtc)
- **Phrases** *Bom dia* (good morning); *obrigado/a* (thank you – m/f speaker)
- **Population** 21 million

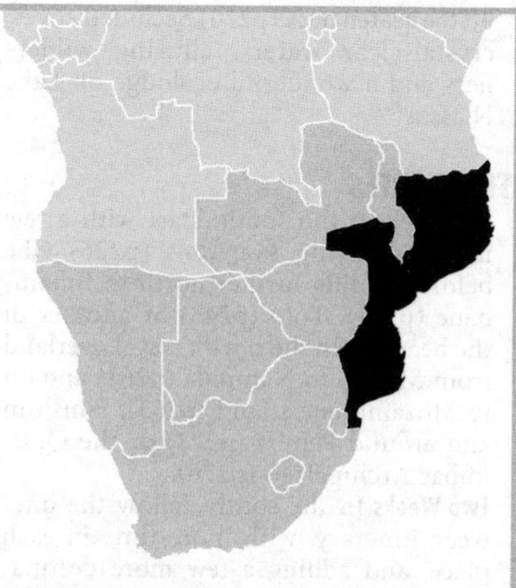

HOW MUCH?

- **Plate of grilled prawns** Mtc300
- **Single-day dive** US$50
- **Short taxi ride** Mtc100
- **Day dhow safari** about Mtc1500
- **Maputo-Inhambane bus fare** Mtc350

LONELY PLANET INDEX

- **1L of petrol** Mtc30
- **1.5L of bottled water** Mtc30
- **Bottle of 2M beer** Mtc40
- **Souvenir T-shirt** Mtc300
- **Plate of xima and sauce** Mtc40

HIGHLIGHTS

- **Mozambique Island** (p263) Quiet, cobbled streets, pastel-painted mansions, whitewashed churches and waving palm trees.
- **Quirimbas Archipelago** (p276) Luxurious Indian Ocean getaways, enchanting Ibo, with its crumbling mansions covered with creepers, and the chance to island-hop on a dhow.
- **Maputo** (p226) Jacaranda- and flame-tree-lined streets, lively sidewalk cafes, art galleries and pumping salsa bars.
- **Bazaruto Archipelago** (p249) A quintessential tropical paradise with turquoise and jade waters full of colourful fish.
- **Off the beaten track** (p270) Secluded coves, crystal-clear waters, alluring wilderness and a wonderful ecolodge on Lake Niassa.

ITINERARIES

- **One Week** In the south: start with a few nights enjoying Maputo's (p226) vibe before heading further north to Inhambane (p241), Tofo (p243) or another of the beaches. In the north: travel overland from Malawi to Nampula (p261) and on to Mozambique Island (p263). Finish in and around Pemba (p273) or the Quirimbas Archipelago (p276).
- **Two Weeks** In the south: follow the one-week itinerary, with more time in each place, and adding a few more destinations, including Vilankulo (p246) and a dhow safari or snorkelling around the Bazaruto Archipelago (p249). In the north: proceed as under the one-week itinerary, finishing with time in both Pemba (p273) and on the Quirimbas Archipelago (p276), including Ibo Island. Alternatively, combine the southern and northern one-week itineraries.
- **One Month** Follow the previous itineraries' southern routings, and add Ponta d'Ouro (p237), Maputo Special Reserve (p239), or another beach or two. From Vilankulo, continue to Beira (p250) or Chimoio (p254) and then to Gorongosa National Park (p253). Alternatively, head to Nampula and Mozambique Island and continue with the northern two-week itinerary. Another option: travel by train from Nampula to Cuamba (p268), and then to Lichinga (p269) and Lake Niassa (p270), from where there are straightforward connections to Malawi and Tanzania.

CLIMATE & WHEN TO GO

Sunshine, blue skies and temperatures averaging between 24°C and 27°C along the coast are the norm, except during the wet summer season from about December/January until April when the heavy rains arrive and everything gets soggy. Temperatures are also higher during the rainy season – averaging 30°C and above in some areas. The hottest areas are in the north around Pemba, in the dry west around Tete and along the Zambezi Valley. Rainfall averages 750mm annually in Maputo.

The best time to visit is from May/June to November, during the cooler dry season, although Mozambique can be visited enjoyably at any time of year. At the height of the rainy season during February and March, be prepared for washed-out roads in more remote areas, and flooding in parts of the south and centre. During the Christmas/New Year holidays, around Easter and again in August, the southern resorts and Pemba fill up with vacationing South Africans.

HISTORY

From Bantu-speaking farmers and fishers to Arabic traders, Goan merchants and adventuring Europeans, Mozambique has long been a crossroads of cultures. For more on the country's early history, along with the history of Southern Africa, see p32.

MOZAMBIQUE

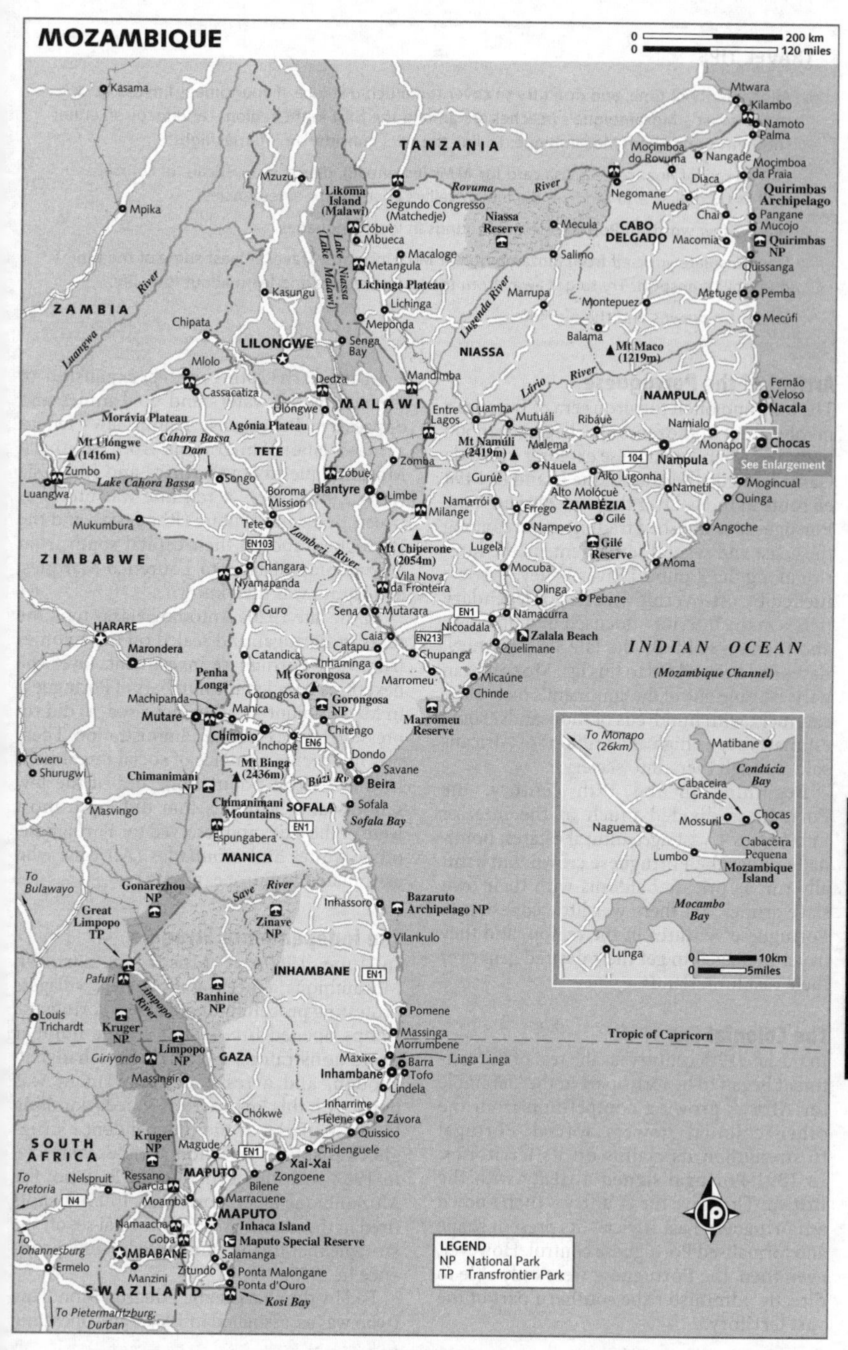
MOZAMBIQUE
0 200 km
0 120 miles
TANZANIA
ZAMBIA
MALAWI
ZIMBABWE
SOUTH AFRICA
SWAZILAND
INDIAN OCEAN
(Mozambique Channel)
NIASSA
CABO DELGADO
NAMPULA
ZAMBÉZIA
TETE
MANICA
SOFALA
INHAMBANE
GAZA
MAPUTO
LILONGWE
HARARE
MAPUTO
MBABANE
Tropic of Capricorn
See Enlargement
LEGEND
NP National Park
TP Transfrontier Park
To Monapo (26km)
Matibane
Condúcia Bay
Cabaceira Grande
Chocas
Mossuril
Naguema
Lumbo
Cabaceira Pequena
Mozambique Island
Mocambo Bay
Lunga
0 10km
0 5miles
MOZAMBIQUE

TRAVEL TIPS

- Allow plenty of time, and don't try to cover too much distance. If your time is limited, stick to the coast – Mozambique's beaches are among the best in the region – and focus on either southern or northern Mozambique. To link the two, consider an internal flight.
- Carry a mix of finances – a Visa card for ATMs (essential!), plus cash (meticais, of course, as well as US dollars and rand), and a few travellers cheques for emergencies.
- Learn a few words of Portuguese or greetings in local languages.
- Don't insulate yourself from Mozambique or Mozambicans. Travel at least some of the time on public transport. Try to get away from the tourist resorts and learn about local life.
- Enjoy the prawns and the nightlife.

Arrival of the Portuguese

The long and often torturous era of European involvement in Mozambique began over 500 years ago when Portuguese explorer Vasco da Gama landed at Mozambique Island in 1498 en route to India. Over the next 200 years, the Portuguese established trading enclaves along the coast and several settlements in the interior along the Zambezi River Valley. Trade – fuelled by oft-overblown tales of legendary riches in the interior – focused first on ivory, and then on gold. By the late 18th century, slaves had been added to this list. Mozambican ports became one of the continent's main slave channels, with hundreds of thousands (some estimates say as high as a million) of Africans sold through them into slavery.

Beginning in the 17th century, the Portuguese divided much of the interior into *prazos* – vast agricultural estates, nominally under the Portuguese crown, but actually run as private fiefdoms with their own slave armies. Yet there was little cohesion to Portuguese ventures in the region, and they never managed to get their desired grip over their vast hinterlands.

The Colonial Era

In the late 19th century, as the rest of the continent began to be torn apart in the 'Scramble for Africa', growing competition from the other colonial powers forced Portugal to strengthen its claims on its territories. In 1891 Portugal signed a treaty with the British. This gave the country – then known as Portuguese East Africa – its present shape and formalised Portuguese control. However, even then, the Portuguese were only able to directly administer the southern part of the vast territory.

In the early 20th century, expansion of the nearby Witwatersrand gold mines and oppressive Portuguese labour laws led to a mass labour migration from southern Mozambique to South Africa and Rhodesia (now Zimbabwe). A rail line was built between Beira and Mutare (Rhodesia), and the Portuguese moved their capital south from Mozambique Island to Lourenço Marques, as Maputo was then known.

In the late 1920s António Salazar took the reins in Portugal, and sealed off the colonies from non-Portuguese investment. Over the next three decades, the numbers of Portuguese in Mozambique steadily increased, as did repression by the colonial administration. There was not even a pretence of social investment in the African population, and of the few schools and hospitals that did exist, most were in the cities and reserved for Portuguese, other whites and *asimilados* (Africans who assimilated to European ways).

The Independence Struggle

In June 1960, at Mueda in northern Mozambique, a meeting was held by villagers protesting peacefully about taxes. Portuguese troops opened fire, killing a large number of demonstrators. Mozambicans had had enough, and a resistance movement was born, with this 'massacre of Mueda' kindling the first sparks of the independence struggle. Resistance to colonial rule coalesced in 1962 with the formation of Frelimo, the Mozambique Liberation Front. In 1964, shots fired in the northern village of Chai set off the struggle that finally culminated in independence in 1975.

Led by the charismatic Eduardo Mondlane (who was assassinated in 1969), and operating from bases in Tanzania, Frelimo's aim was the complete liberation of Mozambique. By 1966 it had freed two northern provinces, but progress was slow and the war dragged on into the 1970s. The Portuguese attempted to eliminate rural support for Frelimo with a scorched-earth campaign and by resettling people in fenced villages. However, squabbling within Portugal's colonial empire and increasing international criticism sapped the government's resources. The final blow for Portugal came in 1974 with the overthrow of the Salazar regime. On 25 June 1975 the independent People's Republic of Mozambique was proclaimed with wartime commander Samora Machel as president.

The Early Years of Independence

The Portuguese pulled out almost overnight, sinking ships and pouring cement down wells as they went, and leaving Mozambique in a state of chaos, with few skilled professionals and virtually no infrastructure. Frelimo found itself faced with the task of running the country, and threw itself headlong into a policy of radical social change. Ties were established with the former USSR and East Germany, private land ownership was replaced with state farms and peasant cooperatives, and schools, banks and insurance companies were nationalised.

However, Frelimo's socialist program proved unrealistic, and by 1983 the country was almost bankrupt. The crisis was compounded by a disastrous three-year drought and by South African and Rhodesian moves to destabilise Mozambique because the African National Congress (ANC) and Zimbabwe African People's Union (ZAPU) – both fighting for majority rule – had bases there.

Onto this scene emerged the Mozambique National Resistance (Renamo). Renamo had been established in the mid-1970s by Rhodesia as part of its destabilisation policy, and was later backed by the South African military and certain sectors in the West.

Ravages of War

Renamo had no desire to govern – its only objective was to paralyse the country. Roads, bridges, railways, schools and clinics were destroyed. Villagers were rounded up, anyone with skills was shot, and atrocities were committed on a massive scale. Many commentators have pointed out that the war that went on to ravage the country for the next 17 years was not a 'civil' war, but one between Mozambique's Frelimo government and Renamo's external backers.

Faced with this situation, Frelimo opened Mozambique to the West in return for Western aid. On 16 March 1984 South Africa and Mozambique signed the Nkomati Accord, under which South Africa undertook to withdraw its support for Renamo and Mozambique agreed to expel the ANC and open the country to South African investment. While Mozambique abided by the agreement, South Africa exploited the situation to the full and Renamo activity continued unabated.

Samora Machel died in a plane crash in 1986 in questionable circumstances, and was succeeded by the more moderate Joaquim Chissano. While the war between the Frelimo government and the Renamo rebels continued, by the late 1980s political change was sweeping through the region. The collapse of the USSR altered the political balance, and the new president of South Africa, FW de Klerk, made it more difficult for right-wing factions to supply Renamo.

By the early 1990s, Frelimo had disavowed its Marxist ideology and announced that multiparty elections were to be scheduled. After protracted negotiations in Rome during 1990, a cease-fire was arranged, followed by a formal peace agreement in October 1992 and a successful UN-monitored disarmament and demobilisation campaign.

Peace at Last

In October 1994 Frelimo won Mozambique's first democratic elections against a surprisingly strong showing by Renamo. Results were similar in the 1999 elections. However, unlike the first elections, which earned Mozambique widespread acclaim as an African model of democracy and reconciliation, the 1999 balloting sparked protracted discord. Renamo protested its loss, boycotted the presidential inauguration and held demonstrations in northern Mozambique that led to a wave of rioting and several dozen deaths.

Mozambique Today

Since then, things have settled down. In December 2004 Frelimo insider Armando Guebuza was elected to succeed Chissano, who had announced his intention to step down. Since taking the reins, Guebuza has

> **HER MAJESTY'S TROPICAL GETAWAY**
>
> Since 1995 Mozambique has been part of the Commonwealth of Nations, to which all its neighbours belong. It is the first member not to have been ruled by Britain at some point.

pursued a more hard-line approach than Chissano, and tensions between Frelimo and Renamo have sharpened. Frelimo has also increased its dominance of political life in the country, and is expected to win in the December 2009 national elections.

Although Mozambique still wins acclaim (and donor funding) as a successful example of postwar reconciliation and democracy-building in Africa, it has a long list of challenges, including widespread corruption and Renamo's ongoing struggles to prove itself as a viable political party. Natural calamities also take their toll, with frequent severe flooding and destructive cyclones. Yet Mozambique has shown a remarkable ability to rebound in the face of adversity, and most observers still count the country among the continent's bright spots.

THE CULTURE

The National Psyche

You don't need to travel far in Mozambique before hearing the word *paciência* (patience). It's the great Mozambican virtue, and most Mozambicans have it in abundance, with each other and with outsiders. You'll be expected to display some in return, especially in dealings with officialdom, and Western-style impatience is always counterproductive. Yet don't let the languid, tropical pace sway you completely: underlying it is a rock-hard determination that has carried Mozambique from complete devastation following two decades of war to near the top of the list of Africa's success stories.

Daily Life

About 80% of Mozambicans are involved at least part-time in subsistence agriculture, tending small plots with cassava, maize and other crops, and you'll see these *machambas* (farm plots) wherever you travel. Fishing is also a major source of income.

Tourism has become increasingly important, and the overall economy is growing. Yet daily life continues to be an economic struggle for many. If one family member is lucky enough to have a good job, it is expected that their good fortune will filter down to even distant relatives and others in the community.

HIV/AIDS infection rates are highest in the south and centre, where they exceed 20% in some areas (27% in Gaza province, which has the highest prevalence rates in the country). Public discussion has opened up in recent years, thanks in part to a dynamic tradition of social theatre in which skits are used to get the AIDS message across. Deaths, however, are still often explained away as 'tuberculosis' or with silence.

Population

There are 16 main ethnic groups. The Makua – who are the largest group, and who are often further divided into various subgroups – live primarily in the provinces of Cabo Delgado, Niassa, Nampula and parts of Zambézia. Other major groups include the Makonde in Cabo Delgado; the Sena in Sofala, Manica and Tete; and the Shangaan, who dominate the southern provinces of Gaza and Maputo. Although Mozambique is relatively free of tribal rivalries, there has long been an undercurrent of north–south differences, with geographically remote northerners often feeling neglected by powerhouse Maputo.

About 1% of Mozambique's population is of Portuguese extraction, most of whom are at least second generation and consider themselves Mozambicans first. There are also small numbers of other Europeans and of Asians, particularly from the Indian subcontinent.

SPORT

Football (soccer) is a national passion and Mozambicans were among the first to start gearing up for the 2010 World Cup in neighbouring South Africa.

Second to football is basketball, which also draws crowds, both for the men's and women's leagues.

The track-and-field scene is still overshadowed by the past successes of the internationally acclaimed runner Maria de Lurdes Mutola, who in 2000 became Mozambique's first Olympic gold medallist.

RELIGION

About 35% of Mozambicans are Christians, about 25% to 30% are Muslims, and the remainder are adherents to traditional religions based on animist beliefs. Among Christians, the major denomination is Roman Catholicism. However, membership of evangelical Protestant churches is growing rapidly, particularly in the south. The majority of Muslims live in the northern provinces of Nampula, Cabo Delgado and Niassa, with the highest number living on the coast and along old trading routes.

ARTS & CRAFTS

Mozambique has rich artistic traditions that continue to thrive despite decades of colonial occupation and civil war.

Dance

Mozambique has a superb tradition of dance, and experiencing the rhythms and moves – whether in a Maputo nightclub or at a traditional dance performance in the provinces – is an opportunity not to be missed.

Along the northern coast, watch for *tufo* – a slower-paced dance of Arabic origin, generally performed only by women, all usually wearing matching *capulanas* (sarongs) and scarves.

Masked dancing is done primarily by the Makonde in northern Mozambique (see the boxed text, p280) and the Chewa-Nyanja in Tete province, who are known for their Nyau masks.

Literature

Mozambican literary developments have closely paralleled the country's independence struggle. During the colonial era, local literature focused on nationalist themes. Two famous poets of this period were Rui de Noronha and Noémia de Sousa.

In the late 1940s José Craveirinha (1922–2003) began to write poetry focusing on the social reality of the Mozambican people and calling for resistance and rebellion. Today, he is honoured as Mozambique's greatest poet, and his work, including *Poem of the Future Citizen*, is recognised worldwide.

As the independence struggle gained strength, Frelimo freedom fighters began to write poems reflecting their life in the forest, their marches and the ambushes. One of the finest of these guerrilla poets was Marcelino dos Santos.

Post-independence freedom was shattered by Frelimo's war against the Renamo rebels, but new writers emerged. They included the prolific Mia Couto, whose works include *Voices Made Night* and *Every Man is a Race*, and who continues to dominate Mozambican literary circles. Other writers from this period include Ungulani Ba Ka Khosa, Heliodoro Baptista and Eduardo White.

One of Mozambique's contemporary female writers is Lilia Momplé, known for *Neighbours – The Story of a Murder* and *The Eyes of the Green Cobra*. Paulina Chiziane's *Balada de Amor ao Vento* (1990) was the first novel published by a Mozambican woman.

For a sampling of Mozambican poetry, try *Poets of Mozambique – A Bilingual Anthology*, edited by Frederick Williams.

Music

Traditional music is widespread. The Makonde are noted for their *lupembe* (wind instruments), made from animal horn or sometimes from wood or gourds. In the south, Chopi musicians play the *timbila*, a form of marimba or xylophone, and are famed for their *timbila* orchestras.

Marrabenta is Mozambique's national music, with a light, upbeat style and distinctive beat inspired by the traditional rural *majika* rhythms of Gaza and Maputo provinces. One of *marrabenta*'s best-known proponents was Orchestra Marrabenta, formed in the 1980s by members of another popular band, Grupo RM, together with dancers from Mozambique's National Company of Song and Dance. When Orchestra Marrabenta split in 1989, several members formed Ghorwane, which became noted as much for its fusion of traditional rhythms with Afropop as for its often-critical social and political commentary.

Well-known new generation bands include Kapa Dêch and Mabulu, a multi-generational band that combines classic *marrabenta* rhythms and hip-hop.

Sculpture & Painting

Mozambique is famed for its woodcarvings, particularly for the sandalwood carvings found in the south and the ebony carvings of the Makonde. The country's most famous sculptor is the late Alberto Chissano, whose work inspired many younger artists.

Makonde carving is centred in Cabo Delgado province, around Mueda, with carving communities also around Pemba and in Nampula province.

The country's most famous painter is Malangatana (see the boxed text, p224). Other internationally famous artists include Bertina Lopes, whose work reflects her research into African images, colours, designs and themes, and Roberto Chichorro, known for his paintings dealing with childhood memories. All have exhibits in Maputo's National Art Museum (p227).

ENVIRONMENT

Mozambique spreads out over about 800,000 sq km, or more than three times the size of the UK, and has a 2500km coastline. It's bordered to the east by a wide lagoon-fringed plain that rises to lush mountains and plateaus on the borders with Zimbabwe, Zambia and Malawi. The highest peak is Mt Binga (2437m) on the Zimbabwe border.

Major rivers include the Zambezi, the Limpopo, the Savé and the Rovuma.

Wildlife

ANIMALS

Mozambique doesn't have the animal herds that you'll see in neighbouring Tanzania or South Africa, and many of its large animal populations were decimated during the war. Yet wildlife is on the rebound, and there is plenty to see. Difficult access, dense vegetation and skittishness on the part of the animals often make spotting challenging, and the country shouldn't be viewed as a 'Big Five' destination. However, if you are seeking something wildlife-related that's different and adventurous, Mozambique is the place to come.

The largest wildlife concentrations are found in the Niassa Reserve, with vast herds of elephants, buffaloes and zebras. Modest and slowly increasing populations of elephants, hippos and other large mammals also live in Gorongosa National Park. With the reopening of Limpopo National Park and the establishment of open borders with South Africa's Kruger, work is underway to encourage wildlife populations in the south to rebound.

Mozambique's marine life includes dolphins, seasonal whales, five of the world's seven species of sea turtles and the region's largest dugong population.

Mozambique is an ornithologist's paradise, with close to 600 bird species, including several near endemics and rare or endangered species, such as the wattled crane and the Cape vulture.

PLANTS

Mozambique's flora includes lavender jacarandas, brilliant red flamboyants and other flowering trees, plus large stands of coconut palms, especially in Inhambane and Zambézia provinces. Large tracts of central and north-central Mozambique are covered by miombo or light woodland. Highly biodiverse areas include the Chimanimani

MOVERS & SHAKERS: MALANGATANA

Malangatana Valente Ngwenya – universally known as 'Malangatana' – has almost single-handedly put Mozambique on the international artistic and cultural stage. He is considered to be one of Mozambique's and Africa's greatest painters, and continues to be a major force in Mozambican cultural and political circles.

Malangatana was born in Matalana village, near Marracuene, in 1936. After spending his early years as a herd boy and attending local mission schools, he began working as an *empregado* (house help) in colonial-era Maputo. Along the way, he began to develop his artistic talents, and in 1959 displayed his first paintings.

Since then, he has continued painting, drawing and creating with a prodigious output, despite an almost two-year interlude as a colonial-era political prisoner, and later post-independence political involvement. Although best known for his paintings on canvas, Malangatana has also worked in various other media, including murals and sculptures. His work is characterised by its dramatic figures and dramatic yet restrained use of colour, and by its highly symbolic social and political commentary on everything from colonialism and war to peacetime rebuilding to the universality of the human experience.

In addition to his artworks, Malangatana has left his mark across a broad swath of Mozambican cultural life. This has included playing founding roles in the establishment of the National Art Museum (p227) and setting up a cultural centre (still in process, and where Malangatana now spends most of his time) in his natal Matalana.

MOZAMBIQUE

GOING GREEN

Here's a sampling of what's happening in Mozambique (see also the GreenDex, p999):

- **Ibo Eco School** (www.iboecoschool.be) gives Ibo island children a good start in their crucial early years. (It also takes volunteers.)
- **Feliciano dos Santos** and his renowned band, the Niassa province-based **Massukos** (www.massukos.org), have received international acclaim for their work promoting social change and sanitation awareness.
- **Eco-Micaia** (www.micaia.org) is working to establish community-based tourism in the Chimanimani Mountains.
- The **Carr Foundation** and staff at **Gorongosa National Park** are doing extensive and impressive work in collaboration with the communities surrounding the park, including in the areas of health, education and literacy.
- **Quirimbas National Park** boasts a number of community tourism initiatives that train locals to be bird guides, and establish community-run campsites, home-stay programs and a tourist information centre.

Mountains, with at least 45 endemic plant species, and the Maputaland area south of Maputo, which is considered a site of global botanical significance.

National Parks

Mozambique has six national parks: Gorongosa, Zinave, Banhine and Limpopo in the interior; Bazaruto offshore; and Quirimbas, encompassing coastal and inland areas in the north.

Bazaruto (p249) is famed for its coral reefs, fish and dugong. Various islands within the Quirimbas Archipelago (p276) can now also be easily visited, and diving can be arranged with the island lodges there and on Bazaruto.

Gorongosa (p253), which has received a major boost thanks to the involvement of the US-based Carr Foundation, is now also straightforward to visit, as is Limpopo (p240), which shares a border with South Africa's Kruger park.

There are several wildlife reserves, including Niassa Reserve (p271) and the Maputo Special Reserve (p239). Gile Reserve, in Zambézia province, is being rehabilitated with assistance from the French government. The Chimanimani National Reserve (p254) is ideal for hiking.

Environmental Issues

Exciting progress is being made in protecting Mozambique's marine resources. Highlights here include ongoing conservation work in Quirimbas National Park and in the Primeiras and Segundas islands off the coast near Angoche.

On the terrestrial side, as conservation measures and antipoaching efforts have begun to show success, with increasing populations of elephants and other wildlife, the instances of human–elephant conflict are also increasing, especially in the north. In addition to fences, more sustainable techniques have been introduced. These include encouraging cultivation of Mozambique's famous piri-piri (hot peppers), which elephants don't like, and roping off crop areas with strings soaked in a mixture of oil and chilli peppers.

Other issues include beach driving (illegal in Mozambique), illegal commercial fishing, and both land-use policy and an economic climate that discourage long-term investment.

Central Mozambique's Nhambita Community Carbon Project (see above) has won international acclaim, and Northern Mozambique's Feliciano dos Santos won a Goldman Environmental prize (www.goldmanprize.org/2008/africa) for his environmental sanitation work.

FOOD & DRINK

Mozambican cuisine blends African, Indian and Portuguese influences, with a dash of piri-piri (hot pepper sauce) topping things off. It's noted for its seafood, including excellent *camarões* (prawns), *lagosta* (crayfish) and the ubiquitous *peixe grelhada* – grilled catch of the day. The cassava- and

MOZAMBIQUE

maize-based staples are *xima* and *upshwa*. One local speciality is *matapa*, cassava leaves cooked in peanut sauce, often with prawns or other additions. *Caril* (curry) dishes are common, as are *chamusas* (samosas – triangular wedges of fried pastry, filled with meat or vegetables) and other snacks. Wash everything down with a cold Dois M (2M) – the national lager.

All larger towns have several restaurants. In major centres, there are sidewalk cafes or *pastelarias* where you can enjoy a light meal or snack with a cup of tea *(chá)*. Everywhere, you'll find small food stalls *(barracas)*, often along the roadside or at markets, where you can get a plate of local food such as *xima* and sauce for less than Mtc100.

Self-catering is easy in Maputo, Beira, Chimoio, Nampula (all with branches of Shoprite) and in major towns. Along the coast, buy seafood at the fish markets and ask your hotel to grill it for you.

MAPUTO

☎ 21

With its Mediterranean-style architecture, wide avenues lined by jacaranda and flame trees and waterside setting, Maputo is easily one of Africa's most attractive capitals. In the bustling, low-lying baixa (port and commercial area), *galabiyya*-garbed men gather in doorways for a chat, and women wrapped in colourful *capulanas* sell everything from seafood to spices at the massive Municipal Market. Along the seaside Avenida Marginal, fishermen hawk the day's catch while banana vendors loll on their carts in the shade. High-rises dot the skyline, lively sidewalk cafes line the streets and there's an array of cultural offerings and great nightlife. Don't miss spending time here before heading north.

ORIENTATION

Maputo sits on a low escarpment overlooking Maputo Bay, with the long avenues of its upper-lying residential sections spilling down into the busy baixa.

Many businesses, the train station, banks, post and telephone offices and some budget accommodation are in the busy baixa, on or near Avenida 25 de Setembro, while embassies and most better hotels are in the city's quieter upper section, especially in and around the Sommerschield diplomatic and residential quarter. A good landmark is the 33 Storey Building *('trinta e três andares')*, in the baixa on the corner of Avenida 25 de Setembro and Rua da Imprensa. At the northernmost end of the Marginal and about 7km from the centre is Bairro Triunfo and Costa do Sol, with a small beach that gets packed with locals on weekends and several places to stay and eat.

Maps

City maps are widely available at bookshops, including a slightly dated but excellent city map put out by Conselho Municipal and Coopération Française, and the Páginas Amarelas *Maputo Guide* map. The backpackers hostels and some hotels also have free photocopied city maps.

INFORMATION

Bookshops

Livraria Europa-América (☎ 21-494692; peamoz@tdm.co.mz; 377 Avenida 24 de Julho) Next to the Geology Museum, with maps and a good selection of English-language books and magazines.

Cultural Centres

Centro Cultural Franco-Moçambicano (☎ 21-314590; www.ccfmoz.com; Praça da Independência) An excellent place, with art exhibitions, music and dance performances, films, theatre and more.

Centro Cultural Português (Instituto Camões; ☎ 21-493892; ccp-maputo@instituto-camoes.pt; 720 Avenida Julius Nyerere) Art and photography exhibits; opposite the South African high commission.

Centro de Estudos Brasileiros (☎ 21-306840; ceb.eventos@tvcabo.co.mz; cnr Avenida Karl Marx & Avenida 25 de Setembro) Exhibitions by artists and Portuguese-language courses.

Emergency

Official emergency numbers are listed following, but they rarely work. It's better to seek help from your hotel or embassy. For emergency medical treatment, see Medical Services, opposite.

Central Hospital (☎ 21-320011/8, 21-325000; cnr Avenidas Eduardo Mondlane & Salvador Allende)

Fire (☎ 21-322222, 800-198198)

Police Station (☎ 21-325031, 21-322002)

Internet Access

There are many wi-fi spots, noted in the sleeping and eating listings.

Mundo's Internet Café (Avenida Julius Nyerere; per hr Mtc50; 🕑 8.30am-9pm Mon-Sat, 10am-4pm Sun) Next to Mundo's restaurant.

Pizza House Internet Café (Avenida Mao Tse Tung; per hr Mtc40; 🕑 8am-10pm) Upstairs at Pizza House (p233).

Teledata (Avenida 24 de Julho; per hr Mtc30; 🕑 7.30am-8pm Mon-Fri, 9am-7pm Sat) One block west of Avenida Vladimir Lenine at corner of Rua das Malotas.

Medical Services

Clínica 222 (☎ 82-000 2220, 21-312222; cnr Avenida 24 de Julho & Rua Augusto Cardoso; 🕑 24hr) Lab, and a doctor on call; Visa card accepted.

Clínica de Sommerschield (☎ 82-305 6240, 21-493924/5/5; 52 Rua Pereira do Lago; 🕑 24hr) Just off Avenida Kim Il Sung, with a lab and a doctor on call. Advance payment required (meticais, rand, dollars or Visa card).

Farmácia Capital Avenida Mao Tse Tung (☎ 82-301 4056; Avenida Mao Tse Tung; 🕑 24hr); Franca Centro Comercial (☎ 82-301 4055; ground fl, Franca Centro Comercial, cnr Avenidas 24 de Julho & Amilcar Cabral; 🕑 24hr) The Mao Tse Tung branch is just up from Pizza House.

Money

There are 24-hour ATMs all over town, including at the airport, at Shoprite, at **Millennium BIM** (cnr Avenidas Mao Tse Tung & Tomás Nduda), and at **Standard Bank** Praça 25 de Junho (Headquarters, Praça 25 de Junho); Avenida Julius Nyerere (Avenida Julius Nyerere, opposite Hotel Avenida) which dispenses up to Mtc10,000 per transaction. **Cotacambios** (Airport ; 🕑 open for all international flights) changes cash only.

Post

Main post office (CTT; Avenida 25 de Setembro; 🕑 8am-6pm Mon-Sat, 9am-noon Sun)

Telephone

Talk-and-pay service is available at the **main post office** (Mtc1 per impulse; 🕑 8am-5pm Mon-Fri) – you can see the amount you'll owe as you speak. MCel and Vodacom have representatives everywhere – on street corners and in shops – for buying starter packs and recharge cards.

Travel Agencies

Dana Agency (☎ 21-484300; travel@dana.co.mz; 1170 Avenida Kenneth Kaunda) Sister agency to Dana Tours, and in the same compound; does domestic and international flight bookings.

Dana Tours (☎ 21-495514; info@danatours.net; 1170 Avenida Kenneth Kaunda) A top-notch agency specialising in the coast. Can also sort you out for destinations throughout Mozambique (plus in Swaziland and South Africa). Midrange and up, with occasional budget offerings.

DANGERS & ANNOYANCES

Although most tourists visit Maputo without mishap, be vigilant when out and about both during the day and at night, and take the precautions discussed on p284. In particular, avoid carrying a bag, wearing expensive jewellery or otherwise giving a potential thief reason to think that you might have something of value. Don't put yourself in isolating situations, and at night, always take a taxi. Areas to avoid during the day include the isolated stretches of the Marginal between Praça Robert Mugabe and the Southern Sun hotel, and the access roads leading down to the Marginal from Avenida Friedrich Engels. Also avoid the area below the escarpment just south of Avenida Patrice Lumumba.

Carry a notarised copy of your passport (photo and Mozambique visa pages) when out and about (see the boxed text, p287). It's rarely checked, but when it is, it's usually by underpaid policemen looking to top up their meagre salaries with bribes. Keep the notarised copy handy (and away from your other valuables). If you do get stopped, always insist on going to the nearest police station *(esquadrão)*, and try to avoid handing over your actual passport. Ask at your hotel where the nearest notary is. Many embassies also provide notary service. The more you can do to minimise the impression that you're a newly arrived tourist, the lower your chances of getting stopped for a document check.

There are several restricted areas that are off-limits to pedestrians (no photos). These include the eastern footpath on Avenida Julius Nyerere in front of the president's residence and the Ponta Vermelha zone in the city's southeastern corner.

SIGHTS

National Art Museum

The **art museum** (Museu Nacional de Arte; ☎ 21-320264; artemus@tvcabo.co.mz; 1233 Avenida Ho Chi Min; admission Mtc20; 🕑 11am-6pm Tue-Fri, 2-6pm Sat, Sun & holidays), half a block west of Avenida Karl Marx, has a collection of paintings and sculptures by Mozambique's finest contemporary artists.

Núcleo de Arte

At this long-standing **artists' cooperative** (☎ 21-492523; www.africaserver.nl/nucleo; 194 Rua da Argélia; 🕑 10-5pm Mon-Sat), housed in a dilapidated colonial-era mansion, you can see

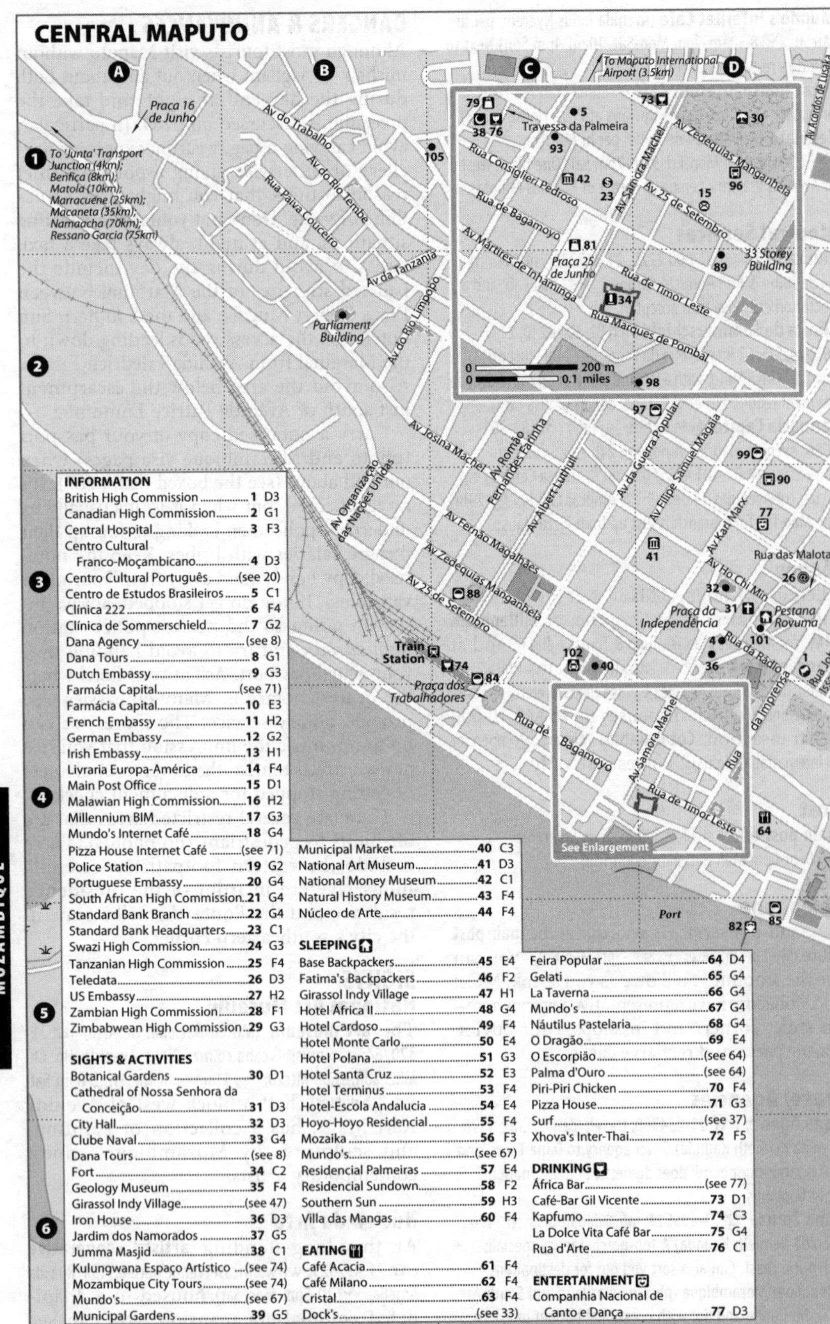
CENTRAL MAPUTO
Praca 16 de Junho
To 'Junta' Transport Junction (4km); Benfica (8km); Matola (10km); Marracuene (25km); Macaneta (35km); Namaacha (70km); Ressano Garcia (75km)
Av do Trabalho
Av do Rio Tembe
Rua Paiva Couceiro
Av da Tanzania
Av do Rio Limpopo
Parliament Building
To Maputo International Airport (3.5km)
Travessa da Palmeira
Rua Consiglieri Pedroso
Rua de Bagamoyo
Av Mártires de Inhaminga
Praça 25 de Junho
Rua de Timor Leste
Rua Marques de Pombal
Av Samora Machel
Av Zedequias Manganhela
Av 25 de Setembro
Av Acordos de Lusaka
33 Storey Building
200 m
0.1 miles
Av Josina Machel
Av Romão Fernandes Farinha
Av Albert Luthuli
Av da Guerra Popular
Av Filipe Samuel Magaia
Av Karl Marx
Av Ho Chi Min
Rua das Malotas
Av Organização das Nações Unidas
Av Fernão Magalhães
Praça da Independência
Pestana Rovuma
Rua da Rádio
Rua John Issa
Train Station
Praça dos Trabalhadores
Rua da Imprensa
Rua
See Enlargement
Port
INFORMATION
British High Commission 1 D3
Canadian High Commission 2 G1
Central Hospital 3 F3
Centro Cultural Franco-Moçambicano 4 D3
Centro Cultural Português (see 20)
Centro de Estudos Brasileiros 5 C1
Clínica 222 6 F4
Clínica de Sommerschield 7 G2
Dana Agency (see 8)
Dana Tours 8 G1
Dutch Embassy 9 G3
Farmácia Capital (see 71)
Farmácia Capital 10 E3
French Embassy 11 H2
German Embassy 12 G2
Irish Embassy 13 H1
Livraria Europa-América 14 F4
Main Post Office 15 D1
Malawian High Commission 16 H2
Millennium BIM 17 G3
Mundo's Internet Café 18 G4
Pizza House Internet Café (see 71)
Police Station 19 G2
Portuguese Embassy 20 G4
South African High Commission 21 G4
Standard Bank Branch 22 G4
Standard Bank Headquarters 23 C1
Swazi High Commission 24 G3
Tanzanian High Commission 25 F4
Teledata 26 D3
US Embassy 27 H2
Zambian High Commission 28 F1
Zimbabwean High Commission 29 G3
SIGHTS & ACTIVITIES
Botanical Gardens 30 D1
Cathedral of Nossa Senhora da Conceição 31 D3
City Hall 32 D3
Clube Naval 33 G4
Dana Tours (see 8)
Fort 34 C2
Geology Museum 35 F4
Girassol Indy Village (see 47)
Iron House 36 D3
Jardim dos Namorados 37 G5
Jumma Masjid 38 C1
Kulungwana Espaço Artístico (see 74)
Mozambique City Tours (see 74)
Mundo's (see 67)
Municipal Gardens 39 G5
Municipal Market 40 C3
National Art Museum 41 D3
National Money Museum 42 C1
Natural History Museum 43 F4
Núcleo de Arte 44 F4
SLEEPING
Base Backpackers 45 E4
Fatima's Backpackers 46 F2
Girassol Indy Village 47 H1
Hotel Àfrica II 48 G4
Hotel Cardoso 49 F4
Hotel Monte Carlo 50 E4
Hotel Polana 51 G3
Hotel Santa Cruz 52 E3
Hotel Terminus 53 F4
Hotel-Escola Andalucia 54 E4
Hoyo-Hoyo Residencial 55 F4
Mozaika 56 F3
Mundo's (see 67)
Residencial Palmeiras 57 E4
Residencial Sundown 58 F2
Southern Sun 59 H3
Villa das Mangas 60 F4
EATING
Café Acacia 61 F4
Café Milano 62 F4
Cristal 63 F4
Dock's (see 33)
Feira Popular 64 D4
Gelati 65 G4
La Taverna 66 G4
Mundo's 67 G4
Náutilus Pastelaria 68 G4
O Dragão 69 E4
O Escorpião (see 64)
Palma d'Ouro (see 64)
Piri-Piri Chicken 70 F4
Pizza House 71 G3
Surf (see 37)
Xhova's Inter-Thai 72 F5
DRINKING
Àfrica Bar (see 77)
Café-Bar Gil Vicente 73 D1
Kapfumo 74 C3
La Dolce Vita Café Bar 75 G4
Rua d'Arte 76 C1
ENTERTAINMENT
Companhia Nacional de Canto e Dança 77 D3

MOZAMBIQUE

0 1 km
0 0.5 miles
E
F
G
H
To Shoprite (500m); Maputo International Airport (3.5km)
Praça da OMM
Eduardo Mondlane University
To Café Do Sol (200m)
Telecomunicações de Moçambique
Sommerschield
Rua Dom Sebastião
To Coconuts Live (500m); Mercado da Peixe (2km); Supermares (3km); Bairro Triunfo (4km); Residencial Belsol (4km); Maputo Backpackers (4.2km); Kurhula Parque Self-Catering Chalets (4.8km); Hotel & Restaurante Costa do Sol (5km)
Av Julius Nyerere
Av Milagre Mabore
Rua Malhangalene
Rua da Resistência
Av Vladimir Lenine
Rua da Base N'Tchinga
Av Cahora Bassa
Rua Pereira Marinho
Rua Fernão Melo e Castro
Rua Pereira do Lago
Av Kenneth Kaunda
Av do Zimbabwe
Rua Damião de Gois
Av Marginal
Rua 1301
Av Kim Il Sung
Rua Duarte Galvão
Av Olof Palme
Jardim Donaberta
Av Paulo Samuel Kankhomba
Av Kwame Nkrumah
Av Mao Tse Tung
Av Agostinho Neto
Av Emília Daússe
Av de Maguiguana
Av Amílcar Cabral
Av Salvador Allende
Av Eduardo Mondlane
Av Ahmed Sekou Toure
Rua Alfredo Keil
Av 24 de Julho
Rua Luis Pasteur
President's Residence
Av Tomás Nduda
Av Mártires de Machava
Av Armando Tivane
Rua de Mukumbura
Rua José Siduno
Rua Augusto Cardoso
Av Francisco Magumbwe
Xenon Cinema
Hotel Avenida
Av Patrice Lumumba
Campo do Desportivo
Jardim dos Professores
Praça Travessa de Zambezi
Av José Mateus
Rua da Argélia
Rua Mateus Muthemba
Rua de Nachingwea
Av Friedrich Engels
Av 25 de Setembro
Praça Robert Mugabe
Av Mártires de Mueda
Av Marginal
Av 10 de Novembro
Facim Complex
Maputo Bay
1
2
3
4
5
6
SHOPPING
Artedif ... 78 H3
Bazart ... (see 4)
Casa Elefante ... 79 C1
Craft Vendors ... 80 G4
Craft Vendors ... (see 51)
Saturday Morning Craft Market ... 81 C1
TRANSPORT
Catembe Ferry Pier ... 82 D5
Chapas to Costa do Sol ... 83 G3
Chapas to Costa do Sol ... 84 C3
Chapas to Junta ... (see 43)
Chapas to Ponta d'Ouro ... 85 D5
Cheetah Express Departures ... 86 G4
Europcar ... 87 G3
Fábrica de Cerveja Laurentina ... 88 C3
Golden Travel ... 89 D2
Greyhound ... 90 D3
Hertz ... (see 51)
Imperial ... 91 F2
Kenya Airways ... 92 G3
LAM ... 93 C1
LAM Sales Office ... 94 G3
MozBus ... (see 8)
Museu Transport Stand ... 95 F4
Panthera Azul ... 96 D1
Ponto Final ... 97 D2
Porto da Pesca ... 98 D2
Ronil ... 99 D2
South African Airways ... 100 H2
TAP Air Portugal ... 101 D3
Taxi Rank ... 102 C3
Taxi Rank ... (see 51)
Taxi Rank ... (see 67)
TCO Turismo & Buses to Beira ... 103 E2
Translux ... 104 E3
Tuk-Tuk Stand ... (see 59)
Tuk-Tuk Stand ... (see 51)
Tuk-Tuk Stand ... (see 49)
Vodacom Ferry to Inhaca ... (see 98)
Xipamanine Market (Chapas to Bilene) ... 105 C1

MOZAMBIQUE

MAPUTO IN...

Two Days

After breakfast at your hotel or a sidewalk cafe, head to **Praça da Independência** (below) and get an early start on some of the sights. Walk to the **Municipal Market** (below), buying some textiles at the nearby shops. Then hire a tuk-tuk to take you on a ride along Avenida Marginal to **Restaurante Costa do Sol** (p233) for lunch.

The **National Art Museum** (p227) is an essential afternoon stop, before resting up for an evening sampling Maputo's **nightlife** (p234).

Spend day two visiting more sights – **Núcleo d'Arte** (p227) is a good choice, as are any of the other museums – and **craft shopping** (p234). For dinner, take your pick of one of Maputo's many restaurants before heading out for another night on the town (or getting to bed early to catch an early bus north).

Four Days

Follow the two-day itinerary. On day three, take an excursion to **Maputo Special Reserve** (p239). Consider spending the night there. Alternatively, on day four go to **Inhaca Island** (p236) and from there to nearby Portuguese Island to relax on the beach or to Cabo Santa Maria for snorkelling.

guns transformed into sculptures, chat with the artists and purchase some of their work. Afternoons are best for watching the artists at work. Adjoining is a small cafe.

Natural History Museum

The **Natural History Museum** (Museu da História Natural; ☎ 21-490879; Praça Travessa de Zambezi; per adult/child Mtc50/10, Sun free; ⏰ 9am-3.30pm Tue-Fri, 10am-5pm Sat & Sun), opposite the Hotel Cardoso, is worth a stop to see its Manueline architecture and its garden with a mural by Malangatana. Inside are some moderately interesting taxidermy specimens and what is probably the region's only collection of elephant foetuses.

Geology Museum

The recently renovated **Geology Museum** (Museu da Geologia; ☎ 21-498053; museugeologia@tvcabo.co.mz; cnr Avenidas 24 de Julho & Mártires de Machava; admission Mtc50; ⏰ 9am-5pm Tue-Fri, 9am-2pm Sat, 2-5pm Sun) has mineral exhibits and a geological relief map of the country.

Other Sights

Maputo's **fort** (Praça 25 de Junho; admission free; ⏰ 8am-5pm) was built by the Portuguese in the mid-19th century near the site of an earlier fort. Inside are a garden and a small museum with remnants from the era of early Portuguese forays to the area.

Several blocks west is the landmark pale-green **train station** – recently voted by *Newsweek* as one of the 10 most beautiful in the world. It dates from 1910, with a dome designed by an associate of Alexandre Gustav Eiffel (of Eiffel Tower fame). Inside (to the left, at the end of the platform, at 'Sala de Espera', is the **Kulungwana Espaço Artístico** (☎ 21-333048; kulungwana@clubnet.co.mz; ⏰ 10am-5pm Tue-Fri, to 3pm Sat & Sun), with a small exhibition of works by local and visiting artists, and sculptures and paintings for sale.

Between the fort and the station is the oldest part of town, centred around **Rua de Bagamoyo**, with the new **Jumma Masjid** just around the corner on the site of what was once Maputo's oldest mosque. Nearby is the **National Money Museum** (Museu Nacional da Moeda; Praça 25 de Junho; admission Mtc20; ⏰ 9am-noon & 2-5pm Tue-Thu & Sat, 9am-noon Fri, 2-5pm Sun), in a restored colonial-era house, with exhibits of local currency ranging from early barter tokens to modern-day bills.

Near the train station is the lively **Municipal Market** (Mercado Municipal; Avenida 25 de Setembro) with colourful stalls overflowing with fruit, vegetables and spices.

Northeast of the market is **Praça da Independência**, fringed by the white, spired **Cathedral of Nossa Senhora da Conceição**, the hulking, neoclassical **City Hall** building, the overgrown **Botanical Gardens** (Jardim Tunduru), and the **Iron House** (Casa de Ferro). This house was designed (also by Eiffel or an associate) in the late 19th century as the governor's residence, but its metal-plated exterior proved unsuitable for tropical conditions.

MAPUTO FOR CHILDREN

There's a large lawn, a playground and several eateries at **Jardim dos Namorados** (Avenida Friedrich Engels). Just next door are the **municipal gardens**, overlooking the bay and a large, not-yet-open water-slide complex. There's also a tiny playground attached to **Mundo's restaurant** (cnr Avenidas Julius Nyerere & Eduardo Mondlane; 8am-midnight). Another good bet is the **swimming pool** (per adult/child Mtc300/125) and small, attached play area at **Girassol Indy Village** (99 Rua Dom Sebastião). In the same compound, in the central gymnasium building, is an indoor playroom, where you can also leave your child with a nanny while working out.

Longer-term visitors can consider a temporary membership at the swimming pool at **Clube Naval** (☎ 21-492690; www.clubenaval.intra.co.mz; Avenida Marginal; per person per month Mtc720).

TOURS

Dana Tours (☎ 21-495514; info@danatours.net; 1170 Avenida Kenneth Kaunda) organises half-day city tours, and 'A Day in the Life' tours, both recommended. The latter takes in a visit to a local school and village, traditional dancing and a local meal, and offers glimpses into local life and culture. Dana Tours also organises 'Maputo by Night' tours, and excursions to various sites around Maputo, including Inhaca Island, Maputo Special Reserve and South Africa's Kruger park.

Mozambique City Tours (www.mozambiquecitytours.com), with a kiosk at the train station entrance, has a hop-on-hop-off 'train' that runs in a two-hour loop to all the city's main sites, with 10 scheduled stops, and four circuits daily. A ticket costs US$36/18 per adult/child, and is valid all day.

FESTIVALS & EVENTS

There's almost always an art or music festival going in Maputo. The best contacts to see what's on include Centro-Cultural Franco-Moçambicano (p226), Rua d'Arte (p234), Kulungwana Espaço Artístico (opposite) and posters around town.

SLEEPING

If you want to be in the thick of things, choose somewhere in or near the baixa or in the central area just above the baixa. For more tranquillity, head to the Sommerschield residential area, or to Avenida Marginal and Costa do Sol, where you'll also have sea breezes. Except as noted, continental breakfast is included with all budget and midrange listings, and full breakfast buffet with the top-end listings.

Budget

You can pitch a tent in the small, enclosed grounds at Fatima's Place (below), Base Backpackers (below) and across the bay in Catembe at Kingston House (p236). The closest camping grounds are well north of town, near Marracuene (see p237).

None of the backpackers have signs – just the house numbers.

Fatima's Backpackers (☎ 82-414 5730; www.mozambiquebackpackers.com; 1317 Avenida Mao Tse Tung; campsites per person Mtc200, dm Mtc300, d Mtc750-1100) In the upper part of town, Fatima's has an outdoor kitchen-bar, a tiny area for camping and a mix of rooms. The same management runs Fatima's Nest in Tofo (p243), although its shuttle service between the two comes with lots of complaints.

Base Backpackers (☎ 21-302723, 82-452 6860; thebasebp@tvcabo.co.mz; 545 Avenida Patrice Lumumba; dm/d Mtc220/600) Small but justifiably popular and often full, with a convenient, quiet location on the edge of the baixa, Base has a kitchen, a backyard bar, and a terrace and braai (barbecue) area with views to the port in the distance. Via public transport from 'Junta', take a 'Museu' chapa to the final Museu stop, from where it's a short walk.

Maputo Backpackers (☎ 21-451213, 82-467 2230; 95 Quarta Avenida, Bairro Triunfo; dm/d/tr Mtc300/1500/1500, d with shared bathroom Mtc1000) A small, quiet place near Costa do Sol, with a handful of clean rooms – including eight- and 10-bed dorms – with fans but no nets. Cooking is permitted if the house isn't too crowded. Chapas to/from town (Mtc7.50) stop nearby, though getting an early one to catch a bus north can be difficult – arrange a taxi the day before.

Other than the backpackers, good, safe shoestring accommodation in Maputo is scarce, and most people opt to pay a bit more for one of the places hovering between budget and midrange. Some recommendations:

Hotel Santa Cruz (☎ 21-303004/6; www.teledata.mz/hotelsantacruz; 1417 Avenida 24 de Julho; s/d with shared bathroom Mtc700/1000, d/ste Mtc1250/1375;) The most basic of the bunch, with clean, reasonable rooms in a nondescript high-rise near the corner of Avenida Amilcar Cabral. Not optimal for solo women travellers.

MOZAMBIQUE

Hotel-Escola Andalucia (☎ 21-323051/4; 508 Avenida Patrice Lumumba; s/d Mtc1000/1625;) Just up from Base Backpackers, this hotel training school has a large wood staircase, basic, mostly spacious rooms with clean linens but sagging mattresses, and a restaurant.

Hotel Costa do Sol (☎ 21-450115; rcs@teledata.mz; Avenida Marginal; s/d US$37/70; P) Above Restaurante Costa do Sol, with straightforward rooms with fan, and the beach across the road.

Hotel África II (☎ 21-488729; safilaher@tvcabo.co.mz; 322 Avenida Julius Nyerere; s/d with shared bathroom Mtc1300/1700, s/d Mtc1600/2200;) Straightforward but soulless rooms – the ones with bathrooms are nice – in a central location.

Residencial Belsol (☎ 82-860 7960; belsol@intra.co.mz; 65 Segunda Avenida, Bairro Triunfo; r Mtc1500) Clean, straightforward rooms above a restaurant featuring Portuguese specialities. It's just in from Avenida Marginal near Costa do Sol.

Midrange

Hoyo-Hoyo Residencial (☎ 21-490701; www.hoyohoyo.odline.com; 837 Avenida Francisco Magumbwe; s/d US$40/55; P) This solid, no-frills hotel rather lacks in pizazz, but rooms are quite decent and fairly priced. The in-house restaurant, O Petisco, is known for its Goan cuisine.

Mundo's (☎ 21-494080; www.mundosmaputo.com; cnr Avenidas Julius Nyerere & Eduardo Mondlane; s/d US$40/70;) Four large rooms next to Mundo's restaurant. Breakfast isn't included in the rates.

our pick **Residencial Palmeiras** (☎ 21-300199, 82-306 9200; www.palmeiras-guesthouse.com; 948 Avenida Patrice Lumumba; s/d US$55/70; P) A recommended place with bright decor, comfortable, good-value rooms – all but one with private bathroom, and all with TV – and a small garden. It's near the British high commission, and about 10 minutes on foot from the Panthera Azul office if you're coming from Johannesburg. If it's full, there are several other hotels further uphill on the same street.

Residencial Sundown (☎ 21-497543; www.hotelmaputo.com; 107 Rua 1301; s/d incl full breakfast from Mtc1820/2340;) A popular, efficient place with good-value, well-appointed rooms in a small apartment block on a quiet street in the Sommerschield residential area. Meals are available on request, as is help arranging excursions.

Mozaika (☎ 21-303939, 21-303965; www.mozaika.co.mz; 769 Avenida Agostinho Neto; s/d Mtc2000/2250, executive d Mtc2750; P) This boutique hotel – convenient to the Hospital Central, in case you're feeling ill – is justifiably popular, with eight small rooms, each decorated with its own theme and set around a small, green garden courtyard. Note that there's just one nonexecutive room. There's a bar, though no restaurant. Advance bookings recommended.

Hotel Monte Carlo (☎ 21-304048; www.montecarlo.co.mz; 620 Avenida Patrice Lumumba; r/ste Mtc2000/2500; P) Convenient central location, dark but tidy rooms and a restaurant. Favoured by local business travellers.

Hotel Terminus (☎ 21-491333; www.terminus.co.mz; cnr Avenidas Francisco Magumbwe & Ahmed Sekou Touré; s/d from Mtc2000/2900; P) This three-star establishment in the upper part of town has small but spotless and well-appointed rooms with TV, plus good service and facilities, a business centre, a garden and a restaurant. It's popular with business travellers and often fully booked.

Villa das Mangas (☎ 21-497078; villadasmangas@tvcabo.co.mz; 401 Avenida 24 de Julho; s/d from Mtc2350/2850;) Villa das Mangas offers a busy albeit convenient location, and tiny, overpriced rooms around a small garden. Rooms come with TV, lots of mosquitoes and a rather mediocre breakfast, and there's an adjoining restaurant and bar. Check 'extras' such as the air-conditioner before settling on a room to be sure everything is working.

Kurhula Parque Self-Catering Chalets (☎ 21-450115; rcs@teledata.mz; Avenida Marginal; 4-person chalets US$119; P) Under the same management as Hotel Costa do Sol and just next door, with serviced self-catering chalets – each with a double bed and a loft with two twin beds – set behind a fence on the inland side of the beach road.

Top End

Hotel Cardoso (☎ 21-491071; www.hotelcardoso.co.mz; 707 Avenida Mártires de Mueda; s/d US$140/155, with sea view from US$160/175;) Opposite the Natural History Museum, and on the clifftop overlooking the bay, this 130-room hotel is a Maputo classic, with good service, lovely, well-appointed rooms – most recently renovated – a business centre and a bar with views over the water and port area.

Hotel Polana (☎ 21-491001; www. www.serenahotels.com/mozambique/polana/home.asp; 1380 Avenida Julius Nyerere; s/d from US$265/290; P) In a prime location on the clifftop with uninterrupted views over the sea, the Polana is

MOZAMBIQUE

Maputo's classiest hotel. It has rooms in the elegant main building or in the 'Polana Mar' section closer to the water – all currently undergoing refurbishment. There's a large pool set amid lush gardens, a business centre, and a restaurant with daily breakfast and weekend dinner buffets.

Other recommendations:

Girassol Indy Village (☎ 21-498765; www.girassolhoteis.co.mz; 99 Rua Dom Sebastião; r from Mtc2895; P 💻 ❄ 🏊) Well-appointed rooms and apartments (also for long-term rental) set in expansive, manicured, enclosed gardens with a pool and children's play area. There's also a gym and a restaurant.

Southern Sun (☎ 21-495050; www.southernsun.com; Avenida Marginal; s/d from US$215/245; P ❄ 💻 🏊) An attractive setting directly on the water (though there's no beach or swimming), with rooms and services on a par with those of other regional Southern Sun hotels.

EATING

Cafes & Quick Eats

Pizza House (☎ 21-485257; 601/607 Avenida Mao Tse Tung; pizzas & light meals Mtc100-200; 🕑 6.30am-10.30pm) Popular with locals and expats, this place has outdoor seating, plus pastries, sandwiches, burgers, grilled chicken and other meals – all very reasonably priced – and a small convenience store. Upstairs is an internet cafe.

Piri-Piri Chicken (Avenida 24 de Julho; meals from Mtc150) A Maputo classic, with the namesake chicken (also available without piri-piri), spicy shrimp curry, cold beers and a good local vibe.

There are dozens of sidewalk cafes (all open from about 8am to 9pm daily) where you can get pastries and light meals, and watch the passing scene. These include **Náutilus Pastelaria** (cnr Avenidas Julius Nyerere & 24 de Julho; light meals Mtc150; 🕑 6am-9pm; ❄), with indoor seating; **Surf** (Jardim dos Namorados, Avenida Friedrich Engels; snacks from Mtc50) with indoor and garden seating, and a children's play area; **Cristal** (554 Avenida 24 de Julho; snacks from Mtc50, meals from Mtc230), with indoor and outdoor seating; **Café Acacia** (Jardim dos Professores, Avenida Patrice Lumumba; snacks from Mtc50), near Hotel Cardoso, with a garden setting, children's play area and bay views; and, the very Western **Café do Sol** (98 Rua Beijo da Mulata; snacks from Mtc50; 🕑 6.30am-7.30pm Mon-Fri, 7.30am-7.30pm Sat & Sun; ❄ 📶), just off the extension of Avenida Julius Nyerere, with connoisseur-quality coffees (including bags of its own blend for sale), pastries and sandwiches. For Italian gelato, try **Gelati** (Avenida Julius Nyerere), next to Xenon cinema.

Restaurants

Maputo has dozens of good restaurants.

Café Milano (Avenida 24 de Julho; meals from Mtc150) Just off Rua Augusto Cardoso, this place has a large streetside eating area and tasty falafel, shawarma, freshly baked pita bread and other Lebanese snacks and light meals, plus the usual array of standards. It also does takeaways.

our pick Restaurante Costa do Sol (☎ 21-450038, 21-450115; Avenida Marginal; meals from Mtc200; 🕑 11am-10.30pm Sun-Thu, to midnight Fri & Sat; P) A Maputo classic, this beachside place draws the crowds on weekend afternoons. There's seating on the large sea-facing porch or indoors, and an array of seafood dishes and grills. It's about 5km from the centre at the northern end of Avenida Marginal.

Feira Popular (Avenida 25 de Setembro; admission Mtc20; 🕑 lunch & dinner; P) Another Maputo institution, with small, informal bars and restaurants inside a large, walled compound. O Escorpião (☎ 21-302180; meals from Mtc200), with hearty Portuguese dishes, and Palma d'Ouro (meals from Mtc200), with *galinha á Zambeziana* (chicken with a sauce of lime juice, garlic, pepper and piri-piri) and other traditional dishes, are two of the best. Taxis wait outside until the wee hours.

Dock's (☎ 21-493204; Avenida Marginal; meals from Mtc200; 🕑 9am-2am) At Clube Naval, with seafood grills and burgers, a breezy, waterside setting and an informal ambience. There's live music most Thursday evenings (jazz – advance reservations required) and Friday evenings, and a late-night bar. The Mtc20 compound entry is deducted from your meal bill.

Mundo's (☎ 21-494080; www.mundosmaputo.com; cnr Avenidas Julius Nyerere & Eduardo Mondlane; meals Mtc200-350; 🕑 8am-midnight; 📶) Chicken wings, nachos, burgers, pizzas, all-day breakfasts and more, served in generous portions at indoor bar seating or wooden tables set around a street-side verandah.

Xhova's InterThai (Rua Mateus Sansão Muthemba; meals from Mtc250; 🕑 closed Mon evening) Delicious Thai food in garden surroundings, complete with a fish pond. It's between Avenida Julius Nyerere and Hotel Cardoso.

Taverna (☎ 84-445550; 995 Avenida Julius Nyerere; meals Mtc250-400; 🕑 lunch & dinner Tue-Sat, dinner Sun) This small place has delicious Portuguese cuisine and rather dark surroundings. It's just up from Mundo's restaurant.

Self-Catering

Maputo's markets and street vendors sell an abundance of tropical fruits and vegetables. For self-catering, try the pricey but well-stocked **Supermares** (Avenida Marginal, Costa do Sol; 9am-7pm Mon-Sat, to 1pm Sun), with an ATM inside the store; or **Shoprite** (Avenida Acordos de Lusaka; 9am-8pm Mon-Sat, to 1pm Sun), with an ATM next door. At our pick **Mercado da Peixe** (off Avenida Marginal), en route to Costa do Sol, you can buy your fish fresh. The adjoining restaurants will cook it for you, and there are tables where you can sit and enjoy it.

DRINKING & ENTERTAINMENT

Bars & Nightclubs

Thursday to Saturday are the main nights, with things getting going only after 11pm.

La Dolce Vita Café-Bar (822 Avenida Julius Nyerere; 10am-late Tue-Sun) A sleek tapas and late-night place near Xenon cinema, with live music on Thursday evenings. By day, try its juices and smoothies.

Rua d'Arte (ruadarte@gmail.com; www.facebook.com/group.php?gid=26252677204; Travessa de Palmeira) Drinks and dancing in the small street opposite the Central Market; check its website first to see what's on.

Café-Bar Gil Vicente (43 Avenida Samora Machel) A constantly changing array of groups; check www.mozhits.com for upcoming performances.

África Bar (☎ 21-322217; www.africabar.blogspot.com; 2182 Avenida 24 de Julho; admission Mtc50; from 5pm Wed-Sun) This long-standing spot draws the crowds on Thursday (jazz night, admission free).

Kapfumo (Train Station; Thu-Sat, evenings only) This unsignposted jazz cafe at the train station has old-world ambience and a mix of live music and CDs.

Coconuts Live (☎ 21-322217; Complexo Mini-Golfe, Avenida Marginal; admission disco Mtc200, lounge free; disco Fri & Sat, lounge Wed-Sun) A weekend disco, plus a popular chill-out lounge.

Traditional Music & Dance

Check with the Centro Cultural Franco-Moçambicano (p226) for upcoming music and dance performances.

Companhia Nacional de Canto e Dança (National Company of Song & Dance; http://myspace.com/cncdmoz; Cine Teatro África, 2182 Avenida 24 de Julho) This renowned national dance company has regular rehearsals – usually between 8am and 3pm Monday to Friday – that are open to the public.

SHOPPING

In addition to the **Saturday morning craft market** (Praça 25 de Junho; about 8am-1pm Sat) and the craft vendors in front of Hotel Polana and on the corner of Avenidas 24 de Julho and Julius Nyerere, shops include the following:

Artedif (Avenida Marginal; 9am-2.30pm Tue, to 3.30pm Wed-Mon) A cooperative for disabled people, selling well-crafted carvings and basketry.

Casa Elefante (Avenida 25 de Setembro; Mon-Sat) A good place to buy *capulanas*; opposite the Municipal Market.

GETTING THERE & AWAY

Air

For domestic and international flights to/from Maputo, see p288. Airline offices include the following:

Kenya Airways (☎ 21-483144/5, 82-303 5931; sales@kenya-airways.co.mz; Aquarium Travel, 252 Avenida Mao Tse Tung)

LAM central reservations (LAM; ☎ 800 147 000, 82-147, 84-147, 21-468000, 21-326001, 21-465074; www.lam.co.mz; cnr Avenidas 25 de Setembro & Karl Marx); sales office (☎ 21-490590; cnr Avenidas Julius Nyerere & Mao Tse Tung)

South African Airways (☎ 21-488970/3, 84-389 9287; www.flysaa.com; Avenida do Zimbabwe, Sommerschield) Near the South African high commissioner's residence.

TAP Air Portugal (☎ 21-303927/8, 431006/7; www.flytap.com; Hotel Pestana Rovuma, Rua da Sé, just off Praça da Independência)

TransAirways (☎ 21-465108; Maputo airport)

Bus & Chapa

For upcountry fares and journey times, see the town headings.

TRANSPORT STANDS

Benfica (Avenida de Moçambique) Chapas to Marracuene.

Fábrica de Cerveja Laurentina ('Feroviario'; cnr Avenidas 25 de Setembro & Albert Luthuli) Chapas to

> **BAZART**
>
> While in Maputo, don't miss stopping by the **Bazar de Arte** (Bazart; Centro Cultural Franco-Moçambicano, Praça da Independência; 10am-7pm Mon-Fri, to 3pm Sat), with an excellent selection of crafts, textiles, artwork, traditional instruments and more – from Mozambique and elsewhere in southern Africa – and a focus on promoting Mozambican and African cultural identity through art.

Swaziland (Mtc250), South Africa, Namaacha, Boane and Goba depart from behind the beer factory from about 6am.
'Junta' (Avenida de Moçambique) Maputo's chaotic long-distance bus depot about 7km (Mtc300 in a taxi) from the centre; most departures are at about 5am. Coming into Maputo, some buses continue into the city to Ponto Final (cnr Avenidas Eduardo Mondlane & Guerra Popular), from where it's about Mtc100 in a taxi to the central area.
'Museu' (Natural History Museum, Praça Travessa de Zambezi) Chapas to the airport and Junta.

OTHER TRANSPORT

TCO Turismo (☎ 82-768 4410; Avenida Vladimir Lenine, just down from Avenida Emília Dausse) runs an aircon bus to Beira departing from its office at Jardim Donaberta (Jardim Nangade). Book direct or through **Golden Travel** (☎ 82-305 1741, 21-309421/2; Rua Baptista Carvalho, just off Avenida 25 de Setembro).

MozBus (www.mozbus.com; at Dana Tours, 1170 Avenida Kenneth Kaunda) provides reliable, insured group transport to most destinations in southern Mozambique, as well as to Kruger park, Nelspruit and Swaziland.

Private, reasonably priced minivan transport for individuals or groups to Inhambane (about Mtc500) and Massinga can be arranged through Residencial Palmeiras (p232).

Departure and ticketing points for express buses to Johannesburg include the following (see p289 for times and prices).
Greyhound (☎ 21-355700; www.greyhound.co.za; 1242 Avenida Karl Marx) At Cotur Travel & Tours.
Panthera Azul (☎ 21-302077/83; panthera@tvcabo.co.mz; 273 Avenida Zedequias Manganhela) Behind the main post office.
Translux (☎ 21-303825, 21-303829; www.translux.co.za; 1249 Avenida 24 de Julho) At Simara Travel & Tours.

Cheetah Express to Nelspruit (p289) departs from Avenida Eduardo Mondlane next to Mundo's restaurant.

GETTING AROUND

To/From the Airport

Maputo International Airport is 6km northwest of the city centre (Mtc300 in a taxi, more at night).

Bus & Chapa

Buses have name boards with their destination. City rides cost about Mtc3.

Chapas go everywhere, with the average price for town trips from Mtc5. Most are marked with route start and end points, but also listen for the destination called out by the conductor. To get to Junta, look for a chapa going to 'Jardim'; coming from Junta into town, look for a chapa heading to 'Museu'.

Useful transport stands:
Museu (Natural History Museum) Chapas to the airport and 'Junta' (Mtc5 from Museu to Junta).
Ponto Final (cnr Avenidas Eduardo Mondlane & Guerra Popular) Terminus for some upcountry buses, and for chapas running along Avenida Eduardo Mondlane.
Praça dos Trabalhadores Chapas to Costa do Sol; these also depart from the corner of Avenidas Mao Tse Tung and Julius Nyerere.
Ronil (cnr Avenidas Eduardo Mondlane & Karl Marx) Chapas to 'Junta', Benfica and Matola.

Car

As in other major cities in the region, car crime happens in Maputo, and it's advisable to park in guarded lots when possible, or tip the young boys on the street to watch your vehicle. Rental agencies include the following:
Avis (☎ 21-465497/8, 21-494473; maputo.airport@avis.co.za; airport)
Europcar (☎ 82-300 2410, 21-497338, 21-466172; www.europcar.co.mz; 1418 Avenida Julius Nyerere) Next to Hotel Polana and at the airport. Currently the only company offering unlimited kilometres.
Hertz (☎ 21-303172/3, 82-327 6220; http://hertz-moz.info) At the airport and at Hotel Polana.
Imperial (☎ 21-465250, 82-300 5180; imperialmaputo@hotmail.com, info@interrent.co.mz; 1516 Avenida Mao Tse Tung) Diagonally opposite Mercado Janeta and at the airport.

Taxi & Tuk-Tuk

There are taxi ranks at Hotel Polana, at most other top-end hotels, at the Municipal Market and on Avenida Julius Nyerere in front of Mundo's restaurant. Town trips start at Mtc100. From central Maputo to Costa do Sol costs about Mtc250. From Junta to anywhere in the city centre costs about Mtc300.

Maputo also has several fleets of tuk-tuks – three-wheelers that can be chartered for daytime sightseeing or rides along Avenida Marginal. Most have meters, with prices roughly equivalent to city taxi prices, or about Mtc50 per kilometre, though this is negotiable for longer distances. You can find them at Hotel Cardoso, Southern Sun, Hotel Polana and other major hotels, or call the **tuk-tuk central booking number** (☎ 84-410 0001).

AROUND MAPUTO

CATEMBE

☎ 21

Across the bay from Maputo is the quiet town of Catembe, with views of Maputo's skyline and a taste of upcountry life for those who won't have a chance to leave the capital.

Kingston House (☎ 82-817 9918; ineedatent@hotmail.com; campsites Mtc200, s/d Mtc300/400) A small local B&B-type place with a couple of rooms sharing bathroom, space to pitch a tent and meals on request. It's about 30 minutes on foot from the ferry (go left when exiting the ferry) – shortly after the bakery, and before reaching Pensão Catembe – look for the yellow house on the beach side of the road.

Pensão Catembe (☎ 21-380050; www.catembe.net; d without bathroom US$60) has a waterside setting and reasonable rooms, but erratic service and standards. It's 4km north of the ferry dock.

Getting There & Away

A ferry runs daily from the dock near the Ministry of Finances in Maputo (per person Mtc5, per large vehicle weekdays/weekends Mtc150/200, 20 minutes). The first boat from Maputo departs at 5am, then 6am, 7am, 8.30am and thereafter every few hours or so until 10pm. From Catembe, the first departure is at 5.30am; evening departures are at 5pm, 6pm, 7.30pm, 9.30pm, 10.45pm and 11.30pm (the final boat sometimes leaves early). Smaller, passenger-only boats (Mtc5) also run throughout the day between about 7am and 7pm.

INHACA ISLAND

☎ 21

Inhaca, about 40km east of Maputo, is an important marine research centre and a popular weekend getaway. Its offshore coral reefs are among the most southerly in the world, and parts of the island and surrounding waters have been designated a protected reserve. The island itself is also notable for its birding. On Inhaca's southwestern edge at the research station is a small **museum** (admission Mtc75; ⏰ 8.30-11.30am & 2-3.30pm Mon-Fri, 9.30-11.30am & 2-3.30pm Sat, Sun & holidays) with specimens of local fauna.

On arrival at Inhaca, you'll be brought to the somewhat congested ferry dock and village area, which is also where the accommodation is. Away from here, the island is much quieter, and lovely. For real beach, head to tiny **Portuguese Island**, a patch of white sand surrounded by crystal-clear waters about 3km northwest of Inhaca, or to **Cabo Santa Maria**, south of Inhaca, with quiet beaches and good snorkelling. Transfers to Portuguese Island are easily arranged once on Inhaca with either the hotels or local fishermen, and most boat charters from Maputo stop there en route. For Cabo Santa Maria, you can arrange a boat transfer (about 45 minutes) with the hotels. Alternatively to the cape, there's an overland route through the Maputo Special Reserve and a self-catering camp; see p239.

Diving (for qualified divers only, no instruction), kayak rental and watersports can be arranged at the watersports centre near the ferry pier.

Sleeping & Eating

Inhacazul (www.inhacazullodge.itgo.com; 6-/8-person chalets US$180/240) Clean, self-catering chalets just back from the water, and an easy walk from the ferry pier. Discounted midweek rates are available. Bring your own nets and towels.

Pestana Inhaca Lodge (☎ 21-760003; www.pestana.com; s/d/f with half board US$245/372/392; ❄ 🏊) The most upmarket option, with bright rooms with mosquito nets, fan and air-con, and larger family rooms, most of which are wheelchair-friendly. There's also a restaurant, and a two-night minimum stay during peak periods.

Restaurante Lucas (☎ 21-760007; meals Mtc250-400; ⏰ from 7am) Pricey but delicious seafood grills and slow service, next to Pestana Inhaca Lodge.

Getting There & Away

AIR

There are daily flights to/from Maputo on **TransAirways** (☎ 21-465108, 21-465011; round-trip per person Mtc2000), departing Maputo at 3.45pm Monday through Friday, at 8am Saturday and at 4pm Sunday. Departures from Inhaca are about 30 minutes later.

BOAT

The Vodacom ferry departs from Maputo's Porto da Pesca (off Rua Marques de Pombal) at 8am on Saturday and Sunday (one way/return Mtc750/1250, two hours). Departures from Inhaca are at about 3pm.

For speedboat charters (about one hour) to Inhaca – with a stop at Portuguese Island en route – or to Cabo Santa Maria, contact **Mozambique Charters** (☎ 84-323 6420; www.mozambiquecharters.com). Dana Tours (p227) also organises Inhaca excursions.

MARRACUENE & MACANETA BEACH

☎ 21

Macaneta is the closest open-ocean beach to Maputo and an easy day trip from the capital. It's on a narrow peninsula divided from the mainland by the Nkomati River, and reached via the colonial-era town of Marracuene, 35km north of Maputo along the N1. Marracuene is also the site of the annual Gwaza Muthini festival; see p285.

Sleeping & Eating

Macaneta Lodge (Complexo Turístico de Macaneta; ☎ 82-715 2813; macanetalodge@tdm.co.mz; 2-/4-person bungalows US$75/150;) Popular with day visitors, with a beachside restaurant, cramped rondavels and a weekend discotheque.

Tan n' Biki (☎ 82-388 5142; www.tanbiki.co.za; campsites per person US$12; 4-/6-person chalet US$87/119;) Just back from the beach near Macaneta Lodge, with camping, self-catering chalets and a restaurant.

Getting There & Away

Take any northbound chapa from Benfica (Mtc50, one hour) to Marracuene, from where it's a 10-minute walk through the town to the Nkomati River ferry (round trip per person/vehicle Mtc4/180, five minutes, runs from 6am until 6pm). On the other side, follow the rutted road for approximately 5km to a junction of sorts, from where most of the Macaneta places are about 5km to 8km further, and signposted. There's no public transport; hitching is slow except at weekends. For self-drivers, 4WD is recommended, although 2WD is usually feasible as well.

NORTH OF MARRACUENE

About 20km north of Marracuene and signposted just off the N1 are several useful places for breaking up your travel if you're doing a self-drive visit from South Africa, including the family-run **Blue Anchor Inn** (☎ 82-308 4290; www.blueanchorinn.com; per adult/child Mtc600/300), with rooms and cottages in large grounds, and a restaurant.

THE SOUTHERN COAST

Long, dune-fringed stretches of white sand, heaping plates of prawns, diving and snorkelling, an established tourism infrastructure, and straightforward road and air access from South Africa make Mozambique's southern coast an ideal destination if you're seeking a beach holiday.

PONTA D'OURO & PONTA MALONGANE

☎ 21

Ponta d'Ouro – a small town with a couple of shops, a petrol station, a few restaurants, hotels and dive camps and a long, wide beach – is the first Mozambique stop for many travellers doing a larger Southern Africa loop (or the only stop, for those just wanting to put their foot over the border from South Africa). Offshore waters host abundant sea life, including dolphins, whale sharks and – from July to October – whales. Thanks to the area's proximity to South Africa, it fills up on holiday weekends.

About 5km north is the quieter Ponta Malongane, with a beautiful and seemingly endless stretch of windswept coastline fringed by high, vegetated dunes.

Activities

DIVING

Visibility that's consistently better than it is just over the border, a profusion of corals, and the chance to see dolphins and sharks have made Ponta d'Ouro one of Mozambique's diving hubs. The Tandje Beach Resort compound is the base for a number of operators that run dive camps. All offer simple tented and/or reed- or wooden-hut accommodation sharing ablutions with the camping ground, catered or self-catering options, diving courses and equipment rental. Most offer low-season and midweek discounts. They include the following:

Simply Scuba (☎ in South Africa 011-678 0972; www.simplyscuba.co.za)

Scuba Adventures (☎ in South Africa 011-648 9648; www.scubatravel.co.za)

Whaler (☎ in South Africa 011-213 0213; www.thewhaler.co.za)

In addition to the operators based at Tandje Beach Resort, local dive bases include **Devocean Diving** (www.devoceandiving.com) and Ponta Malongane (p238).

DOLPHIN TOURS

Dolphins frequent the nearby waters, and catching a glimpse of them can be a beautiful experience. However, remember that dolphins are wild creatures, and sightings can't be guaranteed. The best tours are with **Dolphin Encountours** (☎ 84-330 3859, in South Africa 011-462 8103; www.dolphin-encountours.co.za), which is based in the Tandje Beach Resort compound, and which also offers simple, well-maintained accommodation. The tours are generally part of a three-night package from the Kosi Bay border post, priced from about US$450 per person.

KITE SURFING

Kite surfing can be organised through Moya Kite/Surf, based at Dolphin Encountours.

Sleeping

PONTA D'OURO

Tandje Beach Resort (campsites per person Mtc350, per vehicle Mtc10) In addition to the facilities of the dive camps located on its grounds, Tandje also has a beachside camping area with shared ablutions. It's at the southern end of town.

BougainVilla Sol (☎ 82-310 4360, 82-306 9090; bougainvillasol@gmail.com; d US$80, 5-person self-catering house US$200;) A cosy guesthouse with nicely decorated rooms set around a garden, with braai facilities, and the beach just a five-minute walk away. There's also a self-catering house. It's near the police station, and signposted from the entrance to town. Breakfast costs US$10 extra (order in advance).

Motel do Mar (☎ 21-650000; www.pontadoouro.co.za; 4-person chalets with/without sea view US$102/85) In a good location directly on the beach in the town centre, this motel is a throwback to colonial days, with blocks of faded but well-maintained two-storey self-catering chalets, each with two twin-bedded rooms, and a restaurant.

Praia de Ouro Sul (☎ in South Africa 012-348 2690; www.pontadoouro.co.za; d/q tent from US$150/168;) Well-appointed safari-style tents set on a forested hillside, and a restaurant. It's about 5km south of Ponta d'Ouro town, and signposted from town.

PONTA MALONGANE

Ponta Malongane (☎ in South Africa 013-741 1975; www.malongane.co.za; campsites per person US$14, dive camp tents from US$30, log hut d US$42, self-catering chalets US$90) A sprawling, shaded compound with camping, small twin-bedded log cabins, self-catering chalets, a restaurant and a self-catering area. There's also an in-house dive operator.

Tartaruga Marítima Luxury Camp (☎ in South Africa 083-309 3469, www.tartaruga.co.za; s/d US$100/155;) About 2km further north is this lovely and tranquil retreat, with safari-style tents tucked away in the coastal forest behind the dunes, and a raised self-catering area with sea views. There's no restaurant.

Ponta Mamoli (☎ in South Africa 083-444 6346; www.pontamamoli.com; sea-facing chalet s/d with half board US$168/225;) Log-cabin chalets, plus a restaurant, bar and braai area in a beautiful setting 11km north of Ponta Malongane. Diving, fishing and horse riding can be arranged.

Eating

The following listings are all in Ponta d'Ouro.

Café del Mar (☎ 21-650048; cafedelmarponta@tropical.co.mz; meals from Mtc200; lunch & dinner Wed-Mon) Crêpes and other French fare, plus live music at weekends until dawn. It also has rooms (per person with half board US$52). Look for the orange building on the hilltop in the town centre.

Also recommended:

Scandals (meals Mtc50-150) Just outside Tandje Beach Resort, with all-day breakfasts, omelettes and light meals.

Fishmonger Barracas (☎ 21-650026; meals from Mtc150) Down the hill from and opposite Café del Mar, with filling breakfasts and seafood platters.

Getting There & Away

Ponta d'Ouro is 120km south of Maputo (3½ hours in a private vehicle), about 60km of which is soft, deep sand (4WD only).

Direct chapas depart from Maputo's Catembe ferry pier at 8am on Tuesday and Friday (Mtc150, five hours), and from Ponta d'Ouro at 8am Wednesday and Saturday. Otherwise, go in stages: take the ferry to Catembe, where you can find transport to Salamanga (Mtc75, 1½ hours) or Zitundo (Mtc120, 4½ hours). From Zitundo, there's sporadic transport to Ponta d'Ouro (Mtc30), 20km further south.

Kosi Bay border post is 11km south of Ponta d'Ouro (4WD), but there's no public transport. Coming from South Africa, there's a guarded lot at the border where you can leave your vehicle (about US$4 per day). All the hotels do pick-ups from the border, and it's easy hitching at weekends.

MOZAMBIQUE

MAPUTO SPECIAL RESERVE

En route to Ponta d'Ouro and two hours from Maputo is the wild and beautiful **Maputo Special Reserve** (Reserva Especial de Maputo; adult/child/vehicle per entry Mtc200/100/200), which was gazetted in 1969 to protect the local elephant population and several turtle species. Due to the war and poaching, it's estimated that only about 180 elephants remain, most of which are skittish and seldom seen. A main attraction is the rugged beauty and the wilderness feel of the place. While upscale developments are planned, it offers for now a true bush adventure close to the capital. Another attraction is the birdwatching, with 300-plus species, including fish eagles and many wetland species. The coastline here is also an important nesting area for loggerhead and leatherback turtles; peak breeding season is November to January. At the **reserve camping ground** (campsites per adult/child Mtc200/100), on the beach at Milibangalala, there are no facilities – bring all food, water and supplies with you.

Continuing within the reserve past its northern boundary and on to the tip of the Machangula Peninsula brings you to **Ponta Torres Camp** (☎ 82-252 4670; www.africaafrica.co.za/Pontatorres.htm; 3-bed tent US$81), a self-catering place on Cabo Santa Maria (p236) with safari-style tents that's targeted at anglers and birders; 4WD is essential. Also on Cabo Santa Maria, the same management runs **Nhonguane Lodge** (☎ 82-252 4670; www.nhonguanelodge.co.za; chalets per person US$50), with well-equipped self-catering chalets. For both places, bring all food and drink.

Getting There & Away

Dana Tours (p227) operates day and overnight trips to the elephant reserve. Otherwise, you'll need your own transport (4WD). The main entrance, known as *campeamento principal*, is about 65km from Catembe along the Ponta d'Ouro road. From here, it's 3km to the park gate, and then about 35km further through the reserve to the coast and the camping ground.

NAMAACHA

☎ 21

Namaacha sits on the Swaziland border 70km west of Maputo, with an ornate colonial-era church and streets shaded by jacaranda and flame trees.

Xisaka (☎ 21-960330; s/d/ste Mon-Thu Mtc2210/2600/2750, Fri-Sun Mtc1950/2495/2600;), situated behind the church, has amenable rooms and a restaurant.

Chapas run frequently to/from Maputo (Mtc50).

BILENE

☎ 282

This small resort town – awash with quad bikes during the high season – sits on a large lagoon separated from the open sea by a sandy spit. Its calm waters are good for swimming, although conditions vary with the seasons. If you're based in Maputo and have a car at your disposal, it's an enjoyable weekend excursion, but if you're touring and want some beach, it's better to head further north towards Tofo or south to Ponta d'Ouro. With 4WD (or by chartering a boat – possible at most hotels), it's possible to reach the other side of the lagoon and beach on the open sea.

Sleeping & Eating

Complexo Palmeiras (☎ 282-59019; http://complexopalmeiras.blogspot.com; campsites Mtc170, plus per person Mtc150, 2-/4-person chalets Mtc2200/2550) At the northern edge of town on the beach, this place offers camping, no-frills chalets with refrigerator, braai facilities and a restaurant. Bring your own towels, linens, pans and cutlery. It's about 500m past the market and transport stand: follow the main road into town to the final T-junction, then go left for 1km.

Praia do Sol (☎ 82-3193040; www.pdsol.co.za; chalets or r with half board per person Mtc750) Rustic reed chalets overlooking the lagoon, plus some double rooms, located about 4km south of town along the beach. All come with bathroom and nets, and there's a bar-restaurant (no self-catering), diving, canoeing, quad bikes and boat trips across the lagoon. Turn right at the T-junction onto the beachfront road and continue for 3km, staying right at the fork.

Complexo Aquarius (☎ 282-59000; www.aquariusbilene.co.mz; r Mtc2000;) Just to the right (south) of the main T-junction on a nice, semishaded section of beach are these red-roofed stone chalets and a restaurant. Worth checking out.

Eateries – all on the beachfront road – include **Estrela do Mar** (meals from Mtc75), with seafood grills, **Tchin-Tchin** (meals Mtc75), with grilled chicken and chips, and **Café O Bilas** (pizzas from Mtc120), next to the petrol station.

Getting There & Away

Bilene is 140km north of Maputo and 35km off the main road at the end of a paved access

MOZAMBIQUE

road. A direct chapa departs from Maputo's Xipamanine market (beyond the western end of Avenida Eduardo Mondlane) at about 7am (Mtc100, five hours). Otherwise, go to Junta and have any northbound transport drop you at Macia junction, from where pick-ups run to the transport stand/market area along Bilene's main street (Mtc25, 30 minutes).

To Maputo, a bus departs Bilene daily at 6am, and sometimes again at 1pm (Mtc100, four to five hours). Otherwise, take a chapa (from either the market or the roundabout at the entrance to Bilene, about 1.5km from the beach) to Macia, and wait there for onward transport.

XAI-XAI

☎ 282

Xai-Xai (shy-shy), the capital of Gaza province, is a long town stretched out along the N1. It's of little interest to tourists, but its **beach** (Praia do Xai-Xai or Xai-Xai Beach), about 10km from the town centre, has invigorating sea breezes and makes an agreeable overnight stop. It's usually quiet, except on weekends, when it's packed.

There are several ATMs, including at **Barclay's** (N1), opposite the church, and **Millennium BIM** (N1), further south. Around the corner from Millennium BIM is the central market, and just behind the market is TDM, with an internet connection.

Sleeping & Eating

Kaya Ka Hina (☎ 282-22391; N1; s/d with shared bathroom Mtc400/500, tw/d with air-con from Mtc700/800) Convenient if you're trying to catch an early bus or if you don't want to drive down to the beach, with plain but clean rooms, and an inexpensive restaurant below. It's on the main road about 100m north of the *praça* transport stand. The hotel entrance is around to the side of the restaurant.

Complexo Halley (☎ 282-35003; complexohalley1@yahoo.com.br; Xai-Xai Beach; d Mtc1000-1750;) This long-standing beachfront hotel is the first place you reach at Xai-Xai Beach when coming from town. It has a seaside esplanade, a good restaurant, pleasant, homey rooms (ask for one that's sea-facing), and a weekend discotheque.

Restaurante Kapulana (meals from Mtc150), in town near the market, and **Restaurante-Bar M3** (just south of the N1; meals Mtc200), at the far northern end of town, have meals and M3 also has pizzas. Coming from town, the turn-off for M3 is near the Vodacom-painted building shortly before reaching Motel Concha (on the left).

Getting There & Away

The main '*praça*' transport stand is near the old Pôr do Sol complex on the main road at the southern end of town. Buses to Maputo depart daily at about 6am (Mtc200, four hours). It's marginally faster to take one of the north–south through buses, although getting a seat can be a challenge. Wait by the Pôr do Sol complex on the main road at the southern end of town or, better, take a chapa to the bridge control post *(pontinha)*, where all traffic needs to stop.

To Xai-Xai Beach (Mtc5), chapas depart from the *praça* transport stand (or catch them anywhere along the main road) and go to within at least 700m of the beach.

AROUND XAI-XAI

The lagoon-studded coast north and south of Xai-Xai has a string of attractive beaches, which are all quiet (except during South African school holidays) and popular angling destinations. The area is particularly suited to travellers with their own vehicle, as many of the lodges are located well off the N1, although some offer transfers.

The beach is particularly lovely at **Chidenguele**, about 70km north of Xai-Xai and just 5km off the N1 down an easy access road. The coast here is fringed by high, vegetated dunes stretching to the horizon in each direction.

Paraíso de Chidenguele (☎ 84-390 9999; www.chidbeachresort.com; r per person Mtc925, 4-/6-/8-person chalets Mtc3895/4920/5710;) is a lovely place with accommodation in simple, twin-bedded 'overnight' rooms, or in spacious, well-equipped self-catering cottages – some perched on the dune top with stunning views over the sea, others nestled in the coastal forest. There's a restaurant-bar and a large, sparkling-clean swimming pool. It's ideal for families. It also rents snorkelling equipment for excursions to King's Pool, a sheltered tidal pool about 12km north.

LIMPOPO NATIONAL PARK

Well away from the coast, but a possible stopover for self-drivers combining South Africa and Mozambique, or for intrepid travellers on public transport, is **Limpopo National Park** (Parque

Nacional do Limpopo; ☎ 21-713000; www.limpopopn.gov.mz; per adult/child/vehicle Mtc200/100/200). Together with South Africa's Kruger and Zimbabwe's Ghonarezhou National Park, this park forms part of the **Great Limpopo Transfrontier Park** (www.greatlimpopopark.com; see the boxed text, p62). Ghonarezhou connections are still in the future, but Kruger and Limpopo are linked via two fully functioning border posts. Room rates are payable in meticais, South African rand or US dollars.

Wildlife on the Mozambique side can't compare with that in South Africa's Kruger, and sightings are still very hit and miss. Yet, Limpopo's bush ambience is alluring, and the park area also offers the chance for cultural and adventure tourism.

Sleeping

Campismo Aguia Pesqueira (campsites per person Mtc100, tent rental per day Mtc100) This good park-run camping ground is along the edge of the escarpment overlooking Massingir Dam, about 50km from Giriyondo border post. All camping sites have views over the dam, plus grill facilities, and there's a communal kitchen and ablutions.

Campismo Albufeira (campsites per person Mtc100, s or d chalets Mtc1900) Just inside Massingir gate and near the dam wall, with four simple, clean self-catering reed chalets with bathroom and braai facilities, plus a camping ground with communal ablutions and kitchen.

Covane Community Lodge (☎ 82-760 7830; www.covanelodge.com; campsites Mtc250, d in traditional house Mtc900, 5-person self-catering chalet Mtc1900) This community-run place is about 13km outside Limpopo's Massingir gate on a rise overlooking the dam. For camping, it's better to stay at the nicer park campsites, but for cultural activities this is a good bet, with simple, clean local-style bungalows, including one with self-catering facilities. Staff can help you organise boat trips on the lake, traditional dancing, village walks and visits to the park, and local-style meals are available with advance notice. Advance bookings are recommended. Chapas run daily from Maputo's Junta to Massingir town (Mtc175), where staff will come and collect you.

Machampane Wilderness Camp (www.dolimpopo.com; s or d tent with full board per person US$312) The upmarket Machampane has five spacious, well-appointed safari tents in a tranquil setting directly overlooking a section of the Machampane River where you're likely to see (or at least hear) hippos plus a variety of smaller wildlife and many birds. Activities are the highlights here, including short guided walks from camp, a four-day hiking trail from Massingir Dam west along the Machampane River, and (best) a four-day canoe expedition along the Elefantes (Olifants) River from its confluence with the Shingwedzi River to its confluence with the Limpopo River. The camp is about 20km from Giriyondo border post, and pick-ups can be arranged from Massingir village or from Kruger park's Letaba camp. The camp also offers the five-day Shingwedzi 4WD trail between Kruger's Punda Maria camp through Limpopo park to the Lebombo/Ressano Garcia border post (book through www.dolimpopo.com or www.sanparks.org).

Getting There & Away

The main park entrance on the Mozambique side is **Massingir Gate** (🕒 6am-6pm), about 5km from Massingir town. It's reached via a signposted turnoff from the N1 at Macia junction that continues through Chokwé town (where there's an ATM and a petrol station) on to Massingir.

To enter Limpopo from South Africa's Kruger park, you'll also need to pay Kruger park entry fees, and Kruger's gate quota system (see www.sanparks.org for information) applies. For border crossing information, see p289.

LINDELA

This junction village is where the road to Inhambane splits off the N1. **Quinta de Santo António** (☎ 82-489 2420, 84-490 5105; www.stayonthebeach.co.za/Mozambique_Lindela.htm; N1; campsites per person Mtc175, 1-/2-/4-/6-person chalet Mtc650/1300/2200/2700; Ⓟ) has well-equipped self-catering chalets with fans, nets and microwaves, a shop selling a few basics, a resident parrot, sandwiches, meals with advance notice, and among the cleanest bathrooms along this stretch of the coastal road.

INHAMBANE

☎ 293

Inhambane is one of Mozambique's oldest and most charming towns. Well before the Portuguese arrived, it was a stop for Muslim dhows plying the coast, and from the 18th century, Inhambane was an important trading port for ivory and slaves.

Today, it's a sleepy place with quiet, shaded streets lined with old houses and buildings, conducive to leisurely strolling.

Information

Barclay's Bank (Avenida da Independência) ATM.
Centro Provincial de Recursos Digitais de Inhambane (per min Mtc0.50; 8am-8pm Mon-Fri, 9am-4pm Sat) Internet access.
Millennium BIM (Avenida Acordos de Lusaka) ATM.
Tourist Information Centre (293-56149; info@inhambane-info.net; at Litanga Agência de Viagems) At the entrance to the central market, with city info, walking tours, dhow trips and more.
Verdinho's (Avenida da Independência; per hr Mtc80; 8am-10pm Mon-Sat) Broadband internet.

Sights

Apart from the general ambience and the bayside setting, Inhambane's attractions include the 18th-century **cathedral of Nossa Senhora de Conceição** near the water, and the old and 'new' **mosques**. There's also a tiny **museum** (Avenida da Vigilância; admission free, donations welcome; 9am-5pm Tue-Fri, 2pm-5pm Sat & Sun) near the new mosque.

Sleeping

Pensão Pachiça (293-20565, 82-355 9590; www.barralighthouse.com; Rua 3 de Fevereiro; dm US$15, s/d US$25/40, meals Mtc140-240) This recommended backpackers on the waterfront has clean rooms and dorm beds, a restaurant-bar serving pizzas and local cuisine and a rooftop terrace overlooking the bay. From the ferry, take a left coming off the jetty and continue about 300m. The same management runs campgrounds at Tofinho and Barra lighthouse, and can help with bus travel info between Mozambique and South Africa – see www.inhambane.co.za.

Sensasol (r about Mtc500) A row of small rooms facing a tiny garden – all with double bed, fan and net, and some with TV and minifridge – that were set to open soon at the time of research. It's just off Avenida da Independência.

Casa Jensen (293-20883, 82-859 6150; casajenseninhambane@gmail.com; r Mtc900-1800; P) A recommended stopover for business or midrange travellers. Rooms have internet, cable TV and minifridge and breakfasts are large and good. Takeaway meals can be arranged for lunch and dinner. It's just off the airport road; the turnoff is opposite Mercado Gilo.

Hotel Inhambane (293-20855; (Avenida da Independência; s/d Mon-Thu Mtc1345/1905, Fri-Sun Mtc975/1345;) Simple, clean rooms with minifridge, TV and hot water in the town centre.

Eating

Restaurante Tic-Tic (227a Avenida da Revolução; meals from Mtc80) A good spot for inexpensive local meals, diagonally opposite the market.

Bistro-Café Sem Ceremônias (meals from Mtc180; 7am-10pm;) At the eastern end of Avenida da Independência across from the post office, with indoor and outdoor seating, pizzas, chicken and fish dishes and salads.

Verdinho's (Avenida da Independência; salads from Mtc100, meals from Mtc200; 8am-10pm Mon-Sat;) Currently the 'in' place in Inhambane with a large menu, including meze, gourmet salads and burgers and continental dishes – all delicious – and indoor seating or shaded tables outside on the patio where you can watch the passing scene.

> **LAND OF THE GOOD PEOPLE**
>
> On arrival in Inhambane, the 15th-century Portuguese explorer Vasco da Gama was reportedly so charmed by the locals that he gave the area the name *terra da boa gente* or 'land of the good people'.

Getting There & Away

AIR

LAM has four flights weekly connecting Inhambane with Maputo, Vilankulo and Johannesburg.

Air Travelmax (in South Africa 011-701 3222; www.airtravelmax) flies between Inhambane and Johannesburg's Lanseria airport.

BOAT

Small motorised passenger boats operate from sunrise to sundown between Inhambane and Maxixe (Mtc12.50, 25 minutes). The pier on the Maxixe side is just across the N1 from the main bus stand. Sailing dhows do the trip more slowly for Mtc5.

BUS

The bus station is behind the market. Chapas to Tofo run throughout the day (Mtc20, one hour). There are two direct buses to Maputo daily, departing at 5.30am and 11am (Mtc350, seven hours, 450km). For other southbound buses, and for all northbound transport, you'll need to head to Maxixe.

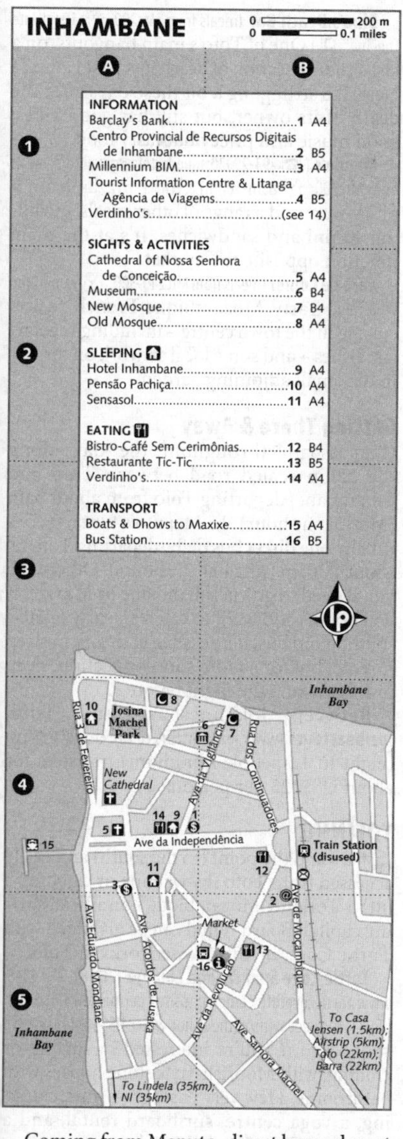

Coming from Maputo, direct buses depart Junta between 5am and 7am, or any northbound bus to Maxixe can be taken.

TOFO

☎ 293

Tofo has long been legendary on the Southern Africa holidaymakers' scene, with its azure waters, long arc of beach, easy access and party-time atmosphere.

Tofo On-Line (upstairs at Dino's Beach Bar; per hr Mtc100; 10am-6pm Thu-Tue) has internet access. The closest ATMs and banks are in Inhambane.

Activities

Diving is excellent from Tofo, with the surrounding waters known particularly for their manta rays and whale sharks. Operators (both PADI Gold Palm) include **Diversity Scuba** (☎ 293-29002; www.diversityscuba.com) in the town centre and **Tofo Scuba** (☎ 293-79030, 82-826 0140; www.tofoscuba.com), about 1km down the beach. Further on, at Bamboozi Beach Lodge, is **Liquid Adventures** (☎ 293-29046, 84-545 3094; www.divingtofo.com). All also organise whale shark snorkelling safaris.

Waterworks Surf & Coffee Shop (town centre) next to Diversity Scuba rents kayaks and surfboards.

Sleeping

BUDGET

Fatima's Nest (☎ 82-414 5730; www.mozambiquebackpackers.com; campsites per person Mtc150, dm Mtc300, s/d tent Mtc500/650; s/d/tr bungalows Mtc500/650/950, s/d with bathroom Mtc750/1150) A makeshift, crowded place about 1.5km south of Bamboozi's on low dunes overlooking the beach, worth noting primarily because it's one of Tofo's cheapest options. On offer: camping, small safari-style tents, no-frills reed bungalows, a kitchen, bar, pool table and evening beach bonfires.

Bamboozi Beach Lodge (☎ 293-29040; www.bamboozibeachlodge.com; dm Mtc330, per person in open/closed hut Mtc300/350, 3-person chalets Mtc2000, d sea-view chalet Mtc3000;) Good dorm beds and basic reed huts – some with floor mattresses and others with beds – all behind the dunes. There are also five stilted ensuite reed A-frame 'chalets' (a couple of which are self-catering) and a nicer chalet up on the dune with sea views. All accommodation has mosquito nets, and the dune-top bar-restaurant has magnificent views. It's 3km north of town along a sandy road. Wednesday and Friday are party nights, and there's an on-site dive operator.

Nordin's Lodge (☎ 293-29009, 82-868 5950; 2-/4-person chalets Mtc1250/2500) The unassuming Nordin's is at the northern edge of town in a shaded location directly on the beach. It has rustic, slightly run-down thatched chalets that come with hot water, fridge and self-catering facilities, and the venerable Nordin himself ensuring that everything is OK. There are no meals.

Mango Beach (☎ 82-943 4660; www.mangobeach.co.za; d hut Mtc690, d Mtc1400, 4-/6-person chalets Mtc1500/3200) A large place behind the dunes about 4km north of town and about 2km beyond Bamboozi Beach Lodge. It has a cluster of basic huts, plus some simple but well-equipped self-catering chalets – all behind the dunes, and all with nets. There's a good dune-top restaurant with views.

Mundo's (☎ 293-29020; mundostofo@gmail.com; s/d from Mtc1200/1800; ❄) Formerly Restaurante Ferroviário, this sister-restaurant to Mundo's in Maputo has a row of small, clean rooms (with nets) next to the restaurant and across from the market at Tofo's main junction. Check that your air-con is working first, as the rooms aren't well ventilated otherwise. Transfers from Inhambane can be arranged.

MIDRANGE

Annex of Aquático Ocean Lodge (☎ 82-857 2850; www.aquaticolodge.com; tr US$68) Five attached self-catering rooms directly on the beach next to Tofo Scuba, all with one double and one single bed and a tiny minicooker. Good location and good value.

Hotel Tofo Mar (☎ 293-290443; www.hotel-tofomar.com; s/d Mtc1250/2500, with sea view Mtc1600/2600; ❄) Situated in a prime location directly on the beach in the town centre, this is the only 'proper' hotel (ie nonbungalow-style place) in Tofo. Rooms are on the modest side, but spacious and recently renovated. The sea-view rooms are worth the price difference.

Casa Barry (☎ 293-29007; www.casabarry.com; d reed casita Mtc1800, 4-/6-person chalets Mtc4920/5800, 4-person cabanas Mtc5600) Well located on the beach at the southern end of town, Casa Barry has a camping area and basic double huts on the back of the property without sea views, as well as a collection of large, closely spaced reed-and-thatch self-catering chalets and newer 'cabanas' and a beachfront restaurant.

Eating

Waterworks Surf & Coffee Shop (breakfasts & light meals from Mtc100; 🕑 7am-5pm Tue-Sun) All-day breakfasts featuring muesli, waffles, porridge and more, plus sandwiches and other light meals. It's next to Diversity Scuba in the town centre.

Tofo Scuba (www.tofoscuba.com; light meals from Mtc150) Head here for salads and other fresh, crunchy food – a good bet for vegetarians.

Dino's Beach Bar (meals from Mtc200; 🕑 10am-late Thu-Tue; 💻) One of Tofo's main hangouts, on a fast-eroding section of beach just past Fatima's Nest. It's struggling a bit these days after the death of its owner, but still has good vibes, good music and pricey but tasty food.

Mundo's (☎ 293-29020; mundostofo@gmail.com; meals from Mtc200; 🕑 8am-10pm) Good pizzas from a pizza oven, and a range of other meals, including panini and sandwiches. It's at the main junction opposite the market.

Casa de Comer (meals from Mtc240-300; 🕑 9am-10pm Wed-Mon) Tasty Mozambique-French fusion cuisine in the town centre – including vegetarian dishes – and some local artwork on display in the small adjoining garden.

Getting There & Away

Chapas run throughout the day along the 22km sealed road between Tofo and Inhambane, departing Tofo from about 5am (Mtc15, one hour). To Maputo's Junta, there's usually one direct bus daily, departing Tofo by about 4.30am (Mtc400; 7½ hours). Otherwise, you'll need to go via Inhambane or Maxixe. If you do this and want to catch an early north–southbound bus, it's possible in theory to sleep in Tofo, but for a more sure connection, sleep in Inhambane the night before.

Between Johannesburg and Tofo, **Jozibeartours** (www.jozibeartours.co.za) does group (eight to 12 people minimum) transfers for about US$125 per person.

TOFINHO

Just around the point (to the south) and easily accessed from Tofo (by walking or catching a lift) is Tofinho, Mozambique's unofficial surfing capital. Board rental can be arranged with Turtle Cove, or with Waterworks in Tofo.

Turtle Cove Surf & Yoga Lounge (☎ 82-719 4848; www.turtlecovetofo.com; campsites per person US$6, dm US$11, d chalet with/without hot water US$60/44) is the spot to go if you're interested in surfing or chilling, with Moorish-style stone houses with bathrooms, a few very basic grass huts, camping, a yoga centre, surfboard rental, and a restaurant featuring sushi nights, among other delicacies. Breakfast costs extra.

Under the same management as Inhambane's Pensão Pachiça, **Tofinho Back Door Campsite** (www.barralighthouse.com; campsites per person US$10, d casitas US$30) has camping overlooking the sea – all sites have *barracas*, power point and water. There are also simple reed *casitas* or bungalows with hammocks and mosquito nets and shared hot-water ablutions.

Just back from cliff near the Frelimo monument, **Café no Mar** (☎ 84-826 1953; www.cafenomar.com; d Mtc3600) has four small but well-appointed and classy rooms with nets, fan and mini-fridge, and meals. Rates include morning and afternoon transfers to/from the beach at Tofo.

Casa de John (Casa Amarela; ☎ in South Africa 082-451 7498; www.casajohn.co.za; 2-/3-bedroom house US$125/187;), next door, has lovely, well-appointed two- and three-bedroom self-catering houses in a breezy setting on the cliff overlooking the sea.

BARRA

☎ 293

Barra sits at the tip of the Barra Peninsula, where the waters of Inhambane Bay mix with those of the Indian Ocean. It's beautiful, but unlike Tofo, there's no town, and everything's spread out. Many self-drivers prefer Barra's quieter scene and its range of midrange accommodation options, but Tofo is a better bet if you're relying on public transport.

Barra Dive Resorts (www.barradiveresorts.com; Barra Lodge) offers diving and instruction.

Sleeping & Eating

Barra Lighthouse (Farol de Barra; ☎ 82-960 3550; www.barralighthouse.com; campsites per adult/child US$10/5) Camping and views next to the lighthouse at Barra Point. Take the signposted 4WD-only road off the Barra road.

Barra Lodge (☎ 293-20561, 82-320 6070; www.barralodge.co.za; bunkhouse d US$59, casita s/d with half board US$147/247, 6-person self-catering cottages US$213;) One of Barra's largest, longest-running and most outfitted places offers a range of accommodation – from small twin-bedded reed *casitas* with bathroom to larger, well-equipped self-catering cottages – plus a beachside bar-restaurant, a full range of activities and excursions to its sister lodge at Pomene, further up the coast. For backpackers, there's a divers' bunkhouse with hot showers and a cooking area.

Flamingo Bay Water Lodge (☎ 293-56001/5; www.barraresorts.com; s/d with half board US$228/374;) Well-appointed wood-and-thatch stilt houses lined up in a row directly over the bay, and a restaurant. No children under 12 years of age permitted. It's under the same management as the nearby Barra Lodge, and it provides transfers to/from the Barra Lodge beach.

Bar Babalaza (meals from Mtc100) About 6km from Barra at the junction where the roads to Tofo and Barra diverge, with meals, drinks and air for your tyres.

Getting There & Away

Barra Lodge and Flamingo Bay offer fly-in packages from Johannesburg.

The turn-off for Barra is about 15km from Inhambane en route to Tofo – go left at Bar Babalaza. There are daily chapas between Inhambane and Conguiana village along the Barra road, from where you'll need to sort out a pick-up or walk (about 4km to Barra Lodge).

MAXIXE

☎ 293

Maxixe (ma-sheesh), about 450km northeast of Maputo on the N1, has little to recommend it to travellers except its convenient location as a stopping point for traffic up and down the coast. It's also the place to get off the bus and onto the boat if you're heading to Inhambane, across the bay. There's an ATM at Millennium BIM, just off the N1.

Maxixe Camping (☎ 293-30351; N1; campsites per person Mtc150), next to the jetty, has an enclosed, rather scruffy camping ground overlooking the bay. You can leave your vehicle here while visiting Inhambane or Ponta Linga Linga for Mtc75 per vehicle per day.

Stop (☎ 293-30025; N1; meals from Mtc125; 6am-10pm), next to the jetty, has meals. It also rents clean rooms (room/suite Mtc900/1500) with air-con and hot water nearby.

Getting There & Away

Buses to Maputo (Mtc300, 6½ hours, 450km) depart from the bus stand by the Tribunal from 6am. There are no buses to Beira originating in Maxixe – you'll need to try to get space on one of those coming from Maputo that stop at Maxixe's main bus stand (Mtc850 from Maxixe to Beira). Thirty-seater buses to Vilankulo originating in Maputo depart Maxixe from about 10am from the main bus stand. Otherwise, chapas to Vilankulo (Mtc175, 3½ hours) depart throughout the day from Praça 25 de Setembro (Praça de Vilankulo), just a couple of blocks north of the bus stand in front of the Conselho Municipal.

MASSINGA & MORRUNGULO

☎ 293

Massinga has several ATMs, including **Millennium BIM** (one block west of the N1) and **BCI** (N1), at the southern end of town. There's accommodation at **Dalilo's Hotel** (☎ 293-71043, 82-816 8950; N1; tw with/without bathroom from Mtc750/500, air-con ste Mtc1500;) at the northern end of town, and meals at **Dalilo's Restaurant** (N1; meals from Mtc150), just south of Dalilo's Hotel.

Several kilometres further north is the signposted turn-off for lovely Morrungulo beach and the equally lovely **Ponta Morrungulo** (www.pontamorrungulo.co.za; campsites per adult/child Mtc320/160, 4-person chalet Mtc3500-3800), with a mix of beachfront and garden self-catering reed-and-thatch chalets and camping – all on a large, manicured bougainvillea-dotted lawn. There's also a restaurant (closed Monday). About 1.5km north of here is **Sylvia Shoal** (www.mozambique1.com; campsites per person US$12, barracas US$14, 2-/4-person chalet US$66/103), with camping, a few self-catering chalets set in large palm-studded grounds behind the dunes and a restaurant (open during low season with advance bookings only).

Getting There & Away

Most north–south buses stop at Massinga. Morrungulo is 13km from the main road; sporadic chapas (Mtc25) run from the Massinga transport stand (on the N1) to Morrungulo village – close to Ponta Morrungulo and Morrungulo Bay, and within a few kilometres' walk of Sylvia Shoal.

POMENE

Pomene, the site of a colonial-era beach resort, is known for its fishing, its birdwatching and its stunning, remote setting between the estuary and the open sea.

Pomene Lodge (☎ 82-369 8580, in South Africa 011-314 3355; www.pomene.co.za; campsites per person US$16, 4-/6-person self-catering bungalow US$120/160, s/d water chalet with half board US$160/282;), in a fine setting on a spit of land between the estuary and the sea, has basic self-catering reed bungalows just back from the beach, plus a row of newer, spacious and very lovely 'water chalets' directly over the estuary – a great splurge. There's also camping (hot and cold water), and a restaurant–bar.

On a rise amid the mangroves and coastal vegetation on the mainland side of the estuary, **Pomene View** (☎ in South Africa 083-962 9818; www.pomeneview.co.za; 3-/5-person chalets US$56/94;) is small and tranquil, with its own special appeal and wide views. Accommodation is in self-catering brick-and-thatch chalets, and there's a bar and restaurant. Take the same signposted turn-off north of Massinga as for Pomene Lodge, and then follow the Pomene View signs.

Getting There & Away

The Pomene turn-off is about 11km north of Massinga, and signposted immediately after the Morrungulo turnoff. From the turn-off (which is also the end of the tarmac), it's about 58km (allow 1½ to two hours) further along an unpaved road to Pomene Lodge, and about 54km to Pomene View (branch left at the small signpost). In the dry season, it's possible to reach Pomene View with a 2WD with clearance. For Pomene Lodge, you'll need 4WD. There's an airstrip for charter flights from Inhambane and Vilankulo.

Via public transport, there are one or two chapas weekly from Massinga to Pomene village (Mtc100), which is a few kilometres before Pomene Lodge. Most locals prefer to take a chapa from Massinga to Mashungo village (Mtc105, daily), and then a boat across the estuary to Pomene Lodge and village. However, the chapa departs Massinga about 3pm, only reaching Mashungo about 8pm or 9pm. There is nowhere in Mashungo village to sleep, although you could try your luck asking locally for permission to camp.

VILANKULO

☎ 293

Vilankulo is a sprawling town that's usually very sleepy, except during South African holidays, when it fills up. It's the finishing (or starting) point of Mozambique's southern tourist circuit with good facilities, and is also the main gateway for visiting the Bazaruto Archipelago.

Orientation

The bus stand, market and ATMs are at the southwestern end of town near the main junction. About 3km northwest of here following the tarmac Avenida Eduardo Mondlane is Bairro Mukoke, with another ATM, the old Dona Ana Hotel (currently being refurbished) and a cluster of sleeping options within easy reach. The beachfront road, with more sleeping places along it or just inland, parallels Avenida Eduardo Mondlane to the east.

Information

Barclay's Bank (Avenida Eduardo Mondlane) ATM (Visa only); near the town entrance.

BCI (Avenida Eduardo Mondlane) ATM (Visa only); near the town entrance, just down from Barclay's.

Millennium BIM (Avenida Eduardo Mondlane; Bairro Mukoke) ATM (Visa and MasterCard).

Telecomunicações de Moçambique (TDM; per min Mtc1; 🕒 7am-5pm Mon-Fri) Internet access and telephone calls in the town centre.

Tourist Information (www.vilankulo.com; 🕒 9am-noon & 1-4pm Mon-Fri, 8am-noon Sat) A helpful stop, with town maps and general info. It's at the *'município'* in the town centre.

Activities

The diving here is very good, although the main sites are well offshore (about 45 minutes' boat ride), around the Bazaruto Archipelago. The main operator is **Odyssea Dive** (www.odysseadive.com), based at Baobab Beach Backpackers.

For day or overnight dhow safaris around the Bazaruto Archipelago, try **Sail Away** (☎ 293-82385, 82-387 6350; www.sailaway.co.za), on the road paralleling the beach road, about 400m south of the old Dona Ana Hotel. Prices average US$80 per person for a day snorkelling excursion to Magaruque, including park fees, lunch, snorkelling equipment, protective footwear (important, as the rock ledges can be sharp), lunch, and usually motoring there and sailing back. Two-day safaris cost from US$210. Day trips to Bazaruto are possible to arrange, but not usually done, given the comparatively long travel distance from Vilankulo. There's officially no camping on the islands in the park, although some dhow safari operators camp on Bangue, while others – more environmentally responsible – camp along the mainland coast.

Sleeping

BUDGET

Baobab Beach Backpackers (campsites per person Mtc150, dm Mtc200, bungalow with/without bathroom Mtc1000/500) Rather scruffy these days, and still showing the effects of the 2007 cyclone, Baobab

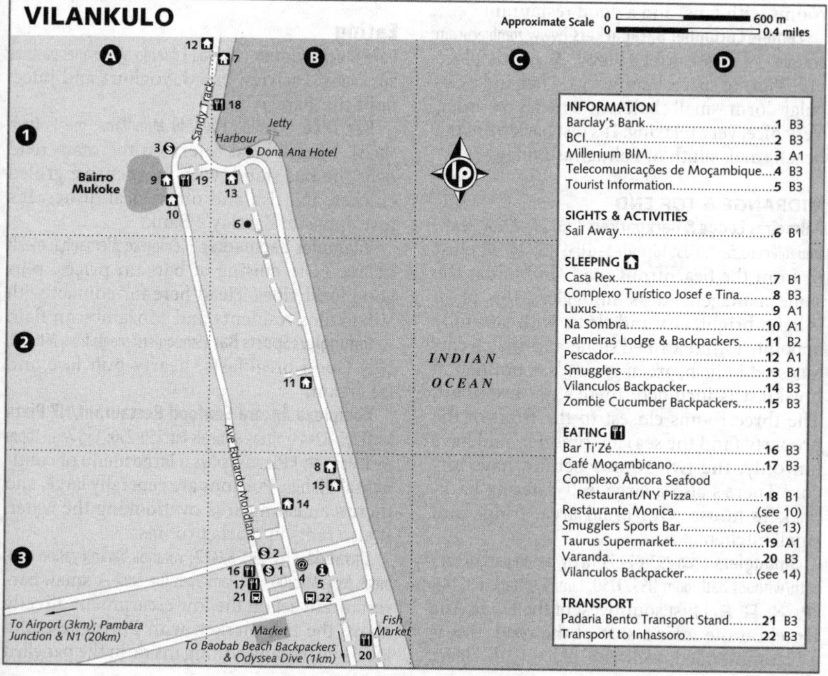

Beach remains nevertheless a decent spot to pitch a tent, with a good setting by the water. It's also the place to come if you're after the party scene.

Complexo Turístico Josef e Tina (☎ 82-965 2130, 82-406 3904; www.joseftina.com; campsites per person Mtc150, chalet r Mtc800, r Mtc1200, guesthouse Mtc3900) Just up from Zombie Cucumbers is this good local-run place with camping, no-frills rooms in reed chalets sharing bathrooms, and simple rooms in a small self-catering guesthouse – all in a garden just back from the sea. All rooms have nets, there's a small self-catering kitchen area and meals also available on order.

Vilanculos Backpacker (Complexo Alemanha; www.vilanculosbackpacker.com; dm Mtc170, d bungalow with shared bathroom Mtc600) On the escarpment in the central part of town, and an easy walk from the market/bus-stand area, with dorm beds, plus small stone-and-thatch double cottages – all sharing bathrooms. There's a small self-catering area and a good restaurant. The turn-off is signposted near Barclay's, and the compound is unmissable, with a huge German flag painted on the wall. There's no camping.

Na Sombra (☎ 293-82429; Bairro Mukoke; s/tw/d/q with shared bathroom Mtc280/350/380/530) Tiny, simple rooms with fans, and a good restaurant.

Zombie Cucumber Backpackers (www.zombiecucumber.com; dm Mtc280, chalet d Mtc850;) This place offers lots of space, hammocks, a bar and a circular dorm, small chalets and meals on order. Very nice, very relaxing. It's just back from the beach road, south of Palmeiras Lodge.

MIDRANGE & TOP END

Palmeiras Lodge & Backpackers (☎ 293-82257; www.smugglers.co.za; dm US$16; cottage d US$105;) Just in from the beachfront road, and under the same management as Smugglers, this place is light, bright, airy and clean, with tastefully appointed whitewashed stone-and-thatch cottages set in lush, green grounds. Continental breakfast is included; there's no restaurant. The three rooms closest to the front of the property (and the sea) are breezier, and have fan only, the two rooms behind have air-con. There's also a large, self-catering backpackers house with braai area, fridge and small kitchen.

Smugglers (☎ 293-82253; www.smugglers.co.za; r with/without bathroom US$71/50, family cottage US$143;) Just southwest of the Dona Ana Hotel on the inland side of the road, this is a recommended, well-run place with clean, pleasant rooms around large, cool, lush gardens, and a popular restaurant and sports bar. Ideal for families.

Luxus (☎ 82-851 1301; s/d Mtc1500/2000;) Spacious, functional rooms with window screens, located in a small shopping mall at the end of the main street, just opposite Taurus Supermarket. In the same mall and under the same management is a restaurant with burgers and fries.

Casa Rex (☎ 293-82048; www.casa-rex.com; s/d from US$140/220, acacia r 180/300, ste US$210/360;) A lovely upmarket midsized boutique place in peaceful, manicured grounds about 500m north of the old Dona Ana Hotel. It has a range of rooms and suites, all with sea views. Meals are homemade and excellent, and the hotel is known for its personalised style.

Pescador (☎ 293-82312; www.pescadormoz.com; s/d US$140/230;) This boutique place is just up from and diagonally opposite Casa Rex, without a beachfront, although the rooms have views of the sea. It has six well-appointed rooms, classical music piped through the lobby and a poolside restaurant.

Eating

Café Moçambicano (Avenida Eduardo Mondlane; pastries from Mtc15) Pastries, bread, yoghurt and juice; opposite Barclay's.

Bar Ti'Zé (Avenida Eduardo Mondlane; meals from Mtc75) A small local eatery on the main road near the bus stand, with inexpensive grilled chicken and fish and other local dishes. It's just opposite Barclay's Bank.

Vilanculos Backpacker (Complexo Alemanha; meals Mtc100) Tasty cuisine at bargain prices, plus good local vibes. Head here for contact with Vilankulos residents and Mozambican flair.

Smugglers Sports Bar (Smugglers; meals from Mtc150;) Good breakfasts, hearty pub fare and ice cream.

Complexo Âncora Seafood Restaurant/NY Pizza (☎ 293-82444; pizzas & meals Mtc150-250; 7am-10pm Wed-Mon;) Pizzas, plus a large menu of continental dishes. Portions are generally large, and there's an eating area overlooking the water. It also rents upmarket rooms.

Varanda (☎ 293-82412; varanda.barko@yahoo.com; meals from Mtc200; 7am-9pm Tue-Sun) A small bar-restaurant set on the low escarpment directly above the fish market, with Portuguese and local cuisine, and seating inside in the panelled bar area or at a few tables outside overlooking the beach below. It also rents a few rooms.

Restaurante Monica (Na Sombra; meals about Mtc300) This long-standing place is renowned for its delicious local curries and seafood dishes.

For self-catering, try **Taurus supermarket** (Avenida Eduardo Mondlane), near the end of the tarmac road and diagonally opposite Millennium BIM.

Getting There & Away

AIR

Offices for all airlines are at the airport, 3km from town and just off the Pambara access road. LAM flies four times weekly to/from Maputo, with connections also to Inhambane and Johannesburg. **Pelican Air** (☎ 293-82483, 293-84050, in South Africa 011-973 3649; www.pelicanair.co.za) flies daily between Johannesburg and Vilankulo (from US$262 one way), sometimes via Nelspruit.

Air Travelmax (☎ in South Africa 011-701 3222; www.airtravelmax) flies several times weekly between Vilankulo and Johannesburg's Lanseria airport.

BUS

Vilankulo is 20km east of the N1 down a tarmac access road, with the turn-off at Pambara junction. Chapas run between the two throughout the day (Mtc15). Except as noted, all transport departs from Vilankulo's main road just down from Padaria Bento and just up from the market.

To Maputo (Mtc500, nine to 10 hours), there are two to three buses daily, departing from in front of Bar TiZé by 4.30am, and sometimes as early as 3am – check with the bus drivers the afternoon before. Coming from Maputo, get to Junta by about 4am.

To Beira (Mtc550, 10 hours), buses depart Vilankulo at 4.30am; book the afternoon before.

To Chimoio, there's no direct bus. You'll need to take a Beira bus as far as Inchope junction (Mtc500 from Vilankulo), and then get a minibus from there.

To Maxixe (for Inhambane and Tofo), several minibuses depart each morning (Mtc175, three hours).

To Inhassoro, minibuses depart from just east of the market (Mtc65, 1½ hours).

Getting Around

Vilankulo is very spread out. For a taxi, try contacting **Junior** (☎ 82-462 4700) directly, or through your hotel and for car rental, try **Merkin 4x4** (☎ 82-012 9430; amiesmael@tdm.co.mz). Occasional chapas run along the main road, but not out to the beach places on the northeastern edge of town.

BAZARUTO ARCHIPELAGO

The Bazaruto Archipelago offers clear, turquoise waters filled with colourful fish, excellent diving and snorkelling and good birdwatching. It makes a fine upmarket holiday if you're looking for the quintessential Indian Ocean getaway.

The archipelago consists of five main islands – Magaruque (Santa Isabel), Benguera (Santo António), Santa Carolina (Paradise Island), Bazaruto and tiny Bangué – spread out 10km to 25km offshore between Vilankulo and Inhassoro. Much of it is protected as **Bazaruto National Marine Park** (adult/child per entry Mtc200/100).

Magaruque – the closest island to Vilankulo and the main destination for day sailing/snorkelling safaris from the mainland – has a rock shelf with many fish, although only isolated coral patches, on its western side. Surf shoes (most operators provide these) or other protective footwear are essential, as there are many sharp edges.

Sleeping & Eating

There is no budget accommodation on the islands. The best options if you have a limited budget are arranging an island dhow cruise from Vilankulo (see p247), or visiting in the off-season, when some of the lodges offer special deals.

Pestana Bazaruto Lodge (☎ 84-308 3120; www.pestana.com; Bazaruto Island; s/d with full board from US$423/570;) An unpretentious four-star getaway on a tranquil bay with A-frame chalets amid lush gardens beneath the sand dunes, and a honeymoon suite. There's a two-night minimum stay.

Indigo Bay Island Resort & Spa (☎ in South Africa 011-467 1277; www.indigobayonline.com; Bazaruto Island; r per person with full board from US$555;) A large lodge, with a mix of villas and beachfront chalets, and a range of activities.

Benguerra Lodge (☎ in South Africa 011-452 0641; www.benguerra.co.za; Benguera Island; r per person with full board from US$590;) An intimate place, with spacious luxury chalets near the beach, and a few honeymoon suites.

Azura (☎ in South Africa 011-258 0180; www.azura-retreats.com; r per person with full board from US$775;

MOZAMBIQUE

) On Benguerra Island, with accommodation in villas in varying degrees of luxury.

Getting There & Away

AIR

Pelican Air flies between Johannesburg, Nelspruit and Vilankulo, from where you can arrange island transfers with the lodges with connections to Benguera and Bazaruto islands; see p249. For scheduled and charter flights connecting the Bazaruto Archipelago with Gorongosa National Park and with Maputo, contact **CFA Charters** (☎ 293-82055; www.cfa.co.za; Vilankulo airport).

BOAT

If you should choose not to fly in, all the top-end lodges can arrange speedboat transfers for their guests. Most day visitors reach the islands by dhow from Vilankulo, where there are a number of sailing safari operators; see p247.

For nonmotorised dhows, allow plenty of extra time to account for wind and water conditions; from Vilankulo to Benguera or Magaruque takes two to six hours under sail.

INHASSORO

Sleepy Inhassoro – the last of the 'main' coastal towns before the N1 turns inland – is a popular destination for South African anglers. Its sunbaked, white-sand shoreline is uncluttered and inviting, although there's no surf or breeze, except during storms when the wind stirs up the waves a bit. Boat transfers to Bazaruto and Santa Carolina islands, both visible offshore, can be arranged with any of the hotels, often on the spot, but better with advance notice. Prices vary, but expect to pay at least Mtc5000/6000 per day per six-person boat to Santa Carolina/Bazaruto.

About 35km north along the coast, and reached (low tide only) via a sandy 4WD track branching north just before Complexo Turístico Seta, is **Bartolomeu Dias Point**, a lovely, tranquil spot with dunes, birdwatching and fishing. There are no ATM or internet facilities in Inhassoro – Vilankulo has the next closest banking.

Complexo Turístico Seta (☎ 293-91000/1, 82-302 0990; hotelseta@hotmail.com; campsites per adult/child Mtc250/125, tw chalets Mtc1000-2000, six-person self-catering chalets Mtc4000;), a long-standing place at the end of the main road leading into town from the N1, has large, quiet grounds, a pleasant restaurant-bar overlooking the sea, camping (towards the back of the property), and accommodation in small sea-facing chalets (several sizes available). There are also basic self-catering cottages in an unappealing setting behind the parking lot–reception area.

At Bartolomeu Dias, there's **BD Lodge** (www.bdlodge.co.za; 2-/6-person self-catering bungalows from Mtc1900/4600), with reed-and-thatch stilt cottages between the lagoon and the sea.

Getting There & Away

Inhassoro is 15km east of the main road. Chapas run daily to/from Vilankulo (Mtc65, 45 minutes). To Beira, go to Vulanjane (the junction with the N1, Mtc10 in a chapa) and wait for passing northbound buses from there – ask staff at your hotel to help with the timing so you're not sitting there all day. Driving northwards, there's a bridge across the Save River.

CENTRAL MOZAMBIQUE

Central Mozambique – Sofala, Manica, Tete and Zambézia provinces – doesn't draw the tourist crowds, although it's a convenient transit zone and has several attractions. These include lovely Gorongosa National Park, hill landscapes and hiking, Cahora Bassa lake and dam, and prime birdwatching.

BEIRA

☎ 23

Beira, Mozambique's second-largest city and busiest port, is as known for its steamed crabs and prawns as for its tawdry nightlife.

About 40km south of the city is the site of the ancient gold-trading port of Sofala. In its 15th-century heyday, it was one of East Africa's most influential centres, with links to Madagascar, India and beyond, although nothing remains of this today.

Orientation

At the heart of the city are the adjacent squares of Praça do Município and Praça do Metical, with shops, banks and internet nearby. North of here is the old commercial area and the port. Various streets lead south and east from Praça do Município through

POUNDS STERLING

Unlike Portuguese-dominated Maputo, British influence was strong in late-19th- and early-20th-century Beira, and for a time the Bank of Beira even circulated sterling currency.

the shady Ponta Gêa residential area to Avenida das FPLM, which runs for several kilometres along the ocean to Makuti Beach and the lighthouse.

Information

There are many ATMs, including at the airport, at Shoprite, at **BCI** (Rua Major Serpa Pinto) opposite LAM, and at **Standard Bank** (Praça do Metical).

Clínica Avicena (☎ 23-327990; Avenida Poder Popular; 24hr) Try here for medical emergencies if the Clínica Universitária is closed; just north of Praça do Metical.

Clínica Universitária (☎ 23-311823; just off Avenida das FLPM; 8am-4pm Mon-Fri, paediatrics to noon Tue) In the pink multistorey building just across the canal from Clube de Sporting da Beira, and about 700m east of Praça da Independência; the best bet for medical treatment.

Post office (Rua Correia de Brito)

Telecomunicações de Moçambique (Rua Companhia de Moçambique; 7am-10pm) Domestic and international telephone calls. Just off Praça do Município.

Teledata (Rua Companhia de Moçambique; per hr Mtc60; 8am-6pm) Internet; diagonally opposite the telecom office.

Sights & Activities

For relaxing, try **Makuti beach**, with breezes and sunset views, or the swimming pool at **Clube Náutico** (Avenida das FPLM; per day on weekdays/weekend Mtc100/150).

Beira's **cathedral** (Avenida Eduardo Mondlane) was built in the early 20th century with stones from the old San Caetano fort (1505) in Sofala. The streets around the **port** are lined with faded colonial-era buildings.

Sleeping

BUDGET

Rio Savane (☎ 23-323555, 82-385 7660; campsites per person US$10, 4-person barracas US$15 plus per person US$8, self-catering bungalows d/q US$50/100) About 40km north of town on the Savane River and very relaxing, with camping, *barracas* with mattresses and bedding, a couple of self-catering chalets and meals. Take the Dondo road past the airport to the signposted turn-off. Continue 35km to the estuary, where there's secure parking and a boat (until 5pm) to take you to the camp. Pick-ups from Beira can be arranged.

Pensão Moderna (☎ 23-329901; Rua Alferes da Silva; d with/without bathroom Mtc980/750, tr with shared bathroom Mtc950) One of the better local-style budget bets, with adequate rooms – most with fan and shared bathroom. It's two blocks south of the cathedral.

Hotel Infante (☎ 23-326603; Rua Jaime Ferreira; s/d from Mtc900/1050;) In a high-rise building in a congested section of town a few blocks from LAM, with small, clean rooms – some with fan and shared bathroom, others with air-con and private bathroom – and a restaurant.

MIDRANGE & TOP END

Jardim das Velas (☎ 23-312209; jardimdasvelas@yahoo.com; 282 Avenida das FPLM, Makuti Beach; d/f US$75/85;) This quiet and very nice place near the lighthouse has spotless, well-equipped rooms with views to the sea from upstairs, and a couple of four-person family rooms with bunk beds downstairs. All rooms have mosquito nets. There are no meals, but there's filtered water and a small garden with braai facilities, and the beach is just across the street. It's very popular and often full; advance bookings recommended.

Residencial BeiraSol (☎ 23-236420; 168 Rua da Madeira; r Mtc1500;) Opposite Hotel Tivoli, with clean, modern rooms, although most have only interior windows, opening onto the hallway or onto other walls (ask for one to the front for more views). Despite this drawback, it is, however, a clean, secure option in the baixa.

Beira Guest House (☎ 23-324030, 82-315 0460; 1311 Avenida Eduardo Mondlane; s/tw incl breakfast Mtc2300/2550;) Another good place, this cosy residential-style B&B in the Ponta Gêa area has pleasant, well-appointed rooms with minifridge, TV and laundry service. There's no food other than breakfast. It's diagonally opposite the Cathedral.

Guest House BeiraSol, (☎ 23-327202; Rua Fernão de Magalhães; r Mtc2500-3500, ste Mtc3750;) Spacious, well-appointed rooms in a restored private villa with polished wood floors and lots of windows. It's just off Avenida Eduardo Mondlane, on the side street immediately next to the governor's residence (*'palácio do governador'*).

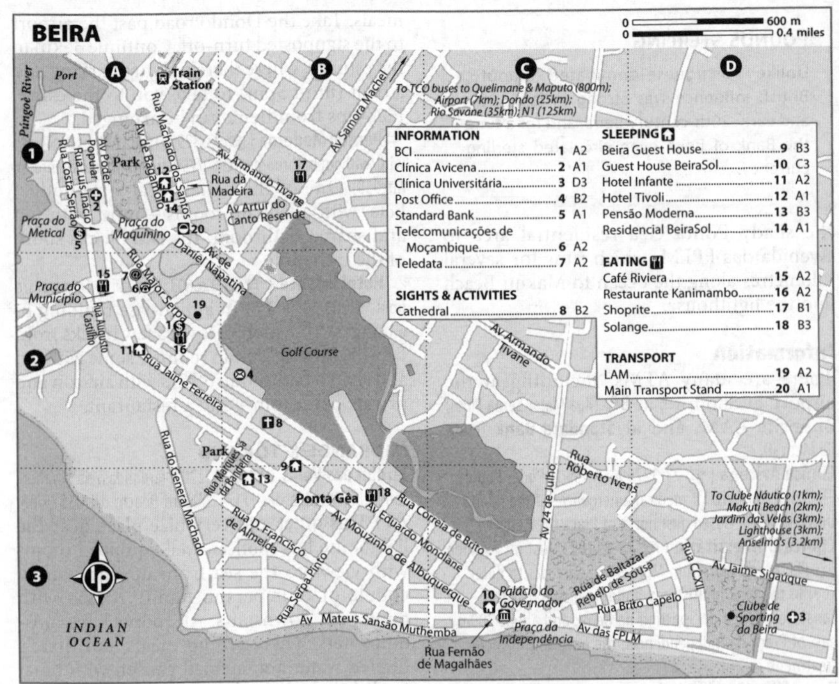

Hotel Tivoli (☎ 23-320300; h.tivoli-beira@teledata.mz; cnr Avenida de Bagamoyo & Rua da Madeira; s/d US$109/141; P ❄ 🖳) Small and tidy albeit rather faded rooms with TV and amenities, in a high-rise in the baixa. Downstairs is a restaurant-bar.

Eating

Café Riviera (Praça do Município; snacks & light meals from Mtc70; 🕑 7.30am-9pm) Sit here with a cup of coffee and *bolo de mandioca* (almond cake) and watch the passing scene.

Restaurante Kanimambo (☎ 23-323132; Rua Pêro de Alenquer; meals from Mtc150; 🕑 lunch & dinner Sun-Fri) Down the small side street opposite LAM, with tasty Chinese food.

Anselmo's (Avenida das FPLM; meals about Mtc200) This small, unsignposted local place past the lighthouse and opposite the old Hotel Estoril does tasty local food. Stop by in the afternoon to place an order for dinner.

Solange (cnr Avenida Eduardo Mondlane & Rua Serpa Pinto; meals from Mtc220; 🕑 lunch & dinner; ❄) Well-prepared meat and seafood grills in a dark, air-con interior.

Clube Náutico (☎ 23-311720; Avenida das FPLM; meals from Mtc200, plus per person entry Mtc20; 🕑 lunch & dinner) Slow service, but a good beachside setting and a good menu selection.

For self-catering, try **Shoprite** (cnr Avenidas Armando Tivane & Samora Machel).

Getting There & Away

AIR

There are flights on **LAM** (☎ 23-324141/2, 23-306000, 23-303112; 85 Rua Major Serpa Pinto) twice weekly to/from Johannesburg, daily to/from Maputo, and several times weekly to/from Tete, Nampula, Quelimane, Pemba, Vilankulo and Lichinga. **SAAirlink** (☎ 23-301569/70; www.saairlink.co.za; airport) flies four times weekly between Beira and Johannesburg.

BUS & CHAPA

Beira's main transport hub in the Praça do Maquinino area. There's no real order to things – ask locals where to go for buses to your destination.

TCO (☎ 82-509 2180, 82-775 0554) departs at 4am daily except Saturday to Maputo (Mtc1300, 15 hours), and at 5am on Monday,

Wednesday and Friday to Quelimane (Mtc690, nine hours). All departures are from its office on Rua dos Irmãos Roby in Bairro dos Pioneiros, 1km north of the centre.

To Vilankulo (Mtc550, 10 hours), there's a direct bus daily departing from the main transport stand by about 4.30am.

To Chimoio (Mtc150, three hours) and Machipanda (Mtc175, four hours), minibuses go throughout the day from the main transport stand.

Another option, for any northbound or southbound transport, is to go to Inchope, a scruffy junction 130km west of Beira (Mtc100, two to three hours via chapa), where the EN6 joins the N1, and try your luck with passing buses there.

Getting Around

The airport is 7km northwest of town (Mtc200 in a taxi).

Chapas to Makuti (Mtc5) depart from the main transport stand.

For vehicle rentals, head to **Imperial** (☎ 23-302650/1, 82-300 5190; imperialbeira@hotmail.com), which has an office at the airport.

GORONGOSA NATIONAL PARK

About 170km northwest of Beira is **Gorongosa National Park** (Parque Nacional de Gorongosa; www.gorongosa.net; adult/child/vehicle Mtc200/100/200; 🕑 6am-6pm May-Nov) once one of Southern Africa's premier wildlife parks, and now getting a second wind thanks to assistance from the US-based Carr Foundation. Entry fees are payable in meticais only.

While animal numbers still pale in comparison with those of the park's heyday, wildlife is making a definite comeback. The park is also beautiful, with a mix of jade-green floodplains, savanna country and woodlands, forests of fever trees, stands of palm and hanging vines. It is well worth a visit. While wildlife doesn't compare with South Africa's Kruger or other Southern Africa safari destinations, it's likely that you will see impalas, waterbucks, sable antelopes, warthogs, hippos, crocodiles and perhaps elephants and lions, and the bird life (with over 300 species, including endemics and near endemics) is wonderful. The park's rehabilitation also involves a strong community development element, and the chance to see some of this work is another highlight.

Vehicle rental, guides for wildlife drives and excursions to visit a nearby village can be arranged at **park headquarters** (☎ 23-535010; travel@gorongosa.net) in Chitengo, about 15km east of the entry gate.

Highly recommended multinight bush walks and (in the wetter months) canoe trips can be arranged through Explore Gorongosa.

Sleeping & Eating

At Chitengo park headquarters, there's a shaded **camping ground** (campsites per person Mtc210), a good restaurant, a swimming pool and pleasant **rondavels** (s/d Mtc2250/2990; ❄) scattered around an expansive, grassy fenced compound.

Explore Gorongosa (www.exploregorongosa.com; s/d all-inclusive US$500/800) runs walking safaris and canoe trips from its base in a semipermanent tented camp in one of the most scenic sections of the park (although the whole park is so beautiful that it's difficult to narrow it down). It also operates several fly camps, and is the best bet for experiencing the bush.

Getting There & Away

AIR

At the time of research, **CFA Charters** (☎ 21-466881, 293-82055; www.cfa.co.za) was planning twice-weekly flights from Maputo to Gorongosa National Park via the Bazaruto Archipelago imminently (about US$540/270 one-way from Maputo/Bazaruto to Gorongosa).

ROAD

The park is reached by turning off the N6 at Inchope (about 130km west of Beira), from where it's 43km north along good tarmac to Nota village and then 17km east along an all-weather gravel road to the park gate. Within the park, 4WD is necessary. Chapas going to Gorongosa town (Vila Gorongosa), about 25km north past the park turn-off, will drop you at the junction, from where you can arrange a pick-up with park staff (advance booking essential). Pick-ups are also possible from Beira and Chimoio. Chapas cost Mtc160/50/20 from Beira/Inchope/Gorongosa town to the park turn-off.

MT GORONGOSA

Just northwest of Gorongosa park is Mozambique's fourth-highest mountain, Mt

Gorongosa (1864m). It's steeped in local lore, and known for its lovely waterfalls and its rich plant and bird life (it's the only place in Southern Africa for spotting the green-headed oriole).

The Carr Foundation, which is financing the rehabilitation of Gorongosa National Park, is also supporting a community-based ecotourism and reforestation project on the mountain, centred on day or multinight hiking trails and birdwatching. A base camp for hikers and birders has been established near **Morrumbodzi Falls**, which are on the mountain's western side at about 950m. From the camp, there are paths to the falls, birdwatching walks and overnight climbs to the summit (about six hours one way). Hikes and excursions should be organised through Gorongosa park headquarters at travel@gorongosa.net. Note that the climb is quite steep on the mountain's upper reaches, and good shoes and a reasonable level of fitness are essential.

To get to the Morrumbodzi base camp area, follow the EN6 from Beira to the turn-off at Inchope. Continue north along the sealed road, passing the turn-off for Gorongosa park and continuing about 25km further to Gorongosa town. About 10km beyond Gorongosa town, turn off the main highway to the right, and continue 10km along an unpaved track to the base camp. Transfers can be arranged at park headquarters.

CHIMOIO

☎ 251

Low-key Chimoio, in the centre of a rich agricultural area, is the jumping-off point for exploring the Chimanimani Mountains, well southwest on the Zimbabwe border.

There are many ATMs, including at **Standard Bank** (cnr Avenida 25 de Setembro & Rua Patrice Lumumba) and at Shoprite. For internet, try the **Internet Café** (Rua Dr Araújo de la Cerda; per hr Mtc60) next to Barclay's Bank, or the slower connection at **Teledata** (cnr Avenida 25 de Setembro & Rua Mossurize; per min Mtc1; 8.30am-6pm Mon-Fri, 9am-noon Sat), which also has wireless.

Sights & Activities

About 5km northeast of town is **Cabeça do Velho**, a large rock resembling the face of an old man at rest. To get here, continue past Magarafa market on Rua do Bárue. It takes about 10 minutes to climb.

There's a **swimming pool** (per adult/child Mtc150/100) at Hotel Milpark.

To the southwest on the Zimbabwe border are the **Chimanimani Mountains** and Mt Binga (2437m), Mozambique's highest peak. Much of the range is encompassed by the Chimanimani National Reserve, which is part of the larger **Chimanimani Transfrontier Conservation Area** (ACTF; www.actf.gov.mz/reserva_chimanimani.html). It is possible to climb Mt Binga from the Mozambique side (allow two to three days from Chimoio via public transport) and to hike throughout the range, with plenty of suitable camping sites on the high plateaus close to mountain streams, and with hike options ranging from a day to a week or more. In addition to a good level of fitness (hikes begin at about 700m in altitude, while the highlands are around 1800m and the highest peaks well above 2000m), you will need to be entirely self-sufficient and be prepared for sudden change in weather, especially mist, rain and cold. The best contact for getting started exploring the mountains and the Chimanimani region in general is the highly recommended **Mozambique EcoTours** (www.mozecotours.com), which is working on establishing several community-run camps, including one as a base camp for climbing Mt Binga. Check its website or call or visit the Micaia office in Chimoio (☎ 251-23759; just off Rua Josina Machel, and behind the International School) for more information.

Sleeping

BUDGET

Pink Papaya (☎ 82-555 7310; http://pinkpapaya.atspace.com; cnr Ruas Pigivide & 3 de Fevereiro; dm Mtc300, s/d Mtc550/700; P) The best budget option, with helpful management, a convenient central location, clean dorm beds and doubles, a well-equipped kitchen and braai area and breakfast available on request. The owner can also help with information on excursions to the Chimanimani Mountains and Gorongosa National Park. It's about 10 minutes on foot from the bus stand: with the bus stand to your right and train station to your left, walk straight and take the fourth right into Rua 3 de Fevereiro. Go one block to Rua Pigivide. On request, staff will accompany you to the bus stop for early-morning departures.

Residencial Safari (☎ 251-22894, 84-239 0234; Rua dos Trabalhadores; s/tw with shared bathroom Mtc700/1000, d Mtc1200) Another option, targeted at local business clientele and worth checking out if you're travelling on a budget. There's an internet connection if you have your own laptop. Breakfast is included, otherwise there are no meals.

Residencial Dabhad (☎ 251-23264, 82-385 5480; cnr Rua do Bárue & Rua dos Agricultores; s/d/tw Mtc1150/1350/1350) This is a friendly, no-frills place, and worth checking if Pink Papaya is full. Other than continental breakfast (included), there are no meals.

MIDRANGE & TOP END

Hotel Milpark (☎ 82-763 2313, 23-910021; milparkhotel@hotmail.com; d Mtc1600-2100, ste Mtc2750) About 7km outside town along the Beira road, with straightforward rooms around expansive grounds, a restaurant and a pool.

Complexo Hoteleiro Vila Pery (☎ 251-24391, 82-501 4520; vilapery@tdm.co.mz; Rua Pigivide; d/tw Mtc1800/1900) Bright paintings give a bit of ambience to this otherwise rather soulless hotel. Rooms – around a central cement courtyard – are clean and fine.

Hotel-Residencial Castelo Branco (☎ 251-23934, 82-522 5960; Rua Sussundenga; s/d Mtc1850/2000; P ❄) Catering to business travellers, this place has modern twin-bed rooms around a small garden, and a good breakfast buffet. It's signposted just off Praça dos Heróis.

Hotel Inter (☎ 251-24200, 84-242 0000; interchimoio@gmail.com; Avenida 25 de Setembro, near Avenida Cidade de Lichinga; r Mtc2200, ste from Mtc2750; ❄) This newish multistorey place is trying to edge out Castelo Branco for the best rooms in town, though it's debatable whether it succeeds. There's also a restaurant.

Eating

Pizzeria Vapor (Rua do Mercado; pizza from Mtc120) Just down from Castelo Branco, this place has Chimoio's best pizzas. Take the first left after Castelo Branco; Pizzeria Vapor will be on your right-hand side.

Restaurante-Bar Jumbo (Rua do Bárue; meals from Mtc150) A basic but reliable place with tasty pizzas and continental dishes, and ice cream for dessert.

For cheap local meals, try **Café Chimoio** (Rua Dr Araújo de la Cerda; snacks & meals from Mtc150) or **Café Atlântida** (cnr Ruas do Bárue & Dr Araújo de la Cerda).

For self-caterers there's **Shoprite** (EN6), about 2km east of the town centre, and the central market near the bus stand.

Getting There & Away

AIR

LAM (☎ 251-22531; Mafúia Comercial, Rua dos Operários) flies several times weekly to Tete and Maputo. The airfield is 10km from town, and signposted about 5km west of Chimoio off the Manica road.

BUS & CHAPA

All transport leaves from near the train station. Buses depart daily at 4am to Tete (Mtc350, seven hours) and between 2.30am and 4am to Maputo (Mtc900, 14 hours). For Vilankulo, there's currently no direct bus – you'll need to take the Maputo bus and get dropped at Pambara junction. While the price should be tallied pro rata, it's difficult from Chimoio to get the drivers to come down from the full Mtc900. Chapas to Beira (Mtc150, three hours) and Manica (Mtc20, one hour) run throughout the day.

MANICA

☎ 251

Tiny Manica, 70km west of Chimoio, lies in what was once the heart of the kingdom of Manica and an important gold-trading area.

Millennium BIM (EN6) has an ATM.

About 5km from town and signposted (as *pinturas rupestres*) are the **Chinamapere rock paintings**.

About 20km north of Manica and straddling the Zimbabwe border is the scenic **Penha Longa** area, where there is good walking (stick to the beaten path).

SACRED FORESTS

The foothills of the Chimanimani Mountains are dotted with sacred areas. One of these is the *dzimbahwe* or chief's compound. Each chiefdom has its own spot, generally in a densely forested area, to which access is strictly limited. Another is the *gwasha*, a forest area used by chiefs, elders and spirit mediums for rainmaking and other ceremonies. Both the *dzimbahwe* and the *gwasha* are treated with great respect by local communities, and no development, wood cutting or harvesting are permitted. Hunting is under the control of the chiefs, as is the gathering of medicinal and other plants.

EXPLORING MANICA PROVINCE

Chimanimani National Reserve is the highlight, but Manica province has many other attractions, including stunning terrain and a wealth of historical and rock art sites. It is ideal for exploration and for combination itineraries west to Zimbabwe or east into Sofala province and the coast.

The excellent **Mozambique EcoTours** (www.mozecotours) is the best contact for information on the latest developments, and for help with suggested routes and itineraries, as well as for information on combining exploration of Manica with visits to off-the-beaten-track coastal destinations in Sofala province. It can also be contacted in Chimoio through the Micaia office (☎ 251-23759; just off Rua Josina Machel, behind the International School).

Sleeping & Eating

Pensão Flamingo (☎ 251-62385; EN6; r Mtc750) Spiffy, no-frills rooms with fan, and a restaurant.

Manica Lodge (☎ 251-62452; d in small rondavel Mtc1200, s/d in large rondavel Mtc1500/1750) About 400m off the main road at the western end of town, with a restaurant and stone rondavels (the large ones are much nicer than the small ones) scattered around tranquil, manicured grounds.

Quinta da Fronteira (campsites Mtc100, r Mtc200) In Penha Longa, this old mansion has camping and a few basic rooms. Bring all food and drink.

Getting There & Away

All transport departs from the market, diagonally opposite Millennium BIM. Chapas run frequently to/from Chimoio (Mtc50, one hour) and to the Zimbabwe border (Mtc20, 30 minutes), and several times daily between Manica and Penha Longa (Mtc40, one hour). From the chapa terminus in Penha Longa, it's a 20-minute walk to the Mutombomwe area, and then from there about 3km further to Quinta da Fronteira.

TETE

☎ 252

Tete was an important trading outpost well before the arrival of the Portuguese and today continues to be a major transport junction and business hub. Apart from the suspension bridge over the Zambezi River, there are few attractions, and Tete's reputation as one of the hottest places in Mozambique discourages visitors. Yet the baobab-studded landscape cut by the wide swath of the Zambezi gives it a unique charm and an atmosphere quite unlike that of Mozambique's other provincial capitals.

Information

Embondeiro Digital (Avenida Julius Nyerere; per hr Mtc60; 8.30am-6pm Mon-Fri, 9am-noon Sat) Internet; just up from Univendas.

Standard Bank (cnr Avenida Julius Nyerere & Avenida Eduardo Mondlane) ATM; next to Hotel Zambeze.

Sleeping

There's camping at the very basic **Campismo Jesus é Bom** (campsites per person Mtc100), just over the bridge (on the north side), and 300m to your right.

Prédios Univendas (☎ 252-23198/9, 252-22670; Avenida Julius Nyerere; s/d with shared bathroom US$25/35, s/d from US$45/55) Near Standard Bank, with clean, spacious rooms, most sharing bathrooms. There's no food.

Smart Naira (☎ 82-686 4815; amadsatar@tdm.co.mz; Avenida da Independência just up from Avenida 24 de Julho; r Mtc1800-2750) A small place catering to local business travellers. The clean, aircon rooms would be nothing special anywhere else, but they're a nice change of pace in Tete.

Motel Tete (☎ 252-22345; N103; r Mtc2000; P) On the river about 25 minutes' walk from town along the Changara road, this longstanding place has simple, pleasant rooms and a riverside restaurant (no alcohol) serving large portions.

Hotel Zambeze (☎ 252-23101, 252-24000; Avenida Eduardo Mondlane; s/d Mtc2500/3500) A large, multistorey place in the centre of town that's been recently renovated and now vies for the honour of having the best rooms in Tete (though there's not much competition). Rooms have TV, and there's a restaurant and snack bar. It's next to Standard Bank.

Eating

Le Petit Café (cnr Avenidas Julius Nyerere & Liberdade; snacks & light meals from Mtc50; 7.30am-8pm Mon-Sat) In Centro Comercial Fatima, with light meals, pastries, snacks and juices.

Pino's Restaurant (cnr Avenidas Julius Nyerere & Liberdade; pizzas & meals from Mtc180; dinner) Just down from Le Petit Café at Clube de Chingale, with pizzas and Italian dishes.

Getting There & Away

AIR

LAM (☎ 252-22056; Avenida 24 de Julho) flies a few times weekly to/from Maputo, Beira, Lichinga, Nampula, Quelimane and Chimoio. The airport is 6km from town; take any chapa heading to Moatize.

BUS & CHAPA

For Chimoio (Mtc350, six to seven hours), transport leaves from opposite Prédio Emose on Avenida da Independência, just down from Smart Naira hotel and near Univendas. The first departures are between 4.30am and 5am.

To Songo (for Cahora Bassa dam), several pick-ups daily depart from the old Correios (post office) building near the cathedral (Mtc120).

Chapas to Moatize (Mtc10) depart throughout the day from Rua do Qua.

For Malawi, chapas run to Zóbuè (Mtc70, two hours) and Dedza from Mercado da OUA on the western side of town.

For Harare (Zimbabwe), take a chapa to Changara (Mtc90, 1½ hours) from Mercado 1 de Maio, and get transport from there.

For Zambia, take a Moatize chapa over the bridge past the SOS compound to the petrol station, where you'll find chapas to Matema, and then on to the border.

The helpful and efficient **Imperial Car Rental** (☎ 252-20261, 82-302 1344; imperialtete@hotmail.com) is at the airport.

CAHORA BASSA DAM & SONGO

☎ 252

About 150km northwest of Tete at the head of a magnificent gorge in the mountains is Cahora Bassa, the fifth-largest dam in the world. It harnesses the waters of the Zambezi River, creating the massive Cahora Bassa Lake, a prime angling destination.

To arrange visits to the dam, contact **Hidroeléctrica de Cahora Bassa** (HCB; ☎ 252-82157, 252-82221/4) in nearby Songo town and ask for Relações Públicas.

Sleeping & Eating

Centro Social do HCB (☎ 252-82454, 252-82508; r/ste Mtc1000/1250;) Comfortable twin-bed rooms overlooking green lawns in the centre of Songo, and the O Teles restaurant.

Ugezi Tiger Lodge (☎ 82-599 8410, in South Africa 082-539 6411; www.ugezitigerlodge.com; campsites per person Mtc290, s/d Mtc1025/1580;) An appealingly rustic fishing camp on a wooded hillside overlooking Lake Cahora Bassa, 14km from Songo town and 6km beyond the dam. It has camping, basic chalets, two eight- to 12-person self-catering houses, a restaurant with grilled fish, and boat charters.

Getting There & Away

Chapas run daily between Tete and Songo (Mtc120, three to four hours). From Songo town, it's 7km down to the dam (walk or hitch). Ugezi Tiger Lodge does pick-ups from Tete.

CAIA

This village is the main north–south crossing point over the Zambezi River. About 32km south of Caia along the main road in Catapu is the good **M'phingwe Camp** (www.dalmann.com; cabins s/d with shared bathroom Mtc500/650, cabin s/d Mtc750/1000), which has spotless double cabins, meals and fine birdwatching.

The new Armando Emílio Guebuza toll bridge over the Zambezi River at Caia had just been inaugurated as this book was researched. Tolls are Mtc80/800 for passenger vehicles/trucks.

QUELIMANE

☎ 24

Quelimane is the capital of Zambézia province and heartland of the Chuabo people. It stands on the site of an old Muslim trading settlement built on the banks of the Bons Sinais (Qua Qua) River in the days when it was linked to the Zambezi River. At one time it was the main entry port to the interior. Few traces of Quelimane's long history remain, but the town's compact size and energetic atmosphere make it an agreeable enough stop for a night or two.

Information

Millennium BIM (Avenida Josina Machel) ATM.

Quelimane Internet Café (Avenida Samora Machel; per min Mtc1; 8am-6pm Mon-Fri, 9am-noon Sat) Diagonally opposite Hotel Chuabo.

Zambézia Travels (☎ 24-216174; Avenida Kwame Nkrumah) Help with flight bookings and local travel arrangements. Diagonally opposite Hotel Chuabo.

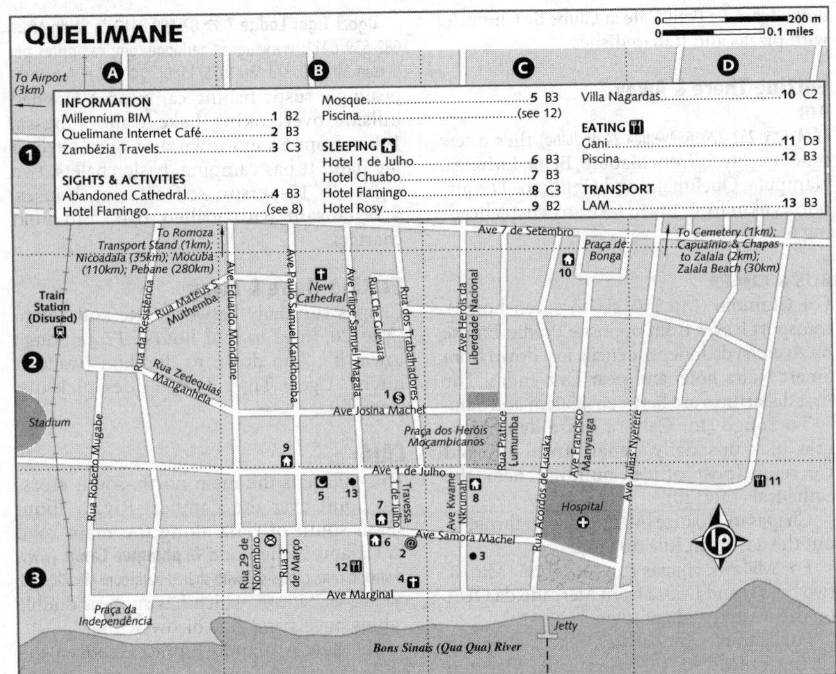

Sights & Activities

The main sights are the abandoned Portuguese **cathedral** on the waterfront and the nearby **old mosque**. About 30km northeast of town through the coconut plantations is the wide **Zalala beach**, although the waters are brown, rather than the aqua and turquoise of further north, thanks to run-off from the Zambezi river.

The swimming pools at Hotel Flamingo and at Piscina make a refreshing dip.

Sleeping

Hotel 1 de Julho (cnr Avenidas Samora Machel & Filipe Samuel Magaia; tw with shared bathroom Mtc500, with air-con Mtc850;) Near the old cathedral, with reasonable, plain rooms, and a small restaurant downstairs. Breakfast costs extra.

Hotel Rosy (☎ 24-214969; cnr Avenidas 1 de Julho & Paulo Samuel Kankhomba; s/d Mtc850/1000;) Near the old mosque, with musty albeit reasonable-value rooms with bathrooms, breakfast and air-con (downstairs) or fan (upstairs).

Hotel Flamingo (☎ 24-215602; www.hflamingo.com; cnr Avenidas Kwame Nkrumah & 1 de Julho; s/d Mtc1550/1900;) Recently renovated midrange rooms, plus full breakfasts and a restaurant.

Villa Nagardas (☎ 24-212046; 79 Praça de Bonga; small/large r Mtc1900/2700;) One of Quelimane's better bets, with African decor, pleasant rooms and a restaurant. It's near the municipal library.

Hotel Chuabo (☎ 24-213181/2; Avenida Samora Machel; s/d Mtc2100/2750;) An ageing Quelimane institution, with spacious rooms, most river-facing, and a usually empty rooftop restaurant (worth visiting for the views).

Eating

Gani (Náutica; Avenida Marginal; meals from Mtc120; lunch & dinner) Quelimane's best dining, with riverside seating, good meals and good vibes, including music in the evenings. It's at the easternmost end of Avenida Marginal, near where it turns in to Avenida Maputo.

Piscina (Rua Filipe Samuel Magaia just off Avenida Samora Machel; meals from Mtc150) Quite decent meals, and a popular spot for drinks in the evening. There's also a clean pool.

Getting There & Away

AIR

LAM (☎ 24-212801; Avenida 1 de Julho) flies several times weekly to/from Maputo, Beira, Nampula and Tete. The airport is 3km northwest of town along Avenida 25 de Junho.

BUS & CHAPA

The transport stand (known locally as 'Romoza') is at the northern end of Avenida Eduardo Mondlane. Chapas run frequently to/from Nicoadala at the junction with the main road (Mtc30, 45 minutes).

To Nampula, a Grupo Mecula bus departs daily at 4.30am (Mtc350, 10 hours). Several vehicles also run daily to Mocuba (Mtc120, two to three hours), for onward transport to Nampula via Alto Molócuè, or to Milange (Malawi border).

To Gurúè (Mtc300, six hours), there's a bus daily at 4.30am; buy your ticket the day before.

To Beira (Mtc690, nine hours), the best bet is TCO, which departs at 5am Tuesday, Thursday and Saturday from its office at Zambézia Travels.

Chapas to Zalala (Mtc25) depart Quelimane from the Capuchin mission *(capuzínio)*, about 1km from the cemetery on the Zalala road.

MOCUBA

☎ 24

Mocuba – known for its dirty water and for being nobody's favourite Mozambican town – is the junction for travel between Quelimane and Nampula or Malawi. Do what you can to avoid overnighting here.

Pensão Cruzeiro (☎ 24-810184; Avenida Eduardo Mondlane; r about Mtc400) on the main street has basic rooms and meals. **Muhamud's Take-Away** (snacks from Mtc50), near Millennium BIM, has samosas, burgers and, sometimes, yoghurt.

Transport to Quelimane (Mtc120, two to three hours) leaves from the market throughout the day. For Nampula, the best bet is to try to get a seat on the Mecula bus from Quelimane, which passes Mocuba from about 7am. There are several vehicles daily in the morning between Mocuba and Milange (Mtc200, four hours) departing from Mocuba's market, though you'll maximise your chances of a lift by walking west past the airstrip to the Milange road junction. Mocuba to Gurúè costs Mtc200.

MILANGE

Milange is a busy town sharing the border with southeastern Malawi with more than its share of hustlers. Millennium BIM has an ATM.

Pensão Reis (r Mtc500-1000), with hot running water, and the more basic **Pensão Fernandinho** (r Mtc500), with running water, although it's not always hot, are both centrally located and recommended as safe, with no-frills rooms and meals with advance notice.

The road between Milange and Mocuba is well travelled, and finding a lift usually isn't a hard. To Gurúè, there's sporadic public transport along a rehabilitated road to Molumbo, and from there to Lioma, from where you can get a chapa to Gurúè. Also see p288.

GURÚÈ

Gurúè sits picturesquely amid the hills and tea plantations in one of the coolest, highest and rainiest parts of the country. There are some lovely walks in the surrounding area, including a stroll through the jacarandas on the northern edge of town.

Millennium BIM (Avenida da República) has an ATM, and **Greenside Café** (per min Mtc1), nearby, has broadband internet access.

Pensão Gurúè (☎ 24-910050; s/d Mtc500/600) on the main street is the best of the local-style guesthouses. Rooms have bathrooms, and meals can be arranged with lots of advance notice, as can guides for climbing Mt Namúli. Nicer is the **Catholic Mission** (Artes e Ofício; r with half board Mtc400) on the edge of town, which is clean and tranquil with good meals and hot water, although the gates close at 9pm.

For meals away from these places, try Café Domino, just up from Pensão Gurúè, or Restaurante Zamzam. There's also inexpensive food in the large concrete building behind the market. The owners of Greenside Café are planning to open a supermarket soon; check with them. Meanwhile, for self-catering, try Aquíl Comercial near Restaurante Namúli.

Getting There & Away

From Nampula, take the Mecula bus to Alto Molócuè (Mtc150), where you can then get a waiting chapa on to Gurúè (Mtc200). Going in the other direction, you'll need to depart Gurúè by 5am at the latest for Nampevo junction to get a connection on to Nampula.

For connections to/from Quelimane, there's a daily direct chapa departing at 4.30am (Mtc300; six hours); buy tickets the day before. Otherwise, there are several vehicles daily to Mocuba (Mtc200, 3½ to four hours), from where you can continue to Quelimane.

CLIMBING MT NAMÚLI

Rising up about 15km northeast of Gurúè are the mist-shrouded slopes of Mt Namúli (2419m), Mozambique's second-highest peak, which make a scenic but challenging climb for which you'll need a good level of fitness and no fear of heights (as there are several near-vertical spots where you'll need to clamber on all fours). The mountain is considered sacred by the local Makua people, so while climbing is permitted, you'll need to observe the local traditions. Guides can be arranged in Gurúè through Pensão Gurúè, but allow several extra days to sort out the logistics. The going rate for a guide is from about Mtc300.

Before setting out, buy some *farinha de mapira* (sorghum flour), rice and sugar at the market in Gurúè (it shouldn't cost more than Mtc50 for everything) for appeasing the spirits and the local *régulo* (chief). Also set aside an additional Mtc300 per person for further appeasement of the chief, and pack some water purification tablets for yourself.

The climb begins about 6km outside Gurúè near UP5, an old tea factory: head south out of Gurúè along the Quelimane road, go left after about 2km and continue several kilometres further to UP5.

Shortly before reaching UP5 you'll see a narrow but obvious track branching left. Follow this through unrehabilitated tea plantations and stands of bamboo and forest until a high valley about 800m below the summit. On the edge of this valley is Mugunha Sede, where you should seek out the chief and request permission to climb further. The sorghum flour that you bought in Gurúè should be presented to the chief as a gift, who may save some to make traditional beer, and scatter the remainder on the ground to appease the ancestors. The chief will then assign someone to accompany you to the top of the mountain.

About two-thirds of the way from the village is a spring where you can refill your water bottle, although it's considered a sacred spot and it may take some effort to persuade your guide to show you where it is. After the spring, the climb steepens with some sections where you'll need to use your hands to clamber up. Once near the summit, the path evens out and then gradually ascends for another 1.5km to the mountain's highest point. After descending the mountain, present the rice that you bought at the Gurúè market to the chief as thanks.

It's theoretically possible to do the climb in a long day from Gurúè if you get an early start and drive as far as Mugunha Sede (about 40km from Gurúè by road), from where it's about three hours on foot to the summit. However, in practice this often doesn't work out as you need to allow time to track down and talk with the chief; it's better to plan on at least an overnight. To do the entire climb on foot from Gurúè, allow three days, walking the first day as far as Mugunha Sede (seven to eight hours from Gurúè), where the *régulo* will show you a spot to camp. The second day, head up to the summit and back, sleeping again in Mugunha Sede, and returning the next day to Gurúè. With an early start, it's possible to combine the second and third stages into one long day. Camping on the summit isn't permitted. Be prepared for rain, cold and rapidly changing conditions during the climb.

It's possible to take the train from either Nampula or Cuamba to Mutuali, where you'll find a waiting open-backed pick-up truck on to Gurúè (Mtc150, four to five hours). This works best coming from Cuamba; from Nampula, most of the journey to Gurúè will be at night.

To Milange, it's fastest to go via Mocuba.

Transport in Gurúè departs from near the market.

ALTO MOLÓCUÈ

This agreeable town is a refuelling point between Mocuba and Nampula.

Pensão Santo António (d Mtc450) on the main square has clean doubles and meals. Several vehicles daily go to/from Nampula (3½ hours) and Mocuba (four hours).

NORTHERN MOZAMBIQUE

Lake Niassa to the west, wild Niassa Reserve in the centre and palm-fringed beaches and magical archipelagos along the coast combine to make the north one of Mozambique's most alluring and adventurous destinations.

NAMPULA

☎ 26

Nampula is a crowded city with a hard edge – although these negatives are redeemed somewhat by the lush surrounding countryside dotted with soaring inselbergs, and by its proximity to Mozambique Island.

Information

Centro Comercial de Nampula (Avenida Eduardo Mondlane) ATM inside.

Farmácia Calêndula (Avenida Eduardo Mondlane; 8am-8pm Mon-Sat, 9am-1pm Sun) One block up from the museum.

Millennium BIM (cnr Avenidas da Independência & Francisco Manyanga) ATM.

Standard Bank (Avenida Eduardo Mondlane) ATM; near the museum.

Telecomunicações de Moçambique (Rua Monomotapa) Telephone calls; near the cathedral.

Teledata (Centro Comercial de Nampula, Avenida Eduardo Mondlane; per hr Mtc80; 8am-noon & 2-8pm Mon-Fri, 9am-1pm & 3-7pm Sat) Internet access.

Sights & Activities

The **National Ethnography Museum** (Avenida Eduardo Mondlane; per person Mtc100; 9am-5pm Tue-Fri, 2-5pm Sat & Sun) has a modest collection on local culture (English and Portuguese explanations).

There are swimming pools at **Clube CFM** (Rua 3 de Fevereiro; admission Mtc70) and (cleaner) **Complexo Bamboo** (admission Mtc100); see right.

Sleeping

BUDGET

Hotel Brasília (☎ 26-212127; 26 Rua dos Continuadores; s/d/tw Mtc700/750/960;) Near Shoprite, and a 20-minute hike from the bus and train depots, with clean, no-frills rooms and a restaurant.

Residencial da Universidade Pedagógica (840 Avenida 25 de Setembro; s/tw Mtc800/1000) In a relatively quiet area next to Hotel Milénio, with simple, clean, secure, good-value rooms and breakfast.

Residencial A Marisqueira (☎ 26-213611; cnr Avenidas Paulo Samuel Kankhomba & Eduardo Mondlane; s/d/tw Mtc800/850/1010;) In a central but hectic location, this place has relatively cleanish, cold-water-only rooms (ask for one of the 'newer' ones). There's also a restaurant downstairs.

Residencial Farhana (☎ 26-212527; Avenida Paulo Samuel Kankhomba; s/d/tw Mtc800/850/1010;) Formerly Pensão Marques, this large, rather dingy edifice has a row of straightforward rooms – the double rooms come with a rattling air-conditioner and musty private bathroom – plus hot water and TV. There's no food. The rooms at the front have small balconies, but they get the street noise; those to the back are less noisy, but ventilation isn't as good.

MIDRANGE & TOP END

Residencial Expresso (☎ 26-218808/9; Avenida da Independência; s/d from Mtc1450/1750; P) Six large, spotless rooms available, each with a fridge and TV.

Complexo Bamboo (☎ 26-217838; www.teledata.mz/bamboo; Ribáué Rd; s/d/tw Mtc1500/2000/2000; P) This is a good option for families, with well-maintained rooms (the twins are nicer than the doubles) in expansive grounds and a restaurant. It's 5km west of town – follow Avenida do Trabalho west from the train station, then right onto the Ribáuè Rd for 1.5km.

Hotel Executivo (☎ 26-219001/2; hotelexecutivo@tdm.co.mz; 370 Rua de Tete; s/d/tw incl breakfast Mtc1990/2250/2250;) An efficient, newish place about two blocks down from Shoprite. All rooms have a view to the pool (which was closed at the time of research) and come with full buffet breakfast. There's also a restaurant.

Hotel Milénio (☎ 26-218877, 26-218989; hotelmilenio@teledata.mz; 842 Avenida 25 de Setembro; tw/d/ste Mtc1950/1850/2500;) Another newish, modern place with large rooms and a restaurant downstairs. Wireless access is in the lobby only.

Hotel Girassol (☎ 26-216000; www.girassolhoteis.co.mz; 326 Avenida Eduardo Mondlane; s/d from Mtc2400/2750; P) In the Centro Comercial de Nampula high-rise, this four-star place has Nampula's priciest rooms, although standards seem to have declined somewhat in recent times and the price difference with the other options in this category simply isn't justified. Ask for a room with views over the cathedral and town.

Eating

Café Atlântico (Centro Comercial de Nampula, Avenida Eduardo Mondlane; snacks & meals from Mtc50; 6am-9pm) *Pregos* (thin steak sandwiches), burgers, pizzas and other light meals.

Frango King (Avenida Eduardo Mondlane; half/whole chicken Mtc75/150; 7.30am-4am) Grilled chicken to go.

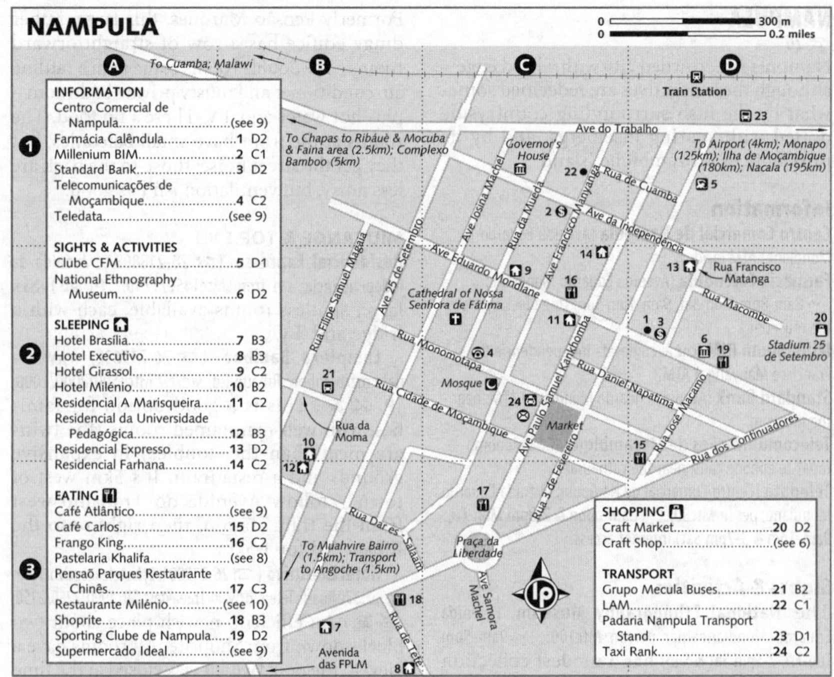

Pastelaria Khalifa (Rua de Tete; snacks from Mtc55) Coffees, sandwiches, snacks and milkshakes next to Hotel Executivo.

Pensão Parques Restaurante Chinês (Avenida Paulo Samuel Kankhomba; meals Mtc100-180) Reasonably priced Chinese food in a rather busy, unappealing location downstairs at Pensão Parques.

Café Carlos (☎ 26-217960; Rua José Macamo; meals from Mtc200; 🕑 Mon-Sat) A small courtyard place just off Rua dos Continuadores; it does reasonable meat and seafood grills and has a pizza oven.

Sporting Clube de Nampula (Avenida Eduardo Mondlane; meals from Mtc170; 🕑 8am-10pm) Next to the museum, with chicken and fish grills and *feijoada* (a traditional Brazilian bean and sausage dish).

Restaurante Milénio (Avenida 25 de Setembro; meals Mtc175-250, Sunday buffet Mtc400; 🕑 6am-10pm; ❄) Short on ambience, but the food in this hotel restaurant – Indian vegetarian dishes, pizzas, Chinese and Portuguese – is good, and the English menu translation provides humour while you wait (try jab of shrimp, pizza of daisy, beef in the track brag or grilled thread).

Self-caterers can try **Shoprite** (Rua dos Continuadores; 🕑 9am-8pm Mon-Sat, to 3pm Sun) or **Supermercado Ideal** (326 Avenida Eduardo Mondlane) in the Girassol hotel building.

Shopping

There's a Sunday morning **craft market** (🕑 dawn-dusk) in the stadium field downhill from the old Hotel Tropical (best from about 7am), and a tiny craft shop behind the museum with Makonde carvings and clay pots.

Getting There & Away

AIR

LAM (☎ 26-213322, 26-212801; Avenida Francisco Manyanga) flies to Maputo (daily), Beira, Lichinga, Quelimane, Tete and Pemba (several times weekly).

The airport is 4km northeast of town (Mtc150 in a taxi).

BUS & CHAPA

Grupo Mecula buses go daily to Pemba (Mtc250, seven to eight hours) and Quelimane (Mtc350, 11 hours), departing at 5am from the Grupo Mecula garage on Rua da Moma.

To Mozambique Island (Mtc120, three to four hours), chapas depart between 5am and 11am from the Padaria Nampula transport stand along Avenida do Trabalho east of the train station. Look for one that's going direct – many go only to Monapo, where you'll need to stand on the roadside and wait for another vehicle. The best connections are on one of the *'tanzaniano'* chapas, which depart Nampula between 7am and 10am, depending on how early they arrive from Mozambique Island. The Padaria Nampula transport stand is also the place to find chapas to Mossuril, Namapa, and other points north and east.

Vehicles to Angoche (Mtc120, three hours) – all go via Nametil – depart from about 5am from Muahvire *bairro,* along the extension of Avenida das FPLM. Go over the small bridge and continue all the way uphill to the start of the Angoche road.

Chapas to Mocuba leave from the 'Faina' area, about 2.5km west of the train station along Avenida do Trabalho near the Ribáuè road junction, but it's faster to take the Mecula bus to Quelimane and have it drop you.

TRAIN

A six-times-weekly passenger train connects Nampula and Cuamba; see p269.

Getting Around

The main **taxi rank** (Avenida Paulo Samuel Kankhomba) is near the market. For car rentals, the best bet is **Imperial** (☎ 26-216312, 82-300 5170; imperialnampula@hotmail.com; Airport).

ANGOCHE

☎ 26

Angoche, an old Muslim trading centre dating from at least the 15th century, was one of the earliest settlements in Mozambique, an important gold- and ivory-trading post and, in the 18th century, one of the major centres along the northern coast. Today, little evidence of this history remains, although the area, and especially the nearby islands, is caught in an intriguing time warp.

About 7km north of Angoche is the long, wide **Praia Nova** ('New Beach'), with some of the whitest sand you'll see anywhere. It has no shade or facilities. Just offshore are the **Primeiras and Segundas Islands**, soon to be Mozambique's newest protected area.

Intra BroadBand (Avenida Liberdade; per min Mtc1) has internet access. Next door is **Millennium BIM** (Avenida Liberdade), which has an ATM. There's a small but lively **fish market** afternoons near the Catholic church. Go left and down towards the water after passing the church.

Sleeping & Eating

Pensão Mafamete (s/d/tw with shared bathroom Mtc200/300/400) Very basic but the best of the local *pensões,* with a few clean rooms in a building under renovation. All have fan, but no nets (although the windows are screened), and all share bathrooms without water, although staff can usually arrange to bring you a bucket. There's no food. When entering town, turn off the main road to the left at the first round marker in front of the Governo building. Go three blocks down, and Mafamete is on your left, on the final block before reaching a small park.

Hesada Apartments (☎ 026-720327/8, 82-666 8880; www.hesadapartments.webs.com; d Mt500, apt Mtc1000; ❄) A much better option, consisting of several rooms in the city centre, plus two self-catering apartments in a quiet area on the outskirts of town – all clean and pleasant, and all with reliable water supplies (a rarity in Angoche).

Restaurante O Pescador (☎ 84-470 8481; meals from Mtc150; 🕑 lunch & dinner Mon-Sat) Good meals, a cool interior and shaded parking. On Sundays, it's sometimes possible to arrange meals in advance with the proprietor. It's around the corner from Pensão Mafamete on the park.

Getting There & Away

Chapas go daily to/from Nampula (Mtc120, four hours) from the transport stand at the top entrance to town, about 1km from the central area. Dhows or motorised boats to the islands can be arranged at the *capitania* (maritime office), at the base of the main road near the Praça dos Heróis. Dhows also leave frequently from the fish market.

The start of the road to Praia Nova is a few blocks past the far (northern) end of the park, past O Pescador, from where it's 7.5km further – you'll need to walk or hitch.

MOZAMBIQUE ISLAND

☎ 26

Mozambique Island (Ilha de Moçambique), about 3km off the mainland, is a Unesco World Heritage Site and one of Mozambique's most fascinating destinations. In the staid

Stone Town, quiet, cobbled streets lead onto graceful *praças* rimmed by once-grand churches and stately colonial buildings. In the adjoining Makuti Town, narrow alleyways echo with the sounds of playing children and squawking chickens, while fishermen sit on the sand repairing their nets.

History

As early as the 15th century Mozambique Island was an important boat-building centre, and its history as a trading settlement – with ties to Madagascar, Persia, Arabia and elsewhere – dates back well before that. Vasco da Gama landed here in 1498, and in 1507 a Portuguese settlement was established on the island. Unlike Sofala to the south, where the Portuguese established a settlement at about the same time, Mozambique Island prospered as both a trading station and a naval base. In the late 16th century, the fort of São Sebastião was constructed. The island soon became the capital of Portuguese East Africa – a status that it held until the end of the 19th century when Lourenço Marques (now Maputo) moved into the spotlight.

Over the years various small waves of immigration from East Africa, Goa, Macau and elsewhere have all contributed to the ethnic mix on the island. Today this heterogeneity continues to be one of Mozambique Island's most marked characteristics, although Muslim influence, together with local Makua culture, now dominates.

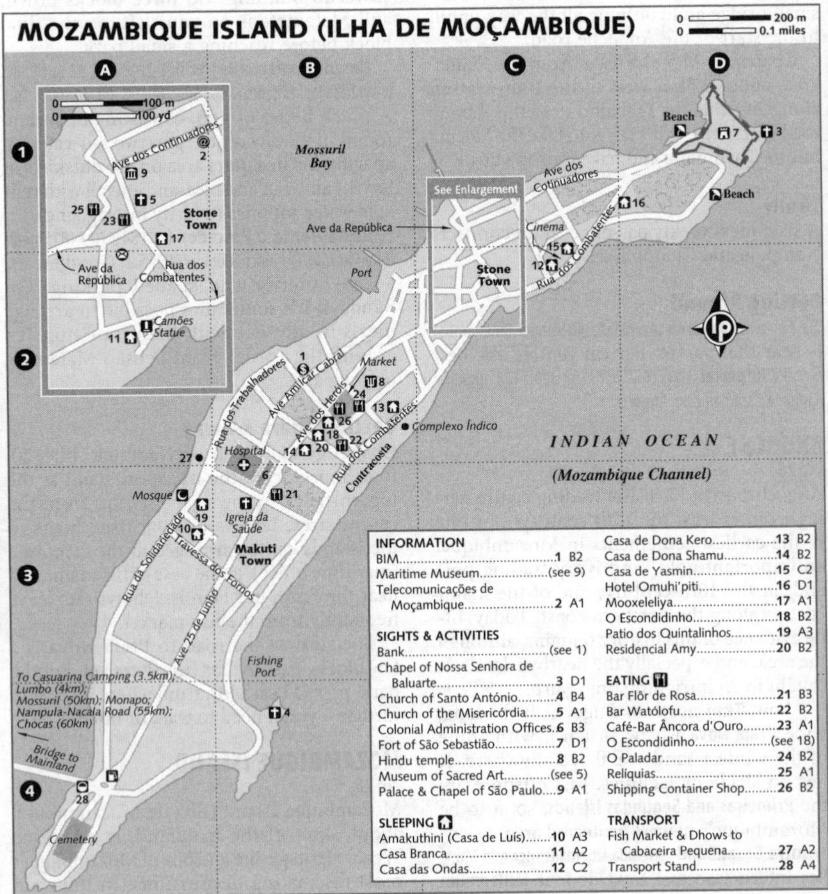

Information

BIM (Avenida Amilcar Cabral) Has an ATM, and changes cash US dollars, euro and rand.

Telecomunicações de Moçambique (per min Mtc1; 7.30am-8pm) Just down from the palace museum; internet access and international calls.

Sights

Just walking around Mozambique Island and soaking up the time-warp ambience is the best way to get a feel for the island and its long history. However, it's also worth putting in time to see some of the main sights.

PALACE & CHAPEL OF SÃO PAULO

This imposing **edifice** (Palácio de São Paulo; ☎ 26-610081; adult/child Mtc100/25; 9am-4pm) – the former governor's residence and now a museum – dates from 1610 and is the island's historical showpiece. The renovated interior gives a glimpse into what upper-class life must have been like during the island's 18th-century heyday. In addition to a collection of knick-knacks from Portugal, Arabia, India and China, there are pieces of original furniture, including an important collection of heavily ornamented Indo-Portuguese pieces. In the chapel, don't miss the altar and the pulpit, which was made in the 17th century by Chinese artists in Goa. On the ground floor is the small **Maritime Museum** (Museu da Marinha), closed at the time of writing, and behind the palace are the **Church of the Misericórdia** and the **Museum of Sacred Art** (Museu de Arte Sacra), with religious ornaments, paintings and carvings. The ticket price includes entry to all three museums.

OTHER SIGHTS

Dominating the island's northern end, the **Fort of São Sebastião**, closed for renovations at the time of research, is the oldest complete fort still standing in sub-Saharan Africa. Immediately beyond, on the island's tip, is the **Chapel of Nossa Senhora de Baluarte**, built in 1522 and considered to be the oldest European building in the southern hemisphere.

At the island's southern end is the **Church of Santo António**, while in the Stone Town are many interesting buildings, including the restored **bank** (Avenida Amilcar Cabral) and the ornate **colonial administration offices**. Nearby is a **Hindu temple**.

> **MUSIRO**
>
> On Mozambique Island and along the northern coast, you'll often see women with their faces painted white. The paste is known as *musiro,* and is used as a facial mask to beautify the skin, and sometimes as a medicinal treatment (though the medicinal paste usually has a yellowish tinge).

Activities

Excursions to nearby **Goa Island** (or Watólofu, as it's known locally) can be arranged through most hotels, or directly at the *capitania* (about Mtc1500/2500 per five-/seven-person boat plus about Mtc750 for petrol).

For beaches, it's best to head across Mossuril Bay to Chocas and Cabaceira Pequena.

Sleeping

BUDGET

Casuarina Camping (☎ 82-446 9900; casuarina09@hotmail.com, helenaabelali@gmail.com; campsites per person Mtc150, r per person Mtc700) On the mainland opposite Mozambique Island, and a two-minute walk from the bridge, Casuarina offers a well-maintained camping ground on a small beach, simple bungalow-style rooms, ablution blocks with bucket-style showers, and meals. Entry costs Mtc120 for vehicles; day visitors pay Mtc25.

Otherwise, the cheapest options are in local homes, most with small, simple rooms in the family quarters. These include the following:

Amakuthini (Casa de Luís; ☎ 82-436 7570, 82-540 7622; dm Mtc300, s/d with shared bathroom incl breakfast Mtc350/700) Very basic, but tidy and welcoming, and the closest you can come to experiencing daily life in Makuti Town. It has an eight-bed dorm and several small, dark rooms with fan in a tiny garden behind the family house. All accommodation has nets. There are also rustic cooking facilities, laundry service and a refrigerator. Meals can be arranged with advance notice. It's on the edge of Makuti Town: take the first left after passing the green mosque (to your right), and watch for the signpost.

Casa de Dona Kero (☎ 26-610034; Contracosta; r Mtc400) Small rooms with fans but no nets, and continental breakfast. It's opposite Complexo Índico.

Residencial Amy (Avenida dos Heróis; d Mtc450) Near the park, with several basic, dark rooms, most without exterior windows. Breakfast costs extra.

Casa de Dona Shamu (Avenida dos Heróis; r Mtc500) Just down from Residencial Amy, and of a similar standard.

Casa de Yasmin (☎ 26-610073; Rua dos Combatentes; r from Mtc500) Near the cinema at the island's northern end, with a handful of small rooms – some with bathroom and some being upgraded to have air-con – in an annex next to the family house. There's no food.

MIDRANGE

Patio dos Quintalinhos (Casa de Gabriele; ☎ 26-610090; www.patiodosquintalinhos.com; Rua do Celeiro; s/d with shared bathroom US$20/25, d/q/ste US$30/35/35; P) A lovely, cosy place opposite the unmissable green mosque, with creatively designed rooms around a small courtyard, including a suite with a star-view skylight and a private rooftop balcony. Staff can help with bicycle and vehicle rental, and excursions. There's also secure garage parking.

Casa das Ondas (☎ 82-438 6400; Rua dos Combatentes; r with/without bathroom Mtc750/600) Another good-value place, just to the left of the cinema and unmarked, with three rooms (one with private bathroom), a sitting area, a kitchen and a bougainvillea-bedecked courtyard. Look for the arched windows.

Casa Branca (☎ 26-610076; flora204@hotmail.com; Rua dos Combatentes; r Mtc750, with minifridge & bathroom Mtc1000) In a prime setting overlooking the sea near the Camões statue, this small, well-maintained place has three simple, bright rooms – one with bathroom – a kitchen and a garden.

Mooxeleliya (☎ 26-610076, 82-454 3290; flora204@hotmail.com, ia_petersson@hotmail.com; d with/without air-con Mtc1500/750, family r Mtc1500) Under the same management as Casa Branca, and also recommended, with simple but spacious high-ceilinged rooms upstairs and two darker, somewhat musty family-style rooms downstairs, all with bathroom. It's just down from the Church of the Misericórdia, and opposite Immigration. There's also a small cooking area with refrigerator, and a communal TV/sitting area

O Escondidinho (☎ 26-610078; ilhatur@teledata.mz; Avenida dos Heróis; r Mtc1000-1950) The atmospheric Escondidinho has high-ceilinged rooms, some with bathroom, and all with nets and ceiling fans, plus a garden courtyard and a good restaurant. It's near the public gardens. Breakfast costs extra.

Hotel Omuhi'piti (☎ 26-610101; h.omuhipiti@teledata.mz; s/d from Mtc1900/2200) Attractively set at the island's northern tip, this three-star establishment has quiet, modern rooms with sea views, and a restaurant.

Eating

O Paladar (meals from Mtc100; lunch & dinner) At the eastern corner of the old market, unmarked, and the place to go for local cuisine. Stop by in the morning and place your order with Dona Maria for lunch or dinner.

Bar Watólofu (off Rua dos Combatentes; meals Mtc130-250; lunch & dinner) A quiet place tucked into an unsignposted walled compound behind O Escondidinho, with grilled chicken, squid, shrimp and other local dishes.

Bar Flôr de Rosa (☎ 82-745 7380; snacks/meals from Mtc50/200; 5pm-midnight Wed-Mon) A small, chic Italian-run place with delicious coffees, a selection of pastas, soups and snacks, and a wonderful rooftop terrace for sundowners. It's near the hospital.

Café-Bar Âncora d'Ouro (☎ 26-610006; light meals from Mtc150; 8am-11pm Wed-Mon) Muffins, pizzas, sandwiches, soups, homemade ice cream, waffles and other goodies, plus prompt service and airy seating diagonally opposite the Church of the Misericórdia.

Relíquias (Avenida da República; meals Mtc160-230; 10am-10pm Tue-Sun) Well-prepared seafood and meat dishes, plus prawn curry, *matapa* and coconut rice. It's near the museum, and has seating indoors or outside overlooking the water.

O Escondidinho (☎ 26-610078; Avenida dos Heróis; meals about Mtc350) French-influenced seafood and meat dishes. Pricey but tasty.

For self-caterers, there's a reasonably well-stocked shop in an old shipping container next to the market.

Getting There & Away

Mozambique Island is joined by a 3.5km bridge to the mainland. Most chapas stop about 1km before the bridge in Lumbo, where you'll need to get into a smaller pick-up to cross over Mossuril Bay (due to vehicle weight restrictions on the bridge).

Leaving Mozambique Island, all transport departs from the bridge. The only direct cars to Nampula (Mtc120, three hours) are the *tanzaniano* minibuses, departing daily between 3am and 5am. Go the day before to the minibus stop in Lumbo and arrange with the driver to be picked up at your hotel, or, better, ask your hotel to get a message to the driver. After about 6am, the only option is open pick-up trucks to Monapo (Mtc40, one hour), where you can get transport on to

Nampula or Nacala. Once in Nampula, there are daily buses north to Pemba and south to Quelimane, though both leave early so you'll need to overnight in Nampula. To head direct to Pemba, take the 4am *tanzaniano* as far as Namialo, where – with luck – you can connect with the Mecula bus from Nampula, which passes Namialo about 6am.

Chapas to Lumbo cost Mtc5. Wide vehicles won't pass over the bridge, and maximum weight is 1.5 tonnes. There's a Mtc10 per vehicle toll payable on arrival on the island. Chartering a vehicle from Nampula to Mozambique Island costs about Mtc3000 one-way.

CHOCAS & AROUND

☎ 26

Diagonally opposite Mozambique Island across Mossuril Bay is the old Portuguese holiday town of Chocas, with an attractive beach and a few places to stay. Continuing from here along a sandy track roughly paralleling the beach, you come to **Cabaceira Pequena**, the point of a narrow peninsula, with a beautiful white-sand beach and views across the bay to Mozambique Island. Just inland are the ruins of an old Swahili-style mosque and the ruins of a cistern used as a watering spot by Portuguese sailors. Further along from here is **Cabaceira Grande**, with a small treasure-trove of ruins, including a late-16th-century church and the ruins of the mid-19th-century governor-general's palace. You can carefully climb up in the latter for superb views.

The Cabaceira Grande area is also notable as the site of Lisa St Aubin de Terán's (author of *Mozambique Mysteries*) Colégio de Turismo e Agricultura, housed in the restored Câmara Municipal. Next door is the small **Dois Coqueiros** (meals from Mtc90) – a small restaurant, run by staff of the community-focused Terán Project, with inexpensive local-style meals.

The next major village is Mossuril, which you'll pass through en route to Chocas by road.

Pensão-Restaurant Sunset Boulevard (r Mtc500) is in the São João area of Mossuril, about 0.8km from the Mossuril Governo building, and a good half-hour walk from the Mossuril transport junction. It's a restored residence with surprisingly nice rooms (given its unlikely location on the road to nowhere) and meals, and lots of information on and help with organising exploration of the surrounding area. It's part of the Téran Foundation's tourism activities, designed to provide local tourism training, and is a fine chill-out spot if you're interested in seeing Mozambique well away from any sort of established routes. Nearby is a small patch of beach, and Mossuril village has a good Saturday market. On Saturday evenings, there are open-air dinners with traditional dancing (per person Mtc450).

Carrusca Mar & Sol (☎ 82-516 0173, 26-213302; r.falcao@idppe.org; 4-/7-person bungalows Mtc1250/2750) has a handful of large, spotless, nicely outfitted bungalows with terraces, all set on a rise between the mangroves and one of the best stretches of beach. There's also a restaurant featuring seafood, pasta and pizza (meals about Mtc260) and a small children's playground. It's about 2km south of Chocas town, en route to Cabaceira Pequena.

Getting There & Away

BOAT

Dhows depart every morning for Cabaceira Pequena from the fish market near the green mosque on Mozambique Island (Mtc15). To return the same day, you'll need to charter a boat (about Mtc600 for a motorised dhow). Hotels on Mozambique Island can also organise Chocas/Cabaceira excursions. There's also a daily dhow between Mozambique Island and Mossuril, departing the island at about midday and departing Mossuril about 6am (Mtc20). If there's no wind, the trip across the bay can take five hours or more. Ask them to drop you at 'São João' for Sunset Boulevard – just a short walk up from the beach. From Mossuril, it's about 1½ hours on foot to Cabaceira Grande.

BUS

There's a daily direct chapa between Nampula and Chocas, departing Nampula between 10am and noon, and departing Chocas about 4am (Mtc150, five hours). Otherwise, take any transport between Nampula or Monapo and Mozambique Island to the signposted Mossuril junction 25km southeast of Monapo (Mtc100 from Nampula to the Mossuril junction). Sporadic chapas go from here to Mossuril (20km), and on to Chocas (12km further, Mtc40), with no vehicles after about 3pm. From Chocas, it's a 30-minute walk at low tide to Cabaceira Pequena, and from one hour to 1½ hours to Cabaceira Grande.

NACALA

☎ 26

Nacala is northern Mozambique's busiest port, and a gateway to diving and beaches, including **Fernão Veloso**, 10km from town.

The main street runs from Nacala-Porto (the port) to Nacala-Alta (the higher town). There are ATMs at **Barclay's Bank** (cnr Rua Principal & Rua 8) in the town centre and at the petrol station in Nacala-Alta. **Telecomunicações de Moçambique** (just off Rua Principal; per min Mtc1; 8am-8pm Mon-Fri, to 1pm Sat), diagonally opposite Hotel Maiaia, has internet access.

Sleeping & Eating

NACALA TOWN

Hotel Maiaia (☎ 26-526842; inturhoteis@teledata.mz; Rua Principal; s/d from Mtc1855/2150;) A centrally located three-star place catering to business travellers, with straightforward rooms and a restaurant. It's on the hill leading down to the port.

AROUND NACALA

Libélula (☎ 84-538 7742; www.divelibelula.com; Fernão Veloso; campsites per person US$8, dm US$10, d with shared bathroom US$30, 2- to 4-person chalets US$45-60;) This place, in a fine setting on an escarpment overlooking the beach and Nacala Bay, had just reopened under new ownership as this book was being written, and early reports are promising. On offer: rustic but comfortable reed-and-thatch chalets, dorm beds, camping, a restaurant, snorkelling, diving (including, soon, diving instruction). To get here, follow directions to Fernão Veloso (see Getting There & Away, right), and then follow the Libélula signs. Pick-ups can be arranged from Nacala town or Nampula.

Nuarro Lodge (www.nuarro.com; per person all-inclusive except drinks US$295) This new and promising place was set to open imminently at the time of research with lovely, upmarket chalets, diving, and lots of opportunities to get to know the surrounding community and environment. It's 90km from Nacala on the Baixa do Pindo peninsula; transfers can be arranged from Nacala, Nampula and Pemba.

Getting There & Away

Grupo Mecula buses to Pemba (Mtc250, seven hours) depart Nacala every other day at 5am from the Mecula garage in the town centre, uphill from the large roundabout near Mozstar.

There are chapas each morning to Nampula (Mtc125), Namialo (Mtc75) and Monapo (Mtc60, one hour), departing from the big tree next to TDM. From Monapo, there's onward transport to Mozambique Island and Namialo (the junction town for Pemba).

To Fernão Veloso: after entering Nacala, the road splits – follow the left fork, and continue for 2km to the unmarked airport and military base turnoff to the right. Go right here. After about 9km watch for the signposted Libélula left-hand turnoff opposite the base, from where it's another 1.5km.

Chapas run frequently from the port area, past Hotel Maiaia and on to Nacala Alta (Mtc5) – the best place to catch these is from the blue container opposite Hotel Maiaia – and then from Nacala-Alta to Fernão Veloso (Mtc10).

CUAMBA

☎ 271

This lively rail and road junction, with its dusty streets, flowering trees and large university student population, is the economic centre of Niassa province and a convenient stopping point if you're travelling between Malawi and the coast. **Millennium BIM** (Avenida Eduardo Mondlane) near the post office has an ATM, and there's internet access just a few doors up at **Telecomunicações de Moçambique** (Avenida Eduardo Mondlane; per min Mtc1.50; 9am-noon, 2-7pm Mon-Sat).

Pensão São Miguel (☎ 271-62701; r with shared bathroom Mtc500, r with bathroom & fan Mtc800, with air-con Mtc1000;) has small, clean rooms crowded behind the restaurant-bar area. Each has one small double bed, and some have been recently renovated. While not the most luxurious, it's currently the best value-for-price option in the town centre, and an easy 10-minute walk from the train station and bus stand.

About 2.5km from town and signposted, **Quinta Timbwa** (☎ 82-692 0250, 82-300 0752; quinta timbwa@yahoo.com.br; tw with shared bathroom Mtc500, d Mtc750, rondavel with/without air-con Mtc1200/1000;) is tranquil and good value, with spotless, pleasant rooms – some in attached rows, some in small rondavels – on expansive grounds around a small lake. It's ideal for families, or for anyone with their own transport. There's also a restaurant.

At the main intersection, **Hotel Vision 2000** (☎ 271-62632; h-vision2000@teledata.mz; cnr Avenidas

Eduardo Mondlane & 25 de Junho; s/d US$50/75;) is not the newest of hotels, as its name betrays, and it's rather down-at-heel these days, although the shower-bidet combo in many of the rooms might be an attraction for some. The attached restaurant has a small selection of meals, and visits to the nearby garnet mines (about 5km from town) can be arranged.

Supermercado Pêra-Doce (town centre), just down from Pensão Namaacha, has basics, and is good for stocking up before the train ride.

Getting There & Away

BUS, CAR & CHAPA

Most transport leaves from Maçaniqueira market, at the southern edge of town. Chapas also come to meet arriving trains.

To Gurúè, the best routing is via train to Mutuali, from where you can find waiting pick-ups on to Gurúè. This generally works best going from Cuamba to Gurúè; going in the other direction entails long waits and travel at night. There's also a direct pick-up most days to Gurúè (Mtc250 to Mtc300, five hours), departing Cuamba by about 6am. Once in Gurúè, you can connect to Mocuba (Mtc200 Gurúè to Mocuba, 3½ to four hours) and Nampula (Mtc120 Mocuba to Nampula, seven to eight hours) the same day. At the time of research, there were no direct vehicles from Cuamba to Nampula. You'll need to take the train, or to go via Gurúè (Mtc300 Gurúè to Nampula direct).

To Lichinga (Mtc350, eight to nine hours), there are several trucks daily via Mandimba (Mtc175, about four hours), with the first departure at about 4am.

To Malawi, there is at least one pick-up daily from Cuamba to Entre Lagos (Mtc150, 1½ hours). Once at Entre Lagos, you'll need to walk across the border, where there's a weekly train on the Malawi side to Liwonde. For travel via Mandimba, see the following Mandimba section, and p288.

TRAIN

The Cuamba–Nampula train (2nd/economy class Mtc332/132, 10 to 12 hours) departs in each direction daily except Monday at 5am. First class has been temporarily discontinued, as has the dining car (although this is scheduled to resume 'soon'), and 2nd class only runs in each direction on alternate days (currently from Cuamba on Wednesday, Friday and Sunday). It's well worth planning your travels to coincide with a day when 2nd class is running. Tickets can only be purchased one day before travel, between 2pm and 5pm.

To transport your vehicle on the train (about US$90), you'll need to load it the night before and arrange a guard. During the journey you can ride with the car.

MANDIMBA

If you get stuck in this border town with Malawi, **Bar-Restaurante Ngame** (Sr Liton's; d Mtc350) near the transport stop has basic rooms lined up along a small courtyard, and meals with advance notice.

Vehicles go daily to Lichinga (Mtc175) and Cuamba (Mtc175). For border information, see p288. Expect to pay Mtc30/50/100 for a bicycle/motorbike/taxi lift to cover the approximately 4km from Mandimba to the border, and Mtc30 to Mtc40 for a bicycle taxi across the 1500m of no-man's-land to the Malawi border post.

LICHINGA

☎ 271

'Fim do mundo' ('the end of the world') is how many Mozambicans describe Niassa – the least populated of Mozambique's provinces – and as far as the rest of the country is concerned, it might as well be. Yet, if you're after adventure and time in the bush, it's an ideal destination, with scenic, rugged terrain and the beautiful Lake Niassa coastline.

A convenient jumping-off point to these attractions is Lichinga, the low-key provincial capital that's set at an altitude of about 1300m amid jacarandas and pine groves.

Information

Barclay's (main roundabout) ATM.

BCI (Avenida Filipe Samuel Magaia) ATM; in the Hotel Girassol complex, next to the entrance.

Lúrio Empreendimentos (☎ 271-21705, 82-492 3780, 84-308 4080; lempreendimentos@teledata.mz; main roundabout) Next to Barclay's, this efficient, reliable outfit is the the best bet for car rentals, LAM bookings and help organising travels anywhere in Niassa, including to the Niassa Reserve, to Cóbuè and Nkwichi, and to Meponda, southwest of Lichinga on the lakeshore, where it will soon be opening its own little lodge.

Meshi Internet Café (Avenida Samora Machel; per hr Mtc60) Internet; next door to the Provincial Tourism Directorate.

MOZAMBIQUE

Millennium BIM (cnr Avenida Samora Machel & Rua Filipe Samuel Magaia) ATM.
Millennium BIM (Avenida Samora Machel) ATM.
Sarifo's Net Café (Avenida Samora Machel; per hr Mtc80) Internet; opposite Hotel 2+1 and MCel.
Standard Bank (Avenida Filipe Samuel Magaia) ATM.
Sycamore Services (Avenida Samora Machel; per hr Mtc100; ⏲ 10am-6pm Mon-Fri, to noon Sat) Internet access.

Sleeping

Ponto Final (☎ 271-20912, 82-304 3632; Avenida Filipe Samuel Magaia; s with shared bathroom Mtc650, d with bathroom & hot water Mtc1000) At the northeastern edge of town, this place has clean, reasonable, low-ceilinged rooms, a big zebra painting in the courtyard and a popular restaurant-bar. Turn down the road at the small green-and-white TDM satellite office.

Residencial 2+1 (☎ 82-381 1070; Avenida Samora Machel; s/d Mtc1200/1500) Clean, efficient and central – within easy walking distance of the bus stand. There is a restaurant attached.

Hotel Girassol Lichinga (☎ 271-21280; www.girassolhoteis.co.mz; Rua Filipe Samuel Magaia; s/d Mtc2000/2300 with advance booking; ⊠ ⊡ ⊡) Hovering between three and four stars, this is Lichinga's most upmarket option, with satellite TV, huge rooms, most with large windows, and a restaurant. Walk-in rates are higher.

Eating

In addition to the hotel restaurants, there are several other good options.

Padaria Mária (Avenida Samora Machel; snacks & light meals from Mtc50) Opposite Residencial 2+1, with a good selection of pastries, plus light meals and yoghurt.

O Chambo (☎ 271-21354, 84-319 8800; meals from Mtc120) A cosy place in the Feira Exposição Niassa (FEN) compound next to the market, with great soups and local meals. The owner also rents some rooms (single/double Mtc1100/1500) in her house, on the Cuamba road just after Socin supermarket.

Supermercado Socin (Cuamba road; ⏲ 9am-1pm & 3-7pm Mon-Fri; 9am-noon Sat) For self-catering.

Getting There & Away

AIR

LAM (☎ 271-20434, 271-20847; Rua da LAM), just off the airport road, operates four flights weekly to/from Maputo, going via Tete (weekly) or Nampula (three times weekly) and sometimes Beira.

BUS & TRUCK

All transport departs from beside the market, with vehicles to most destinations leaving by around 6am. There are daily trucks to Cuamba (Mtc350, eight hours) via Mandimba (Mtc175), to Metangula (Mtc120, 2½ hours) and to Meponda (Mtc60, 1½ hours). The first vehicle to Cuamba departs between 3am and 4am. There's also at least one pick-up truck daily to Segundo Congresso/Matchedje and the Rovuma River (Mtc500, six hours), leaving anywhere between 7am and noon from the dusty street just before the transport stand – look for the blue barracas near Safi Comercial and inquire there. Once over the bridge, you can get transport to Songea for about US$5. In both directions, you'll need to have your visa in advance if using this crossing.

To Marrupa, there's a daily vehicle (Mtc350, three hours), but no public transport from there onwards, either to Niassa Reserve or to Montepuez.

LAKE NIASSA

The Mozambican side of Lake Niassa (Lake Malawi) is much less developed than the Malawian side, and sees a small but steady stream of adventure travellers.

Metangula

Metangula is the largest Mozambican town along the lakeshore, with little to offer visitors. However, about 8km north is the attractive **Chuwanga Beach**, a popular weekend getaway for Lichinga residents.

Chuwanga Beach Hotel (Catawala's; Chuwanga Beach; campsites per person Mtc150, d wihtout bathroom Mtc400) is a low-key place directly on the sand with camping, simple bungalows sharing ablutions, a restaurant and a grill. There are occasional chapas between Metangula and Chuwanga, and hitching is easy at weekends. Otherwise, you can take the Cóbuè chapa and get off at the junction, from where it's about 2km further to Chuwanga Beach.

About 15km south of Metangula, **Mbuna Bay** (☎ 82-536 7782; www.mbunabay.ch; s/d with full board in bush bungalow US$125/190, in beach chalet US$165/250) is more upmarket, with lakeshore bungalows, a restaurant and the chance to organise canoeing and other local excursions.

GETTING THERE & AWAY

Daily chapas connect Metangula and Lichinga (Mtc120, 2½ hours), most departing Lichinga by about 8am or earlier. There's also one chapa daily between Metangula and Cóbuè (Mtc150, four hours). Departures in Metangula are from the fork in the road just up from the market at Bar Triângulo – look for the yellow Mcel wall. Transfers to Mbuna Bay can be organised from Lichinga.

For information on the *Ilala* ferry between Metangula and Malawi, see p289. For more on the *Dangilila* between Metangula and Cóbuè, see right. Both these boats depart Metangula from the small dhow port just down from Bar Triângulo and below the Catholic church.

Cóbuè

Tiny Cóbuè is the gateway into Mozambique if you're travelling from Malawi via Likoma Island, 10km offshore.

It's also the jumping-off point to reach the highly recommended **Nkwichi Lodge** (www.mandawilderness.org; s/d with full board US$375/580) – one of the most unique, appealing and most genuinely community-integrated lodges we've seen in the region, and absolutely worth the splurge. It's about 15km south of Cóbuè on the lakeshore, and linked with the Manda Wilderness Community Conservation Area – a privately initiated conservation area that also promotes community development and responsible tourism. It offers the chance to explore an area of Southern Africa that's about as remote as it gets while enjoying all the comforts. Accommodation is in six spacious handcrafted chalets – each one unique, all with private outdoor bathrooms and many with their own little white-sand coves. The lake here is crystal clear, safe for swimming and with squeaky, white sands, and the lodge has several canoes. The surrounding bush is full of birds and small wildlife, and walks, boating and village excursions can be arranged, as can a visit to the lodge's demonstration farm. Boat transfers from Cóbuè take about one hour. It's also possible to arrange pick-ups from Likoma Island. Advance bookings are essential. All in all, an idyllic getaway. Oh – and delicious meals are also part of the deal.

If your budget doesn't stretch to Nkwichi Lodge, there are several other options in Cóbuè town. **Khango Beach** (☎ in Malawi 88-856 7885, 99-962 0916, from Mozambique, dial 00-265-856 7885; r with shared bathroom per person Mtc200; (P)) has simple reed bungalows directly on the sand – all with nets and shared ablutions – and meals. **Rest House Mira Lago** (Pensão Layla; r without bathroom Mtc200; (P)), a five-minute walk away in the village centre, has solar-powered lighting and a row of rooms, each with one small double bed.

About 8km south of Cóbuè along the lakeshore, at Mbueca village, is Mchenga Wede. It was closed when we passed through, though it's worth inquiring at Khango Beach in Cóbuè if it has reopened. When operating, it has camping, basic bungalows and meals, plus bush walks and canoe trips.

GETTING THERE & AWAY

Air

There's an airstrip in Cóbuè for charter flights.

Boat

The *Ilala* ferry (weekly, in theory) no longer stops at Cóbuè – you'll need to take it to either Metangula or Likoma Island and arrange transfers from there; see p289. It's possible to get a Mozambique visa in Cóbuè, and if you're travelling to/from Malawi, you'll need to go to immigration – on the hill near the large antenna – to get your passport stamped.

The *Dangilila*, a local boat that plies the waters on the Mozambican side of the lakeshore between Metangula and Ngofi village (north of Cóbuè) stops almost everywhere on demand, including at Nkwichi Lodge, Cóbuè, Mbuna Bay and Mbueca village. It departs Metangula early Thursday mornings, arriving in Cóbuè at about 2pm. Departures from Cóbuè are at about 3am on Saturdays, arriving in Metangula about midday (Mtc150 between Metangula and Cóbuè). Buy your tickets when boarding.

Bus & Car

A daily chapa runs between Metangula and Cóbuè, departing Metangula about 7am and Cóbuè about 8am (Mtc150, four hours).

The road between Cóbuè and Metangula (75km) is unpaved but in good condition, and there's secure parking at Khango Beach and Mira Lago in Cóbuè. Walking between Cóbuè and Metangula takes about two days, going along the river via the villages of Ngoo and Chia.

NIASSA RESERVE

About 160km northeast of Lichinga on the Tanzanian border is the **Niassa Reserve** (Reserva do Niassa; www.niassa.com; per adult/child/vehicle per day

US$25/10/25, discounts for longer stays, & for Mozambican & other SADC nationals). It's a vast, wild tract notable as much for its ruggedly beautiful scenery as for its large wildlife populations, although these can be challenging to spot. In addition to the wildlife, there are also many communities still living within the reserve area.

It is possible in theory to do drive-in visits. However, given the lack of a developed network of tracks, this is only recommended for the adventure and the wilderness, rather than for the safari or 'Big Five' aspects. There is currently no official public camping ground, although there is a very rudimentary area near Mbatamila headquarters where you can pitch a tent. Bring all food, drinking water and supplies with you. Note that Niassa's tsetse flies are very aggressive and very numerous. They are attracted by the dust and heat of moving vehicles, so any vehicle safaris will need to be done with windows up.

At the time of research, fees were not being collected at the reserve entrance, but rather are payable in advance – in person or via cheque – through the Maputo office of the **Sociedade para a Gestão e Desinvolvimento da Reserva do Niassa** (SGN; ☎ 21-329807; sgdrn.map@tvcabo.co.mz; 1031 Avenida Mao Tse Tung) – the entity charged with managing the reserve. The receipt should then be presented when you reach the reserve. That said, the entire reserve infrastructure is still in very early stages, and we haven't heard of anyone being turned away at the gate for lack of a receipt.

Lugenda Bush Camp (www.raniresorts.com), on the Lugenda River near the eastern edge of the park, caters primarily to fly-in guests, and offers a unique safari experience that's likely to appeal to well-heeled safari connoisseurs seeking an 'unpackaged' experience with all the amenities. There's a set of maintained roads around the camp to facilitate wildlife tracking.

The recommended **Moja Safari Wilderness** (www.mojasafariwilderness.com; s/d all-inclusive US$425/700), which was about to commence operations as this book was published, offers multinight canoeing along the Lugenda River, hiking up an inselberg and the chance to explore the bush on foot and by boat under the expert guidance of the owner-managers Rob and Jos. The camp itself consists of one semipermanent camp – about a five-hour drive from Mecula – together with a series of bush fly camps set up along the river.

GETTING THERE & AWAY

Charter flights from Pemba (per person one-way US$560) can be arranged with Lugenda Bush Camp, Moja Safari Wilderness, or with Kaskazini in Pemba (opposite).

Via road, it's possible to reach Mbatamila in the dry season via Montepuez, Balama and Marrupa, although the Balama–Marrupa section is in extremely poor condition. Allow up to two days from Pemba, and plan on bush camping en route. It is better to approach the reserve from Lichinga, where you have good tarmac as far as Marrupa. Once at Marrupa, the remaining stretch up to the Lugenda River and on into the reserve is dirt but in reasonable shape. The unpaved road from Cuamba to Marrupa is another doable option, especially during the dry season. Petrol is generally available on the roadside in Mecula, however this should not be relied upon, and plenty of extra supplies should be carried along from either Cuamba, Pemba or Lichinga.

Once across the Lugenda, you'll need to sign in at the reserve, before continuing on towards Mecula and Mbatamila park headquarters – set in the shadow of the 1441m-high Mt Mecula – where you can arrange a guide.

MONTEPUEZ

☎ 272

Until the stretch of road leading west from Montepuez to Marrupa is paved, this busy district capital remains very much the end of the road, with little to attract tourists. It will, however, seem like a first-world mecca and is an essential stocking-up point if you are headed to/from Lichinga or the Niassa Reserve.

Residencial do Geptex (☎ 272-51114; Avenida Julius Nyerere; r Mtc400) has very basic rooms with double beds, bucket baths, fan and no nets. It's at the western end of town, two blocks north of the main road.

Vivenda Angelina (Avenida Julius Nyerere; r Mtc500) has clean, quiet rooms in a private house sharing a bathroom that often has running water. There's no food and no signpost. Coming from the main road, turn right at the Plexus signboard at the western end of town, go two short blocks, and then turn left onto Avenida Julius Nyerere. It's the second house on the left.

For meals, there's a **refrigerator** (🕒 from 7am Mon-Sat) next to the bakery – which is on a side street one block before the bus stand – with juice, yoghurt and (sometimes) apples. Also try the small **cafe** (light meals from Mtc80) behind the park with the aeroplane.

The transport stand is two blocks south of Avenida Eduardo Mondlane – turn down the street with Millennium BIM. Several chapas daily go between Pemba and Montepuez (Mtc150, three hours). Heading west, there's regular transport to Balama (Mtc150), but from there to Marrupa (for Niassa Reserve) there is no option other than hitching a lift with a tractor or a truck.

PEMBA

☎ 272

Pemba is a sleepy port town set on a peninsula jutting into the enormous Pemba Bay. It was established in 1904 as administrative headquarters for the Niassa Company. Today, it's the capital of Cabo Delgado province and the main town in Mozambique's far north. Although lacking the charm to be a destination in itself, the town makes a relaxing, enjoyable stop, and it's also the main gateway to the islands of the Quirimbas Archipelago. The hub of tourist activity is Wimbi (Wimbe) Beach, a one-street town with a permanent holiday atmosphere.

Orientation

At the peninsula's southwestern tip is the low-lying baixa area around the port and old town. East of here and up the hill is the modern-day town centre, with a few hotels and restaurants. About 5km further east is Wimbi Beach.

Information

On Wimbi Beach, Complexo Náutilus also has an ATM.

Clínica Cabo Delgado (☎ 272-21462; Rua Modesta Neva 10) For medical treatment.

Farmácia São Carlos Lwanga (🕒 7am-6.30pm Mon-Fri, 8am-5pm Sat) Well-stocked pharmacy; one block behind Avenida 25 de Setembro, and just down from the Grupo Mecula bus office.

Kaskazini (☎ 272-20371, 82-309 6990; www.kaskazini.com; Pemba Beach Hotel, Avenida Marginal, Wimbi Beach; 🕒 8am-3pm Mon-Fri, 8.30am-noon Sat) An excellent first stop, with lots of info on Pemba and the surrounding area, plus flight and accommodation bookings.

Millennium BIM (Avenida Eduardo Mondlane) ATM.

Standard Bank (Avenida Eduardo Mondlane) ATM.

Sycamore Services (☎ 272-21999; 1282 Avenida 25 de Setembro; per hr Mtc100; 🕒 7am-9pm Mon-Sat, 8am-noon Sun) Internet connection; it's just after Mcel.

Activities

There is good diving in Pemba Bay, and beyond around the Quirimbas Archipelago. **CI Divers** (☎ 272-20102; www.cidivers.com; Complexo Náutilus, Avenida Marginal, Wimbi Beach) has PADI instruction and equipment rental, plus windsurfing and other watersports-equipment rental and boat charters.

Kaskazini arranges day trips around Pemba Bay and dhow safaris to the islands of the Quirimbas Archipelago.

You can use the pool and small playground at **Clube Naval** (☎ 272-21770; Avenida Marginal, Wimbi Beach; 🕒 10am-midnight) for free if you eat a meal there.

Sleeping

BUDGET

Pemba Magic Lodge (Russell's Place; ☎ 82-686 2730; www.pembamagic.com; Wimbi Beach; campsites per person US$8, dm US$15, rental tent per person US$15, chalet d US$60; 📶) About 3.5km beyond Complexo Náutilus along the beach-road extension, this recently renovated lodge has camping with ablutions (although no self-catering), a handful of rustic but new and comfortable chalets with fan with fan and bathroom, tents for rent, a bar-restaurant with pizzas and a large menu, information for overlanders, and the beach (high-tide swimming only). Coming soon: a dorm and a pool.

Pemba Dive & Bushcamp (Nacole Jardim; ☎ 82-661 1530; www.pembadivecamp.com; campsites per person US$10, dm US$20, d/q chalet US$100/140) A tranquil camping ground that's good for families. There are also dorm beds, several screened-in chalets, a beachside bar and braai area, and botanical walking tours on request. It's about 10 minutes from town (Mtc200 in a taxi), behind the airport on the bay, and about 3km off the main road down an unpaved track.

Pensão Baía (cnr Rua 1 de Maio & Rua Base Beira; d with shared bathroom & fan Mtc500, with private bathroom & air-con Mtc600) Spartan budget rooms in the town centre, and breakfast on request.

MIDRANGE

Wimbi Sun Residencial (☎ 82-318 1300; wimbisun@teledata.mz; 7472 Avenida Marginal; r/ste Mtc1250/1600; ❄) Clean, modern rooms (ask for a 'suite') diagonally opposite Complexo Náutilus. Breakfast costs Mtc150 extra.

Complexo Turístico Caraçol (☎ 272-20147; sulemane@teledata.mz; Avenida Marginal; r Mtc1000, 1-/2-room

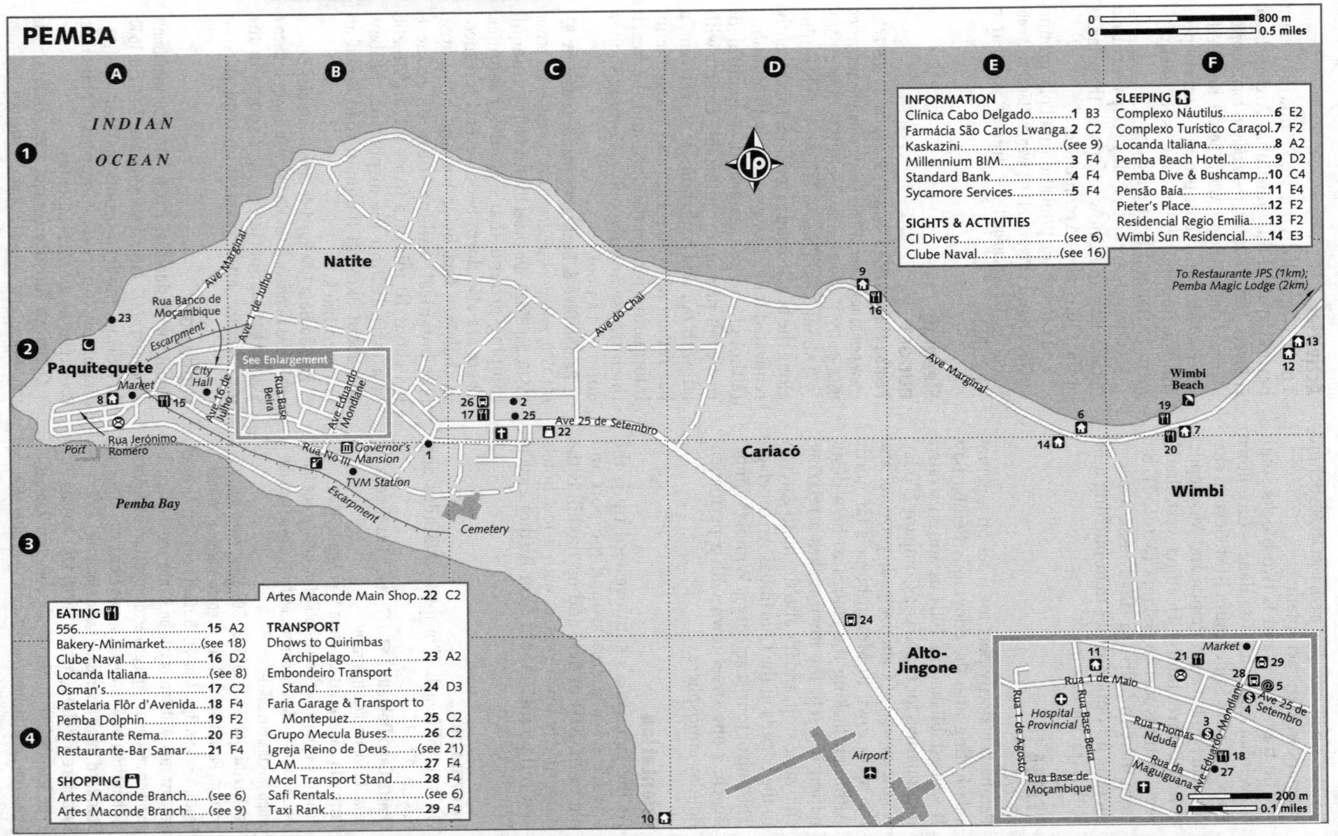

INFORMATION
Clínica Cabo Delgado....................1 B3
Farmácia São Carlos Lwanga.2 C2
Kaskazini..........................(see 9)
Millennium BIM....................3 F4
Standard Bank......................4 F4
Sycamore Services................5 F4

SIGHTS & ACTIVITIES
CI Divers...........................(see 6)
Clube Naval........................(see 16)

SLEEPING
Complexo Náutilus................6 E2
Complexo Turístico Caraçol.7 F2
Locanda Italiana...................8 A2
Pemba Beach Hotel...............9 D2
Pemba Dive & Bushcamp...10 C4
Pensão Baía........................11 E4
Pieter's Place......................12 F2
Residencial Regio Emilia.....13 F2
Wimbi Sun Residencial......14 E3

EATING
556.......................................15 A2
Bakery-Minimarket..........(see 18)
Clube Naval.........................16 D2
Locanda Italiana.................(see 8)
Osman's...............................17 C2
Pastelaria Flôr d'Avenida....18 F4
Pemba Dolphin....................19 F2
Restaurante Rema..............20 F3
Restaurante-Bar Samar......21 F4

SHOPPING
Artes Maconde Branch......(see 6)
Artes Maconde Branch......(see 9)
Artes Maconde Main Shop..22 C2

TRANSPORT
Dhows to Quirimbas Archipelago....................23 A2
Embondeiro Transport Stand...........................24 D3
Faria Garage & Transport to Montepuez....................25 C2
Grupo Mecula Buses.........26 C2
Igreja Reino de Deus........(see 21)
LAM.....................................27 F4
Mcel Transport Stand........28 F4
Safi Rentals.....................(see 6)
Taxi Rank...........................29 F4

apt Mtc1500/1700;) On the inland side of the beach road just beyond Complexo Náutilus, with straightforward, musty rooms that are reasonable value for the price, and small apartments, some with kitchenettes.

Pieter's Place (☎ 272-20102; cidivers@teledata.mz; Avenida Marginal; d about US$70) Along the extension of the Wimbi Beach road with two small, airy rooms in shaded grounds and dorm rooms planned. There's no food, although a restaurant is also planned.

our pick **Residencial Regio Emilia** (☎ 272-21297, 82-928 5510; www.wix.com/akeelz/Residencial-Reggio-Emilia; 8696 Avenida Marginal; r US$80, per r in self-catering chalets US$80;) A lovely, tranquil spot with spacious, spotless rooms – all with hot water, air-con, DSTV and minifridge – and a few self-catering chalets in the green, quiet grounds. All are nicely decorated with locally sourced materials such as Palma mats, and all also have mosquito screening in the windows. Breakfast costs extra. A restaurant is planned.

Complexo Náutilus (☎ 272-21520; nautiluscas@teledata.mz; Avenida Marginal; s/d/q bungalows Mtc2500/3000/3500;) Accommodation is in closely spaced bungalows with TV and minifridge (ask for one of the 'newer' ones), and there's a restaurant. The effect of the good beachside setting here is marred by indifferent management.

Locanda Italiana (☎ 272-20672, 82-688 9050; locandaitaliana@tdm.co.mz; 487 Rua Gerónimo Romero; r Mtc2900-3500;) A cosy boutique and business travellers' hotel in the baixa with six very well-appointed, spacious rooms – one with a sunken bathtub built around a spreading fig tree – and a restaurant. Very nice.

TOP END

Pemba Beach Hotel (☎ 272-21770; www.pembabeachresort.com; Avenida Marginal; s/d from US$165/330;) This five-star establishment has expansive grounds overlooking the water, well-equipped rooms, a restaurant (closed at the time of research) and a yacht for charters around the Quirimbas Archipelago. Package deals from Johannesburg are available that also include sister lodges in the Quirimbas and Bazaruto Archipelagos.

Eating

TOWN CENTRE

Restaurante-Bar Samar (☎ 272-20415; Avenida 25 de Setembro; meals from Mtc150; 9am-10pm Sun-Fri) In the parking lot of the Igreja Reino de Deus, with hearty Portuguese cuisine served on a shaded porch.

Pastelaria Flôr d'Avenida (☎ 272-20514; Avenida Eduardo Mondlane; meals from Mtc100) A no-frills eatery with a wide selection of standard dishes and pastries served at tables on a small streetside plaza.

556 (☎ 272-21487; Rua No 1; meals Mtc180-400; 10am-10pm Mon-Sat;) On the hill overlooking the port and the bay, with South African meats, plus chicken grills, pizzas, hamburgers, grilled prawns, squid, pub food and ice cream.

Locanda Italiana (☎ 272-20672; 487 Rua Gerónimo Romero; meals about Mtc250; from 5pm Mon-Sat) Delicious and reasonably priced Italian cuisine served in a quiet courtyard. It makes a calming retreat from the heat and bustle of town.

For self-catering, try **Osman's** (Avenida 25 de Setembro), about 1.5km east of the main junction, or the **bakery-minimarket** (Avenida Eduardo Mondlane), next to Pastelaria Flôr d'Avenida.

WIMBI BEACH

Restaurante JPS (Avenida Marginal extension; half chicken & chips Mtc150; lunch & dinner Tue-Sun) A local haunt on the inland side of the road, with grilled chicken, *matapa* and other local dishes, and screened-in eating areas. Service isn't speedy, but the price is right, and the food is good.

Restaurante Rema (Avenida Marginal; meals from Mtc120) Another good spot for local meals and vibes. It's just opposite Pemba Dolphin.

Pemba Dolphin (Avenida Marginal; seafood grills from Mtc180) Directly on the beach, with a beach-bar ambience and seafood grills.

Clube Naval (☎ 272-21770; Avenida Marginal; meals from Mtc250; 10am-midnight) Next door to Pemba Beach Hotel, this beachside place has salads, seafood, chicken, ribs, pizzas and desserts, a small pool and a children's playground.

Getting There & Away

AIR

LAM (Avenida Eduardo Mondlane; 7am-4.30pm Mon-Fri, 9.30-11.30am Sat) flies daily to/from Maputo (via Nampula and/or Beira), and three times weekly to/from Dar es Salaam (Tanzania). **SAAirlink** (☎ 272-21700; www.saairlink.co.za; airport) flies twice weekly between Johannesburg and Pemba.

For charters to the Quirimbas Archipelago or Lake Niassa, contact Kaskazini (see Information, p273). For the Quirimbas, also see the boxed text, p278.

BUS & CHAPA

Grupo Mecula (☎ 272-20821) has daily buses to Nampula (Mtc250, seven hours), Moçimboa da Praia (Mtc250, 7½ hours) and Mueda (Mtc250, 10 hours) – with the same bus going first to Moçimboa da Praia and then on to Mueda. There's a direct bus every other day to Nacala (Mtc250, seven hours); otherwise take the Nampula bus to Namialo junction and wait there for onward transport. For Mozambique Island, the best bet is to continue to Nampula, and then get onward transport from there the next day. You can also try your luck getting out at Namialo junction and looking for onward transport from there, but the timing often doesn't work out, and Namialo is unappealing as an overnight spot. All Pemba departures are at 4.45am from the Grupo Mecula office, just off the main road and about 1.5km from the centre on a small side street behind Osman's supermarket. All buses also pass by the Mcel office (corner of Avenidas 25 de Setembro and Eduardo Mondlane) before departing town by around 5am.

Otherwise, try your luck with other transport at Mcel, or head to Embondeiro transport stand, 3km from the centre (Mtc75 in a taxi). Alternatively, '*tanzaniano*' chapas depart in all directions from Igreja Reino de Deus from 4am, with high speeds and prices only marginally cheaper than those of the Mecula buses.

To Montepuez (Mtc130, two hours), minibuses depart from Faria garage, on Avenida 25 de Setembro opposite the Catholic church, from around 4.30am.

Getting Around

There are taxi ranks on Avenida Eduardo Mondlane just down from Mcel and nearby along Avenida 25 de Setembro, on the other side of the junction with Avenida Eduardo Mondlane. Town to Wimbi beach costs from Mtc150. There's also a public bus that runs between 6am and 7pm from town to Wimbi Beach and beyond (Mtc10).

Safi Rentals (☎ 82-380 8630; 82-684 7770; www.pembarentacar.com) comes highly recommended, offering reliable car rentals for very reasonable prices. Rates include unlimited kilometres, and open the door to many attractions in the north that would be otherwise inaccessible for budget and midrange travellers. It is currently based at the Náutilus, but if you don't find it there, give a phonecall or email.

It's also possible to arrange car rentals through Kaskazini (p273).

AROUND PEMBA

About 12km south of Pemba is Murrebue, a lovely stretch of sand known for its optimal kite-surfing conditions.

Il Pirata (www.murrebue.com; d US$80-110) is the hub of activity, and also has some lovely bungalows and delicious Italian meals. Airport transfers cost a very reasonable US$30 return.

QUIRIMBAS ARCHIPELAGO

☎ 272

The Quirimbas Archipelago consists of about two dozen islands and islets strewn among the turquoise waters along the 400km stretch of coastline between Pemba and the Rovuma River. Some are waterless and uninhabited, while others have histories as long as the archipelago itself.

Ibo, the best known of the islands, was already an important Muslim trading post when the Portuguese arrived in the 15th century, and by the late 18th century, it had become a major slave-trading port and the second-most important town in Mozambique after Mozambique Island. Today, it's a fascinating place with wide streets lined with dilapidated villas and crumbling, moss-covered buildings. At its northern end is the star-shaped fort of São João dating from the late 18th century,

MOZAMBIQUE

CRAFT SHOPPING

Even if you don't think you want to buy crafts, it's worth stopping in at the excellent **Artes Maconde** (☎/fax 272-21099; artesmaconde@tdm.co.mz; Town Centre Avenida 25 de Setembro; Wimbi Beach Pemba Beach Hotel; Wimbi Beach At CI Divers), especially its main shop in the town centre, which is packed with a wide range of quality carvings, crafts and textiles sourced from throughout Mozambique, as well as from elsewhere in the region. It's one of the best craft shops in the country, as far as quality of the artistry and uniqueness of the art are concerned, and craftsmen come from outlying villages throughout Cabo Delgado and as far away as the DR Congo (Zaïre) to deliver their wares. It does international air and sea shipping, and also takes orders.

CABO DELGADO

Cabo Delgado province was the birthplace of Mozambique's independence struggle, which was supported from bases in nearby Tanzania. At the height of the war, it could take up to a month to travel – convoy-style, and moving only at night – between Pemba and Moçimboa da Praia. One legacy of this era: many of the most unlikely towns still have huge, tarmac landing strips long enough to accommodate a jet.

known now for its silversmiths. While there are no good beaches near town, there are several secluded spots around the island where you can swim.

Other islands include **Quirimba**, with extensive coconut plantations, and **Matemo** and **Quisiva**, both sites of large Portuguese plantation houses. Tiny **Rolas**, between Matemo Island and Pangane, is uninhabited except for some seasonal fishing settlements and a population of giant coconut-eating land crabs. **Quilaluia** is now a protected marine sanctuary. **Vamizi**, **Rongui** and **Macaloé Islands** are part of the **Maluane Project** (www.maluane.com) – a privately funded community-based conservation project that will ultimately also encompass an adjoining coastal strip, and an inland area where wildlife safari-tropical island combinations will be possible.

While there are many beautiful patches of white, soft sand, the archipelago is also known for its vegetation, and many of the islands are fringed in part by mangroves. Dense mangrove forests also link some of the islands to each other, and with the coast. Only skilled dhow captains are able to navigate among the intricate channels that were cut during Portuguese times. The archipelago is also known for its diving, and for its birdwatching.

Many of the southern islands, including Ibo and Matemo, are part of **Quirimbas National Park** (Parque Nacional das Quirimbas; adult/child Mtc200/100), which also includes areas on the fringing coastline. Fees are currently collected by hotels within the park area, though this may change.

Information

A Quirimbas National Park and **tourist information office** has just opened on Ibo Island opposite the church and near the dhow port, where you can get information and arrange guides, and pay park entry fees. Various community-based tourism activities are also planned, including dhow excursions, traditional dancing and guided tours. Once the program is up and going, you can arrange these here as well. Meanwhile, the hotels should be able to help.

Activities

There is so much to do on Ibo and around the islands that you just might have trouble finding time to relax. Among the options are **wandering around Ibo** town and soaking up the time-warp ambience; taking a day **excursion to a nearby sandbank** for snorkelling; or, **sailing around the archipelago** on a live-aboard dhow (see the boxed text, p278). If you speak Portuguese or have a translator, don't miss **visiting Senhor João Baptista** – Ibo's official historian, and a wealth of information of the island. His house – marked by a signpost – is along the shaded path leading from town to the fort of São João.

Sleeping & Eating

IBO ISLAND

It's possible to arrange **homestays** (☎ 82-551 1919; r Mtc250) with local families. Contact Ibraimo Assane directly at this booking number, or arrange through Kaskazini (p273) in Pemba. You'll get a taste for how locals live, and get to sample local meals. Be prepared for extremely basic conditions.

Campsite do Janine (campsites per person Mtc150) A simple campsite just up from Ibo Island Lodge and the dhow port. Check with Kaskazini in Pemba first to confirm it's still operating.

Tikidiri (Airfield road; s/tw Mtc150/300) This community-run place, about 2km from the dhow port opposite the old cemetery along the path leading to the airfield, has no-frills but clean stone-and-thatch bungalows, all with nets and private bucket baths. There's no electricity and no breakfast, but good local meals can be arranged, as can guides for exploring the island and elsewhere in the archipelago.

Self-catering house This three-bedroom self-catering house with adjoining garden was being rehabilitated as part of community-based tourism initiatives on Ibo. It can be rented by room or in its entirety. It's near the small St Antonio fort and the antenna.

Check with the Ibo tourist information centre or with Kaskazini (p273) in Pemba for an update.

TDM Casa de Hospedes (s/d without bathroom from Mtc400/700, ste Mtc900) Cleanish, basic with fan and nets, and all sharing bathroom. It's just around the corner from Miti Miwiri, at the start of the road leading to the airfield.

Miti Miwiri (☎ 26-960530, 82-543 5864; www.mitimiwire.com; dm US$20, d US$50-80) A lovely, atmospheric place in a restored house with a handful of spacious, good-value rooms with private bathrooms and fan, including one 'dorm' room with two double beds, and a large, walled garden with two large swings. There's also a bar, a sheesha lounge, a restaurant, and help with tourist information, flight bookings and excursions. It's in the heart of the town, and about 10 minutes on foot from the dhow port – ask any of the children who come to meet the boat to show you the way. Continental/full breakfast costs Mtc100/150 extra.

Cinco Portas (www.cincoportas.com; s US$35-60, d US$60-100, 8-person house US$240;) Another atmospheric, good-value place in a restored mansion with a lovely garden. It's just up the road from Miti Miwiri and has a variety of rooms, some with sea-facing verandahs, and a restaurant (breakfast costs extra). It's also possible to rent out the 8-person main house.

Ibo Island Lodge (www.iboisland.co.za; s/d with half board from US$435/670;) This nine-room luxury boutique hotel – the most upmarket accommodation on Ibo – is housed in two restored mansions in a prime setting overlooking the water near the dhow port. Relax on the sea-facing verandahs, enjoy a sundowner overlooking the water, or luxuriate in the comforts of the rooms.

OTHER ISLANDS

Matemo Community Campsite (Matemo Island; campsites per person about Mtc100) This place was just getting started as this book was researched. It's on the southern coast of Matemo Island near Muanancombo village, with four simple A-frame bungalows and a camping area, all with shared ablutions and communal cook-

ISLAND HOPPING

If you've ever dreamed of sailing around tropical islands surrounded by turquoise waters and past deserted white sandbanks, the Quirimbas Archipelago is the place to come. **Fim do Mundo Safaris** (☎ 82-511 6925, 82-304 2908; www.fimdomundosafaris.com) offers liveaboard trips departing from Ibo Island on their handcrafted 13m wooden sailing and motorised dhow (six persons, maximum). Apart from sailing, days are spent snorkelling, diving (certified divers only), kayaking and exploring deserted beaches and islands. Prices are a very reasonable US$120 per person per day including meals, and the sailing calendar is posted on their website. The owners are longtime Mozambique residents and divers and very knowledgeable on the area, and the ambience is laid-back and convivial. All in all, it's an excellent experience.

If you're in a group or aren't feeling up to the rigours of public transport to reach Ibo, or are simply wondering how to reach the other islands, there's now a **private transfer service** (☎ 82-724 4437; jorickv@gmail.com) based out of Ibo. It costs US$200 to charter a vehicle (up to six passengers) for a one-way transfer in either direction between Pemba and Tandanhangue or US$30 per person to hitch a lift if the vehicle is going anyway between the two towns. The same operator also offers transfers in a motorised boat between Tandanhangue and Ibo (US$30 one-way), as well as island-hopping services from Ibo to Matemo or Pangane (US$60 and 1½ hours Ibo to Matemo, US$90, 2½ hours Ibo to Pangane). Alternatively, for a US$10 organising fee, they can help you sort out a reliable local nonmotorised dhow to any of these destinations or other spots in the archipelago, including to Rolas Island. Expect to pay Mtc1000/2000 per boat from Ibo to Matemo/Pangane.

Yet another option is **private dhow charter** to cruise around the Quirimbas. Stephane has a six-sleeper cabin dhow for charter anywhere in the archipelago, and also runs regular trips from Pemba to Ibo with an overnight stop at Mefunvo Island, where you rough camp on the beach (per person US$80 for the entire trip with three meals). Dimitri has motorised and nonmotorised boats available for dive charters or transfers. Both of these can be contacted through the private transfer service (above), through Miti Miwiri hotel (above) on Ibo, or through Kaskazini (p273) in Pemba.

COCONUT CRABS

Tiny Rolas Island is known for its fascinating population of giant, coconut-eating land crabs. These nocturnal creatures, considered to be the largest arthropods in the world, sometimes grow up to 1m long. Coconut crabs get their name from their proclivity for climbing coconut palms, shaking down the nuts, and then prying the cracked shells open to scoop out the flesh.

ing facilities. An informal 'restaurant' (meals cooked by local ladies) and a small shop selling some basics are planned.

Vamizi Island Lodge (www.vamizi.com; Vamizi Island; r per person with full board & activities US$770) A 24-bed luxury getaway on a long arc of white sand.

Medjumbe Island Resort (www.medjumberesort.com; Medjumbe Island; per person all-inclusive from US$515;) and **Matemo Island Resort** (www.matemoresort.com; Matemo Island; per person all-inclusive from US$460;) are luxurious getaways operated by Rani Africa, which also runs the Pemba Beach Hotel in Pemba and Lugenda Safari Camp in Niassa Reserve.

Getting There & Away

AIR

All lodges organise charters, and individual seats are often available (US$110 per person one-way from Pemba to Ibo). Book through Kaskazini (p273)(☎ 272-20371, 82-309 6990; www.kaskazini.com; Pemba Beach Hotel, Avenida Marginal, Wimbi Beach; 8am-3pm Mon-Fri, 8.30am-noon Sat) in Pemba.

BOAT

First – read the boxed text, opposite. If none of those options suit, you'll need to go first to Quissanga, on the coast north of Pemba. A direct chapa departs Pemba from the fish market behind the mosque in Paquitequete *bairro* (Mtc200, four to five hours) at about 4am daily. From Quissanga, most vehicles continue on to Tandanhangue village (Mtc200 from Pemba), 5km further, which is the departure point for dhows to Ibo (Mtc100). In the dry season, it's sometimes possible to find a vehicle from Pemba going via Metuge (Mtc150), which saves a bit on time.

For drivers (4WD), there's secure parking at Gringo's Place next to the Tandanhangue dhow port for Mtc50 per day, and at Casa de Isufo (signposted 2km before the Tandanhangue port) for Mtc70 per day. The latter is a bit of a walk, but useful if you're visiting when rains or high water make the intervening stretch of mud flats impassable for a vehicle. (A bridge is planned over the flats, but it's still well in the future.)

Dhows leave Tandanhangue only at high tide (with a window of about two hours on either side of the high-tide point), and nonmotorised boats take from one to six hours to Ibo (about 45 minutes with motor). There's no accommodation in Tandanhangue, but if you get stuck waiting, Isufo (at Casa de Isufo) can help you find a meal (allow plenty of time), and has an enclosed area where you can sleep on the ground or set up a tent. Chartering a motorised boat for yourself to Ibo will cost about Mtc800 to Mtc1000 one-way.

For speedboat charters from Pemba direct to the islands, contact the upmarket lodges or Kaskazini (p273). For those with plenty of time, there's a dhow (nonmotorised) that sails with some regularity from Paquitequete in Pemba to Ibo (Mtc100, about 12 hours). To hire a Paquitequete-to-Ibo dhow for yourself, expect to pay about Mtc2500.

MACOMIA

Macomia is the turn-off point for the beach at Pangane and the end of the good tarmac if you're heading north. About 40km north along the main road is the large village of **Chai**, where Frelimo's military campaign against colonial rule began in 1964 with an attack on a Portuguese base.

Pensão-Residencial Caminho do Norte (r Mtc350), on the main road just north of the junction, has no-frills rooms. **Bar Chung** (at the junction) has a few very basic rooms in the family compound to rent, and can help with meals.

For transport to Mucojo and on to Pangane, see p280.

PANGANE

This large village sits on a long, palm-fringed beach that – while sometimes rather littered – remains nevertheless an ideal chilling-out spot just on the edge of paradise.

Hashim's Camp (campsites per person Mtc200, bungalow s/d with shared bathroom Mtc400/600) is a laid-back camp on the point that's run by the helpful Hashim and his family, with reed bungalows on the sand, and local-style grilled fish meals.

Situated 15km south of Mucojo on an idyllic stretch of white sand, **Guludo** (☎ in UK 01323-766 655; www.guludo.com; r per person with full board from US$285) is an upmarket fair-trade camp that makes a fine base if you want to combine a beach holiday with support for local community development initiatives. Accommodation is in well-appointed safari-style tents or more upmarket 'adobe bandas'. There's also a spacious family banda, and the chance for island excursions, diving and more. Transfers can be arranged from Pemba and Macomia.

Getting There & Away

Pangane is 50km off the main north–south road (the turn-off is at Macomia), and 9km north of Mucojo – a tiny junction village on the coast. There is at least one daily chapa between Macomia and Pangane (Mtc100), departing Pangane at about 5am. Departures from Macomia are at about 9am – the chapa waits until the Pemba–Moçimboa da Praia and Moçimboa da Praia–Pemba through buses arrive. There are also several chapas daily from Macomia to Mucojo, from where you can usually find a pick-up on to Pangane. Dhows to the Quirimbas Islands can be arranged at Hashim's Camp and Guludo; for dhows from Ibo or the other islands to Pangane, see p278.

MUEDA

Mueda, the main settlement on the cool Makonde Plateau, was the site of the infamous 'massacre of Mueda' (see p220), and there's a statue commemorating its role in Mozambican independence at the western end of town. Many Makonde carvers live in the outlying villages.

Pensão Takatuka (Rua 1 de Maio; r Mtc200, annexe r Mtc250) and the nearby and better **Motel Sanzala** (Rua 1 de Maio; r Mtc250), both along the main road, have basic rooms sharing bathrooms. Motel Sanzala also has meals and bucket baths.

Grupo Mecula has a daily bus between Pemba and Mueda via Moçimboa da Praia (Mtc250, 10 hours), departing at 5am. Several vehicles go each morning between Mueda and Moçimboa da Praia (Mtc120, two hours). All transport leaves from the main road opposite the market.

MOÇIMBOA DA PRAIA

☎ 272

This bustling outpost, with its lively dhow port, is the last major town before the Tanzanian border. If you're travelling by dhow and enter or leave Mozambique here, have your passport stamped at the immigration office near Complexo Miramar. **Barclays Bank** (Avenida 7 de Março) has an ATM (Visa card); **Telecomunicações de Moçambique** (Avenida 7 de Março; per min Mtc1) has internet access.

Sleeping & Eating

Pensão Leeta, at the town entrance opposite the transport stand, was leased out long-term in its entirety when this book was researched, but you may still be able to pitch a tent in its grounds.

Pensão-Residencial Magid (☎ 272-81099; Avenida Samora Machel; r Mtc350) A short walk downhill

MAPIKO DANCING

If you hear drumming in the late afternoons while travelling around Cabo Delgado, it likely means *mapiko* – the famed masked dancing of the Makonde.

The dancer – always a man – wears a special wooden mask or *lipiko* (plural: *mapiko*), decorated with wildly exaggerated features, hair (often real) and facial etchings. Before *mapiko* begins, the dancer's body is completely covered with large pieces of cloth wrapped around the legs, arms and body so that nothing can be seen other than the fingers and toes. All evidence that there is a person inside is supposed to be hidden. *Mapiko* supposedly grew out of male attempts to limit the power of women in matrilineal Makonde society. The idea is that the dancer represents the spirit of a dead person who has come to do harm to the women and children, from which only the men of the village can protect them. While boys learn the secret of the dance during their initiation rites, women are never supposed to discover it, remaining in fear of the *mapiko*.

Once the dancer is ready, distinctive rhythms are beaten on special *mapiko* drums. The dance is usually performed on weekend afternoons, and must be finished by sunset. Watch for *mapiko* dancing in and around Mueda, and in Macomia. To take a mask home, look in craft shops in Pemba and Nampula.

THE MAKONDE

Like many ethnic groups in the north of the country, Mozambique's Makonde are matrilineal. Children and inheritances normally belong to the woman, and it's common for husbands to move to the village of their wives after marriage, setting up house near their mother-in-law.

from the transport stand, with basic rooms sharing facilities.

Complexo Miramar (Complexo Natasha or Dona Bebe; ☎ 272-81135/6; r Mtc1000) Directly on the water at the lower end of town, with three very basic rondavels that likely haven't received a lick of maintenance since they were constructed, although there is usually a trickle of running water. Meals are available with advance notice. Follow the main road – Avenida Samora Machel – downhill to the water (about 10 minutes' walk from the transport stand).

Hotel Chez Natalie (☎ 272-81092, 82-439 6080; natalie.bockel@gmail.com; campsites per person Mtc300, 4-person chalets Mtc1800) The best bet in town if you have your own transport, with a tranquil atmosphere and large grounds overlooking the estuary, camping, a handful of spacious family-style four-person chalets with running water and mosquito nets, and a grill. Breakfast and other meals are available with advance arrangement only. It's 2.5km from the town centre; watch for the barely signposted left-hand turn-off from Avenida Samora Machel onto Avenida Eduardo Mondlane just after passing Clube de Moçimboa. Continue along Avenida Eduardo Mondlane past the small Praça do Paz on your left for 400m. Turn left next to a large tree onto a small dirt path, and continue about 1km past a row of local-style houses to Chez Natalie. With advance notice, *mapiko* dancing can be arranged.

Restaurante Estrelha (Avenida Samora Machel) Opposite the police station and on the right, just before the park. There's outdoor seating and – with luck – a choice of grilled chicken or fish. Otherwise, try the cheap and reliable **Take Away** (Avenida Samora Machel), just down from and opposite Clube de Moçimboa.

Getting There & Away

The transport stand is near the market at the town entrance near the large tree. Pick-ups go daily to/from the Rovuma ('Namoto') via Palma, leaving Moçimboa da Praia between 2.30am and 3.30am (Mtc300, four hours); arrange with the driver the afternoon before to be collected from your hotel. Coming from Tanzania, the last vehicle to Moçimboa da Praia leaves the Rovuma by about noon.

To Pemba, there's a daily Mecula bus departing at 4.30am sharp (Mtc250, seven hours). Get it at its 'garage', midway between Complexo Miramar and the bus stand, or at the main transport stand. A few chapas also do the journey, departing by 7am from the main road in front of the market.

The not-so-nice Maningue Nice bus goes between Moçimboa da Praia and Nampula several times weekly, and several vehicles go daily to/from Mueda (Mtc120, two hours).

PALMA

This large fishing village is nestled among coconut groves about 45km south of the Tanzania border. The surrounding area is known for basketry, mat weaving and boat making. Offshore are Rongui and Vamizi Islands, both privately owned as part of the Maluane Project. The immigration office is in the upper part of town.

Casa do Antigo Administrador (Casa de Mahmud; r Mtc500), opposite the church at the town entrance, is the place to stay. Meals can be arranged with advance notice.

All transport leaves from the Boa Viagem roundabout at the town entrance. For travel to/from Tanzania, see p290. From Palma to the Rovuma River, chapas charge Mtc200, and depart from about 6am. Transport to Moçimboa da Praia (Mtc150, 2½ hours) passes Palma (returning from the Rovuma) between about 11am and 2pm. Dhows to the islands can be arranged from the harbour in the lower part of town, about 3km from the Boa Viagem roundabout; bring shade, food and water with you.

MOZAMBIQUE DIRECTORY

ACCOMMODATION

Mozambique accommodation tends to be pricier than elsewhere in the region. Once away from the southern beaches, midrange options are more limited, although there are

PRACTICALITIES

- Mozambique's main daily is *Notícias*. For English-language news, try the website of **Mozambique News Agency** (AIM; www.poptel.org.uk/mozambique-news).
- **Radio Mozambique** is state run, with programming in Portuguese, English and local languages.
- TV stations include TVM (state run), RTK (commercial), RTP (Portuguese TV).
- Electricity is 220V to 240V AC, 50Hz, accessed with South African–style three-round-pin plugs or two-round-pin plugs. Adaptors are easily found in major cities.
- Weights, measures are in the metric system.

a number of budget backpacker places in the south, and some upmarket island lodges. Coastal accommodation fills up during the South African school holidays (see p571); try to book in advance.

When quoting prices, many places distinguish between a *duplo* (room with two twin beds) and a *casal* (double bed), with the former usually slightly more expensive. Many hotels offer midweek and low-season discounts, and most have children's discounts.

Prices in this book have been quoted in dollars when the hotel itself quotes in dollars, but payment can always also be made in the meticais equivalent.

Budget

The cheapest options – from about Mtc300 per room – are small local hotels or *pensões,* usually with shared bathrooms and bucket baths.

Backpacker hostels are found mostly along the southern coast. Dorm beds average Mtc300.

There are many camping grounds, especially along the coast. Per-person prices range from Mtc100 to Mtc250. Away from established campsites, always ask the village *régulo* (chief) first for permission to camp.

Midrange & Top End

For midrange standards, including a private bathroom, hot running water, electricity, air-conditioning (sometimes) and a restaurant on the premises, expect to pay from about Mtc1500 per room.

Top-end hotels offer all the amenities you would expect from around Mtc3000 per room, and often have special weekend and low-season deals.

ACTIVITIES

Birdwatching

Prime birdwatching areas include the Bazaruto Archipelago, Gorongosa National Park and nearby Mt Gorongosa, the Chimanimani Mountains, Mt Namúli, the southern coastal wetlands and Maputo Special Reserve. Recommended contacts for bird lists and birding trips include the Pretoria-based **Indicator Birding** (www.birding.co.za), **Southern African Birding** (www.sabirding.co.za) and the **African Bird Club** (www.africanbirdclub.org).

Dhow Safaris & Boating

The best places for arranging dhow safaris are Ibo (for sailing around the Quirimbas Islands, see p278) and Vilankulo (to the islands of the Bazaruto Archipelago, see p247).

In Pemba, Kaskazini (p273) can arrange upmarket yacht charters. In Maputo, contact Mozambique Charters (p237).

Diving & Snorkelling

Quality equipment, instruction and certification are readily available in the main coastal areas, including Ponta d'Ouro (known for its sharks and corals); Tofo and Barra (manta rays and whale sharks); Vilankulo and the Bazaruto Archipelago (dolphins, dugongs and fantastic fish diversity, plus snorkelling); Nacala (corals and dhow-based diving); Pemba; and the Quirimbas Archipelago (excellent fish diversity and coral gardens, wall dives and snorkelling). Prices are comparable to what you would pay elsewhere in East Africa, though higher than in South Africa. Humpback whales are seen all along the coast between about July and September. The best time to see whale sharks is between about November and March. For a preview, look for a copy of the beautifully photographed *Gone Diving Mozambique* by Jean-Paul Vermeulen.

Fishing

Popular fishing areas include the southern coast between Ponta d'Ouro and Inhassoro,

MOZAMBIQUE

the far north around Pemba, and Lake Cahora Bassa, near Tete. Contacts include Ugezi Tiger Lodge (p257) for Lake Cahora Bassa; Mozambique Charters (p237, for Maputo and Inhaca area); Benguerra Lodge (p249) or the other Bazaruto lodges; Pomene Lodge (p246); BD Lodge (p250); and **Pensão Inhassoro** (www.inhass oro.co.za).

Hiking

The most easily arranged mountain climbs are up Mt Gorongosa (p253) and Mt Namúli (see the boxed text, p260). For hiking, head to the Chimanimani Mountains (p254).

Surfing

The best waves are at Tofinho (see p244), where you can also rent boards. There's also a surfing community at Ponta d'Ouro. For kite surfing, contact **Pirate Kites** (www.murrebue.com) or Moya Kite/Surf at Ponta d'Ouro.

Wildlife Watching

Mozambique has plenty of wildlife, although you'll often need to spend considerable time, effort and money to seek it out, and the country shouldn't be considered a 'Big Five' destination. However, if it is genuine bush adventure and beautiful wilderness terrain that you're after, coupled with the opportunity to see wildlife, Mozambique is an optimal destination. Niassa Reserve, Maputo Special Reserve, and Gorongosa and Limpopo parks are the main locations.

BOOKS

Kalashnikovs and Zombie Cucumbers: Travels in Mozambique by Nick Middleton and *With Both Hands Waving – A Journey Through Mozambique* by Justin Fox are highly entertaining travelogues with many historical snippets. *Drawn from the Plains – Life in the Wilds of Namibia & Moçambique* by Lynne Tinley has alluring descriptions of Gorongosa National Park. *Mozambique Mysteries* by Lisa St Aubin de Terán is as much about the author as it is about Mozambique, but it offers insights into a little-visited corner of the country (the area around Chocas). *At the Mercy of the River* by Peter Stark is a good read before visiting the Niassa Reserve.

BUSINESS HOURS

Banks are open from 8am to 3pm Monday to Friday, with a few open also on Saturday morning. Shops open from about 8am to noon and from 2pm to 6.30pm Monday to Friday, and from 8am to 1pm Saturday. Most forex bureaus *(casas de câmbio)* are open from about 8.30am to 5pm Monday to Friday, and on Saturday until about noon. Restaurants are generally open daily – many from about 9am, otherwise from noon – until about 10pm (earlier in smaller towns). Some close between lunch and dinner.

CHILDREN

For general information, see p745.

The southern beach resorts – many of which have a swimming pool, in addition to the beach – are ideal for visiting with young children, and most offer children's discounts.

Powdered full-cream milk is available in most towns, as is bottled water. Nappies (diapers) and wipes are available in Maputo, Beira, Chimoio and Nampula, as is prepared baby food, but not elsewhere. Shoprite branches and well-stocked pharmacies are the best places to find baby supplies in all these towns. Cots and spare beds are easily arranged at most midrange and top-end places. For infants, pushchairs (strollers) are not practical. Much better is some sort of harness or cloth that allows you to carry the baby on your back, Mozambican style, or in front of you.

In beach areas, be aware of the risk of hookworm infestation in populated areas, as well as the risk of bilharzia in lakes. Other things to watch out for are sea urchins at the beach – beach shoes are a good idea for children and adults – and thorns and the like in the brush.

For malaria protection, bring nets from home for your children and ensure that they sleep under them. Also bring mosquito repellents from home, and check with your doctor regarding the use of prophylactics. Long-sleeved shirts and trousers are the best protection at dawn and dusk.

Child care is easy to arrange informally through your hotel.

CUSTOMS REGULATIONS

It's illegal to export any endangered species or their products, including anything made from ivory or tortoiseshell. If you bring a bicycle, laptop computer or major camping and fishing equipment into Mozambique, you'll need to fill out a temporary import permit. You'll then be given a receipt, which you'll need to present again (with the item/s declared) when leaving the country. You're also supposed to declare imported cash in excess of US$5000. Local currency cannot be exported. Import of food and other consumables is limited to a maximum value of US$50 per person.

DANGERS & ANNOYANCES

Mozambique is a relatively safe place, and most travellers shouldn't have any difficulties. That said, there are a few areas where caution is warranted. Also see p293.

Crime

Petty theft and robbery are the main risks: watch your pockets in markets, and avoid carrying a bag; don't leave personal belongings unguarded on the beach or elsewhere; and minimise (or eliminate) trappings such as jewellery, watches, headsets and external money pouches. Don't hold your wallet or money in your hand while bargaining for prices. If you leave your vehicle unguarded, don't be surprised if windscreen wipers and other accessories are gone when you return. Don't leave anything inside a parked vehicle. When at stop lights or slowed in traffic, keep your windows up and doors locked, and don't leave anything on the seat next to you where it could be snatched.

In Maputo and southern Mozambique, due to the proximity to South African organised crime rings, carjackings and more violent robberies do occur, although the situation is nowhere near as bad as in Johannesburg, and most incidents can be avoided by taking the usual precautions – avoid driving at night, don't wander around isolated or dark streets, and don't put yourself in isolating situations, including on the beach. If you are driving and your car is hijacked, hand over the keys straight away. All this said, don't let these warnings deter you; simply be a savvy traveller. The vast majority of visitors travel through this beautiful country without incident.

Hassles & Bribes

More likely to occur than crime are simple hassles such as underpaid authorities in search of bribes. If you do get stopped you shouldn't have any problem as long as your papers are in order. Being friendly and respectful helps, as does trying to give the impression that you know what you're doing and aren't new in the country. Sometimes the opposite tack is also helpful – feigning complete ignorance if you're told that you've violated some regulation, and apologising. If you are asked to pay a *multa* (fine) for a trumped-up charge, playing the game a bit (asking to speak to the supervisor or *chefe*, and requesting a receipt) helps to counteract some of the more blatant attempts, as does insisting on going to the nearest police station or *esquadrão*. (You should always do both of these things anyway.)

Land Mines

Thanks to a massive de-mining effort, many of the unexploded land mines littering Mozambique – a legacy of the country's long war – have been eliminated. The northern provinces of Niassa, Cabo Delgado, Nampula and Zambézia have officially been declared free of known mined areas. However, mines are still a risk in some areas. To be on the safe side, stick to well-used paths, and don't free-camp or go wandering off into the bush without first seeking local advice.

EMBASSIES & CONSULATES

Except as noted, most are open from about 8.30am to 3pm, often with a midday break. The closest Australian representation is in South Africa.

Canada (Map pp228-9; ☎ 21-492623; www.canadainternational.gc.ca/mozambique/index.aspx; 1138 Avenida Kenneth Kaunda)

France (Map pp228-9; ☎ 21-484600; www.ambafrance-mz.org; 2361 Avenida Julius Nyerere)

Germany (Map pp228-9; ☎ 21-482700; www.maputo.diplo.de; 506 Rua Damião de Gois)

Ireland (Map pp228-9; ☎ 21-483524/5; 3332 Avenida Julius Nyerere)

Malawi (Map pp228-9; ☎ 21-492676; 75 Avenida Kenneth Kaunda)

Netherlands (Map pp228-9; ☎ 21-484200; www.hollandinmozambique.org; 324 Avenida Kwame Nkrumah)

Portugal (Map pp228-9; ☎ 21-490316; embaixada@embpormaputo.org.mz; 720 Avenida Julius Nyerere)

South Africa (Map pp228-9; ☎ 21-490059, 21-491614; consular@tropical.co.mz, sahc_cs@satcom.co.mz; 41 Avenida Eduardo Mondlane)

Swaziland (Map pp228-9; ☎ 21-491601; swazimoz@teledata.mz; Rua Luís Pasteur) Behind Netherlands embassy.

Tanzania (Map pp228-9; ☎ 21-491051; Avenida Mártires de Machava) Near the corner of Avenida Eduardo Mondlane.

UK (Map pp228-9; ☎ 21-356000; http://ukinmozambique.fco.gov.uk; 310 Avenida Vladimir Lenine)
USA (Map pp228-9; ☎ 21-492797; http://maputo.usembassy.gov; 193 Avenida Kenneth Kaunda)
Zambia (Map pp228-9; ☎ 21-492452; 1286 Avenida Kenneth Kaunda)
Zimbabwe (Map pp228-9; ☎ 21-490404, 21-486499; 1657 Avenida Mártires de Machava)

FESTIVALS & EVENTS

For concerts, art displays and performances, watch for posters around town, and check with the Centro Cultural Franco-Moçambicano (p226). Local festivals include **Gwaza Muthini**, held in Marracuene in early February to commemorate the Battle of Marracuene and the start of the *ukanhi* (traditional brew) season and the Chopi **Timbilas Festival**, held sporadically around August in Quissico, in southern Mozambique. The **Mozambique Jazz Festival** (www.mozjazzfest.com) is held around April in Maputo. Also in Maputo: the **Cedarte National Art & Crafts Fair** (www.cedarte.org.mz), held annually in December, and the **Maputo International Music Festival** (www.maputo music.com).

HOLIDAYS

New Year's Day 1 January
Mozambican Heroes' Day 3 February
Women's Day 7 April
International Workers' Day 1 May
Independence Day 25 June
Lusaka Agreement/Victory Day 7 September
Revolution Day 25 September
Christmas/Family Day 25 December

INTERNET ACCESS

Internet access is easy and fast in Maputo, where there are numerous internet cafes. Elsewhere, there are internet cafes in most provincial capitals and some larger towns – often at the local Telecomunicações de Moçambique (TDM) office, though connections are slow. Rates average Mtc1 per minute. Broadband connections are cropping up in the most unlikely places (such as Angoche and Gurúè), and many midrange and upmarket hotels and eateries have wi-fi.

INTERNET RESOURCES

African Studies Centre Mozambique Page (www.africa.upenn.edu/Country_Specific/Mozambique.html) Many links.
Club of Mozambique (www.clubofmozambique.com) A Mozambique business portal, but with several free tourism-related newsletters plus events listings.
Images du Mozambique (www.imagesdumozambique.com) Check out the 'Gallery' section of this site when planning your trip for a preview of what's to come.
Moçambique (www.visitmozambique.net) The Ministry of Tourism's official site.
Mozambique News Agency (www.poptel.org.uk/mozambique-news/) Mozambique news in English.
MozHits (www.mozhits.com) A music portal dedicated to Mozambican musicians and music, created by students at Maputo's Eduardo Mondlane University.

LEGAL MATTERS

Use or possession of recreational drugs is illegal in Mozambique. However, marijuana and more are readily available in several places along the coast. If you're offered anything, it will invariably be part of a set-up, and if you're caught, penalties are very stiff. At the least, expect to pay a large bribe to avoid arrest or imprisonment.

Driving on the beach, driving without a seatbelt (for all occupants of the vehicle), exceeding speed limits, driving while using your mobile phone, turning without using your indicator lights and driving without two red hazard triangles in the boot are all illegal, and are common ways of attracting police attention and demands for a bribe or fine *(multa)*.

MAPS

The detailed Reise Know-How *Mosambik & Malawi* map (1:1,200,000) shows altitude gradients and many obscure roads and villages (in addition to major destinations), and is readily available outside Mozambique. The Globetrotter *Mozambique* map (1:2,300,000) is less detailed, but readily available in Maputo and abroad.

MONEY

Mozambique's currency is the metical (plural meticais, pronounced me-ti-caish) *nova família,* abbreviated in this book Mtc. Note denominations include Mtc20, Mtc50, Mtc100, Mtc200, Mtc500 and Mtc1000, and coins include Mtc1, Mtc2, Mtc5 and Mtc10. One metical is equivalent to 100 centavos (Ct), and there are also coins of Ct1, Ct5, Ct10, Ct20 and Ct50, plus a few old metical coins floating around. For exchange rates, see the inside front cover of this guide.

Payment can always be made in meticais. Dollars are also readily accepted, especially by midrange and top-end places, and South African rand are widely accepted in southern Mozambique.

Outside Maputo, the best way to travel in Mozambique is with a good supply of cash in a mixture of US dollars (or South African rand in the south) and meticais (including a supply of small-denomination notes, as nobody ever has change). Supplement this with a Visa card for withdrawing meticais at ATMs (the best way of accessing money), and a few travellers cheques for emergencies (though they are difficult to change – see right).

ATMs

All larger and many smaller towns have ATMs for accessing cash meticais. Most accept Visa card only, although some also take MasterCard. Useful ones include: Millennium BIM (Visa, MasterCard); Standard Bank (Visa, MasterCard); Barclay's (Visa); BCI (Visa). Many machines have a limit of Mtc3000 (US$120) per transaction. Standard Bank's limit is Mtc10,000 (US$400) per transaction.

Black Market

There's essentially no black market. Never change on the street; if you are offered good rates, assume it's a set-up.

Cash

US dollars are easily exchanged everywhere, and – together with South African rand – are the best currency to carry. Euros are easy to change in major cities, but elsewhere you're likely to get a poor exchange rate. Other major currencies can be changed in Maputo.

Most banks don't charge commission for changing cash, and together with forex bureaus *(casas de câmbio)*, these are the best places to change money, although some banks (including most Millennium BIM branches) will let you change cash only if you have an account.

In Maputo and other larger cities there are foreign exchange bureaus, which usually give a rate equivalent to or slightly higher than the banks, and are open longer hours. Changing money on the street isn't safe anywhere, and is illegal – ask shopkeepers if you're stuck.

Credit Cards

Credit cards are accepted at most top-end hotels and car-rental agencies, and at some midrange places in the south (sometimes with a 5% commission), but otherwise are of only limited use apart from ATMs. Visa is the most useful, and is also the main (often only) card for accessing money from ATMs.

Travellers Cheques

When this book was researched, only Standard Bank changed travellers cheques, with a minimum US$40 commission per transaction, and original purchase receipts and lots of time required. We've heard from some travellers who had luck with BCI, so it may be worth inquiring there. The bottom line: while it's OK to bring some cheques along as an emergency standby, they shouldn't be relied on as a ready source of funds in Mozambique.

TELEPHONE

The cheapest international dialling is with the Telecomunicações de Moçambique (TDM) Bla-Bla Fixo card, sold at all TDM branches. It's a prepaid card for fixed lines (including those at TDM offices), and is cheaper than dialling internationally from TDM directly.

Domestic calls cost about Mtc3 per impulse; most short calls won't use more than two or three impulses. Calls to Europe, the USA and Australia cost from about Mtc130 for the first three minutes (minimum), plus Mtc50 for each additional minute. Regional calls cost about Mtc100 for the first three minutes. Rates are cheaper on weekends and evenings.

All landline telephone numbers have eight digits, including provincial area codes, which must always be dialled (even when calling a number in the same city). Codes are included with all telephone numbers in this book, and are also listed at the beginning of each town section. *No initial zero is required* (and the call won't go through if you use one).

Mobile Phones

Mobile phone numbers are seven digits, preceded by ☎ 82 for **Mcel** (www.mcel.co.mz) or ☎ 84 for **Vodacom** (www.vm.co.mz). No initial zero is required. Seven-digit mobile numbers listed with zero at the outset are in South Africa, and must be preceded by the South Africa country code (☎ 27) when dialling. Check the Mcel and Vodacom websites for coverage *(cobertura)* maps. Both companies have outlets in all major towns where you can buy SIM-card starter packs (Mtc50 or less) and top-up cards.

Telephone Codes

When calling Mozambique from abroad, dial the international access number (☎ 09 from South Africa), then the international code for Mozambique (☎ 258), followed by the provincial or city code (no zero) and the number. For mobile numbers, dial the international access number, followed by the international code, the mobile prefix (no zero) and the seven-digit number.

VISAS

Visas are required by all visitors except citizens of South Africa, Swaziland, Zambia, Tanzania, Botswana, Malawi, Mauritius and Zimbabwe. Single-entry visas (only) are available at most major land and air entry points – but not anywhere along the Tanzania border – for US$25 for one month. Your passport must be valid for at least six months, and have at least three blank pages. To avoid sometimes long visa lines at busy borders, or for a multiple-entry visa, you'll need to arrange your visa in advance. If you're arriving in Maputo via bus from Johannesburg it's recommended, though not essential, to get your visa in advance; see p289.

Fees vary according to where you buy your visa and how quickly you need it, and range from US$20 to US$70 for a one-month single-entry tourist visa outside Africa. Note that for getting a visa in Johannesburg, you'll need to go first to a branch of Nedbank and make a cash deposit of the visa fee. Then, take the deposit slip with you to the embassy and make your visa application. Call the embassy for bank account details.

Visa Extensions

Visas can be extended at the immigration office *(migração)* in all provincial capitals provided you haven't exceeded the three-month maximum stay. Processing takes one to three days and is usually straightforward. Hefty fines (US$100 per day) are levied for overstays.

> **DOCUMENTOS (DOCUMENTS)**
>
> All foreigners are required to carry a copy of their passport when out and about. Rather than carrying the original, it's much better to carry a notarised copy of the name and visa pages, plus notarised copies of your driving licence, and to hand these over if you're stopped. Ask at your hotel for recommendations of nearby notaries.

VOLUNTEERING

Most volunteer work is in teaching or health care, and school construction. Initial contacts include **InterAction** (www.interaction.org), whose subscriber newsletter advertises both paid and volunteer positions internationally, including in Mozambique; the Mozambique page of **Volunteer Abroad** (www.volunteerabroad.com/Mozambique.cfm); **Voluntary Service Overseas** (VSO; www.vso.org.uk), which provides placements for young professionals, and the similar US-based **Peace Corps** (www.peacecorps.gov); and **Frontier** (www.frontier.ac.uk).

There are also several volunteer holiday opportunities included in the Mozambique listings of **ResponsibleTravel.com** (www.responsibletravel.com). Also check out **Idealist.org** (www.idealist.org) and **Travel Tree** (www.traveltree.co.uk). Smaller Mozambique entities that accept volunteers include the **Téran Foundation** (www.teranfoundation.org), **Ibo Eco School** (www.iboecoschool.be) and **DolphinCare-Africa** (www.dolphincare.org).

There is extensive missionary work in Mozambique, so another possibility would be to make inquiries through your local church.

TRANSPORT IN MOZAMBIQUE

GETTING THERE & AWAY

This section covers access to Mozambique from neighbouring countries. For getting to Southern Africa from outside the region, see p755).

Entering the Country

A valid passport and visa are required to enter, plus the necessary vehicle paperwork if you are driving (p291), and a yellow-fever vaccination certificate if coming from an infected area (p773).

Air

Maputo's **Maputo International** (MPM; ☎ 21-465827/8; www.aeroportos.co.mz) is the main airport. Regional flights also go to the airports at **Vilankulo** (VNX), **Beira** (BEW), **Nampula** (APL) and **Pemba** (POL).

The national carrier is **Linhas Aéreas de Moçambique** (LAM; code TM; ☎ 21-4680000, 21-490590; www.lam.co.mz; hub Maputo International), which has flights connecting Johannesburg with

Maputo (daily), Beira (five weekly); Dar es Salaam with Pemba (five weekly); and Lisbon (Portugal) with Maputo (five weekly). Other airlines flying into Mozambique:

Air Travelmax (☎ in South Africa 011-701 3222; www.airtravelmax) Several times weekly from Johannesburg's Lanseria to both Inhambane and Vilankulo.

Kenya Airways (code KQ; ☎ 21-320337/8; www.kenya-airways.com; hub Jomo Kenyatta International, Nairobi) Twice weekly between Maputo and Nairobi.

Pelican Air Services (code 7V; ☎ in South Africa 011-973 3649; www.pelicanair.co.za; hub OR Tambo International, Johannesburg) Daily between Johannesburg and Vilankulo via Kruger Mpumalanga International Airport.

SAAirlink (code SA; ☎ 21-495483, 21-495484; www.saairlink.co.za; hub OR Tambo International, Johannesburg) Four times weekly between Beira and Johannesburg, and between Maputo and Durban; twice weekly between Johannesburg and Pemba.

South African Airways (SAA; code SA; ☎ 21-488970, 84-389 9287, 21-465625; www.flysaa.com; hub OR Tambo International, Johannesburg) Daily between Maputo and Johannesburg.

TAP Air Portugal (code TP; ☎ 21-303927/8, 21-431006/7; www.flytap.com; hub Lisbon) Five flights weekly between Maputo and Lisbon.

Border Crossings

Everyone entering Mozambique overland needs to pay an immigration tax of US$2 or the equivalent in meticais, rand or the local currency of the country from which you're arriving. Have exact change, and get a receipt. For additional fees and requirements for drivers, see p291. Except as noted, most borders are open from 6am to 6pm.

For information on getting to Mozambique from outside Southern Africa, see p755.

MALAWI

The busiest border is at Zóbuè, on the Tete Corridor route linking Blantyre (Malawi) and Harare (Zimbabwe). Others include crossings at Dedza (85km southwest of Lilongwe), Milange (120km southeast of Blantyre), Entre Lagos (southwest of Cuamba), Mandimba (northwest of Cuamba), Vila Nova da Fronteira (at Malawi's southern tip), and Cóbuè and Metangula (both on Lake Niassa).

To/From Blantyre

The Zóbuè crossing – which is open until at least 9pm – has good roads and public transport connections on both sides. There are daily vehicles from Blantyre to the border via Mwanza. Once on the Mozambique side there are daily chapas to Tete.

Vila Nova da Fronteira sees a reasonable amount of traffic, although it's still an off-the-beaten track journey. There are daily minibuses from Blantyre to Nsanje and on to the border. Once across, you can find chapas along a reasonable road via Mutarara to Sena, and from there on to Caia on the main north–south road.

The Milange border is convenient for Quelimane and Gurúè. There are regular buses from Blantyre via Mulanje to the border. Once across, there are several vehicles daily to Mocuba, and then frequent transport south to Quelimane and north to Nampevo junction (for Gurúè) and Nampula. It's worth noting that on Sundays, passports aren't checked in either direction at the Milange border – which is handy if you want to leave Mozambique and return the same day. If you are leaving for good, though, you'll need to ask for a stamp.

The crossing at Entre Lagos (for Cuamba and northern Mozambique) is possible with your own 4WD (allow about 1½ hours to cover the 80km from Entre Lagos to Cuamba), or via chapa between the border and Cuamba, and is currently the preferred route for Cuamba residents, given the poor state of the road between Cuamba and Mandimba. On the Malawi side, there are minibuses from the border to Liwonde. Another option is the weekly Malawi train to the border – currently Thursdays – from where you'll need to take a chapa to Cuamba.

At the Mandimba crossing, there's frequent transport on the Malawi side to Mangochi, from where you can get minibuses to Namwera, and on to the border at Chiponde. Once in Mozambique (bicycle taxis bridge the approximately 1.5km of no-man's-land for about Mtc30, and then vehicles take you on to Mandimba town), there are several vehicles daily from Mandimba to both Cuamba and Lichinga.

To/From Lilongwe

The Dedza border is convenient for Lilongwe, and is linked with the N103 to/from Tete by a tarmac road. From Tete, there's usually at least one chapa daily to Ulongwé and on to Dedza. Otherwise, go in stages from Tete via Moatize and the junction about 15km southwest of Zóbuè. Once across the border, it's easy to find transport for the final 85km to Lilongwe.

If planning to enter Mozambique at this border, arrange your visa in advance.

By Boat

The *Ilala* ferry services several Mozambican ports (but no longer Cóbuè) on its way up and down Lake Niassa, departing Monkey Bay (Malawi) at 10am Friday, arriving in Metangula (via Chipoka and Nkhotakota in Malawi) early Saturday morning, then departing by about 9am or 10am and reaching Likoma Island (Malawi) about 3pm Saturday, and Nkhata Bay (Malawi) at around 1am Sunday. Southbound, departures are at 8pm Monday from Nkhata Bay and at 6.30am Tuesday from Likoma Island, reaching Metangula late Tuesday afternoon. The schedule changes frequently; get an update from **Malawi Lake Services** (ilala@malawi.net). Fares are about US$35/15 for a 1st-class/economy class between Likoma Island and Metangula. (First-class fare gets you a cabin.)

There are immigration posts in Metangula and Cóbuè (and on Likoma Island and in Nkhata Bay, for Malawi). You can get a Mozambique visa at Cóbuè, but not at Metangula. Slow sailing boats also go between Likoma Island, Cóbuè and Metangula; guests of Nkwichi Lodge (p271) can arrange boat transfers with the lodge.

SOUTH AFRICA

The busiest crossing is **Lebombo/Ressano Garcia** (6am-10pm), northwest of Maputo, which is soon to be a one-stop border. Others include **Kosi Bay/Ponta d'Ouro** (8am-4pm), 11km south of Ponta d'Ouro; and the two Kruger park borders.

To/From Johannesburg

The best option between Johannesburg and Maputo is one of the large 'luxury' buses that do the route daily (US$30 to US$35 one-way, eight to nine hours), listed here (see p235 for Maputo location and contact details). All lines also service Pretoria. It's best to organise your Mozambique visa in advance. That said, some of the companies will take you without a visa (especially if you don't advertise the fact that you don't have one). However, if you do this, and if lines at the border are long, the bus may not wait, in which case you'll need to take a chapa the remaining 85km to Maputo.

Greyhound (in South Africa 083-915 9000; www.greyhound.co.za) Daily from Johannesburg's Park Station complex at 6.45am, and from Maputo at 7.30am.

Panthera Azul (in South Africa 011-618 8811/2; panthera@tvcabo.co.mz) Daily from Johannesburg (Hotel Oribi, 24 Bezuidenhout Ave, Troyville) at 7.30am; from Maputo at 6.45am, though schedule was being modified at the time of research, so check in advance. Between Maputo and Nelspruit/Johannesburg is Mtc570/750.

Translux (in South Africa 011-774 3333; www.translux.co.za) Daily from Johannesburg at 8.45am; from Maputo at 7.45am.

For drivers, there's a good toll road connecting Maputo with Johannesburg via Ressano Garcia.

To/From Nelspruit

In addition to the Johannesburg services listed above, which allow you to travel in each direction between Maputo and Nelspruit, but not between Nelspruit and Johannesburg, there is the good **Cheetah Express** (82-410 1213, 21-486 3222; cheetahexpress@tdm.co.mz), which goes daily between Maputo and Nelspruit (Mtc660 one-way), departing Maputo at 7am from Avenida Eduardo Mondlane next to Mundo's, and departing Nelspruit at about 4pm from Mediclinic, Crossings and Riverside Mall.

To/From Kruger National Park

There are two border points between Mozambique and South Africa's Kruger park: **Pafuri** (6am-5.30pm), 11km east of Kruger's Pafuri Camp; and **Giriyondo** (8am-4pm Oct-Mar, 8am to 3pm Apr-Sep), 75km west of Massingir town and 95km from Kruger's Phalaborwa Gate. Neither is accessible via public transport. Visas are available on both sides of both borders. Officially, you're required to have a 4WD to cross both borders, and 4WD is essential for the Pafuri crossing, which involves an unbridged crossing of the Limpopo River near Mapai that's only possible during the dry season, and a rough bush track thereafter via Mabote and Mapinhane to Vilankulo. Allow two full days between Pafuri and Vilankulo; there's a **campsite** (per person US$5) with hot-water showers near Mapai.

For those without their own transport, Dana Tours (p227) and several Maputo hotels offer day and overnight trips to Kruger (although using the Ressano Garcia border).

Other routes

Between Durban and Maputo, **Panthera Azul** (in Durban 031-309 7798) has buses via Namaacha and Big Bend in Swaziland

(Mtc810, 8½ hours) departing Maputo at 6.30am Tuesday, Thursday and Saturday, and Durban at 6.30am Wednesday, Friday and Sunday.

For travel via the Kosi Bay border, see p238).

SWAZILAND

The main crossing is at **Lomahasha/Namaacha** (7am-8pm) in Swaziland's northeast corner, with another post at **Goba/Mhlumeni** (7am-6pm).

To/From Manzini

Minibuses depart Maputo throughout the day for Namaacha (Mtc50, 1½ hours), with some continuing on to Manzini.

The Namaacha border is notoriously slow at holiday weekends; the quiet border at Goba makes a good alternative. The good road from Swaziland's Mananga border, connecting north to Lebombo/Ressano Garcia, is another option.

TANZANIA

The main crossing is at Kilambo (Namiranga or Namoto on the Mozambique side), with other crossings further west at Negomane and south of Songea (crossing to Segundo Congresso/Matchedje in Mozambique). On the coast, there are Mozambique border and customs officials at Palma and Moçimboa da Praia for those arriving in the country from Tanzania by dhow.

To/From Mtwara

Pickups depart Moçimboa da Praia daily between 2.30am and 3.30am (Mtc300, four hours) for the Rovuma ('Namoto'), which is crossed – adventurously or dangerously, depending on your perspective and water levels – via dugout canoe. There is no longer a vehicle ferry. Once across, pick-ups go to Mtwara (Tsh3000, one hour).

Further west, the Unity Bridge (at Negomane) should be finished within the lifetime of this book, and possibly also some of the road work planned to link this with Mueda on the Mozambique side and Mtwara in Tanzania.

To/From Songea

Still further west, there's a vehicle bridge and passport/customs posts at Segundo Congresso/Matchedje, with road links (and public transport) north to Songea and south to Lichinga. One or two chapas daily depart Lichinga from about 8am for the Rovuma (Mtc500, six hours). Once across, there's Tanzanian transport to Songea. See p270 for more.

ZAMBIA

The main crossing is at **Cassacatiza** (7am-5pm), 290km northwest of Tete. There's another crossing at **Zumbo** (7am-5pm), at the western end of Lake Cahora Bassa.

To/From Lusaka

The road on both sides of the Cassacatiza/Chanida border crossing is reasonably good, but the crossing is seldom used as most travellers combining Mozambique and Zambia go via Malawi. If you want to try it, chapas go daily from Tete to Matema, from where there's sporadic transport to the border. On the other side, there are daily vehicles to Katete (Zambia), and then on to Lusaka or Chipata.

The rarely used crossing at Zumbo is difficult to access from Mozambique – the route goes via Fíngoè – and is of interest primarily to anglers and birdwatchers heading to the western reaches of Lake Cahora Bassa.

ZIMBABWE

The main crossing points are at Nyamapanda on the Tete Corridor, linking Harare with Tete and Lilongwe (Malawi), and at Machipanda on the Beira Corridor linking Harare with the sea. Other crossings are at Espungabera, in the Chimanimani mountains, and at **Mukumbura** (7am-5pm), west of Tete.

To/From Harare

Both the Nyamapanda and Machipanda border crossings have reasonably good tarmac access roads, and are easy to cross using public transport or hitching.

From Tete there are frequent vehicles to Changara and on to the border at Nyamapanda, where you can get transport to Harare.

From Chimoio there is frequent transport to Manica and from there to the border, from where you'll need to take a taxi for the 12km to Mutare, and then get Zimbabwe transport to Harare.

The seldom-used route via Espungabera is slow and scenic, and an interesting dry-season alternative for those with a 4WD. Public transport on the Mozambique side is scarce.

Mukumbura, best done with 4WD, is of interest mainly to anglers heading to Cahora Bassa dam. There is no public transport on the Mozambique side.

Tours

For tour operators who organise travel to and within Mozambique, see p293.

GETTING AROUND

Air

AIRLINES IN MOZAMBIQUE

The national airline is **Linhas Aéreas de Moçambique** (LAM; ☎ 800 147 000, 82-147, 84-147, 21-468000; www.lam.co.mz), which has flights linking Maputo with Inhambane, Vilankulo, Beira, Chimoio, Quelimane, Tete, Nampula, Lichinga and Pemba. Service has improved markedly in recent years, and flights are generally reliable though it's essential to reconfirm your ticket, and to check in well in advance.

Fares are expensive, especially last-minute fares, although LAM offers occasional specials on domestic routes; always inquire before booking.

There are various small charter companies, including Rani Aviation (book through Kaskazini, p273) for getting around the Quirimbas Archipelago.

Bicycle

Allow plenty of time to cover the long distances, plan the trip legs carefully and carry almost everything, as there are long stretches with nothing en route, including no water supplies. Avoid cycling in central Maputo and along main roads whenever possible, as there's often no shoulder, traffic is fast and drivers have little respect for cyclists. Carrying a tent is essential; always check in with the local *régulo* (chief) before pitching it. Bicycles can be transported on buses (Mtc50 to Mtc150, depending on the journey).

Bus

Bus travel is the most economical way to get around, and direct services connect all major towns at least daily, although vehicle maintenance and driving standards leave much to be desired.

A large bus is called a *machibombo*, and sometimes also *autocarro*. All buses have just one class. The main companies are Grupo Mecula in the north and TCO in central Mozambique. Otherwise, most routes are served by freelancers/no-names. Ask staff at your hotel for recommendations about the best connections.

Most towns don't have central bus stations. Rather, transport usually leaves from the bus company garage, or from the start of the road towards the destination (which frequently involves a hike of 1km to 2km from the centre of town). Long-distance transport in general, and all transport in the north, leaves early – between 3am and 7am. And, Mozambican transport usually leaves quickly and close to the stated departure time. If a driver tells you they will be departing at 4.30am, get there by 4am, at the latest. Showing up on the morning of travel (about an hour prior to departure for heavily travelled routes) is generally enough to ensure you get a place. If you are choosy about your seat (best is at the front, on the shady side), get to the departure point earlier.

Sample journey fares and times: Maputo to Inhambane (Mtc350, seven hours); Nampula to Pemba (Mtc250, seven hours); Maputo to Beira (Mtc1300, 16 hours).

Car & Motorcycle

BRING YOUR OWN VEHICLE

In addition to a passport and driving licence, drivers need third-party insurance, a temporary import permit, the original vehicle registration papers and an authorisation document from the rental agency or registered vehicle owner, plus two red hazard triangles in the boot and a reflector vest. If you're towing a trailer or boat, a hazard triangle needs to be displayed on your front bumper and at the back of the trailer, and trailers also require reflective tape. You'll also need a sticker on the back of the vehicle (or at the end of the trailer) showing the country of registration (eg ZA for South Africa).

Temporary import permits (about US$2) and third-party insurance (about US$25 for 30 days, depending on vehicle size) are available at most land borders, or if not, then in the nearest large town. You'll be required to show the paperwork at all checkpoints (and will be fined if you can't produce it). Fees can be paid in meticais, US dollars or the local currency of the country you are leaving. As some smaller border posts don't always issue third-party insurance, it's worth arranging this in advance with your local automobile association if planning to enter Mozambique via an out-of-the-way routing. If you find yourself in Mozambique without it, contact **Hollard Seguros** (☎ 21-313114; www.hollard.co.za) to help you sort it out.

DRIVING LICENCE

You'll need either a South African or an international driving licence to drive in Mozambique. Those staying longer than six months will need a Mozambique driving licence.

FUEL & SPARE PARTS

Petrol *(gasolina)* is a scarce commodity off main roads, especially in the north. Diesel *(gasóleo)* supplies tend to be more reliable. Always carry an extra jerry can or two and tank up at every opportunity, as filling stations sometimes run out, especially in more remote areas. Or sometimes the fuel may be there but, if there's a power outage, it may not be accessible. In remote areas, sometimes the only choice will be petrol sold from roadside *barracas* (stalls); watch out for petrol that has been mixed with water or kerosene. Fuel prices in Mozambique range from Mtc24 to Mtc34 per litre for petrol, and from Mtc29 to Mtc35 for diesel. At an increasing number of petrol stations in the south along the N1, it's possible to pay for your gas with Visa or MasterCard, but don't count on this.

A limited supply of spare parts is available in Maputo and in major towns. Otherwise, they'll need to be ordered from South Africa. In the south, Massinga (especially) and Vilankulo both have good repair facilities. A number of petrol stations don't have air for tyres, but in every major town you'll be able to find a tyre shop – look for old tyres stuck in the ground, usually under a large, shady tree – that can fill up your tyres or help with punctures.

MOZAMBIQUE

HIRE

There are rental agencies in Maputo, Beira, Nampula, Tete and Pemba, most of which take credit cards. Sticking with the major agencies (ie, those listed in this book) is recommended. Elsewhere, you can usually arrange something with upscale hotels. Rates start at US$100 per day for 4WD, excluding fuel. At the time of research, only Europcar (p235) was offering unlimited kilometres. With the appropriate paperwork, rental cars from Mozambique can be brought into South Africa and Swaziland, but not into other neighbouring countries. Note, however, that most South African rental agencies don't permit their vehicles to enter Mozambique.

INSURANCE

All private vehicles entering Mozambique are required to purchase third-party insurance at the border (see Bring Your Own Vehicle, p291), which covers you to some degree in the event of hitting a pedestrian or another Mozambican vehicle. It's also advisable to take out good insurance coverage at home or (for rental vehicles) with the rental agency to cover damage to the vehicle, yourself and your possessions. Car-rental agencies in Mozambique have wildly differing policies (some offer no insurance at all, those that do often have high deductibles and most won't cover off-road driving) so inquire before signing any agreements. If renting in South Africa, ask whether Mozambique is included in the coverage.

ROAD CONDITIONS

Mozambique's road network is steadily improving, and most southern coastal areas between Maputo and Vilankulo are reachable with 2WD, with the exception of some sandy resort access roads. A 2WD vehicle is also fine for the roads connecting Nampula, Nacala, Mozambique Island and Pemba, for the Beira corridor, and for the Tete corridor between Harare (Zimbabwe) and Tete. For most other routes, you'll need 4WD with high clearance. However, all it takes is a heavy rainstorm or some flooding to change the road map, so ask around to get the latest updates, and don't place too much reliance on what your map says.

ROAD HAZARDS

Drunk driving, excessive speeds and road accidents are common. Armed robberies and carjackings are a risk, especially in Maputo. Throughout the country, travel as early in the day as possible, and avoid driving at night. If you must drive at night, use appropriate speeds, watch for pedestrians and obstacles (including parked vehicles with no lights) in the middle of the road and keep the doors locked and windows up. Tree branches in the road are the local version of flares or hazard lights, and mean there's a stopped vehicle, crater-sized pothole or similar calamity ahead.

For public transport, where there's a choice, always take buses rather than chapas.

ROAD RULES

In theory, traffic in Mozambique drives on the left. At roundabouts, traffic in the roundabout has the right of way (again, in theory). There's a seatbelt requirement for the driver and all passengers. Other relevant provisions of Mozambique's new traffic law (in effect since April 2009) include a prohibition on driving while using a mobile phone, a requirement to drive with the vehicle's insurance certificate, and a requirement to carry a reflector jacket in addition to two hazard triangles. Speed limits (usually 100km/h on main roads, 80km/h on approaches to towns and 60km/h or less when passing through towns) are enforced by radar, and should be strictly adhered to as controls are frequent, especially in the south. Fines for speeding and seatbelt and other traffic infringements vary, and should always be negotiated (in a polite, friendly way), keeping in mind that official speeding fines range from Mtc1000 up to Mtc24,000, depending on how far above the speed limit you are travelling and where the infringement occurs. In addition to avoiding fines, another reason to limit your speed is to escape axle-shattering potholes that can appear out of nowhere, or children or livestock running unexpectedly into the road.

Although the rule is frequently violated, driving on the beach is illegal.

Hitching

In parts of rural Mozambique, your only transport option is hitching a lift. See p765 for general considerations. In Mozambique, hitching is usually easy, though often slow off main routes. Payment for lifts is usually not expected, though clarify before getting in, and a small token of thanks, such as paying for a meal or making a contribution for petrol, is always appreciated. To flag a vehicle down, hold your hand out at about waist level and wave it up and down. Try to avoid hitching alone, especially women. Throughout the country, the prevalence of drunk driving makes it worth trying to assess the driver's condition before getting into a vehicle.

Local Transport

The main form of local transport is the chapa – the name given to converted minivans or any other public transport that isn't a bus or truck. On some routes, your only option will be a *camião* (truck). Many have open backs, and on long journeys the sun and dust can be brutal unless you get a seat in the cab.

Chapas can be hailed down anywhere, and prices are fixed. Intracity fares average Mtc5; long-haul fares are usually slightly higher than the bus fare for the same route. Chapa drivers aren't known for their safe driving, and there are many accidents. If you have a choice (which you often won't), bus is always a better option.

Tours

All of the following companies organise travel to Mozambique, as well as in-country itineraries.

Dana Tours (www.danatours.net) Long-established and highly reliable, Dana Tours covers most of Mozambique, plus Mozambique–South Africa combination itineraries, focusing particularly on midrange and upmarket.

Makomo Safaris (www.makomo.com) Combination itineraries for northern Mozambique, southern Tanzania and Malawi. Recommended for budget and adventure travellers, and for getting off the beaten track.

Mozaic Travel (www.mozaictravel.com) Another long-standing and reliable operator catering to all budgets.

Mozambique Collection (www.themozambiquecollection.com) A collection of environmentally conscious upmarket Mozambique lodges and experiences.

Mozambique Connection (www.mozambiqueconnection.co.za) Covers most of the country and all price ranges.

Ocean Island Safaris (www.oceanislandsafari.com) Luxury itineraries to the Quirimbas and other Indian Ocean islands.

Tanzania Yachts (www.tanzaniayachts.com) Tanzania–Mozambique combination sailing itineraries.

Train

The only passenger train regularly used by tourists is the line between Nampula and Cuamba; see p269.

Namibia

Wedged between the Kalahari and the South Atlantic, Namibia enjoys both vast potential and promise as among the youngest countries in Africa. One of Africa's hidden gems, Namibia remains a frontier realm for intrepid travellers to discover. Here you will find the oldest rust-red desert in the world, quintessential African landscapes teeming with wildlife, preternaturally blue skies stretching above vast open horizons, and silent spaces where emptiness and desolation can quickly become overwhelming. Namibia is also a photographer's dream, boasting wild seascapes, rugged mountains, lonely deserts, stunning wildlife, colonial cities and nearly unlimited elbow room.

A predominantly arid country, Namibia can be divided into four main topographical regions: the Namib Desert and coastal plains in the west, the eastward-sloping Central Plateau, the Kalahari along the borders with South Africa and Botswana, and the densely wooded bushveld of the Kavango and Caprivi regions. This defining geography fosters one of the largest animal congregations on the planet, alongside one of the lowest human population densities, a rare combination that yields unequalled opportunities for wildlife watching. At Etosha National Park, one of the world's grandest safari parks, a single watering hole can foster literally dozens of species.

Namibia also draws its identity – and indeed its name – from the Namib, one of the oldest and driest deserts in the world. This is in marked contrast to the Kalahari, a semi-arid landscape that is covered with trees and criss-crossed by ephemeral rivers and fossil watercourses. It is one of the continent's most prominent geographical features, and stretches across parts of Congo, Angola, Zambia, Botswana, Zimbabwe and South Africa.

FAST FACTS

- **Area** 825,000 sq km
- **Capital** Windhoek
- **Country code** ☎ 264
- **Famous for** Namib Desert, Kalahari, Etosha Pan
- **Languages** English, Afrikaans, German, Oshivambo, Herero, Nama
- **Money** Namibian dollar (N$)
- **Phrase** Howzit? (How are you?)
- **Population** 2.1 million

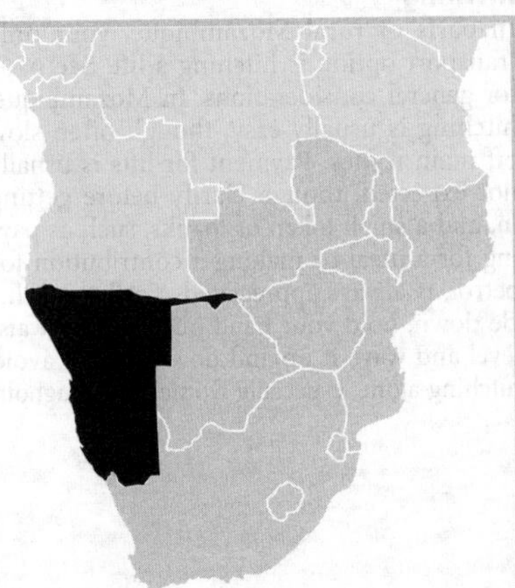

HIGHLIGHTS

- **Sossusvlei** (p362) Watch the sun rise from the tops of flaming red dunes on the edge of ephemeral salt pans.
- **Etosha National Park** (p321) Go on a self-drive safari in one of the continent's premier wildlife venues.
- **Swakopmund** (p346) Get your adrenaline fix at this popular extreme-sports capital of Namibia.
- **Fish River Canyon** (p374) Test your endurance on the five-day hike through one of the world's largest canyons.
- **Off the beaten track** (p340) Have a face-to-face encounter with the Himba, one of Namibia's most iconic peoples.

ITINERARIES

- **Three days** Namibia's tourist highlight is the expansive sand sea of the Namib (p364) and, if you have only a few days to visit, this is where you'll want to focus. From Sesriem (p363), spend a day hiking through the dunes, or arrange for a scenic flyover from the beach town of Swakopmund (p346).
- **One week** Combine a visit to the Namib with a safari through Etosha National Park (p321), one of the continent's most distinctive safari experiences. Splurge on a rental car, and get ready for some hair-raising, self-driven good times.
- **One month** With a month, you can hire a 4WD or use a reputable safari company and see the best of the country: in addition to sights listed above, you could also hike the Fish River Canyon (p374), visit the Himba in Opuwo (p340) and go on an expedition along the Skeleton Coast (p344) and through Khaudom Game Reserve (p329) in the Kalahari.

CLIMATE & WHEN TO GO

Namibia's climatic variations correspond roughly to its geographical subdivisions. In the arid Central Namib, summer daytime temperatures may climb to over 40°C, but can fall to below freezing at night. Rainfall is heaviest in the northeast, which enjoys a subtropical climate, and along the Okavango River, it reaches over 600mm annually. The northern and interior regions experience the 'little rains' between October and December. The main stormy period occurs from January to April.

HOW MUCH?

- **Dune surfing** N$340
- **Foreign newspaper** N$30
- **Night in a budget hotel** N$80
- **Package of kudu biltong** N$15
- **Traditional German dinner** N$65

LONELY PLANET INDEX

- **1L of petrol** N$7
- **1L of bottled water** N$3
- **Bottle of beer** N$8
- **Souvenir T-shirt** N$90
- **Snack** N$12

Note that accommodation is frequently booked out in national parks and other tourist areas, especially during public holidays. The busiest times are consistently during the Namibian, South African (see p570) and European school holidays. See p745 for more on the climate in Southern Africa.

HISTORY

For information on the general history of Southern Africa, see p32.

The Scramble for Africa

The Germans, under Chancellor Otto von Bismarck, were late entering the European scramble for Africa. Bismarck had always been against colonies; he considered them an expensive illusion, famously stating, 'My map of Africa is here in Europe. Here is Russia and here is France and here we are in the middle. That is my map of Africa'. But he was to be pushed into an ill-starred colonial venture by the actions of a Bremen merchant called Adolf Lüderitz.

Having already set up a trading station in Lagos (Nigeria) in 1881, Lüderitz convinced the Nama chief, Joseph Fredericks, to sell Angra Pequena, where Lüderitz established his second station, trading in the stinking guano of thousands of cormorants that nest along the coast. He then petitioned the German chancellor for protection. Bismarck, still trying to stay out of Africa, politely requested the British at Walvis Bay to say whether they had any interest in the matter but they never bothered to reply and in 1884 the newly named Lüderitz was officially declared part of the German Empire.

Initially, German interests were minimal, and between 1885 and 1890 the colonial administration amounted to three public administrators. Their interests were served largely through a colonial company (along the lines of the British East India Company in India prior to the Raj), but the organisation couldn't maintain law and order.

So in the 1880s, due to renewed fighting between the Nama and Herero, the German government dispatched Curt von François and 23 soldiers to restrict the supply of arms from British-administered Walvis Bay. This seemingly innocuous peacekeeping regiment slowly evolved into the more powerful Schutztruppe (Imperial Army), which constructed forts around the country to aid its efforts to put down opposition.

At this stage of its history, Namibia became a fully fledged protectorate known as German South-West Africa. The first German farmers arrived in 1892 to take up expropriated land on the Central Plateau, and were soon followed by merchants and other settlers. In the late 1890s, the Germans, the Portuguese in Angola and the British in Bechuanaland (now Botswana) agreed on Namibia's boundaries.

Colonial Atrocities

Once the Germans had completed their inventory of Namibia's natural resources, it is dif-

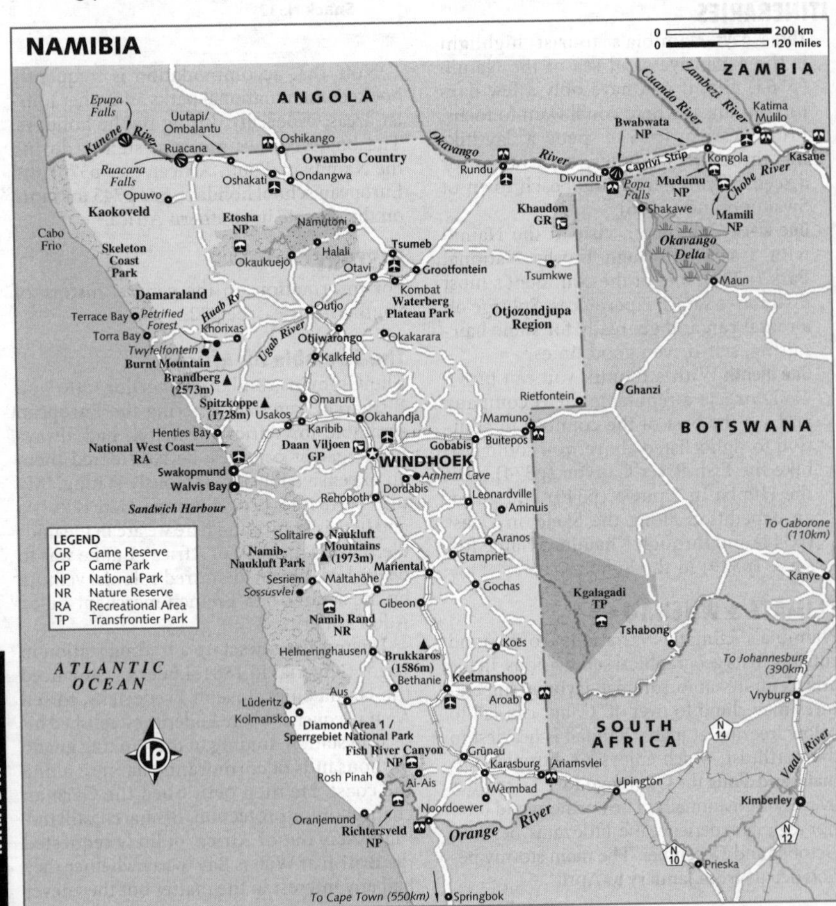

WHAT'S YOUR BUDGET?

If you're camping or staying in backpackers' hostels, cooking your own meals and hitching or using local combis (minibuses), you'll get by on as little as US$20 per day. A plausible midrange budget, which would include staying in a B&B or in doubles in backpackers' accommodation, public transport and at least one restaurant meal daily, would be around US$50 to US$100 per person (if accommodation costs are shared between two people). In the upper range, accommodation at hotels, meals in restaurants and escorted tours will cost upwards of US$300 per person per day.

To reach Namibia's most popular tourist sites, you'll have to take an organised tour or hire a vehicle (see p385). Car hire may be expensive for budget travellers but, if you can muster a group of four people and share costs, you can squeak by on an additional US$20/50 per day for a 2WD/4WD vehicle, including petrol, tax, insurance and 200 free kilometres per day.

ficult to see how they could have avoided the stark picture that presented itself. Their new colony was a drought-afflicted land enveloped by desert, with a nonexistent transport network, highly restricted agricultural opportunities, unknown mineral resources and a sparse, well-armed indigenous population. It was hardly the stuff of empirical dreams. In fact, the only option that readily presented itself was to follow the example of the Herero and pursue a system of seminomadic pastoralism. The problem with this was that all the best land fell within the territories of either the Herero or the Nama and they weren't about to give it up without a fight.

In 1904 the paramount chief of the Herero invited his Nama, Baster and Owambo counterparts to join forces with him to resist the growing German presence. This was an unlikely alliance between traditional enemies, especially considering that warring between the Herero and Nama had been a catalyst for increased involvement by the colonial powers. Driven almost all the way back to Windhoek, the German Schutztruppe brought in reinforcements and under the ruthless hand of General von Trotha went out in force to meet the Herero forces at their Waterberg camp.

On 11 August 1904 the Battle of Waterberg commenced. The general's plan was to surround the Herero position and with their massively superior firepower 'annihilate these masses with a simultaneous blow'. Although the casualties on the day were fairly light, Von Trotha ordered the pursuit and extermination of some 65,000 survivors over the following four weeks, only desisting when his troops began to die from exhaustion and typhoid, which they contracted from polluted water holes littered with human bodies. In all, some 80% of the entire Herero population was wiped out.

At this stage, the Nama, under Hendrik Witbooi, took up the resistance cause and launched a large-scale rebellion but, after their defeat at the Battle of Vaalgras on 29 October 1905, the 68-year-old Witbooi died of his wounds. Still, it was to be another three years before the Germans could fully defeat the remaining guerrilla forces in the south.

Reaping the Whirlwind

Meanwhile, in the south of the country, diamonds had been discovered at Grasplatz, east of Lüderitz, by a South African labourer, Zacharias Lewala. Despite the assessment of De Beers that the find probably wouldn't amount to much, prospectors flooded in to stake their claims. By 1910, the German authorities had branded the entire area between Lüderitz and the Orange River a *Sperrgebiet* (closed area), thrown out the prospectors and granted exclusive rights to Deutsche Diamanten Gesellschaft.

Despite their efforts to control the bounty, with dire consequences for the local populace, Germany was never to benefit from the diamond riches they found. The advent of WWI in 1914 marked the end of German colonial rule in southwest Africa. By this time, though, the Germans had all but succeeded in devastating the Herero societal structures and taken over all Khoikhoi and Herero lands. The more fortunate Owambo, in the north, managed to avoid German conquest, but were subsequently overrun during WWI by Portuguese forces fighting on the side of the Allies.

In 1914, at the beginning of WWI, Britain pressured South Africa into invading Namibia. Under the command of Prime Minister Louis Botha and General Jan Smuts, the South Africans pushed northwards, forcing the outnumbered Schutztruppe to retreat. In May 1915, the Germans faced their final defeat at Khorab, near Tsumeb, and a week later a South African administration was set up in Windhoek.

By 1920, many German farms had been sold to Afrikaans-speaking settlers and the German diamond-mining interests in the south were handed over to the South Africa-based Consolidated Diamond Mines (CDM), which retains the concession rights to the present day.

South African Occupation

Under the Treaty of Versailles in 1919, Germany was required to renounce all its colonial claims, and in 1921 the League of Nations granted South Africa a formal mandate to administer Namibia as part of the union. After a brief rebellion in 1924, the Basters at Rehoboth, who were descendants of liaisons between the Cape Colony Dutch and indigenous African women, were granted some measure of autonomy, and the following year the territorial constitution was amended to permit South Africa to set up a territorial legislature.

The mandate was renewed by the UN following WWII. However, South Africa was more interested in annexing southwest Africa as a full province in the union and decided to scrap the terms of the mandate and rewrite the constitution. In response, the International Court of Justice determined that South Africa had overstepped its boundaries and the UN established the Committee on South-West Africa to enforce the original terms of the mandate. In 1956, the UN decided that South African control should be terminated.

Undeterred, the South African government tightened its grip on the territory, and in 1949 granted the white population parliamentary representation in Pretoria. The bulk of Namibia's viable farmland was parcelled into some 6000 farms for white settlers, while other ethnic groups were relegated to newly demarcated 'tribal homelands'. The official intent was ostensibly to 'channel economic development into predominantly poor rural areas', however, the direct consequence of the policy was to maintain the majority of the country for white settlement and ranching.

As a result, a prominent line of demarcation appeared between the predominantly white ranching lands in the central and southern parts of the country, and the poorer but better-watered areas to the north. Perhaps the only positive result of this effective imposition of ethnic boundaries was the prevention of territorial disputes between previously mobile groups now forced to live under the same political entity. This arrangement was retained until Namibian independence in 1990, and to some extent continues up to the present day.

Swapo

Throughout the 1950s, despite mounting pressure from the UN, South Africa refused to release its grip on Namibia. This intransigence was based on its fears of having yet another antagonistic government on its doorstep and of losing the income that it derived from the mining operations there.

Forced labour had been the lot of most Namibians since German annexation, and was one of the main factors that led to mass demonstrations and the increasingly nationalist sentiments during the late 1950s. Among the parties was the Owamboland People's Congress, founded in Cape Town under the leadership of Samuel Daniel Shafiishuna Nujoma and Adimba Herman Toivo ja Toivo.

In 1959, the party's name was changed to the Owamboland People's Organisation and Nujoma took the issue of South African occupation to the UN in New York. By 1960, his party had gathered the support of several others and they eventually coalesced into the South West African People's Organisation (Swapo) with its headquarters in Dar es Salaam (Tanzania). Troops were sent to Egypt for military training and the organisation prepared for war.

In 1966, Swapo took the issue of South African occupation to the International Court of Justice. The court upheld South Africa's right to govern South-West Africa, but the UN General Assembly voted to terminate South Africa's mandate and replace it with a Council for South-West Africa (renamed the Commission for Namibia in 1973) to administer the territory.

In response, on 26 August 1966 (now called Heroes' Day), Swapo launched its campaign of guerrilla warfare at Ongulumbashe in the Owambo region of northern Namibia. The next year, one of Swapo's founders, Toivo ja Toivo, was convicted of terrorism and imprisoned in South Africa, where he would remain until 1984; Nujoma stayed in Tanzania. In 1972, the UN finally declared the South African occupation of southwest Africa officially illegal and called for a withdrawal, proclaiming Swapo the legitimate representative of the Namibian people.

In 1975 the independence of Angola finally gave Swapo a safe base just across the border from the action in Namibia, which enabled them to step up their guerrilla campaign. South Africa responded by invading Angola in support of the opposition party Unita (National Union for the Total Independence of Angola). The attempt failed, and by March 1976 the troops had been withdrawn, although incursions continued well into the 1980s.

In the end, however, it was not the activities of Swapo alone or international sanctions that forced the South Africans to the negotiating table. People were growing tired of the war and the economy was suffering badly. South Africa's internal problems also had a significant effect. By 1985, the war was costing some R480 million (around US$250 million) per year and conscription was widespread. Mineral exports, which once provided around 88% of the country's GDP, had plummeted to just 27% by 1984.

Independence

In December 1988 a deal was finally struck between Cuba, Angola, South Africa and Swapo that provided for the withdrawal of Cuban troops from Angola and South African troops from Namibia. It also stipulated that the transition to Namibian independence would formally begin on 1 April 1989, and would be be followed by UN-monitored elections in November 1989 on the basis of universal suffrage. Although minor score-settling and unrest among some Swapo troops threatened to derail the whole process, the plan went ahead and, in September, Samuel Nujoma returned from his 30-year exile. In the elections, Swapo garnered two-thirds of the votes but the numbers were insufficient to give the party the sole mandate to write the new constitution, an outcome that went some way to allaying fears that Namibia's minority groups would be excluded from the democratic process.

Following negotiations between the Constituent Assembly (which was soon to become the National Assembly) and international advisers including the USA, France, Germany and the former USSR, a constitution was drafted. The new constitution established a multiparty system and an impressive bill of rights, covering provisions for protection of the environment, the rights of families and children, freedom of religion, speech and the press, and a host of other matters. It also limited the presidential executive to two five-year terms. The new constitution was adopted in February 1990 and independence was granted a month later, with Samuel Nujoma being sworn in as Namibia's first president.

In 1999, Swapo won 76.8% of the vote, although concerns arose when President Nujoma amended the constitution to allow himself a rather unconstitutional third presidential term. Five years later, the world watched warily to see if Nujoma would cling to the office of power for a fourth term, and an almost audible sigh of relief could be heard in Namibia when he announced that he would finally be stepping down in favour of his chosen successor, Hifikepunye Pohamba.

Namibia has also profited considerably in the last few years from the extraction and processing of minerals for export. Rich alluvial diamond deposits alongside uranium and other metal reserves put the country's budget into surplus in 2007 for the first time since independence. Compared to other sub-Saharan countries, Namibia has one of the highest per capita GDPs, though this statistic masks one of the world's most unequal income distributions.

THE CULTURE

The National Psyche

On a national level, Namibia is still struggling to attain a cohesive identity. History weighs heavily on generations who grew up during the struggle for independence. As a result, some formidable tensions endure between various social and racial groups. Although most travellers will be greeted with great warmth and curiosity, some people may experience unpleasant racism or apparently unwarranted hostility (this is not confined to black/white relations but can affect travellers of all ethnicities, as Namibia's ethnic groups are extremely varied in colour).

MOVERS & SHAKERS: SAMUEL NUJOMA

Samuel Daniel Shafiishuna Nujoma was born on 12 May 1929 in the small village of Ongandjera in Owambo. His first rise to power was in the 1950s when he assumed control of the Owamboland People's Organisation (OPO), which aimed to end the South African occupation of southwest Africa and to resist the implementation of apartheid. In 1960, OPO developed into the South West African People's Organisation (Swapo), and began its multi-decade campaign of guerrilla warfare under the helm of Nujoma and other Namibia patriots. During the struggle, Nujoma took the combat name 'Shafiishuna', which means lightning in the Owambo language.

Following independence, Nujoma was unanimously declared president after Swapo's victory in a UN-supervised election in 1989, and was sworn in by UN Secretary-General Javier Pérez de Cuéllar on 21 March 1990. Nujoma was re-elected in 1994 and in 1999 after changing the constitution of Namibia to allow a third five-year term. In 2005, he stepped down despite having an approval rating of over 75%, and hand-picked his successor, the current Namibian president ,Hifikepunye Pohamba.

The defining issues of the Nujoma presidency were the Zimbabwe-style expropriation of a few dozen commercial farms, Namibia's HIV/AIDS crisis and a nascent secessionist movement in the Caprivi Strip. After retiring from public office, Nujoma stepped out of the limelight, and began pursuing a graduate degree in geology at the University of Windhoek in the hopes of improving Namibia's lucrative mining sector. At the time of research, Nujoma's portrait in a gown and mortarboard was splashed across every newspaper in the country, though it remains to be seen what his next move will be.

Acquainting yourself with Namibia's complex and often turbulent past will hopefully alert you to potentially difficult or awkward situations. Taking care to follow basic etiquette such as dressing appropriately (see right), greeting people warmly or learning a few words of the local languages will also stand you in good stead.

Socially, Namibians enjoy a rock-solid sense of community thanks to the clan-based system. Members of your clan are people you can turn to in times of need. Conversely, if someone from your clan is in trouble you are obligated to help; this may mean providing food for someone who is hungry, caring for someone who is sick, or even adopting an orphaned child in some cases. This inclusivity also extends to others – any traveller who is willing is sure to be asked to participate in a spontaneous game of football or a family meal.

Such an all-embracing social structure also means that the family nucleus is less important. Indeed many Namibian 'families' will include innumerable aunts and uncles, some of whom might even be referred to as mother or father. Likewise, cousins and siblings are interchangeable and in some rural areas men may have dozens of children, some of whom they might not even recognise. In fact, it is this fluid system that has enabled families to deal in some way with the devastation wreaked by the AIDS crisis.

Daily Life

On the whole, Namibians are conservative and God-fearing people (90% of the country is Christian, with about 10% of people following indigenous belief systems). Education is technically compulsory for all children (the literacy rate is 84%) and the motivation to get a good education is high. Since independence the government has built some 832 classrooms and 700 literacy centres around the country and now at least 80% of the population is receiving a basic primary-school education. But getting an education is by no means easy for everyone, and for families living in remote rural areas it often means that very young children must be sent to schools far away, where they board in hostels.

Most Namibians still live in homesteads in rural areas and lead typical village lives. Villages tend to be family- and clan-based and are presided over by an elected *elenga* (headman). The *elenga* is responsible for local affairs – everything from settling disputes to determining how communal lands are managed. He in turn reports to a senior headman, who represents a larger district comprising several dozen villages. This system functions alongside Namibia's regional government bodies and enables traditional lifestyles to flourish side by side with the country's modern civic system.

Modesty in dress and manner are important in Namibia. T-shirts and shorts are unheard of and while foreign men may *just* be able to pull it off, you may feel like the only person at the wedding who came in casual dress! Modest dress is required of women, probably to an even greater degree. Keeping up appearances is also all-important and extends from dressing well, behaving modestly, performing religious and social duties to fulfilling all essential family obligations.

A Woman's Place

Namibian society is unquestionably patriarchal, although women have traditionally worked hard to contribute to the family income. As head of the family, men are expected to project their authority through material wealth, charisma or often just their own physical size. Status – according to profession, wealth and family – is also important. One of the key obstacles to the AIDS outreach program was convincing men with local status to get tested, the objection being that they were 'uncomfortable with youngsters or junior officers coming to them and telling them to go for testing'. Being disrespectful to or undermining one's elders or social and professional superiors is a heinous social crime.

In a culture where male power is mythologised, it's unsurprising that women's rights lag behind. It's not uncommon for men to have multiple partners and, until recently, in cases where women and their children were abandoned by their husbands, there was very little course for redress. Part of the problem was that Namibia inherited the rather backward Roman Dutch law that governed the country during apartheid. However, since independence the Namibian government has been committed to improving women's rights with bills like the Married Persons Equality Act (1996), which equalised property rights and gave women equal rights of custody over their children.

However, the government acknowledges that achieving gender equality is more about changing grassroots attitudes than passing laws, as a survey into domestic violence in 2000 revealed. Of the women interviewed for the survey in Lüderitz, Karasburg and Keetmanshoop, 25% said they had been abused or raped by their husbands. Endemic social problems, such as poverty, alcohol abuse and the feeling of powerlessness engendered by long-term unemployment, only serve to increase feelings of disaffection and fuel the flames of abuse. And although the government passed one of the most comprehensive rape acts in the world in the same year, it remains to be seen how effectively the laws are enforced.

Population

Namibia's population in 2009 was estimated to be 2.1 million. This figure takes into account the effects of excess mortality due to AIDS, which became the leading cause of death in Namibia in 1996. With approximately two people per square kilometre, Namibia has one of Africa's lowest population densities, with an annual population growth rate of over 2.3% according to the World Health Organization (WHO) in 2006.

The population of Namibia comprises 11 major ethnic groups. The majority of people come from the Owambo (50%), with the other ethnic groups making up a relatively small percentage of the population: Kavango (9%), Herero/Himba (7%), Damara (7%), Caprivian (4%), Nama (5%), Afrikaner and German (6%), Baster (6.5%), San (1%) and Setswana (0.5%); the remaining 4% is mixed.

Although this ethnic diversity is overlain with Western cultural influences, since independence there have been efforts to emphasise the history and traditions of each group. About 75% of the people inhabit rural areas, but urban drift in search of work or higher wages has resulted in increased homelessness, unemployment and crime in the capital and other towns.

Like nearly all other African nations Namibia is struggling to contain its HIV/AIDS epidemic, which is impacting heavily on average life expectancy and population-growth rates. According to the CIA Factbook, life expectancy in Namibia has dropped to a shocking 51 years, and in 2007 it was estimated that about 15% of the population were HIV-positive.

RELIGION

About 80% to 90% of Namibians profess to being Christians, and German Lutheranism is the dominant sect in most of the country. As a result of early missionary activity and

Portuguese influence from Angola, there is also a substantial Roman Catholic population, mainly in the central and northern areas.

Most non-Christian Namibians – mainly Himba, San and some Herero – live in the north and continue to follow animist traditions. In general, their beliefs are characterised by ancestor-veneration, and most practitioners believe that deceased ancestors continue to interact with the living and serve as messengers between their descendants and the gods.

ARTS & CRAFTS

Namibia is still in the process of developing a literary tradition, but its musical, visual and architectural arts are fairly well established. The country also enjoys a wealth of amateur talent in the production of material arts, including carvings, basketware and tapestry, along with simple but resourcefully designed and produced toys, clothing and household implements.

Music

Namibia's earliest musicians were the San, whose music probably emulated the sounds made by their animal neighbours, and was sung to accompany dances and storytelling. The early Nama, who had a more developed musical technique, used drums, flutes and basic stringed instruments, also to accompany dances. Some of these techniques were later adapted by Bantu peoples, who added marimbas, gourd rattles and animal-horn trumpets to the range. A prominent European contribution to Namibian music is the choir; the German colonists also introduced their traditional 'oom-pah-pah' bands, which feature mainly at German festivals.

For more information on music in Southern Africa, see p48.

Architecture

The most obvious architectural contribution in Namibia was made by the German colonists, who attempted to re-create late 19th-century Germany along the desert coast. In deference to the warmer climate, however, they added features such as shaded verandahs to provide a cool outdoor living space. The best examples can be seen in Lüderitz, Swakopmund and Windhoek. The most memorable structures were built in Wilhelminischer Stil and Jugendstil (art nouveau) styles.

Painting & Sculpture

Most of Namibia's renowned modern painters and photographers are of European origin; they mainly interpret the country's colourful landscapes, bewitching light, native wildlife and diverse peoples. Artists include François de Mecker, Axel Eriksson, Fritz Krampe and Adolph Jentsch, as well as colonial landscape artists Carl Ossman and Ernst Vollbehr. Non-European rural Namibians, on the other hand, have generally concentrated on wood and stone sculpture. Township art, which develops sober themes in an expressive, colourful and generally light-hearted manner, first appeared in the townships of South Africa during the apartheid years. Names to watch out for include Tembo Masala and Joseph Madisia, among others.

Dance

Each Namibian group has its own dances, but common threads run through most of them. San dancing tends to mimic the animals they hunt. The Himba *ondjongo* dance is performed only by cattle owners, who dance to demonstrate the care and ownership of their animals. Herero dances feature the *outjina* for women and *otjipirangi* for men, in which dancers strap planks to one foot in order to deliver a hollow, rhythmic percussion. In the Kavango and Caprivi regions, traditional dancing involves rhythmic and exaggerated stamping and gyrating, accompanied by repetitive chanting and a pervasive drumbeat.

ENVIRONMENT

The Land

The oldest desert in the world, the Namib is a garden of burned and blackened-red basalt that spilled out of the earth 130 million years ago in southwest Africa, hardening to form the driest country south of the Sahara. Precious little can grow or thrive in this merciless environment, with the exception of a few uniquely adapted animals and plants, which illustrate the sheer ingenuity of life on earth.

The Namib extends along the country's entire Atlantic coast, and is scored by a number of rivers, which rise in the Central Plateau, but often run dry. Some, like the ephemeral Tsauchab, once reached the sea, but now end in calcrete pans. Others flow only during the summer rainy season but, at some former stage, carried huge volumes of water, and carved out dramatic canyons like Fish River.

In wild contrast are the Kavango and Caprivi regions, which are nothing short of well-watered paradises. Bordering Angola to the north, they are bounded by four great rivers – the Kunene, Okavango, Kwando/Mashi/Linyanti/Chobe and Zambezi – that flow year-round.

Wildlife

Etosha, Namibia's greatest wildlife park, contains a variety of antelope species, as well as other African ungulates, carnivores and pachyderms. Damaraland, in the northwest, is home to antelopes and other ungulates, and also harbours desert rhinos, elephants and other species that have specially adapted to the arid climate. Hikers in the Naukluft massif may catch sight of the elusive Hartmann's mountain zebra, and along the desert coast live jackass penguins, flamingos, Cape fur seals and the rare *Strandwolf* (brown hyena).

As Namibia is mostly arid, its typical vegetation features mainly scrubby bushveld and succulents such as *Euphorbia*. Some unique floral oddities include the kokerboom (quiver tree), which is a species of aloe, and the bizarre *Welwitschia mirabilis* (the welwitschia plant). Along the coastal plain around Swakopmund lie the world's most extensive and diverse lichen fields; in dry weather, they appear to be merely plant skeletons, but with the addition of water they burst into colourful bloom.

National Parks

Despite its harsh climate, Namibia has some of the world's grandest national parks, ranging from the world-famous wildlife-oriented Etosha National Park to the immense Namib-Naukluft Park, which protects vast dune-fields, desert plains, wild mountains and unique flora. There are also the smaller reserves of the Caprivi region, the renowned Skeleton Coast Park and the awe-inspiring Fish River Canyon, which ranks among Africa's most spectacular sights.

In addition to national parks, Namibia has a network of conservancies, which are individual farms supporting either tourist lodges or hunting opportunities. Examples of these are the 200,000-hectare NamibRand Nature Reserve and the 102,000-hectare Gondwana Cañon Park.

Access to most wildlife-oriented parks is limited to enclosed vehicles only; no bicycles or motorcycles are allowed. For some parks, such as Etosha and Namib-Naukluft, a 2WD is sufficient, but you need a 4WD in Mamili National Park and the Khaudom Game Reserve.

Facilities in Namibian national parks are operated by the semiprivate **Namibia Wildlife Resorts** (NWR; ☎ 062-2857200; www.nwr.com.na; Erkrath Bldg, Independence Ave, Windhoek; 🕑 8am-3pm Mon-Fri). When booking park campsites or accommodation by phone, fax or email, include your passport number; the number of people in your group (including the ages of any children); your full address, telephone/fax number or email address; the type of accommodation required; and dates of arrival and departure (including alternative dates).

Bookings may be made up to 12 months in advance, and fees must be paid by credit card before the bookings will be confirmed. Camping fees are good for up to four people; each additional person up to eight people will be charged extra. Parks also charge a daily admission fee per person and per vehicle, payable when you enter the park.

Booking is always advised for national parks. While you may be able to pick up accommodation at the last minute by just turning up at the park gates, it isn't recommended (especially for Etosha and Sossusvlei). Note that pets aren't permitted in any wildlife-oriented park.

Environmental Issues

With a small human population spread over a large land area, Namibia is in better environmental shape than most African countries, but challenges remain. Key environmental issues include water schemes and water quality, uneven population distribution, bush and wildlife management, trophy-hunting policies, attitudes of farmers and villagers towards wildlife, conservation methods and ecotourism issues.

In recent years, Namibia's energy crisis has deepened to worrying levels. Since 2006, NamPower has been at the forefront of an energy conservation awareness campaign, and the Windhoek City Council has jumped on board by asking residents to switch off gas-fired water heaters in an attempt to manage the power shortages. But this barely begins to tackle the problem, especially since Namibia continues to import more than 45% of its energy from South Africa. It is this looming crisis that lies behind Namibia's many dam proposals, like the Epupa and Popa Falls dams, the hydroelectric plant proposal on the Kunene River, and the proposal for a pipeline diverting water from the Okavango River direct to Windhoek.

See p20 for information on travelling responsibly in Southern Africa.

FOOD & DRINK

Food

Traditional Namibian food consists of a few staples, the most common of which is *oshifima*, a dough-like paste made from millet, and usually served with a stew of vegetables or meat. Other common dishes include *oshiwambo*, a rather tasty combination of spinach and beef, and *mealie pap*, an extremely basic porridge.

As a foreigner you'll rarely find such dishes on the menu. Most Namibian restaurants serve a variation on European-style foods, like Italian or French, alongside an abundance of seafood dishes. Such gourmet pretensions are confined to big towns like Windhoek, Swakopmund and Lüderitz; outside of these you'll rapidly become familiar with fried-food joints and pizza parlours.

More than anything else, German influences can be found in Namibia's *konditoreien* (cake shops), where you can pig out on *Apfelstrudel* (apple strudel), Sachertorte (a rich chocolate cake with apricot jam in it), Schwarzwälder Kirschtorte (Black Forest cake) and other delicious pastries and cakes. Several places in Windhoek and Swakopmund are national institutions. You may also want to try Afrikaners' sticky-sweet *koeksesters* (small doughnuts dripping with honey) and *melktart* (milk tart).

Cooked breakfasts include bacon and *boerewors* (farmer's sausage), and don't be surprised to find something bizarre – curried kidneys, for example – alongside your eggs. Beef in varying forms also makes an occasional appearance at breakfast time.

Evening meals feature meat – normally beef or game. A huge beef fillet steak or a kudu cutlet will set you back no more than N$75. Fish and seafood are best represented by kingklip, kabeljou and several types of shellfish. These are available all over Namibia, but are best at finer restaurants in Windhoek, Swakopmund and Lüderitz, where they'll normally be fresh from the sea.

Drinks

NONALCOHOLIC DRINKS

Tap water is generally safe to drink, but in some locations it may be salty or otherwise unappealing, especially in desert areas and around Windhoek and Etosha. Packaged fruit juices provide an alternative. Every cafe and takeaway serves coffee and tea, as well as the strong herbal tea known as *rooibos* (red bush).

ALCOHOLIC DRINKS

Namibia's dry heat means big sales for Namibia Breweries. The most popular drop is Windhoek Lager, a light and refreshing lager-style beer, but the brewery also produces Tafel Lager, the stronger and more bitter Windhoek Export and the slightly rough Windhoek Special. Windhoek Light (a tasty beer with just 2% alcohol) and the similarly light Das Pilsner are both drunk as soft drinks. The same brewery also produces a 7% stout known as Urbock.

Namibia Breweries' main competitor is Hansa, in Swakopmund, which produces both standard and export-strength beer. South African beers such as Lion, Castle and Black Label are widely available and you'll also find a range of refreshing spirit coolers and typically excellent and great-value South African wines. The best place to buy beer, wine or spirits is a *drankwinkel* (bottle store), but small convenience shops may also sell beer and coolers.

In the rural areas – especially the Owambo regions – people socialise in tiny makeshift bars, enjoying such traditional local brews as *oshikundu* (millet beer), *mataku* (watermelon wine), *tambo* (fermented millet and sugar), *mushokolo* (a beer made from small seeds), and *walende*, which is distilled from the makalani palm and tastes similar to vodka. Apart from *walende*, all of these rural confections are brewed in the morning and drunk the same day, and they're all dirt cheap – around N$2 a glass.

WINDHOEK

☎061 / pop 240,000

Largely influenced by its German colonial heritage, Windhoek's architecture is colourful and inspiring, and there are a few streets in the capital where colonial styling still predominates. Neo-baroque cathedral spires, as well as a few seemingly misplaced German castles, punctuate the skyline and complement the steel and glass high-rises that rose from Namibia's rapid growth and development. Indeed, Windhoek is an extremely well-heeled city that stands in marked contrast to the desolate hinterlands that serve as Namibia's main tourist drawcards.

With so much open space lying beyond the borders of the capital, most foreign visitors treat Windhoek as little more than a springboard for their onward travels. But a few days in the capital can be viewed as an opportunity to gain perspective on the complexities of one of the world's youngest nations. From the posh bars and exclusive eateries dotting the eastern suburbs, to the bustling markets and heaving streets of the black townships, Windhoek is where rich and poor alike give shape and form to the face of modern Namibia.

HISTORY

Windhoek has only existed for just over a century. The modern name Windhoek, or 'windy corner', was corrupted from the original 'Winterhoek' during the German colonial occupation. At that time, it became the headquarters for the German Schutztruppe, which was ostensibly charged with brokering peace between the warring Herero and Nama. For over 10 years around the turn of the 20th century, Windhoek served as the administrative capital of German South-West Africa.

ORIENTATION

Central Windhoek is bisected by Independence Ave, where most shopping and administrative functions are concentrated. The shopping district is focused on the pedestrianised Post St Mall and the nearby Gustav Voigts Centre, Wernhill Park Centre and Levinson Arcade. Zoo Park, beside the main post office, provides a green lawn and shady lunch spots.

Maps

Free city plans are available from the tourist offices. You can purchase topographic sheets of much of Namibia for a small fee from the map section of the **Office of the Surveyor General** (Map p308; ☎ 245055; cnr Robert Mugabe Ave & Korn St).

INFORMATION

Emergency

Ambulance & Fire Brigade (☎ 211111)
Crime report (☎ 290 2239) 24-hour phone service.
National police (☎ 10111)
Police (☎ 228328)

Internet Access

Virtually all hotels and hostels now offer cheap and reliable internet access, with wireless becoming increasingly the norm. If you're out and about, net cafes can be found in every mall in the city.

Medical Services

Rhino Park Private Hospital (Map p306; ☎ 225434; Sauer St) Provides excellent care and service, but patients must pay up front.
Windhoek State Hospital (Map p306; ☎ 303 9111) An option for those who are short of cash but have time to wait. Located just off Harvey Rd.

Money

Major banks and bureaux de change are concentrated around Independence Ave, and all will change foreign currency and travellers cheques and give credit-card advances. First National Bank (FNB) and Standard Bank's ATM systems handle Visa, MasterCard and home ATM transactions.

Post & Telephone

The modern **main post office** (Map p308; Independence Ave) can readily handle overseas post. It also has telephone boxes in the lobby, and next door is the **Telecommunications Office** (Map p308; Independence Ave), where you can make international calls and send or receive faxes.

Tourist Information

Namibia Tourism Board (Map p308; ☎ 290 6000; www.namibiatourism.com.na; cnr Frans Indongo & Fidel Castro) The national tourist office can provide information from all over the country.
Namibia Wildlife Resorts (NWR; Map p308; ☎ 285 7200; www.nwr.com.na; Erkrath Bldg, Independence Ave) Books national park accommodation and hikes.
Windhoek Information & Publicity Office (Map p308; ☎ 290 2058; www.cityofwindhoek.org.na; Post St Mall) This friendly office answers questions and distributes local publications, including *What's On in Windhoek*.

Travel Agencies

Cardboard Box Travel Shop (Map p308; ☎ 256580; www.namibian.org) Attached to the backpacker hostel of

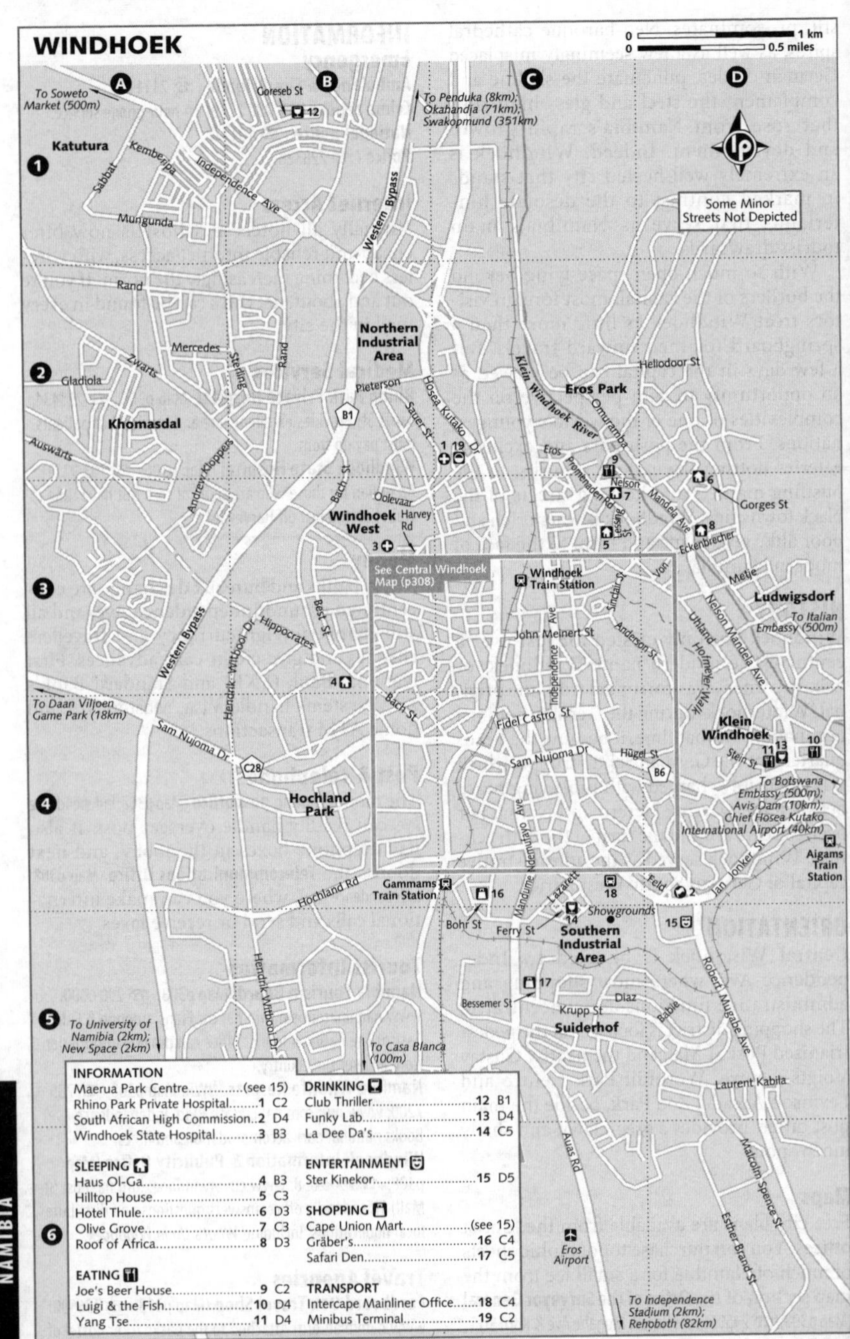
WINDHOEK
0 1 km
0 0.5 miles
A
B
C
D
1
2
3
4
5
6
Some Minor Streets Not Depicted
To Soweto Market (500m)
To Penduka (8km); Okahandja (71km); Swakopmund (351km)
To Italian Embassy (500m)
To Botswana Embassy (500m); Avis Dam (10km); Chief Hosea Kutako International Airport (40km)
To Daan Viljoen Game Park (18km)
To University of Namibia (2km); New Space (2km)
To Casa Blanca (100m)
To Independence Stadium (2km); Rehoboth (82km)
See Central Windhoek Map (p308)
Katutura
Khomasdal
Northern Industrial Area
Windhoek West
Eros Park
Ludwigsdorf
Klein Windhoek
Hochland Park
Southern Industrial Area
Suiderhof
Showgrounds
Windhoek Train Station
Gammams Train Station
Aigams Train Station
Eros Airport
Klein Windhoek River
Goreseb St
Kemberipa
Sabbat
Independence Ave
Mungunda
Western Bypass
Rand
Mercedes
Sterling
Zwarts
Gladiola
Pieterson
Auswärts
Andrew Kloppers
Bach St
Hosea Kutako Dr
Sauer St
Oolevaar
Harvey Rd
Best St
Hippocrates
Hendrik Witbooi Dr
Sam Nujoma Dr
Heliodoor St
Omuramba
Eros
Promenaden Rd
Nelson
Mandela Ave
Gorges St
Lessing St
Eckenbrecher
Metje
Von
Sinclair St
John Meinert St
Anderson St
Uhland
Hofmeyer Walk
Nelson Mandela Ave
Fidel Castro St
Hügel St
Stein St
Jan Jonker St
Feld
Mandume Ndemufayo Ave
Lazarett
Hochland Rd
Bohr St
Ferry St
Bessemer St
Krupp St
Diaz
Babie
Robert Mugabe Ave
Laurent Kabila
Auas Rd
Malcolm Spence St
Esther Brand St
B1
B6
C28
INFORMATION
Maerua Park Centre (see 15)
Rhino Park Private Hospital 1 C2
South African High Commission 2 D4
Windhoek State Hospital 3 B3
SLEEPING
Haus Ol-Ga 4 B3
Hilltop House 5 C3
Hotel Thule 6 D3
Olive Grove 7 C3
Roof of Africa 8 D3
EATING
Joe's Beer House 9 C2
Luigi & the Fish 10 D4
Yang Tse 11 D4
DRINKING
Club Thriller 12 B1
Funky Lab 13 D4
La Dee Da's 14 C5
ENTERTAINMENT
Ster Kinekor 15 D5
SHOPPING
Cape Union Mart (see 15)
Gräber's 16 C4
Safari Den 17 C5
TRANSPORT
Intercape Mainliner Office 18 C4
Minibus Terminal 19 C2

the same name (p310), this recommended travel agency can arrange both budget and upmarket bookings all over the country.

Chameleon Safaris (Map p308; ☎ 247668; www.chameleonsafaris.com) Attached to the backpacker hostel of the same name (p310), this travel agency is also recommended for all types of safaris around the country.

DANGERS & ANNOYANCES

Windhoek is generally safe by day, but avoid going out alone at night, and be wary of newspaper sellers, who may shove the paper in your face as a distracting ruse. Don't use bum bags or carry swanky camera or video totes, and never leave anything of value visible in a vehicle. Parts of Katutura and other northwestern suburbs, where boredom and unemployment are rife, should be avoided unless you have a local contact and/or a specific reason to go there.

SIGHTS

Post St Mall & Gibeon Meteorite Exhibit

The throbbing heart of the Windhoek shopping district is the bizarrely colourful **Post St Mall** (Map p308), an elevated pedestrian walkway lined with vendors selling curios, artwork, clothing and practically anything else that may be of interest to tourists. Scattered around the centre of the mall is a display of **meteorites** from the Gibeon meteor shower, which some time in the distant past deposited upwards of 21 tonnes of mostly ferrous extraterrestrial boulders around the town of Gibeon in southern Namibia.

Zoo Park

Although this leafy **park** (Map p308; 🕑 dawn-dusk) served as a public zoo until 1962, today it functions primarily as a picnic spot and shady retreat for lunching office workers. Of course, 5000 years ago the park was the site of a Stone Age elephant hunt, as evidenced by the remains of two elephants and several quartz tools found here in the early 1960s. This prehistoric event is honoured by the park's prominent **elephant column**, designed by Namibian sculptor Dörthe Berner.

Christuskirche

Windhoek's best-recognised landmark, and something of an unofficial symbol of the city, this German Lutheran **church** (Map p308; Peter Müller St) stands on a traffic island and lords over the city centre. This unusual building, which was constructed from local sandstone in 1907, was designed by architect Gottlieb Redecker in conflicting neo-Gothic and art-nouveau styles. The resulting design looks strangely edible, and is somewhat reminiscent of a whimsical gingerbread house.

Tintenpalast

The former administrative headquarters of German South-West Africa have been given a new mandate as the Namibian **parliament building** (Map p308; ☎ 2882583; www.parliament.gov.na; admission free; 🕑 tours Mon-Fri 9-11am, 3-4pm). As a fitting homage to the bureaucracy of government, the name of the building means 'Ink Palace', in honour of all the ink spent on typically excessive official paperwork.

Hofmeyer Walk

This **walking track** (Map p306) through Klein Windhoek Valley starts from either Sinclair or Uhland Sts, and heads south through the bushland to finish at the point where Orban St becomes Anderson St. The walk takes about an hour at a leisurely pace, and affords panoramic views over the city as well as a close-up look at the aloes that characterise the hillside vegetation. These cactus-like plants are at their best in winter, when their bright red flowers attract tiny sunbirds, mousebirds and bulbuls.

Hikers have been robbed along this route, so don't go alone, and avoid carrying valuables.

State House

The residence of the German colonial governor once graced the present site of the **State House** (Map p308; Robert Mugabe Ave), though the mansion was razed to the ground in 1958. Soon after, it was replaced by the present building, which was occupied by yet another colonist, the South African Administrator. After independence, control of the State House finally returned to Namibia as it became the official residence of the Namibian president. All that remains of the original building is part of the old garden wall.

Gathemann's Complex

Along Independence Ave are three colonial-era buildings, all designed by the German architect Willi Sander. The one furthest south was built in 1902 as the Kronprinz Hotel, which later joined Gathemann House (now

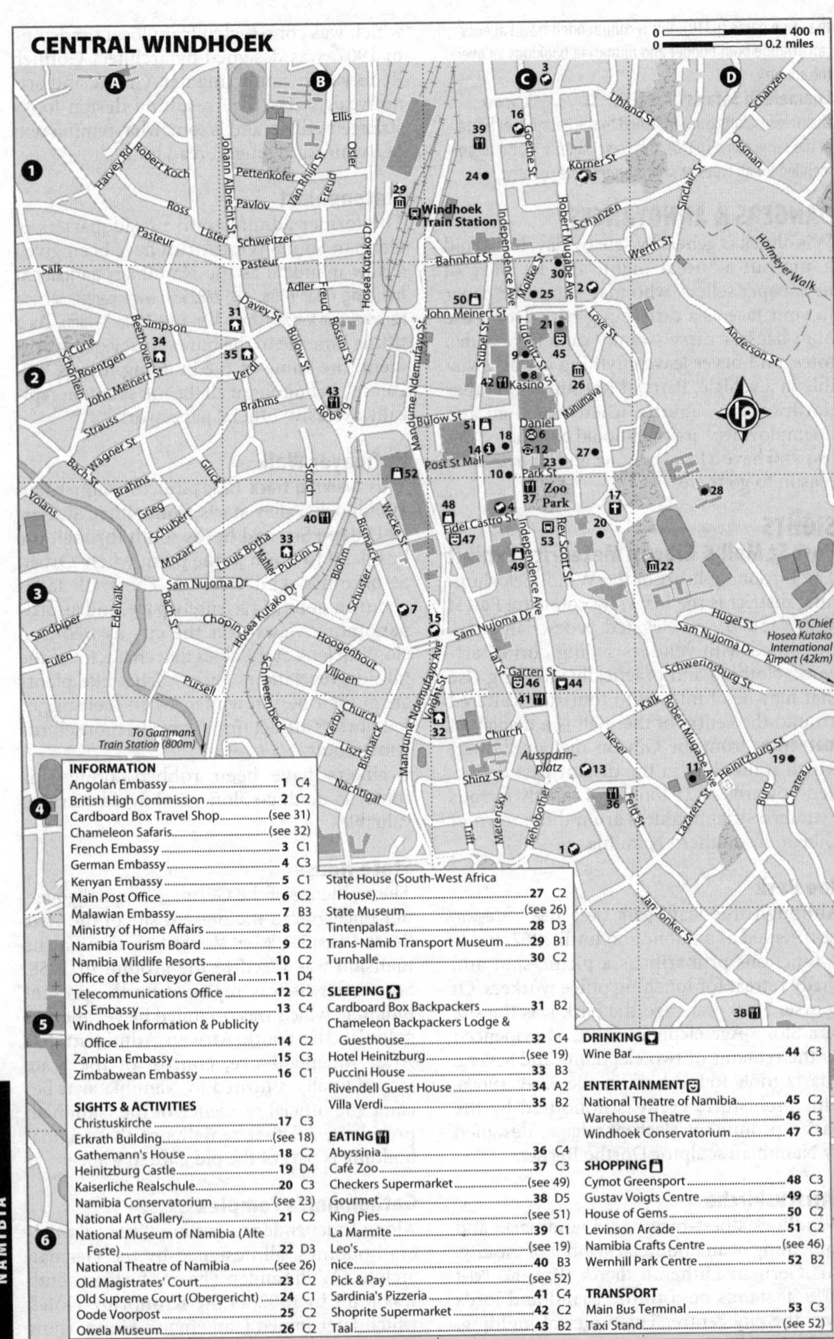
CENTRAL WINDHOEK
0 400 m
0 0.2 miles
A
B
C
D
1
2
3
4
5
6
Harvey Rd
Robert Koch
Johann Albrecht St
Pettenkofer
Ellis
Osler
Van Rhijn St
Freud
Ross
Pavlov
Lister
Schweitzer
Pasteur
Salk
Pasteur
Adler
Freud
Hosea Kutako Dr
Windhoek Train Station
Davey St
Simpson
Beethoven
Curie
Roentgen
Schönlein
John Meinert St
Verdi
Bülow St
Rossini St
Brahms
Roberg
Strauss
Wagner St
Bach St
Brahms
Glück
Grieg
Schubert
Storch
Volans
Mozart
Louis Botha
Mahler
Puccini St
Sam Nujoma Dr
Bach St
Edelvalk
Sandpiper
Eulen
Chopin
Hosea Kutako Dr
Pursell
Schmerenbeck
Hoogenhout
Viljoen
Kerby
Church
Liszt
Bismarck
Nachtigal
Blohm
Schuster
Bismarck
Wecke St
To Gammans Train Station (800m)
Goethe St
Körner St
Uhland St
Schanzen
Ossman
Robert Mugabe Ave
Independence Ave
Schanzen
Sinclair St
Werth St
Hofmeyer Walk
Bahnhof St
Moltke St
John Meinert St
Mandume Ndemufayo St
Love St
Anderson St
Stübel St
Lüderitz St
Kasino St
Manumava
Bülow St
Daniel
Post St Mall
Park St
Zoo Park
Fidel Castro St
Independence Ave
Rev Scott St
Sam Nujoma Dr
Hügel St
Sam Nujoma Dr
To Chief Hosea Kutako International Airport (42km)
Schwerinsburg St
Tal St
Garten St
Mandume Ndemufayo Ave
Voigts St
Church
Kalk
Robert Mugabe Ave
Neser
Heinitzburg St
Ausspann-platz
Shinz St
Merensky
Tritt
Rehobother
Feld St
Lazarett St
Burg
Chateau
Jan Jonker St
INFORMATION
Angolan Embassy 1 C4
British High Commission 2 C2
Cardboard Box Travel Shop (see 31)
Chameleon Safaris (see 32)
French Embassy 3 C1
German Embassy 4 C3
Kenyan Embassy 5 C1
Main Post Office 6 C2
Malawian Embassy 7 B3
Ministry of Home Affairs 8 C2
Namibia Tourism Board 9 C2
Namibia Wildlife Resorts 10 C2
Office of the Surveyor General 11 D4
Telecommunications Office 12 C2
US Embassy 13 C4
Windhoek Information & Publicity Office 14 C2
Zambian Embassy 15 C3
Zimbabwean Embassy 16 C1
SIGHTS & ACTIVITIES
Christuskirche 17 C3
Erkrath Building (see 18)
Gathemann's House 18 C2
Heinitzburg Castle 19 D4
Kaiserliche Realschule 20 C3
Namibia Conservatorium (see 23)
National Art Gallery 21 C2
National Museum of Namibia (Alte Feste) 22 D3
National Theatre of Namibia (see 26)
Old Magistrates' Court 23 C2
Old Supreme Court (Obergericht) 24 C1
Oode Voorpost 25 C2
Owela Museum 26 C2
State House (South-West Africa House) 27 C2
State Museum (see 26)
Tintenpalast 28 D3
Trans-Namib Transport Museum 29 B1
Turnhalle 30 C2
SLEEPING
Cardboard Box Backpackers 31 B2
Chameleon Backpackers Lodge & Guesthouse 32 C4
Hotel Heinitzburg (see 19)
Puccini House 33 B3
Rivendell Guest House 34 A2
Villa Verdi 35 B2
EATING
Abyssinia 36 C4
Café Zoo 37 C3
Checkers Supermarket (see 49)
Gourmet 38 D5
King Pies (see 51)
La Marmite 39 C1
Leo's (see 19)
nice 40 B3
Pick & Pay (see 52)
Sardinia's Pizzeria 41 C4
Shoprite Supermarket 42 C2
Taal 43 B2
DRINKING
Wine Bar 44 C3
ENTERTAINMENT
National Theatre of Namibia 45 C2
Warehouse Theatre 46 C3
Windhoek Conservatorium 47 C3
SHOPPING
Cymot Greensport 48 C3
Gustav Voigts Centre 49 C3
House of Gems 50 C2
Levinson Arcade 51 C2
Namibia Crafts Centre (see 46)
Wernhill Park Centre 52 B2
TRANSPORT
Main Bus Terminal 53 C3
Taxi Stand (see 52)
NAMIBIA

home to a gourmet restaurant) to function as a private business. The most notable of the three is the Erkrath Building, which was constructed in 1910 as a private home and business, but now serves as the headquarters of **Namibian Wildlife Resorts** (NWR; see p305).

Turnhalle

The **Turnhalle** (Map p308; Bahnoff St) was built in 1909 as a practice hall for the Windhoek Gymnastic Club, though in 1975 it was modernised and turned into a conference hall. On 1 September of that year, it served as the venue for the first Constitutional Conference on Independence for South-West Africa, which subsequently – and more conveniently – came to be called the Turnhalle Conference. Unfortunately, a fire ravaged the Turnhalle in 2007, which calls into question its future role in state affairs.

Old Magistrates' Court

This old **courthouse** (Map p308; cnr Lüderitz & Park Sts; 8am-1pm & 2pm-5pm Mon-Fri, 8am-1pm Sat) was built between 1897 and 1898 for Carl Ludwig, the state architect, though it was never used and was eventually drafted into service as the magistrates' court. Take a look at the verandah on the south side, which provided a shady sitting area for people waiting for their cases to be called. The building has been given new life as the Namibia Conservatorium.

Kaiserliche Realschule

Windhoek's first German **primary school** (Map p308; Robert Mugabe Ave) was built in 1908, and opened the following year with a class size of 74 students. Notice the curious turret with wooden slats, which was designed to provide ventilation for European children unaccustomed to the African heat. The building later housed Windhoek's first German high school, an English middle school and today the administrative headquarters of the National Museum.

Castles

Believe it or not, Windhoek is home to no less than three castles, which serve as austere reminders of German colonisation. Uphill from Robert Mugabe Ave are **Schwerinsburg Castle** (1913; Map p308), which now serves as a private home, **Sanderburg Castle** (1917; Map p308), which is the Italian ambassador's stately residence, and **Heinitzburg Castle** (1914; Map p308), which now houses a fine hotel and restaurant (see Sleeping, p311, and Eating, p312).

Oode Voorpost

This classically elegant **building** (Map p308; John Meinert St) dates from 1902, and originally held the colonial surveyors' offices. Today, it's more famous for the nearby bronze **kudu statue** (cnr Independence Ave & John Meinert St), which honours the many kudu who died from the 1896 rinderpest epidemic – only in Namibia!

Museums

NATIONAL MUSEUM OF NAMIBIA

The whitewashed ramparts of Alte Feste, Windhoek's oldest surviving building, date from the early 1890s, and originally served as the headquarters of the German Schutztruppe. Today it houses the historical section of the **National Museum of Namibia** (Map p308; ☎ 293 4437; Robert Mugabe Ave; admission free; 9am-6pm Mon-Fri, 3-6pm Sat & Sun), which contains memorabilia and photos from the colonial period as well as indigenous artefacts.

OWELA MUSEUM & NATIONAL THEATRE OF NAMIBIA

The other half of the National Museum of Namibia, about 600m from the main building, is known as the **Owela Museum** (Map p308; State Museum; ☎ 293 4358; 4 Lüderitz St; admission free; 9am-6pm Mon-Fri, 3-6pm Sat & Sun). Exhibits focus on Namibia's natural and cultural history.

Practically next door is the **National Theatre of Namibia** (Map p308; ☎ 237966; 12 John Meinert St), built in 1960 by the Arts Association of Namibia, and which continues to serve as one of Windhoek's major cultural centres.

TRANS-NAMIB TRANSPORT MUSEUM

Windhoek's beautiful old Cape Dutch-style **train station** on Bahnhof St was constructed by the Germans in 1912, and was expanded in 1929 by the South African administration. Across the driveway from the entrance is the German steam locomotive 'Poor Old Joe,' which was shipped to Swakopmund in 1899, and reassembled for the treacherous journey across the desert to Windhoek. Upstairs in the train station is the small but worthwhile **Trans-Namib Transport Museum** (Map p308; ☎ 2982186; admission N$5; 9am-noon & 2-4pm Mon-Fri) outlining Namibian transport history, particularly that of the railway.

NATIONAL ART GALLERY

This **art gallery** (Map p308; ☎ 240930; cnr Robert Mugabe Ave & John Meinert St; admission free; ⏰ 8am-5pm Mon-Fri, 8am-1pm Sat) contains a permanent collection of works reflecting Namibia's historical and natural heritage.

Around Windhoek

DAAN VILJOEN GAME PARK

This beautiful **game park** (Map p316; admission per person N$40, per vehicle N$10; ⏰ sunrise-6pm) sits in the Khomas Hochland, about 18km west of Windhoek, though unfortunately it was being juggled between owners at the time of research. Once operated under the jurisdiction of Namibian Wildlife Resorts (NWR), the property is currently under private ownership and is no longer open to overnight guests. However, there are rumours circulating that a much-needed facelift is underway, and that the campsite and resort will reopen in the years to come.

Because there are no seriously dangerous animals (eg big cats), you can walk to your heart's content through lovely wildlife-rich desert hills, and spot gemsboks, kudus, mountain zebras, springboks, hartebeests, warthogs and elands. Daan Viljoen is also known for its birdlife, and over 200 species have been recorded, including the rare green-backed heron and pin-tailed whydah.

Daan Viljoen's hills are covered with open thorn-scrub vegetation that allows excellent wildlife viewing, and three walking tracks have been laid out. The 3km **Wag-'n-Bietjie Trail** follows a dry riverbed from near the park office to Stengel Dam. A 9km circuit, the **Rooibos Trail**, crosses hills and ridges and affords great views back to Windhoek in the distance. The 34km **Sweet-Thorn Trail** circuits the empty eastern reaches of the reserve.

To get to Daan Viljoen, take the C28 west from Windhoek; Daan Viljoen is clearly signposted off the Bosua Pass Hwy, about 18km from the city.

FESTIVALS & EVENTS

Windhoek's annual cultural bash is September's **/Ae//Gams Festival**, which features colourful gatherings of dancers, musicians and people in ethnic dress. True to its partially Teutonic background, Windhoek also stages its own **Oktoberfest** in late October. Similarly, the German-style **Windhoek Karnival** (or WIKA) is held in late April and features a week of events.

SLEEPING

Budget

Cardboard Box Backpackers (Map p308; ☎ 228994; www.cardboardbox.com.na; 15 Johann Albrecht St; campsite N$40, dm N$80, r from N$220; 💻 🏊) 'The Box' has been doing it for years, namely rocking the spot as Windhoek's wildest backpackers. Centred on a dreamy swimming pool that fronts a fully stocked bar, travellers have a tough time leaving this oasis of affordable luxury, though no one seems to be bothered in the slightest! If you do decide to get motivated, the city centre is just a short walk away. The excellent onsite Travel Shop gives unbiased information, and can help sort out all your future travel plans.

Chameleon Backpackers Lodge & Guesthouse (Map p308; ☎ 244347; www.chameleonbackpackers.com; 5-7 Voight St; campsite N$50, dm from N$90, r from N$325; 💻 🏊) This well-matched rival to the Cardboard Box caters to a slightly more subdued crowd, offering luxurious African chic en suite rooms and spic-and-span dorms at shoestring prices. Of course, Chameleon is a backpackers at its core, so you can be sure that the bar sees plenty of action, and its onsite safari centre offers some of the most affordable trips in Namibia. Here's the best part: you can check your eco-guilt at the door thanks to the solar-heated showers, a comprehensive recycling program and a compost heap!

Puccini House (Map p308; ☎ 236355; www.puccini-namibia.com; 4 & 6 Puccini St; s/d with shared bathroom N$215/360, s/d/tr N$385/450/630; 💻 🏊) The closest backpacker option to the city centre is conveniently near the Wernhill Park Centre, yet retains its intimate atmosphere with only 14-rooms and a very welcoming management.

Rivendell Guest House (Map p308; ☎ 250006; www.rivendell.com; 40 Beethoven St; s/d with shared bathroom from N$265/340, s/d N$345/460; 💻 🏊) A very relaxed guest house in a shady suburb within easy walking distance of the centre, Rivendell is a quieter alternative to some of the more bustling backpackers.

Haus Ol-Ga (Map p306; ☎ 235853; 91 Bach St; s/d N$300/400) Haus Ol-Ga enjoys a nice, quiet garden atmosphere in Windhoek West, and is a good choice if you're looking for accommodation that is more reminiscent of a home-stay.

KATUTURA – A PERMANENT PLACE?

In 1912, during the days of the South African mandate – and apartheid – the Windhoek town council set aside two 'locations', which were open to settlement by black Africans working in the city: the Main Location, which was west of the centre, and Klein Windhoek, to the east. The following year, people were forcibly relocated to these areas, which effectively became haphazard settlements. In the early 1930s, streets were laid out in the Main Location, and the area was divided into regions. Each subdivision within these regions was assigned to an ethnic group and referred to by that name (eg Herero, Nama, Owambo, Damara), followed by a soulless numerical reference.

In the 1950s, the Windhoek municipal council, with encouragement from the South African government (which regarded Namibia as a province of South Africa), decided to 'take back' Klein Windhoek, and consolidate all 'location' residents into a single settlement northwest of the main city. There was strong opposition to the move, and in early December 1959 a group of Herero women launched a protest march and boycott against the city government. On 10 December, unrest escalated into a confrontation with the police, resulting in 11 deaths and 44 serious injuries. Frightened, the roughly 4000 residents of the Main Location submitted and moved to the new settlement, which was ultimately named 'Katutura'. In Herero the name means 'We Have No Permanent Place', though it can also be translated as 'The Place We Do Not Want To Settle'.

Today in independent Namibia, Katutura is a vibrant Windhoek suburb – Namibia's Soweto – where poverty and affluence brush elbows. The town council has extended municipal water, power and telephone services to most areas of Katutura, and has also established the colourful and perpetually busy Soweto Market, where traders sell just about anything imaginable. Unlike its South African counterparts, Katutura is relatively safe by day, assuming of course you find a trustworthy local who can act as a guide. The **Namibia Community Based Tourism Association** (Nacobta; ☎ 250558; www.nacobta.com.na) sponsors township tours with **Face-to-Face Tours** (☎ 265446; www.face2face.co.za), which can be arranged by phoning ahead or sending them an email. Alternatively, you can simply book through your accommodation, and the backpacker hostels in particular run extremely worthwhile tours.

Midrange & Top End

Casa Blanca (off Map p306; ☎ 249623; www.casablancahotelnamibia.com; 52 Fritsche St; s/d from N$540/740;) This Spanish Moorish-influenced 'white house' is more akin to a castle, complete with wrought-iron balustrades, terracotta tiling and impeccable gardens brimming with verdant plants and vibrant flowers.

Olive Grove (Map p306; ☎ 234971; www.olivegrove-namibia.com; 20 Promenaden Rd; standard s/d N$595/695, luxury N$795/925, ste from N$1350;) Refined elegance is the order of the day at this boutique hotel in Klein Windhoek, which features 10 individually decorated rooms and two suites awash in fine linens, handcrafted furniture and all-round good taste.

Roof of Africa (Map p306; ☎ 254708; www.roofofafrica.com; 124-126 Nelson Mandela Ave; standard s/d N$595/795, deluxe N$695/895, luxury N$895/1095;) A pleasant haven about 30 minutes by foot from the city centre, Roof of Africa has a rustic barnyard feel, offering well-designed rooms of varying price and luxury that attract laid-back travellers looking for a quiet retreat from the city.

Hilltop House (Map p306; ☎ 249116; www.thehilltophouse.com; 12 Lessing St; r per person from N$625;) A historic Bavarian mansion built into the side of a hill decades ago, this tiny guest house oozes personality at every turn, and atmospheric rooms reflect the house's past history as an artists' studio.

Villa Verdi (Map p308; ☎ 221994; www.leadinglodges.com/villaverdi.htm; 4 Verdi St; standard s/d N$670/1080, luxury N$815/1340;) This utterly unique Mediterranean-African hybrid features whimsically decorated rooms complete with original paintings and artsy finishing.

Hotel Thule (Map p306; ☎ 371950; www.thule-namibia.com; 1 Gorges St; s/d from N$935/1380;) Perched on a towering hilltop in Eros, which is something along the lines of the Beverly Hills of Windhoek, Hotel Thule has cavernous rooms with a touch of European elegance.

Hotel Heinitzburg (Map p308; ☎ 249597; www.heinitzburg.com; 22 Heinitzburg St; s/d from N$1620/2480;) This is Windhoek's most royal B&B

option – quite literally – as it's located inside Heinitzburg Castle, which was commissioned in 1914 by Count von Schwerin for his fiancée, Margarethe von Heinitz.

EATING

Budget

King Pies (Map p308; ☎ 248978; Levinson Arcade; pies N$10-15) If you're looking for a quick and filling bite, this popular Namibian chain sells a variety of filled meat and vegetable pies.

Cafe Zoo (Map p308; ☎ 223479; Zoo Park, Independence Ave; coffee N$10-15, light meals $25-50) A storied Windhoeker cafe that is part of a long line of cafes stretching back nearly a century, this sheltered spot beneath a giant rubber tree on the edge of Zoo Park is just lovely for a cappuccino accompanied by a light meal.

Sardinia's Pizzeria (Map p308; ☎ 225600; 39 Independence Ave; dishes N$20-50) An energetic restaurant that sells decent pizza by the slice and other Italian classic dishes as well as strong coffee and sugary gelato.

Yang Tse (Map p306; ☎ 234779; /Ae//Gams Shopping Centre, 351 Sam Nujoma Dr; mains N$30-60) This cheap Chinese joint, which has a long list of traditional mainland dishes and more Westernised treats, is a nice change if you're growing tired of standard Namibian fare.

Midrange & Top End

Gourmet (Map p308; ☎ 232360; Kaiserkrone Centre, Post St Mall; mains N$40-70) Tucked away in a nondescript courtyard just off Post St Mall, this alfresco bistro has one of the most comprehensive menus you've ever seen.

Taal (Map p308; ☎ 221958; 416 Independence Ave; mains N$45-85) Offering the full set of Indian dishes from the subcontinent, Taal introduces some much-needed spice and heat into Windhoek's restaurant scene.

Abyssinia (Map p308; ☎ 254891; Lossen St; mains N$50-90) Drawing its name from the ancient kingdom that eventually became modern Ethiopia, Abyssinia offers spongy *njera* (sourdough bread) alongside family-style meat and veggie stews.

Luigi & the Fish (Map p306; ☎ 256399; 320 Sam Nujoma Dr; mains N$50-100) Often described as the ocean equivalent to Joe's Beer House, this equally famous Windhoek institution specialises in (you guessed it!) fish, serving up Namibian regulars such as hake, butterfish, mussel hotpots and crayfish cocktails alongside meats, pizza, game dishes and vegetarian fare.

La Marmite (Map p308; ☎ 248022; Independence Ave; mains N$60-120) Here you can sample wonderful North and West African cuisine, including Algerian, Senegalese, Ivorian, Cameroonian and Nigerian dishes, all of which are prepared with the finesse of the finest French haute cuisine.

nice (Map p308; ☎ 300710; cnr Mozart St & Hosea Kutako Dr; mains N$65-11) The Namibian Institute of Culinary Education – or 'nice' for short – operates this wonderfully conceived 'living classroom' where apprentice chefs can field test their cooking skills.

Leo's (Map p308; ☎ 249597; www.heinitzburg.com; 22 Heinitzburg St; mains N$175-300) Arguably Windhoek's finest restaurant, Leo's takes its regal setting in Heinitzburg Castle to heart by welcoming diners into its banquet hall, which has previously served royalty.

Self-Catering

The big names are Pick & Pay in the Wernhill Park Centre and Checkers in the Gustav

EAT AT JOE'S

Joe's Beer House (Map p306; ☎ 232457; Green Market Sq, 160 Nelson Mandela Ave; beers N$10-30, mains N$50-100; 🕔 5pm-late) A legendary Windhoek institution that is something of an obligatory stop for foreign visitors, Joe's Beer House is where you can indulge in flame-broiled fillets of all those amazing animals you've seen on safari! Seriously. We're talking huge cuts of zebra tenderloin, ostrich skewers, peppered springbok steak, oryx medallions, crocodile on a hotplate and, the house speciality, sliced and marinated kudu. (And in case you're worried, all game meats in Namibia are farm raised, so the industry is sustainable and generates a significant amount of employment.)

True to its moniker, Joe's also stocks a wide assortment of Namibian and German beers, and you can count on prolonged drinking here until early in the morning. Sure, it's touristy, but there's a lot of fun to be had here, especially on a warm evening when you can kick back a few cold ones underneath a faux African hut. Reservations are recommended.

Voigts Centre. The cheapest supermarket is the crowded Shoprite on lower Independence Ave. The Mini-Markt in Klein Windhoek is larger than it sounds and is open from 7am to midnight daily. The well-stocked OK supermarket at Hidas Centre is the best place for foreign and ethnic ingredients.

DRINKING

Club Thriller (Map p306; Goreseb St, Katutura; admission charge varies; ☎ 11pm-late) Lies in a rough area, but beyond the weapons search at the door, the music is Western and African the atmosphere is upbeat and it's relatively secure.

El Cubano (Map p308; ☎ 2917192; cnr Sam Nujoma & Tal St; ☎ 5:30pm-late) Offering up a little bit of Havana, El Cubano is a popular lounge as well as the preferred nightspot for lovers of fine cigars and expertly crafted mojitos.

Funky Lab (Map p306; ☎ 271946; /Ae//Gams Centre; 4pm-late Sun-Thu, 2pm-late Fri & Sat) This very popular club is one of Windhoek's hottest night-time dancing spots, especially if you're craving a little disco in your life.

La Dee Da's (Map p306; ☎ 0812 434 432; Ferry St near Patterson, Southern Industrial Area; admission charge varies; 10.30pm-4am Thu-Sat) Another traditional stalwart on the Windhoek clubbing scene, here you can dance to Angolan *kizomba* (fast-paced Portuguese-African music), hip hop, rave, traditional African, rock and commercial pop accompanied by special effects.

Wine Bar (Map p308; ☎ 226514; 3 Garten St; 5:30-11pm) Wine Bar occupies a historic mansion on a quiet side street and strives to satiate your palate with one of the city's best wine selections, paired with Mediterranean-style tapas and small snacks.

ENTERTAINMENT

National Theatre of Namibia (Map p308; ☎ 237966; John Meinert St; www.namibiatheatre.org) Located south of the National Art Gallery, the national theatre stages infrequent theatre presentations; for information see the Friday edition of the *Namibian*.

New Space (Map p306; ☎ 206 3111; University of Namibia complex) New Space sometimes stages theatre productions.

Ster Kinekor (Map p306; ☎ 249267; Maerua Park Centre, off Robert Mugabe Ave) This place shows recent films and has half-price admission on Tuesday.

Warehouse Theatre (Map p308; ☎ 225059; old South-West Brewery Bldg, 48 Tal St; admission varies) A delightfully integrated club staging live African and European music and theatre productions.

Windhoek Conservatorium (Map p308; ☎ 293 3111; Fidel Castro St) The conservatorium occasionally holds classical concerts.

SHOPPING

Mall culture is alive and well in Windhoek, and you'll find them scattered throughout the city centre and out in the 'burbs. Most of the stores are South African standards, which generally offer high-quality goods at a fraction of the price back home. Katutura's **Soweto Market** (p311) is more reminiscent of a traditional African market, though it's best to visit either with a local or as part of an organised tour.

Namibia Crafts Centre (Map p308; ☎ 222236; 40 Tal St; 9am-5.30pm Mon-Fri & 9am-1pm Sat) This place is an outlet for heaps of wonderful Namibian inspiration – leatherwork, basketry, pottery, jewellery, needlework, hand-painted textiles and other material arts – and the artist and origin of each piece is documented. The attached snack bar is well known for its coffee and healthy snacks.

House of Gems (Map p308; ☎ 225202; scrap@iafrica.com.na; 131 Stübel St) This is the most reputable shop in Windhoek for buying both raw and polished minerals and gemstones.

Penduka (Map p306; ☎ 257210; www.penduka.com) Penduka, which means 'wake up', operates a nonprofit women's needlework project at Goreangab Dam, 8km northwest of the centre. You can purchase needlework, baskets, carvings and fabric creations for fair prices and be assured that all proceeds go to the producers. To get there, take the Western Bypass north and turn left on Monte Cristo Rd, left on Otjomuise Rd, right on Eveline St and right again on Green Mountain Dam Rd. Then follow the signs to Goreangab Dam/Penduka.

Camping Gear

Cymot Greensport (Map p308; ☎ 234131; 60 Mandume Ndemufayo Ave) is good for quality camping, hiking, cycling or vehicle outfitting equipment, as is **Cape Union Mart** (Map p306; Maerua Park Centre). Gear for 4WD expeditions is sold at **Safari Den** (Map p306; ☎ 231931; 20 Bessemer St); alternatively, try **Gräber's** (Map p306; ☎ 222732; Bohr St) in the Southern Industrial Area.

GETTING THERE & AWAY

Air

Chief Hosea Kutako International Airport, which is about 40km east of the city centre, serves most international flights into and out of Windhoek. **Air Namibia** (☎ 299 6333; www.airnamibia.com) operates flights daily between Windhoek and Cape Town and Johannesburg, as well as twice-weekly flights to/from Frankfurt. (Flights to London were suspended at the time of writing). Several airlines also offer international services to/from Maun, Botswana, and Victoria Falls, Zimbabwe. For more information, see p383.

Eros airport, immediately south of the city centre, serves most domestic flights into and out of Windhoek. Air Namibia offers occasional flights to/from Katima Mulilo, Lüderitz, Ondangwa, Rundu, Swakopmund/Walvis Bay and Tsumeb.

Coming from Windhoek, make sure the taxi driver knows which airport you are going to.

Other airlines with flights into and out of Windhoek include the following:

British Airways (☎ 248528; www.ba.com)
Lufthansa Airlines (☎ 226662; www.lufthansa.com)
South African Airways (☎ 237670; www.flysaa.com)

Bus

From the main long-distance bus terminal (Map p308), at the corner of Fidel Castro St and Rev Michael Scott St, the **Intercape Mainliner** (www.intercape.co.za) runs to/from Cape Town, Johannesburg, Victoria Falls and Swakopmund, serving a variety of local destinations along the way. Tickets can be purchased either through your accommodation, or over the internet – given the popularity of these routes, advance reservations are recommended. For specific fare information, see the various destination chapters.

Local combis (minibuses) leave when full from the Rhino Park petrol station and can get you to most urban centres in Namibia. However, these routes do not serve the vast majority of Namibia's tourist destinations, which are located well beyond major population centres. Still, they're a great way to travel if you want to visit some of the country's smaller towns and cities, and it's great fun to jump on the bus with the locals. Again, for specific fare information, see the various destination chapters.

Car & Motorcycle

Windhoek is literally the crossroads of Namibia – the point where the main north–south (the B1) and east–west routes (B2 and B6) cross – and all approaches to the city are extremely scenic, passing through beautiful desert hills. Roads are clearly signposted and those travelling between northern and southern Namibia can avoid the city centre by taking the Western Bypass.

Train

Windhoek station has a **booking office** (☎ 2982175; 🕑 7.30am-4pm Mon-Fri) where you can reserve seats on any of the country's public rail lines. Routes are varied, and include overnight trains to Keetmanshoop, Tsumeb and Swakopmund, though irregular schedules, lengthy travel times and far better bus connections make train travel of little interest for the vast majority of overseas travellers.

GETTING AROUND

City buses have been phased out in favour of inexpensive shared taxis and combis. Collective taxis from the main ranks at Wernhill Park Centre follow set routes to Khomasdal and Katutura and, if your destination is along the way, you'll pay around N$5 to N$10. With taxis from the main bus terminals or by radio dispatch, fares are either metered or calculated on a per kilometre basis, but you may be able to negotiate a set fare per journey. Plan on N$25 to N$50 to anywhere around the city.

If you're arriving at Chief Hosea Kutako International Airport, taxis typically wait outside the arrivals area. It's a long drive into the city, so you can expect to pay anywhere from N$250 to N$300 depending on your destination. For Eros airport, fares are much more modest at around N$30 to N$50, though in all instances you're going to need to negotiate hard.

NORTH-CENTRAL NAMIBIA

The tourist trail in North-Central Namibia leads directly to Etosha National Park, one of the world's pre-eminent wildlife areas. Unlike most safari parks in Africa, roads inside Etosha are 2WD-accessible and open to private vehicles. This of course means that if you've been fortunate enough to rent your own vehicle, you're in for one of the most memorable safaris of your life. Anyone can tell their friends and family back home how quickly their guide spotted a leopard in a tree, but how many people can say they drove on the edges of a salt pan while spotting elephant herds in the distance?

OKAHANDJA & AROUND

☎ 062

Okahandja is the administrative centre for the Herero people, and the main service centre and highway junction between Windhoek, Swakopmund and the north.

At the southern end of Church St is **Friedenskirche**, the Rhenish mission church, which was consecrated in 1876. Both in the churchyard and over the road are the **graves** of several historical figures, including those of Herero leader Willem Maherero, Nama leader Jan Jonker Afrikaner and Hosea Kutako, the 'father of Namibian independence'. Okahandja's big events are **Maherero Day** in August and the **gathering** of the Green Flag Herero people in June.

Located 26km southwest of Okahandja, the former mission station of **Gross Barmen Recreation Resort** (Map p316; ☎ 501091; www.nwr.com.na; admission per person N$80, per vehicle N$10, campsite N$50, 2-/4-bed chalet N$450/600) is Namibia's most popular hot-spring resort. Known as Otikango or 'weak spring in the rocks' in Herero, the site is home to naturally occurring mineral springs, through there have been plenty of more recent additions, including tennis courts, heated pools and an open-air bar and restaurant – the whole package feels something like a cross between an oasis and a health farm.

Sylvanette Guesthouse (☎ 501213; www.sylvanette.com; Anderson St; s/d from N$390/600;) is in a quiet and gardenlike suburban setting, and centred on a refreshing swimming pool surrounded by all manner of potted plants.

Bäckerei Dekker & Café (☎ 501962; Main St; meals & snacks N$20-45) This German cafe and bakery serves full breakfasts, toasted sandwiches, healthy snacks, pies, light lunches and desserts.

There are several weekly buses between Windhoek and Okahandja (fares from N$150, one hour) on the **Intercape Mainliner** (www.intercape.co.za) service. Combis also run up and down the B1 with fairly regular frequency, and a ride between Windhoek and Okahandja shouldn't cost more than N$75.

Trans-Namib (☎ 061-298 2175) runs trains on Monday and Wednesday between Windhoek and Okahandja (fares from $75), though very limited.

ERONGO MOUNTAINS (ERONGOBERG)

☎ 064

The volcanic Erongo Mountains, often referred to as the Erongoberg, rise as a 2216m massif north of Karibib and Usakos. The site was occupied in prehistory by the San, who left behind a rich legacy of cave paintings and rock art that has weathered remarkably well throughout the ages.

The Erongo range is best known for its caves and rock paintings, particularly the 50m-deep **Phillips Cave** (Map p316; day permit N$30). This cave, 3km off the road, contains the famous hump-backed white elephant painting. Superimposed on the elephant is a large hump-backed antelope (perhaps an eland), and around it frolic ostriches and giraffes.

Ameib Ranch (Map p316; ☎ 530803; www.natron.net/tour/ameib; campsite per person N$70, half/full board per person from N$500;) is a historic farmhouse that is adjacent to a landscaped pool, a *lapa* (a circular area with a firepit, used for socialising) and a well-maintained campsite. Ameib Ranch owns the concessions on Phillips Cave, and issues permits for the site in addition to providing guided hikes and day tours.

Erongo Wilderness Lodge (Map p316; ☎ 570537; www.erongowilderness.com; s/d tented bungalows with full board per person from N$1350;) is a highly acclaimed wilderness retreat that combines spectacular mountain scenery, wildlife viewing, birdwatching and environmentally sensitive architecture to create one of Namibia's most memorable lodges. To get to the lodge, go to Omaruru, turn west on the D2315 (off the Karabib road 1km south of town) and continue for 10km.

North of Ameib, the D1935 skirts the Erongo Mountains before heading north into Damaraland. Alternatively, you can head east towards Omaruru on the D1937. This route virtually encircles the Erongo massif and provides access to minor 4WD roads into the heart of the mountains.

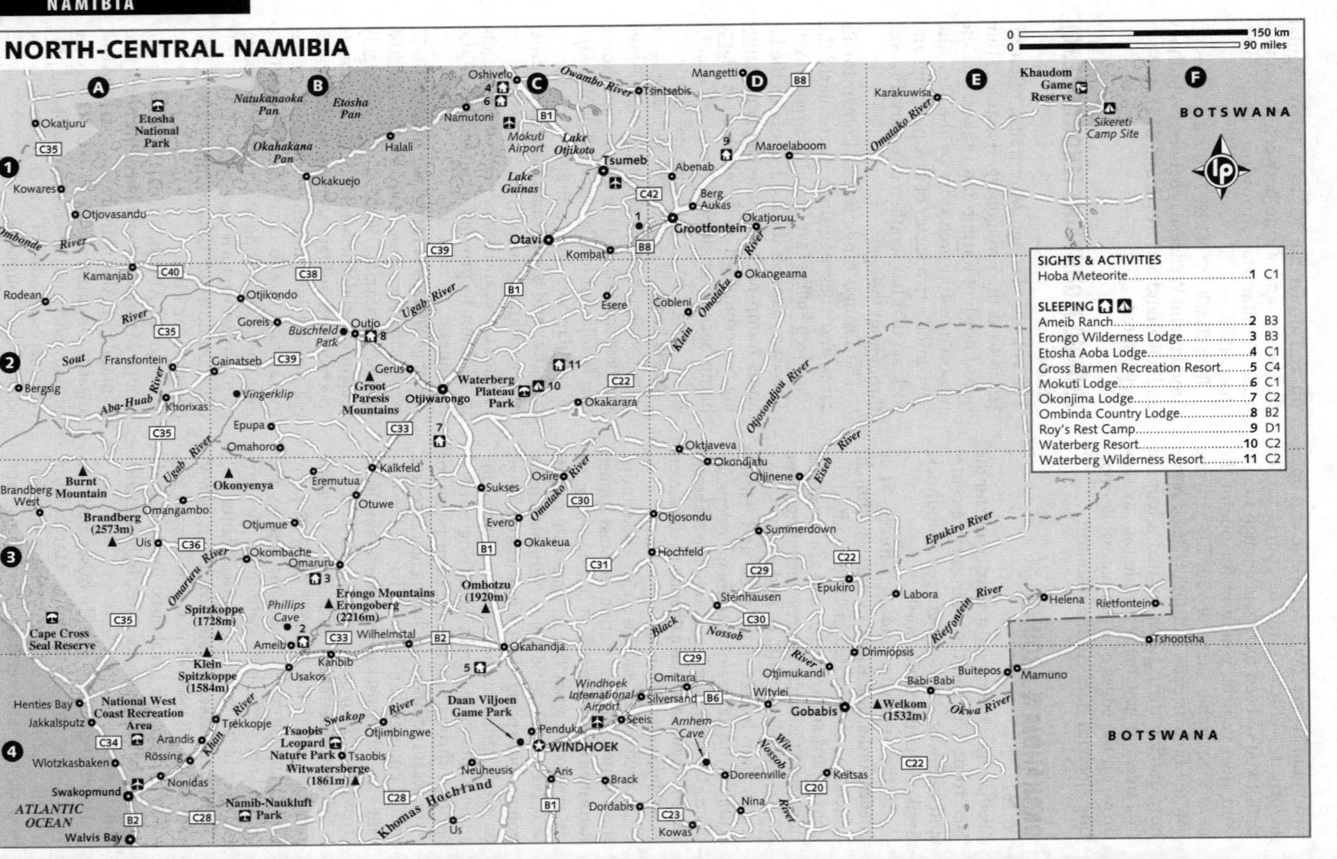
NORTH-CENTRAL NAMIBIA
0 150 km
0 90 miles
SIGHTS & ACTIVITIES
Hoba Meteorite 1 C1
SLEEPING
Ameib Ranch 2 B3
Erongo Wilderness Lodge 3 B3
Etosha Aoba Lodge 4 C1
Gross Barmen Recreation Resort 5 C4
Mokuti Lodge 6 C1
Okonjima Lodge 7 C2
Ombinda Country Lodge 8 B2
Roy's Rest Camp 9 D1
Waterberg Resort 10 C2
Waterberg Wilderness Resort 11 C2
BOTSWANA
ATLANTIC OCEAN
WINDHOEK

OTJIWARONGO

☎ 067

The roads between Windhoek, Swakopmund, Outjo and the Golden Triangle converge at the agricultural and ranching centre of Otjiwarongo. Known as the 'Pleasant Place' in Herero, Otjiwarango is particularly pleasant in September and October when the town explodes with the vivid colours of blooming jacaranda and bougainvillea.

Otjiwarongo is home to Namibia's first **crocodile ranch** (☎ 302121; cnr Zingel & Hospital Sts; admission N$20; 9am-4pm Mon-Fri, 11am-2pm Sat-Sun). This ranch produces skins for export, though you can score some cheap prices on high-quality belts, wallets, shoes and even jackets.

The **Out of Africa Town Lodge** (☎ 303397; www.out-of-afrika.com; Long St; s/d N$270/350;) is an attractive whitewashed, colonial-style affair with lofty rooms that still retain their historical accents.

Named after a common French expression that translates to 'it's so good', **C'est Si Bon Hotel** (☎ 301240; Swembad St; s/d N$670/885;) is a charmer of a hotel that takes its moniker to heart, blending Namibian design with European flourishes.

Okonjima Lodge (Map p316; ☎ 304563; www.okonjima.com; low season/high season per person with full board from N$990/2000) or the 'Place of Baboons' is home to the AfriCat Foundation, which sponsors a cheetah and leopard rehabilitation centre as well as a sanctuary for orphaned or problem lions, cheetahs and other cats. Guests are able to participate in cheetah and leopard tracking expeditions, in addition to more relaxing activities including hiking, birdwatching and wildlife drives. To reach Okonjima, turn west onto the D2515, 49km south of Otjiwarongo; follow this road for 15km and then turn left onto the farm road for the last 10km.

The Intercape Mainliner service between Windhoek and Victoria Falls passes through Otjiwarongo, and combis between Windhoek and the north stop at the Engen petrol station. All train services between Tsumeb and Windhoek or Walvis Bay (via Swakopmund) also pass through.

OUTJO

☎ 067

Bougainvillea-bedecked Outjo, settled in 1880, was never a mission station, but in the mid-1890s it did a short, uneventful stint as a German garrison town. For visitors, it best serves as a staging point for trips to Okakuejo, in Etosha National Park. The 1899 military residence, Franke House, now houses the **Outjo Museum** (admission free; 10am-12.30pm & 3-5pm Mon-Fri).

The **Etosha Garden Hotel** (☎ 313130; www.etosha-garden-hotel.com; s/d N$390/660;) is an Austrian-run oasis, just a short walk from the town centre. It has attractively decorated rooms filled with curios, which surround plush greenery and a sparkling clear swimming pool.

The **Ombinda Country Lodge** (Map p316; ☎ 313181; ombinda@ovt.namib.com; campsite per person US$90, s/d from N$455/785;) is studded with jacarandas, and consists of traditional reed-and-thatch chalets that have been brought up to date with amenities such as satellite TV and air-con.

Something of an obligatory stop for German tour buses en route to Etosha, the **Outjo Cafe-Bäckerei** (☎ 313055; light meals N$35-55) is an Outjo institution famous for its bread and sweet treats, and is also a good choice for light meals including chicken, schnitzels and burgers.

Combis run between the OK supermarket in Outjo to towns and cities around North-Central Namibia, though there is no public transport leading up to Okakuejo and the Andersson Gate of Etosha National Park. If you're driving, however, the paved route continues north as far as the park gate, but keep your speed under control as wildlife is frequently found along the sides of the highway – smashing into a warthog (or worse yet, an impala) can seriously ruin your onward safari plans.

WATERBERG PLATEAU PARK

Waterberg Plateau Park takes in a 50km-long, 16km-wide Etjo sandstone plateau, looming 150m above the desert plains. Rainwater is absorbed by the sandstone layers, and percolates through the strata until it reaches the southwest tilting mudstone, forming an aquifer that emerges in springs at the cliff base.

Around this sheer-sided 'lost world' is an abundance of watering holes that support a mosaic of lush trees and rare wildlife. In addition to the standard complement of African herbivores, the park protects rare and threatened species, including sable and roan antelopes, white and black rhinos and even wild dogs.

Information

Waterberg Plateau Park (daily admission per person N$80 plus per vehicle N$10, game drive N$450 per person) is accessible by private vehicle, though visitors must explore the plateau either on foot, or as part of an official game drive conducted by Namibia Wildlife Resorts (NWR).

Open-top safari vehicles driven by park rangers depart from the visitors centre at 7am and 3pm, and advanced reservations must be made through the NWR office in Windhoek (see p305).

With the exception of walking trails around the NWR resort, both unguided and guided hiking routes in Waterberg must be booked well in advance. For more information, see the Activities section below.

Activities

HIKING

Waterberg Wilderness Trail

From April to November, the four-day guided Waterberg Wilderness Trail operates every second, third and fourth Thursday of the month. The walks, which are led by armed guides, accommodate groups of six to eight people. They begin at 2pm on Thursday from the visitors centre, and end early on Sunday afternoon. They cost N$100 per person and must be booked through NWR in Windhoek. There's no set route, and the itinerary is left to the whims of the guide.

The first day begins at the visitors centre and follows the escarpment for 13km to Otjozongombe shelter. The second day's walk to Otjomapenda shelter is just a three-hour, 7km walk. The third day comprises an 8km route that loops back to Otjomapenda for the third night. The fourth and final day is a six-hour, 14km return to the rest camp.

Waterberg Unguided Hiking Trail

A four-day, 42km unguided hike around a figure-eight track begins at 9am every Wednesday from April to November. It costs N$50 per person, and groups are limited to between three and 10 people. Book through NWR in Windhoek.

Hikers stay in basic shelters along the course and don't need to carry a tent, but must otherwise be self-sufficient (food, sleeping bag, torch etc). Shelters have drinking water, but you'll need to carry enough bottles – plan on drinking 3L to 4L per day, especially in the hot summer months.

Resort Walking Trails

Around the pink-sandstone-enclosed rest camp are nine short walking tracks, including one up to the plateau rim at Mountain View. They're great for a pleasant day of easy walking, but watch for snakes, which sun themselves on rocks and even on the tracks themselves. No reservations are required for these trails.

Sleeping

The Waterberg Resort must be booked in advance through NWR in Windhoek. The Waterberg Wilderness Lodge is privately owned and accepts walk-ins, though advance reservations are recommended given its popularity.

Waterberg Resort (Map p316; campsite N$100, s/d N$650/1000, s/d bush chalet from N$800/1300) Together with its sibling properties in Etosha, the Waterberg Resort is part of NWR's Classic Collection, which has benefited from significant investment and total refurbishment over the past several years. At Waterberg, campers can pitch a tent in any number of immaculate sites (complete with power points) scattered around hot-water ablution blocks, braai (barbecue) pits and picnic tables. If you're looking for a bit of bush luxury, newly constructed luxury chalets benefit from good design sense.

Waterberg Wilderness Resort (Map p316; ☎ 687018; www.waterberg-wilderness.com; campsite N$120, s/d with half board from N$1070/2100;) While it's considerably more expensive than the NWR resort, Waterberg Wilderness occupies a vast private concession within the park and is a wonderful upmarket alternative if you've got a bit of extra cash to burn. Despite the resort's former life as a cattle farm, the Rust family has painstakingly transformed the property by repopulating game animals, and allowing nature to return to its pre-grazed state. The main lodge rests in a sun-drenched meadow at the end of a valley, where you'll find red-sandstone chalets adorned with rich hardwood furniture.

Getting There & Away

Waterberg Plateau Park is only accessible by private car – motorcycles are not permitted anywhere within the park boundaries. From Otjiwarango, it's about 90km to the park gate via the B1, the C22 and the gravel D512. While this route is passable to 2WD vehicles, go slow in the final stretches as the road is torn apart in several spots. If you have a high-clearance 4WD (and a bit of extra time on your hands), you might want to leave or arrive on the particularly scenic D2512, which runs between Waterberg and Grootfontein.

GROOTFONTEIN

☎ 067

With a pronounced colonial feel, Grootfontein (Afrikaans for 'Big Spring') has an air of uprightness and respectability, with local limestone constructions and avenues of jacaranda trees that bloom in the autumn. The springboard for excursions out to Khaudom National Park and the San villages in Otjozondjupa (p334), Grootfontein is the last town of any real significance before heading out into the deep, deep bush.

Sights

GROOTFONTEIN SPRING

The Herero knew this area as 'Otjiwanda tjongue', or 'Leopard's Crest', but the current name, Afrikaans for 'Big Spring', parallels the Nama name 'Gei-aus', which means the same thing. This reliable source of water has attracted both people and wildlife for thousands of years, and also became a halt for European hunters as early as the 1860s.

AROUND GROOTFONTEIN

Hoba Meteorite

Near the Hoba Farm, 25km west of Grootfontein, the world's largest **meteorite** (Map p316; admission N$10; ⏲ dawn-dusk) was discovered in 1920 by hunter Jacobus Brits. This cuboid bit of space debris is composed of 82% iron, 16% nickel and 0.8% cobalt, along with traces of other metals. No one knows when it fell to earth (it's thought to have been around 80,000 years ago), but since it weighs around 54,000kg, it must have made a hell of a thump.

From Grootfontein, follow the C42 towards Tsumeb. After 4km, turn west on the D2859 and continue 18km to the Hoba Farm; then follow the clearly marked signs until you reach the complex.

Sleeping & Eating

Roy's Rest Camp (Map p316; ☎ 240302; campsite per person N$100, s/d N$550/920;) Accommodation in this recommended place looks like a fairy-tale illustration – the handmade wood furnishings are all fabulously rustic, while the thatched bungalows sit tranquilly beneath towering trees. Hiking and mountain biking possibilities include 3km and 5km trails, and there are also opportunities for multi-day camping trips led by San guides. Roy's is 43km outside of Grootfontein on the road towards Rundu, and it's a convenient stop if you're heading to Tsumkwe (p334).

Meteor Hotel (☎ 242078; Okavango Rd; s/d from N$250/400;) Conveniently located in the centre of town, this long-standing Grootfontein establishment has rooms that have seen better years, but they'll suffice if you're not too fussy.

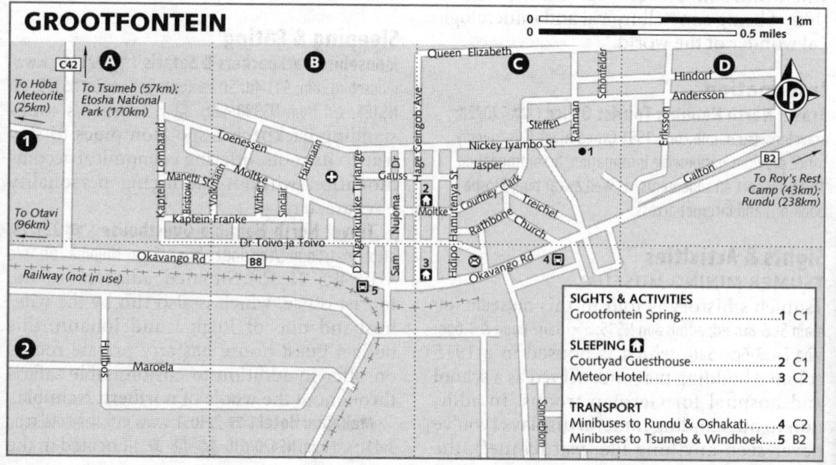

Courtyard Guesthouse (☎ 240027; www.natron.net/tour/courtyard; 2 Gauss St; s/d N$425/605;) The top spot in Grootfontein is modest by any standard, but its truly enormous rooms leave you plenty of space to unpack your bag and take stock of your gear.

Getting There & Away

Combis run frequently between Grootfontein and Tsumeb, Rundu, Katima Mulilo and Windhoek, departing when full from informal bus stops along Okavango Rd at the appropriate ends of town. The Intercape Mainliner bus between Windhoek and Victoria Falls also passes through.

If you're heading out to Tsumkwe, you will need a private vehicle. The gravel road into town is accessible by 2WD if you take it slow, but you will need a high-clearance vehicle to reach the various villages in Otjozondjupa, and a 4WD might be necessary in the rainy season. If you're heading to Khaudom, a sturdy 4WD is a requirement, as is travelling as part of a well-equipped convoy.

TSUMEB

☎ 067

The prosperity of this mining town is based on the presence of 184 known minerals, including 10 that are unique to this area. Its deposits of copper ore and a phenomenal range of other metals and minerals (lead, silver, germanium, cadmium and many others), brought to the surface in a volcanic pipe, as well as Africa's most productive lead mine (the world's fifth largest), give it the distinction of being a metallurgical and mineralogical wonder of the world.

Information

Travel North Namibia Tourist Office (☎ 220728; travelnn@tsu.namib.com; 1551 Omeg Alee) This friendly office provides nationwide information, accommodation and transport arrangements, as well as car hire, Etosha bookings and internet access.

Sights & Activities

TSUMEB MINING MUSEUM

Tsumeb's history is told in this **museum** (cnr Main St & 8th Rd; admission N$15; 9am-noon & 3-6pm Mon-Fri, 3-6pm Sat), which is housed in a 1915 colonial building that once served as a school and hospital for German troops. In addition to outstanding mineral displays (you've never seen anything like psitticinite!), the museum also houses mining machinery, stuffed birds and Himba and Herero artefacts and weapons.

TSUMEB ARTS & CRAFTS CENTRE

This **craft centre** (☎ 220257; 18 Main St; 8.30am-1pm & 2.30-5.30pm Mon-Fri, 8.30am-1pm Sat) markets Caprivian woodwork, San arts, Owambo basketry, European-Namibian leatherwork, karakul weavings and other traditional northern Namibian arts and crafts.

ST BARBARA'S CHURCH

Tsumeb's distinctive Roman Catholic **church** (cnr Main St & Omeg Allee) was consecrated in 1914 and dedicated to St Barbara, the patron saint of mineworkers. It contains some fine colonial murals and an odd tower, which makes it look less like a church than a municipal building in some small German town.

OMEG MINENBÜRO

Due to its soaring spire, the **OMEG Minenbüro building** (Otavi Minen und Eisenbahn Gesellschaft Bldg; 1st St) is frequently mistaken for a church – in fact, it looks more like a church than St Barbara's. It's probably Tsumeb's most imposing building – and few would guess that it dates back to 1907.

TSUMEB CULTURAL VILLAGE

This **complex** (☎ 220787; admission N$10; 8.30am-1pm Mon-Fri, 2.30-5.30pm Sat), 3km outside town on the road to Grootfontein, showcases examples of housing styles, cultural demonstrations and artefacts from all major Namibian traditions.

Sleeping & Eating

Mousebird Backpackers & Safaris (☎ 221777; www.mousebird.com; 533 4th St; campsite per person N$125, dm N$185, s/d from N$390/420;) Tsumeb's longstanding backpacker spot continues to stay true to its roots, offering economical accommodation without sacrificing personality or character.

Travel North Namibia Guesthouse (☎ 220728; http://natron.net/tnn/index.htm; Sam Nujoma Dr; s/d N$350/480;) Situated adjacent to the tourist office, which is also run by the wife/husband duo of Regina and Johann, this budget guest house has airy private rooms on offer in addition to customisable safaris throughout the whole of northern Namibia.

Makalani Hotel (☎ 221051; www.makalanihotel.com; 3rd St; s/d from N$420/610) Located in the

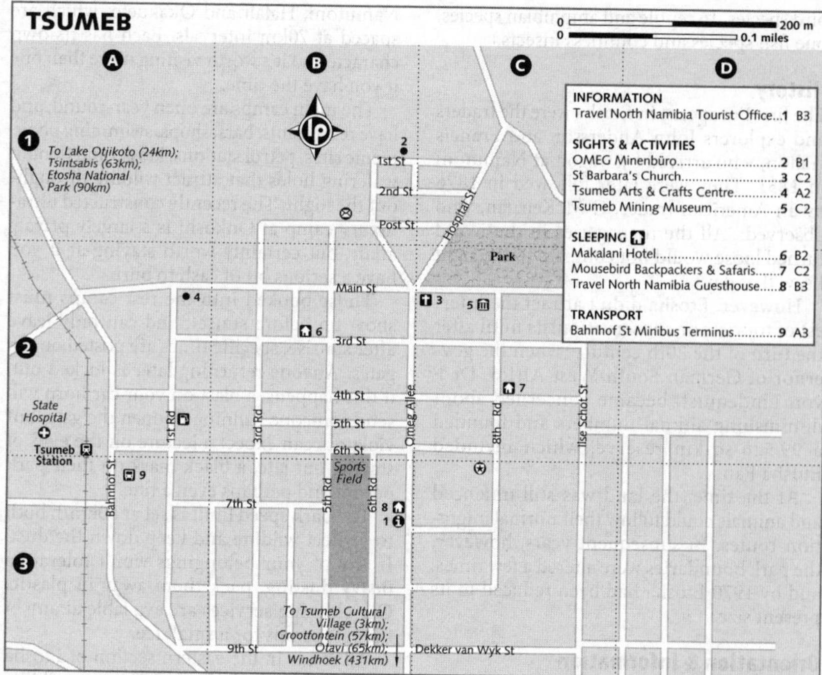

town centre, the upmarket Makalani Hotel exudes a positively Caribbean vibe, complete with shady palms, tranquil (pool) waters and vibrant shades of yellow, blue and red.

Getting There & Away

BUS

There are several weekly buses between Windhoek and the Travel North office (fares from N$350, six hours) on the **Intercape Mainliner** (www.intercape.co.za). Book your tickets in advance online as this service continues on to Victoria Falls and fills up quickly.

Combis also run up and down the B1 with fairly regular frequency, and a ride between Windhoek and Tsumeb shouldn't cost more than N$200. If you're continuing on to Etosha National Park, be advised that there is no public transportation serving this route.

CAR

Tsumeb is an easy day's drive from Windhoek along paved roads, and serves as the jumping-off point for Namutoni and the von Lindequist gate of Etosha National Park. The paved route continues north as far as the park gate, but keep your speed under control as wildlife is frequently found along the sides of the highway.

TRAIN

Trans-Namib (☎ 061-298 2175) operates trains on Monday and Wednesday between Windhoek and Tsumeb (fares from N$175), though very limited early-morning and late-night departures are inconvenient for most.

ETOSHA NATIONAL PARK

Covering an area of more than 20,000 sq km, Etosha National Park ranks as one of the world's greatest wildlife-viewing venues. Its name, which means 'Great White Place of Dry Water', is taken from the vast greenish-white Etosha Pan, an immense, flat, saline desert covering over 5000 sq km that for a few days each year is converted by the rains into a shallow lagoon teeming with flamingos and pelicans. However, it's the surrounding bush and grasslands that provide habitat for Etosha's diverse wildlife. Although it may look barren, the landscape surrounding the pan is home to 114 mammal species as well as 340 bird species, 16 reptile and amphibian species, one fish species and countless insects.

History

The first Europeans in Etosha were the traders and explorers John Andersson and Francis Galton, who arrived by wagon at Namutoni in 1851. They were later followed in 1876 by an American trader, G McKeirnan, who observed: 'All the menageries in the world turned loose would not compare to the sight I saw that day'.

However, Etosha didn't attract the interest of tourists or conservationists until after the turn of the 20th century, when the governor of German South-West Africa, Dr F von Lindequist, became concerned about diminishing animal numbers and founded a 99,526-sq-km reserve, which included Etosha Pan.

At the time, the land was still unfenced and animals could follow their normal migration routes. In subsequent years, however, the park boundaries were altered a few times, and by 1970 Etosha had been reduced to its present size.

Orientation & Information

Only the eastern two-thirds of Etosha are open to the general public; the western third is reserved exclusively for tour operators. Etosha's three main entry gates are von Lindequist (Namutoni), west of Tsumeb; King Nehale, southeast of Ondangwa; and Andersson (Okaukuejo), north of Outjo.

Visitors are encouraged to check in at either von Lindequist or Andersson Gate (King Nehale Gate is frequently closed), where you then must purchase a permit costing N$80 per person plus N$10 per vehicle per day. The permits are then to be presented at your reserved rest camp, where you pay any outstanding camping or accommodation fees.

Although fees are normally prepaid through Namibia Wildlife Resorts (NWR) in Windhoek (see p305), it is sometimes possible to reserve accommodation at either gate. However, be advised that the park can get very busy on weekends, especially during the dry season – if you can, booking is recommended.

Etosha is open to day visitors, but it's impossible to see much of the park in less than two or three days. Most visitors spend a couple of nights at one of its three rest camps, Namutoni, Halali and Okakuejo, which are spaced at 70km intervals. Each has its own character, so it's worth visiting more than one if you have the time.

The main camps are open year-round, and have restaurants, bars, shops, swimming pools, picnic sites, petrol stations, kiosks and floodlit watering holes that attract wildlife throughout the night. The recently constructed ultra-luxury camp at Onkoshi is a largely private affair, but certainly worth staying at if you have a serious bit of cash to burn.

Those booked into the rest camps must show up before sunset, and can only leave after sunrise; specific times are posted on the gates. Anyone returning later is locked out; if this happens, a blast on your car horn will send someone running to open the gate, but violators can expect a lecture on the evils of staying out late, a black mark on their park permit and perhaps even a fine.

The park speed limit is set at 60km/h both to protect wildlife and keep down the dust. If any of your belongings won't tolerate a heavy dusting, pack them away in plastic. Car-cleaning services are available at any of the rest camps for a small fee.

All roads in the eastern section of Etosha are passable to 2WD vehicles, but wildlife viewing is best from the vantage point offered by a high-clearance vehicle. The park road between Namutoni and Okakuejo skirts Etosha Pan, providing great views of its vast spaces. Driving isn't permitted on the pan, but a network of gravel roads threads through the surrounding savannas and mopane (woodland) and even extends out to a viewing site, the Etosha Lookout, in the middle of the salt desert.

The best time for wildlife drives is at first light and late in the evening, though visitors aren't permitted outside the camps after dark. While self-drivers should definitely wake up at twilight when animals are most active, guided night drives (N$600 per person) can be booked through any of the main camps, and are your best chance to see lions hunting as well as various nocturnal species. Each of the camps also has a visitor register, which describes any recent sightings in the vicinity.

Pedestrians, bicycles, motorcycles and hitching are prohibited in Etosha, and open trucks must be screened off. Outside the rest camps, visitors must stay in their vehicles (except at toilet stops).

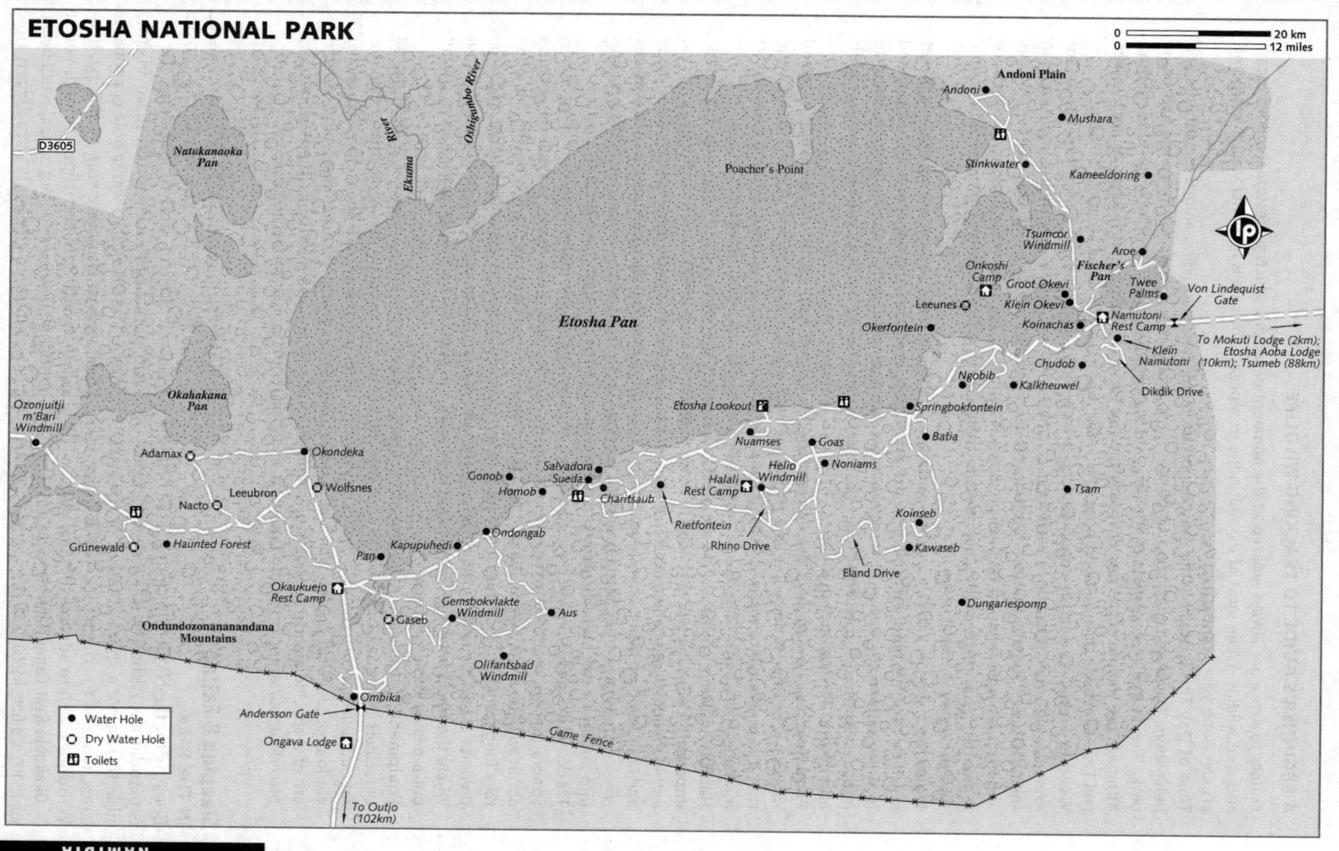
ETOSHA NATIONAL PARK
0 20 km
0 12 miles
D3605
Natukanaoka Pan
Ekuma River
Oshigambo River
Poacher's Point
Andoni Plain
Andoni
Mushara
Stinkwater
Kameeldoring
Tsumcor Windmill
Aroe
Fischer's Pan
Onkoshi Camp
Groot Okevi
Klein Okevi
Twee Palms
Von Lindequist Gate
Leeunes
Namutoni Rest Camp
Koinachas
Okerfontein
Etosha Pan
To Mokuti Lodge (2km); Etosha Aoba Lodge (10km); Tsumeb (88km)
Klein Namutoni
Chudob
Ngobib
Kalkheuwel
Dikdik Drive
Okahakana Pan
Ozonjuitji m'Bari Windmill
Etosha Lookout
Springbokfontein
Batia
Nuamses
Goas
Adamax
Okondeka
Noniams
Helio Windmill
Salvadora
Gonob
Sueda
Halali Rest Camp
Tsam
Wolfsnes
Homob
Leeubron
Charitsaub
Nacto
Rietfontein
Koinseb
Rhino Drive
Grünewald
Haunted Forest
Ondongab
Kawaseb
Kapupuhedi
Pan
Eland Drive
Okaukuejo Rest Camp
Gemsbokvlakte Windmill
Aus
Dungariespomp
Gaseb
Ondundozonananandana Mountains
Olifantsbad Windmill
Ombika
Water Hole
Andersson Gate
Dry Water Hole
Ongava Lodge
Game Fence
Toilets
To Outjo (102km)

Book your stay at lonelyplanet.com/hotels

A BEGINNER'S GUIDE TO TRACKING WILDLIFE

Visitors to Africa are always amazed at the apparent ease with which professional guides locate and spot wildlife. While most of us can't hope to replicate their skills in a brief visit, a few pointers can hone your approach.

Time of Day This is possibly the most important factor for determining animal movements and behaviours. Dawn and dusk tend to be the most productive periods for mammals and many birds. They're the coolest parts of the day, and also produce the richest light for photographs. Although the middle of the day is usually too hot for much action, this is when some antelope feel less vulnerable at a watering hole, and when raptors and reptiles are most obvious.

Weather Prevailing weather conditions can greatly affect your wildlife-viewing experience. For example, high winds may drive herbivores and birds under cover, so concentrate your search in sheltered areas. Summer thunderstorms are often followed by a flurry of activity as insect colonies and frogs emerge, followed by their predators. Overcast or cool days may prolong activity such as hunting by normally crepuscular predators, and extremely cold winter nights force nocturnal species to stay active at dawn.

Water Most animals drink daily when water is available, so water sources are worthwhile places in which to invest time, particularly in the dry season. Predators and very large herbivores tend to drink early in the day or at dusk, while antelopes tend to drink from the early morning to midday. On the coast, receding tides are usually followed by the appearance of wading birds and detritus feeders such as crabs.

Food Sources Knowing what the different species eat will help you to decide where to spend most of your time. A flowering aloe might not hold much interest at first glance, but knowing that it is irresistible to many species of sunbirds might change your mind. Fruiting trees attract monkeys while herds of herbivores with their young are a predator's dessert cart.

Habitat Knowing which habitats are preferred by each species is a good beginning, but just as important is knowing where to look in those habitats. Animals aren't merely randomly dispersed within their favoured habitats. Instead, they seek out specific sites to shelter – hollows, trees, caves and high points on plains. Many predators use open grasslands, but also gravitate towards available cover such as large trees, thickets or even grass tussocks. 'Ecotones' – where one habitat merges into another – can be particularly productive because species from both habitats overlap.

Tracks and Signs Even when you don't see animals, they leave many signs of their presence. Spoors (tracks), scat (droppings), pellets, nests, scrapes and scent marks provide information about wildlife, and may even help to locate it. Check dirt and sand roads when driving – it won't take long for you to recognise interesting spoor. Elephant footprints are unmistakable, and large predator tracks are fairly obvious. Also, many wild cats and dogs use roads to hunt, so look for where the tracks leave the road – often they mark the point where they began a stalk or sought out a nearby bush for shade.

Equipment Probably the most important piece of equipment you can have is a good pair of binoculars. These not only help to spot wildlife, but also to correctly identify it (this is essential for birding). Binoculars are also useful for viewing species and behaviours where close approaches are impossible. Field guides, which are pocket-sized books that depict mammals, birds, flowers etc of a specific area with photos or colour illustrations, are also invaluable. These guides also provide important identification pointers and a distribution map for each species.

Sleeping & Eating

IN THE PARK

Booking for the NWR-run camps listed below is mandatory. Although it is sometimes possible to reserve a space at either of the park gates, it's best to contact the NWR office in Windhoek well in advance of your visit.

Okakuejo Rest Camp (campsite N$200 plus per person N$100, s/d from N$800/1300, chalet from N$900/1500, luxury chalet per person N$1600;) Pronounced 'o-ka-kui-yo,' this is the site of the Etosha Research Station, and functions as the official park headquarters and main visitors centre. The Okakuejo water hole is probably Etosha's best rhino-viewing venue, particularly between 8pm and 10pm, though you're almost guaranteed to spot zebra, wildebeest, jackals and even elephants virtually any time of day. Okakuejo's camping ground can get very crowded, but the shared facilities are excellent, and include washing stations, braai pits, and bathroom and toilet facilities with hot water. The self-catering accommodation is the nicest in the park (excluding Onkoshi), and includes older but recently refurbished rooms alongside stand-alone chalets. If you want to splurge, the luxury chalet is a stunning two-storey affair complete with a furnished centre stage balcony boasting unmatched views of animals lining up to drink.

Halali Rest Camp (campsite N$200 plus per person N$100, s/d from N$800/1300, chalet from N$900/1500;) Etosha's middle camp, Halali, nestles between several incongruous dolomite outcrops. The name is derived from a German term for the ritual horn-blowing to signal the end of a hunt, and a horn now serves as Halali's motif. The short Tsumasa hiking track leads up Tsumasa Kopje, the hill nearest the rest camp, from where you can snap wonderful panoramic shots of the park. The best feature of Halali is its floodlit water hole, which is a 10-minute walk from the rest camp, and is sheltered by a glen of trees with huge boulders strewn about. While it's not as dramatic in scope as Okakuejo, it's a wonderfully intimate setting where you can savour a glass of wine in peace, all the while scanning the bush for rhinos and lions, which frequently stop by to drink in the late evening hours. Like Okakuejo, there is a very well serviced campsite here, in addition to a fine collection of luxury chalets that make for a wonderfully relaxed night of sleep despite being deep in the middle of the African bush.

Namutoni Rest Camp (campsite N$200 plus per person N$100, s/d from N$1400/1800, chalet from N$2000/3000;) Etosha's easternmost camp is defined by its landmark whitewashed German fort, a colonial relic that casts a surreal shadow on the rest camp. The structure originally served as an outpost for German troops, but it was later fortified in 1899 by the German cavalry in order to quell Owambo uprisings. In the battle of Namutoni, on 28 January 1904, seven German soldiers unsuccessfully tried to defend the fort against 500 Owambo warriors. Two years later, the damaged structure was renovated and pressed into service as a police station. In 1956, it was restored to its original specifications, and two years later was opened as tourist accommodation. In recent years, the entire interior has been painstakingly updated, and now serves as Etosha's boutique accommodation.

Onkoshi Camp (s/d incl activities, entrance fees & transfers from Namutoni from N$5500/9000;) Although it's an enormous splash-out that requires some serious purchasing power, the brand-new Onkoshi Camp at Etosha National Park is the shining crown jewel of NWR's Premier Collection. Upon arrival in Namutoni, you will be chauffeured to a secluded peninsula on the rim of the pan, and then given the keys to one of only 15 thatch and canvas chalets that rest on elevated wooden decks, and occupy exclusive locations well beyond the standard tourist route. The interiors, which blend rich hardwoods, delicate bamboo, elaborate metal flourishing, finely crafted furniture, hand-painted artwork and fine porcelain fixtures, create an overwhelmingly opulent atmosphere.

OUTSIDE THE PARK

There are literally dozens and dozens of top-end lodges on the periphery of Etosha, though only a few are listed below. At all of these properties, booking is essential, and access is via private vehicle or charter flight.

Etosha Aoba Lodge (Map p316; ☎ 229100; www.etosha-aoba-lodge.com; s/d from N$895/1390;) Situated on a 70-sq-km private concession about 10km east of von Lindequist Gate, this tranquil lodge is in Tamboti forest, next to a dry riverbed, and has 10 cottages that blend effortlessly into the surrounding riverine forest.

Mokuti Lodge (Map p316; ☎ 229084; www.namibsunhotels.com.na; s/d from N$965/1375;) This sprawling lodge, just 2km from von Lindequist Gate, has over 100 rooms as well as several swimming pools and tennis courts, though the low-profile buildings create an illusion of intimacy.

Ongava Lodge (☎ 061-274500; www.wilderness-safaris.com; from per person N$2530;) The most exclusive luxury lodge in the Etosha area is on a private game reserve near Andersson Gate that protects several prides of lions, a few black and white rhinos and your standard assortment of herd animals.

Getting There & Away

There's no public transport into or around the park, which means that you must visit either in a private vehicle or as part of an organised tour.

NORTHERN NAMIBIA

Known as the 'Land of Rivers', northern Namibia is bounded by the Kunene and Okavango Rivers along the Angolan border, and in the east by the Zambezi and the Kwando/Mashe/Linyanti/Chobe river systems. Although Windhoek may be the capital, northern Namibia, which is the country's most densely populated region, is undeniably its cultural heartland.

ONDANGWA

☎ 065

The second-largest Owambo town is known for its large number of warehouses, which provide stock to the 6000 tiny *cuca* (small bush shops named after the brand of Angolan beer they once sold) that serve the area's rural residents. Aside from being a population and distribution centre, Ondangwa is also the region's major transportation hub, with combis fanning out from here to other cities and towns in the north.

The main attraction in the area is **Lake Oponono**, a large wetland fed by the *Culevai oshanas* (underground river channels). Also worthwhile is the **Nakambale House** (admission N$5; 8am-1pm & 2-5pm Mon-Fri, 8am-1pm Sat, noon-5pm Sun), which was built in the late 1870s by Finnish missionary Martti Rauttanen, and is believed to be the oldest building in northern Namibia.

Sleeping

Nakambale Campsite (Map pp326-7; ☎ 245668; www.nacobta.com.na; campsite N$50, hut per person N$100) Here's your opportunity to sleep in a basic hut that would have been used historically by an Owambo chief or one of his wives. A member of Nacobta, a collective of various organisations that aims to foster increased community-based tourism, Nakambale is on the outskirts of Olukonda village, 6km southeast of Ondangwa on the D3606.

Protea Hotel Ondangwa (Map pp326-7; ☎ 241900; www.proteahotels.com; s/d from N$730/915;) This plush business hotel features bright rooms decorated with tasteful artwork as well as modern furnishings.

Getting There & Away

AIR

Air Namibia flies to and from Windhoek's Eros airport daily. Note that the airstrip in Oshakati is for private charters only, which means that Ondangwa serves as the main access point in the north for airborne travellers.

BUS

Combis also run up and down the B1 with fairly regular frequency, and a ride between Windhoek to Ondangwa shouldn't cost more than N$150. From Ondangwa, a complex network of combi routes serves population centres throughout the north, with fares typically costing less than N$30 a ride.

NORTHERN NAMIBIA

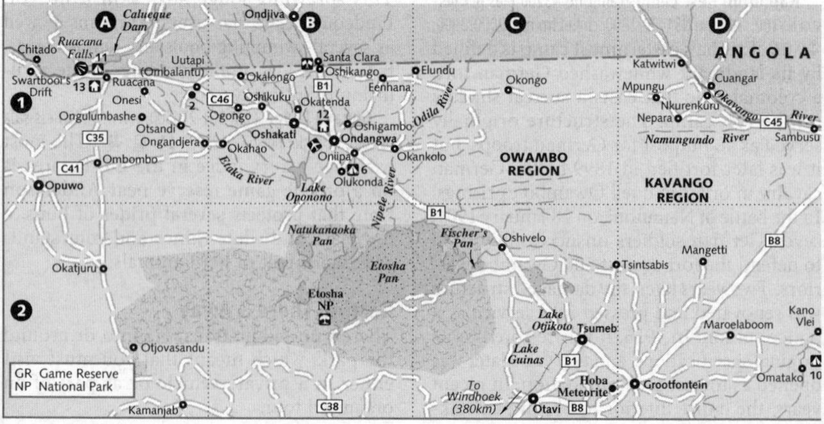

GR Game Reserve
NP National Park

NAMIBIA

CAR

The B1 is paved all the way from Windhoek to Ondangwa and out to Oshakati.

The Oshikango border crossing to Santa Clara in Angola, 60km north of Ondangwa, is open and carries frequent cross-border truck traffic. During the day, you may be able to hop across for a quick look around, but to stay overnight or travel further north you'll need an Angolan visa that allows overland travel.

TRAIN

Trans-Namib (☎ 061-2982175) operates a new passenger line between Windhoek and Ondangwa (fares from N$110). Overnight trains leave Windhoek at 5:30pm on Friday, and return from Ondangwa at 1pm on Sunday.

UUTAPI (OMBALANTU)

Uutapi (also known as Ombalantu), which lies on the C46 between Oshakati and Ruacana, is home to a number of widely revered national heritage sites, and warrants a quick visit if you've got your own wheels and are passing through the area.

The most famous attraction in Uutapi is the former **South African Defence Force (SADF) base** (Map pp326–7), which is dominated by an enormous baobab tree. This tree, known locally as *omukwa*, was once used to shelter cattle from invaders, and later as a turret from which to ambush invading groups. It didn't work with the South African forces, however, who invaded and used the tree for everything from a chapel to a coffee shop. To reach the fort, turn left at the police station 350m south of the Total petrol station, and look for an obscure grassy track winding between desultory buildings towards the conspicuous baobab.

Another famous destination is the town of **Ongulumbashe**, which is regarded as the birthplace of modern Namibia. On 26 August 1966, the first shots of the war for Namibian independence were fired from this patch of scrubland. The site is also where the People's Liberation Army of Namibia enjoyed its first victory over the South African troops, who had been charged with rooting out and quelling potential guerrilla activities. From Uutapi, turn south on the D3612 to the village of Otsandi (Tsandi). At the eastern edge of the village, turn west down an unnumbered track and continue 20km to Ongulumbashe. Be advised that this area is considered politically sensitive – you will need permission to visit the site from the Swapo office in Uutapi.

Ongandjera lies on the D3612, 52km southeast of Uutapi near Okahao. It's also accessible via the C41 from Oshakati.

RUACANA

☎ 065

The tiny Kunene River town of Ruacana (the name comes from the Herero words *orua hakahana* – 'the rapids'), was constructed as a company town to serve the 320-megawatt underground Ruacana hydroelectric project, which currently supplies more than half of Namibia's power requirements.

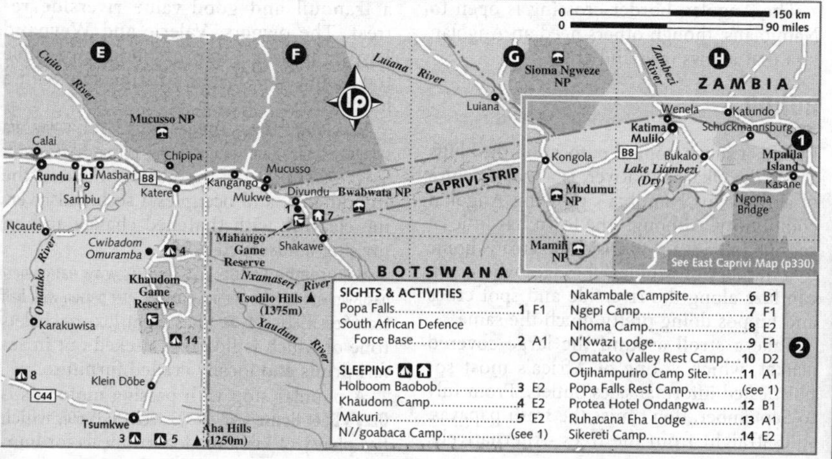

The dramatic 85m-high **Ruacana Falls** was once a great natural wonder, but thanks to Angola's Calueque Dam the water flows only during heavy rains, when the power station is satisfied and excess water is released over the dam. In 2001 and 2002, the falls roared to life in March and April, presenting a spectacle comparable to Victoria Falls – if you hear that it's flowing, you certainly won't regret a side trip to see it. To enter the border area, visitors must sign the Namibian immigration register.

Otjihampuriro Camp Site (Map pp326-7; ☎ 270120; www.nacombta.com.an; campsite per person N$50) is next to the Hippo Pools. Local community members can organise trips to Ruacana Falls or to nearby Himba villages for a small fee.

Ruacana Eha Lodge (Map pp326-7; ☎ 271500; www.ruacanaehalodge.com.na; Springbom Ave; campsite per person N$55; hut per person N$180, s/d N$630/860;) appeals to travellers of all budgets by offering manicured campsites and rustic A-frame huts alongside its polished rooms.

Ruacana is near the junction of roads between Opuwo, the Owambo country and the rough 4WD route along the Kunene River to Swartbooi's Drift. Note that mileage signs along the C46 confuse Ruacana town and the power plant, which are 15km apart. Both are signposted 'Ruacana' – don't let them throw you too badly.

For westbound travellers, the 24-hour BP petrol station is the last before the Atlantic; it's also the terminal for afternoon combis to and from Oshakati and Ondangwa, costing around N$30.

The Angolan border crossing is open to Namibians, though others need an Angolan visa that allows overland entry.

RUNDU

☎ 066

Rundu, a sultry tropical outpost on the bluffs above the Okavango River, is a major centre of activity for Namibia's growing Angolan community. Although the town has little of specific interest for tourists, the area is home to a number of wonderful lodges where you can laze along the riverside and spot crocs and hippos doing pretty much the same.

Take a stroll around the large covered **market**, which is one of Africa's most sophisticated informal sales outlets. From July to September, don't miss the fresh papayas, sold straight from the trees. Alternatively,

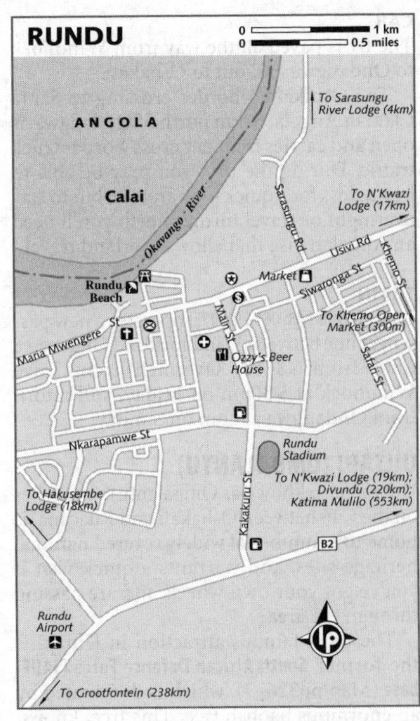

head for the **Khemo Open Market**, where you can shop for both African staples and Kavango handicrafts.

Situated on the banks of the Okavango, about 20km from Rundu's town centre, is the **N'Kwazi Lodge** (Map pp326-7; ☎ 255467; nkwazi@iafrica.com.na; campsite per person N$110, s/d N$520/590), a tranquil and good-value riverside retreat. The owners, Valerie and Weynand Peyper, are active in promoting responsible travel, and have begun a partnership with a local school.

Sarasungu River Lodge (☎ 255161; www.sarasunguriverlodge.com; campsite per person N$70, s/d/tr N$445/620/830;) is the newest lodge in the Rundu area, and occupies a secluded riverine clearing with thatched chalets and an inviting landscaped pool.

Hakusembe Lodge (☎ 257010; www.natron.net/hakusembe; campsite per person N$80, per person with half board from N$880;) has eight luxury chalets (one of which is floating) decked out in safari prints and locally crafted furniture.

A popular stop with passing motorists is **Ozzy's Beer House** (☎ 256723; meals N$35-60), which has plenty of kilojoule-loaded meals for hungry drivers, as well as ice-cold draught beer if you're retiring in Rundu for the night.

Getting There & Away

BUS

There are several weekly buses between Windhoek and Rundu (fares from N$365, seven hours) on the **Intercape Mainliner** (www.intercape.co.za). Book your tickets online as this service continues on to Victoria Falls and fills up quickly.

Combis connect Windhoek and Rundu with fairly regular frequency, and a ride shouldn't cost more than N$200. From Rundu, routes fan out to various towns and cities in the north, with fares costing less than N$30 a ride.

CAR & MOTORCYCLE

Drivers travelling to and from Grootfontein should take special care due to the many pedestrians, animals and potholes that create road hazards. Note that military convoys along the Caprivi Strip are no longer necessary, and the route has been considered safe for self-drivers since the end of the Angolan Civil War in 2002.

FERRY

The rowboat ferry between Rundu and Calai in Angola operates on demand from the riverbanks.

KHAUDOM GAME RESERVE

☎ 066

Exploring the largely undeveloped 384,000-hectare Khaudom Game Reserve is an intense wilderness challenge that is guaranteed not to disappoint. Meandering sand tracks lure you through pristine bush and across *omiramba* (fossil river valleys), which run parallel to the east–west-oriented Kalahari dunes. With virtually no signage, and navigation largely based on GPS coordinates and topographic maps, few tourists make the effort to extend their safari experience beyond the secure confines of Etosha.

But that is precisely why Khaudom is worth exploring – as one of Namibia's most important game reserves, Khaudom is home to one of only two protected populations of lions, and it's the only place in the country where African wild dogs can be spotted. The reserve also protects large populations of elephants, zebras, giraffes, wildebeests, kudu, oryx and *tsessebes*, and there's a good chance you'll be able to spot large herds of roan antelopes here. If you're an avid birder, Khaudom supports 320 different species, including summer migratory birds such as storks, crakes, bitterns, orioles, eagles and falcons.

Orientation & Information

In order to explore the reserve by private 4WD vehicle, you will have to be completely self-sufficient as petrol and supplies are only available in towns along the Caprivi Strip. Water is available inside the reserve, though it must be boiled or treated prior to drinking. As a bare minimum, you will need a GPS unit, a proper topographic map and compass as well as lots of common sense and genuine confidence and experience in driving a 4WD.

Tracks in the reserve are mostly sand, though they deteriorate into mud slicks after the rains. As a result, NWR requires that parties travel in a convoy of at least two self-sufficient 4WDs, and are equipped with enough food, water and petrol to survive for at least three days. Caravans, trailers and motorcycles are prohibited.

Wildlife viewing is best from June to October when herds congregate around the water holes and along the *omiramba*. November to April is the richest time to visit for birdwatchers, though you will have to be prepared for a difficult slog through muddy tracks.

Sleeping

In the past, NWR used to administer two official campsites in the park, though after one too many episodes of elephants gone wild, they've decided to close down shop. The remains of the camps are still present, and you're still encouraged to camp there (the alternative is pitching a tent in the bush), though once again we need to stress that you must be completely self-sufficient before visiting Khaudom.

Sikereti Camp (Map pp326–7) 'Cigarette' camp is in shady grove of terminalia trees, though full appreciation of this place requires sensitivity to its subtle charms, namely isolation and silence.

Khaudom Camp (Map pp326–7) This dune-top camp overlooks an ephemeral water hole, and is somewhat akin to the Kalahari in miniature.

Getting There & Away

From the north, take the sandy track from Katere on the B8 (signposted 'Khaudom'), 120km east of Rundu. After 45km you'll reach the Cwibadom Omuramba, where you should turn east into the park.

From the south, you can reach Sikereti Camp via Tsumkwe. From Tsumkwe, it's 20km to Groote Döbe and another 15km from there to the Dorslandboom turning. It's then 25km north to Sikereti Camp.

BWABWATA NATIONAL PARK

☎ 066

First gazetted in 1999, but only very recently recognised as a national park, Bwabwata was established to rehabilitate local game populations. Prior to the 2002 Angolan ceasefire, this area saw almost no visitors, and wildlife populations had been virtually wiped out by rampant poaching instigated by ongoing conflict. Now that peace has returned, the animals are miraculously back again, and tourism is starting to pick up once more.

Orientation

Bwabwata includes five main zones: the Divundu area, the West Caprivi Triangle, the Mahango Game Reserve, Popa Falls and the now-defunct West Caprivi Game Reserve. The Mahango Game Reserve presently has the largest concentrations of wildlife, and consequently is the focus of most safaris in the area.

Sights

MAHANGO GAME RESERVE

This small but diverse 25,000-hectare **park** (admission per person N$40, per vehicle N$10; sunrise-sunset) occupies a broad flood plain north of the Botswana border and west of the Okavango River. It attracts large concentrations of thirsty elephants and herd animals, particularly in the dry season. Like Khaudom Game Reserve, you are permitted to leave your vehicle, but exercise caution at all times.

With a 2WD vehicle, you can either zip through on the Mahango transit route or follow the Scenic Loop Drive past Kwetche picnic site, east of the main road. With a 4WD, you can also explore the 20km Circular Drive

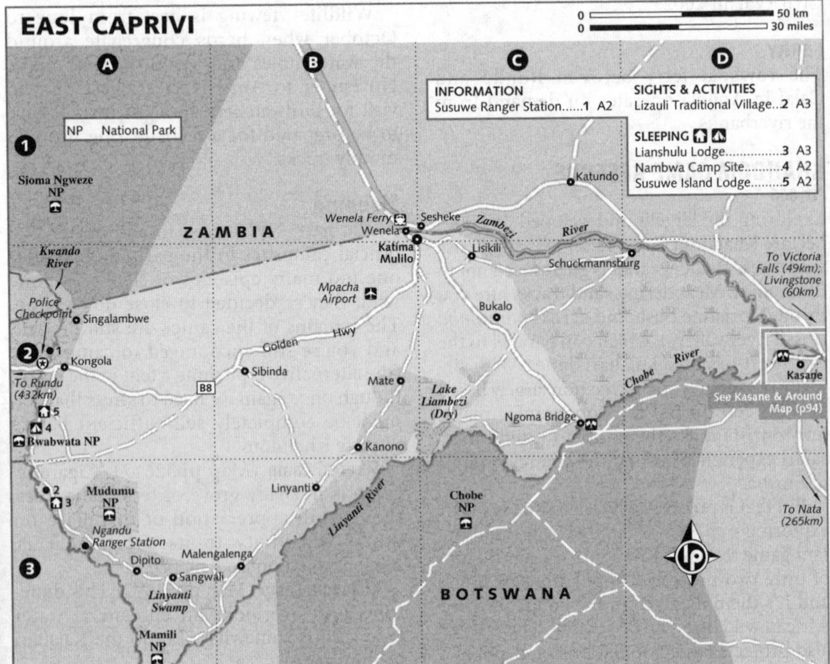

Loop, which follows the *omiramba*, and offers the best wildlife viewing. It's particularly nice to stop beside the river in the afternoon and watch the elephants swimming and drinking among hippos and crocodiles.

POPA FALLS

Near Bagani, the Okavango River plunges down a series of cascades known as **Popa Falls** (Map pp326-7; admission per person N$40, per vehicle N$10; sunrise-sunset). The falls are nothing to get steamed up about, especially if Victoria Falls lies in your sights. In fact, the falls are actually little more than large rapids, though periods of low water do expose a drop of 4m. Aside from the 'falls', there are good opportunities here for hiking and birdwatching, though swimming is definitely not safe as there are hungry crocs about.

Sleeping

While private concessions here handle their own bookings, the campsite at Popa Falls is run by Namibia Wildlife Resorts (NWR) and must be booked through the main office in Windhoek (see p305).

WESTERN SECTION

Ngepi Camp (Map pp326-7; ☎ 259903; www.ngepicamp.com; campsite per person N$50, bush/tree huts per person N$300/430) Travellers rave about this place, and we agree: it's probably one of the best backpacker lodges in Namibia. You can swim in the Okavango River 'cage' (it keeps you and the crocs at a safe distance from one another), and spend evenings in the inviting bush bar. Crash for the night in a bush or tree hut, or pitch a tent by the river, and let the sounds of hippos splashing ease you into a restful sleep. Ngepi is not a luxury camp – showers are rough and there's no TV – but this all adds to the rustic charm. The camp is 4km off the main road, though the sandy access can prove difficult without a high clearance vehicle.

Popa Falls Rest Camp (Map pp326-7; campsite per person N$50, s/d cabin N$350/500) Recent renovations have turned this humble rest camp into a sparkling riverside spot. A small onsite shop sells the essentials while a field kitchen is available for self-catering. Facilities include hot showers, sit-down flush toilets and braai pits.

N//goabaca Camp (Map pp326-7; www.nacobta.com.na; campsite per person N$50, s/d cabins N$350/500) This leafy community-run campsite sits beside the Okavango River opposite the Popa Falls Rest Camp. Any money spent here supports local Kxao (Bushmen) communities, and there are trackers on staff who can arrange walking ventures out into the bush.

EASTERN SECTION

Nambwa Camp Site (Map p330; campsite per person N$50) Nambwa, 14km south of Kongola, lacks facilities, but it's the only official camp in the park, and provides easy access to the wildlife-rich oxbow lagoon, about 5km south. Book and pick up a permit at the Susuwe ranger station, about 4km north of Kongola (4WD access only) on the west bank of the river. To reach the camp, follow the 4WD track south along the western bank of the Kwando River.

Susuwe Island Lodge (Map p330; ☎ South Africa 27-11-706 7207; www.islandsinafrica.com; low/high season per person from N$2480/3220;) This posh safari lodge is on a remote island in the Kwando River, and surrounded by a diverse habitat of savanna, woodland and wetland. Accommodation is in six stylish brick and thatch chalets adorned in soft earth tones. Susuwe is accessible only by charter flight or 4WD; booking is mandatory.

Getting There & Away

The paved road between Rundu and Katima Mulilo is perfectly suited to 2WD vehicles, as is the gravel road between Divundu and Mohembo (on the Botswana border). Drivers may transit the park without charge, but incur national park entry fees to use the loop drive through the park.

KATIMA MULILO

☎ 066

Out on a limb at the eastern end of the Caprivi Strip lies remote Katima Mulilo, which is as far from Windhoek (1200km) as you can get in Namibia. Once known for the elephants that marched through the village streets, Katima is devoid of wildlife these days – apart from the hippos and crocodiles in the Zambezi – though it continues to thrive as a border town and minor commercial centre.

Sleeping & Eating

Mukusi Cabins (☎ 253255; Engen petrol station; campsite N$50, s/d from N$300/350;) Although it lacks the riverside location of other properties in the area, this oasis behind the petrol station has a good range of accommodation from simple rooms with fans to small but comfortable air-con cabins.

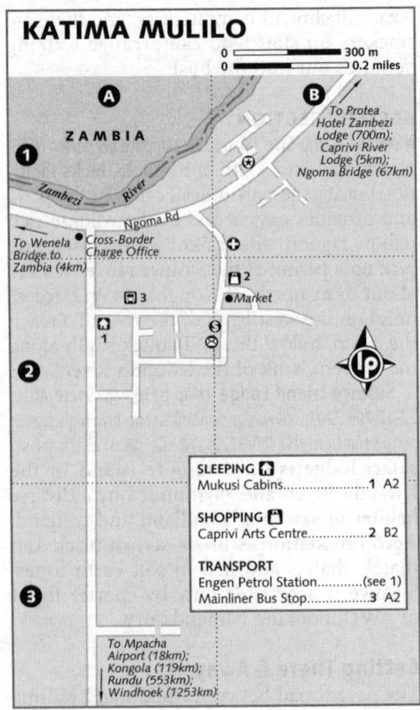

Caprivi River Lodge (☎ 253300; www.capriviriver lodge.info; campsite per person N$50; s N$305-800, d N$445-1075;) This diverse lodge offers options to suit travellers of all budgets, from a grassy campsite and rustic chalets with shared bathrooms to slightly more luxurious wooden cabins with bathrooms.

Protea Hotel Zambezi Lodge (☎ 253149; http://namibweb.com/zambezilodge.htm; campsite per person N$50, s/d from N$650/955;) This stunning, riverside lodge is perched on the banks of the Zambezi, and features a floating bar where you can watch the crocs and hippos below.

Shopping

The **Caprivi Arts Centre** (8am-5.30pm), run by the Caprivi Art & Cultural Association, is a good place to look for local curios and crafts, including elephant and hippo woodcarvings, baskets, bowls, kitchen implements and traditional knives and spears.

Getting There & Away

AIR

Air Namibia has several weekly departures between Windhoek's Eros airport and Katima's Mpacha airport, located 18km southwest of town.

BUS & MINIBUS

There are several weekly buses between Windhoek and Katima Mulilo (fares from N$350, 17 hours) on the **Intercape Mainliner** (www.intercape.co.za). Book your tickets online as this service continues on to Victoria Falls and fills up quickly.

Combis connect Windhoek and Katima with fairly regular frequency, and a ride shouldn't cost more than N$225. From Katima, routes fan out to various towns and cities in the north, with fares costing less than N$30 a ride.

CAR

The paved Golden Hwy runs between Katima Mulilo and Rundu, and is accessible to all 2WD vehicles.

TO BOTSWANA & ZAMBIA

For information on border crossings, see p383.

MPALILA ISLAND

☎ 066

Mpalila (Impalilia) Island, a wedge driven between the Chobe and Zambezi Rivers, represents Namibia's outer limits at the 'four-corners meeting' of Zimbabwe, Botswana, Namibia and Zambia. The island itself, which is within easy reach by boat of Chobe National Park, is home to a handful of exclusive lodges catering to upmarket tourists in search of luxurious isolation.

Booking for all accommodation on the island is essential. All lodges offer a variety of activities for guests including cruises on the Chobe River, guided game drives, fishing expeditions, island walks and mokoro trips. Rates include full board and transfers.

Overlooking the impressive Mombova rapids, the **Impalila Island Lodge** (☎ South Africa 27-11-706-7207; www.islandsinafrica.com; low/high season per person US$350/550;) is a stylish retreat of eight luxury chalets built on elevated decks at the water's edge. The centrepiece of the lodge is a pair of ancient baobab trees, which tower majestically over the grounds.

The most famous spot on the island is the **Chobe Savannah Lodge** (☎ 686 1243; www.desertdelta.com; low/high season per person US$375/650;), which is renowned for its panoramic views of the game-rich Puku Flats. Each stylishly decorated room has a private verandah where you can spot wildlife without ever having to change out of your pyjamas.

Access to Mpalila Island is either by charter flight or by boat from Kasane, Botswana, though lodges will organise all transport for their booked guests.

MUDUMU NATIONAL PARK

☎ 066

Mudumu National Park has a tragic history of environmental abuse and neglect, though it's back on the maps once again thanks largely to the efforts of Grant Burton and Marie Holstensen of Lianshulu Lodge (right). As the owners of a vast private concession within the park boundaries, Grant and Marie have worked closely with both local communities and the Ministry of Environment and Tourism (MET) to link conservation, sustainable land use and economic development in the Caprivi.

Although Mudumu was once one of Namibia's most stunning wildlife habitats, by the late 1980s, the park had become an unofficial hunting concession gone mad. In under a decade, the wildlife was decimated by trophy hunters, which prompted the MET to gazette Mudumu National Park in a last-ditch effort to rescue the area from total devastation. Mudumu's wildlife has begun to return but it will take years of wise policy making and community awareness before it approaches its former glory. In the meantime, a visit here lends further support to an ambitious project that aims to improve the local economy while restoring some of Mudumu's former splendour.

Sights

A joint partnership between the owners of Lianshulu Lodge, MET, private benefactors and the Lizauli community, the **Lizauli Traditional Village** (Map p330; admission N$20; 9am-5pm Mon-Sat) was established to educate visitors about traditional Caprivian lifestyles, and to provide insight into the local diet, fishing and farming methods, village politics, music, games, traditional medicine, basketry and tool making. After the guided tour, visitors can shop for good-value local handicrafts without the sales pressure.

The aforementioned partnership also recruits Mudumu game scouts from Lizauli and other villages, and has been given responsibility for community conservation and anti-poaching education. Most importantly, the project provides a forum in which locals can interact with tourists, and benefit both economically and culturally from the adoption of a strict policy of environmental protection.

Sleeping

Lianshulu Lodge (Map p330; ☎ South Africa 27-11-257-5111; r per person from N$3299;) Dominated by an impressive bar and dining area that overlooks the surrounding wetlands, Lianshulu Lodge has some of the most beautifully situated accommodation in all of Namibia. Around lunchtime, leguaans (water monitors) can be seen about, while at dinnertime, hippos emerge from the river to graze on the lawns. In the late evening, you will be serenaded by an enchanting wetland chorus of both insects and the haunting 'tink-tink' of bell frogs, before falling asleep in one of only 10 exclusive stand-alone chalets. The lodge offers a range of excursions, which includes the popular pontoon river cruise, where you will likely see herds of elephants as well as nesting colonies of carmine bee-eaters.

Getting There & Away

To reach Lianshulu Lodge, follow the D3511 about 40km south of Kongola, and then turn west on the signposted track.

MAMILI NATIONAL PARK

In years of good rains, this wild, seldom-visited **national park** (per person N$40, per vehicle N$10) becomes Namibia's equivalent of Botswana's Okavango Delta. Forested islands fringed by reed and papyrus marshes foster some of the country's richest birdwatching, with more than 430 recorded species to count. Poaching has taken a toll, though Mamili's wildlife, mainly semiaquatic species such as hippos, crocodiles, pukus, red lechwes, sitatungas and otters, will still impress.

Birding is best from December to March, though the vast majority of the park is inaccessible during this time. Wildlife viewing is best from June to August, and is especially good on Nkasa and Lupala Islands.

There is a sparse network of unmaintained wilderness campsites in the park, though you must bring in everything, including your own water, and be prepared for extremely rough road conditions. Although there is generally a ranger to collect park fees at the entrance gate, you're all alone once inside, and it's highly recommended that you travel as part of a convoy.

Access to the park is by 4WD track from Malengalenga, northeast of the park, or from Sangwali village, which is due north.

OTJOZONDJUPA

Otjozondjupa is commonly referred to as Bushmanland, a pejorative term that unfortunately seems to resist dying away. A largely flat landscape of scrub desert lying at the edge of the Kalahari, Otjozondjupa is part of the traditional homeland of the Ju/hoansi San, who were among the original inhabitants of Southern Africa. Following a spurt in worldwide interest in Kalahari cultures, tourist traffic has increased throughout the region, though any expectations you might have of witnessing an entirely self-sufficient hunter-gatherer society will sadly not be met here.

For some people, witnessing the stark reality of the modern Ju/hoansi San lifestyle is a sobering experience wrought with disappointments. Hunting is forbidden throughout the region, and most communities have largely abandoned foraging in favour of cheap, high-calorie foods such as pap (corn meal) and rice, which are purchased in bulk from shops. With the right attitude and mindset, most travellers try to look beyond the dire realities of their economic situation, and attempt to use the experience as a rare chance to interact with the modern-day descendants of perhaps all of our ancestors.

Tsumkwe & Around

☎ 064

Tsumkwe is the only real permanent settlement in the whole of Otjozondjupa, though it's merely a wide spot in the sand that consists of a few rust-covered buildings. Originally constructed as the regional headquarters of the SADF, Tsumkwe has been given a new mandate as the administrative centre of the Ju/hoansi San community, and home to the Nyae Nyae Conservancy. While organised tourism in the region is still something of a work in progress, Tsumkwe is where you can arrange everything from bush walks to hunting safaris, and inject some much needed cash into the local community.

INFORMATION

If you're visiting the region as a tourist, you are required to stop by the office of the **Nyae Nyae Conservancy** (☎ 244011; irregular hours) in central Tsumkwe. Although travellers sometimes complain that the office is extremely disorganised, it's still recommended that you book activities through the official channels rather than striking off on your own. This practice ensures that the money you spend ends up in the community fund rather than in the pockets of one or two individuals.

There are no officially posted prices for activities, though you can expect to be charged a reasonably modest amount for every person that accompanies you. English-speaking guides command the largest fee, generally in the realm of N$200 to N$250 per day plus food, while hunters and foragers expect around N$75 to N$100 per outing. You need to be very clear from the outset how many people you plan to pay as the conservancy will sometimes assign as many as five hunters and gatherers to accompany you on an outing. It is also possible to arrange overnight stays in villages, and traditional music and performances are also on offer.

SIGHTS & ACTIVITIES

Village Visits

While stereotypes of the San abound, from misleading Hollywood cinematic representations to misconstrued notions of a primitive people living in the bush, San society is extremely complex. Before visiting a San village, take some time to read up on their wonderfully rich cultural heritage – doing so will not only provide some context to your visit, but will also help you better engage with your hosts.

Decades of anthropological research have provided incredible insight into the nature of hunter-gather societies. In the case of the San, one of the most amazing findings was that traditional communities were non-hierarchical and egalitarian, and grouped together based on kinship and ethnic membership. Since groups were never able to build up a surplus of food, full-time leaders and bureaucrats never emerged.

Although village elders did wield a measure of influence over the mobile group, the sharpest division in status was between the sexes. Men provided for their families by hunting game, while women supplemented this diet by foraging for wild fruits, vegetables and nuts.

While Thomas Hobbes famously noted in the 17th century that this lifestyle was 'solitary, poor, nasty, brutish and short,' recent ethnographic data has shown that hunter-gatherers worked fewer hours, and enjoyed more leisure time than members of industrial societies.

Hunting and foraging trips are the highlight of any visit to Otjozondjupa. Much as they have for generations, the San still use traditional gear, namely a bow with poisoned arrows for men, and a digging stick and sling for women. In the past, men would be gone for several days at a time in pursuit of herds, so you shouldn't expect to take down any big game on an afternoon excursion. But, it's fascinating to see trackers in pursuit of their quarry, and you're likely to come across scat and spoors and maybe even an antelope or two.

Unlike hunting, foraging is very likely to turn up edible roots and tubers, wild fruits and nuts, and even medicinal plants. At the end of your excursion, the women will be more than happy to slice up a bush potato for you, which tastes particularly wonderful when roasted over a bed of hot coals. Baobab fruit is also surprisingly sweet and tangy, while protein-rich nuts are an exotic yet nutritious desert treat.

SLEEPING & EATING

Nyae Nyae Conservancy Camp Sites (campsite per person from N$50) The Nyae Nyae Conservancy has set several campsites, the most popular being the **Holboom Baobab** (Map pp326–7) at Tjokwe, southeast of Tsumkwe; **Makuri** (Map pp326–7), a few kilometres east of that, and **Khebi Pan** (Map pp326–7), well out in the bush south of Tsumkwe. Water is sometimes available in adjacent villages, but generally it's best to carry in all of your supplies and be entirely self-sufficient. Avoid building fires near the baobabs – it damages the trees' roots.

Omatako Valley Rest Camp (Map pp326-7; ☎ 255977; www.nacobta.com.na; campsite per person N$50) Outside the conservancy at the junction of the C44 and D3306, this community-run camp has solar power, a water pump, hot showers and a staff of local San. It offers both hunting and gathering trips as well as traditional music presentations.

Tsumkwe Country Lodge (☎ 061-37475; www.namibialodges.com/tsumkwe.html; campsite per person N$115, s/d from N$720/1040;) The only tourist lodge in Tsumkwe proper changed hands in 2008 and is now run under the umbrella of the upmarket Country Lodge Association. At the time of research, there were promises of a wider network of affiliated luxury campsites deep in the bush. In the meantime, guests can easily base themselves here and visit surrounding villages as part of an organised tour.

Nhoma Camp (Map pp326-7; ☎ 2734606; www.tsumkwel.iway.na/NhomaCamp.htm; half/full board per person N$1199/2399;) The former owners of the Tsumkwe Country Lodge, Arno and Estelle, have lived in the area for much of their lives, and are well respected by the local San communities. Their new project is a luxury-tented camp that is perched between a fossilised river valley and a verdant teak grove, though the main attraction continues to be their wonderful excursions into local San villages. The camp is 280km east of Grootfontein and 80km west of Tsumkwe along the C44.

GETTING THERE & AWAY

There are no sealed roads in the region, and only the C44 is passable to 2WD vehicles. Petrol is sometimes available at the Tsumkwe Country Lodge, though it's best to carry a few jerry cans with you. If you're planning to explore the bush around Tsumkwe, it is recommended that you hire a local guide and travel as part of a convoy.

The Dobe border crossing to Botswana requires 4WD and extra fuel to reach the petrol stations at Maun or Etsha 6, which are accessed by a difficult sand track through northwestern Botswana.

NORTHWESTERN NAMIBIA

For 4WD explorers, Namibia is synonymous with the Skeleton Coast, a formidable desert coastline engulfed by icy breakers. Here, seemingly endless stretches of foggy beach are punctuated by rusting shipwrecks and flanked by wandering dunes. As one moves inland, the sinister fogs give way to the wondrous desert wildernesses of Damaraland and the Kaokoveld. The former is sparsely populated by the Damara people, and is known for its unique geological features; the latter is known as one of the last great wildernesses in Southern Africa, as well as the home of the oft-photographed Himba people.

DAMARALAND

The territory between the Skeleton Coast and Namibia's Central Plateau has traditionally been known as Damaraland, after the people who make up much of its population. Although it's not an officially protected area, its wild open spaces are home to many desert-adapted species, including giraffes, zebras, lions, elephants and rhinos. In addition to its sense of freedom, the region is rich in both natural and cultural attractions, including Brandberg, Namibia's highest massif, and the rock engravings of Twyfelfontein.

The Spitzkoppe

☎ 064

The 1728m **Spitzkoppe** (Map pp338-9; Groot Spitzkoppe village; admission per person N$50 & per car N$10; ⌚ sunrise-sunset), one of Namibia's most recognisable landmarks, rises miragelike above the dusty pro-Namib plains of southern Damaraland. Its dramatic shape has inspired its nickname, which is the Matterhorn of Africa, but similarities between this granite inselberg and the glaciated Swiss Alps begin and end with its sharp peak. Beside the Spitzkoppe rise the equally impressive Pondoks, another inselberg formation that comprises enormous granite domes.

Spitzkoppe Rest Camp (Map pp338-9; ☎ 530879; www.nacobta.com.na; Groot Spitzkoppe village; campsite per person N$35, bungalow per person N$100) is an excellent community-run camp that includes a number of sites that are dotted around the base of the Spitzkoppe and surrounding outcrops – most are set in magical rock hollows and provide a sense of real isolation.

Under normal dry conditions, a 2WD is sufficient to reach the mountain. Turn northwest off the B2 onto the D1918 towards Henties Bay, then after 1km, turn north on the D1930. After 27km (you actually pass the mountain) turn southwest on the D3716 until you reach Groot Spitzkoppe village; here you turn west into the site.

The Brandberg

☎ 064

The Brandberg (Fire Mountain) is named for the effect created by the setting sun on its western face, which causes the granite massif to resemble a burning slag heap. Its summit, Königstein, is Namibia's highest peak at 2573m.

Its best-known attraction, the gallery of rock art in **Tsisab Ravine**, features the **White Lady of the Brandberg**. The figure, which isn't necessarily a lady (it's still open to interpretation), stands about 40cm high, and is part of a larger painting that depicts a bizarre hunting procession. In one hand, the figure is carrying what appears to be a flower or possibly a feather. In the other, the figure is carrying a bow and arrows. However, the painting is distinct because 'her' hair is straight and light-coloured – distinctly un-African – and the body is painted white from the chest down.

The first assessment of the painting was in 1948 when archeologist Abbé Henri Breuil speculated that the work had Egyptian or Cretan origins, based on similar ancient art he'd seen around the Mediterranean. However, this claim was eventually dismissed, and recent scholars now believe the white lady may in fact be a San boy, who is covered in white clay as part of an initiation ceremony.

At the **Brandberg White Lady Lodge** (Map pp338-9; ☎ 684004; www.brandbergwllodge.com; campsite per person N$50, bungalow/chalet from N$300/450) campers can pitch a tent along the riverine valley, all the while taking advantage of the lodge's upmarket facilities, while lovers of creature comforts can choose from rustic bungalows and chalets that are highlighted by their stone interiors and wraparound patios.

To reach Tsisab Ravine from Uis, head 15km north on the D2369 and turn west on the D2359, which leads 26km to the Tsisab car park. To reach Numas Ravine from the westward turning 14km south of Uis, follow the D2342 for 55km, where you'll see a rough track turning eastward. After about 10km, you'll reach a fork; the 4WD track on the right leads to the Numas Ravine car park.

Twyfelfontein & Around

☎ 067

Twyfelfontein (Doubtful Spring), at the head of the grassy Aba Huab Valley, is one of the most extensive rock-art galleries on the continent. The original name of this water source was /Ui-//Ais (Surrounded by Rocks), but in 1947 it was renamed by European settler D Levin, who deemed its daily output of 1 cu metre of water insufficient for survival. To date, over 2500 individual engravings have been discovered, which led Twyfelfontein to became a national monument in 1952. In 2007, Twyfelfontein was declared a Unesco World Heritage Site, the first such distinction in the whole of Namibia.

SIGHTS

Rock Engravings

Most dating back at least 6000 years to the early Stone Age, Twyfelfontein's **rock engravings** (admission N$50; sunrise-sunset) were probably the work of ancient San hunters, and were made by cutting through the hard patina covering the local sandstone. In time, this skin reformed over the engravings, protecting them from erosion. From colour differentiation and weathering, researchers have identified at least six distinct phases, but some are clearly the work of copycat artists, and probably date from the 19th century. Guides are compulsory, and remember that tips are their only source of income.

Burnt Mountain & Organ Pipes

Southeast of Twyfelfontein rises a barren 12km-long volcanic ridge, at the foot of which lies the hill known as **Burnt Mountain**, an expanse of volcanic clinker that appears to have been literally exposed to fire. Virtually nothing grows in this eerie panorama of desolation. Burnt Mountain lies beside the D3254, 3km south of the Twyfelfontein turn-off. Over the road, you can follow an obvious path into a small gorge that contains a 100m stretch of unusual 4m-high dolerite (coarse-grained basalt) columns known as the **Organ Pipes**.

Petrified Forest

The **petrified forest** (admission N$50; sunrise-sunset) is an area of open veld scattered with petrified tree trunks up to 34m long and 6m in circumference, which are estimated to be around 260 million years old. The original trees belonged to an ancient group of cone-bearing plants that are known as *Gymnospermae*, which includes such modern plants as conifers, cycads and welwitschias. The Petrified Forest, signposted 'Versteende Woud', lies 40km west of Khorixas on the C39.

SLEEPING & EATING

Aba Huab Camp (Map pp338-9; ☎ 697981; www.nacobta.com.na; campsite per person N$50, A-frame from N$300) This popular community-run campsite is attractively perched beside the Aba Huab riverbed immediately north of the Twyfelfontein turn-off.

Twyfelfontein Country Lodge (Map pp338-9; ☎ 374750; www.namibialodges.com; s/d from N$1150/1730;) Over the hill from Twyfelfontein, this architectural wonder is embedded in the red rock. On your way in, be sure not to miss the ancient rock engravings, as well as the swimming pool with its incongruous desert waterfall.

Mowani Mountain Camp (Map pp338-9; ☎ 232009; www.mowani.com; tent per person with full board from N$2600;) There's little to prepare you for this beautiful lodge – hidden among a jumble of boulders, its domed buildings seem to disappear into the landscape and you don't see it until you're there, The mountain camp is 5km north of the Twyfelfontein turn-off from the D2612.

GETTING THERE & AWAY

There's no public transport in the area and little traffic. Turn off the C39, 73km west of Khorixas, turn south on the D3254 and continue 15km to a right turning signposted as Twyfelfontein. It's 5km to the petroglyph site.

Sesfontein

Damaraland's most northerly outpost is almost entirely encircled by the Kaokoveld, and is somewhat reminiscent of a remote oasis in the middle of the Sahara.

Ever fancy spending the night in a colonial fort out in the middle of the desert? At **Fort Sesfontein** (☎ 065-275534; www.fort-sesfontein.com; r per person N$780;), you and 63 other guests can live out all your Lawrence of Arabia fantasies! Accommodation is basic, but incredibly atmospheric, and there is a good restaurant here that serves German-inspired dishes.

The road between Palmwag and Sesfontein is good gravel, and you'll only have problems if the Hoanib River is flowing. Unless it has been raining, the gravel road from Sesfontein to Opuwo is accessible to all vehicles.

KAOKOVELD

☎ 065

The northwest corner of the country represents Namibia at its most primeval. The Kaokoveld (also known as the Kaokoland) is a vast repository of desert mountains that is crossed only by sandy tracks laid down by

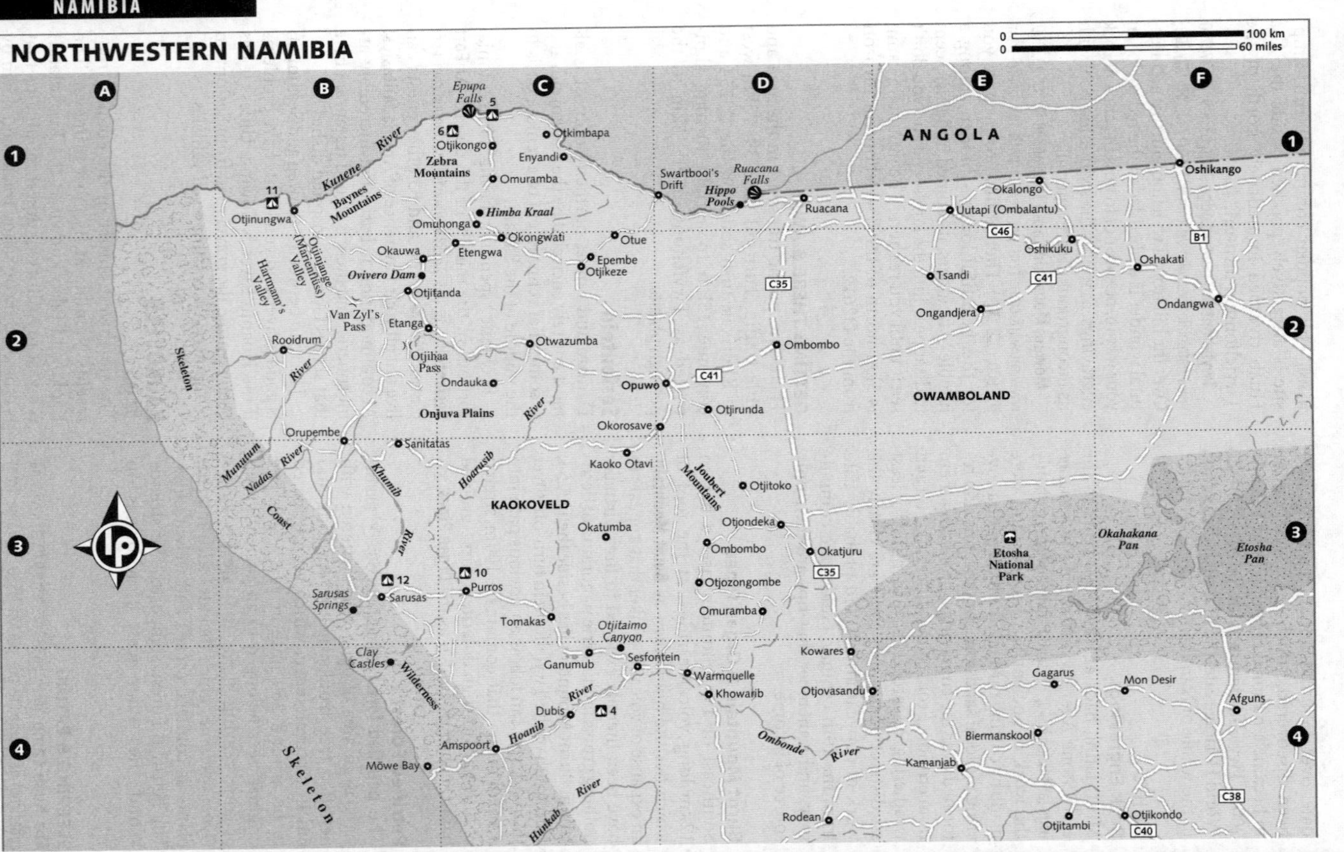
NORTHWESTERN NAMIBIA
0 100 km
0 60 miles
A
B
C
D
E
F
1
2
3
4
ANGOLA
Epupa Falls
5
6
Otkimbapa
Otjikongo
Enyandi
Zebra Mountains
Omuramba
Kunene River
Baynes Mountains
11
Otjinungwa
Himba Kraal
Omuhonga
Okongwati
Otue
Okauwa
Etengwa
Epembe
Otjikeze
Ovivero Dam
Otjitanda
Otjinjange (Marienflüss) Valley
Hartmann's Valley
Van Zyl's Pass
Etanga
Rooidrum
River
Otwazumba
Otjihaa Pass
Ondauka
Onjuva Plains
River
Skeleton
Swartbooi's Drift
Ruacana Falls
Hippo Pools
Ruacana
C35
Ombombo
C41
Opuwo
Otjirunda
Okorosave
Kaoko Otavi
Oshikango
Okalongo
Uutapi (Ombalantu)
C46
Oshikuku
B1
Oshakati
Tsandi
C41
Ongandjera
Ondangwa
OWAMBOLAND
Orupembe
Sanitatas
Munutum
Nadas River
Khumib
Hoarusib
Coast
KAOKOVELD
River
Joubert Mountains
Otjitoko
Otjondeka
Okatumba
Ombombo
Okatjuru
C35
Etosha National Park
Okahakana Pan
Etosha Pan
12
Sarusas Springs
Sarusas
10
Purros
Otjozongombe
Omuramba
Tomakas
Otjitaimo Canyon
Ganumub
Sesfontein
Kowares
Clay Castles
Wilderness
Warmquelle
Khowarib
Otjovasandu
Gagarus
Mon Desir
Afguns
River
Dubis
4
Hoanib
Amspoort
Möwe Bay
Skeleton
Ombonde River
Biermanskool
Kamanjab
Hunkab River
Rodean
Otjitambi
Otjikondo
C38
C40

Terrace Bay
C34
Torra Bay
Uniab River
Springbokwater
C39
Bergsig
Palmwag
C43
Skeleton Coast Park
Toscanini
Huab River
Ugabmund
Skeleton Coast Park Gate
Ugab River
Brandberg West
Messum Crater
Wondergat Sinkhole
Twyfelfontein
Organ Pipes
Burnt Mountain
Petrified Forest
Aba Huab River
Khorixas
Fransfontein
Gainatseb
C35
Vingerklip
Goreis
C39
Outjo
Ugab River
DAMARALAND
Brandberg (2573m)
Uis
C36
Okombache
Omaruru
C33
Neineis
Uigaran
Omaruru River
Spitzkoppe (1728m)
Klein Spitzkoppe (1584m)
Usakos
Karibib
To Windhoek (172km)
C32
Tsaobis Leopard Sanctuary
Tsaobis
Witwatersberge (1861m)
National West Coast Recreational Area
Cape Cross Seal Reserve
Henties Bay
B2
Trekkopje
Khan River
Arandis
Rössing
Nonidas
Swakop River
C28
Namib-Naukluft Park
Swakopmund
Walvis Bay
Wlotzkasbaken
C34
Coast
ATLANTIC OCEAN

SLEEPING

Aba Huab Camp	1	D5
Brandberg White Lady Lodge	2	E6
Cape Cross Lodge	3	D7
Elephant Song Camp	4	C4
Epupa Camp	5	C1
Epupa Falls Camp Site	6	C1
Jakkalsputz Camp Site	7	E8
Mile 108 Camp Site	8	D7
Mowani Mountain Camp	9	E5
Ngatutunge Pamwe Camp Site	10	C3
Okarohombo Camp Site	11	B1
Omarunga Camp	(see 6)	
Skeleton Coast Wilderness Camp	12	B3
Spitzkoppe Rest Camp	13	E7
Twyfelfontein Country Lodge	14	D6
Ugab River Camp Site	15	D6

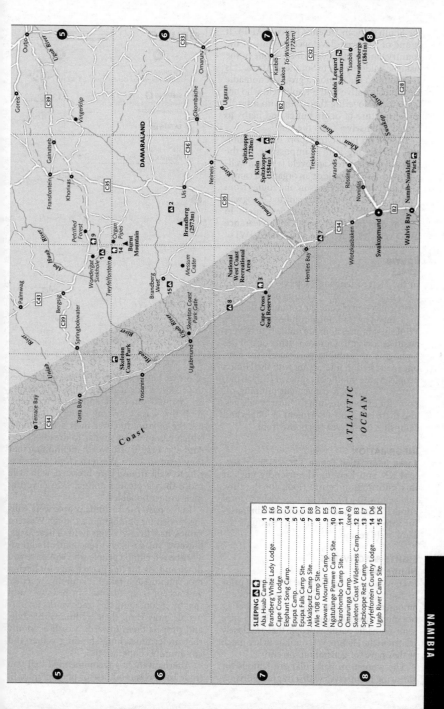

the South African Defence Force (SADF). It is one of the least-developed regions of the country, and is often described as one of the last true wildernesses in Southern Africa. It is also home to the Himba, a group of nomadic pastoralists native to the Kaokoveld who are famous for covering their skin with a traditional mixture of ochre butter and herbs to protect themselves from the sun.

There's no public transport in the region and hitchhiking is near impossible, so the best way to explore Kaokoveld is with a well-outfitted 4WD vehicle or an organised camping safari. In the dry season, the routes from Opuwo to Epupa Falls, Ruacana to Okongwati (via Swartbooi's Drift) and Sesfontein to Purros may be passable with high-clearance 2WD vehicles, otherwise, you'll need 4WD.

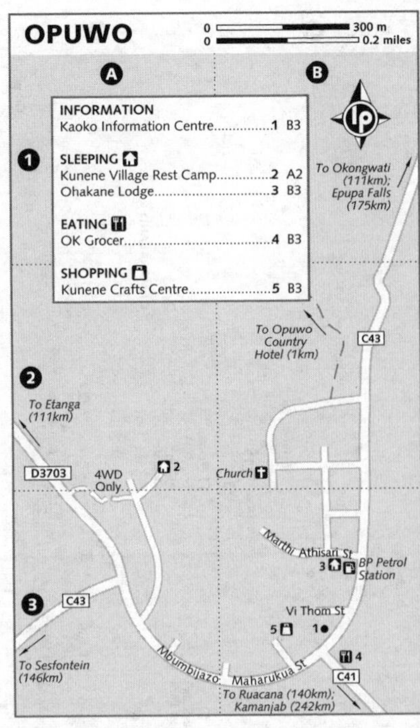

Opuwo

☎ 065

In the Herero language, Opuwo means 'the end', which is certainly a fitting name for this dusty collection of concrete commercial buildings ringed by traditional rondavels and huts. While first impressions are unlikely to be very positive, a visit to Opuwo is truly one of the highlights of Namibia, particularly for anyone interested in interacting with the Himba people. As the unofficial capital of Himbaland, Opuwo serves as a convenient jumping-off point for excursions into the nearby villages, and there is a good assortment of lodges and campsites in the area to choose from.

INFORMATION

Kaoko Information Centre (☎ 273420; 8am-6pm) KK and Kemuu, the friendly guys at this information centre (look for the tiny, tiny yellow shack), can arrange visits to local Himba villages in addition to providing useful information for your trip through the Kaokoveld region.

SIGHTS & ACTIVITIES

Himba Visits

Even if you've never heard of the Himba prior to visiting Namibia, you'll quickly become enamoured of them. An ethnic group numbering not more than 50,000 people, the Himba are a semi-nomadic pastoral people that are closely related to the Herero, yet continue to live much as they have for generations on end.

The women in particular are famous for smearing themselves with a fragrant mixture of ochre, butter and bush herbs, which dyes their skin a burnt-orange hue, and serves as a natural sun block and insect repellent. As if this wasn't striking enough, they also use the mixture to cover their braided hair, which has an effect similar to dreadlocking. And of course, it also worth mentioning that they tend to shun Western clothes, preferring to walk around bare-breasted, with little more than a pleated-animal skin covering their unmentionables.

In the past, rural Himba people were willing models for photography, though Western values had firmly taken hold. These days, however, you are likely to encounter traditionally dressed Himba people who will wave you down and ask for tips in exchange for having their photograph taken. Naturally, whether you accept is up to you, but bear in mind that by encouraging this trade works to draw people away from their traditional lifestyle, and propels them towards a cash economy that undermines long-standing values and community cooperation.

Alternatively, it's recommended that you trade basic commodities for photographs. In times of plenty, Himba grow maize to supplement their largely meat- and milk-based diet, though rain is highly unpredictable in Namibia. Pap (mealie meal) is a very desirable gift for the Himba, as are rice, bread, potatoes and other starches. Try to resist giving sugar, soft drinks and other sweets as the majority of Himba may never meet a dentist in their lifetime.

All throughout Opuwo, you will see Himba wherever you go – they will be walking the streets, shopping in the stores and even waiting in line behind you at the supermarket! However tempting it might be, please do not sneak a quick picture of them as no one appreciates having a camera unwillingly waved in front of their face.

If you would like to have free rein with the camera, visiting a traditional village – if done in the proper fashion – can yield some truly amazing shots. Needless to say, a guide who speaks both English and the Himba language is essential to the experience. There are a few ways to go about this: you can either join an organised tour through your accommodation, stop by the Kaoko Information Centre (opposite) or find an independent guide somewhere in Opuwo.

Before arriving in the village, please do spend some time shopping for gifts – entering a village with food items will garner a warm welcome from the villagers, who will subsequently be more willing to tolerate photography. At the end of your time in the village, buying small bracelets and trinkets direct from the artisans is also a greatly appreciated gesture.

Finally, don't be afraid to ask lots of questions with the aid of your translator, and spend some time interacting with the Himba rather than just photographing them. Showing respect and admiration helps the Himba reinforce their belief that their traditions and way of life are something worth preserving.

SLEEPING

Kunene Village Rest Camp (☎ 273043; www.nacobta.com.na; campsite per person N$40, s/d huts N$140/170) This amenable community-run rest camp has well-groomed campsites with adequate facilities as well as basic thatched huts with shared bathrooms. Follow the signposted turn-off from the government housing project at the edge of town, en route to Sesfontein.

Opuwo Country Hotel (☎ 61-374750; www.namibialodges.com/opuwo.html; campsite per person N$125, s/d N$1234/1748;) This enormous thatched building elegantly lords over the town below. Accommodation is in a handful of exclusive bungalows facing out across the valley towards the Angolan foothills, though most of your time here will be spent soaking your cares away in the infinity edge pool. Even if you can't afford a bungalow here, consider pitching a tent in their secluded campsite, which grants you full access to the hotel's amenities, including a fully stocked wine bar and a regal dining hall.

Ohakane Lodge (☎ 273031; www.natron.net/tour/ohakane/lodgee.html; s/d N$450/800;) This well-established and centrally located lodge sits along the main drag in Opuwo, and has fairly standard but fully modern rooms.

SHOPPING

Kunene Crafts Centre (☎ 273209; 8am-5pm Mon-Fri, 9am-1pm Sat) Opuwo's brightly painted self-help curio shop sells local arts and crafts on consignment. You'll find all sorts of Himba adornments smeared with ochre: conch-shell pendants, wrist bands, chest pieces and even the head-dresses worn by Himba brides. There's also a range of original jewellery, appliquéd pillowslips, Himba and Herero dolls, drums and wooden carvings.

GETTING THERE & AWAY

The marvellously paved C41 runs from Outjo to Opuwo, which makes Himbaland accessible even to 2WD vehicles. Although there is a temptation to speed along this long and lonely highway, keep your lead foot off the pedal north of the veterinary control fence as herds of cattle commonly stray across the road. If you're heading deeper into the Kaokoveld, be advised that Opuwo is the last opportunity to buy petrol before Kamanjab, Ruacana or Sesfontein.

Epupa Falls

At Epupa, which means 'Falling Waters' in Herero, the Kunene River fans out into a vast floodplain, and is ushered through a 500m-wide series of parallel channels, dropping a total of 60m over 1.5km. The greatest single drop, an estimated 37m, is commonly identified as the Epupa Falls. Here the river tumbles into a dark, narrow, rainbow-wrapped cleft, which is a spectacular sight.

SIGHTS & ACTIVITIES

During periods of low water, the **pools** above the Epupa Falls make fabulous natural

LOCAL VOICES: THE HIMBA IN THEIR OWN WORDS

Queen Elizabeth is a Himba woman who was born in a small village just outside Opuwo, but now works in town as an independent tour guide. While showing us around her birthplace, she helped us understand a bit more about what it means to be Himba.

What do the Himba like to eat? We keep all sorts of animals, so there is always milk and meat in the villages. Our water is only from rain. No rain, no crops. But this year we had so much rain, so look at all this maize we have now! You see this structure here? It's made from sand and cow dung and mopane wood, the same as our houses. We dry the corn here, and keep it for eating and for planting. We also mash the maize on stones to make mealie meal, which we boil and mix with bush herbs. Of course we prefer to eat meat, but maize keeps our bellies full when we get hungry.

What beliefs are important to the Himba? The holy fire at the centre of each village is very important to us. Our chief watches over the holy fire and talks to our ancestors through the flame. When you get married, you pray to the holy fire for good life. When a baby is born, you ask the holy fire to give the child a good name. Actually, today is a special day because twin calves were born, which is very lucky for us! So, tonight we will light the holy fire and have a ceremony to honour them. You see, cows are very important to our people. When you turn 11, we take out the bottom four teeth. It's painful my dear! But we admire cows and we take after the cows so we like to have the same mouth as them. We also circumcise our boys. They don't like it of course! They can't walk for a few days, but we rub mopane leaves on the cut to stop infection.

What is the secret to your beauty? We Himba women have pride because of our beauty. We still cover our bodies with powdered ochre, which we get from a few secret places. Actually, the best stuff comes from Angola! We never take a shower, forever. So, we mix the powder with cow butter and special perfume we make from herbs, so we can smell nice. The colour is also important to us. Our bodies turn the same colour as the red earth, which is where all life comes from. We also like big, big hair. We style our hair with oil and ochre, but it's not always big enough. So we can buy extensions in the market place and we weave this into our hair.

What about your jewellery? Our jewellery is made from beads and wires and cowrie shells. You see these ankle bracelets – one stripe means you have no children or one baby, two stripes means you have two or more. These anklets also protect our legs from snakebites when we're out in the bush. After a woman's first menstruation, we have a big party, and the woman goes to the special menstruation hut. Then we make her a special head-dress and sometimes a skirt out of lambskin. She can also start wearing metal belts instead of plastic belts. So you see, you can tell a lot about a woman just by looking at her dress!

If you'd like to visit a local Himba village with the Queen, you can either phone her at ☎ 081-2138326, or look for her outside the OK Grocer at the entrance to Opuwo.

Jacuzzis. You're safe from crocodiles in the eddies and rapids, but hang onto the rocks and keep away from the lip of the falls; once you're caught by the current, there's no way to prevent being swept over. Every couple of years, some unfortunate locals and foreign tourists drown in the river, and it's difficult at best to retrieve their bodies. Swimming here is most definitely not suitable for children.

There's also excellent **hiking** along the river west of the falls, and plenty of mountains to climb, affording panoramic views along the river and far into Angola. Keen hikers can manage the route along the 'Namibian Riviera' from Swartbooi's Drift to Epupa Falls (93km, five days) or from Ruacana to Epupa Falls (150km, eight days). You're never far from water, but there are lots of crocodiles and, even in the winter, the heat can be oppressive and draining. It's wise to go by the full moon, when you can beat the heat by walking at night.

SLEEPING

Epupa Falls Campsite (Map pp338-9; ☎ 695 1065; www.nacobta.com.na; campsite per person N$50) This community-run camp has hot showers and flush toilets, and is conveniently located right at the falls. Unfortunately, it can get very crowded and extremely noisy as it tends to get colonised by the overland crowd.

Omarunga Camp (Map pp338-9; ☎ 064-403096; www.natron.net/omarunga-camp/main.html; campsite per person N$80, s/d tents with half board N$935/1610) This German-run camp operates through a concession granted by a local chief, and has a well-groomed campsite with modern facilities as well as a handful of luxury tents.

Epupa Camp (Map pp338-9; ☎ 061-232740; www.epupa.com.na; s/d full board N$1499/1999; 🍴) Located 800m upstream from the falls, this former engineering camp for a now-shelved hydroelectric project has been converted into a beautifully situated luxury camp among a grove of towering baobab trees.

GETTING THERE & AWAY

The road from Okongwati is accessible to high-clearance 2WD vehicles, but it's still quite rough. The rugged 93km 4WD river route from Swartbooi's Drift may take several days, and it's far quicker to make the trip via Otjiveze/Epembe.

The Northwest Corner

West of Epupa Falls is the Kaokoveld of travellers' dreams: stark, rugged desert peaks, vast landscapes, sparse scrubby vegetation, drought-resistant wildlife and nomadic bands of Himba people and their tiny settlements of beehive huts. This region, which is contiguous with the Skeleton Coast Wilderness, has now been designated as the Kaokoveld Conservation Area.

SIGHTS

Van Zyl's Pass

The beautiful but frightfully steep and challenging Van Zyl's Pass forms a dramatic transition between the Kaokoveld plateaus and the vast, grassy expanses of Marienflüss. This winding 13km stretch isn't suitable for trailers and may only be passed from east to west, which means you'll have to return either via Otjihaa Pass or through Purros.

Otjinjange & Hartmann's Valleys

Allow plenty of time to explore the wild and magical Otjinjange (better known as Marienflüss) and Hartmann's Valleys – broad sandy and grassy expanses descend gently to the Kunene River. Note that camping outside campsites is prohibited at either valley.

SLEEPING

Except for in Otjinjange and Hartmann's Valleys, unofficial bush camping is possible throughout the Northwest Corner.

Okarohombo Camp Site (Map pp338-9; www.nacobta.com.na; campsite per person N$50) This community-run campsite is at the mouth of the Otjinjange Valley. Facilities are limited to long-drop toilets and a water tap, and you must be entirely self-sufficient.

Ngatutunge Pamwe Camp Site (Map pp338-9; www.nacobta.com.na; campsite per person N$50; 🍴) Another community-run campsite, Ngatutunge is perched along the Hoarusib River in Purros, and surprisingly has hot showers, flush toilets, well-appointed bungalows, a communal kitchen and (believe it or not!) a swimming pool.

Elephant Song Camp (Map pp338-9; ☎ 064-403829; www.nacobta.com.na; campsite per person N$50) Yet another community-run campsite, Elephant Song is in the Palmwag Concession, a very rough 25km down the Hoanib River from Sesfontein.

GETTING THERE & AWAY

From Okongwati, the westward route through Etengwa leads to either Van Zyl's Pass or Otjihaa Pass. From Okauwa (with a landmark broken windmill) to the road fork at Otjitanda (which is a Himba chief's *kraal*), the route is extremely rough and slow-going – along the way, stop for a swim at beautiful Ovivero Dam. From Otjitanda, you must decide whether you're heading west over Van Zyl's Pass (which may only be traversed from east to west) into Otjinjange and Hartmann's Valleys, or south over the equally beautiful but much easier Otjihaa Pass towards Orupembe.

You can also access Otjinjange and Hartmann's Valleys without crossing Van Zyl's Pass by turning north at the three-way junction in the middle of the Onjuva Plains, 12km north of Orupembe. At the T-junction in Rooidrum (Red Drum), you can decide which valley you want. Turn right for Otjinjange and left for Hartmann's. West of this junction, 17km from Rooidrum, you can also turn south along the fairly good route to Orupembe,

Purros (provided that the Hoarusib River isn't flowing) and on to Sesfontein.

SKELETON COAST

The term 'Skeleton Coast' is derived from the treacherous nature of the coast – a foggy region with rocky and sandy coastal shallows that has long been a graveyard for unwary ships and their crews. Early Portuguese sailors called it *As Areias do Inferno* (the Sands of Hell) as once a ship washed ashore, the fate of the crew was sealed.

Although it has been extrapolated to take in the entire Namib Desert coastline, the Skeleton Coast actually refers to the coastal stretch between the mouths of the Swakop and Kunene Rivers. For our purposes, it covers the National West Coast Recreation Area and the Skeleton Coast Park (including the Skeleton Coast Wilderness). These protected areas stretch from just north of Swakopmund to the Kunene River, taking in nearly two million hectares of dunes and gravel plains to form one of the world's most inhospitable waterless areas.

National West Coast Recreation Area

☎ 064

A 200km-long, 25km-wide strip from Swakopmund to the Ugab River, the National West Coast Recreation Area makes up the southern end of the Skeleton Coast. It's extremely popular with anglers and wildlife watchers alike, and it's convenient to visit since you don't need to arrange a permit in advance, unlike other destinations along the Skeleton Coast.

Most visitors head for the **Cape Cross Seal Reserve** (admission N$45; 10am-5pm), where the seal population has grown large and fat by taking advantage of the rich concentrations of fish in the cold Benguela Current. The sight of more than 100,000 seals basking on the beach and frolicking in the surf is an impressive sight to behold, though you're going to have to contend with overwhelming piles and piles of stinky seal poo. There's a basic snack bar with public toilets. No pets or motorcycles are permitted and visitors may not cross the low barrier between the seal-viewing area and the rocks where the colony lounges.

For keen hikers, a new **40km trail** begins at the southern end of Henties Bay and follows the coast south to Jakkalsputz (Jackals' Well), then back north to the Omaruru River mouth. Highlights include the sand dunes, freshwater springs and fields of desert lichen that flank the route.

SLEEPING

Jakkalsputz Campsite (Map pp338-9; per person N$30) Around 9km south of Henties Bay is a bleak strip of beach that is completely exposed to the wind, sand and drizzle. Having said that, this is one of the world's more unusual places to pitch a tent.

De Duine Country Hotel (☎ 061-374750; www.namibialodges.com; s/d from N$485/700) The most established hotel in Henties Bay, sits on the coast, though not a single room has a sea view – go figure that! The German colonial-style property does, however, feature rooms with swimming pool and garden views.

Cape Cross Lodge (Map pp338-9; ☎ 064-694012; www.capecross.org; standard/luxury r with half board per person from N$750/935) The odd but strangely appealing architecture is self-described as a cross between Cape Dutch and fishing village style, but it's actually very well designed and properly sheltered from the bleating seal colony.

Skeleton Coast National Park

At Ugabmund, 110km north of Cape Cross, the salt road passes through the entry gate to the Skeleton Coast National Park. UK journalist Nigel Tisdall once wrote: 'If hell has a coat of arms, it probably looks like the entrance to Namibia's Skeleton Coast Park'. If the fog is rolling in and the sand is blowing, you're likely to agree with that assessment.

Despite the enduring fame of this coastline, surprisingly few travellers ever reach points north of Cape Cross. The reason: in order to preserve this incredibly fragile environment, Namibian Wildlife Resorts (NWR) imposes very strict regulations on individual travellers seeking to enter the park.

Although this can be a deterrent for some people, permits are easily obtainable if you do a bit of advance planning. And, while you may have to sacrifice a bit of spontaneity to gain admittance to the park, the enigmatic Skeleton Coast really does live up to all the hype.

ORIENTATION & INFORMATION

The zone south of the Hoanib River is open to individual travellers, but you will need a permit, which costs N$80 per person and N$10 per vehicle per day. These are available through the NWR office in Windhoek (p305).

Accommodation is available only at Terrace Bay and Torra Bay (the latter is open only in December and January), either of which must be booked at NWR concurrently with your permit. To stay in either camp, you must pass the Ugabmund entrance before 3pm and/or Springbokwater before 5pm.

No day visits to the park are allowed, but you can obtain a transit permit to pass between Ugabmund and Springbokwater, which can be purchased at the gates. To transit the park, you must pass the entry gate before 1pm, and exit through the other before 3pm the same day. Note that transit permits aren't valid for Torra Bay or Terrace Bay.

ACTIVITIES

The 50km-long **Ugab River Guided Hiking Route** is open to groups of between six and eight people on the second and fourth Tuesday of each month from April to October. Hikes start at 9am from Ugabmund and finish on Thursday afternoons. Most hikers stay 40km south of Ugabmund on Monday night at the **Mile 108 Campsite** (Map pp338-9; per person N$30), which allows you to arrive at Ugabmund in time for the hike. The hike costs N$200 per person and must be booked through NWR – hikers must provide and carry their own food and camping equipment. The route begins by crossing the coastal plain, then climbs into the hills and follows a double loop through lichen fields and past caves, natural springs and unusual geological formations.

SLEEPING

All accommodation (with the exception of the Ugab River Camp Site) must be booked through NWR.

Ugab River Camp Site (Map pp338-9; www.rhino-trust.org.na; campsite per person N$50) Outside the Skeleton Coast Park, this campsite is administered by the Save the Rhino Trust. It's also one of the best places in Namibia to see the elusive black rhino – multiday rhino tracking expeditions can be arranged, though you must book in advance and supply your own food, water and camping gear. To get there, turn east onto the D2303, 67km north of Cape Cross; it's then 76km to the camp.

Torra Bay Camping Ground (per person N$50; ⌚ Dec & Jan only) This campsite, which is open to coincide with the Namibian school holidays, is flanked by a textbook field of barchan dunes. Torra Bay is 215km north of Cape Cross.

Terrace Bay Resort (s/d N$950/1400, 8-person beach chalet N$3200) Open year-round, this resort is a luxurious alternative to camping at Torra Bay. Terrace Bay is 49km north of Torra Bay.

GETTING THERE & AWAY

The Skeleton Coast Park is accessed via the salt road from Swakopmund, which ends 70km north of Terrace Bay. The park is also accessible via the C39 gravel road that runs between Khorixas and Torra Bay. Note that motorcycles are not permitted in the Skeleton Coast Park. Hitchhikers may be discouraged by the bleak landscape, cold sea winds, fog, sandstorms and sparse traffic.

Skeleton Coast Wilderness Area

The Skeleton Coast Wilderness Area, stretching between the Hoanib and Kunene Rivers, makes up the northern third of the Skeleton Coast. This section of coastline is among the most remote and inaccessible areas in Namibia, though it's here in the wilderness that you can truly live out your Skeleton Coast fantasies. Since the entire area is a private concession, you're going to have to part with some serious cash to visit.

If your budget stretches this far, the **Skeleton Coast Wilderness Camp** (Map pp338-9; ☎ 061-274500; www.wilderness-safaris.com; 4-/5-day trips per person from US$2500/3000) offers mind-blowing activities including viewing desert elephants along the Hoarusib, ocean fishing, dune climbing, hiking through the Clay Castles and basking in veritable isolation.

The Skeleton Coast Wilderness Area is closed to private vehicles. Access is restricted to fly-in trips operated by **Wilderness Safaris** (www.wilderness-safaris.com). The flights in and out travel one way over the Kaokoveld highlands and the other way along the Skeleton Coast.

CENTRAL NAMIBIA

Central Namibia is defined by the barren and desolate landscapes of the Namib Desert. The Nama word 'Namib', which inspired the name of the entire country, rather prosaically means 'Vast Dry Plain'. Nowhere is this truer than at Sossusvlei, Namibia's most famous strip of sand, where gargantuan dunes tower more than 300m above the underlying strata. Although it's difficult to imagine that civilisation could flourish in such a harsh and unforgiving environment, Central Namibia is home to two large cities, Walvis Bay and Swakopmund, which were originally established as port towns during the colonial era.

SWAKOPMUND

☎ 064

Often described as being more German than Germany, Swakopmund is a quirky mix of German-Namibian residents and overseas German tourists, who feel right at home with the town's pervasive *Gemütlichkeit*, a distinctively German appreciation of comfort and hospitality. With its seaside promenades, half-timbered homes and colonial-era buildings, it seems that only the wind-blown sand and the palm trees distinguish Swakop from holiday towns along Germany's North Sea and Baltic coasts.

Swakop is Namibia's most popular holiday destination, and it attracts surfers, anglers and beach lovers from all over Southern Africa. However, the city has recently reinvented itself as the adventure sports capital of Namibia, and now attracts adrenaline junkies jonesing for a quick fix. Whether you slide down the dunes on a greased-up snowboard, or go against your survival instincts by hurling yourself out of a Cessna, Swakop has no shortage of gut-curdling activities to choose from.

Information

BOOKSHOPS

CNA Bookshop (Hendrick Witbooi St) Sells popular paperbacks.

Die Muschel Book & Art Shop (☎ 402874; Roon St) Esoteric works on art and local history are available here.

Swakopmunder Buchhandlung (☎ 402613; Sam Nujoma Ave) A wide selection of literature from various genres.

EMERGENCY

Ambulance (☎ 405731)

Fire brigade (☎ day 402411, after-hours pager 405544).

Police (☎ 10111)

INTERNET ACCESS

Swakopmunder I-café (Tobias Hainyeko St; per hr US$2; ⏰ 7am-10pm Mon-Sat, 10am-10pm Sun)

MEDICAL SERVICES

Bismarck Medical Centre (☎ 405000; Bismarck St) For doctors' visits, see the recommended Drs Swiegers, Schikerling, Dantu and Biermann, all at this centre.

MONEY

Bureau de Change (Sam Nujoma Ave; ⏰ 7am-7pm daily) The most convenient option for changing money. Charges no commission to change travellers cheques – the catch is that you'll need the slips verifying proof of purchase.

POST

Main post office (Garnison St) Also sells telephone cards and offers fax services.

TOURIST INFORMATION

Namib-i (☎ 404827; www.namibi.org; Sam Nujoma Ave, PO Box 829; ⏰ 8am-1pm & 2-5pm Mon-Fri, 9am-noon & 3.30-5.30pm Sat, 9.30am-noon & 3.30-5pm Sun) This tourist information centre is a very helpful resource. In addition to helping you get your bearings, they can also act as a booking agent for any activities and tours that happen to take your fancy.

Namibia Wildlife Resorts (NWR; ☎ 204172; www.nwr.com.na; Woermannhaus, Bismarck St; ⏰ 8am-1pm & 2-5pm Mon-Fri) Like its big brother in Windhoek (see p305), this office sells Namib-Naukluft Park and Skeleton Coast permits, and can also make reservations for any NWR-administered property in the country.

Dangers & Annoyances

Although the palm-fringed streets and cool sea breezes in Swakopmund are unlikely to make you tense, you should always keep your guard up in town. Regardless of how relaxed the ambience might be, petty crime is unfortunately on the rise.

If you have a private vehicle, never leave your car unattended. Also, when you're choosing a hotel or hostel, be sure that the security precautions (ie an electric fence and/or a guard) are up to your standards. Finally, although Swakopmund is generally safe at night, it's best to stay in a group and, when possible, take a taxi to and from your accommodation.

Sights

HISTORICAL BUILDINGS

Woermannhaus

From the shore, the delightful German-style Woermannhaus, on Bismarck St, stands out from surrounding buildings. Built in 1905 as the main offices of the Damara & Namaqua Trading Company, it was taken over four years later by the Woermann & Brock Trading Company, which supplied the current name. In the 1920s, it was used as a school dormitory, and later served as a merchant sailors' hostel. It now houses the **Swakopmund Military Museum**

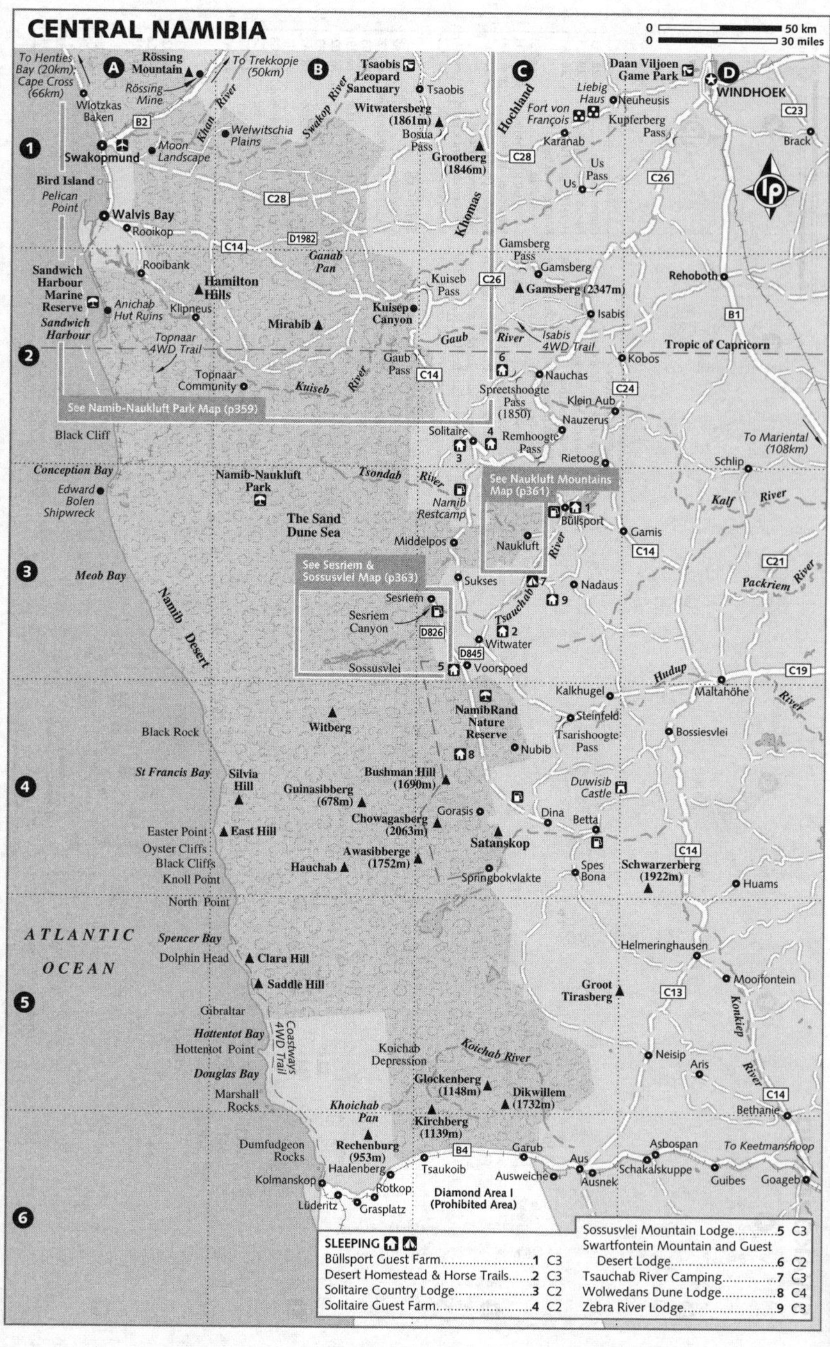
CENTRAL NAMIBIA
0 50 km
0 30 miles
To Henties Bay (20km); Cape Cross (66km)
Rössing Mountain
Rössing Mine
To Trekkopje (50km)
Tsaobis Leopard Sanctuary
Tsaobis
Wlotzkas Baken
Swakopmund
Moon Landscape
Welwitschia Plains
Khan River
Swakop River
Witwatersberg (1861m)
Bosua Pass
Grootberg (1846m)
Hochland
Daan Viljoen Game Park
WINDHOEK
Liebig Haus
Neuheusis
Fort von François
Kupferberg Pass
Karanab
Us Pass
Us
Brack
Bird Island
Pelican Point
Walvis Bay
Rooikop
Khomas
Ganab Pan
Gamsberg Pass
Gamsberg
Gamsberg (2347m)
Rooibank
Sandwich Harbour Marine Reserve
Hamilton Hills
Kuiseb Pass
Rehoboth
Anichab Hut Ruins
Klipneus
Sandwich Harbour
Kuisep Canyon
Mirabib
Isabis
Isabis 4WD Trail
Topnaar 4WD Trail
Gaub River
Tropic of Capricorn
Kobos
Gaub Pass
Nauchas
Topnaar Community
Kuiseb River
Spreetshoogte Pass (1850)
Klein Aub
See Namib-Naukluft Park Map (p359)
Nauzerus
Black Cliff
Solitaire
Remhoogte Pass
To Mariental (108km)
Rietoog
Schlip
Conception Bay
Namib-Naukluft Park
Tsondab River
See Naukluft Mountains Map (p361)
Edward Bolen Shipwreck
Namib Restcamp
Kalf River
Büllsport
The Sand Dune Sea
Gamis
Middelpos
Naukluft
River
Meob Bay
See Sesriem & Sossusvlei Map (p363)
Sukses
Nadaus
Packriem River
Sesriem
Sesriem Canyon
Tsauchab
Namib Desert
Witwater
Sossusvlei
Voorspoed
Hudup
Maltahöhe
Kalkhugel
River
Steinfeld
NamibRand Nature Reserve
Tsarishoogte Pass
Bossiesvlei
Black Rock
Witberg
Nubib
St Francis Bay
Silvia Hill
Bushman Hill (1690m)
Guinasibberg (678m)
Duwisib Castle
Gorasis
Dina
Betta
Chowagasberg (2063m)
Easter Point
East Hill
Satanskop
Oyster Cliffs
Awasibberge (1752m)
Black Cliffs
Hauchab
Springbokvlakte
Spes Bona
Schwarzerberg (1922m)
Knoll Point
Huams
North Point
ATLANTIC OCEAN
Spencer Bay
Helmeringhausen
Dolphin Head
Clara Hill
Saddle Hill
Mooifontein
Groot Tirasberg
Gibraltar
Konkiep River
Hottentot Bay
Coastways 4WD Trail
Hottentot Point
Koichab Depression
Koichab River
Neisip
Douglas Bay
Aris
Glockenberg (1148m)
Marshall Rocks
Dikwillem (1732m)
Khoichab Pan
Kirchberg (1139m)
Bethanie
Dumfudgeon Rocks
Rechenburg (953m)
Garub
Asbospan
To Keetmanshoop
Haalenberg
Tsaukoib
Aus
Schakalskuppe
Ausweiche
Ausnek
Guibes
Goageb
Kolmanskop
Rotkop
Diamond Area I (Prohibited Area)
Lüderitz
Grasplatz
B2 C28 C14 D1982 C26 C23 B1 C24 C21 D826 D845 C19 C14 C13 B4
SLEEPING
Büllsport Guest Farm 1 C3
Desert Homestead & Horse Trails 2 C3
Solitaire Country Lodge 3 C2
Solitaire Guest Farm 4 C2
Sossusvlei Mountain Lodge 5 C3
Swartfontein Mountain and Guest Desert Lodge 6 C2
Tsauchab River Camping 7 C3
Wolwedans Dune Lodge 8 C4
Zebra River Lodge 9 C3
NAMIBIA

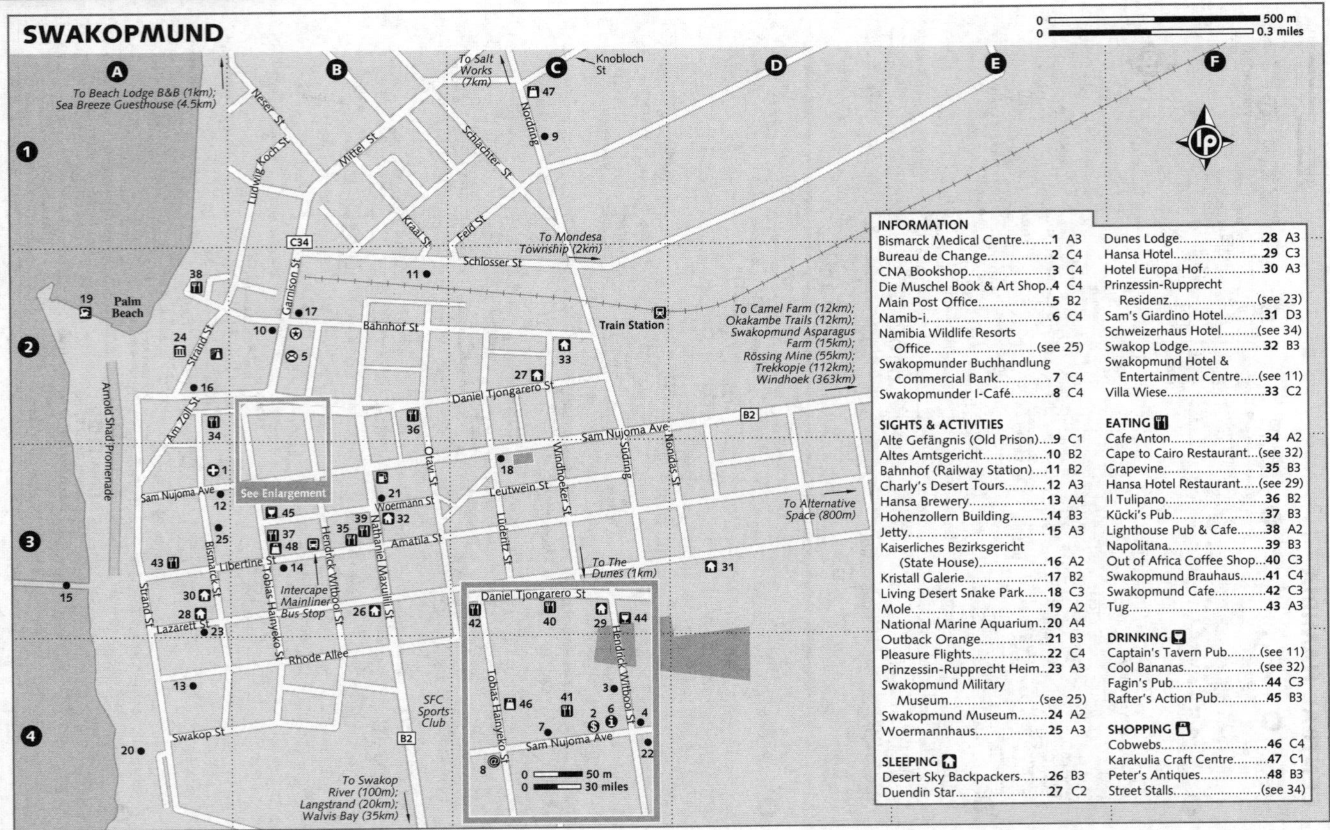
SWAKOPMUND
0 500 m
0 0.3 miles
A B C D E F
1 2 3 4
To Beach Lodge B&B (1km); Sea Breeze Guesthouse (4.5km)
To Salt Works (7km)
Knobloch St
Neser St
Ludwig Koch St
Mittel St
Schlachter St
Nordring
Kraal St
Feld St
To Mondesa Township (2km)
C34
Garnison St
Schlosser St
Palm Beach
Bahnhof St
Train Station
To Camel Farm (12km); Okakambe Trails (12km); Swakopmund Asparagus Farm (15km); Rössing Mine (55km); Trekkopje (112km); Windhoek (363km)
Strand St
Arnold Shad Promenade
Am Zoll St
Daniel Tjongarero St
B2
Sam Nujoma Ave
Otavi St
Südring
Nonidas St
Windhoeker St
See Enlargement
Leutwein St
Woermann St
Lüderitz St
To Alternative Space (800m)
Bismarck St
Libertine St
Tobias Hainyeko St
Hendrick Witbooi St
Nathaniel Maxuilili St
Amatila St
Intercape Mainliner Bus Stop
To The Dunes (1km)
Lazarett St
Rhode Allee
SFC Sports Club
Swakop St
To Swakop River (100m); Langstrand (20km); Walvis Bay (35km)
0 50 m
0 30 miles
INFORMATION
Bismarck Medical Centre.......1 A3
Bureau de Change.......2 C4
CNA Bookshop.......3 C4
Die Muschel Book & Art Shop..4 C4
Main Post Office.......5 B2
Namib-i.......6 C4
Namibia Wildlife Resorts Office.......(see 25)
Swakopmunder Buchhandlung Commercial Bank.......7 C4
Swakopmunder I-Café.......8 C4
SIGHTS & ACTIVITIES
Alte Gefängnis (Old Prison)....9 C1
Altes Amtsgericht.......10 B2
Bahnhof (Railway Station)....11 B2
Charly's Desert Tours.......12 A3
Hansa Brewery.......13 A4
Hohenzollern Building.......14 B3
Jetty.......15 A3
Kaiserliches Bezirksgericht (State House).......16 A2
Kristall Galerie.......17 B2
Living Desert Snake Park......18 C3
Mole.......19 A2
National Marine Aquarium..20 A4
Outback Orange.......21 B3
Pleasure Flights.......22 C4
Prinzessin-Rupprecht Heim..23 A3
Swakopmund Military Museum.......(see 25)
Swakopmund Museum.......24 A2
Woermannhaus.......25 A3
SLEEPING
Desert Sky Backpackers.......26 B3
Duendin Star.......27 C2
Dunes Lodge.......28 A3
Hansa Hotel.......29 C3
Hotel Europa Hof.......30 A3
Prinzessin-Rupprecht Residenz.......(see 23)
Sam's Giardino Hotel.......31 D3
Schweizerhaus Hotel.......(see 34)
Swakop Lodge.......32 B3
Swakopmund Hotel & Entertainment Centre.....(see 11)
Villa Wiese.......33 C2
EATING
Cafe Anton.......34 A2
Cape to Cairo Restaurant...(see 32)
Grapevine.......35 B3
Hansa Hotel Restaurant.....(see 29)
Il Tulipano.......36 B2
Kücki's Pub.......37 B3
Lighthouse Pub & Cafe.......38 A2
Napolitana.......39 B3
Out of Africa Coffee Shop...40 C3
Swakopmund Brauhaus.......41 C4
Swakopmund Cafe.......42 C3
Tug.......43 A3
DRINKING
Captain's Tavern Pub.......(see 11)
Cool Bananas.......(see 32)
Fagin's Pub.......44 C3
Rafter's Action Pub.......45 B3
SHOPPING
Cobwebs.......46 C4
Karakulia Craft Centre.......47 C1
Peter's Antiques.......48 B3
Street Stalls.......(see 34)

(admission N$10; ⌚ 10am-noon Mon & Tue, Thu-Sat & 3-6pm Mon-Thu) and a gallery of historic paintings.

The Jetty

In 1905, the need for a good cargo- and passenger-landing site led Swakopmund's founders to construct the original wooden pier. In the years that followed, it was battered by the high seas and damaged by woodworm, and in 1911 construction began on a 500m iron jetty. When the South African forces occupied Swakopmund, the port became redundant (they already controlled Walvis Bay), so the old wooden pier was removed in 1916, and the unfinished iron pier was left to the elements.

The Mole

In 1899, architect FW Ortloff's sea wall (better known as the Mole) was intended to enhance Swakopmund's poor harbour and create a mooring place for large cargo vessels. But Mr Ortloff was unfamiliar with the Benguela Current, which sweeps northwards along the coast, carrying with it a load of sand from the southern deserts. Within less than five years, the harbour entrance was choked off by a sand bank, and two years later the harbour itself had been invaded by sand to create what is now called Palm Beach. The Mole is currently used as a mooring for pleasure boats.

Altes Amtsgericht

This gabled building, on the corner of Garnison and Bahnhof Sts, was constructed in 1908 as a private school. When the funds ran out, the government took over the project and requisitioned it as a magistrates' court. In the 1960s it functioned as a school dormitory, and now houses municipal offices. Just so no one can doubt its identity, the words 'Altes Amtsgericht' (German for 'Old Magistrates' Court') are painted across the front.

Kaiserliches Bezirksgericht (State House)

This rather stately building on Daniel Tjongarero St was constructed in 1902 to serve as the district magistrates' court. It was extended in 1905 and again in 1945, when a tower was added. After WWI it was converted into the official holiday home of the territorial administrator. In keeping with that tradition, it's now the official Swakopmund residence of the president.

Bahnhof (Railway Station)

This ornate railway station, built in 1901 as the terminal for the Kaiserliche Eisenbahn Verwaltung (Imperial Railway Authority), connected Swakopmund to Windhoek. In 1910, when the railway closed down, the building assumed the role as main station for the narrow-gauge mine railway between Swakopmund and Otavi.

Prinzessin Rupprecht Heim

The single-storey Prinzessin Rupprecht Heim, on Lazarett St, was constructed in 1902 as a military hospital. In 1914 it was transferred to the Bavarian Women's Red Cross, which named it after its patron, Princess Rupprecht, wife of the Bavarian crown prince. The idea was to expose convalescents to the healthy effects of the sea breeze. The building currently operates as a hotel (see p353).

Alte Gefängnis (Old Prison)

This impressive 1909 structure, on Nordring St, was built as a prison, but if you didn't know this, you'd swear it was either an early train station or a health-spa hotel. The main building was used only for staff housing, while the prisoners were relegated to much less opulent quarters on one side.

Hohenzollern Building

This imposing baroque-style building, situated on Libertine St, was constructed in 1906 to serve as a hotel. Its rather outlandish decor is crowned by a fibreglass cast of Atlas supporting the world, which replaced the precarious cement version that graced the roof prior to renovations in 1988.

MUSEUMS & GALLERIES

Swakopmund Museum

When ill winds blow, head for this **museum** (☎ 402046; www.swakopmund-museum.org.na/english.htm; Strand St; adult/student N$18/12; ⌚ 10am-12.30pm & 3-5.30pm), at the foot of the lighthouse, where you can hole up and learn about the town history. The museum occupies the site of the old harbour warehouse, which was destroyed in 1914 by a 'lucky' shot from a British warship.

National Marine Aquarium

This waterfront **aquarium** (Strand St; admission N$30; ⌚ 10am-6pm Tue-Sat, 11am-5pm Sun, closed Mon except public holidays) provides an excellent introduction to the cold offshore world in the South Atlantic. Most impressive is the tunnel through the largest aquarium, which allows close-up views of graceful rays, toothy sharks (you can literally count all the teeth!) and other little marine beasties found on Namibia's seafood platters.

Kristall Galerie

This architecturally astute **gallery** (☎ 406080; Bahnhof St; admission N$20; 🕑 9am-5pm Mon-Sat) features some of the planet's most incredible crystal formations, including the largest quartz crystal that has ever been found. The adjacent shop sells lovely mineral samples, crystal jewellery, and intriguing plates, cups and wine glasses that are carved from the local stone.

Living Desert Snake Park

This **park** (☎ 405100; Sam Nujoma Ave; admission N$15; 🕑 8:30am-5pm Mon-Fri, 8.30am-3pm Sat & Sun) houses an array of serpentine sorts. The owner knows everything you'd ever want to know – or not know – about snakes, scorpions, spiders and other widely misunderstood creatures.

BEACHES & DUNES

Swakopmund is Namibia's main beach resort, but even in summer, the water is never warmer than around 15°C (remember, the Benguela Current sweeps upwards from Antarctica). Swimming in the sea is best in the lee of the Mole sea wall.

At the lagoon at the Swakop River mouth you can watch ducks, flamingos, pelicans, cormorants, gulls, waders and other birds. North of town you can stroll along miles and miles of deserted beaches stretching towards the Skeleton Coast. The best surfing is at Nordstrand or 'Thick Lip' near Vineta Point.

A fascinating short hike will take you across the Swakop River to the large dune fields south of town. The dune formations and unique vegetation are great for solo exploring.

HANSA BREWERY

Aficionados of the amber nectar will want to visit the **Hansa Brewery** (☎ 405021; 9 Rhode Allee; admission free), which is the source of Swakopmund's favourite drop. Free tours – with ample opportunity to sample the product – run on Tuesday and Thursday, but advance reservations are necessary.

AROUND SWAKOPMUND

Welwitschia Drive

This worthwhile excursion by vehicle or organised tour is recommended if you want to see one of Namibia's most unusual desert plants, the welwitschia. Welwitschias reach their greatest concentrations on the Welwitschia Plains east of Swakopmund, near the confluence of the Khan and Swakop Rivers, where they're the dominant plant species.

In addition to this wilted wonder, Welwitschia Drive also takes in grey and black **lichen fields**, which were featured in the BBC

THE MARTIN LUTHER

In the desert 4km east of Swakopmund, a lonely and forlorn steam locomotive languished for several years. The 14,000kg machine was imported to Walvis Bay from Halberstadt, Germany, in 1896 to replace the oxwagons used to transport freight between Swakopmund and the interior. However, its inauguration into service was delayed by the outbreak of the Nama–Herero wars and, in the interim, its locomotive engineer returned to Germany without having revealed the secret of its operation.

A US prospector eventually got it running, but it consumed enormous quantities of locally precious water. It took three months to complete its initial trip from Walvis Bay to Swakopmund, and subsequently survived just a couple of short trips before grinding to a halt just east of town. Clearly, this particular technology wasn't making life easier for anyone, and it was abandoned and dubbed the *Martin Luther,* in reference to the great reformer's famous words to the Diet of Reichstag in 1521: 'Here I stand. May God help me, I cannot do otherwise'.

Although the *Martin Luther* was partially restored in 1975, and concurrently declared a national monument, it continued to suffer from the ravages of nature. Fortunately, in 2005 students from the Namibian Institute of Mining and Technology restored the locomotive to its former grandeur. They also built a protective encasement that should keep the *Martin Luther* around at least for another century.

production *The Private Life of Plants*. It was here that David Attenborough pointed out these delightful examples of plant–animal symbiosis, which burst into 'bloom' with the addition of fog droplets. If you're not visiting during a fog, sprinkle a few drops of water on them and watch the magic.

Another interesting stop is the **Baaiweg (Bay Rd)**, the ox-wagon track that was historically used to move supplies between the coast and Central Namibia. The tracks remain visible because the lichen that were destroyed when it was built have grown back at a rate of only 1mm per year, and the ruts aren't yet obscured.

Further east is the **Moon Landscape**, a vista across eroded hills and valleys carved by the Swakop River. Here you may want to take a quick 12km return side trip north to the farm and oasis of **Goanikontes**, which dates from 1848. It lies beside the Swakop River amid fabulous desert mountains, and serves as an excellent picnic site.

To the east along the main loop is further evidence of human impact in the form of a **campsite** used by South African troops for a few days in 1915. They were clearly not minimum-impact campers!

A few kilometres beyond the South African troop camp, the route turns north. Shortly thereafter, you'll approach a prominent black **dolerite dyke** splitting a ridgetop. This was created when molten igneous material forced its way up through a crack in the overlying granite and cooled.

Camping is available at the **Welwitschia campsites** (campsite N$50, plus per person N$10), near the Swakop River crossing on the Welwitschia Plains detour, to parties of up to eight people. Book through Namibia Wildlife Resorts in either Windhoek (p305) or Swakopmund (p346).

The Welwitschia Drive, which turns off the Bosua Pass route east of Swakopmund, lies inside the Namib-Naukluft Park. Most often visited as a day trip from Swakopmund, the drive can be completed in two hours, but allow more time to experience this other-worldly landscape.

Swakopmund Salt Works

When the Klein family began extracting salt from here in 1933, it was thought that the area was nothing more than a low, salty depression along the desert coast. But when the **salt works** (☎ 402611; 🕑 Mon-Fri, reservations necessary) lasted for 20 years, they decided to excavate a series of shallow evaporation pans to concentrate and extract the minerals. Now, water is pumped into the pans directly from the sea and the onshore breeze provides an ideal catalyst for evaporation.

Rössing Mine

This **mine** (☎ 402046), 55km east of Swakopmund, is the world's largest open-cast uranium mine. Uranium was first discovered here in the 1920s by Peter Louw, though his attempts at developing the mine quickly failed. In 1965, the concession was transferred to Rio Tinto-Zinc, and comprehensive surveys determined that the formation measured 3km long and 1km wide. Ore extraction came on line in 1970, but didn't reach capacity for another eight years. The current scale of operations is staggering: at full capacity the mine produces one million tonnes of ore per week.

Three-hour **mine tours** (admission N$50) leave from Cafe Anton at 10am on the first and third Friday of each month; book in advance at the Swakopmund Museum. You can also arrange a visit through any of the companies listed under Tours, p352.

Swakopmund Asparagus Farm

You surely never thought that an **asparagus farm** (☎ 405134; admission free; 🕑 9am-4pm Mon-Fri) could be a tourist attraction, but Swakopmund's delicious green gold grows in the wildest desert, and makes for an interesting quick visit and taste test. To reach the farm, take the Windhoek road 11km east of town and turn off at El Jada; it's 4km from there.

Activities

After aspiring for years to become a dry version of Victoria Falls, Swakopmund is one of the top destinations in Southern Africa for extreme sports enthusiasts. Although filling your days with adrenaline-soaked activities is certainly not cheap, there are few places in the world where you can climb up, race down and soar over towering sand dunes.

Most activity operators don't have offices in town, which means that you need to arrange all of your activities through either your accommodation or the **Namib-i** (p346) tourist information centre.

Alternatively, you can stop by **Outback Orange** (p352). Although they specialise in quad biking (motorcycle-style 4WD), the friendly staff members here are more than happy to phone a few operators for you.

SANDBOARDING

Sandboarding with **Alter Action** (☎ 402737; lie-down/stand-up N$340/550) is certain to increase your heart rate while going easy on your wallet. If you have any experience snowboarding or surfing, it's highly recommended that you have a go at the stand-up option. You will be given a snowboard, gloves, goggles and enough polish to ensure a smooth ride. While you can't expect the same speeds as you would on the mountain, you can't beat the experience of carving a dune face, and falling on sand hurts a lot less than ice!

QUAD BIKING

Outback Orange (☎ 400968; www.outback-orange.com; 42 Nathaniel Maxulili St; 1-/2-hour trip N$250/395) offers stomach-dropping tours on quad bikes through the enormous dune field adjacent to Swakop. If you've ever wanted to re-create the *Star Wars* experience of riding a speeder through the deserts of Tatooine, this is your chance! In two hours, you'll travel over 60km and race up and down countless dunes, all the while enjoying panoramic views of sand and sea. These tours are definitely not for the weak-hearted as you can pick up some serious speed on these bikes, and there are plenty of hairpin turns and sheer drops to contend with throughout the trip.

SKYDIVING

Ground Rush Adventures (☎ 402841; www.skydiveswakop.com.na; tandem jump N$1900; handycam/professional video N$450/850) provides the ultimate rush, and skydiving in Swakopmund is sweetened by the outstanding dune and ocean backdrop. The crew at Ground Rush has an impeccable safety record to date, and they make even the most nervous participant feel comfortable about jumping out of a plane at 3000m and freefalling for 30 seconds at 220km/h. If you're having second thoughts about taking the plunge, know that your tandem master has been pulling the cord several times a day for years and years on end!

SCENIC FLIGHTS

Pleasure Flights (☎ 404500; www.pleasureflights.com.na; Sam Nujoma Ave; prices variable) One of the most reputable light-plane operators in Namibia, Pleasure Flights has been offering scenic aerial cruises for more than 15 years. Considering that so much of the South Atlantic coastline is inaccessible on the ground, taking to the skies is a wonderful way to appreciate the wild nature that typifies most of the region. Several uniquely designed routes are available for your choosing, which take in a range of destinations, including the Salt Works, Sandwich Harbour, Welwitschia Drive, the Brandberg mountains, Sossusvlei, the Skeleton Coast and beyond.

HORSE RIDING

Okakambe Trails (☎ 402799; www.okakambe.iway.na; prices variable) Meaning 'horse' in the local Herero and Oshivambo languages, Okakambe specialises in horse riding and trekking through the desert. The German owner cares immensely for her horses, so you can be assured that they're well fed and looked after. It's 12km east of Swakopmund on the D1901.

CAMEL RIDING

If you want to live out all your Lawrence of Arabia-inspired Saharan fantasies, visit the **Camel Farm** (Map p359; ☎ 400363; 🕑 2-5pm), which is adjacent to Okakambe Trails. After donning the necessary amount of Bedouin kitsch, you can mount your dromedary and make haste for the horizon. While camels run the gamut from uncouth to downright mean-tempered, don't underestimate their speed and grace!

Tours

If you've arrived in Swakopmund by public transport, and don't have access to a private vehicle, then consider booking a tour through one of the operators listed below. Downtown Swakop is compact and easy to walk around, but you need to escape the city confines if you really want to explore the area.

Prices are variable depending on the size of your party and the length of tour. As with activities in Swakop, money stretches further if you get together with a few friends, and combine a few destinations to make a longer outing.

Possible tours include a sundowner on the dunes, the Cape Cross Seal Reserve, Rössing Mine gem tours, Welwitschia Drive, Walvis Bay Lagoon and various destinations in the Namib Desert and Naukluft Mountains.

The most popular operators are **Charly's Desert Tours** (☎ 404341; www.charlysdeserttours.com; Sam Nujoma Ave), **Namib Tours and Safaris** (☎ 404072; www.namibia-tours-safaris.com) and **Turnstone Tours** (☎ 403123; www.turnstone-tours.com). With the exception of Charly's, the operators listed in this section do not have central offices, so it's best to make arrangements through your accommodation.

If you're interested in arranging a visit to the Mondesa township, **Hata-Angu Cultural Tours** (☎ 461118; www.culturalactivities.in.na) runs a variety of different excursions that provide insight into how the other half of Skakopmunders live.

Sleeping

BUDGET

Desert Sky Backpackers (☎ 402339; dsbackpackers@swakop.com; 35 Lazarett St; campsite per person N$50, dm N$60, r per person N$160;) This centrally located backpackers' haunt is an excellent place to drop anchor in Swakopmund. The indoor lounge is simple and homey, while the outdoor picnic tables are a nice spot for a cold beer and warm conversation.

Dunes Lodge (☎ 463139; www.dunes.com.na; 12 Lazarett St; campsite per person N$50, dm N$110, r from N$300;) The Dunes Lodge is an upmarket backpackers featuring a number of attractive perks, including an indoor pool and billiards table, as well as traditional backpacker amenities, such as a communal kitchen, internet, TV lounge and laundry service.

Villa Wiese & Duendin Star (☎ 407105; www.villawiese.com; cnr Bahnhof & Windhoeker Sts; dm N$110, s/d N$330/385;) Villa Wiese and the nearby Duendin Star are friendly and funky guest lodges occupying historic colonial mansions complete with vaulted ceilings, rock gardens and period furniture.

Swakop Lodge (☎ 402030; 14 Nathaniel Maxuilili St; dm N$135, s/d N$415/600;) This backpacker-orientated hotel is the epicentre of the action in Swakopmund, especially since this is where many of the adrenaline activities depart from and return to, and where many of the videos are screened each night.

Prinzessin-Rupprecht Residenz (☎ 412540; www.prinzrupp.com.na; 15 Lazarett St; s/d from N$290/570) Housed in the former colonial military hospital, this *pension* (boarding house) appeals to history buffs looking to catch a glimpse of the Swakopmund of old.

Alternative Space (☎ 402713; nam0352@mweb.com.na; 46 Dr Alfons Weber St; s/d from N$300/400;) On the desert fringe, 800m east of town, this delightfully alternative budget choice is run by Frenus and Sybille Rorich. The main attractions are the castle-like architecture, saturation artwork and an industrial scrap-recycling theme.

MIDRANGE & TOP END

Sea Breeze Guesthouse (☎ 463348; www.seabreeze.com.na; Turmalin St; s/d/tr N$260/520/780;) This very affordable guest house is right on the beach about 4.5km north of town, and is an excellent option if you're looking for a secluded retreat.

Schweizerhaus Hotel (☎ 400331; www.schweizerhaus.net; 1 Bismarck St; s/d from N$510/850;) Although it's best known for the landmark institution that is Cafe Anton (p354), the Schweizerhaus Hotel is itself a class act. Standard but comfortable rooms benefit from spectacular views of the beach and the adjacent lighthouse.

Hotel Europa Hof (☎ 405061; www.europahof.com; 39 Bismarck St; s/d N$610/915;) The Europa Hof resembles a proper Bavarian chalet, and overflows with Continental atmosphere, complete with colourful flower boxes, a German-style beer garden and European flags flying from the windows.

Beach Lodge B&B (☎ 400933; www.beachlodge.com.na; Stint St; s/d from N$640/870;) This boat-shaped place, which sits right on the sand about 1km north of town, allows you to watch the sea through your very own porthole.

Sam's Giardino Hotel (☎ 403210; www.giardino.com.na; 89 Lazarett St; s/d from N$900/1150;) A slice of central Europe in the desert, Sam's Giardino Hotel mixes Swiss and Italian hospitality and architecture while emphasising fine wines, fine cigars and relaxing in the rose garden with a Saint Bernard named Ornelia.

Hansa Hotel (☎ 400311; www.hansahotel.com.na; 3 Hendrick Witbooi St; s/d from N$1230/1730;) Swakopmund's most established upmarket hotel bills itself as 'luxury in the desert', and offers individually decorated rooms with lofty ceilings and picture windows that are tasteful and elegant.

Eating

BUDGET

Out of Africa Coffee Shop (☎ 404752; 13 Daniel Tjongarero St; snacks & coffee N$15-35) This inviting spot welcomes you in the morning with some of Namibia's best coffee – espresso, cappuccino, latte and other caffeinated specialities – served up in French-style cups, along with freshly baked muffins and light meals.

Swakopmund Cafe (☎ 402333; 5 Tobias Hainyeko St; light meals N$35-55) At this excellent bistro, you can tuck into imaginative breakfasts, lunches and dinners, including a variety of salads, crêpes, *gyros*, steaks and seafood specials.

Cafe Anton (☎ 402419; 1 Bismarck St; light meals N$35-65) This much-loved local institution, in the Schweizerhaus Hotel, serves superb coffee, apple strudel, *kugelhopf* (cake with nuts and raisins), *mohnkuchen* (poppy-seed cake), *linzertorte* (cake flavoured with almond meal, lemon and spices, and spread with jam) and other European delights.

MIDRANGE

Napolitana (☎ 402773; 33 Nathaniel Maxuilili St; mains N$50-85) This quaint and intimate Italian bistro specialises in gourmet pizzas and pasta, as well as heartier meat and seafood dishes.

Swakopmund Brauhaus (☎ 402214; 22 Sam Nujoma Ave; mains N$60-90) This excellent restaurant and boutique brewery offers one of Swakopmund's most sought-after commodities, namely authentic German-style beer.

Cape to Cairo Restaurant (☎ 463160; 7 Nathaniel Maxuilili St; mains N$60-95) This popular tourist restaurant serves a wide variety of dishes from across the African continent, though the specialty here is game meat, served up in filets, stews and burgers.

Kücki's Pub (☎ 402407; Tobias Hainyeko St; meals N$60-100) Another Swakopmund institution, Kücki's has been in the bar and restaurant biz for a couple of decades running – everything is masterfully prepared, and the warm and congenial atmosphere is a welcome complement.

Lighthouse Pub & Cafe (☎ 400894; Palm Beach; mains US$60-110) With a postcard-perfect view of the beach and crashing surf, the Lighthouse Pub & Cafe is an atmospheric choice for lovers of fine seafood – you'll find everything from kingklip and lobster to kabeljou and calamari.

Tug (☎ 402356; mains US$75-125) Housed in the beached tugboat *Danie Hugo* near the jetty, the Tug is something of an obligatory destination for any diner-goer in Swakopmund. Regarded by many as the best restaurant in town, the Tug is an atmospheric, upmarket choice for meat and seafood, though a sundowner cocktail will do just fine. Due its extreme popularity and small size, bookings are recommended.

TOP END

Grapevine (☎ 404770; Libertine St; mains N$80-155) True to its moniker, the emphasis at this upmarket bistro is on the fruit of the vine, and you'll be allotted plenty of time to select your vintage from the veritable novel of a wine list.

Il Tulipano (☎ 400122; 37 Daniel Tjongarero St; mains N$95-165) At Il Tulipano, you can expect the real deal, namely handmade semolina pasta, light and fluffy risotto and fragrant lamb and veal dishes, topped off with fresh-baked breads, carefully chosen wines, strong coffees and sugary sweets.

Hansa Hotel Restaurant (☎ 400311; www.hansahotel.com.na; 3 Hendrick Witbooi St; mains N$95-215) In the main dining hall at this classic colonial spot, you can indulge in culinary excesses such as Kalahari-truffle-topped ostrich steak, oryx medallions in wildberry sauce and bacon-wrapped monkfish fillets drenched in herbed butter.

Drinking & Entertainment

Fagin's Pub (Hendrick Witbooi St) This extremely popular, down-to-earth watering hole is reminiscent of a US truckies' stop, complete with jocular staff, faithful clientele and evening videos of your day's adrenaline activities.

Cool Bananas (14 Nathaniel Maxuilili St) Housed inside the Swakop Lodge, this bar–club is packed when the overland trucks roll into town, which means you can be assured of plenty of drunken revelry well into the morning hours.

Rafter's Action Pub (cnr Moltke & Woermann Sts) At Rafter's, it's a safe bet that the music is always pounding, the strobes are always flashing and everyone is strutting their stuff on the dance floor, regardless of the time of night.

Captain's Tavern Pub (2 Bahnhof St) This upmarket tavern attracts highbrow clientele from the Swakopmund Hotel & Entertainment Centre, and sometimes features live music.

Shopping

Street stalls sell Zimbabwean crafts on the waterfront by the steps below Cafe Anton on Bismarck St.

Karakulia Craft Centre (☎ 461415; www.karakulia.com.na; 3 Knobloch St) This local carpet factory produces original and beautiful African rugs, carpets and wall-hangings in karakul wool and offers tours of the spinning, dyeing and weaving processes.

Cobwebs (☎ 404024; brigadon@iafrica.com.na; 10 Tobias Hainyeko St) This arts shop sells African masks, crafts and other traditional artefacts.

Peter's Antiques (☎ /fax 405624; 24 Moltke St) An Ali Baba's cave of treasures, Peter's Antiques specialises in colonial relics, historic literature, West African art, politically incorrect German paraphernalia and genuine West African fetishes and other artefacts from around the continent.

Getting There & Away

AIR

Air Namibia (☎ 405123; www.airnamibia.com.na) has several flights a week between Windhoek's Eros airport and Walvis Bay (see below), from where you can easily catch a bus or taxi to Swakopmund.

BUS

There are several weekly buses between Windhoek and Swakopmund (fares from N$180, five hours) on the **Intercape Mainliner** (www.intercape.co.za). You can easily book your tickets online.

Town Hopper (www.namibiashuttle.com) runs private shuttle buses between Windhoek and Swakop (N$220) and also offers door-to-door pick-up and drop-off service.

Finally, combis run this route with fairly regular frequency, and a ride between Windhoek and Swakopmund shouldn't cost more than N$100. Swakopmund is also a minor public transport hub, serving various regional destinations including Walvis Bay by combi, with fares averaging between N$15 and N$30.

CAR

Swakopmund is about 400km west of Windhoek on the B2, the country's main east–west highway.

TRAIN

Trans-Namib (☎ 061-2982175) operates daily night trains, though they're not very convenient or popular, especially given the ease of bus travel. Fares to Windhoek from N$75.

WALVIS BAY

☎ 064 / pop 65,000

Walvis Bay (pronounced 'vahl-fis bay') is 30km south of Swakopmund and is the only real port between Lüderitz and Luanda (Angola). The natural harbour at Walvis Bay is the result of the sand spit Pelican Point, which forms a natural breakwater and shelters the city from the strong ocean surge.

Due to the city's strategic location, Walvis Bay has a long and storied history of British and South African occupation. Since 1992, however, the city has rested firmly in Namibian hands, and is the country's second-largest city after Windhoek. Today, Walvis Bay boasts a tanker berth, a dry dock and container facilities as well as a lucrative salt works and fish-processing industry.

Information

Computerland I-café (Sam Nujoma Ave; per hr N$20) Internet access.

Police (☎ 10111; cnr 11th St & 13th Rd)

Post office (Sam Nujoma Ave) Provides public telephones and fax services.

Viggo-Lund Bookseller (Sam Nujoma Ave) Has a modest selection of popular fiction.

Walvis-i (☎ 209170; Shop 6, Hickory Creek Spur Bldg, Theo-Ben Gurirab St; 9am-5pm Mon-Fri, 9am-1pm Sat) Provides visitor information.

Welwitschia Medical Centre (13th Rd; 24hr)

Sights

DUNE 7

In the bleak expanse just off the C14, 6km by road from town, Dune 7 is popular with locals as a slope for sandboarding and skiing. A picnic site, which is now being engulfed by sand, has several shady palm trees tucked away in the lee of the dune.

RHENISH MISSION CHURCH

Walvis Bay's oldest remaining building, the **Rhenish Mission Church** (5th Rd) was prefabricated in Hamburg, Germany, reconstructed beside the harbour in 1880 and consecrated the following year. Because of machinery sprawl in the harbour area, it was relocated to its present site in the mid-20th century, and functioned as a church until 1966.

WALVIS BAY MUSEUM

The town **museum** (Nangolo Mbumba Dr; admission free; 9am-12.30pm & 3-4.30pm Mon-Fri) is in the library. It concentrates on the history and maritime background of Walvis Bay, but also has archaeological exhibits, a mineral collection and natural history displays on the Namib Desert and the Atlantic Coast.

BIRD ISLAND

Along the Swakopmund road, 10km north of Walvis Bay, take a look at the offshore wooden platform known as Bird Island. It was built to provide a roost and nesting site for sea birds and a source of guano for use as fertiliser. The annual yield is around 1000 tonnes, and the smell from the island is truly unforgettable.

AROUND WALVIS BAY

Sandwich Harbour

Historically, Sandwich Harbour, 56km south of Walvis Bay, served as a commercial fishing and trading port. Some historians suggest that the name may be derived from an English whaler, the *Sandwich,* whose captain produced the first map of this coastline. Still, others contend that the name may also be a corruption of the German word *Sandfische*, a type of shark often found here. History aside, at present the harbour is a total wilderness devoid of any human settlement.

While few people would think of visiting such a remote destination, 4WD enthusiasts regard an excursion to Sandwich Bay as a true test of their off-road mettle. If you think you have what it takes, the **Topnaar 4WD Trail** extends from Walvis Bay through the sand sea to Sandwich Harbour, Conception Bay and the fabulous *Edward Bolen* shipwreck.

Assuming you have a sturdy high-clearance 4WD vehicle, follow the left fork 5km south of Walvis Bay. When the road splits at the salt works, bear left again and continue across the marshy Kuiseb Delta. After 15km, you will be entering the Namib-Naukluft Park and must purchase a permit at the gate.

For the final 20km into Sandwich Harbour you can either continue straight along the sandy beach (time your journey for low tide) or bear left past the control post and follow the tracks further inland. However, dune shifts may present tedious stretches of deep sand or alter the route entirely. Bring a shovel, a towrope and a couple of planks in case you get stuck.

Activities

KAYAKING

Run by the very amenable Jeanne Mientjes, **Eco-Marine Kayak Tours** (☎ 203144; www.em

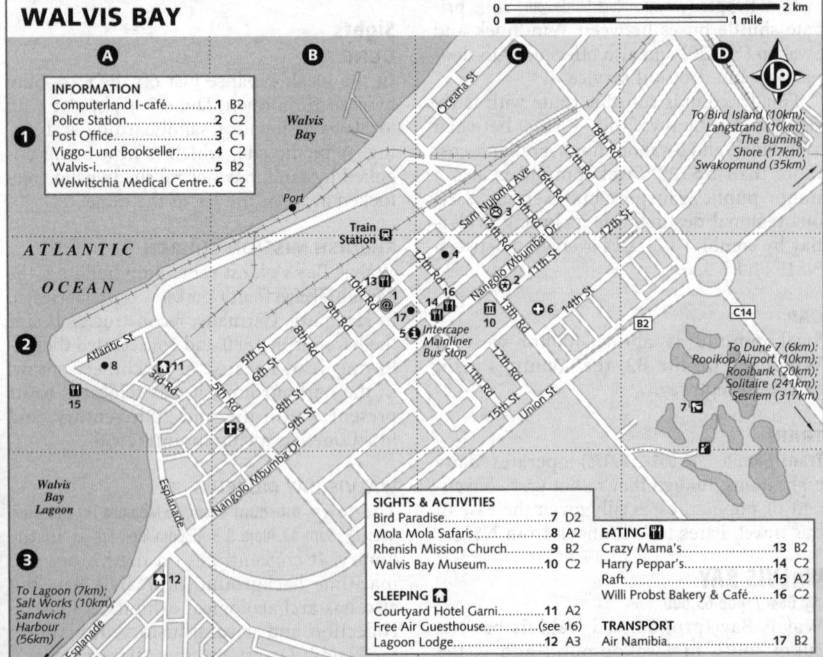

FLAMINGOS AT WALVIS BAY

Lesser and greater flamingos flock in large numbers to pools along the Namib Desert coast, particularly around Walvis Bay and Lüderitz. They're excellent fliers, and have been known to migrate up to 500km overnight in search of proliferations of algae and crustaceans.

The lesser flamingo filters algae and diatoms (microscopic organisms) from the water by sucking in, and vigorously expelling water from its bill. The minute particles are caught on fine hair-like protrusions, which line the inside of the mandibles. The suction is created by the thick ,fleshy tongue, which rests in a groove in the lower mandible, and pumps back and forth like a piston. It has been estimated that a million lesser flamingos can consume over 180 tonnes of algae and diatoms daily.

While lesser flamingos obtain food by filtration, the greater flamingo supplements its algae diet with small molluscs, crustaceans and other organic particles from the mud. When feeding, it will rotate in a circle while stamping its feet in an effort to scare up a tasty potential meal.

The greater and lesser flamingos are best distinguished by their colouration. Greater flamingos are white to light pink, and their beaks are whitish with a black tip. Lesser flamingos are a deeper pink – often reddish – colour, with dark-red beaks.

Located near Walvis Bay are three diverse wetland areas, namely, the lagoon, the salt works and the Bird Paradise at the sewage works. Together, they form Southern Africa's single most important coastal wetland for migratory birds, with up to 150,000 transient avian visitors stopping by annually, including massive flocks of both lesser and greater flamingos. The three wetland areas are as follows:

- **The Lagoon** This shallow and sheltered 45,000-hectare lagoon, southwest of town and west of the Kuiseb River mouth, attracts a range of coastal water birds in addition to enormous flocks of lesser and greater flamingos. It also supports chestnut-banded plovers and curlew sandpipers, as well as the rare Damara tern.
- **The Salt Works** Southwest of the lagoon is this 3500-hectare salt-pan complex, which currently supplies over 90% of South Africa's salt. As with the one in Swakopmund, these pans concentrate salt from sea water with the aid of evaporation. They also act as a rich feeding ground for shrimp and larval fish.
- **Bird Paradise** Immediately east of town along the C14, at the municipal sewage-purification works, is this nature sanctuary, which consists of a series of shallow artificial pools, fringed by reeds. An observation tower and a short nature walk afford excellent birdwatching.

kayak.iway.na; 3-hour tour from N$495) operates sea-kayaking trips around the beautiful Walvis Bay wetlands. Note that although there is no central office, you can make bookings over the phone or through your accommodation.

MARINE SAFARI

Mola Mola Safaris (☎ 205511; www.mola-namibia.com; cnr Esplanade & Atlantic St; prices variable) This marine safari company offers fully customisable boating trips around the Walvis Bay and Swakopmund coastal areas, where you can expect to see dolphins, seals and countless birds. Prices are dependent on your group size and length of voyage. Mola Mola also offers a variety of land safaris, including guided 4WD trips to Sandwich Harbour and sights beyond.

Sleeping

Asgard House (☎ 209595; www.gateway-africa.com/asgard; cnr Esplanade & 2nd St; s/d N$220/288) Basic rooms that are kept clean and tidy, and there is a breezy dining area where you can have a quality home-cooked meal without worrying about breaking the bank.

Courtyard Hotel Garni (☎ 206252; 16 3rd Rd; s/d from N$600/680; 💻 🏊) The Courtyard is one of the better hotels in Walvis Bay, yet still occupies an affordable price bracket – elegant rooms with polished hardwood floors surround two manicured courtyards, and guests can access the indoor heated pool and sauna.

Free Air Guesthouse (☎ 202247; www.namibia-walvisbay-guesthouse.com; 12th Rd; s/d N$655/919; 💻) Free Air occupies a visually arresting building with sharp lines and smooth surfaces, and minimalist rooms with carefully selected design flourishes are comfortable and soothing.

Lagoon Lodge (☎ 200850; www.lagoonlodge.com.na; 2 Nangolo Mbumba Dr; s/d N$710/1060;) This French-run lodge commands a magnificent location next to the lagoon, and features individually decorated rooms with private terraces facing out towards the sand and sea.

Burning Shore (☎ 207568; www.burningshore.na; s/d from N$895/1380;) This once little-known resort, located south of Walvis Bay along the Langstrand (Long Beach), received a huge publicity boost in 2006 following Angelina Jolie's and Brad Pitt's surprise trip to Namibia. While much of the hype has since dissipated, the Burning Shore remains a secluded retreat where you can soak up the beauty and serenity of the dunes and the ocean.

Eating

Willi Probst Bakery & Café (☎ 202744; cnr 12th Rd & 9th St; light meals N$15-35) If you're feeling nostalgic for Swakopmund (or Deutschland for that matter), take comfort in knowing that Probst specialises in stodgy German fare: pork, meatballs, schnitzel and the like.

Harry Peppar's (☎ 203131; cnr 11th Rd & Nangolo Mbumba Dr; pizzas N$40-55) Harry comes up with all sorts of creative thick-crust pizzas, and if you're feeling lazy, and don't want to stop by and say hi, he'll deliver his mad creations right to your hotel.

Crazy Mama's (☎ 207364; cnr Sam Nujoma Ave & 11th Rd; mains N$45-65) This funky little bistro, which is centred on an enormous hewn tree, gets rave reviews for its warm vibes, friendly service and ever-changing menu offering varied food items that span the culinary globe.

Raft (☎ 204877; Esplanade; mains N$75-125) This Walvis Bay landmark sits on stilts offshore, and has a great front-row view of the ducks, pelicans and flamingos.

Getting There & Away

AIR

Air Namibia (☎ 203102; www.airnamibia.com.na) has several flights a week between Windhoek's Eros airport and Walvis Bay's Rooikop airport, located 10km southeast of town on the C14.

BUS & COMBI

All buses and combis to Walvis Bay run via Swakopmund – for more information, see p355.

NAMIB-NAUKLUFT PARK

The present boundaries of Namib-Naukluft Park, one of the world's largest national parks, were established in 1978 by merging the Namib Desert Park and the Naukluft Mountain Zebra Park with parts of Diamond Area 1 and bits of surrounding government land. Today, it takes in over 23,000 sq km of arid and semi-arid land, and protects various areas of vast ecological importance in the Namib and the Naukluft, including Sossusvlei, Sandwich Harbour and Welwitschia Drive. The Namib-Naukluft Park also abuts the NamibRand Nature Reserve, the largest privately owned property in Southern Africa, forming a massive wildlife corridor that promotes migratory movement.

Namib Section

While most people associate the Namib solely with Sossusvlei, the desert sweeps across most of Central Namibia, and is characterised by a large array of geological formations. Given the extremes of temperature and environment, you will need a 4WD vehicle in addition to good navigation skills in order to properly explore the Namib. However, a surprisingly comprehensive network of bush campsites provides a reliable safety net, and truly this is one place where the journey itself is worth much more than the destination.

SIGHTS

Kuiseb Canyon

Located on the Gamsberg Pass route west of the Khomas Hochland, Kuiseb Canyon contains the ephemeral Kuiseb River, which is no more than a broad, sandy riverbed for most of the year. Although it may flow for two or three weeks during the rainy season, it only gets as far as Gobabeb before seeping into the sand.

Hamilton Hills

The range of limestone hills known as the Hamilton Hills, south of Vogelfederberg campsite, rises 600m above the surrounding desert plains. It provides lovely desert hikes, and the fog-borne moisture supports an amazing range of succulents and other botanical wonders.

SLEEPING

The Namib-Naukluft Park has eight exclusive camps, some of which have multiple

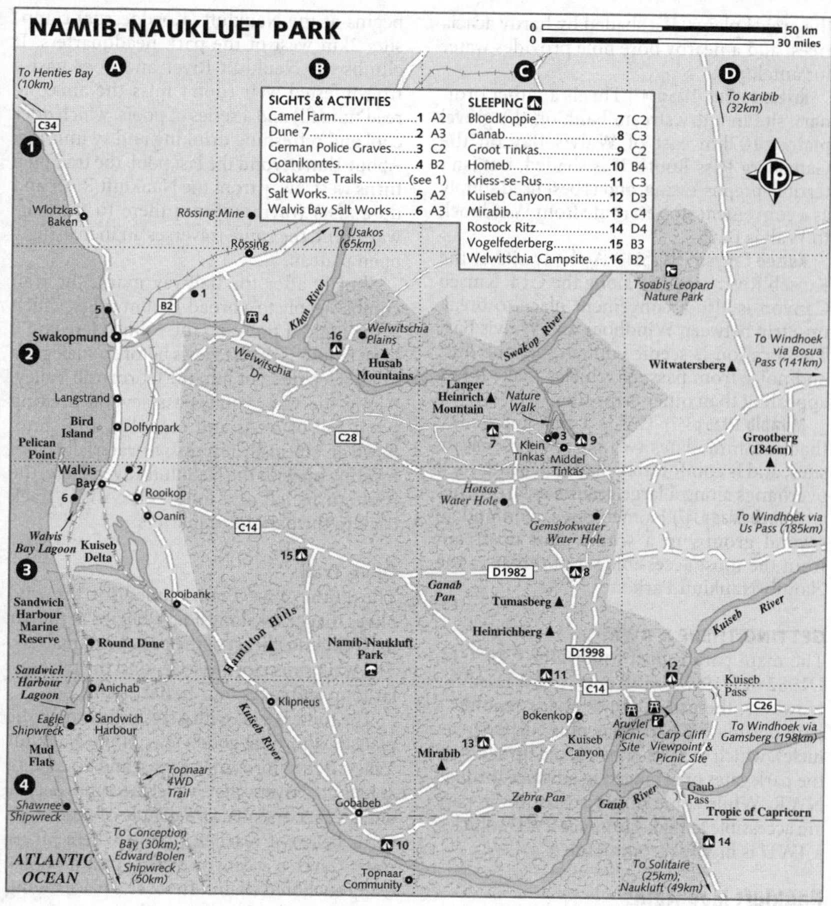

but widely spaced campsites. Sites have tables, toilets and braais, but no washing facilities. Brackish water is available for cooking and washing but not drinking – be sure that you bring enough water. All sites must be booked through NWR in Windhoek (p305) or Swakopmund (p346). Camping costs US$100 per site plus N$50 per person, and fees are payable when the park permit is issued.

Bloedkoppie (Map p347) Otherwise known as 'Blood Hill', Bloedkoppie has among the most beautiful and popular sites in the park. If you're coming from Swakopmund, they lie 55km northeast of the C28, along a signposted track. The northern sites may be accessed with 2WD, but they tend to be more crowded. The southern sites are quieter and more secluded, but can be reached only by 4WD.

Groot Tinkas (Map p347) This camp must be accessed with 4WD and rarely sees much traffic. It enjoys a lovely setting beneath shady rocks, and the surroundings are super for nature walks. During rainy periods, the brackish water in the nearby dam attracts a variety of birdlife.

Vogelfederberg (Map p347) A small facility, 2km south of the C14, Vogelfederberg makes a convenient overnight camp just 51km from Walvis Bay, but it's more popular for picnics or short walks.

Ganab (Map p347) Translating to 'Camelthorn Acacia', Ganab is a dusty, exposed facility that sits beside a shallow stream bed on the gravel plains. It's shaded by hardy acacia trees, and a nearby bore hole provides water for antelopes.

Kriess-se-Rus (Map p347) This is a rather ordinary site in a dry stream bank on the gravel plains, 107km east of Walvis Bay on the Gamsberg Pass Route. It is shaded, but isn't terribly prepossessing, and is best used simply as a convenient stop en route from Windhoek to Walvis Bay.

Kuiseb Canyon (Map p347) A shady site at the Kuiseb River crossing along the C14, Kuiseb Canyon is also a convenient place to break up a trip between Windhoek and Walvis Bay. The location is scenic enough, but the dust and noise from passing vehicles make it less appealing than other campsites.

Mirabib (Map p347) This is a pleasant facility that accommodates two parties at separate sites, and is comfortably placed beneath rock overhangs along a large granite escarpment.

Homeb (Map p347) Homeb can accommodate several groups in a scenic spot upstream from the most accessible set of dunes in the Namib-Naukluft Park.

GETTING THERE & AWAY

The main park transit routes, the C28, C14, D1982 or D1998, are all open to 2WD traffic. However, the use of minor roads requires a park permit (N$40 per day plus N$10 per vehicle), which can either be picked up at any of the park gates or arranged in advance through NWR. While some minor roads in the park are accessible to high-clearance 2WD vehicles, a 4WD is highly recommended.

Naukluft Mountains

☎ 063 / elev 1973m

The Naukluft Mountains, which rise steeply from the gravel plains of the Central Namib, are characterised by a high plateau bounded by gorges, caves and springs cut deeply from dolomite formations. The Tsondab, Tsams and Tsauchab Rivers all rise in the massif, and the relative abundance of water creates an ideal habitat for mountain zebras, kudus, leopards, springboks and klipspringers. In addition to wildlife watching, the Naukluft is home to a couple of challenging hikes that open up this largely inaccessible terrain.

SIGHTS & ACTIVITIES

Waterkloof Trail

This lovely 17km anticlockwise loop takes a total of about seven hours to complete, and begins at the Naukluft (Koedoesrus) campsite, 2km west of the park headquarters. It climbs the Naukluft River and goes past a frog-infested weir (don't miss the amazing reed tunnel!) and a series of pools, which offer cool and refreshing drinking and swimming. About 1km beyond the last pool, the trail then turns west, away from the Naukluft River and up a *kloof* (ravine). From there to the halfway point, the route traverses an increasingly open plateau.

Shortly after the halfway mark, the trail climbs steeply to a broad 1910m ridge, which is the highest point on the route. Here you'll have fabulous desert views before you begin a long, steep descent into the Gororosib Valley. Along the way, you'll pass several inviting pools full of reeds and tadpoles, and climb down an especially impressive waterfall before meeting up with the Naukluft River. Here, the route turns left and follows the 4WD track back to the park headquarters.

Olive Trail

The 11km Olive Trail, named for the wild olives that grow alongside it, begins at the car park 4km northeast of the park headquarters. The walk runs clockwise around the triangular loop and takes four to five hours.

The route begins with a steep climb onto the plateau, affording good views of the Naukluft Valley. It then turns sharply east and descends a constricted river valley, which becomes deeper and steeper and makes a couple of perfect U-turns before it reaches a point where hikers must traverse a canyon wall – past a pool – using anchored chains. In several places along this stretch, the dramatic geology presents an astonishing gallery of natural artwork. Near the end of the route, the trail strikes the Naukluft 4WD route and swings sharply south, where it makes a beeline back to the car park.

Four-Day & Eight-Day Loops

The two big loops through the massif can be hiked in four and eight days. For many people the Naukluft is a magical place, but its charm is more subtle than that of Fish River Canyon in southern Namibia. For example, some parts are undeniably spectacular, such as the Zebra Highway, Ubusis Canyon and Die Valle (look for the fantastic stallion profile on the rock beside the falls). However, a couple of days involve walking in relatively open country or along some maddeningly rocky riverbeds.

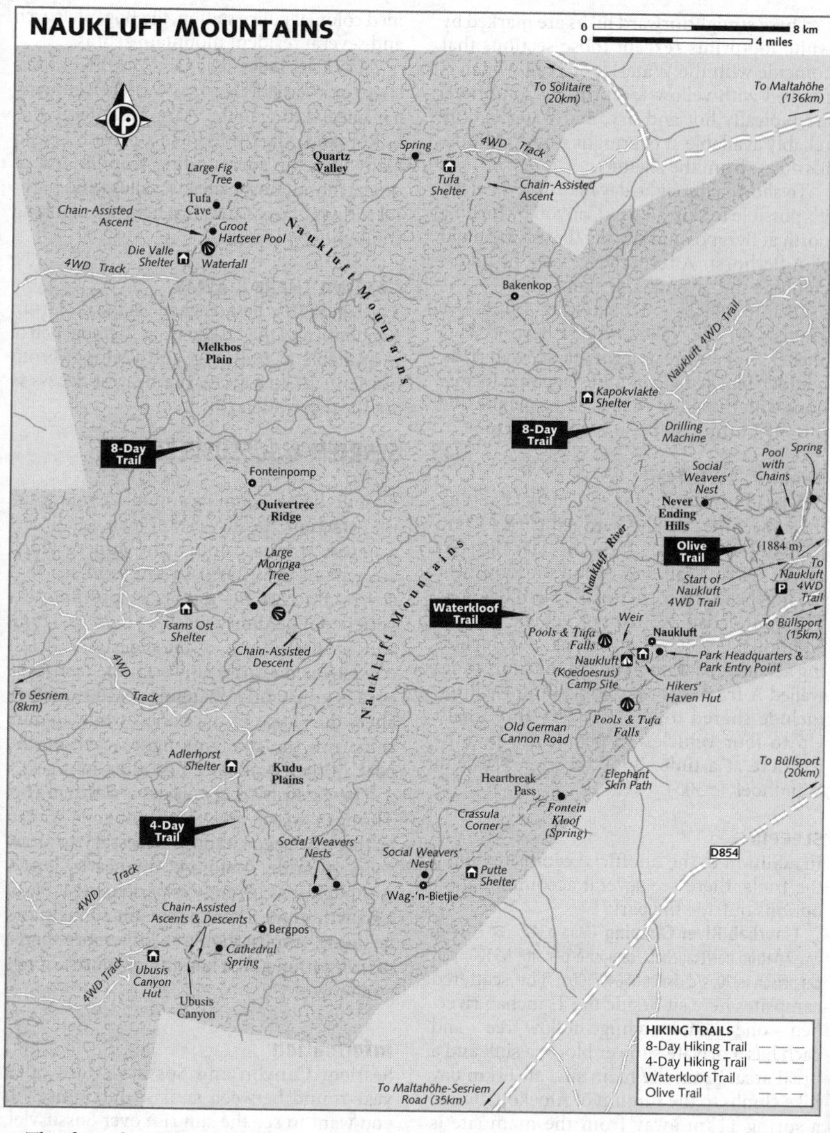

The four-day 60km loop is actually just the first third of the eight-day 120km loop, combined with a 22km cross-country jaunt across the plateau back to park headquarters. It joins up with the Waterkloof Trail at its halfway point, and follows it the rest of the way back to park headquarters. Alternatively, you can finish the four-day route at Tsams Ost Shelter, midway through the eight-day loop, where a road leads out to the Sesriem–Solitaire Rd. However, you must arrange to leave a vehicle there before setting off from park headquarters. Note that hikers may not begin from Tsams Ost without obtaining special permission from the rangers at Naukluft.

These straightforward hikes are marked by white footprints (except those sections that coincide with the Waterkloof Trail, which is marked with yellow footprints). Conditions are typically hot and dry, and water is only reliably available at overnight stops (at Putte, it's 400m from the shelter).

To shorten the eight-day hike to seven days, it's possible to skip Ubusis Canyon by turning north at Bergpos and staying the second night at Adlerhorst. Alternatively, very fit hikers combine the seventh and eighth days.

In four places – Ubusis Canyon, above Tsams Ost, Die Valle and just beyond Tufa Shelter – hikers must negotiate dry waterfalls, boulder-blocked *kloofs* and steep tufa formations with the aid of chains. Some people find this off-putting, so be sure you're up to it.

Naukluft 4WD Trail

Off-road enthusiasts can now exercise their machines on the national park's 73km Naukluft 4WD Trail. It begins near the start of the Olive Trail and follows a loop near the northeastern corner of the Naukluft area. The route costs N$220 per vehicle plus an additional US$50 per person per day, including accommodation in one of the four stone-walled A-frames at the 28km point. Facilities include shared toilets, showers and braais. Up to four vehicles/16 people are permitted here at a time. Book through NWR in Windhoek (p305).

SLEEPING

In addition to the unofficial campsites along the trails, there are several accommodation options outside the park.

Tsauchab River Camping (Map p347; ☎ 293416; www.natron.net/tsauchab; campsite per site N$100, plus per person N$70, s/d chalet N$640/1060) The scattered campsites here sit beside the Tsauchab riverbed – one occupies a huge hollow tree – and each has a private shower block, a sink and a braai area. From the main site, an 11km day hike climbs to the summit of Aloekop. Beside a spring 11km away from the main site is the 4WD-exclusive site, which is the starting point for the wonderful 21km Mountain Zebra Hiking Trail.

Büllsport Guest Farm (Map p347; ☎ 693371; www.natron.net/tour/buellspt; s/d with half board N$660/990) This scenic farm, owned by Ernst and Johanna Sauber, occupies a lovely, austere setting below the Naukluft massif, and features a ruined colonial police station, the Bogenfels arch and several resident mountain zebras.

Zebra River Lodge (Map p347; ☎ 693265; www.zebrariver.com; s/d with full board N$850/1580) Occupying a magical setting in the Tsaris Mountains, this is Rob and Marianne Field's private Grand Canyon – the surrounding wonderland of desert mountains, plateaus, valleys and natural springs is accessible on a network of hiking trails and 4WD tracks.

GETTING THERE & AWAY

The Naukluft is best reached via the C24 from Rehoboth and the D1206 from Rietoog; petrol is available at Büllsport and Rietoog. From Sesriem, 103km away, the nearest access is via the dip-ridden D854.

SESRIEM & SOSSUSVLEI

☎ 063

Despite being Namibia's number one tourist attraction, Sossusvlei still manages to feel isolated. Hiking through the dunes, which are part of the 32,000-sq-km sand sea that covers much of the region, is a sombre experience. The dunes reach as high as 325m, and are part of one of the oldest and driest ecosystems on earth. However, the landscape here is constantly changing – wind forever alters the shape of the dunes, while colours shift with the changing light, reaching the peak of their brilliance just after sunrise.

The gateway to Sossusvlei is Sesriem (Six Thongs), which was the number of joined leather ox-wagon thongs necessary to draw water from the bottom of the nearby gorge. Although it's currently experiencing a bit of a growth spurt, Sesriem remains a lonely and far-flung outpost, home to little more than a petrol station and a handful of tourist hotels and lodges.

Information

Sesriem Canyon and Sossusvlei are open year-round between sunrise and sunset. If you want to see the sun rise over Sossusvlei, you must stay inside the park, either at the Sesriem campsite or the Sossus Dune Lodge. From both places, you are allowed to start driving to Sossusvlei about 15 minutes before the general public is allowed through the main gates. If you're content with simply enjoying the morning light, however, you can stay in Sesriem or Solitaire, and simply pass through the park gate once the sun rises above the horizon.

All visitors headed for Sossusvlei must check in at the park office and secure a park entry permit.

Sights & Activities

SOSSUSVLEI

Sossusvlei, a large ephemeral pan, is set amid red sand dunes that tower up to 200m above the valley floor and more than 300m over the underlying strata. It rarely contains any water, but when the Tsauchab River has gathered enough volume and momentum to push beyond the thirsty plains to the sand sea, it's completely transformed. The normally cracked, dry mud gives way to an ethereal blue-green lake, surrounded by greenery and attended by aquatic birdlife, as well as the usual sand-loving gemsbok and ostriches.

At the end of the 65km 2WD road from Sesriem is the 2x4 Car Park, and only 4WDs can drive the last 4km into the Sossusvlei Pan itself. Visitors with lesser vehicles park at the 2x4 Car Park and walk, hitch or catch the shuttle (N$150 round trip) to cover the remaining distance. If you choose to walk, which really is the best way to take in all the desert scenery, allot about 90 minutes, and carry enough water for a hot, sandy slog in the sun.

SESRIEM CANYON

The 1km-long, 30m-deep Sesriem Canyon, 4km south of the Sesriem headquarters, was carved by the Tsauchab River through the 15-million-year-old deposits of sand and gravel conglomerate. There are two pleasant walks: you can hike upstream to the brackish pool at its head or 2.5km downstream to its lower end. Check out the natural sphinx-like formation on the northern flank near the canyon mouth.

DUNE 45

The most accessible of the large red dunes along the Sossusvlei road is Dune 45, so-called because it's 45km from Sesriem. It rises over 150m above the surrounding plains, and is flanked by several scraggly and often photographed trees.

ELIM DUNE

This often-visited red dune, 5km north from the Sesriem campsite, can be reached with 2WD vehicles, but also makes a pleasant morning or afternoon walk.

HIDDEN VLEI

The rewarding 4km return hike from the 2x4 Car Park to Hidden Vlei, an unearthly dry vlei (low, open landscape) amid lonely dunes, makes a rewarding excursion. The route is marked by white-painted posts. It's most intriguing in the afternoon, when you're unlikely to see another person.

DEAD VLEI

The rugged 6km return walk from Sossusvlei to Dead Vlei is popular with those who think

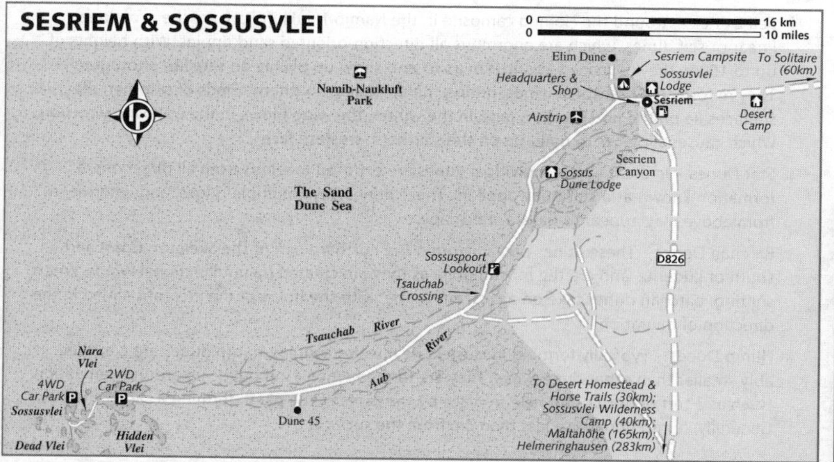

the former is becoming overly touristy. Despite the name, it's a lovely spot and is just as impressive as its more popular neighbour.

Sleeping

Reservations are essential at all of the places listed here, especially during the high season, school holidays and busy weekends.

Sesriem Camp Site (Map p347; campsite N$300, plus per person N$150) With the exception of the upmarket Sossus Dune Lodge, this is the only accommodation inside the park gates – staying here guarantees that you will be able to arrive at Sossusvlei in time for sunrise. Given its popularity, you must book at the NWR office in Windhoek (p305) and arrive by sunset or the camp staff will reassign your site on a stand-by basis; anyone who was unable to book a site in Windhoek may get in on this nightly lottery.

Sossus Dune Lodge (Map p347; ☎ 061-2857200; s/d US$600/835, with full board from N$2300/3600;) If money is no object, then splash out on this brand-new and ultra-exclusive lodge, which is administered by the NWR, and is one of only two properties inside the park gates. Constructed entirely of local materials, the lodge consists of elevated bungalows that run alongside a curving promenade, and face out to towards the silent desert plains.

Desert Camp (Map p347; ☎ 683205; www.desertcamp.com; s/d N$730/900;) Desert Camp consists of 20 East African–style canvas tents, complete with bathrooms, kitchenettes and braai pits, which fan out from the central communal area. Here's the best part: if you place your dinner order with reception, in the evening you will be hand delivered game steaks, mixed salads and other tasty treats.

Desert Homestead & Horse Trails (Map p347; ☎ 293243; www.deserthomestead-namibia.com; s/d N$825/1325;) This reader-recommended lodge, about 30km southeast of Sesriem, specialises in horse riding through the Namib-Naukluft Park – whether you're keen for a sundowner or an overnight desert 'sleep-out' ride, the professional staff and exceptional horses will make your experience a memorable one.

Sossusvlei Lodge (Map p347; ☎ 293223; www.sossusvleilodge.com; s/d from N$1915/2550;)

THE NAMIB DUNES

The following is a list of the major types of dunes found in the Namib:

- Parabolic Dunes – Along the eastern area of the dune sea (including those around Sossusvlei), the dunes are classified as parabolic or multi-cyclic, and are the result of variable wind patterns. These are the most stable dunes in the Namib, and therefore the most vegetated.
- Transverse Dunes – The long, linear dunes along the coast south of Walvis Bay are transverse dunes, which lie perpendicular to the prevailing southwesterly winds. As a result, their slipfaces are oriented towards the north and northeast.
- Seif Dunes – Around the Homeb campsite in the Namib-Naukluft Park are the prominent linear or seif dunes, which are enormous all-direction-oriented sand ripples. With heights of up to 100m, they're spaced about 1km apart and show up plainly on satellite photographs. They're formed by seasonal winds; during the prevailing southerly winds of summer, the slipfaces lie on the northeastern face. In the winter, the wind blows in the opposite direction, which causes slipfaces to build up on the southern–western faces.
- Star Dunes – In areas where individual dunes are exposed to winds from all directions, a formation known as a star dune appears. These dunes have multiple ridges, and when seen from above may appear to have a star shape.
- Barchan Dunes – These dunes prevail around the northern end of the Skeleton Coast and south of Lüderitz, and are the most mobile as they are created by unidirectional winds. When shifting, barchan dunes take on a crescent shape, with the horns of the crescent aimed in the direction of migration.
- Hump Dunes – Typically forming in clusters near water sources, hump dunes are considerably smaller than other dune types. They are formed when sand builds up around vegetation (such as a tuft of grass), and held in place by the roots of the plant, forming a sandy tussock. Generally, hump dunes rise less than 3m from the surface.

Accommodation is in self-contained chalets with private verandahs, and guests can mingle with one another in the swimming pool, bar-restaurant and observatory. Despite the high price tag, this lodge is outside the park gate, so arriving at Sossusvlei in time for sunrise is not possible.

Getting There & Away

Sesriem is reached via a signposted turn-off from the C14, and petrol is available in town. There is no public transport leading into the park, though hotels can arrange tours if you don't have your own vehicle.

In 2006, the road leading from the park gate to the 2WD car park was paved, though the speed limit remains 60km/h. Although the road is conducive to higher speeds, there are oryx and springbok dashing about, so drive with extreme care.

SOLITAIRE & AROUND

Solitaire is a lonely and aptly named settlement of just a few buildings about 80km north of Sesriem along the A46. Although the town is nothing more than an open spot in the desert, the surrounding area is home to several guest farms and lodges, any of which serve as an alternative base for exploring Sossusvlei.

Sleeping

Solitaire Guest Farm (Map p347; ☎ 062-572024; www.solitaireguestfarm.com; campsite N$70, r per person N$430;) This inviting guest farm, 6km east of Solitaire on the C14, is peaceful with bright rooms, home-cooked meals and relaxing surroundings, making it a good choice.

Solitaire Country Lodge (Map p347; ☎ 061-256598; www.namibialodges.com; campsite N$100, s/d N$465/665;) Despite being only a few years old, the property was designed to evoke images of a colonial-era farmhouse, albeit one with a large swimming pool in the backyard!

Swartfontein Mountain and Desert Guest Lodge (Map p347; ☎ 062-572004; s/d with half board N$650/1150;) The lodge occupies a farmhouse constructed by a German colonial soldier in 1900, though the stylish decor is Italian all the way. In addition to the dramatic location, perks include pasta dinners, guided hikes and wildlife drives through the reserve.

Rostock Ritz (Map p347; ☎ 064-403622; kuecki@mweb.com.na; s/d chalets N$1069/1669;) Established by the owner of Kücki's Pub in Swakopmund, this unique accommodation is known for its bizarre water gardens and cool and cave-like cement-domed chalets.

Getting There & Away

Solitaire is connected to Sesriem by the unpaved C19, and petrol is available in town.

NAMIBRAND NATURE RESERVE

Boarding the Namib-Naukluft Park, this reserve is essentially a collection of private farms that together protect over 200,000 hectares of dunes, desert grasslands and wild, isolated mountain ranges. Currently, several concessionaires operate on the reserve, offering a range of experiences amid one of Namibia's most stunning and colourful landscapes. A surprising amount of wildlife can be seen here, including large herds of gemsbok, springboks and zebras, as well as kudus, klipspringers, spotted hyenas, jackals, and Cape and bat-eared foxes.

Access by private vehicle is restricted in order to maintain the delicate balance of the reserve. Accommodation prices are also extremely high, which seeks to limit the tourist footprint. As a result, you must book through either of the lodges listed below, and then arrange either a 4WD transfer or a chartered fly-in.

Sleeping

Wolwedans Dune Lodge (Map p347; ☎ 061-230616; www.wolwedans.com; chalet with full board & activities per person from N$2855;) One of the more affordable lodges in the NamibRand (at this price bracket, affordable is a relative term), Wolwedans features an architecturally arresting collection of raised wooded chalets that are scattered amid towering red sand dunes.

Sossusvlei Mountain Lodge (Map p347; ☎ in Johannesburg 27-11-809 4300; www.andbeyond.com; chalet with full board & activities per person from N$4995;) This fashionable accommodation, dubbed by *Condé Nast* as one of the top lodges in the world, has only 10 chalets, which are nothing short of regal and feature personal fireplaces, marble baths and linen-covered patios.

SOUTHERN NAMIBIA

The deserts of southern Namibia sparkle beneath the sun – quite literally – as they're filled with millions of carats of diamonds.

Since the Germans first unearthed vast treasure troves resting beneath the sands, much of the region has been dubbed the *Sperrgebeit* (Forbidden Area). Following the very recent declaration of Namibia's newest national park, this virtually pristine biodiversity hotspot is now open to the general public for the first time in more than a century.

While Sperrgebeit National Park has been grabbing all the headlines recently, the nearby port of Lüderitz has long been many a traveller's favourite. A surreal colonial relic that has been largely disregarded by the 21st century, Lüderitz clings fiercely to its European roots, astounding travellers with its traditional German architecture set against a backdrop of fiery sand dunes and deep blue seas.

BRUKKAROS

With a 2km-wide crater, this extinct volcano dominates the skyline between Mariental and Keetmanshoop. It was formed some 80 million years ago when a magma pipe encountered ground water about 1km below the earth's surface and caused a series of violent volcanic explosions.

From the car park, it's a 3.5km hike to the crater's southern entrance; along the way, look for the remarkable **quartz formations** embedded in the rock. From here, you can head for the other-worldly **crater floor**, or turn left and follow the southern rim up to the abandoned sunspot research centre, which was established by the US Smithsonian Institute in the 1930s.

Brukkaros Campsite (Map p367: ☎ 061-255977; www.nacobta.com.na; campsite per person N$35), a Spartan spot that is administered by the local community, is literally carved out of the volcano, and offers some truly stunning views across the valley.

Brukkaros rises 35km west of Tses on the B1. Follow the C98 west for 40km and then turn north on to the D3904 about 1km east of Berseba. It's then 8km to the car park. Note that a 4WD is required to access some of the higher campsites at Brukkaros Campsite.

KEETMANSHOOP

☎ 063

Keetmanshoop (*kayt*-mahns-*hoo*-up) sits at the main crossroads of southern Namibia, but it's the surrounding countryside that draws most travellers' attention. The area is home to large concentrations of *kokerboom* (quiver trees), which belong to the aloe family, and can grow to heights of 8m.

In the town itself, there are a few examples of German colonial architecture, including the 1910 **Kaiserliches Postampt** (Imperial Post Office; cnr 5th Ave & Fenschel St), and the **town museum** (☎ 221256; cnr Kaiser St & 7th Ave; admission free; 🕑 7.30am-12.30pm & 2.30-4.30pm Mon-Fri), which is housed in the 1895 Rhenish Mission Church and outlines the history of Keetmanshoop with old photos, early farming implements, an old wagon and a model of a traditional Nama home.

About 25km north of town, **//Garas Park** (Map p367; ☎ 223217; morkel@namibnet.com; campsite per person N$35 plus per vehicle N$5, day admission per person N$10 plus per vehicle N$5) has stands of *kokerboom*, lots of hiking tracks and drives through a fantasy landscape of stacked boulders as well as some zany sculptures made from junk.

About 14km east of town, the **Quivertree Forest Rest Camp** (Map p367; ☎ 222835; www.quivertreeforest.com; campsite per person N$80, s/d/tr/q bungalows N$330/465/555/800, day admission per person N$50) proudly boasts Namibia's largest stand of *kokerboom*.

Getting There & Away

BUS

There are several weekly buses between Windhoek and Keetmanshoop (fares from N$288, seven hours) on the **Intercape Mainliner** (www.intercape.co.za). Book your tickets online as this service continues on to Cape Town and fills up quickly.

Combis also run up and down the B1 with fairly regular frequency, and a ride between Windhoek and Keetmanshoop shouldn't cost more than N$100. Less regular combis connect Keetmanshoop to the black township in Lüderitz, with fares averaging around N$175.

TRAIN

Trans-Namib (☎ 061-298 2175) also operates a daily night train between Windhoek and Keetmanshoop (fares from N$90).

DUWISIB CASTLE

☎ 063

A curious neo-baroque structure, 70km south of Maltahöhe and smack dab in the middle of the barren desert, this full-on

NAMIBIA

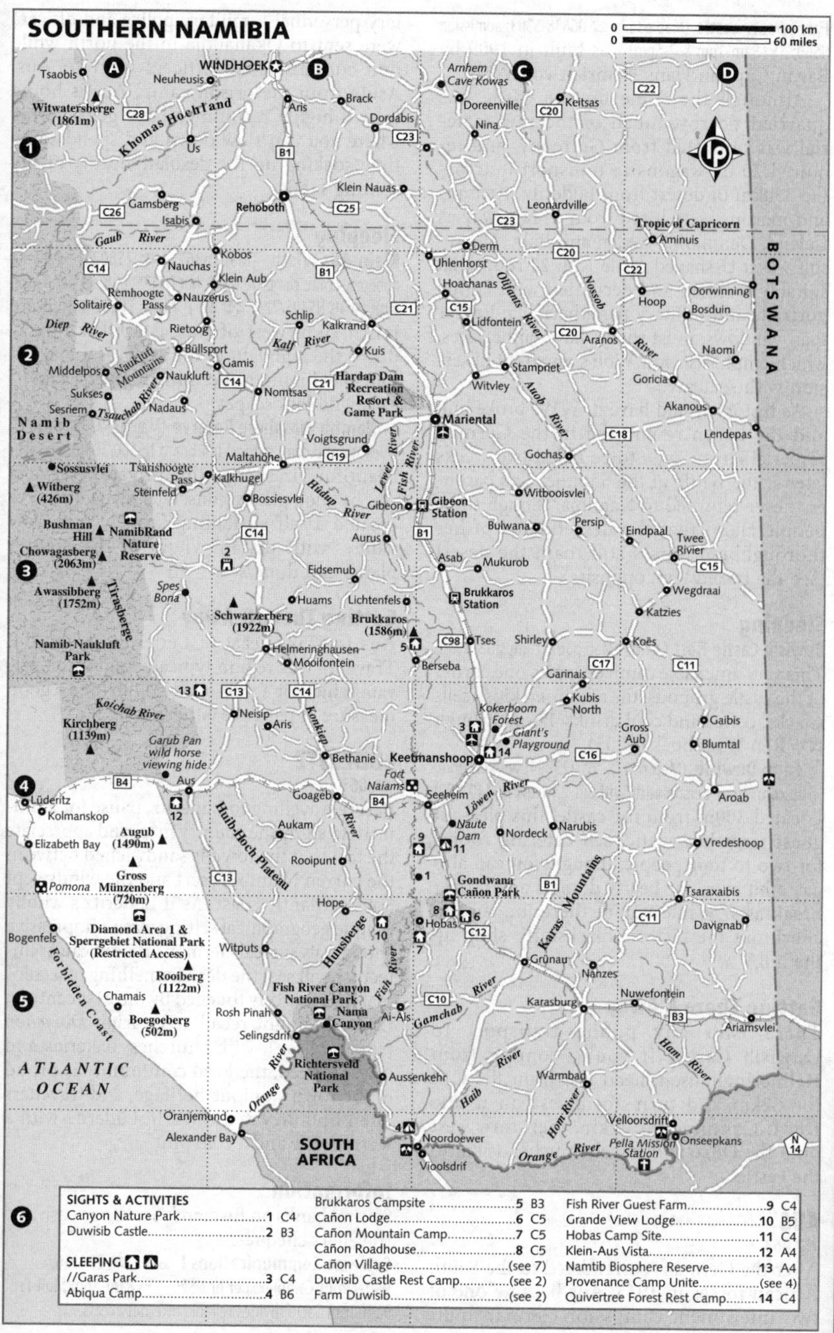
SOUTHERN NAMIBIA
0 100 km
0 60 miles
A
B
C
D
1
2
3
4
5
6
Tsaobis
WINDHOEK
Neuheusis
Witwatersberge (1861m)
C28
Khomas Hochland
Us
Aris
Brack
Dordabis
B1
C23
Arnhem Cave Kowas
Doreenville
Nina
Keitsas
C20
C22
Klein Nauas
Rehoboth
C25
Gamsberg
C26
Isabis
Leonardville
C23
Tropic of Capricorn
Aminuis
Gaub River
Kobos
Derm
Uhlenhorst
C20
C14
Nauchas
B1
Klein Aub
Hoachanas
C15
Olifants River
Nossob
C22
Hoop
Oorwinning
Bosduin
BOTSWANA
Remhoogte Pass
Solitaire
Nauzerus
Schlip
Kalkrand
C21
Lidfontein
C20
Aranos
Diep River
Rietoog
Kalf River
Kuis
Naomi
Büllsport
Naukluft Mountains
Gamis
Stampriet
Middelpos
Naukluft
C14
C21
Hardap Dam Recreation Resort & Game Park
Witvley
Goricia
Sukses
Tsauchab River
Nomtsas
Auob River
Sesriem
Nadaus
Akanous
Namib Desert
Mariental
Voigtsgrund
C18
Lendepas
Maltahöhe
C19
Lower Fish River
Gochas
Sossusvlei
Tsarishoogte Pass
Kalkhugel
Witberg (426m)
Steinfeld
Hudup River
Witbooisvlei
Bossiesvlei
Gibeon
Gibeon Station
Bushman Hill
NamibRand Nature Reserve
C14
B1
Aurus
Bulwana
Persip
Eindpaal
Twee Rivier
Chowagasberg (2063m)
2
Asab
Mukurob
C15
Eidsemub
Awassibberg (1752m)
Tirasberge
Spes Bona
Wegdraai
Huams
Lichtenfels
Brukkaros Station
Schwarzerberg (1922m)
Brukkaros (1586m)
Katzies
Namib-Naukluft Park
5
C98
Tses
Shirley
Koës
Helmeringhausen
Mooifontein
Berseba
C17
C11
13
C13
C14
Garinais
Kubis North
Koichab River
Neisip
Kokerboom Forest
Kirchberg (1139m)
Aris
Konkiep
3
Giant's Playground
Gross Aub
Gaibis
Garub Pan wild horse viewing hide
Bethanie
Keetmanshoop
14
C16
Blumtal
B4
Aus
Fort Naiams
Löwen River
Lüderitz
Goageb
Seeheim
Aroab
Kolmanskop
12
B4
Huib-Hoch Plateau
Aukam
River
Naute Dam
Nordeck
Narubis
Elizabeth Bay
Augub (1490m)
9
11
Vredeshoop
Rooipunt
Gross Münzenberg (720m)
C13
1
Gondwana Cañon Park
B1
Karas Mountains
Pomona
Tsaraxaibis
Hope
8
6
Diamond Area 1 & Sperrgebiet National Park (Restricted Access)
Hobas
C11
Davignab
Bogenfels
10
C12
Huns berge
7
Witputs
Fish River
Grünau
Nanzes
Forbidden Coast
Rooiberg (1122m)
Chamais
Fish River Canyon National Park
Nama Canyon
C10
River
Karasburg
Nuwefontein
Rosh Pinah
Ai-Ais
Gamchab
B3
Ariamsvlei
Boegoeberg (502m)
Selingsdrif
Ham River
ATLANTIC OCEAN
Richtersveld National Park
River
Aussenkehr
Warmbad
Orange
Haib
Hom River
Oranjemund
Velloorsdrift
Alexander Bay
4
Noordoewer
Onseepkans
SOUTH AFRICA
Orange River
Pella Mission Station
N14
Vioolsdrif
SIGHTS & ACTIVITIES
Canyon Nature Park 1 C4
Duwisib Castle 2 B3
SLEEPING
//Garas Park 3 C4
Abiqua Camp 4 B6
Brukkaros Campsite 5 B3
Cañon Lodge 6 C5
Cañon Mountain Camp 7 C5
Cañon Roadhouse 8 C5
Cañon Village (see 7)
Duwisib Castle Rest Camp (see 2)
Farm Duwisib (see 2)
Fish River Guest Farm 9 C4
Grande View Lodge 10 B5
Hobas Camp Site 11 C4
Klein-Aus Vista 12 A4
Namtib Biosphere Reserve 13 A4
Provenance Camp Unite (see 4)
Quivertree Forest Rest Camp 14 C4

NAMIBIA

European **castle** (Map p367; ☎ 06638-5303; admission N$60; ⏰ 8am-1pm & 2-5pm) was built in 1909 by Baron Captain Hans Heinrich von Wolf.

Although the stone for the castle was quarried nearby, much of the raw material was imported from Germany, and required 20 ox wagons to transport it across the 330km of desert from Lüderitz. Artisans and masons were hired from as far away as Ireland, Denmark, Sweden and Italy. The result was a U-shaped castle with 22 rooms, all suitably fortified and decorated with family portraits and military paraphernalia. Rather than windows, most rooms have embrasures, which emphasise von Wolf's apparent obsession with security.

As history would have it, WWI broke out, and the baron re-enlisted in the German Imperial Army, only to be killed two weeks later at the Battle of the Somme. The baroness never returned to Namibia, though some people claim that the descendants of her thoroughbred horses still roam the desert (see the boxed text, opposite).

Sleeping

Duwisib Castle Rest Camp (Map p367; campsites N$50) This very amenable camp occupies one corner of the castle grounds; the adjoining kiosk sells snacks, coffee and cool drinks. Book through NWR in Windhoek (p305).

Farm Duwisib (Map p367; ☎ 223994; www.farmduwisib.com; r per person with/without 2 meals N$440/390) Located 300m from the castle, this pleasant guest farm has rustic, self-catering rooms for two to four people, though you can also pay a bit extra for hearty dinners and proper breakfasts. While you're there, be sure to check out the historic blacksmith shop up the hill.

Getting There & Away

There isn't any public transport to Duwisib Castle. If you're coming from Helmeringhausen, head north on the C14 for 62km and turn northwest on to the D831. Continue for 27km, then turn west onto the D826 and travel a further 15km to the castle.

AUS

☎ 063

After the Germans surrendered to the South African forces in 1915, Aus became one of two internment camps for German military personnel – military police and officers were sent to Okahandja in the north while non-commissioned officers went to Aus. Aside from the prison camp, Aus is home to two highly recommendable guest farms where you can slow down and spend some time soaking up the desolate beauty of the shifting sands.

Sleeping

Klein-Aus Vista (Map p367; ☎ 258021; www.namibhorses.com; campsite N$75, hut N$125, r/chalet per person with meals N$495/725; ✿ ⛰) This 10,000-hectare ranch, 3km west of Aus, is a hiker's paradise – the highlight of the ranch is a magical four-day hiking route, which traverses fabulous wild landscapes.

Namtib Biosphere Reserve (Map p367; ☎ 683055; www.namtib.com; s/d incl full board N$600/1030) In the beautiful Tirasberge, this private reserve is run by ecologically conscious owners who've created a self-sustaining farm in a narrow valley, with distant views of the Namib plains and dune sea.

Getting There & Away

Aus is 125km east of Lüderitz on the B4. Travel in this region typically requires a private vehicle or a well-oiled thumb (and a good measure of patience either way).

LÜDERITZ

☎ 063

Before travelling to Lüderitz, pause for a moment to study the country map, and appreciate the fact that the town is sandwiched between the barren Namib Desert and the windswept South Atlantic coast. As if Lüderitz's wholly unique geographical setting wasn't impressive enough, its surreal German art nouveau architecture will seal the deal. Something of a colonial relic scarcely touched by the 21st century, Lüderitz might recall a Bavarian *Dorfchen* (small village), with churches, bakeries and cafes. Indeed, the local community is proud of the town's unique heritage, and travellers often find they're greeted in Lüderitz with a warm smile and a cold pint.

Information

Several banks on Bismarck St change cash and travellers cheques.

Extreme Communications I-café (☎ 204256; Waterfront Complex; per hr N$20; ⏰ 8am-5pm Mon-Fri, 9am-1pm Sat) Provides reliable internet access.

WILD HORSES

On the desert plains west of Aus live some of the world's only wild desert-dwelling horses. The origin of these eccentric equines is unclear, though several theories abound. One theory suggests that the horses are descended from Schutztruppe (German Imperial Army) cavalry horses abandoned during the South African invasion in 1915, while others claim they were brought in by Nama raiders moving north from beyond the Senqu (Orange) River. Yet another theory asserts that they descended from a load of shipwrecked horses en route from Europe to Australia. Still others maintain that the horses descended from the stud stock of Baron Captain Hans Heinrich von Wolf, the original owner of the Duwisib Castle.

These horses, whose bony and scruffy appearance belies their probable high-bred ancestry and apparent adaptation to the harsh conditions, are protected inside the Diamond Area 1. In years of good rain, they grow fat and their numbers increase to several hundred. Their only source of water is Garub Pan, which is fed by an artificial borehole. The horses may also be valuable for scientific purposes. For instance, they urinate less than domestic horses and are smaller than their supposed ancestors. The horses are also able to go without water for up to five days at a time. These adaptations may be valuable in helping scientists understand how animals cope with changing climatic conditions.

Lüderitz Safaris & Tours (☎ 202719; ludsaf@africaonline.com.na; Bismarck St; ⌚ 8am-1pm & 2-5pm Mon-Fri, 8am-noon Sat, 8.30-10am Sun) Provides reliable tourist information, organises visitor permits for the Kolmanskop ghost town (p373), books seats on the schooner *Sedina*, which sails past the Cape fur seal sanctuary at Diaz Point and the penguin colony on Halifax Island, and sells curios, books, stamps and phone cards.

Namibia Wildlife Resorts Office (NWR; ☎ 202752; Schinz St; ⌚ 7.30am-1pm & 2-4pm Mon-Fri) This local office can help with national park information.

Dangers & Annoyances

Stay well clear of the Sperrgebiet as the vast majority of the area is still strictly off-limits. The northern boundary is formed by the B4 and extends almost as far east as Aus. The boundary is vigorously patrolled, and trespassers will be prosecuted (or worse).

Sights

LÜDERITZ TOWN

Lüderitz is chock-a-block with colonial buildings, and every view reveals something interesting. The curiously intriguing architecture, which mixes German Imperial and art nouveau styles, makes this bizarre little town appear even more other-worldly.

Goerke Haus

Lieutenant Hans Goerke came to Swakopmund with the Schutztruppe in 1904, though he was later posted to Lüderitz, where he served as a diamond company manager. His **home** (Diamantberg St; admission N$16), designed by architect Otto Ertl and constructed in 1910 on Diamond Hill, was one of the town's most extravagant.

Felsenkirche

The prominent **Evangelical Lutheran church** (Kirche St; admission free), dominates Lüderitz from high on Diamond Hill. It was designed by Albert Bause, who implemented the Victorian influences he'd seen in the Cape. With assistance from private donors in Germany, construction of the church began in late 1911 and was completed the following year.

Lüderitz Museum

This **museum** (☎ 202582; Diaz St; admission N$10; ⌚ 3.30-5pm Mon-Fri) contains information on the town's history, including displays on natural history, local indigenous groups and the diamond-mining industry. Phone to arrange a visit outside standard opening hours.

LÜDERITZ PENINSULA

The Lüderitz Peninsula, much of which lies outside the Sperrgebiet, makes an interesting half-day excursion from town.

Agate Bay, just north of Lüderitz, is made of tailings from the diamond workings. There aren't many agates these days, but you'll find fine sand partially consisting of tiny grey mica chips.

The picturesque bay, **Sturmvogelbucht**, is a pleasant place for a braai, though the water temperature would be amenable only to a

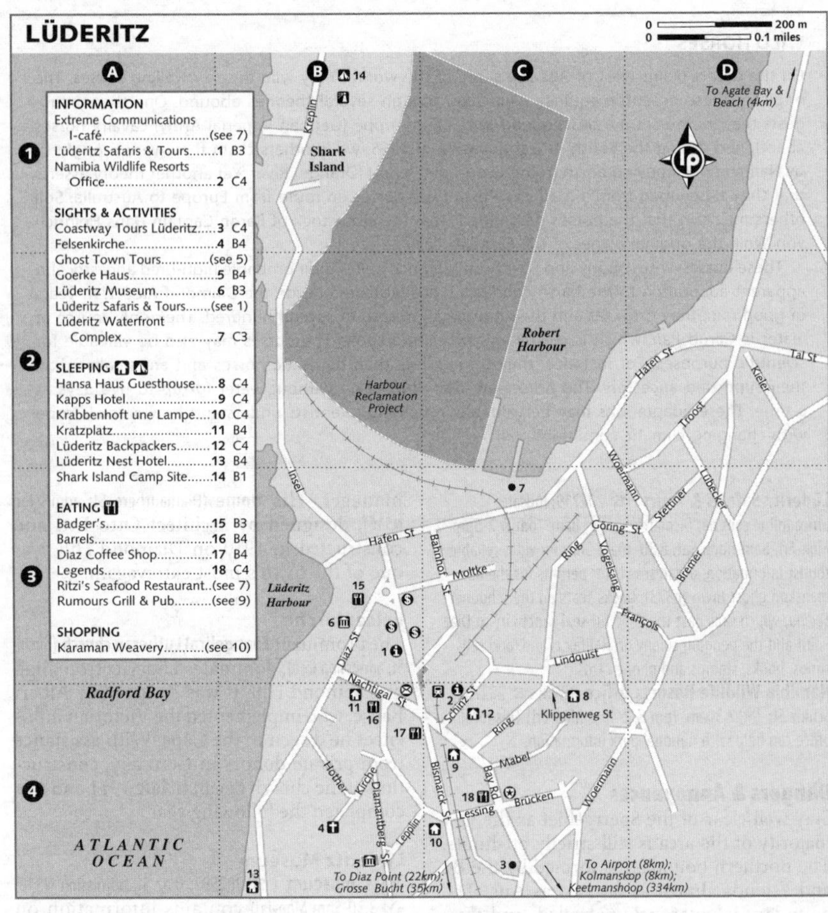

penguin or polar bear. The rusty ruin in the bay is the remains of a 1914 Norwegian whaling station; the salty pan just inland attracts flamingos and merits a quick stop.

At **Diaz Point**, 22km by road from Lüderitz, is a classic lighthouse and a replica of the cross erected in July 1488 by Portuguese navigator Bartolomeu Dias on his return from the Cape of Good Hope.

Halifax Island, a short distance offshore south of Diaz Point, is home to Namibia's best-known jackass penguin colony.

Grosse Bucht (Big Bay), at the southern end of Lüderitz Peninsula, is a wild and scenic beach favoured by flocks of flamingos, which feed in the tidal pools.

Just a few kilometres up the coast is **Klein Bogenfels**, a small rock arch beside the sea. When the wind isn't blowing a gale, it makes a pleasant picnic spot.

Tours

With the exception of the Kolmanskop ghost town, allow at least five days to plan any excursion into the Sperrgebiet as tour companies need time to fill out all of the paperwork and acquire all of the necessary permits.

Coastway Tours Lüderitz (☎ 202002; www.coastways.com.na; Bay Rd) This highly reputable company runs multi-day self-catering 4WD trips deep into the Sperrgebiet.

Ghost Town Tours (☎ 204033; www.ghosttowntours.com; Goerke Haus) This company operates day trips to Kolmanskop, Elizabeth Bay and other sights in the Sperrgebiet.

Lüderitz Safaris & Tours (☎ 202719; ludsaf@africaonline.com.na; Bismarck St; 🕑 8am-1pm & 2-5pm Mon-Fri, 8am-noon Sat, 8.30-10am Sun) See p368.

Sleeping

Shark Island Camp Site (day entry N$40, campsite N$50 plus per person N$20, 6-person bungalow N$450, lighthouse N$850) This is a beautifully situated but aggravatingly windy locale. Shark Island is connected to the town by a causeway but is no longer an island, thanks to the harbour reclamation project that attached it to the mainland. Book accommodation through Namibia Wildlife Resorts (NWR) in Windhoek (p305) or in Lüderitz.

Lüderitz Backpackers (☎ 202000; www.namibweb.com/backpackers.htm; 7 Schinz St; campsite N$115, dm/d N$145/365) Housed in a historic colonial mansion, this friendly place is the only true backpacker spot in town – the vibe is congenial and low-key, and the friendly management is helpful in sorting out your onward travels.

Krabbenhoft une Lampe (☎ 202674; info@klguesthouse.com; 25 Bismarck St; s/d from N$150/250) One of the more unusual sleeping options in town, the Krabbenhoft is a converted carpet factory that now offers a number of basic rooms and self-catering flats upstairs from a weaver.

Hansa Haus Guesthouse (☎ 203581; mcloud@africaonline.com.na; Klippenweg St; s/d from N$200/400) This imposing hilltop home, which dates back to 1909 and is presently splashed out in regal blues and rich woods, boasts dramatic sea views and quiet surroundings.

Kapps Hotel (☎ 202345; pmk@mweb.com.na; Bay Rd; r per person from N$225) This is the town's oldest hotel, dating back to 1907, though a recent renovation has managed to retain the historical ambience while adding a touch of modernity.

Kratzplatz (☎ 202458; kratzmr@iway.na; 5 Nachtigal St; s/d from N$350/450) Housed in a converted church complete with vaulted ceilings, this centrally located B&B offers a variety of different rooms to choose from.

Lüderitz Nest Hotel (☎ 204000; www.nesthotel.com; 820 Diaz St; r per person from N$580; ❄ 🏊) Lüderitz's oldest upmarket hotel occupies a jutting peninsula in the southwest corner of town complete with its own private beach.

Eating

Diaz Coffee Shop (☎ 203147; cnr Bismarck St & Nachtigal St; snacks & meals N$10-30) The cappuccinos are strong and the pastries are sweet, and the ambiance wouldn't look out of place in Munich.

Badger's (☎ 202855; Diaz St; meals N$20-45) An excellent choice for a cold lager and some hot pub grub, Badger's is a lively spot where you can count on finding good company.

Rumours Grill & Pub (☎ 202655; Bismarck St; meals $25-55; 🕑 lunch & dinner) Part bustling sports bar, part German-style beer garden, Rumours is something of a Lüderitz institution that has been in business for decades.

Barrels (☎ 202458; 5 Natchtigal; mains N$35-75) A wonderfully festive restaurant accented by occasional live music, Barrels offers rotating daily specials highlighting fresh seafood and German staples.

Legends (☎ 203110; Bay Rd; mains N$45-85) This understated restaurant has a relaxed atmosphere and serves up a healthy mix of seafood, grilled meats, pizzas and burgers, as well as the odd vegetarian option or two.

Ritzi's Seafood Restaurant (☎ 202818; Waterfront; mains N$85-215) Occupying a choice location in the new waterfront complex, Ritzi's is the town's top spot for amazing seafood matched with equally amazing sunset views.

Shopping

Karaman Weavery (☎ 202272; 25 Bismarck St) This shop specialises in locally woven high-quality rugs and garments in pastel desert colours, with Namibian flora and fauna the favoured designs. It accepts special orders and can post them worldwide.

Getting There & Away

AIR

Air Namibia travels several times a week between Windhoek and Lüderitz, at least once weekly to/from Swakopmund, and at least twice weekly to/from Walvis Bay. The airport is 8km southeast of town.

BUS

Somewhat irregular combis connect Lüderitz to Keetmanshoop, with fares averaging around N$175. Buses depart from the southern edge of town at informal bus stops along Bismarck St.

CAR & MOTORCYCLE

Lüderitz and the scenery en route are worth the 334km trip from Keetmanshoop via the tarred B4.

SPERRGEBIET NATIONAL PARK

Although it's been off-limits to the public for most of the last century, in 2008 the Namibian government inaugurated its newest national park, the Sperrgebiet. Known as the source of Namibia's exclusive diamonds, the Sperrgebiet (forbidden area) is set to become the gem of Namibia's protected spaces. The park encompasses the northern tip of the Succulent Karoo Biorne, an area of 26,000 sq km of dunes and mountains that appear dramatically stark, but represent one of 25 outstanding global hotspots of unique biodiversity.

The Sperrgebiet originally consisted of two private concessions: Diamond Area 1 and Diamond Area 2. The latter, home to the Kolmanskop ghost town and Elizabeth Bay, has been open to the public for some time now. Since 2004, parts of the former have also been opened up to specialist conservation groups, though given the diamond industry's security concerns, access has been carefully controlled.

At the time of research, the Namibian Ministry of Environment and Tourism (MET) announced its intention to open up further tourism concessions within Area 1. While it may be another couple of years before travel restrictions are fully eased, the chance to be one of the first civilians to step foot in this zone is an enticing prospect.

Orientation & Information

The 'forbidden area' was established in 1908 following the discovery of diamonds near

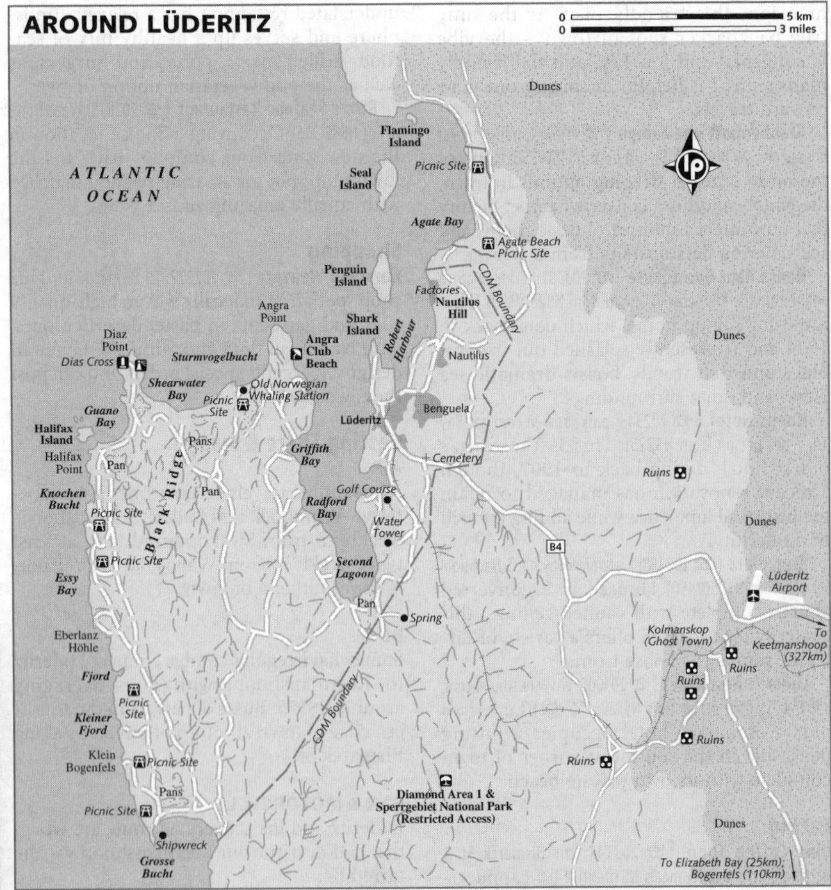

Lüderitz. Although mining operations were localised along the coast, a huge swath of southern Namibia was sectioned off in the interest of security.

As a diamond mining concession, the Sperrgebiet has been off-limits to the public and scientists for most of the last century, and the tight restrictions on access have helped to keep much of the area pristine. De Beers Centenary, a partner in De Beers Consolidated Diamond Mines, continues to control the entire area until the Ministry of the Environment and Tourism establishes a management plan for the park.

Around 40% of the park is desert and 30% is grassland; the rest is rocks, granite mountains and moonscape. Though the area has yet to be fully explored, initial scientific assessments have discovered 776 plant species, 230 of which are thought to be unique to the park. There are also populations of gemsboks, brown hyenas and rare, threatened reptile species, including the desert rain frog. Bird species are extremely varied, and include the dune lark, the black-headed canary and the African oystercatcher.

The area has been identified as a priority area for conservation in the **Succulent Karoo Ecosystem Plan** (SKEP; www.skep.org). SKEP is a joint Namibian and South African initiative that brings together all the stakeholders in the region, from government ministries to local populations. The program is supported by the **Critical Ecosystem Partnership Fund** (CEPF; www.cepf.net), which acts as its locally based coordination team.

Also involved is the **Namibian Nature Foundation** (NNF; www.nnf.org.na), which will eventually take over the planning for the park and will focus on community-based initiatives to ensure that locals benefit. The development of tourism in the Sperrgebiet is expected to stimulate the economy of Lüderitz, which will serve as the main gateway to the park.

Sights

KOLMANSKOP GHOST TOWN

Given that permits can be arranged from Namdeb (Namdeb Diamond Corporation Limited) with relative ease, the most popular excursion from Lüderitz is the ghost town of Kolmanskop. Named after an early Afrikaner trekker, Jani Kolman, whose ox wagon became bogged in the sand here, Kolmanskop was originally constructed as the Consolidated Diamond Mines (CDM) headquarters. Although Kolmanskop once boasted a casino, bowling alley and theatre with fine acoustics, the slump in diamond sales after WWI and the discovery of richer pickings at Oranjemund ended its heyday. By 1956, the town was totally deserted and left to the mercy of the shifting desert sands. Today, Kolmanskop has been partially restored as a tourist attraction, and the sight of decrepit buildings being invaded by dunes is simply too surreal to describe.

You can turn up at any time, and you're not required to arrive as part of an organised tour, though you do need to purchase a permit (N$40) in advance through either Namibian Wildlife Resorts in Lüderitz (p368) or a local tour operator. To photograph Kolmanskop you can purchase an additional permit for N$125. Guided tours (in English and German), which are included in the price of the permit, depart from the museum in Kolmanskop at 9.30am and 11am Monday to Saturday, and at 10am Sunday and public holidays. After the tour, you can return to the museum, which contains relics and information on the history of Namibian diamond mining.

ELIZABETH BAY

In 1986, CDM again began prospecting in the northern Sperrgebiet, and found bountiful diamond deposits around Elizabeth Bay, 30km south of Kolmanskop. The estimated 2.5 million carats weren't expected to last more than 10 years, but CDM installed a full-scale operation and, rather than duplicate their Lüderitz facilities here, they provided their workers with daily transport from the town. Half-day tours to Elizabeth Bay, which must be booked through tour operators in Lüderitz, also take in Kolmanskop and the Atlas Bay Cape fur seal colony.

BOGENFELS SEA ARCH

One-third of the way down the Forbidden Coast, between Lüderitz and Oranjemund, is the 55m natural sea arch known as Bogenfels (Bow Rock). Bogenfels has only been opened to private tours for a few years, which also take in the mining ghost town of Pomona, the Maerchental Valley, the Bogenfels ghost town and a large cave near the arch itself. Again, you must book this trip through tour operators in Lüderitz.

DIAMOND DEMENTIA

Diamonds are the best-known allotrope (form) of carbon, and are characterised by their extreme hardness (they are the hardest naturally occurring mineral) and high dispersion of light (diamonds are prismatic when exposed to white light). As a result, they are valued for industrial purposes as abrasives since they can only be scratched by other diamonds, and for ornamental purposes since they retain their lustre when polished. It's estimated that 130 million carats (or 26,000kg) of diamonds are mined annually, yielding a market value of over US$9 billion.

Diamonds are formed when carbon-bearing materials are exposed to high pressures and temperatures for prolonged periods of time. With the exception of synthetically produced diamonds, favourable conditions only occur beneath the continental crust, starting at depths of about 150km. Once carbon crystallises, a diamond will then continue to grow in size so long as it is exposed to both sufficiently high temperatures and pressures. However, size is limited by the fact that diamond-bearing rock is eventually expelled towards the surface through deep-origin volcanic eruptions. Eventually, they are forced to the surface by magma, and are expelled from a volcanic pipe.

Since the early 20th century the quality of a diamond has been determined by four properties, now commonly used as basic descriptors of a stone – carat, clarity, colour and cut. The carat weight measures the mass of a diamond, with one carat equal to 200mg. Assuming all other properties are equal, the value of a diamond increases exponentially in relation to carat weight since larger diamonds are rarer.

Clarity is a measure of internal defects known as inclusions, which are foreign materials or structural imperfections present in the stone. Higher clarity is associated with value, and it's estimated that only about 20% of all diamonds mined have a high enough clarity rating to be sold as gemstones.

Although a perfect diamond is transparent with a total absence of hue, virtually all diamonds have a discernable colour due to chemical impurities and structural defects. Depending on the hue and intensity, a diamond's colour can either detract from or enhance its value (yellow diamonds are discounted, while pink and blue diamonds are more valuable).

Finally, the cut of a diamond describes the quality of workmanship and the angles to which a diamond is cut.

Tours

Until the park loosens its tight restrictions on public access, it's in your own best interest to have a healthy respect for the boundaries. Armed guards in the Sperrgebiet have a lot of time on their hands – don't make their day. Select sights in the national park are open to visitors on private tours – for listings of approved operators, see p370.

Sleeping

There are no tourist lodges within the national park, and bush camping is strictly forbidden. It's likely that some form of accommodation will be constructed in the years to come; in the meantime your best option is to base yourself in Lüderitz (see p371).

Getting There & Away

Do not attempt to access the Sperrgebiet in a private vehicle as you will be inviting a whole mess of trouble. The only exception to this statement is Kolmanskop, which can be accessed if you have a sturdy 4WD along with the necessary permits.

FISH RIVER CANYON NATIONAL PARK

☎ 063

Nowhere else in Africa will you find anything quite like Fish River Canyon, part of the |Ai-|Ais/Richtersveld Transfrontier Park. Despite the enormity of this statement, the numbers don't lie: the canyon measures 160km in length and up to 27km in width; the dramatic inner canyon reaches a depth of 550m. The figures are impressive but it's difficult to get a sense of perspective without actually witnessing the enormous scope of the canyon, which means embarking on a monumental five-day hike traversing half the length of the canyon that will ultimately test the limits of your physical and mental endurance.

Information

The main access points for Fish River Canyon are at Hobas, near the northern end of the park, and Ai-Ais, near the southern end. Both are administered by Namibian Wildlife Resorts (NWR). Accommodation must be booked in advance through the Windhoek office (p305). Daily park permits (N$80 per person and N$10 per vehicle) are valid for both Hobas and Ai-Ais.

The **Hobas Information Centre** (7.30am-noon & 2-5pm) at the northern end of the park is also the check-in point for the five-day canyon hike. Packaged snacks and cool drinks are available here, but little else.

Sights

HOBAS

From Hobas, it's 10km on a gravel road to the **Hikers' Viewpoint** (start of the hiking route), which has picnic tables, braai pits and toilets. Just around the corner is a good overview of the northern part of the canyon. The **Main Viewpoint**, a few kilometres south, has probably the best – and most photographed – overall canyon view. Both these vistas take in the sharp riverbend known as Hell's Corner.

AI-AIS

The **hot springs** (per person N$15; 9am-9pm) at Ai-Ais (Nama for 'Scalding Hot') are beneath the towering peaks at the southern end of Fish River Canyon National Park. Although the 60°C springs have probably been known to the San for thousands of years, the legend goes that they were 'discovered' by a nomadic Nama shepherd rounding up stray sheep. They're rich in chloride, fluoride and sulphur, and are reputedly therapeutic for sufferers of rheumatism or nervous disorders. The hot water is piped to a series of baths and Jacuzzis as well as an outdoor swimming pool.

CANYON NATURE PARK

Technically outside Fish River National Park, this **nature park** (Map p367; ☎ 683005; www.canyonnaturepark.com) is a private concession situated in the confluence of the Löwen and Fish River Canyons amid some of the most amazing geology imaginable. The best part of visiting is that the area falls outside the jurisdiction of NWR, which means you don't need to book through Windhoek if you want to hike here.

Activities

FISH RIVER HIKING TRAIL

The five-day **hike** (per person N$100) from Hobas to Ai-Ais is Namibia's most popular long-distance walk – and with good reason. The magical 85km route, which follows the sandy riverbed past a series of ephemeral pools, begins at Hikers' Viewpoint, and ends at the hot spring resort of Ai-Ais.

Due to flash flooding and heat in summer months, the route is open only from 1 May to 30 September. Groups of three to 30 people may begin the hike every day of the season, though you will have to book in advance as the trail is extremely popular. Reservations can be made at the NWR office in Windhoek (p305).

Officials may need a doctor's certificate of fitness, issued less than 40 days before your hike, though if you look young and fit they may not ask. Hikers must arrange their own transport to and from the start and finish as well as accommodation in Hobas and Ai-Ais.

Thanks to the typically warm, clear weather, you probably won't need a tent, but you must carry a sleeping bag and food. In Hobas, check on water availability in the canyon. In August and September, the last 15km of the walk can be completely dry and hikers will need several 2L water bottles to manage this hot, sandy stretch. Large plastic soft-drink bottles normally work just fine.

Sleeping

Accommodation inside the national park must be prebooked through the NWR office in Windhoek (p305).

Hobas Camp Site (per person N$20, campsite N$50;) Administered by NWR, this pleasant and well-shaded camping ground near the park's northern end is about 10km from the main viewpoints.

Ai-Ais Hot Springs Resort (Map p367; per person N$20, campsite N$50, flats from N$600;) Also administered by NWR, amenities include washing blocks, braai pits and use of the resort facilities, including the hot springs.

Fish River Guest Farm (Map p367; ☎ 683005; www.canyonnaturepark.com; r with shared bathroom per person from N$250) Located near the eastern rim in the Canyon Nature Park concession off the C12, this historic farmhouse serves self-catering hikers of all skill levels.

Grande View Lodge (Map p367; ☎ 683005; www.canyonnaturepark.com; r per person from N$1550;)

Perched on the western rim in the Canyon Nature Park concession along the D463, the Grande View is by far the most luxurious lodge in the region.

Getting There & Away

There's no public transport to Hobas or Ai-Ais.

GONDWANA CAÑON PARK

Founded in 1996, the 100,000-hectare Gondwana Cañon Park was created by amalgamating several former sheep farms and removing the fences to restore the wilderness country immediately northeast of Fish River Canyon National Park. Water holes have been established and wildlife is now returning to this wonderful, remote corner of Namibia. In the process, the park absorbed the former Augurabies-Steenbok Nature Reserve, which had been created earlier to protect not only steenboks but also Hartmann's mountain zebras, gemsboks and klipspringers.

Information

Funding for the park is derived from a 5% bed levy applied to all four Cañon lodges. Any and all of these properties can be booked through the **reservation centre** (☎ 061-230066; www.gondwana-canyon-park.com). A wide range of activities, from 4WD excursions and guided hikes to horse riding and scenic flights, are available at all of the lodges.

Sleeping

Cañon Roadhouse (☎ 061-230066; www.gondwana-canyon-park.com; campsite per person N$85, s/d from N$620/990;) This wonderfully unique place attempts to recreate a roadhouse out on the wildest stretches of Route 66 – at least as it exists in the collective imagination.

Cañon Mountain Camp (☎ 061-230066; www.gondwana-canyon-park.com; r per person from N$295) One of the more budget-oriented properties in the Cañon collection, this remote mountain camp occupies a high altitudinous setting amid dolerite hills.

Cañon Village (☎ 061-230066; www.gondwana-canyon-park.com; s/d from N$995/1590;) Drawing inspiration from the Cape Dutch villages of yesteryear, this wonderfully bucolic spot hugs a rock face on the outskirts of Fish River Canyon.

Cañon Lodge (☎ 061-230066; www.gondwana-canyon-park.com; s/d from N$995/1590;) This mountain retreat is one of Namibia's most stunning accommodation options, consisting of red-stone bungalows perfectly integrated into its boulder-strewn backdrop.

Getting There & Away

Gondwana Cañon Park can be accessed via private vehicle along the C37.

NOORDOEWER

☎ 063

Noordoewer sits astride the Orange River, which has its headwaters in the Drakensberg Mountains of Natal (South Africa) and forms much of the boundary between Namibia and South Africa. The river was named not for its muddy colour, but for Prince William V of Orange, the Dutch monarch in the late 1770s. Although the town primarily exists as a border post and a centre for viticulture, it serves as a good base for organising a canoeing or rafting adventure on the Orange River.

Activities

RIVER TRIPS

Canoe and rafting trips are normally done in stages and last three to six days. The popular trips from Noordoewer north to Aussenkehr aren't treacherous by any stretch – the white water never exceeds Class II – but they do provide access to some wonderfully wild canyon country. Other possible stages include Aussenkehr to the Fish River mouth; Fish River mouth to Nama Canyon (which has a few more serious rapids); and Nama Canyon to Selingsdrif.

Amanzi Trails (☎ South Africa 27-21-559 1573; www.amanzitrails.co.za) This well-established South African company is based in Abiqua Camp (see Sleeping below), and specialises in four-/five-day guided canoe trips down the Orange River costing N$1950/2250 per person. It can also arrange shorter self-guided trips and longer excursions up Fish River for more experienced clients.

Felix Unite (South Africa ☎ 27-21-670-1300; www.felixunite.com) Another highly reputable South African operator, Felix Unite is based in Provenance Camp, and specialises in four-/six-day guided canoe and rafting trips down the Orange River costing N$2200/2450 per person. It can also combine these excursions with lengthier trips around the Western Cape of South Africa.

Sleeping

Abiqua Camp (Map p367; ☎ 297255; www.amanzitrails.co.za; campsite per person N$55, s/d/tr chalet N$300/355/410)

This friendly and well-situated camp, 15km down Orange River Rd, sits on the riverbank opposite some interesting sedimentary formations. This is the launching point for Amanzi Trails, so you can stock up on supplies, indulge in a hot meal and get a good night's rest before embarking on your canoe trip.

Provenance Camp Unite (Map p367; ☎ South Africa 27-21-670-1300; www.felixunite.com; campsite per person N$70, permanent twin tent N$350, twin cabana N$650) Approximately 10km west of Noordoewer is this chic safari river camp and launching point for Felix Unite. Purists can pitch their own tent on the grassy field, while lovers of creature comforts can bed down in a permanent tent or chalet, and stockpile their reserves for the paddling ahead.

Getting There & Away

The town is just off the B1 near the South African border, and is only accessible by private transport.

NAMIBIA DIRECTORY

ACCOMMODATION

Namibia has an exhaustive (and growing) array of hotels, rest camps, camping grounds, caravan parks, guest farms, backpackers' hostels, B&Bs, guest houses and safari lodges. It would take an enormous volume to mention everything that's available, so those included in this book are recommended and/or provide accommodation in areas with few options. Note, however, that the lack of a mention here doesn't mean that an establishment *isn't* recommended.

For further information, see the following annual publications, which are distributed at tourist offices: *Where to Stay – Namibia; Welcome to Namibia – Tourist Accommodation & Info Guide; Namibia Holiday & Travel* and the listings and accompanying map published by the Hospitality Association of Namibia (HAN).

Hotels and most other establishments are graded using a star system; awards are based on guidelines from the Ministry of Environment and Tourism. The accommodation rates listed in this chapter are rack rates for overseas bookings and include 15% value-added tax (VAT). In most cases, you'll get the best rates when booking from within Namibia.

The accommodation breakdown used in this chapter is budget (less than N$450), midrange (N$450 to N$900), and top end (above N$900).

Camping

Most towns have caravan parks with bungalows or rondavels (round African-style huts) where

PRACTICALITIES

- Namibia uses the metric system for weights and measures.
- Plugs have three round pins; the current is 220/240V, 50Hz. If you don't have the right adaptor, you can always buy a plug locally and connect it yourself. Note that a voltage adaptor is needed for US appliances.
- While Namibia ostensibly enjoys freedom of the press, no Namibian newspaper is known for its coverage of international events, and none takes a controversial stance on political issues. There are a decent number of commercial newspapers, of which the *Namibian* and the *Windhoek Advertiser* are probably the best. The *Windhoek Observer*, published on Saturday, is also good. The two main German-language newspapers are *Allgemeine Zeitung* and *Namibia Nachrichten*.
- The Namibian Broadcasting Corporation (NBC) operates a dozen or so radio stations broadcasting on different wavebands in nine languages. The two main stations in Windhoek are Radio Energy and Radio; the best pop station is Radio Wave, at 96.7FM in Windhoek.
- The NBC broadcasts government-vetted television programs in English and Afrikaans. News is broadcast at 10pm nightly. Most top-end hotels and lodges with televisions provide access to satellite-supported DSTV, which broadcasts NBC and a cocktail of cable channels: MNET (a South African-based movie and entertainment package), CNN, ESPN, MTV, BBC World, Sky, Supersport, SABC, SATV, NatGeo, Disney and Discovery, among other channels.

you can stay for very reasonable rates. For information on camping in national parks, see below. Anyone is welcome to camp on communal lands but, if you can't get out of sight, it's polite to ask locals to direct you to an unobtrusive place to set up. On private land, you must secure permission from the landowner.

Guest Farms

A growing number of predominantly German-Namibian private farms welcome guests, and provide insight into the white rural lifestyle. Many of these farms have also established hiking routes and set aside areas as wildlife and hunting reserves. In all cases, bookings are essential.

Hostels & B&Bs

Backpacker hostels now operate in Windhoek, Swakopmund, Walvis Bay, Outjo, Keetmanshoop and Lüderitz, and more are planned. They provide dorm accommodation and cooking facilities. B&B establishments are also emerging around the country; for listings, contact the **Budget & Home Association of Namibia** (☎ 061-222899; www.bed-breakfast-namibia.com; PO Box 90270, Klein Windhoek).

Hotels

The Namibian hotel-classification system rates everything from small guest houses to four-star hotels. Most are locally owned and managed, and most have at least a breakfast room, if not a dining room and a bar. Any hotel with a name that includes the word *garni* lacks a full dining room, but does offer a simple breakfast. The most luxurious hotels include the Kalahari Sands and Windhoek Country Club, both in Windhoek, and the Swakopmund Hotel & Entertainment Centre.

National Parks Accommodation

Namibia Wildlife Resorts (NWR) oversees accommodation in the national parks and offers a range of campsites, bungalows, chalets and 'bus quarters' (for bus tours). Most sites include access to a swimming pool, shop, kiosk, restaurant, braai facilities and well-maintained ablutions (amenities) blocks. During school holidays, visitors may be limited to three nights at each of the three Etosha National Park camps and 10 nights at other camps. Pets aren't permitted in any camp, but kennels are available at the gates of Daan Viljoen, Von Bach Dam, Gross Barmen, Ai-Ais and Hardap Dam. For booking information, see p303.

Safari Lodges

Most of Namibia's lodges offer luxury accommodation and superb international cuisine. Rates are very reasonable when compared with similar places in other countries in the region and there's little multi-tier pricing. Even around the popular Etosha National Park, you'll pay a third of what you'd pay for similar lodges in the Okavango Delta. Other areas are even more reasonably priced.

ACTIVITIES

Hiking is a highlight in Namibia, and a growing number of private ranches have established wonderful hiking routes for their guests to enjoy; the finest ones include Klein-Aus Vista, near Aus, and Canyon Adventures Guest Farm, south of Keetmanshoop. You'll also find superb routes in the national parks: Daan Viljoen, Namib-Naukluft, Fish River Canyon, Waterberg Plateau and the Ugab River area of the Skeleton Coast.

A burgeoning craze is sandboarding, which is commercially available in Swakopmund. In the same area, operators offer horse and camel riding, quad biking, deep-sea fishing, sea kayaking, birdwatching and skydiving. A growing number of 4WD routes are opening up for a largely South African market, including several popular routes along remote sections of the Namib Desert. White-water rafting is available on the Kunene River, but it's extremely expensive; more down to earth is the white-water canoeing along the Orange River, on the South African border.

BOOKS

Guide to Namibian Game Parks, by Willie and Sandra Olivier, has the lowdown on national parks, wildlife reserves and other conservation areas, with useful maps and advice on wildlife viewing. It's available locally.

Horns of Darkness – Rhinos on the Edge, by conservationists Carol Cunningham and Joel Berger, describes a journey through the Namibian wilds to find and protect the country's remaining desert rhinos. *The Sheltering Desert*, by Henno Martin, is a Namibian classic recounting the adventures of German geologists Henno Martin and Hermann Korn, who spent two years in the Namib Desert avoiding Allied forces during WWII.

The Colonising Camera, by Wolfram Hartmann et al (eds), is part of the new historical writings. This book is an illustrated history of the country. *To Free Namibia: The Life of the First President of Namibia,* by Sam Nujoma, is an autobiography of the president. *Herero Heroes,* written by JB Gewald, blends oral and written accounts to provide a fascinating history of Namibia's Herero people. *Namibia – The Struggle for Liberation,* by Alfred T Moleah, is an account of Swapo's independence struggle and describes the situation before success was certain.

The Burning Shore, by Wilbur Smith, is highly entertaining and is probably the best novel set in Namibia. *Kaokoveld – the Last Wilderness,* by Anthony Hall-Martin, J du P Bothma and Clive Walker, is a breathtaking compilation of beguiling photos that will have you heading for northwestern Namibia.

BUSINESS HOURS

Normal business hours are from 8am to 1pm and 2.30pm to 5pm weekdays. In winter, when it gets dark early, some shops open at 7.30am and close at around 4pm. Lunchtime closing is almost universal. On Saturday, most city and town shops open from 8am to 1pm. Banks, government departments and tourist offices also keep these hours, but some petrol stations, especially along highways, are open 24 hours.

Restaurant opening hours vary according to the type of establishment – as a rule cafes and cheap eats will be open all day, closing in the early evening. More expensive restaurants will be open from around 10.30am to 11pm Monday to Saturday, usually with a break between lunch and dinner. Run-of-the-mill bars open from around 5pm until late, while nightclubs and late-night drinking spots open their doors at around 9pm (or 10pm) and keep going until 5am.

CHILDREN

Although Namibia is a safe place for children to travel in, be advised that child-related goods and services are extremely limited, particularly in the far fringes of the country.

CUSTOMS REGULATIONS

Any item (except vehicles) from elsewhere in the Southern African Customs Union – Botswana, South Africa, Lesotho and Swaziland – may be imported duty free. From elsewhere, visitors can import duty free 400 cigarettes or 250g of tobacco, 2L of wine, 1L of spirits and 250mL of eau de cologne.

DANGERS & ANNOYANCES

Theft isn't particularly rife in Namibia, but in Windhoek and Swakopmund avoid walking alone at night and conceal your valuables. Similarly, don't leave anything in sight inside a vehicle or at campsites, and keep valuables inside your sleeping bag at night.

Kavango and Caprivi have malarial mosquito problems, and bilharzia is present all over northern Namibia; in the eastern Caprivi, the tsetse fly is especially active at dusk, and all of northern Namibia's rivers harbour very large crocodiles.

East of Lüderitz, keep well clear of the Sperrgebiet, the prohibited diamond area, as well-armed patrols can be overzealous. The area begins immediately south of the Lüderitz–Keetmanshoop road and continues to just west of Aus, where the off-limits boundary turns south towards the Orange River.

EMBASSIES & CONSULATES

All of the following representations are in Windhoek (area code ☎ 061); opening hours are weekdays only:

Angola (Map p306; ☎ 227535; 3 Dr Agostino Neto St; 🕑 9am-1pm)
Botswana (Map p306; ☎ 221941; 101 Klein Windhoek; 🕑 8am-12.30pm)
Canada (Map p308; ☎ 251254; Suite 1118, Sanlam Centre, 154 Independence Ave; 🕑 8am-12.30pm)
Finland (Map p308; ☎ 221355; 5th fl, Sanlam Centre, 154 Independence Ave; 🕑 9am-noon Mon, Wed & Thu)
France (Map p308; ☎ 229021; 1 Goethe St; 🕑 8.30am-12.30pm & 2-5pm Mon-Thu, 8.30am-12.30pm Fri)
Germany (Map p308; ☎ 273100; 6th fl, Sanlam Centre, 154 Independence Ave; 🕑 9am-noon)
Italy (Map p306; ☎ 228602; Anna & Gevers Sts, Ludwigsdorf; 🕑 8.30am-12.30pm & 2-5pm Mon-Thu, 8.30am-12.30pm Fri)
Kenya (Map p308; ☎ 226836; 5th fl, Kenya House, 134 Robert Mugabe Ave; 🕑 9am-12.30pm & 2-5pm)
Malawi (Map p308; ☎ 221391; 56 Bismarck St, Windhoek West; 🕑 8am-noon & 2-5pm)
South Africa (Map p306; ☎ 205 7111; RSA House, cnr Jan Jonker St & Nelson Mandela Dr, Klein Windhoek; 🕑 8.15am-12.15pm)
UK (Map p308; ☎ 223022; 116A Robert Mugabe Ave; 🕑 8am-1pm & 2-4pm Mon-Thu, 8am-noon Fri)
USA (Map p308; ☎ 221601; www.usembassy.namib.com; 14 Lossen St; 🕑 8.30am-noon Mon, Wed & Fri)

Zambia (Map p308; ☎ 237610; cnr Sam Nujoma Dr & Mandume Ndemufeyo Ave; 🕑 8am-1pm & 2-4pm)
Zimbabwe (Map p308; ☎ 228134; Gamsberg Bldg, cnr Independence Ave & Grimm St; 🕑 9am-12.30pm & 2-3pm)

FESTIVALS & EVENTS

A major local event is **Maherero Day**, on the weekend nearest 26 August, when the Red Flag Herero people gather in traditional dress at Okahandja for a memorial service for the chiefs killed in the German-Nama wars. A similar event, also at Okahandja, is staged by the Mbanderu (Green Flag Herero) on the weekend nearest 11 June. On the weekend nearest 10 October, the White Flag Herero gather in Omaruru to honour their chief, Zeraua.

Among the ethnic European community, events include the **Windhoek Karnival** (WIKA) in late April/early May; the **Küska** (Küste Karnival) at Swakopmund in late August/early September; the **Windhoek Agricultural Show** in late September; and the **Windhoek Oktoberfest** in late October.

HOLIDAYS

Resort areas are busiest over the Namibian and South African school holidays, which normally occur from mid-December to mid-January, around Easter, from late July to early August, and for two weeks in mid-October.

New Year's Day 1 January
Independence Day 21 March
Good Friday March or April
Easter Sunday March or April
Easter Monday March or April
Ascension Day April or May, 40 days after Easter
Workers' Day 1 May
Cassinga Day 4 May
Africa Day 25 May
Heroes' Day 26 August
Human Rights Day 10 December
Christmas 25 December
Family/Boxing Day 26 December

INTERNET ACCESS

Email and internet access are available at backpacker hostels, internet cafes and hotels in larger towns, and also at several tourist offices and remote lodges.

INTERNET RESOURCES

Cardboard Box Travel Shop (www.namibian.org) Namibia's best budget and adventure travel agency is the place for a range of travel options, excellent background information and efficient bookings.
Gorp Travel (www.gorp.com) This is another useful trip-planning site, with links to adventure outfits featuring Namibia.
Namibia Holiday & Travel (www.holidaytravel.com.na) This site provides information from the glossy publication of the same name.
Namibia Tourism (www.tourism.com.na) The national tourist office site provides a wide range of local travel information.
Namibia Wildlife Resorts (www.namibiawildliferesorts.com) Includes guidelines on booking national parks, permits and accommodation.
Namibian (www.namibian.com.na) For up-to-date news from Namibia, try the *Namibian* newspaper site.
Natron.net (www.natron.net/etour.htm) This is a good tourism site, with useful links.

For more information, see p23.

LANGUAGE

At independence in 1990, the official language of Namibia was designated as English, but the first language of most Namibians is either a Bantu language, which would include Owambo, Kavango, Herero and Caprivian languages; or a Khoisan language, including Khoikhoi (Nama/Damara) and San dialects. In addition, Afrikaans is used as a lingua franca, and is the first language of more than 100,000 Namibians of diverse ethnic backgrounds. German is also widely spoken but is the first language of only about 2% of the population. In the far north, Portuguese is the first language of an increasing number of Angolan immigrants. (See p775 for some useful words and phrases.)

MAPS

The Shell *Roadmap – Namibia* is probably the best reference for remote routes; it also has an excellent Windhoek map. Shell also publishes the *Kaokoland-Kunene Region Tourist Map,* which depicts all routes and tracks through this remote area. It's available at bookshops and tourist offices for US$3.

The Macmillan *Namibia Travellers' Map,* at a scale of 1:2.4 million, has clear print and colour-graded altitude representation, but minor routes aren't depicted.

Beautiful but generally outdated government survey topographic sheets and aerial photos are available from the **Office of the**

Surveyor General (Map p308; ☎ 061-245055; Ministry of Justice, Robert Mugabe Ave, Windhoek).

MONEY

The Namibian dollar (N$) equals 100 cents, and in Namibia it's pegged to the South African rand (in South Africa, it fetches only about R0.70), which is also legal tender at a rate of 1:1. This can be confusing, given that there are three sets of coins and notes in use, all with different sizes: old South African, new South African and Namibian. Namibian dollar notes come in denominations of N$10, N$20, N$50, N$100 and N$200, and coins in values of 5¢, 10¢, 20¢ and 50¢, and N$1 and N$5.

ATMs

ATMs are common in major cities and towns, and accept most major Western cards.

Credit Cards

Most major credit cards (especially Visa and MasterCard) are accepted at tourist hotels and restaurants in the larger cities and towns.

Moneychangers

To change cash, both Barclays and Standard Chartered banks charge 3% commission, while the former also charges 3% to change travellers cheques.

Tipping

Tipping is expected only in upmarket tourist establishments, but many places add a service charge as a matter of course. Tipping is officially prohibited in national parks and reserves, and bargaining is only acceptable when purchasing arts and handicrafts directly from the artist or artisan.

Travellers Cheques

Travellers cheques are falling into disuse in Namibia, though they can still be changed in large cities.

POST

Domestic post generally moves slowly; for example, it can take several weeks for a letter to travel from Windhoek to Lüderitz or Katima Mulilo. Overseas airmail post is normally more efficient, and is limited only by the time it takes the letter to get from where you post it to Windhoek. Poste restante works best in Windhoek (Poste Restante, GPO, Windhoek, Namibia). Photo identification is required to collect mail.

TELEPHONE & FAX

Namibian area codes all have three digits and begin with ☎ 06. When phoning Namibia from abroad, dial the international access code (☎ 09 from South Africa, ☎ 011 from the US and ☎ 00 from most other places), then the country code (☎ 264), followed by the area code (without the leading zero) and the desired number. To phone out of Namibia, dial ☎ 00 followed by the country code, area code and number.

Telecom Namibia Flexicards (you buy only as much time as you want) are sold at post offices and some retail shops, and most internet cafes also have fax services. Mobile coverage is usually fine in major towns and cities, and is improving out on the open road.

TOURIST INFORMATION

Local Tourist Offices

The level of service in Namibia's tourist offices is generally high, and everyone speaks impeccable English, German and Afrikaans.

Namibia's national tourist office, **Namibia Tourism** (☎ 061-220640, 284 2360; www.namibiatourism.com.na; Independence Ave, Private Bag 13346) is in Windhoek, where you'll also find the local **Windhoek Information & Publicity Office** (☎ 061-290 2058; Post St Mall), for more city-specific information.

Also in Windhoek is the office of **Namibia Wildlife Resorts** (Map p308; ☎ 061-285 7200; www.nwr.com.na; Erkrath Bldg, Independence Ave) where you can pick up information on the national parks and make reservations at any NWR campsite.

Other useful tourist offices include **Lüderitz Tours & Safaris** (p368) in Lüderitz, **Namib-i** (p346) in Swakopmund and **Travel North** (p320) in Tsumeb.

Tourist Offices Abroad

The Ministry of the Environment and Tourism maintains a number of tourist offices abroad. The staff are friendly, professional and eager to promote Namibia as a tourist destination.

France (☎ 01 40 50 88 63; 20 Ave Recteur Poincaré, Paris)

Germany (☎ 069-133 7360; 42-44 Schillerstrasse, Frankfurt)

South Africa Johannesburg (☎ 011-785 4626; 1 Orchard Lane, Rivonia) Cape Town (☎ 021-422 3298; Ground fl, The Pinnacle, Burg St)

UK (☎ 0870 330 9333; Suite 200, Parkway House, Sheen Lane, London)

VISAS

All visitors require a passport from their home country that is valid for at least six months after their intended departure date from Namibia. You may also be asked for an onward plane, bus or rail ticket, although checks are rarely made. Nationals of the following countries do not need visas to visit Namibia: Angola, Australia, Botswana, Brazil, Canada, EU countries, Iceland, Japan, Kenya, Mozambique, New Zealand, Norway, Russia, Singapore, South Africa, Switzerland, Tanzania, the USA, Zambia, Zimbabwe and most Commonwealth countries. Citizens of most Eastern European countries do require visas.

Tourists are granted an initial 90 days, which may be extended at the **Ministry of Home Affairs** (☎ 061-292 2111; info@mha.gov.na; cnr Kasino St & Independence Ave, Private Bag 13200, Windhoek). For the best results, be there when the office opens at 8am, and submit your application at the 3rd-floor offices (as opposed to the desk on the ground floor).

VOLUNTEERING

Namibia has a good track record for grassroots projects and community-based tourism. The largest organisation in the country is **Nacobta** (Namibia Community Based Tourism Association; ☎ 061-250558; www.nacobta.com.na), which runs various campsites.

However, it's seldom possible to find any volunteering work in-country due to visa restrictions and restricted budgets. Any organisations that do offer volunteer positions will need to be approached well in advance of your departure date. It also has to be said that many conservation outfits look for volunteers with specific skills that might be useful in the field.

International organisations that offer volunteering in Namibia include the youth development charity **Raleigh International** (www.raleighinternational.org) and **Project Trust** (www.projecttrust.org.uk) in the UK, and **World Teach** (www.worldteach.org) in the US. Another very worthwhile organisation, which you can support from the comfort of your own home, is the **Namibian Connection Youth Network** (www.namibiaconnection.org). You can register with them as a professional affiliate and offer your mentorship and advice to young Namibians via email.

WOMEN TRAVELLERS

On the whole Namibia is a safe destination for women travellers, and we receive few complaints from women travellers about any sort of harassment. Having said that, Namibia is still a conservative society. Many bars are men only (by either policy or convention) but, even in places that welcome women, you may be more comfortable in a group or with a male companion. Note that accepting a drink from a local man is usually construed as a come-on.

The threat of sexual assault isn't any greater in Namibia than in Europe, but women should still avoid walking alone in parks and back streets, especially at night. Hitching alone is not recommended. Also, never hitch at night and, if possible, find a companion for trips through sparsely populated areas. Use common sense and things should go well.

In Windhoek and other urban areas, wearing shorts and sleeveless dresses or shirts is fine. However, if you're visiting rural areas, wear knee-length skirts or loose trousers and shirts with sleeves. If you're poolside in a resort or lodge where the clientele is largely foreign, then somewhat revealing swimwear is acceptable, though it's best to err on the side of caution at locally owned hotels.

TRANSPORT IN NAMIBIA

GETTING THERE & AWAY

This section covers access into Namibia from neighbouring countries. You'll find information about reaching Southern Africa from elsewhere in Africa and other continents on p755.

Entering Namibia

All visitors entering Namibia must hold a passport that is valid for at least six months. Also, allow a few empty pages for stamp-happy immigration officials, especially if you're crossing over to Zimbabwe and/or Zambia to see Victoria Falls.

Members of the EU, USA, South Africa, Scandinavia, Balkan countries and all members of the Commonwealth (with the exception of Ghana, India, Sri Lanka, Nigeria and Mauritius) will be granted a one-month entry permit on arrival (passport photos required). Other nationalities will need to obtain a visa before they arrive in the country.

Air

Most international flights into Namibia arrive at Windhoek's **Chief Hosea Kutako International Airport** (WDH; ☎ 061-299 6602; www.airports.com.na), 42km east of the capital. Shorter-haul international flights may also use Windhoek's in-town **Eros airport** (ERS; ☎ 061-299 6500), although this airport mainly serves internal flights and light aircraft.

The main carrier is Air Namibia, which flies routes within Southern Africa as well as to Frankfurt. Reservations are best handled via the internet or telephone.

AIRLINES FLYING TO/FROM NAMIBIA

Air Namibia (☎ 299 6000; www.airnamibia.com.na; hub Windhoek)
British Airways (☎ 248528; www.ba.com)
Lufthansa (☎ 238205; www.lufthansa.com)
South African Airways (☎ 237670; www.flysaa.com)
TAAG Angola (☎ 226625; www.taag.com.br)

Border Crossings

Thanks to the Southern African Customs Union, you can drive through Namibia, Botswana, South Africa and Swaziland with a minimum of ado. To travel further to the north needs serious consideration as it requires a *carnet de passage*, which can mean heavy expenditure.

If you're driving a hire car into Namibia you will need to present a letter of permission from the rental company saying the car is allowed to cross the border. For more information on taking a vehicle into Namibia see p759.

ANGOLA

To enter Namibia overland, you'll need an Angolan visa permitting overland entry. At Ruacana Falls, you can enter the border area temporarily without a visa to visit the falls by signing the immigration register (see p327).

BOTSWANA

The most commonly used crossing is at Buitepos/Mamuno, between Windhoek and Ghanzi, although the border post at Mohembo/Mahango is also popular. The only other real option is the crossing at Ngoma Bridge across the Chobe River. The Mpalila Island/Kasane border is only available to guests who have booked accommodation at upmarket lodges on the island.

Drivers crossing the border at Mahango must secure an entry permit for Mahango Game Reserve at Popa Falls. This is free if you're transiting, or US$3 per person per day plus US$3 per vehicle per day if you want to drive around the reserve (which is possible in a 2WD).

By Bus

On Monday and Friday you can catch a very useful shuttle-bus service from Windhoek to Maun, via Ghanzi, with **Audi Camp** (p101). Other than this, the public transport options between the two countries are few and far between. The Trans-Kalahari Hwy from Windhoek to Botswana, via Gobabis, crosses the border at Buitepos/Mamuno. Unfortunately, passengers on the Intercape Mainliner between Windhoek and Victoria Falls may not disembark in Botswana.

SOUTH AFRICA

By Bus

The **Intercape Mainliner** (☎ South Africa 27-21 380 4400; www.intercape.co.za) service runs between Windhoek and Cape Town. Students and seniors receive a 15% discount. Bus tickets can be easily booked by phone or via the internet.

ZAMBIA

A new kilometre-long bridge (open from 7am to 6pm) spans the Zambezi between Katima Mulilo and Wenela, providing easy access to Livingstone and other destinations in Zambia. If you're heading to the falls, the road is now tarred all the way to Livingstone and is accessible by 2WD vehicle, even in the rainy season.

By Bus

The **Intercape Mainliner** (☎ South Africa 27-21 380 4400; www.intercape.co.za) service also runs between Windhoek and Livingstone.

ZIMBABWE

There's no direct border crossing between Namibia and Zimbabwe. To get there you must take the Chobe National Park transit route from Ngoma Bridge through northern Botswana to Kasane/Kazungula, and from there to Victoria Falls.

By Bus

At the time of research, the only public transport between Namibia and Zimbabwe was the weekly **Intercape Mainliner** (☎ South Africa 27-21 380 4400; www.intercape.co.za), which travels between Windhoek and Victoria Falls.

Bus

There's only really one main inter-regional bus service connecting cities in Namibia with Botswana and South Africa. Intercape Mainliner has services between Windhoek and Johannesburg and Cape Town (South Africa). They also travel northeast to Victoria Falls, and between larger towns within Namibia.

Car & Motorcycle

Crossing land borders with your own vehicle or hire car is generally straightforward as long as you have the necessary paperwork – the vehicle registration documents, proof of insurance and a letter from the hire company stating that you have permission to take the car over the border. You won't need a *carnet de passage* to drive around Namibia and other countries in the Southern African Customs Union (SACU), ie Lesotho, Botswana, South Africa and Swaziland, although if you're planning on travelling further north you will need to obtain one.

A vehicle registered outside Namibia can be driven around the country so long as you have proof of insurance and a letter from the hire-car agency giving you permission to cross the border with the car. Everyone entering Namibia with a foreign-registered car must pay a Cross Border Charge (CBC). Passenger vehicles carrying fewer than 25 passengers are charged N$70. Keep the receipt, because you may be asked to produce it at police roadblocks.

GETTING AROUND

Air

Air Namibia has an extensive network of local flights operating out of Eros airport (see p383). There are regular flights to Tsumeb; Rundu and Katima Mulilo; Lüderitz and Alexander Bay (South Africa); and Swakopmund and Oshakati/Ondangwa. Passengers are allowed a baggage limit of 20kg; additional weight will set you back around N$20 per kilogram. For details of Air Namibia's local offices, log on to www.airnamibia.com.na.

CHARTER FLIGHTS

Charter flights are often the best – and sometimes the only – way to reach remote lodges. In the past it was possible to 'hitch a ride' on charter flights around the country, but in recent years the industry has become more regulated, and it is now virtually impossible to book a flight without also booking a safari package.

Some companies, however, do offer 'scenic' flights that enable you to enjoy the heady sensation of flying over Namibia's dramatic dunescapes. Pleasure Flights (p352) in Swakopmund is just such an operation, offering flight-seeing tours along the Skeleton Coast and over Fish River Canyon. To get the best price you'll need a group of five people.

Bicycle

Namibia is a desert country and totally unsuitable for a biking holiday. Distances are great and horizons are vast; the climate and landscapes are hot and very dry; and, even along major routes, water is scarce and villages are widely spaced. What's more, the sun is intense, and prolonged exposure to the burning ultraviolet rays is hazardous to your health. As if all of this wasn't enough of a deterrent, also bear in mind that bicycles are not permitted in any national parks.

Of course, loads of Namibians do get around by bicycle, and cycling around small cities and large towns is much easier than a cross-country excursion. With that said, be wary of cycling on dirt roads as punctures from thorn trees are a major problem. Fortunately, however, many local people operate small repair shops, which are fairly common along populated roadsides.

Bus

Namibia's bus services aren't extensive. Luxury services are limited to the **Intercape Mainliner** (☎ 061-227847; www.intercape.co.za), which has scheduled services from Windhoek to Swakopmund, Walvis Bay, Grootfontein, Rundu and Katima Mulilo. You're allowed only two items of baggage, which must not exceed a total of 30kg. Fares include meals. For details of prices see the relevant regional chapters.

There are also local combis, which depart when full and follow main routes around the country. From Windhoek's Rhino Park petrol station they depart for dozens of destinations. For more details on local routes see the Getting There & Away sections in this chapter.

In Windhoek, a few cheap local buses connect the city centre with outlying townships, but they're rapidly being phased out in favour of the more convenient shared taxis.

Car

The easiest way to get around Namibia is in your own car, and an excellent system of sealed roads runs the length of the country from the South African border at Noordoewer to Ngoma Bridge on the Botswana border and Ruacana in the northwest. Similarly, sealed spur roads connect the main north–south routes to Buitepos, Lüderitz, Swakopmund and Walvis Bay. Elsewhere, towns and most sites of interest are accessible on good gravel roads. Most C-numbered highways are well maintained and passable to all vehicles, and D-numbered roads, although a bit rougher, are mostly (but not always) passable to 2WD vehicles. In the Kaokoveld, however, most D-numbered roads can only be negotiated with a 4WD.

Nearly all the main car-rental agencies have offices at the airport. Ideally, you'll want to hire a car for the duration of your holiday, but if cost is an issue you might consider a shorter hire from either Windhoek or Swakopmund. If you can muster a group of four, hiring a car will undoubtedly work out cheaper than an organised tour.

DRIVING LICENCE

Foreigners can drive in Namibia on their home driving licence for up to 90 days, and most (if not all) car-hire companies will accept foreign driving licences for car hire. If your home licence isn't written in English then you'd be better off getting yourself an International Driving Permit (IDP) before you arrive in Namibia.

FUEL & SPARE PARTS

The cost of fuel (petrol) is relatively expensive in Namibia at around US$0.75 per litre, but prices vary according to the remoteness of the petrol station. Although the odd petrol station is occasionally open 24 hours, most are open from 7am to 7pm.

As a general rule you should never pass a petrol station without filling up, and it is advisable to carry an additional 100L of fuel (either in long-range tanks or jerry cans) if you're planning on driving in more remote areas.

Spare parts are readily available in most major towns, but not elsewhere. If you are planning on some 4WD driving it is advisable to carry the following: two spare tyres, jump leads, tow rope and cable, a few litres of oil, a wheel spanner and a complete tool kit.

HIRE

For a compact car, the least expensive companies charge US$40 to US$60 per day (the longer the hire period, the lower the daily rate) with unlimited kilometres. Hiring a 4WD vehicle opens up remote parts of the country, but it can get expensive at US$85 to US$100 per day.

Most companies include insurance and unlimited kilometres in their standard rates, but some require a minimum rental period before they allow unlimited kilometres. Note that some internationally known companies, such as Avis and Budget, charge amenable daily rates, but sometimes only allow 200 free kilometres per day. If one company's rates seem quite a bit higher than another's, check whether it includes VAT, which would otherwise add 15.5% to the quoted figure. Most companies also require a N$1000 deposit, and won't hire to anyone under the age of 23 (although some go as low as 21).

It's cheaper to hire a car in South Africa and drive it into Namibia, but you need permission from the rental agency, as well as the appropriate paperwork to cross the borders. Drivers entering Namibia in a foreign-registered vehicle must pay a N$70 road tax at the border. Most major international car-rental companies will allow you to take a vehicle to neighbouring South Africa, Botswana and Zimbabwe, but only if you clear it with the company beforehand so they can sort out the paperwork. Rental companies are less happy about drivers going to Zambia, and will not allow you to go anywhere else in Africa.

Naturally, you should always check the paperwork carefully, and thoroughly examine the vehicle before accepting it. Car-rental agencies in Namibia have some very high excesses due to the general risks involved in driving on the country's gravel roads (for driving tips, see p766). You should also carefully check the condition of your car and never *ever* compromise if you don't feel totally happy with its state of repair.

It is probably best to deal with one of the major car-rental companies listed below.

Avis (www.avis.com) Offices in Windhoek, Swakopmund, Tsumeb and Walvis Bay as well as at the airport.
Budget (www.budget.co.za) Another big agency with offices in Windhoek and Walvis Bay as well as at the airport.
Imperial (www.imperialcarrental.co.za) Offices in Windhoek, Swakopmund, Tsumeb, Lüderitz, Walvis Bay and at both Chief Hosea Kutako and Eros airports.
Triple Three Car Hire (www.333.com.na) A competitive local car-rental firm with offices in Swakopmund and Walvis Bay.

Additional charges will be levied for the following: dropping off or picking up the car at your hotel (rather than the car-rental office); each additional driver; a 'cleaning fee' (which can amount to US$50!) may be incurred – at the discretion of the rental company; and a 'service fee' may be added.

Always give yourself plenty of time when dropping off your hire car to ensure that the vehicle can be checked over properly for damage etc. The car-rental firm should then issue you with your final invoice before you leave the office.

It is nearly always advisable to pay with a 'gold level' credit card, which will offer you some protection should anything go wrong, and will possibly cover you for collision as well. American Express cards have a good reputation among travellers for providing comprehensive insurance for rental vehicles.

INSURANCE

Although insurance is not compulsory it is *strongly* recommended. No matter who you hire your car from, make sure you understand what is included in the price (unlimited kilometres, tax, insurance, collision-waiver and so on) and what your liabilities are. Most local insurance policies do not include cover for damage to windscreens and tyres.

Third-party motor insurance is a minimum requirement in Namibia. However, it is also advisable to take Damage (Collision) Waiver, which costs around US$20 extra per day for a 2WD; and about US$40 per day for a 4WD. Loss (Theft) Waiver is also an extra that is worth having. For both types of insurance, the excess liability is about US$1500 for a 2WD and US$3000 for a 4WD. If you're only going for a short period of time it may be worth taking out the Super Collision Waiver, which covers absolutely everything, albeit at a price.

PURCHASE

Unless you're going to be staying in Namibia for several years, it's not worth purchasing a vehicle in-country. The best place to buy a vehicle is across the border in South Africa.

If you do buy a car with hard currency and resell it in Namibia, you can remit the same amount of hard currency to your home country without hassles – just keep the papers and inform the bank in advance.

ROAD HAZARDS

In addition to its fantastic system of tarred roads, Namibia has everything from high-speed gravel roads to badly maintained main routes, farm roads, bush tracks, sand tracks and challenging 4WD routes. Driving under these conditions requires special techniques, appropriate vehicle preparation, a bit of practice and a heavy dose of caution; see p766 for some tips.

ROAD RULES

To drive a car in Namibia, you must be at least 21 years old. Like most other Southern African countries, traffic keeps to the left side of the road. The national speed limit is 120km/h on paved roads, 80km/h on gravel roads and 40km/h in all national parks and reserves. When passing through towns and villages, assume a speed limit of 60km/h, even in the absence of any signs.

Highway police use radar and love to fine motorists (about US$10, plus an additional US$1 for every 10km you exceed the limit) for speeding. Sitting on the roof of a moving vehicle is illegal, and wearing seat belts (where installed) is compulsory in the front (but not back) seats. Drink-driving is also against the law, and your insurance policy will be invalid if you have an accident while drunk. Driving without a licence is also a serious offence.

If you have an accident causing injury, it must be reported to the authorities within 48 hours. If vehicles have sustained only minor damage and there are no injuries – and all parties agree – you can exchange names and addresses and sort it out later through your insurance companies.

Hitching

Hitching is possible in Namibia, but it's illegal in national parks, and even main highways see relatively little traffic. Truck drivers generally expect to be paid around US$1.50 per 100km, so agree on a price before climbing in. Your best options for lifts are Windhoek backpacker lodges, where you can post notices about rides wanted or offered. (For warnings about hitching, see p765.)

Tours

Namibia's public transport system will get you to population centres, but not the sites most visitors want to see: the Skeleton Coast, Damaraland, the Kaokoveld, the Kunene River, Fish River Canyon, Sossusvlei, the Naukluft and so on. Therefore, even those who would normally spurn organised tours may want to consider joining an inexpensive participation safari or a more luxurious option:

Afro Ventures (☎ 064-463812; www.afroventures.com) Afro Ventures offers several Namibian highlights tours, focusing on fine lodges and 4WD tours. Its five- and seven-day Namib Desert tours explore the desert coast and dunes.

Campfire Safaris (☎ 062-523946; namibia@bigfoot.com) This economically priced company offers combi tours through a range of Namibian highlights.

Cardboard Box Travel Shop (☎ 061-256580; www.namibian.org) This friendly agency offers bookings (including last-minute options) for all budget safaris; lodge, safari, car-hire and transport bookings; national parks bookings; good advice; and other travel services.

Chameleon Safaris (☎ 247668; www.chameleonsafaris.com) This budget safari company is geared to backpackers and does a range of good-value safaris.

Crazy Kudu Safaris (☎ 222636; www.crazykudu.com; Windhoek) One of Namibia's friendliest and most economical safari companies, Crazy Kudu does a variety of package trips around the country, as well as custom safaris to the Okavango Delta, Victoria Falls, Fish River and Kaokoveld, for the best possible price.

Enyandi Safaris (☎ 061-255103; enyandi@iafrica.com.na) This recommended company runs budget tours mainly in northwestern Namibia.

Felix Unite (☎ 061-255488; www.felixunite.com) This water-oriented company runs river-rafting and canoeing adventures on the Kunene and Orange Rivers.

Kaokohimba Safaris (☎ 061-222378; www.kaoko-namibia.com) Kaokohimba organises cultural tours through Kaokoveld and Damaraland and wildlife-viewing trips in Etosha National Park. A highlight is Camp Syncro, in remote Marienflüss.

Magic Bus Safaris (☎ 061-259485, 0811 298 093; magicbus@iafrica.com.na) This small company runs budget trips from Windhoek to Sossusvlei, Etosha and other combinations.

Muramba Bushman Trails (☎ 067-220659; bushman@natron.net) This popular company, owned by Reinhard Friedrich in Tsumeb, provides a unique introduction to the Heikum San people.

Namib Sky (☎ 063-683188; www.namibsky.com) For those who dream of looming over the dunes in a balloon, this company offers Namib Desert balloon flights. The early-morning flight departs before sunrise, when not a breath of wind is stirring.

Okakambe Trails (☎ 064-40279; www.okakambe.iway.na) With Okakambe, you can ride on horses along the Swakop River to a moon landscape; it also organises a good variety of longer riding trips.

Outside Adventures (☎ 061-245595; www.namibia-adventures.com) These folks run excellent day tours from Windhoek: brewery tours, mountain biking in Daan Viljoen, Arnhem Caves, Katutura township and tours to see cheetahs, leopards and rhinos on private reserves in the capital area.

Turnstone Tours (☎ 064-403123; www.turnstone-tours.com) Turnstone runs 4WD camping tours around Swakopmund, including Sandwich Harbour and Damaraland.

West Coast Safaris (☎ 061-256770; www.westcoast.demon.nl) The company runs camping participation safaris averaging one week in length to a variety of destinations, including Kaokoveld, Etosha, Damaraland, Bushmanland and the Waterberg Plateau.

Wild Dog Safaris (☎ 061-257642; www.wilddog-safaris.com) This friendly operation runs Northern Namibia Adventures and Southern Swings, Etosha or Sossusvlei circuits as well as longer participation camping safaris and accommodated excursions.

Train

Trans-Namib Railways (☎ 061-298 2032; www.transnamib.com.na) connects some major towns, but trains are extremely slow – as one reader remarked, moving 'at the pace of an energetic donkey cart'. In addition, passenger and freight cars are mixed on the same train, and trains tend to stop at every post, which means that rail travel isn't popular and services are rarely fully booked.

Windhoek is Namibia's rail hub, with services south to Keetmanshoop and Upington (South Africa); north to Tsumeb, west to Swakopmund and east to Gobabis. Trains carry economy and business-class seats but, although most services operate overnight, sleepers are not available. Book at train stations or through the Windhoek booking office (p314); tickets must be collected before 4pm on the day of departure.

South Africa

South Africa has always been a country that has made headlines. When apartheid crumbled and Nelson Mandela walked free, just three months after the Berlin Wall was torn down, it was a pivotal, hopeful moment in history. More recently, the news coming from the rainbow nation has included President Zuma's election, and new stadiums appearing, along with improved infrastructure, in preparation for the 2010 World Cup.

One of the first things travellers notice about South Africa is that, despite the rise of 'black diamonds' (middle-class black folk), racial inequality persists here. Black and coloured townships face problems such as a horrific HIV/AIDS rate and xenophobic tensions caused by economic refugees from nearby countries.

Nonetheless, Africa's southernmost nation is capable of worming deep into the imagination. Indeed, with South Africa's unique mix of epic landscapes, a healthy travelling scene, and vibrant cultures, you can easily have inspiring African experiences here. Whether you head into a national park on a wildlife-spotting mission, sample some homebrew in a township *shebeen* (unlicensed bar), or hike through landscapes such as the Drakensberg, this mind-bogglingly diverse country rewards travellers' exploratory efforts.

Once you've recovered from that, or from adrenaline-pumping activities such as the world's highest bungee jump, reflect on it all over a bottle in the Winelands, a braai (barbecue) in the wilderness, a beach session on the Wild Coast or a tour of Cape Town's galleries. Whatever you choose, it will probably be, as South Africans like to say, *lekker* (tasty).

FAST FACTS

- **Area** 1.2 million sq km
- **Capital** Pretoria (administrative), Bloemfontein (judicial), Cape Town (legislative)
- **Country code** ☎ 27
- **Famous for** Nelson Mandela, ending apartheid, Zululand, cosmopolitan Cape Town, Big Five wildlife
- **Languages** English, Afrikaans, Ndebele, Xhosa, Zulu, Sepedi, Sesotho, Venda, Setswana, Swati and Tsonga
- **Money** Rand (R)
- **Phrases** *Dumela/Sawubona* (hello; Setswana & Sesotho/Zulu & Swati), *howzit* (hello; English), *sala sentle/sala hantle/sala kahle* (goodbye; Setswana/Sesotho/Zulu & Swati)
- **Population** 49 million

HIGHLIGHTS

- **Cape Town** (p403) Meet the Mother City, where Table Mountain looks down on Atlantic beaches and Long St's nightlife.
- **Kruger National Park** (p513) Don some khaki and join the rangers on a safari of the most involving kind – on foot.
- **Drakensberg range** (p504) Hike towards the peaks for a view of the Amphitheatre, an 8km mountain curtain.
- **Soweto** (p532) See where two Nobel Peace Prize winners were once neighbours, and learn about township life.
- **Wild Coast** (p477) Choose between a hammock and the beach at one of the laid-back hostels.

ITINERARIES

- **Two weeks** Touching down in Johannesburg (Jo'burg), spend a few hours at the moving Apartheid Museum (p530) before heading northeast to safari showpiece Kruger National Park (p513). The teeming wildlife here and in the adjoining private wildlife reserves (p518) will hold you captivated for several days. If time is tight, Madikwe Game Reserve (p556) and Pilanesberg National Park (p555) are easily reached from Jo'burg via Rustenburg. From Kruger, head south into KwaZulu-Natal, where the dramatic peaks and valleys of the Drakensberg range (p502) provide an endless array of hikes. Head up the Sani Pass (p507) to the Lesotho border for breathtaking views before returning to the throbbing heart of the country to get a taste of township life in Soweto (p532).
- **One month** After a few days in Cape Town (p403) and a trip up Table Mountain (p410), tear yourself away from the wonderful Mother City before you slip into a 'Cape coma'. Head to the fertile valleys of the Winelands, with a couple of nights in Stellenbosch (p429) or Franschhoek (p433), then continue the wine tour along scenic Rte 62 (p439) through the Little Karoo to ostrich-mad Oudtshoorn (p440). Possible coastal detours include Hermanus (p436) for whale watching (between June/July and November); Cape Agulhas (p437) for the thrill of standing at Africa's southernmost point; or De Hoop Nature Reserve (p437). Make your way south from Oudtshoorn to the Garden Route (p441), joining the N2 near arty, lagoon-side Knysna (p446) and Plettenberg Bay (p448), a relaxed beach town. Recommended parks on the coast include Tsitsikamma National Park Area (p461) and, past Port Elizabeth, Addo Elephant National Park (p467). Move northeastwards through the striking Wild Coast (p477), and don't succumb to 'Pondo fever' in Pondoland, but carry onto Durban (p481) for more beaches. Head north to President Zuma's birthplace, Zululand (p496), or east to the Drakensberg range (p502); or hit the park-packed Elephant Coast (p497), where the wilderness areas include Hluhluwe-iMfolozi Park (p498) and uMkhuze Game Reserve (p500), before returning to Durban or making your way to Jo'burg for the flight home.

HOW MUCH?

- **Bottle of red wine** R55-80
- **Car hire per day** R200-300
- **Kilogram of biltong and droëwors** R140-160
- **Township tour** R350
- **Surfboard** R3000

LONELY PLANET INDEX

- **1L petrol** R8
- **1L bottled water** R13
- **Can of Black Label beer** R7
- **Souvenir T-shirt** R70
- **Roasted mealie (corn)** R2

CLIMATE & WHEN TO GO

South Africa has a temperate climate compared with many African countries, and it can be visited comfortably any time. However, depending on what you plan to do, it's worth paying attention to the seasons, which are the reverse of those in the northern hemisphere. Winter (June to September) is cooler, drier and ideal for hiking and outdoor pursuits. Because vegetation is less dense, and thirsty animals congregate around rivers and other permanent water sources, winter is also the best time for wildlife watching. In the eastern

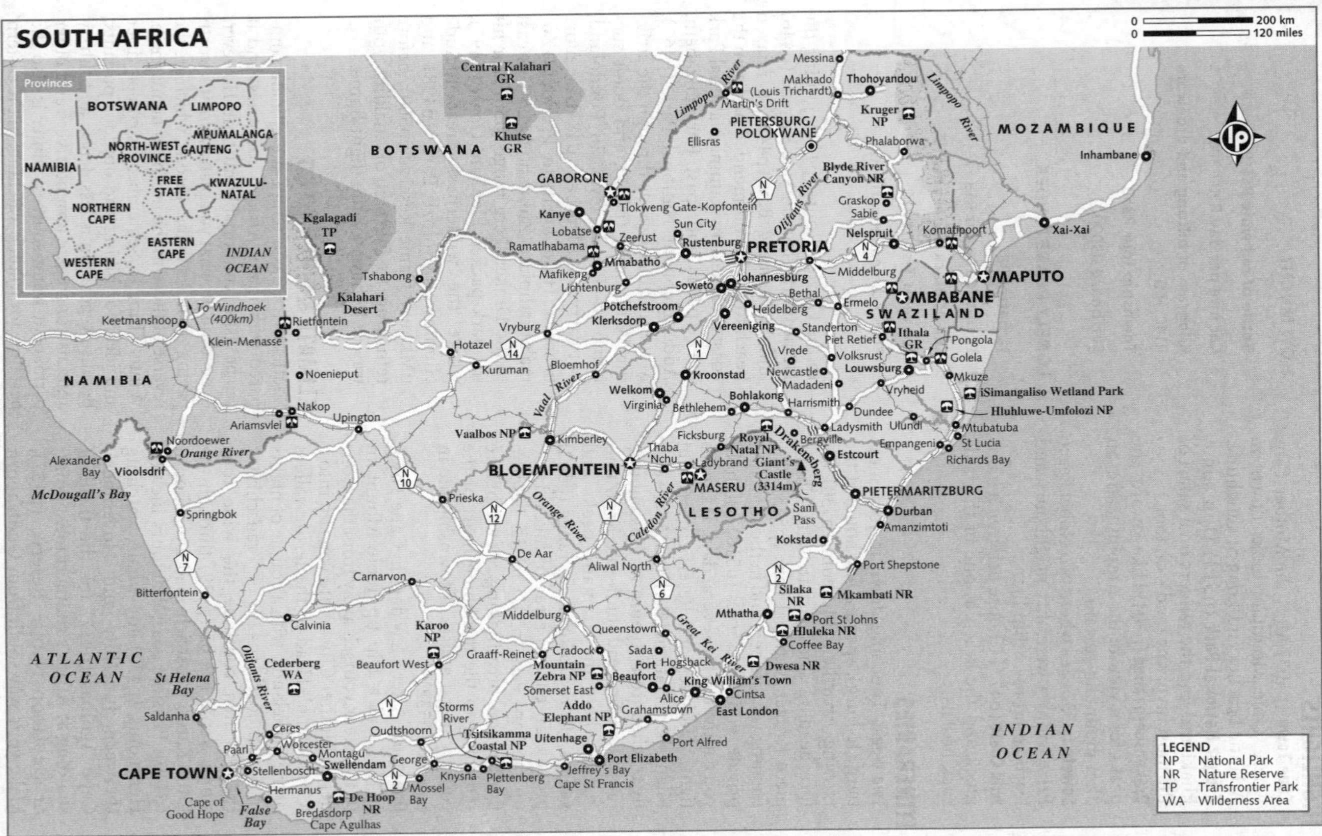
SOUTH AFRICA
0 200 km
0 120 miles
Provinces
BOTSWANA
LIMPOPO
MPUMALANGA
NORTH-WEST PROVINCE
GAUTENG
NAMIBIA
FREE STATE
KWAZULU-NATAL
NORTHERN CAPE
EASTERN CAPE
WESTERN CAPE
INDIAN OCEAN
Central Kalahari GR
Khutse GR
BOTSWANA
GABORONE
Kanye
Lobatse
Ramatlhabama
Tlokweng Gate-Kopfontein
Zeerust
Mmabatho
Mafikeng
Lichtenburg
Kgalagadi TP
Tshabong
Kalahari Desert
Keetmanshoop
To Windhoek (400km)
Klein-Menasse
Rietfontein
Noenieput
NAMIBIA
Nakop
Ariamsvlei
Upington
Noordoewer
Orange River
Alexander Bay
Vioolsdrif
McDougall's Bay
Springbok
Bitterfontein
ATLANTIC OCEAN
St Helena Bay
Saldanha
Olifants River
Cederberg WA
Calvinia
Ceres
Worcester
Paarl
Montagu
Stellenbosch
Swellendam
CAPE TOWN
Hermanus
De Hoop NR
Cape of Good Hope
False Bay
Bredasdorp
Cape Agulhas
Oudtshoorn
George
Mossel Bay
Knysna
Plettenberg Bay
Tsitsikamma Coastal NP
Storms River
Beaufort West
Karoo NP
Carnarvon
Middelburg
Graaff-Reinet
Cradock
Mountain Zebra NP
Somerset East
Addo Elephant NP
Uitenhage
Port Elizabeth
Jeffrey's Bay
Cape St Francis
Port Alfred
Grahamstown
Queenstown
Sada
Fort Beaufort
Hogsback
Alice
King William's Town
Cintsa
East London
Great Kei River
Dwesa NR
Coffee Bay
Hluleka NR
Port St Johns
Mthatha
Silaka NR
Mkambati NR
Port Shepstone
Kokstad
Amanzimtoti
Durban
PIETERMARITZBURG
Sani Pass
LESOTHO
MASERU
Giant's Castle (3314m)
Drakensberg
Royal Natal NP
Ladybrand
Thaba 'Nchu
Ficksburg
Caledon River
Aliwal North
De Aar
Orange River
Prieska
BLOEMFONTEIN
Kimberley
Vaalbos NP
Vaal River
Bloemhof
Kuruman
Hotazel
Vryburg
Klerksdorp
Potchefstroom
Welkom
Virginia
Bethlehem
Bohlakong
Kroonstad
Vereeniging
Soweto
Johannesburg
Heidelberg
Rustenburg
Sun City
PRETORIA
Middelburg
Bethal
Ermelo
Standerton
Piet Retief
Vrede
Volksrust
Newcastle
Madadeni
Harrismith
Ladysmith
Bergville
Estcourt
Dundee
Ulundi
Vryheid
Louwsburg
Empangeni
Richards Bay
St Lucia
Mtubatuba
Hluhluwe-Umfolozi NP
iSimangaliso Wetland Park
Mkuze
Golela
Pongola
Ithala GR
SWAZILAND
MBABANE
MAPUTO
Komatipoort
Nelspruit
Sabie
Graskop
Blyde River Canyon NR
Olifants River
Ellisras
PIETERSBURG/ POLOKWANE
Martin's Drift
Limpopo River
Makhado (Louis Trichardt)
Messina
Thohoyandou
Kruger NP
Phalaborwa
Limpopo River
MOZAMBIQUE
Inhambane
Xai-Xai
INDIAN OCEAN
LEGEND
NP National Park
NR Nature Reserve
TP Transfrontier Park
WA Wilderness Area

highveld, nights are often crisp and clear, with occasional frosts.

Summer (late November to March) brings rain, mists and – in the lowveld – some uncomfortably hot days. Along the Indian Ocean coast, conditions are sultry and tropical, with high humidity.

More of a consideration than weather are school holidays. From mid-December to January, waves of vacationers stream out of the cities, with foreign tourists adding to the crush. The absolute peak is from Christmas to mid-January, followed by Easter. Accommodation in tourist areas and national parks is heavily booked, and prices can more than double. Bookings and prices will also skyrocket around the 2010 World Cup (11 June to 11 July).

Spring (mid-September to November) and autumn (April and May) are ideal almost everywhere. Spring is also the best time to see vast expanses of Northern Cape carpeted with wildflowers.

HISTORY

South Africa's history extends back to around 40,000 BC when the San people first settled Southern Africa. By AD 500, Bantu-speaking peoples had arrived from West Africa's Niger Delta. Competing colonial European powers began settling here in small numbers from the 17th century, mostly in the Cape. Widespread colonial settlement of South Africa began in the 19th century.

The Great Trek

From 1836, groups of Boers dissatisfied with British rule in the Cape Colony trekked off into the interior in search of freedom. In a decade of migration known as the Great Trek, increasing numbers of Voortrekkers (Fore-trekkers – pioneers) abandoned their farms and crossed the Senqu (Orange) River. Reports from early missions told of vast, uninhabited – or at least poorly defended – grazing lands.

Tensions between the Boers and the government had been building for some time, but the reason given by many trekkers for leaving was the 1833 act banning slavery.

The Great Trek coincided with the *difaqane* (forced migration; see p36) and the Boers mistakenly believed that what they found – deserted pasture lands, disorganised bands of refugees and tales of brutality – was the normal state of affairs. This gave rise to the Afrikaner myths that the Voortrekkers moved into unoccupied territory or arrived at much the same time as black Africans.

The Voortrekkers Meet the Zulu

The Great Trek's first halt was at Thaba 'Nchu, near present-day Bloemfontein, where a republic was established. Following disagreements among their leadership, the various Voortrekker groups split, with most crossing the Drakensberg into Natal to try and establish a republic there. As this was Zulu territory, the Voortrekker leader Piet Retief paid a visit to King Dingaan, and was promptly massacred by the suspicious Zulu. This massacre triggered others, as well as a revenge attack by the Boers. The culmination came at the Battle of Blood River (1838) in Natal. While the Boers sustained some injuries, more than 3000 Zulu were killed, reportedly causing the Ncome River to run red.

After this victory (the result of vastly superior weapons), the Boers felt their expansion really did have that long-suspected stamp of divine approval. The 16 December victory was celebrated as the Day of the Vow until 1994, when it was renamed the Day of Reconciliation.

The Boer Republics

Several short-lived Boer republics sprang up but soon the only serious contenders were the Orange Free State and the Transvaal. The republics' financial position was always precarious and their economies depended entirely on cattle. Most trade was by barter. Just when it seemed that the republics, with their thinly spread population of fiercely independent Boers, were beginning to settle into stable states, diamonds were discovered near Kimberley in 1869. Britain stepped in quickly and annexed the area.

The Boers were disturbed by the foreigners, both black and white, who poured in following the discovery and were angry that their impoverished republics were missing out on the money the mines brought in.

Anglo-Boer Wars

Long-standing Boer resentment became a full-blown rebellion in the Transvaal and the first Anglo-Boer War, known by Afrikaners as the War of Independence, broke out. It was over almost as soon as it began, with a crushing Boer victory at the Battle of Majuba Hill in 1881, and the republic regained its independence as the Zuid-Afrikaansche Republiek (ZAR; South African Republic).

With the discovery of a huge reef of gold in the Witwatersrand (the area around Johannesburg) in 1886 and the ensuing explosive growth of Jo'burg itself, the ZAR was suddenly host to thousands of *uitlanders* (foreigners), black and white.

This only intensified the Boers' grievances that had begun during the earlier diamond rush. In 1899 the British demanded voting rights for the 60,000 foreign whites on the Witwatersrand. Paul Kruger (ZAR president 1883–1900) refused, and demanded that British troops be withdrawn from the republic's borders, leading to the second Anglo-Boer War.

The conflict was more protracted than its predecessor, as the British were better prepared. By mid-1900, Pretoria, the last of the major Boer towns, had surrendered. Yet resistance by Boer *bittereinders* (bitter enders) continued for two more years with guerrilla-style battles, which in turn were met by scorched-earth tactics by the British. In May 1902, the Treaty of Vereeniging brought a superficial peace. Under its terms, the Boer republics acknowledged British sovereignty.

British Rule

The British response after their victory was a mixture of appeasement and insensitive imperialism. It was essential for the Boers and British to work together. The nonwhites were scarcely considered, other than as potential labour, despite the fact that they constituted more than 75% of the combined population of the provinces.

Political awareness was growing, however. Mohandas (later Mahatma) Gandhi was working with the Indian populations of the Natal and Transvaal, and men such as John Jabavu, Walter Rubusana and Abdullah Abdurahman laid the foundations for new nontribal, black political groups.

Afrikaners found themselves in the position of being poor farmers in a country where big mining ventures and foreign capital rendered them irrelevant. As a backlash, Afrikaans came to be seen as the *volkstaal* (people's language) and a symbol of Afrikaner nationhood.

The former Boer republics were given representative government in 1906–07, and moves towards union began almost immediately.

Union of South Africa

The Union of South Africa was established in 1910. The British High Commission Territories of Basotholand (now Lesotho), Bechuanaland (now Botswana), Swaziland and Rhodesia (now Zimbabwe) continued to be ruled directly by Britain.

English and Dutch became the official languages – Afrikaans was not recognised as an official language until 1925.

The first government of the new Union was the South African National Party (later known as the South African Party, or SAP). A diverse coalition of Boer groups under General Louis Botha, with General Jan Smuts as his deputy, the party followed a generally pro-British, white-unity line.

General Barry Hertzog raised divisive issues, championing Afrikaner interests, advocating separate development for the two white groups and independence from Britain. He and his supporters formed the National Party (NP).

Soon after the union was established a barrage of repressive legislation was passed. It became illegal for black workers to strike; skilled jobs were reserved for whites; blacks were barred from military service; and pass laws, restricting black freedom of movement, were tightened.

In 1912, Pixley ka Isaka Seme formed a national democratic organisation to represent blacks. It was initially called the South African Native Congress, but from 1923 it was known as the African National Congress (ANC).

In 1913 the Natives Land Act set aside 8% of South Africa's land for black occupancy. Blacks were not allowed to buy, rent or even become sharecroppers outside their designated areas. Thousands of squatters were evicted from farms and forced into increasingly overcrowded reserves, or into the cities.

In 1914 South Africa, as a part of the British Empire, was drawn into war with Germany and saddled with the responsibility of dealing with German South West Africa (now Namibia). After the war, South West Africa became part of South Africa under 'mandate' from the League of Nations.

Coalitions

In 1924 Hertzog and the NP came to power in a coalition government, and Afrikaner nationalism gained a greater hold. The dominant issue of the 1929 election was the *swaart gevaar* (black threat).

Hertzog joined briefly in a coalition with the more moderate Jan Smuts in the mid-1930s, after which Smuts took the reins. However, any hopes of turning the tide of Afrikaner nationalism were dashed by the rise of DF Malan and the Purified National Party, which quickly became the dominant force in Afrikaner political life. The Afrikaner Broederbond, a secret ultranationalistic Afrikaner brotherhood, became an extraordinarily influential force behind the NP.

Due to the booming WWII economy, black labour became increasingly important to the mining and manufacturing industries, and the black urban population nearly doubled. Enormous squatter camps grew up on the outskirts of Johannesburg and, to a lesser extent, the other major cities.

Apartheid

The NP, led by DF Malan in a coalition with the Afrikaner Party (AP), won the 1948 election on a platform of establishing apartheid (literally, the state of being apart). With the help of creative electoral boundaries the NP held power right up to the first democratic election in 1994.

Mixed marriages were prohibited and interracial sex was made illegal. Every individual was classified by race. The Group Areas Act enforcing the physical separation of residential areas was promulgated. The Separate Amenities Act created separate public facilities – separate beaches, separate buses, separate toilets, separate schools and separate park benches. The pass laws were further strengthened and blacks were compelled to carry identity documents at all times and were prohibited from remaining in towns, or even visiting them, without specific permission.

Black Action

In 1949 the ANC for the first time advocated open resistance in the form of strikes, acts of public disobedience and protest marches. These continued intermittently throughout the 1950s, with occasional violent clashes.

In June 1955, at a congress held at Kliptown near Johannesburg, a number of organisations, including the Indian Congress and the ANC, adopted a Freedom Charter setting out a vision of a nonracial democratic state.

In 1960 the Pan African Congress (PAC), a breakaway group from the ANC, called for nationwide protests against the hated pass laws. When demonstrators surrounded a police station in Sharpeville police opened fire, killing at least 67 people and wounding 186. To onlookers in South Africa and the rest of the world, the struggle had now crossed a crucial line – there could no longer be any doubts about the nature of the white regime.

Soon after, the PAC and ANC were banned and the security forces were given the right to detain people indefinitely without trial. Prime Minister Verwoerd announced a referendum on whether the country should become a republic. A slim majority of white voters gave their approval to the change and in May 1961 the Republic of South Africa came into existence.

Nelson Mandela became the leader of the underground ANC and Oliver Tambo went abroad to establish the organisation in exile. As more black activists were arrested, the ANC and PAC began a campaign of sabotage through the armed wings of their organisations, respectively Umkonto We Sizwe (Spear of the Nation; usually known as MK) and Poqo (Pure). In 1963 Nelson Mandela, along with a number of other ANC and communist leaders, was arrested, charged with fomenting violent revolution and later sentenced to life imprisonment.

The Homelands

Verwoerd was assassinated in parliament in 1966 (there was apparently no political motive) and was succeeded by BJ Vorster, who was followed in 1978 by PW Botha. Both men continued to pursue the dream of separate black Homelands and a white South Africa.

The plan was to restrict blacks to Homelands that were, according to the propaganda, to become self-sufficient, self-governing states on the traditional lands of particular ethnic groups. In reality, they had little infrastructure and no industry and were therefore incapable of producing sufficient food for the burgeoning black population. Under the plan, 14% of the country's total land area was to be the home to some 80% of the population.

Intense and widespread suffering was the result as blacks could not even leave their Homeland without a pass and permission. The situation was further worsened by internal political strife. In an effort to garner more power for themselves, some homeland leaders became collaborators with the government, accepting 'independence' while crushing all resistance to their rule and to the South African government.

Decades of Darkness

As international opinion turned decisively against the white regime, the government (and most of the white population) increasingly saw the country as a bastion besieged by communism, atheism and black anarchy. Considerable effort was put into circumventing international sanctions, and the government even developed nuclear weapons (since destroyed).

On 16 June 1976 the Soweto Students' Representative Council protested against the use of Afrikaans (considered the language of the oppressor) in black schools. Police opened fire on a student march, sparking nationwide demonstrations, strikes, mass arrests and riots that, over the following 12 months, took more than 1000 lives.

Steve Biko, the charismatic leader of the Black Consciousness movement, which stressed the need for psychological liberation and black pride, was killed in 1977. The security police beat him until he lapsed into a coma – he went without medical treatment for three days and finally died in Pretoria. At the subsequent inquest, the magistrate found that no one was to blame.

South Africa was never the same again – a generation of young blacks committed themselves to a revolutionary struggle against apartheid and black communities were politicised.

President PW Botha, telling white South Africans to 'adapt or die', instituted numerous reforms, including repeal of the pass laws. But he stopped well short of full reform, and many blacks (as well as the international community) felt the changes were only cosmetic. International pressures increased as economic sanctions began to dig in harder, and the value of the rand collapsed. In 1985, the government declared a state of emergency that was to stay in force for the next five years. The media were strictly censored and, by 1988, 30,000 people had been detained without trial. Thousands were tortured.

Reform

In late 1989, FW de Klerk succeeded a physically ailing Botha. At his opening address to the parliament in February 1990 De Klerk announced that he would repeal discriminatory laws and legalise the ANC, PAC and Communist Party. Media restrictions were lifted, and political prisoners not guilty of common-law crimes were released. On 11 February, Nelson Mandela was freed after 27 years in jail. During 1990 and 1991 virtually all the old apartheid regulations were repealed.

In December 1991 the Convention for a Democratic South Africa (Codesa) began negotiations on the formation of a multiracial transitional government and a new constitution extending political rights to all groups.

Months of wrangling produced a compromise and an election date, although at considerable human cost. Political violence exploded across the country during this time, particularly in the wake of the assassination of Chris Hani, the popular leader of the South African Communist Party.

Free Elections

Finally, at midnight on 26–27 April 1994, the old national anthem 'Die Stem' (The Call) was sung across the country and the old flag was lowered. Then the new rainbow flag was raised and the new anthem, 'Nkosi Sikelele Afrika' (God Bless Africa), was sung.

In the country's first democratic elections, the ANC won 62.7% of the vote, less than the 66.7% that would have enabled it to rewrite the interim constitution. As well as deciding the national government, the election also decided the provincial governments, and the ANC won in all but two of the provinces. The NP captured most of the white and coloured vote and became the official opposition party.

Rewriting History

After the elections, focus turned to the Truth & Reconciliation Commission (1994–99), which worked to expose crimes of the apartheid era under the dictum of Archbishop Desmond Tutu: 'Without forgiveness there is no future, but without confession there can be no forgiveness'. Many stories of horrific brutality and injustice were heard by the commission, offering some catharsis to people and communities shattered by their past.

The commission operated by allowing victims to tell their stories and perpetrators to confess their guilt, with amnesty on offer to those who made a clean breast of it. Those who chose not to appear before the commis-

MOVERS & SHAKERS: NELSON MANDELA

Nelson Rolihlahla Mandela is without doubt one of the global leaders of the millennium. Once vilified by South Africa's ruling whites and sentenced to life imprisonment, he emerged from 27 years of incarceration calling for reconciliation and forgiveness, and was able to rally together all South Africans at the most crucial of times.

Mandela, son of a Xhosa chief, was born on 18 July 1918 in the village of Mveso on the Mbashe River. When he was young the family moved to Qunu, south of Mthata in what is now Eastern Cape. He grew up living a typical rural life, while being groomed for a future position in the ethnic leadership. After attending the University College of Fort Hare, Mandela headed to Johannesburg (Jo'burg), where he soon became immersed in politics. He finished his law degree and, together with Oliver Tambo, opened South Africa's first black law firm.

Meanwhile, in 1944, together with Tambo and Walter Sisulu, Mandela formed the Youth League of the African National Congress (ANC), which worked to turn the ANC into a nationwide grass-roots movement. During the 1950s, Mandela was at the forefront of the ANC's civil disobedience campaigns. Various arrests and detention followed.

After the ANC was banned in the wake of the Sharpeville massacre, Mandela advocated establishing its underground military wing, Umkhonto we Sizwe. In 1964, he stood trial for sabotage and fomenting revolution in the widely publicised Rivonia Trial. After brilliantly arguing his own defence, he was sentenced to life imprisonment, and spent the next 18 years in the infamous Robben Island prison, before moving to jails on the mainland.

Throughout his incarceration, Mandela repeatedly refused to compromise his political beliefs in exchange for freedom, saying that only free men can negotiate. He rejected offers of release in exchange for recognising the independence of the Transkei (and thereby giving tacit approval of the legitimacy of the apartheid regime).

On 18 February 1990, Mandela was released and in 1991 he was elected president of the ANC. From this position, he continued the negotiations (which had started secretly while he was in prison) to demolish apartheid and bring an end to minority rule. In 1993, Mandela shared the Nobel Peace Prize with FW de Klerk and, in the country's first democratic elections the following year, was elected president of South Africa. In his much-quoted speech, 'Free at Last!', made after winning the 1994 elections, he focused the nation's attention on the future, declaring, 'This is the time to heal the old wounds and build a new South Africa'.

Now in his early 90s, Mandela – or Madiba, his traditional Xhosa name – stepped down as ANC president in 1997, although he continues to be revered as an elder statesman.

sion would face criminal prosecution if their guilt could be proven. Yet, while some soldiers, police and 'ordinary' citizens confessed their crimes, many of the human-rights criminals who gave the orders and dictated the policies failed to present themselves (PW Botha is one famous no-show).

After Madiba

In 1999, South Africa held its second democratic elections. In 1997 Mandela had handed over ANC leadership to his deputy, Thabo Mbeki, and there was speculation that the ANC vote might therefore drop. In fact, it increased to put the party within one seat of the two-thirds majority that would allow it to alter the constitution.

The NP, restyled as the New National Party (NNP), lost two-thirds of its seats, as well as official opposition status to the Democratic Party (DP) – traditionally a stronghold of liberal whites, with new support from conservatives disenchanted with the NP, and from some middle-class blacks. Coming in just behind the DP was the KwaZulu-Natal–based Inkatha Freedom Party (IFP), historically the voice of Zulu nationalism.

While Mbeki was viewed with far less affection by the ANC grassroots than the beloved 'Madiba' (Mandela), he proved himself a shrewd politician, maintaining his political pre-eminence by isolating or coopting opposition parties. He led the ANC to victory in the 2004 elections, the black middle class significantly expanded under his tenure, and he promoted the country's regional engagement as part of his vision of an 'African renaissance'.

Yet it was not all clear sailing. In the early days of his presidency, Mbeki's effective denial of the HIV/AIDS crisis invited global criticism, and his conspicuous failure to condemn the forced reclamation of white-owned farms in neighbouring Zimbabwe unnerved both South African landowners and foreign investors.

South Africa Today

Mbeki resigned as president after almost 10 years in 2008, and Kgalema Motlanthe stepped in as 'caretaker president' until the April 2009 elections. Mbeki had lost his party's support after a power struggle with his former deputy Jacob Zuma, a fellow one-time ANC exile whose theme song is 'Bring Me My Machine Gun'.

As the political dramas were playing out, long-simmering social discontent boiled over in rioting in May 2008 in a Jo'burg township. The violence – which reflected competition for scarce jobs and housing – was targeted primarily at immigrants from Mozambique, Zimbabwe and other neighbouring nations, and soon spread to other parts of the country, resulting in several dozen deaths and the displacement of thousands of immigrants. Army forces were deployed on the streets in affected areas of Gauteng and calm was restored, but many commentators argue that the riots' causes have not been properly addressed and similar incidents could happen again.

A controversial figure, Jacob Zuma (also known as JZ) was assured of victory in the 2009 elections when charges against him, relating to a US$4.8 billion arms deal, were dropped just weeks before the polls opened. The reasons for dropping the charges involved the alleged compromising of the evidence by those opposed to him. Zuma initially had a strong following, with people seeing the Zulu polygamist as more of a common man's champion than academic Mbeki. He promised in his first state-of-the-nation speech to create 500,000 new jobs by the end of 2009, although the *Sowetan* newspaper responded with a mocking headline: '2380 jobs a day for the rest of the year!' In July, rubber bullets flew as union strikes sparked violent expressions of general discontent with continuing deprivation in the townships.

Although the 2010 World Cup is set to lessen the blow of South Africa's first recession in 17 years, the ANC still faces major challenges in areas such as crime, economic inequality, education and, especially, HIV/AIDS. An estimated 5.7 million South Africans are affected – more than in any other country in the world.

In recent years, efforts by AIDS activists and NGOs have focused on urging the government to make antiretroviral drugs available for treatment for all AIDS sufferers, and on reducing the major social stigma associated with infection. While huge strides have been made – many provinces now provide widespread access to treatment – there is still a long way to go.

THE CULTURE

The National Psyche

More than 15 years has passed since South Africa's first democratic elections, and the country is still finding its way. While the streets pulsate with the same determination and optimism that fuelled the liberation struggle, the beat is tempered by the sobering social realities that are mostly the legacy of the oppression and bloodshed seen under apartheid. Freedom has also brought with it a whole new set of challenges.

Unemployment, crime and HIV/AIDS are the top concerns of most South Africans, and the nation is fast becoming a society divided by class rather than colour. The gap between rich and poor is vast – one of the highest in the world, according to World Bank statistics. Manicured suburbs rub shoulders with squalid townships where domestic violence and abuse of the drug 'tik' (crystal meth) are just two of the many social problems, and palatial residences overlook cramped, tin-roofed shanties. Violent crime has reached unacceptably high levels, and a generation that saw almost daily brutality and uncertainty during its formative years is now coming of age. Although the formal racial divisions of apartheid have dissolved, shadows and old ways of interacting remain, and suspicion and distrust still run high.

While crime continues to grab headlines and undermine South Africa's reputation as a tourism destination, it's important to keep it in perspective. The slowly and often fitfully emerging new South Africa is a unique and refreshing country to visit, and one of the most inspiring and hope-filled places on the continent. Visiting is a rare chance to experience a nation that is rebuilding itself after profound change. A backdrop to all this is the magnificent natural scenery, and the deep bond that most South Africans feel for their land.

Daily Life

It's difficult to present a unified picture of everyday life in South Africa. Many middle-class and wealthy families live in heavily secured homes and spend their leisure time in equally fortified shopping centres. Guards patrol the walkways and shops to keep criminals at bay; the lingering sense of fear and loss, connected with the passing of the old regime, is giving away to anxiety about the future; and conversations are peppered with gloomy predictions about the government and even the 2010 World Cup.

Life is very different for the millions of South Africans and immigrants who live in poverty. Tiny matchbox houses are home to large extended families, clean drinking water remains a luxury in some areas, and health facilities are not uniformly available.

Yet, township life is vibrant and informal. People gather on street corners and in local bars known as '*shebeens*'. Weddings are big events, and frequently spill onto the streets with plenty of dancing. If you're passing by, don't be surprised if you're encouraged to join in.

Unfortunately, funerals are becoming one of the most common gatherings in South Africa, and on weekends, cemeteries are routinely crowded with mourners. Many of those who are dying are youths, and people spend their time attending the funerals of one relative after the next.

Thousands of South African households are now headed by children whose parents have died from AIDS, which causes almost half of all deaths in the country according to some estimates. Sometimes the only survivors from an entire family are the eldest children, who were born before their parents became infected. A large number of grandparents who have nursed and lost their adult offspring to AIDS are also looking after their orphaned grandchildren, many of whom are also HIV-positive.

Population & People

During the apartheid era, the government attempted to categorise everyone into one of four major groups – easily enough said, perhaps, but disastrous to implement. The classifications – as African (at various times also called 'native' and 'Bantu', and sometimes now also 'black'), coloured, Asian or white – were often arbitrary and highly contentious. They were used to regulate where and how people could live and work, and became the basis for institutionalised inequality and intolerance.

These times are fading into history, although discrimination based on wealth is threatening to replace racial discrimination. While the apartheid-era classification terms continue to be used, and we've also used them in this chapter, they work only to a certain extent; within each of the four major categories are dozens of subgroups that are even more subjective and less clearly defined.

Most of the 'coloured' population, descended from mixed ancestors as diverse as Afrikaners and Khoisan peoples, lives in Northern Cape and Western Cape. A major subgroup is the Cape Malays, who are mostly Muslim and can trace their roots to places as widely dispersed as India, Indonesia and parts of East Africa. Most South Africans of Indian descent live in KwaZulu-Natal.

Rural provinces such as Limpopo and the Free State are the Afrikaner heartlands. People of British descent are concentrated in KwaZulu-Natal, Western Cape and Eastern Cape.

The Zulu have maintained the highest-profile ethnic identity; about 24% of South Africans speak Zulu as a first language and the Inkatha Freedom Party wants an autonomous Zulu state. The second-largest group, the Xhosa, has traditionally formed the heart of the black professional class and been influential in politics (numerous figures in the apartheid struggle, including Mandela, were Xhosa). About 18% of the population uses Xhosa as a first language. Other major groups include the Basotho, the Setswana, and the distinct Ndebele and Venda peoples.

South Africa's Gauteng province, which includes Jo'burg and Pretoria, is the most densely populated and urbanised province. At the other end of the scale is the rural and underdeveloped Eastern Cape, where up to 20% of adults have never received any formal schooling.

Millions of immigrants from across the continent make their way to South Africa to take advantage of its powerhouse economy. Many of those who are considered illegal live in Jo'burg's impoverished inner city, causing resentment among some South Africans who accuse the outsiders of taking jobs and housing.

South Africa has the highest incidence of reported rape in the world, with approximately 55,000 cases reported to the police annually. Some women's groups say the real figures are much worse, because many women are too afraid to report the crime. Even more saddening is the fact that at least 20% – some places the figure is closer to 40% – of reported rapes and attempted rapes are of girls below 18 years of age.

Women are statistically more likely than men to be infected with HIV, and many women become infected at an early age because they are having sex with older men. Worsening the situation is the threat of sexual violence, which often undermines the ability of young women to ensure their partner is wearing a condom.

SPORT

South Africans are sports fanatics, and after decades of being shut out of international competition, the national teams are hungry for glory. Football (soccer), followed by rugby and cricket, is the most popular spectator sport. The majority of football fans are black, while cricket and rugby attract predominately white crowds, although this is slowly changing.

The 2010 World Cup will take place at 10 venues from Cape Town to Polokwane/Pietersburg in June and July. The national football team, Bafana Bafana, has had mixed fortunes, winning the 1996 African Nations Cup but not qualifying for the tournament in 2010. The big local match is the Soweto Derby, pitting Jo'burg's Orlando Pirates and Kaizer Chiefs teams against each other. In the townships, football stars enjoy pop-star status.

The South African cricket team, known as the Proteas, ranks number one in the world in One Day International competition; and second in Test cricket. Having beaten England (in England) and drawn against India (in India) in 2008, South Africa became the first team to defeat Australia in a Test series on Australian soil in 16 years.

South African rugby, in particular, is still struggling to shake its reputation as a whites-only domain, despite the inclusion of black players and officials. Victory in the 1995 Rugby World Cup was a turning point, and the image of President Nelson Mandela celebrating while wearing a Springboks jersey became a symbol of reconciliation. The 'Boks' won the tournament again in 2007.

RELIGION

Religion plays a central role in the lives of most South Africans, more than 75% of whom identify themselves as Christians. Major denominations include the Dutch Reformed Churches, which have a national congregation of more than 3.5 million people and 1200-plus churches nationwide; and the flamboyant Zion Christian Church (ZCC), with more than four million followers. More than one million ZCC members gather at Zion city near Polokwane/Pietersburg during festivals at Easter and in September.

Despite their large social influence in cities such as Durban, Muslims, Hindus and Jews combined make up less than 6% of the population. About 15% are atheist and agnostic, and some 2% follow traditional African beliefs.

Up to two-thirds of South Africa's Indians have retained their Hindu faith, and Islam has a small but growing following, particularly in the Cape. The Jewish community is estimated to number around 70,000, mostly in Jo'burg and the Cape.

Traditional African beliefs and practices have a significant influence on the cultural fabric and life of the region. The use of *muti* (traditional medicine) is widespread, even among those who practise Christianity.

ARTS & CRAFTS

For information on music in South Africa and the region, see p48.

Literature

Many of the first black South African writers were missionary-educated, including Solomon Tshekisho Plaatje, who was also the first Secretary-General of the ANC. In 1930, his epic romance, *Mhudi*, became one of the first books published in English by a black South African.

In 1948, Alan Paton's *Cry, the Beloved Country* became an international bestseller. This beautifully crafted, lyrical tale of a black priest who comes to Jo'burg to find his son is still one of the country's most widely recognised titles. Another Paton classic is *Too Late the Phalarope*, which looks at the Afrikaner psyche and the inhumanity of apartheid.

During the 1950s, *Drum* magazine became the focal point of lively satire, fiction and comment, and routinely drew attention as a major anti-apartheid mouthpiece, eventually launching the careers of numerous prominent journalists and authors.

In the 1960s, future Nobel laureate Nadine Gordimer published her first books; her most famous novel, *July's People* (1981), depicts the collapse of white rule.

It was also in the 1960s and into the '70s that Afrikaner writers such as Breyten Breytenbach and André Brink began to gain prominence as powerful voices for the opposition. Brink's classic novel, *A Dry White Season*, portrays the lonely struggles of a white South African who discovered the truth about a black friend who died in police custody. Another Brink title, *The Rights of Desire*, is a tale of postapartheid South Africa.

The 1970s also gave rise to several influential black poets, including Mongane Wally Serote, a veteran of the liberation struggle. His work, including the moving epic poem 'No Baby Must Weep', served as a rallying force for those living under apartheid.

John Maxwell (JM) Coetzee was also published in the 1970s, although it wasn't until two decades later that he gained international acclaim, eventually winning the Nobel Prize for Literature in 2003. His novel *Disgrace* (1999) – a powerful, brittle and complex look at South African social realities – won Coetzee his second Booker Prize.

One of the most prominent contemporary authors is Zakes Mda. With the publication of *Ways of Dying* (1995), he made a successful transition from poetry and plays to become an acclaimed novelist. Phaswane Mpe – whose hard-hitting debut, *Welcome to Our Hillbrow*, deals with life in inner-city Jo'burg – sadly died in 2004, at the age of 34.

Visual Arts

South African art had its beginnings with the San, who left their distinctive designs on rock faces and cave walls throughout the region. When European painters arrived, many of their early works centred on depictions of Africa for colonial enthusiasts back home, although with time, a more South Africa-centred focus developed.

Black artists were sidelined for many decades. Gerard Sekoto was one of the first to break through the barriers. At about the same time that Sekoto was gaining prominence, a Sophiatown neighbour, John Koenakeefe Mohl, began spearheading artistic instruction and schooling for young black artists. In 1960, he was one of the founding members of the Artists' Market Association, which was set up to provide a showcase for young talent, continued in Artists Under the Sun.

Theatre & Dance

During the colonial era, South African theatre was dominated by European and American plays staged for local audiences. But homegrown playwrights, performers and directors gradually emerged, particularly in the 1930s, when theatre began to gain popularity in the townships. One of the first black South African writers to have his work published in English was Herbert Dhlomo, who won acclaim for *The Girl Who Killed to Save* (1936).

Athol Fugard played a crucial role in developing black theatrical talent by establishing troupes in Port Elizabeth and Jo'burg during the 1950s. By the 1960s and '70s, theatre and politics were inextricably intertwined, and several artists were arrested and others had their work banned. The innovative two-man show *Woza Albert!*, portraying Jesus Christ arriving in apartheid-era South Africa, won rave reviews and international acclaim.

In 1974, run-down buildings at Jo'burg's old 'Indian' fruit market were converted to become the Market Theatre, with patrons and performers defying the apartheid government's notorious Group Areas Act to ensure that it become an all-race venue. The Market Theatre is still one of the best-known performance spaces in the country (see p536).

ENVIRONMENT

The Land

South Africa occupies over 1.23 million sq km – five times the size of the UK – and is Africa's ninth-largest and fifth-most populous country. On three sides, it's edged by a windswept and stunningly beautiful coastline, winding down the Atlantic seaboard in the west, and up into the warmer Indian Ocean waters to the east.

Much of the country consists of the highveld, a vast plateau averaging 1500m in height. To the east is the lowveld, while to the northwest is the low-lying Kalahari basin. The dramatic Drakensberg Escarpment marks the point where the highveld plummets down towards the eastern lowlands.

Wildlife

ANIMALS

South Africa boasts some of the most accessible wildlife viewing on the continent; you probably have a better chance of seeing the Big Five (rhinos, buffaloes, elephants, leopards and lions) here than anywhere else. On even a short visit to the country's parks you are almost guaranteed to see dozens of creatures, and the chance to spot the big cats and great herd animals is one of the region's prime attractions. See the boxed text, p58, for tips on wildlife viewing.

The best time for wildlife watching is the cooler, dry winter months (June to September), when foliage is less dense and animals congregate at water holes. Summer (late November to March) is rainy and hot, with the animals more widely dispersed and often difficult to see, although the landscape turns beautiful shades of green.

South Africa's 800-plus bird species include the world's largest bird (ostrich), the heaviest flying bird (Kori bustard) and the smallest raptor (pygmy falcon). Birdwatching is good year-round, with spring (September to November) and summer the best.

Endangered Species

Endangered species include the black rhino (sometimes spotted in uMkhuze Game Reserve, p500, and Hluhluwe-iMfolozi Park, p498); the riverine rabbit (found only near rivers in the central Karoo); the wild dog (Hluhluwe-iMfolozi Park); and the roan antelope.

Endangered bird species include the wattled crane and the blue swallow; the African penguin and the Cape vulture are threatened.

PLANTS

More than 20,000 plant species sprout from South Africa's soil – an amazing 10% of the world's total, although the country constitutes only 1% of the earth's land surface.

Dozens of flowers that are domesticated elsewhere grow wild here, including gladioli, proteas, birds of paradise and African lilies. South Africa is also the only country with one of the world's six floral kingdoms within its borders.

In the drier northwest, there are succulents (dominated by euphorbias and aloes) and annuals, which flower brilliantly after the spring rains.

In contrast to this floral wealth, South Africa has few natural forests. They were never extensive, and today only remnants remain. Temperate forests occur on the southern coastal strip between George and Humansdorp, in the KwaZulu-Natal Drakensberg and in Mpumalanga. Subtropical forests are found northeast of Port Elizabeth in areas just inland from the Wild Coast, and in KwaZulu-Natal.

In the north are large savanna areas, dotted with acacias and thorn trees.

National Parks & Reserves

South Africa has close to 600 national parks and reserves, collectively boasting spectacular scenery, impressive fauna and flora, excellent facilities and reasonable prices. Visiting them will likely be the highlight of your visit. You'll generally only see their fences when you drive through the park gates – the animals are satisfyingly wild. The most famous contain wildlife, while others are primarily wilderness sanctuaries or hiking areas.

Wildlife tourism is one of the main sources of revenue for conservation efforts in South Africa. The money you spend in national parks and reserves is ploughed back into these areas, thus ensuring that future visitors will be able to collect their own unforgettable memories. Try to book ahead during holiday periods, as accommodation and organised activities in parks and reserves fill up.

Most of the larger wildlife parks are under the jurisdiction of **South African National (SAN) Parks** (☎ 012-428 9111; www.sanparks.org), except for those in KwaZulu-Natal, which are run by **Ezemvelo KZN Wildlife** (☎ 033-845 1000; www.kznwildlife.com). Other provinces also have conservation bodies that oversee areas within their boundaries. **Komatiland Forests Eco-Tourism** (☎ 013-754 2724; www.komatiecotourism.co.za) oversees forest areas, promotes ecotourism and manages hiking trails around Mpumalanga. **Cape Nature** (☎ 021-426 0723; www.capenature.org.za) is responsible for permits and bookings for Western Cape reserves.

All South African national parks charge a daily entry ('conservation') fee. Amounts vary; see individual park listings for details. One way to save is to purchase a **Wild Card** (www.wildinafrica.com; per adult/couple/family R940/1640/2210) online or at the parks. The version of the card for foreign tourists, which is valid for a year, gives you unlimited entry into any of the parks and reserves

TOP PARKS & RESERVES

Location (Park)	Features	Activities	Best time to visit	Page
Cape Peninsula				
Table Mountain National Park	rocky headlands, seascapes; water birds, bonteboks, elands, African penguins	hiking, mountain biking	year-round	p410
Western Cape				
Cederberg Wilderness Area	mountainous & rugged; San rock art, bizarre sandstone formations, abundant plant life	hiking	year-round	p451
Mpumalanga/ Limpopo				
Kruger National Park	savanna, woodlands, thornveld; the Big Five & many more	vehicle safaris, guided wildlife walks	Jun-Oct	p513
Blyde River Canyon Nature Reserve	canyon, caves, river; stunning vistas	hiking, kloofing (canyoning)	year-round	p522
Northern Cape				
Augrabies Falls National Park	desert, river, waterfalls; klipspringers, rock dassies; striking scenery	hiking, canoeing, rafting	Apr-Sep	p458
|Ai-|Ais/Richtersveld Transfrontier Park	mountainous desert; haunting beauty; klipspringers, jackals, zebras, plants, birds	hiking	Apr-Sep	p461
Eastern Cape				
Addo Elephant National Park	dense bush, coastal grasslands, forested kloofs (ravines); elephants, black rhinos, buffalo	vehicle safaris, walking trails, horse riding	year-round	p467
Tsitsikamma National Park	coast, cliffs, rivers, ravines, forests; Cape clawless otters, baboons, monkeys, birdlife	hiking	year-round	p461
KwaZulu-Natal				
Hluhluwe-iMfolozi Park	lush, subtropical vegetation, rolling savanna; rhinos, giraffes, lions, elephants, lots of birds	wildlife watching, wilderness walks	May-Oct	p498
iSimangaliso Wetland Park	wetlands, coastal grasslands; elephants, birds, hippos	wilderness walks, vehicle/boat safaris	Mar-Nov	p498
uMkhuze Game Reserve	savanna, woodlands, swamp; rhinos & almost everything else, hundreds of bird species	guided walks, bird walks, vehicle safaris	year-round	p500
uKhahlamba-Drakensberg Park	awe-inspiring Drakensberg Escarpment; fantastic scenery & wilderness areas	hiking	year-round	p502
Free State				
Golden Gate Highlands National Park	spectacular sandstone cliffs & outcrops; zebras, jackals, rheboks, elands, birds	hiking	year-round	p551

in the Wild Card system. It's an excellent deal if you're a frequent parkgoer, or even if you're just planning more than five days in one of the more expensive parks such as Kruger.

In addition to its national parks, South Africa is also party to several transfrontier conservation areas. These include Kgalagadi Transfrontier Park (p456), combining Northern Cape's old Kalahari Gemsbok National Park with Botswana's Gemsbok National Park; and the ambitious Great Limpopo Transfrontier Park, which will ultimately encompass 35,000 sq km across South Africa, Mozambique and Zimbabwe.

Private wildlife reserves also abound and while entry to these generally costs more than their public equivalents, you can often get closer to the animals.

In total, just under 3% of South African land has national park status. The government has started teaming up with private landowners to bring private conservation land under government protection, with the goal of ultimately increasing the total amount of conservation land to over 10%.

Environmental Issues

South Africa is the world's third-most biologically diverse country. It's also one of Africa's most urbanised, with over 50% of the population living in towns and cities. Major challenges for the government include managing increasing urbanisation while protecting the environment. The picture is complicated by a distorted rural-urban settlement pattern – a legacy of the apartheid era – with huge population concentrations in townships that generally lack adequate utilities and infrastructure.

Land degradation is one of the most serious problems, with about 25% of South Africa's land considered to be severely degraded. In former homeland areas, years of overgrazing and overcropping have resulted in massive soil depletion. This, plus poor overall conditions, is pushing people to the cities, further increasing urban pressures.

South Africa receives an average of only 500mm of rainfall annually, and droughts are common. To meet demand, all major South African rivers have been dammed or modified. While this has improved water supplies to many areas, it has also disrupted local ecosystems and caused increased silting.

South Africa is ranked in the top 15 worldwide contributors to global warming. With about 90% of the country's electricity coming from coal-firing plants, electricity generation is the main culprit in the production of greenhouse gases. The Kuyasa Project, spearheaded by the nonprofit development organisation **SouthSouthNorth** (www.southsouthnorth.org), has taken small but widely lauded steps towards minimising greenhouse gas emissions through introducing alternative energy sources to residences in Khayelitsha.

For a list of green initiatives, see the GreenDex near the back of the book.

FOOD & DRINK

It's only since the dismantling of apartheid that anyone has talked of South African cuisine as a unified whole. Earlier, the Africans had their mealie pap (maize porridge), the Afrikaners their *boerewors* (spicy farmers sausages), and the Indians and Cape Malays their curries.

Today, along with divisions in other aspects of life, the culinary barriers are starting to fall. Now, a simmering *potjie* (pot) of culinary influences awaits the visiting gastronome – described by the well-known foodie writer Lannice Snyman as 'a bit of black magic, a dash of Dutch heartiness, a pinch of Indian spice and a smidgen of Malay mystery'.

Perhaps more than anything else, it's the braai (barbecue) – an Afrikaner institution that has broken across race lines – that defines South African cuisine. It's as much a social event as a form of cooking, with the essential elements meat, corncobs and beer. The Winelands and Cape Town remain the best places to eat well.

Food

BILTONG & BOEREWORS

The Afrikaner history of trekking led to their developing portable food: hence the traditional biltong (dried strips of salted meat); rusks (hard biscuits) for dunking; dried fruit; and *boerewors*, where meat is preserved with spices and vinegar, also found dried *(droëwors)*.

CAPE CUISINE

Cape cuisine is a fusion of Malay and Dutch influences (the former introducing tastes from Madagascar and Indonesia). You'll find dishes such as *bobotie* (curried-mince pie topped with savoury egg custard, served on a bed of yellow rice with chutney), chicken pie and *waterblommetjie bredie* (lamb stew with Cape Pondweed flowers, lemon juice and sorrel). Puddings can be the delicious *malva* sponge dessert or *melktert* (rich, custardlike tart), usually brightened up with a sprinkling of cinnamon.

CURRIES

South African Indian cuisine includes delicious curries and *breyanis* (similar to biryanis), and fuses with Malay cooking, so that you'll get hotter curries in Durban and milder ones in Cape Town. In Durban, fill up on bunny chow (a half, quarter or full loaf of bread hollowed out and filled with beans or curry stew).

MEALIE PAP

The most widely eaten food in South Africa, mealie pap is thinner or stiffer depending on where you eat it, and is completely bland. However, it's ideal if you want something filling and economical, and can be quite satisfying served with a good sauce or stew.

Drink

BEER

Beer is the national beverage. It comes in bottles (or cans) at around R15, and bars serve draught from around R25. The world's largest brewer, SAB Miller, is based in Jo'burg, so there's no shortage of brands, with Amstel the favourite. Boutique brewers such as Millers and Birkenhead are found in the Cape. Windhoek, made in Namibia, is a crisp premium lager.

WATER

Tap water is generally safe in South Africa's cities. However, in rural areas (or anywhere that local conditions indicate that water sources may be contaminated), use bottled water and purify stream water.

WINE

Since it made its debut in 1659, South African wine has had time to age to perfection, and is both of a high standard and reasonably priced. Dry whites are particularly good – try sauvignon blanc, riesling, colombard and chenin blanc – while popular reds include cabernet sauvignon, pinotage (a local cross of pinot and cinsaut, which was known as hermitage), shiraz and pinot noir.

White/red wine prices average from around R25/55 in a bottle store, twice that in a restaurant. Wine by the glass is often available from around R12.

CAPE TOWN

☎ 021 / pop 3.1 million

Prepare to fall in love, as South Africa's 'Mother City' is an old pro at capturing people's hearts. And who wouldn't swoon at the sight of magnificent Table Mountain, its summit draped with cascading clouds, its flanks coated with unique flora and vineyards, its base fringed by golden beaches? Few cities can boast such a wonderful national park at their heart or provide the range of adventurous activities that take full advantage of it.

Accentuating this natural majesty is the Capetonians' imaginative flair with design and colour. From the Bo-Kaap's brightly painted facades to the contemporary Afro-chic decor of the city's treasure trove of guest houses, restaurants and bars, this is one good-looking metropolis. The new Green Point Stadium, a bold architectural statement, is being built for the 2010 World Cup, complemented by improved infrastructure.

Counterbalancing these splendid assets are some obvious flaws. One academic has gone as far as to dub this the most unequal city in the world; comparing the mansions of Constantia with the shacks of Crossroads, you'd be tempted to agree. However, Capetonians don't lack charity or compassion and there's an admirable can-do spirit that results in many small miracles being achieved.

Above all it's a multicultural city where nearly everyone has a fascinating, sometimes heartbreaking, story to tell. When the time comes to leave, you may find your heart breaking too.

HISTORY

Long before the Dutch East India Company (Vereenigde Oost-Indische Compagnie; VOC) established a base here in 1652, the Cape Town area was settled by the San and Khoikhoi nomadic peoples, collectively known as the Khoisan. The indigenous people shunned the Dutch, so the VOC imported slaves from Madagascar, India, Ceylon, Malaya and Indonesia to deal with the colony's chronic labour shortage. Women were in even shorter supply, so the Europeans exploited the female slaves and the local Khoisan for both labour and sex. In time the slaves also intermixed with the Khoisan. The offspring of these unions formed the basis of sections of today's coloured population – and help explain the unique character of the city's Cape Muslim population.

In the 150-odd years of Dutch rule, Kaapstad, as the Cape settlement became known, thrived and gained a wider reputation as the 'Tavern of the Seven Seas', a riotous port used by sailors travelling between Europe and the East. Following the British defeat of the Dutch in 1806 at Bloubergstrand, 25km north of Cape Town, the colony was ceded to the Crown on 13 August 1814. The slave

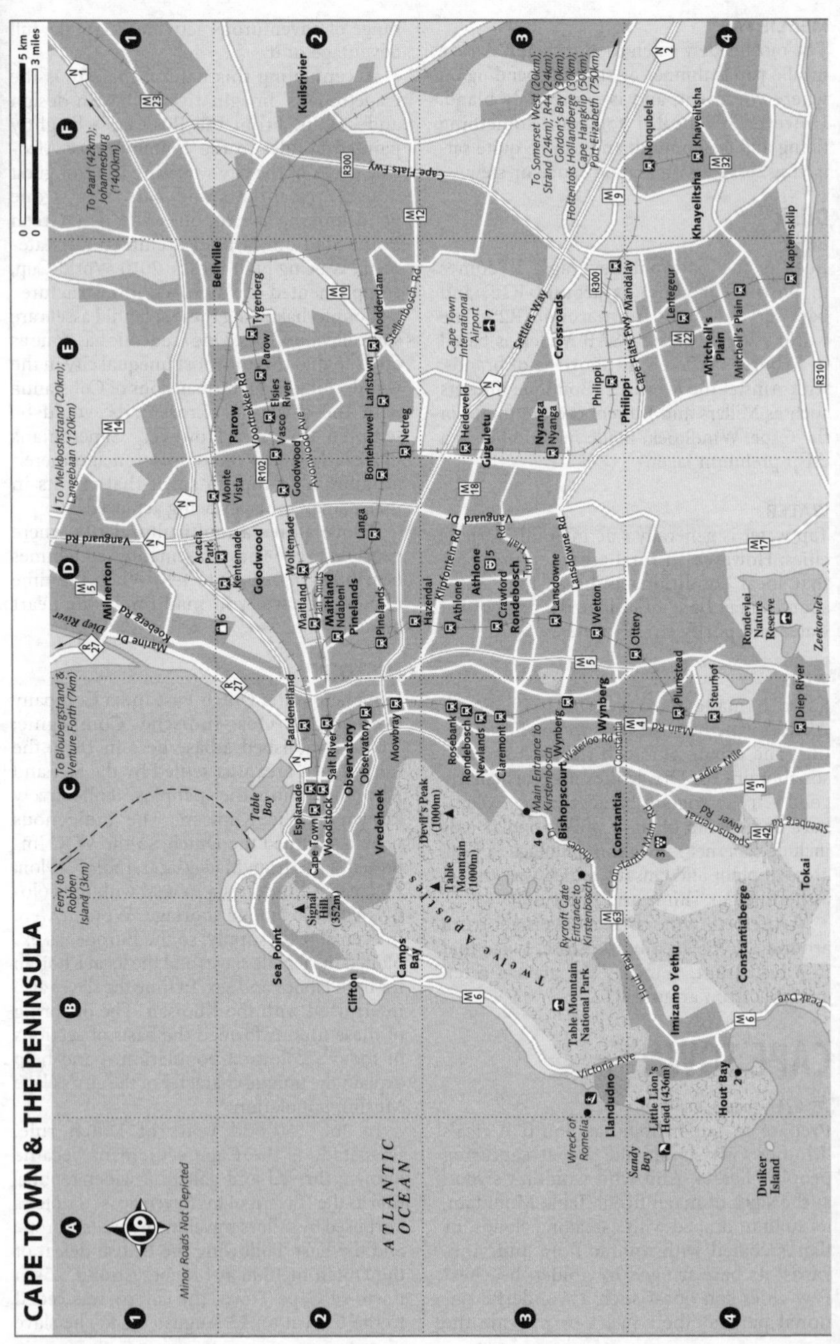
CAPE TOWN & THE PENINSULA
Minor Roads Not Depicted
0 5 km
0 3 miles
ATLANTIC OCEAN
Table Bay
Ferry to Robben Island (3km)
To Bloubergstrand & Venture Forth (7km)
To Melkbosstrand (20km); Langebaan (120km)
To Paarl (42km); Johannesburg (1400km)
To Somerset West (20km); Strand (24km); R44 (24km); Gordon's Bay (30km); Hottentots Hollandberge (30km); Cape Hangklip (50km); Port Elizabeth (750km)
Sea Point
Signal Hill (352m)
Clifton
Camps Bay
Twelve Apostles
Table Mountain (1000m)
Devil's Peak (1000m)
Table Mountain National Park
Llandudno
Wreck of Romelia
Little Lion's Head (436m)
Sandy Bay
Hout Bay
Duiker Island
Imizamo Yethu
Constantiaberge
Tokai
Constantia
Bishopscourt
Rycroft Gate Entrance to Kirstenbosch
Main Entrance to Kirstenbosch
Cape Town
Esplanade
Woodstock
Salt River
Paardeneiland
Observatory
Vredehoek
Mowbray
Rosebank
Rondebosch
Newlands
Claremont
Wynberg
Plumstead
Steurhof
Diep River
Ottery
Wetton
Lansdowne
Crawford
Athlone
Hazendal
Pinelands
Ndabeni
Maitland
Jan Smuts
Woltemade
Kentemade
Acacia Park
Goodwood
Monte Vista
Vasco
Elsies River
Parow
Tygerberg
Bellville
Kuilsrivier
Langa
Bonteheuwel
Netreg
Heideveld
Laristown
Modderdam
Cape Town International Airport
Gugulethu
Nyanga
Crossroads
Philippi
Mandalay
Lentegeur
Mitchell's Plain
Kapteinsklip
Khayelitsha
Nonqubela
Milnerton
Rondevlei Nature Reserve
Zeekoevlei
Marine Dr
Koeberg Rd
Diep River
Vanguard Rd
Vanguard Dr
Voortrekker Rd
Avonwood Ave
Klipfontein Rd
Turf Hall Rd
Lansdowne Rd
Stellenbosch Rd
Settlers Way
Cape Flats Fwy
Main Rd
Waterloo Rd
Ladies Mile
Spaanschemat River Rd
Steenberg Rd
Constantia Main Rd
Rhodes Dr
Hout Bay
Victoria Ave
Peak Dve
R27
N1
N2
N7
M3
M4
M5
M6
M9
M10
M12
M14
M17
M18
M22
M23
M32
M42
M63
R102
R300
R310
1
2
3
4
5
6
7
A
B
C
D
E
F

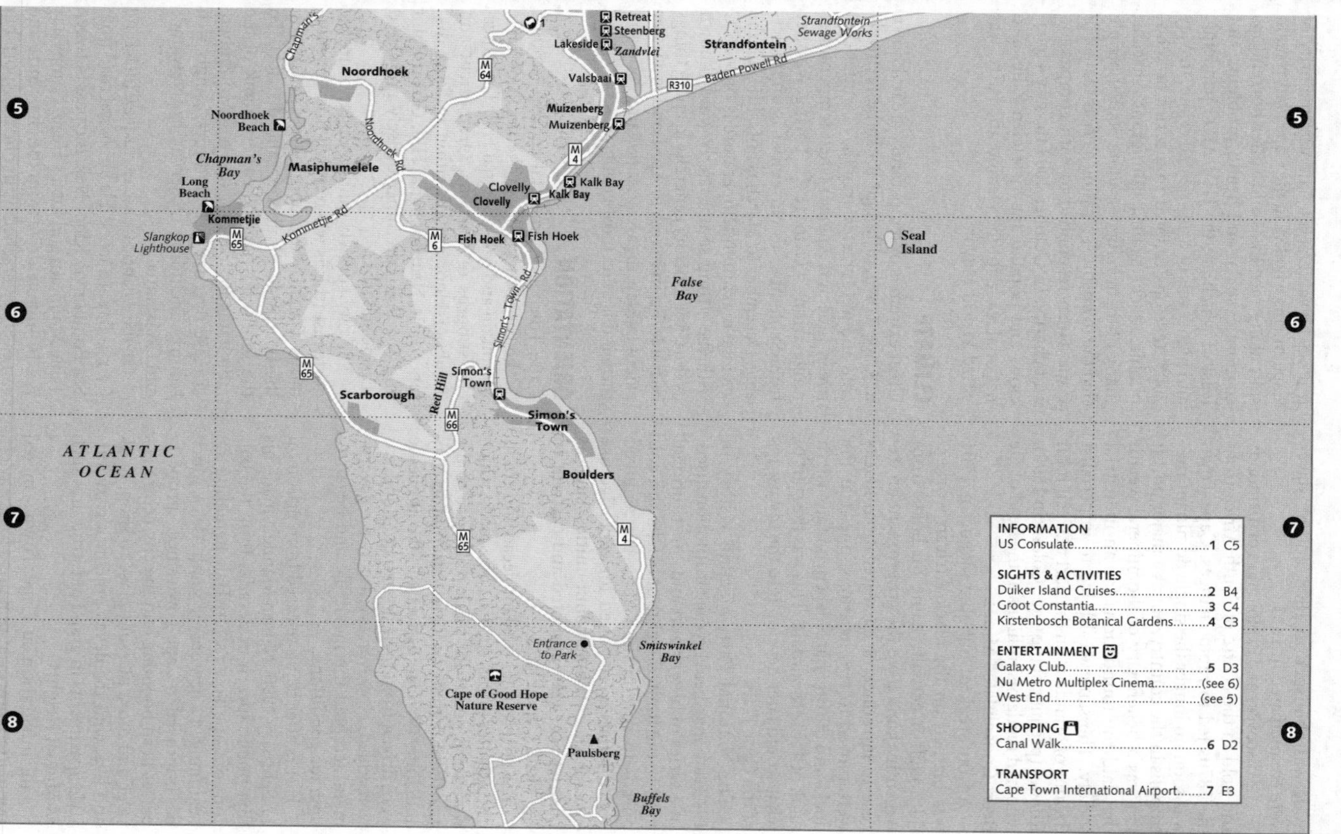

Retreat
Steenberg
Lakeside
Zandvlei
Strandfontein
Strandfontein Sewage Works
Baden Powell Rd
R310
Valsbaai
Chapman's
Noordhoek
Noordhoek Beach
Noordhoek Rd
Chapman's Bay
Masiphumelele
Long Beach
Kommetjie
Kommetjie Rd
Slangkop Lighthouse
Muizenberg
Kalk Bay
Clovelly
Fish Hoek
Simon's Town Rd
Seal Island
False Bay
Simon's Town
Red Hill
Scarborough
Boulders
ATLANTIC OCEAN
Entrance to Park
Smitswinkel Bay
Cape of Good Hope Nature Reserve
Paulsberg
Buffels Bay
M4
M6
M64
M65
M66
5
6
7
8
INFORMATION
US Consulate 1 C5
SIGHTS & ACTIVITIES
Duiker Island Cruises 2 B4
Groot Constantia 3 C4
Kirstenbosch Botanical Gardens 4 C3
ENTERTAINMENT
Galaxy Club 5 D3
Nu Metro Multiplex Cinema (see 6)
West End (see 5)
SHOPPING
Canal Walk 6 D2
TRANSPORT
Cape Town International Airport 7 E3

trade was abolished in 1808, and all slaves were emancipated in 1833.

The discovery and exploitation of diamonds and gold in the centre of South Africa from the 1870s led to rapid changes. Cape Town was soon no longer the single dominant metropolis in the country, but as a major port it too was a beneficiary of the mineral wealth that laid the foundations for an industrial society. The same wealth led to imperialist dreams of grandeur on the part of Cecil John Rhodes (premier of the Cape Colony in 1890), who had made his millions at the head of De Beers Consolidated Mines.

An outbreak of bubonic plague in 1901 was blamed on the black African workers (although it actually came on boats from Argentina) and gave the government an excuse to introduce racial segregation. Blacks were moved to two locations, one near the docks and the other at Ndabeni on the eastern flank of Table Mountain. This was the start of what would later develop into the townships of the Cape Flats.

The National Party election victory in 1948 saw apartheid become institutionalised. In a series of bitter court and constitutional battles, the limited rights of blacks and coloureds to vote in the Cape were removed and districts were zoned for exclusive use by each race. Whole communities, such as District Six, were uprooted and cast out to the bleak Cape Flats.

The government tried for decades to eradicate squatter towns, such as Crossroads, which were focal points for black resistance to the apartheid regime. In its last attempt in May and June 1986, an estimated 70,000 people were driven from their homes and hundreds were killed. However, eventually the government accepted the inevitable and began to upgrade conditions.

Hours after being released from prison on 11 February 1990, Nelson Mandela made his first public speech in decades from the balcony of Cape Town's City Hall, heralding the beginning of a new era for South Africa. Much has improved in Cape Town since – property prices keep booming and the city centre is a safer and more pleasant place to shop, work and live, with the development of ritzy loft-style apartments in grand old structures such as Mutual Heights.

Full integration of Cape Town's mixed population, however, remains a long way off, if it's achievable at all. The vast majority of Capetonians who live in the Cape Flats remain split along race lines and suffer horrendous economic, social and health problems, not least of which are the HIV/AIDS pandemic and high levels of drug-related crime. In May 2008, tensions erupted in a series of xenophobic attacks against immigrant Africans, many of them refugees; some 30,000 people fled the townships, creating a crisis that all of Cape Town responded to with compassion and charity. In October 2008 the city's tenacious and popular mayor Helen Zille, also national leader of the Democratic Party, was voted World Mayor.

CLIMATE

Great extremes of temperature are unknown in Cape Town, although it can be relatively cold and wet for a few months in winter (between June and August) when temperatures range from 7°C to 18°C. Spring weather from September to November is unpredictable. December to March is hot, although the average maximum temperature is only 26°C with the strong southeasterly wind (known as the Cape Doctor) generally keeping things bearable. From March to April, and to a lesser extent in May, the weather remains good and the wind is at its most gentle.

ORIENTATION

Cape Town's commercial centre – known as the City Bowl – lies to the north of Table Mountain and east of Signal Hill. The inner-city suburbs of Gardens, Oranjezicht and Tamboerskloof are all within walking distance of it. Near to Signal Hill, Green Point and Sea Point are other densely populated seaside suburbs.

The city sprawls quite a distance to the northeast (this is where you'll find the enormous Canal Walk Shopping Centre and the beachside Bloubergstrand district). To the south, skirting the eastern flank of the mountains and running down to Muizenberg at False Bay, are leafy and increasingly rich suburbs including Observatory, Newlands and Constantia.

On the Atlantic Coast, exclusive Clifton and Camps Bay are accessible by coastal road from Sea Point or via Kloof Nek, the pass between Table Mountain and Lion's Head. Camps Bay is a 10-minute drive from the city centre and can easily be reached by public transport, but as you go further south, the communities of Llandudno, Hout Bay and Noordhoek are better explored with your own car or bike.

INFORMATION

Bookshops

The main mass-market bookshop and newsagent is CNA, with branches around the city.

Clarke's Bookshop (Map pp412-13; ☎ 021-423 5739; 211 Long St, City Bowl) Stocks an unsurpassed range on South Africa and the continent.

Exclusive Books Lifestyles on Kloof (Map p420; Kloof St); Waterfront (Map pp416-17; ☎ 021-419 0905; Victoria Wharf) Has an excellent range, with magazines and some books in German.

Emergency

In an emergency call ☎ 107, or ☎ 112 if using a mobile phone. Other useful phone numbers:

Ambulance (☎ 10177)
Fire brigade (☎ 021-535 1100)
Mountain Rescue Services (☎ 021-948 9900)
Police (☎ 10111)

Internet Access

Cape Town is one of Africa's most wired cities. Most hotels and hostels offer internet facilities and you'll seldom have to hunt far for a wi-fi network or internet cafe. Rates are pretty uniform at R20 per hour. There is a handful of cafes in and around the mall **Lifestyles on Kloof** (Map p420; Kloof St) and access is available at Cape Town Tourism's City Bowl office (see right) at R10 per hour.

Medical Services

Groote Schuur Hospital (Map pp412-13; ☎ 021-404 9111; http://capegateway.gov.za/gsh; Main Rd, Observatory) In an emergency, you can go directly to the casualty department.

Netcare Christiaan Barnard Memorial Hospital (Map pp412-13; ☎ 021-480 6111; www.netcare.co.za; 181 Longmarket St, City Bowl) The best private hospital; reception is on the 8th floor.

Netcare Travel Clinic (Map pp408-9; ☎ 021-419 3172; www.travelclinics.co.za; Room 1107, 11th fl, Picbel Parkade, 58 Strand St, City Bowl; 🕐 8am-4pm Mon-Fri) For vaccinations and travel health.

Money

Money can be changed at the airport, most commercial banks and at Cape Town Tourism (below). Rennies Travel (below), the local agent for Thomas Cook, has foreign-exchange offices.

There are ATMs all over town; see p747 for information on scams.

American Express City Bowl (Map pp412-13; ☎ 021-425 7991; Thibault Sq); Waterfront (Map pp416-17; ☎ 021-419 3917; V&A Hotel Mall, Waterfront)

Post

Waterfront (Map pp416-17; ☎ 021-421 4551; upper fl, Victoria Wharf; 🕐 9am-7pm Mon-Fri, to 4pm Sat, 10am-2pm Sun) Next to ATMs.

Tourist Information

Cape Town Tourism (www.capetown.travel) City Centre (Map pp412-13; ☎ 021-487 6800; cnr Castle & Burg Sts, City Bowl; 🕐 8am-5.30pm Mon-Fri, 8.30am-1pm Sat, 9am-1pm Sun); Waterfront (Map pp412-13; ☎ 021-408 7600; Clock Tower Centre; 🕐 9am-6pm Oct-Mar, 8am-5pm Apr-Sep) Well-run centres where you'll find advisers who can book accommodation, tours and rental cars. The City Centre branch offers a Computicket booth, a free phone for ordering Rikkis (see p428), and advice on Cape Nature reserves (☎ 021-426 0723) and national parks.

Western Cape Tourism (Map pp412-13; ☎ 021-405 4500; www.thewesterncape.co.za; 🕐 9am-7pm) Shares the Waterfront office with Cape Town Tourism.

Travel Agencies

Africa Travel Centre (Map p420; ☎ 021-423 5555; www.backpackers.co.za; The Backpack, 74 New Church St, Tamboerskloof) Books all sorts of tours and activities, including day trips, hire cars and extended African expeditions.

Flight Centre (Map p420; www.flightcentre.co.za; ☎ 021-461 8658; Gardens Centre, Mill St, Gardens) There are other branches around the city.

Rennies Travel (www.renniestravel.co.za) City Bowl (Map pp412-13; ☎ 021-423 7154; 101 St George's Mall); Sea Point (Map pp408–9; ☎ 021-439 7529; Adelphi Centre, 182 Main Rd); Waterfront (Map pp412-13; ☎ 021-418 3744; Victoria Wharf) Handles international and domestic bookings and can arrange visas for neighbouring countries.

STA Travel (Map pp408-9; ☎ 021-686 6800; www.statravel.co.za; 14 Main Rd, Rondebosch)

DANGERS & ANNOYANCES

Cape Town's relaxed vibe can instil a false sense of security. Thefts are most likely to happen when visitors do something foolish such as leaving their gear on a beach while they go swimming.

Paranoia is not required, but common sense is. There is tremendous poverty on the

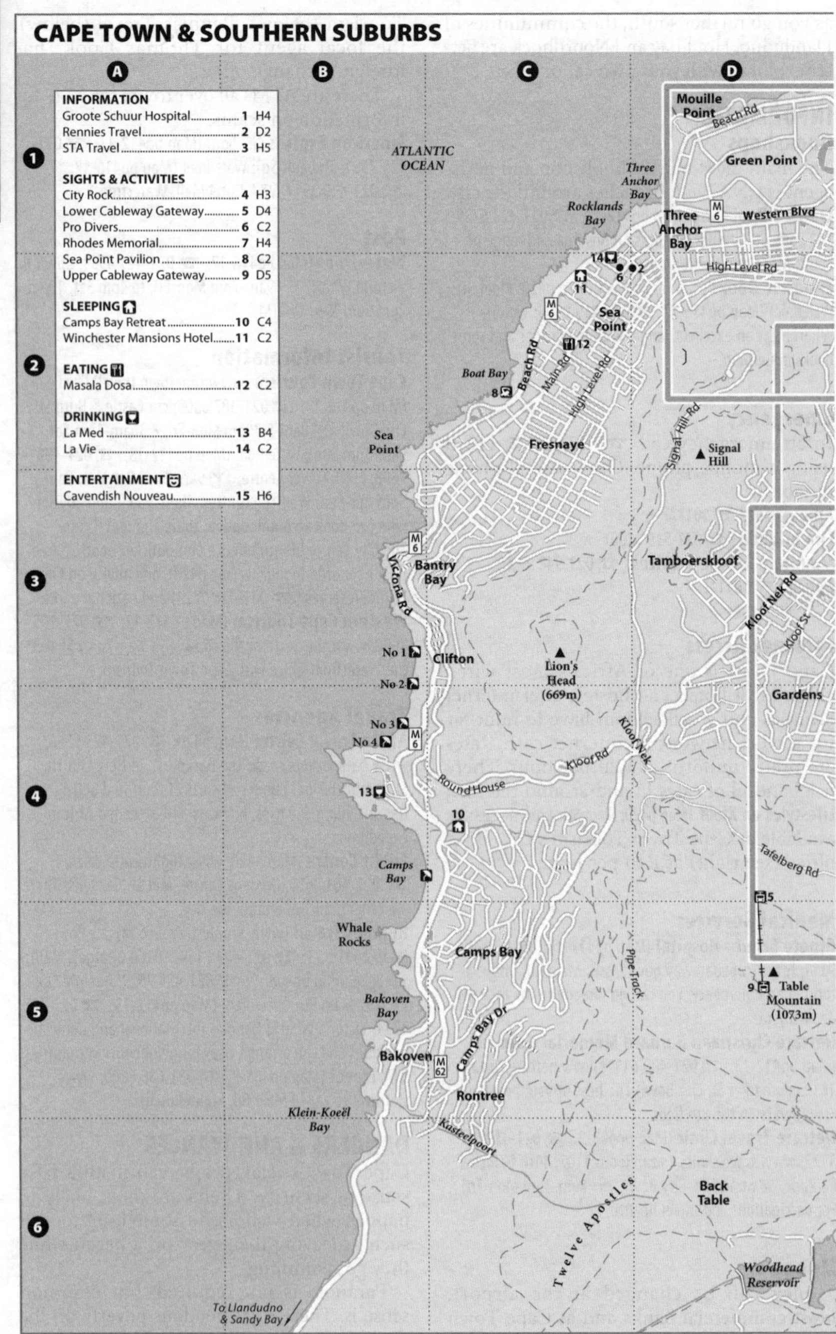
CAPE TOWN & SOUTHERN SUBURBS
INFORMATION
Groote Schuur Hospital 1 H4
Rennies Travel 2 D2
STA Travel 3 H5
SIGHTS & ACTIVITIES
City Rock 4 H3
Lower Cableway Gateway 5 D4
Pro Divers 6 C2
Rhodes Memorial 7 H4
Sea Point Pavilion 8 C2
Upper Cableway Gateway 9 D5
SLEEPING
Camps Bay Retreat 10 C4
Winchester Mansions Hotel 11 C2
EATING
Masala Dosa 12 C2
DRINKING
La Med 13 B4
La Vie 14 C2
ENTERTAINMENT
Cavendish Nouveau 15 H6
ATLANTIC OCEAN
Mouille Point
Beach Rd
Green Point
Western Blvd
Three Anchor Bay
High Level Rd
Rocklands Bay
Sea Point
Boat Bay
Main Rd
Fresnaye
Signal Hill Rd
Signal Hill
Bantry Bay
Victoria Rd
Tamboerskloof
Kloof Nek Rd
Kloof St
Clifton
No 1
No 2
No 3
No 4
Lion's Head (669m)
Kloof Nek
Kloof Rd
Round House
Gardens
Tafelberg Rd
Camps Bay
Whale Rocks
Pipe Track
Table Mountain (1073m)
Bakoven Bay
Bakoven
Camps Bay Dr
Rontree
Klein-Koeël Bay
Kasteelpoort
Back Table
Twelve Apostles
Woodhead Reservoir
To Llandudno & Sandy Bay

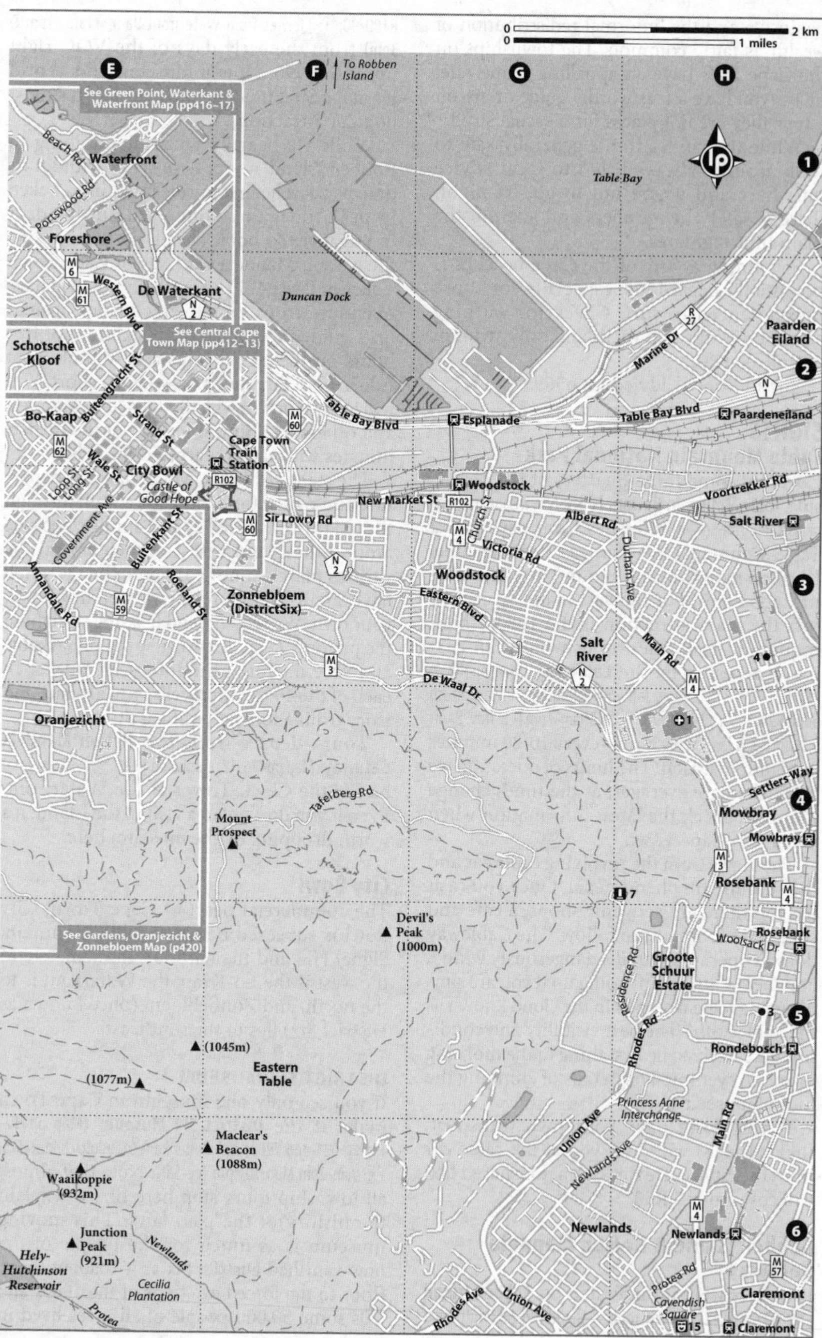
To Robben Island
See Green Point, Waterkant & Waterfront Map (pp416–17)
Table Bay
Beach Rd
Waterfront
Portswood Rd
Foreshore
Western Blvd
De Waterkant
Duncan Dock
See Central Cape Town Map (pp412–13)
Schotsche Kloof
Marine Dr
Paarden Eiland
Buitengracht St
Bo-Kaap
Strand St
Table Bay Blvd
Esplanade
Paardeneiland
Cape Town Train Station
Wale St
City Bowl
Loop St
Long St
Castle of Good Hope
Woodstock
New Market St
Voortrekker Rd
Sir Lowry Rd
Albert Rd
Salt River
Government Ave
Buitenkant St
Church St
Victoria Rd
Durham Ave
Annandale Rd
Roeland St
Zonnebloem (DistrictSix)
Eastern Blvd
Main Rd
De Waal Dr
Oranjezicht
Settlers Way
Tafelberg Rd
Mowbray
Mount Prospect
Rosebank
Woolsack Dr
Devil's Peak (1000m)
See Gardens, Oranjezicht & Zonnebloem Map (p420)
Groote Schuur Estate
Residence Rd
Rhodes Rd
Rondebosch
(1045m)
Eastern Table
(1077m)
Princess Anne Interchange
Union Ave
Maclear's Beacon (1088m)
Newlands Ave
Waaikoppie (932m)
Newlands
Junction Peak (921m)
Hely-Hutchinson Reservoir
Cecilia Plantation
Protea Rd
Claremont
Cavendish Square
Rhodes Ave
Union Ave
Protea
0 2 km
0 1 miles

peninsula and the 'informal redistribution of wealth' is fairly common. The townships on the Cape Flats have an appalling crime rate; unless you have a trustworthy guide or are on a tour they are not places for a casual stroll.

While the city centre is generally safe to walk around, always listen to local advice on where and where not to go. At night, there is safety in numbers and stick to the main thoroughfares.

Swimming at any of the Cape beaches is potentially hazardous, especially for those inexperienced in surf. Check for warning signs about rips and rocks and only swim in patrolled areas.

For additional advice see p569.

SIGHTS

Table Mountain National Park

Covering some three-quarters of the peninsula, **Table Mountain National Park** (www.sanparks.org/parks/table_mountain) stretches from flat-topped Table Mountain (*Hoerikwaggo*, its indigenous Khoisan name, means 'mountain in the sea') to Cape Point. For the vast majority of visitors the main attraction is the 1086m-high mountain itself, the top of which can easily be accessed by the **Cableway** (Map pp408-9; ☎ 021-424 8181; www.tablemountain.net; 1-way/return adult R74/145, child R38/76; 🕐 8.30am-7pm Feb-Nov, 8am-9.30pm Dec & Jan), which runs every 10/20 minutes in high/low season. The hours of operation we have listed are averages, as the times change monthly; check the latest information when you are in Cape Town.

The views from the revolving cable car and the summit are phenomenal. Once you're at the top there are souvenir shops, a cafe and some easy footpaths to follow. The Cableway doesn't operate when it's dangerously windy, and there's little point going up if you are simply going to be wrapped in the cloud known as the 'tablecloth'. The best visibility and conditions are likely to be first thing in the morning or in the evening. For details of climbing the mountain see p418.

If you don't have your own transport, Rikkis (p428) will drop you at the cable car from the city centre for R30; a nonshared taxi will cost around R60.

Robben Island & Nelson Mandela Gateway

Prisoners were incarcerated on **Robben Island** (☎ 021-413 4220; www.robben-island.org.za; adult/child R180/90; 🕐 ferries from Waterfront 9am, 11am, 1pm & 3pm) from the early days of the VOC right up until 1996. Now a museum and World Heritage Site, it is one of Cape Town's most popular attractions.

While we heartily recommend going to Robben Island, a visit here is not without its drawbacks. The first hurdle is getting a ticket; in peak times these often sell out for days in advance, so book ahead via the website, the Nelson Mandela Gateway or Cape Town Tourism (see p407). Most likely you will have to endure crowds and being hustled around on a guided tour that at a maximum of two hours on the island (plus a 30-minute boat ride in both directions) is woefully short. You will learn much of what happened to Mandela and others like him, since one of the former inmates will lead you around the prison.

The standard tours, which have set departure and return times, include a walk through the old prison, as well as a 45-minute bus ride around the island with commentary on the various places of note. If you're lucky, you'll have about 10 minutes to wander around on your own. We recommend heading straight to the prison's A-section to view the remarkable and very moving exhibition *Cell Stories*. In each of the 40 isolation cells is an artefact and story from a former political prisoner.

Tours depart from the **Nelson Mandela Gateway** (Map pp416-17; admission free; 🕐 7.30am-9pm) beside the Clock Tower at the Waterfront. Even if you don't plan a visit to the island, it's worth dropping by the museum here.

City Bowl

The commercial heart of Cape Town, City Bowl is squeezed between Table Mountain, Signal Hill and the harbour. Immediately to the west is the Bo-Kaap, the Waterkant is to the north, and Zonnebloem (once known as District Six) lies to the southeast.

DISTRICT SIX MUSEUM

If you see only one museum in Cape Town make it the **District Six Museum** (Map pp412-13; ☎ 021-466 7208; 25A Buitenkant St; adult/child R15/5; 🕐 9am-2pm Mon, to 4pm Tue-Sat). Note that almost all township tours stop here first to explain the history of the pass laws. This moving museum is as much for the people of the now-vanished District Six as it is about them. Prior to the forced evictions of the 1960s and '70s some 50,000 people of all races lived in the area. Displays include a floor map of District Six on which former residents have labelled where their demolished homes and features of their neighbourhood once stood.

You can also arrange a **walking tour** (☎ 021-466 7208; per person R50) of the old District Six (10 people minimum).

CASTLE OF GOOD HOPE

Built between 1666 and 1679 to defend the city, this stone-walled pentagonal **castle** (Map pp412-13; ☎ 021-787 1249; Buitenkant St; adult/child R20/10; 9am-4pm, tours 11am, noon & 2pm) is commonly touted as the city's oldest building. A tour is worthwhile, but you can quite easily find your own way around. The noon tour on weekdays coincides with the changing of the guard; also, at the castle gate, keys to the gate are handed over in an orchestrated ceremony at 10am Monday to Friday.

HOUSES OF PARLIAMENT

Although it sounds unlikely, visiting South Africa's **parliament** (Map pp412-13; ☎ 021-403 2266; Parliament St; admission free; tours by appointment 9am-noon Mon-Fri) can be fascinating, especially if you're interested in the country's modern history. Opened in 1885, the hallowed halls have seen some momentous events, including when president Hendrik Verwoerd, architect of apartheid, was stabbed to death in 1966. You must present your passport to gain entry.

LONG ST

Whether you come to browse the antique shops, secondhand bookshops and the streetwear boutiques, or to party at the bars and clubs that crank up at night, a stroll along Long St (Map pp412–13) is an essential element of a Cape Town visit. The most attractive section, lined with Victorian-era buildings with lovely wrought-iron balconies, runs from the junction with Buitensingle St north to around the Strand.

SIGNAL HILL & NOON GUN

Once also known as Lion's Rump, as it's attached to Lion's Head by a 'spine' of hills, Signal Hill (Map pp412–13) separates Sea Point from the City Bowl. There are magnificent views from the 350m-high summit, especially at night.

At noon Monday to Saturday, a cannon known as the Noon Gun (Map pp412–13) is fired from the lower slopes of Signal Hill. Traditionally this allowed the burghers in the town below to check their watches. It's a stiff walk up here through the Bo-Kaap – take Longmarket St and keep going until it ends.

IZIKO SLAVE LODGE

One of the oldest buildings in South Africa, dating from 1660, **Iziko Slave Lodge** (Map pp412-13; ☎ 021-460 8242; 49 Adderley St; adult/child R15/free; 10am-5pm Mon-Sat) has a fascinating history. Until 1811 the building was home, if you could call it that, to as many as 1000 slaves, who lived in damp, insanitary, crowded conditions. Up to 20% died each year. The slaves were bought and sold just around the corner on Spin St.

The museum today is mainly devoted to the history and experience of slaves and their descendants in the Cape, although the displays on the 2nd floor, including artefacts from ancient Egypt, Greece and Rome, hark back to the building's former use as the Cultural History Museum.

IZIKO BO-KAAP MUSEUM

Giving some insight into the history and lifestyle of the people of the Bo-Kaap is this small but engaging **museum** (Map pp412-13; ☎ 021-481 3939; 71 Wale St, Bo-Kaap; adult/child R10/free; 10am-5pm Mon-Sat). It's worth a stroll around the area (during the day) to admire the traditional architecture.

COMPANY'S GARDENS

These shady green **gardens** (Map pp412-13; 7am-7pm) in the heart of the city are a lovely place to relax during the heat of the day. The surviving 6 hectares of what started as the vegetable patch for the Dutch East India Company are found around Government Ave.

Gardens & Around

Rising up Table Mountain's slopes are the ritzy suburbs of Gardens, Tamboerskloof, Oranjezicht and Vredehoek. Most of the major sights here are clustered around Company's Gardens (above).

IZIKO SA NATIONAL GALLERY

South Africa's premier **gallery** (Map p420; ☎ 021-467 4660; Government Ave, Gardens; adult/child R15/free; 10am-5pm Tue-Sun) is a must for art lovers. The permanent collection harks back to Dutch

CENTRAL CAPE TOWN

INFORMATION

American Express 1 F2
Botswana Consulate 2 G1
British Consulate .... (see 2)
Cape Town Tourism 3 E3
Clarke's Bookshop 4 D5
Flight Centre .... (see 40)
German Consulate 5 F2
Mozambican Consulate 6 E3
Namibia Tourism .... (see 6)
Netcare Christiaan Barnard Memorial Hospital 7 D3
Netcare Travel Clinic 8 F3
Netherlands Consulate 9 E2
Rennies Travel 10 E3

SIGHTS & ACTIVITIES

Abseil Africa 11 C5
Castle of Good Hope 12 G5
Company's Gardens 13 D5
District Six Museum 14 F5
Houses of Parliament 15 E5
Iziko Bo-Kaap Museum 16 C3
Iziko Slave Lodge 17 E4
Noon Gun 18 B1

SLEEPING

Cape Diamond Hotel 19 F4
Daddy Long Legs Apartments 20 C5
Daddy Long Legs Hotel 21 D4
Grand Daddy Hotel 22 E3
Long Street Backpackers 23 D5
Penthouse on Long 24 D4
Scalabrini Guesthouse 25 F6
St Paul's Guesthouse 26 C5
Urban Chic 27 D4

EATING

Addis in Cape 28 D4
Birds Café 29 D3
Bizerca Bistro 30 G2
Crush 31 E4
Jardine 32 C4
Lola's 33 C5
Masala Dosa 34 D4
Noon Gun Tearoom & Restaurant 35 C1
Royale Eatery 36 C5

DRINKING

Julep Bar 37 D5
Marvel 38 C5
Neighbourhood Bar & Restaurant 39 D4
Vida e Caffé 40 E4
Waiting Room .... (see 36)

ENTERTAINMENT

Artscape 41 H2
Assembly 42 F6
Hemisphere 43 F3
Old City Hall 44 F5
Zula Sound Bar 45 D5

SHOPPING

African Image 46 E4
Greenmarket Square 47 E4
Pan African Market 48 E3

TRANSPORT

Bus Terminus 49 G3
Golden Acre Terminal 50 G4
Greyhound .... (see 49)
Intercape .... (see 49)
SA Roadlink .... (see 49)
Translux .... (see 49)

A B C D
1 2 3 4 5 6

Signal Hill
Schotsche Kloof
Bo-Kaap
Heritage Sq
Van Riebeeck Sq
Company's Gardens
To Signal Hill
Vredenburg La
De Smit St
Napier St
Jarvis St
Dixon St
Loader St
Waterkant St
Hudson St
Ella St
August St
Longmarket St
Strand St
Chiappini St
Rose St
Berg St
Astana St
Yusuf Dr
Church St
Shortmarket St
Pentz Rd
Wale St
Upper Pepper St
Upper Bloem St
Upper Leeuwen St
Bree St
Lion St
Jordan St
Service St
Buitengracht St
Dorp St
Leeuwen St
New Church St
Pepper St
Bryant St
Bloem St
Loop St
Upper Buitengracht St
Buiten St
Long St
Keerom St
Queen Victoria St
Orphan St
Buitensingel St
Carisbrook St
Jamieson Rd
Dean St
Grey's Pass
Orange St
Museum St
Government Ave
Kloof St
Dorman St
Park Rd
Paddock Ave
Gallery
Hatfield St
Rheede St
Kohling St
Faure St
Vrede St

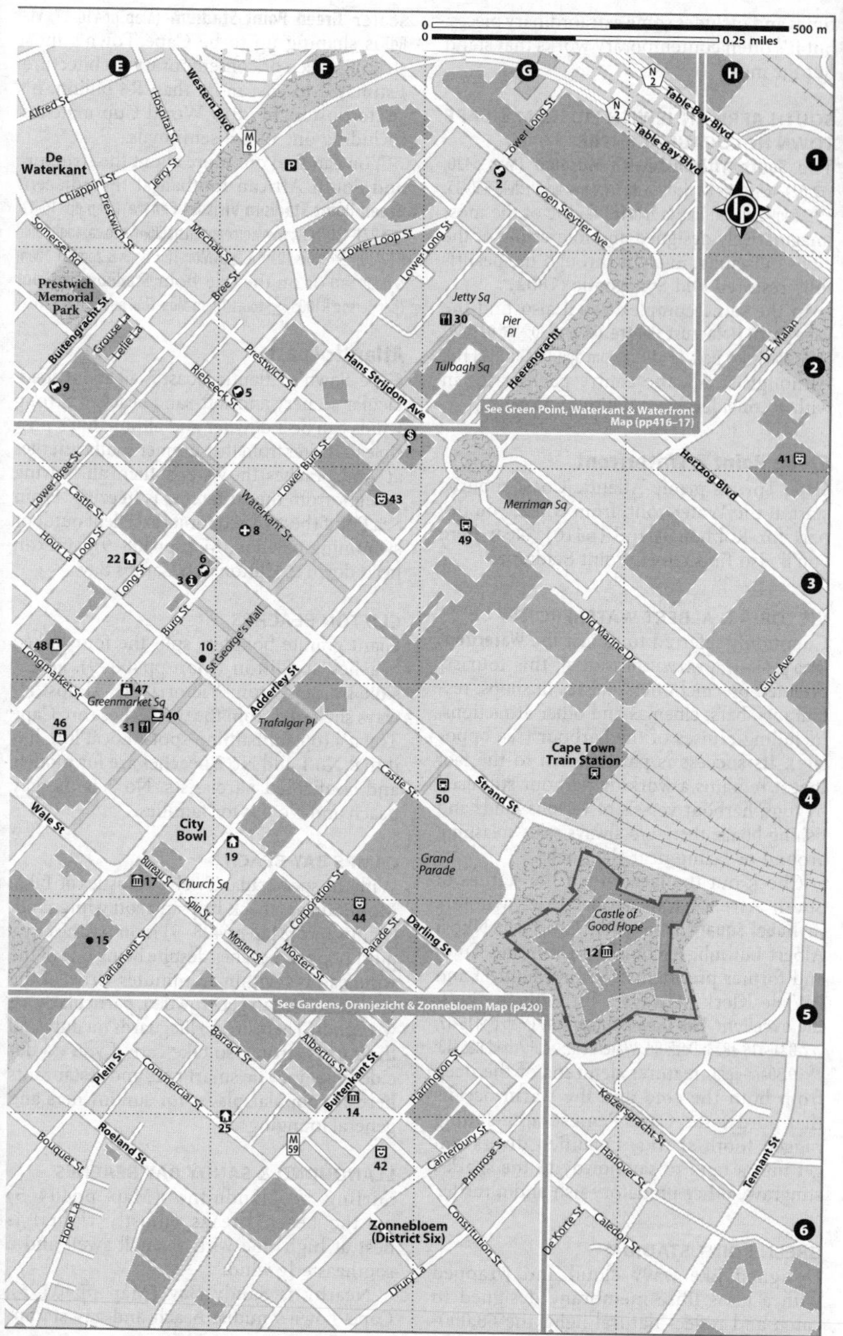
0
500 m
0
0.25 miles
E
F
G
H
1
2
3
4
5
6
Alfred St
Hospital St
Western Blvd
De Waterkant
Chiappini St
Jerry St
Prestwich St
Somerset Rd
Mechau St
Bree St
Prestwich Memorial Park
Buitengracht St
Grouse La
Lellie La
Riebeeck St
Prestwich St
Lower Loop St
Lower Long St
Coen Steytler Ave
Table Bay Blvd
Jetty Sq
Pier Pl
Tulbagh Sq
Hans Strijdom Ave
Heerengracht
D F Malan
See Green Point, Waterkant & Waterfront Map (pp416–17)
Hertzog Blvd
Lower Bree St
Castle St
Hout La
Loop St
Lower Burg St
Waterkant St
Merriman Sq
Long St
Burg St
St George's Mall
Old Marine Dr
Civic Ave
Longmarket St
Greenmarket Sq
Adderley St
Trafalgar Pl
Cape Town Train Station
Castle St
Strand St
Wale St
City Bowl
Grand Parade
Bureau St
Church Sq
Spin St
Corporation St
Castle of Good Hope
Parliament St
Mostert St
Parade St
Darling St
See Gardens, Oranjezicht & Zonnebloem Map (p420)
Barrack St
Albertus St
Plein St
Commercial St
Buitenkant St
Harrington St
Roeland St
Keizersgracht St
Bouquet St
Canterbury St
Primrose St
Hanover St
Tennant St
Hope La
Constitution St
Zonnebloem (District Six)
De Korte St
Caledon St
Drury La

times and includes some extraordinary pieces, but it's often contemporary works that stand out the most.

SOUTH AFRICAN JEWISH MUSEUM & CAPE TOWN HOLOCAUST CENTRE

The **South African Jewish Museum** (Map p420; ☎ 021-465 1546; 88 Hatfield St, Gardens; adult/child R50/15; 🕑 10am-5pm Sun-Thu, to 2pm Fri) is one of the most imaginatively designed and interesting of the city's museums. Entry is through the beautifully restored Old Synagogue (1862).

In the same complex you'll also find the **Cape Town Holocaust Centre** (Map p420; ☎ 021-462 5553; admission free; 🕑 10am-5pm Sun-Thu, to 1pm Fri). Although small, the centre packs a lot in with a considerable emotional punch.

Green Point & Waterfront

Cape Town's prime Atlantic Coast suburbs start at the Waterfront, from where you depart for Robben Island (p410). Near here you'll also find Green Point Stadium.

VICTORIA & ALBERT WATERFRONT

Commonly referred to as just the **Waterfront** (Map pp416-17; www.waterfront.co.za), this tourist-oriented precinct offers masses of shops, restaurants, bars, cinemas and other attractions, including cruises of the harbour (see opposite). Its success is partly down to the fact that it remains a working harbour still used by tugs, harbour vessels of various kinds and fishing boats; there are always seals splashing around or lazing near the docks.

Check out the larger-than-life statues of South Africa's four Nobel Prize winners in **Nobel Square** (Map pp416-17; Dock Rd): Nkosi Albert Luthuli, Archbishop Desmond Tutu, and former presidents Nelson Mandela and FW de Klerk. Always a hit with the kids, the excellent **Two Oceans Aquarium** (Map pp416-17; ☎ 021-418 3823; Dock Rd, Waterfront; adult/child R85/40; 🕑 9.30am-6pm) features denizens of the deep from both the cold and the warm oceans that border the Cape Peninsula, including ragged tooth sharks. Qualified divers can get into a tank to say howdy to the sharks, stingrays, other predatory fish and a turtle.

GREEN POINT STADIUM

Designed like wavy cloud and wrapped with a glass-fibre membrane designed to catch and reflect natural light, the 68,000-seater **Green Point Stadium** (Map pp416-17; Vlei Rd) is shaping up to be Cape Town's most striking piece of contemporary architecture. Estimated to cost more than R4 billion, it's set to host eight 2010 World Cup matches, including one of the semifinals.

You can find out more about the structure and South African football at the adjacent **Green Point Stadium Visitors Centre** (Map pp416-17; ☎ 021-430 0410; www.greenpointstadiumvc.co.za; adult/child R40/20; 🕑 tours 10am & 2pm Mon-Thu, noon & 2pm Fri, 10am & noon Sat) or on the one-hour **Stadium Site Tour** (per person R100; 🕑 tours 10am Mon-Thu, noon Fri & Sat).

Atlantic Coast

Cape Town's Atlantic Coast is all about spectacular scenery and soft-sand beaches. Strong winds can be a downer and although it's possible to shelter from the summer southeasterlies at some beaches, the water at them all, flowing straight from the Antarctic, is freezing. From Sea Point (best visited for its excellent outdoor swimming pavilion, Map pp408–9), you can head down to Clifton and Camps Bay.

CLIFTON BEACHES

Giant granite boulders split the four linked beaches at Clifton (Map pp408–9), accessible by steps from Victoria Rd. Almost always sheltered from the wind, these are Cape Town's top sunbathing spots. Local lore has it that No 1 and No 2 beaches are for models and confirmed narcissists, No 3 is the gay beach and No 4 is for families.

CAMPS BAY BEACH

With the spectacular Twelve Apostles of Table Mountain as a backdrop and soft white sand, Camps Bay (Map pp408–9) is one of the city's most popular beaches despite being one of the windiest. It's within 15 minutes' drive of the city centre so can get crowded, particularly on weekends. There are no lifeguards on duty and the surf is strong, so take care if you do decide to swim. The smart bars and restaurants here are popular places for sundowners and general lounging.

LLANDUDNO & SANDY BAY BEACHES

Surfing at Llandudno (Map pp404–5) on the beach breaks (mostly rights) is best at high tide with a small swell and a southeasterly wind.

Nearby is Sandy Bay (Map pp404–5), Cape Town's nudist beach and gay stamping ground. It's a particularly beautiful stretch of sand and there's no pressure to take your clothes off if you don't want to. Like many such beaches, Sandy Bay has no direct access roads.

Southern Suburbs

Heading east around Table Mountain along Sir Lowry Rd (Map pp404–5) will bring you to the Southern Suburbs, beginning with the bohemian, edgy areas of Woodstock and Observatory and moving south below Devil's Peak to Rondebosch, Newlands and wealthy Constantia, home to South Africa's oldest vineyards and wine estates.

KIRSTENBOSCH BOTANICAL GARDENS

Location and unique flora combine to make Cape Town's **botanical gardens** (Map pp404-5; ☎ 021-799 8783; Rhodes Dr, Newlands; adult/child R32/10; 🕑 8am-7pm Sep-Mar, to 6pm Apr-Aug) among the most beautiful in the world. The 36-hectare landscaped section seems to merge almost imperceptibly with the 492 hectares of *fynbos* (fine-leafed bush) vegetation cloaking the mountain slopes.

The gardens are at their best between mid-August and mid-October.

You can hire a Rikki (p428) to get you here or hop on the City Sightseeing Cape Town bus (see p419).

GROOT CONSTANTIA

A superb example of Cape Dutch architecture, **Groot Constantia** (Map pp404-5; ☎ 021-794 5128; Groot Constantia Rd, High Constantia; tastings incl glass R25; 🕑 10am-6pm) is set in a beautiful wine estate. Not surprisingly, it can become busy with tour groups, but the grounds are big enough for you to escape the crowds. In the 18th century, Constantia wines were exported around the world and were highly acclaimed. The beautifully restored homestead is now a **museum** (adult/child R15/free; 🕑 10am-5pm).

RHODES MEMORIAL

This impressive granite **memorial** (Map pp408-9; 🕑 7am-7pm) to the mining magnate and former prime minister stands on the eastern slopes of Table Mountain. There are sweeping views of the Cape Flats and the mountain ranges beyond, and, behind the memorial, a pleasant tearoom. The exit for the memorial from the M3 is at the Princess Anne Interchange.

ACTIVITIES

Abseiling & Kloofing

Abseil Africa (Map pp412-13; ☎ 021-424 4760; www.abseilafrica.co.za; Long St, City Bowl; abseiling R495) is the company to see if you want to shimmy 112m down a rope off the top of Table Mountain.

Abseil Africa also offers canyoning trips around Cape Town (R695). The sport of clambering into and out of kloofs (gorges) also entails abseiling, climbing, hiking, swimming and jumping.

Another reliable operator is Day Trippers (see p419).

Cruises

DUIKER ISLAND CRUISES

From Hout Bay's (Map pp404–5) harbour you can catch regular daily cruises to Duiker Island, also known as Seal Island because of its colony of Cape fur seals. Three companies run these cruises daily, usually with guaranteed sailings in the mornings. The cheapest is **Circe Launches** (☎ 021-790 1040; www.circelaunches.co.za; adult/child R42.50/15).

HARBOUR CRUISES

If only to take in the panoramic view of Table Mountain from the water, a cruise into Table Bay should not be missed. **Waterfront Boat Company** (Map pp416-17; ☎ 021-418 5806; www.waterfrontboats.co.za; Quay 5, Waterfront) offers a variety of cruises, including highly recommended 1½-hour sunset cruises (R200). Other operators tout their services in the same area; check www.waterfront.co.za/play/Pages/Home.aspx for more info.

Cycling

Thrill meisters **Downhill Adventures** (Map p420; ☎ 021-422 0388; www.downhilladventures.com; cnr Orange & Kloof Sts, Gardens) offers a variety of cycling trips and adventures. Try a mountain-bike descent from the lower Cableway station on Table Mountain (R495), or ride through the Constatntia winelands and the Cape of Good Hope (R655). Day Trippers (p419) includes cycling on its trip to Cape Point.

Diving

Cape Town offers some excellent shore and boat dives, although the shark-cage diving

GREEN POINT, WATERKANT & WATERFRONT

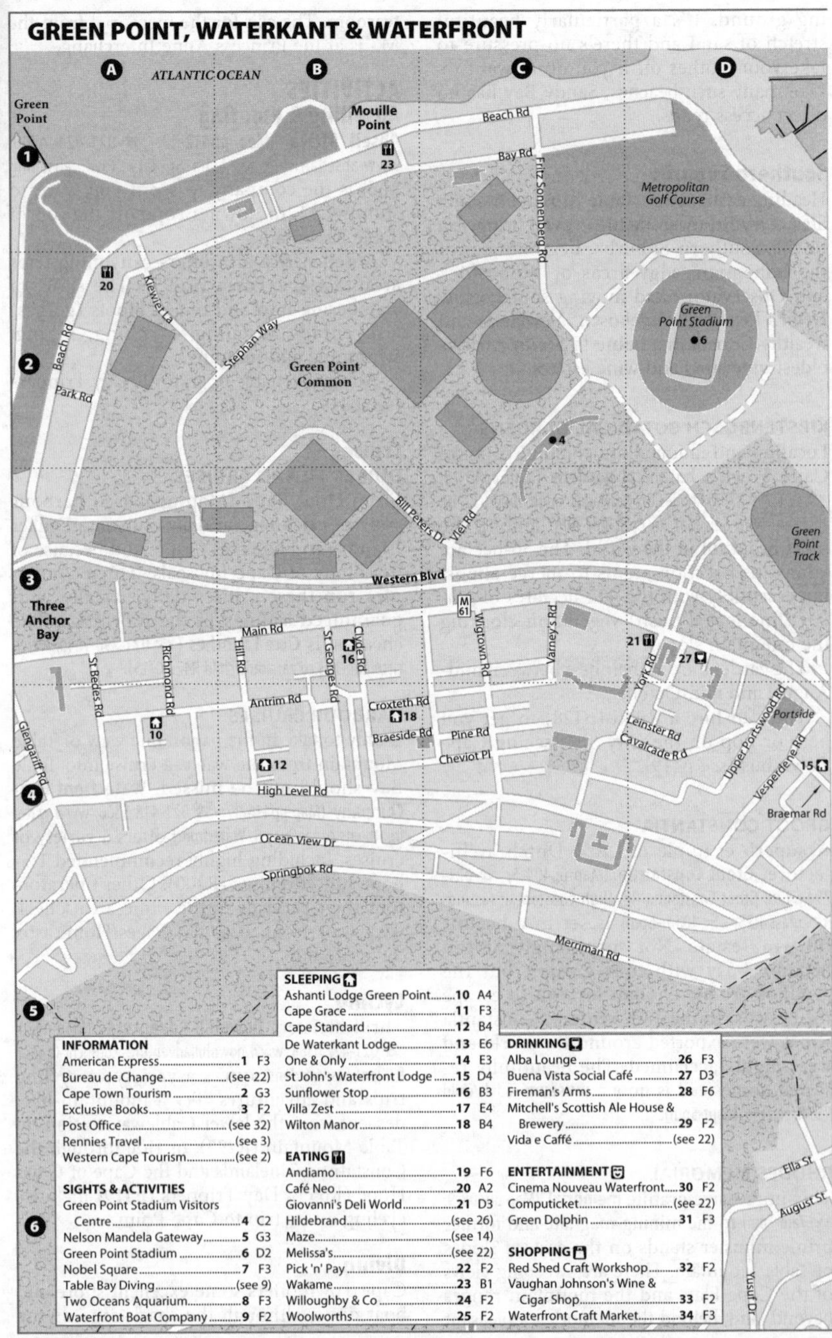

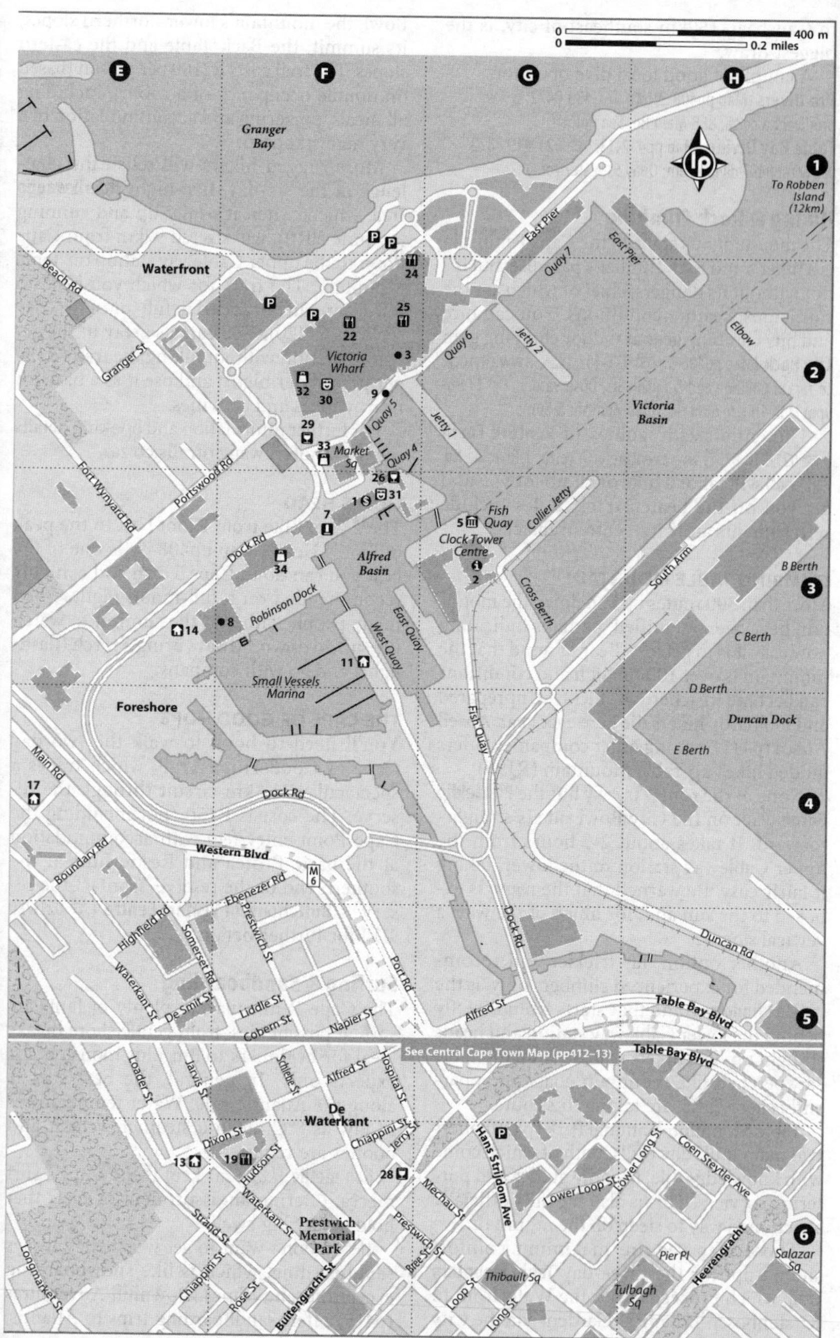
400 m
0.2 miles
Granger Bay
To Robben Island (12km)
Waterfront
Beach Rd
Granger St
Victoria Wharf
East Pier
Quay 7
Quay 6
Jetty 2
Elbow
Victoria Basin
Quay 5
Jetty 1
Market Sq
Quay 4
Fort Wynyard Rd
Portswood Rd
Fish Quay
Collier Jetty
Clock Tower Centre
Dock Rd
Alfred Basin
South Arm
B Berth
Robinson Dock
Cross Berth
East Quay
West Quay
C Berth
Small Vessels Marina
Foreshore
D Berth
Duncan Dock
E Berth
Fish Quay
Main Rd
Dock Rd
Boundary Rd
Western Blvd
M6
Ebenezer Rd
Highfield Rd
Prestwich St
Somerset Rd
Waterkant St
Port Rd
Dock Rd
Duncan Rd
De Smit St
Liddle St
Cobern St
Napier St
Alfred St
Table Bay Blvd
See Central Cape Town Map (pp412–13)
Table Bay Blvd
Loader St
Jarvis St
Schiebe St
Alfred St
Hospital St
De Waterkant
Chiappini St
Jerry St
Hans Strijdom Ave
Dixon St
Hudson St
Coen Steytler Ave
Lower Long St
Lower Loop St
Mechau St
Waterkant St
Strand St
Prestwich Memorial Park
Prestwich St
Heerengracht
Salazar Sq
Pier Pl
Longmarket St
Chiappini St
Rose St
Buitengracht St
Bree St
Loop St
Thibault Sq
Long St
Tulbagh Sq

in Gansbaai, 150km southeast of city, is the biggest draw.

A couple of good local dive operators:

Pro Divers (Map pp408-9; ☎ 021-433 0472; www.prodiverssa.co.za; 88B Main Rd, Sea Point)

Table Bay Diving (Map pp412-13; ☎ 021-419 8822; www.tablebaydiving.com; Quay 5, Waterfront)

Hiking & Rock Climbing

The mountainous spine of the Cape Peninsula is a hiker's and rock climber's paradise, but it's not without its dangers, chief of which are the capricious weather conditions. You can hire and buy climbing gear at indoor climbing gym **City Rock** (Map pp408-9; ☎ 021-447 1326; www.cityrock.co.za; cnr Collingwood & Anson Sts, Observatory; 🕑 11am-9pm Mon-Thu, to 6pm Fri, 10am-6pm Sat & Sun).

The enthusiastic guides of **Venture Forth** (☎ 021-510 6707; www.ventureforth.co.za; 1 Riverine Rd, Parklands) will tailor a hike or climb for you and get you off the beaten track. Rates include refreshments and city-centre transfers.

CLIMBING TABLE MOUNTAIN

More than 300 routes up and down the mountain have been identified, perhaps indicating how easy it is to get lost. Bear in mind that the mountain is over 1000m high and conditions can become treacherous quickly. Unprepared and foolhardy hikers die here ever year. Abseil Africa (p415), among other companies, offers guided hikes up Table Mountain (R195).

None of the routes is easy but the **Platteklip Gorge** walk on the City Bowl side is straightforward. It takes about 2½ hours from the upper Cableway station to the lower, taking it fairly easy. Be warned that the route is exposed to the sun and, for much of the way, a vertical slog.

Another option, far trickier and recommended for experienced climbers only, is the **Indian Windows** route that starts from directly behind the lower Cableway station and heads straight up. The hikers you see from the cable car, perched like mountain goats on apparently sheer cliffs, are taking this route.

Table Mountain National Park (p410) offers two main multiday trails, both of which come with knowledgeable, friendly guides and portering services. This is also the only officially sanctioned way to sleep on the mountain.

Those who require maximum comfort should opt for the three-day **Table Mountain Trail**, which proceeds from the Waterfront to Kirstenbosch Botanical Gardens via the City Bowl, the mountain's lower northern slopes, its summit, the Back Table and the eastern slopes. The trail costs R2100 per person (based on double occupancy of a room), including all meals, portering and accommodation of a very high standard.

More rugged hikers will relish the challenge of the six-day, five-night **Hoerikwaggo Trail**, which, when it's fully up and running (by June 2010), will stretch 97km from Cape Point to the upper Cableway station on Table Mountain. The trail, for which you need to self-cater, can be tackled in full- or in two-day sections (R420). You can also stay in the accommodation without hiking the trail (R350 per person per night) and use it as a base for nearby hikes and activities.

For further information and booking details see www.hoerikwagg otrails.co.za.

LION'S HEAD

The 2.2km hike from Kloof Nek to the peak of Lion's Head (Map pp408–9) is one of the best you can do in Cape Town and is highly recommended on a full-moon night, when many people gather at the summit to watch the sun go down. Always bring a torch (flashlight) and go with company.

THE CAPE OF GOOD HOPE

You'll need to book to walk the two-day Cape of Good Hope Trail, which traces a spectacular 33.8km circuit through the reserve. The cost is R150 (not including the Cape Point entry fee) with accommodation at the basic Protea and Restio huts at the southern end of the reserve. Contact the reserve's **Buffelfontein Visitors Centre** (☎ 021-780 9204) for further details.

Surfing & Sandboarding

The Cape Peninsula has plenty of fantastic surfing possibilities, from gentle shore breaks ideal for beginners to 3m-plus monsters for experts only. In general, the best surf is along the Atlantic side. Water temperatures as low as 8°C mean a steamer wetsuit and booties are required.

Kommetjie (*kom*-mi-kee) is the Cape's surf mecca, offering an assortment of reefs that hold a very big swell.

If you don't want to get wet there's always sandboarding, which is like snowboarding except on sand dunes. Downhill Adventures (p415) offers sandboarding trips to Atlantis, north of the city centre, and introductory surfing courses (both cost R495/655 for a half-/full day).

TOURS

Cape Town Tourism (p407) should be your first stop to find out about the many tours on offer in and around the city.

The double-decker bus tour **City Sightseeing Cape Town** (☎ 021-511 6000; www.city-sightseeing.com; adult/child R120/60) is good for a quick orientation on a fine day. The hop-on, hop-off services run at roughly half-hourly intervals between 8.30am and 3.30pm, with extra services in high season. The Red Route (which takes about two hours) starts at the Waterfront in front of the Two Oceans Aquarium, then heads into the city centre, up to the Table Mountain Cableway, down to Camps Bay and back along Sea Point promenade. The Blue Route (2¼ hours) also starts and finishes at the Two Oceans Aquarium, but goes via Kirstenbosch and Hout Bay.

Andulela (☎ 021-790 2592; www.andulela.com) This innovative company arranges offbeat adventures including cookery, jazz and football tours.

Day Trippers (☎ 021-511 4766; www.daytrippers.co.za) Many of the tours include cycling. Most cost around R495, and include Cape Point, the Winelands and whale watching (in season).

Ferdinand's Tours & Adventures (☎ 021-987 8888; www.fgroup.co.za) This backpacker-focused Winelands tour takes in at least four wineries and includes lunch.

Gateway to Newlands (☎ 021-686 2150; www.newlandstours.co.za) Tours of the main cricket and rugby stadiums, the Sports Science Institute of South Africa and the South African Rugby Museum (from adult/child R25/12).

Grassroute Tours (☎ 021-464 4269; www.daytours.co.za/htownship.htm) One of the most experienced operators of townships tours (half-day/evening R360/450).

Sam's Cultural Tours (☎ 021-555 1468; ntimba@telkomsa.net) Sam Ntimba's half-day trip (R320) includes visits to a dormitory and *shebeen* in Langa and a crèche project in Crossroads.

FESTIVALS & EVENTS

A short list:

Kaapse Klopse (Cape Minstreal Carnival; ☎ 021-696 9538) The local equivalent of Rio's Mardi Gras; the main parades are held on 1 and 2 January.

Cape Town Pride (☎ 021-425 6463; www.capetownpride.co.za) The two-week gay and lesbian shindig in February flies the Mother City's rainbow colours with pride.

Cape Town International Jazz Festival (☎ 021-422 5651; www.capetownjazzfest.com) Cape Town's biggest jazz event, held at the end of March.

Obz Festival (☎ 082 885 0018; www.obzfestival.com) On the first weekend in December, South Africa's biggest street festival brings live music and DJs, comedy, film and a street market to Observatory.

SLEEPING

Whether you're into lively hostels, characterful guest houses or unfettered luxury, Cape Town has it. If you have transport, then anywhere is OK, but inquire about parking and note that city-centre establishments often charge R20 to R50 per day for a bay.

Advance booking is recommended, especially during the school holidays from

STEVEN OTTER

Few white South Africans visit the townships and even fewer actually choose to live there. Someone who did is journalist Steven Otter, who wrote about his experiences in *Khayelitsha,* a humorous and insightful memoir.

Why did you decide to live in Khayelitsha? If people are living in our country like this, I felt I should experience it too. My first night in Khaya I was terrified. It took a few months to break down the old fears, but now I feel very safe.

It seems like you spent a lot of time in the shebeens... In Khaya there's not much else for the average guy to do. Drinking is a big thing, but so is going to church – and what do people do in the [white] suburbs? Pretty similar things.

What didn't you like about living there? The separation culturally between women and men is difficult. In the winter it's cold and damp and in the summer there are flies – millions of them. I also experienced stomach problems.

What did you like? Living in the shack was incredible – there are people around all the time. There's a similar sense of community in the Bo-Kaap. I feel the only part of Cape Town that is truly Africa is Khaya.

As told to Simon Richmond.

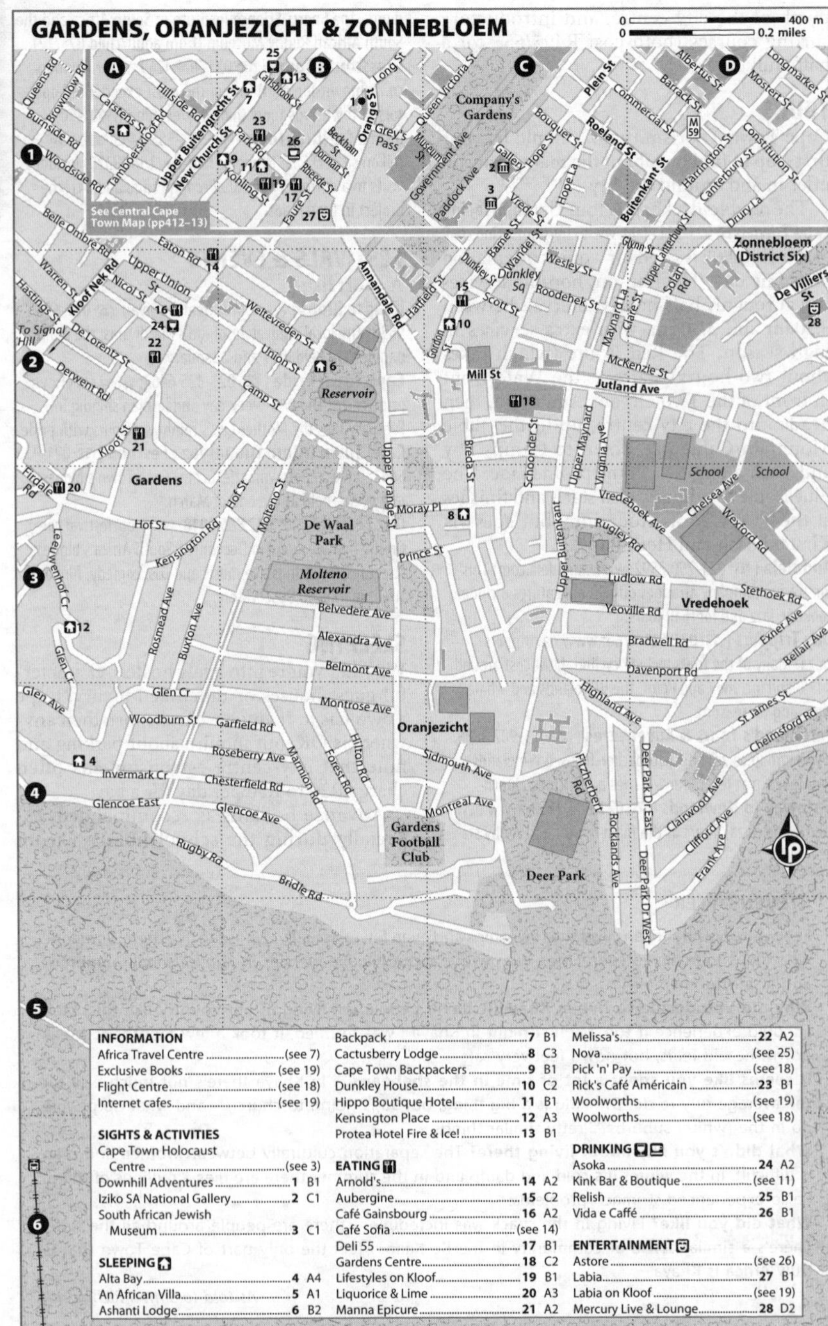
GARDENS, ORANJEZICHT & ZONNEBLOEM
400 m
0.2 miles
See Central Cape Town Map (pp412–13)
Company's Gardens
Zonnebloem (District Six)
Gardens
De Waal Park
Molteno Reservoir
Reservoir
Vredehoek
Oranjezicht
Gardens Football Club
Deer Park
School
To Signal Hill
Queens Rd
Brownlow Rd
Burnside Rd
Woodside Rd
Carstens St
Tamboerskloof Rd
Hillside Rd
Upper Buitengracht St
New Church St
Kohling St
Park Rd
Carisbrook St
Beckham St
Dorman St
Rheede St
Faure St
Orange St
Long St
Grey's Pass
Queen Victoria St
Museum St
Government Ave
Paddock Ave
Gallery
Hope St
Bouquet St
Plein St
Commercial St
Roeland St
Buitenkant St
Barrack St
Albertus St
Longmarket St
Mostert St
Harrington St
Constitution St
Canterbury St
Drury La
Upper Canterbury St
Glynn St
Solan Rd
Belle Ombre Rd
Eaton Rd
Kloof Nek Rd
Warren St
Nicol St
Upper Union St
Hastings St
De Lorentz St
Weltevreden St
Union St
Annandale Rd
Hatfield St
Dunkley St
Barnet St
Wandel St
Vrede St
Hope La
Dunkley Sq
Wesley St
Roodehek St
Scott St
Gordon St
Maynard La
Clare St
De Villiers St
McKenzie St
Mill St
Jutland Ave
Derwent Rd
Camp St
Kloof St
Firdale Rd
Hof St
Molteno St
Upper Orange St
Breda St
Schoonder St
Upper Maynard
Virginia Ave
Vredehoek Ave
Chelsea Ave
Wexford Rd
Moray Pl
Kensington Rd
Leeuwenhof Cr
Prince St
Upper Buitenkant
Rugley Rd
Ludlow Rd
Stethoek Rd
Yeoville Rd
Belvedere Ave
Alexandra Ave
Belmont Ave
Rosmead Ave
Buxton Ave
Bradwell Rd
Exner Ave
Bellair Ave
Davenport Rd
Glen Cr
Glen Ave
Montrose Ave
Highland Ave
St James St
Woodburn St
Garfield Rd
Chelmsford Rd
Roseberry Ave
Marmion Rd
Forest Rd
Hilton Rd
Sidmouth Ave
Fitzherbert Rd
Deer Park Dr East
Invermark Cr
Chesterfield Rd
Clairwood Ave
Glencoe East
Glencoe Ave
Montreal Ave
Rocklands Ave
Clifford Ave
Frank Ave
Rugby Rd
Bridle Rd
Deer Park Dr West
INFORMATION
Africa Travel Centre (see 7)
Exclusive Books (see 19)
Flight Centre (see 18)
Internet cafes (see 19)
SIGHTS & ACTIVITIES
Cape Town Holocaust Centre (see 3)
Downhill Adventures 1 B1
Iziko SA National Gallery 2 C1
South African Jewish Museum 3 C1
SLEEPING
Alta Bay 4 A4
An African Villa 5 A1
Ashanti Lodge 6 B2
Backpack 7 B1
Cactusberry Lodge 8 C3
Cape Town Backpackers 9 B1
Dunkley House 10 C2
Hippo Boutique Hotel 11 B1
Kensington Place 12 A3
Protea Hotel Fire & Ice! 13 B1
EATING
Arnold's 14 A2
Aubergine 15 C2
Café Gainsbourg 16 A2
Café Sofia (see 14)
Deli 55 17 B1
Gardens Centre 18 C2
Lifestyles on Kloof 19 B1
Liquorice & Lime 20 A3
Manna Epicure 21 A2
Melissa's 22 A2
Nova (see 25)
Pick 'n' Pay (see 18)
Rick's Café Américain 23 B1
Woolworths (see 19)
Woolworths (see 18)
DRINKING
Asoka 24 A2
Kink Bar & Boutique (see 11)
Relish 25 B1
Vida e Caffé 26 B1
ENTERTAINMENT
Astore (see 26)
Labia 27 B1
Labia on Kloof (see 19)
Mercury Live & Lounge 28 D2

mid-December to the end of January, and at Easter; prices can double and many places are fully booked. Rates will also spike for the 2010 World Cup, when advance booking will be essential. Hostels typically don't include breakfast; for other properties, unless otherwise mentioned rates also include breakfast.

For longer-term stays or if you wish to self-cater a serviced apartment or villa can work out as a good deal. Some reliable agencies include the following:

Cape Town Budget Accommodation (☎ 021-447 4398; www.capetownbudgetaccommodation.co.za)

Nox Rentals (☎ 021-424 3353; www.noxrentals.co.za) Apartments and villas in Camps Bay.

Platinum Places (☎ 021-425 5922; www.platinumplaces.co.za) Luxurious pads including a tree house.

City Bowl

BUDGET

Long Street Backpackers (Map pp412-13; ☎ 021-423 0615; www.longstreetbackpackers.co.za; 209 Long St; dm/s/d R100/180/250) This pick of the backpackers dotting Long St occupies a block of 14 small flats, with four beds and a bathroom in each. They're arranged around a leafy courtyard where you'll find funky mosaics, chillaxing music and likeable staff.

Scalabrini Guesthouse (Map pp412-13; ☎ 021-465 6433; www.scalabrini.org.za; 47 Commercial St; dm/s/d without breakfast R200/320/470; 🖳) At the base of an Italian monastic order that provides welfare services to Cape Town's poor and refugees, this wonderful guest house has immaculately clean rooms with bathrooms, plus a great kitchen with satellite TV.

St Paul's Guesthouse (Map pp412-13; ☎ 021-423 4420; www.stpaulschurch.co.za/theguesthouse.htm; 182 Bree St; s/d R300/500; P) These simply furnished rooms, set around a vine-shaded courtyard, are a quiet alternative to a backpackers.

Penthouse on Long (Map pp412-13; ☎ 021-424 8356; www.penthouseonlong.com; 6th fl, 112 Long St; dm/r with shared bathroom R110/350, r R400; P 🖳) Doing amazing things with former office space, the Penthouse's private rooms have colourful themes such as Hollywood, the Orient or Moroccan nights. In the rafters is a spacious bar and lounge.

MIDRANGE & TOP END

Cape Diamond Hotel (Map pp412-3; ☎ 021-461 2519; www.capediamondhotel.co.za; cnr Longmarket & Parliament Sts; s/d without breakfast from R825/1090; P 🖳) Good-value hotel that has kept some features of its art-deco building such as the wood-panelled floors. It's short on natural light but there's a rooftop jacuzzi with a view of Table Mountain.

Daddy Long Legs (Map pp412-13; ☎ 021-422 3074; www.daddylonglegs.co.za; 134 Long St; r R945; ❄ 🖳) A stay at this boutique hotel–cum–art installation is anything but boring. Thirteen artists were given free rein to design the boudoirs of their dreams, with results ranging from a bohemian garret to a hospital ward! It also offers superstylish apartments (from R1045) at 263 Long St, an ideal choice if you crave hotel-suite luxury and want to self-cater.

Urban Chic (Map pp412-13; ☎ 021-426 6119; www.urbanchic.co.za; cnr Long & Pepper Sts; s/d from R1233/1369; P ❄ 🖳) Rooms with fabulous floor-to-ceiling views towards Table Mountain feature at this stylish boutique hotel. Its Gallery Café is one of Long St's more polished watering holes.

our pick **Grand Daddy Hotel** (Map pp412-13; ☎ 021-424 7247; www.daddylonglegs.co.za/grand-daddy.html; 38 Long St; r/ste R1500/2000; P ❄ 🖳) Daddy Long Legs' sister operation takes creativity to new heights with its rooftop trailer park of penthouse suites, made from seven vintage Airstream trailers. The silver caravans were decorated by artists and designers, with themes including the John and Yoko bed-in or Goldilocks and the Three Bears. Incorporating playful references to South African culture, the regular rooms are also very stylish; the bar, blinged to the max, is named Daddy Cool.

Gardens & Around

BUDGET

Ashanti Lodge (Map p420; ☎ 021-423 8721; www.ashanti.co.za; 11 Hof St, Gardens; campsites R75, dm/s/d with shared bathroom R140/300/420, r R600; P 🖳 🏊) One of Cape Town's premier party hostels. For something quieter, opt for the excellent rooms with bathroom in two heritage-listed houses around the corner.

Cape Town Backpackers (Map p420; ☎ 021-426 0200; www.capetownbackpackers.com; 81 New Church St, Tamboerskloof; dm/r with shared bathroom R120/400, s/d R450/550; P 🖳) The backpackers grows up at this stylish place with pleasant dorms and chic rooms with bathrooms. Parking per day R10.

Ashanti Green Point (☎ 021-433 1619; www.ashanti.co.za/ashanti_greenpoint.htm; 23 Antrim Rd; dm/s/d with shared bathroom R150/400/550, r R700; 🏊 🖳) Quieter and more sophisticated than the original.

Backpack (Map p420; ☎ 021-423 4530; www.backpackers.co.za; 74 New Church St, Tamboerskloof; dm/s/tw with shared bathroom R145/500/650, dm/s/d R270/550/800; P) Occupying four houses, including a former commune, Cape Town's longest-running backpackers sits at the boutique end of the hostel spectrum, with stylish dorms and rooms, a buzzy vibe and fantastic staff. It has Fair Trade accreditation, supporting youth projects on the Cape Flats (ask about getting involved), and the barman makes a mean springbok.

MIDRANGE

Cactusberry Lodge (Map p420; ☎ 021-461 9787; www.cactusberrylodge.com; 30 Breda St, Oranjezicht; s/d from R640/820; P) There are just six rooms at this red-wine-coloured lodge with a striking contemporary interior design, mixing arty photography, African crafts and Euro style. The sun deck looks over to Table Mountain and there's a splash pool in the courtyard.

Dunkley House (Map p420; ☎ 021-462 7650; www.dunkleyhouse.com; 3B Gordon St, Gardens; s/d from R650/850, apt s/d R1100/1450;) Ultrastylish guest house tucked away on a quiet street. The rooms are decorated in neutral tones, all with CD players and satellite TV, and there's a plunge pool in the courtyard.

Protea Hotel Fire & Ice! (Map p420; ☎ 021-488 2555; www.proteahotels.com/protea-hotel-fire-and-ice.html; cnr New Church & Victoria Sts, Tamboerskloof; r excl breakfast R1000-1700; P) The Protea chain really thought outside of the box with this fun place that takes Cape Town's adventurous spirit as inspiration. The stylish rooms are slightly cramped, especially the standard ones, but we love the cable-car lift and the hilarious toilets off the vibey bar.

An African Villa (Map p420; ☎ 021-423 2162; www.capetowncity.co.za/villa; 19 Carstens St, Tamboerskloof; r from R1100;) There's a sophisticated and colourful 'African Zen' look at this appealing guest house, sheltering behind the facades of three 19th-century terrace houses.

Hippo Boutique Hotel (Map p420; ☎ 021-423 2500; www.hippotique.co.za; 5-9 Park Lane, Gardens; r/ste excl breakfast R1290/2200; P) This appealing boutique property offers spacious, stylish rooms with kitchenettes. Gadget lovers will also smile at each room's computer and music system. Larger suites have mezzanine-level bedrooms and funky theme designs.

TOP END

Alta Bay (Map p420; ☎ 021-487 8800; www.altabay.com; 12 Invermark Cres, Higgovale; r R2500-3000; P) Cascading down the hillside, Alta Bay is a haven of tranquillity as well as a designer heaven. The six luxury rooms mix locally handcrafted furnishings (including king-size beds) with European artworks.

Kensington Place (Map p420; ☎ 021-424 4744; www.kensingtonplace.co.za; 38 Kensington Cres, Higgovale; r from R2860; P) This fine boutique property offers eight spacious and tastefully decorated rooms, all with balconies and beautifully tiled bathrooms. There's free internet access, fresh fruit and flowers, a small pool and faultless service.

Green Point, Waterkant & Waterfront

BUDGET

St John's Waterfront Lodge (Map pp416-17; ☎ 021-439 1404; www.stjohns.co.za; 6 Braemar Rd, Green Point; dm/s/d with shared bathroom R115/250/300, r R350; P) Don't be put off by the unwelcoming facade. This large, relaxed and friendly place has freshly painted rooms, a wicker-furniture-enhanced bar, lovely floorboards, a huge TV, and a deck overlooking one of the two pools.

Sunflower Stop (Map pp416-17; ☎ 021-434 6535; www.sunflowerstop.co.za; 179 Main Rd, Green Point; dm R120, r with/without bathroom R400/490;) Set far enough back from Main Rd to offer tranquillity, this sunny, spacious hostel is an adequate retreat from the city and Green Point Stadium – just 400m away. The large bathrooms feel rather institutional, but the lounge, poolside bar and braai, and attractive rooms with bathroom get the thumbs up.

MIDRANGE

De Waterkant Lodge (Map pp416-17; ☎ 021-419 2476; www.dewaterkantplace.com; 35 Dixon St, Waterkant; s/d from R650/950;) An appealing guest house offering good-value, antique-decorated, fan-cooled rooms. There's a lovely view from the roof, and self-catering units are available from R1800.

Cape Standard (Map pp416-17; ☎ 021-430 3060; www.capestandard.co.za; 3 Romney Rd, Green Point; s/d R895/1150; P) This secluded boutique hotel, one of Cape Town's nicest, offers whitewashed beach-house-chic rooms, or more edgy, contemporary upstairs rooms. The showers are big enough to dance in.

Wilton Manor (Map pp416-17; ☎ 021-434 7869; www.wiltonmanor.co.za; 15 Croxteth Rd, Green Point; r R1150-2000; P) This charming house with a wooden verandah has been converted into a stylish guest house with seven African-themed rooms. The owners also run other properties in the area, including the more contemporary Wilton Place higher up Signal Hill.

Villa Zest (Map pp416-17; ☎ 021-433 1246; www.villazest.co.za; 2 Braemar Rd, Green Point; s/d from R1290/1590; P ⊠ 💻 🏊) The lobby at this Bauhaus-style home is lined with an impressive collection of '60s and '70s groovy electronic goods, including radios, phones, Polaroid cameras and View-Masters. The seven individual rooms have bold retro furniture and wallpaper-covered walls – very *Austin Powers*, but in a good way.

TOP END

Cape Grace (Map pp416-17; ☎ 021-410 7100; www.capegrace.com; West Quay, Waterfront; s/d from R5590/5750; P ⊠ 💻 🏊) Clint Eastwood et al reportedly loved this Waterfront stalwart when they were in town filming *Invictus*. With its winning combination of antiques and artsy decor – including handpainted bed covers and curtains – the luxurious hotel provides a unique sense of place and Cape Town's history.

One & Only (Map pp416-17; ☎ 021-431 5800; www.oneandonlyresorts.com; Dock Rd, Waterfront; r/ste from R6900/7900; P ⊠ 💻 🏊) The latest peacock feather in the cap of South African hotel magnate Sol Kerzner is a 131-room colossus that dominates even the showy Waterfront, with 41 suites on an artificial island and a Gordon Ramsay restaurant, Maze (p425). Locals remain loyal to Cape Grace, but we loved the original art adorning the walls and the entrance is a knockout, offering a full frontal of Table Mountain beyond a glowing bar and an imposing chandelier.

Atlantic Coast

TOP END

Winchester Mansions Hotel (Map pp408-9; ☎ 021-434 2351; www.winchester.co.za; 221 Beach Rd, Sea Point; s/d R1640/2120; P ⊠ 💻 🏊) Although parts of it could do with an upgrade, the Winchester Mansions offers a good combination of seaside position, old-fashioned style and affordable rates. The lovely courtyard restaurant with its central fountain is popular for its Sunday brunch (R195) with live jazz – book ahead.

Camps Bay Retreat (Map pp408-9; ☎ 021-437 8300; www.campsbayretreat.com; 7 Chilworth Rd, Camps Bay; r/ste from R2800/4100; P ⊠ 💻 🏊) Based in the grand Earl's Dyke Manor, this is a splendid option with a choice of 14 rooms in either the main house or the contemporary Deck House, reached by a rope bridge over a ravine.

EATING

Dining in the Mother City is a pleasure, with places to suit practically everyone's taste and budget, from chic restaurants to neighbourhood cafes. Don't miss the opportunity to sample traditional Cape Malay food, or to dine at one of the city's good African restaurants.

Most restaurants are licensed but some allow you to bring your own wine for little or no corkage charge. Self-caterers and picnickers can stock up at the major supermarkets Pick 'n' Pay and Woolworths, which have branches all over the city including at Victoria Wharf (Map pp412–13) and Gardens Centre (Map p420); or at delis such as Gionvanni's Deli World (p425) and **Melissa's** (☎ 021-424 5540; 🕑 8.30am-8pm), with branches at 94 Kloof St, Gardens (Map p420) and Victoria Wharf (Map pp416–17).

City Bowl & Bo-Kaap

Long St has many great places to eat, plus fantastic street life. Head to the Bo-Kaap to sample authentic Cape Malay dishes in unpretentious surroundings.

CAFES & QUICK EATS

Lola's (Map pp412-13; ☎ 021-423 0885; 228 Long St, City Bowl; mains R30-40; 🕑 8am-midnight) Groovy veggie institution where the only meat is the beefcake photos on the menu. Come for breakfast, coffee or a late-night wine or beer and watch Long St's passing parade.

Crush (Map pp412-13; ☎ 021-422 5533; 100 St George's Mall, City Bowl; mains R30-40) Deservedly packed during weekday lunchtimes, Crush offers freshly squeezed juices, smoothies and tasty wraps, proving healthy eating need not be boring.

Birds Café (Map pp412-13; ☎ 021-426 2534; 127 Bree St, City Bowl; mains R50-60; 🕑 8am-4pm) This delightful cafe's sophisticated rustic style (think milk-bottle crate seats in a grand old Dutch building, and handmade crockery) matches the artisan food, including delicious homemade pies, strudels and chunky scones.

RESTAURANTS

Masala Dosa (Map pp412-13; ☎ 021-424 6772; 167 Long St, City Bowl; mains R38-79; 🕑 noon-10.30pm Mon-Sat) Bollywood chic rules at this South Indian cuisine outpost serving pretty decent dosas (lentil pancakes) and thalis (set meals with a variety of curries). There's also a Sea Point branch (Map pp408–9, ☎ 021-434 2612; 154 Main Rd).

Royale Eatery (Map pp408-9; ☎ 021-422 4536; 279 Long St, City Bowl; mains R60-70; ⌚ noon-11.30pm Mon-Sat) Gourmet burgers grilled to perfection; for something different try the Big Bird ostrich burger. Downstairs is casual and buzzy while upstairs is a restaurant where you can book a table.

Noon Gun Tearoom & Restaurant (Map pp408-9; ☎ 021-424 0529; 273 Longmarket St, Bo-Kaap; mains R65-80; ⌚ 10am-10pm Mon-Sat) High on Signal Hill, this is a fine place to sample Cape Malay dishes such as *bobotie*.

Addis in Cape (Map pp408-9; ☎ 021-424 5722; 41 Church St, City Bowl; mains R75-90) Sit at a low basket-weave *mesob* table and enjoy tasty Ethiopian cuisine served traditionally on plate-sized *injera* (sourdough pancakes), which you rip and use to eat instead of cutlery.

our pick **Bizerca Bistro** (Map pp408-9; ☎ 021-418 0001; Jetty St, Foreshore; mains R105) French chef Laurent Deslandes and his South African wife Cyrillia run this fantastic bistro. The atmosphere is contemporary and friendly, the expertly prepared food bursting with flavour. Signature dishes include butternut pumpkin gnocchi and braised pigs trotter.

Jardine (Map pp408-9; ☎ 021-424 5640; 185 Bree St, City Bowl; 2-/3-course meal R240/280; ⌚ 7-10pm Tue-Sat) Award-winning chef George Jardine concocts amazing dishes such as twice-cooked crispy duck with honeyed parsnip puree or chalmar beef fillet stuffed with roasted garlic. You also can't go wrong with one of the gourmet sandwiches (R35) and pastries available from the bakery (open 9am to 3pm Monday to Saturday) with streetside tables.

Gardens & Around

Kloof St in Gardens has a high concentration of eateries and the street's two malls have pleasant cafes.

CAFES & QUICK EATS

Liquorice & Lime (Map p420; ☎ 021-423 6921; 162 Kloof St, Higgovale; sandwiches R38-50) Pause at this convivial cafe-deli on your way down from climbing Table Mountain or Lion's Head; the French toast with grilled banana is yummy.

Deli 55 (Map p420; ☎ 021-424 6463; 55 Kloof St, Gardens; mains R40; ⌚ 7.30am-5pm Mon-Fri, to 3pm Sat) Light and funky, this deli attached to the Love Project clothes shop does a good line in soups, schwarmas, freshly squeezed juices and jumbo health muffins.

Arnold's (Map p420; ☎ 021-424 4344; 60 Kloof St, Gardens; mains R50-100; ⌚ 8am-late) With an appealing neighbourhood feel (half the customers greet the boss like old friends), Arnold's has a covered street-front beer garden. It has a good breakfast menu, and lunch and dinner dishes range from the recommended chicken curry to crocodile or warthog ribs.

Manna Epicure (Map p420; ☎ 021-426 2413; 151 Kloof St, Tamboerskloof; mains R55-90; ⌚ 9am-6pm Tue-Sat, to 4pm Sun) Join the style set for a scrumptious breakfast or lunch at this trendy cafe and bakery, or come for late-afternoon cocktails and tapas on the street-front verandah.

Café Gainsbourg (Map p420; ☎ 021-422 1780; 64 Kloof St, Gardens; mains R60-95) This minimalist-decorated cafe is a great spot for a snack or any of the day's meals, with the lamb shank, burgers and salads especially worth a try.

RESTAURANTS

Café Sofia (Map p420; ☎ 021-426 0801; 60 Kloof St, Gardens; tapas R42-89, mains R89-109; ⌚ breakfast, lunch & dinner) Pinstripe wallpaper and customers plugged into laptops are a backdrop for tapas, meze, sangria and cocktails (R20 between 5pm and 7pm) at this branch of the small chain.

Rick's Café Américain (Map p420; ☎ 021-424 1100; 2 Park Lane, Gardens; mains R70-100) Popular with everyone from backpackers to models (we only just snagged a table on a Monday night), Rick's evokes the nightclub of the same name in *Casablanca*. Tagines and tapas, steaks and seafood are on the menu and the surroundings are inviting, from the rooftop terrace to the three fireplaces.

Nova (Map p420; ☎ 021-422 3585; 70 New Church St, Tamboerskloof; mains R95-135; ⌚ 7-10pm Mon-Sat) Chef Richard Carstens, who dabbles in molecular gastronomy, is tickling Capetonians' tastebuds with this elegant new venture, serving dishes such as tempura prawns with prawn ravioli and a scoop of apple ice cream.

Aubergine (Map p420; ☎ 021-465 4909; 39 Barnet St, Gardens; mains R160, 3-/4-/5-course degustation menu R295/350/450; ⌚ 5-10pm Mon-Sat, noon-2pm Wed-Fri) Harald Bresselschmidt is one of Cape Town's most consistent chefs, producing highly creative yet unfussy dishes – his soufflés are divine. Service and ambience are equally impeccable.

Green Point, Waterkant & Waterfront

The Waterfront's many restaurants and cafes have nice ocean views, although it's essentially a giant tourist trap. Better value and a less touristy dining experience are on offer a short walk away in Green Point and Mouille Point; closer to the city is Waterkant's expanding Cape Quarter complex.

CAFES & QUICK EATS

Gionvanni's Deli World (Map pp416-17; ☎ 021-434 6983; 103 Main Rd, Green Point; mains R20-40; 🕑 7.30am-8.30pm) A mainstay of the Green Point parade, Giovanni's can make any sandwich you fancy – ideal for a picnic. The adjoining espresso bar is a popular hang-out.

Café Neo (Map pp416-17; ☎ 021-433 0849; 129 Beach Rd, Mouille Point; mains R55; 🕑 6.30am-7.30pm) Our favourite seaside cafe has a relaxed vibe and a contemporary design. Sit at the big communal table or relax on the deck overlooking the red-and-white lighthouse.

RESTAURANTS

Wakame (Map pp416-17; ☎ 021-433 2377; cnr Beach Rd & Surrey Pl, Moullie Point; sushi R40, mains R75-100) Tucking into Wakame's salt-and-pepper squid or sushi platter while gazing at the glorious coastal view is a wonderful way to pass an afternoon. On the 2nd level it specialises in dim sum and, between noon and 7pm on Friday, R25 cocktails on the deck.

Hildebrand (Map pp416-17; ☎ 021-425 3385; Pierhead, Waterfront; mains R70) Set in a historic building, this Italian restaurant offers better value than many Waterfront eateries, attracting locals in the evening as well as tourists during the day. Pasta options range from bolognese to seafood dishes and the house red is recommended.

Andiamo (Map pp416-17; ☎ 021-421 3687; Shop C2, Cape Quarter, 72 Waterkant St, Waterkant; mains R70; 🕑 9am-10.30pm) Andiamo's chairs colonise a chunk of the Cape Quarter, confirming its popularity as one of the best casual eateries in the area, serving pizza, pasta, salads and the like. There's a well-stocked deli and, during the week, the meal deals are excellent value.

Willoughby & Co (Map pp416-17; ☎ 021-418 6115; Shop 6132, Victoria Wharf, Waterfront; mains R60-100; 🕑 noon-11pm) Huge servings of sushi are the standout in the good-value menu at this casual eatery-cum-fishmongers on the ground floor of Victoria Wharf. Commonly acknowledged as one of the better places to eat at the Waterfront.

Maze (Map pp416-17; One & Only, Dock Rd, Waterfront, mains R95-750; ☎ breakfast, lunch & dinner) Gordon Ramsay's restaurant blends in with its coolly contemporary surroundings in Sol Kerzner's hotel (p423), with huge orange lights and a boxy carpet design. Although modelled on its British namesake, it focuses on South African dishes and ingredients. Choices include Cape Malay mussels, white onion risotto with roasted local mushrooms, and, for R750, a 200g, ninth-grade Australian wagyu fillet steak.

DRINKING

Cape Town didn't become known as the 'Tavern of the Seven Seas' for nothing. Head out on a Friday or Saturday night to Long St, the Waterkant or Camps Bay for an eye-opening experience of how the locals like to party. Most bars open around 3pm and close after midnight, and much later Friday and Saturday; exceptions are noted below.

Need a caffeine fix? Homegrown chain **Vida e Caffé** (☎ 021-426 0627) serves freshly brewed coffee, orange juice, Portuguese-style pastries and filled rolls, ideal for breakfast or a quick lunch. You'll find branches at locations including 34 Kloof St (Map p420), St George's Mall (Map pp412–13 and the Waterfront (Map pp416–17).

City Bowl

Julep Bar (Map pp412-13; ☎ 021-423 4276; Vredenburg Lane; 🕑 5pm-2am Mon-Sat) Occupying the ground floor of a former brothel, this hidden gem, a favourite with local hipsters, will set you apart from the riff-raff on nearby Long St. Select cocktails are R15 from 5.30pm to 7.30pm Monday to Saturday.

Marvel (Map pp412-13; ☎ 021-426 5880; 236 Long St; 🕑 1pm-4am Mon-Sat) This is where cool kids of all colours rub shoulders (not to mention practically everything else). Grab one of the cosy booths, or linger on the pavement and enjoy the foot-tapping grooves from the DJ.

Neighbourhood Bar & Restaurant (Map pp412-13; ☎ 021-424 7260; 163 Long St; 🕑 4pm-2am Mon-Thu, 2pm-4am Fri-Sun) From the guys behind Royale Eatery comes this relaxed bar and casual restaurant where the colour divide melts away. The long balcony is good place to cool off and keep tabs on Long St.

our pick **Waiting Room** (Map pp412-13; ☎ 021-422 4536; 273 Long St; Fri & Sat cover R30; 🕑 6pm-2am Mon-Sat) Climb the narrow stairway beside Royale

Eatery to find this hip bar, complete with retro furniture and DJs spinning funky tunes. Head even higher and you'll eventually reach the roof deck, the perfect spot from which to admire the city's glittering nightlights.

Gardens & Around

Asoka (Map p420; ☎ 021-422 0909; 68 Kloof St, Gardens) There's a party going on at this Buddhist-themed preclub bar. Ice cubes clink in big drinks, bottles poke out of buckets, dance music moves the crowd and a wooden deck overlooks Kloof St.

Kink Bar & Boutique (Map p420; ☎ 021-424 0757; 3 Park Lane, Gardens; bar 5pm-2am Tue-Sat) Next to popular fajita and margarita stop Fat Cactus is this cafe-bar with a difference. Downstairs, it specialises in 'sensual' food and drinks (think cocktails with names such as the G-Spot, Anonymous Fondle and The Fetish), with a hidden garden courtyard to the rear. Once you're in the mood, go upstairs to peruse the lacy lingerie and sex toys (including leather paddles, whips and cuffs made in South Africa). Burlesque shows are promised!

Relish (Map p420; ☎ 021-422 3584; 70 New Church St, Tamboerskloof; 5pm-late Mon-Sat) You'll get panoramic views of Table Mountain and Lion's Head from this trendy cocktail bar and pizza joint with a wide outdoor deck.

Green Point, Waterkant & Waterfront

Alba Lounge (Map pp416-17; ☎ 021-425 3385; 1st fl, Hildegards, Pierhead, Waterfront) The views across the harbour are grand from this contemporary-designed cocktail bar where the drinks are inventive and there's a roaring fire in winter to add to that inner alcoholic glow.

Buena Vista Social Café (Map pp416-17; ☎ 021-433 0611; Exhibition Bldg, 81 Main Rd, Green Point) Staff mix a nice mojito at this Cuban-themed bar and restaurant, taking inspiration from the famous album. Book a seat on the airy balcony and come on Sunday if you want to salsa, or Monday from 9pm for live Cuban music.

Fireman's Arms (Map pp416-17; ☎ 021-419 1513; 25 Mechau St, Waterkant) A traditional pub that's been here for eons; check out its memorabilia including a tie collection and colonial-era flags.

Mitchell's Scottish Ale House & Brewery (Map pp416-17; ☎ 021-419 5074; East Pier Rd, Waterfront; mains R50; 10am-2am) Check all airs and graces at the door of South Africa's oldest microbrewery (established 1983 in Knysna), serving freshly brewed ales and good pint-and-a-meal deals.

Atlantic Coast

La Med (Map pp408-9; ☎ 021-438 5600; Glen Country Club, Victoria Rd, Clifton; noon-late Mon-Fri, 9am-late Sat & Sun) Sinking a sundowner and munching pizza at this alfresco bar with a killer view down the length of the Twelve Apostles is a Cape Town ritual. Keep an eye out for the easily missed turn-off, on the way to Clifton from Camps Bay.

La Vie (Map pp408-9; ☎ 021-439 2061; 205 Beach Rd, Sea Point; 7.30am-midnight) One of the very few places where you can have anything from breakfast to late-night cocktails within sight of Sea Point promenade.

ENTERTAINMENT

Check the weekly arts guide in the *Mail & Guardian* (www.theguide.co.za) to find out what's going on.

You can book seats for practically anything through **Webtickets** (www.webtickets.co.za) or **Computicket** (Map pp416-17; ☎ 083 915 8000; www.computicket.com), which has branches in locations including the Waterfront.

Cinemas

The big multiplexes can be found in Victoria Wharf at the Waterfront, Cavendish Sq and Canal Walk.

Labia (Map p420; ☎ 021-424 5927; www.labia.co.za; 68 Orange St, Gardens; tickets R25), together with the two-screen **Labia on Kloof** (Map p420; ☎ 021-424 5727) nearby, is the best cinema for 'mainstream alternative' films.

Live Music

For listings of music events and to buy tickets check out **Tunegum** (www.tunegum. com/Events).

CLASSICAL

The incredibly active **Cape Town Philharmonic** (☎ 021-410 9809; www.cpo.org.za) leads the way on the Mother City's classical-music scene, performing concerts mainly at **Old City Hall** (Map pp412-13; Darling St, City Bowl) as well as the performing-arts complex **Artscape** (Map pp412-13; ☎ 021-410 9800; www.artscape.co.za; DF Malan St, Foreshore), the Waterfront and elsewhere around the Cape. Consisting of three different-sized auditoria, Artscape is the hub of classical and theatrical performances in Cape Town. Walking around this area at night is not recommended.

JAZZ

Green Dolphin (Map pp412-13; ☎ 021-421 7471; Waterfront; cover R30-35) There's a consistently good line-up of artists at this upmarket jazz venue and restaurant (serving decent food). Shows kick off at 8.15pm daily.

West End (Map pp404-5; ☎ 021-637 9132; http://superclubs.co.za; Cine 400 Bldg, College Rd, Rylands Estate, Athlone; cover R30; 🕑 5pm-4am Fri & Sat) Mainstream jazz is the name of the game here. This is one of Cape Town's top venues, attracting a well-heeled clientele and top performers. There's plenty of security, if you drive.

ROCK & POP

Mercury Live & Lounge (Map p420; ☎ 021-465 2106; www.mercuryl.co.za; 43 De Villiers St, Zonnebloem; cover R20-50) This long-running rock venue plays host to top South African bands and overseas visitors. The sound quality is good and there's the DJ bar Mercury Lounge below and the Shack bar next door.

Assembly (Map pp412-13; ☎ 021-465 7286; www.theassembly.co.za; 61 Harrington St, Zonnenbloem; cover R30-50) In an old furniture assembly factory, this live-music and DJ-performance space has made its mark with an exciting, eclectic line-up of local and international artists.

Pick up a flyer from the boutique **Astore** (Map p420; Shop 2, Mooikloof Centre, 34 Kloof St, Gardens), which sells tickets for gigs.

Nightclubs

The major nightclubs are concentrated in the City Bowl around Long St and in Waterkant. Cover charges vary between R30 and R60. The big nights are Wednesday, Friday and Saturday.

Galaxy Club (Map pp404-5; ☎ 021-637 9132; http://superclubs.co.za; College Rd, Rylands Estate, Athlone) Thirty years young, this legendary Cape Flats dance venue is where you can get down to R&B, hip-hop and live bands with a black and coloured crowd. Women often get in for free. The West End jazz venue is next door.

Hemisphere (Map pp412-13; ☎ 021-421 0581; www.hemisphere.org.za; 31st fl, ABSA Centre, Riebeeck St, City Bowl; 🕑 10pm-3am Thu-Sat) Twinkling views of the city are part of the deal at this superstylish club atop the ABSA Centre. It's velvet-rope-and-glamour-model stuff, so dress to the nines.

Zula Sound Bar (Map pp412-13; ☎ 021-424 2442; www.zulabar.co.za; 194 Long St, City Bowl) Funky venue that hosts an interesting range of events, including live bands, DJs, stand-up comedy (Monday night), acoustic musicians (Tuesday) and open-mike poetry sessions (last Wednesday of the month).

SHOPPING

There are craft shops all over town but few of the traditional African items come from the Cape Town area itself. Great buys include the local township-produced items, such as beadwork dolls, toys made from recycled tin cans and wire sculptures.

Canal Walk (Map pp404-5; ☎ 0860-101 165; Century Blvd, Century City, Milnerton; 🕑 9am-9pm) Shops in the city centre and the Waterfront stock most things you'll need, but if you hunger for a sub-urban mall, visit Africa's largest mall, about 5km north of the city centre.

Vaughan Johnson's Wine & Cigar Shop (Map pp412-13; ☎ 021-419 2121; Dock Rd, Waterfront; 🕑 10am-5pm) Want to take some pinotage home? This shop sells practically every quality South African wine you could wish to buy (plus a few from other countries).

Central markets include **Pan African Market** (Map pp412-13; ☎ 021-426 4478; www.panafrican.co.za; 76 Long St, City Bowl; 🕑 9am-5pm Mon-Fri, to 3pm Sat) and **Greenmarket Square** (pp412-13; cnr Shortmarket & Burg Sts, City Bowl; 🕑 9am-6pm), which is in a great area for galleries and shops; a good one is **African Image** (Map pp412-13; ☎ 021-423 8385; cnr Church & Burg Sts; 🕑 9am-5pm Mon-Fri, to 1.30pm Sat), which stocks a range of ancient African artefacts and township crafts, as well as wildly patterned shirts.

At the Waterfront there's **Red Shed Craft Workshop** (Map pp412-13; ☎ 021-408 7708; Victoria Wharf, Waterfront; 🕑 9am-9pm Mon-Sat, 10am-9pm Sun) and **Waterfront Craft Market** (Map pp412-13; ☎ 021-408 7884; Dock Rd, Waterfront; 🕑 9.30am-6pm), also known as the Blue Shed.

GETTING THERE & AWAY

Air

Cape Town International Airport (CPT; Map pp404-5; ☎ 021-937 1200; www.airports.co.za) is 20km east of the city centre, approximately 20 minutes' drive depending on traffic.

Apart from **South African Airways** (☎ 0861-359 722; www.flysaa.com), three budget airlines operate out of Cape Town: **Kulula.com** (☎ 0861-444 144; www.kulula.com), **Mango** (☎ 0861-162 646; ww5.flymango.com) and **1time** (☎ 0861-345 345; www.1time.aero), all flying to the major South African cities. During the summer, you could pick up a one-way flight to Durban for a little over R400; to Jo'burg for less than R700.

Bus

Four major long-distance bus lines operate out of Cape Town. Their booking offices and main arrival and departure points are at the Merriman Sq end of Cape Town train station (City Bowl, Map pp412–13).

Greyhound (☎ 083 915 9000; www.greyhound.co.za)
Intercape (☎ 021-380 4400; www.intercape.co.za)
SA Roadlink (☎ 021-425 0203; www.saroadlink.co.za)
Translux (☎ 021-449 6209; www.translux.co.za)

For more information on bus routes and fares, and on the Baz Bus, see p578.

Minibus Taxi

Most long-distance minibus taxis start picking up passengers around Cape Town train station in City Bowl before heading out to the Cape Flats and the townships. It's preferable to take a reliable local guide as the townships are not always safe for outsiders to wander around. Langa is relatively safe and long-distance taxis leave from the Langa shopping centre early in the morning. A local-area minibus taxi from Cape Town train station to Langa costs about R7.

Train

Long-distance trains depart and arrive at the **central train station** (Map pp412-13; Strand St). Be prepared for queues at the **booking office** (☎ 021-449 4596; 🕑 7.30am-4.55pm Mon-Fri, to 10.30am Sat).

Destinations include Pretoria, Jo'burg and Durban via Kimberley; and East London (economy-class only). For more information, see p581.

GETTING AROUND

To/From the Airport

Backpacker Bus (☎ 021-439 7600; www.backpackerbus.co.za) picks up from hostels and hotels in the city and offers airport transfers for R150 per person (R170 between 5pm and 8am).

Expect to pay from R200 for a nonshared taxi; the officially authorised airport taxi company is **Touch Down Taxis** (☎ 021-919 4659). If there are two or more of you, consider making a booking with Rikkis (right), which charges from R180 for transfers to/from the City Bowl area.

Bus

For local bus services the main station is the **Golden Acre Terminal** (Map pp412-13; Grand Parade, City Bowl). From here **Golden Arrow** (☎ 0800-656 463; www.gabs.co.za) buses run, with most services stopping early in the evening. Buses are most useful for getting along the Atlantic Coast from the city centre to Hout Bay. When travelling short distances, most people wait at the bus stop and take either a bus or a shared taxi, whichever arrives first. A tourist-friendly alternative is the City Sightseeing Cape Town service (p419).

Destinations and off-peak fares (applicable from 8am to 4pm) from the city include the Waterfront (R4), Sea Point (R4) and Kloof Nek (R4). Peak fares are about 30% higher. If you're using a particular bus regularly, it's worth buying 'clipcards', with 10 discounted trips.

Minibus Taxi

Minibus taxis (see also left) cover most of the city with an informal network of routes and are a cheap way of getting around. Useful routes are from Adderley St (opposite the Golden Acre Centre) to Sea Point along Main Rd (R4), and up Long St to Kloof Nek (R3).

Hail them from the side of the road and ask the driver where they're going. The main stop is on the upper deck of the main train station, accessible from a walkway in the Golden Acre Centre or from stairways on Strand St.

Rikkis

A cross between a taxi and a shared taxi are **Rikkis** (☎ 0861-745 547; www.rikkis.co.za; 🕑 6.30am-2am Mon-Thu, 24hr service 6.30am Fri-2am Mon). They offer shared rides most places around the City Bowl, and down the Atlantic coast to Camps Bay, for R15 to R30.

Although cheap, Rikkis are not the quickest way to get around, as there is usually a certain amount of meandering as passengers are dropped off, and they are notoriously slow to turn up to a booking.

Taxi

Consider taking a private taxi late at night or if you're in a group. Rates are typically R10 to R12 per kilometre. Call **Marine Taxi** (☎ 021-434 0434), **SA Cab** (☎ 0861-172 222) or **Unicab Taxis** (☎ 021-447 4402).

Train

Metrorail (☎ 0800-656 463; www.capemetrorail.co.za) commuter trains are a handy way to get around, although there are few (or no) trains after 6pm.

Metro trains have 1st- and economy-class carriages only. The difference in price and comfort is negligible, and you'll find the 1st-class compartments to be safer on the whole.

The most important line for visitors is the Simon's Town line, which runs through Observatory (1st/economy class R5.50/4.20) and around the back of Table Mountain through upper-income suburbs, then on to Muizenberg (R8.50/5.50) and the False Bay coast. There's a R25 ticket allowing unlimited travel between Cape Town and Simon's Town and all stations in between from 8am to 4.30pm daily.

Trains run at least every hour from 5am to 7.30pm Monday to Friday (to 6pm on Saturday), and from 7.30am to 6.30pm on Sunday. Other services from Cape Town include those to Strand on the eastern side of False Bay, and into the Winelands to Stellenbosch (R12/7.50) and Paarl (R14.50/8.50). They are the cheapest and easiest means of transport to these areas; security is best at peak times.

WESTERN CAPE

The Western Cape is without a doubt one of the world's premier destinations, a place often so picture-perfect it's hard to describe without using clichés. The diversity of the landscape is unparalleled and the number of adventures to experience almost overwhelming. Dive with sharks, jump out of an aeroplane, surf some of Southern Africa's best breaks, cruise with whales, eat fresh crayfish at a beachside barbecue, stand at the southernmost tip of Africa and sample some of the world's finest wines.

The region is the country's most popular tourist destination, so at times you may feel a bit like a zebra in a herd travelling around here, particularly along the Garden Route. But it's a magical place, with ample opportunity to flee the crowds. Whichever way you go, however, in the Western Cape there's no escaping the beauty.

WINELANDS

The Boland, stretching inland and upwards from Cape Town, is not South Africa's only wine-growing region, but it's certainly the most famous. Its name means 'Upland', a reference to the dramatic mountain ranges that shoot up to over 1500m, on whose fertile slopes the vineyards form a patchwork.

With its centuries-long history of colonial settlement, there's a distinctly European feel to the Boland, particularly in French-themed culinary hot spot Franschhoek (French Corner). Lively student-town Stellenbosch offers the most activities, while Paarl is a busy commercial centre with excellent estates.

Stellenbosch

☎ 021 / pop 220,000

South Africa's second-oldest European settlement, established on the banks of the Eerste River in 1679, Stellenbosch wears many faces. At times it's a rowdy joint for Stellenbosch University students and at others it's a stately monument to colonial architectural splendour. But most times it's just plain busy, as Capetonians, vineyard workers and tourists descend on its museums, markets, quality hotels and varied eating and nightlife options.

INFORMATION

Java Café (☎ 021-887 6261; cnr Church & Andringa Sts; per hr R27; 🕑 8am-10pm, 9am-10pm Sun) Stylish cafe offering Stellenbosch's cheapest internet access, and a wi-fi hot spot.

Rennies Foreign Exchange (Mill St) Has a Thomas Cook foreign-exchange office and MoneyGram.

Stellenbosch Tourism (☎ 021-883 3584; www.tourismstellenbosch.co.za; 36 Market St; 🕑 8am-6pm Mon-Fri, 9am-4pm Sat, to 3pm Sun Sep-Apr, to 5pm Mon-Fri, 9.30am-2pm Sat, 10am-2pm Sun May-Aug) The staff is extremely helpful and various brochures and maps are available, covering both the town and wine routes.

SIGHTS & ACTIVITIES

Village Museum

Charming gardens and a group of exquisitely restored and period-furnished houses dating from 1709 to 1850 make up this must-see **museum** (☎ 021-887 2902; 18 Ryneveld St; adult/child R20/5; 🕑 9am-5pm Mon-Sat, 10-4pm Sun), which occupies the entire city block bounded by Ryneveld, Plein, Drostdy and Church Sts.

Sasol Art Museum

Featuring one of the country's best selections of local art, both famous and emerging, this **museum** (☎ 021-808 3693; 52 Ryneveld St; adult/child R5/2; 🕑 9am-4.30pm Tue-Sat, from 10am Mon) also contains

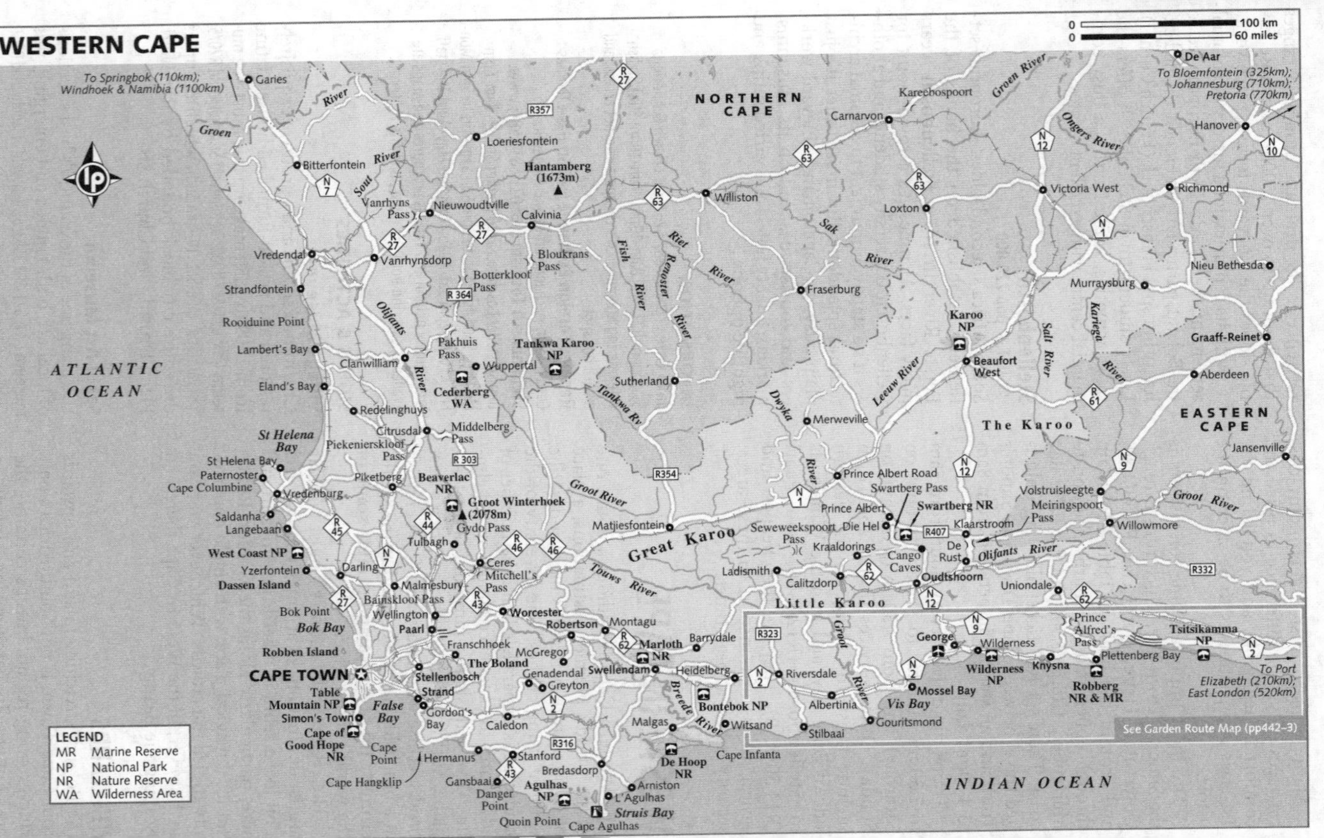
WESTERN CAPE
0 100 km
0 60 miles
To Springbok (110km); Windhoek & Namibia (1100km)
To Bloemfontein (325km); Johannesburg (710km); Pretoria (770km)
To Port Elizabeth (210km); East London (520km)
See Garden Route Map (pp442-3)
ATLANTIC OCEAN
INDIAN OCEAN
NORTHERN CAPE
EASTERN CAPE
The Karoo
Great Karoo
Little Karoo
Garies
Bitterfontein
Vredendal
Strandfontein
Rooiduine Point
Lambert's Bay
Eland's Bay
St Helena Bay
Paternoster
Cape Columbine
Vredenburg
Saldanha
Langebaan
West Coast NP
Yzerfontein
Dassen Island
Darling
Bok Point
Bok Bay
Robben Island
CAPE TOWN
Table Mountain NP
Simon's Town
Cape of Good Hope NR
Cape Point
False Bay
Cape Hangklip
Gordon's Bay
Strand
Stellenbosch
Paarl
Wellington
Franschhoek
Malmesbury
Bainskloof Pass
Tulbagh
Piketberg
Redelinghuys
Clanwilliam
Citrusdal
Piekenierskloof Pass
Middelberg Pass
Cederberg WA
Wuppertal
Pakhuis Pass
Botterkloof Pass
Vanrhynsdorp
Vanrhyns Pass
Nieuwoudtville
Loeriesfontein
Calvinia
Hantamberg (1673m)
Bloukrans Pass
Tankwa Karoo NP
Beaverlac NR
Groot Winterhoek (2078m)
Gydo Pass
Ceres
Mitchell's Pass
Worcester
Robertson
McGregor
The Boland
Genadendal
Greyton
Caledon
Hermanus
Stanford
Gansbaai
Danger Point
Quoin Point
Agulhas NP
Cape Agulhas
Struis Bay
L'Agulhas
Arniston
Bredasdorp
De Hoop NR
Malgas
Swellendam
Marloth NR
Montagu
Barrydale
Heidelberg
Bontebok NP
Witsand
Cape Infanta
Stilbaai
Riversdale
Albertinia
Gouritsmond
Vis Bay
Mossel Bay
George
Wilderness
Wilderness NP
Knysna
Robberg NR & MR
Plettenberg Bay
Prince Alfred's Pass
Tsitsikamma NP
Uniondale
Oudtshoorn
De Rust
Cango Caves
Klaarstroom
Meiringspoort Pass
Swartberg NR
Swartberg Pass
Prince Albert
Die Hel
Prince Albert Road
Kraaldorings
Seweweekspoort Pass
Calitzdorp
Ladismith
Matjiesfontein
Sutherland
Merweville
Fraserburg
Williston
Carnarvon
Loxton
Kareebospoort
Victoria West
Richmond
Hanover
De Aar
Murraysburg
Nieu Bethesda
Graaff-Reinet
Aberdeen
Jansenville
Willowmore
Volstruisleegte
Beaufort West
Karoo NP
Olifants River
Groot River
Breede River
Touws River
Dwyka River
Leeuw River
Sak River
Riet River
Renoster River
Fish River
Tankwa Rv
Salt River
Kariega River
Ongers River
Groen River
Sout River
LEGEND
MR Marine Reserve
NP National Park
NR Nature Reserve
WA Wilderness Area

an irreplaceable collection of African anthropological treasures.

Braak

At the north end of the **Braak** (Town Square), an open stretch of grass, you'll find the neo-Gothic **St Mary's on the Braak Church**, completed in 1852. To the west is the **VOC Kruithuis** (Powder House), which was built in 1777 to store the town's weapons and gunpowder. On the northwest corner is **Fick House**, also known as the Burgerhuis, a fine example of Cape Dutch style from the late 18th century. It's not the safest part of town if you're by yourself or it's late.

Wineries

There are too many good wineries in the Stellenbosch area to list all of them, so it's sometimes best to drive around and stop on a whim. We do, however, recommend a visit to **Villiera** (☎ 021-865 2002; Koelenhof; tastings free; 🕑 8.30am-5pm Mon-Fri, to 3pm Sat), which produces several excellent Méthode Cap Classique wines. It also works with M'hudi Wines, a black-owned neighbouring wine farm, producing a sauvignon blanc, pinotage and merlot.

Try to make it to **Neethlingshof** (☎ 021-883 8988; tastings R30; 🕑 9am-5pm Mon-Fri, 10am-4pm Sat & Sun), where a beautiful tree-lined avenue leads to a charming estate with a rose garden and **restaurant** (mains R58 to R115; 🕑 lunch Mon-Sun, dinner Wed-Sat Oct-Apr, lunch Tue-Sun May-Sep). There are cellar and vineyard tours, and its pinotage and cabernet sauvignon have won several awards.

Thanks to a favourable microclimate, the **Hartenberg Estate** (☎ 021-865 2541; tastings free; 🕑 9am-5.15pm Mon-Fri, to 3pm Sat, 10am-3.30pm Sun) also produces a top cabernet and shiraz. Lunch is available from noon to 2pm (bookings essential).

TOURS

If you need to walk off all that cheese and wine, explore town with the brochure *Stellenbosch on Foot* (R5), available at Stellenbosch Tourism, or head to the same office to take the **guided walk** (per person R80; 🕑 tours 11am & 3pm Mon-Fri), with a minimum of two people.

Easy Rider Wine Tours (☎ 021-886 4651; Stumble Inn, 12 Market St) Long-established company offering good value for a full-day trip at R350 including lunch and all tastings.

Madiba (☎ 083 479 2801; per person R120) Walking tours of Kayamandi township.

Vine Hopper (☎ 021-882 8112; per person R170) Hop-on, hop-off bus with two routes each covering six estates, departing hourly from Stellenbosch Tourism.

SLEEPING

Stellenbosch Traveller's Lodge (☎ 021-886 9290; www.stellenlodge.co.za; 8 Stadler St; dm/s/d R90/220/300; 💻 🏊) A fallback plan if the other budget options are full, this shabby but secure place has spacious rooms. The downstairs showers work better than those upstairs.

Stumble Inn (☎ 021-887 4049; www.stumbleinnstellenbosch.hostel.com; 12 Market St; dm R90, r with shared bathroom R250; 💻 🏊) With a lively and welcoming atmosphere, this place is split over two old houses, one with a small pool and the other with a pleasant garden. The owners, travellers and wine lovers themselves, also run Easy Rider Wine Tours (left).

Banghoek Place (☎ 021-887 0048; www.banghoek.co.za; 193 Banghoek Rd; dm/r R100/400; 💻 🏊) The recreation area of this modern, comfortable option has satellite TV and a pool table. A good place to organise transport and tours.

De Oude Meul (☎ 021-887 7085; www.deoudemeul.com; 10A Mill St; s/d incl breakfast R700/900; ❄) Above an antiques shop in the centre of town, the accommodation here is very good and some rooms have balconies. Guests breakfast in the modern Mill Coffee House nearby.

Stellenbosch Hotel (☎ 021-887 3644; www.stellenbosch.co.za/hotel; cnr Dorp & Andringa Sts; s/d R795/1090; ❄) A comfortable country-style hotel with a variety of rooms, including some with self-catering facilities and others with four-poster beds. A section dating from 1743 houses the Jan Cats Brasserie, a good spot for a drink.

D'Ouwe Werf (☎ 021-887 4608; www.ouwewerf.com; 30 Church St; s/d incl breakfast from R1425/1650; ❄ 🏊) This is an appealing, old-style hotel (dating back to 1802) with an uninspiring restaurant. The luxury rooms are furnished with antiques and brass beds. Cleanliness of the swimming pool had been questioned by some readers, but we found it perfectly inviting.

EATING

Greengate (☎ 021-886 6111; 44 Ryneveld St; snacks from R25; 🕑 8am-5pm Mon-Fri, to noon Sat) An epicure's delight, this deli-cum-cafe by the Sasol Art Museum has a fine breakfast menu, featuring croissant, omelettes, and a pay-by-weight muesli and fruit salad option.

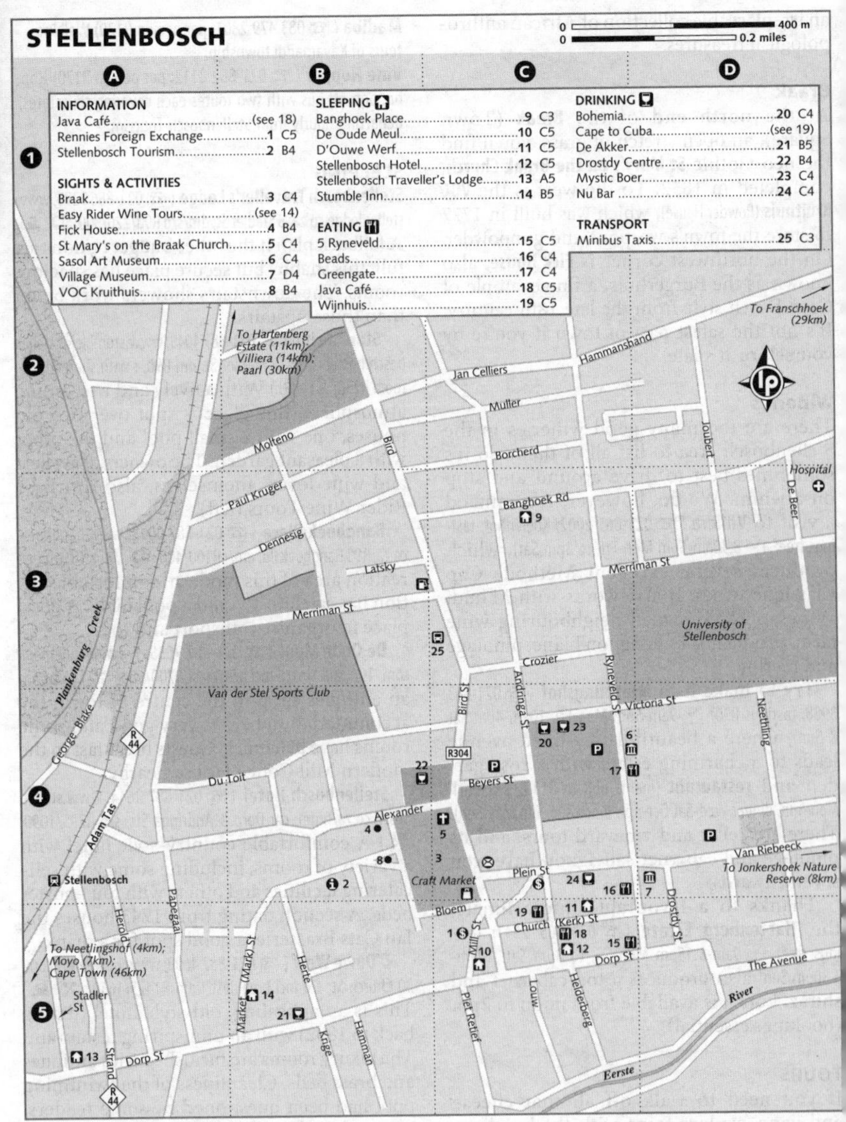

Beads (☎ 021-886 8734; cnr Church & Ryneveld Sts; mains R50-100; ⏰ breakfast, lunch & dinner) This popular à la carte restaurant, with outside seating opposite the Village Museum, attracts the great and the good of Stellenbosch. The menu includes 10 salads, *bobotie* and the recommended chicken pot with pineapple chutney.

5 Ryneveld (☎ 021-886 4842; 5 Ryneveld St; mains R60; ⏰ breakfast, lunch & dinner) Living up to its address, this award-winning gourmet burger restaurant has five rooms with five themes. Ostrich and chicken and oak-smoked beef are available and there's an intimate courtyard at the rear.

Wijnhuis (☎ 021-887 5844; cnr Church & Andringa Sts; mains R120) Restaurants come and go in

Stellenbosch but Wijnhuis has been one of the town's classier options for years. You eat in a loft space among wine-stacked cabinets, chandeliers and ornate mirrors. The food, which includes a good range of fish and meat dishes, falls down on presentation but is certainly delicious.

Moyo (☎ 021-809 1137; Spier Estate, Lynedoch Rd; buffet R225) This tourist-pleasing place brings a fantasy vision of Africa, face paint and all, to the middle of a wine estate. It's a lot of fun, with roving musicians and dancers, and alfresco dining in tents and up in the trees (you're given a blanket in winter).

DRINKING

Stellenbosch's nightlife scene is geared largely towards the interests of the university students, but there are classier options.

Cape to Cuba (☎ 021-887 3559; 13 Andringa St; mains R90) Love or hate its over-the-top Cuban furnishings, this bar-restaurant is a fun place for a drink with Cuban beers and a long list of cocktails (R30).

Mystic Boer (☎ 021-886 8870; 3 Victoria St) Cool kids hang out here in surroundings perhaps best described as post-transformation-era retro-Boer chic.

Nu Bar (☎ 021-886 8998; 51 Plein St) Beyond its gothic exterior, this place has a nightclub feel, with a long bar, a small dance floor and DJs pumping out hip-hop and house.

Two classic student watering holes are **Bohemia** (☎ 021-882 8375; cnr Andringa & Victoria Sts) and **De Akker** (☎ 021-883 3512; 90 Dorp St), which has an upstairs cellar for live music.

Lively bars are also found in the **Drostdy Centre** (off Bird St), north of the Braak.

GETTING THERE & AWAY

Bus

Long-distance bus services charge high prices for the short sector to Cape Town and do not take bookings. You're better off using **Backpacker Bus** (☎ 021-439 7600), which charges R80 to R210 per person (depending on the size of your party), and will pick you up from where you are staying. Madiba (see p431) offers a slightly more expensive shuttle service.

Minibus Taxi

A minibus taxi ride to Paarl is about R20 (45 minutes), but you may have to change in Klapmuts or Pniel; for Franschhoek (R20) you may have to change in Pniel.

Train

Metrorail (☎ 0800-656 463; www.capemetrorail.co.za) trains run the 46km between Cape Town and Stellenbosch (1st/economy class R12/7.30, about one hour). To be safe, travel in the middle of the day.

GETTING AROUND

Stellenbosch is navigable on foot and, being largely flat, this is good cycling territory. Bikes can be hired from the **Adventure Centre** (☎ 021-882 8112; per day R120) at Stellenbosch Tourism; ask about the 20km return ride on the Jonkershoek Rd, taking in two wine estates, Jonkershoek Nature Reserve and restaurants.

Franschhoek

☎ 021 / pop 13,000

The toughest decision you'll face in Franschhoek, which bills itself as the country's gastronomic capital, is where to eat. It certainly has one of the loveliest settings in the Cape and with a clutch of art galleries, wine farms and stylish guest houses thrown in, it can feel a little like a tourist theme park. Nevertheless, if you have transport this a good base from which to visit both Stellenbosch and Paarl.

Franschhoek Wine Valley Tourism (☎ 021-876 3603; www.franschhoek.org.za; Huguenot St; 🕑 9am-6pm Mon-Fri, to 5pm Sat & Sun Oct-Apr, to 5pm Mon-Fri, 10am-4pm Sat & Sun May-Sep) has maps of local walks and wineries, and issues permits (R20) for trails in nearby forestry areas.

SIGHTS & ACTIVITIES

Huguenot Memorial Museum

This engrossing **museum** (☎ 021-876 2532; Lambrecht St; adult/child R10/5; 🕑 9am-5pm Mon-Sat, 2-5pm Sun) celebrates South Africa's Huguenots and houses the genealogical records of their descendants.

Horse Riding

Mont Rochelle Equestrian Centre (☎ 083 300 4368) offers outrides or a three-hour ride with wine tasting.

Wineries

Many of Franschhoek's wineries are within cycling distance of the town centre.

Cabrière Estate (☎ 021-876 8500; Pass Rd; tastings with cellar tour R30; 🕑 9am-5pm Mon-Fri, 10am-4pm Sat, tours 11am & 3pm Mon-Fri, 11am Sat) offers tastings

SOUTH AFRICA

that include a couple of sparkling wines and one of the vineyard's excellent range of white, red and dessert wines and brandies.

Grande Provence (☎ 021-876 8600; Main Rd; tastings R20, cellar tours R15; ⏰ 10am-6pm, tours 11am & 3pm Mon-Fri), a beautifully revamped, 18th-century manor house off Rte 45, is home to a stylish restaurant and a splendid gallery showcasing contemporary South African art.

Northwest of town is **Chamonix** (☎ 021-876 8426; Uitkyk St; tastings R15, cellar tours R25; ⏰ 9.30am-5pm, tours by appointment), where the tasting room is in a converted blacksmith's. In addition to its wines, **Dieu Donné** (☎ 021-876 2493; Uitkyk St; tastings R15; ⏰ 9am-4pm Mon-Fri, 10.30am-4pm Sat & Sun), further up the hill, has a microbrewery producing stout, pilsner and ale.

SLEEPING

Sunny Lane (☎ 083 581 9686; www.sunnylane.za.net; 30 Akademie St; s/d from R250/350; 🅿) Pleasantly furnished and close to all the village action, these good-value units are in a pretty garden.

Chamonix Guest Cottages (☎ 021-876 8400; www.chamonix.co.za; Uitkyk St; cottages per person from R250) Pleasant cottages sleeping up to four are set in the winery's vineyards, a 20-minute walk uphill north of Huguenot St.

Reeden Lodge (☎ 021-876 3174; www.reedenlodge.co.za; off Cabriere St; cottage from R500; 🅿) A good-value, terrific option for families, with well-equipped, self-catering cottages sleeping up to eight people, situated on a farm about 10 minutes' walk south of town.

La Fontaine (☎ 021-876 2112; www.lafontainefranschhoek.co.za; 21 Dirkie Uys St; s/d/tr incl breakfast from R650/1300/1800; 🅿) Offering quiet accommodation off the main drag, this stylishly appointed, comfortable family home has 12 spacious rooms with wooden floors and mountain views. There is a downstairs room that would be suitable for disabled travellers.

Le Quartier Français (☎ 021-876 2151; www.lequartier.co.za; 16 Huguenot St; r incl breakfast from R3950; ❄ 💻 🅿) This is one of the best places to stay in the Winelands. Set around a leafy courtyard and pool, guest rooms are very large with fireplaces, huge beds and stylish decor. There's a bistro, Ici, and the Tasting Room restaurant (see right).

EATING

Essence (☎ 021-876 4135; Huguenot Sq; mains R49-98) With all those bistros around, it can be hard to find somewhere for a straightforward coffee and light meal. Essence plugs that gap, serving grub from Thai fish cakes to pancakes in unpretentious surroundings soundtracked by jazzy music.

Kalfi's (☎ 021-8876 2520; 17 Huguenot St; mains R52-110; ⏰ breakfast, lunch & dinner) You can watch the world go by from the verandah of this family-orientated restaurant, or check out the black-and-white photos of old Franschhoek. There's a fire inside on winter evenings and a children's menu, but not much for vegetarians.

Dieu Donné (☎ 021-876 3384; Uitkyk St; mains R75-145) The winery (see left) offers a free local shuttle service to its two-year-old restaurant, which serves world cuisine with sweeping views down the valley.

Reuben's (☎ 021-876 3772; 19 Huguenot St; mains R78-125; ⏰ breakfast, lunch & dinner) Locals vote this restaurant as the best in the valley. There's a deli-style eatery and courtyard for breakfast and lunch, and dinner is served in the restaurant.

Franschhoek stalwart **Ici** (☎ 021-876 2151; 16 Huguenot St; mains R100; ⏰ breakfast, lunch & dinner), a beautifully decorated bistro, offers dishes such as truffled Jerusalem artichoke soup and bacon-wrapped quail. Also here is the **Tasting Room** (5-/8-course meal R550/700; ⏰ dinner), the best restaurant in Africa and the Middle East (according to one gastronomic guidebook).

GETTING THERE & AWAY

The best way to reach Franschhoek is in your own vehicle. Some visitors choose to cycle the 32km from Stellenbosch, but roads are winding and can be treacherous. Catching a minibus taxi from Stellenbosch or Paarl (R20) will likely involve a few changes. A private taxi operator is **Isak de Wet** (☎ 078-587 4061).

Paarl

☎ 021 / pop 165,000

Less touristy and more spread out than Stellenbosch, Paarl is a large commercial centre, surrounded by mountains and vineyards, on the banks of the Berg River. It's not really a town to tour on foot, because Main St is more than 11km long, but there is still quite a lot to see and do, including vineyards within town limits. There are some great walks in the Paarl Mountain Nature Reserve, some excellent Cape Dutch architecture and some significant monuments to Afrikaner culture.

INFORMATION

Paarl Tourism (☎ 021-872 4842; www.paarlonline.com; 216 Main St; ⌚ 8am-5pm Mon-Fri, 10am-1pm Sat & Sun) Information on the whole region.

SIGHTS & ACTIVITIES

Paarl museum (☎ 021-872 2651; 303 Main St; admission R5; ⌚ 9am-5pm Mon-Fri, to 1pm Sat) is housed in the *Oude Pastorie* (Old Parsonage), built in 1714. It has a fascinating collection of Cape Dutch antiques and relics of Huguenot and early Afrikaner culture.

Paarl is considered the wellspring of the Afrikaans language, a fact covered well by the interesting **Afrikaans Language Museum** (☎ 021-872 3441; 11 Pastorie Ave; adult/child R12/2; ⌚ 9am-4pm Mon-Fri).

The three giant granite domes that dominate the popular **Paarl Mountain Nature Reserve** and loom over the western side of town glisten like pearls if they are caught by the sun after a rainfall. The reserve has mountain *fynbos*, a cultivated wildflower garden, and numerous walks with excellent views over the valley.

Bainskloof Pass is one of the country's great mountain passes, with a superb caravan park halfway along. It's a magical drive, which, if you have the lungs for it, would be even better experienced on a bicycle. Rte 303 runs from Wellington across Bainskloof to meet Rte 43, which runs south to Worcester and north to Ceres.

There are several nearby **walks**, ranging from the Murasie trail (7km, three hours) to the Happy Valley trail (10km, six hours). You need to buy a permit (adult/child R25/12), which is available from the **Wellington Tourist Information Office** (☎ 021-873 4604; Main Rd, Wellington; ⌚ 8am-5pm Mon-Fri, 10am-1pm Sat & Sun) along with maps (R20).

SLEEPING

Berg River Resort (☎ 021-863 1650; www.bergriverresort.co.za; campsites R205, d chalets R485;) An attractive municipal camping ground beside the Berg River, 5km from Paarl on Rte 45 towards Franschhoek. Facilities include canoes, trampolines and a cafe.

Bakkies B&B (☎ 021-873 5161; www.bakkiesbb.co.za; Bainskloof Rd, Wellington; s/d R275/460;) This place, next to a gated housing development at the foot of the Bainskloof Pass, is an excellent budget base for exploring the area, where activities including horse riding and mountain biking are on offer. Breakfast is R55.

Rodeberg Lodge (☎ 021-863 3202; www.rodeberglodge.co.za; 74 Main St; s/d incl breakfast R390/700;) Good rooms are sensibly located away from the busy main road, and breakfast is taken in the conservatory, opening onto a leafy garden.

Pontac Manor (☎ 021-872 0445; www.pontac.com; 16 Zion St; s/d incl breakfast R995/1430;) A small, stylish hotel in a delightful Victorian house with good views over the valley. The rooms are comfortable and have underfloor heating. The restaurant (mains R50 to R125) is recommended.

EATING

Several of the local vineyards have restaurants or do picnic lunches and they are among the best places to eat.

Kikka (☎ 021-872 0685; 217 Main St; mains R20-60; ⌚ 7.30am-6pm Mon-Fri, to 3pm Sat) Watch florists at work in this delightful deli and cafe with funky, retro decor. There's a buffet lunch on offer during the week.

Marc's Mediterranean Cuisine & Garden (☎ 021-863 3980; 129 Main St; mains R60-125) A light and bright place with food to match and a Provençal-style garden to dine in.

Noop (☎ 021-863 3925; 127 Main St; mains R70-120; ⌚ lunch Mon-Sat, dinner Mon-Fri) Recommended by locals all over the Winelands, this restaurant and wine bar has a small but excellent menu and really fresh salads.

GETTING THERE & AWAY

Bus

All the major long-distance bus companies offer services going through Paarl, making it easy to build into your itinerary. The bus segment between Paarl and Cape Town is R150, so consider taking the cheaper train to Paarl and then linking up with the buses.

Train

Metrorail (☎ 0800-656 463; www.capemetrorail.co.za) trains run roughly every hour (less frequently at weekends) between Cape Town and Paarl (1st/economy class R14.50/8.50, 1¼ hours). It's safer to travel on trains during the busy part of the day.

You can travel by train from Paarl to Stellenbosch: take a Cape Town–bound train and change at Muldersvlei.

THE OVERBERG

Almost all roads heading east from Cape Town suddenly hit a rocky barrier, forcing drivers into the lower gears. Once you're up and over the top, you're 'over the mountain', the literal meaning of Overberg. The landscape here is quite different to the Cape Flats, with rolling wheat fields bordered by mountains, the Breede River and the coast.

Ballooning east from Cape Hangklip to the coastal De Hoop Nature Reserve and elegant Swellendam, the area is reached from Cape Town via the N2 over the scenic Sir Lowry's Pass or (slower) via Rte 44 from Strand, a breathtaking coastal drive. The first major stop is Hermanus, a seaside resort famous for the whales that frequent its shores.

This region's wealth of *fynbos* is unmatched; most species flower somewhere in the period between autumn and spring.

Hermanus

☎ 028 / pop 45,000

Hermanus (hair-*maan*-es) was founded as a fishing village, and while it retains vestiges of its heritage, its proximity to Cape Town (122km) has made it a day-tripper's paradise, in part thanks to its being considered the world's best land-based whale-watching destination. As a result, the town can get crowded, particularly during the **Hermanus Whale Festival** (www.whalefestival.co.za) in September and during school holidays in December and January.

Hermanus is highly recommended at quieter times of year; respite from whale-seeking hordes can also be found on the appealing beaches and in the surrounding rocky hills, which offer good walks and a nature reserve protecting some of the prolific *fynbos*.

INFORMATION

Computer Connections (☎ 028-312 4683; Waterkant Bldg, 38 Main Rd; per hr R15; 🕒 8am-6.30pm Mon-Fri, 8.30am-4.30pm Sat, 9am-3pm Sun) Offers reliable and speedy internet connections.

Hermanus Tourism (☎ 028-312 2629; www.hermanus.co.za; Old Station Bldg, Mitchell St; 🕒 9am-5pm Mon-Sat, also open Sun in whale season) East of the town centre.

SIGHTS & ACTIVITIES

Between June/July and November, southern right whales come to Walker Bay to calve. There can be up to 70 whales in the bay at once and the numbers visiting seem to grow every year. Humpback whales are also sometimes seen.

Whales often come very close to shore and there are some excellent vantage points from the cliff paths that run from one end of Hermanus to the other. The best places are Gearings Point and Kraal Rock.

Shark Cage Diving

Many operators in Hermanus heavily promote this, but most boats actually depart from Gansbaai, some 53km along the coast (all companies transport you there). There has been much controversy over the last few years, as it was thought that operators used bait to attract sharks to the cages, thereby teaching these killer-fish to associate boats and humans with food. However, the operators actually throw 'chum' into the water – fish blood and guts; the sharks are attracted by the smell but there's nothing for them to eat.

You do not need to be able to scuba-dive or snorkel to take part; the diver holds their breath and submerges into the water to watch the fish. Underwater visibility is best from May to September.

Two recommended operators are **Brian McFarlane** (☎ 028-384 1418; www.sharkcagediving.net; trips excl transport adult/child R1250/650) and **Shark Diving Unlimited** (☎ 082-441 4555; www.sharkdivingunlimited.com; trips excl transport R1200). Tours generally include breakfast, lunch and diving gear.

Walking

The **Cliff Path Walking Trail** meanders for 10km from town along the sea to the mouth of the Klein River. Along the way you'll pass Kwaaiwater, a good whale-watching lookout, Langbaai and Voelklip beaches, and Grotto Beach, the most popular beach with excellent facilities. The 1400-hectare **Fernkloof Nature Reserve** (☎ 028-313 8100; Fir Ave; admission free; 🕒 7am-7pm) has some 1500 species of *fynbos* and trails lasting up to two hours (including one to a waterfall).

SLEEPING

Zoete Inval Travellers Lodge (☎ 028-312 1242; www.zoeteinval.co.za; 23 Main Rd; dm R95, r with shared bathroom from R250) An excellent budget option for those wanting less of a party atmosphere, this is a quieter place with good amenities (including a jacuzzi) and neatly furnished rooms.

Hermanus Backpackers (☎ 028-312 4293; www.hermanusbackpackers.co.za; 26 Flower St; dm R100, d with shared bathroom R300, d R330; 💻) This is a smashing place with clued-up staff, great decor and facilities including a reed-roof bar. Free breakfast is served in the morning.

Moby's Travellers Lodge (☎ 028-313 2361; www.mobys.co.za; 9 Mitchell St; dm R100, s/d R300/400; 💻 🅿) Centrally situated, this place is loads of fun and travellers love it. There's a big bar for partying, a great rock pool for chillaxing and pub meals are available.

Hermanus Esplanade (☎ 028-312 3610; www.hermanusesplanade.com; 63 Marine Dr; d apt R300-900) Some of these cheery, self-catering apartments with colourful furniture overlook the sea. The lowest rates on offer actually cover the whale-watching season from May to October.

Windsor Hotel (☎ 028-312 3727; www.windsorhotel.co.za; 49 Marine Dr; s/d incl breakfast from R650/960; 💻) A sea-facing room at this old stalwart situated on an oceanside cliff means you'll be able to whale-watch from your bed.

Auberge Burgundy (☎ 028-313 1201; www.auberge.co.za; 16 Harbour Rd; s/d incl breakfast R780/1040; 🅿) This wonderful place has just about the most perfect position overlooking the sea and in the centre of town. Built in the style of a Provençal villa, it has art on the walls and a shady courtyard.

EATING & DRINKING

There's no shortage of eateries in Hermanus, many offering views within whale range.

Zebra Crossing (☎ 028-312 3906; 121 Main Rd; mains R30-85; 🕑 breakfast, lunch & dinner) This bar with a funky zebra theme is a great late-night party spot on weekends, and popular with backpackers.

Cubana (☎ 028-313 1178; Village Sq, Marine Dr; mains R40-98; 🕑 breakfast, lunch & dinner) *The* place for the cocktail crowd to be seen, this large restaurant-cum-lounge has a wide menu and wider windows overlooking the water.

Annie se Kombuis (Annie's Kitchen; ☎ 028-313 1350; Warrington Pl; mains R50-85; 🕑 lunch Tue-Sun, dinner Tue-Sat) This cosy place in an arcade off Harbour Rd serves traditional cuisine at reasonable prices, including the recommended *smoorsnoek* (fish curry) and a tasting plate. There's a Sunday lunchtime buffet (R100).

Paradiso (☎ 028-313 1153; 83 Marine Dr; mains R60-120; 🕑 dinner) This Italian restaurant offers a wide range of pizzas and pasta dishes, with seafood making an appearance in both, and a different risotto every night. Canvases hang on the stone walls and there are intimate dining areas and plenty of ocean-facing windows.

Bientang's Cave (☎ 028-312 3454; mains R95-125) Nestling in the cliffs beside the water in an actual cave off Marine Dr, this restaurant's remarkable setting overshadows the so-so food.

GETTING THERE & AWAY

Trevi's Tours (☎ 072-608 9213) offers daily shuttles to Gansbaai (two or more people R150, 30 minutes) and Cape Town (two or more people R300, 1½ hours).

All three hostels run a shuttle service to the Baz Bus drop-off point in Botrivier, 50km west of town; otherwise there are no regular bus services to Hermanus from Cape Town.

Cape Agulhas

☎ 028

The Cape of Good Hope isn't Africa's southernmost point; it's actually Cape Agulhas, which is part of **Agulhas National Park** (☎ 028-435 6222; www.sanparks.org.za). This rugged, windswept coastline, where the Atlantic and Indian Oceans meet, has been a graveyard for many a ship. South Africa's second-oldest lighthouse (1848) houses the **Lighthouse Museum** (☎ 028-435 6222; adult/child R15/7.50; 🕑 9am-5pm).

Just east of Cape Agulhas is the small town of **L'Agulhas**, where the **tourism bureau** (☎ 028-435 7185; agulhastourism@omail.co.za) can help if you'd like to stay over.

De Hoop Nature Reserve

Covering 36,000 hectares, plus 5km out to sea, is **De Hoop Nature Reserve** (☎ 028-542 1253; www.capenature.org.za; admission R25; 🕑 7am-6pm). One of Cape Nature's best reserves, it includes a scenic coastline with stretches of beach, huge dunes and exceptional *fynbos,* plus a freshwater lake and Potberg Mountain. Fauna includes the endangered Cape mountain zebra, the bontebok (antelope) and a wealth of birdlife, with one of the only remaining breeding colonies of the rare Cape vulture. The coast is a key breeding and calving area for the southern right whale.

Although there are numerous day walks, an overnight mountain-bike trail and good snorkelling along the coast, the reserve's most interesting feature is the five-day **Whale Route** (per person R990). Covering 55km, it offers excellent opportunities to see whales between June and December. Accommodation is in modern fully equipped self-catering cottages. The trail needs to be booked in advance, and only groups of six to 12 are accepted.

Most of the wide variety of accommodation in the reserve is managed by **De Hoop Collection**

(☎ 028-542 1253; www.dehoopcollection.co.za; campsites/rondavels for 2 with shared bathroom R275/500, cottages for 6 from R1600, luxury r per person R1250).

The reserve is about 260km from Cape Town. The only access to the reserve is via Wydgeleë on the road between Bredasdorp and Malgas. At Malgas a manually operated pont (river ferry) on the Breede River still operates (between dawn and dusk).

Swellendam

☎ 028 / pop 30,000

One of South Africa's oldest towns (dating back to 1776), rapidly growing Swellendam offers an unbeatable menu of heritage and culture, architecture, wildlife and outdoor adventures. It's a disarming town – dotted with old oaks and surrounded by rolling wheat country and mountains – which makes a great base for exploring the Overberg and the Little Karoo. It's also a handy stopover between Cape Town and the Garden Route.

The town backs up against a spectacular ridge, part of the Langeberge range, and is impressive on a cloudy day when the mist rolls in over the mountains.

Swellendam Tourism Bureau (☎ 028-514 2770; www.swellendamtourism.co.za; Voortrek St; 9am-5pm Mon-Fri, to 1pm Sat & Sun) is in the old mission on the main street.

SIGHTS

The main sight in town is the excellent **Drostdy Museum** (☎ 028-514 1138; 18 Swellengrebel St; adult/child R15/2; 9am-4.45pm Mon-Fri, 10am-3.45pm Sat & Sun). The centrepiece is the beautiful *drostdy* (official's residence) itself, which dates from 1746. The museum ticket also covers entrance to **Mayville**, a residence dating back to 1853, with a formal Victorian garden (and a shop selling stylish African curios); the **Old Gaol**, the **Gaoler's Cottage** and a **watermill**. The Old Gaol Coffee Shop, a wonderful little cafe where staff members are shareholders, has moved to 8A Voortrek St, opposite the Dutch Reformed Church, and is now known as Old Gaol on Church Square.

You can't miss the enormous **Dutch Reformed Church** (Voortrek St) in the centre of town; Swellendam residents swear every visitor takes a photograph of it.

ACTIVITIES

Swellendam has adventures for all ages, budgets and tastes. **Harvey World Travel** (☎ 028-514 3040; 19 Swellengrebel St; 9am-6pm Mon-Fri, to 2pm Sat & Sun) offers a plethora of activities; even star-gazing (with dinner R260).

For day permits (adult/child R25/12) to walk in **Marloth Nature Reserve** in the Langeberge, a few kilometres north of town, contact the **Nature Conservation Department** (☎ 028-514 1410) at the entrance to the reserve. Trails include the demanding **Swellendam Hiking Trail** (☎ reservations 021-659 3500; www.capenature.co.za; admission R38), regarded as one of South Africa's top 10 hikes.

Two Feathers Horse Trails (☎ 082-494 8279; 5 Lichtenstein St; per hr R180) caters for inexperienced and experienced riders.

SLEEPING

Swellendam Backpackers Adventure Lodge (☎ 028-514 2648; www.swellendambackpackers.co.za; 5 Lichtenstein St; campsites per person R50, dm R100, d with shared bathroom R200) Set on a huge plot of land with its own river, lots of horses and Marloth Nature Reserve next door, this is an excellent hostel with enthusiastic management and delicious, homemade dinners (around R70). Horse riding, permits for the reserve and day trips to Cape Agulhas (R450) can be arranged.

Roosje Van de Kaap (☎ 028-514 3001; www.roosjevandekaap.com; 5 Drostdy St; s/d R395/590;) Take a swim with a mountain view. This Cape-country inn has 10 cosy rooms and an excellent restaurant (mains R80 to R135) serving Cape Malay dishes and wood-fired pizzas.

Cypress Cottage (☎ 028-514 3296; www.cypresscottage.info; 3 Voortrek St; s/d R420/640;) There are six individually decorated rooms in this 200-year-old house with a gorgeous garden and a refreshing pool.

Braeside B&B (☎ 028-514 3325; www.braeside.co.za; 13 Van Oudtshoorn Rd; s/d incl breakfast R550/800;) This quiet, gracious Cape Edwardian home boasts a beautiful garden, fantastic views and knowledgeable, friendly hosts.

Bloomestate (☎ 028-514 2984; www.bloomestate.com; 276 Voortrek St; s/d incl breakfast R865/1500;) A modern guest house set on a beautiful 2.5-hectare property, which offers Zen-like privacy to go with the luxurious, colourful rooms. There's an outside jacuzzi, heated salt-water pool and treatment room.

EATING

La Belle Alliance (☎ 028-514 2252; 1 Swellengrebel St; mains R30-80) This appealing tearoom, a good spot for lunch, is an old Masonic lodge with shaded outdoor tables beside the Koringlands River.

Mattsen's Steak House (☎ 028-514 2715; 25 Swellengrebel St; mains R40-165) The pizzas here are delicious and, if you're not starving, large enough for two.

Milestone (☎ 028-514 3565; cnr Voortrek & Andrew Whyte Sts; mains R69-110; 🕑 breakfast, lunch & dinner Mon-Fri, breakfast & lunch Sat) Fresh salads, daily specials and decadent cakes are on offer at this Victorian house with a shady garden.

Koornlands Restaurant (☎ 082 430 8188; 5 Voortrek St; mains R80-120; 🕑 dinner) An eclectic menu of mostly African meat – from kudu fillet to crocodile sashimi – is served in an intimate candlelit setting.

GETTING THERE & AWAY

Most of the major bus companies pass through Swellendam on their runs between Cape Town and Port Elizabeth, stopping opposite the Swellengrebel Hotel on Voortrek St. The Baz Bus stops at Swellendam Backpackers Adventure Lodge.

Minibus taxis depart from Station Rd by the Caltex petrol station. Services include Cape Town (R120, 2½ hours, daily) and Mossel Bay (R100, two hours).

Bontebok National Park

Some 6km south of Swellendam is **Bontebok National Park** (☎ 028-514 2735; adult/child R36/18; 🕑 7am-7pm Oct-Apr, to 6pm May-Sep), established in 1931 to save the remaining 30 bontebok. The project was successful, and bontebok as well as other antelopes and mountain zebras are found here. *Fynbos* (which flowers in late winter and spring), rare *renosterveld* plants and an abundance of birdlife also feature. Swimming is possible in the Breede River.

A lot of thought has gone into the park's accommodation. Ten new chalets (for four R625), incorporating 'Touch the Earth Lightly' principles, include two geared towards people with special needs. Campsites (with/without electricity R160/130) are also available.

ROUTE 62

This area, promoted as the longest wine route in the world, provides an excellent hinterland alternative to the N2 for travel between Cape Town and the Garden Route. Breathtaking mountain passes and intensively cultivated valleys, perfectly preserved 18th-century towns and vast stretches of semi-arid plains dotted with ostriches provide eye-candy, while delectable wine, country cafes, charming B&Bs and even a hot-springs resort enchant the palate and relax the body.

The Little (Klein) Karoo, east of the Breede River Valley, is more fertile and better watered than the harsher Great Karoo to the north.

Montagu

☎ 023 / pop 9500

Coming into Montagu along Rte 62 from Robertson, the road passes through a narrow arch in the Cogmanskloof mountains, and suddenly the town appears before you. With wide streets bordered by 24 restored national monuments, including some fine art-deco architecture, Montagu has an air of calm dignity that attracts romantics and artists alike. There's a wide range of activities, including hot springs, easy walks and more serious hikes, and excellent accommodation and restaurants.

The **tourism bureau** (☎ 023-614 2471; www.tourismmontagu.co.za; 24 Bath St; 🕑 8.30am-6pm Mon-Fri, 9am-5pm Sat, 9.30am-5pm Sun) is extremely efficient and helpful. Opening hours are slightly shorter between May and October.

SIGHTS & ACTIVITIES

Water from the **hot mineral springs** (☎ 023-614 1150; adult/child Mon-Fri R30/20, Sat & Sun R60/40; 🕑 8am-11pm) finds its way into the Avalon Springs Hotel's swimming pools, about 3km from town. Renowned for its healing properties, the water gushes from a rock face in an underground cavern at a constant 43°C. The pools are a lively place at weekends.

A great way to get there (storm damage permitting) is to hike along the 2.2km **Lover's Walk Trail**, which starts at the car park at the end of Barry St. Pick up the *Hiking Trails* leaflet from the tourism bureau. The route leads past Montagu's top rock-climbing spots.

Interesting displays and some good examples of antique furniture can be found at the **Montagu Museum** (☎ 023-614 1950; 41 Long St; adult/child R5/3; 🕑 9am-1pm & 2-5pm Mon-Fri, 10.30am-12.30pm Sat & Sun) in the old mission church. **Joubert House** (☎ 023-614 1774; 25 Long St; adult/child R5/3; 🕑 9am-1pm & 2-4.30pm Mon-Fri, 10.30am-12.30pm Sat, 10am-noon Sun), a short walk away, is Montagu's oldest house (built in 1853) and has been restored to its Victorian glory.

For hikers, the 15.6km-long **Bloupunt Trail** (admission R20) can be walked in six to eight hours;

it traverses ravines and mountain streams, and climbs to 1000m. The 12.1km **Cogmanskloof Trail** (admission R20) can be completed in four to six hours. Both trails start from the car park at the end of Tanner St. The tourism bureau handles bookings for overnight cabins near the start of the trails.

SLEEPING

De Bos (☎ 023-614 2532; www.debos.co.za; Bath St; campsites per person R30, dm R60, s/d R150/240;) A genuine farmstay for backpackers – there's a river, chickens and pecan-nut trees in this 7-hectare property, where colourful old workers' cottages have been converted into self-catering cottages (from R250).

Montagu Caravan Park (☎ 023-614 3034; Bath St; campsites for 2 R120, 4-person cabins/chalets R300/400) This park, in a pleasant location with apricot trees and lots of shade and grass, has chalets with cooking equipment and TVs, and hikers' cabins (for four R260).

7 Church Street (☎ 023-614 1186; www.7churchstreet.co.za; 7 Church St; s/d incl breakfast R450/750;) A friendly, upmarket guest house in a charming Karoo building with a manicured garden. The stylish interior doubles as a gallery of the owner's personal art collection.

Airlies Guest House (☎ 023-614 2943; www.airlies.co.za; Bath St; s/d incl breakfast R520/740;) Quaint accommodation in a roomy, thatched-roof house with spacious wood-floored rooms looking out on the mountains. The hosts are obliging and the breakfast excellent.

EATING

Cottage Café (☎ 023-614 1932; 78 Bath St; mains R20-45) Light lunches are served in a grassy garden. The daily specials are usually tasty and good value; sweet-toothed diners will enjoy the ice cream.

Jessica's (☎ 023-614 1805; 47 Bath St; mains R75-115; dinner) Named after the family dog, cosy Jessica's serves up inventive bistro dishes, such as game loin encrusted with garlic, ginger and served with a black pepper and thyme jus.

Templeton's @ Four Oaks (☎ 023-614 2778; 46 Long St; mains R85-105) Set in a lovely old house, the style is minimalist, rather than the usual country decor, and the food and service are impeccable. One of South Africa's top restaurants.

GETTING THERE & AROUND

Translux (☎ 021-449 3333; www.translux.co.za) buses and the company's cheaper City to City services stop at Ashton, 9km from Montagu, on the run between Cape Town (from R100, 2½ to three hours, daily) and Port Elizabeth (R270, eight hours, daily).

Munnik's (☎ 021-637 1850; per person R80; runs Wed & Fri-Sun) runs a shuttle between Montagu and Cape Town.

Most accommodation establishments offer (prebooked) shuttles from Ashton to Montagu, but you can also jump in one of the minibus taxis (R10) that ply this route, leaving from the **OK Supermarket** (Bath St) in Montagu.

Oudtshoorn

☎ 044 / pop 85,000

That Oudtshoorn bills itself as the ostrich capital of the world is no overstatement. The birds have been bred hereabouts since the 1860s, and at the turn of the 20th century fortunes were made from the fashion for ostrich feathers. Oudtshoorn boomed, and the so-called 'feather barons' built gracious homes and other grand edifices such as the sandstone building housing the CP Nel Museum.

The town still turns a pretty penny from breeding the birds for meat and leather. The ostriches also pay their way with tourists – you can buy ostrich eggs, feathers and biltong all over town – but more importantly Oudtshoorn is a great base for exploring the different environments of the Little Karoo, the Garden Route (it's 55km to George along the N12) and the Great Karoo.

The helpful **Oudtshoorn Tourism Bureau** (☎ 044-279 2532; www.oudtshoorn.com; Baron van Rheede St; 8.30am-5pm Mon-Fri, to 1pm Sat) is next to the CP Nel Museum.

SIGHTS & ACTIVITIES

There are three show ostrich farms that offer guided tours of 45 minutes to 1½ hours. There's little to choose between them; we found the staff at **Highgate Ostrich Show Farm** (☎ 044-272 7115; off Rte 328; adult/child R50/25; 7.30am-5pm) very knowledgeable.

Extensive displays about ostriches, as well as Karoo history, make up the large and interesting **CP Nel Museum** (☎ 044-272 3676; 3 Baron van Rheede St; adult/child R12/3; 8am-5pm Mon-Sat). Included in the ticket price is admission to the **Le Roux Townhouse** (☎ 044-272 3676; cnr Loop & High Sts; 9am-1pm & 2-5pm Mon-Fri), as good an example of a 'feather palace' as you're likely to see.

Everyone loves a meerkat, but none with as much devotion as Grant McIlrath, the world's foremost expert on the endearing animals. On his **meerkat experience** (☎ 082 413 6895; admission R600; ⏰ sunrise on sunny days) at a natural meerkat colony a few kilometres west of town, you will get to see up close how these curious, highly intelligent creatures communicate and live. No children under 10 are admitted. If you have only one wildlife encounter in the Western Cape, make it this one. To book, send Grant a text message.

If you're heading north to the Cango Caves or Cango Ostrich Farm, carry on driving and take the **Swartberg Pass** all the way to Prince Albert (p449), then return via the **Meiringspoort Pass**. Both are engineering masterpieces, and halfway down the latter there is a waterfall and small visitor centre.

Named after the Khoisan word for 'a wet place', the **Cango Caves** (☎ 044-272 7410; adult/child R55/30; ⏰ 9am-4pm), 30km north of Oudtshoorn, are heavily commercialised but impressive. There's a choice of tours on offer.

SLEEPING

Oasis Shanti (☎ 044-279 1163; www.oasisshanti.com; 3 Church St; campsites per person R40, dm R70, d with shared bathroom from R200; 💻 🏊) A bit of a hike up from the centre of town, this friendly hostel is in a large house with a spacious braai and swimming pool area, and shady camping spots.

Backpackers Paradise (☎ 044-272 3436; www.backpackersparadise.net; 148 Baron van Rheede St; campsites per person R50, dm R90, r from R240, d from R280; 💻 🏊) In a large old house, this lively hostel has a separate dorm-bed annexe and free ostrich-egg breakfasts (in season). There's an adventure centre attached.

Kleinplaas Resort (☎ 044-272 5811; kleinpls@mweb.co.za; cnr North & Baron van Rheede Sts; campsites R217, 4-person chalets R640; 🏊) A terrific caravan park with a restaurant (open for breakfast only).

Oakdene Guesthouse (☎ 044-272 3018; www.oakdene.co.za; 99 Baron van Rheede St; s/d R495/790; ❄ 🏊) Elegant cottage furniture, wooden floors, ostrich eggs and quality linen make each room special. There's lush gardens and an excellent pool.

Adley House (☎ 044-272 4533; www.adleyhouse.co.za; 209 Jan van Riebeeck Rd; s/d incl breakfast R715/1100; ❄ 🏊) Rooms, all with private entrance, in this 1905 'Feather Palace' have bags of charm. Try to stay in the house rather than the garden cottages. There are a couple of pools and a beautiful outdoor braai and bar area.

EATING

As you'd expect, most places serve ostrich in one form or another.

Montague House (☎ 044-272 3208; cnr Baron van Rheede & Olivier Sts; mains R49-98; ⏰ breakfast, lunch & dinner) Breakfast is served until 2.30pm; otherwise dine on pasta, salads or sandwiches under umbrellas in the large flowery garden.

Kalinka (☎ 044-279 2596; 93 Baron van Rheede St; mains R80-160; ⏰ dinner Mon-Sun) Little touches of Kalinka's Russian heritage show in the imaginative menu at this stylish, upmarket restaurant.

Jemima's (☎ 044-272 0808; 94 Baron van Rheede St; mains from R85; ⏰ lunch Mon-Fri, dinner Mon-Sun) With a small menu specialising in traditional Cape fare, this restaurant is set in an attractive old house and garden.

GETTING THERE & AROUND

Intercape (☎ 0861-287 287; www.intercape.co.za) serves Jo'burg (R532, 14½ hours, daily) and Cape Town (R238, eight hours). Cheaper **City to City** (☎ 021-449 3333; www.translux.co.za) runs to Jo'burg and to Mossel Bay (R90, two hours, daily), from where you can get to multiple destinations.

The Baz Bus stops at George, from where you can arrange a transfer to Oudtshoorn with Backpackers' Paradise (R50).

Minibus taxis leave from behind Spar (Adderley St) en route to George (R35, 30 minutes) or Cape Town (R180, three hours). The area east of Adderley St has a dodgy feel to it, so be careful.

GARDEN ROUTE

The Garden Route is perhaps South Africa's most internationally renowned destination after Cape Town and the Kruger National Park, and with good reason. Within a few hundred kilometres, the range of topography, vegetation, wildlife and outdoor activities is breathtaking.

Roughly encompassing the coastline from Mossel Bay in the west to just beyond Plettenberg Bay in the east, it caters to all kinds of travellers. Backpackers are taken care of with plenty of hostels, and midrange and top-end folk will be pleased with the range of swanky hotels and charming guest houses.

There are excellent beaches providing activities from boating to good surfing and fishing. Inland are picturesque lagoons and lakes,

GARDEN ROUTE

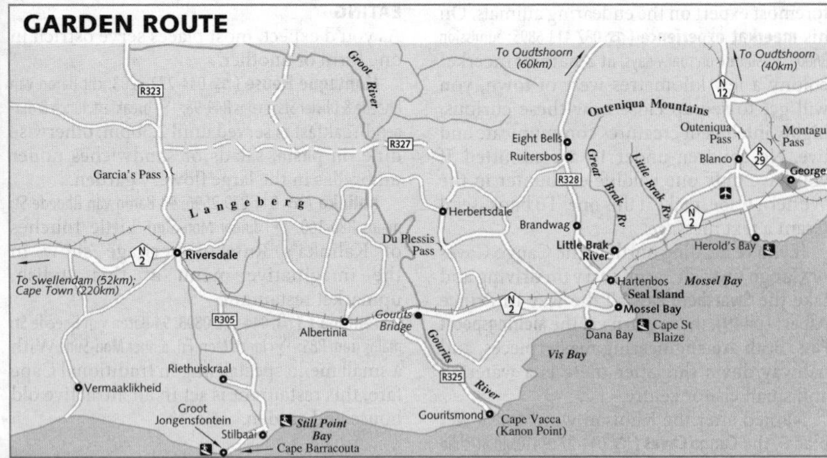

rolling hills and eventually the mountains of the Outeniqua and Tsitsikamma ranges that divide the Garden Route from the arid Little Karoo. The ancient indigenous forests that line the coast from Wilderness to Knysna offer adventure trails and hiking, birding, canoeing the rivers, sliding through the tree canopy or simply taking an easy walk between the trees.

Knysna and Plettenberg Bay are most commonly used as bases, though we prefer less-crowded Wilderness and Buffalo Bay. In recent years development has seemingly spiralled out of control, and at times you might feel like you're a cog in a huge tourist machine. All in all, the Garden Route is great, but if you leave South Africa without having seen it, it isn't a disaster. If you leave having seen nothing else, it might be.

Mossel Bay

☎ 044 / pop 96,000

Once one of the jewels of the Garden Route, Mossel Bay was marred by rampant industrial sprawl in 1980s. Today the town is enjoying a revival, thanks to its historic buildings, excellent places to stay, plentiful activities, fine beaches and gnarly surf spots. Compared with the Garden Route's more developed spots, it's a pleasantly low-key place to wander in the footsteps of its original tourists, Bartholomeu Dias and Vasco da Gama.

The **tourism bureau** (☎ 044-691 2202; www.visitmosselbay.co.za; Market St; 🕑 8am-6pm Mon-Fri, 9am-5pm Sat & Sun) is extremely helpful.

SIGHTS & ACTIVITIES

The highlight of the **Bartholomeu Dias Maritime Museum complex** (☎ 044-691 1067; Market St; adult/child R10/3; 🕑 Maritime, History & Shell Museums 9am-4.45pm Mon-Fri, to 3.45pm Sat & Sun) is the replica of the vessel that Dias, the first European to visit the bay, used on his 1488 voyage of discovery. You can also see the **postal tree** where 16th-century explorers left letters for fellow swashbucklers – the first South African post office.

Mossel Bay is chock-full of activities. From the harbour, there are regular boat trips on the **Romonza** (☎ 044-690 3101) and the **Seven Seas** (☎ 044-691 3371) to view the seal colony, birds and dolphins around Seal Island. One-hour trips cost R100. In late winter and spring the *Romonza* also runs whale-watching trips (R550, 2½ hours).

White Shark Africa (☎ 044-691 3796; Commercial Slipway, Mossel Bay Harbour; dives R1200) organises cage dives and snorkelling to view great white sharks.

Hikers can tackle the **Oystercatcher Trail** (☎ 044-699 1204; www.oystercatchertrail.co.za) to Dana Bay via Cape St Blaize, where you're likely to see the endangered black oystercatcher (three/five days including accommodation, meals and portering R2950/5450).

If all the action is wearing you out, **Back Road Safaris** (☎ 083-262 2307) offers a variety of tours, including **Meet the People** (per person R450). This four-hour itinerary offers home visits, with traditional meals on request, in nearby Friemersheim and KwaNonqaba townships; immensely preferable to the

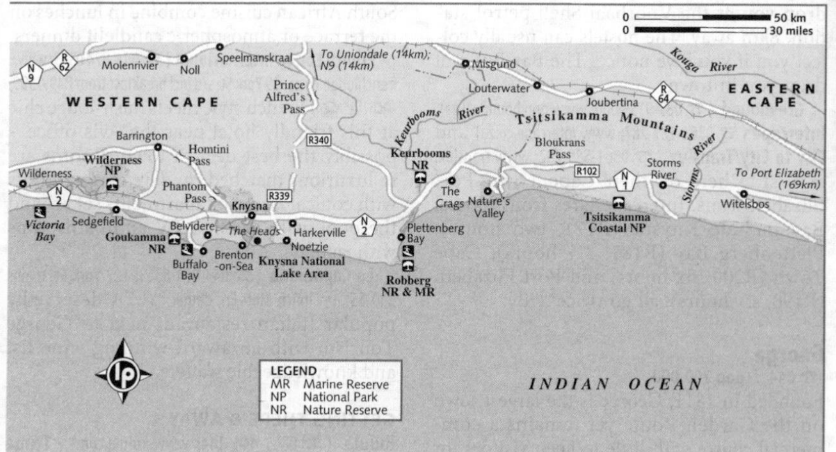

sometimes voyeuristic township tours offered in the cities.

SLEEPING

Santos Express (☎ 044-691 1995; www.santosexpress.co.za; Santos Beach; dm R85, s/d with shared bathroom & breakfast R130/230) The novelty value and position of this converted train on the beach can't be beaten, although the two-bed coupés are cramped and creaky (four-bed compartments are also available). There's an attached bar-restaurant (mains R40 to R75) overlooking the water.

Park House Lodge (☎ 044-691 1937; www.park-house.co.za; 121 High St; dm R120, s/d with shared bathroom from R235/300, s/d from R285/340) This place, in a gracious old sandstone house next to the park, is friendly, smartly decorated and has beautiful gardens, though some doubles have a bathroom between them so can be noisy. Breakfast and braais are available and the on-site travel centre organises activities.

Huis te Marquette (☎ 044-691 3182; www.marquette.co.za; 1 Marsh St; s/d incl breakfast from R480/780) This comfortable, long-running guest house, near the Point, has its more expensive rooms facing the pool. Some rooms come with spa baths, and there's disabled access.

Point Hotel (☎ 044-691 3512; www.pointhotel.co.za; Point Rd; s/d R820/1080) This modern hotel boasts a spectacular location, right above the wave-pounded rocks. There's a decent restaurant and the spacious rooms have balconies with ocean views.

Cape St Blaize Lighthouse (☎ 021-449 2400; cottage for 6 R995) The lighthouse, up on the rocks off Point Rd with dramatic coastal views, has a well-appointed cottage.

There are three municipal **caravan parks** (☎ 044-691 2915; campsites/chalets from R130/360), as well as **Mossel Bay Backpackers** (☎ 044-691 3182; www.mosselbayhostel.com; 1 Marsh St; campsites per person R70, dm R120, r with shared bathroom from R300, r R350), which is attached to Huis te Marquette.

EATING

Marsh St and Point Rd are where it all happens in Mossel Bay.

Big Blu (☎ 044-691 2010; Point Rd; mains R40-90) This ramshackle place right on the rocks draws a young crowd with its prime sundowner potential. Burgers, baskets, seafood and daily specials are dished up.

Pavilion (☎ 044-690 4567; Santos Beach; mains R40-129) In a 19th-century bathing pavilion, this is a fine choice for a beachside meal. The menu offers just about everything.

Jazzbury's (☎ 044-691 1923; 11 Marsh St; mains R60-110; dinner) Locally produced ostrich, available in marinated wing or fillet form, is one of the stars of the culinary show at this 'modern traditional' restaurant. Karoo lamb shank, fish and Cape Malay dishes are also on the menu, and African art decorates the maroon walls.

GETTING THERE & AWAY

Mossel Bay is off the highway, so long-distance buses don't come into town; they drop you at the Voorbaai Shell petrol station, 8km away. The hostels can usually collect you if you give notice. The Baz Bus will drop you in town.

Greyhound (☎ 083-915 9000; www.greyhound.co.za), **Intercape** (☎ 0861-287 287; www.intercape.co.za) and **City to City/Translux** (☎ 0861-589 282; www.translux.co.za) stop here on their Cape Town–Port Elizabeth runs. Intercape fares from Mossel Bay include Knysna (R171, two hours), Plettenberg Bay (R181, 2½ hours), Cape Town (R200, six hours) and Port Elizabeth (R190, six hours); all go twice daily.

George

☎ 044 / pop 200,000

Founded in 1811, George is the largest town on the Garden Route yet remains a commercial centre with little to keep visitors for long. It has some attractive old buildings, but it's 8km from the coast; for most people its chief draw is the *Outeniqua Choo-Tjoe* steam train, which runs to Mossel Bay although it was set to close when we visited.

George Tourism (☎ 044-801 9295; www.visitgeorge.co.za; 124 York St; 🕓 8am-5pm Mon-Fri, 9am-1pm Sat) has a wealth of information.

SIGHTS

George was the hub of the indigenous timber industry and thus the **George Museum** (☎ 044-873 5343; Courtenay St; admission by donation; 🕓 9am-4.30pm Mon-Fri, to 12.30pm Sat) contains related artefacts, as well as exhibits covering other aspects of 19th-century life.

The **George Transport Museum** (☎ 044-801 8288; cnr Courtenay & York Sts; adult/child R10/5; 🕓 7.30am-6pm Mon-Sat) is worth a visit if you're interested in trains.

SLEEPING & EATING

Outeniqua Backpackers (☎ 082-316 7720; www.outeniqua-backapckers.com; 115 Merriman St; dm 100, s/d with shared bathroom R200/260; 💻) Travellers have recommended this backpackers hostel. While it is a bit out of the way in a commercial district, the hostel is clean and well equipped. Staff is keen to arrange local tours.

Het Vijfde Seizoen (☎ 044-870 7320; www.hetvijfdeseizoen.co.za; 3 Maitland St, Blanco; s/d R380/700; 🏊) This guest house offers tranquil accommodation in leafy Blanco, just outside George. Springbok carpaccio is on the menu in the restaurant (mains R80), where European and traditional South African cuisine combine in lunches on the terrace or atmospheric candlelit dinners.

French Lodge International (☎ 044-874 0345; www.frenchlodge.co.za; 29 York St; s/d incl breakfast from R499/599; ❄ 💻 🏊) French style meets bush-lodge chic at this friendly hotel near the Avis office – possibly the best deal in town. Rooms are in luxurious thatched *rondavels* (round huts with conical roofs) or apartments set around the pool, with satellite TV and bathrooms with jacuzzis.

La Capannina (☎ 044-874 5313; 122 York St; mains R40-85; 🕓 lunch Mon-Fri, dinner daily) A deservedly popular Italian restaurant next to George Tourism with an award-winning wine list and knowledgeable waiters.

GETTING THERE & AWAY

Kulula (☎ 0861-444 144; www.kulula.com), **1time** (☎ 0861-345 345; www.1time.aero), **SAAirlink** (☎ 011-961 1700; www.saairlink.co.za) and **SA Express** (☎ 011-978 9900; www.saexpressco.za) fly to **George airport** (☎ 804-476 9310), which is about 15km west of town.

Bus services stop in George on their runs between Cape Town and Port Elizabeth and between Jo'burg and the Garden Route. **Greyhound** (☎ 083-915 9000; www.greyhound.co.za) and **Citiliner** (☎ 072-424 4679; www.citiliner.co.za) services stop in St Mark's Sq behind the Spar supermarket on the main street, while **Intercape** (☎ 0861-287 287; www.intercape.co.za) and **Translux** (☎ 0861-589 282; www.translux.co.za) stop at the train station 2km south of George Tourism. Intercape fares include Knysna (R266, 1½ hours), Plettenberg Bay (R124, two hours), Port Elizabeth (R220, 5½ hours), Cape Town (R260, seven hours), Bloemfontein (R440, 10 hours) and Jo'burg (R1000, 15½ hours); these services are mostly daily.

The Baz Bus drops off in town and you can call the hostels in Oudtshoorn for shuttle services there.

Wilderness

☎ 044

The name says it all: dense old-growth forests and steep hills run down to a beautiful stretch of coastline of rolling breakers, kilometres of white sand, bird-rich estuaries and sheltered lagoons. All this has made Wilderness very popular, but thankfully it doesn't show. The only drawback is everything is quite widely scattered, which can be problematic if you don't have a vehicle.

INFORMATION

Internet Café (☎ 044-877 1124; Wilderness Centre; per hr R40; ⌚ 8am-5pm Mon-Fri, to noon Sat)

Wilderness Tourism Bureau (☎ 044-877 0045; Milkwood Village, Beacon Rd; ⌚ 8am-5pm Mon-Fri, 9am-1pm Sat) Just off the N2 as you pull into the village.

ACTIVITIES

Wilderness is jam-packed with activities. You can try **Eden Adventures** (☎ 044-877 0179; www.eden.co.za; Wilderness National Park) if you're looking to rent a canoe (from R60 per hour) or try your hand at abseiling (R345) or canyoning (from R450). The company also organises guided hikes.

The beach here is beautiful, but be warned: a strong rip means bathing is not advised.

SLEEPING & EATING

Fairy Knowe Backpackers (☎ 044-877 1285; www.wildernessbackpackers.com; Dumbleton Rd; campsites per person R70, dm R100, s/d with shared bathroom R230/300, r R400; 💻) Overlooking a river, set in spacious, leafy grounds, this 1874 farmhouse has yellowwood floors and some original fittings. The *lapa* (circular thatched building) bar and cafe, which serves breakfast and dinner, are a discreet distance away across the lawn. It's 3km east of town but the Baz Bus comes to the door.

Beach House Backpackers (☎ 044-877 0549; www.wildernessbeachhouse.com; Wilderness Beach; dm from R115, d with shared bathroom from R300, r R460; 💻) Southwest of town, this breezy hostel lives up to its name, providing prime beach views, accommodation ranging from dorms to a self-contained cottage, and a *lapa* bar and cafe (serving breakfast and dinner).

Village Inn (☎ 044-877 1187; www.villageinn.co.za; George Rd; per person R450) This bright and airy place behind Wilderness Grille has a beach-house feel. Some rooms have sea views, but with that comes a view of the N2.

Palms Wilderness Retreat & Guesthouse (☎ 044-877 1420; www.palms-wilderness.com; 1 Owen Grant St; s/d incl breakfast R1193/1590; ❄ 💻 🏊) This stylish place has African decor and its gallery stocks African art and jewellery. Rooms are luxurious and it's a two-minute walk from the beach. The emphasis is on local produce in the restaurant (three-course set dinner R195), Wilderness' best.

Pomodoro (☎ 044-877 1403; George Rd; mains R40-90; ⌚ breakfast, lunch & dinner) The local people-watching spot of choice is a good place to sit on the *stoep* (verandah) and enjoy a *panino*, pasta or pizza. Accommodation is available upstairs.

Wilderness Grille (☎ 044-877 0808; George Rd; mains R70; ⌚ breakfast, lunch & dinner) Sit outside among the trees and murals in the garden area. There is an interesting selection of steaks, from blackened sirloin to Cajun, as well as decent pizzas.

Milkwood Village has a number of eateries, such as friendly **Mikado's** (☎ 044-877 1474; mains R70; ⌚ breakfast, lunch & dinner Mon-Sat), which serves German and Afrikaner dishes. There's a **food and craft market** (⌚ 4-9pm) on Friday.

Wilderness National Park

This **national park** (☎ 044-877 1197; adult/child R64/32; ⌚ 24hr) covers a unique system of lakes, rivers, wetlands and estuaries that are vital for the survival of many species. The rich bird life includes the beautiful Knysna lourie and five species of kingfisher.

There are several nature trails taking in the lakes, the beach and the indigenous forest. The lakes offer anglers, canoeists, windsurfers and sailors an ideal venue.

Two similar **camps** (campsites from R125, d rondavels with/without bathroom R245/215, forest cabins R405, 4-person log cottages R705) in the park offer basic but comfortable accommodation with disabled access. A 20% discount applies from 3 May to 30 November. It's possible to walk to the park from Wilderness, 5km west.

Buffalo Bay

☎ 044

Buffalo Bay, 20km southwest of Knysna, is distinctly un–Garden Route: a long, almost deserted surf beach, only a tiny enclave of holiday homes, a beach-shack backpackers hostel and a nature reserve. That's about it, and it's more that enough.

The term 'chillax', often heard on the South African coast, could have been invented for friendly **Buffalo Bay Backpackers** (☎ 044-383 0608; www.buffalobaybackpackers.co.za; campsites per person R60, dm R100, d with shared bathroom R250; 💻), formerly Wildside Backpackers. Kick back in the lounge overlooking the ocean or brave the waves; you can hire a board (R100 per day) or a paddle ski (R50), or take a Rasta township tour. You won't find a lot of luxury – it's right on the beach and there's a constant battle to keep the sand out. Breakfast (R15) and dinner (R60) are available.

Knysna

☎ 044 / pop 54,000

Perched on the edge of a serene lagoon and surrounded by forests, Knysna's (*ny*-znah) sylvan setting, gay-friendly vibe, good places to eat, drink and sleep, and wide range of activities, make it the major stop on the Garden Route. But if you're after something quiet and undeveloped, you should look elsewhere, particularly in season, when the number of visitors swells and getting around can be hell.

There's an **oyster festival** in July, while in mid-September you can pig out at the **Gastronomica Festival** (www.gastronomicakny.co.za). In late April/early May the town confirms its gay-friendly credentials with the **Pink Loerie Festival** (www.pinkloerie.com).

INFORMATION

3@1 (☎ 044-382 2057; Main St; per hr R40; 8am-6pm Mon-Fri, 9am-2pm Sat, 10am-1pm Sun) Internet access opposite Knysna Tourism.

Knysna Tourism (☎ 044-382 5510; www.visitknysna.co.za; 40 Main St; 8am-5pm Mon-Fri, 8.30am-1pm Sat year-round, plus 8.30am-1pm Sun Dec-Jan & Jul) An excellent office with knowledgeable staff.

SIGHTS & ACTIVITIES

Knysna Lagoon

Although regulated by **SAN Parks** (☎ 044-302 5600; www.sanparks.org; Long St, Thesen Island), Knysna Lagoon (13 sq km) is not a national park or wilderness area. Much is still privately owned, and the lagoon is used by industry and for recreation. The lagoon opens up between two

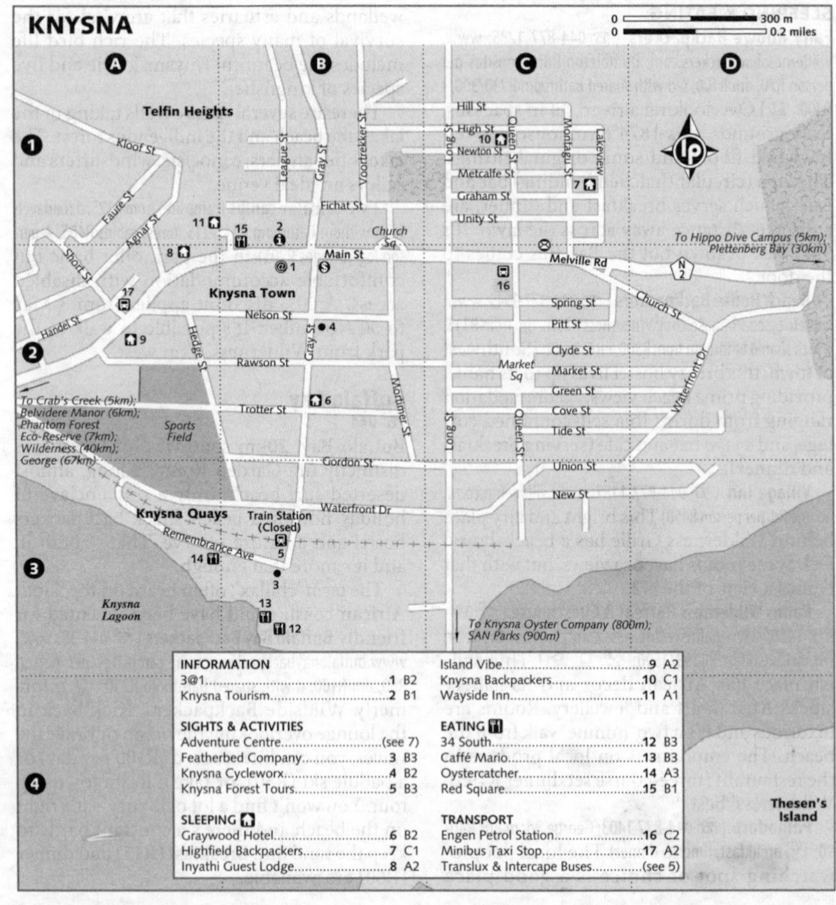

sandstone cliffs, known as the Heads. There are good views from a lookout on the eastern head, and the privately owned Featherbed Nature Reserve on the western head.

The best way to appreciate the lagoon is to take a cruise. The **Featherbed Company** (☎ 044-382 1697; www.featherbed.co.za; Waterfront) has several vessels, including the **John Benn** (adult/child R120/50; departs 12.30pm & 5pm in winter, 6pm in summer) that takes you to Featherbed Nature Reserve.

Township Tours & Homestays

Sprawling across the hills above Knysna is the township of Concordia, best visited on a two-hour tour (R250 to R300) run by operators including **Eco Afrika Tours** (☎ 082 925 0716; 9.30am & 2pm). Knysna's townships have a different look from others in South Africa: homes are built mostly with timber from the nearby forests. The tour takes you through the usual township sites but then add a twist. You'll also get to visit the Grass Routes neighbourhood, the country's largest community of Rastafarians.

If you want to stay overnight in either the Rastafarian community or in the township (R180 to R220), contact Knysna Tourism.

Other Activities

Walking or cycling in the forests around the town is delightful; visit Knysna Tourism or **Knysna Cycleworx** (☎ 044-382 5153; 13 Nelson St; per day R125) for more information.

There are plenty of other activities on offer in the area; start by making inquiries at **Hippo Dive Campus** (☎ 044-384 0831; the Heads). Among the possibilities are boat- and shore-entry scuba dives (R100 to R250) to some of South Africa's best spots. Snorkelling equipment can be rented for R150.

Adventure Centre (☎ 083-260 7198; Highfields Backpackers, 2 Graham St) offers activities including canoe safaris and kloofing.

Knysna Forest Tours (☎ 044-382 6130; Remembrance Ave) offers a range of tours by foot, mountain bike and canoe (and combinations thereof) from R350.

SLEEPING

Budget

Highfield Backpackers (☎ 044-382 6266; www.highfieldsbackpackers.co.za; 2 Graham St; dm R90, d with shared bathroom from R250;) In a spacious old house, Highfield feels like a B&B with its focus on doubles with hardwood floors. A range of activities is on offer.

Island Vibe (☎ 044-382 1728; www.islandvibe.co.za; 67 Main St; dm R100, r with shared bathroom R270, s/d R224/320;) More laid-back than its party-orientated sibling in Jeffrey's Bay, this central backpackers has a bar and a great view from the deck. Bikes can be rented for R50 per day.

Knysna Backpackers (☎ 044-382 2554; www.knysnabackpackers.co.za; 42 Queen St; dm R100, r with shared bathroom R280, d R350) You'll find mainly dorm beds at this large, spruce Victorian house on the hill a few blocks up from the main street. It's quieter and more relaxing than other places.

Midrange

Wayside Inn (☎ 044-382 6011; www.waysideinn.co.za; Pledge Sq; s/d incl breakfast R550/780;) Intimate and well managed, the Wayside Inn has nicely decorated rooms and is in a handy location just off Main St by the cinema.

Inyathi Guest Lodge (☎ 044-382 7768; www.inyathi-sa.com; 52 Main St; d incl breakfast R620) This is Knysna's most imaginatively designed guest house, with accommodation in uniquely decorated timber lodges – some with Victorian bathtubs, others with stained-glass windows.

Graywood Hotel (☎ 044-382 5850; www.graywood.co.za; cnr Gray & Trotter Sts; s/d incl breakfast R750/1190;) Still with its locomotive theme, this hotel has been refurbished and is much improved. It now has decent-sized rooms, set around a leafy pool area. There's disabled access.

Top End

Belvidere Manor (☎ 044-387 1055; www.belvidere.co.za; Belvidere Estate; s/d incl breakfast from R785/1310;) An impressive collection of luxury guest cottages, some with lagoon views, in a garden setting with a gorgeous pool and gazebo. There is also a restaurant (mains R65 to R100) serving regional dishes.

Phantom Forest Eco-Reserve (☎ 044-386 0046; www.phantomforest.com; s/d incl breakfast from R2050/3100;) This 137-hectare private ecoreserve, 7km west of Knysna, overlooks the lagoon and comprises 14 cleverly designed and elegantly decorated tree houses built with sustainable materials. An award-winning six-course African dinner (R250) is served in the Forest Boma from 7pm daily; booking is essential.

EATING

Red Square (☎ 044-382 4052; Pledge Sq, Main St; mains R45-119) This small restaurant with a romantic, old-fashioned feel, has an interesting menu and wines rated by the *John Platter Wine Guide*.

Knysna Oyster Company (☎ 044-382 6941; Thesen Island; 6 oysters from R46, mains R80; ⏰ tours 10am-4.30pm Mon-Sat) This company, opened in 1949, grows its own oysters out in the lagoon; you can take a tour of the processing plant and have a tasting of a cultivated and wild oyster with a glass of wine for R45 at its restaurant afterwards.

Oystercatcher (☎ 044-382 9995; Remembrance Ave; mains R50) Overlooking the fishermen on the pier, this little blue shack serves farmed oysters and other light dishes in a waterside setting.

34 South (☎ 044-382 7331; Waterfront; mains R50-100; ⏰ breakfast, lunch & dinner) With outdoor tables overlooking the yachts and a cheaper takeaway counter at the rear, this food palace has deli and sushi sections heaving with goodies from lavish salads to seafood pâtés.

Caffé Mario (☎ 044-382 7250; Waterfront; mains R50-100; ⏰ breakfast, lunch & dinner) Italianate, deservedly popular Caffé Mario is, like 34 South, a superb lunch option in the Knysna Quays centre.

Crab's Creek (☎ 044-386 0011; 29 Belvidere Rd; mains R70; ⏰ breakfast, lunch & dinner) This is a favourite local watering hole, in a chilled-out setting right on the lagoon, off the N2. There's a buffet lunch (R65) on Sunday and daily specials. Children will enjoy the sandpit and climbing frames.

GETTING THERE & AWAY

Bus

Translux (☎ 021-449 3333; www.translux.co.za), and **Intercape** (☎ 0861-287 287; www.intercape.co.za) stop at the old train station at the Waterfront. **Greyhound** (☎ 021-505 6363; www.greyhound.co.za) stops at the **Engen petrol station** (Main St); Baz Bus will drop you where you want. For travel between nearby towns on the Garden Route, you're better looking for a minibus taxi than travelling with the major bus lines, which are expensive on short sectors.

Intercape destinations include George (R124, one hour), Mossel Bay (R233, two hours), Port Elizabeth (R228, four hours), Cape Town (R295, eight hours) and Jo'burg (R760, 17½ hours); these services depart daily at least.

Minibus Taxi

The main minibus taxi stop is at the Shell petrol station near the tourist office. Routes include Plettenberg Bay (R20, 30 minutes, daily) and Cape Town (R150, 7½ hours, daily).

Plettenberg Bay

☎ 044 / pop 34,000

Plettenberg Bay, or 'Plett' as it's more commonly known, is a resort town through and through, with mountains, white sand and crystal-blue water making it one of the country's top local tourist spots. As a result, things can get very busy and somewhat overpriced, but the town retains a relaxed, friendly atmosphere and has good-value hostels. The scenery to the east in particular is superb, with some of the best coast and indigenous forest in South Africa.

INFORMATION

Internet Café (☎ 044-533 6010; Melville's Corner Shopping Centre, Main St; per hr R30; ⏰ 8.30am-5pm Mon-Fri, 9am-2pm Sat)

Plett Tourism (☎ 044-533 4065; www.plettenberg bay.co.za; Melville's Corner Shopping Centre, Main St; ⏰ 8.30am-5pm Mon-Fri year-round, plus 9am-1pm Sat Apr-Oct)

ACTIVITIES

Apart from lounging on the beaches or hiking on the Robberg Peninsula (see opposite) there's a lot to do in Plett.

Boat trips to view dolphins and whales in season are available with **Ocean Blue** (☎ 044-533 5083; Central Beach) and **Ocean Safaris** (☎ 044-533 4963; Central Beach). Regular two-hour trips cost R400; close encounters with whales cost R650.

Equitrailing (☎ 044-533 0599; off Wittedrift Rd), located northwest of Plett via the N2, offers horse riding through the forest for R150 per hour. Those wanting to try surfing can take a lesson through the **International Surf School** (☎ 082-636 8431; 3½hr lesson incl equipment R350), which caters to all levels of surfers.

At the Crags, east of Knysna, you'll find three 'wildlife' parks in close proximity:

Birds of Eden (☎ 082-979 5683; adult/child R120/60; ⏰ 8am-5pm)

Elephant Sanctuary (☎ 044-534 8145; tours adult/child R295/150, rides adult/child over 8yr R670/350; ⏰ 8am-5pm)

Monkeyland (☎ 044-534 8906; adult/child R120/60; ⏰ 8am-5pm)

SLEEPING

Albergo for Backpackers (☎ 044-533 4434; www.al bergo.co.za; 8 Church St; campsites per person R75, dm R100, s/d with shared bathroom R300/350, s R350; 💻) Well run and friendly, Albergo encourages activities in and around Plett Bay and can organise just about anything. Try for the upstairs dorm with huge windows and stellar ocean views from the balcony.

Amakaya Backpackers (☎ 044-533 4010; www.amakaya.co.za; 1 Park Lane; dm from R100, s/tw with shared bathroom R125/250, d R500) The outside of this house is a bit severe, but its pretty blue rooms are clean and bright and the roof bar has mountain views.

our pick **Nothando Backpackers Hostel** (☎ 044-533 0220; www.nothando.com; 5 Wilder St; dm R120, r with shared bathroom R320, r R365;) This centrally located, five-star budget option, YHA-affiliated and award-winning, is owner-run and it shows. There's a great bar area with satellite TV, yet the large grounds are quiet and peaceful.

Periwinkle Guest Lodge (☎ 044-533 1345; www.periwinkle.co.za; 75 Beachy Head Dr; d incl breakfast from R2024) This white beachfront guest house in the suburbs west of the town centre offers individually decorated rooms, all with great views; you might even be able to spot whales and dolphins.

Plettenberg (☎ 044-533 2030; www.plettenberg.com; Church St; s/d from R2150/3600;) The heated pool here alone is worth the stay – it gives the illusion of ending in the sea. Built on a rocky headland with breathtaking vistas, this five-star palace is pure decadence, with fantastic rooms, a spa and a top-class restaurant.

EATING

Cranzgot's Pizzeria (☎ 044-533 1660; 9 Main St; mains R36-80) This family-friendly Plett stalwart serves mouth-watering pizzas, pastas and char-grilled steaks. You might have to wait for a table in the evenings, but there is also a bar.

Europa (☎ 044-533 6942; cnr Church & Main Sts; mains R42-99; breakfast, lunch & dinner) This large, snazzy resto-bar has a great deck. There's a good range of salads and interestingly filled bagels.

Miguel's (☎ 044-533 5056; Melville Corner Shopping Centre, Main St; mains R70-150; breakfast, lunch & dinner) A modern place with an eclectic menu, it's busy and smart with floor-to-ceiling windows and patio seating.

Lookout (☎ 044-533 1379; Lookout Rocks; mains R75; breakfast, lunch & dinner) With a deck overlooking the beach, this bar-restaurant is a great place for a simple meal and perhaps views of dolphins or whales.

GETTING THERE & AWAY

All the major buses stop at the Shell Ultra City on the N2; the Baz Bus will come into town. **Intercape** (☎ 0861-287 287; www.intercape.co.za) destinations from Plett include George (R228, two hours), Port Elizabeth (R228, 3½ hours) and Cape Town (R323, 9½ hours), all twice daily; Jo'burg (R684, 18 hours), Graaff-Reinet (R333, five hours) and Bloemfontein (R437, 12 hours), all daily.

If you're heading to Knysna you're better off taking a minibus taxi (R20, 30 minutes) – services leave from the corner of Kloof and High Sts.

Gecko (☎ 044-533 3705; www.geckotours.co.za) provides transfers; for example George airport to Plett is R530 for one passenger.

Robberg Nature & Marine Reserve

This **reserve** (☎ 021-659 3500; www.capenature.org.za; adult/child R25/12; 7am-5pm Feb-Nov, to 8pm Dec-Jan), 9km southeast of Plettenberg Bay, protects a 4km-long peninsula with a rugged coastline of cliffs and rocks. There are three circular walks of increasing difficulty, with rich intertidal marine life and coastal-dune *fynbos*, but it's very rocky and not for the unfit or anyone with knee problems! There are overnight shacks (R360) at the Point and the Fountain. To get here head along Robberg Rd, off Piesang Valley Rd, until you see the signs.

CENTRAL KAROO

The seemingly endless Karoo has a truly magical feel. It's a vast, semi-arid plateau (its name is a Khoisan word meaning 'land of thirst') that features stunning sunsets and starscapes. Inhabited for more than half a million years, the region is rich in archaeological sites, fossils, San paintings, wildlife and some 9000 plant species.

In this land of blazing summers and icy winters, life is slow. Off the main highways you can drive for hours without seeing another car. If you need a break from the crowds of the Garden Route, head over the magnificent Swartberg Pass to unwind in the quaint, peaceful villages and towns.

The region is often split into the Great Karoo (north) and Little Karoo (south), but it doesn't respect provincial boundaries; for our purposes it's the Central Karoo here, and Eastern Karoo in the Eastern Cape section.

Prince Albert & Around

☎ 023 / pop 2500

To many urban South Africans, Prince Albert – a charming village dating back to 1762 and dozing at the foot of the Swartberg Pass – represents an idyllic life in the Karoo. Despite being surrounded by very harsh country, Prince Albert is green and fertile (producing peaches, apricots, grapes and olives), thanks to the run-off from the mountain springs. There's an **Olive Festival** each May.

If you have your own transport and are short on time, you can easily visit on a day trip from Oudtshoorn (p440) or even from the coast.

Contact the helpful **tourist information office** (☎ 023-541 1366; www.patourism.co.za; Church St; 9am-5pm Mon-Fri, to 1pm Sat) for more information.

SIGHTS & ACTIVITIES

Prince Albert is a good base for exploring the Karoo and hiking on the more than 100km of trails in the **Swartberg Nature Reserve** (☎ 044-203 6325; www.capenature.org.za). Overnight walks have to be booked through **Cape Nature** (☎ 044-659 3500).

There's a good drive east to **Klaarstroom**, a tiny *dorp* (small town) along the foot of the mountains. The road runs along a valley, beneath the Groot Swartberg range, which is cut by dramatic gullies, clefts and waterfalls. On Rte 407 between Prince Albert (40km) and Klaarstroom (10km), **Remhoogte Hiking Trail** can be walked in about five hours, although there is a camping place on the trail.

SLEEPING & EATING

Swartberg Hotel (☎ 023-541 1332; www.swartberg.co.za; 70 Church St; s/d incl breakfast R380/553;) Swartberg is a three-star country inn; you can choose from thatched-roof huts or rooms in the main hotel. There are amazing gardens to relax in and the hotel organises activities locally. The attached coffee shop (mains R30 to R47) and Swartberg Arms (mains from R50) are popular with locals.

Karoo Lodge (☎ 023-541 1467; www.karoolodge.com; 66 Church St; s/d from R430/760;) This lodge is an owner-run guest house with a large garden and beautiful antique furniture. The hosts are knowledgeable about the area and the restaurant (mains R50 to R85) offers Karoo-Mediterranean fusions.

Prince Albert of Saxe-Coburg Lodge (☎ 023-541 1267; www.saxecoburg.co.za; 60 Church St; s/d from R600/800;) This place offers lovely garden rooms with satellite TV; its owners are a great source of information and offer guided hikes in the area.

Koggelmander Eatery & Art Gallery (☎ 023-541 1900; 61 Church St; mains R45-95; lunch Tue-Sun, dinner daily) From the art on the walls to the Karoo lamb and ostrich on its inventive menu, this eclectic venue specialises in everything local.

GETTING THERE & AWAY

Most people visit by driving over one of the area's passes from Oudtshoorn, or from the N1 between Cape Town and Jo'burg. **Shosholoza Meyl** (☎ 0860-008 888; www.shosholoza meyl.co.za) trains from Cape Town to Jo'burg stop at the Prince Albert Road station (sitting class only; R90, daily), 45km northwest of Prince Albert. Long-distance buses, which are more expensive than the train, also stop at Prince Albert Road. A taxi from there to Prince Albert costs R70, but most accommodation will pick you up.

Karoo National Park

Just 5km north of Beaufort West, the **Karoo National Park** (☎ 023-415 2828; www.sanparks.org; adult/child R76/38; 5am-10pm) covers 33,000 hectares of impressive Karoo landscapes and representative flora.

The park has 61 species of mammal, the most common of which are dassies (agile, rodentlike mammals, also called hyraxes) and bat-eared foxes. The antelope population is small but growing. Mountain zebras have been reintroduced, as has the odd black rhino. There are a great many reptiles and birds, including black eagles.

Facilities include a shop and restaurant. There are two short nature trails and an 11km day walk. There are also vehicle routes and day or overnight 4WD guided trails.

Accommodation is at pleasant **campsites** (per person R130) or in Cape Dutch–style **cottages** (d R640).

You cannot get out of your vehicle in the park, except at designated spots, so hiking the 10km from the gate to the rest camp is not an option. You'll need your own transport.

WEST COAST & SWARTLAND

If you're keen to do the Western Cape the way locals do it, head north of Cape Town and explore the windswept coastline, rugged mountains and undulating hills of the West Coast and Swartland, a peaceful and undeveloped paradise. You'll come across quiet whitewashed fishing villages, unspoilt beaches, a lagoon and wetlands teeming with birds, fascinating country towns and one of the best hiking regions in the country.

West Coast National Park

Encompassing the clear, blue waters of the Langebaan Lagoon and home to an enormous number of birds is the **West Coast National Park** (☎ 022-772 2144; www.sanparks.org; adult/child Aug-Oct R88/44, Nov-Jul R64/32; 🕑 7am-7.30pm Apr-Sep, 6am-8pm Oct-Mar). The park covers around 31,000 hectares and protects wetlands of international significance and important seabird breeding colonies. Wading birds flock here by the thousands in summer. The offshore islands are home to colonies of jackass penguins.

The park is famous for its wildflower display, which is usually between August and October. The park is only about 120km from Cape Town, 7km south of Langebaan. The return trip from Langebaan to the northern end of the Postberg section is more than 80km. The rainy season is between May and August.

The **Geelbek Visitor's Centre & Restaurant** (☎ 022-772 2134; West Coast National Park; mains R65-95; 🕑 breakfast & lunch) has a wide menu specialising in traditional fare. The information centre can help with accommodation options, which include the chalets at **Duinepos** (☎ 022-707 9900; duinepos@telkomsa.net; 2-/4-person chalets R550/700; ♿), two of which have disabled access and the romantic lagoon **houseboats** (☎ 021-689 9718; www.houseboating.co.za; 4-person boats R1200) moored at Kraalbaai.

Olifants River Valley

The scenery changes dramatically at the Piekenierskloof Pass; coming north on the N7 you suddenly overlook the intensively cultivated Olifants River Valley. On the valley floor are some acclaimed wineries and co-ops, which specialise in white wine. The eastern side is largely bounded by the spectacular Cederberg range. Citrusdal and Clanwilliam, to the southwest and northwest of Cederberg Wilderness Area, are the region's two main towns.

CEDERBERG WILDERNESS AREA

Bizarrely shaped, weathered sandstone formations, San rock art, craggy and rugged mountains and green valleys all make the desolate Cederberg a must-see. The peaks and valleys extend roughly north–south for 100km, between Citrusdal and Vanrhynsdorp. A good proportion is protected by the 83,000-hectare Cederberg Wilderness Area, which is administered by **Cape Nature** (☎ 022-931 2900; www.capenat ure.org.za).

Spring is the best time to see the wildflowers, although there's plenty of interest at other times of the year. There are small populations of baboons, rheboks, klipspringers and grysboks; and predators such as caracals, Cape foxes, honey badgers and the elusive leopard.

Orientation & Information

The Cederberg is divided into three excellent hiking areas of around 24,000 hectares, each with a network of trails. Two of the most popular hikes are to the Maltese Cross and the Wolfberg Cracks and Arch. Permits, required for all hikes, vary in price and are obtainable from Cape Nature in Cape Town, Algeria Forest Station (below) or **Dwarsrivier Farm** (☎ 027-482 2825). To be certain you'll get a permit, apply well in advance; the maximum group size is 12 and the minimum is two adults. Outside school holidays and weekends you may be able to get one on the spot, but phone before arriving to make sure. Maps are essential. There's no real season for walking; from May to the end of September expect rain and possibly snow. From December to April water is scarce.

There is a buffer zone of conserved land between the wilderness area and the farmland, and here more intrusive activities such as mountain biking are allowed.

The entrance to the Algeria campsite closes at 4.30pm (9pm on Friday). You won't be allowed in if you arrive late. You can only collect your permit (if you haven't already organised it) during office hours, so if you're arriving on Friday evening you'll need to make arrangements.

There are no eating places in the area so you will need to bring your own food.

Sleeping

See Citrusdal & Around and Clanwilliam & Around (both p452) for places to stay outside the Cederberg Wilderness Area.

Algeria (☎ 027-482 2404; 6-person campsites R95, d cottages R380) This is the main camping spot, with exceptional grounds in a beautiful, shaded site alongside the Rondegat River. There is a swimming hole, plus lovely spots to picnic and fully equipped stone cottages for noncampers.

The major drawback is guests have reported a chronic problem with baboons, which have even been sighted rummaging in tents. Rates do not include the park-entry fee. If Algeria is full, call Cape Nature for other camping areas. The site can become overcrowded at weekends and during school holidays.

Gecko Creek Wilderness Lodge (☎ 027-482 1300; www.geckocreek.com; tents/caves/cabins per person R160/190/220;) Highly recommended by readers, Gecko's ecofriendly ethos shows in the materials used in its solar-powered buildings. There are magnificent views, San art in caves on the ridge and hiking trails over 1000 hectares. Meals are available, and the owner can arrange flights over the Cederberg or West Coast. No visitors under 16 are allowed. Take the Algeria turn-off on the N7 and look out for the sign on the right.

Getting There & Away

The Cederberg range is about 200km from Cape Town, accessible from Citrusdal, Clanwilliam and the N7.

Public transport to Algeria is nonexistent. There are several roads to the campsite, all offering magnificent views. It's not signposted from Clanwilliam, about 45 minutes away by car, but you just follow the road above the dam to the south. Algeria *is* signposted from the N7 and it's only 20 minutes from the main road.

Citrusdal & Around

☎ 022 / pop 9000

The small town of Citrusdal is a good base for exploring the Cederberg. August to September is wildflower season, and the displays can be spectacular. This is also one of the best times for hiking.

The **tourism bureau** (☎ 022-921 3210; www.citrusdal.info; 39 Voortrekker St; 8.30am-5pm Mon-Fri, 9am-noon Sat) can help find accommodation and provides information on mountain biking and hiking trails.

There are several interesting and beautiful places to stay in the surrounding mountains, including the **Baths** (☎ 022-921 8026/7; www.thebaths.co.za; campsites per person R70, d from R450;), a hot-water-spring resort about 18km from Citrusdal, and the hard-to-reach but unforgettable camping spot of **Beaverlac** (☎ 022-931 2945; Beaverlac Nature Reserve; admission R5; campsites per person R30).

Intercape (☎ 0861-287 287; www.intercape.co.za) buses stop at the Sonop petrol station on the N7 outside town. Destinations include Cape Town (R352, three hours) and Springbok (R276, five hours).

Clanwilliam & Around

☎ 027 / pop 37,000

The adjacent dam and some adventurous dirt roads into the Cederberg make the compact town of Clanwilliam a popular weekend resort. Well-preserved examples of Cape Dutch architecture and trees line the main street.

The **information centre** (☎ 027-482 2024; 8.30am-5pm Mon-Fri, to 12.30pm Sat & Sun in season) is at the top end of the main street, across from the old *tronk* (jail in Afrikaans), which doubles as the town's museum.

A 120-year-old banyan tree looms over **Saint du Barrys Country Lodge** (☎ 027-482 1537; www.saintdubarrys.com; 13 Augsburg Dr; s/d incl breakfast R500/960;), a pleasant thatch-roofed guest house with a charming garden.

Buses that go through Citrusdal also serve Clanwilliam; it's about 45 minutes between the two. Minibus taxis running between Springbok (R140, five hours) and Cape Town (R120, three hours) stop at Clanwilliam post office.

NORTHERN CAPE

Welcome to South Africa's last great frontier. The republic's largest, least-populated and downright strangest province is a playground for off-the-grid explorers. A journey through this supersized land of half-human trees and singing sands, of big orange-ball sunsets and bright starry nights, is like stepping into the pages of a swashbuckling adventure.

Not content with straightforward national parks, two of its protected wildernesses sprawl across the country's northern borders. In the harsh but rewarding |Ai-|Ais/Richtersveld Transfrontier Park you can hike across surreal moonscapes, and in the Kgalagadi Transfrontier Park, search for black-maned lions in the remote and crimson outback.

Filled with unexpected twists and trivia (the Khoisan, Nama and Griqua are the world's oldest ethnic groups), the Northern Cape is also a talented magician, capable of pulling wildflower carpets, buckets of diamonds and even bottles of wine from her parched and barren desert hat. For a few weeks in spring, Namakwa's scorched lunar landscape transforms into a rainbow-coloured wildflower blanket.

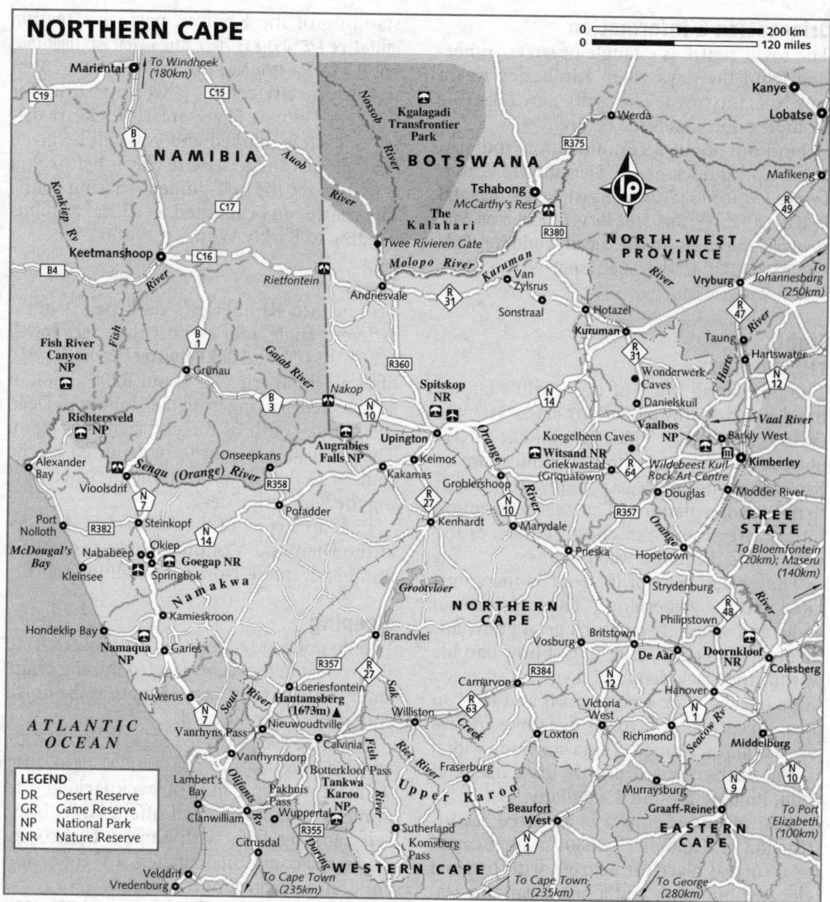

As in the Western Cape, coloured people, rather than black people, make up the majority of the province's population. Afrikaans is the most widely spoken language with more than 60% of the province speaking it, although English is understood everywhere.

KIMBERLEY

☎ 053 / pop 170,500

Whether you are drinking in saloons dating back to the raucous diamond days, visiting the world's largest hand-dug hole or spending the night in one of South Africa's oldest townships, Kimberley is a great place to lose yourself in the country's history for a few days.

It's nearly a century since mining stopped in the Northern Cape's capital, but Kimberley remains synonymous with diamonds. Step inside an atmospheric old pub, with a dark smoky interior, scarred wooden tables and last century's Castle Lager posters, and you'll be transported back in time to the rough-and-ready mining heyday. Spend a night in the period-perfect Victorian guest house inside the recently renovated Big Hole complex, and you'll wake up thinking it's the late 19th century. Or visit sights of ghastly mine-shaft accidents and gruesome murders on a ghost tour to really grasp the city's bawdy Wild West past.

The province's only real city is also home to fantastic galleries and museums, and lots of lovely hotels and guest houses to rest your head after an action-packed day.

Orientation & Information

The town centre is a tangle of streets inherited from the days when Kimberley was a rowdy shantytown. The spiffy new Big Hole Complex dominates the centre.

Find out about accommodation and area tours and guides at the **Diamantveld Visitors Centre** (☎ 053-832 7298; www.northerncape.co.za; 121 Bultfontein Rd; 8am-5pm Mon-Fri, 8am-noon Sat); browse the web at the **Small World Net Café** (☎ 053-831 3484; 42 Sidney St; per hr R30; 8am-5.30pm Mon-Fri, 9am-2pm Sat).

Sights

THE BIG HOLE

The hour-long tours of the world's largest hand-dug hole, the **Big Hole** (☎ 053-830 4417; West Circular Rd; admission R70; 8am-5pm, closed Dec 25 & Good Fri, tours on the hour), start with a 20-minute film on Kimberley's mining legacy, followed by a visit to the viewing platform. The steel contraption jutting over the 800m chasm enhances the view to the turquoise water below.

The coolest part of the tour is the simulated mining experience. Through special audio and visual effects you'll get a pretty authentic (but safe) picture of just how bad life was for the black diamond diggers. Get ready to be freaked – we won't ruin it and tell you how, except that it involves dynamite and we jumped and screamed. Tours conclude with a visit to the heavily guarded De Beers diamond vault, holding around 3500 diamonds.

Also on the premises is a partial reconstruction of Kimberley's 1880s mining camp. It's a surreal place for a stroll, with original relocated buildings and a hotel, bar and restaurant (see right).

GALESHEWE TOWNSHIP

One of South Africa's oldest townships, Galeshewe rates with Soweto as an important source of activists in the struggle against apartheid. Although poor and overcrowded, it is not particularly dangerous; if you have transport and go during the day you'll likely be met more with smiles than trouble. Alternatively, walking tours can be arranged through the Diamantveld Visitors Centre (above) or you can stay at Ekhaya Guesthouse (right).

WILDEBEEST KUIL ROCK ART TOURISM CENTRE

Built to help create jobs for poor local communities and promote a renewed understanding of the Khoisan past, this **tourism initiative** (☎ 053-833 7069; Barkly West Rd; adult/child R10/5; 9am-4pm Mon-Fri, 10am-4pm Sat), 10km west of the city centre, is worth visiting for the cause alone. There are 10 rock-art displays; each is marked and you will be given headphones and a cassette player before you start out on the self-guided walking tours. The centre can be reached on a local minibus heading to Barkly West.

Tours

To tap into Kimberley's dark past from a different angle, join a ghost tour. **Jaco Powell** (☎ 093-256 4795) and **Dirk Potgieter** (☎ 053-861 4983) offer 3½-hour trips for about R200 (book in advance), departing from the Honoured Dead Memorial, south of the city centre, at 6pm. The vault here is said to be haunted by the souls of 27 British soldiers who perished during the Kimberley siege.

Pick up a copy of the *Kimberley Meander* at the Diamond Visitors Centre; it details a number of interest-oriented walking tours.

Sleeping

You do not need to tour the Big Hole (left) to sleep or eat in the reconstructed mining camp; enter through the green side gate at the north end of West Circular Rd.

Gum Tree Lodge (☎ 053-832 8577; fax 831 5409; cnr Hull St & Bloemfontein Rd; dm from R100, s/d R120/240;) Attracting a mix of backpackers and families, this former jail offers large, basic self-catering flats with shared bathroom. There is a communal kitchen, TV room and children's playground.

Heerengracht Guesthouse (☎ 053-831 1531; www.kelesedi.co.za; 42 Heerengracht St, Royldene; r incl breakfast R400-1200;) This award-winning black-owned guest house has tasteful rooms with satellite TV and minibar on grassy grounds. Service is professional and the pool sparkling.

Ekhaya Guesthouse (☎ 053-874 3795; www.ekhaya.co.za; cnr Hulana & Montshiwa St, Galeshewe; r incl breakfast R720;) An award-winning boutique guest house in Galeshewe township, Ekhaya has modern *rondavels*, rooms done up like a corrugated-iron shack, and a restaurant serving traditional meals.

Australian Arms Guesthouse (☎ 053-830 4402; Big Hole Complex; r incl breakfast R800;) A surreal, living history experience. In original late-19th-century diamond rush buildings, rooms are perfectly Victorian down to the claw-foot tub, doorknobs and thick draperies. When you tire of watching satellite TV from your mahogany four-poster, walk out the door and travel back 100 years.

Eating

George & Dragon (☎ 053-833 2075; 187 Du Toitspan Rd; mains R30-60) This classy old-fashioned darkwood pub attracts a professional crowd, offering a multicourse Sunday lunch (R30) and two-for-one burger and pizza nights.

Star of the West Hotel (☎ 053-832 6463; North Circular Rd; mains R40-50; breakfast, lunch & dinner) Step back into Kimberley's mining heyday at this atmospheric city staple that serves up hearty pub grub.

Occidental Grill Bar (☎ 083 284 6225; Big Hole Complex; mains R40-65; lunch & dinner) Offering plenty of veggie options (we loved the stuffed feta and spinach pancakes) alongside pizza, pasta, meat and seafood, this picture-perfect Victorian-era restaurant is a treat.

Getting There & Away

AIR

You can fly to Kimberley from Jo'burg (one-way from R600, 1½ hours) on **SA Express** (☎ 011-978 9900; www.flysax.com). **SAAirlink** (☎ 053-838 3339; www.saairlink.co.za) has a direct service to Cape Town (one-way from R900, 1¾ hours).

Kimberley airport is about 7km south of the city centre. A taxi costs about R200.

BUS

Translux (☎ 011-774 3333; www.translux.co.za) is one of three companies that stop in Kimberley daily en route to Jo'burg/Pretoria (R170, seven hours) and Cape Town (R360 to R480, 12 hours).

Buses stop at the Shell Ultra City long-distance bus terminal on the N12, from where minibuses take you into town.

MINIBUS TAXI

The main minibus taxi area in Duncan St is around the Indian shopping centre in the city centre. Destinations from Kimberley include Bloemfontein (R60, 2½ hours), Kuruman (R85, two hours), Jo'burg (R130, seven hours), Upington (R85, four hours) and Cape Town (R145, 10 hours).

TRAIN

Kimberley is an important junction for tourist-class trains (see p581) travelling between Cape Town, Durban and Jo'burg. The Blue Train and Rovos Rail (see p582) stop here and tour the mine.

UPINGTON

☎ 054 / pop 53,000

On the banks of the Senqu (Orange) River, orderly and prosperous Upington is a good place to catch your breath at either end of a long Kalahari slog. Wide boulevards slightly cluttered with supermarkets and chain stores fill the centre of town, but on the side streets, lazy river views and endless rows of date palms create a calm and quiet atmosphere perfect for an afternoon stroll (if the heat is not too stifling).

The helpful **tourist office** (☎ 054-332 6046; greenkal@mweb.co.za; Schröder St; 8am-5pm Mon-Fri, 9am-noon Sat) is in the Kalahari Oranje Museum.

Tours

Upington's central location makes it a good place to organise a remote desert adventure. Reader-recommended **Kalahari Safaris** (☎ 054-332 5653; www.kalaharisafaris.co.za; 3 Oranje St) runs small-group trips to Kgalagadi Transfrontier Park (three days R5500), Augrabies Falls National Park and Witsand Nature Reserve.

Sakkie se Arkie (☎ 082 564 5447; www.arkie.co.za; Park St) offers two-hour sunset cruises in a wooden barge on the Senqu (Orange) River.

Sleeping & Eating

Die Eiland Holiday Resort (☎ 054-334 0286; tourism@kharahais.gov.za; campsites R100, r from R200;) The town's best budget option offers a range of huts and bungalows and shaded camping spots on tranquil grounds adjacent to the eastern bank of the river.

Affinity Guesthouse (☎ 054-331 2101; www.affinityguesthouse.co.za; 4 Budler St; s/d R380/480;) Right on the river, this place is great value for money. The rooms are small, but very comfortable with firm mattresses.

A Riviera Garden B&B (☎ 054-332 6554; 16 Budler St; s/d R400/590;) The gardens at this friendly lodge with two cosy rooms are a fairy-tale creation, and run all the way down to the river.

Le Must River Residence (☎ 054-432 3971; www.lemustupington.com; 14 Budler St; r from R980;) This five-star guest house has luxurious, African-themed rooms with antique furnishings and crisp white linens. Nearby, Le Must's three-star River Manor (rooms from R365) boasts the same professional service.

Le Must Restaurant (☎ 054-332 3971; 11 Schröder St; mains R75-125) Follow Nelson Mandela's lead and sample this renowned restaurant's mouth-watering Kalahari creations. Considering the professional service, sleek decor and phenomenal food, which fuses Cape Malay and Karoo cooking, the prices are low.

Getting There & Away

AIR

Upington's airport accommodates connecting flights from around the world. For domestic tickets from Jo'burg or Cape Town, book through **SAAirlink** (☎ 011-961 1700; www.saairl ink.co.za).

BUS

For tickets go to the **Intercape office** (☎ 054-332 6091; www.intercape.co.za; Lutz St). Buses run to Jo'burg and Pretoria (R360, 10 hours, daily), Windhoek, Namibia (R350, 12 hours, four times weekly) and Cape Town (R320, 10½ hours, four times weekly).

CAR RENTAL

There's an agent for **Avis** (☎ 054-332 4746; www.avis.co.za) at Upington airport, which rents 4WDs (about R1000 per day) and compact cars (about R450). Rates are generally cheaper in Jo'burg or Cape Town, or through an online consolidator.

MINIBUS TAXI

You'll find minibus taxis near the Checkers supermarket near the corner of Mark and Basson Sts. Daily services from Upington include Jo'burg (R230, 10 hours), Cape Town (R220, 10 hours) and Windhoek (R240, 10 hours).

VIP Taxis (☎ 027-851 8780) operates a weekday taxi service between Upington and Port Nolloth (R140) via Springbok, departing at 8am.

KGALAGADI TRANSFRONTIER PARK

A visit to the otherworldly **Kgalagadi Transfrontier Park** (☎ 054-561 0021; www.sanparks.org; adult/child R140/70), in your own vehicle or on a tour, is more than worth the effort it takes to reach Africa's first multinational park. The scenery is phenomenal in this land of harsh extremes and frequent droughts, where shifting red-and-white sands meet thorn trees and dry riverbeds. Even the drive in, a seemingly endless jostle down dusty crimson roads, is an invigorating trip, evoking images of the grand African safaris of lore. The romance only intensifies inside the 9591-sq-km South African section of the park, thanks to orange-ball sunsets, black-velvet skies studded with millions of twinkling stars, and predators from prides of black-maned lions to packs of howling spotted hyenas.

Proclaimed a national park in 1999, Kgalagadi is the result of a merger between the former Kalahari-Gemsbok National Park in South Africa and the Mabuasehube-Gemsbok National Park in Botswana, forming one of Africa's largest protected wilderness areas.

Although the countryside is described as semidesert, it is richer than it appears and supports large populations of birds, reptiles,

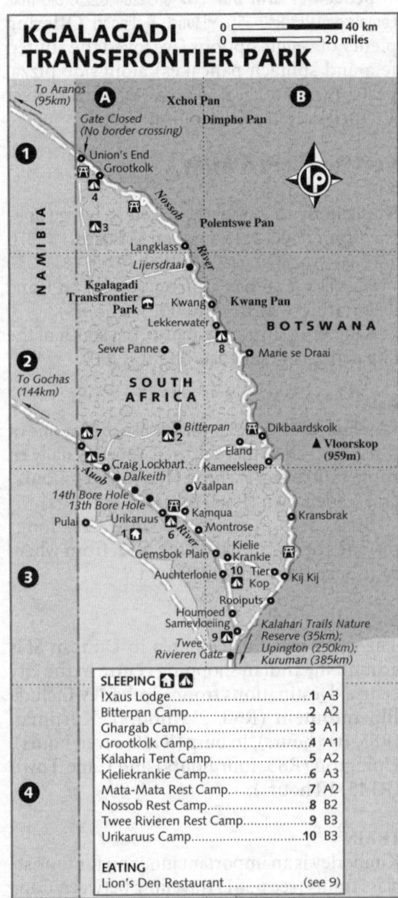

rodents, small mammals and antelopes. These in turn support more than 1100 predators. Most of the animals are remarkably tolerant of cars, allowing you to get extremely close.

Orientation & Information

Visitors are restricted to four gravel-sand roads, two running up the beds of the Nassob and Auob Rivers. Make sure to take one of the roads linking the rivers for unobstructed views of the empty expanses of the Kalahari. Visitors must remain in their cars, except at a small number of designated picnic spots.

The best time to visit is in June and July when the days are coolest (below freezing at night) and the animals have been drawn to the bores along the dry river beds. September to October is the wet season and if it does rain, many of the animals scatter out across the plain to take advantage of the fresh pastures.

All the rest camps have shops selling basic groceries, soft drinks and alcohol, open from 7am until 30 minutes after the gates close. Petrol and diesel are available at each camp; Twee Rivieren (right) also has public phones, a pub, a swimming pool and a good information centre.

The gate opening hours generally follow the rising and setting sun, opening between 5.30am and 7.30am and shutting between 6pm and 7pm.

The minimum travelling time from the entrance gate at Twee Rivieren to Nossob rest camp is 3½ hours; to Mata-Mata Rest Camp it's 2½ hours. No driving is permitted after dark.

Venturing into the Botswana side of the park is possible on a 4WD trail; make arrangements with the **Botswana Department of Wildlife & National Parks** (☎ 09-267 580 774; Gabarone). Visitors can enter Namibia through the Mata-Mata gate border crossing, but you need to be booked into the Mata-Mata Rest Camp to do so.

Sights

WILDLIFE

More than 215 species of bird have been spotted in the park, including the sociable weaver and the pygmy falcon. There are 19 predator species, including black-maned Kalahari lions, cheetahs, leopards and hyenas; plus antelopes, including the large, striking gemsbok, an emblem of the park, and the hyperactive little suricate (meerkat).

Tours

Early morning, sunset and night **wildlife drives** (adult/child R110/55) depart from Twee Rivieren, Nossob, Mata-Mata and Kalahari Tented Camp. You have a better chance of spotting animals, especially big cats, when accompanied by a ranger. At least four people are needed for a tour to depart.

See also p455.

Sleeping & Eating

Inside the park are three rest camps and seven luxury wilderness camps, which fill up during the December/January school holidays and can be booked through **SAN Parks** (☎ 012-428 9111; www.sanpa rks.org).

All of the rest camps have **campsites** (per 2 people R130, extra person R42) without electricity and with shared ablutions facilities. The camps also have a range of huts, bungalows and cottages equipped with bedding, towels, cooking and eating utensils, and with kitchens and bathrooms.

Twee Rivieren Rest Camp (cottages R600-1000;), the closest camp to the park's entrance and the one with the most facilities, is the only rest camp with a swimming pool and air-con; hence the higher-than-average rates.

The wilderness camps give you the opportunity to really get off the beaten path. None is fenced, which means animals are able to wander in at will, although a ranger is on duty at all times. Make sure to stock up on petrol and drinking water before visiting. The focus at **!Xaus Lodge** (☎ 021-701 7860; www .xauslodge.co.za; all-inclusive rates from R2250;), which is owned by the Khomani San (Bushmen) and Mier people, is on interaction, from wildlife walks to campfire chats where locals share secrets of the night sky and natural medicine. Blending beautifully into the red-sand environs and overlooking an enormous salt pan, accommodation is in creatively decorated chalets with decks facing a water hole.

Outside the park are a few interesting options on the road to Twee Rivieren gate, including the **Kalahari Trails Nature Reserve** (☎ 054-902 906, ask for 91634; www.kalahari-trails.co.za; campsites R100, r from R400).

The park's only restaurant, **Lion's Den Restaurant** (Twee Rivieren; breakfast/dinner from R50/80; 7.30-9am & 6.30-9pm), also has a snack bar selling takeaways.

SOUTH AFRICA

Getting There & Away

It's a solid, 385km, six-hour drive from Kuruman to Twee Rivieren. The drive from Upington to Twee Rivieren gate is 250km with about 60km on dirt roads.

We've had several letters from travellers who wrecked their cars on this trip. Petrol is not available between Upington and Twee Rivieren.

It's important to carry water, as you may have to wait a while for help if you break down.

UPINGTON TO NAMAKWA

The N14 southwest of Upington follows the course of the Senqu (Orange) River, passing through an area that produces 10% of the country's wines. The first towns you come to are palm-tree-lined **Keimos** and, surrounded by cotton fields and vineyards, **Kakamas**.

In Kakamas, the **Kalahari Gateway Hotel** (☎ 054-431 0838; www.kalaharigateway.co.za; Main Rd; r from R350;) has massive rooms and a zebra-themed **bar-restaurant** (mains from R40, dinner).

Augrabies Falls National Park

☎ 054

The Khoisan people called it 'Aukoerbis', meaning place of great noise. And when the waterfall for which this **park** (☎ 054-452 9200; www.sanparks.org; adult/child R76/38; dawn-dusk) is named is fat with rainy season run-off, its thunderous roar is nothing short of spectacular. You won't find any big predators here, but this is the world's sixth-tallest waterfall. The park, set in a rocky mosaic around an 18km ravine through which the Senqu (Orange) River flows, has a harsh climate and fascinating desert-riverine ecosystems.

The three-hour, 9km **Dassie Trail** is well worth doing, particularly if your time is short. It involves clambering over rocks through some magical landscape. The popular three-day, 37km **Klipspringer Hiking Trail** (R140; Apr–mid-Oct) runs along the southern bank of the Senqu (Orange) River and the **Gariep 3-in-1 Route** (adult/child R180/90) includes canoeing, walking and mountain biking.

Accommodation in the park can be booked through **SAN Parks** (☎ 012-428 9111; www.sanparks.org); options include **campsites** (per 2 people R130) and **chalets** (from R525).

The friendly **Kalahari Backpackers-Augrabies Falls** (☎ 054-451 0177; www.kalahari.co.za; Rte 359; r from R100) has a great reed bar serving ice-cold beer and is about 10km before the park on the road from Kakamas.

The park is 38km northwest of Kakamas and 120km from Upington.

NAMAKWA

In the Northern Cape's rugged northwestern corner the roads stretch on forever, the stars seem bigger and brighter than anywhere else and you can tumble off the map without anyone noticing. From exploring the misty shipwrecked diamond coastline on the country's far western edge to four-wheeling through an otherworldly mountain desert in remote |Ai-|Ais/Richtersveld Transfrontier Park, experiences pile up fast here. Every spring, Namakwa's sunbaked desert sprouts a multihued wildflower blanket so spectacular you'll leave believing miracles do happen.

Springbok

☎ 027 / pop 15,000

Springbok sits in a valley surrounded by harsh rocky hills that explode with colour in flower season. When the flowers aren't blooming, there's little to see or do, although the town's remoteness, desolate landscape and 300-plus days of sunshine are alluring. After dark, with little light pollution, the stars are brilliantly bright and nights are dramatically quiet and still.

From an edgy frontier town, Springbok has been transformed into a busy service centre for the copper and diamond mines in the region. Visit the **tourism information office** (☎ 027-718 2985; Voortrekker St; 7.30am-4.15pm Mon-Fri, 9am-noon Sat & Sun) for flower-season info.

SLEEPING

Cat Nap Accommodation (☎ 027-718 1905; Voortrekker St; dm R80, r from R400;) The walls of the spacious old house are adorned with nature photos and original art, and rooms are cosy African-themed affairs. Backpackers can shack up in dorm beds in the barn.

Mountain View Guest House (☎ 027-712 1438; 2 Overberg Ave; www.mountview.co.za; d incl breakfast from R550;) Check out the mountain views from the attractive pool; rooms are four-star elegant.

Annie's Cottage (☎ 027-712 1451; annie@springbokinfo.com; 4 King St; r incl breakfast R600-1600;) Each of the 10 rooms in this beautifully restored four-star guest house is decorated differently. The pool and garden area is quaint with fountains, trees, flowers and benches.

Old Mill Lodge (☎ 027-718 1705; www.oldmilllodge.com; 69 Van Riebeeck St; d incl breakfast from R610;) Pleasantly situated in a peaceful garden up against the rocks on a quiet side street; the rooms here are plush and done up with modern art.

EATING

Titbits Pizza Restaurant (☎ 027-718 1455; cnr Namaqua & Voortrekker Sts; mains R25-50; breakfast, lunch & dinner) Despite the big-breasted mural, Titbits has a certain titillating atmosphere with loads of tasty options, including sandwiches, steak, pasta, pizzas and breakfasts.

Godfather Restaurant (☎ 027-718 1877; Voortrekker St; mains R25-50) This simple, small place has a large menu, featuring everything from meat to sandwiches, and a fun bar.

Tauren Steak Ranch (☎ 027-718 21900; 2 Hospital St; mains from R50; dinner) Meat lovers rejoice, Tauren's serves steaks weighing 1kg and pizzas topped with biltong. The salad bar gets good reviews.

GETTING THERE & AWAY

Intercape (☎ 086-128 7287; www.intercape.co.za) has buses to Cape Town (R350, 7½ hours) and Windhoek, Namibia (R450, 12 hours) that depart four times weekly from opposite the Springbok Lodge near the *kopje* (small hill).

For 4WD hire, contact Cat Nap Accommodation or the tourism information office. Rental starts at about R1000 per day; online consolidators usually offer cheaper rates.

Minibus taxis depart from the rank opposite the First National Bank near the *kopje*. Destinations include Cape Town (R250, five hours, daily), Upington (R100, 3½ hours) and Port Nolloth (R80, 2½ hours, five times weekly).

VIP Taxis (p456) goes to Upington and Port Nolloth.

Goegap Nature Reserve

This 7000-hectare semidesert **nature reserve** (☎ 027-712 1880; admission R10; 7.45am-4.15pm) is famous for its extraordinary display of spring flowers and a nursery of 200 amazing Karoo and Namakwa succulents at the **Hester Malan Wildflower Garden**.

There are a few driving routes around the reserve, but you'll see more on one of the circular walks (4km, 5.5km and 7km). There are two **mountain-biking routes** (14km and 20km), which are particularly memorable during flower season. Bring your own bike.

Vioolsdrif

This town is at the 24-hour border crossing with Namibia on the N7, 677km north of Cape Town. The 65km drive from Steinkopf, with its views of the Senqu (Orange) River carving its way through desolate mountains, is spectacular.

Kamieskroon & Around

☎ 027

Out amid the tumbleweed and scrub brush, forgotten-looking Kamieskroon sits in the heart of wild country. Craggy mountains and boulder-strewn hills surround the remote and desolate place. It's a great spot to get away from it all and to explore the area, especially in flower season.

About 18km southwest of Kamieskroon is the **Namaqua National Park** (☎ 027-672 1948; www.sanparks.org; admission R35; 8am-5pm), where the shrubland and old wheat fields burst into flower in spring. Their clarity and prevalence often surpass all other areas in the region, making this one of the best places to photograph the flowers (Kamieskroon Hotel runs photographic workshops).

The new Skilkop Rest Camp offers chalet digs for travellers with a disability, starting at R350. Alternatively, just off the N7 (follow the signs), you'll find the comfortable and popular **Kamieskroon Hotel** (☎ 027-672 1614; www.kamieskroonhotel.com; r incl breakfast R220-350;), which offers dinner for R80.

Kamieskroon is 80km south of Springbok on the N7.

EASTERN CAPE

It may be the poorest of South Africa's nine provinces, but the Eastern Cape has the country's widest range of topography, climate, flora and fauna. Between the wild northeastern highlands and the lush Tsitsikamma National Park in the southwest, you'll find the spectacular semi-arid Karoo, seriously good surfing and hiking along the Wild Coast, charming towns such as Graaff-Reinet and Grahamstown and some excellent wildlife viewing.

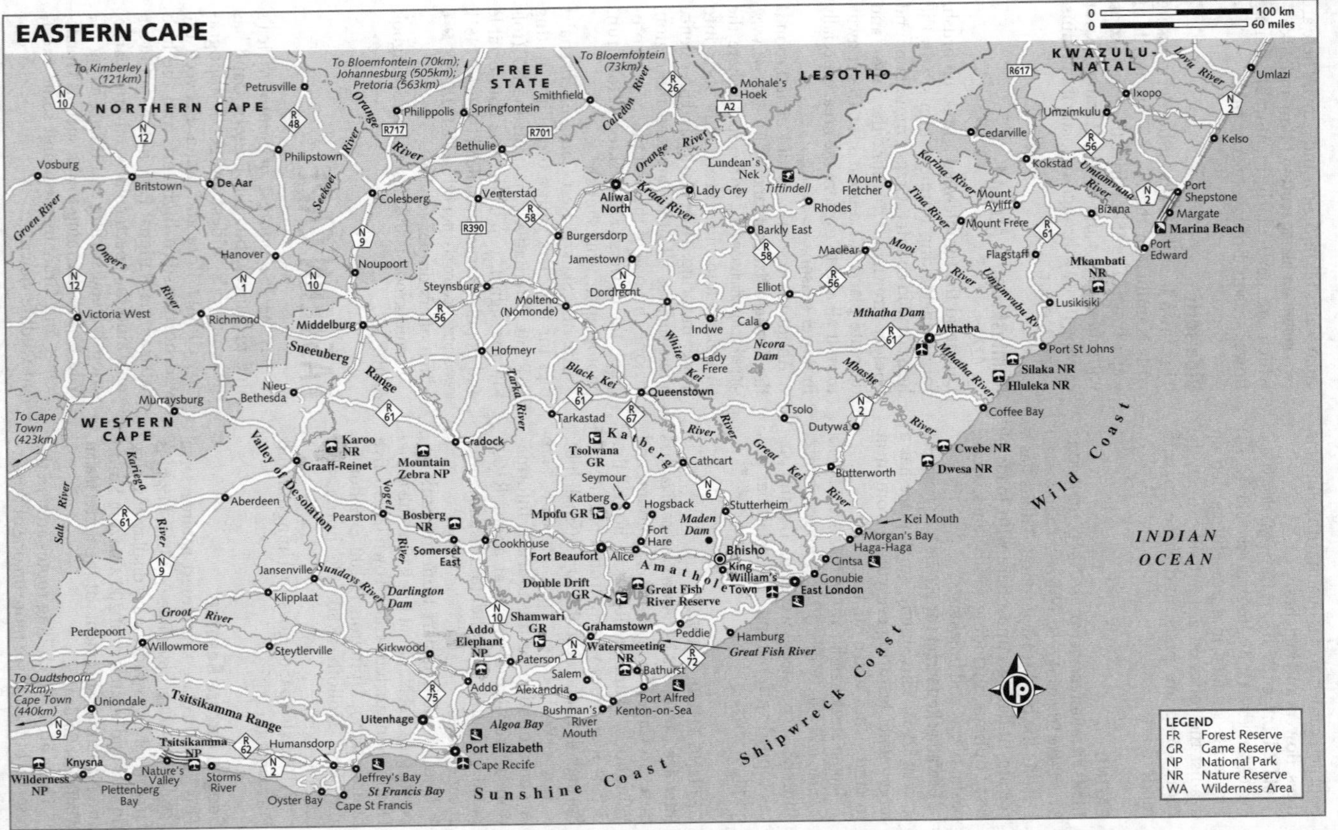
EASTERN CAPE
0 100 km
0 60 miles
LEGEND
FR Forest Reserve
GR Game Reserve
NP National Park
NR Nature Reserve
WA Wilderness Area
INDIAN OCEAN
Wild Coast
Shipwreck Coast
Sunshine Coast
KWAZULU-NATAL
LESOTHO
FREE STATE
NORTHERN CAPE
WESTERN CAPE
To Kimberley (121km)
To Bloemfontein (70km); Johannesburg (505km); Pretoria (563km)
To Bloemfontein (73km)
To Cape Town (423km)
To Oudtshoorn (77km); Cape Town (440km)
Umlazi
Kelso
Port Shepstone
Margate
Marina Beach
Port Edward
Ixopo
Umzimkulu
Bizana
Kokstad
Cedarville
Mount Ayliff
Mount Frere
Flagstaff
Lusikisiki
Mkambati NR
Port St Johns
Silaka NR
Hluleka NR
Coffee Bay
Mthatha
Mthatha Dam
Mthatha River
Cwebe NR
Dwesa NR
Kei Mouth
Morgan's Bay
Haga-Haga
Cintsa
Gonubie
East London
Butterworth
Dutywa
Tsolo
Mount Fletcher
Maclear
Rhodes
Tiffindell
Barkly East
Elliot
Cala
Ncora Dam
Mohale's Hoek
Lundean's Nek
Lady Grey
Indwe
Lady Frere
Queenstown
Cathcart
Stutterheim
Bhisho
King William's Town
Maden Dam
Hogsback
Fort Hare
Alice
Amathole
Great Fish River Reserve
Hamburg
Great Fish River
Peddie
Port Alfred
Bathurst
Kenton-on-Sea
Watersmeeting NR
Grahamstown
Double Drift GR
Fort Beaufort
Katberg
Seymour
Tsolwana GR
Mpofu GR
Katberg
Tarkastad
Dordrecht
Jamestown
Burgersdorp
Aliwal North
Kraai River
Orange River
Caledon River
Smithfield
Springfontein
Bethulie
Venterstad
Molteno (Nomonde)
Hofmeyr
Tarka River
Cradock
Cookhouse
Somerset East
Bosberg NR
Mountain Zebra NP
Shamwari GR
Paterson
Salem
Alexandria
Bushman's River Mouth
Addo Elephant NP
Addo
Algoa Bay
Port Elizabeth
Cape Recife
Uitenhage
Kirkwood
Darlington Dam
Sundays River
Jeffrey's Bay
St Francis Bay
Cape St Francis
Humansdorp
Oyster Bay
Steytlerville
Klipplaat
Jansenville
Pearston
Vogel River
Karoo NR
Graaff-Reinet
Valley of Desolation
Aberdeen
Nieu Bethesda
Sneeuberg Range
Middelburg
Steynsburg
Noupoort
Colesberg
Philippolis
Philipstown
Petrusville
Seekoei River
De Aar
Hanover
Richmond
Britstown
Murraysburg
Victoria West
Ongers River
Kariega River
Vosburg
Groen River
Salt River
Willowmore
Groot River
Perdepoort
Uniondale
Tsitsikamma Range
Tsitsikamma NP
Storms River
Nature's Valley
Plettenberg Bay
Knysna
Wilderness NP
Lovu River
Umtamvuna River
Umzimvubu Rv
Karina River
Tina River
Mooi River
Mbashe River
Great Kei River
White Kei
Black Kei
R617
R56
R61
R58
R26
A2
R701
R390
R717
R48
R67
R72
R75
R62
N2
N6
N9
N10
N12
N1

WORTH THE TRIP

A seemingly barren wilderness of lava rocks and sandy moonscapes studded with semiprecious stones, the **|Ai-|Ais/Richtersveld Transfrontier Park** (☎ 027-831 1506; www.sanparks.org; adult/child R96/48; 7am-6pm) is South Africa's final wild frontier. Straddling the Namibian border (where it's also called Fish River Canyon National Park), it's most beautiful during the spring flower season, when the park turns into a technicolour wonderland. The three hiking trails (42km, 23km and 15km) are challenging but spectacular, traversing jagged peaks, grotesque rock formations, deep ravines and gorges.

Sendelingsdrift rest camp (2-person campsites R130, chalets from R475;) is surprisingly luxurious for such a remote area. There are also two remote **wilderness camps** (chalets or cabins R480), where you must bring your own water, and four **camping areas** (per 2 people R130). All should be booked in advance with **SAN Parks** (☎ 012-428 9111; www.sanparks.org).

Most of the park is virtually inaccessible without a properly equipped 4WD vehicle and maybe a local guide. Tours can be organised at Cat Nap Accommodation in Springbok (p458).

The Eastern Cape provides an insight into Xhosa culture, particularly in Nelson Mandela's birthplace, the former Transkei apartheid-era 'homeland' that's now known as the Wild Coast. Brightly painted, round, thatch-roofed huts dot the hills that roll inland from the region's rugged coastline.

The northeastern highlands, tucked under the southern edge of Lesotho and south of the Senqu (Orange) River, are relatively unexplored. Little-known valleys, interesting small towns and magnificent mountains (you can even go skiing) lie almost untouched by travellers.

History

In the 19th century, Trekboers (nomadic pastoralists descended from the Dutch) clashed with the Xhosa along the Great Kei River, and later with the British in a series of guerrilla wars. Intrepid settlers arrived in the 1820s to farm the land, establishing towns and cities including Port Elizabeth and East London. More recently the province has been a wellspring of resistance heroes including Nelson Mandela, Steve Biko, Robert Mangaliso Sobukwe, Chris Hani, Oliver Tambo and Thabo Mbeki.

Xhosa culture dominates the former apartheid 'homelands' of Transkei (the Wild Coast) and Ciskei, nominally independent republics that were used as a dumping ground for economically unviable populations.

NATURE'S VALLEY TO PORT ELIZABETH

☎ 044

Nature's Valley is a small village nestled in yellowwood forest next to a magnificent beach in the west of Tsitsikamma National Park. This is where the Otter Trail ends and the Tsitsikamma Trail begins (see p462), but if you don't want to walk for that long, there are plenty of shorter hikes possible in the area.

A popular place to stay is **Nature's Valley Rest Camp** (☎ 044-531 6700, bookings 012-428 9111; www.sanparks.org; 1-2 person campsites R125, forest huts d R275), on the edge of a river east of town.

There's no public transport to Nature's Valley, although the Baz Bus stops at the village.

Tsitsikamma National Park Area

This **park** (adult/child R80/40) protects 80km of coast between Plettenberg Bay and Humansdorp, including a Marine Protected Area 5km out to sea. Located at the foot of the Tsitsikamma Range and cut by rivers that have carved deep ravines into the ancient forests, it's a spectacular area to walk through.

Elusive Cape clawless otters, after which the Otter Trail is named, inhabit this park; there are also baboons, monkeys and small antelopes. Bird life is plentiful.

Several short day walks give you a taste of the coastline. The waterfall circuit (four hours) on the first part of the Otter Trail is recommended; the suspension bridge over the river mouth is closed due to fire damage, but should be open by the time you read this.

ORIENTATION & INFORMATION

The main information centre for the national park is Storms River Mouth Rest Camp (p462), 68km from Plettenberg Bay, 99km from Humansdorp and 8km from the N2. The park gate is 6km from the N2. It's 2km from the gate to the main camp, which is open 24 hours. You can also pay park entrance fees and get information at Nature's Valley Rest Camp (see p461).

OTTER, TSITSIKAMMA & DOLPHIN TRAILS

The 42km **Otter Trail** (☎ 012-426 5111; www.sanparks.org; per person R560) is one of the country's most acclaimed hikes, hugging the coastline from Storms River Mouth to Nature's Valley. The walk, which lasts five days and four nights, involves fording a number of rivers and gives access to some superb stretches of coast. A good level of fitness is required.

The trail is usually booked up one year ahead, but there are often cancellations so it's always worth trying. Single hikers are not permitted.

Accommodation is in six-bed rest huts with mattresses but without running water. Camping is not allowed.

The 60km **Tsitsikamma Trail** (☎ 042-281 1712; ivy@cyberperk.co.za; per day R80) commences at Nature's Valley and ends at Storms River, taking you inland through the forests and mountains. This hike takes up to six days and five nights, but you can opt for two, three, four or five days. Porterage is available as well as guided day walks and mountain-bike trails.

The **Dolphin Trail** (☎ 012-428 9111; www.dolphintrail.co.za; per person R3300) is ideal for hikers who don't want to carry heavy equipment or sleep in huts. Accommodation on this three-day, two-night hike, which runs from Storms River Mouth to Forest Fern, is in comfortable hotels, and luggage is carried on vehicles. The price includes accommodation and meals, guides and a boat trip into the Storms River Gorge on the way back. Book at least a year in advance.

SLEEPING

Storms River Mouth Rest Camp (☎ 012-428 9111; www.sanparks.org; campsites/forest huts/family cottages R195/295/950) As well as a small shop and a restaurant (mains R55 to R135; open breakfast, lunch and dinner), the main camp offers forest huts, chalets, cottages and 'oceanettes'. All except the forest huts are equipped with kitchens, bedding and bathrooms.

Tsitsikamma Falls Adventure Park (☎ 042-280 3770; www.tsitsikammaadventure.co.za; Witelsbos; per person incl breakfast from R220) This family-run guest house, near a beautiful waterfall about halfway between Nature's Valley and Jeffrey's Bay, offers a range of activities.

Misty Mountain Reserve (☎ 042-280 3699; www.misty-sa.co.za; chalets per person R450, 4-person cottage R1200) A great place to stay if hiking the Dolphin Trail, Misty Mountain has luxury wooden cottages or chalets with wonderful views and full amenities, and a restaurant (three-course menu R150).

GETTING THERE & AWAY

Greyhound (☎ 083-915 9000; www.greyhound.co.za), **Intercape** (☎ 0861-287 287; www.intercape.co.za) and **Translux** (☎ 0861-589 282; www.translux.co.za) buses run along the N2, from where it's an 8km walk to Storms River Mouth. The Baz Bus stops at Nature's Valley.

Storms River

☎ 042

Storms River is an odd little hamlet with tree-shaded lanes, a few places to stay and an outdoor centre. From the N2 the Storms River signpost points to this village, which lies outside the national park. The turn-off is 4km east of the turn-off to the national park, which is signed as Storms River Mouth (or Stormsriviermond in Afrikaans).

Tsitsikamma Tourism Information Office (☎ 042-280 3561; www.tsitsikamma.info) is at the PetroPort petrol station, 4km east on the N2.

Most activities on offer are organised by the Fair Trade–accredited **Storms River Adventures** (☎ 042-281 1836; www.stormsriver.com; Darnell St, Storms River), including a tree-canopy slide (R395), 'woodcutter's journey' and forest tractor ride (R175 with lunch).

The world's highest bungee jump (216m) is at the **Bloukrans River Bridge** (☎ 042-281 1458; www.faceadrenalin.com; per jump R590), 21km west of Storms River.

If you're after a postbungee rest try the jacuzzi on the upper deck at **Dijembe Backpackers** (☎ 042-281 1842; www.dijembebackpackers.com; cnr Formosa & Assegai Sts; campsites R60, dm R110, d with/without bathroom R310/270; 💻), or **Ploughman's Rest** (☎ 042-281 1726; www.ploughmansrest.co.za; 31 Formosa St; s/d incl breakfast R350/600), a friendly B&B.

The Baz Bus stops at Storms River; otherwise buses and minibus taxis could drop you at Bloukrans River Bridge or Tsitsikamma Lodge, 2km away on the N2.

Jeffrey's Bay

☎ 042 / pop 25,000

Once just a sleepy seaside town, 'J-Bay' is now one of the world's top surfing destinations. Boardies from all over the planet flock here to ride waves such as the famous Supertubes, once described as 'the most perfect wave in the world'. June to September are the best months for experienced surfers, but novices can learn year-round.

Development is raging at a furious pace, with shopping in the myriad clothing stores almost overtaking surfing as the main leisure activity, but so far the local board-waxing vibe has been retained. The biggest surf crowd comes to town every July for the Billabong Pro championship.

INFORMATION

Atlantic Internet Café (☎ 042-293 2399; Da Gama Rd; per hr R22; ⏲ 8am-5pm Mon-Fri, to 4pm Sat, 9am-3pm Sun) Internet access.

Jeffrey's Bay Tourism (☎ 042-293 2923; jbaytourism@telkomsa.net; Da Gama Rd; ⏲ 9am-5pm Mon-Fri, to noon Sat)

SLEEPING

Peggy's Place (☎ 042-293 2160; pegjbay@yahoo.com; 8A Oribi St; campsites/dm/d R40/70/200) A wonderfully rustic, friendly place in a comfortable, old house on the outskirts of town, near the surf area and justifiably loved by readers.

Island Vibe (☎ 042-293 1625; www.islandvibe.co.za; 10 Dageraad St; campsites/dm/d R60/90/200) J-Bay's most popular backpackers hostel is 500m south of the city centre. Activities on offer include surf lessons (R180), plus of course plenty of drinking and partying. There's an open-air restaurant and a beautifully decorated beach house with double rooms (R300) and a separate kitchen.

Lazee Bay (☎ 042-296 2090; lazeebay@worldonline.co.za; 25 Mimosa St; d incl breakfast R400;) One of J-Bay's best guest houses, up on a hill above Da Gama Rd, is memorable for its funky decor and great sea views. There's a pool deck, a braai area and a bar.

Supertubes Guesthouse (☎ 042-293 2957; supertubes@agnet.co.za; 6/10/12 Pepper St; s/d incl breakfast from R550/760;) A stalwart of J-Bay accommodation, right in the prime surfing spot, Supertubes offers luxurious accommodation and various activities.

African Perfection (☎ 042-293 1401; www.africanperfection.co.za; 20 Pepper St; s/d incl breakfast R750/1100;) A massive circular staircase is the centrepiece of this impressive luxury option, with African-themed rooms offering stunning sea views. There's a self-catering four-sleeper loft (R2400) and shuttles from Port Elizabeth airport are available (two people R400).

EATING

Kitchen Windows (☎ 042-293 4230; Diaz Rd; mains R36-50) One of the town's best eateries, with a small but excellent menu; bookings are essential. A great sea view complements superb fresh fish and a good selection of salads.

Wax Café (☎ 042-293 2674; cnr Da Gama Rd & Goedehoop St; mains R44-60) This is a laid-back venue attracting the local beautiful people. Sip a cappuccino while you peruse the interesting menu.

Die Walskipper (☎ 082-800 9478; Marina Martinique; seafood platters R155; ⏲ lunch & dinner Tue-Sat, lunch Sun) This alfresco restaurant specialising in seafood, and crocodile and ostrich steaks, is just metres from the lapping sea at the Marina Martinique beach.

Getting There & Away

The Baz Bus stops daily at hostels in both directions. Travelling to Cape Town costs R950 (12 hours); Port Elizabeth to Jeffrey's Bay costs R170 (one hour). The **J-Bay Sunshine Express** (☎ 082-449 5735) runs door-to-door between Port Elizabeth and Jeffrey's Bay (R175).

PORT ELIZABETH

☎ 041 / pop 1.5 million

At the time of research, Port Elizabeth's downtown area, like many city centres throughout the country, was mostly run-down and full of fast-food chains and cheap stores. The more upmarket shops, bars and restaurants had moved out to suburban shopping centres such as the Boardwalk and Dolphin's Leap.

However, this will hopefully change with the construction of the Nelson Mandela Stadium, in the central North End area, for the 2010 World Cup. With the huge amount of revamping that was underway, North End and neighbouring Central will hopefully become safer and more accessible.

'PE', as it's dubbed, lies on the Sunshine Coast and certainly has some of the Eastern Cape's best bathing beaches, and the surf's good too. It's worth exploring the interesting South End and Port Elizabeth museums or the vibrant *shebeen* scene in the surrounding townships.

Information

Amex (☎ 041-583 2025; The Boardwalk, Marine Dr; ⏲ 9am-8pm Mon-Fri, 10am-4pm Sat & Sun)

Bay Tourism & Tours (☎ 041-584 0056; www.baytours.co.za; Beach Rd; ⏲ 8am-5pm) In the white building below Brookes Pavilion.

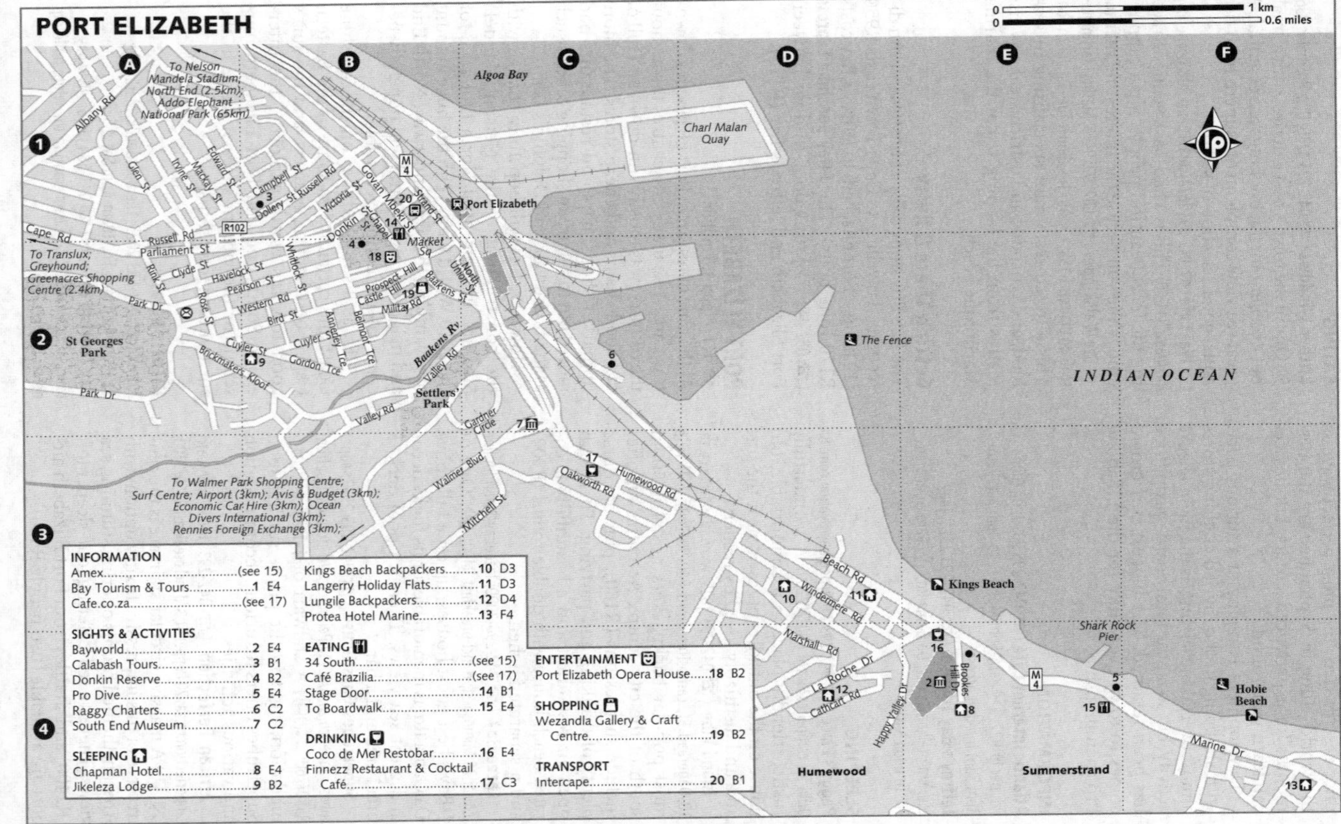
PORT ELIZABETH
0 1 km
0 0.6 miles
INDIAN OCEAN
Algoa Bay
Charl Malan Quay
The Fence
Kings Beach
Shark Rock Pier
Hobie Beach
Summerstrand
Humewood
Port Elizabeth
St Georges Park
Settlers' Park
Baakens Rv
Brookes Hill Dr
Happy Valley Dr
Marine Dr
Beach Rd
Windermere Rd
Marshall Rd
La Roche Dr
Cathcart Rd
Humewood Rd
Oakworth Rd
Walmer Blvd
Mitchell St
Gardner Circle
Valley Rd
Govan Mbeki St
Strand St
Market Sq
North Union St
Chapel St
Donkin St
Baakens St
Prospect Hill
Castle Hill
Military Rd
Belmont Tce
Annerley Tce
Gordon Tce
Cuyler St
Whitlock St
Bird St
Western Rd
Pearson St
Havelock St
Clyde St
Rose St
Rink St
Park Dr
Parliament St
Russell Rd
Cape Rd
Albany Rd
Glen St
Irvine St
Mackay St
Edward St
Campbell St
Dollery St
Victoria St
Brickmakers Kloof
To Nelson Mandela Stadium; North End (2.5km); Addo Elephant National Park (65km)
To Translux; Greyhound; Greenacres Shopping Centre (2.4km)
To Walmer Park Shopping Centre; Surf Centre; Airport (3km); Avis & Budget (3km); Economic Car Hire (3km); Ocean Divers International (3km); Rennies Foreign Exchange (3km);
INFORMATION
Amex (see 15)
Bay Tourism & Tours 1 E4
Cafe.co.za (see 17)
SIGHTS & ACTIVITIES
Bayworld 2 E4
Calabash Tours 3 B1
Donkin Reserve 4 B2
Pro Dive 5 E4
Raggy Charters 6 C2
South End Museum 7 C2
SLEEPING
Chapman Hotel 8 E4
Jikeleza Lodge 9 B2
Kings Beach Backpackers 10 D3
Langerry Holiday Flats 11 D3
Lungile Backpackers 12 D4
Protea Hotel Marine 13 F4
EATING
34 South (see 15)
Café Brazilia (see 17)
Stage Door 14 B1
To Boardwalk 15 E4
DRINKING
Coco de Mer Restobar 16 E4
Finnezz Restaurant & Cocktail Café 17 C3
ENTERTAINMENT
Port Elizabeth Opera House 18 B2
SHOPPING
Wezandla Gallery & Craft Centre 19 B2
TRANSPORT
Intercape 20 B1

Cafe.co.za (☎ 041-585 6142; Humerail Centre, Humewood Rd; per hr R25; ⏰ 8am-8pm Mon-Fri, 9am-6pm Sat, to 5pm Sun) Internet access.

Rennies Foreign Exchange (☎ 041-368 5890; Walmer Park Shopping Centre; ⏰ 8.30am-4.30pm Mon-Fri, to noon Sat) About 3km from the city centre.

Dangers & Annoyances

The city centre can be dangerous at night; take a taxi if you're going out. The main beachfront, however, is considered one of the safest in the country.

Sights

The small but fascinating **South End Museum** (☎ 041-582 3325; cnr Walmer Blvd & Humewood Rd; admission free, South End tour adult/child R40/15; ⏰ 9am-4pm Mon-Fri, 10am-3pm Sat & Sun) records multicultural Port Elizabeth, a vibrant district once known as South End. The apartheid bulldozers put an end to the neighbourhood during forced removals between 1965 and 1975 under the infamous Group Areas Act.

One of the best and largest museum complexes in the country, **Bayworld** (☎ 041-584 0650; Beach Rd; adult/child R45/20; ⏰ 9am-4.30pm) incorporates the Port Elizabeth Museum, an oceanarium and a snake park. Trained dolphins and seals perform at 11am and 3pm daily.

In the **Donkin Reserve**, on a hill behind the town centre, you can climb up inside the **lighthouse** (☎ 041-585 8884; Nelson Mandela Bay Tourism; admission adults/children R5/3; ⏰ 8am-4.30pm Mon-Fri, 9.30am-3.30pm Sat &Sun) for views over the bay.

Activities

The wide sandy beaches to the south of central Port Elizabeth make the town a major watersports venue. Kings Beach stretches from the harbour to Humewood and there are more at Summerstrand which are all fairly sheltered.

The **Surf Centre** (☎ 041-585 6027; Walmer Park Shopping Centre) sells and hires surfboards and body boards. Its surf school will teach you how to use them for R200 per two-hour lesson.

Good diving sites around Port Elizabeth include some wrecks and the St Croix Islands, a marine reserve. Contact either **Ocean Divers International** (☎ 041-581 5121; www.odipe.co.za; 10 Albert Rd) or **Pro Dive** (☎ 041-583 5316; www.prodive.co.za; Shark Rock Pier, Beach Rd; per dive US$37).

Tours

Bay Tourism & Tours (p463) runs tours to destinations including Addo Elephant National Park (from R600), the city (from R250) and townships (from R350). **Calabash Tours** (☎ 041-585 6162; 8 Dollery St; ⏰ 9am-5pm) runs similar trips for similar prices.

The township tours generally give the opportunity to visit squatter camps, *shebeens* and *abakhwetha* (initiation camps for boys). The guides are locals who are proud of the Port Elizabeth townships' part in the anti-apartheid struggle, and highlight places of historical and political interest along the way.

Raggy Charters (☎ 073-152 2277; Algoa Bay Yacht Club) offers cruises led by a qualified marine biologist to St Croix, Jahleel and Benton Islands. You can see penguins, Cape fur seals, dolphins and whales on its half-day tour, which departs at 8.30am daily (R800).

Sleeping

Most of Port Elizabeth's accommodation choices are lined up along the beachfront.

BUDGET

Jikeleza Lodge (☎ 041-586 3721; www.jikelezalodge.co.za; 44 Cuyler St; campsites/dm R55/75, s/d with shared bathroom R140/190; 💻) A favourite with readers, the cheery Jikeleza Lodge has recently been refurbished. There's a big garden and braai area, and it's a good place to organise township visits and other local tours.

Lungile Backpackers (☎ 041-582 2042; www.lungilebackpackers.co.za; 12 La Roche Dr; campsites/dm/d with shared bathroom R60/100/240, r R320; 💻 🏊) Port Elizabeth's most popular and busy backpackers hostel is contained in an airy, A-frame home minutes from the beachfront. The large entertainment area rocks most nights, and the dorms and tiny campsite can fill up when the Baz Bus arrives, so book ahead.

Kings Beach Backpackers (☎ 041-585 8113; kingsb@agnet.co.za; 41 Windermere Rd; dm/d with shared bathroom R90/200, d R230; 💻) A quieter, more intimate backpackers hostel, with some cottage rooms and comfortable doubles. Staff can help organise tours in the area, and satellite TV keeps you connected to the world outside PE.

MIDRANGE

Chapman Hotel (☎ 041-584 0678; www.chapman.co.za; 1 Lady Bea Cres, Brookes Hill Dr; s/d incl breakfast R580/785; ❄ 💻 🏊) South of the city centre, the family-run Chapman has a waterfall, rim-flow pool, and modern rooms with private balconies and sea views. It sometimes offers special deals on rooms and its Blackbeards restaurant (mains R75) is popular.

Protea Hotel Marine (☎ 041-583 2101; www.proteahotels.com; Marine Dr; s/d R770/970;) The Protea Marine, one of Port Elizabeth's most expensive hotels, suffers from a tiny swimming pool, which is right next to the road. There's another one, though, in the 3rd-floor gym. Other features include a jazzy bar and comfortable, if characterless, rooms with a bathroom and personal safe. There's disabled access.

There are dozens of self-catering flats along the beachfront. If you're looking for a clean, no-frills apartment, head to **Langerry Holiday Flats** (☎ 041-585 2654; www.langerry.co.za; 31 Beach Rd; 1-/2-bedroom flats from R290/500). All flats have TV, telephone and kitchen with a microwave, and the company has other blocks in the area.

Eating

Many of Port Elizabeth's best cafes are in the Boardwalk casino complex in Summerstrand, at the far end of Beach Rd. The atmosphere is a bit artificial, but you can at least sip a cappuccino in peace away from the plastic fast-food joints of the beachfront.

Stage Door (☎ 041-586 3553; Phoenix Hotel, 5 Chapel St; mains R22-66; lunch & dinner) With its unpretentious, if-you-don't-like-the-service-don't-tell-us attitude, this atmospheric old pub dishes up snacks, specials and politically incorrect posters galore. A much-loved PE institution, it has live music Wednesday to Saturday.

34 South (☎ 041-583 1085; The Boardwalk, Marine Dr; deli dishes per 100g R25, mains R80; 10am-10pm) Past the tacky sailing-boat art, moccasins and nautical T-shirts in its shop, this large airy deli-bistro has a menu including lots of fish dishes, curries and Smørrebrød (a Danish sandwich, preferably consumed with schnapps). You can also pick your own ingredients from the goodies served up at its counter.

Café Brazilia (☎ 041-585 1482; Humerail Centre, Humewood Rd; mains R80; 10am-10pm Mon-Fri, to 2.30pm & 5-10pm Sat, 10am-2.30pm Sun) The sweeping bay view is the main highlight, but the international cuisine's also good, with dishes ranging from French pepper fillet steak to Mauritian kingclip. Breakfasts and *tramezzini* (Italian tea sandwiches) are also on the menu.

Drinking & Entertainment

Wednesday seems to be the biggest night in the pubs and clubs, although Friday and Saturday are popular as well.

Finnezz Restaurant & Cocktail Café (☎ 041-586 3233; Humerail Centre, Humewood Rd; mains R30-78; 9am-2am Mon-Sat, 10am-1am Sun) Finnezz is a snappy joint to try a cocktail overlooking the harbour and marina.

Coco de Mer Restobar (☎ 041-585 0507; Dolphin's Leap Centre, Beach Rd; mains R70-105; noon-late) Coco de Mer is a slick, upmarket restaurant and cocktail lounge with a black-and-white theme and an imaginative menu including tapas and fondues. There's dancing and hubbly-bubblies in the separate lounge, with DJs every Wednesday, Friday and Saturday.

Port Elizabeth Opera House (☎ 041-586 2256; White's Rd) Port Elizabeth's opera house is the oldest in South Africa, with a beautiful 19th-century interior. It shows a lively program of concerts, ballets, plays and jazz recitals – drop into the box office for the latest.

Shopping

Wezandla Gallery & Craft Centre (☎ 041-585 1185; 27 Baakens St) Brightly coloured, this has a huge array of artefacts made by local groups and a small cafe. Staff can also help with tourist information.

Getting There & Away

AIR

South African Airways (☎ 041-507 1111; www.flysaa.com) has daily flights between Jo'burg (R2144 return), Durban (R1618), Cape Town (R1504) and Port Elizabeth. **SAAirlink** (☎ 011-961 1700; www.saairlink.co.za) flies daily from Port Elizabeth to East London (R627 one-way), Durban (R809) and Cape Town (R752). **Kulula** (☎ 0861-444 144; www.kulula.com) flies daily to Jo'burg. One-way fares start at around R500.

BUS

Greyhound (☎ 041-363 4555; www.greyhound.co.za) departs from opposite Checkers at Greenacres Shopping Centre, around 3km from Humewood. **Translux/City to City** (☎ 041-392 1333; www.translux.co.za) also operates out of the Greenacres Shopping Centre. **Intercape** (☎ 0861-287 287; www.intercape.co.za) departs from the bus stop on the corner of Fleming and North Union Sts, behind the old post office.

The 12-hour-or-so trip to Cape Town averages around R250. The Baz Bus runs daily from Port Elizabeth to Cape Town (R1110 one-way – hop-on, hop-off).

All three bus companies serve Jo'burg; the 15-hour trip averages around R360.

Translux runs to Durban daily (R380, 13 hours) via Grahamstown (R80, 1½ hours), East London (R140, four hours), Mthatha (R240, seven hours) and Port Shepstone (R310, 11½ hours); City to City offers a cheaper overnight service. Greyhound goes to Durban daily (R375, 12½ hours).

The Baz Bus runs Monday, Tuesday, Thursday, Friday and Sunday from Port Elizabeth to Durban, and returns on Monday, Wednesday, Thursday, Saturday and Sunday.

CAR

All the big car-hire operators have offices in Port Elizabeth or at the airport, including **Avis** (☎ 041-501 7200; www.avis.co.za), **Budget** (☎ 041-581 4242; www.budget.co.za) and **Imperial** (☎ 0861-131 000; www.imperialcarrental.co.za). Also try **Economic Car Hire** (☎ 041-581 5826; www.economiccarhire.co.za; 104 Heugh Rd).

MINIBUS TAXI

J-Bay Sunshine Express (☎ 082-449 5735) runs door-to-door to/from Jeffrey's Bay (R175) and other coastal areas.

TRAIN

Shosholoza Meyl (☎ 0860-008 888; www.shosholozameyl.co.za) runs tourist- and economy-class services to Jo'burg (R420, 20 hours) via Cradock, Bloemfontein and Kroonstad. Shosholoza Meyl also runs a weekly **Premier Classe** (www.premierclasse.co.za) service to Cape Town (R1250, 8½ hours) via Oudtshoorn.

Getting Around

The **airport** (Allister Miller Rd) is about 5km from the city centre. Taxis (around R65) and hire cars are available at the airport.

PORT ELIZABETH TO KEI RIVER

Addo Elephant National Park

This **national park** (☎ 042-233 8600; www.sanparks.org; adult/child R100/50; ⏲ 7am-7pm) is 72km north of Port Elizabeth, near the Zuurberg range in the Sundays River Valley. Addo now encompasses five biomes over 164,000 hectares of malaria-free wildlife viewing, and there are plans to expand it further.

The park protects the remnants of the huge elephant herds that once roamed Eastern Cape. When Addo was proclaimed a national park in 1931, there were only 11 elephants left. Today there are more than 450 in the park, and you'd be unlucky not to see some. A day or two at Addo is a highlight of any visit to this part of the Eastern Cape, not only for the elephants but for the zebras, black rhinos, Cape buffalo, leopards, lions, myriad birds, unique flightless dung beetles, great white sharks and southern right whales (in season).

INFORMATION

The park is closed if there has been heavy rain. There is a well-stocked **shop** (⏲ 8am-7pm) at the park headquarters, 7km from Addo village on Rte 335. Midsummer heat can be intolerable.

For optimum wildlife spotting, pick up one of the **Eyethu Hop-on Guides** (☎ 072-034 8349/076-813 7085; 2hr per car R110; ⏲ 8am-5pm) at the gate; they can give you advice on where to go and explain what you're looking at in interesting detail. The park's own **vehicle** (2hr drive per person R190) can also be used for wildlife-spotting drives.

SLEEPING

Homestead B&B (☎ 042-233 0354; homestead@webmail.co.za; campsites R90, per person backpackers/B&B R75/250;) Homestead has a few backpackers rooms and self-catering units, as well as camping, alongside the normal B&B accommodation.

Addo Rest Camp (☎ 012-428 9111; www.sanparks.org; campsites/safari tents/forest cabins with shared bathroom R130/325/425, 4-person chalets R700) At the park headquarters, Addo's main campsite is a great spot with a picnic area, and some of the accommodation overlooks a water hole where elephants come to drink. Most of the sleeping options are excellent value, sleeping two to six people.

Chrislin African Lodge (☎ 042-233 0022; www.chrislin.co.za; s/d incl breakfast R780/900;) Chrislin has friendly owners and pretty African-style huts on an ecofriendly farm. A three-course dinner (per person R135) can be provided and wildlife drives, mountain tours and paddles on the river are offered.

GETTING THERE & AWAY

The park is signposted from the N2. Alternatively you can travel via Uitenhage on Rte 75.

Port Alfred

☎ 046 / pop 32,500

Port Alfred is leaving behind its old image of unkempt seaside town and is fast becoming 'the new Knysna', with a delightful marina. It's still pretty quiet out of season, but there are huge developments of shopping malls, tourist accommodation and housing that even attracts foreign investment. The town remains popular with students from Grahamstown for its beaches and pubs, but these days budget accommodation is scarce. In season (mid-December to January) the place bustles with life as people arrive from other parts of the country to soak up the holiday atmosphere, and prices surge.

Ndlambe Tourism (Tourism Port Alfred; ☎ 046-624 1235; www.portalfred.co.za; Causeway Rd; 🕒 8am-4.30pm Mon-Fri, 8.30am-noon Sat) is near the municipal offices on the western bank of the Kowie River.

ACTIVITIES

Fish River Horse Safaris (☎ 046-675 1271; 2½/5hr trails R250/500) offers daily horse rides on the beach or through a private reserve.

For **surfers**, there are good right- and left-hand breaks at the river mouth. There's an 8km **walking trail** through the Kowie Nature Reserve and **Rufanes River Trails** (☎ 041-624 1469) has mountain-bike trails.

Outdoor Focus (☎ 046-624 4432) offers scuba-diving courses (diving is between May and August), rents out canoes (per two hours R60) and mountain bikes (per day R150), and organises river and sea cruises. You can also book the two-day **Kowie Canoe Trail** (per person R125), a fairly easy 21km canoe trip upriver from Port Alfred, with an overnight stay in a hut.

SLEEPING

Medolino Caravan Park (☎ 046-624 1651; www.caravanparks.co.za/medolino; 23 Stewart Rd; campsites per person R80, 2-/4-person chalets R475/650; ♿) This disabled-friendly park, in town off Princes Ave, is near both Kowie River and Kelly's Beach, and is one of the best in the country.

Residency (☎ 046-624 5382; www.theresidency.co.za; 11 Vroom Rd; s/d incl breakfast R420/800) The Residency is a gracious B&B in a magnificently restored Victorian house built in 1898. A big breakfast is served on the wide verandah every morning.

Fort D'Acre Reserve (☎ 046-675 1091; www.fortdacre.com; s/d R600/900; 💻 ♿) With smart, African-themed accommodation, this upmarket wildlife reserve is home to white rhinos, buffalo, giraffes, zebras, wildebeests and antelopes. It's off Rte 72, 24km north of Port Alfred.

Bretton Beach Crest (☎ 046-624 1606; www.brettonbeach.co.za; Freshwater Rd; 2- or 4-person self-catered cottages R690) A charming collection of self-contained beach cottages 3km from the Kowie River mouth with wonderful sea views and neat rooms.

EATING

Guido's Restaurant (☎ 046-624 5264; West Beach Dr; mains R42-120) Guido's is a pizza-and-pasta restaurant on the beach that's popular with Grahamstown students during the week and families on weekends.

Butler's (☎ 046-624 3464; 25 Van der Riet St; mains R43-125; 🕒 lunch & dinner Wed-Mon) Port Alfred's top dining experience, Butler's imaginative, oft-changing menu always features a great fish and seafood selection.

Highlander Pub & Thistle Restaurant (☎ 046-624 1379; 19 St Andrews Rd; mains R48-90) The pub and restaurant at the Royal St Andrews Lodge has a cosy, Scottish ambience and serves good-quality food, including an excellent king-prawn platter.

GETTING THERE & AWAY

The Baz Bus stops at Beavis Restaurant on its run from Port Elizabeth (two hours) to Durban (13 hours) on Monday, Tuesday, Thursday, Friday and Sunday.

The **minibus taxi rank** (Biscay Rd), outside the Heritage Mall, offers daily services to Port Elizabeth (R75), Grahamstown (R25) and East London (R75). Local daily services include Bathurst (R12).

Shipwreck Coast

The coast between the Great Fish River and East London is also known as the Shipwreck Coast, as it is the graveyard for many ships. The 69km **Shipwreck Hiking Trail** (per person R600) leads from Port Alfred to the Fish River Mouth near East London and includes canoeing. The six-day, five-night trip rewards walkers with wild, unspoilt sections of surf beach, rich coastal vegetation and beautiful estuaries. The trail can be booked through **Dave Marais** (☎ 082 391 0647; adrift@mweb.co.za), who also runs the two-day Kleinemonde West River Canoe Trail.

East London

☎ **043 / pop 980,000**

East London is the country's only river port, situated on a spectacular bay that curves round to huge sand hills. Downtown is downright ugly: it's dotted with large Victorian churches, ugly 1960s and '70s buildings, modern glass monstrosities and a great deal of new development. Queenstown Park (containing the zoo) is pretty, and the beaches and surf are excellent, but there's not a lot to keep you here. The city is a good base for moving on to holiday spots along the Sunshine or Wild Coasts.

Its Khoisan name means 'Place of Buffalo', and the whole area has been named 'Buffalo City' by the tourism authorities.

INFORMATION

Portal (☎ 043-726 2535; cnr Sansom St & Deveureux Ave; per hr R20; 🕑 8am-8pm Mon, Wed & Thu, 9am-9pm Tue, 8am-6pm Fri, 9am-4pm Sat, 10am-2pm Sun) has internet access.

There are two tourist offices in East London, both in **King's Tourist Centre** (cnr Longfellow & Aquarium Rds) on the beachfront and both not especially helpful:

Eastern Cape Tourism Board (☎ 043-701 9600; www.ectourism.co.za; 🕑 8am-4.30pm Mon-Fri) Covers the wider area.

Tourism Buffalo City (☎ 043-042-722 6015; 🕑 8am-4.30pm Mon-Fri, 9am-2pm Sat, to 1pm Sun) Deals with matters relating to the city and neighbouring townships.

DANGERS & ANNOYANCES

The eastern end of Eastern Beach and the area around Nahoon River mouth are not considered safe to walk on. Take care on the Esplanade and get a taxi home from anywhere in East London after dark. Watch out for pickpockets if you end up in the area around Buffalo St and the minibus taxi ranks.

SIGHTS & ACTIVITIES

The **East London Museum** (☎ 043-743 0686; Dawson Rd; admission R10; 🕑 9am-4pm Mon-Fri, 10am-1pm Sat, to 3pm Sun) displays a stuffed coelancanth, a strange-looking fish that, until one was discovered in the harbour in 1938, was thought to have been extinct for 50 million years. Other exhibits include trace-fossil human footprints and a living beehive.

If you have children, there's the small **East London Zoo** (☎ 043-722 1171; adult/child R19/11; 🕑 9am-5pm Mon-Sun) at Queen's Park, and a small **aquarium** (☎ 043-705 2637; Esplanade; adult/child R18/11; 🕑 9am-5pm Mon-Sun) on the beachfront.

The best **surfing** is at Nahoon Reef at the southern end of Nahoon Beach.

SLEEPING

Sugarshack Backpackers (☎ 043-722 8240; www.sugarshack.co.za; Eastern Esplanade, Eastern Beach; campsites/dm/d with shared bathroom R50/80/190; 💻) With the beach just metres away, the surf's always up at this lively backpackers. Surfboard hire (R50) and two-hour lessons (R90) are available. This is a place to cut loose, not to sleep, although the wooden garden cottages offer some privacy.

East London Backpackers (☎ 043-722 2748; www.elbackpackers.co.za; 11 Quanza St; dm/s/d with shared bathroom R70/110/170; 💻 🏊) This well-maintained place is quieter and less vibey than Sugarshack, but has spacious and clean chilling areas and dorms, a braai area and a plunge pool. There are also good-quality doubles with their own bathroom (R200).

Gonubie Caravan Park (☎ 043-705 9748; fax 043-740 5937; Beachfront, Gonubie; 4-person campsites/1-bedroom chalets R214/839) A great escape from the city, with log-cabin-style chalets right on the beachfront of rustic, outer suburb Gonubie, 20km from town.

White House (☎ 043-740 0344; www.thewhitehousebandb.co.za; 10 Whitthaus St, Gonubie; s/d incl breakfast R495/595; 🏊) A stylish guest house with glass windows for panoramic views of cliffs and sea – you can watch whales and dolphins passing by while you're having breakfast!

Hemingway's Hotel (☎ 043-707 8000; www.southernsun.com; cnr Western Bypass & Two Rivers Dr, Cambridge; s/d incl breakfast R1620/1840; 💻 🏊) East London's only upper-end option, this Southern Sun hotel has all the usual amenities as well as a casino next door.

Kat Leisure (☎ 0800-422 433; www.katleisure.co.za; r from R265), which runs mostly midrange accommodation, has a virtual monopoly on the hotels and apartments in East London. Places that include breakfast provide a prepacked, airline-style continental affair.

EATING

Guido's Family Restaurant (☎ 043-743 4441; Kennaway's Hotel, Esplanade; mains R40-70) This Italian chain, complete with faux-Grecian columns and a water feature, is a good standby for pizza and pasta.

Imbizo (☎ 043-722 0155; 22 Currie St; mains R55) This is a fun place to sample genuine African cuisine such as *ulusu* (Xhosa-style tripe), *mleqwa* (chicken) and *sadza ne nyama* (Shona cornmeal with meat).

Buccaneers (☎ 043-743 5171; Eastern Esplanade; mains R60-80) Next to Sugarshack Backpackers, this

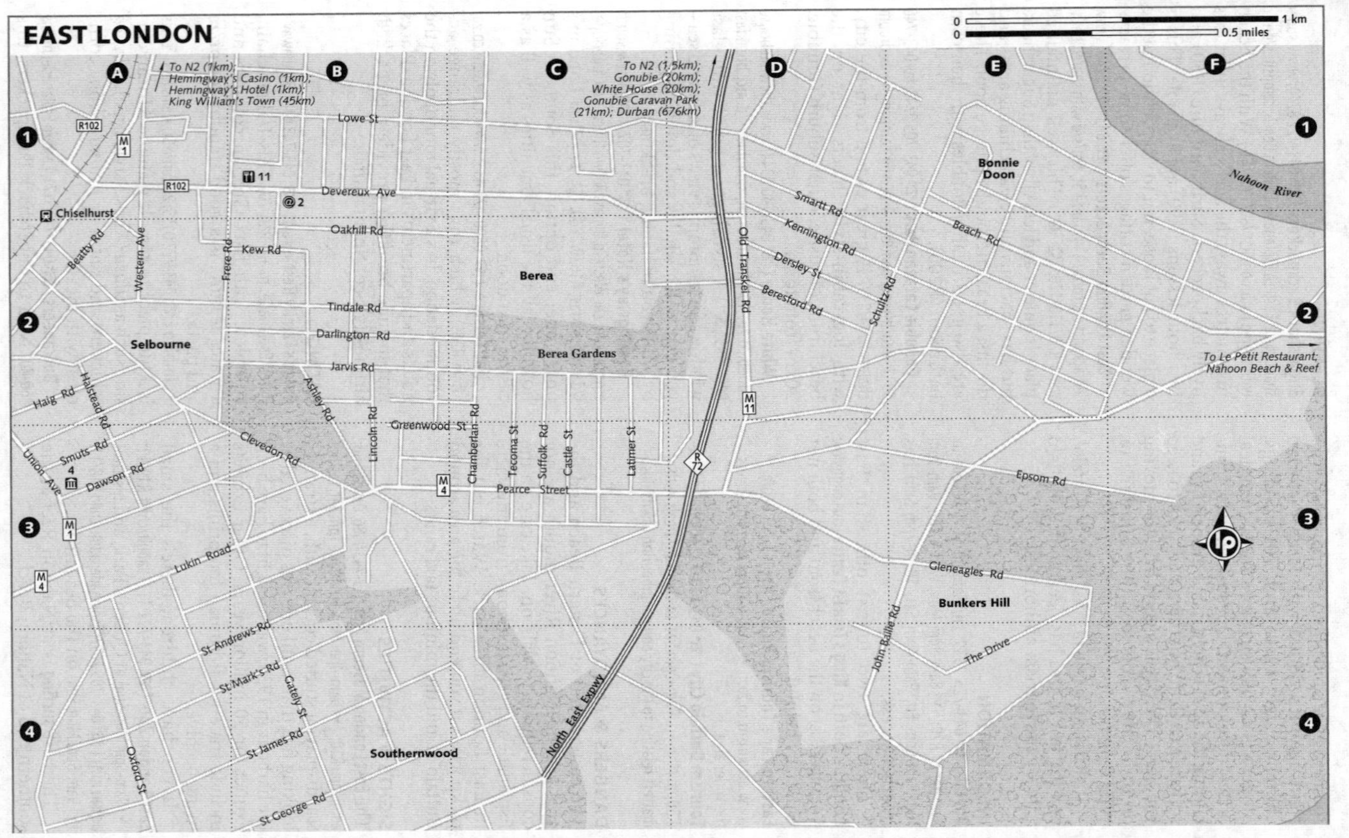
EAST LONDON
0 1 km
0 0.5 miles
To N2 (1km); Hemingway's Casino (1km); Hemingway's Hotel (1km); King William's Town (45km)
To N2 (1.5km); Gonubie (20km); White House (20km); Gonubie Caravan Park (21km); Durban (676km)
To Le Petit Restaurant; Nahoon Beach & Reef
Nahoon River
Bonnie Doon
Berea
Berea Gardens
Selbourne
Bunkers Hill
Southernwood
Chiselhurst
11
2
4
Lowe St
Devereux Ave
Oakhill Rd
Kew Rd
Frere Rd
Western Ave
Beatty Rd
Tindale Rd
Darlington Rd
Jarvis Rd
Ashley Rd
Lincoln Rd
Greenwood St
Chamberlain Rd
Tecoma St
Suffolk Rd
Castle St
Latimer St
Pearce Street
Haig Rd
Halstead Rd
Smuts Rd
Dawson Rd
Union Ave
Clevedon Rd
Lukin Road
St Andrews Rd
St Mark's Rd
Gately St
St James Rd
St George Rd
Oxford St
Old Transkei Rd
Smartt Rd
Kennington Rd
Dersley St
Beresford Rd
Schultz Rd
Beach Rd
Epsom Rd
Gleneagles Rd
John Bailie Rd
The Drive
North East Expwy
R102
R72
M1
M4
M11

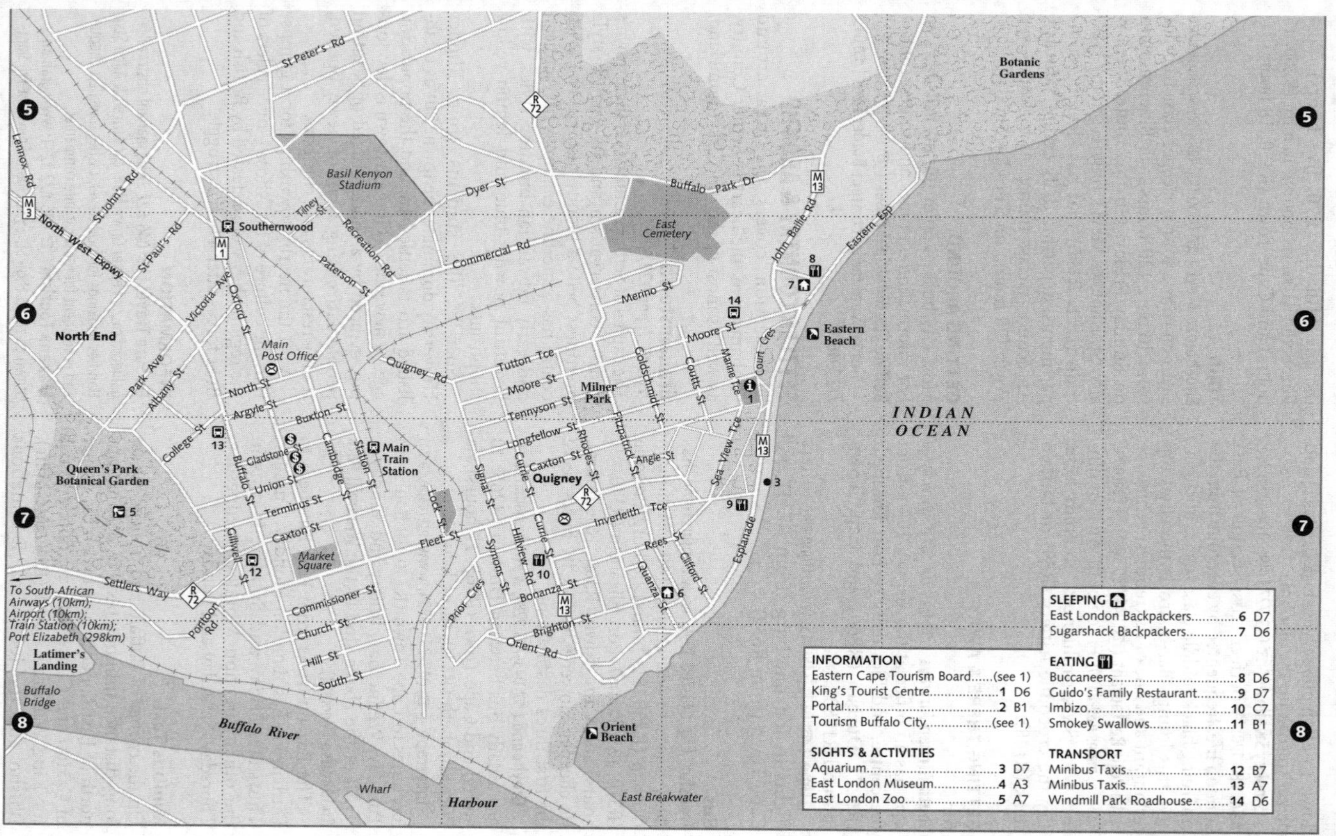
Botanic Gardens
INDIAN OCEAN
Eastern Beach
Orient Beach
East Breakwater
Harbour
Wharf
Buffalo River
Buffalo Bridge
Latimer's Landing
Queen's Park Botanical Garden
North End
Quigney
Milner Park
East Cemetery
Basil Kenyon Stadium
Southernwood
Main Post Office
Main Train Station
Market Square
St Peter's Rd
Dyer St
Buffalo Park Dr
John Bailie Rd
Eastern Esp
Commercial Rd
Recreation Rd
Tiley St
Paterson St
Merino St
Lennox Rd
St John's Rd
North West Expwy
St Paul's Rd
Victoria Ave
Oxford St
Park Ave
Albany St
College St
North St
Argyle St
Buxton St
Gladstone St
Union St
Buffalo St
Terminus St
Caxton St
Gillwell St
Cambridge St
Station St
Quigney Rd
Tutton Tce
Moore St
Tennyson St
Longfellow St
Goldschmidt St
Coutts St
Marine Tce
Court Cres
Fitzpatrick St
Rhodes St
Angle St
Sea View Tce
Signal St
Currie St
Lock St
Fleet St
Inverleith Tce
Symons St
Hillview Rd
Rees St
Clifford St
Quanza St
Esplanade
Bonanza St
Prior Cres
Brighton St
Orient Rd
Commissioner St
Church St
Hill St
South St
Settlers Way
Pontoon Rd
To South African Airways (10km); Airport (10km); Train Station (10km); Port Elizabeth (298km)
SLEEPING
East London Backpackers 6 D7
Sugarshack Backpackers 7 D6
INFORMATION
Eastern Cape Tourism Board (see 1)
King's Tourist Centre 1 D6
Portal 2 B1
Tourism Buffalo City (see 1)
EATING
Buccaneers 8 D6
Guido's Family Restaurant 9 D7
Imbizo 10 C7
Smokey Swallows 11 B1
SIGHTS & ACTIVITIES
Aquarium 3 D7
East London Museum 4 A3
East London Zoo 5 A7
TRANSPORT
Minibus Taxis 12 B7
Minibus Taxis 13 A7
Windmill Park Roadhouse 14 D6

down-to-earth pub serves steaks, burgers and pizzas to soak up the alcohol.

Smokey Swallows (☎ 043-727 1349; 20 Devereux Ave; mains R80-120) A perfect cross-section of East London life, frequented by everyone from the emerging black middle class to jazz aficionados, this lounge-bar-bistro is the city's top restaurant and one of its trendiest venues.

Le Petit Restaurant (☎ 043-735 3685; 54 Beach Rd, Nahoon; mains R89-R150) Fine South African dining, with Swiss influences, abounds here. Try the crocodile fritters (R59) or buffalo steak (R148).

GETTING THERE & AWAY

Air

South African Airways (☎ 043-706 0203; www.flysaa.com) has an office at the airport, 10km from the centre, and flies daily to Port Elizabeth (R627), Durban (R866) and Cape Town (around R1083).

1time (☎ 0861-345 345; www.1time.aero) offers flights to Johannesburg (from R734) and Cape Town (from R632).

Bus

Translux (☎ 043-700 1999; www.translux.co.za) has daily buses to Mthatha (R140, 2½ hours), Durban (R250, 8½ hours), Jo'burg/Pretoria (R310, 13½ hours), Port Elizabeth (R140, 4½ hours) and Cape Town (R360, 16½ hours). Its cheaper, slower City to City buses serve the first three destinations.

Greyhound (☎ 043-743 9284; www.greyhound.co.za) has a daily bus between Durban (R265, 10 hours) and Cape Town (R365, 17 hours) via Port Elizabeth (R110, three hours).

Intercape (☎ 043-743 9284; www.intercape.co.za) has buses to Cape Town (R340, 19 hours) on Tuesday, Wednesday, Friday and Sunday.

All of the above stop at the **Windmill Park Roadhouse** (Moore St).

The Baz Bus runs from Port Elizabeth to Durban via East London Monday, Tuesday, Thursday, Friday and Sunday. It runs in the other direction Monday, Wednesday, Thursday, Saturday and Sunday.

Minibus Taxi

On the corner of Buffalo and College Sts are long-distance minibus taxis to destinations north of East London. Nearby, on the corner of Caxton and Gillwell Sts, are minibus taxis for King William's Town (R18, one hour), Bhisho and the local area. Destinations include Mthatha (R70, five hours), Port Elizabeth (R100, six hours), Jo'burg (R250, 15 hours) and Cape Town (R350, 18 hours).

Train

Shosholoza Meyl (☎ 0860-008 888; www.shosholozameyl.co.za) runs a tourist-sleeper class train to/from Jo'burg (20 hours) via Bloemfontein on Sunday/Friday. On this route, there is also Shosholoza Meyl's only economy-class train (seats R190) that has sleeping compartments, departing daily except Saturday. An economy-class train runs to/from Cape Town (28 hours) on Tuesday/Sunday.

GETTING AROUND

Most city buses stop at the **city hall** (Oxford St). For information on times and routes, contact **Buffalo City Municipal Buses** (☎ 043-705 2666).

For private taxis, contact **Border Taxis** (☎ 043-722 3946).

SETTLER COUNTRY & AROUND

This section covers the area around Grahamstown, the heart of Settler Country, as well as most of the old Ciskei homeland.

Grahamstown

☎ 046 / pop 120,000

The capital of Settler Country, Grahamstown's genteel conservatism and its English-style prettiness belie a bloody history. The town centre has some fine examples of Victorian and early Edwardian building styles, with beautiful powder-blue and lemon-yellow shopfronts.

Socially, the students from Rhodes University dominate the town. But as established artists settle here and the population ages, a new side of Grahamstown is developing, evinced by a sudden breed of beautiful people patronising a raft of newly opened, trendy restaurants and chic bars.

Visit the nearby townships for a glimpse into the culture of the Xhosa – once rulers of the region, they were defeated by British and Boer forces after a fierce struggle.

INFORMATION

Go Sure Travel (☎ 046-622 2235; marianl.gbstravel@galileosa.co.za; Pepper Grove Mall, cnr African & Allen Sts) Handles bookings for local travel, cashes travellers cheques and is an agent for most car-hire companies.

Makana Tourism (☎ 046-622 3241; www.grahamstown.co.za; 63 High St; ⏲ 8.30am-5pm Mon-Fri, 9am-

1pm Sat) This office is also an agent for Translux buses and has internet access (R30 per hour).

SIGHTS & ACTIVITIES

Grahamstown is rightly proud of its museums, four of which are administered by the **Albany Museum Group** (☎ 046-622 4450). The most interesting is the eccentric **Observatory Museum** (☎ 046-622 2312; Bathurst St; adult/child R8/5; ⏰ 9am-1pm & 2-5pm Mon-Fri, 9am-1pm Sat), with its Victorian memorabilia.

The **Albany History Museum** (Somerset St; admission R5; ⏰ 9am-1pm & 2-5pm Mon-Fri, 9am-1pm Sat) details the history and art of the peoples of the Eastern Cape.

There's also the **National English Literary Museum** (Beaufort St; admission free; ⏰ 8.30am-1pm & 2-5pm Mon-Fri), which contains the 1st editions of just about every work by famous South African writers.

The best examples of preserved Victorian and Edwardian shopfronts are on Church Sq: **Grocott's Mail**, still a working newspaper office, and **Birch's Gentlemen's Outfitters**.

For a taste of local student life, head to the **Dam** up Grey St on the way out of town. It's a place to chill out and have a swim, and on Friday there are drumming sessions.

A Rhodes University research project into *iQhilika* (African mead) has spawned the **Makana Meadery** (☎ 046-636 1227; Old Power Station, Highlands Industrial Area; ⏰ 9am-4pm), off the N2 on the way to Port Elizabeth.

TOURS

Umthathi (☎ 046-622 4450; Station Bldg, High St), with an office in the old train station building, organises township visits including a traditional Xhosa meal (R50), and visits to a herbal nursery in Rhini township.

FESTIVALS & EVENTS

Grahamstown bills itself as 'Africa's Festival Capital', with events of various kinds happening several times a year. The biggest is the hugely popular **National Arts Festival** (☎ 046-603 1103; www.nafest.co.za) and its associated **Fringe Festival**, which run for 10 days at the beginning of July. Accommodation at this time can be booked out a year in advance, and nights can be freezing.

Held in late April, the **Makana Freedom Festival** (☎ 082-932 1304) is a festival of song and dance, with live bands playing in the townships.

SLEEPING

Entabeni Homestays (☎ 046-622 3241; enthomestay@yahoo.co.uk) Vuyane Njovane at Makana Tourism organises overnight homestays in rooms of a good standard in Grahamstown's townships. Tours can also be arranged.

Old Gaol Backpackers (☎ 046-636 1001; www.oldgaol.co.za; 40 Somerset St; dm/s/d with shared bathroom R100/150/250) This former jail, now a national monument, offers the chance to feel like an inmate, complete with fingerprinting upon registration. The cells are all considerably more comfortable than in their previous incarnation, though you'll probably spend most of your time in the atmospheric bar-restaurant anyway.

Lantern Hill (☎ 046-622 8782; www.lanternhill.co.za; 4 Thompson St; s/d R400/600; 💻) This friendly, wheelchair-accessible B&B has cosy, comfy wooden-floored rooms with TV and safe. The owners speak German.

Cock House (☎ 046-636 1287; www.cockhouse.co.za; 10 Market St; s/d incl breakfast R475/830) Named after one of the 1820 settlers, today this national monument houses a hugely popular guest house with comfortable rooms in converted stables and a pretty garden. The restaurant (mains R65 to R85) is highly regarded.

7 Worcester Street (☎ 046-622 2843; www.worcesterstreet.co.za; 7 Worcester St; s/d incl breakfast R1120/1790; ❄ 🏊) This luxurious guest house is filled with sumptuous period furniture and priceless artworks. Three-course dinner is available for R160.

EATING

Gino's Italian Restaurant (☎ 046-622 7208; 8 New St; mains R30-60) Grahamstown's most popular student restaurant is a very average pizza and pasta joint with an attached bar.

Bella Vita (☎ 046-622 3007; 131 High St; mains R35-75; ⏰ breakfast & lunch Mon-Sun, dinner Wed, Fri & Sat) This stylish New York–style cafe offers buffet dishes (per 100g R14) and a small á la carte menu. There's live music on Saturday nights and an outdoor cocktail bar.

Maxwell's (☎ 046-622 5119; cnr Somerset St & High St; mains R50-95) Offering excellent service and hearty Eastern Cape food such as venison pie, kudu steak and ostrich carpaccio, Maxwell's has a well-earned reputation. Booking is essential.

Calabash (☎ 046-622 2324; 123 High St; mains R50-100; ⏰ breakfast, lunch & dinner) Calabash offers traditional South African food and specialities such as Xhosa hotpots and *samp* (broken dried corn kernels) and beans.

GETTING THERE & AWAY

Buses depart from the **terminus** (cnr High & Bathurst Sts). **Mini-Lux** (☎ 043-741 3107) runs to East London and Port Elizabeth. Check with the tourist office for prices and times.

Translux (☎ 046-622 3241; www.translux.co.za) runs daily between Cape Town (R300, 12½ hours), Port Elizabeth (R80, 1½ hours) and Durban (R320, 12 hours), via East London and Mthatha. Its cheaper, slower City to City buses runs twice daily to Cape Town, Port Elizabeth and Durban.

Greyhound (☎ 046-622 2235; www.greyhound.co.za) also serves Durban (R335, 12½ hours) and Port Elizabeth (R115, two hours).

You'll find minibus taxis on Raglan St, but most leave from Rhini township. Destinations include Fort Beaufort (R30, two hours), King William's Town (R42, three hours), Port Elizabeth (R40, 2½ hours) and East London (R60, four hours).

King William's Town

☎ 043

Established by the London Missionary Society in 1826, King William's Town (known as 'King') was a colonial capital and an important military base in the interminable struggle with the Xhosa. The main reason for a visit is the excellent **Amathole Museum** (☎ 043-642 4506; 3 Albert Rd; adult/child R5/free; 🕑 8am-4.30pm Mon-Fri), one of the finest in the region, with an excellent Xhosa Gallery featuring in-depth explanations of Xhosa culture, mysticism and history.

The **library** (☎ 043-642 3391; Ayliff St; 🕑 9am-5.30pm Mon-Fri, to 1pm Sat) has a list of guest houses and B&Bs.

Bhisho

pop 171,000

Bhisho, once capital of Ciskei, is now the administrative capital of Eastern Cape. The centre of Bhisho was built to house Ciskei's bureaucrats and politicians, so there is a compact bunch of suitably grandiose and ugly public buildings, which are now in the service of the new provincial bureaucracy.

Regular minibuses travel from the King William's Town train station to Bhisho (R12, 20 minutes).

Amathole & Katberg Mountains

The area north and west of King William's Town is partly degraded grazing land and partly rugged mountains with remnant indigenous forest. There are some good walks. When the mists are down on the Amathole Mountains, the forests take on an eerie silence.

The easiest way into this area is via King William's Town or Queenstown. There are occasional minibus taxis, but otherwise you're going to need your own vehicle.

The 121km, six-day **Amathole Trail** (per person per night R135.70) ranks as one of South Africa's top mountain walks, but is pretty tough and should only be attempted if you are reasonably experienced and fit.

The trail must be booked with the **Department of Water Affairs & Forestry** (☎ 043-642 2571; www.dwaf.gov.za; 2 Hargreaves Ave, King William's Town).

HOGSBACK

☎ 045 / pop 1500

There's something about Hogsback, improbably located 1300m up in the beautiful Amathole Mountains above Alice, that makes you half expect to meet a hobbit. Promoters of the village will tell you it inspired JRR Tolkien, who came here on childhood holidays from Bloemfontein. Its English climate (four distinct seasons), organic food, and mind-boggling views of mountains and forested valleys in all directions, make it an ecodestination *par excellence*.

There are some great walks, bike rides and drives in the area. Snow falls, though rarely heavy, in 11 out of 12 months. Be prepared for rain at any time, and in winter for temperatures that can drop to -1°C.

Away with the Fairies (☎ 045-962 1031; www.backpackers@awaywiththefairies.co.za; Hydrangea Lane; campsites/dm R55/95, d with/without bathroom R325/220; 🍴) is a delightful backpackers, where care and attention to detail (along with terrific views) have paid dividends.

Another option is **Granny Mouse House** (☎ 045-962 1259; www.grannymousehouse.co.za; 1 Nutwoods Dr; per person incl breakfast/dinner R325/425; 🍴), a charming guest house with rooms in an old wattle-and-daub house, plus a self-catering garden cottage.

The easiest way to get to Hogsback without a car is by shuttle bus (R65 one way) from Sugarshack Backpackers (East

London, p469), Buccaneer's Backpackers (Chintsa, p478) or Old Gaol Backpackers (Grahamstown, p473).

EASTERN KAROO

This is the southeastern extension of the vast semidesert that stretches across the great South African plateau, inland from the Cape coast. It's one of the region's most intriguing areas, with an overwhelming sense of space and peace that stands in sharp contrast to the cheery, sometimes overdeveloped coastline.

See p449 for more information.

Graaff-Reinet

☎ 049 / pop 44,317

Cradled in a curve of the Sundays River and within walking distance of the Camdeboo National Park, Graaff-Reinet is often referred to as the 'jewel of the Karoo'. It's no exaggeration: this is an exquisite, fascinating town that should not be missed.

It's the fourth-oldest European town in South Africa, and it has a superb architectural heritage with more than 220 buildings designated as national monuments. These range from Cape Dutch houses, with their distinctive gables, to classic, flat-roofed Karoo cottages and ornate Victorian villas. Added to all this beauty is a charming small-town quirkiness, some excellent-value accommodation and a variety of eccentric local characters who add to the benignly surreal feel of the whole place.

INFORMATION

Graaff-Reinet Tourism (☎ 049-892 4248; www.graaffreinet.co.za; 13A Church St; 8am-5pm Mon-Fri, 9am-noon Sat) Offers an abundance of maps and information about the area.

Karoo Connections (☎ 049-892 3978; Church St; per hr R30; 8am-5pm Mon-Fri, 9am-noon Sat) Internet access.

SIGHTS

The **Hester Rupert Art Museum** (☎ 049-892 2121; Church St; adult/child R5/free; 9am-12.30pm & 2-5pm Mon-Fri, 9am-noon Sat & Sun) was originally a Dutch Reformed Mission church, consecrated in 1821. The beautiful interior space and art collection are refreshingly contemporary after the Victoriana found elsewhere in town.

The **Old Library** (☎ 049-892 3801; cnr Church & Somerset Sts; adult/child R5/4; 8am-12.30pm & 2-5pm

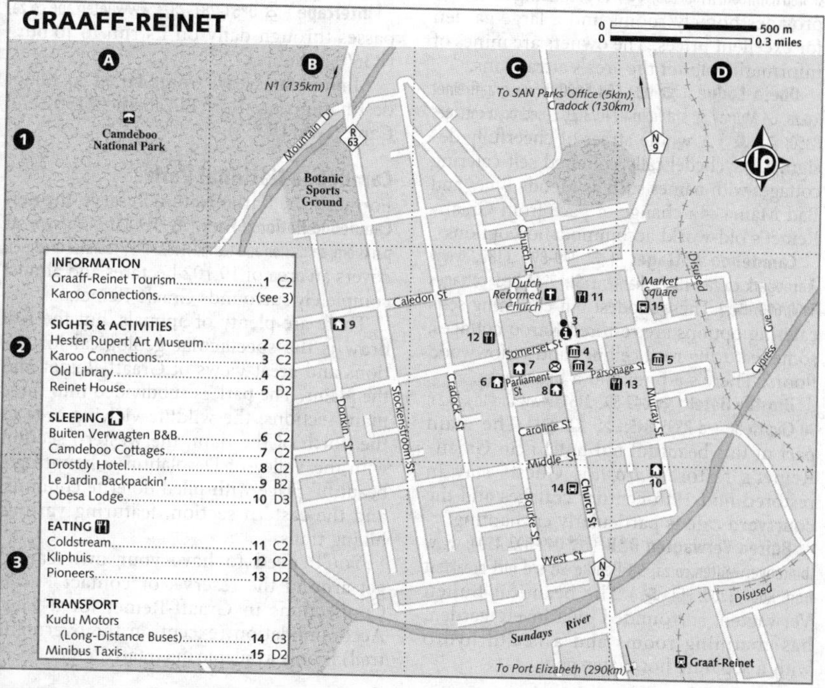

SOUTH AFRICA

Mon-Fri, 9am-3pm Sat, to 4pm Sun) houses a collection of photographs, historical clothing, rock art and fossils from the Karoo.

Reinet House (☎ 049-892 3801; Murray St; adult/child R7/2; 8am-5pm Mon-Fri, 9am-3pm Sat, to 4pm Sun), the Dutch Reformed parsonage built between 1806 and 1812, is a beautiful example of Cape Dutch architecture and the rear courtyard has one of the largest grapevines in the world.

TOURS

Several readers have recommended **Irhafu Tours** (☎ 082 844 2890; irhafutours@yahoo.com); its 1½-hour township tour (R100) gives an insight into both Xhosa culture and history and modern township life. The company can also organise homestays and group meals.

Karoo Connections (☎ 049-892 3978; Church St) operates tours in the area including to the Camdeboo National Park (R275). It can also arrange township walks, nature walks and city tours.

SLEEPING

Le Jardin Backpackin' (☎ 049-892 5890, 082 644 4938; nitagush@telkomsa.net; cnr Donkin & Caledon Sts; s/d with shared bathroom R100/200;) Welcoming Le Jardin provides homely rooms and a large garden for excellent prices. The owners are mines of information about the area's attractions.

Obesa Lodge (☎ 082-588 5900; www.graaffreinet.co.za; 64 Murray St; s/d from R210/300, 2-bedroom cottages R350;) A whole street of cheerfully designed, psychedelically coloured self-catering cottages with names such as Moody Blues and Bad Mama – a change of pace from Graaff-Reinet's old-world accommodation options.

Camdeboo Cottages (☎ 049-892 3180; www.karoopark.co.za; 16 Parliament St; 2-/4-bed cottages R400/600;) These modest but charming self-catering options are restored Karoo cottages, some featuring reed ceilings and yellowwood floors. There's a pool and a braai area.

Drostdy Hotel (☎ 049-892 2161; www.drostdy.co.za; 30 Church St; s/d R595/845;) The main part of this beautiful old hotel is in Graaff-Reinet's restored *drostdy*. Guests stay in restored mid-19th-century cottages and the courtyard cafe is particularly enchanting.

Buiten Verwagten B&B (☎ 049-892 4504; www.buitenverwagten.co.za; 58 Bourke St; s/d incl breakfast from R600/1200;) The beautiful Buiten Verwagten, surrounded by a lovely garden, has charming rooms and a health hydro with a separate hot-water pool.

EATING

Coldstream (☎ 049-891 1181; 3 Church St; mains R60-100; breakfast, lunch & dinner Mon-Sat) An excellent restaurant in a converted family home specialising in old favourites, such as the beloved 'trio' platter of beef, ostrich and kudu or springbok. There's a kiddies menu too.

Pioneers (☎ 049-892 6059; 3 Parsonage St; mains R72-85; lunch & dinner) This cafe-restaurant serves fare including sandwiches, delicious cakes, and *boontjiesop* (bean soup; free if you order something else). There's streetside seating and a small curio shop.

Kliphuis (☎ 049-892 2345; 46 Bourke St; mains R70-120; breakfast, lunch & dinner Tue-Sat, lunch & dinner Sun) Kliphuis is one of Graaff-Reinet's most popular eating spots, with good country fare. Try the salad of roasted butternut, biltong and feta.

GETTING THERE & AWAY

Long-distance buses stop at **Kudu Motors** (Church St). The tourist office acts as the agent for Translux, which stops here en route from Cape Town (R260, 8½ hours) to Queenstown (R160, three hours) via Cradock (R110, 1½ hours), and on the way to Port Elizabeth (R150, three hours).

Intercape (☎ 0861-287 287; www.intercape.co.za) passes through daily on its run to Jo'burg (R360, 11 hours).

Minibus taxis leave from Market Sq. Major destinations are Port Elizabeth (R150) and Cape Town (R350).

Camdeboo National Park

Formerly the Karoo Nature Reserve, the new **Camdeboo National Park** (☎ 049-892 3453; www.sanparks.org; admission adult/child R48/24; sunrise to sunset) covers an area of 19,102 hectares and almost completely surrounds Graaff-Reinet.

There are plenty of animals, but the real draw is the spectacular geological formations and great views of Graaff-Reinet and the plains. The park is subdivided into three main sections: the wildlife-viewing area to the north of the dam; the western section with the Valley of Desolation, a hauntingly beautiful place with piled dolerite columns and the eastern section, featuring various hiking trails.

You'll need to have your own car to get around the reserve, or contact Karoo Connections in Graaff-Reinet for a tour. Accommodation (except on the overnight trail) is only available in Graaff-Reinet.

WILD COAST

With its rugged cliffs plunging into the sea, remote coves sheltering sandy beaches and a history of shipwrecks and stranded sailors, the aptly named Wild Coast is a place for adventure and intrigue.

The Wild Coast stretches for 350km from East London to Port Edward. Dotted along its shore are tiny Xhosa settlements and the occasional holiday resort or backpackers hostel.

You may hear some people refer to the area as the 'Transkei', which was the name of the apartheid-era homeland that once covered this part of the country. Today, 'the Wild Coast' is increasingly used to refer not just to the shoreline, but to the nearby inland areas as well.

Whatever the name of the region, the Xhosa people are some of the friendliest you'll meet anywhere in South Africa, and chances are you'll be invited inside a few of their brightly painted homes that dot the landscape.

This is the place to forego the bus or your car for a while and make use of the walking paths that connect the coastal villages. There are a number of trails, some making use of hotels along the way and offering porterage, and some where you can stay with locals.

If you plan to hike or drive around inland on the Wild Coast, always ask permission before camping. Don't drive after dark, and remember that many of the roads here don't appear on maps, and signposts are few and far between. Drive slowly and watch out for cattle, pedestrians and maniacal drivers.

Chintsa

☎ 043 / pop 2000

Heading up the N2, the sea spray starts to hit your face at an unspoilt stretch of white-sand beach called Chintsa, 38km from East London. Chintsa comprises two small, pretty villages, Chintsa East and Chintsa West. It's definitely the best place on this part of the coast to hang out for a few days (or weeks). Also in the area is the private, upmarket **Inkwenkwezi Game Reserve** (☎ 043-734 3234; www.inkwenkwezi.com; wildlife drive morning/afternoon R595/495, tented bush camp incl meals & activities per person deluxe/luxury R1600/2300; 🕐 8am-4pm), which contains

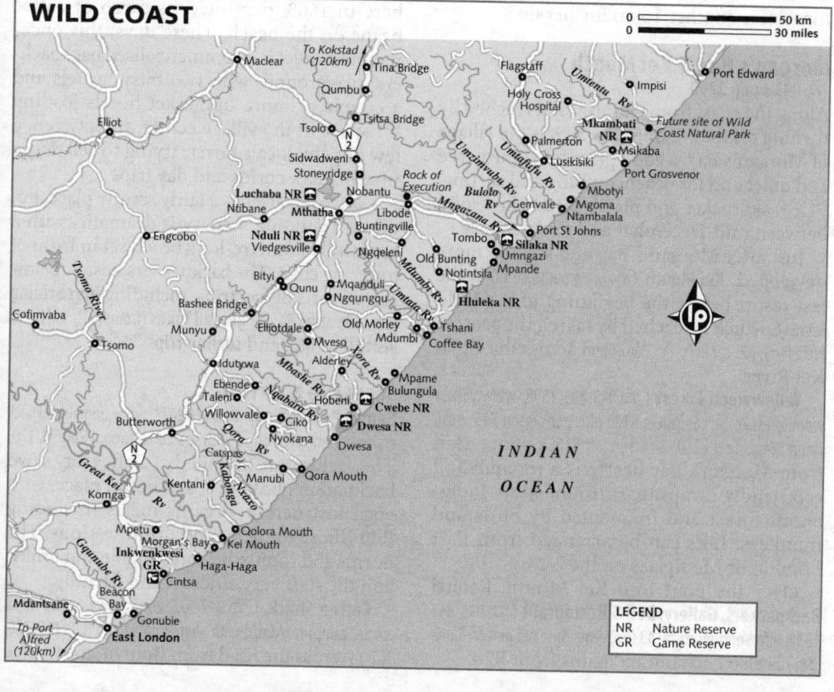

all the Big Five (although the elephants are not wild). The morning wildlife drive includes elephant interaction and both drives include lunch.

SLEEPING

Buccaneer's Backpackers (☎ 043-734 3012, 043-734 3749; www.cintsa.com; Chintsa West; campsites/dm/d incl breakfast R55/110/395; 💻 🏊) Something of a rarity, 'Bucks' is a sort of all-inclusive holiday resort for backpackers offering every imaginable outdoor activity, from surfing to school visits. The dorms and rooms are comfortable, and safari tents (R200) and cottages (for four R750) are also available.

Crawfords Lodge & Cabins (☎ 043-738 5000; www.crawfordscabins.co.za; Chintsa East; s/d incl breakfast & dinner R550/990, self-catering cottages R700; ❄ 💻 🏊) This attractive midrange resort has 23 cottages plus three B&B apartments. It has a pool, good beach access and tennis courts.

GETTING THERE & AWAY

To reach Chintsa from East London, take Exit 26 (East Coast Resorts) off the N2. Go over the overpass and follow the road for 1km to the Chintsa East turn-off. The Chintsa West turn-off is another 16km further on.

Morgan's Bay & Kei Mouth

☎ 043 / pop 2200

Along the coast from Chintsa, and reached by turning off the N2 onto Rte 349, is the village of Morgan's Bay, a good place for some peace and quiet and for beachcombing and surfing. Prices skyrocket and places get booked solid between mid-December and mid-January.

Just after Morgan's Bay and slightly more developed, **Kei Mouth** (www.keimouth.co.za) is the last resort before the beginning of the Wild Coast, which is reached by taking the **pont** (vehicle ferry; per car R60; 🕑 7am-6pm) across the Great Kei River.

Yellowwood Forest (☎ 043-841 1598; www.yellowwoodforest.co.za; campsites R120 plus per person R15, bush camp campsite d R150, 2-person loft R165), about 1km from Morgan's Bay beach, is a tranquil and ecofriendly campsite, surrounded by indigenous forest and frequented by birds and monkeys. Lifts can be arranged from East London or Mooiplaas on the N2.

Over the pont into Kei Mouth, **Naturel Backpackers, Gallery, Deli & Restaurant** (☎ 043-841 1332; info@naturel.co.za; 43 Grosvenor Sq; r per person R200; 🏊) is also enchanting; mains from R70.

Alternatively, the **Morgan Bay Hotel** (☎ 043-841 1062; Beach Rd, Morgan's Bay; r with half board R555; 💻 🏊) is a light and airy family hotel with a bar serving pub grub and a **campsite** (campsites R60-215) nearby.

Strandloper Trail

The 57km, four-day **Strandloper Hiking Trail** (☎ bookings 043-841 1046; www.strandlopertrails.org.za; trail R400) runs between Kei Mouth and Gonubie, just outside East London. The hiking trail is fairly easy, but good fitness is required. Profits are channelled into environmental education for local children. The Strandlopers (meaning 'Beach Walkers') were a Khoisan ethnic group who lived on the coast but disappeared as a distinct group after white settlement.

There are three overnight huts and the cost of staying in these is included in the booking fee. Camping on the beach is prohibited, but most of the coastal hotels have campsites.

Coffee Bay

☎ 047 / pop 600

No one is sure how tiny Coffee Bay got its name, but there is a theory that a ship, wrecked here in 1863, deposited its cargo of coffee beans on the beach. These days, this once-remote hamlet is a commercialised backpackers' playground, with two busy hostels and a couple of more upmarket hotels jostling for space in the village centre. In between, a few hopeful locals hover, trying to sell *dagga* (marijuana), curios and day trips.

Coffee Bay itself is a fairly scruffy place, but the surrounding scenery is dramatic, with a beautiful kilometre-long beach set in front of towering cliffs. The backpackers hostels below run all sorts of day trips, including **horse riding** (2hr treks about R150), **guided hikes** (from R50), **cultural visits** (from R60) and **surfing trips** (R60).

SLEEPING & EATING

Bomvu Paradise (☎ 047-575 2073; www.bomvubackpackers.com; campsites/dm/d with shared bathroom R60/90/170) This is the more hippified of Coffee Bay's two backpackers hostels. It's a soulful place, with yoga instruction, organic meals (including R40 Xhosa dinners) and drum sessions. The dorms and rooms are comfortable and funky and the staff very efficient and friendly.

Coffee Shack (☎ 047-575 2048; www.coffeeshack.co.za; campsites/dm/d with shared bathroom R70/110/260; 💻) Across the road from Bomvu, the Coffee

Shack has a definite party vibe, with regular live local music in the evenings. There are dorms in the main block, but the *rondavels* across the river offer a little more privacy. If you're coming from elsewhere on the Wild Coast, the hostel offers a shuttle service (Mthatha R55; Bulungula R30). Dinner is R60.

Ocean View Hotel (☎ 047-575 2005; www.oceanview.co.za; s/d with half board R910/1400;) Ocean View has good-quality, chalet-style rooms, with a deck overlooking the ocean. There is a restaurant (set dinner R100) and seafood snacks are served in the bar in the evenings.

You can buy mussels, crayfish and other seafood from locals and there's a well-stocked grocery shop.

GETTING THERE & AWAY

If you're driving to Coffee Bay, take the sealed road that leaves the N2 at Viedgesville. A minibus taxi from Mthatha to Coffee Bay costs R25 and takes one hour. The backpackers hostels meet the Baz Bus at the Shell Ultra City, 4km south of Mthatha.

Around Coffee Bay

BULUNGULA BACKPACKERS

This **backpackers hostel** (☎ 047-577 8900, 083 391 5525; www.bulungula.com; campsites per person/dm/d with shared bathroom R60/100/250) has legendary status for its stunning location, community-based activities and ecofriendly ethos. It's 40% owned by the local Xhosa community, which runs tours including horse riding, hiking and canoeing. There's an overall mellow vibe, and the beach parties take place well away from the main camp. Xhosa-style *rondavels* serve as quarters.

Bulungula is two hours' drive southwest of Coffee Bay; phone ahead to get directions or to arrange pick-ups from locations including Mthatha (R60).

Port St Johns

☎ 047 / pop 2100

In the laid-back, idyllic town of Port St Johns, you may well succumb to 'Pondo Fever' – you'll fall in love with it all and won't be able to drag yourself away. The tropical vegetation, dramatic cliffs and great beaches with terrific surf are certainly very attractive, particularly to hippies both young and old. Set on the coast at the mouth of the Umzimvubu River, the town has recently drawn a number of film crews.

SLEEPING & EATING

Amapondo Backpackers (☎ 047-564 1344, 083 315 3103; www.amapondo.co.za; Second Beach Rd; campsites/dm/d with shared bathroom R50/100/250) Four kilometres from the town centre, this is a beautiful hostel with a great view of Second Beach, genial staff, and activities from lounging in hammocks to horse riding and volunteering at community projects. Breakfast (R30), lunch (R25) and dinner (R50) are available and the bar gets lively at night. When we visited, self-contained cottages (from R350) were being built out of recycled materials on the hillside.

Jungle Monkey (☎ 047-564 1517; www.junglemonkey.co.za; 2 Berea Rd; campsites/dm/r with shared bathroom R50/100/250, log cabin R270;) We've had mixed reports about this backpackers hostel and its more upmarket sister next door, Island Backpackers Lodge. Jungle Monkey certainly has the 'party hostel' routine nailed, with a great pool, a garden full of hammocks and a pool table in the always-lively bar. Breakfast (R30), pizzas for dinner (R50) and activities are offered.

Lodge on the Beach (☎ 047-564 1276; www.wildcoastlodge.com; Second Beach; d incl breakfast R500) The two doubles and one twin in this idyllic thatched house open onto decks with unbeatable views of the beach and Bulolo River. It's next to the recommended Delicious Monster cafe-restaurant.

Outspan Inn (☎ 047-564 1057; www.outspaninn.co.za; s/d incl breakfast R325/590, self-catering per person R195;) A favourite with movie crews, this friendly inn has comfortable rooms set around a garden. You can hear the sea, but can't see it – a path through the trees leads to the beach.

GETTING THERE & AWAY

Most backpacker places will pick you up from the Shell Ultra City, 4km south of Mthatha (where the Baz Bus stops) for around R60, but it's essential to book ahead. There are also regular minibus taxis to Port St Johns from here (R40, two hours) that drop you at the roundabout.

If you have your own vehicle, the roads from Mthatha and Port Edward are now mostly sealed, but you still need to drive slowly.

NORTH-EASTERN HIGHLANDS

Roughly comprising the out-of-the-way area that stretches from the lush valleys of the Wild Coast to the sharply ascending peaks of Lesotho, the North-Eastern Highlands enjoys the best of both worlds: stunning scenery and tourist scarcity. Summer brings excellent hiking and fishing, while snowfalls in winter provide the opportunity to ski (albeit on mostly artificial pistes). In the more remote parts, you'll need your own vehicle.

Rhodes

☎ 045 / pop 700

In a spectacular mountain setting alongside the Bell River, Rhodes was declared a conservation area in 1997 and, as a result, the architecture remains as it was when the town was established in 1891.

Tiffindell Ski Resort (☎ 045-974 9005, 011-787 9090; www.snow.co.za), at a height of 2800m and around 23km up a mountain pass (4WD only unless you're very brave) from Rhodes, is a purpose-built winter-sports resort. Its snow-making facilities make a season of 100 days (May to August) possible. Enjoy an après-ski in Ice Station 2720 (elevation: 2720m), South Africa's highest pub.

Tours of **Zakhele township**, housing 569 people, are organised by **Hilda Konzaphi** (☎ 076-856 6062; per person R25).

SLEEPING & EATING

Rhodes Campsite & Caravan Park (☎ 045-974 9290; campsites R45) The park is right in the middle of town and offers shady sites, braai facilities and reasonable ablutions.

our pick **Walkerbouts Inn** (☎ 045-974 9290; www.walkerbouts.co.za; per person with full board R450) Walkerbouts has cosy, comfortable rooms in an interesting house full of old artefacts. There's a friendly bar and the food is good (including build-your-own pizza for around R30).

Rhodes Hotel (☎ 045-974 9305; www.rhodesvillage.co.za; Muller St; s/d with full board R525/850) Rhodes' only hotel is located in an atmospheric old house with well-appointed rooms. There's a convivial bar and a restaurant (mains R45 to R70). Horse riding, tennis and volleyball are on offer.

GETTING THERE & AWAY

The road from to Rhodes from Barkly East (60km, 1½ hours), passing through gob-smacking scenery, is untarred but fine for 2WD cars. The route from Maclear is best undertaken in a 4WD vehicle. The road to Tiffindell is 2WD-friendly but extremely steep in parts; there's a shuttle from Walkerbouts Inn (R200 return).

Aliwal North

☎ 051 / pop 30,000

Aliwal North was in the early 20th century a major tourist drawcard because of its thermal spas. Its appeal dwindled, but today it is enjoying something of a renaissance as a centre of local government.

The **Hot Springs Spa Complex** (admission R18; 🕒 6am-10pm) has a dilapidated indoor pool, but the gardens with picnic facilities, outdoor pools and supertube have been revamped.

Conville Guest Farm (☎ 051-634 2203; www.conville-farm.com; s/d R250/350), an exquisite 1908 farmhouse designed by Sir Herbert Baker, sits in stunning gardens overlooking a lake just outside town, and inside it's all rather grand, with brass beds and antique furniture.

Translux/City to City (☎ 0861-589 282; www.translux.co.za) and **Greyhound** (☎ 083-915 9000; www.greyhound.co.za) stop at the Shell petrol station near General Hertzog Bridge in the north of town. Translux and City to City have daily services to Jo'burg (from R200, eight hours); Greyhound stops here daily en route from Port Elizabeth to Jo'burg/Pretoria (R305, eight hours) via Bloemfontein (R145, two hours). The minibus taxi stop is on Grey St, near the corner of Somerset St.

KWAZULU-NATAL

Rough and ready, smart and sophisticated, rural and rustic, KwaZulu-Natal (KZN) is as eclectic as its cultures, people and landscapes. It has its metropolitan heart in the port of Durban and its nearby historic capital, Pietermaritzburg. The beaches along this coast attract local holiday-makers and visitors wishing to soak up the sand, sea, surf and sun. Head north and you enter President Zuma's birthplace, Zululand, home to some of Africa's most evocative traditional settlements and cultural sites, which proudly display Zulu culture and heritage. The Elephant Coast (Maputaland) boasts the alluring iSimangaliso Wetland Park, encompassing remote wilderness areas.

Head northwest of Durban, and you enter another realm: the historic heartland where the province's history was thrashed out on the Battlefields during the Anglo-Zulu and Anglo-Boer Wars. On the province's western border, the heritage-listed uKhahlamba-Drakensberg Park features awesome peaks, unforgettable vistas and excellent hiking opportunities.

History

Battled over by Boers, Brits and Zulus, Natal was named by Portuguese explorer Vasco da Gama, who sighted the coastline on Christmas Day 1497, and named it for the natal day of Jesus. It took the British Empire more than 300 years to set its sights on the region, proclaiming it a colony in 1843. Briefly linked to the Cape Colony in 1845, Natal again became a separate colony in 1856, when its European population numbered fewer than 5000.

The introduction of Indian indentured labour in the 1860s – sections of the province still retain a subcontinental feel – and the subsequent development of commercial agriculture (mainly sugar) boosted development, and the colony thrived from 1895, when train lines linked Durban's port with the booming Witwatersrand.

The recorded history of the province up until the Union of South Africa is full of conflict: the forced migration of South African ethnic groups, the Boer-Zulu and the Anglo-Zulu Wars, which subjugated the Zulu kingdom; and the two Anglo-Boer wars.

Following the 1994 elections, Natal Province was renamed KwaZulu-Natal, in recognition of the fact that KwaZulu, the Zulu homeland, comprises a large part of the province. Ulundi (the former KwaZulu capital) and Pietermaritzburg (the former Natal homeland capital) were then the joint capitals of the KwaZulu-Natal, until Pietermaritzburg became the province's official capital in 2005.

DURBAN

☎ 031 / pop 3.5 million

Like a maturing adolescent, KwaZulu-Natal's metropolitan hub is ever-changing and taking steps to be more sophisticated. There's more to her than meets the eye yet she is often passed over for her traditionally 'cooler' counterparts such as Cape Town.

South Africa's third-largest city (known as eThekweni in Zulu) is increasingly frequented for her stylish cafes, good shopping and cultural offerings, and justifiably claims to be the country's sporting capital. Thanks to the smart new Moses Mabhida Stadium, a swath of butter yellow sand and balmy water temperatures, Durban is a great city for spectator sports and outdoor enthusiasts.

Despite ongoing efforts to improve the city centre – including five police stations in the dodgy Point neighbourhood and tourist 'ambassadors' walking the streets – the downtown area loses its shimmer when the sun goes down. During the day, however, the beachfront remains a city trademark for activities; the Sun Coast Casino and uShaka Marine World are among the more popular areas.

Northwest of the city centre much is hidden on the pretty, leafy streets of the sophisticated suburbs collectively known as Berea, where there's a plethora of accommodation options, funky bars and stylish eateries.

Durban is renowned for its mix of colours and creeds. The gritty city centre, peppered with some grandiose colonial buildings and art-deco architecture, throbs to a distinctly African beat. Home to the country's largest concentration of people of Indian descent, Durban also has an Asian twang, with the Indian area's marketplaces and streets teeming with the sights, sounds and scents of the subcontinent.

History

Natal Bay, around which Durban is located, provided refuge for seafarers at least as early as 1685, and it's thought that Vasco da Gama anchored here in 1497.

In 1837 the Voortrekkers crossed the Drakensberg and founded Pietermaritzburg, 80km northwest of Durban. The next year, after Durban was evacuated during a Zulu raid, the Boers claimed control. It was reoccupied by a British force later that year, but the Boers stuck by their claim. The British sent troops to Durban but they were defeated at the Battle of Congella in 1842.

The Boers retained control for a month until a British frigate arrived and dislodged them. The next year Natal was annexed by the British and Durban began its growth as an important colonial port city.

In 1860 the first indentured Indian labourers arrived to work the cane fields. Despite the inequitable system – slave labour by another name – many more Indians arrived, including, in 1893, Mohandas Gandhi.

Orientation

In 2007–08 Durban's municipal council controversially renamed many of the city's streets

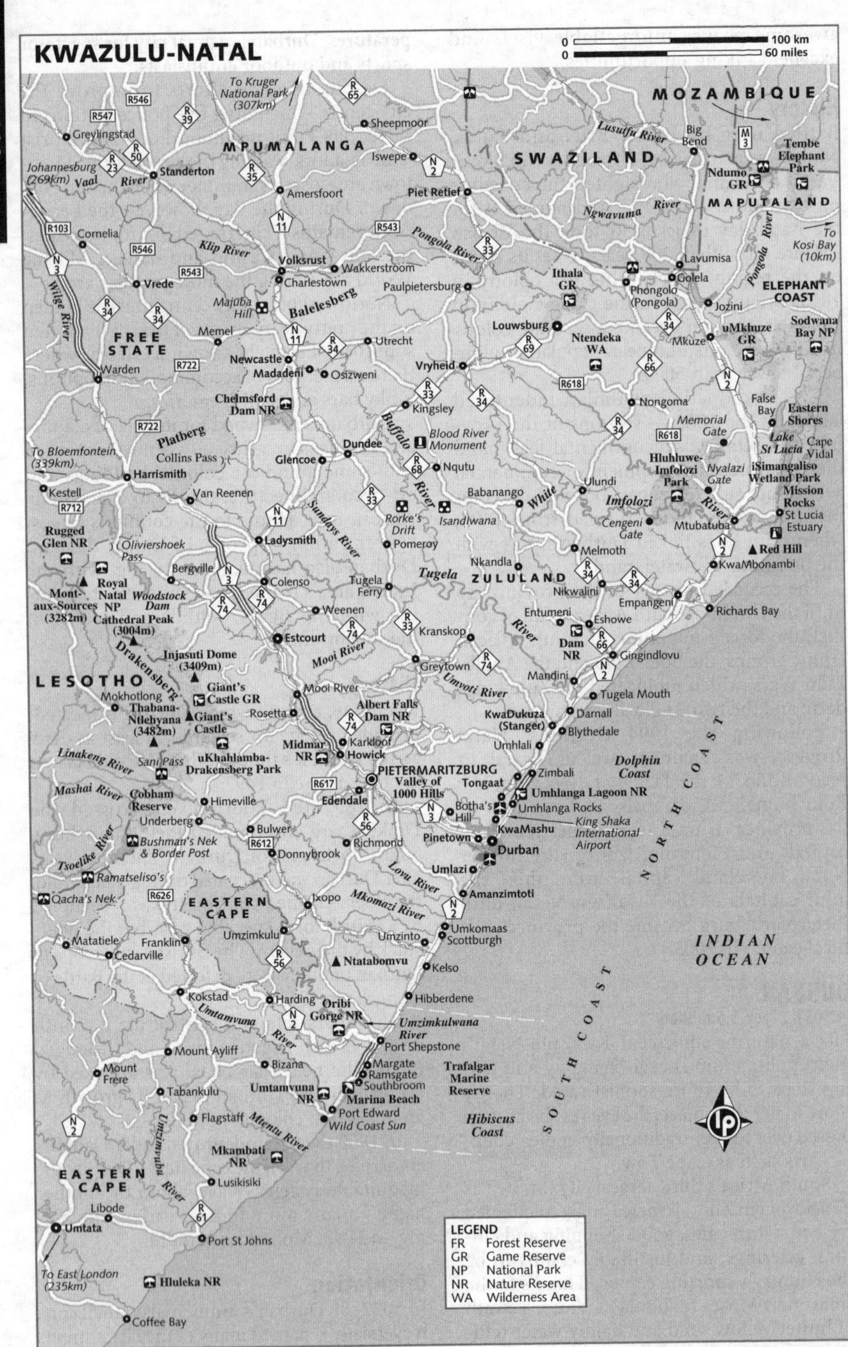
KWAZULU-NATAL
0 100 km
0 60 miles
To Kruger National Park (307km)
MPUMALANGA
MOZAMBIQUE
SWAZILAND
MAPUTALAND
Sheepmoor
Greylingstad
Standerton
Johannesburg (269km)
Vaal River
Amersfoort
Iswepe
Piet Retief
Lusutfu River
Big Bend
Tembe Elephant Park
Ndumo GR
Ngwavuma River
To Kosi Bay (10km)
Cornelia
Klip River
Volksrust
Wakkerstroom
Charlestown
Pongola River
Lavumisa
Golela
Phongolo (Pongola)
Ithala GR
Jozini
ELEPHANT COAST
Vrede
Majuba Hill
Balelesberg
Paulpietersburg
Louwsburg
Ntendeka WA
Mkuze
uMkhuze GR
Sodwana Bay NP
FREE STATE
Memel
Utrecht
Newcastle
Madadeni
Osizweni
Vryheid
Wilge River
Warden
Chelmsford Dam NR
Kingsley
Nongoma
False Bay
Eastern Shores
Memorial Gate
Platberg
Buffalo River
Blood River Monument
Lake St Lucia
Cape Vidal
To Bloemfontein (339km)
Collins Pass
Glencoe
Dundee
Nqutu
Hluhluwe-Imfolozi Park
Nyalazi Gate
iSimangaliso Wetland Park
Harrismith
Kestell
Van Reenen
Babanango
White
Ulundi
Imfolozi
Mission Rocks
St Lucia Estuary
Rorke's Drift
Isandlwana
Cengeni Gate
Mtubatuba
River
Rugged Glen NR
Olivershoek Pass
Ladysmith
Sundays River
Pomeroy
Melmoth
Red Hill
KwaMbonambi
Royal Natal NP
Mont-aux-Sources (3282m)
Bergville
Woodstock Dam
Colenso
Tugela Ferry
Tugela
Nkandla
ZULULAND
Nkwalini
Empangeni
Richards Bay
Cathedral Peak (3004m)
Weenen
Entumeni
Eshowe
Dam NR
Drakensberg
Injasuti Dome (3409m)
Estcourt
Mooi River
Kranskop
Greytown
Umvoti River
Gingindlovu
Mandini
Tugela Mouth
LESOTHO
Mokhotlong
Giant's Castle GR
Thabana-Ntlenyana (3482m)
Giant's Castle
Rosetta
Albert Falls Dam NR
KwaDukuza (Stanger)
Darnall
Blythedale
Umhlali
Linakeng River
Sani Pass
uKhahlamba-Drakensberg Park
Midmar NR
Karkloof
Howick
PIETERMARITZBURG
Valley of 1000 Hills
Tongaat
Zimbali
Dolphin Coast
Mashai River
Cobham Reserve
Himeville
Edendale
Umhlanga Lagoon NR
Umhlanga Rocks
Botha's Hill
KwaMashu
King Shaka International Airport
Underberg
Bulwer
Richmond
Pinetown
Durban
Bushman's Nek & Border Post
Tsoelike River
Donnybrook
Umlazi
Lovu River
Ramatseliso's
Qacha's Nek
EASTERN CAPE
Ixopo
Mkomazi River
Amanzimtoti
NORTH COAST
Matatiele
Franklin
Umzimkulu
Umzinto
Umkomaas
Scottburgh
Cedarville
Ntatabomvu
Kelso
INDIAN OCEAN
Kokstad
Harding
Oribi Gorge NR
Hibberdene
Umtamvuna River
Umzimkulwana River
Port Shepstone
Mount Ayliff
Bizana
Margate
Ramsgate
Southbroom
Trafalgar Marine Reserve
Mount Frere
Tabankulu
Umtamvuna NR
Marina Beach
SOUTH COAST
Flagstaff
Port Edward
Wild Coast Sun
Hibiscus Coast
Mtentu River
Umzimvubu River
Mkambati NR
EASTERN CAPE
Lusikisiki
Libode
Umtata
Port St Johns
To East London (235km)
Hluleka NR
Coffee Bay
LEGEND
FR Forest Reserve
GR Game Reserve
NP National Park
NR Nature Reserve
WA Wilderness Area

to reflect a 'new South Africa'; debate still rages over the changes. Many streets are now labelled twice: with the old sign – with a red line through it – as well as the new one.

Some new street names are awaiting the rubber stamp. We have provided, where possible, both the new and former street names; the old names, which many people still use, are listed second.

OR Tambo/Marine Pde, which fronts the beach, is one of Durban's seaside focal points. Formerly derelict, the Point, which runs along the spit south of OR Tambo/Marine Pde, is slowly being revived. The area's huge uShaka Marine World theme park has a patrolled beach, but venturing beyond there is not recommended.

Dr Pixley KaSeme/West St starts as a mall, but further west it becomes one of central Durban's main streets. The City Hall and the centre of town are about 1km west of the beach, straddling Dr Pixley KaSeme/West St and Anton Lembede/Smith St.

On the western side of the city centre, around Dr Yusuf Dadoo/Grey and Berta Mkhize/Victoria Sts, is the Indian area. There is a bustle and vibrancy here that is missing from most commercial districts in South Africa.

Near the Indian area, around Berea train station, is Warwick Triangle. This jumble of overpasses, minibus taxi ranks and markets is a fascinating, but in-your-face, gritty place, and should be visited with a tour guide.

Northwest of the city, starting at a ridge and spreading beyond, is the area known as Berea. This incorporates the beginnings of the wealthier suburbs (including Greyville, Morningside, Musgrave and Berea itself), rich with pubs, clubs, eateries and hostels. Across the Umgeni River, Durban North is an upmarket residential suburb dotted with guest houses.

Suburbs sprawl all the way up the coast to Umhlanga Rocks, a big resort and retirement town. On Durban's western fringe is the suburb of Pinetown, one of the former townships that surround the city and house most of its mainly black population.

Information

EMERGENCY

Ambulance (☎ 10177)

General emergency (☎ 031-361 0000)

Main police station (Map pp486-7; ☎ 10111; Stalwart Simelane/Stanger St) North of the city centre.

Police station (Map pp486-7; ☎ 031-368 3399; OR Tambo/Marine Pde) Near Funworld on the beach.

INTERNET ACCESS

Europa cafe (see p491) offers wi-fi access. Most accommodation has wi-fi and/or a computer for guest use; charges start at about R40 per hour.

Cityzen (Map p489; ☎ 031-303 9169; 161 Gordon Rd, Morningside; per hr R20; 8am-midnight) A stylish cafe for surfing the net or just hanging out over coffee.

MEDICAL SERVICES

Entabeni Hospital (Map p484; ☎ 031-204 1300; 148 South Ridge Rd, Berea)

Umhlanga Hospital (off Map p484; ☎ 031-560 5500; 323 Umhlanga Rocks Dr, Umhlanga) Handy to the north coast and northern Durban.

MONEY

There are banks with ATMs and change facilities across the city – including Standard Bank, FNB and Nedbank.

American Express (Map p484; ☎ 031-202 8733; FNB House, 151 Musgrave Rd, Musgrave)

Rennies Foreign Exchange Central Durban (Map pp486-7; ☎ 031-305 5722; ground fl, 333 Anton Lembede/Smith St); Musgrave Centre (Map p484; ☎ 031-202 7833; Shop 311, Level 3, Musgrave Centre, Musgrave Rd; 9am-5pm Mon-Fri, to 1pm Sat)

POST

Main post office (Map pp486-7; cnr Dr Pixley KaSeme/West & Dorothy Nyembe/Gardiner Sts; 8am-5pm Mon-Fri, to 1pm Sat)

TOURIST INFORMATION

Durban Tourism airport (☎ 031-408 1000; Arrivals Hall; 7am-9pm); Tourist Junction (Map pp486-7; ☎ 031-304 4934; www.durbanexperience.co.za, www.durban.gov.za; 1st fl, Tourist Junction); An extremely useful information service on Durban and surrounds. It can help with accommodation bookings and arrange tours of the city and beyond.

Ezemvelo KZN Wildlife (Map pp486-7; ☎ 031-304 4934; www.kznwildlife.com; 1st fl, Tourist Junction) Here you can reserve accommodation in Ezemvelo KZN Wildlife parks and reserves (at least 48 hours' notice required).

SAN Parks Reservations (Map pp486-7; ☎ 031-304 4934; www.sanparks.org; 1st fl, Tourist Junction) Takes accommodation bookings for national parks across the country.

Tourist Junction (Map pp486-7; ☎ 031-304 4934; 160 Monty Naicker Rd/Pine St; 8am-4.30pm Mon-Fri, 9am-2pm Sat) On the corner of Soldier's Way, the main tourist

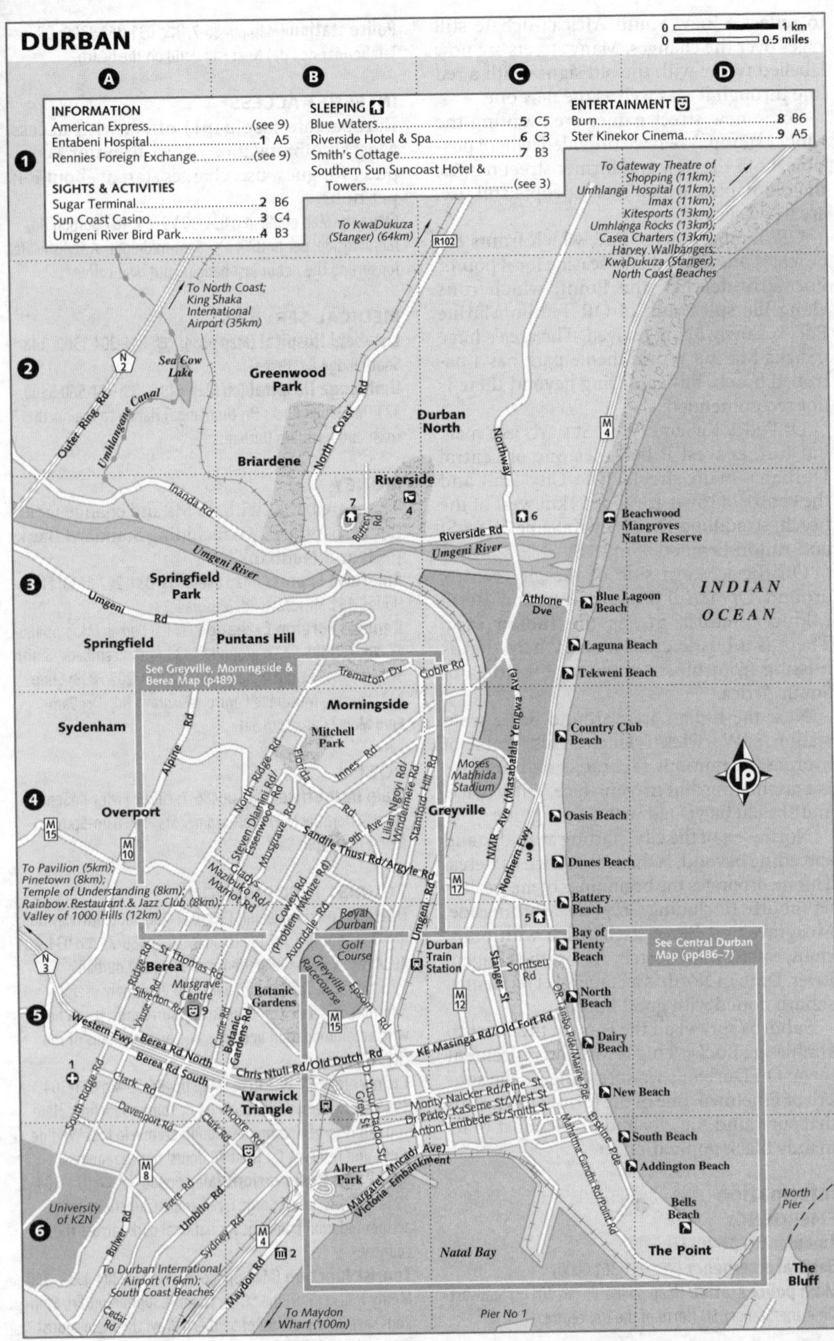

DURBAN
INFORMATION
American Express (see 9)
Entabeni Hospital 1 A5
Rennies Foreign Exchange (see 9)
SIGHTS & ACTIVITIES
Sugar Terminal 2 B6
Sun Coast Casino 3 C4
Umgeni River Bird Park 4 B3
SLEEPING
Blue Waters 5 C5
Riverside Hotel & Spa 6 C3
Smith's Cottage 7 B3
Southern Sun Suncoast Hotel & Towers (see 3)
ENTERTAINMENT
Burn 8 B6
Ster Kinekor Cinema 9 A5
To Gateway Theatre of Shopping (11km); Umhlanga Hospital (11km); Imax (11km); Kitesports (13km); Umhlanga Rocks (13km); Casea Charters (13km); Harvey Wallbangers; KwaDukuza (Stanger); North Coast Beaches
To KwaDukuza (Stanger) (64km)
To North Coast; King Shaka International Airport (35km)
Sea Cow Lake
Umhlangane Canal
Outer Ring Rd
Greenwood Park
North Coast Rd
Durban North
Northway
Briardene
Riverside
Inanda Rd
Buttery Rd
Riverside Rd
Umgeni River
Beachwood Mangroves Nature Reserve
INDIAN OCEAN
Springfield Park
Umgeni Rd
Athlone Dve
Blue Lagoon Beach
Laguna Beach
Tekweni Beach
Springfield
Puntans Hill
See Greyville, Morningside & Berea Map (p489)
Trematon Dv
Goble Rd
Morningside
Sydenham
Mitchell Park
Country Club Beach
Alpine Rd
North Ridge Rd
Florida Rd
Innes Rd
Moses Mabhida Stadium
NMR Ave (Masabalala Yengwa Ave)
Overport
Steven Dlamini Rd/Essenwood Rd
Musgrave Rd
9th Ave
Lillian Ngoyi Rd/Windermere Rd
Stamford Hill Rd
Greyville
Oasis Beach
Sandile Thusi Rd/Argyle Rd
Northern Fwy
Dunes Beach
To Pavilion (5km); Pinetown (8km); Temple of Understanding (8km); Rainbow Restaurant & Jazz Club (8km); Valley of 1000 Hills (12km)
Gladys Mazibuko Rd/Marriott Rd
Cowey Rd (Problem Mkhize Rd)
Avondale Rd
Battery Beach
Royal Durban Golf Course
Umgeni Rd
Bay of Plenty Beach
See Central Durban Map (pp486–7)
Berea
St Thomas Rd
Ridge Rd
Musgrave Centre
Silverton Rd
Greyville Racecourse
Epsom Rd
Durban Train Station
Stanger St
Somtseu Rd
North Beach
Botanic Gardens
Vause Rd
Currie Rd
Botanic Gardens Rd
OR Tambo Pde/Marine Pde
Western Fwy
Berea Rd North
Berea Rd South
KE Masinga Rd/Old Fort Rd
Dairy Beach
Chris Ntuli Rd/Old Dutch Rd
Clark Rd
South Ridge Rd
Warwick Triangle
Dr Yusuf Dadoo St/Grey St
Monty Naicker Rd/Pine St
Dr Pixley KaSeme St/West St
Anton Lembede St/Smith St
New Beach
Davenport Rd
Moore Rd
Clark Rd
Erskine Pde
South Beach
Mahatma Gandhi Rd/Point Rd
Albert Park
Margaret Mncadi Ave)
Victoria Embankment
Addington Beach
Frere Rd
Umbilo Rd
University of KZN
Bulwer Rd
Sydney Rd
Natal Bay
Bells Beach
The Point
North Pier
The Bluff
To Durban International Airport (16km); South Coast Beaches
Maydon Rd
Cedar Rd
To Maydon Wharf (100m)
Pier No 1
0 1 km
0 0.5 miles

information centre for Durban and the region is in the city's original train station (built in 1894).

Zulu Kingdom Tourist Junction (KZN Tourism; Map pp486-7; ☎ 031-366 7500; www.zulu.org.za; ground fl, Tourist Junction); uShaka Marine World (Map pp486-7; ☎ 031-337 8099; 🕑 9am-9pm) Information office dealing with the whole province; offers a smorgasbord of reference and promotional brochures.

Dangers & Annoyances

Muggings and pickpockets are a problem around the beach esplanade and some central areas; do not walk around here at night. Mahatma Gandhi Point Rd, south of Anton Lembede/Smith St, should be avoided. Extra care should also be taken around the Umgeni Rd side of the train station and the Warwick Triangle markets.

At night, with the exception of the Casino and around the Playhouse Theatre (if something is on), central Durban becomes a ghost town as people head to the suburbs for entertainment. Always catch a cab to/from nightspots (and with others, if possible).

If you have a car, parking is generally OK outside suburban restaurants, but don't leave it in the street all night; use off-street parking (most accommodation options offer this).

Sights

BEACHFRONT

If you dip into the city's summer surf and sun, you have a playground of more than 6km of warm-water beaches (protected by the requisite shark nets). The 'Golden Mile' beaches run from Blue Lagoon (at the mouth of the Umgeni River) to uShaka Marine World on the Point.

The beachfront isn't for everyone, of course; to some, it's a smorgasbord of garish and tacky bars and restaurants. If you do take the plunge, always swim in patrolled areas, which are indicated by flags.

Divided into several areas (Sea World, Wet'n'Wild World and uShaka Beach), **uShaka Marine World** (Map pp486-7; ☎ 031-368 6675/328 8000; www.ushakamarineworld.co.za; Addington Beach, the Point; Wet'n'Wild adult/child/senior R79/62/62, Sea World R100/70/70, combination R152/100/100; 🕑 9am-5pm) boasts one of the world's largest aquariums, the biggest collection of sharks in the southern hemisphere, a seal stadium, a dolphinarium, a mock-up 1940s steamer wreck housing restaurants and a bar, enough freshwater rides to make you seasick, and a beach featuring activities from surfing lessons to snorkelling.

The **Promenade** is the pedestrianised tourist superhighway running up the beach from Anton Lembede/Smith St north of uShaka. On the other side of the road, particularly along OR Tambo/Marine Pde, you will find the canyon of high-rise hotels, bars, restaurants and nightclubs typical of modern seaside cities.

In summer, **rickshaws** ply their trade along the beachfront, many sporting exotic Zulu regalia. A 15-minute ride costs about R30 (plus R10 for a happy snap).

The glitzy, nouveau art deco of **Sun Coast Casino** (Map p484; ☎ 031-328 3000; www.suncoastcasino.co.za; Snell Pde) is popular among the locals and features slot machines, cinemas and some well-attended restaurants. The casino's beachside **relaxation area** (admission R5; 🕑 8.30am-5pm) is a safe and pleasant spot to lie and bake. It has a lawn, deck chairs and umbrellas.

A planned promenade will link the beachfront near the Casino to the new **Moses Mabhida Stadium**, with shops and cafes near the base of the stadium. A **cable car** will ascend to a viewing platform at the top of the stadium's 105m-high arch.

MARGARET MNCADI AVE/VICTORIA EMBANKMENT

Maydon Wharf, which runs along the southwestern side of the harbour and south of Margaret Mncadi Ave/Victoria Embankment, contains the **Sugar Terminal** (Map p484; ☎ 031-365 8153; 51 Maydon Rd; adult/concession R15/7; 🕑 tours 8.30am, 10am & 11.30am Mon-Fri, 2pm Mon-Wed & Fri), which offers an insight into the former importance of the sugar trade.

Further north, waterside development **Wilson's Wharf** (Map pp486-7) has decent eateries and bars, boat-charter outfits, shops and a theatre.

The **Port Natal Maritime Museum** (Map pp486-7; ☎ 031-311 2230; Maritime Pl; adult/child R3/1.50; 🕑 8.30am-3.30pm Mon-Sat, 11am-3.30pm Sun) is on a service road running parallel to Margaret Mncadi Ave. You can explore two former steam tugs and see the huge wicker basket once used for hoisting passengers onto ocean liners.

BAT Centre (Map pp486-7; ☎ 031-332 0451; 45 Maritime Pl) is a colourful bohemian arts centre housing art and craft shops, artists' studios and a bar-restaurant, all cut through with a lively trans-Africa theme.

Durban's harbour is the busiest in Southern Africa (and the ninth busiest in the world). The channel mouth is currently being extended by 100m.

SOUTH AFRICA

CENTRAL DURBAN

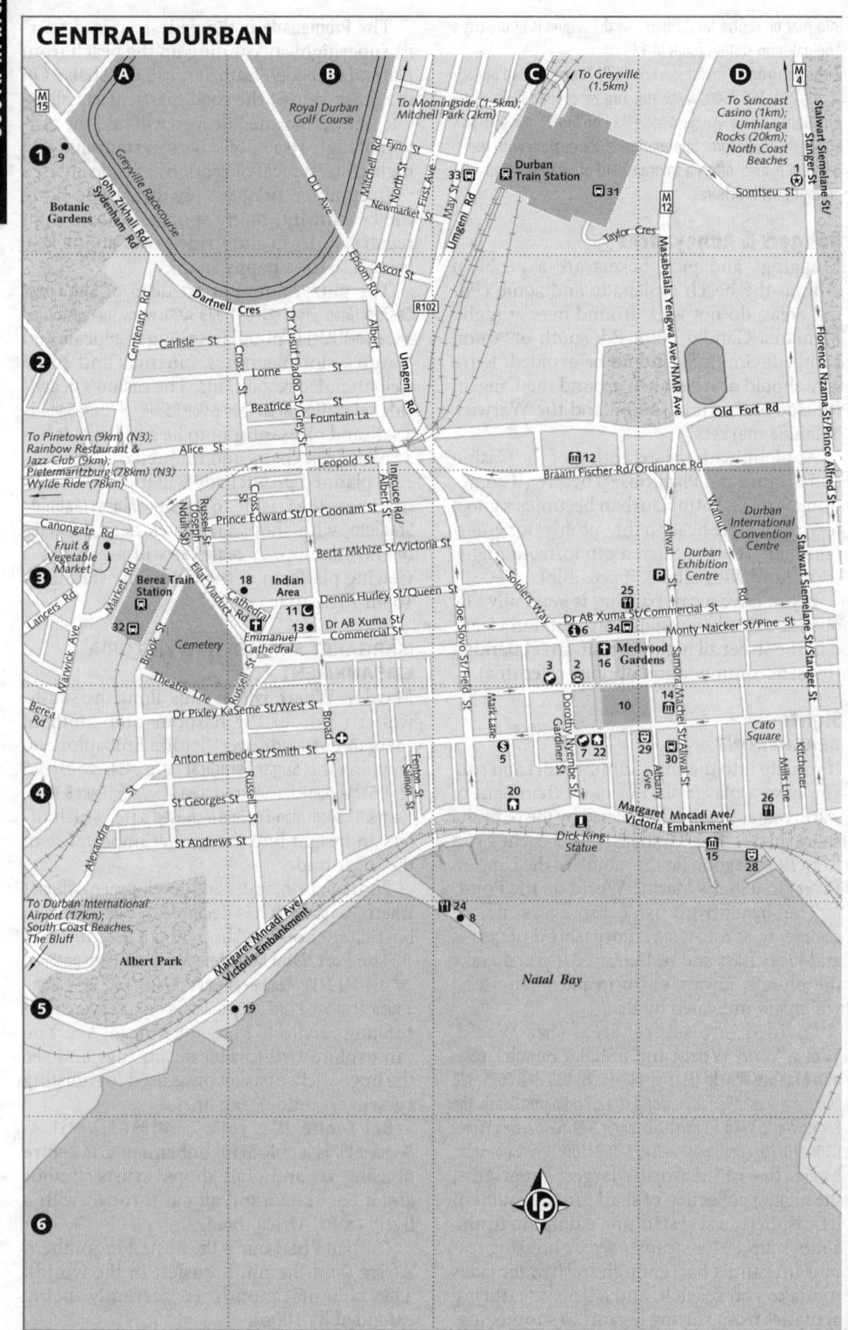

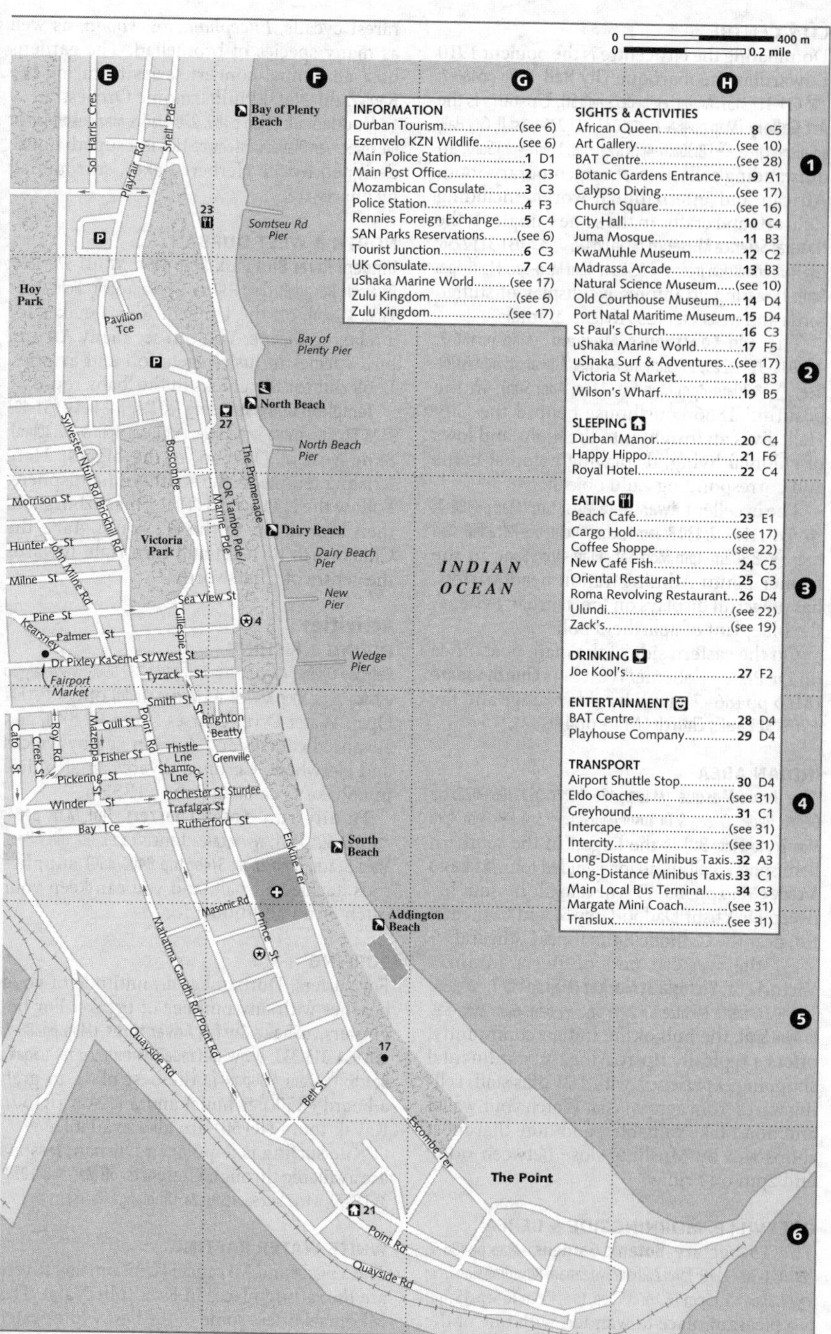
0 400 m
0 0.2 mile
E
F
G
H
1
2
3
4
5
6
INFORMATION
Durban Tourism....................(see 6)
Ezemvelo KZN Wildlife...........(see 6)
Main Police Station.................1 D1
Main Post Office......................2 C3
Mozambican Consulate............3 C3
Police Station............................4 F3
Rennies Foreign Exchange.......5 C4
SAN Parks Reservations.........(see 6)
Tourist Junction.......................6 C3
UK Consulate............................7 C4
uShaka Marine World..........(see 17)
Zulu Kingdom..........................(see 6)
Zulu Kingdom........................(see 17)
SIGHTS & ACTIVITIES
African Queen..........................8 C5
Art Gallery.........................(see 10)
BAT Centre...........................(see 28)
Botanic Gardens Entrance........9 A1
Calypso Diving....................(see 17)
Church Square.....................(see 16)
City Hall.................................10 C4
Juma Mosque.........................11 B3
KwaMuhle Museum...............12 C2
Madrassa Arcade...................13 B3
Natural Science Museum.....(see 10)
Old Courthouse Museum......14 D4
Port Natal Maritime Museum..15 D4
St Paul's Church....................16 C3
uShaka Marine World............17 F5
uShaka Surf & Adventures...(see 17)
Victoria St Market.................18 B3
Wilson's Wharf......................19 B5
SLEEPING
Durban Manor........................20 C4
Happy Hippo..........................21 F6
Royal Hotel............................22 C4
EATING
Beach Café.............................23 E1
Cargo Hold.........................(see 17)
Coffee Shoppe....................(see 22)
New Café Fish.........................24 C5
Oriental Restaurant.................25 C3
Roma Revolving Restaurant...26 D4
Ulundi.................................(see 22)
Zack's..................................(see 19)
DRINKING
Joe Kool's...............................27 F2
ENTERTAINMENT
BAT Centre.............................28 D4
Playhouse Company...............29 D4
TRANSPORT
Airport Shuttle Stop...............30 D4
Eldo Coaches.......................(see 31)
Greyhound..............................31 C1
Intercape.............................(see 31)
Intercity...............................(see 31)
Long-Distance Minibus Taxis..32 A3
Long-Distance Minibus Taxis.33 C1
Main Local Bus Terminal.........34 C3
Margate Mini Coach............(see 31)
Translux...............................(see 31)
Bay of Plenty Beach
Sol Harris Cres
Playfair Rd
Snell Pde
Somtseu Rd Pier
Hoy Park
Pavilion Tce
Bay of Plenty Pier
North Beach
North Beach Pier
Sylvester Ntuli Rd/Brickhill Rd
Boscombe
The Promenade
OR Tambo Pde/ Marine Pde
Morrison St
Hunter St
John Milne Rd
Victoria Park
Dairy Beach
Dairy Beach Pier
Milne St
Sea View St
New Pier
INDIAN OCEAN
Pine St
Kearsney
Palmer St
Gillespie
Dr Pixley KaSeme St/West St
Wedge Pier
Fairport Market
Tyzack St
Smith St
Brighton Beatty
Cato St
Creek St
Roy Rd
Mazeppa St
Gull St
Point Rd
Fisher St
Thistle Lne
Grenville
Shamrock Lne
Pickering St
Rochester St
Sturdee
Winder St
Trafalgar St
Bay Tce
Rutherford St
Erskine Ter
South Beach
Masonic Rd
Prince St
Addington Beach
Mahatma Gandhi Rd/Point Rd
Quayside Rd
Bell St
Escombe Ter
The Point
Point Rd
Quayside Rd

CITY CENTRE

Dominating the city centre is the opulent 1910 Edwardian neobaroque **City Hall** (Map pp486-7; ☎ 031-311 2137; Anton Lembede/Smith St). Upstairs is the **Art Gallery** (Map pp486-7; ☎ 031-311 2264; 1st fl, City Hall; admission free; 8.30am-4pm Mon-Sat, 11am-4pm Sun), an outstanding collection of contemporary South African and international works, including Zulu arts and crafts. In the same complex is the **Natural Science Museum** (Map pp486-7; ☎ 031-311 2256; City Hall; admission free; 8.30am-4pm Mon-Sat, 11am-4pm Sun), boasting an impressive display of stuffed birds and insects, plus African animals.

The **Old Courthouse Museum** (Map pp486-7; ☎ 031-311 2229; 77 Samora Machel/Aliwal St; admission free; 8.30am-4pm Mon-Sat, 11am-4pm Sun), in the beautiful 1866 courthouse behind the City Hall, gives an insight into the highs and lows of colonial living, displaying colonial items and corresponding Zulu objects.

The excellent **KwaMuhle Museum** (Map pp486-7; ☎ 031-311 2237; 130 Braam Fischer/Ordinance Rd; admission free; 8.30am-4pm Mon-Sat, 11am-4pm Sun), in the former Bantu Administration headquarters, has powerful displays on the 'Durban System', the blueprint of apartheid policy.

On the eastern side of the main post office on Dr Pixley KaSeme/West St is **Church Square** (Map pp486–7), with its old vicarage and the 1909 **St Paul's Church** (Map pp486–7).

INDIAN AREA

The **Juma Mosque** (Map pp486-7; ☎ 031-306 0026; cnr Dennis Hurley/Queen & Dr Yusuf Dadoo/Grey Sts; 9am-4pm Mon-Fri, to 11am Sat) is the largest in the southern hemisphere; call ahead for a guided tour. **Madrassa Arcade** (Map pp486–7) is next to the mosque between Dr Yusuf Dadoo/Grey St and Cathedral Rd, near the Catholic Emmanuel Cathedral.

At the western end of Berta Mkhize/Victoria St, **Victoria St Market** (Map pp486-7; ☎ 031-306 4021, Berta Mkhize/Victoria St; 6am-6pm Mon-Sat, to 4pm Sun), the hub of the Indian community, offers a typically rip-roaring, subcontinental shopping experience, with 160-plus stalls selling wares from across Asia. Watch your wallet and don't take valuables, and note that most shops run by Muslims close between noon and 2pm on Friday.

GREYVILLE, MORNINGSIDE & BEREA

The 15-hectare **Botanic Gardens** (Map pp486-7; ☎ 031-309 1170; John Zikhali/Sydenham Rd; admission free; 7.30am-5.15pm 16 Apr-15 Sep, to 5.45pm 16 Sep-15 Apr) is a pleasant place to wander, with one of the rarest cycads, *Encephalartos woodii,* as well as many species of bromeliad. The gardens host an annual concert series featuring the KwaZulu-Natal Philharmonic Orchestra.

Muckleneuk (Map p489; 220 Gladys Mazibuko/Marriot Rd, cnr Steven Dlamini/Essenwood Rd) is a superb house designed by Sir Herbert Baker, surrounded by gnarly trees.

NORTH & WEST DURBAN

Umgeni River Bird Park (Map p484; ☎ 031-579 4600; Riverside Rd; adult/child R30/25; 9am-5pm, flight shows 11am & 2pm), on the Umgeni River, makes for a relaxing escape. You can see many African bird species in lush vegetation and aviaries. Look out for the chicks in the 'baby room'.

Temple of Understanding (off Map p484; ☎ 031-403 3328; Bhaktieedanta Sami Circle; 10am-1pm & 4-7.30pm), 8km west of Durban, is the biggest Hare Krishna temple in the southern hemisphere. Follow the N3 towards Pietermaritzburg and then branch off to the N2 south. Take the Chatsworth turn-off and turn right towards the centre of Chatsworth.

Activities

DIVING & FISHING

Calypso Diving (Map pp486-7; ☎ 031-332 0905; www.calypsoushaka.co.za; Shop K8, uShaka Marine World) offers PADI Open Water Diver courses (from R2400), and advanced courses and dives in nearby wrecks and elsewhere. Certified divers can also dive in uShaka's ocean aquarium (R350).

Family-run **Casea Charters** (off Map p484; ☎ 031-561 7381; www.caseacharters.co.za; Grannies Pool, Main Beach, Umhlanga; 3/4hr trip R400/450) supplies rods, tackle and bait, and you can keep your catch at no additional fee.

SURFING

For surfers, Durban has a multitude of good beaches with any number of breaks. For beginners, **uShaka Surf & Adventures** (Map pp486-7; ☎ 031-313 333; www.surfandadventures.co.za; uShaka Beach; 7am-4.30pm) is the best place to grab a board (R50 per hour) and a lesson (R150). Kayak tours (R150) are also available.

Kite surfing is popular in Durban; lessons are available through **Kitesports** (off Map p484; 079-353 9472; www.kitesports.co.za; Umhlanga Rocks).

WHITE-WATER RAFTING

The Tugela and Mkomazi (Umkomaas) Rivers are *the* rafting places in KwaZulu-Natal. The Mkomazi offers some of the best white-water

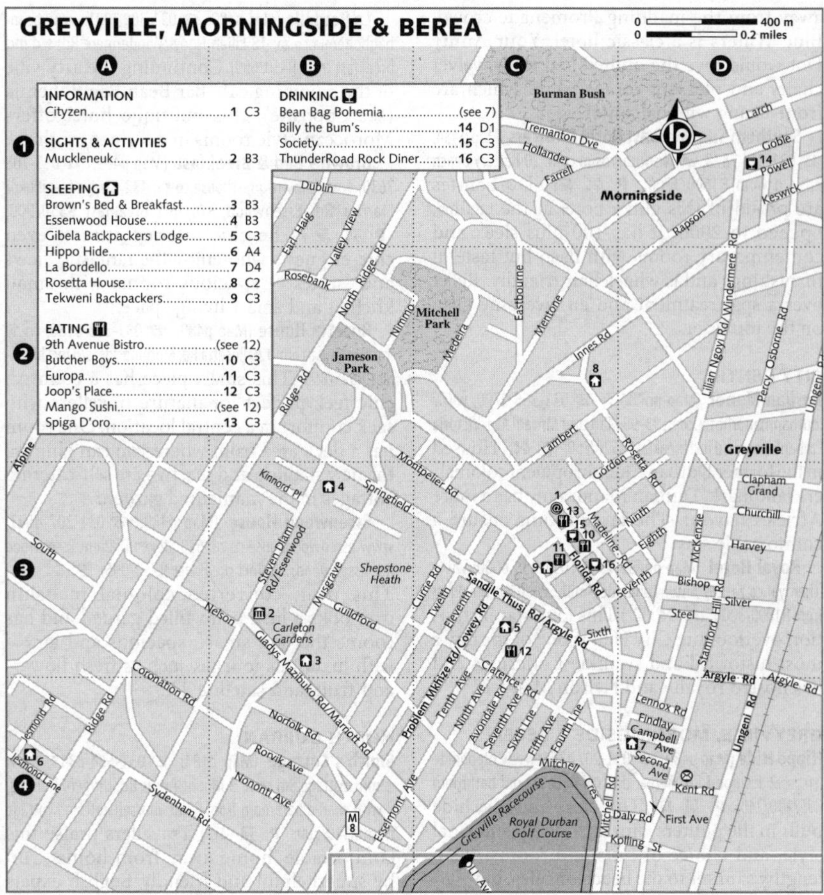

rafting, especially from November to April, when you can rip through Grade II–IV rapids. **Wylde Ride** (off Map pp486-7; ☎ 082 561 5660, 082 455 8323; 80 Leinster Rd, Scottsville, Pietermaritzburg) runs trips (from R515) with great scenery and rapids.

CRUISES

The luxury yacht **African Queen** (Map pp486-7; ☎ 032-305 3099; Wilson's Wharf; adult/child from R50/30; departs 10am-4pm) cruises the harbour for half an hour or goes out to sea for an hour (departing 12.30pm and 2.30pm).

Sleeping

Durban Africa's accommodation website, www.bookabedahead.co.za, allows you to browse and book online.

Despite the hotel-lined beachfront promenade, much of Durban's accommodation is in the western and northwestern suburbs. Unless you have come for the sun and sand alone, accommodation in the suburbs is better value than the beachfront options.

BEACHFRONT

Happy Hippo (Map p484; ☎ 031-368 7181; www.happy-hippo.info; 222 Mahatma Ghandi/Point Rd; dm/s/d with shared bathroom R100/250/270, r R390;) Hippo Hide's spacious, warehouse-style sister lodge is close to the beach and uShaka Marine World, but in the dodgy Point area.

Blue Waters (Map p484; ☎ 031-327 7000; www.bluewatershotel.co.za; 175 Snell Pde; s/d incl breakfast R770/870; P) At the northern end of the beachfront, away from the madding Promenade crowd, Blue Waters is a classic hotel. Your Aunty Dot would love the quilted bedheads, velvet chairs and pleasant rooms, all of which are front-facing with balconies.

Southern Sun Suncoast Hotel & Towers (Map p484; ☎ 031-314 7878; www.southernsun.com; 20 Battery Beach Rd; s/d from R1600/1700; P) Durbanites are proud of this glitzy hotel at the casino, opened in 2006. It has 100-plus sleek and contemporary rooms with flash but tasteful furnishings and is wheelchair friendly. Relax over a spa treatment and an awesome vista on the top floor.

CITY CENTRE

Durban Manor (Map pp486-7; ☎ 031-366 0700; www.durbanmanorhotel.com; 93-96 Margaret Mncadi Ave/Victoria Embankment; s/d incl breakfast R520/750; P) Housed in the former Durban Club, an opulent colonial-era landmark, Durban Manor now has a more African flavour. The large rooms ensure a comfortable stay.

Royal Hotel (Map pp486-7; ☎ 031-333 6000; www.theroyal.co.za; 267 Anton Lembede/Smith St; s/d incl breakfast from R1800/3000; P) This four-star institution overlooking City Hall is one of the city's most historical and swankiest offerings and has hosted royalty and Nelson Mandela.

GREYVILLE, MORNINGSIDE & BEREA

Hippo Hide (Map p489; ☎ 031-207 4366; www.hippohide.co.za; 2 Jesmond Rd, Berea; dm/s/d with shared bathroom R95/190/240; P) This clean and cosy hide pulls in the punters with its friendly, informal style, and choice of huts and rooms. It's a lengthy saunter to the beach or cafes, but staff helps organise outings.

Tekweni Backpackers (Map p489; ☎ 031-303 1433; www.tekwenibackpackers.co.za; 169 Ninth Ave, Morningside; dm/s/d with shared bathroom from R105/220/300; P) This old dog 'keeps on keeping on'; it's a slightly saggy place that nevertheless attracts party animals who like raucous, gregarious surrounds. Its friendly staff is in the 'nightlife know' and you're just off Florida Rd.

Gibela Backpackers Lodge (Map p489; ☎ 031-303 6291; www.gibelabackpackers.co.za; 119 Ninth Ave, Morningside; dm/s/tw with shared bathroom incl breakfast R150/300/400; P) If this hostel, a tastefully converted 1950s Tuscan-style home, were a B&B, it would be described as 'boutique'. Once you're past the fortresslike exterior, it has sparkling surfaces and rooms neat enough to pass an army major's inspection.

La Bordello (Map p489; ☎ 031-309 1001; www.beanbagbohemia.co.za; 18 Lilian Ngoyi/Windermere Rd; s/d incl breakfast from R450/650) Continuing the arty vibe of the adjoining cafe-bar Bean Bag Bohemia (see opposite), this boutique hotel offers Moroccan-style rooms in a former brothel.

Brown's Bed & Breakfast (Map p489; ☎ 031-208 7630; www.brownsguesthouse.co.za; 132 Gladys Mazibuko/Marriot Rd, Essenwood; s/d incl breakfast R550/900; P) The chic interior attracts even chic-er guests who enjoy the fantastic views and 'suites' – spacious rooms with small kitchen and smart living space.

Rosetta House (Map p489; ☎ 031-303 6180; www.rosettahouse.com; 126 Rosetta Rd, Morningside; s/d incl breakfast R625/850) This smart place has a country-chic feel, perfect for mature travellers who seek comfort in a central location. One room has a deck area from where you can glimpse the new stadium and sea; two are self-catering cottages in the manicured garden.

Essenwood House (Map p489; ☎ 031-207 4547; www.essenwoodhouse.co.za; 630 Steven Dlamini/Essenwood Rd, Essenwood; s/d incl breakfast R750/995; P) This neat, converted colonial mansion overlooks a lush palm-filled garden and has rooms that are smart, spacious and airy – with luxurious touches such as fresh flowers and fruit, and satellite TV.

NORTH DURBAN

Smith's Cottage (Map p484; ☎ 031-564 6313; www.smithscottage.8m.com; 5 Mount Argus Rd, Umgeni Heights; d with shared bathroom from R300, dm/self-catering cottage from R110/700; P) Travellers praise this comfortable 'home away from home', run by superhelpful and friendly English expats Keith and Pat. Accommodation comes in all shapes and sizes, with a laid-back atmosphere and poolside bar and braai. It's a bit further out, though within chirping distance of Umgeni River Bird Park.

Riverside Hotel & Spa (Map p484; ☎ 031-310 6900; www.riversidehotel.co.za; 10 Northway, Durban North; s/d from R1610/2140) The corridors have a touch of bling in this white behemoth, but the rooms are tastefully decorated with plush fittings and flat-screen TVs. It's in a good location, accessible to the city and Durban's north coast, and there are fabulous views from the poolside cocktail bar.

Eating

Look out for the local Indian speciality, bunny chow (a half, quarter or full loaf of bread hollowed out and filled with beans or curry stew).

BEACHFRONT

On the beachfront, you'll be hard-pressed to find much more than eateries serving the usual spread of burgers, pizza and candy floss. You are better off heading to the uShaka Marina or the Casino, both of which have some reasonable choices.

Beach Café (Map pp486-7; ☎ 031-332 8302; Bay of Plenty Beach; snacks R30-45; 7am-6pm) Durbs' hot beach hang-out. Soak up the sun at the tables planted in the sand, or chill out with a cocktail on the deck (until 8pm).

Cargo Hold (Map pp486-7; ☎ 031-328 8065; uShaka Marina; mains R70-125; lunch & dinner) On the Phantom Ship at uShaka Marina, your dining companions are fish with very large teeth – the glass tank forms one of the walls to a shark aquarium. In the hold beneath the cheaper Upper Deck restaurant and outdoor Shark Bar, it's well-known for casting some high-quality fish dishes with international flavours.

MARGARET MNCADI AVE/VICTORIA EMBANKMENT

Zack's (Map pp486-7; ☎ 031-305 1677; Wilson's Wharf; mains R50-100; breakfast, lunch & dinner) Offering cafe-style dining, this stylish (chain) eatery serves bistro fare washed down with good smoothies and blasts of fresh sea air.

New Café Fish (Map pp486-7; ☎ 031-305 5062; 31 Yacht Mole, Margaret Mncadi Ave/Victoria Embankment; mains R50-75) At this distinctive green-and-blue construction, the seafood dishes are as appealing as the views of the city and surrounding moored yachts. The upstairs bar offers nautical baskets aplenty.

CITY CENTRE

Around Dr Yusuf Dadoo/Grey St you'll find Indian takeaways (ask around). Otherwise, there are limited eating options in the centre.

Oriental Restaurant (Map pp486-7; ☎ 031-304 5110; The Workshop, 99 Samora Machel/Aliwal St; mains R30-100; breakfast, lunch & dinner) With seating in the shopping centre and a smarter restaurant section, the Oriental is popular with workers at lunchtime and is a good place to try bunny chow.

Roma Revolving Restaurant (Map pp486-7; ☎ 031-332 3337; 22nd fl, John Ross House, Margaret Mncadi Ave/Victoria Embankment; mains R55-150; lunch & dinner) One of only 40 or so revolving restaurants worldwide, it's worth enduring the stodgy Italian fare and chaotic service for the views.

The Royal Hotel (Map pp486–7, see opposite) has half a dozen restaurants: the **Coffee Shoppe** (sandwiches R40, 6am-11pm) is great for a luncheon snack or relaxing cuppa; **Ulundi** (meals R150; dinner) is the place to sample a Bombay fish curry or Western dishes.

GREYVILLE, MORNINGSIDE & BEREA

Florida Rd and nearby Lilian Ngoyi/Windermere Rd are the best places to forage for a meal.

Mango Sushi (Map p489; ☎ 031-312 7054; Avonmore Centre, Ninth Ave; mains & sushi R15-70; lunch Mon-Fri, dinner Mon-Sat) In an unlikely location on the edge of a shopping centre, with outdoor tables overlooking the car park, Mango Sushi serves a range of sushi and Thai dishes between red and black canvas walls.

Spiga D'oro (Map p489; ☎ 031-303 9511; 200 Florida Rd; mains R35-70; breakfast, lunch & dinner) Locals mention this in an 'of-course-you-already-know-about-Spiga-D'oro' tone. The restaurant serves up hearty helpings of Italian food, with some tables under the arches outside, and the waiters even say *ciao*.

Europa (Map p489; ☎ 031-312 1099; 167 Florida Rd; mains R40-70; breakfast, lunch & dinner) This friendly local franchise offers the best coffee in the area, plus a fabulous range of salads and wraps, and a front verandah for people watching.

Butcher Boys (Map p489; ☎ 031-312 8248; 170 Florida Rd; mains R95-125; lunch & dinner) This carnivore's paradise is much more than a typical 'meat market', attracting business people and the 'in' set to its stylish surrounds with creative cuts and combos.

The nondescript Avonmore Centre hides some other recommended eateries near Mango Sushi, including the friendly, highly regarded **9th Avenue Bistro** (☎ 031-312 9134; Avonmore Centre, Ninth Ave, Morningside; mains R75-130; lunch Tue-Fri, dinner Mon-Sat) and unpretentious **Joop's Place** (☎ 031-312 9135; Avonmore Centre, Ninth Ave, Morningside; mains R65-100; dinner Mon-Sat, lunch Fri), popular for its high-quality steaks.

Drinking

The best options are found in the suburbs.

Bean Bag Bohemia (Map p489; ☎ 031-309 6019; 18 Lilian Ngoyi/Windermere Rd; mains R40-120) Doing a good line in pizzas and dim sum (the *char siu sou* is recommended) among mosaics, chandeliers and gothic decor, this hip cafe-bar shares a building with an elegant restaurant and La Bordello (p490).

ThunderRoad Rock Diner (Map p489; ☎ 031-303 3440; 136 Florida Rd) Compare favourite bands and get to know local rockers and backpackers at this grungy, rock-soundtracked bar, which has open-mic nights on Tuesday and live music at weekends.

Billy the Bum's (Map p489; ☎ 031-303 1988; 504 Lilian Ngoyi/Windermere Rd, Morningside) Attracting Durban's upwardly mobile (the sign above the bar says 'elegantly wasted'), this reliably raucous suburban cocktail bar has DJs on Friday and Saturday.

Joe Kool's (Map pp486-7; ☎ 031-332 9698; Lower OR Tambo/Lower Marine Pde, North Beach; 🕑 10am-late Fri, Sat & Sun) Rated by locals as a legendary night out, Joe Kool's seemed to us like a tacky joint with cheesy music and epileptic strobes, although it is right on the beach. If leaving at night, grab one of the taxis that wait outside; do not wander in this area.

Entertainment

Many events, from Natal Sharks games to theatre shows, can be booked through **Computicket** (☎ 083-915 8000; www.computicket.com), with outlets at the Playhouse Company (right) and MTN shops in the Pavilion and Gateway malls.

CINEMAS

There are cinemas in all of the major malls:

Imax (off Map p484; ☎ 031-566 4415; Gateway Theatre of Shopping, 1 Palm Blvd, Umhlanga Ridge) Big-screen action in the Gateway mall.

Ster Kinekor Gateway Theatre of Shopping (off Map p484; ☎ 031-566 3222; www.sterkinekor.com); Musgrave Centre (Map p484; ☎ 0860-300 222; Musgrave Centre, Musgrave Rd)

LIVE MUSIC

KwaZulu-Natal Philharmonic Orchestra (☎ 031-369 9438; www.kznpo.co.za) The orchestra has an interesting spring concert program with weekly performances in the City Hall (Map pp486–7).

BAT Centre (Map pp486-7; www.batcentre.co.za) One of Durban's more interesting haunts (see p485), this venue features performances including poetry (5pm to 7pm Wednesday and Thursday) and jazz (Friday evening and Sunday afternoon). The area is isolated; never walk here at night.

Rainbow Restaurant & Jazz Club (off Map pp486-7; ☎ 031-702 9161; 23 Stanfield Lane) In Pinetown, 8km west of the centre, decades-old Rainbow is still considered the centre of Durban's jazz scene and the preferred local haunt. It features concerts and headline acts on the first or last Sunday of the month.

NIGHTCLUBS

Burn (Map p484; ☎ 082 325 9746; 112 Umbilo Rd) Heavy rock and a sizzling dance floor.

Clapham Grand (Map p489; 672 Umgeni Rd, Berea) The new two-storey nightclub is part of an international chain. Tuesday night is student night.

Harvey Wallbanger's (off Map p484; Broadway, Durban North) A trendy top-floor spot, above its own restaurant.

THEATRE

Playhouse Company (Map pp486-7; ☎ 031-369 9555; www.playhousecompany.com; Anton Lembede/Smith St) Opposite City Hall, Durban's central theatre is an attractive venue featuring dance, drama and music performances.

Getting There & Away

AIR

King Shaka International Airport (off Map p484; ☎ 011-921 6262; www.airports.co.za; La Mercy), currently under construction 35km north of the city, is set to open shortly before the 2010 World Cup, when it will supersede **Durban International Airport** (DUR; off Map p484; ☎ 031-451 6666; www.airports.co.za), which is off the N2, 16km south of the city.

Internet fares to Jo'burg start at around R400, but vary depending on the day of the week, month, and even time of day.

1time (☎ 031-451 6710; www.1time.aero) Great deals to Jo'burg.

Kulula.com (☎ 0861-444 144; www.kulula.com) Links Durban with Jo'burg, Cape Town and Port Elizabeth.

Mango (☎ 0861-162 646; ww5.flymango.com) Flights to Jo'burg and Cape Town.

SAAirlink (☎ 011-961 1700; www.saairlink.co.za) Flies daily to Port Elizabeth, Bloemfontein, George and Nelspruit.

South African Airways (☎ 0861-359 722; www.flysaa.com) Flies daily to Jo'burg, Port Elizabeth, East London, Cape Town, George and Nelspruit.

BUS

The Baz Bus (see p578) serves Durban.

Long-distance buses leave from the bus stations near Durban train station (Map pp486–7). It's safest to enter from Masabalala Yengwa/NMR Ave, not Umgeni Rd. The following companies have offices here:

Eldo Coaches (Map pp486-7; ☎ 031-307 3363) has three buses daily to Jo'burg (from R130, eight hours).

Greyhound (Map pp486-7; ☎ 083 915 9000; www.greyhound.co.za) has daily buses to Richards Bay (R165, 2½ hours), Jo'burg (from R240, eight hours), Cape Town (R530, from 22 hours), Port Elizabeth (R395, 15 hours), Port Shepstone (R165, 1¾ hours), Pietermaritzburg (from R160, one hour), Estcourt (from R155, 2½ hours), Ladysmith (from R235, four hours), Newcastle (R260, 5½ hours) and Vryheid (R260, six hours).

Intercape (Map pp486-7; ☎ 0861-287 287; www.intercape.co.za) has several similarly priced daily services to Jo'burg and Cape Town, and to Gaborone, Botswana (R345, 15½ hours) and Maputo, Zimbabwe (R400, 15 hours).

Intercity (Map pp486-7; ☎ 031-305 9090; www.intercity.co.za) operates daily services to Margate (R100, 2½ hours), Jo'burg International Airport and Park Station (R250, 8½ hours), and Pretoria (R240, nine hours).

The **Margate Mini Coach** (☎ 039-312 1406; Greyhound office) links Durban and Margate three times a day (one-way R100, 2½ hours).

Translux (Map pp486-7; ☎ 0861-589 282; www.translux.co.za) runs daily buses to Jo'burg (from R200, eight hours) and Cape Town (R510, 27 hours); its cheaper City to City buses go to destinations across the country.

CAR

Most major car-hire companies (see p579) have offices at the airport:

Avis (☎ 031-304 1741; www.avis.co.za)

Imperial (☎ 031-337 3731; www.imperialcarrental.co.za)

MINIBUS TAXI

Some long-distance taxis leave from stops in the streets opposite the Umgeni Rd entrance to the train station (Map pp486–7). Others running mainly to the south coast and the Wild Coast region of Eastern Cape leave from around Berea train station (Map pp486–7). The areas in and around the minibus taxi ranks are unsafe and extreme care should be taken if entering them.

TRAIN

Durban train station (Map pp486–7) is huge. Use the Masabalala Yengwa/NMR Ave entrance, 1st level. The local inner-city or suburban trains are not recommended for travellers; even hardy travellers report feeling unsafe.

Contrastingly, tourist-class, long-distance **Shosholoza Meyl** (☎ 0860-008 888; www.shosholozameyl.co.za) services are recommended. They include the Saturday service to Jo'burg (R170, 12½ hours) via Ladysmith and Pietersmaritzburg, and the more luxurious Friday service to Cape Town (high/low season R740/460, 38 hours) via Bloemfontein and Kimberley. There is an seated-economy-class-only service between Durban and Jo'burg daily except for Tuesday; the part of this trip that involves overnight travel is not recommended.

Shosholoza Meyl's **Premier Classe** (www.premierclasse.co.za) has Durban–Jo'burg departures on Wednesday and Sunday, and Jo'burg–Durban departures on Tuesday and Friday. Tickets should be booked in advance.

Rovos Rail (p582) runs to Pretoria, stopping en route for safaris.

Getting Around

TO/FROM THE AIRPORT

Some hostels run their own taxi shuttle services for clients at competitive prices. By taxi, the same trip should cost about R225. The **Airport Shuttle Bus** (☎ 031-465 1660) departs the airport regularly for major hotels (R30) at the beach and in the city centre. Buses return to the airport on the hour between 5am and 10pm from outside Shell House near the corner of Samora Machel/Aliwal and Anton Lembede/Smith Sts (Map pp486–7).

BUS

The **Durban People Mover** (☎ 031-309 5942; www.durbanpeoplemover.co.za) is a useful shuttle-bus service that operates along three routes within the city (with more planned). It currently links the beachfront to the city centre and runs the length of the beachfront from uShaka Marine World to Suncoast Casino with designated stops (including the Victoria Street Market and City Hall) along the way. Day passes (R15) and single-journey tickets (R4) can be purchased on the buses, which run daily between 6.30am and 11pm.

The main bus station and information centre (Map pp486–7) for inner-city and metropolitan buses is on Dr AB Xuma/Commercial St across from the Workshop shopping centre.

Durban Transport (☎ 031-309 5942) runs the Mynah bus service, which covers most of the city and local residential areas.

Trips cost around R5. Its larger Aqualine buses run through the outer-lying Durban metropolitan area.

TAXI

A taxi between the beach and Florida Rd, Morningside, costs about R30. **Mozzie Cabs** (☎ 0860-669 943) runs a reliable 24-hour service.

AROUND DURBAN

A pleasant and hassle-free (if slightly kitsch) getaway from the steamy streets of Durban, the **Valley of 1000 Hills** (also known as the Umgeni Valley) runs from the city's western outskirts to Nagle Dam, east of Pietermaritzburg. The area abounds in touristy craft shops and eateries, but the rolling hills, sleepy villages and traditional Zulu communities make for an interesting visit. The routes are outlined in the *1000 Hills Experience* brochure, available from Durban Tourism (p483); routes 5 and 6 offer the most authentic experience. You can drive there via the N13 towards Pietermaritzburg, then the M13 past Pinetown to Kloof, where the routes start.

On Rte 2, it's a pleasant winding drive to the beautiful 600-hectare **Krantzkloof Nature Reserve** (adult/child R10/5; 🕑 6am-6pm), with its variety of stunning gorge, wetland and grassland walks of between one and six hours' duration. Maps of self-guided trails are available from the security guard (R5).

SOUTH OF DURBAN

The South Coast is a 160km-long string of seaside resorts and suburbs running from Amanzimtoti to Port Edward, near the Eastern Cape border. There's a bit of a Groundhog Day feel about this mass of shoulder-to-shoulder getaways along the N2 and Rte 102, albeit a pleasant one. The region is a surfers' and divers' delight (see the boxed text, below), and in summer there ain't much room to swing a brolly. The stunning Oribi Gorge Nature Reserve, inland from Port Shepstone, provides beautiful forest walks, eating and accommodation options.

The first stop for information is **Amanzimtoti Tourism** (☎ 031-903 7498; www.southernexplorer.co.za; 95 Beach Rd, Amanzimtoti; 🕑 8am-4pm Mon-Fri, 9am-2pm Sat).

South of Amanzimtoti's high-rise jungle of apartment blocks, Warner Beach is less built-up and more relaxed. Umkomaas and Scottburgh are good diving-off points for the Aliwal Shoal (see the boxed text, below). The bustling, industrial town of Port Shepstone is of little interest to tourists, but there are some pleasant sleeping options on the coastal strip to the north. You may prefer Ramsgate or Southbroom to nearby Margate, a claustrophobic holiday hub. The last main centre in the region is Port Edward, where the lush surrounds and some reasonable accommodation make a pleasant escape from the concrete jungle.

Oribi Gorge Nature Reserve

☎ 039

This **nature reserve** (☎ 039-679 1644; www.kznwildlife.com; admission R10; 🕑 6am-6pm summer, 7.30am-4.30pm winter) is inland from Port Shepstone, off the N2. The spectacular gorge, on the

SOUTH COAST DIVING

The highlight of this strip is the Aliwal Shoal – touted as one of the world's 10 best dive sites – named after the wrecked ship, the *Aliwal,* which ran aground on the reef in 1849. Other ships have since met a similar fate here. Today the shoal's ledges, caves and pinnacles are home to wrecks, rays, turtles, 'raggies' (ragged-mouth sharks), tropical fish and soft corals.

Numerous operators along the South Coast offer day dives and four-day courses with dives, equipment hire and air-tank refills. Rates range from R2000 to R2500. Always speak to other travellers about their experiences, as safety standards vary.

2nd Breath (☎ 039-317 2326; www.2ndbreath.co.za; cnr Bank St & Berea Rd, Margate) PADI professional who takes classes and safety issues seriously.

African Watersports (☎ 039-973 2505; www.africanwatersports.co.za; Umkomaas) Major focus is sharks; for experienced divers.

Aliwal Dive Centre (☎ 039-973 2233; www.aliwalshoal.co.za; 2 Moodie St, Umkomaas) Also has pleasant rooms available.

Quo Vadis (☎ 039-978 1112; www.raggiecave.com; Cutty Sark Hotel, Scottburgh) Recommended for its charters.

Umzimkulwana River, is one of the highlights of the South Coast with beautiful scenery, animals and birds. On the south side of the gorge is **accommodation** (campsites R66, 2-bed chalets R130).

Wild 5 Extreme Adventures (☎ 082-566 7424; Oribi Gorge Hotel) offers a 100m Wild Swing (free-fall jump and swing) off Lehr's Falls (R350), abseiling (R250), and white-water rafting (R495). It's 11km off the N2 along the Oribi Flats Rd.

Oribi Gorge Hotel (☎ 039-687 0253; www.oribigorge.co.za; s/d incl breakfast R610/1020;) is a large pine place with a nearby gorge viewpoint (R10).

Margate & Around

☎ 039 / pop 34,000

The south coast's tourist hub is a concrete jungle with a string of loud and lively bars. If it's too much, you're better off heading to Ramsgate, with a nice little beach, or to the lush green confines of Southbroom, the posh neck of the woods, but delightfully located within a bushbuck conservancy.

SLEEPING

Southbroom Backpackers Lodge (☎ 039-316 8448; 11 Cliff Rd, Southbroom; dm/s/d from R120/180/280;) Joy oh joy – an affordable option in this upmarket area, a beautiful neck of the (subtropical) woods and a 10-minute walk from the beach. This comfortable, laid-back choice resembles a large holiday home with light and airy rooms.

Wailana Beach Lodge (☎ 039-314 4606; www.wailana.co.za; 436 Ashmead Dr, Ramsgate; s/d incl breakfast from R430/700;) This svelte guest house, 200m from the sea, has five designer bedrooms with contemporary, individual styling and private sun decks, leafy gardens and a bar.

GETTING THERE & AWAY

The Margate Mini Coach (p493) links Durban and Margate. Book through **Hibiscus Coast Tourism** (☎ 039-312 2322; www.tourismsouthcoast.co.za; Panorama Pde, Main Beach, Margate).

Intercity Express (☎ 031-305 9090; www.intercity.co.za; Hibiscus Coast Tourism) runs regular buses between Margate and Jo'burg (R330, 10 hours).

NORTH OF DURBAN

The stretch of coast from Umhlanga Rocks north to the Tugela River is a profusion of upmarket timeshare apartments and retirement villages with some pleasant beaches. The section from Zimbali, slightly north of Umhlanga, to the Tugela is known as the Dolphin Coast because of the bottlenose dolphins that favour the area.

Sangweni Tourism Centre (☎ 032-946 1997; www.northcoast.org.za; cnr Ballito Dr & Link Dr; 7.45am-4.30pm Mon-Fri, 9am-1pm Sat), which lists accommodation in the area, is near the BP petrol station, where you leave the N2 to enter Ballito.

The region is home to a fascinating mix of peoples: the descendants of colonialists, indentured labourers from the Indian subcontinent and French Mauritian sugarcane growers, plus colourful Zulu cultures.

Metropolitan buses run between Durban and Umhlanga Rocks, and buses and minibus taxis also run between Durban and KwaDukuza (Stanger) and other inland towns.

Umhlanga Rocks

☎ 031

The buckle of Durban's chichi commuter belt, Umhlanga (the 'h' is pronounced something like a 'sh') is a cosmopolitan mix of upmarket beach resort, moneyed suburbia and small malls.

SIGHTS & ACTIVITIES

The **Natal Sharks Board** (☎ 031-566 0400; www.shark.co.za; 1A Herrwood Dr; audiovisual & dissection adult/child R25/12; 8am-4pm Mon-Fri, noon-6pm Sun) is a research institute dedicated to studying sharks, specifically in relation to their danger to humans. There are audiovisual presentations and shark dissections at 9am and 2pm Wednesday to Thursday and 2pm Sunday. The public can accompany the Sharks Board personnel on their boat trips.

Umhlanga Lagoon Nature Reserve

This **nature reserve** (admission free, parking R5; 6am-9pm) is on a river mouth just north of town. Despite its small size (26 hectares) there are many bird species. Trails lead through stunning dune forest, across the lagoon and onto the beach.

SLEEPING & EATING

Umhlanga is crowded with holiday apartments and B&Bs, mostly close to the beach. A two-bedroom serviced apartment in low/high season starts at about R500/700 per night (a minimum number of nights often applies); enquire at **Umhlanga Tourism Information Centre** (☎ 031-561 4257; www.umhlanga-rocks.com; Chartwell Centre, Chartwell Dr).

Beverley Hills Sun Intercontinental (☎ 031-561 2211; www.southernsun.com; Lighthouse Rd; s/d incl breakfast R3500/3800;) They didn't pull out the stops on the exterior, but this top-notch classic is deliciously stylish on the inside, with an award-winning restaurant (mains R90 to R380).

There are eating options galore and many pleasant pavement cafes, including the chic eatery **Ile Maurice** (☎ 031-561 7609; 9 McCausland Cres; mains R90-270), for a special seaside splurge with a Gallic touch.

GETTING THERE & AWAY

Metro buses 716 and 706 run between Umhlanga and Durban.

ZULULAND

Evoking images of wild landscapes and tribal rhythms, this beautiful swath of KwaZulu-Natal offers a different face of South Africa, where fine coastline, mist-clad hills and traditional settlements contrast with the ordered suburban developments around Durban. Dominated by the Zulu ethnic group, the region offers a fascinating historical and contemporary insight into one of the country's most enigmatic, and best-known, cultures. Intense poverty and all the social problems that come with it are still commonplace.

President Zuma's birthplace, the region is most visited for the spectacular Hluhluwe-Imfolozi Park and its many traditional Zulu villages. Here, you can learn about Zulu history and the legendary King Shaka.

Richards Bay

☎ 035 / pop 115,000

The industrial port of Richards Bay, a mass of modern suburbia, aluminium smelters and a web of roads linking very little, is included mainly because Greyhound buses stop here. **BirdLife South Africa** (☎ 035-753 5644; www.birdlife.org.za; Imvubu Log Cabins, cnr Hibberd & Davidson Lane, Meerensee) is based here, and many bird species favour the surrounding lakes and marshes.

If you do need to overnight here, **Woodpecker Inn** (☎ 035-786 1230; fax 786 1243; Pelican Pde; s/d R375/520;) offers thatched, lodge-style country comforts in a garden setting near the airport.

Greyhound (☎ 083-915 9000; www.greyhound.co.za) runs daily to Durban (R175, 2½ hours) and Jo'burg (R280, eight hours). Most of the surrounding towns can be reached by minibus taxi.

Eshowe

☎ 035 / pop 14,700

Situated around a beautiful indigenous forest and surrounded by green rolling hills, Eshowe typifies idiosyncratic Zululand. The centre has a rural, rough-and-tumble atmosphere, but the suburbs are leafy and quiet. It is well placed for exploring the wider region and there are many decent attractions and accommodation options on offer.

SIGHTS & ACTIVITIES

The **Fort Nongqayi Museum Village** (☎ 035-473 3474; Nongqayi Rd; adult/child R25/5; 7.30am-4pm Mon-Fri, 9am-4pm Sat & Sun), based around the fort built by the British in 1883, includes access to the Zululand Historical Museum, a Zulu basketry collection and the Zululand Missionary Museum.

From the museum you can also walk to **Mpushini Falls** (40 minutes return), but note that bilharzia has been reported here in the past.

When war approached, King Shaka is said to have hidden his wives in the thick stand of forest that now makes up the 200-hectare **Dlinza Forest Reserve** (☎ 035-474 4029; admission free; 6am-6pm Sep-Apr, 7am-5pm May-Aug). There is prolific bird life as well as some walking trails.

The 125m-long **Dlinza Forest Aerial Boardwalk** (adult/child R25/5) offers some great views of the canopy and bird life. This is the start of the Prince Dabulamanzi Trail, a three-day circuit through nature reserves and rivers. **Entumeni Nature Reserve** (☎ 035-474 5084; admission free; 6am-6pm) is larger than Dlinza, and preserves indigenous mist-belt forest in a sugarcane region. It's 16km west of town, off the road to Entumeni and Nkandla.

SLEEPING

George Hotel & Zululand Backpackers (☎ 035-474 4919; www.eshowe.com; 38 Main St; dm R100, s/d incl breakfast R295/395;) This attractive, whitewashed building boasts some recently renovated bathrooms, and a colonial feel. The hotel's own beer brand flows on Friday night in particular; also on tap are the owner's 101 activities.

Eshowe Guesthouse (☎ 035-474 2362; dlinza@tlkomsa.net; 3 Oftebro St; s/d R300/760) Backing onto the chirping Dlinza Forest and opposite Dlinza Forest Accommodation (single/double R300/380), this sparkling new place offers airy, spacious rooms with a shared kitchen and dining area. Breakfasts cost R60 per person.

GETTING THERE & AWAY

Minibus taxis leave from the bus and taxi rank (downhill from KFC near the Osborne/Main Sts roundabout; go across the bridge and to the right) to Empangeni, (R40, one hour), the best place to catch taxis deeper into Zululand, and Durban (R70, 1½ hours).

Nikwalini Valley

King Shaka's *kraal* (fortified village), KwaBulawayo, once loomed over this beautiful valley but today Nikwalini is regimented with citrus orchards and cane fields rather than Zulu warriors. From Eshowe head north for 6km on Rte 66, and turn right onto Rte 230 (a dirt road that eventually leads to Rte 34).

Across the road from the KwaBulawayo marker is **Coward's Bush**, now just another marker, where warriors who returned from battle without their spears, or who had received wounds in the back, were executed.

Shakaland & Simunye

☎ 035

Created as a set for the telemovie *Shaka Zulu*, the slightly Disney-fied **Shakaland** (☎ 035-460 0912; Nandi Experience R285; display 11am & noon) beats up a touristy, but entertaining, blend of perma-grin performance and informative authenticity. The Nandi Experience (Nandi was Shaka's mother) is a display of Zulu culture and customs; the Zulu dance performance is said to be the best in the country. You can also stay overnight in luxury beehives at the four-star **hotel** (www.shakaland.com; s/d incl Nandi Experience & full board R1700/2872).

Shakaland is at Norman Hurst Farm, Nikwalini, 3km off Rte 66 and 14km north of Eshowe.

Simunye Zulu Lodge (☎ 035-450 3111; www.simunyelodge.co.za; per person from R1100), a collection of cottages, beehive huts and *rondavels*, is owned by renowned 'white Zulu' Barry Leitch. It's located between Melmoth and Eshowe, and nestled at the bottom of cliffs on the banks of the Mfuli River. Guests meet local Zulus and learn about their traditional and contemporary culture.

Ulundi & Around

☎ 035 / pop 15,200

Formerly the hub of the powerful Zulu empire and the joint capital of KZN (with Pietermaritzburg), Ulundi is an unattractive, merely functional place, and its small centre-cum-shopping mall has a temporary feel. For Zulu fanatics, however, there are still plenty of historic sites to explore in the immediate area.

SIGHTS & ACTIVITIES

Established as Cetshwayo's capital in 1873, **Ondini** (High Place; ☎ 035-870 2050; admission R20/10; 8am-4pm Mon-Fri, 9am-4pm Sat & Sun) was razed by British troops after the Battle of Ulundi, the final engagement of the 1879 Anglo-Zulu War. The royal *kraal* section of the Ondini site has been rebuilt and you can see where archaeological digs have uncovered the floors of identifiable buildings.

The **KwaZulu Cultural-Historical Museum**, part of the site, has good exhibits on Zulu history and culture, including one of the country's best collections of beadwork.

The **Emakhosini Ophathe Heritage Park** (Valley of the Kings; admission free) is of great significance to the Zulu. The great *makhosi* (chiefs) Nkhosinkulu, Senzangakhona (father of Shaka, Dingaan and Mpande) and Dinizulu are buried here. A monument, the **Spirit of eMakhosini** (8am-4pm Mon-Fri, 9am-4pm Sat & Sun), sits on a hill.

SLEEPING

uMuzi Bushcamp (☎ 035-450 2531; www.umuzibushcamp.co.za; dm R210, s/d with shared bathroom R275/440, s/d R460/600) Inside the Ondini complex is this privately run group of traditional beehive huts. Dinner (R90) can be arranged.

Southern Sun Garden Court (☎ 035-870 1012; www.southernsun.com; Princess Magogo St; r incl breakfast R1049;) Catering to passing dignitaries and bureaucrats, this offers the predictably safe comforts of a chain hotel. Ask about the weekend specials.

GETTING THERE & AWAY

The minibus taxi rank is opposite the Southern Sun Garden Court, with services to destinations including Vryheid (R60, 1½ hours) and Eshowe (R65, 1½ hours).

THE ELEPHANT COAST

Up there with the world's great ecotourist destinations, the Elephant Coast is a must-see stretch of natural beauty, with a fabulously diverse mix of environments and wildlife. Incorporating the northern region known as Maputaland, it's bound in the south by the Imfolozi River just below the

St Lucia Estuary, and to the northwest by the Lebombo Mountains.

Mtubatuba & Around

☎ 035

For travellers, the only real reason to visit this chaotic place is that minibus taxis run through here on their way to Durban (R70, two hours), Phongolo (from R80, two hours; via Hluhluwe and Mkuze) and west into Zululand. Coming from those destinations, Mtubatuba is the stop for St Lucia (St Lucia Estuary is 25km east; take Rte 6188 by minibus taxi).

Mtubatuba B&B (☎ 035-550 0538; www.bnbmtuba.co.za; 243 Celtis Dr; per person from R350;) has smart, contemporary rooms with stylish African touches. Set around a lovely 2-hectare garden, it serves excellent breakfasts.

Hluhluwe-iMfolozi Park

☎ 035

Hluhluwe-iMfolozi Park (☎ 035-550 8476; www.kznwildlife.com; adult/child R90/45; 5am-7pm Nov-Feb, 6am-6pm Mar-Oct) is one of South Africa's best-known and most evocative parks. Covering 96,000 hectares, the park has lions, elephants, rhinos (black and white), leopards, giraffes, buffaloes and wild dogs. It's best visited in winter, when the animals range widely without congregating at water sources (the White iMfolozi and Black iMfolozi Rivers flow here), although the vegetation sometimes makes viewing difficult. Summer visits can be rewarding in the open savanna country areas.

The **Centenary Centre** (8am-4pm), a wildlife-holding centre with an attached museum and information centre, is in the eastern section of iMfolozi.

Hilltop Camp (☎ 035-562 0848) offers morning and night wildlife drives, while Mpila Camp offers night drives only. The drives (R200 per person) are very popular, although open to resort residents only.

The reserves are in a (low-risk) malarial area and there are lots of mosquitoes – come prepared.

WILDERNESS TRAILS

One of iMfolozi's main attractions is its (seasonal) trail system, in a special 24,000-hectare wilderness area. The **Base Trail** (three nights/four days, R3080) is, as the name suggests, at a base camp.

The **Short Wilderness Trail** (two nights/three days, R1870) is at satellite camps, which have no amenities (bucket shower only) but are fully catered. Similar is the **Extended Wilderness Trail** (three nights/four days, R2750) but guests must carry their gear for 7km into camp. On the **Primitive Trail** (four nights/five days, R2300), you carry equipment, help prepare the food (provided) and sit up in 1½-hour watches during the night.

SLEEPING & EATING

You must book accommodation in advance through **KZN Wildlife** (☎ 033-845 1000; www.kznwildlife.com) in Pietermaritzburg or at Durban's Tourist Junction (p483). Last-minute bookings (those made 48 hours ahead) should be made directly with the camps.

Hilltop Camp (☎ 035-562 0848; rest huts/chalets per person R276/550, 2-bed units with full board per person R466) is the signature resort on the Hluhluwe side, with stupendous views, a restaurant and a much-needed bar.

If you want peace and quiet, try one of the private and sedate bush lodges, which are fully equipped and reasonably upmarket.

Muntulu Bush Lodge (8-bed bush lodges per person R595, minimum R3570) is perched high above the Hluhluwe River; **Munywaneni Bush Lodge** (8-bed bush lodges per person R595, minimum R3570) is secluded and self-contained.

The main accommodation centre on the iMfolozi side is spectacular **Mpila Camp** (per person 4-bed rest huts R230, 2-bed safari camps R310) in the centre of the reserve; **Masinda Lodge** (6-bed lodge incl wildlife drives & walks per person R550), near the Centenary Centre, is fully hosted and catered.

Be warned: all accommodation options are billed per person but are subject to a minimum charge.

GETTING THERE & AWAY

The main entrance, Memorial Gate, is about 15km west of the N2, about 50km north of Mtubatuba. The second entrance, the Nyalazi Gate, is accessed by turning left off the N2 onto Rte 618 just after Mtubatuba towards Nongoma. The third, Cengeni Gate, on iMfolozi's western side, is accessible by road (tarred for 30km) from Ulundi.

iSimangaliso Wetland Park

☎ 035

This Unesco World Heritage Site stretches for 200 glorious kilometres, from the

Mozambican border to Maphelana, at the southern end of Lake St Lucia. With the Indian Ocean on one side, and a series of lakes on the other (including Lake St Lucia), the 328,000-hectare park protects five distinct ecosystems, offering everything from offshore reefs and beaches, to lakes, wetlands, woodlands and coastal forests. The wildlife ranges from dolphins to zebras and the ocean beaches pull big crowds during the holiday season.

Lake St Lucia is Africa's largest estuary. Despite its past healthy water levels, it is currently at its lowest level for 55 years, due to a severe drought. The estuary mouth is currently closed; controversy surrounds a long-term solution to the management of the lake, with both animal and plant species being affected by changing ecological factors.

Unless otherwise specified, all Ezemvelo KZN Wildlife accommodation must be booked at **Ezemvelo KZN Wildlife** (☎ in Pietermaritzburg 033-845 1000, in Durban 031-304 4934; www.kznwildlife.com) with 48 hours' notice. Less than 48 hours before, try your luck directly with the lodges and campsites. Minimum charges often apply.

Activities & Tours

As part of the iSimangaliso Wetlands Park Authority's responsible tourism practices, every few years, an ecotour operator must officially apply to be an approved operator; the following were current at the time of research.

Advantage Tours (☎ 035-590 1250; www.advantagetours.co.za; trip per person R700) Runs daily whale-watching boat tours between June and September, weather permitting. You can also head up river on boat tours to view hippos and crocodiles.

Bhangazi Horse Safaris (☎ 035-550 4898; www.horsesafari.co.za; 1/2½hr beach or wildlife rides R190/450, safari trips per person R1360-2900) Its two specialities are week-long safari trips, the 'adventure safari' and 'true safari'. The latter is a luxury experience – colonial-style safari tents (with hot bucket showers), real beds and dinner served with silver and crystal.

Euro Zulu Safaris (☎ 035-590 1635; info@eurozulu.com; per person R600) Fascinating night turtle-watching tours operate from Cape Vidal and Kosi Bay.

Shakabarker Tours (☎ 035-590 1162; 43 Hornbill St, St Lucia) Operates out of St Lucia and conducts a range of excellent wildlife tours, including a chameleon tour.

St Lucia Kayak Safaris (☎ 035-590 1047; www.kayaksafaris.co.za; half-/full day R250/425) Full-day outings include lunch and snorkelling at Cape Vidal.

Themba's Birding & Eco Tours (☎ 071-413 3243; St Lucia; per person from R100) Minimum two people per tour.

At the time of research, an operator was being appointed to run the superb multiday Mziki and Emoyeni hiking trails; contact iSimangaliso Wetland Park Information office (below) for details. There are also guided and self-guided trails throughout the park

ST LUCIA

Although not officially within the iSimangaliso Wetland Park, the pleasant village of St Lucia is a useful base to explore the park's southern sections. In high season, the village is a hotbed of activity as the population swells from 600 to the thousands. Hippos sometimes amble down the quieter streets (beware, these are not cute).

Information

There are FNB, Nedbank and Standard Bank ATMs on the main street.

BiB's International Backpackers (310 MacKenzie St; per hr R4; 🕒 7am-10pm) The hostel has by far the best internet service.

iSimangaliso Wetland Park Information office (☎ 035-590 1633; www.isimangaliso.com)

Sleeping

BiB's International Backpackers (☎ 035-590 1056; www.bibs.co.za; 310 MacKenzie St; campsites R75, dm R115, d R245, self-catering d R315; P 💻 🏊) Occupying a series of sprawling buildings (forever, it seems, under renovation), BiB's offers all the backpacker staples – a busy bar, a huge kitchen, and organised fun.

Hornbill House (☎ 035-590 1162; 43 Hornbill St; s/d incl breakfast R475/750; ❄ 🏊) A pleasant place to nest, with homey B&B comforts, plus pool and deck. The knowledgeable owner, also a tour-company operator, offers many ecofriendly trips and activities.

Sunset Lodge (☎ 035-590 1197; www.sunsetstlucia.co.za; d R595-795) Located on the estuary, these dark wood-lined log cabins have a safari theme.

In St Lucia Estuary, you can camp at three sites run by **Ezemvelo KZN Wildlife** (☎ 033-590 1340; www.kznwildlife.com; Pelican St). Eden Park and the pretty Sugarloaf, both R70 per person, are on the estuary; the former is near the Ezemvelo KZN Wildlife office.

Getting There & Away

The Baz Bus drops backpackers off several times a week. If you're not doing tours out of St Lucia, the only way of getting around is to have your own wheels.

EASTERN SHORES

☎ 035

One of the most accessible areas from St Lucia, the **Eastern Shores** (☎ 035-590 1633; www.isimangaliso.com; adult/child/vehicle R20/15/35; 5am-7pm Nov-Mar, 6am-6pm Apr-Oct) has four scenic routes – pan, *vlei* (marshland), coastal dune and grassland – that reflect their different features and ecosystems. About 14km north of the entrance is **Mission Rocks**, a rugged and rock-covered shoreline where, at low tide, you can view a fabulous array of sea life in the rock pools (you cannot swim here). At low tide, you can walk 5km north to **Bats Cave**, a bat-filled cave. About 4km before Mission Rocks, the Mission Rocks lookout (signed) provides a wonderful view of Lake St Lucia and the Indian Ocean.

CAPE VIDAL

☎ 035

Twenty kilometres north of Mission Rocks (30km from St Lucia), taking in the land between Lake Bhangazi and the ocean, is **Cape Vidal**. Some of the forested sand dunes are 150m high and the beaches are excellent for swimming.

There is accommodation at the pretty **Cape Vidal Camp** (campsites R80, 5-bed log cabins per person R256, bush lodges R490), near the shores of Lake Bhangazi.

WESTERN SHORES & FALSE BAY

This stretch desperately needs the rainbird to sing; parts have been closed due to the drought. Two stunning lakeside spots you can access are **Charters Creek** (entrance is off the N2, 18km north of Mtubatuba and 32km south of Hluhluwe), a region of dense coastal forest and grasslands; and **False Bay** (adult/child R70/35), accessed via Rte 22 east of Hluhluwe village, and offering forest walks and an attractive **campsite** (adult/child R90/45).

UMKHUZE GAME RESERVE & AROUND

☎ 035

A possible trip highlight is the **uMkhuze Game Reserve** (☎ 031-845 1000; www.kznwildlife.com; adult/child/vehicle R35/18/35; 5am-7pm Nov-Mar, 6am-6pm Apr-Oct). Established in 1912, this reserve of dense scrub and open acacia plains covers 36,000 spectacular hectares. It may lack lions, but just about every other sought-after animal is represented, as well as 400-plus bird species.

Better still, the reserve has hides at water holes, which offer some of the best wildlife viewing in the country. It's 15km from Mkuze town. Evening wildlife drives (R180) and an escorted forest walk across suspension bridges (R90) are available.

Ezemvelo KZN Wildlife runs a fabulous bush lodge at **Nhlonhlela** (per person R325) and various accommodation options at **Mantuma** (rest huts per person R190, 2- & 4-bed safari camps per person R286, chalets per person R320).

The town of Mkuze is west of the Lebombo range on the N2. **Ghost Mountain**, south of the town, was an important burial place for the Ndwandwe people; occasionally human bones, which date from a big battle between rival Zulu factions in 1884, are found near Ghost Mountain.

Ghost Mountain Inn (☎ 035-573 1025; www.ghostmountaininn.co.za; s/d incl breakfast R715/1160) is an old-school colonial place with a modern and luxurious touch, indoor-outdoor lounge areas and blooming gardens. It's an excellent base for explorations, with tours on offer.

SODWANA BAY

☎ 035

Spectacular **Sodwana Bay** (24hr; adult/child R20/15) is bordered by lush forest on one side, and glittering sands on another. Popular activities include guided walking and birding trails, especially along the 5km **Mgobozeleni Trail**, which features coastal forest and grassland. Serious deep-sea fishing also occurs here, but it's best known for its **scuba-diving**. The diversity of underwater seascapes and marine flora and fauna makes it one of South Africa's diving capitals.

Avoid the silly season (summer holidays) when thousands throng here to take the plunge – literally. At all other times it's a peaceful place.

Tour and dive operators, accommodation and cafes sprawl along the road leading to the park entrance. Facilities inside the park include a campsite plus a couple of lodge-cum-diving-operators.

There is an ATM in the general store at the park entrance; otherwise you'll need to head to Mbazwana, 14km west.

Sleeping & Eating

The following two places offer accommodation and dive packages.

Triton Dive Charters (☎ 082-4948761; www.tritondiving.co.za; per person R180-310) Two kilometres off the main road and surrounded by a landscaped indigenous garden, Triton offers neat wooden cabins and more upmarket brick ones. A kitchen and braai area ensures a social ambience.

Coral Divers (☎ 033-345 6531; www.coraldivers.co.za; Sodwana Bay; tent per person R160, cabin d with/without bathroom from R640/520;) This factory-style operation continues to net the shoals with its large dining-area-cum-bar and tadpole-sized pool. The tents and smaller cabins are a bit run-down, but the more upmarket cabins are pleasant.

Ezemvelo KZN Wildlife (☎ 033-590 1340; www.kznwildlife.com; Pelican St; campsites per person R60-90, 5-bed cabins per person R330) has hundreds of campsites and cabins within the park in coastal forest.

Getting There & Away

Turn off the N2 at Hluhluwe village heading to Mbazwana, and continue about 20km to the park. Minibus taxis ply this route.

LAKE SIBAYA & COASTAL FOREST

Remote grassland plains, lush forests and pristine beaches are the main features of the Ezemvelo KZN Wildlife–administered **Coastal Forest**, a magical area accessible by 4WD (along the coastal sandy track between Kosi Bay and Sodwana Bay or from KwaNgwanase). Highlights include **Black Rock**, a rugged rocky peninsula reached by climbing over sand dunes, and **Lala Nek**, a beautiful and seemingly never-ending stretch of sand.

Further south sits **Lake Sibaya**, South Africa's largest freshwater lake, with hippos, crocs and more than 280 bird species. Canoeing trips can arranged through the luxurious beachside **Thonga Beach Lodge** (☎ 035-474 1473; www.isibindiafrica.co.za; s/d with full board from R2925/4500;), which transfers guests from the main road.

KOSI BAY

☎ 033

The jewel of iSimangaliso Wetland Park, **Kosi Bay** (☎ 035-845 1000; 6am-6pm Apr-Sep, 5am-7pm Oct-Mar) features a string of four lakes starting from an estuary lined with some of South Africa's most beautiful and quiet beaches. Within the estuary mouth, there's excellent snorkelling. There are hippos, Zambezi sharks and some crocs in the lake system, and the rare palmnut vulture is one of 250-plus bird species that have been identified here.

You will find shops and an ATM in the nearest service centre, **KwaNgwanase**, some 10km west of the reserve. There are two entrances to the reserve: Kosi Bay Camp (7km north of KwaNgwanase) and **Kosi Bay Mouth** (adult/child/vehicle R20/10/15), 19km north of KwaNgwanase. Permits for both are obligatory, and can be arranged through Utshwayelo Campsite (see below) or by calling ☎ 035-592 0236.

Sleeping & Eating

Most lodge accommodation is dispersed around the region's sandy dunes several kilometres from KwaNgwanase. In many cases 4WDs are needed to negotiate the sandy tracks.

Utshwayelo Campsite (☎ 084 531 2173; www.kosi-bay.co.za; campsites per person R70, hut s/d R200/300) This lovely community-run camp offers basic but neat bamboo-lined chalets with communal kitchen. Right by the Kosi Bay Mouth entrance to the park, it's 30 minutes' walk from one of the country's best beaches.

Maputaland (☎ 035-592 0654; stay@maputalandlodge.co.za; Posbus 757, KwaNgwanase; s/d incl breakfast R450/600;) These 23 more suburban, yet pleasant, self-catering chalets have all the mod cons including DSTV, bar and restaurant. A good option in a creature-free zone.

Kosi Forest Lodge (☎ 035-474 1473; www.isibindiafrica.co.za; s/d R1350/1650;) The only private lodge in this region, and surrounded by the sand forest's Umdoni trees, this intimate 16-bed lodge offers a dreamy, luxurious – given the remote circumstances and lack of electricity – experience. There are activities on tap, and guest transfers available.

Getting There & Away

A 4WD is required to access both Kosi Bay Mouth and Kosi Bay Camp, but some lodges in other areas organise trips here.

If you are driving, Rte 22 runs north to Kosi Bay from Hluhluwe and the N2. If heading from Sodwana Bay, continue up Rte 22; if you have a 4WD, the sandy coastal route is not to be missed.

Tembe Elephant Park

☎ 035

Heading westwards along a dirt road to the N2 from Kosi Bay, South Africa's last free-ranging elephants are protected in the sandveld (dry, sandy belt) forests of **Tembe Elephant Park** (☎ 035-592 0001; www.tembe.co.za; adult/child/vehicle R30/15/35; 6am-6pm), straddling the Mozambique border. There are about 230 elephants in its 30,000 hectares; the only indigenous elephant in KZN and the largest in the world, weighing up to 7000kg. The park also boasts the Big Five and more than 300 bird species.

Tembe Lodge (☎ 031-267 0144; www.tembe.co.za; per person with full board & activities R800;) offers accommodation in delightful, secluded safari tents built on wooden platforms and with bathrooms.

There's a sealed road to the park entrance, but only 4WD vehicles are allowed to drive inside the park.

Ndumo Game Reserve

☎ 033

A little further west, the **Ndumo Game Reserve** (☎ 035-845 1000, 035-591 0004; www.kznwildlife.com; adult/child/vehicle R40/20/35; 5am-7pm) is beside the Mozambique border and close to the Swaziland border, about 100km north of Mkuze. On some 10,000 hectares, there are black and white rhinos, hippos, crocodiles and antelope species, but it is the bird life on the Phongola and Usutu Rivers, and their flood plains and pans, which attracts visitors. This is the southernmost limit of the range of many bird species. The reserve is known locally as a 'mini Okavango'.

Wildlife viewing and birdwatching, guided walks (R85) and vehicle tours (R180) are available.

Fuel and limited supplies are usually available 2km outside the park gate. Camping and rest huts are offered by **Ezemvelo KZN Wildlife** (☎ 033-845 1000; www.kznwildlife.com; per person campsites R106, 2-bed rest huts R286).

DRAKENSBERG

If any landscape lives up to its airbrushed, publicity-shot alter ego, it is the jagged, green sweep of the tabletop peaks of the Drakensberg range. This forms the boundary between South Africa and the mountain kingdom of Lesotho, and offers some of the country's most awe-inspiring landscapes.

Within the area is uKhahlamba-Drakensberg Park, a vast 243,000-hectare sweep of basalt summits and buttresses that was granted World Heritage status in November 2000. The famous vistas here include the unforgettable curve of the Amphitheatre in the Royal Natal National Park.

Drakensberg means 'Dragon Mountains'; the Zulu named it Quathlamba, meaning 'Battlement of Spears'. The Zulu word is a more accurate description of the sheer escarpment but the Afrikaans name captures something of the Drakensberg's otherworldly atmosphere. People have lived here for thousands of years – this is evidenced by the many San rock-art sites – yet many of the peaks were first climbed little more than 50 years ago.

There's no single road linking all the main areas of interest, so you're better off selecting one place (or perhaps a few) and enjoying what it has to offer – from hiking to birdwatching – rather than spending most of your time behind the wheel.

CLIMATE

The frosts come in winter, but the rain falls in summer, and snow has been recorded on the summits every month of the year. While the summer weather forecasts, posted in Ezemvelo KZN Wildlife park offices, often make bleak reading for those hoping for blue skies and sunshine, you can often bet on clear, dry mornings, with the thunderheads only rolling in during the afternoon. Whenever you visit, always carry wet-weather gear, and be prepared for icy conditions and snowfalls.

INFORMATION

In general, you must book **Ezemvelo KZN Wildlife** (☎ Pietermaritzburg 033-845 1000, Durban 031-304 4934; www.kznwildlife.com) accommodation in advance. Minimum charges often apply. Other information offices:

Central Drakensberg Information Centre (☎ 036-488 1207; www.cdic.co.za; 9am-6pm) This helpful private enterprise is based in the Thokozisa complex, 13km outside Winterton on Rte 600.

Okhahlamba Drakensberg Tourism (☎ 036-448 1557; www.drakensberg.org.za; Tatham Rd, Bergville; 9am-4.30pm Mon-Fri, to 1pm Sat) Covers the northern and central Drakensberg; not particularly helpful.

Southern Berg Tourism (☎ 033-701 1471; www.drakensberg.org; Clocktower Centre, Old Main Rd, Underberg; 8am-4pm Mon-Fri, 9am-1pm Sat & Sun) Has the useful *Southern Drakensberg Pocket Guide*.

HIKING

The Drakensberg range is one of Africa's best hiking destinations. Valleys, waterfalls, rivers,

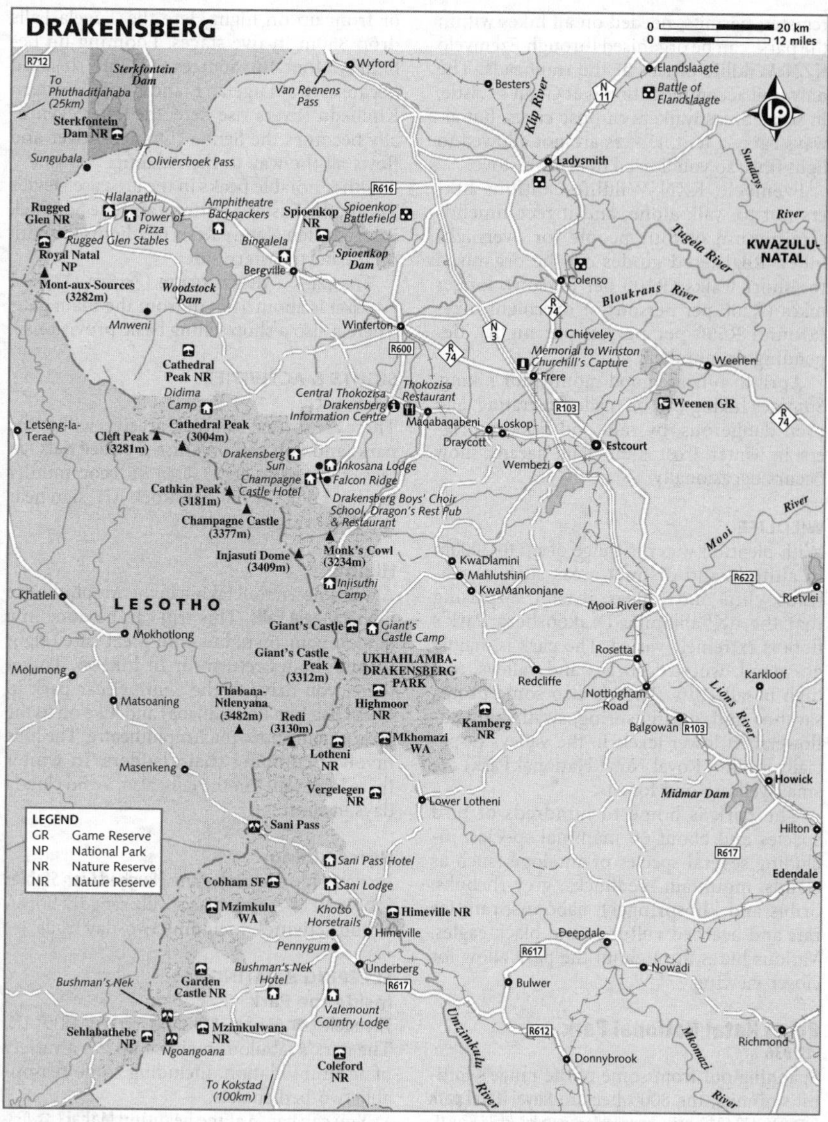

caves and the escarpment provide wonderful opportunities and spectacular wilderness experiences for walkers of all levels, but only experienced climbers should attempt peaks.

There are gentle day walks, moderate half-day hikes, strenuous 10- to 12-hour hikes, and multiday hikes for more serious and experienced hikers.

The trails are accessed through Royal Natal National Park (renowned for its excellent day walks), Cathedral Peak, Monks Cowl, Injisuthi and Giants Castle, and the Southern Drakensberg's remote wilderness areas.

Make sure you obtain the relevant 1:50,000 scale maps and seek advice on the current status of the trail. You must always fill in a register; permits, needed on all hikes within the park, can be organised through Ezemvelo KZN Wildlife offices at the trailheads. The only trail accommodation is at Giant's Castle; in some areas walkers can use caves, but always carry a tent. Hikers are not allowed to light fires, so you'll need to bring a stove.

Ezemvelo KZN Wildlife cautions hikers not to walk alone, and it recommends a minimum of four people for overnight hikes. Registered guides can be organised for short walks (R100 per person), longer hikes (R200 per person) or overnight hikes (around R500 per person per night), depending on numbers.

April to July are good months for hiking. Summer hiking can be made frustrating, and even dangerous, by rain and flooding rivers; in winter, frost is the main hazard; snow occurs occasionally.

WILDLIFE

With plentiful water, a range of up to 3000m in altitude and distinct areas such as plateaus, cliffs and valleys, it isn't surprising that the uKhahlamba-Drakensberg Park's flora is extremely varied. The park is mainly grassland, wooded gorges and valleys, and high basalt cliffs. There's also some protea savanna and, during spring, swaths of wildflowers. At lower levels in the valleys (especially around Royal Natal National Park) are small yellowwood forests.

The park is home to hundreds of bird species and about 60 mammal species, including several species of antelope (such as elands, mountain reedbucks, grey rheboks, oribis and klipspringer), baboons, rare ice rats and bearded vultures, and black eagles. Various hides throughout the park allow for closer viewing.

Royal Natal National Park

☎ 036

Spanning out from some of the range's loftiest summits, the 8000-hectare **Royal Natal park** (☎ 036-438 6310; www.kznwildlife.com; adult/child R30/15; 🕑 5am-7pm) has a presence that far outstrips its relatively meagre size, with many of the surrounding peaks rising as high into the air as the park stretches across. With some of the Drakensberg's most dramatic and accessible scenery, the park is crowned by the sublime Amphitheatre, an 8km wall of cliff and canyon, which is spectacular from below or from up on high. Here the Tugela Falls drop 850m in five stages. Looming up behind is Mont-aux-Sources (3282m), so called because the Tugela, Elands and Western Khubedu Rivers rise here; the latter eventually becomes the Senqu (Orange) River and flows all the way to the Atlantic.

Other notable peaks in the area are Devil's Tooth, the Eastern Buttress and the Sentinel. Rugged Glen Nature Reserve adjoins the park on the northeastern side.

The park's **visitors centre** (🕑 8am-12.30pm & 2-4.30pm) is about 1km in from the main gate. There's also a shop selling basic provisions.

SIGHTS & ACTIVITIES

Rock Art

There are several San rock-art sites within the park, and you can organise a **guided walk** (per person R10; 🕑 walks 10am-3.30pm) with community guides. Look for the 'San Rock Art' sign near the first bridge after entry.

Hiking

A well-known trail taking in the Amphitheatre is the **Tugela Falls**. This trip can be done in a day on your own, but with great care (eight to nine hours return for fit hikers). To get there, you drive to the Sentinel car park in Qwa Qwa (via Phutadijaba) and hike on to the escarpment above the Amphitheatre. The hike involves climbing chain ladders. In winter there is no water in the falls; also, avoid cloudy days in summer.

Horse Riding

Just outside the park gates, **Rugged Glen Stables** (☎ 036-438 6422) organises a wide range of horse-riding activities, including two-day trails.

SLEEPING & EATING

Inside the Park

Thendele (☎ 033-845 1000; chalets per person R360-420) The park's fabulous main camp has a variety of accommodation, including some reasonable two-bed chalets.

You can camp at the beautiful **Mahai** (☎ 033-845 1000, 036-438 6303; fax 036-438 6231; campsites per person R80), or in the more rustic **Rugged Glen Nature Reserve** (☎ 033-845 1000, 033-438 6303; fax 438 6231; campsites per person R80).

Outside the Park

Hlalanathi (☎ 036-438 6308; www.hlalanathi.za.net; campsites per person R50, 2-/4-bed chalets R390/690;

) With a location lifted straight from an African chocolate-box lid, this pretty resort offers camping and excellent accommodation on a finger of land overlooking the Tugela River.

Amphitheatre Backpackers (☎ 036-438 6675; www.amphibackpackers.co.za; campsites R55, dm R85, d R240-280;) Facing out over the Amphitheatre, this hostel is 21km north of Bergville on Rte 74. The busy bar, pool and activities galore will keep you occupied.

Sungubala Mountain Camp (☎ 036-438 6000, 082 781 3476; www.sungubala.com; per person R600) 'Glamping' (glamorous camping) best describes the experience offered by this intimate self-catering option, with six safari tents (with thatched gazebos and beds) and three A-frame units. A 4WD is required; arrange transport with the office.

Coyote Café (☎ 036-438 6220; snacks R18-60; 8am-9.30pm Tue-Sat, to 4pm Sun & Mon) This sleek modern place at the entrance to Little Switzerland serves up gourmet snacks.

Tower of Pizza (☎ 036-438 6480; mains R27-50;) Yep, there really is a tower, where very good oven-fired pizza is prepared. It also offers quaint cottages (doubles including breakfast from R580) and internet access.

GETTING THERE & AWAY

The road into Royal Natal runs off the Rte 74, about 30km northwest of Bergville and about 5km from Oliviershoek Pass.

Bergville

☎ 036

Small and rough around the edges, Bergville is nevertheless a useful jumping-off point for the northern Drakensberg.

If you've arrived late, **Bingalela** (☎ 036-448 1336; s/d R310/560), 3km from Bergville on Rte 74, is one of the few places worth staying. Attractive double and family-sized *rondavels* are set in dusty, car-park-like surrounds, under lovely eucalypts. Locals rate the restaurant, and the bar can get lively.

Further from Bergville, along dirt roads in the Mnweni Valley, the community-run **Mnweni Cultural Centre** (☎ 072-712 2401; campsites per person R35, dm R110) has basic but comfortable self-catering huts, each with four pine beds. San rock art and a dam for canoeing are nearby. It's the registration point for walks into the valley, and guides can be hired.

You'll have to get to Ladysmith and take a minibus taxi from there (R20, 45 minutes). A daily Greyhound bus stops at Estcourt and Ladysmith.

Central Berg

Crowned with some of the Drakensberg's most formidable peaks, including Giant's Castle Peak (3312m), the Monk's Cowl (3234m) and Champagne Castle (3377m), the Central Berg is loved by hikers and climbers. But with its dramatic scenery, this region is just as popular with those who prefer to admire mountains from a safe distance.

The quaint, sedate little town of **Winterton** is the gateway to the Central Drakensberg and makes a pleasant stopover. **Winterton Museum** (☎ 036-488 1885; Kerk St; admission by donation; 9am-3pm Mon-Fri, to noon Sat) offers an excellent insight into San rock art, Zulu history and the Spioenkop battle.

There are accommodation options on the main street, but you're better off driving the 20km to 30km into the Champagne Valley, en route to Monk's Cowl.

There are minibus taxis to Cathedral Peak (30 minutes), Bergville (15 minutes) and Estcourt (45 minutes).

CATHEDRAL PEAK NATURE RESERVE

☎ 036

A beautifully photogenic area in the shadow of the ramparts of Cathedral Peak, **Cathedral Peak Nature Reserve** (☎ 036-488 8000; www.kznwildlife.com; adult/child R25/13; 6am-6pm) backs up against a colossal escarpment of peaks, with the Bell (2930m), the Horns (3005m) and Cleft Peak (3281m) on the horizon.

Obtain instructions and times regarding the hikes, including that to Cathedral Peak, at the **park office** (☎ 036-488 8000; Didima Camp), which also sells permits for the scenic drive (4WD only) up Mike's Pass (R50 per person) and arranges guides.

The **Didima San Art Centre** (☎ 036-488 1332; adult/child R40/20; 8am-4pm), at Didima Camp 1km into the park, offers an excellent, multimedia insight into San rock art.

You can camp near the main gate or at **Didima Camp** (☎ 033-845 1000; www.kznwildlife.com; campsites per person R80, chalets per person R420-460;), one of Ezemvelo KZN Wildlife's swankiest offerings, with huge views, a restaurant, tennis courts, lashings of elegant style and excellent self-catering chalets.

MONK'S COWL

☎ 036

Monk's Cowl (☎ 036-468 1103; www.kznwildlife.com; adult/child R30/15; 6am-6pm), another stunning slice of uKhahlamba-Drakensberg Park, offers superb hiking and rock climbing. Within Monk's Cowl are the two peaks Monk's Cowl and Champagne Castle.

The **park office** (☎ 036-468 1103; campsites per person R74) is 3km beyond Champagne Castle Hotel, which is at the end of Rte 600 running southwest from Winterton. The office takes bookings for camping and **overnight hiking** (adult/child R40/20).

Inkosana Lodge (☎ 036-468 1202; www.inkosana.co.za; campsites R100, dm/d with shared bathroom R150/400, 2-person thatched rondavels with/without bathroom R500/400;), one of the best backpackers hostels in Africa, boasts an indigenous garden and clean rooms. Excellent cuisine and heaps of activities and walks are on offer. It's on Rte 600, en route to Champagne Castle.

One of the best-known resorts in the area is the **Champagne Castle Hotel** (☎ 036-468 1063; www.champagnecastle.co.za; s/d with full board R795/1030;), conveniently located in the mountains at the end of the road to Champagne Castle peak, off Rte 600.

Giant's Castle

☎ 036

Rising up to Injasuti Dome (3409m), **Giant's Castle** (☎ 033-845 1000, 353 3718; www.kznwildlife.com; adult/child R25/13; 5am-7pm) is one of the Drakensberg's loftiest sections – even its lowest point sits at 1300m above sea level. Established in 1904, mainly to protect the eland, it is a rugged, remote and popular destination, with huge forest reserves to the north and south and Lesotho's barren plateau over the escarpment to the west.

Giant's Castle Day Walks (R5), available at Giant's Castle Camp, gives details and has a basic map of the trails.

Limited supplies (including fuel) are available at Giant's Castle Camp and there's a kiosk selling limited provisions.

SIGHTS & ACTIVITIES

Wildlife

The rare lammergeier, or bearded vulture, which is found only in the Drakensberg, nests in the reserve. Reserve staff sometimes give guests bones to put out to encourage the birds to feed here. The **Lammergeyer Hide** (☎ 036-353 3718; giants@kznwildlife.com; per person R170, minimum R510; May-Sep), the best place to see the vultures, is extremely popular so it's necessary to book in advance.

Rock Art

The area is rich in San rock art, with at least 26 sites. It is thought that the last San lived here at the beginning of the 20th century.

To see the paintings, you can visit only **Main Cave** (adult/child R25/10; tours 9am-4pm), 2.3km south of Giant's Camp (a 30-minute walk), which must be visited as part of a tour that departs from Giant's Camp on the hour.

SLEEPING

There are several accommodation centres inside the reserve, as well as trail huts and caves for hikers. There's a small shop at reception with basic supplies only.

Injisuthi Camp (☎ 033-845 1000, 036-431 7849; campsites per person R65, safari camps R120, chalets R240) This secluded and pleasant spot on the northern side of Giant's Castle (accessed from Loskop, northwest of Estcourt) has self-contained cabins and campsites. The area has caves for overnight hikers (check on their state before departing).

Giant's Castle Camp (☎ 033-845 1000, 353 3718; www.kznwildlife.com; trail huts per person R45, chalets R360-400) The camp has well equipped two-, four- and six-bed chalets, and eight-bed mountain huts.

GETTING THERE & AWAY

The roads from both Mooi River and Estcourt are sealed – do not take the unsealed back roads as they can become impassable and in the past, robberies have been reported.

Infrequent minibus taxis run from Estcourt to villages near the main entrance (KwaDlamini, Mahlutshini and KwaMankonjane), but these are still several kilometres from Giant's Castle Camp.

Southern Berg

Best accessed from the pleasant towns of Himeville and Underberg, the Southern Berg boasts one of the region's highlights: the journey up to Lesotho over the Sani Pass. It is renowned as a serious hiking area, offering a smorgasbord of wilderness areas and some great walks including the fabulous Giant's Cup Trail.

COBHAM STATE FOREST

The Mzimkulu Wilderness Area and the Mzimkulwana Nature Reserve are in this

state forest (☎ 033-702 0831; www.kznwildlife.com; adult/child R20/10; ⌚ 6am-6pm). The park office, about 15km from Himeville on the D7, is a good place to get information on the many hiking trails, some with **trail huts** (per person R60). Basic **campsites** (per person R40) are available.

GARDEN CASTLE

The park office of **Garden Castle Nature Reserve** (☎ 033-701 1823; adult/child R20/10; campsites per person R46, huts R60; ⌚ 6am-6pm) is 30km west of Underberg – carry along the road past Khotso Horsetrails.

This reserve incorporates beautiful **Bushman's Nek Valley**, dominated by the 3051m Rhino Peak. The area has many sandstone buttresses and rock-art sites, and a good (long) day walk.

Overnight hikers can use trail huts, campsites or caves (check on their condition before departing).

HIGHMOOR NATURE RESERVE

The park office of **Highmoor Nature Reserve** (☎ 033-845 1000, 033-263 7240; www.kznwildlife.com; adult/child R20/10, campsites per person R50, caves R30; ⌚ 8am-4pm) is off the road from Rosetta to Giant's Castle and Kamberg. Turn off to the south just past the sign to Kamberg, 31km from Rosetta. It's more exposed and less dramatic than some of the Drakensberg region, but its undulating hills make for pleasant walks. There are two caves, both 2.5km from the main office, and Fultons Rock, which has rock art (a 4km easy walk).

KAMBERG NATURE RESERVE

Southeast of Giant's Castle and a little away from the main escarpment area, **Kamberg Nature Reserve** (☎ 033-267 7251; www.kznwildlife.com; ⌚ 6am-6pm) has a number of antelope species and guided **rock-art walks** (adult/child R25/13).

The new **rock-art centre** (video R15, guided walk to waterfall R15, guided walk to waterfall & shelter R25; ⌚ tours 9am, 11am, 12.30pm) is well worth visiting. Allow three hours for the tour, which is an easy 3.5km walk, if a little steep at the end. Two documentaries are shown, including a visual tour, aimed at disabled visitors who are unable to walk to the site.

Well-equipped, self-catering **chalets** (tw R250) with floor-to-ceiling windows in a quaint garden setting can be booked through the reserve office.

You can reach the reserve from Rosetta, off the N3 south of Mooi River, travelling via either Nottingham Road or Redcliffe.

LOTHENI NATURE RESERVE

Lotheni (☎ 033-702 0540; www.kznwildlife.com; adult/child R20/10; ⌚ 6am-6pm) has a Settlers' Museum and some very good day walks.

Contact **Ezemvelo KZN Wildlife** (☎ Pietermaritzburg 033-845 1000, Durban 031-304 4934; www.kznwildlife.com; campsites R50, 3-bed chalets per person R164) for accommodation.

The access road runs from Lower Lotheni, about 30km northeast of Himeville or 65km southwest of Nottingham Road. The roads are some of the most scenic you'll find, but they aren't great and heavy rain can close them.

MKHOMAZI WILDERNESS AREA & VERGELEGEN NATURE RESERVE

The **Mkhomazi Wilderness Area** (033-266 6444; www.kznwildlife.com; adult/child R25/13; ⌚ 6am-6pm) is one of the few places where you can hike for days without seeing anyone else. The **Vergelegen Nature Reserve** (☎ 033-702 0712; www.kznwildlife.com; adult/child R20/10; ⌚ 6am-6pm) has trout fishing. There are no established campsites in the area, but you can camp on hikes (R40). The turn-off is 44km from Nottingham Rd, off the Lower Lotheni–Sani Pass road, at the Mzinga River. From there the area is another 2km.

SANI PASS

☎ 033

The drive up the Sani Pass is a trip to the roof of South Africa: a spectacular ride around hairpin bends into the clouds to the kingdom of Lesotho. At 2865m, this is the highest pass in the country and the vistas (on a clear day!) are magical. There are hikes in almost every direction and inexpensive horse rides are available. Amazingly, this is also the only road link between Lesotho and KwaZulu-Natal.

At the top of the pass, just beyond the Lesotho border crossing, is the Sani Top Chalet. Various operators run 4WD trips up to the chalet. You need a passport to cross into Lesotho. The border is open from 6am to 6pm daily, but check beforehand; times alter.

At the bottom of the pass, **Sani Lodge** (☎ 033-702 0330; www.sani-lodge.co.za; campsites US$6; dm/d with shared bathroom US$9/11, 2-bed rondavels US$30) tops the pops in the local-knowledge stakes, offering a range of fabulous tours and activities and insider tips about the region through its tour company. Some of the rooms are basic (*rondavels* are nicer) but the communal, ski-lodge-style atmosphere makes up for it. The lodge can pick up guests from Himeville or Underberg.

GIANT'S CUP TRAIL

Without doubt, the Giant's Cup Trail (68km, five days and five nights), running from Sani Pass to Bushman's Nek, is one of the nation's great walks. Any reasonably fit person can walk it. Early booking, through Ezemvelo KZN Wildlife (p499), is advisable in local holiday seasons. Fees are based on the composition of the hiking party.

Highlights include the **Bathplug Cave** with San rock art and the breathtaking mountain scenery on day four. Accommodation is in limited **shared huts** (adult/child per trail R65/50). No firewood is available so you'll need a stove and fuel. Sani Lodge (p507), which sells maps (R45), is almost at the head of the trail.

BUSHMAN'S NEK

☎ 033

This is a South Africa–Lesotho border crossing (no vehicles!). From here there are hiking trails up into the escarpment, including to Lesotho's Sehlabathebe National Park. You can trot through the border and into Lesotho on horseback with **Khotso Horsetrails** (☎ 033-701 1502).

Accommodation options include the **Silverstreams Caravan Park** (☎ 033-701 1249; www.silverstreams.co.za; campsites per person R120-300, cottages from R350), right next to the border, and **Bushman's Nek Hotel** (☎ 033-701 1460; www.bushmansnek.co.za; r R589;), a full-on resort about 2km east of the border crossing.

Underberg

☎ 033 / pop 1500

Clustered in the foothills of the southern Drakensberg, this small farming town fills up in summer, when Durbanites head to the peaks for a breath of the fresh stuff. It has good infrastructure, and is the place to go for money, shopping and to organise activities in the region.

Sani Pass Tours (☎ 033-701 1064; www.sanipasstours.com; Underberg Village Mall) offers day tours up the Sani Pass (from around R420 excluding lunch), as well as packages tailored to more specialist interests.

The large, thatched farmhouse B&B **Valemount Country Lodge** (☎ 033-701 1686; www.valemountafrica.com; s/d incl breakfast R495;) oozes graceful charm, and has 48 hectares of grounds to explore. It's 8km from Underberg on the Kokstad road.

Underberg Express (☎ 086-111 4924; www.underbergexpress.co.za) operates regular shuttles between Underberg and Durban (from R200), Pietermaritzburg (R130) and Kokstad (R180; where you can catch ongoing connections). You must book these services. Minibus taxis run to Himeville (R6, 10 minutes), Sani Pass Hotel (R25, 30 minutes) and Pietermaritzburg (R55, 1½ hours).

Himeville

☎ 033

A skip and a jump from Underberg, Himeville is a pretty, more sedate jumping-off point for the southern Drakensberg. The **Himeville Museum** (☎ 033-702 1184; admission by donation; 9am-12.30pm Mon-Sat), one of the best rural museums in the country, contains an incredible array of bric-a-brac.

For accommodation, the **Himeville Arms** (☎ 033-702 1305; www.himevillehotel.co.za; Main Rd, Himeville; dm with/without bathroom R150/120, incl breakfast s R340, d R620-680) is a homey inn with a cosy bar, three eating options and lashings of rustic, village-green atmosphere.

Minibus taxis run to Underberg (R6, 10 minutes).

THE MIDLANDS

The Midlands run northwest from Pietermaritzburg, KwaZulu-Natal's capital, to Estcourt, skirting the Battlefields to the northeast. West of Pietermaritzburg is picturesque, hilly country, originally settled by English farmers. The region is promoted as the Midlands Meander, a slightly contrived concoction of craft shops, artistic endeavours, teashops and B&Bs.

Pietermaritzburg

☎ 033 / pop 457,000

Billed as the heritage city, Pietermaritzburg's (usually known as PMB) grand historic buildings hark back to an age of pith helmets and midday martinis. Today, they proudly house museums and refurbished hotels. By day, KZN's administrative and legislative capital is vibrant: its large Zulu community sets a colourful flavour and the Indian community brings echoes of the subcontinent to its busy streets. A large student population adds to the city's vitality.

INFORMATION

Ezemvelo KZN Wildlife Headquarters (☎ 033-845 1000; www.kznwildlife.com; Queen Elizabeth Park, Peter Brown Dr; 🕑 reception 8am-4.30pm Mon-Fri, reservations to 5.30pm Mon-Thu, to 4.30pm Fri, to 12.30pm Sat) Provides information and accommodation bookings for all Ezemvelo KZN Wildlife parks and reserves.

Orange Ring (☎ 033-342 9254; 31 Chief Albert Luthuli Rd; 🕑 7am-9pm) Surf the internet, do your laundry and drink coffee.

Pietermaritzburg Tourism (☎ 033-345 1348; www.pmbtourism.co.za; Publicity House, 117 Chief Albert Luthuli Rd; 🕑 8am-5pm Mon-Fri, to 1pm Sat) Has excellent information on the city and surrounds.

SIGHTS & ACTIVITIES

One of the city's finest sights is the **Tatham Art Gallery** (☎ 033-342 1804; Chief Albert Luthuli Rd; admission free; 🕑 10am-6pm Tue-Sun), a fine collection of French and English 19th- and early-20th-century works housed in the beautiful Old Supreme Court. The nearby, colonial-era **City Hall** (cnr Church St & Commercial Rd) is the largest load-bearing red-brick building in the southern hemisphere.

The **Msunduzi Museum** (☎ 033-394 6834; 351 Lanagalibalele St; adult/child/student R5/2/3; 🕑 9am-4pm Mon-Fri, to 1pm Sat) incorporates Voortrekker, Zulu and Indian displays as well as buildings including the Church of the Vow (1841), built to fulfil the Voortrekkers' promise to God at the Battle of Blood River.

Three **Hindu temples** grace the northern end of Langalibalele St and the main **mosque** (East St) is nearby. A **statue of Gandhi**, who was famously ejected from a 1st-class carriage at Pietermaritzburg station, stands defiant opposite the old colonial buildings on Church St.

SLEEPING

Sleepy Hollow (☎ 033-342 1758; 80 Leinster Rd; www.wylderide.co.za; campsites R60, dm/s/d R100/125/250) In the heart of the student precinct, this rambling mint-coloured 1940s abode has a cosy preloved feel, and a communal kitchen. The owners run rafting and cycling adventures.

Prince Alfred Street Backpackers (☎ 033-345 7045, www.chauncey.co.za; 312 Prince Alfred St; per person R120; P 💻) This bright place, with multicoloured mosquito-net extravaganzas and ethnic adornments, is handy to the centre and offers gourmet cuisine.

Smith Grove (☎ 033-345 3963; www.smithgrove.co.za; 37 Howick Rd; s/d R350/500) This renovated Victorian home offers English-style B&B comforts with decorated, individually styled rooms.

Briar Ghyll (☎ 033-342 2664; www.bglodge.co.za; George MacFarlane Lane; s/d R495/650) This historic and stunning home, set on 20 hectares of farm and garden, has large, luxurious rooms, plump pillows, stylish antique interiors and miles of green lawn, trees and bird life.

Redlands Hotel & Lodge (☎ 033-394 3333; www.guestnet.co.za; cnr Howick Rd & George MacFarlane Lane; s/d from R545/675; ❄ 🏊) A favourite among dignitaries, this elegant place offers contrived but tasteful colonial-style surrounds and an escape-from-it-all ambience.

EATING

Rosehurst (☎ 033-394 1443; 239 Boom St; mains R45-55; 🕑 8.30am-4pm Mon-Fri, to 2pm Sat) Behind a chintzy gift shop in a delightful Victorian house, an English garden hides in the middle of 'Maritzburg. Relax under blossom and pink bougainvillea while munching on tasty salads, sandwiches, pastries or breakfasts.

Butchery (☎ 033-342 5239; www.thebutchery.co.za; 101 Roberts Rd; mains R46-70; 🕑 noon-late) Ladies' (200g) and gents' (300g) steaks of every type, racks of drying biltong, wall-to-wall wine racks and a packed deck of eaters make for a sizzling night out. Vegetarians are also catered for.

Chef's Plate (☎ 033-342 8327; Chief Albert Luthuli St; lunches R60-90) Upstairs at the Tatham Art Gallery, and following the same opening hours, this arty little cafe with an outdoor verandah whips up creative and fresh, healthy fare.

Eaton's on Eighty (☎ 033-342 3280; 80 Roberts Rd, Clarendon; mains R70-130; 🕑 lunch Wed-Fri, dinner Tue-Sat) Mellow and romantic, Eaton's draws a slightly older and sedate crowd, but the menu (which leans towards seafood) is contemporary fusion, offering creative, colourfully presented dishes.

GETTING THERE & AWAY

Air

SAAirlink (☎ 033-3869 2861; www.saairlink.co.za), with an office at the airport, flies to Jo'burg daily (high season R1130).

Bus

Most bus companies' head offices are on Burger St, or directly opposite in McDonalds Plaza. **Greyhound/Citiliner** (☎ 083-915 9000;

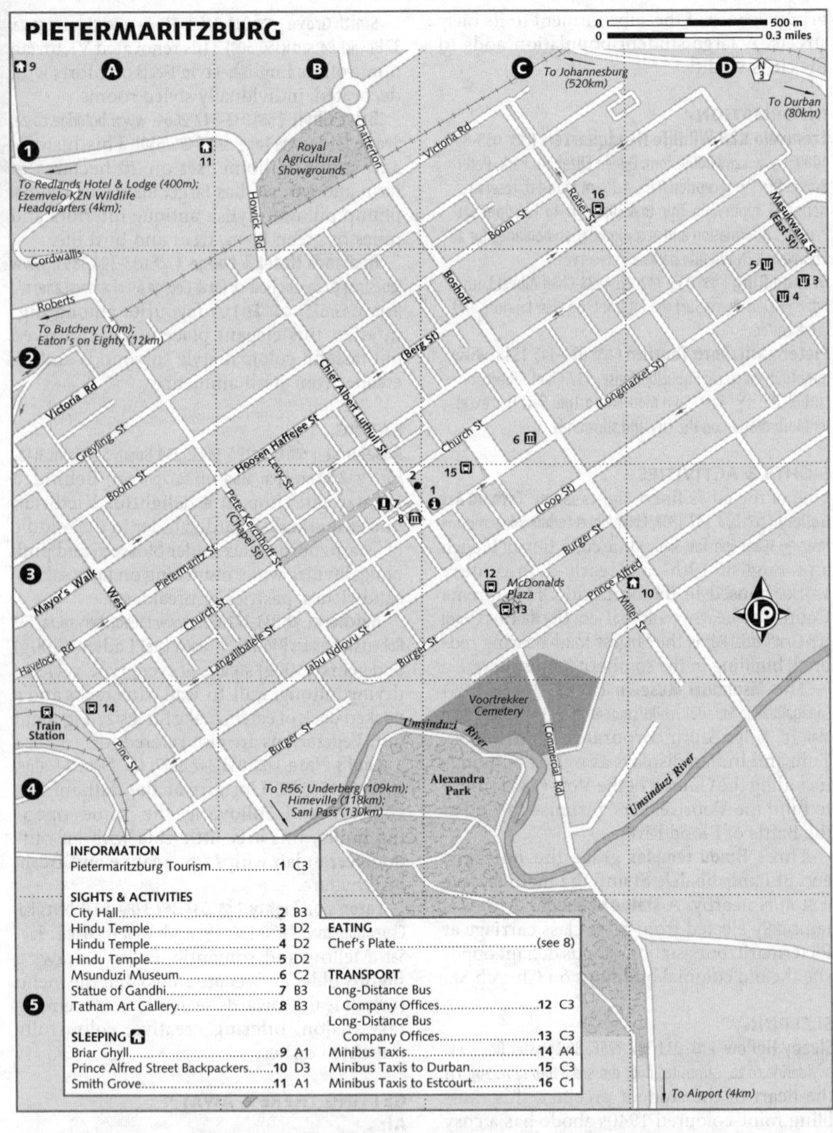

www.greyhound.co.za), **Translux/City to City** (☎ 033-345 0165; www.translux.co.za), **Luxliner** (☎ 011-914 4321; www.luxliner.co.za) and **Intercape** (☎ 0861-287 287; www.intercape.co.za) offer similar prices depending on the level of onboard services. Destinations from Pietermaritzburg include Jo'burg (from R140, six to seven hours), Pretoria (R200, seven to eight hours), Port Elizabeth (R320, 15 hours) and Durban (from R160, 1½ hours).

Underberg Express (☎ 033-701 2750, 086-111 4924; www.underbergexpress.co.za) offers a daily service to Durban Airport (R160) and Durban Central (R130). The Baz Bus travels between Durban and Pietermaritzburg three times a week.

African Link Travel (☎ 033-345 3175; www.africanlink.co.za; 267 Burger St) does transfers from Durban International Airport to Pietermaritzburg (R590).

Car

Most of the major car-hire companies have agents here and are based at the airport.

Minibus Taxi

Minibus taxis generally congregate in Church St in front of the train station. Destinations from Pietermaritzburg include Ladysmith (R75, 2½ hours), Underberg (R60, 2½ hours), Newcastle (R100, 3½ hours), Jo'burg (eight hours), Durban (R40, one hour, from behind City Hall) and Estcourt (R55, 1¾ hours, from the corner of Retief and Hoosen Haffejee Sts, not a safe part of town).

Train

Shosholoza Meyl (☎ 0860-008 888; www.shosholozameyl.co.za) runs once a week to Jo'burg (sleeper class R240, 10 hours) via Ladysmith, and to Durban (R50, 2½ hours); to Cape Town (1st and 2nd class, 36 hours) via Ladysmith and Bloemfontein on Friday.

Shosholoza Meyl's **Premier Classe** (www.premierclasse.co.za) runs to Jo'burg on Wednesday and Sunday, to Durban on Tuesday and Friday.

Economy-class (seats only) trains also service these routes.

BATTLEFIELDS

KwaZulu-Natal's history is intrinsically linked to its Battlefields, the stage on which many of the country's bloodiest scenes were played out. The province's northwestern region is where some 500 Voortrekkers avenged the murder of their leader Piet Retief by defeating a force of 12,000 Zulu at the Battle of Blood River, and a Zulu army crushed the British Empire at Isandlwana. The Brits subsequently staged the heroic defence of Rorke's Drift, and slogged it out against the Boers at Ladysmith and Spioenkop.

The *Battlefields Route* brochure is available at Durban's Tourist Junction (p483) and tourist offices across the region.

Tours

Some recommended guides for touring the Battlefields:

Dave Sutcliffe (☎ 072-271 1766; dave.sutcliffe@telkomsa.net)
Elisabeth Durham (☎ 079-7795949; cheznous@dundeekzn.co.za)
Ken Gillings (☎ 083-654 5880; ken.gillings@mweb.co.za)
Pat Rundgren (☎ 082-6907812; gunners@trustnet.co.za)

Estcourt & Around

☎ 036

Once a thriving town, Estcourt today is a rough-and-tumble place, although it's surrounded by pleasant farming communities. It has an interesting museum, and is on the Durban–Jo'burg/Pretoria bus route.

Around 25km northeast of Estcourt is the 5000-hectare undulating thornveld of the **Weenen Game Reserve** (☎ 036-354 7013; www.kznwildlife.com; adult/child/vehicle R20/10/20; 🕑 6am-6pm), which has black and white rhinos, giraffes and several antelope species. There are two short self-guided trails, **campsites** (per person R66) and a five-bed **cottage** (per person R170).

A lovely colonial villa ringed by tropical gardens, homey **Ashtonville Terraces** (☎ 036-352 7770; dlsa@telkomsa.net; 76 Albert St; s/d incl breakfast R370/520;) boasts large rooms and massive breakfasts.

Greyhound (☎ 031-334 9720; www.greyhound.co.za) stops outside the uMtshezi Tourism Information Bureau, on Upper Harding St. Tickets are available from the **Christian Bookshop** (☎ 036-352 5972; 140 Victoria St). Buses run daily to Durban (from R170, 2½ hours) and Jo'burg (R275, 7½ hours).

Minibus taxis run from the main rank, at the bottom of Phillips St in the town centre, to destinations including Winterton (R14, 30 minutes), Ladysmith (R25, one hour), Pietermaritzburg (R55, 1¾ hours), Durban (R80, 2½ hours) and Jo'burg (R135, eight hours).

Spioenkop Nature Reserve

☎ 036

The 6000-hectare **Spioenkop Nature Reserve** (☎ 036-488 1578; www.kznwildlife.com; admission R20; 🕑 6am-6pm;) is based on the Spioenkop Dam on the Tugela River. The reserve is handy for most of the area's battlefield sites and not too far from the Drakensberg for day trips into the range. Animals include white rhinos, giraffes, various antelope species and 290-plus bird species. There's horse riding, a vulture hide and guided walks.

Inside the reserve in a valley, **iPika** (campsites/bush camp per person R60/190) offers campsites and one four-bed tented bush camp.

Spionkop Lodge (☎ 036-488 1404; www.spionkop.co.za; s/d with full board R1400/2200, 4-/6-person cottages per person R890/990;), overlooking the Spioenkop Battlefield, is a luxury 'barracks' owned by a raconteur and Battlefield guide.

The reserve is northeast of Bergville but the entrance is on the eastern side, 13km from Winterton off Rte 600. You will need a car to get here. If coming by car, the Spioenkop Battlefield is accessed from the Rte 616 (not the Rte 600; follow the signs).

Ladysmith

☎ 036

Named after the wife of Cape governor Sir Harry Smith, Ladysmith achieved fame during the 1899–1902 Anglo-Boer War, when it was besieged by Boer forces for 118 days. The famous vocal group, Ladysmith Black Mambazo, has its roots here. Apart from the historical aspect – several buildings were here during the siege – Ladysmith is a reasonable base for the area's Battlefield tours.

Local information is available at the new **Emnambithi Cultural Centre** (☎ 036-637 2331; www.ladysmith.co.za; 316 Murchison St; 9am-4pm Mon-Fri, to 1pm Sat).

SIGHTS & ACTIVITIES

The excellent **Siege Museum** (☎ 036-637 2231; adult/child R10/5; 9am-4pm Mon-Fri, to 1pm Sat), next to the town hall in the old Market House (built in 1884), was used to store rations during the siege.

At the Emnambithi Cultural Centre, the small but excellent **Cultural Museum** (9am-4pm Mon-Fri) has displays including a Ladysmith Black Mambazo tribute and a reconstruction of a Zulu hut.

Outside the town hall are two guns, **Castor** and **Pollux**, used by the British in defence of Ladysmith. Nearby is a replica of **Long Tom**, a Boer gun capable of heaving a shell 10km.

SLEEPING

Budleigh Guesthouse (☎ 036-635 7700; 12 Berea Rd; s/d R350/550;) This mansion with its verandahs and trim garden has neat, smart rooms with wooden bedsteads and faux antiques.

Buller's Rest Lodge (☎ 036-637 6154; www.bullersrestlodge.co.za; 61 Cove Cres; s/d incl breakfast R410/595;) At this smart thatched abode, the snug 'Boer War' pub completes with Battlefields artefacts, scrumptious home cooking, and views from the sundeck-cum-bar.

Royal Hotel (☎ 036-637 2176; www.royalhotel.co.za; 140 Murchison St; s/d incl breakfast R410/640;) With a resident pub, these slightly tired but pleasant historical digs combine old-style touches (floral borders) with 1980s renovations (shag-pile carpet).

GETTING THERE & AWAY

Bus

Bus tickets can be purchased from Shoprite/Checkers in the Oval Shopping Centre. Buses depart from the Guinea Fowl petrol station (not to be confused with the restaurant) on Murchison Rd, and run to Durban (R255, four hours), Pretoria (R265, seven hours) and Cape Town (R485, 19 hours).

Minibus Taxi

The main taxi rank is east of the town centre near the corner of Queen and Lyell Sts. Destinations include Pietermaritzburg (R75, 1½ hours) and Durban (R100, 2½ hours). Taxis bound for Jo'burg (R130, five hours) are nearby on Alexandra St.

Train

Durban–Cape Town and Durban–Jo'burg/Pretoria **Shosholoza Meyl** (☎ 0860-008 888; www.shosholozameyl.co.za) trains stop here, as does Shosholoza Meyl's **Premier Classe** (www.premierclasse.co.za) service.

Isandlwana & Rorke's Drift

☎ 034

If you have seen *Zulu*, the film that made Michael Caine a star, you will have doubtless heard of Rorke's Drift, a victory of the misty-eyed variety, where on 22–23 January 1879, 139 British soldiers successfully defended a small mission station from around 4000 Zulu warriors. Queen Victoria lavished Victoria Crosses on the survivors and the battle was assured its dramatic place in British military history.

For the full picture, however, you must travel 15km across the plain to Isandlwana, the precursor of Rorke's Drift, where only hours earlier the Zulu dealt the Empire one of its great battlefield disasters by annihilating the main body of the British force in devastating style. Tellingly, *Zulu Dawn* (1979), the film made about the Battle of

Isandlwana, never became the cult classic *Zulu* (1964) is now.

Ideally, the two battlefields should be visited together. Start at the **Isandlwana Visitors Centre** (☎ 034-271 8165; adult/child R20/10; ⏲ 8am-4pm Mon-Fri, 9am-4pm Sat & Sun), where there is a small museum. The battlefield itself is extremely evocative, with white cairns and memorials marking the spots where British soldiers fell.

Zulu was filmed in the Drakensberg, but the scenery around Rorke's Drift is nonetheless beautifully rugged, and the **Rorke's Drift Orientation Centre** (☎ 034-642 1627; adult/child R20/10; ⏲ 8am-4pm Mon-Fri, 9am-4pm Sat & Sun), on the site of the original mission station, is excellent. The Zulu know this site as Shiyane, their name for the hill at the back of the village.

SLEEPING

Rorke's Drift Lodge (☎ 034-642 1805; www.rorkesdriftlodge.co.za; Rorke's Drift; per person incl half board R750;) Mixing old-world hospitality and contemporary design, this place is 5km up a rough track near the Rorke's Drift Orientation Centre. Call ahead to check on road conditions and for pick-ups.

Isandlwana Lodge (☎ 034-271 8301; www.isandlwana.co.za; s/d with full board from R2550/3400;) For such a modern construction, the lodge ingeniously blends into the landscape. Its stunning rooms have expansive views over Mt Isandlwana, the Anglo-Zulu battle site.

GETTING THERE & AWAY

The battle sites are both southeast of Dundee (Isandlwana is 70km southeast and Rorke's Drift is 42km) and accessible from Rte 66. The roads to both can be dusty and rough, and a dirt road connects them.

Blood River Monument

☎ 034

On 16 December 1838, some 500 Voortrekkers avenged the massacre of Piet Retief's diplomatic party by crushing a 12,000-strong Zulu army. More than 3000 Zulu died – the Ncome River ran red with their blood – while the Voortrekkers sustained barely a few casualties. The Battle of Blood River became a seminal event in Afrikaner history, seen as proof that the Boers had a divine mandate to conquer and 'civilise' Southern Africa. Afrikaners still visit the site on 16 December, but the former 'Day of the Vow' is now the 'Day of Reconciliation'.

The battle site is marked by a full-scale bronze re-creation of the Voortrekkers' 64-wagon *laager* (wagon circle). The monument and the nearby **Blood River Museum** (☎ 034-632 1695; adult/child R20/10; ⏲ 8am-4.30pm) are 20km southeast of Rte 33; the turn-off is 27km from Dundee and 45km from Vryheid.

The interesting **Ncome Museum** (☎ 034-271 8121; admission by donation; ⏲ 8am-4.30pm), on the other side of the river, gives the Zulu perspective of events.

MPUMALANGA

Apart from Kruger National Park, Mpumalanga's major draw is the Blyde River Canyon, which carves its way spectacularly through the Drakensberg Escarpment. Surrounding it are mountains, rivers, waterfalls and thick tracts of pine forest – which make the region a prime target for outdoor enthusiasts.

Those not into death-defying pursuits can soak up the region's gold-mining history in Baberton or the living museum of Pilgrim's Rest. The dry, hot lowveld surrounding Kruger is home to Mpumalanga's answer to the big smoke, Nelspruit.

Many travellers zip through the province en route to Kruger, but it's worth setting aside a few days to explore the area.

EASTERN LOWVELD

The hot and dry Eastern Lowveld lacks the obvious appeal of the Drakensberg Escarpment and is mostly used as a staging post on the way into and out of Kruger National Park. However, the region has its attractions. You can learn about the history of the gold rush in laid-back Barberton, get your big-city fix in Nelspruit and whet your appetite for the mighty Kruger in country lodges.

Kruger National Park

Kruger is one of South Africa's national symbols, and for many visitors, the park is *the* 'must-see' wildlife destination in the country. Little wonder: in an area the size of Wales, enough elephants wander around to populate a major city, giraffes nibble on acacia trees, hippos wallow in the rivers, leopards prowl through the night and a multitude of birds sing, fly and roost.

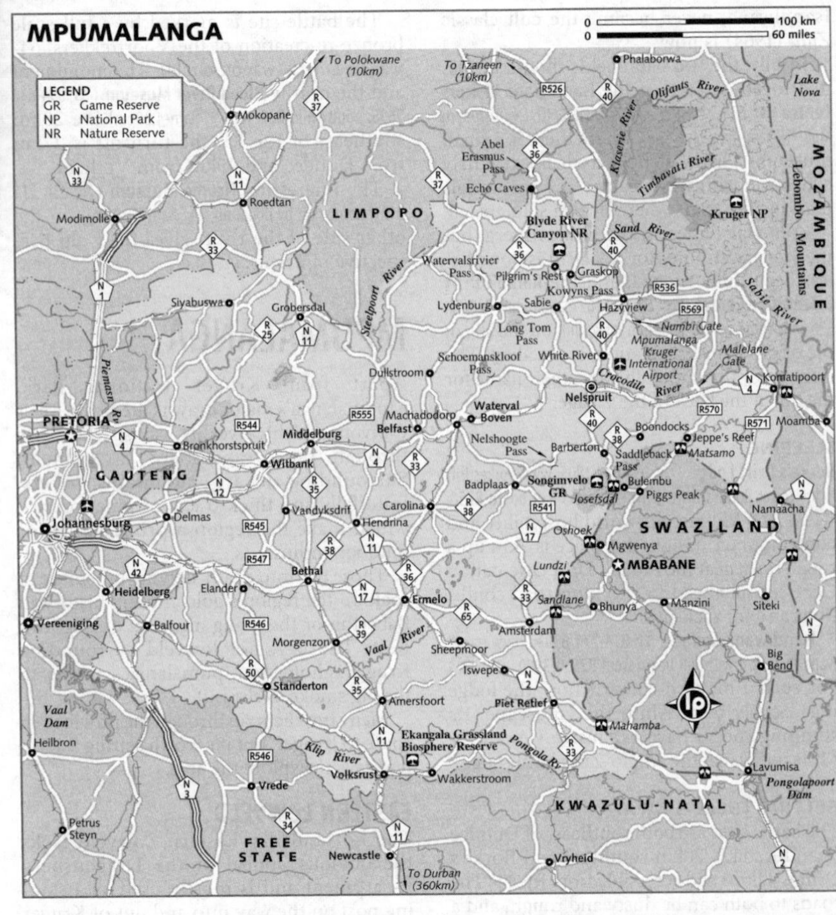

Kruger is one of the world's most famed protected areas – known for its size, conservation history, wildlife diversity and ease of access. It's a place where the drama of life and death plays out on a daily basis. One morning you may spot lions feasting on a kill, and the next a newborn impala struggling to take its first steps.

The park has an extensive network of sealed roads and comfortable camps, but if you prefer to keep it rough, there are also 4WD tracks and hiking trails. Even when you stick to the tarmac, the sounds and scents of the bush are never far away. And, if you avoid weekends and holidays, or stay in the north and on gravel roads, it's easy to travel for an hour or more without even seeing another vehicle.

Southern Kruger is the most popular section, with the highest animal concentrations and easiest access. The park is at its best in the far north, around Punda Maria and Pafuri Gates. Here, although animal concentrations are somewhat lower, the bush setting and wilderness atmosphere are all-enveloping.

ORIENTATION

Kruger is a long, narrow wedge (about 65km across, and 350km long), bordered by Zimbabwe to the north, Limpopo to the west, Mpumalanga to the west and south, and Mozambique to the east. Rimming the park to the west, and sharing the same unfenced terrain, is a chain of private wildlife reserves.

Terrain ranging from the flat to the gently undulating covers the majority of the park, with the Lebombo Mountains rising up to the east along the Mozambique border. Major rivers flowing across Kruger from west to east include the Limpopo, Luvuvhu, Shingwedzi, Letaba, Olifants, Timbavati and Sabie.

There are nine South African *heks* (entry gates). On the park's southern edge are **Malelane** (☎ 013-735 6152) and **Crocodile Bridge** (☎ 013-735 6012). Both are readily accessible from the N4 from Pretoria. The **Numbi** (☎ 013-735 5133), **Phabeni** (☎ 013-735 5890) and **Paul Kruger** (☎ 013-735 5107) gates are easily accessed from Hazyview (turn off the N4 before Nelspruit); Paul Kruger Gate is the closest to Skukuza, Kruger's main rest camp. Towards the park's central section, **Orpen** (☎ 013-735 6355) is convenient if you're coming from the Blyde River area. **Phalaborwa** (☎ 013-735 6509) is nearest to Polokwane; **Punda Maria** (☎ 013-735 6870) can be reached via Louis Trichardt (Makhado) and the Venda region; and **Pafuri** (☎ 013-735 5574), in the far north, is near the Zimbabwe border. It is also possible to enter Kruger from Mozambique at the Giriyondo and Pafuri Gates, which double as international border crossings (visas are available on both sides).

INFORMATION

Bookings

Accommodation can be booked through **SAN Parks** (☎ 012-428 9111; www.sanparks.org), which has offices in Pretoria (p542) and Durban (p483), and **Lowveld Tourism** (013-755 1988/9; www.lowveldtourism.com), which has offices in Nelspruit (p519) and Cape Town.

Except in the high season (school holidays, Christmas and Easter) and at weekends, bookings are advisable but not essential.

Entry

Day or overnight entry to the park costs R160/80 per adult/child, with significant discounts available for South African citizens and residents, and for South African Development Community (SADC) nationals. The Wild Card (p400) also applies to Kruger.

Bicycles and motorcycles are not permitted to enter the park. During school holidays you can stay in the park for a maximum of 10 days, and at any one rest camp for five days (10 days if you're camping). Park authorities restrict the total number of visitors, so in the high season it pays to arrive early if you don't have a booking.

Entry gate opening times vary slightly according to the season, and are currently as follows:

Month	Gates/camps open (am)	Gates/camps close (pm)
Jan	5.30/4.30	6.30
Feb	5.30	6.30
Mar	5.30	6
Apr	6	6
May-Jul	6	5.30
Aug & Sep	6	6
Oct	5.30	6
Nov & Dec	5.30/4.30	6.30

It's an offence to arrive late at a camp and you can be fined for doing so (the camps are fenced). There are strictly enforced speed limits of 50km/h on sealed roads and 40km/h on dirt roads.

Wildlife

Impalas, buffaloes, Burchell's zebras, blue wildebeests, kudus, waterbucks, baboons, vervet monkeys, cheetahs, leopards and other smaller predators are all widespread. Bird life is prolific along the rivers and north of the Luvuvhu River.

Rainfall is highest (700mm a year) in the southern section of the park, leading to grasslands and thick woods with a variety of trees. This terrain is particularly favoured by white rhinos, zebras and buffaloes, but less so by antelope and, therefore, by predators.

The central eastern sections of the park, to the south of the Olifants River on the plains around Satara rest camp and south to the Crocodile River, experience reasonable rainfall (600mm). In this region there are large populations of impalas, zebras, wildebeests, giraffes and black rhinos. Joining them are predators, particularly lions (which prey on impalas, zebras and blue wildebeests) and cheetahs.

North of the Olifants River the rainfall drops below 500mm and the dominant tree is mopane (mopani), a favoured food of elephants – which are common north of Olifants River, around Olifants and Letaba rest camps. The mopaneveld also attracts tsessebes, elands, roans and sables.

Perhaps the most interesting area is in the far north around Punda Maria and Pafuri, which lies completely in the tropics and has a higher rainfall (close to 700mm at Punda

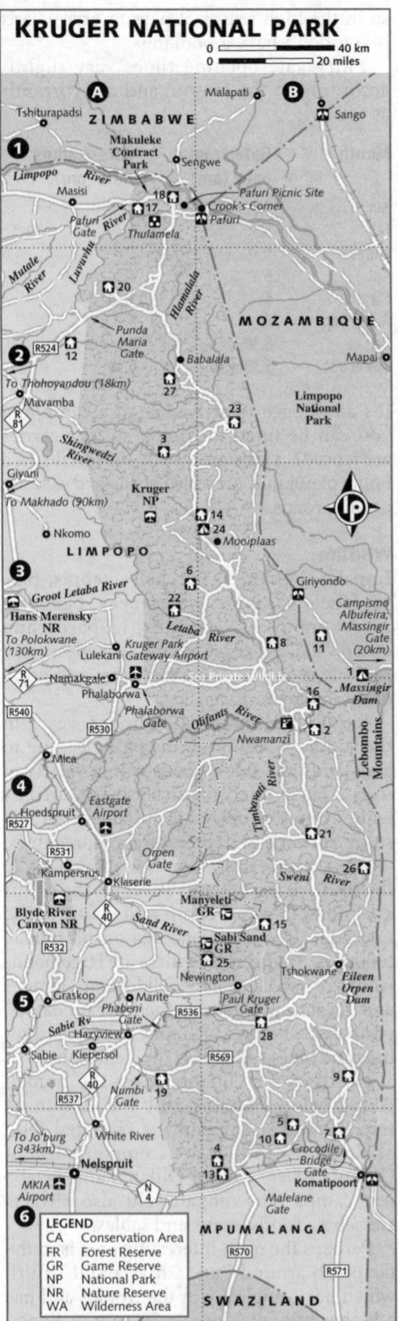

SLEEPING

Aguia Pesqueira Campsite	1	B3
Balule Satellite Camp	2	B4
Bateleur Bushveld Camp	3	A2
Berg-en-dal Rest Camp	4	B6
Biyamiti Bushveld Camp	5	B6
Boulders Bush Lodge	6	A3
Crocodile Bridge Rest Camp	7	B6
Letaba Rest Camp	8	B3
Lower Sabie Rest Camp	9	B5
Lukimbi Safari Lodge	10	B6
Machampane Wilderness Camp	11	B3
Makuleke Community Centre & Homestay	12	A2
Malelane Satellite Camp	13	B6
Mopani Rest Camp	14	B3
Nkorho Bush Lodge	15	B5
Olifants Rest Camp	16	B4
Outpost	17	A1
Pafuri Camp	18	A1
Pretoriuskop Rest Camp	19	A5
Punda Maria Rest Camp	20	A2
Satara Rest Camp	21	B4
Shimuwini Bushveld Camp	22	A3
Shingwedzi Rest Camp	23	B2
Shipandani Overnight Hide	24	B3
Singita	25	B5
Singita Lebombo Lodge	26	B4
Sirheni Bushveld Camp	27	A2
Skukuza Rest Camp	28	B5

Maria) than the mopaneveld. There is woodland, bushveld, grass plains and, between the Luvuvhu and Limpopo Rivers, a tropical riverine forest. Baobabs abound, elephants, lions and leopards are encountered, and there's an exceptional array of birds.

Note that even outside the park borders there are areas that support wildlife, such as along the Olifants River to the south of Phalaborwa.

ACTIVITIES

Although it's possible to get a sense of Kruger in a day, the park merits at least four to five days, and ideally a week. The closer you get to the bush, and the more time you devote to becoming acquainted with its sounds, smells and rhythms, the more rewarding your experience will be. Activities need to be booked in advance, except short bush walks and wildlife drives, which can be booked at the gates and camps.

4WD Trails

Kruger's longest 4WD trail is the **Lebombo Motorised Eco Trail**, a rough, rugged 500km route along the eastern boundary of the park. The trail lasts five days and costs R6870 per vehicle (maximum four people). You'll need to provide your own vehicle, food and drink. Only five vehicles are permitted at a time on the trail (plus the accompanying ranger's vehicle).

There are four shorter 'adventure trails', all averaging about four hours, and costing R460 per vehicle plus a R100 refundable deposit. They (and the points where you can reserve them) are: **Northern Plains Adventure Trail** (Shingwedzi or Punda Maria camps); **Nonokani Adventure Trail** (Phalaborwa Gate); **Mananga Adventure Trail** (Satara camp); **Madlabantu Adventure Trail** (Pretoriuskop camp). All are closed after rains, and can only be booked on the morning of the day that you want to drive.

Bush Walks

Recommended guided morning and afternoon **bush walks** (morning/afternoon per person R310/240) are possible at all the larger camps, many smaller ones and some gates. Accompanied by two armed rangers, the excellent walks both get you into the bush and offer the chance of up-close encounters with animals. You have a better chance of seeing wildlife on the move in the morning.

Wilderness Trails

Kruger's seven wilderness walking trails are one of the park's highlights, offering a superb opportunity for an intimate experience of the bush. The three-day walks, done in small groups (maximum eight people) with highly knowledgeable armed guides, are not particularly strenuous, covering about 20km per day at a modest pace.

Trails cost R3120 per person, including accommodation in rustic huts, plus food and equipment, and depart on Wednesday and Sunday afternoon. All are extremely popular, and should be booked well in advance through central reservations (see p515). No children under 12 are allowed.

Wildlife Drives

Dawn (three hours), midmorning (two hours), sunset (three hours) and night (two hours) wildlife drives in 10- or 20-seat vehicles are available at most rest camps, and offer good chances to maximise your safari experience. They cost between R140 and R210 per person, depending on time and vehicle size.

TOURS

At the budget level, the best places to contact are the backpacker lodges in Hazyview (p521), Nelspruit (p519) and Graskop (p524), most of which organise tours into Kruger from about R800 per day, plus entry fees and meals.

At the upper end of the spectrum, or if you're on a tight schedule, **eHolidaysTours** (www.airlinktours.com) runs flight-accommodation packages between Jo'burg and central Kruger. Other operators include **Wildlife Safaris** (☎ 011-791 4238; www.wildlifesaf.co.za), which has four-day panorama tours taking in the Blyde River and Kruger for R6125 per person, including half board.

SLEEPING & EATING

Most visitors stay in one of the park's 12 main rest camps. These offer camping, plus a range of huts, bungalows and cottages (self-catering or sharing cooking facilities), as well as shops, restaurants and other facilities. Several of the rest camps have satellite camps, which are set a few kilometres away, and are much more rustic, with only an ablutions block, kitchen and braai area.

Huts (2 people from R315) are the cheapest non-camping option, with shared ablutions and communal cooking facilities; **bungalows** (2 people from R670) range from simple to luxurious, and generally have bathroom; **cottages** (up to 4 people R1240), the next step up in comfort and price, usually have a living area.

Some camps also offer **safari tents** (R350, with bathroom & kitchen R780), all of which are furnished and have a refrigerator and fan.

For those with tents or caravans, **camping** (campsites from R150) is available at many rest camps. As with other types of accommodation, book in advance during the high season.

There are cash-only petrol stations at the 12 main rest camps, which also have swimming pools apart from Crocodile Bridge, Punda Maria and Orpen; ATMs at Skukuza, Letaba, Satara and Punda Maria (the latter two dispense up to R300 maximum, during shop hours only, and depending on cash availability); and internet access at Berg-en-dal and Skukuza.

There are also five **bushveld camps** (cottages for up to 4 people R1035-1475) – smaller, more remote clusters of self-catering cottages without shops or restaurants – and two **bush lodges** (lodges for up to 4 people R2100-2175), which are set in the middle of the wilderness, and must be booked in their entirety by a single group.

At the opposite end of the spectrum, there's luxurious accommodation in the private reserves bordering Kruger to the west (p518). Another possibility is to stay outside the park. For budget travellers, the best places for this are Hazyview (p521) and Nelspruit (p521).

GETTING THERE & AROUND

Air

SAAirlink (☎ 011-961 1700; www.saairlink.co.za) has daily flights linking both Jo'burg and Cape Town with Mpumalanga Kruger International Airport (MQP) near Nelspruit (for Numbi, Malelane and Crocodile Bridge Gates), and with Kruger Park Gateway Airport in Phalaborwa (2km from Phalaborwa Gate). Sample one-way fares and flight times: Jo'burg to Phalaborwa (R1500, one hour); Jo'burg to MQP (R900 to R1600, one hour); and Cape Town to MQP (R2020, 2¼ hours). Daily SAAirlink flights also connect Cape Town with Hoedspruit (for Orpen Gate) via Jo'burg (R2080, 3¼ hours).

South African Airways (☎ 0861-359 722; www.flysaa.com) flies six times weekly between Durban and MKIA (R1100 to R1800, 1½ hours), while **SA Express** (☎ 011-978 9900; www.flysax.com) flies daily between Jo'burg and Hoedspruit Eastgate Airport (from R1000, 1½ hours), with connections to Cape Town.

Bus & Minibus Taxi

For most visitors, Nelspruit is the most convenient large town near Kruger, and is well served by buses and minibus taxis to and from Jo'burg (see p520). Numbi Gate is about 50km away, and Malelane Gate about 65km away. Phalaborwa (for Phalaborwa Gate) and, to a lesser extent, Hoedspruit (70km from Orpen Gate) are connected to Polokwane, Pretoria and Jo'burg by bus.

Car

Skukuza is 500km from Jo'burg (six hours) and Punda Maria about 620km (eight hours). **Avis** (☎ 013-735 5651; www.avis.co.za) has a branch at Skukuza, and there is car hire from the Nelspruit, Hoedspruit and Phalaborwa airports.

Most visitors drive themselves around the park, and this is the best way to experience Kruger. There are petrol stations at the biggest camps.

Train

An economy-class-only **Shosholoza Meyl** (☎ 0860-008 888; www.shosholozameyl.co.za) service runs from Jo'burg via Nelspruit to Komatipoort, about 12km from Kruger's Crocodile Bridge Gate, but you would need to arrange vehicle hire or a tour to visit the park.

Private Wildlife Reserves

Spreading over a vast lowveld area just west of Kruger is a string of private reserves that offer comparable wildlife watching to what you'll experience in the park. The main reserves – Sabi Sand, Manyeleti and Timbavati – directly border Kruger (with no fences), and the same Big Five populations that roam the park are also at home here.

There are around 200 lodges and camps in the private reserves and most are expensive. However, together with the private concessions within the park, the private reserves offer among Africa's best opportunities for safari connoisseurs, and are the place to go for those who want to experience the bush in the lap of luxury.

Prices tend to be seasonal so it's best to have a look at their websites for the most accurate costs. Note that many of these places like to call themselves 'game reserves'. They're not. They are simply lodges inside a designated wildlife reserve.

Because of the personalised safari attention, rangers can train you in the art of wildlife watching before you head to Kruger for a self-guided trip. Many operators run tours and offer packages with accommodation in this area, so it's worth talking to a travel agent such as Africa Unlimited (p564) to help you find a good deal. Hoedspruit is a convenient gateway to the private lodges.

The best known, most luxurious options are found within the large **Sabi Sand Game Reserve** (www.sabisand.co.za), including **Nkorho Bush Lodge** (☎ 013-735 5367; www.nkorho.com; all-inclusive s/d R2418/3720;), one of the more moderately priced lodges, and top-end favourite **Singita** (☎ 021-683 3424; www.singita.com; per person all-inclusive r R9950;).

Nelspruit

☎ 013 / pop 235,000

Nelspruit, Mpumalanga's largest town and provincial capital, sprawls along the Crocodile River Valley and has plenty of green open spaces. Unless you've come for the four 2010 World Cup matches taking place here, it's more of a place to get things done than a tourist destination. There are, however, some decent shopping malls, good accommodation and excellent restaurants, making it a reasonable stop-over on the way elsewhere.

INFORMATION

Lowveld Tourism (☎ 013-755 1988/9; www.lowveld.info; cnr Madiba & Samora Machel Drs; 🕑 8am-5pm Mon-Fri, to 1pm Sat) This helpful office at Nelspruit Crossing Mall takes bookings for all national parks, and can help arrange accommodation and tours.

Mozambican consulate (☎ 013-752 7396; mozconns@mweb.co.za; 32 Bell St; 🕑 8am-3pm Mon-Fri) Does same-day, single-entry visa processing for R750. At the border you'll pay R180.

SIGHTS

At **Chimpanzee Eden** (☎ 013-745 7406; Rte 40; www.janegoodall.co.za), a sanctuary for rescued chimpanzees, you can see chimps in a semi-wild environment and learn about primate behaviour and their plight. Alternatively, you can meet prehistoric creatures face to face at the **Croc River Reptile Park** (☎ 013-752 5511; Rte 40; adult/child R30/15; 🕑 8am-5pm). Also out of town, the 150-hectare **Lowveld National Botanical Gardens** (☎ 013-752 5531; Rte 40; adult/child R10/5; 🕑 8am-6pm), home to tropical African rainforest, are a nice place for a stroll.

SLEEPING

Funky Monkey Backpackers (☎ 013-744 1310; www.funkymonkeys.co.za; 102 Van Wijk St; campsites per person R40, dm R130, d or tw with shared bathroom R600; 💻 🅿) A little out of town, this is Nelspruit's best backpackers, with clean rooms in a rambling house and a spacious garden. Meals are available and the in-house tour operator can take you to Kruger or the Blyde River Canyon.

Old Vic Travellers Inn (☎ 013-744 0993; www.krugerandmore.co.za; 12 Impala St; dm R100, d with shared bathroom from R260, s/d R240/360, self-catering house per 1-7 people R320-740; 💻 🅿) A friendly, somewhat upscale backpackers hostel, with self-catering facilities or meals on request, tents for rent and a big riverside garden. It's about 3km south of the centre, near an extension of Sonheuwel Nature Reserve, and a Baz Bus stop.

Auberge Guest Lodge (☎ 013-741 2866; www.aubergeguestlodge.com; 3 de Villiers St; s/d incl breakfast from R350/520; 💻 🅿) A quiet, well-maintained sunny-yellow guest house with a plant-filled courtyard and comfortable rooms.

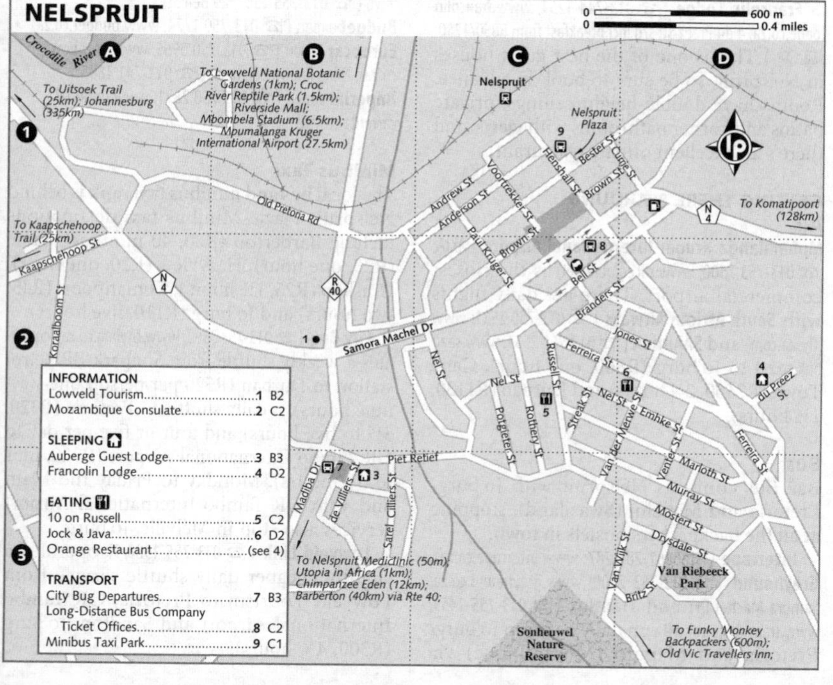

NELSPRUIT'S FAVOURITE EATERIES

Talking to the locals is the best way to get the lowdown on a city's dining scene. We spoke to several Nelspruit residents to help us choose the best restaurants around.

- **10 on Russell** (☎ 013-755 2376; 10 Russell St; mains from R70; 🕑 10am-midnight Mon-Sat) This old award-winner, set in a building dating back to the 1890s, is a real favourite: 'the perfect date-night restaurant' serving 'beautiful handmade pasta' and 'bloody good steaks'.
- **Orange Restaurant** (☎ 013-744 9507; 4 Du Preez St; mains R45-135, 6-course menu R250; 🕑 breakfast, lunch & dinner) At the top of a hill, this place has 'unbelievable views' and 'the most sophisticated food you'll get in Nelspruit'. Think artful plates of guinea fowl, brazed ox cheek and *escargot* (edible snails), and a fine selection of cocktails.
- **Jock & Java** (☎ 013-755 4969; Ferreira St; mains R30-100; 🕑 breakfast, lunch & dinner) The newest hit on the Nelspruit scene at the time of research, this rambling 'outback-style' pub and separate tearoom set in large grassy lawns is a 'great place to bring the kids' with 'a girly dining room' and a revolving cake trolley that's 'bad for the hips'. The whimsical explosion of reds, creams and gingham, and tea served in dainty floral cups, impressed us too.

As told to Nana Luckham.

Utopia in Africa (☎ 013-745 7714; www.theportfoliocollection.com; 6 Daleen St; s/d incl breakfast R550/820; ⊠ ⊡) A beautiful guest house with a grand, double-height, central thatched lodge, thoughtful decor and friendly service. Rooms have balconies overlooking the nearby forest reserve.

Francolin Lodge (☎ 013-744 1251; www.francolinlodge.co.za; 4 du Preez St; s/d incl breakfast from R850/1250; ⊡ ⊡) This is one of the best guest houses in Nelspruit, so be sure to book in advance. Rooms have double-height ceilings, private patios and corner bathrooms with views, and there's an excellent on-site restaurant.

GETTING THERE & AROUND

Air

Mpumalanga Kruger International Airport (MKIA; ☎ 013-753 7500; www.mceglobal.net) is the closest commercial airport. There are daily flights with **South African Airways** (☎ 013-750 2531; www.flysaa.com) and **SAAirlink** (☎ 013-750 2531; www.saairlink.co.za) to Jo'burg (R860, one hour), Cape Town (R2600, 2¾ hours) and Durban (R1130, 1½ hours).

Bus

Baz Bus connects Nelspruit with Jo'burg/Pretoria and Manzini (Swaziland), stopping at all the backpackers hostels in town.

Intercape (☎ 0861-287 287; www.intercape.co.za), **Greyhound** (☎ 013-753 2100; www.greyhound.co.za; Samora Machel Dr) and **Translux** (☎ 013-755 1453; www.translux.co.za) all run daily between Jo'burg/Pretoria and Maputo (Mozambique) via Nelspruit. Greyhound offers the best service, charging about R200 for Jo'burg or Maputo. Its ticket offices are just up from Henshall St, and opposite Promenade Mall.

Car Hire

Avis airport (☎ 013-741 1029; www.avis.co.za); downtown (☎ 013-755 1567; 29 Bell St)
Budget airport (☎ 013-750 1774; www.budget.co.za)
Europcar airport (☎ 013-750 0965; www.europcar.co.za); Orion Promenade Hotel (☎ 013-741 1805)
Imperial airport (☎ 013-750 2871; www.imperialcarrental.co.za)

Minibus Taxi

The local bus and minibus taxi rank is behind Nelspruit Plaza. Minibus taxi destinations include Barberton (R20, 40 minutes), Sabie (R25, one hour), Hazyview (R20, one hour), Graskop (R25, 1½ hours), Komatipoort (R45, two hours) and Jo'burg (R110, five hours).

City Bug (☎ 013-753 3392; www.citybug.co.za) operates a weekly shuttle from Sonpark BP petrol station to Durban (R520 per person one-way, nine hours), a daily shuttle to Pretoria (R320, 3½ to five hours) and four or five per day to OR Tambo International Airport (R320, four to 5½ hours). Monday to Friday the 10am and 4pm OR Tambo International Airport services also stop in Melville, Jo'burg.

Lowveld Link (☎ 013-755 1988/9) operates a slightly cheaper daily shuttle service from Lowveld Tourism to Pretoria, OR Tambo International Airport and Sandton, Jo'burg (R300, 4¾ hours).

Train

Shosholoza Meyl (☎ 0860-008 888; www.shosholozameyl.co.za) runs a seat-only service daily except Saturday between Jo'burg (eight hours) and Komatipoort (2½ hours) via Nelspruit.

Hazyview

☎ 013 / pop 20,000

Strung out along Rte 40, the town of Hazyview acts as a service centre and gateway for nearby Kruger National Park. There are good facilities, but consider it little more than an overnight stop before the early-morning dash to the Phabeni (12km), Numbi (15km) or Paul Kruger (47km) Gates.

For information stop by the **Big 5 Country tourist office** (☎ 013-737 8191; www.big5country.com; 8am-5pm Mon-Sat, 8am-1pm Sun) in the Rendezvous Tourism Centre.

SLEEPING

Kruger Park Backpackers (☎ 013-737 7224; www.krugerparkbackpackers.co.za; campsites per person R40, dm R80, d huts with shared bathroom R170;) A spacious, somewhat rustic place, with trips to Kruger and accommodation in dorms or Zulu huts. It's about 2km south of the four-way stop, and about 500m along the road to Kruger's Numbi Gate.

Chilli Pepper Lodge (☎ 013-737 8373; www.chillipepperlodge.co.za; s/d cottages R400/700) Some 10km out of town on the Sabie Rd is this lovely place on a fruit farm full of sunny-yellow buildings, with great views over the Sabie River Valley and wandering hippos at night. The only let-down is the sad-looking buffet breakfast.

Gecko Lodge (☎ 013-737 8374; www.geckolodge.net; s/d R490/750;) The 27 rooms in this well-equipped lodge have vaulted ceilings, wrought-iron bedsteads and comfy beds, set in sprawling gardens leading through a forest to Sabie River. All manner of adventure activities can be arranged.

Perry's Bridge Hollow Boutique Hotel (☎ 013-737 6784; www.perrysbridgehollow.co.za; s/d incl breakfast from R800/1200;) Worth it for the sheer convenience of being in a retail centre and pretty stylish to boot. All rooms have patio areas overlooking the gardens or the pretty pool area.

GETTING THERE & AWAY

The daily **City to City** (☎ 013-755 1453; www.translux.co.za) Jo'burg–Acornhoek bus stops at the Shell petrol station in Hazyview (R95 from Jo'burg). The backpacker places do pick-ups from Nelspruit from about R15.

Minibus taxis go daily to Nelspruit (R20, one hour) and Sabie (R25, one hour).

Komatipoort

☎ 013 / pop 4700

This border town is at the foot of the Lebombo Mountains, near the confluence of the Komati and Crocodile Rivers and only 10km from Kruger National Park's Crocodile Bridge Gate. It's a convenient stop if you're travelling to/from Mozambique or Swaziland.

Stoep Café (☎ 013-793 7850; 74 Rissik St; s/d incl breakfast R220/400;) is a pretty green and white colonial-style house with a small garden and pool in the heart of things, with three simple rooms and an on-site coffee shop, serving tasty meals, snacks and pancakes.

Minibus taxis leave from just off Rissik St near the Score supermarket, and regularly run between Komatipoort and Maputo (Mozambique; R70, two hours). Exit procedures are fairly swift and on the Mozambique side you can buy a visa for R180.

Shosholoza Meyl (☎ 0860-008 888; www.shosholozameyl.co.za) trains travel daily except Saturday between Jo'burg and Komatipoort (11 hours) via Melelane and Nelspruit.

Barberton

☎ 013 / pop 29,500

The splendid town of Barberton dates to the gold rush days of the late 19th century, when it was a boom town and home to South Africa's first stock exchange. Its prominence later declined, leaving quiet, leafy streets and beautifully preserved old buildings, against a backdrop of green and purple mountains.

The helpful **Tourist Information Centre** (☎ 013-712 2121; www.barberton.co.za; Market Sq, Crown St; 7.30am-4.30pm Mon-Fri, 9am-4pm Sat & Sun) in the town centre can assist with accommodation, tours of historic sites and day hikes in the area.

SLEEPING

Barberton Chalets & Caravan Park (☎ 013-712 3323; www.barbertonchalets.co.za; General St; campsites per person R60, caravan sites R80, s/d/tr cottages R200/280/360;) This caravan park, in large grassy grounds, is conveniently close to the town centre, with camping and self-catering chalets.

Fountain Baths Holiday Guest Cottages (☎ 013-712 2707; www.fountainbaths.co.za; 48 Pilgrim St; cottages per person R200) Centrally located but peaceful, this place has charming, fully equipped self-catering cottages.

Chill Inn (☎ 013-712 3477; cnr De Villiers & Tate Sts; s/d R220/500) A good-value, central lodge, with a communal self-catering kitchen and a braai area.

Kloof House (☎ 013-712 4268; www.kloofhuis.co.za; 1 Kloof St; s/d incl breakfast R300/500; 💻) A lovely old hillside Victorian house with grand views from the wraparound verandah leading to the comfortable rooms.

EATING

Co-co Pan (☎ 013-712 2653; Crown St; mains R25-50; 🕑 9am-5.30pm Mon-Sat) This basic restaurant serves simple burgers, salads and sandwiches at reasonable prices.

Victorian Tea Garden & Restaurant (☎ 013-712 4985; light meals from R40; 🕑 8am-5pm Mon-Fri, to 2pm Sat; 📶) Munch on sandwiches, cakes and more substantial offerings while sitting in a gazebo and watching the world go by. Next to the tourist information office.

Old Rock Café (☎ 013-712 3477; 90 De Villiers St; mains R50-60; 🕑 1pm-late) The large, convivial sports bar has a grill serving meaty specials.

GETTING THERE & AWAY

A few minibus taxis stop in town near Shoprite, but it's better to go to the minibus taxi rank near Emjindini (3km from town on the Nelspruit road). The fare to Nelspruit is R20 (40 minutes). Most departures are in the early morning, by 8am.

DRAKENSBERG ESCARPMENT

The Drakensberg Escarpment marks the point where the highveld plunges down over 1000m, before spilling out onto the eastern lowveld. It's one of South Africa's most scenic areas, with stunning views and an abundance of adventure activities. Elephants, buffaloes and even lions once wandered here in untamed rainforest, but today, it's holidaying South Africans who roam the highlands in their droves. While it's possible to get around via minibus taxi, the going is slow; car hire is the best option.

Blyde River Canyon

The Blyde River's spectacular canyon is nearly 30km long and one of South Africa's most impressive natural features. Much of it is rimmed by the 26,000-hectare **Blyde River Canyon Nature Reserve** (admission per person R20), which snakes north from Graskop, following the escarpment and meeting the Blyde River as it carves its way down to the lowveld. Most visitors drive along the edge of the canyon, with stops at the many wonderful viewpoints, but if you have the time, it's well worth exploring on foot.

Heading north from Graskop, look first for the **Pinnacle**, a striking skyscraperlike rock formation; lock up your vehicle here. Just to the north along Rte 534 (a loop off Rte 532) are **God's Window** and **Wonder View** – two viewpoints with amazing vistas and batteries of craft stalls. At God's Window take the trail up to the rainforest (300 steps).

Back on Rte 532, take a short detour 2km south to the impressive **Lisbon Falls** (or if you are coming back to Graskop, catch it in the afternoon).

The Blyde River canyon starts north of here, near **Bourke's Luck Potholes**. These bizarre cylindrical holes were carved into the rock by whirlpools near the confluence of the Blyde and Treuer Rivers. There's a **visitors centre** (☎ 013-769 6019), where you can pay the reserve entrance fee and find information about the canyon.

Continuing north past Bourke's Luck Potholes and into the heart of the nature reserve, you'll reach a viewpoint overlooking the **Three Rondavels** – huge cylinders of rock with hutlike pointed 'roofs' rising out of the canyon. There are a number of short walks in the surrounding area.

West of here, outside the reserve and off Rte 36, are **Echo Caves** (admission & guided tour adult/child R40/15), where Stone Age relics have been found. The caves get their name from dripstone formations that echo when tapped.

HIKING

The main route is the popular and scenic 2½-day **Blyde River Canyon Hiking Trail** (☎ 013-759 5432; mpbinfo@cis.co.za; R60), which begins at Paradise Camp and finishes at Bourke's Luck Potholes. Bookings can be made at the Bourke's Luck Potholes visitors centre. You'll need to sort out onward transport from the end of the trail.

The short but reasonably strenuous **Belvedere Day Walk** (R5, five hours) takes you in a circular route to the Belvedere hydroelectric

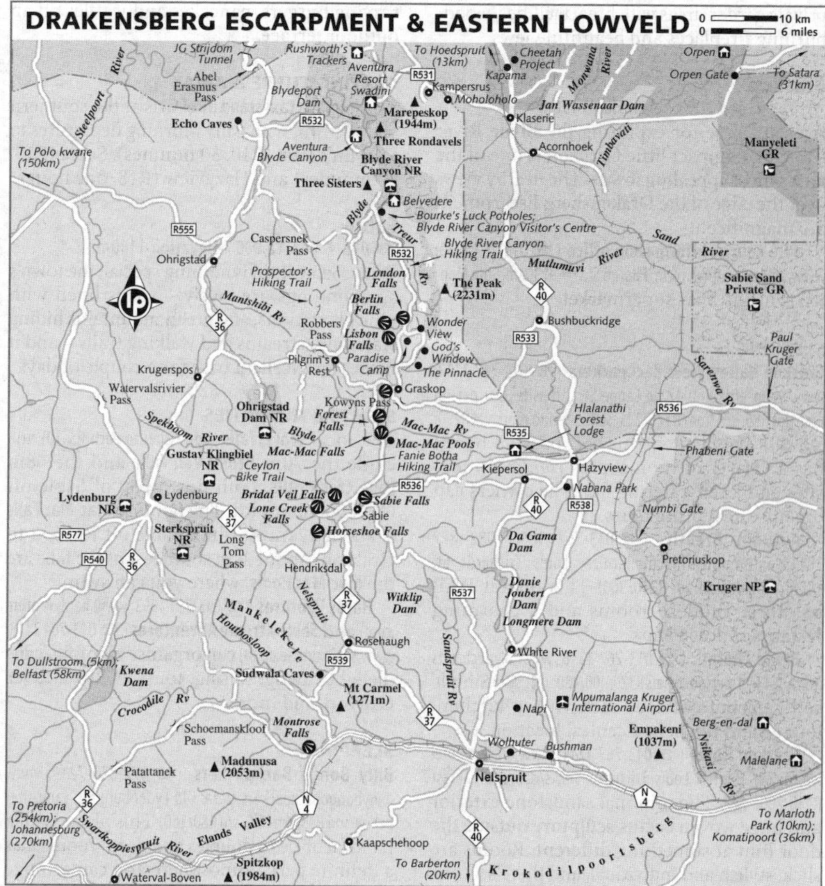

power station at Bourke's Luck Potholes; turn left at the guest house down a path to some beautiful waterfalls and rock pools. Bookings should be made at Potholes.

SLEEPING

It's easy to explore the canyon by car as a day jaunt from Graskop, Sabie or Pilgrim's Rest. If you're continuing further north, a good alternative is to stay in or around the nature reserve.

Forever Blyde Canyon (☎ 0861 226 966; www.foreverblydecanyon.co.za; campsites R55, plus per person R60, 2-/4-person self-catering chalets R405/585, 2-/4-person deluxe chalets from R720/900;) This rambling resort has a wide choice of accommodation, from tent sites to luxury stone chalets (one wheelchair-friendly), a restaurant, bar and supermarket. Hikers can mix and match a series of six routes.

Forever Resort Swadini (☎ 015-795 5141; www.foreverswadini.co.za; campsites R80, plus per person R35, 6-person self-catering chalet from R650;) Uninspiring chalets are improved greatly by the good location and impressive views. It's at the northern end of the reserve along the Blyde River, with a supermarket, liquor store, laundry facilities and activities including abseiling and white-water rafting.

Thaba Tsweni Lodge (☎ 013-767 1380; www.blyderivercanyonaccommodation.com; off Rte 352; double occupancy from R480) Just a short walk from Berlin Falls are several self-catering chalets, with stone walls, African-print bedspreads, kitchens, private garden areas with braai facilities, wood-burning fireplaces and beautiful views.

Graskop

☎ 013 / pop 2000 / elevation 1450m

A useful base for exploring the Blyde River Canyon, compact little Graskop is one of the area's most appealing towns. The nearby views over the edge of the Drakensberg Escarpment are magnificent.

The **tourist information office** (☎ 013-767 1833; www.wildadventures.co.za; Pilgrim St; 8.30am-5pm Mon-Sat) is inside Spar supermarket.

SLEEPING

Graskop Valley View Backpackers (☎ 013-767 1112; www.yebo-afrika.nl; 47 de Lange St; campsites per person R60, dm R85, s/d from R175/225, self-catering rondavel R290;) This Dutch-run backpackers hostel has a variety of rooms, plus *rondavels*, tent sites and a self-catering flat. The owners can organise adventure tours.

Autumn Breath (☎ 013-767 1866, 082 877 2811; autumnbreath@cfmail.co.za; Louis Trichardt St; s/d incl breakfast from R210/360) This quaint B&B has three modern rooms and a charming restaurant downstairs.

Blyde Chalets (☎ 013-767 1316; www.blydechalets.co.za; 2-/3-/4-person chalets R320/400/480;) Simple self-catering cottages each with a kitchen, lounge and braai, in a central location.

Graskop Hotel (☎ 013-767 1244; www.graskophotel.co.za; cnr Hoof & Louis Trichardt Sts; s/d incl breakfast R410/700;) The minimal sandstone exterior and huge woven cactus sculpture outside the door hint at something different. Rooms are slick, stylish and individual, and there's a contemporary art gallery and a haven of a garden and swimming pool.

EATING

Harrie's Pancakes (☎ 013-767 1273; Louis Trichardt St; pancakes R40-60; 8am-7pm) Don't expect breakfast-style pancakes – most have savoury and exotic fillings as well as some sweet offerings.

Wine & Dine Restaurant (☎ 013-767 1030; 3 Pilgrim St; meals R40-80; lunch & dinner Sat-Thu, dinner Fri) Meat is king here; the menu is laden with all manner of tempting flesh for the hungry carnivore. There's a wooden terrace for the summer and a cosy fire indoors in the winter.

Silver Spoon (☎ 013-767 1039; Louis Trichardt St; meals R40-90; 7am-7pm) This log-cabin-style place is popular with locals and tourists alike, serving burgers, pancakes and waffles on an outdoor terrace.

GETTING THERE & AWAY

The **minibus taxi stand** (Hoof St) is at the southern end of town, with daily morning departures to Pilgrim's Rest (R10, 30 minutes), Sabie (R15, 40 minutes) and Hazyview (R18, one hour).

Sabie

☎ 013 / pop 12,000 / elevation 1100m

While Sabie itself is nothing special, the town's surroundings are lovely – roads lined with pine plantations, and green mountains hiding waterfalls, streams and walking trails – and it makes an excellent base for a couple of days.

SIGHTS & ACTIVITIES

The local **waterfalls** (admission to each R5-10) include the 70m **Bridal Veil Falls** and the 68m **Lone Creek Falls**, both northwest of Sabie off Old Lydenburg Rd. The popular **Mac-Mac Falls** is about 12km north of Sabie off Rte 532 to Graskop. About 3km southeast of the falls are the **Mac-Mac Pools**, where you can swim.

Hardy Ventures (☎ 013-751 1693; www.hardyventure.com) and **Sabie Xtreme Adventures** (☎ 013-764 2118; www.sabiextreme.co.za) can organise kloofing, candlelight caving, rafting, tours of Blyde River Canyon, and more.

SLEEPING

Billy Bongo Backpackers (☎ 072-370 7219; www.billybongobackpackers.co.za; Old Lydenburg Rd; campsites per person R45, dm R70, s/d R80/160) This place, with a handful of clean doubles and dorm rooms, has a definite party atmosphere and can arrange adventure tours by day.

Sabie Backpackers Lodge (☎ 013-764 2118; www.sabiextreme.co.za; Main St; campsites per person R60, dm R90, d with/without bathroom R240/210;) The owners work hard to create a convivial atmosphere and it's a good place to meet other travellers, perfect for unwinding after a frenetic day of activities (Sabie Xtreme Adventures is based here). Pick-ups from Nelspruit are available.

Sabie Townhouse (☎ 013-764 2292; www.sabietownhouse.co.za; Power St; s/d R350/700;) This pretty stone house has a terrace with fabulous views over the hills, huge home-cooked breakfasts and lovely hosts. On the downside, the rooms are rather '80s.

Artists' Café & Guest House (☎ 013-764 2309; www.wheretostay.co.za/artistscafe; Hendriksdal; s/d incl breakfast

R380/680) At this wonderfully quirky place, about 15km south of Sabie along Rte 37, old train-station buildings have been converted into rooms, retaining lots of the old signs. The restaurant serves tasty Tuscan-style trattoria food (meals from R50).

EATING

Petena's Pancakes (☎ 013-764 1541; Main St; pancakes from R30; ⏰ 9am-5.30pm) Chow down on your choice of sweet or savoury fillings.

Woodsman (☎ 013-764 2204; Main St; mains R60-100) A lively pub with a big terrace and views over the hills. Greek food is a speciality.

Wild Fig Tree (☎ 013-764 2239; cnr Main & Louis Trichardt Sts; meals R70-110; ⏰ 8am-9pm) The low lighting, candles and African-print wall hangings and tablecloths create a warm atmosphere, and the food is rich, hearty and lacking refinement – for example, a gargantuan slab of ostrich or warthog accompanied by a shovelful of potatoes. There's also a guest house (singles/doubles R350/450).

GETTING THERE & AWAY

There are daily buses from Jo'burg to Nelspruit, from where you can get minibus taxis to Sabie (R25, one hour). Minibus taxis also run frequently to/from Hazyview (R25, one hour). Timetable information is available at the **transport stand** (Main St), behind Spar supermarket.

Pilgrim's Rest

☎ 013 / pop 600

Tiny Pilgrim's Rest appears frozen in time – a perfectly preserved gold-rush town with wood and corrugated-iron houses lining a pretty, manicured main street. Tourists come here by the coachload and the town can feel a little Disney-fied during the height of the day. Come early in the morning, or even stay the night – when you'll be able to soak up the ghosts of the past.

There's an **information centre** (☎ 013-768 1060; Main St, Uptown; ⏰ 9am-12.45pm & 1.15-4.30pm) at the museums building, and an ATM just down the road.

SIGHTS & ACTIVITIES

The information centre sells tickets for the town's four main **museums** (☎ 013-768 1060; total admission R10; ⏰ 9am-12.45pm & 1.45-4pm Mon-Sat), which include a printing shop, a restored Victorian home and a general store. More interesting is historic **Alanglade** (☎ 013-768 1060; admission R20; ⏰ tours 11am & 2pm Mon-Sat), a former mine-manager's residence at the northern edge of town furnished with period objects from the 1920s. Just east of town along the Graskop road is the open-air **Diggings Museum** (guided tours adult/child R10/5) where you can see how gold was panned. Tours are arranged through the information centre.

SLEEPING

Pilgrim's Rest Caravan Park (☎ 013-768 1427; pilgrimscamp@mweb.co.za; campsites per person R65; 🏊) This beautiful spot alongside the Blyde River has large grounds and braai facilities, although the ablutions blocks have seen better days.

Royal Hotel (☎ 013-768 1100; www.royal-hotel.co.za; s/d incl breakfast from R480/700; ✖) It's definitely worth spending the night at this elegant, historical option. Mostly in houses on the main street, rooms have Victorian baths, brass beds and other period features.

GETTING THERE & AWAY

Sporadic minibus taxis run between Pilgrim's Rest and Graskop (R10, 30 minutes).

GAUTENG

Gauteng is the country's commercial and industrial hub, and the quest for profit has been the driving force behind its recent history. Within a decade of the discovery of gold here in the late 1800s, Johannesburg had sprung up from the highveld.

Today Gauteng's provincial capital is an enormous bundle of energy, where New York–style skyscrapers, busy freeways, shiny shopping malls and wealthy, high-security suburbs exist alongside pockets of deprivation. Pretoria, South Africa's political capital, feels like a different world; it's a laid-back city of historic buildings and jacaranda-lined streets.

Gauteng is a region of frenetic activity, and it's predicted that Pretoria and Jo'burg will eventually become one giant urban conglomeration. It's not just a concrete jungle though. Within an hour's drive of both cities you'll find beautiful countryside, cultural villages, wildlife-spotting opportunities and the Cradle of Humankind.

History

The Cradle of Humankind in northwestern Gauteng is thought to have played a key role in human evolution, with sites across the region yielding as many as 850 sets of hominid remains. However, the area now called Gauteng remained a quiet and rural place right through until 1886, when gold was discovered, and it was catapulted into the modern age.

Boers, escaping British rule in the Cape Colony, had been here since the mid-19th century, founding the independent Zuid-Afrikaansche Republiek (ZAR; South African Republic) and establishing its capital in the then frontier village of Pretoria. But as the British turned their attentions to the colossal profits being made in the gold mines, it was only a matter of time before the events that led to the Anglo-Boer War (1899–1902) were set in motion.

After suffering severe losses, particularly in British concentration camps, the Boers conceded defeat, leading to the Treaty of Vereeniging and ultimately the Union of South Africa in 1910. The fledgling city of Jo'burg exploded into life, but little changed for the thousands of black miners. Apartheid would be managed from Pretoria, and the townships surrounding Jo'burg – not least of them Soweto – would become the hub of both the system's worst abuses and its most energetic opponents. Consequently Gauteng, then known as Transvaal, was at centre stage in South Africa's all-too-familiar 20th-century drama.

JOHANNESBURG

☎ 011 / pop 5.7 million

Johannesburg, more commonly known as Jo'burg or Jozi, is a rapidly changing city at the cutting edge of South Africa's development. The city centre is smartening up and Newtown, with its theatres, restaurants, museums and jazz clubs, is already a lively cultural hub.

Jo'burg is the country's corporate capital and a thriving black middle class has risen up here – in both the suburbs and the famous township of Soweto, which is increasingly attracting tourist dollars and investment. However, the city still bears the scars of past oppression and segregation. The glitzy shopping malls and exclusive restaurants of affluent suburbs such as Rosebank and Sandton are just down the road from desperately poor townships such as Alexandra.

Jo'burg's notorious crime rate is another symptom of persisting inequalities, and it can make the city seem like an intimidating sprawl to first-time visitors. Although most serious crime occurs far from the tourist haunts of the northern suburbs, this is certainly a town where you should be on your guard.

That said, Jo'burg is a friendly, unstuffy city, worth tackling if only to see the sobering reminders of the country's recent past in the excellent Apartheid Museum. From Melville's bohemian streets to the buzz of Newtown and the country's biggest township, Soweto, the City of Gold is increasingly cosmopolitan and confident about its future.

Orientation

Jo'burg is big, but not too difficult to negotiate if you have a car. OR Tambo International Airport is 25km northeast of the city and easily accessible (Rte 24 runs out of the CBD past Ellis Park Stadium and becomes the N12 freeway). The main train station, Park Station, is on the northern edge of the city centre. At the time of writing, many of Jo'burg's major roads were being widened and road surfaces improved, causing extra traffic jams and diversions. The worst of these happen, predictably, during the commuter rush hours.

The city centre, laid out on a straightforward grid, is dominated by office blocks. North of the centre, a steep ridge runs west–east from Braamfontein across to the dangerous suburb of Hillbrow. Northeast of the centre is the equally dangerous Yeoville.

To the north are the wealthy and predominantly white suburbs, bordered by the N1 and N3 freeways, and home to tourist accommodation, large shopping malls and fenced-off houses. In the inner-suburban enclaves of Melville, Greenside, Parkhurst and Norwood, restaurants and bars are at street level rather than enclosed in malls.

The black townships ringing the city present a contrast to the northern suburbs, though you'll find all kinds of conditions here, from suburban streets to shanty towns. The main township, Soweto, is west of Soccer City Stadium (formerly known as the FNB Stadium); other big townships include Alexandra (inside the N3 freeway to the northeast of the city centre) and, further out of the city, Thokoza, Kwa-Thema, Tsakane, Daveyton and Tembisa.

Information

EMERGENCY

AIDS line (☎ 0800-012 322)
Fire (☎ 10111)
Police (Map p531; ☎ 10111; Headquarters, Main Rd)
Rape Crisis Line (☎ 011-806 1888)

INTERNET ACCESS

Most accommodation options have internet facilities, charging anything from R20 to R60 per hour, and many offer free wi-fi. Most malls have an internet cafe and wi-fi hot spots are increasingly prevalent, particularly in cafes and eateries in areas such as Melville.

Chroma Copy (Map pp528-9; ☎ 011-483 2320; Norwood; per hr R30; 🕑 8.30am-6pm Mon-Thu, to 5pm Fri, to 1pm Sat) One of a few on Grant Ave.
Jetline.com (Map pp528-9; ☎ 011-726 1520; Shop 63, Campus Square Centre, Melville; per hr R40; 🕑 8.30am-5pm Mon-Fri, 9am-noon Sat) Also has a branch at Rosebank Mall.

MEDICAL SERVICES

Charlotte Maxeke Johannesburg Hospital (Map pp528-9; ☎ 011-488 4911; M1/Jubilee Rd, Parktown) Jo'burg's main public hospital.
Rosebank Clinic (Map pp528-9; ☎ 011-328 0500; 14 Sturdee Ave, Rosebank; 🕑 7am-10pm) A private hospital in the northern suburbs, with casualty, GP and specialist services.

MONEY

There are banks with ATMs and exchange facilities at every commercial centre.

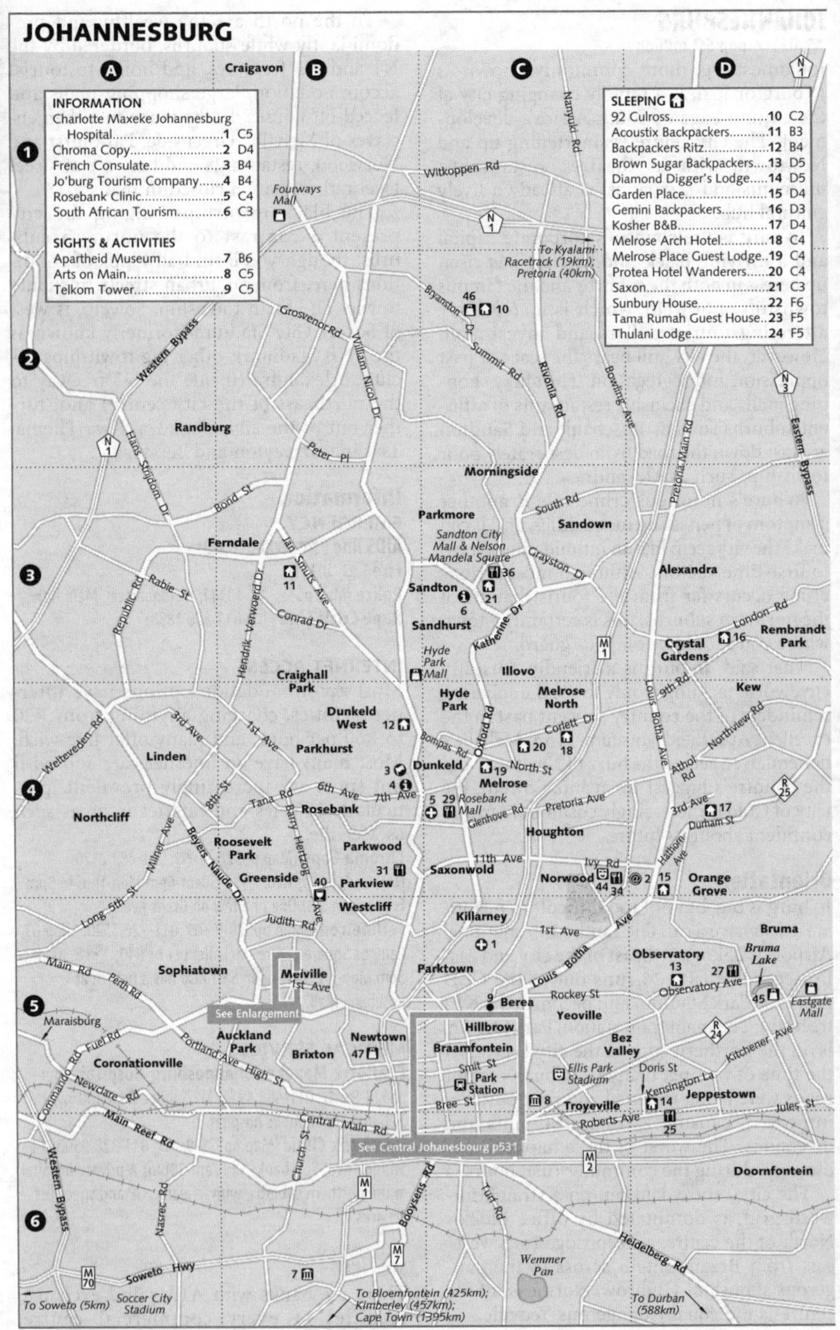
JOHANNESBURG
INFORMATION
Charlotte Maxeke Johannesburg Hospital....1 C5
Chroma Copy....2 D4
French Consulate....3 B4
Jo'burg Tourism Company....4 B4
Rosebank Clinic....5 C4
South African Tourism....6 C3
SIGHTS & ACTIVITIES
Apartheid Museum....7 B6
Arts on Main....8 C5
Telkom Tower....9 C5
SLEEPING
92 Culross....10 C2
Acoustix Backpackers....11 B3
Backpackers Ritz....12 B4
Brown Sugar Backpackers....13 D5
Diamond Digger's Lodge....14 D5
Garden Place....15 D4
Gemini Backpackers....16 D3
Kosher B&B....17 D4
Melrose Arch Hotel....18 C4
Melrose Place Guest Lodge....19 C4
Protea Hotel Wanderers....20 C4
Saxon....21 C3
Sunbury House....22 F6
Tama Rumah Guest House....23 F5
Thulani Lodge....24 F5
Craigavon
Fourways Mall
Witkoppen Rd
Nanyuki Rd
To Kyalami Racetrack (19km); Pretoria (40km)
Bryanston Dr
Summit Rd
Grosvenor Rd
William Nicol Dr
Western Bypass
Rivonia Rd
Bowling Ave
Randburg
Hans Strijdom Dr
Peter Pl
Morningside
Pretoria Main Rd
Eastern Bypass
Bond St
South Rd
Parkmore
Sandown
Ferndale
Sandton City Mall & Nelson Mandela Square
Grayston Dr
Rabie St
Republic Rd
Jan Smuts Ave
Sandton
Alexandra
Conrad Dr
Sandhurst
Katherine Dr
London Rd
Rembrandt Park
Crystal Gardens
Hendrik Verwoerd Dr
Hyde Park Mall
Illovo
Craighall Park
Hyde Park
Melrose North
Kew
9th Rd
Dunkeld West
Louis Botha Ave
Corlett Dr
Northview Rd
3rd Ave
1st Ave
Welteveden Rd
Linden
Parkhurst
Bompas Rd
Oxford Rd
Dunkeld
North St
Melrose
Athol Rd
8th St
Tana Rd
6th Ave
7th Ave
Rosebank Mall
Pretoria Ave
3rd Ave
Northcliff
Rosebank
Glenhove Rd
Houghton
Durham St
Barry Hertzog Ave
Milner Ave
Roosevelt Park
Parkwood
Beyers Naude Dr
11th Ave
Hathorn Ave
Greenside
Parkview
Saxonwold
Ivy Rd
Norwood
Orange Grove
Long 5th St
Westcliff
Judith Rd
Killarney
1st Ave
Bruma
Bruma Lake
Observatory
Main Rd
Sophiatown
Melville
1st Ave
Parktown
Observatory Ave
Eastgate Mall
Perth Rd
Louis Botha Ave
Berea
Rockey St
See Enlargement
Maraisburg
Yeoville
Hillbrow
Fuel Rd
Auckland Park
Newtown
Braamfontein
Bez Valley
Kitchener Ave
Portland Ave
Coronationville
Brixton
High St
Smit St
Park Station
Ellis Park Stadium
Doris St
Kensington La
Commando Rd
Newclare Rd
Jeppestown
Bree St
Troyeville
Jules St
Roberts Ave
Main Reef Rd
Central Main Rd
See Central Johannesburg p531
Church St
Doornfontein
Western Bypass
Booysens Rd
Nasrec Rd
Turf Rd
Heidelberg Rd
Wemmer Pan
Soweto Hwy
To Soweto (5km)
Soccer City Stadium
To Bloemfontein (425km); Kimberley (457km); Cape Town (1395km)
To Durban (588km)

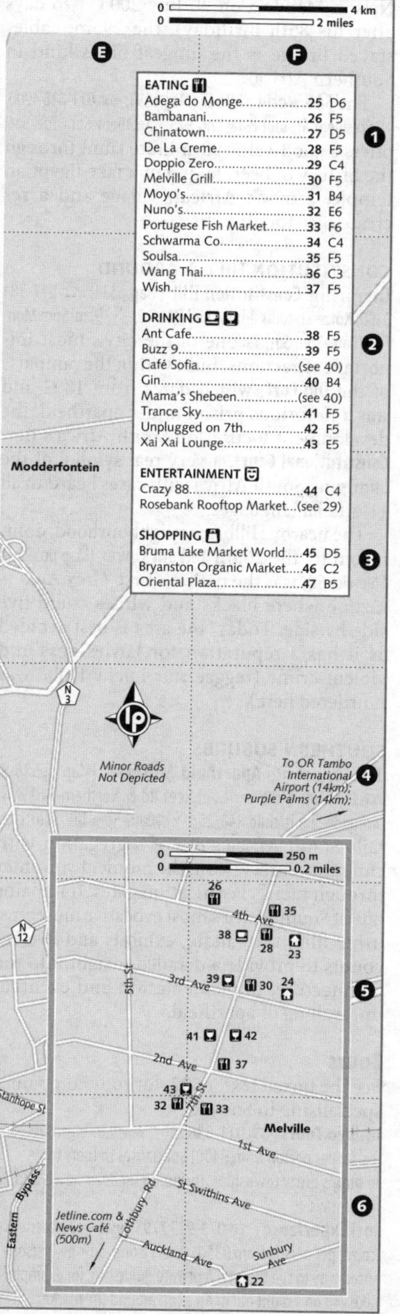

American Express and Rennies Travel (an agent for Thomas Cook) have branches at the airport and in major malls.

POST

Post office (Map pp528-9; ☎ 011-726 8505; Campus Square Centre, Melville; 🕑 8am-5pm Mon, Tue, Thu & Fri, 9am-5pm Wed, 8am-1pm Sat)

TOURIST INFORMATION

Gauteng Tourism Authority (Map p531; ☎ 011-639 1600; www.gauteng.net; 1 Central Pl, cnr Jeppe & Henry Nxumalo Sts, Newtown; 🕑 8am-5pm Mon-Fri) The staff at the tourist body's headquarters in the Newtown Cultural Precinct provides basic information and brochures. You can pick up the monthly *Go Gauteng* magazine here.

Johannesburg Tourism Company (Map pp528-9; ☎ 011-214 0700; www.joburgtourism.com; ground fl, Grosvenor Cnr, 195 Jan Smuts Ave, Parktown North; 🕑 8am-5pm Mon-Fri) A private endeavour; covers the city of Jo'burg.

South African Tourism (Map pp528-9; ☎ 011-895 3000; www.southafrica.net; Bojanala House, 90 Protea Rd, Sandton; 🕑 8am-5pm Mon-Fri) Can be contacted for general South Africa information.

Dangers & Annoyances

Pay careful attention to your personal security in Jo'burg. Daylight muggings in the city centre and other inner suburbs, notably Hillbrow, do happen and you must be constantly on your guard. We've also heard of incidents in the suburban underpasses leading out of Park Station. You'd be crazy to walk around central Jo'burg at night – if you arrive after dark and don't have a car, catch a taxi to your final destination.

Crime is a big problem, but it is important to put things in perspective: remember that most travellers come and go without incident and that much of the crime afflicts parts of the city you would have little reason to stray into. It's when using ATMs that you're most vulnerable.

The secret to success is simple: seek local advice, listen to it and remain aware of what's going on around you.

Illegal immigration from other Southern African countries is a problem here and black travellers might find themselves stopped by police and asked to show identity documents or visas. They will usually let you go once they're convinced you're a tourist.

See p569 for more advice.

Sights & Activities

CITY CENTRE

The city centre choked and largely died in the early 1990s, with many white businesses fleeing to the northern suburbs, leaving the district to vanish under a mountain of squatted buildings and crime statistics. The area retains its edgy atmosphere, but regeneration projects in Newtown to the west and university-oriented Braamfontein to the northwest are helping to boost confidence in the heart of the city.

In Joubert Park (itself a no-go area), entered from King George St near the corner with Noord St, is the **Johannesburg Art Gallery** (Map p531; ☎ 011-725 3130; Joubert Park; admission free; 10am-5pm Tue-Sun). This gallery has a reputable collection of European and South African landscape and figurative paintings, more adventurous contemporary work such as multimedia installations, and retrospectives of black artists.

To view Jo'burg from on high, take the lift to the **Top of Africa** (Map p531; ☎ 011-308 1331; 50th fl, Carlton Centre, 152 Commissioner St; adult/child R10/8; 9am-7pm). The entrance is via a special lift one floor below street level.

Arts on Main (Map p531; ☎ 083 399 9740; 245 Main St; admission free; 11am-4pm Mon-Fri) is a new arts centre occupying a former warehouse, with a mission to generate some cultural vibrancy in the city centre. The Goethe-Institut has opened a gallery and other planned attractions include a rooftop bar, outdoor cinema, restaurant, internet cafe and regular performances.

NEWTOWN

Rejuvenation has made Newtown the most appealing section of the downtown area. Surrounded by museums and cafes, Newtown's cultural precinct, which occupies **Mary Fitzgerald Square** (Map p531; named after South Africa's first female trade unionist), is the best place to focus on.

At the heart of the cultural precinct, **Museum Africa** (Map p531; ☎ 011-833 5624; 121 Bree St; admission free; 9am-5pm Tue-Sun) has several excellent exhibitions, covering diverse subjects including South African photography, geology and Sophiatown.

The lively **Market Theatre** complex (p536), next door, puts on regular shows and has a couple of restaurants and some craft stalls.

Looming over Newtown is the **Nelson Mandela Bridge** (Map p531). Officially opened by Nelson Mandela on 20 July 2003 (two days after his 85th birthday), the 295m, cable-stayed bridge is the longest of its kind in Southern Africa.

The **SAB World of Beer** (Map p531; ☎ 011-836 4900; 15 President St; tour & tasting R25; 10am-6pm Tue-Sat) offers a good-value 90-minute jaunt through the history of beer, taking in a fake Egyptian temple, a mock African village and a re-created Victorian pub.

CONSTITUTION HILL & AROUND

Inspiring **Constitution Hill** (Map p531; ☎ 011-381 3100; Kotze St; tours adult/child R22/10; 9am-5pm Mon-Fri, 10am-3pm Sat) is one of the city's most important attractions. Built within the ramparts of the **Old Fort**, which dates from 1892 and was a notorious prison under apartheid, the development focuses on South Africa's new **Constitutional Court**, a very real symbol of the changing South Africa with cases heard in all 11 official languages.

The nearby Hillbrow neighbourhood, dominated by the 269m **Telkom Tower** (Map pp528-9; Goldreich St), was the nation's first 'Grey Area' – a zone where blacks and whites could live side by side. Today, the area is best avoided as it has a reputation for lawlessness and violent crime (reggae star Lucky Dube was murdered here).

SOUTHERN SUBURBS

The moving **Apartheid Museum** (Map pp528-9; ☎ 011-309 4700; cnr Gold Reef Rd & Northern Parkway, Ormonde; adult/child R40/25; 10am-5pm Tue-Sun) details South Africa's era of segregation with chilling accuracy, from the moment you enter through racial classification gates. It remains one of South Africa's most evocative museums, using film, text, audio, exhibits and live accounts to provide a detailed insight into the architecture, implementation and eventual unravelling of apartheid.

Tours

See the boxed text, p532, for tour companies specialising in Soweto.

Imbizo Tours (☎ 011-838 2667; www.imbizotours.co.za; per person from R400) Specialises in tours to Jo'burg's gritty townships, including *shebeen* crawls and homestays.

Jozi Experience (☎ 073-917 7791; www.joziexperience.co.za; per person from R350) Offers a one-on-one, personalised way to see the city. A private guide can, for example, take you on a night out or on a trip around the markets.

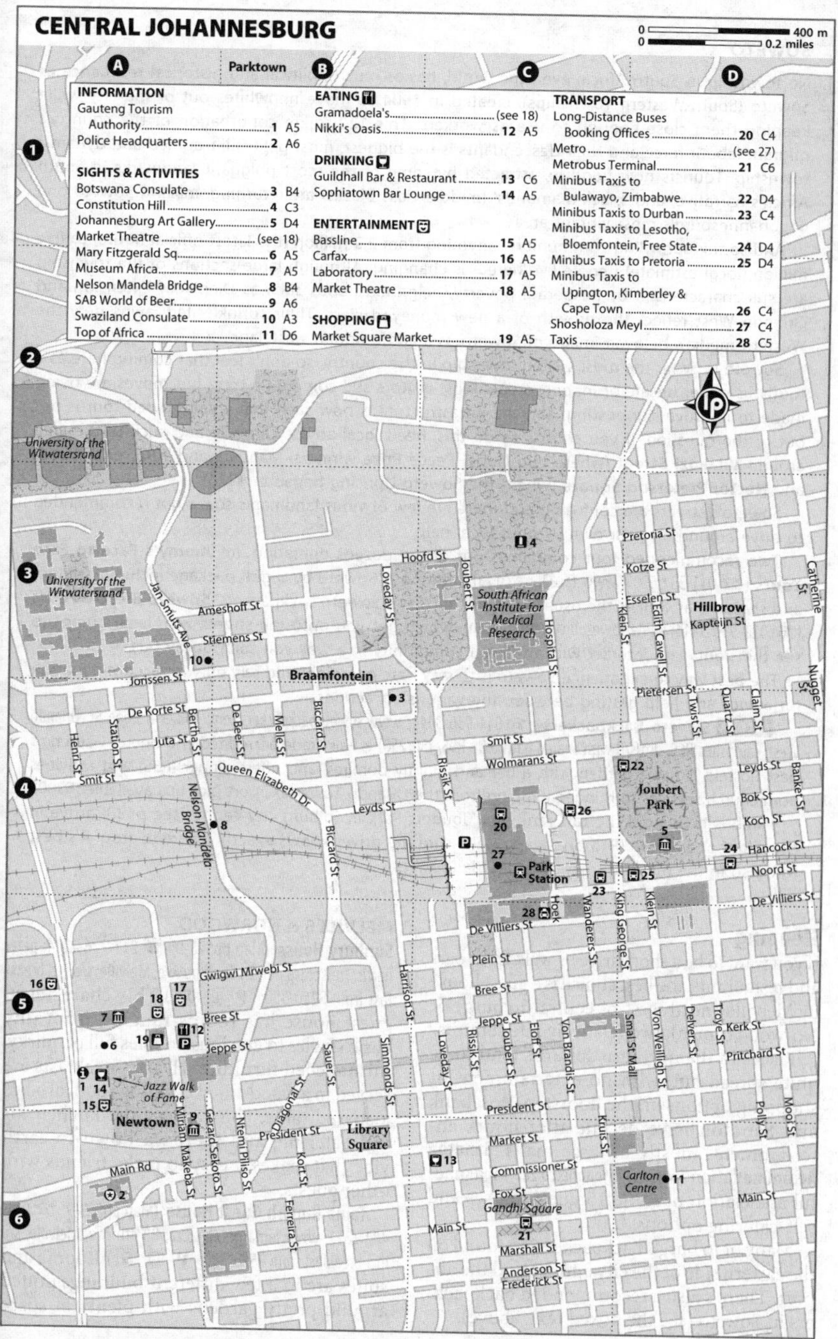
CENTRAL JOHANNESBURG
0 400 m
0 0.2 miles
A
B
C
D
1
2
3
4
5
6
Parktown
INFORMATION
Gauteng Tourism Authority 1 A5
Police Headquarters 2 A6
SIGHTS & ACTIVITIES
Botswana Consulate 3 B4
Constitution Hill 4 C3
Johannesburg Art Gallery 5 D4
Market Theatre (see 18)
Mary Fitzgerald Sq 6 A5
Museum Africa 7 A5
Nelson Mandela Bridge 8 B4
SAB World of Beer 9 A6
Swaziland Consulate 10 A3
Top of Africa 11 D6
EATING
Gramadoela's (see 18)
Nikki's Oasis 12 A5
DRINKING
Guildhall Bar & Restaurant 13 C6
Sophiatown Bar Lounge 14 A5
ENTERTAINMENT
Bassline 15 A5
Carfax 16 A5
Laboratory 17 A5
Market Theatre 18 A5
SHOPPING
Market Square Market 19 A5
TRANSPORT
Long-Distance Buses Booking Offices 20 C4
Metro (see 27)
Metrobus Terminal 21 C6
Minibus Taxis to Bulawayo, Zimbabwe 22 D4
Minibus Taxis to Durban 23 C4
Minibus Taxis to Lesotho, Bloemfontein, Free State 24 D4
Minibus Taxis to Pretoria 25 D4
Minibus Taxis to Upington, Kimberley & Cape Town 26 C4
Shosholoza Meyl 27 C4
Taxis 28 C5
University of the Witwatersrand
University of the Witwatersrand
Jan Smuts Ave
Ameshoff St
Stiemens St
Jorissen St
Braamfontein
De Korte St
Juta St
Smit St
Henri St
Station St
Bertha St
De Beer St
Melle St
Biccard St
Loveday St
Hoofd St
Joubert St
South African Institute for Medical Research
Hospital St
Pretoria St
Kotze St
Esselen St
Klein St
Edith Cavell St
Hillbrow
Kapteijn St
Catherine St
Pietersen St
Twist St
Quartz St
Claim St
Nugget St
Wolmarans St
Rissik St
Leyds St
Banket St
Bok St
Koch St
Hancock St
Noord St
De Villiers St
Joubert Park
Queen Elizabeth Dr
Nelson Mandela Bridge
Park Station
Hoek
Wanderers St
King George St
Plein St
Bree St
Jeppe St
Harrison St
Eloff St
Von Brandis St
Smal St Mall
Von Wielligh St
Delvers St
Troye St
Kerk St
Pritchard St
Gwigwi Mrwebi St
Jazz Walk of Fame
Newtown
Miriam Makeba St
Gerard Sekoto St
Ntemi Piliso St
Diagonal St
Sauer St
Simmonds St
President St
Library Square
Kort St
Ferreira St
Main Rd
Market St
Commissioner St
Fox St
Gandhi Square
Main St
Marshall St
Anderson St
Frederick St
Kruis St
Carlton Centre
Polly St
Mooi St

SOWETO

No township in South Africa, even the world, has as much political and historical resonance as Soweto (South-Western Townships), created in 1904 to move nonwhites out of the city while keeping them close enough to use as workers. This 120-sq-km conurbation of the country's migrant labour force and their descendants is the biggest, most political, troubled and dynamic township. Tourists now flood in, attracted by some of the most poignant landmarks in South Africa's narrative, and 'black diamonds' (middle-class blacks) are returning, making Soweto one of Johannesburg's most vibrant areas.

And so this sprawling community – anything from 2.3 million (the latest official figure) to five million (local estimate) people live here – is changing. Although large sections of the township are still characterised by desperate poverty, neighbourhoods such as Diepkloof Extension and Orlando West reflect the growth of a new moneyed class. Their sprinkler-fed lawns defy the Western media's beloved image of Soweto as a crime-ridden wasteland.

Soweto is by far the most visited township in the country, so don't feel that coming here as a tourist is either unsafe or inappropriate. Most visitors still come on a tour, but moves are being made to improve signposting, and the infrastructure is now such that a self-guided tour is not out of the question. If you choose to do this, heed local advice carefully and stick to the area around **Vilakazi Street** (where two Nobel Peace Prize winners, Mandela and Tutu, once lived) and **Hector Pieterson Square** (where the Soweto Uprising began in 1976).

Soweto's streets are confusing and there are few obvious landmarks so it's not recommended to drive around on your own without local help.

Two recommended tour companies out of the dozens operating are **Jimmy's Face to Face Tours** (☎ 011-331 6109; www.face2face.co.za), offering a 'Soweto by Night' package including dinner and *shebeens* as well as the usual minibus tours; and Soweto Backpackers' **Soweto Bicycle Tours** (☎ 011-936 3444; www.sowetobicycletours.com), which get you onto the streets with local guides to see the sights and interact with the local community in a way you can't do by bus.

The best way to experience Soweto is to stay here overnight and rely on your accommodation for advice and help getting between the various attractions.

our pick **Soweto Backpackers** (☎ 011-936 3444; www.sowetobackpackers.com; 10823 A Pooe St, Orlando West; campsites R65, dm/s/d with shared bathroom R95/150/250) is Fair Trade accredited and one of Gauteng's best hostels. It has a garden with a bar and nightly bonfires, and offers dinner (R55) and activities from church services to bungee jumping from the Orlando Towers. Airport pick-ups available (R300).

Minibus taxis from the taxi rank near Joubert Park in Jo'burg city centre (see p538) arrive in Diepkloof or Orlando (R15 one-way). Make sure the driver knows exactly where to stop; it's best to do so in the more touristy area of Orlando West.

Sleeping

If you want to be a short drive or walk from bars and restaurants, the best choice is a guest house in Melville (northwest of central Jo'burg) or Norwood (north), two relatively safe suburbs.

Places in the northern suburbs tend to be quite spread out, with no entertainment or shopping options on the doorstep. Rosebank and Sandton have decent after-hours entertainment, mostly in large malls. **Sandton Accommodation** (www.sandtonbnb.co.za) is a useful association of some 15 guest houses and self-catering options.

Many of Jo'burg's backpackers are found on the eastern side of the city and around the airport. There's also a recommended backpackers in Soweto (see the boxed text, above).

MELVILLE & NORWOOD

Sunbury House (Map pp528-9; ☎ 011-726 1114; peterharris@telkomsa.net; 24 Sunbury Ave, Melville; s/d incl breakfast from R250/350; P 💻 🅿) This characterful guest house has rooms ranging from tiny basic singles to gracious doubles full of quirky, mismatched furniture. Hearty breakfasts are served in a wood-floored dining room around a shared table, you can use the kitchen for self-catering, and there's a down-to-earth vibe that makes it easy to make friends with other guests.

Tama Rumah Guest House (Map pp528-9; ☎ 011-482 7611; www.tamarumah.co.za; 88 4th Ave, Melville; s/d incl breakfast from R520/730; P 💻 🅿) Rooms and suites are in a few different buildings dotted around pretty gardens with plenty of space to sit out in the sun. African art and crafts decorate the rooms – the bathrooms are particularly gorgeous – and there's always fresh coffee brewing in the lounge.

Thulani Lodge (Map pp528-9; ☎ 011-482 1106; www.thulanilodge.co.za; 85 3rd Ave, Melville; s/d or tw incl breakfast R580/760; P) Thulani offers a peaceful location within staggering distance of the bright lights of 7th St. Comfortable, spacious rooms are arranged in a couple of buildings with a bright garden and pool. There's a cosy lounge, and a warm welcome from the amiable owner, Beat.

Garden Place (Map pp528-9; ☎ 011-485 3800; 53 Garden Rd, Norwood; s/d R799/899; P) This leafy property offers options including self-catering double/triple studios (R999/1099) and two-bedroom luxury cottages (R1099), as well as two pools and a free shuttle service to nearby malls. It's slightly away from Grant Ave.

NORTHERN SUBURBS

Budget

Gemini Backpackers (Map pp528-9; ☎ 011-882 6845; www.geminibackpackers.co.za; 1 Van Gelder Rd, Crystal Gardens; campsites R50, dm/s/d with shared bathroom R80/130/180, d R220; P) This is like a mini-backpackers empire, with a pub, lounges, snooker *and* pool tables, a gym, a travel desk, a tennis court, and a DVD library. It's a bit out of the way though (although there is free pick-up) and the staff isn't the friendliest. Wheelchair accessible.

Acoustix Backpackers (Map pp528-9; ☎ 011-787 8070; www.accoustix.co.za; 477 Jan Smuts Ave, Randburg; dm/s/d with shared bathroom from R70/175/195; P) This small, chaotic hostel makes up for its tiny dorms with a homely vibe and social activities such as regular African drum sessions. It also has a good location about halfway between the city centre and Fourways.

Backpackers Ritz (Map pp528-9; ☎ 011-325 7125; www.backpackers-ritz.co.za; 1A North Rd, Dunkeld West; dm/s/d with shared bathroom R120/200/330; P) The Ritz does a roaring trade with the overland crowd and has top views over the city, a cool little crypt bar and proximity to the Hyde Park Mall. However, the rooms are on the small side and the bathrooms and kitchens aren't too clean. The annexe lacks the main house's facilities.

Midrange

Kosher B&B (Map pp528-9; ☎ 011-485 5006; www.kosherbandb.co.za; 124 3rd Ave, Fairmount; s/d incl breakfast from R650/800; P) Under the supervision of the Johannesburg Beth Din, and claiming to be the country's only kosher guest house, it offers good-sized, if uninspiring, rooms and a fish restaurant.

Protea Hotel Wanderers (Map pp528-9; ☎ 011-770 5500; www.proteahotels.com; cnr Rudd Rd & Corlett Dr, Illovo; s/d incl breakfast R720/810; P) The plain, well-equipped rooms are a good place to base yourself if you're a cricket fan – it's near the Wanderers Stadium.

92 Culross (Map pp528-9; ☎ 011-463 4602; www.92culross.co.za; 92 Culross Rd, Bryanston; s/d incl breakfast from R760/1000; P) Set in a quiet suburb, this place is understated and elegant, full of African masks, woven baskets and Persian rugs. The spacious rooms have underfloor heating in the bathrooms.

Top End

Melrose Place Guest Lodge (Map pp528-9; ☎ 011-442 5231; www.melroseplace.co.za; 12A North St, Melrose; s/d incl breakfast R995/1400; P) With a great spot between Rosebank and Sandton, this place has a handful of quiet guest rooms with private entrances. There's a shady, tree-filled garden and styling straight out of a country homes magazine.

Melrose Arch Hotel (Map pp528-9; ☎ 011-214 6666; www.africanpridehotels.com; 1 Melrose Sq, Melrose Arch; s/d incl breakfast from R2800/3600; P) This spare, slick, ultramodern masterpiece is bursting with cool features including rooms with 20 choices of mood lighting, a Sherlock Holmes–style library bar, and a heated swimming pool where you can dine in the water.

Saxon (Map pp528-9; ☎ 011-292 6000; www.thesaxon.com; 36 Saxon Rd, Sandhurst; r incl breakfast from R5800; P) This gorgeous, all-suite boutique hotel has been voted best in the world on several occasions. Rooms are drop-dead luxurious, and service is impeccable. Nelson Mandela spent six months in the peace and comfort here as he finished off his autobiography.

EASTERN SUBURBS

Diamond Digger's Lodge (Map pp528-9; ☎ 011-624 1676; www.oneandonly.co.za; 36 Doris St, Kensington; dm/d with shared bathroom R80/200, d R300; P) It's slightly worn and gloomy in places, but makes up for it with views of the city towers and Ellis Park Stadium, a variety of dorms and doubles, three kitchens, an outdoor fire pit, a sauna and a bar with a jacuzzi. Free airport pick-ups are offered.

Brown Sugar Backpackers (Map pp528-9; ☎ 011-648 7397; www.brownsugarbackpackers.com; 75 Observatory Ave, Observatory; campsites R100, dm/s/d with shared bathroom from R110/180/250, s/d R240/320; P 💻) The novel building, a pink castellated mansion built by a '70s gangster, is Brown Sugar's main recommendation, but the rooms and cabins are reasonable and there are sweeping views from the bar and pool.

Purple Palms (off Map pp528-9; ☎ 011-393 4393; www.purplepalms.co.za; 1 Boompeiper Ave, Kempton Park; dm/s/d with shared bathroom R100/250/400, d R450; P 💻) In a quiet suburb 2km from the airport, this self-described 'flash-packers' has clean, well-equipped rooms and a garden bar. There's a free airport shuttle and free transport to/from Purple Palms' (less impressive) sister lodge in Pretoria, North South Backpackers.

Eating

Jo'burg is stacked with restaurants to satisfy every whim, craving, occasion and budget. Unfortunately for visitors, especially those without cars, most of the best places are scattered around the northern suburbs.

All of Jo'burg's shopping centres have big supermarkets.

NEWTOWN

Nikki's Oasis (Map p531; ☎ 011-838 9933; 138 Bree St, Newtown; mains R50; lunch & dinner Mon-Sat) Traditional South African favourites such as mutton *potjie* and Western fare are served to a jazz soundtrack, and local musicians play some weekends.

Gramadoela's (Map p531; ☎ 011-838 6960; Bree St, Newtown; mains R70-130; lunch & dinner Tue-Sat, dinner Mon;) This 40-year-old restaurant, in its third incantation at Market Theatre, brims with curios and character, and has been graced by international celebs and royals. The vibrant cuisine is a mixture of authentic African and Cape Malay and there's often a buffet laid on from 6pm.

MELVILLE

Melville's hip 7th St is one of the best places to eat in Jo'burg, with a wide selection of restaurants and cafes, almost all of which have outdoor seating.

Cafes & Quick Eats

Ant Café (Map pp528-9; ☎ 011-726 2614; 7th St; mains R35-50; lunch & dinner) Light lunches, four types of spaghetti and the star attraction – 14 types of thin-crust pizza – draw the local intelligentsia in their droves to this bohemian den, decorated with vintage film posters.

De La Creme (Map pp528-9; ☎ 011-726 7716; cnr 7th St & 4th Ave; mains R60-70; breakfast, lunch & dinner) The counter at the front holds some of the best bread and cakes in Jo'burg, but it's also a restaurant serving breakfasts, sandwiches, burgers and heavier meals. With large windows overlooking the street, it gets busy at weekday lunchtimes.

News Café (Map pp528-9; ☎ 011-726 3748; Campus Square Centre; mains R75; breakfast, lunch & dinner) With outside seating, this branch of the dependable chain serves wraps, burgers, all-day breakfasts, smoothies galore and even chai tea.

Wish (Map pp528-9; ☎ 011-482 1162; cnr 7th St & 2nd Ave; mains R80; 7am-midnight;) A popular meeting place for students and media types, Wish has free (temperamental) wi-fi, a colourful floor dotted with low tables and a sunny rear courtyard. The menu ranges from lamb chops and ostrich fillet to gourmet open sandwiches, soups and salads.

Restaurants

Bambanani (Map pp528-9; ☎ 011-482 2900; 85 4th Ave; mains R40-75; 7.30am-10pm;) With curvy chairs, booths and chandeliers, Bambanini may seem like a trendy hang-out, but at the rear are a family-friendly deck and a garden area with a children's play den. The menu features tapas, Middle Eastern food, homemade desserts and childrens portions.

Nuno's (Map pp528-9; ☎ 011-482 6990; 3 7th St; mains R50-100; 8am-1am) The food sometimes takes a while to arrive at this Mozambican restaurant, but dishes such as the Godfather pizza and the puttanesca are worth the wait, as is the espresso.

Melville Grill (Map pp528-9; ☎ 011-726 2890; cnr 7th St & 3rd Ave; mains R60-150; lunch & dinner Mon-Fri, dinner Sat;) Red-blooded meat-eaters will be in their element here, and can merrily chomp away at superb-quality aged meat cuts. If you don't like steak, there's always pork belly or Ethiopian cuisine.

Portugese Fish Market (Map pp528-9; ☎ 011-726 3801; 7th St; mains R70; breakfast, lunch & dinner Tue-Sun;) Seafood is obviously a good choice at this blue-and-white place with outside tables, where service can be a victim of its popularity. Fishy options range from crab curry to Mozambican fish platters, with many land-based dishes also on offer.

Soulsa (Map pp528-9; ☎ 011-482 5572; 16 7th St; mains R90; breakfast, lunch & dinner Tue-Sun;) Extremely easy on the eye, Soulsa is one of Melville's best restaurants, with a mezzanine floor with views out over the street and a small Zen garden. Food is suitably creative, offering vegetarians some interesting brunch and dinner choices.

NORWOOD

Grant Ave has a string of cafes and restaurants; sushi, Italian and tandoori are a few of the types of cuisine on offer.

our pick **Schwarma Co** (Map pp528-9; ☎ 011-483 1776; 71 Grant Ave; mains R35-115; 10am-11pm) This is a popular place for a Middle Eastern fix. It resembles a regular kebab shop from the outside, but is far from it; excellent-quality ingredients are used in the delicious, filling platters of *schwarma* (Middle Eastern meat wrap) and kebabs (R75).

NORTHERN SUBURBS

The many eating options in these affluent suburbs are centred on the huge shopping malls that form the core of northern suburbs society.

Not far from Melville, around the junction of Gleneagles and Greenway Rds in Greenside, is a variety of restaurants including sushi, Indian and a branch of Adega do Monge (right).

Doppio Zero (Map pp528-9; ☎ 011-447 9538; cnr Baker St & Cradock Ave, Rosebank; mains R60-80; breakfast, lunch & dinner) Next to an upmarket fish restaurant and opposite the Rosebank Mall, this branch of the Italian chain will satisfy diners who know their fettuccine from their farfalle. Gourmet pizzas, pasta dishes such as calamari *alla siciliana* and homemade lemonade are on offer.

Wang Thai (Map pp528-9; ☎ 011-784 8484; Nelson Mandela Sq, Sandton; mains R70-110) Glittering peacocks and dragons adorn this Thai restaurant, where spicy dishes such as chicken, mussel and pineapple in red curry are available in hot or medium form. The *meang khum* starter (build-your-own spinach cones) is fun to share.

Café Sofia (Map pp528-9; ☎ 011-646 4003; 133-135 Greenway Rd, Greenside; mains R89-109; breakfast, lunch & dinner) Tapas, meze, sangria and cocktails are on the ample menu at Jo'burg's first branch of the Capetonian chain (see p424).

EASTERN SUBURBS

Derrick Ave, Cyrildene is an established Chinatown (Map pp528–9), where cheap restaurants offer a range of Asian cuisine. It's off Marcia St (the eastern continuation of Observatory Ave) near Bruma Lake.

Adega do Monge (Map pp528-9; ☎ 011-614 3041; 32 Roberts Ave, Kensington; mains R75-120; lunch & dinner) This upmarket Luso–South African restaurant near Diamond Digger's Lodge attracts the great and the good from the eastern suburbs and further afield. Portions are huge and there are lunch specials during the week.

Drinking

Jo'burg has an ever-evolving bar scene, with options including Bohemian haunts, chic cocktail lounges and conservative wine bars. Newtown has a few lively places, but much of the action is in the northern suburbs, particularly around Melville, Greenside and Rosebank.

CITY CENTRE & NEWTOWN

Guildhall Bar & Restaurant (Map p531; ☎ 011-833 1770; 88 Market St, Marshalltown) One of the city's first hostelries, established in 1888, the Guildhall is a wood-panelled, dimly lit bar with an upstairs dining room serving pub grub and a good range of fish (mains R35 to R50).

our pick **Sophiatown Bar Lounge** (Map p531; ☎ 011-836 5999; 1 Central Pl, cnr Jeppe & Henry Nxumalo Sts, Newtown) With a tin awning overlooking the Jazz Walk of Fame, Sophiatown is a good example of Jo'burg's 'township chic' bars and restaurants. There's an eclectic menu (mains R60 to R90) and live music on Friday and Saturday nights.

MELVILLE

Unplugged on 7th (Map pp528-9; ☎ 011-482 5133; 8 7th St) More casual than many of its neighbours, this open-fronted bar offers amusingly named cocktails and, at weekends, DJs spinning tunes of the deep and dancey variety.

Xai Xai Lounge (Map pp528-9; ☎ 011-482 6990; 3 7th St) This Mozambican bar transports you far from suburban Jo'burg using the power of Laurentina beer and the beach scenes decorating the walls.

Trance Sky (Map pp528-9; ☎ 011-726 2241; 7th St) With table football in the window and walls decorated with bright colours and pebbles, there's normally a party going on at this black-dominated bar.

Buzz 9 (Map pp528-9; ☎ 011-726 2019; 9 7th St) Funky multilevel bar with cosmically decorated metal banisters. There's a large menu of potent cocktails (R30), and light snacks are available (mains R60).

GREENSIDE

Gin (Map pp528-9; ☎ 011-486 2404; 12 Gleneagles Rd) This bar is part shabby Caribbean shack, part gallery, with ramshackle whitewashed furniture, pop art on the walls, an upstairs balcony and tables on the pavement. House and hip-hop keep the crowd happy.

Mama's Shebeen (Map pp528-9; ☎ 082 965 2640; 18 Gleneagles Rd) From the outside seating under a colourfully lit corrugated awning to the tin-shack toilets, Mama's is a flamboyant nod to township cool. The cocktails have names such as Bo-Kaap blues and Cape Flats colada, and the food (mains R60) includes *shebeen* classics such as mopane worms, oxtail stew and epic platters.

Entertainment

The best entertainment guide is in Friday's *Mail & Guardian*. 'Tonight' in the daily *Star* is also good. For bookings by credit card, contact **Computicket** (☎ 011-915 8000; www.computicket.com), which has a booth at Park Station.

CINEMAS

Huge cinemas are found across Jo'burg, with one in almost every shopping centre. **Ster-Kinekor** (☎ central bookings 082 16789; www.sterkinekor.co.za) has the widest distribution of multiplexes, with screens in the Fourways, Westgate, Eastgate, Sandton and Rosebank malls.

LIVE MUSIC & NIGHTCLUBS

The city is home to a thriving live-music scene; on weekends, Jo'burgers really come out to play and regularly hold enormous raves.

Classical

Johannesburg Philharmonic Orchestra (☎ 011-789 2733; www.jpo.co.za) The city's budding orchestra stages a regular circuit of concerts, utilising venues from Wits University to City Hall.

Contemporary

Bassline (Map p531; ☎ 011-838 9145; 10 Henry Nxumalo St, Newtown; admission R60-170) A fantastic live-music venue, Bassline hosts major national and international players. It's known for its jazz and blues performances but you'll also catch world music, hip-hop and rock.

Crazy 88 (Map pp528-9; ☎ 011-728 8417; 1st fl, 114 William Rd, Norwood; admission free-R100) Hosts bands, DJs and comedians from around the country. It's all here: house, hip-hop, rock and jazz; chilled-out Sunday sessions and more raucous fancy-dress parties on Friday and Saturday night.

Carfax (Map p531; ☎ 011-834 9187; 39 Pim St, Newtown; admission R70) This converted factory space has long been one of the most popular joints in town. Local and international DJs play house and hip-hop to an eclectic crowd.

THEATRES

Market Theatre (Map p531; ☎ 011-832 1641; www.markettheatre.co.za; 56 Margaret Mcingana St) The city's most important venue for live theatre, with three live-theatre venues as well as galleries, a cafe and the excellent Kippie's Jazz International.

Other theatres include the **Laboratory** (Map p531; ☎ 011-836 0516; 60 Margaret Mcingana St), an offshoot of the Market Theatre that acts as a showcase for community talent, with free local theatre shows every Saturday at 1pm.

Shopping

ARTS & CRAFTS

Rosebank Rooftop Market (Map pp528-9; ☎ 011-442 4488) One of the most convenient places to shop for traditional carvings, beadwork, jewellery, books and fertility dolls. Held every Sunday in Rosebank Mall's multilevel car park.

Bryanston Organic Market (Map pp528-9; ☎ 011-492 3696; Culross Rd, Bryanston) Arts and crafts are on offer here but the main draw is the stalls bursting with splendid organic produce. Held every Thursday and Saturday.

Bruma Lake Market World (Map pp528-9; ☎ 011-622 9648; Marcia St) This place sells a wide range of crafts and lots of kitsch.

Market Square Market (Map p531; Bree St) Held on Saturday mornings in the car park opposite the Market Theatre; there's a lively, cheerful atmosphere and some reasonable crafts amid the flea-market rubbish.

MALLS

Jo'burg prides itself on its malls jammed with Western consumer goods. They are as much a wealthy white habitat as a place to go shopping. A short walk from Newtown, the **Oriental Plaza** (Map pp528-9; ☎ 011-838 6752; Bree St, Fordsburg; 🕒 9am-5pm Mon-Fri, 8.30am-3pm Sat) is a collection of mostly Indian-owned stores selling everything from spices to cheap watches.

Getting There & Away

AIR

South Africa's major international and domestic airport is **OR Tambo International Airport** (ORTIA; ☎ 011-921 6262; www.airpor ts.co.za).

For regular flights to national and regional destinations try **South African Airways** (☎ 0861-359 722; www.flysaa.com), **SAAirlink** (☎ 011-961 1700; www .saairlink.co.za) and **SA Express** (☎ 011-978 9900; www .flysax.com). All flights can be booked through SAA, which has offices in the airpport's domestic and international terminals.

Smaller budget airlines, including **Kulula.com** (☎ 0861-444 144; www.kulula.com), **1time** (☎ 0861-345 345; www.1time.aero) and **Mango** (☎ 0861-162 646; ww5.flymango.com), also link Jo'burg with major destinations and often offer cheapest fares.

BUS

A number of international bus services leave Jo'burg from the Park Station complex for Botswana, Lesotho, Malawi, Mozambique, Namibia, Swaziland, Zambia and Zimbabwe. The main long-distance bus lines (national and international) also depart from and arrive at the Park Station transit centre, in the northwest corner of the site, where you will also find the booking offices.

The Baz Bus (p578) connects Jo'burg with the most popular destinations including Swaziland, Durban, Garden Route and Cape Town. It stops at most of the city's backpackers hostels.

The most comprehensive range of services to/from Jo'burg is provided by the government-owned **Translux/City to City** (☎ 0861-589 282; www .translux.co.za). For more information about these, plus other major bus lines – **Greyhound** (☎ 012-323 1154; www.greyhound.co.za), **SA Roadlink** (☎ 011-333 2223; www.saroadlink.co.za) and **Intercape** (☎ 0861-287 287; www.intercape.co.za) – see p578.

Except for City to City buses, which start in Jo'burg, all services not heading north commence in Pretoria.

To Cape Town

Translux runs twice daily to Cape Town (R450, 19 hours) via Bloemfontein (R205, five hours), and less frequently via Kimberley (R190, seven hours).

Greyhound has daily buses to Cape Town (R490, 18½ hours) via Bloemfontein (R200, six hours) and Kimberley (R240, seven hours).

Intercape also runs to Cape Town (R560, 19 hours) via Upington (R460, 10 hours), where you can also pick up the Intercape bus to Windhoek, Namibia (R430, 12 hours).

SA Roadlink offers competitive rates on its daily buses to Cape Town (R250, 19 hours).

To Durban & KwaZulu-Natal

Greyhound has six daily buses to Richard's Bay (R250, 10 hours) via Durban (R250, eight hours), including services stopping in Newcastle (R250, seven hours), Ladysmith (R215, 6½ hours) and Estcourt (R240, 5½ hours). Translux has at least one bus a day to Durban (R210, nine hours), as does Intercape (R195, eight hours).

To Mpumalanga & Kruger National Park

Greyhound runs to Maputo, Mozambique (R250, nine hours) via Nelspruit (R190 to R200, five hours), the nearest large town to Kruger National Park, daily. Translux offers a cheaper daily service to Maputo via Nelspruit.

City to City has some slow, cheap services to Nelspruit (R80, seven hours) and Hazyview (R75, eight hours). Closer to Kruger than Nelspruit, Hazyview has backpackers hostels that can arrange trips into the park.

Translux has daily buses to Phalaborwa (R200, eight hours), convenient for central and northern Kruger.

Citybug (☎ 011-753 3392; www.citybug.co.za) and **Lowveld Link** (☎ 013-750 1174; www.lowveldlink.com) run shuttle services to/from Nelspruit (R320, 4½ hours) via Pretoria.

To the North

Several bus services run north up the N1, but some only go as far as Polokwane (Pietersburg), where you need to catch a local bus or minibus taxi to get to the border. Intercape heads north to Gaborone, Botswana (R150, seven hours).

Translux has a daily service to Louis Trichardt (Makhado; R190, 6½ hours) via Mokopane (Potgietersrus; R130, four hours) and Polokwane (Pietersburg; R150, 4½ hours). It also has services that head east through Limpopo, stopping in Tzaneen (R190, 6½ hours) and Phalaborwa (R200, eight hours).

City to City's daily services to Sibasa (R120, eight hours), in Limpopo's Venda region, wind north through townships and ex-homelands, as well as major towns on the N1.

To the South

Translux runs daily to East London (R320, 15 hours) via Bloemfontein (R190, seven hours), and five times a week to Port Elizabeth (R360, 14 hours) and Graaff-Reinet (R320, 15½ hours).

Intercape has daily services to Port Elizabeth via Cradock (R300, 15 hours) and on to Plettenberg Bay (R385, 18 hours).

Greyhound has daily buses that travel overnight to Port Elizabeth (R365, 16 hours) and East London (R355, 13 hours).

Translux runs to Knysna (R610, 17 hours) via Kimberley/Bloemfontein three/four times weekly, stopping in Oudtshoorn, Mossel Bay and George (all R350). Intercape serves Knysna for the same price.

CAR

All the major car-hire operators (see p579) have counters at OR Tambo International Airport and at various locations around the city, including Park Station. A satellite navigation device is a recommended investment for tackling Jo'burg's roads and you can rent them at the airport (but nowhere else in the city).

MINIBUS TAXI

Most minibus taxis use the road-transport interchange in Park Station, over the tracks between the Metro Concourse and Wanderers St. Because of the risk of mugging, it isn't a good idea to go searching for a taxi while carrying your luggage. Store your bags, go down and collect the information, then retrieve your luggage and return in a taxi.

You can also find minibus taxis going in the direction of Kimberley, Cape Town and Upington on Wanderers St near Leyds St; Bulawayo taxis at the northern end of King George St; Pretoria, Lesotho, Bloemfontein (and other Free State destinations) on Noord St; and Durban taxis near the corner of Wandeers and Noord Sts. Take extreme care waiting in these areas; you should ideally be accompanied by a local. Fares fluctuate, but rates from Jo'burg include the following:

Destination	Fare (R)
Cape Town	400
Durban	230
Gaborone (Botswana)	200
Harrismith	120
Kimberley	210
Komatipoort	190
Manzini (Swaziland)	160
Maputo (Mozambique)	250
Nelspruit	190
Polokwane (Pietersburg)	120
Pretoria	40
Thohoyandou (Venda)	150
Tzaneen	145

TRAIN

Shosholoza Meyl (Map p531; ☎ 0860-008 888, 011-774 4555; www.shosholozameyl.co.za, www.premierclasse.co.za; Park Station) trains run to destinations including Pretoria, Cape Town, Bloemfontein, Kimberley, Port Elizabeth, Durban, Nelspruit and Komatipoort. The 'tourist class' services with sleeper compartments are a cheap and scenic way of travelling long-distance. For more information, see p581.

Gautrain (www.gautrain.co.za) is set to link Park Station and Pretoria (40 minutes), stopping en route at Rosebank, Sandton and OR Tambo International Airport.

Getting Around

When you arrive in Jo'burg, most hostels offer free or cheap pick-up from the airport or Park Station. Guest houses and hotels will also arrange pick-ups but you'll be charged about the same as a taxi.

TO/FROM THE AIRPORT

OR Tambo International Airport is about 25km northeast of central Johannesburg in Kempton Park. The 24-hour **Airport Shuttle** (☎ 0861-748 8853; www.airportshuttle.co.za) charges R310 to R390 for most destinations in Jo'burg, but book a day in advance if possible.

Taxis are expensive at around R350 one-way to the northern suburbs. Meters will generally be used, otherwise agree on a price before you get into the cab. Most hostels will collect you from the airport for free.

When its first stage is completed in 2010, the **Gautrain** (www.gautrain.co.za) will offer a direct service between the airport, Sandton, Rosebank and Park Station.

BUS

Metropolitan Bus Services (Metrobus; Map p531; ☎ 011-375 5555; www.mbus.co.za; Gandhi Sq) runs services covering 108 routes in the greater Jo'burg area. The main terminal is at Gandhi Sq, west of the Carlton Centre. Fares work on a zonal system ranging from Zone 1 (R6.50) to Zone 8 (R16). Metrobus prefers you to use their tag system (a starter tag costs R40). Travellers buy tags from the bus station or Computicket (p536).

MINIBUS TAXI

Fares differ depending on routes, but Rte 5 will get you around the inner suburbs and the city centre and Rte 9 will get you almost anywhere (try to make sure you have small change before boarding).

If you take a minibus taxi into central Jo'burg, be sure to get off before it reaches the end of the route and avoid the taxi rank – it's a mugging zone.

TAXI

Taxis are an expensive but necessary evil in this city. They operate meters if they work, but it's wise to ask a local the likely price and agree on a fare at the outset. From the taxi rank at Park Station a trip to Rosebank should cost around R80, and significantly more to Sandton. **Maxi Taxi Cabs** (☎ 011-648 1212) and **Rose's Radio Taxis** (☎ 011-403 9625) are reputable firms.

TRAIN

For inquiries about **Metro** (☎ 011-773 5878) services, call or visit the information office in Park Station. The Metro system is not recommended as it has a reputation for violent crime, particularly its lines connecting with the townships. The Jo'burg–Pretoria Metro line should also be avoided; the Gautrain (opposite) will be faster and safer.

AROUND JOHANNESBURG

Western Gauteng

The area to the northwest of Jo'burg, a World Heritage Site, is thought of as one of the world's most important palaeontological zones, focused around the Sterkfontein hominid fossil fields. The area is part of the **Cradle of Humankind**, and at 47,000 hectares it can be difficult knowing where to visit first. Most Jo'burg-based tour operators offer full- and half-day tours of the area.

Off Rte 563 and on the way to Hekpoort, **Maropeng** (☎ 014-577 9000; adult/child R95/55, with Sterkfontein Caves entry R150/90; 🕑 9am-5pm) is a good place to start. Interactive exhibits, including a boat ride back in time, show how the human race has progressed since its beginnings.

Your next stop should be the visitors centre at the **Sterkfontein Caves** (☎ 011-577 9000; Sterkfontein Caves Rd; adult/child R80/50; 🕑 9am-5pm), where tours down into the caves, one of the world's most significant archaeological sites, leave every 30 minutes.

PRETORIA

☎ 012 / pop 1.65 million

Though only 50km away from Jo'burg, Pretoria, South Africa's administrative centre, lacks its sister city's rough-and-tumble vibrancy. It's slower and more old-fashioned, and many travellers feel safer here than they do in Jo'burg. It's also a handsome city, home to gracious old buildings in the city centre, the stately Union Buildings, leafy suburbs, and wide streets that are lined with a purple haze of jacarandas in October and November.

Culturally, Pretoria feels more like an Afrikaner-dominated country town than a capital city, and its bars and restaurants are less cosmopolitan than Jo'burg's. It was once at the heart of the apartheid regime, and its very name was a symbol of oppression, but these days it's the base of the same black president who was inaugurated here in May 2009.

History

By the time the British granted independence to the ZAR in the early 1850s, there were some 15,000 whites and 100,000 blacks living between the Vaal and Limpopo Rivers. The whites were widely scattered, and in 1853 two farms on the Apies River were bought as the site for the republic's capital.

The ZAR was a shaky institution. There were ongoing wars with the black ethnic groups and violent disputes among the Boers themselves. Pretoria, which was named after Andries Pretorius, hero of the Battle of Blood River, was the scene of fighting during the 1863–69 Boer Civil War.

Pretoria was nothing more than a tiny frontier village with a grandiose title, but the discovery of gold on the Witwatersrand in the late 1880s changed everything. Within about 20 years the Boers would again be at war with the British. Self-government was again granted to the Transvaal in 1906, and Pretoria was made the country's administrative capital following the Union of South Africa in 1910. The city held onto that role in 1961, when the Republic of South Africa came into existence under the leadership of Hendrik Verwoerd.

Orientation

You will likely arrive in Pretoria by road from Jo'burg, or from OR Tambo International Airport. From Jo'burg, the M1 freeway quietens suddenly, and you'll notice the University of South Africa (Unisa) building, looking like a grounded spaceship.

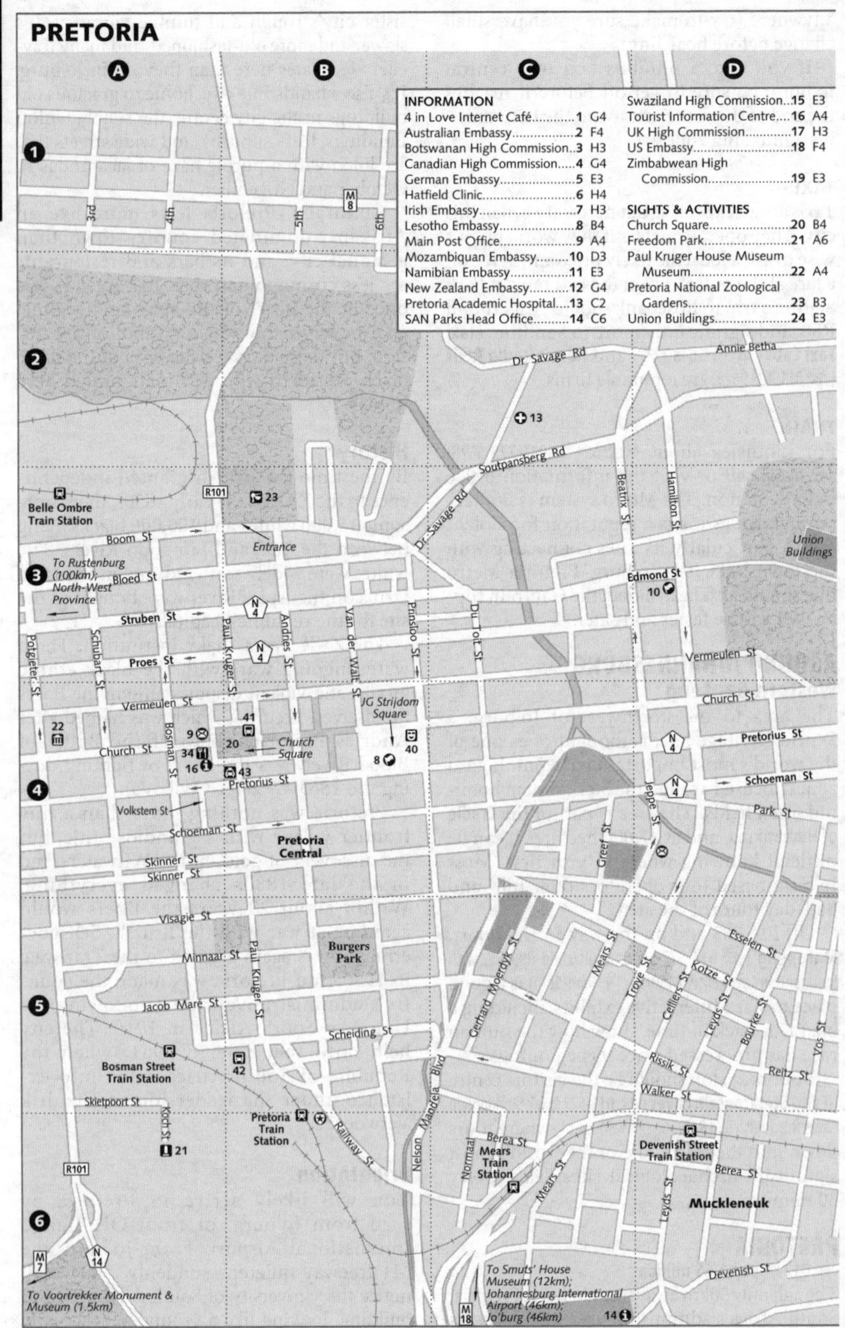
PRETORIA
A
B
C
D
1
2
3
4
5
6
INFORMATION
4 in Love Internet Café............1 G4
Australian Embassy..................2 F4
Botswanan High Commission...3 H3
Canadian High Commission.....4 G4
German Embassy.....................5 E3
Hatfield Clinic..........................6 H4
Irish Embassy...........................7 H3
Lesotho Embassy......................8 B4
Main Post Office......................9 A4
Mozambiquan Embassy.........10 D3
Namibian Embassy.................11 E3
New Zealand Embassy...........12 G4
Pretoria Academic Hospital....13 C2
SAN Parks Head Office..........14 C6
Swaziland High Commission..15 E3
Tourist Information Centre....16 A4
UK High Commission.............17 H3
US Embassy...........................18 F4
Zimbabwean High Commission.......................19 E3
SIGHTS & ACTIVITIES
Church Square.......................20 B4
Freedom Park.........................21 A6
Paul Kruger House Museum Museum..........................22 A4
Pretoria National Zoological Gardens...........................23 B3
Union Buildings.....................24 E3
3rd
4th
5th
6th
M 8
Dr Savage Rd
Annie Betha
13
Soutpansberg Rd
R101
23
Belle Ombre Train Station
Entrance
Boom St
To Rustenburg (100km); North-West Province
Bloed St
Beatrix St
Hamilton St
Union Buildings
Edmond St
10
Struben St
N 4
Paul Kruger St
Andries St
Van der Walt St
Prinsloo St
Du Toit St
Vermeulen St
Church St
Potgieter St
Schubart St
Proes St
JG Strijdom Square
Pretorius St
22
9
41
Bosman St
20
Church Square
40
8
34
16
43
Schoeman St
Park St
Volkstem St
Pretoria Central
Greef St
Jeppe St
Skinner St
Visagie St
Esselen St
Burgers Park
Minnaar St
Mears St
Kotze St
Troye St
Celliers St
Leyds St
Jacob Maré St
Gerhard Moerdyk St
Bourke St
Scheiding St
Vos St
Bosman Street Train Station
42
Rissik St
Reitz St
Walker St
Skietpoort St
Koch St
Pretoria Train Station
Railway St
Nelson Mandela Blvd
Berea St
Mears Train Station
Normaal
Devenish Street Train Station
21
Muckleneuk
M 7
N 14
To Voortrekker Monument & Museum (1.5km)
To Smuts' House Museum (12km); Johannesburg International Airport (46km); Jo'burg (46km)
M 18
14
Devenish St

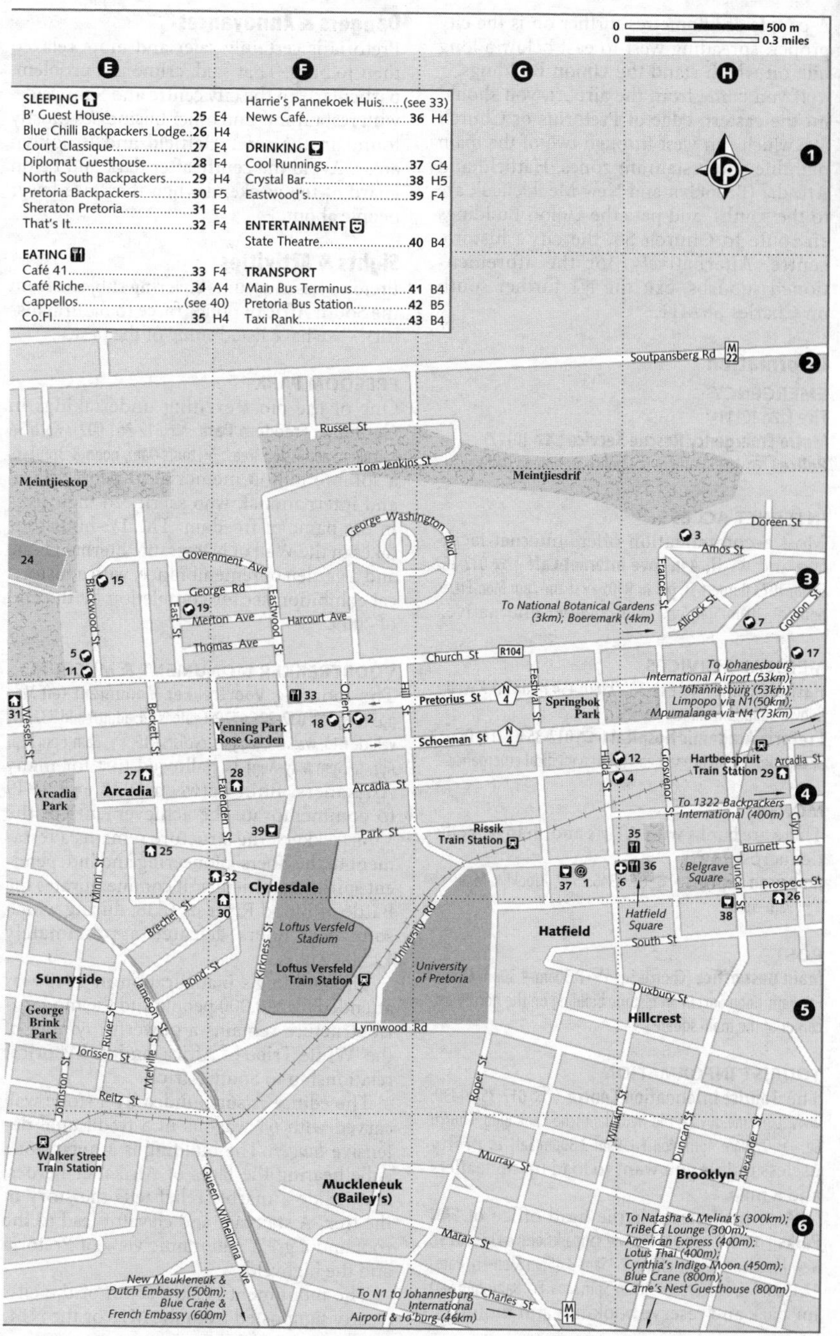
0 500 m
0 0.3 miles
E
F
G
H
1
2
3
4
5
6
SLEEPING
B' Guest House....................25 E4
Blue Chilli Backpackers Lodge..26 H4
Court Classique....................27 E4
Diplomat Guesthouse............28 F4
North South Backpackers.......29 H4
Pretoria Backpackers.............30 F5
Sheraton Pretoria..................31 E4
That's It...............................32 F4
EATING
Café 41................................33 F4
Café Riche............................34 A4
Cappellos.......................(see 40)
Co.Fl...................................35 H4
Harrie's Pannekoek Huis......(see 33)
News Café...........................36 H4
DRINKING
Cool Runnings......................37 G4
Crystal Bar...........................38 H5
Eastwood's...........................39 F4
ENTERTAINMENT
State Theatre.......................40 B4
TRANSPORT
Main Bus Terminus...............41 B4
Pretoria Bus Station.............42 B5
Taxi Rank.............................43 B4
Soutpansberg Rd
M22
Russel St
Tom Jenkins St
Meintjieskop
Meintjiesdrif
George Washington Blvd
Doreen St
Amos St
Frances St
Government Ave
George Rd
East St
Merton Ave
Eastwood St
Harcourt Ave
Thomas Ave
Blackwood St
To National Botanical Gardens (3km); Boeremark (4km)
Allcock St
Gordon St
Church St
R104
To Johanesbourg International Airport (53km); Johannesburg (53km); Limpopo via N1(50km); Mpumalanga via N4 (73km)
Wessels St
Beckett St
Orient St
Hill St
Pretorius St
N4
Festival St
Springbok Park
Venning Park Rose Garden
Schoeman St
Hartbeespruit Train Station
Arcadia St
Hilda St
Grosvenor St
Arcadia Park
Arcadia
Farenden St
To 1322 Backpackers International (400m)
Glyn St
Park St
Rissik Train Station
Burnett St
Minni St
Clydesdale
Belgrave Square
Prospect St
Duncan St
Brecher St
Loftus Versfeld Stadium
University Rd
Hatfield Square
Hatfield
South St
Kirkness St
Bond St
Loftus Versfeld Train Station
University of Pretoria
Sunnyside
Jameson St
Duxbury St
Hillcrest
George Brink Park
Rivier St
Lynnwood Rd
Jorissen St
Melville St
Roper St
Johnston St
Reitz St
William St
Alexander St
Walker Street Train Station
Queen Wilhelmina Ave
Murray St
Brooklyn
Muckleneuk (Bailey's)
To Natasha & Melina's (300km); TriBeCa Lounge (300m); American Express (400m); Lotus Thai (400m); Cynthia's Indigo Moon (450m); Blue Crane (800m); Carne's Nest Guesthouse (800m)
Marais St
New Meukleneuk & Dutch Embassy (500m); Blue Crane & French Embassy (600m)
To N1 to Johannesburg International Airport & Jo'burg (46km)
Charles St
M11

A couple of kilometres further on is the city proper, spreading west to east below a long hill, on which stand the Union Buildings.

If you come from the airport, you should hit the eastern edge of Pretorius or Church Sts, which run west through two of the main nightlife and restaurant zones, Hatfield and Arcadia (Brooklyn and New Meukleneuk are to the south), and pass the Union Buildings en route to Church Sq, the city's historic centre. Alternatively, for the aforementioned suburbs, exit the N1 further south on Charles St/M11.

Information

EMERGENCY

Fire (☎ 10111)
Metro Emergency Rescue Service (☎ 10177)
Police (☎ 10111) There is a police station on Railway St.

INTERNET ACCESS

Most accommodation offers internet facilities and wi-fi; **4 in Love Internet Café** (☎ 012-362 5358; 1077 Burnett St; per hr R10; 9am-7pm Mon-Fri, to 6pm Sat, 10am-5pm Sun) is a cheaper alternative.

MEDICAL SERVICES

Hatfield Clinic (☎ 012-362 7180; 454 Hilda St) A well-known suburban clinic.
Pretoria Academic Hospital (☎ 012-354 1414; Dr Savage Rd) The place to head for in a medical emergency.

MONEY

There are banks with ATMs and change facilities across town.
American Express (☎ 012-346 2599; Brooklyn Mall; 9am-5pm)

POST

Main post office (Church Sq; 8.30am-4.30pm Mon-Fri, 8am-noon Sat) In an historic building on the northwest corner of the main square.

TOURIST INFORMATION

The **Tourist Information Centre** (☎ 012-358 1430; www.tshwane.gov.za; Old Nederlandsche Bank Bldg, Church Sq; 7.30am-4pm Mon-Fri, 9am-3.30pm Sat) is pretty useless unless you want to load up on leaflets and a map.

Also in Pretoria is the head office of **SAN Parks** (☎ 012-428 9111; www.sanparks.org; 643 Leyds St, New Muckleneuk; offices 7.45am-3.45pm Mon-Fri, 8am-12.15pm Sat, call centre 7.30am-5pm Mon-Fri, 8am-2pm Sat) for park and reserve bookings and inquiries.

Dangers & Annoyances

Pretoria is certainly safer and more relaxed than Jo'burg. That said, crime is a problem, particularly in the city centre and Sunnyside, with restaurants and other businesses mostly found in the safer Hatfield and Brooklyn areas. Avoid the centre after dark and be on guard at the weekend when there are fewer people about.

Sights & Activities

Pretoria has museums covering subjects from the South African police force to natural history – we have listed some of the best.

FREEDOM PARK

One of the most exciting undertakings in Gauteng, **Freedom Park** (☎ 012-361 0021; Koch St, Salvokop; admission free; tours 9am, noon & 3pm) is a sombre hilltop memorial to people, local and international, who sacrificed their lives in the name of freedom. The 1½-hour tour takes in the Wall of Names, the Eternal Flame and a garden of remembrance, with a historical exhibition set for completion by the end of 2009.

VOORTREKKER MONUMENT & MUSEUM

The looming **Voortrekker Monument** (off Map pp540-1; ☎ 012-326 6770; Eeufees Rd; adult/child R32/12, vehicle R13, walkers, joggers, cyclists R15; 8am-6pm Sep-Apr, to 5pm May-Aug) is hallowed turf for many Afrikaners. Built between 1938 and 1949 to commemorate the achievements of the Voortrekkers, the structure remains a testament to the Boers' pioneering and independent spirit. In particular, it commemorates the Battle of Blood River in 1838, during which some 500 Boers defeated approximately 12,000 Zulus.

The building's inauguration in 1949 was attended by 250,000 people and the modernist structure remains a powerful symbol of the 'White Tribe of Africa' and its historical relationship to South Africa.

The edifice is surrounded by a stone wall carved with 64 wagons in a traditional defensive *laager*. The building is a huge stone cube bearing the faces of Afrikaner heroes, and inside a marble relief tells the story of the trek. A staircase and elevator lead to the roof and a great panoramic view of Pretoria and the highveld.

The monument is 3km south of the city, clearly signposted from the M18 or the N14.

CHURCH SQUARE

At the heart of Pretoria, the imposing public buildings surrounding **Church Square** include the Ou Raadsaal (Old Government) building on the southern side; the Old Capitol Theatre in the northwestern corner; First National Bank in the northeastern; and the Palace of Justice, where the Rivonia Trial that sentenced Nelson Mandela to life imprisonment was held, on the northern side.

In the centre, a bronze sculpture of the 'Old Lion', Paul Kruger, looks disapprovingly at office workers lounging on the grass.

PAUL KRUGER HOUSE MUSEUM

A short walk west from Church Sq is the **Paul Kruger House Museum** (☎ 012-326 9172; 60 Church St; adult/child R25/10; 8.30am-4.30pm Mon-Fri, 9am-4.30 Mon-Sat), Kruger's former residence. The 19th-century house contains period furniture and an assortment of knick-knacks that belonged to Kruger and his wife Gezina.

PRETORIA NATIONAL ZOOLOGICAL GARDENS

About 1km north of the city centre is the **zoo** (☎ 012-328 3265; cnr Paul Kruger & Boom Sts; adult/child R45/30; 8.30am-5.30pm), a pleasant spot to spend an afternoon, with a reptile park, an aquarium, a vast collection of exotic trees and beautiful picnic spots. The highlight is probably the **cable car** (single/return R5/10), which runs up to the top of a hill overlooking Pretoria.

UNION BUILDINGS

These buildings are the headquarters of government, and home to the presidential offices. The impressive sandstone structures – with a self-conscious imperial grandeur – survey beautiful terraced gardens with indigenous trees.

Sleeping

Backpackers are well served in Hatfield, midrangers will find the best B&Bs in Arcadia, Brooklyn and Hatfield, and upmarket business and boutique hotels tend to be east of the city centre and in Arcadia.

BUDGET

1322 Backpackers International (Map pp540-1; ☎ 012-362 3905; www.1322backpackers.com; 1322 Arcadia St, Hatfield; dm/s/d with shared bathroom from R90/150/230, r R350; P) A friendly, well-organised hostel with comfortable dorm beds, a guest-house-standard double in the main house, and log cabins at the bottom of the garden.

Pretoria Backpackers (☎ 012-343 9754; www.pretoriabackpackers.net; 425 Farenden St, Clydesdale; dm R110, s/d with shared bathroom R200/280; P) This large, well-equipped hostel has a lounge and bar, a travel desk offering tours to Jo'burg and beyond, and several small cabins. There's even a fish pond. The annexe down the road has a self-catering kitchen and pool, but isn't as nice or as convenient.

Two fall-back options are **North South Backpackers** (☎ 012-362 0989; www.northsouthbackpackers.co.za; 355 Glyn St, Hatfield; campsites R70, dm R100, s/d with shared bathroom R220/300; P) and **Blue Chilli Backpackers Lodge** (Map pp540-1; ☎ 082-719 5100; www.bluechillisa.com; 1261 Prospect St, Hatfield; campsites/dm/s/d with shared bathroom R40/80/130/170; P).

MIDRANGE

That's It (☎ 012-344 3404; www.thatsit.co.za; 5 Brecher St, Clydesdale; s/d incl breakfast R370/500; P) Owned by a friendly young couple, this place has pretty unexciting rooms, but there's a wraparound verandah overlooking a large garden, a sofa-filled *lapa* and meals available.

B' Guest House (☎ 012-344 0524; www.bguesthouse.co.za; 751 Park St, Arcadia; s/d R440/660; P) A very pretty house with a fantastic curved stained-glass entrance way. Rooms have private entrances and patios, dinners can be made on request, and there's a cosy lounge in which to sample the contents of the wine cellar.

Crane's Nest Guesthouse (☎ 012-460 7223; www.cranesnest.co.za; 212 Boshoff St, New Muckleneuk; s/d incl breakfast R550/780; P) This place, opposite a bird sanctuary, is set in a large suburban house in a scrupulously manicured garden. Comfortable rooms open on to the garden or have terraces, and there's a hotel vibe to the dedicated reception, fully stocked minibars, good wine selection and overpriced wi-fi.

Diplomat Guesthouse (☎ 012-344 3131; www.thediplomat.co.za; 822 Arcadia St, Arcadia; s/d incl breakfast R660/880; P) A gorgeous wood-floored Victorian manor and its beautiful garden are the setting for this four-star guest house. Rooms are stylish and chintz-free, and there's a two-bedroom self-catering cottage.

TOP END

Court Classique (Map pp540-1; ☎ 012-344 4420; www.courtclassique.co.za; cnr Schoeman & Beckett Sts, Arcadia; s/d from R1220/1300; P) Voted best hotel in

Pretoria three years running in the Tshwane Tourism Awards, this is an excellent top-end choice. The rooms are comfortable suites, with lounges opening onto a patio or balcony, and kitchenettes. Staff will even do your food shopping for you. There's wheelchair access.

Sheraton Pretoria (Map pp540-1; ☎ 012-429 9999; www.sheraton.com; cnr Church & Wessels Sts, Arcadia; r from R1500; P) This monster of a hotel opposite the Union Buildings offers the city's classiest digs. The bathrooms are marble-tastic, and there's all the bend-over-backwards service you'd expect.

Eating

The best eateries are in Hatfield, Brooklyn and New Muckleneuk, generally concentrated along a few streets.

CITY CENTRE

Café Riche (☎ 012-328 3173; www.caferiche.co.za; 2 Church St; mains R40-75; 6am-6pm) This historic bistro, built in 1905 and occupying pride of place in Church Sq, is popular with tourists and visiting dignitaries.

Cappellos (☎ 012-392 4027; cnr Church & Prinsloo Sts; mains R65; breakfast, lunch & dinner) This chic bar-restaurant makes the most of its brutal shell (read: the State Theatre complex) with curvy chairs and alcoves, retro decor and flat-screen TVs. The menu ranges from ciabattas and pasta to steaks and pizzas.

HATFIELD & ARCADIA

If you stumble out of the pubs on Hatfield Sq, there's a Lebanese takeaway joint across the road.

Harrie's Pannekoek Huis (Harry's Pancake House; ☎ 012-342 3613; Eastwood Village Centre, cnr Eastwood & Pretorius Sts; mains R30-65; breakfast, lunch & dinner) Part of a popular chain of pancake houses offering mostly savoury pancakes with fillings such as spicy chicken livers, as well as other meals.

Café 41 (☎ 012-342 8914; Eastwood Village, Eastwood & Pretoria Sts; mains R40-110; breakfast, lunch & dinner) A beautifully designed bistro-style restaurant serving Mediterranean fare from an extensive menu. There's a large outdoor deck, and a sunken lounge that makes you forget you're in a shopping village.

News Café (☎ 012-362 7190; Hatfield Sq, Burnett St; mains R50-100; 8am-late;) This perennially popular branch of the chain has a large terrace, a big-screen TV showing 24-hour news, free wi-fi and an extensive menu.

Co.Fi (☎ 012-342 1726; Burnett St; mains R60-100; breakfast, lunch & dinner) A similar proposition to News Café, this small chain proffers Peroni on tap and a wide range of breakfasts, sandwiches and meat and fish dishes. The service is not as sharp as the glowing blue fridges or tessellated wallpaper.

BROOKLYN & NEW MUCKLENEUK

Blue Crane (☎ 012-460 7615; cnr Boshiff & Melk Sts; mains R40-80; breakfast, lunch & dinner;) Offering Afrikaner dishes as well as the usual roster of steak and seafood, this restaurant overlooks a lake that is the breeding site for the endangered blue crane, South Africa's national bird.

Lotus Thai (☎ 012-346 6230/1; 281 Middle St; mains R60-85; 11am-10pm Mon-Sun;) This Thai restaurant's lotus-themed interior is striking, with a large raised circular sushi bar, but it's not all about the flash design. The food is fresh, authentic and delicious.

Natasha & Melina's (☎ 012-346 5317; Design Sq, Veale St; mains R60-100; breakfast, lunch & dinner) This simple, blue-and-white Greek restaurant offers more character than the nearby chains. Get stuck into white wine and fish or pasta, or pan-fried dishes with Greek-style roast potatoes.

Cynthia's Indigo Moon (☎ 012-346 8926; 283 Dey St; mains R80-100; lunch & dinner Mon-Fri, dinner Sat;) Gently lit, plastered with framed posters of all descriptions and surrounded by a colossal wine cellar, this Pretoria favourite has the buzz of a New York neighbourhood bistro. It's known for the excellent steaks.

Drinking

Hatfield is the safest and best place for a night out, with bars, restaurants and clubs frequented mostly by students, backpackers and young professionals. Head to Hatfield Sq and Burnett St.

TriBeCa Lounge (☎ 012-460 3068; Design Sq, Veale St, Brooklyn) This stylish cafe is the perfect place to chill out with a latte and browse the magazines for a few hours, or sip an exquisite cocktail.

Crystal Bar (☎ 012-362 8888; 525 Duncan St, Hatfield) The place to come to join an attitude-free crowd of locals sipping cocktails in faux Roman glory. There's decent food too.

Cool Runnings (☎ 012-362 0100; 1075 Burnett St, Hatfield) With reggae on the stereo, rustic decor in Rasta colours and a nice line in rum-based cocktails, this place heaves with drunken young bodies at night.

Eastwood's (☎ 012-344 0243; cnr Eastwood & Park Sts, Clydesdale) This Afrikaner-dominated pub, with lots of bright lights, screens and a stage for live music, is often packed, particularly if the Bulls have triumphed. It has lots of steak-and-beer deals.

Entertainment

CINEMAS

There are several large cinema complexes in Pretoria, including the Brooklyn Mall Cinemas. The *Pretoria News* lists screenings daily; **Ster-Kinekor** (☎ central bookings 082 16789; www.sterkinekor.co.za) also provides listings and makes bookings.

LIVE MUSIC & SHEBEENS

Despite being home to a large student population, Pretoria's live-music scene can be a bit uninspiring. Check out the *Pretoria News* for listings or just head to Hatfield.

The surrounding townships, especially Mamelodi and Atteridgeville, have plenty of *shebeens,* best visited with a local resident or as part of a tour.

THEATRES

State Theatre (☎ 012-392 4027; www.statetheatre.co.za; cnr Prinsloo & Church Sts) Hosts a range of productions – including opera, music, ballet and theatre.

Getting There & Away

AIR

OR Tambo International Airport is South Africa's international hub, with flights from across the globe. See p755 for information.

BUS

Most national and international bus services commence in Pretoria before picking up passengers in Jo'burg, unless the general direction is north. **Pretoria Bus Station** (Railway St) is next to Pretoria's train station. You will also find booking and information offices here.

Most **Translux/City to City** (☎ 0861-589 282; www.translux.co.za), **Intercape** (☎ 0861-287 287; www.intercape.co.za), **Greyhound** (☎ 012-323 1154; www.greyhound.co.za) and **SA Roadlink** (☎ 012-323 5105; www.saroadlink.co.za) services running from Jo'burg to Durban, the south coast and Cape Town originate in Pretoria. Services running north up the N1 (see p537) also stop here.

Translux, Greyhound and Intercape fares from Pretoria are identical to those from Jo'burg. If you only want to go between the two cities, it will cost about R60.

The Baz Bus (p578) picks up and drops off at Pretoria hostels.

CAR

Many large local and international car-hire companies (see p579) are represented in Pretoria.

METRO

Because of high incidence of crime, we don't recommend travelling between Pretoria and Jo'burg by Metro. The Gautrain (p538) will be faster and safer.

MINIBUS TAXIS

Minibus taxis go from the main terminal by the train station and travel to a host of destinations including Jo'burg (R25).

TRAIN

Shosholoza Meyl (☎ 0860-008 888; www.shosholozameyl.co.za) has daily economy-class services to Jo'burg, Komatipoort via Nelspruit, and Musina via Polokwane/Pietersburg. The Blue Train and Rovos Rail (see p582) run to Cape Town.

Pretoria train station is about a 20-minute walk from the city centre. Buses run along Paul Kruger St to Church Sq, the main local bus station.

Getting Around

TO/FROM THE AIRPORT

If you call ahead, most hostels, and many hotels, offer free pick-up.

Get You There Transfers (☎ 012-346 3175; www.getyoutheretransfers.co.za) operates shuttle buses between OR Tambo International Airport (Jo'burg) and Pretoria for about R400, the same price as a taxi.

The Gautrain (see p538) will link the airport and Pretoria.

BUS & MINIBUS TAXI

There's an extensive network of local buses. A booklet of timetables and route maps is available from the inquiry office in the main **bus station** (☎ 012-308 0839; Church Sq) or from pharmacies. Fares range from R5 to R10, depending on the distance.

Minibus taxis run pretty much everywhere and the standard fare is about R10.

TAXI

There are taxi ranks on the corner of Church and Van der Walt Sts, and on the corner of Pretorius and Paul Kruger Sts. Or you can get a metered taxi from **Rixi Taxis** (☎ 012-362 6262; per km R10).

AROUND PRETORIA

National Botanical Gardens

Around 9km east of the city centre, these 77-hectare **gardens** (☎ 012-843 5104; Cussonia Ave, Brummeria; adult/child R15/5; ⌚ 6am-6pm) are planted with indigenous flora from around the country.

By car, head east along Church St (Rte 104) for about 8km, then turn right into Cussonia Rd; the gardens are on the left-hand side. Take the Meyerspark or Murrayfield bus from Church Sq.

Smuts' House Museum

General JC Smuts was a brilliant scholar, Boer general, politician and international statesman. An architect of the Union of South Africa, he was the country's prime minister 1919–24 and 1939–48.

Smuts' home, once known as Doornkloof, has been turned into a **museum** (☎ 012-667 1941; Nelmapius Rd, Irene; adult/child R10/5; ⌚ 9.30am-4.30pm Mon-Fri, to 5pm Sat & Sun). Surrounded by a wide verandah and shaded by trees, it has a family atmosphere and gives a vivid insight into Smuts' life.

The house is signposted from both the N14 (Rte 28) and Rte 21. The most direct route from Pretoria is along Louis Botha Ave to Irene.

De Wildt Cheetah Research Centre

Just past Hartbeespoort, about 50km northwest of Pretoria, is the **De Wildt Cheetah Research Centre** (☎ 012-504 1921; Farm 22, Rte 513 Pretoria North Rd; tour R220, cheetah run & guided tour R310; ⌚ tours 8.30am & 1.30pm Tue, Thu, Sat & Sun, cheetah runs summer/winter 7/8am Tue & Thu), famous for breeding rare and endangered animals.

To a large degree it's thanks to the work done here since the 1960s that the cheetah is now off the endangered-species list.

The open-truck tours provide a fascinating insight into some of Africa's most endangered predators. You can also go on a thrilling cheetah run, but only if you're fit! Bookings for all activities are essential and you should call at least a week in advance.

To get to there from Pretoria (via Hartbeespoort), take Rte 513 northwest for 34km – the centre is on the left, about half a kilometre off the main road.

FREE STATE

In this rural state, farmers in floppy hats and overalls drive rusty *bakkies* full of sheep down empty roads, and brightly painted Sotho houses languish by vast fields of sunflowers. The Free State may not boast many not-to-be-missed attractions, but it has a subtle country charm that's easy to fall for.

In this conservative bastion, the colour divide remains stark, and dreams of an Afrikaner Arcadia live on. But the news isn't all bad. Though the state is a long way from racial nirvana, progress is happening; even in the smallest rural enclaves, the colour barrier is slowly starting to dissolve.

BLOEMFONTEIN

☎ 051 / pop 645,000

A spunky, progressive university town, Bloem is the state capital and South Africa's judicial capital. While there is no reason to come here unless you're a *Lord of the Rings* fan (JRR Tolkien was born here) or you're watching one of the six 2010 World Cup matches taking place at the Free State Stadium, the city's location, smack in the middle of the country and at the intersection of a few major highways, means you'll likely pass through at some point.

Although it feels more like a country town than a major city, Bloem has a buzzing atmosphere when the university is in session. The dive bars and eclectic restaurants lining the main streets fill with chattering students and professors, and the mix of black, white and coloured faces sharing the same table is a refreshing sight.

Known as the 'City of Roses', Bloemfontein is home to 4000 rose bushes, and it can smell delightful when the plants bloom.

History

Originally called Mangaung (Place of Cheetahs) by the Setswana people who inhabited it, today Bloemfontein's Afrikaans name translates to 'Fountain of Flowers'. Bloem became the

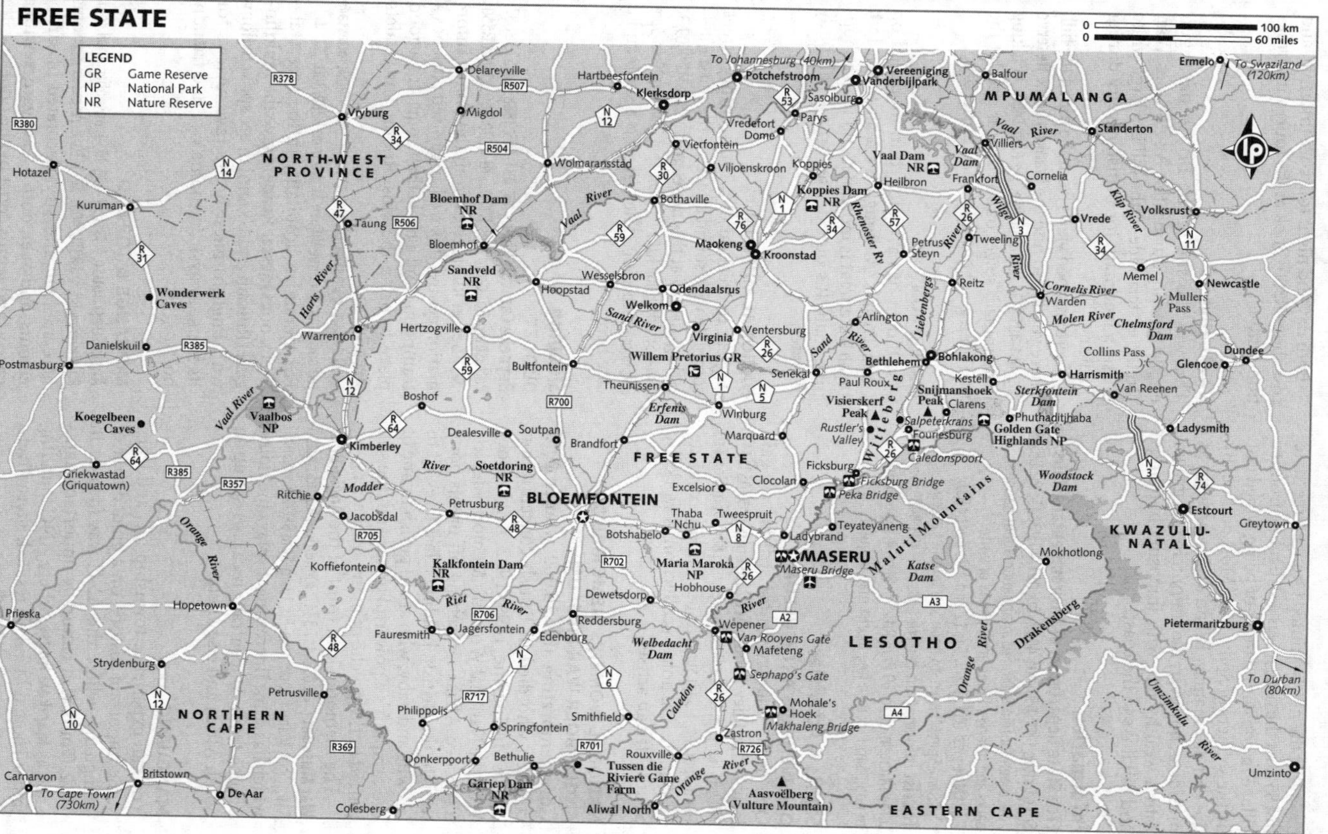
FREE STATE
LEGEND
GR Game Reserve
NP National Park
NR Nature Reserve
0 100 km
0 60 miles
MPUMALANGA
NORTH-WEST PROVINCE
FREE STATE
KWAZULU-NATAL
LESOTHO
EASTERN CAPE
NORTHERN CAPE
BLOEMFONTEIN
MASERU
To Swaziland (120km)
To Johannesburg (40km)
To Durban (80km)
To Cape Town (730km)
Ermelo
Standerton
Balfour
Vereeniging
Vanderbijlpark
Potchefstroom
Klerksdorp
Hartbeesfontein
Delareyville
Vryburg
Hotazel
Kuruman
Wonderwerk Caves
Danielskuil
Postmasburg
Koegelbeen Caves
Griekwastad (Griquatown)
Prieska
Hopetown
Strydenburg
Britstown
De Aar
Carnarvon
Petrusville
Colesberg
Volksrust
Newcastle
Dundee
Glencoe
Ladysmith
Estcourt
Greytown
Pietermaritzburg
Umzinto
Vrede
Cornelia
Villiers
Frankfort
Tweeling
Reitz
Heilbron
Vaal Dam NR
Sasolburg
Parys
Vredefort
Dome
Koppies
Koppies Dam NR
Kroonstad
Maokeng
Viljoenskroon
Vierfontein
Bothaville
Wolmaransstad
Migdol
Bloemhof
Bloemhof Dam NR
Sandveld NR
Hoopstad
Wesselsbron
Odendaalsrus
Welkom
Virginia
Ventersburg
Senekal
Willem Pretorius GR
Winburg
Theunissen
Erfenis Dam
Brandfort
Bultfontein
Soutpan
Dealesville
Boshof
Hertzogville
Kimberley
Warrenton
Taung
Vaalbos NP
Ritchie
Jacobsdal
Petrusburg
Soetdoring NR
Koffiefontein
Kalkfontein Dam NR
Fauresmith
Jagersfontein
Edenburg
Reddersburg
Dewetsdorp
Botshabelo
Thaba 'Nchu
Maria Moroka NP
Excelsior
Tweespruit
Hobhouse
Wepener
Van Rooyens Gate
Mafeteng
Sephapo's Gate
Mohale's Hoek
Makhaleng Bridge
Zastron
Aasvoëlberg (Vulture Mountain)
Rouxville
Tussen die Riviere Game Farm
Aliwal North
Smithfield
Springfontein
Bethulie
Gariep Dam NR
Donkerpoort
Philippolis
Marquard
Clocolan
Ladybrand
Maseru Bridge
Teyateyaneng
Ficksburg
Ficksburg Bridge
Peka Bridge
Rustler's Valley
Visierskerf Peak
Paul Roux
Bethlehem
Arlington
Petrus Steyn
Bohlakong
Kestell
Snijmanshoek Peak
Clarens
Salpeterkrans
Fouriesburg
Caledonspoort
Phuthaditjhaba
Golden Gate Highlands NP
Harrismith
Warden
Memel
Van Reenen
Collins Pass
Mullers Pass
Mokhotlong
Katse Dam
Woodstock Dam
Sterkfontein Dam
Chelmsford Dam
Vaal Dam
Vaal River
Klip River
Wilge River
Cornelis River
Molen River
Rhenoster Rv
Sand River
Harts River
Modder River
Riet River
Orange River
Caledon River
Umzimkulu River
Liebenbergs
Witteberg
Maluti Mountains
Drakensberg
N1
N3
N5
N6
N8
N10
N11
N12
N14
R26
R30
R31
R34
R47
R48
R53
R57
R59
R64
R74
R76
R357
R369
R378
R380
R385
R504
R506
R507
R700
R701
R702
R705
R706
R717
R726
A2
A3
A4

capital of the newly minted Orange Free State in 1854. At the time it was a struggling frontier village in constant danger of being wiped out by the soldiers of Sotho king Moshoeshoe. By the end of Johannes Brand's 25-year term as president, however, Bloemfontein had grown into a wealthy city with imposing buildings and rail links to the coast.

Information

Free State Department of Environmental Affairs & Tourism (☎ 051-405 4062; fax 051-403 3845; PO Box 264, Bloemfontein 9300) For information about national parks and reserves in the area, phone or write.

PostNet (☎ 051-447 9757; 12 2nd Ave; per hr R36; 8am-5pm Mon-Fri, to noon Sat) Internet access.

Tourist information centre (☎ 051-405 8489; www.bloemfontein.co.za; 60 Park Rd; 8am-4.15pm Mon-Fri, to noon Sat) Pick up a free tourist map or guide.

Sights & Activities

OLIEWENHUIS ART MUSEUM

One of the country's most striking art galleries, the **Oliewenhuis Art Museum** (☎ 051-447 9609; 16 Harry Smith St; admission free; 8am-5pm Mon-Fri, 10am-5pm Sat, 1-5pm Sun), housed in an exquisite 1935 mansion, holds a collection of works by South African artists.

NATIONAL WOMEN'S MEMORIAL & ANGLO-BOER WAR MUSEUM

Commemorating the 26,000 women and children who died in British concentration camps during the 1899–1902 Anglo-Boer War, the National Women's Memorial depicts a bearded Afrikaner, setting off on his pony to fight the British, bidding a last farewell to his wife and baby, who are to perish in one of the camps. It's a powerful image and one still buried in the psyche of many Afrikaners.

The memorial is in front of the **Anglo-Boer War Museum** (☎ 051-447 3447; Monument Rd; admission R10; 8.30am-4.30pm Mon-Fri, 10am-5pm Sat, 2-5pm Sun), which has some interesting displays including photos from concentration camps set up in South Africa and elsewhere.

MANGUANG

You can experience township life, and learn some important history, on a guided tour of Manguang, where the ANC was formed in 1912. Tours visit culturally important sights such as **Mapikela House**, where ANC founding father Thomas Mapikela resided; alternatively, evening tours hit the *shebeens*.

Both day and night tours are informal, and cost about R300. Book at the tourist information centre.

NAVAL HILL

This was the site of the British naval-gun emplacements during the Anglo-Boer War. On the eastern side of the hill is a large white horse, a landmark for British cavalry during the war.

There are good views from the top of the hill, where you'll also find the **Franklin Game Reserve** (☎ 051-405 8124; admission free; 8am-5pm). Walking is permitted, so get out of the car and hit the trail for a good old-fashioned bush romp.

WATERFRONT

Yes, Bloem has a Waterfront, modelled on Cape Town's. Although it's a bit tacky, **Loch Logan Waterfront** is more pleasant than a shopping mall. It's outside, set on a small body of water.

NATIONAL MUSEUM

A great re-creation of a 19th-century street, complete with sound effects, is the most interesting display at this **museum** (☎ 051-447 9609; 36 Aliwal St; admission R10; 8am-5pm Mon-Fri, 10am-5pm Sat, noon-5.30pm Sun). There is also a shop and a cafe here.

Sleeping

BUDGET

Reyneke Caravan Park (☎ 051-523 3888; fax 523 3887; Petrusburg Rd; campsites R170, s/d R290/360, chalet R560;) Seven kilometres from the tourist information centre, this well-organised park has a trampoline and a basketball court. It's a good place to bring the kids. Rooms and chalets sleep up to four.

Odessa Guesthouse (☎ 084 966 0200; odessa@telkomsa.net; 4 Gannie Viljoen St; s/d from R280/380;) For Ukrainian hospitality in the Free State, check out Odessa. Readers give the multilingual (Russian and Ukrainian are spoken along with English) guest house rave reviews for its home-away-from-home vibe and friendly hosts.

MIDRANGE & TOP END

Ansu Guesthouse (☎ 051-436 4654; ansugh@gmail.com; 80 Waverley Rd; s/d R350/400;) The modern rooms here are light and airy, decorated in earthy colours, and open onto a leafy garden with a gazebo and tennis court by the pool.

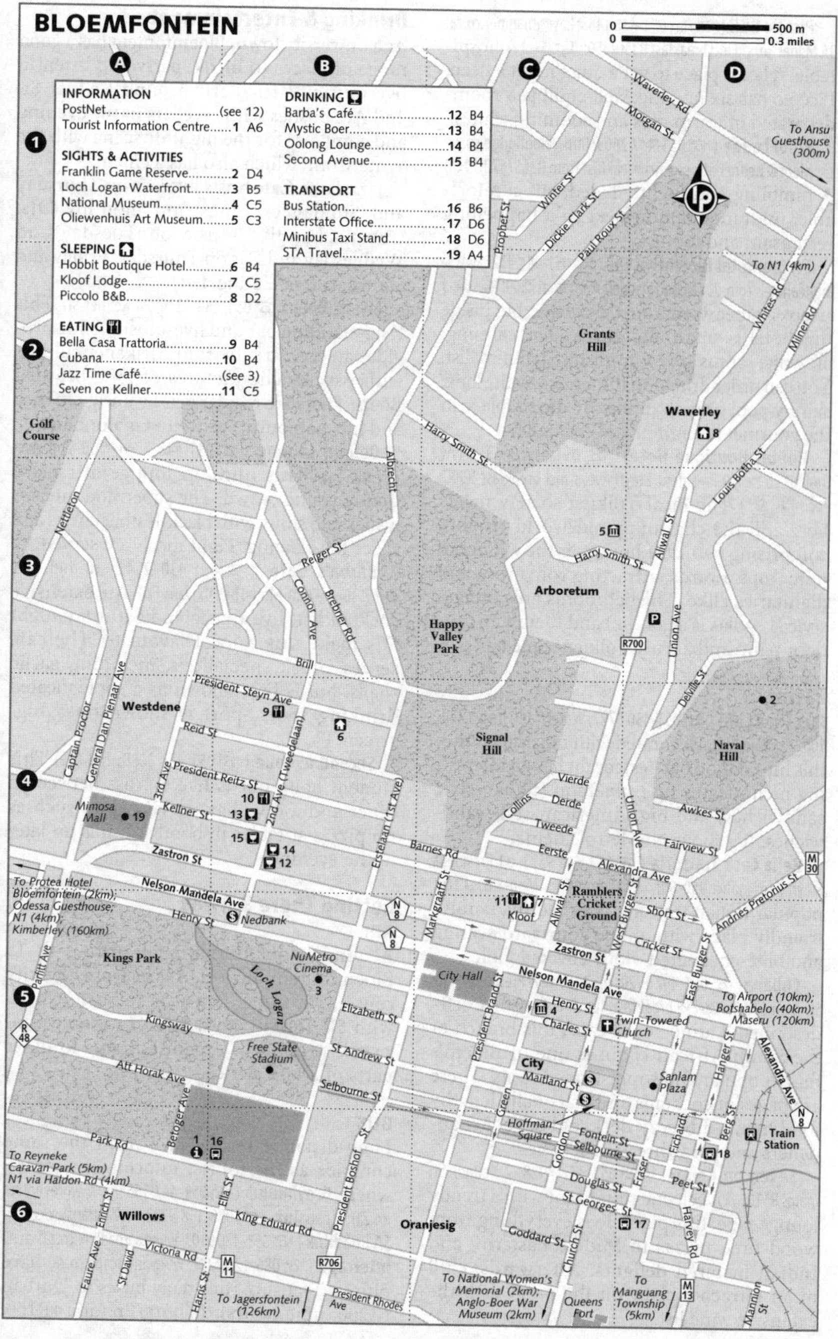
BLOEMFONTEIN
0 500 m
0 0.3 miles
A
B
C
D
1
2
3
4
5
6
INFORMATION
PostNet (see 12)
Tourist Information Centre 1 A6
SIGHTS & ACTIVITIES
Franklin Game Reserve 2 D4
Loch Logan Waterfront 3 B5
National Museum 4 C5
Oliewenhuis Art Museum 5 C3
SLEEPING
Hobbit Boutique Hotel 6 B4
Kloof Lodge 7 C5
Piccolo B&B 8 D2
EATING
Bella Casa Trattoria 9 B4
Cubana 10 B4
Jazz Time Café (see 3)
Seven on Kellner 11 C5
DRINKING
Barba's Café 12 B4
Mystic Boer 13 B4
Oolong Lounge 14 B4
Second Avenue 15 B4
TRANSPORT
Bus Station 16 B6
Interstate Office 17 D6
Minibus Taxi Stand 18 D6
STA Travel 19 A4
Waverley Rd
Morgan St
To Ansu Guesthouse (300m)
Winter St
Dickie Clark St
Paul Roux St
Prophet St
To N1 (4km)
Whites Rd
Milner Rd
Grants Hill
Waverley
Golf Course
Harry Smith St
Albrecht
Louis Botha St
Nettleton
Aliwal St
Reiger St
Connor Ave
Brebner Rd
Arboretum
Happy Valley Park
R700
Union Ave
Brill
President Steyn Ave
Westdene
Delville St
Naval Hill
Signal Hill
Reid St
Captain Proctor
General Dan Pienaar Ave
President Reitz St
2nd Ave (Tweedelaan)
Estelaan (1st Ave)
Vierde
Derde
Tweede
Eerste
Collins
Union Ave
Awkes St
Fairview St
Mimosa Mall
3rd Ave
Kellner St
Barnes Rd
Alexandra Ave
M30
Zastron St
Nelson Mandela Ave
Ramblers Cricket Ground
Andries Pretorius St
To Protea Hotel Bloemfontein (2km); Odessa Guesthouse; N1 (4km); Kimberley (160km)
Henry St
Nedbank
N8
Markgraaff St
Kloof
Short St
West Burger St
Cricket St
Kings Park
Parfitt Ave
Loch Logan
NuMetro Cinema
City Hall
East Burger St
To Airport (10km); Botshabelo (40km); Maseru (120km)
R48
Kingsway
Elizabeth St
President Brand St
Charles St
Twin-Towered Church
Alexandra Ave
Free State Stadium
St Andrew St
City
Maitland St
Sanlam Plaza
Hanger St
Att Horak Ave
Selbourne St
Green
Hoffman Square
Fontein St
Berg St
Train Station
Park Rd
Betoger Ave
Gordon
Eichardt
To Reyneke Caravan Park (5km) N1 via Haldon Rd (4km)
President Boshof St
Douglas St
Fraser
Peet St
Ella St
St Georges St
Willows
King Eduard Rd
Oranjesig
Harvey Rd
Enrich St
Goddard St
Church St
Faure Ave
St David
Victoria Rd
M11
R706
To National Women's Memorial (2km); Anglo-Boer War Museum (2km)
To Manguang Township (5km)
M13
Harris St
To Jagersfontein (126km)
President Rhodes Ave
Queens Fort
Mannion St

Piccolo B&B (☎/fax 051-436 1483; kay@imaginet.co.za; 3A Milner Rd; s/d incl breakfast R350/450;) A hospitable, relaxed place to get a quiet night's sleep, Piccolo has six inviting, well-equipped rooms decorated in warm reds and soothing whites.

Kloof Lodge (☎ 051-447 7603; info@klooflodge.co.za; cnr Kloof & Kellner Sts; s/d incl breakfast from R365/470;) A rambling and slightly faded, but comfortable, midrange option next to a happening restaurant and lounge.

Protea Hotel Bloemfontein (☎ 051-444 4321; www.proteahotels.com; 202 Nelson Mandela Ave; r from R800;) It looks rather worn from the outside, but inside this hotel is smart and glossy. The calming, all-white rooms are Asian-inspired minimalist. You can order drinks on the terrace by the long, skinny pool or grab dinner by the fireplace in the gourmet restaurant and cocktail bar.

Hobbit Boutique Hotel (☎ 051-447 0663; www.hobbit.co.za; 19 President Steyn Ave; r incl breakfast R900;) The local Tolkien society meets here and the charming, old-world Hobbit, comprising two 1921 houses, is the winner of numerous awards, attracting romantics and dignitaries alike. The bedrooms are cottage-style (Legolas is a goodie) and there's an outdoor patio and a truly Tolkienesque bar.

Eating

Jazz Time Café (☎ 051-430 5727; Waterfront; mains R40-100; 9am-late) Decorated with musical photos, this hip rooftop bar-restaurant has an interesting menu featuring *tramezzini* (Italian-style sandwiches) and big, American-style sandwiches. It's above NuMetro cinema.

Bella Casa Trattoria (☎ 051-448 9573; 31 President Steyn Ave; mains R50-80; 10am-10pm Mon-Sat) This popular Italian trattoria is a cheerful, family-friendly place with ample courtyard seating and blue-chequered-cloth-covered tables.

Cubana (☎ 051-447 1920; cnr 2nd Ave & President Reitz St; mains R50-90; breakfast, lunch & dinner) A self-described 'Latino social cafe', this branch of the South African chain is one of Bloem's more popular and sophisticated spots. There are pages of cocktails and an equally lengthy food menu; a breezy deck, old-school chandeliers and gold-threaded couches.

Seven on Kellner (☎ 051-447 7928; 7 Kellner St; mains R110) An eclectic restaurant with a trendy lounge vibe, this place does everything from wood-fired pizzas to Middle Eastern– and Indian-inspired delights. Afterwards, chill in an ultracool chair on the patio with the extensive wine list.

Drinking & Entertainment

As a university town, Bloemfontein has a good range of places to drink, party and listen to live music. Particularly around Kellner St, 2nd Ave bustles with revellers in the evening and competes for the nightlife scene with the Waterfront, which also has a cinema.

Jazz Time Café hosts live jazz on Thursday and Sunday evenings and monthly DJs; Cubana has live music on Tuesday and Wednesday and DJs on Thursday, Friday and Saturday. (See Eating, left).

Mystic Boer (☎ 051-430 2206; 84 Kellner St) This long-standing bar and live-music venue provides an eccentric twist to Afrikaner culture, with psychedelic pictures of long-bearded Boers. There are regular gigs by unsigned rock and hip-hop outfits as well as major bands.

Oolong Lounge (☎ 051-448 7244; 16B 2nd Ave; Tue-Sat) This ultrahip lounge attracts a trendy young crowd. The supermod interior is slick and shiny with black-leather chairs and space for dancing. Light meals are served.

Barba's Café (☎ 051-430 2542; 16 2nd Ave; 7.30am-2am Mon-Thu, to 4am Fri) An extensive cocktail list, live music and Saturday-night DJs make this a local favourite. The cafe serves Greek specialities, including garlic snails, but is best known as a sophisticated drinking spot. Sport is shown on a big-screen TV.

Second Avenue (☎ 051-448 3088; 2nd Ave) This student hang-out is like a cross between a diner and a dive bar, serving grub such as rib pizzas at tables in booths. It fills up later in the evening.

Getting There & Away

AIR

A number of international airlines fly to Bloemfontein airport, 10km from the city centre, via Cape Town or Jo'burg. Check with **STA Travel** (☎ 051-444 6062; laudep@statravel.co.za; Mimosa Mall) to organise flights to other parts of South Africa.

BUS

Long-distance buses leave from the same complex as the tourist information centre, where **Greyhound** (☎ 051-447 1558; www.greyhound.co.za), **Translux** (☎ 086-158 9282; www.translux.co.za), **SA Roadlink** (☎ 051-430 9103; www.saroadlink.co.za) and **Intercape** (☎ 086-128 7287; www.intercape.co.za) have offices. Translux runs daily buses to Durban (R200, nine hours), Jo'burg/Pretoria (R150, five hours), Port Elizabeth (R230, nine hours), East London (R240, seven hours), Knysna (R420, 12 hours) and Cape Town (R380, 10 hours). Greyhound and **Interstate** (☎ 051-448 4951; www.interstate.co.za) have similar routes and prices.

MINIBUS TAXI

Most minibus taxis leave from opposite the train station and head to Maseru, Lesotho (R45, three hours), Kimberley (R70, four hours) and Jo'burg (R100, six hours). There's usually at least one service daily, but times vary.

TRAIN

Shosholoza Meyl (☎ 0860-008 888; www.shosholozameyl.co.za) runs weekly via Bloemfontein between Cape Town (1st/2nd/economy class R510/250/200) and Durban (R350/240/145) via Kimberley; five times weekly via Bloemfontein between Jo'burg (1st/2nd/economy R190/130/75, about seven hours) and Port Elizabeth (R235/160/95); and five times weekly between Jo'burg and East London (R275/190/110).

Getting Around

Bloem's central business district is compact and easy to navigate. There are plenty of metered taxis around; or you can call **GG Taxis** (☎ 051-522 6969).

NORTHERN FREE STATE

Gold was discovered in this area in April 1938 and a rush started immediately. Now the Free State goldfields produce more than a third of the country's output. Unless you're interested in mining or yearning to spend a few days on a farm, there's not much to attract travellers to northern Free State, although the World Heritage–listed Vredefort Dome, near Parys, is the world's oldest and largest meteorite-impact site.

Kroonstad

☎ **056 / pop 111,000**

Kroonstad, on the N1, is a typical large, rural Free State town and makes a good base for exploring nearby Koppies Dam Nature Reserve.

The **old market building** (cnr Mark & Murray Sts), opposite the pretty magistrate's building, is a national monument. You can see the **Celliers statue** in the grounds of the impressive **NG Moederkerk** (Mother Church; Cross St). Sarel Celliers is standing on a gun carriage making the Blood River vow.

The 4000-hectare **Koppies Dam Nature Reserve** (☎ 056-72 2521; 7am-9pm), about 70km northeast of Kroonstad on the Rhenoster River, is popular with anglers.

With classically elegant rooms, four-star **Arcadia Guesthouse** (☎ 056-212 8280; www.arcadiakroonstad.co.za; s/d incl breakfast from R400/500) is in the middle of a large garden scattered with faux Greek statues.

Translux (☎ 058-408 4888; www.translux.co.za) is one of three bus companies doing daily runs to Jo'burg/Pretoria (R200, four hours), East London (R300, 10 hours) and Paarl (R310, 14 hours) from the Shell Ultra petrol station.

Shosholoza Meyl (☎ 0860-008 888; www.shosholozameyl.co.za) trains stop here en route between Jo'burg and East London or Port Elizabeth, and between Cape Town and Durban. All services travel via Bloemfontein.

EASTERN HIGHLANDS

Bumped up against the wild and rugged mountains that guard Lesotho's border, this is the most beautiful portion of the Free State and well worth exploring. The region boasts sandstone monoliths towering above undulating golden fields, fantastic Golden Gate Highlands National Park and South Africa's coolest country-village art destination, trendy Clarens.

Golden Gate Highlands National Park

Don't miss spending a sunset at **Golden Gate Highlands National Park** (☎ 058-255 0012; www.sanparks.org; adult/child R76/38), where jagged outcrops and the Maluti Mountains glow golden in the dying light. The scenery from the western approach is pretty tempting – loads of blazing sandstone and rusting old cars – but only stop here for a few moments; head out into the open instead, taking the turn-off for the Basatho Cultural Village. You'll now be off the main road and in the middle of the grasslands, where you can toast the end of another perfect African day with a good bottle of South African red.

There are plenty of animals in the park, including blesboks, elands, oribis, grey rheboks, Burchell's zebras, jackals, baboons and numerous bird species, including the rare bearded and Cape vulture. Winters (June to August) in the park can be very cold, with frost and snow; summers (January to March) are mild but rainfalls and cold snaps are possible.

SIGHTS & ACTIVITIES

Hiking Trails

The well-maintained, circular, 33km **Rhebok Hiking Trail** (per person R70) is a two-day hike and a great way to see the park, climbing to a viewpoint at 2732m. There are also shorter trails in the foothills, ranging from 45 minutes to half a day.

Basotho Cultural Village

Within the park you'll find the small **Basotho Cultural Village** (☎ 058-721 0300; tours R20; 🕐 8am-4.30pm Mon-Fri, to 5pm Sat & Sun), essentially an open-air museum, peopled by actors depicting aspects of traditional Sotho life. There's a curio shop and an outdoor restaurant, open for lunch and dinner, serving a few Sotho dishes.

A two-hour guided hike (R50 per person) explores medicinal plants and rock art. You can stay in two-person self-catering *rondavels* (R475).

SLEEPING

Glen Reenen Rest Camp (☎ 011-428 9111; 2-person campsites R120, chalets R475-525) Popular with South Africans on holiday, with well-maintained chalets and campsites by the river.

Protea Hotel Golden Gate (☎ 011-428 9111; r & chalets R640-800) This stately old lodge is fabulously located in the heart of the park, boasting great mountain views and a restaurant, bar and coffee shop.

GETTING THERE & AWAY

Rte 712, a sealed road, crosses the park. Minibus taxis running between Bethlehem and Harrismith, via Clarens and Phuthaditjhaba, travel through the park.

Clarens

☎ 058 / pop 4500

The jewel of the Free State, Clarens is one of those places you stumble upon expecting little, then find yourself talking about long after you depart. Set against a backdrop of craggy limestone rocks, green hills, spun-gold fields and the magnificent Maluti Mountains, this town of whitewashed buildings, art galleries and quiet shady streets is a bucolic country retreat.

Mountain Odyssey Tourism (☎ 058-256 1173; www.infoclarens.com; Main St; 🕐 8am-6pm) is a one-stop shop for all things outdoors. Popular excursions include white-water rafting (R500, three hours) and horse riding (R250, two hours).

The town's best budget option, **Clarens Inn & Backpackers** (☎ 058-256 1119; schwim@netactive.co.za; 93 Van Reenan St; campsites R50, dm R100, s/d R150/300), offers single-sex dorms and basic doubles in a tranquil locale, pushed up against a mountain.

The impeccably maintained **Lake Clarens Guesthouse** (☎ 058-256 1436; s/d incl breakfast from R460/880) offers buckets of intimate country charm and luxuriously appointed bedrooms. There are fabulous views from the terrace, where you can enjoy hearty breakfasts and afternoon teas.

There are sporadic minibus taxis to Bethlehem and Harrismith from Clarens, and no set departure point; head towards the outskirts of town and ask around.

Fouriesburg

☎ 058

Entirely surrounded by wild, craggy mountains, Fouriesburg occupies a magnificent spot just 12km north of the Caledonspoort border crossing to Lesotho. Two nearby peaks are the highest in Free State.

Fouriesburg was a stronghold in the Anglo-Boer War and was pronounced the capital of Free State after the British occupied Bethlehem. There are a number of fine old **sandstone buildings** in the town including President Steyn's house.

About 11km outside Fouriesburg, and just 800m from the Lesotho border, **Camelroc Guest Farm** (☎ 058-223 0368; www.camelroc.co.za; campsites R110, s/d incl breakfast R275/450, chalets from R500) sits in a spectacular location against a camel-shaped sandstone outcrop with mountain views. It's a great rustic retreat, offering a variety of sleeping options.

Rustler's Valley

☎ 051

To journey into the wildly beautiful heart of nowhere, ditch the pavement and head down brown-dusty byways to random oases scattered amid this rough-and-ready countryside. This remote valley is located off Rte 26 between Fouriesburg and Ficksburg.

Franshoek Mountain Lodge (☎ 051-933 2828; www.franshoek.co.za; r per person incl breakfast/half board R350/450; 💻 🍴) is a working farm with comfortable sandstone cottages in its garden, a round swimming pool, Zulu steam room and great views of the valley. The lodge has a Thai chef who doubles as a masseuse, and you can sign up for a cookery course. Ask for the two-room honeymoon suite with its open fire.

Ficksburg

☎ 051

Nestled against the purple-hued Maluti Mountains on the banks of the Caledon River, Ficksburg is particularly spectacular in winter when dollops of snow cover the craggy peaks.

The village is the centre of the Free State's cherry industry. There's a **Cherry Festival** (www.cherryfestival.co.za) in November but September and October are the best times to see the trees in bloom. The **Cherry Trail** is a tourist route around the district; get a map and organise farm stays at the **tourist office** (☎ 051-933 2130; 9am-4.30pm Mon-Fri) in the Caltex office on the main road.

African-flavoured **Imperani Guest House & Coffee Shop** (☎ 051-933 3606; www.imperaniguesthouse.co.za; 53 McCabe Rd; s/d incl breakfast from R260/480;) has a country-cottage vibe, with spotless, modern rooms in expansive, beautifully maintained grassy grounds scattered with cheery trees and fountains.

NORTH-WEST PROVINCE

With some of its most revered attractions less than three hours' drive from Jo'burg, the North-West Province is the perfect antidote to Gauteng's big-city clutter. Home to some of the country's best-kept secrets, most notably Madikwe Game Reserve, the region offers something for everyone, from safari addicts to slot-machine wizards.

The Disney-esque Sun City is South Africa's most opulent and kitschy themepark. Once an exclusive sanctuary for the white elite, today the apartheid era's most famous retreat is a multicultural resort, popular with gamblers, golfers and wave riders of all colours.

Nearby Pilanesberg National Park is our pick for a self-drive safari. On the Botswana border, Madikwe is worth a splurge; the 760-sq-km reserve teems with the same animals as Kruger, but sees far fewer visitors.

History

The North-West Province takes in much of the area once covered by the fragmented apartheid homeland of Bophuthatswana (often shortened to 'Bop'), dumping ground for thousands of 'relocated' Setswana people. The nominally independent homeland became famous for the excesses of the white South African men who visited its casinos and pleasure resorts for interracial encounters with prostitutes, which would have been illegal elsewhere in South Africa.

The province was the site of a complex and sophisticated Iron Age civilisation centred on the 'lost city' of Kaditshwene, about 30km north of modern-day Zeerust. The people who lived here had an economy so developed they traded copper and iron jewellery with China. By 1820, when European missionaries first visited the city, it was bigger than Cape Town. In the end Kaditshwene's peace-loving inhabitants proved no match for the aggression of the Sotho, displaced by Zulu incursions into the Free State. The city was sacked by a horde of 40,000 people and fell into ruins.

Diamonds were discovered in the province in the 1870s, resulting in an enormous rush to the fields around Lichtenburg. Mining is still important here and there are extensive platinum mines near Rustenburg.

RUSTENBURG

☎ 014 / pop 130,000

Sitting on the edge of the Magaliesberg mountains, about 115km northwest of Jo'burg, Rustenburg is a big country town with an urban grittiness to its crowded central business district. With three budget sleeping options, it's a handy base for Pilansberg National Park, Sun City and the six 2010 World Cup matches taking place at the Royal Bafokeng Stadium, 15km northwest of town.

The **tourist information centre** (☎ 014-597 0904; Main Rd; 7.30am-5pm Mon-Fri, 8am-1pm Sat), between Plein and Van Staden Sts, is well stocked.

Sleeping & Eating

Bushwillows B&B (☎ 014-537 2333; wjmcgill@lantic.net; s/d incl breakfast R150/300;) This country retreat is about 12km from Rustenberg off Rte 24, set in lovely grounds filled with indigenous trees. The welcoming owner, a wildlife artist, offers birdwatching tours.

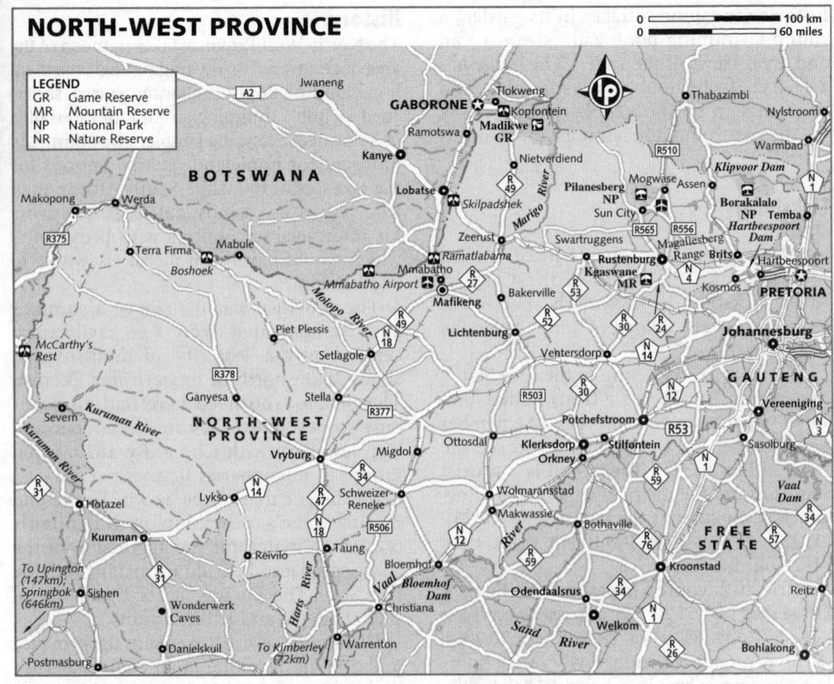

Hodge Podge Lodge Backpackers (☎ 014-537 2963; Rte 24; campsites R50, s/d R180/360;) At the foot of the Magaliesberg Mountains, around 14km south of the city, Hodge Podge is a comfortable farm hostel with colourful rooms, a great pool and a funky bar. Tours to Pilanesberg and Sun City can be arranged.

Traveller's Inn (☎ 014-592 7658; 99 Leyds St; campsites R50, s/d R250/350) Our top choice in town, this family-run hotel has well-appointed and comfy rooms, a friendly staff and a convivial bar. All sorts of activities can be arranged.

Rustenburg's dining scene is pretty much limited to the cafes, restaurants and chain eateries inside the Waterfall Mall (off Rte 30 around 3km south of town), including the local branch of **Cape Town Fish Market** (☎ 014-537 3663; mains R50-200; lunch & dinner).

Getting There & Away

Intercape (☎ 0861-287 287; www.intercape.co.za) stops daily at the **BP petrol station** (cnr Van Staden & Smit Sts) – from where you can catch a minibus taxi into town (about R10) – on its run between Pretoria (R120, three hours) and Gaborone, Botswana (R160, five hours).

SUN CITY

☎ 014

Welcome to Sin City, South African style. At **Sun City** (☎ 014-557 1000; www.suncity.co.za; admission R70), Disneyland collides with ancient Egypt in a demented attempt to look like Vegas. Filled with gilded statues of lions and monkeys, acres of artificial beaches, exploding volcanoes and countless clinking slot machines, this gambling-centric resort is almost grotesquely gaudy, yet a visit here can also be pretty damn fun.

Although it was started as an apartheid-era haven for wealthy whites, these days one of Sun City's best features is the mix of black, white and especially Asian weekenders. Losers at the tables can also console themselves with the thought that they are helping to pay more than 3500 salaries.

If you're travelling with children or on a budget, Sun City is a good bargain. The admission fee covers all the main attractions, and you'll be given R30 in 'Sunbucks', which can be spent at the various restaurants, shops or slot machines. If you've got the cash to splash out, this place boasts one of the world's most luxurious hotels.

Sights & Activities

The best part of Sun City is **Lost City**, entered over a bridge flanked by life-sized fake elephants. The African-themed mega-amusement park mostly consists of **Valley of the Waves** (adult/child R80/40), a pool with a large wave-making machine, a sandy beach, water slides and various rides. It's good, kitsch fun.

You'll find separate smoking and non-smoking casinos in the **entertainment centre**. Done up in a jungle theme with animal murals painted on the dome ceiling, it also houses food courts, shops and cinemas.

Palace of the Lost City is a hotel that could inspire hallucinations, but to which access is prohibited to all but its lucky – and wealthy – guests.

Eighteen holes on the beautiful **Gary Player Country Club** cost R700 (R600 for resort guests).

Sleeping & Eating

If Sun City's hotels are too expensive (and you have your own transport), consider staying at Pilanesberg National Park (right) or Rustenburg (p553) and visiting the complex on a day trip.

The following options can be booked through **Sun International central reservations** (☎ 011-780 7800; www.suninternational.com) or Sun City itself.

Sun City Cabanas (r from R1500; ✱ ⓟ) The cheapest option is laid-back and aimed at family groups. Rooms are modern with all the typical upmarket conveniences.

Sun City Hotel (r from R2400; ✱ ⓟ) The most lively of the hotels, with gambling facilities on the premises, as well as restaurants, a nightclub and an entertainment centre.

Cascades (r from 2900; ✱ ⓟ) The Cascades has been displaced by the Palace of the Lost City as the most luxurious hotel in the complex, but the rooms are still easily described as palatial.

Palace of the Lost City (r from R3900; ✱ ⓟ) This over-the-top property redefines the fantasy of luxury. The rooms are done up with bold-coloured carpets and duvets and hand-painted ceilings, but they seem almost unimaginative compared with the awesome public spaces and water-filled botanical gardens.

All the hotels have a selection of restaurants and there are plenty of fast-food joints in the entertainment centre.

Getting There & Away

Tiny Pilanesberg Airport is about 9km east of the Sun City complex. **SAAirlink** (☎ 011-961 1700; www.saairlink.co.za) operates flights from Jo'burg and Cape Town. From the airport, you'll need to hire a car or arrange for your hotel to pick you up.

From Jo'burg it's less than a three-hour drive. The most straightforward route is via Rustenburg and Boshoek on Rte 565.

PILANESBERG NATIONAL PARK

Don't be fooled into thinking this **national park** (☎ 014-555 1600; adult/child R45/20, per vehicle R20; ⏲ dawn-dusk) is some kind of tacky superannuated zoo just because it's nearly on top of Sun City. In reality, malaria-free Pilanesberg is South Africa's most accessible big-game reserve. Conceptualised as a sort of back-to-nature weekend escape for nearby city dwellers at the end of the 1970s, the park remains a refreshing haven where the animals roaming its extinct volcanic crater confines are 100% wild.

All the big cats are here, as are African wild dogs, jackals, hyenas, white and black rhinos, elephants, giraffes, hippos, buffaloes, zebras, antelopes and 300-plus bird species.

With nearly 200km of excellent gravel roads, Pilanesberg was designed with **self-drive safaris** in mind. Devote at least a few hours to camping out with a cooler of Castles and a pair of binoculars in one of the many public hides, which have been constructed next to the water sources that attract thirsty animals.

If you're staying in the park, check if your lodge offers wildlife drives. Otherwise, **Gametrackers Outdoor Adventures** (☎ 014-552 5020; www.gametrac.co.za), in Sun City and at Bakgatla and Manyane Gates, offers a dizzying range of organised activities and **Mankwe Safaris** (☎ 014-555 7056; www.mankwesafaris.co.za; tours from R400) combines looking for wildlife with Setswana cultural lessons.

Sleeping & Eating

Manyane Complex & Caravan Park (☎ 014-555 5351; www.goldenleopard.co.za; campsites R145, 2-person safari tent R350, d/tr chalet from R750/1150; ✱ ⓟ) Near Manyane Gate, this complex has posh chalets with high-quality facilities, including a shop and a decent restaurant. Rates include a breakfast buffet.

Bakgatla Complex (☎ 014-555 5351; www.goldenleopard.co.za; campsites R165, d safari tent R900, d/tr chalet

R950/1100;) The luxury safari tents at this smaller camp northwest of Manyayne Gate come with full bathrooms and covered porches. Rates include a buffet breakfast.

Tshukudu Lodge (www.south-african-lodges.com/tshukudu-game-lodge/index.php; s/d with full board from R3600/5100;) Tshukudu, or 'place of the rhino', is the park's most exclusive sleeping option, offering six luxury chalets. Rates include wildlife drives with knowledgeable rangers in small vehicles.

Getting There & Away

There are four gates into Pilanesberg. Enter from the direction of Sun City using either Bakubung Gate to the west (via Rte 556) or Manyane Gate to the northeast (via Rte 556 and Rte 510 if you're coming from Pretoria or Jo'burg).

MADIKWE GAME RESERVE

South Africa's most underrated **game reserve** (083 629 8282; adult/child R50/20) comprises 760 sq km of bushveld, savanna grassland and riverine forest on the edge of the Kalahari Desert. Closer to Jo'burg than Kruger, it offers Big Five wildlife viewing and dreamy lodging in striking (and malaria-free) red-sand and thorn-bush environs, and is packed with so many lions that the provincial parks department was in the process of removing some when we visited.

Sleeping & Eating

Madikwe is not open to day visitors, so to visit you'll have to book into one of the lodges within the park. The rates below are per person per day, based on double occupancy, and include meals, wildlife drives and evening sundowners.

Mosethla Bush Camp (011-444 9345; www.thebushcamp.com; per day R1200-1600) There's nothing fancy about this intimate camp with abodes in open-fronted log cabins, especially since there's no electricity or running water; a canvas bucket shower and water boilers ensure it's comfortable.

Tau Game Lodge (011-314 4350; www.taugamelodge.com; per day R2100-2900;) We loved Tau's giant bathtubs and massive outdoor bush showers in the cosy thatched-roof chalets, as well watching the water-hole action from a private deck. The rangers here are bush savvy, humorous and well trained.

Getting There & Away

Madikwe is about 400km from Jo'burg/Pretoria via the N4 and Rte 47/Rte 49. The two main gates are located just off Rte 47/Rte 49, and minibus taxis running between Zeerust and Gaborone (Botswana) will drop you near either gate if you ask.

MAFIKENG

018 / pop 70,000

Mafikeng also comprises Mmabatho, built as the capital of the 'independent' homeland of Bophuthatswana, and famous for the monumental and absurd buildings erected by corrupt Bophuthatswana president, Lucas Mangope. Today Mafikeng is a friendly and relaxed town with a large middle-class black population.

For more information visit the **Mafikeng Tourism Info & Development Centre** (018-381 3155; www.tourismnorthwest.co.za/mafikeng; cnr Licthenburg Rd & Nelson Mandela Dr; 8am-6pm Mon-Fri, to noon Sat).

The excellent **Mafikeng Museum** (018-381 6102; cnr Carrington & Martin Sts; admission by donation; 8am-4pm Mon-Fri, 10am-1pm Sat) has reams of quirky regional information dating from prehistoric times.

Sleeping & Eating

Ferns Country Guesthouse (018-381 5971 www.ferns.co.za; 12 Cooke St; s/d from R300/450;) Ferns is stylish and elegant filled with antiques and modern-style furnishings, gorgeous gardens and multiple swimming pools.

Protea Hotel Mafikeng (018-381 0400; www.proteahotels.com/protea-hotel-mafikeng.html; 80 Nelson Mandela Dr; s/d incl breakfast from R350/550;) Mafikeng's most stylish option has a very cool skinny swimming pool, rooms designed with restful slumber in mind, two restaurants, a lounge and a cocktail bar.

Tony's Corner (018-381 0700; 12 Gemsbok St; mains R30-60) This upmarket pub-restaurant has an interesting menu, including duck, stir-fries and plenty of seafood.

Getting There & Around

Many people pass through Mafikeng on their way to/from Botswana's Ramatlabama border crossing, 24km to the north. The airport is 16km northwest of Mafikeng; **SAAirlink** (011-961 1700; www.saairlink.co.za) has flights four days a week to Jo'burg (R900).

Long-distance minibus taxis leave from the forecourt of Mafikeng train station, headed for destinations including Zeerust (R25, 1½ hours), Gaborone (R40, 2½ hours), Rustenburg (R40, three hours) and locations to the south along the N14.

Local buses depart from near the disused train station for the Megacity shopping mall in Mmabatho.

LIMPOPO

If one thing unites this diverse province's tourist operators, including Fair Trade lodges and art or birding routes, it's that they offer visitors something completely different. So if you visit Polokwane/Pietersburg for the 2010 World Cup, be sure to check out the surrounding countryside.

Subtropical eastern Limpopo, bordering Kruger, packs in areas such as misty Magoebaskloof, where waterfalls crash in the forests. In the traditional Venda region, a python god is believed to live in Lake Fundudzi and artists produce highly original work.

The Soutpansberg is an island of biodiversity in the savanna, and the Big Five are found beneath the Waterberg's red cliffs. However, Limpopo's major star is Mapungubwe National Park. Reached on empty roads lined with baobabs and baboons, the 28,000-hectare wilderness contains traces of a millennium-old civilisation.

History

Sites in the province have offered up an archaeological record stretching back to protohuman times, while the area that is now Mapungubwe National Park was once the heart of one of Africa's most technologically advanced civilisations, holding sway over an area of 30,000 sq km and enjoying its heyday in the 8th and 9th centuries.

The Voortrekkers made this region home in the mid-19th century, founding Pietersburg (now Polokwane) in 1886. Conflict with the local Ndebele people marked a period of resistance against the settlers.

Around the turn of the 20th century, northeastern Limpopo, near the borders with Mozambique and Zimbabwe, earned a reputation as a haven for ivory hunters, gunrunners and other outlaws. It was nicknamed 'Crook's Corner'.

The province, which has one of the highest poverty rates in the country, is also a hot spot of racial tension and farm attacks. In 2008 Musina made headlines worldwide when Zimbabwe's cholera epidemic seeped across the border.

THE N1 HIGHWAY

The wide, straight, but heavily tolled N1 Highway running from Gauteng to the Zimbabwe border divides Limpopo. Most of the province's major towns line this route, including the provincial capital, Polokwane.

Translux/City to City (☎ 0861-589 282; www.translux.co.za) and **Greyhound** (☎ 083-915 9000; www.greyhound.co.za) buses run along the N1, and a daily (except Saturday) economy-class **Shosholoza Meyl** (☎ 0860-008 888; www.shosholozameyl.co.za) train follows a similar route between Jo'burg and Musina (R110, 17 hours). The train is not recommended.

Bela-Bela/Warmbaths

☎ 014 / pop 37,200

The small, soporific town of Bela-Bela has grown on the back of the hot springs discovered by the Setswana in the early 19th century. Around 22,000L of the warm stuff bubble out of the earth every hour and there's no shortage of folk from the big cities to soak it up.

At the **hydro spa** (☎ 014-736 8500; www.aventura.co.za; Chris Hani Dr; day/evening R70/60; 🕑 7am-4pm & 5-10pm), children head to the pools with slides, while those who prefer a relaxing experience can wallow in 52°C water.

The same **Forever Resort** (campsites from R190, r incl breakfast from R1200, 1-/2-bedroom chalet from R1000/1400) also offers a Spur restaurant.

Nylsvley Nature Reserve

The 4000-hectare **Nylsvley Nature Reserve** (☎ 014-743 1074; adult/child/vehicle R10/5/20; 🕑 6am-6pm) is one of the country's best places to see birds (380 species are listed). Chalets and a restaurant were being built at the time of research, joining the basic **campsite** (campsites R50). The reserve, 20km south of Mookgophong/Naboomspruit, is signposted from Rte 101.

Mokopane/Potgietersrus & Around

☎ 015 / pop 120,000

With Voortrekker origins and a local economy driven by mining, Mokopane is a tough Bushveld town. The pubs play Bon Jovi on rotation and, over the weekend, accommodation

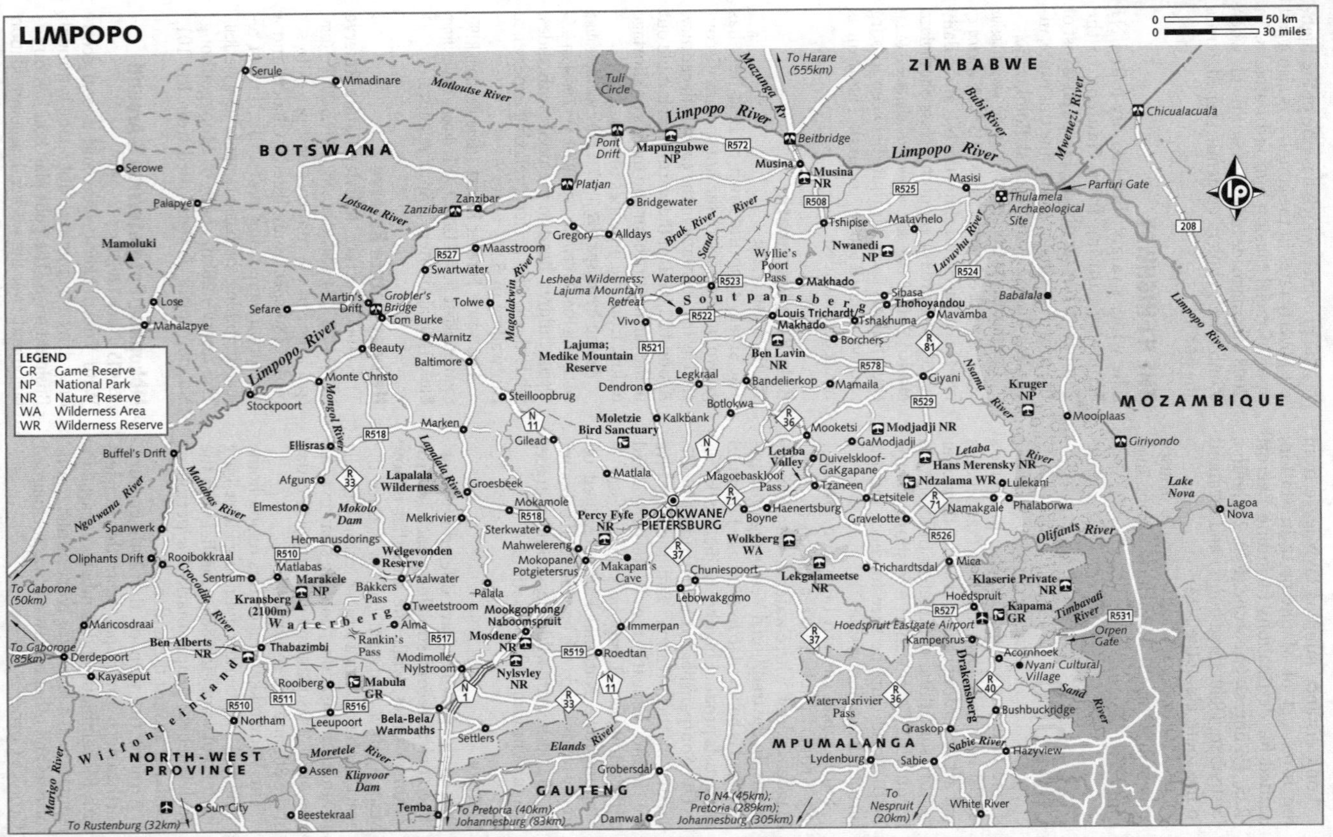
LIMPOPO
0 50 km
0 30 miles
LEGEND
GR Game Reserve
NP National Park
NR Nature Reserve
WA Wilderness Area
WR Wilderness Reserve
ZIMBABWE
BOTSWANA
MOZAMBIQUE
MPUMALANGA
GAUTENG
NORTH-WEST PROVINCE
To Harare (555km)
Serule
Mmadinare
Motloutse River
Tuli Circle
Limpopo River
Mazunga Rv
Bubi River
Mwenezi River
Chicualacuala
Serowe
Palapye
Mamoluki
Lose
Mahalapye
Lotsane River
Zanzibar
Pont Drift
Mapungubwe NP
Platjan
R572
Beitbridge
Musina
Musina NR
Masisi
Parfuri Gate
Thulamela Archaeological Site
208
R525
R508
Tshipise
Matavhelo
Nwanedi NP
Bridgewater
Gregory
Alldays
Brak River
Sand River
Maasstroom
Swartwater
R527
Magalakwin River
Lesheba Wilderness; Lajuma Mountain Retreat
Waterpoor
R523
Wyllie's Poort Pass
Makhado
Luvuvhu River
R524
Sibasa
Thohoyandou
Babalala
Martin's Drift
Grobler's Bridge
Tom Burke
Sefare
Tolwe
Soutpansberg
Vivo
R522
Louis Trichardt/ Makhado
Tshakhuma
Mavamba
Marnitz
Beauty
Baltimore
Lajuma; Medike Mountain Reserve
R521
Ben Lavin NR
Borchers
R81
Limpopo River
Monte Christo
Stockpoort
Mongol River
Steilloopbrug
Dendron
Legkraal
Bandelierkop
R578
Mamaila
Giyani
Nsama River
Kruger NP
Mooiplaas
Giriyondo
Marken
R518
Botlokwa
R529
Ellisras
Gilead
N11
Moletzie Bird Sanctuary
Kalkbank
N1
R36
Mooketsi
Modjadji NR
GaModjadji
Buffel's Drift
Lapalala River
Letaba Valley
Duivelskloof-GaKgapane
Letaba River
Hans Merensky NR
Afguns
R33
Lapalala Wilderness
Groesbeek
Matlala
Magoebaskloof Pass
Ndzalama WR
Lulekani
Lake Nova
Matlabas River
Ngotwana River
Elmeston
Mokolo Dam
Mokamole
R71
Tzaneen
Letsitele
Namakgale
Phalaborwa
Lagoa Nova
Spanwerk
Melkrivier
R518
Sterkwater
Percy Fyfe NR
POLOKWANE/ PIETERSBURG
Boyne
Haenertsburg
Gravelotte
Hermanusdorings
Mahwelereng
Wolkberg WA
R526
Olifants River
Oliphants Drift
Rooibokkraal
R510
Matlabas
Welgevonden Reserve
Mokopane/ Potgietersrus
Makapan's Cave
R37
Mica
Sentrum
Marakele NP
Vaalwater
Chuniespoort
Lekgalameetse NR
Trichardtsdal
Klaserie Private NR
To Gaborone (50km)
Crocodile River
Bakkers Pass
Palala
Lebowakgomo
Hoedspruit
Kransberg (2100m)
Tweetstroom
Mookgophong/ Naboomspruit
R527
Kapama GR
Timbavati River
R531
Maricosdraai
Waterberg
Alma
Immerpan
Hoedspruit Eastgate Airport
Orpen Gate
Ben Alberts NR
Thabazimbi
Rankin's Pass
R517
Mosdene NR
Kampersrus
To Gaborone (85km)
Derdepoort
Modimolle/ Nylstroom
R519
Roedtan
Acornhoek
Kayaseput
Nylsvley NR
Nyani Cultural Village
Drakensberg
R40
Rooiberg
Mabula GR
Sand River
R510
R511
R516
Witfonteinrand
Northam
Leeupoort
Bela-Bela/ Warmbaths
Watervalsrivier Pass
Bushbuckridge
Settlers
Graskop
Elands River
Moretele River
Sabie River
Hazyview
Marigo River
Assen
Klipvoor Dam
Grobersdal
Lydenburg
Sabie
Sun City
Beestekraal
Temba
To Pretoria (40km); Johannesburg (83km)
Damwal
To N4 (45km); Pretoria (289km); Johannesburg (305km)
To Nespruit (20km)
White River
To Rustenburg (32km)

empties as mine workers flood home. Fruit farms are also big business; one of the southern hemisphere's largest citrus farms, the Zebediela Citrus Estate, lies to the southeast.

The **Game Breeding Centre** (☎ 015-491 4314; Thabo Mbeki Dr; adult/child R15/8, tour per vehicle R350; 8am-4pm Mon-Fri, to 6pm Sat & Sun) is a breeding centre for the National Zoo in Pretoria. You can drive through the 1300-hectare reserve. Accommodation (rooms per adult/child R120/60, campsites per person R25) is available.

Makapan's Caves (☎ 079-515 6491; adult/student R25/15), 23km northeast of Mokopane, was declared a World Heritage Site for its palaeontological significance, having yielded the skull of a 3.3-million-year-old humanoid. Chief Makapan and 1000-plus followers were besieged here for a month in 1854 by the Voortrekkers. You must prebook visits.

Polokwane/Pietersburg

☎ 015 / pop 140,000

Football fans who come to watch the four 2010 World Cup matches taking place at the Peter Mokaba Stadium – in an area where wild giraffes and antelopes roamed a few decades ago – will find the provincial capital to be a city of two halves. In the sedate eastern suburbs, sprinklers rotate on tidy lawns and the people circulate between a handful of malls and restaurants; downtown, a healthy dose of African chaos enlivens the streets.

Polokwane Municipality Local Development Office (☎ 015-290 2010; www.polokwane.gov.za; Civic Sq, Landdros Mare St; 7.30am-4.30pm Mon-Fri, 9am-1pm Sat) has local information; **Limpopo Tourism & Parks Board** (☎ 015-290 7300; www.golimpopo.com; cnr Kerk & Grobler Sts; 8am-4.30pm Mon-Fri) covers the whole province.

SIGHTS & ACTIVITIES

Less than 5km south of town, **Polokwane Game Reserve** (☎ 015-290 2331; Dorp St; adult/child/vehicle R14/10/22; 7am-5.30pm May-Sep, to 6.30pm Oct-Apr) is one of the country's largest municipal nature reserves, with wildlife including zebras, giraffes and white rhinos, plus roads and hiking trails. Last entry is two hours before closing.

The **Bakone Malapa Open-Air Museum** (☎ 015-295 2432; adult/child R6.50/4; 8.30am-3pm Mon-Fri, 9am-3.30pm Sat), a re-created village 9km south of Polokwane on Rte 37 to Chuniespoort, evokes Northern Sotho customs.

The **Hugh Exton Photographic Museum** (☎ 015-290 2186; Civic Sq; admission free; 9am-3.30pm Mon-Fri), in a restored 19th-century church, covers early Polokwane and the second Anglo-Boer War.

SLEEPING

Olivia's Place (☎ 015-295 3811; www.oliviasplace.co.za; 162 Suid St; s/d incl breakfast R350/450) Conveniently located for Peter Mokaba Stadium, the Afrikaner-run Olivia's Place offers a similar experience to more expensive options, and a garden with a tiered fountain.

Plumtree Lodge (☎ 015-295 6153; www.plumtree.co.za; 138 Marshall St; r incl breakfast R515) This German-run guest house's bungalow rooms are some of Polokwane's most spacious and appealing, with high ceilings, lounge areas, minibars, DSTV, and desks where you can tap into the free wi-fi.

At the entrance to Polokwane Game Reserve (left) are **campsites** (R112) and **chalets** (2-/4-/6-bed R250/313/451) with twin rooms.

EATING

You can find the usual takeaways in and around Library Gardens, but the Savannah Centre (Rte 71) offers the widest selection of sit-down meals.

Café Pavilion (☎ 015-291 5359, 082 853 4794; Sterkloop Garden Pavilion, Kerk St; mains R30-65; 9am-10pm Mon-Sat, to 3pm Sun) Overlooking a garden centre, the Pavilion's covered outdoor area is the local venue of choice for long, leisurely meals. Food has the usual focus on meat feasts prepared in a variety of styles.

GETTING THERE & AWAY

Air

SAAirlink (☎ 015-288 0166; www.saairlink.co.za), with offices at the airport, flies daily to/from Jo'burg (R1000 to R1580 one-way). **Polokwane airport** (☎ 015-288 0122) is 5km north of town.

WHAT'S IN A NAME?

Many town names in Limpopo, and the name of the province itself, have changed in recent years. We list the new name, followed by the old moniker. However, while all names have been changed on the official record, some road signs and many locals have yet to catch up.

Bus

Translux (☎ 015-295 5548; www.translux.co.za; cnr Joubert & Thabo Mbeki Sts) runs services to Jo'burg (R140, 4½ hours) via Pretoria (R140, 3½ hours) at 10.30am and 11am. Cheaper City to City buses (R100) leave at 10.50am.

North Link Tours (☎ 015-291 1867; 22 Library Gardens, Hans van Rensburg St) runs daily (10.30am) buses to Jo'burg (R150, 4½ hours) via Pretoria (R110, 3½ hours), departing from outside Library Gardens.

Greyhound (☎ 083 915 9000; www.greyhound.co.za) has daily departures for Harare, Zimbabwe (R320, 12 hours). Buses stop at Civic Sq.

Car

Avis (☎ 015-288 0163; www.avis.co.za), **Budget** (☎ 015-288 0169; www.budget.co.za) and **Abba** (☎ 015-288 1510; www.abbacarrental.co.za), which accepts debit cards and cash, have desks at the airport.

Minibus Taxi

Minibus taxis run to destinations including Louis Trichardt/Makhado (R40, 1¼ hours) and Thohoyandou (R55, 2½ hours) from the rank at the Indian Centre, on the corner of Kerk and Excelsior Sts. For Jo'burg and Pretoria, prices are similar to the bus, which is faster and safer.

Train

Shosholoza Meyl trains stop here (see p557).

Louis Trichardt/Makhado

☎ 015 / pop 90,000

Scruffy Louis Trichardt is a little hard on the eyes – a stark contrast to the verdant countryside surrounding it. Treat the town as a springboard to some worthwhile country lodges, nature reserves and hiking trails in the nearby Soutpansberg mountains, which boast an extraordinary diversity of flora and fauna, with one of the continent's highest concentrations of the African leopard.

One reliable tour operator is **Face Africa** (☎ 082 969 3270; per group per day from R1500).

Louis Trichardt changed its name to Makhado, then, following a successful Supreme Court appeal by a group of businesspeople from the town, reverted to its original moniker.

SLEEPING

Makhado Municipal Caravan Park (☎ 015-519 3106; www.makhado.caravanparks.co.za; Grobler St; campsites per person R50.75) A central camping option.

Madi a Thavha (☎ 015-516 0220; http://tinyurl.com/cc2mj7; campsite per person R60, s/d R440/700;) Some 10km west of town, off Rte 522, this Fair Trade–accredited farm lodge offers colourful little cottages with Venda bedspreads and cushions, tea-light candles aplenty and kitchenettes. Dinner is R120.

Louis Trichardt Lodge (☎ 015-516 2222; www.lttlodge.co.za; Hlanganani St; s/d R260/340) This red-brick motel on the main road has basic rooms with kitchenettes and braai areas.

Ultimate Guest House (☎ 015-517 7005; www.wheretostay.co.za/ultimateguesthouse; s/d incl breakfast R390/490;) Set in 78 hectares of land, this quirky, colourful guest house has a bar-restaurant with a verandah overlooking a lush valley.

EATING

Ricky's Takeaway (☎ 015-516 0414; Baobab St; 8am-8pm Mon-Sat) Ricky's fills with people trying to get hold of its locally famous sausages, burgers and sandwiches.

Casa Café (☎ 015-516 3574; 129 Krogh St; mains R30; 8am-5pm) Opening onto a garden with a climbing frame, this cafe and Christian bookshop is a top spot for lazy breakfasts and light lunches.

GETTING THERE & AWAY

The **Louis Trichardt Travel Agency** (☎ 015-516 5042; 8am-1pm & 2-4.30pm Mon-Fri, 9-11am Sat), down an alley off Krogh St (opposite Louis Trichardt Stationers), is the local agent for Greyhound and Translux buses. Most buses to Jo'burg (R190, six hours, 8am, 3.30pm and 5pm), Harare, Zimbabwe (R295, 11 hours, 1.50am and 6.30pm Saturday) and Bulawayo (R255, 18 hours, 1.40pm) stop by the Caltex petrol station on the corner of the N1 and Baobab St.

The minibus taxi rank is in the Shoprite supermarket car park off Burger St, a block northeast of Songozwi Rd.

Shosholoza Meyl trains stop here (see p557).

Around Louis Trichardt/Makhado

SOUTPANSBERG MOUNTAINS

Beginning on the outskirts of town, the two-day, 20.5km **Hanglip Trail** (☎ 013-754 2724; www.komatiecotourism.co.za) climbs through indigenous forest to a 1719m peak. Take precautions against malaria, bilharzia and ticks. Overnight accommodation is in huts (per person R75); alternatively, a 2½-hour walk begins in the same location.

There are a number of remote Soutpansberg hideaways off Rte 522 to Vivo, including hiking- and climbing-focused **Medike** (☎ 015-516 0481; www.wheretostay.co.za/medike; d from R200), with self-catering, paraffin-lamp-lit accommodation; Fair Trade–accredited **Lesheba Wilderness** (☎ 015-593 0076; www.lesheba.co.za; s/d from R599/750, with full board & 1 activity from R1512/2420;), a dreamy resort perched in the clouds and based on a Venda village; and **Lajuma Mountain Retreat** (☎ 015-593 0352; www.lajuma.com; camp/chalet per person R140/200), run by a biologist and a medical sociologist who revel in the local wildlife.

Musina & Around

☎ 015 / pop 20,000

Some 15km south of the Beitbridge border crossing with Zimbabwe, Musina hums with typical border-town tension. The cars, many visiting from Zimbabwe, never seem to stop blowing their horns; groups of economic refugees from the defunct state trudge along the N1, hiking south in search of work.

SLEEPING & EATING

Old Mine Guest House (☎ 015-534 2250; 1 Woodburn Ave; oldmineguesthouse@limpopo.co.za; s/d R350/500;) In a residence built in 1919, this guest house has an old-fashioned feel, with an antelope head surveying the dining room. The stylish rooms have the pleasantest bathrooms for miles around.

Ilala Country Lodge (☎ 015-534 3220; www.places.co.za/html/2175.html; Rte 572; s/d incl breakfast R500/700;) Ilala's thatched rooms have fans, TVs and fridges, and there's an upstairs lounge with sweeping views of the Limpopo River Valley. It's 8km northwest of town.

Lifestyle Tea Garden (☎ 083 295 0012; Lifestyle Corner, 10 Hans van der Merwe Ave; sandwiches R20-30; 7am-5pm Mon-Fri, 8am-noon Sat) Wraps, sushi, pancakes and muffins are on the menu at this tranquil garden cafe.

Frangos (N1; meals R50; 9am-10pm) The chicken den is one of Musina's fast-food eateries.

GETTING THERE & AWAY

The Zimbabwe border at Beitbridge is open 24 hours. If you are coming from Zimbabwe, there is a large taxi rank on the South African side of the border.

Bus

Greyhound (☎ 083-915 9000; www.greyhound.co.za) runs daily from Beitbridge to Harare, Zimbabwe (eight hours) and Bulawayo (4½ hours), picking up at the Beitbridge Hotel.

Car

Car hire is available at **Avis** (☎ 015-534 2220; limpopotrav@lantic.net; Lifestyle Corner, 10 Hans van der Merwe Ave) for about R350 a day.

Minibus Taxi

If you're coming from Zimbabwe and want to take a minibus taxi further south than Musina, catch one at the border as there are many more there than in Musina. Destinations include Louis Trichardt (R30, 1½ hours) and Jo'burg (R140, 7½ hours). Taxis between the border and Musina cost R20 (20 minutes).

Train

Shosholoza Meyl trains stop here (see p557).

Mapungubwe National Park

The call of the wild is perhaps nowhere louder than in **Mapungubwe National Park** (☎ 015-534 2014; adult/child R76/38; 6.30am-6pm), where 28,000 hectares of baobab trees and rock gaze across the Limpopo River delta at Botswana and Zimbabwe.

The World Heritage Site contains South Africa's most significant Iron Age site, as well as animals from white and black rhinos to the rare Pel's fishing owl. The **Heritage Tour** (R115), one of the walks and drives on offer, gives an insight into the civilisation behind the 13th-century graves on Mapungubwe Hill.

Self-catering accommodation ranges from **camping** (per campsite from R130) to the luxury cottages at **Leokwe Camp** (per campsite from R655;). East of the park entrance is the recommended **Mopane Bush Lodge** (☎ 015-534 7906; www.mopanebushlodge.co.za; s/tw with full board R1400/2260;).

Mapungubwe is a 60km drive from Musina on Rte 572 to Pont Drift.

VENDA REGION

The most enigmatic section of the Soutpansberg region, this is the traditional home of the Venda people, who moved to the area from modern-day Zimbabwe in the early 18th century. The last 'homeland' created by the apartheid regime, the Venda region is a world away from the South Africa of uptown Jo'burg; here even a short diversion from the freeway takes you through an Africa of mist-clad hilltops, dusty streets and mud huts, a land where myth and legend continue to play a major role in everyday life.

Elim & Around

☎015

Some 25km southeast of Louis Trichardt, tiny Elim is closer to the N1 than the Venda capital Thohoyandou and makes a more convenient, and pleasanter, base for local tours.

The region is famous for its **art and craft studios**. Noria Mabasa, whose work adorns Pretoria's Union Buildings, and Thomas Kubhayi (see the boxed text, below) are worth visiting, but there are many other artists and cooperatives. **Daniel Khosa** (☎072-235 4543; khosahd@yahoo.com) is a knowledgeable guide.

SLEEPING

Mambedi Country Lodge (☎015-556 7400; mambedi@telkosma.net; Levubu; r from R480; 💻 🏊) Some 25km northeast of Elim, what Mambedi's remote location lacks in atmosphere it makes up for in tranquillity. The well-equipped *rondavels* have TVs and showers, and there's a bar-restaurant.

Shiluvari Lakeside Lodge (☎015-556 3406; www.shiluvari.com; s/d incl breakfast from R609/870; 🏊) This Fair Trade–accredited lodge's chalets, rooms and suite are adorned with zebra-print cushions and bead-decorated portraits. After a sunset cruise on the dam, adjourn to the *lapa* for dinner on the verandah.

GETTING THERE & AWAY

Translux buses serve Jo'burg (R190, seven hours) and Sibasa (R80, one hour). Tickets are available at **Shoprite Checkers** (☎015-295 5548; Hubyeni Shopping Centre).

Lake Fundudzi

Lake Fundudzi is a sacred site that emerges spectacularly from forested hills, a turquoise gem on a bed of green velvet. The python god, who holds an important place in the rites of the Venda's matriarchal culture, is believed to live in the lake.

You can't visit the lake, 35km northwest of Thohoyandou, without permission from its custodians, the Netshiavha people. The easiest way to get permission is to hire a local guide such as **Beth Mashawana** (☎072 401 1832; greatnorthtours@hotmail.com; Thohoyandou). Remember that when you approach the lake you must do so with proper respect; turn your back to it, bend over, and view it from between your legs.

THE WATERBERG

The 150km-long Waterberg range, which makes up part of the Bushveld region, stretches northeast from Thabazimbi in southern Limpopo. Protected by a Unesco biosphere reserve the size of the Okavango Delta, it's a wild and inspirational place etched by rivers.

The rolling terrain of the Waterberg is ideal for exploring on horseback, and several operators and lodges near Vaalwater can set you up with a steed, typically charging R250 to R400 for a two- to three-hour ride. **Horizon Horseback Adventures** (☎014-755 4003; www.ridinginafrica.com) offers adventurous options including a four-day horse safari in the Dinaka Wildlife Reserve.

The mountainous **Marakele National Park** (☎014-777 1745; www.sanparks.org/parks/marakele; adult/child R88/44; 🕐7.30am-5pm May-Aug, to 4pm Sep-Apr) is at the southwestern end of the Waterberg Biosphere Reserve. Elephants, rhinos and many other large wildlife species call the park home, as do one of the world's largest

THOMAS KUBHAYI

Taking a break from sculpting in the shade of a marula tree, the Tsonga sculptor Thomas Kubhayi explains the traditional role of carving in local life.

'When you want a house, you are given cutting tools and carving tools and told to cut down a tree,' he says. 'The same tools are used to make spoons and plates – it is our heritage. Everyone is an artist and carving is the most important art.'

The 40-year-old's studio is full of allegorical woodcarvings that address African problems such as 'war and climate change, and people forgetting their stories, religions and beliefs'.

Kubhayi is also well known for the work he does with young people, and some accomplished pieces by his protégés are on display. 'Children must have vision – where they are going and where they come from. Old people may pass away, but we can keep our traditions going for a long time.'

As told to James Bainbridge.

colonies of the endangered Cape vulture and some imposing sandstone bluffs.

Regular cars can access much of the park, including the sky-high vulture-viewing point, as well as the hard-dirt Bakkers Pass Rd, which runs alongside the mountains from Vaalwater and offers spectacular views.

The **booking office** (7am-5.30pm) is on the Thabazimbi–Alma road, 3km northeast of the intersection with the Matlabas–Rooiberg road.

The park offers **tent sites** (2-person campsite R145, extra adult/child R48/24) and, at **Tlopi Tent Camp** (s & d R775, tr/q R919/1063), 15km from reception, furnished tents with bathroom and open-air kitchen.

THE EAST

Eastern Limpopo is a subtropical, culturally rich area, being the traditional home of the Tsonga-Shangaan and Lobedu peoples. Phalaborwa and Hoedspruit are handy access points to northern and central Kruger, and the latter is a gateway to the many private reserves bordering the park.

Magoebaskloof Pass

The Letaba Valley, east of Polokwane, is lush, with tea plantations and fruit farms overlooked by forested hills. At Haenertsburg, known locally as 'The Mountain', Rte 71 climbs northeast over the steep Magoebaskloof Pass. A less scenic route to Tzaneen is Rte 528, which runs along the gentler George's Valley.

Magoebaskloof is the escarpment on the edge of the highveld, and Rte 71 careers down to Tzaneen and the lowveld, winding through plantations and tracts of thick indigenous forest.

There are a number of waterfalls in the area, including the glorious **Debengeni Falls** (De Hoek State Forest; adult R10; 8am-5pm). Turn left off Rte 71 just after the sign saying 'Tzaneen 15km'.

There are 10 **walking trails** (013-754 2724; www.komatiecotourism.co.za) in the area, and six huts including some above Debengeni Falls. Two recommended options are the two-night, 21km **Debengeni Trail** and the three-night, 40km **Dokolewa Waterfall Trail.**

Some 10km northeast of Haenertsburg, the **Pot 'n Plow** (082 691 5790; Rte 71; pizza R40-55; lunch & dinner) is an essential stop for pizza (No 5's a must), pool and patter. If you get caught chatting, there's accommodation nearby at **Little Haven** (082-452 3708; http://tinyurl.com/n5af7p; s/d R180/360;).

Tzaneen & Around

015 / pop 81,000

Producing most of South Africa's mangoes and avocados, steamy Tzaneen is known as 'the fruit basket' – although one heat-fatigued local we spoke to gave up trying to remember the nickname and settled for 'the tropical place'. This is typical of the slow pace of life in the Letaba Valley's largest town, but you can shake off the stupor at some cool hideaways and quirky sights in the surrounding hills.

SIGHTS & ACTIVITIES

Kings Walden (015-307 3262; Agatha; admission R10; daylight), a 3-hectare formal English garden at 1050m, has Drakensberg views.

It takes 40 tree-huggers with outstretched arms to encircle the **Sunland Baobab** (015-309 9039; Sunland Nursery; adult/child R10/free; 9am-5pm), off the road from Modjadjiskloof/Duivelskloof to Modjadji.

The **Modjadji Nature Reserve** (082 393 5551; adult/vehicle R10/20; 7.30am-6pm) protects forests of ancient 'Modjadji palms' (cycads).

SLEEPING & EATING

Satvik Backpackers Village (015-307 3920; satvik@pixie.co.za; George's Valley Rd; campsites per person R50, dm/r/cottage R90/220/440) These cottages and rooms on a slope above a dam have views of wooded hills, a kitchen and a braai.

Kings Walden (015-307 3262; Agatha; www.kingswalden.co.za; s/d incl breakfast R415/830;) Rooms are available at this garden (see above).

Silver Palms Lodge (015-307 3092; Monument St; r from R435;) This good-value hotel has some pleasant touches such as marula-based shower gel in the smart rooms.

Highgrove Lodge (015-307 7242; Agatha St; mains R20-70; 7am-8.30pm) Highgrove serves dishes including steaks, seafood, pasta and hearty breakfasts, with a dining area on poolside terraces.

GETTING THERE & AWAY

Checkers (012-317 6104; Letaba Blvd shopping centre) sells tickets for the daily Translux buses to Phalaborwa (R100, one hour), and to Jo'burg (R190, 5½ hours) via Pretoria (R190, 4½ hours) and Polokwane (R110, 1¾ hours).

Glosure Shuttles (079-528 0621) runs between Tzaneen and Pretoria (R280, six hours) via Haenertsburg on Monday and Friday.

Most minibus taxis depart from the rank behind the Tzaneng Crossing Mall.

Phalaborwa

☎015 / pop 109,000

Phalaborwa is a stretch of suburban tidiness on the edge of Kruger, with a green belt in the centre and the occasional warthog grazing on a lawn. There's a range of sleeping options thanks to the town's proximity to the park.

Phalaborwa makes an ideal starting point if you're intending to explore central and northern Kruger. For people with limited time in South Africa, it is possible to visit Kruger by flying from Jo'burg to Phalaborwa (or Hoedspruit) and hiring a car at the airport. **Africa Unlimited** (☎015-781 7825; www.africaunltd.co.za) offers activities including astronomy safaris, river cruises, bush walks and Kruger trips.

Phalaborwa is also a gateway to Mozambique, as it's possible to drive across Kruger and into Mozambique via the **Giriyondo Gate** (☎013-735 8919) in a car with good clearance.

The **Fourscore viewpoint** (Selati Rd; 7am-7pm) overlooks the 'Big Hole', one of the planet's largest man-made holes. It's surprisingly exhilarating up there.

SLEEPING & EATING

Daan & Zena's (☎015-781 6049; www.daanzena.co.za; 15 Birkenhead St; s/d from R200/400;) Brought to life by lashings of colourful paint, this place is a tad crumbly, but it's a good spot if you're looking for a comfy bed and a youthful vibe.

Kaia Tani (☎015-781 1358; www.kaiatani.com; 29 Boekenhout St; s/d incl breakfast R350/640;) On one of Phalaborwa's leafy suburban streets, this 'exclusive guest house' has six rooms and a thatched bar-restaurant overlooking the rock swimming pool.

Mfubu Lodge (☎015-769 6252; www.mfubu.com; Grietjie Private Nature Reserve; half board per person R650-950;) At this small lodge 30km southwest of Phalaborwa, safari tents open onto a boardwalk with a prime view of crocodiles and hippos in the river below.

Buffalo Pub & Grill (☎015-781 0829; 1 Lekkerbreek St; mains R60-90; lunch & dinner;) If you've emerged from Kruger feeling like a hungry lion, stop here for some pub grub. There's a terrace for alfresco dining and African trimmings aplenty.

GETTING THERE & AWAY

Air

SAAirlink (☎015-781 5823; www.saairlink.co.za), with an office at the airport, flies daily to Jo'burg (R1000 to R1600). The airport is 2km north of town.

SA Express (☎015-793 3681; www.flysax.com) flies daily from **Hoedspruit Eastgate airport** (Rte 40) to Jo'burg (R1000 to R1400).

Bus

Sure Turn Key Travel (☎015-781 7761; Phalaborwa Mall, Nelson Mandela St) is the local agent for Translux/City to City. Translux connects Phalaborwa with Jo'burg (R220, seven hours) via Tzaneen, Polokwane and Pretoria; City to City travels to Jo'burg (R180, 9½ hours) via Middelburg.

CAR

Hiring a car is often the cheapest way of seeing Kruger. **Avis** (☎015-781 3169; www.avis.co.za), **Imperial** (☎082-566 2428; www.imperialcarrental.co.za), **Budget** (☎082-828 8837; www.budget.co.za), **National** (☎015-881 0376; www.nationalcar.com), **Hertz** (☎082-335 4754; www.hertz.co.za) and **First Car Rental** (☎015-781 1500; www.firstcarrental.co.za) have offices at the airport. The first three also have offices in Hoedspruit.

Minibus Taxi

There aren't many minibus taxis in this area, and most run from the township of Namakgale (R5, 20 minutes). From here, you can catch connections to Tzaneen (R35, 1½ hours).

SOUTH AFRICA DIRECTORY

ACCOMMODATION

Whatever your budget, you'll generally find high standards, often for significantly less than you would pay for the equivalent in Europe or North America. Prices for a double room in this chapter: budget less than R400, midrange R400 to R1000, top end more than R1000. In Cape Town and some other more expensive places on the south coast, these ranges move upward. Except as noted, prices in this chapter refer to rooms with bathroom, excluding breakfast and for high-season weekends.

The main budget options are camping, backpackers hostels, self-catering cottages and indigenous, community-run offerings including homestays. The main caveat is that

PRACTICALITIES

- South Africa uses the metric system for weights and measures.
- Access electricity (220V to 250V AC, 50Hz) with a three-pin adaptor (South Africa has its own unique version with large, round pins), which is easy enough to find. Upmarket accommodation sometimes has European-style sockets.
- Best weekly: *Mail & Guardian*. Best daily: the *Sowetan*. Others to look for: the *Sunday Independent;* the *Sunday Times;* the Johannesburg *Star;* and *Business Day*. Check out *Getaway* magazine for travel news.
- Tune the TV to SABC for the news (SABC3 is mostly English). M-Net offers US films and series; e-TV carries alternative programs.
- SABC radio broadcasts in 11 languages. BBC World Service is available on some FM and AM stations.

there aren't enough places in this category; away from tourist areas, sometimes the best budget option is camping.

Midrange accommodation is particularly good value, especially for B&Bs. Expect a private bathroom and a clean, comfortable room. Self-catering accommodation at national parks, usually in the midrange category, also tends to be good value.

At the top end, South Africa boasts some of the best wildlife lodges on the continent, as well as classic guest houses and superb hotels. Places at this level offer all the amenities you would expect for prices that are similar to, or slightly less than, those you would pay in Europe or North America.

There are significant seasonal price variations, with rates rising steeply during the December–January school break, and again around Easter, when room prices often double, and minimum stays are imposed. Expect prices during the 2010 World Cup (held in June and July) to be at the same level. Advance bookings are essential during these times. The other school holidays are also often classified as high season, although it's more common to have 'midseason' pricing. Conversely, you can get some excellent deals during the winter low season, which is also the best time for wildlife watching.

Minimum charges often apply at accommodation options in national parks and nature reserves, notably those run by Ezemvelo KNZ Wildlife, and at private reserves and lodges.

There have been cases of accommodation discriminating against black and coloured people. Establishments rated by the South African Grading Council can be stripped of their stars if found to be doing so. We urge travellers who experience racial discrimination to share their stories with both local tourism authorities and Lonely Planet.

ACTIVITIES

Thanks to South Africa's diverse terrain and favourable climate, almost anything is possible – from ostrich riding to the world's highest bungee jump. Good facilities and instruction mean that most activities are accessible to all, whatever their experience level.

There are dozens of operators. In addition to the ones listed here, ask other travellers and at hostels. Try to book day or overnight trips as close to your destination as possible.

Aerial Pursuits

Ideal weather conditions and an abundance of high points to launch yourself from make South Africa a fine destination for aerial pursuits. A helpful contact for getting started is the **Aero Club of South Africa** (☎ 0861-018 018; www.aeroclub.org.za).

South Africa is one of the world's best destinations for paragliding, particularly Cape Town's Table Mountain. **South African Hang Gliding & Paragliding Association** (☎ 012-668 1219; www.sahpa.co.za) can provide names of operators, and numerous schools offer courses for beginners. In Cape Town, try **Air Team** (☎ 082 257 0808; www.tandemparagliding.co.za).

Good places to float over the countryside in a hot-air balloon include Hazyview (p521) and the surrounding Mpumalanga area.

South Africa also boasts the world's highest bungee jump at Bloukrans River Bridge (p462), between Plettenberg Bay and Storms River.

Birdwatching

With its enormous diversity of habitats, South Africa is a paradise for birdwatchers. Top spots include the following:

Cape Peninsula & West Coast Cape of Good Hope, within Table Mountain National Park (p410), is excellent for seabird-watching, as is West Coast National Park (p451), about 120km to the north.

Kruger National Park (p513) One of the continent's best areas for birdwatching, especially the south and the far north; known for its raptors and migratory species.

Northern KwaZulu-Natal uMkhuze Game Reserve (p500) hosts more than 400 species; iSimangaliso Wetland Park (p498) protects one of Southern Africa's most significant water-bird breeding grounds.

Soutpansberg (p560) The mountain range attracts some 540 feathered species (55% of South Africa's species).

Canoeing, Kayaking & Rafting

South Africa has few major rivers, but the ones that do flow year-round offer rewarding canoeing and rafting. Popular ones include the Blyde and Sabie Rivers, both in Mpumalanga; the waterways around Wilderness (p444) and Wilderness National Park in the Western Cape; and the Senqu (Orange) River, especially through Augrabies Falls National Park (p458). There's some serene canoeing at the iSimangaliso Wetland Park (p498).

Rafting is highly rain-dependent, with the best months in most areas from December/January to April. Good contacts include **Felix Unite** (☎ 021-670 1300; www.felixunite.com), **Hardy Ventures** (☎ 013-751 1693; www.hardyventure.com) and **Intrapid** (☎ 072-900 0348; www.rafts a.co.za).

For sea kayaking, try the Cape Town–based **Coastal Kayak** (☎ 021-439 1134; www.kayak.co.za) and the **Sea Kayaking Association of South Africa** (☎ 021-790 5611; www.doorway.co.za /kayak/recskasa).

Diving

To the west, the main dive sites are around the Cape Peninsula, known for its wrecks and giant kelp forests. To the east, the main area is the KwaZulu-Natal north coast where – particularly around Sodwana Bay (probably the best choice for beginners) – there's some excellent warm-water diving with beautiful coral reefs and the chance to see dolphins and sometimes whale sharks. There are several sites off the Eastern Cape near Port Elizabeth, and many resort towns along the Garden Route have diving schools.

The best time to dive the KwaZulu-Natal shoreline is from May to September, when visibility tends to be highest. Along the Atlantic seaboard, the water is cold year-round, but at its most diveable, with many days of high visibility, between November and January/February.

With the exception of Sodwana Bay during the warmer months (when a 3mm wetsuit will be sufficient), you will need at least a 5mm wetsuit for many sites, and a drysuit for some sites to the south and west. Strong currents and often windy conditions mean advanced divers can find challenges all along the coast.

Hiking

South Africa is wonderful for hiking, with an excellent system of well-marked trails varied enough to suit every ability. Some trails have accommodation, from camping to simple huts with electricity and running water, and all must be booked well in advance; many have limits as to how many hikers can be on them at any one time. Most longer routes and wilderness areas require hikers to be in a group of at least three or four.

Some designated wilderness areas offer off-trail hiking. Little information is available on suggested routes, and it's up to you to survive on your own.

Ezemvelo KZN Wildlife (☎ 033-845 1000; www.kznwildlife.com) controls most trails in KwaZulu-Natal. Elsewhere, most trails are administered by **SAN Parks** (☎ 012-426 5000; www.sanparks.org) or the various Forest Region authorities. To find out about local hiking clubs, contact **Hiking South Africa** (☎ 083 535 4538; www.hiking-south-africa.info).

Shorter hikes, from an hour up to a full day, are possible almost everywhere and require no advance arrangements. Prime areas include the Cape Peninsula near Cape Point and the Drakensberg. It's also possible to take guided walks in many national parks, accompanied by armed rangers.

Hiking is possible year-round, although you'll need to be prepared in summer for extremes of wet and heat. The best time is March to October.

Kloofing (Canyoning)

Kloofing is a mix of climbing, hiking, swimming and some serious jumping. Places where you can try it include Cape Town and along the Drakensberg Escarpment in Mpumalanga. Companies that can sort you out include **Abseil Africa** (www.abseilafrica.co.za); there's an ele-

SOUTH AFRICA'S TOP HIKES

Following are some of South Africa's top hiking trails and their booking contacts; more details are given throughout the chapter.

Cape Peninsula & Western Cape

Hoerikwaggo Trail (Table Mountain National Park; ☎ 021-465 8515) Three two-day trails running 97km from Cape Point to Table Mountain's upper cable-car station (see p418).

Whale Route (De Hoop Nature Reserve) Five days of hiking along the coastline in De Hoop Nature Reserve, with the added bonus of whale-watching opportunities in season (see p437).

Eastern Cape

Otter Trail Five days on the coast at the end of the Garden Route (see p462; this trail is usually booked out, but there are cancellations).

Tsitsikamma Trail A two- to six-day hike running inland through the forests, parallel to the Otter Trail but walked in the opposite direction (see p462). Porterage is available.

Free State

Rhebok Hiking Trail (Golden Gate Highlands National Park) Two days among the park's sandstone outcrops, with some steep sections (see p552).

KwaZulu-Natal

Giant's Cup (Drakensberg) Five days in the southern Drakensberg. There are also wilderness trails and guided walks in Hluhluwe-iMfolozi, uMkhuze and iSimangaliso Wetland parks and reserves (see p508).

Mpumalanga & Limpopo

Hanglip Trail (Soutpansberg) Up to two days in Limpopo's verdant Soutpansberg range (see p560).

Blyde River Canyon Hiking Trail Two and a half days taking in Mpumalanga's spectacular 30km-long canyon (see p522).

Kruger National Park Wilderness trails and guided bush walks (see p517).

Northern Cape

Klipspringer Hiking Trail (Augrabies Falls National Park) Three days of stunning scenery along the Senqu (Orange) River (see p458).

Kodaspiek Trail (|Ai-|Ais/Richtersveld Transfrontier Park) Two days wandering amid incredible mountain desert landscapes (see p461).

ment of risk to the sport, so check operators' credentials carefully before signing up.

Mountain Biking

There are trails almost everywhere in South Africa. Some suggestions to get you started: De Hoop Nature Reserve (p437), with overnight and day trails; the ride up (and down) Sani Pass, on the South Africa–Lesotho border (p507); Citrusdal (p452), with a network of trails; Cederberg Wilderness Area (p451); and Knysna (p447) and the surrounding area, with a good selection of trails. Cape Town is an unofficial national hub for the activity.

Useful sources of information include **Mountain Bike South Africa** (www.mtbsa.co.za, www.mtb.org.za) and the bimonthly *Ride* (www.ride.co.za), South Africa's main mountain-biking magazine.

Rock Climbing

Some of the most challenging climbing is on the KwaZulu-Natal Drakensberg's close-to-sheer faces. The **South African Climbing Info Network** (www.saclimb.co.za) has listings and photos of many climbing and bouldering sites. For information on regional clubs, contact the **Mountain Club of South Africa** (MCSA; ☎ 021-465 3412; www.mcsa.org.za). **Roc-n-Rope** (☎ 013-257 0363; www.rocrope.com) is another useful contact.

Surfing

Most surfers will have heard of Jeffrey's Bay, but South Africa offers myriad alternatives, particularly along the Eastern Cape coast from Port Alfred northeastwards. The best time of the year for surfing the southern and eastern coasts is autumn and early winter (from about April to July).

For more information check out www.wavescape.co.za and *Zig Zag* (www.zigzag.co.za), South Africa's main surf magazine.

Whale Watching

South Africa is considered one of the world's best spots to sight whales without boarding a boat. Southern right and humpback whales are regularly seen offshore between June/July and November, with occasional spottings of Bryde's and killer whales. Hermanus (p436), where southern right whales come to calve, is the country's whale-watching capital, complete with a whale crier and an annual whale festival.

Other favoured spots include the False Bay shoreline, especially between Cape Point and Muizenberg, and from Gordon's Bay southeast; and Mossel (p442) and Plettenberg (p448) Bays. The whales continue their progress around the Cape and up the KwaZulu-Natal coast, where the cliffs north of Durban and iSimangaliso Wetland Park are good places to spot them.

Wildlife Watching

South Africa's populations of large animals are one of its biggest attractions. In comparison with some nearby countries such as Botswana and Zambia, wildlife watching here tends to be very accessible, with good roads and accommodation for all categories of traveller. It is also comparatively inexpensive, although there are plenty of pricier choices for those seeking a luxury experience in the bush.

BOOKS

Following is a listing of some books – mostly nonfiction – to begin immersing yourself in South African life and culture.

Khayelitsha by white journalist Steven Otter describes living in Cape Town's famous township and confronting his own preconceptions.

In *Beyond the Miracle: Inside the New South Africa*, the distinguished journalist and campaigner Allister Sparks follows his earlier two tomes on apartheid and its aftermath.

Long Walk to Freedom by Nelson Mandela – Madiba's superb and inspirational autobiography – is a good way to prepare for a South African trip.

Country of my Skull is prominent Afrikaaner journalist Antjie Krog's wrenching account of the Truth & Reconciliation Commission hearings.

No Future Without Forgiveness by Desmond Tutu is another, somewhat more hope-filled, chronicling of the work of the Truth & Reconciliation Commission by its chairman.

Indaba, My Children by Credo Mutwa is an excellent compendium of traditional mythology and folktales.

The Whale Caller, a recent novel by Zakes Mda, the acclaimed author of *Ways of Dying*, takes a sceptical look at the new South Africa.

BUSINESS HOURS

Opening hours in South Africa generally follow those listed on the inside front cover, with a few variations. In addition to regular banking hours, many foreign-exchange bureaus remain open until 5pm Monday to Friday, and until noon on Saturday. Shops open until 1pm on Saturday and, in urban areas, supermarkets often open from 9am to noon on Sunday. If a cafe or restaurant has a closing day, it's usually Sunday or Monday. Exceptions have been noted in individual listings.

CHILDREN

South Africa is an eminently suitable destination for travelling with children. With its abundance of national parks, beaches, swimming pools and hiking trails, plus a good collection of museums and a handful of amusement parks, it offers plenty to do for travellers of all ages in a generally hazard-free setting. Most South Africans are welcoming to children, and you should have no shortage of offers for assistance. For some help organising things, and for equipment rental or purchase, try the Cape Town–based **Tiny Tourists** (www.tinytourists.com).

COURSES

Language

There are numerous language schools for learning Xhosa, Zulu and Afrikaans, including the following:

Interlink Cape Town (☎ 021-439 9834; www.interlink.co.za) Afrikaans, Xhosa.

Language Teaching Centre Cape Town (☎ 021-425 0019; www.languageteachingcentre.co.za) Xhosa, Zulu.

University of KwaZulu-Natal (☎ 031-260 2510; www.nu.ac.za/department/default.asp?dept=zuludund; Durban) Zulu.

University of the Witwatersrand (☎ 011-717 4206; www.witslanguageschool.com/aae.aspx; Jo'burg) Afrikaans, Zulu.

A good contact if you want to get beneath South Africa's surface is **TALK** (Transfer of African Language Knowledge; ☎ 011-487 1798; www.phaphama.org). It organises 'immersion visits' in which you live in a homestay arrangement in either a township or rural area while receiving an hour or so daily of instruction in an African language. The main focus is Soweto, but visits can be arranged in other parts of the country.

Other Courses

Bead Merchants of Africa (☎ 021-423 4687; www.beadmerchantsofafrica.com; Cape Town) Beadwork classes.

Cape Wine Academy (☎ 021-889 8844; www.capewineacademy.co.za; Stellenbosch & Cape Town) Wine-tasting courses.

EcoTraining (☎ 013-745 7777; www.ecotraining.co.za; Kruger National Park) Field-guide training and courses in birding and wildlife photography.

CUSTOMS REGULATIONS

You're permitted to bring 1L of spirits, 2L of wine, 200 cigarettes and up to R3000 worth of goods into South Africa without paying duties. The import and export of protected animal products such as ivory is not permitted. Visit www.southafrica.info/travel/advice/redtape.htm for more information.

DANGERS & ANNOYANCES

Crime is the national obsession and, apart from car accidents, it's the major risk that you'll face in South Africa. However, try to keep things in perspective, and remember that despite the statistics and newspaper headlines, the majority of travellers visit the country without incident.

The risks are highest in Jo'burg, followed by some townships and other urban centres. Daylight muggings are common in certain sections of Jo'burg, and the city's metro train system has a problem with violent crime.

See p747 for more advice. No matter where you are, you can minimise the risks by following basic safety precautions, including the following:

- If arriving at OR Tambo International Airport (Jo'burg) keep valuables in your hand luggage and/or vacuum-wrap your baggage, as items are sometimes pilfered from bags before they reach the carousel.
- One of the greatest dangers during muggings or carjackings, especially in Jo'burg, is that your assailants will assume you are armed, and that you will kill them if you get a chance. Stay calm, and don't resist or give them any reason to think you will fight back.
- Listen to local advice on unsafe areas.
- Avoid deserted areas day and night, and especially avoid the commercial business district areas of larger cities at night and weekends.
- If you're going to visit a township – and it will certainly be one of the highlights of your visit to South Africa – go with a trusted guide or as part of a tour.
- If you get a failed transaction or anything irregular happens while making a payment with a card, retrieve your card as quickly as possible and do not try the procedure again.

EMBASSIES & CONSULATES

Most countries have their main embassy in Pretoria, with an office or consulate in Cape Town (which becomes the official embassy during Cape Town's parliamentary sessions). Some countries also maintain consulates in Jo'burg and in Durban.

South Africa is a gold mine for travellers hunting for visas for other African countries.

The following list includes some of the more important embassies and consulates; most are open in the mornings only for visa applications, usually between 9am and noon. For more foreign missions in South Africa see www.dfa.gov.za/foreign/forrep/index.htm; for South African missions abroad visit www.dfa.gov.za/foreign/sa_abroad/index.htm.

Australia embassy in Pretoria (Map pp540–1; ☎ 012-423 6000; www.australia.co.za; 292 Orient St, Arcadia)

Botswana high commission in Pretoria (Map pp540–1; ☎ 012-430 9640; 24 Amos St, Colbyn); Cape Town (Map pp412–13; ☎ 021-421 1045; 13th fl, Metropolitan Centre, City Bowl); Jo'burg (Map p531; ☎ 011-403 3748; 2nd fl, Future Bank Bldg, 122 De Korte St, Braamfontein)

Canada high commission in Pretoria (Map pp540–1; ☎ 012- 422 3000; www.dfait-maeci.gc.ca/southafrica; 1103 Arcadia St, Hatfield)

France embassy in Pretoria (Map pp540–1; ☎ 012-425 1600; france@ambafrance-rsa.org; 250 Melk St, New

Muckleneuk); Cape Town (Map pp412–13; ☎ 021-423 1575; www.consulfrance-lecap.org; 78 Queen Victoria St Gardens); Jo'burg (Map pp528–9; ☎ 011-778 5600; 191 Jan Smuts Ave, Rosebank)

Germany embassy in Pretoria (Map pp540–1; ☎ 012-427 8900; www.pretoria.diplo.de; 180 Blackwood St, Arcadia); Cape Town (Map pp412–13; ☎ 021-405 3000; www.kapstadt.diplo.de; 19th fl, Triangle House, 22 Riebeeck St, City Bowl)

Ireland embassy in Pretoria (Map pp540–1; ☎ 012-342 5062; 1st fl, Southern Life Plaza, 1059 Schoeman St)

Lesotho high commission in Pretoria (Map pp540–1; ☎ 012-460 7648; 391 Anderson St, Menlo Park); Durban (Map pp486-7; ☎ 031-307 2168; 2nd fl, Westguard House, cnr West & Gardiner Sts); Jo'burg (Map p531; ☎ 011-339 3653; 76 Juta St, Indent House, Braamfontein)

Mozambique high commission in Pretoria (Map pp540–1; ☎ 012-401 0300; 529 Edmond St, Arcadia); Cape Town (Map pp412–13; ☎ 021-426 2944; 10th fl, Pinnacle Bldg, 8 Burg St, City Bowl); Durban (Map pp486-7; ☎ 031-304 0200; Room 520, 320 West St); Jo'burg (☎ 011-336 1819; 18 Hurlinghum Rd, Illovo); Nelspruit (Map p519; ☎ 013-752 7396; 43 Brown St)

Namibia high commission in Pretoria (Map pp540–1; ☎ 012-481 9118; www.namibia.org.na; 197 Blackwood St, Arcadia, Pretoria)

Netherlands embassy in Pretoria (Map pp540–1; ☎ 012-425 4500; www.dutchembassy.co.za; 210 Queen Wilhelmina Ave, New Muckleneuk); Cape Town (Map pp412–13; ☎ 021-421 5660; www.dutchconsulate.co.za; 100 Strand St, City Bowl)

New Zealand embassy in Pretoria (Map pp540–1; ☎ 012-342 8656; Block C, Hatfield Gardens, 1110 Arcadia St)

Swaziland high commission in Pretoria (Map pp540–1; ☎ 012-344 1910; 715 Government Ave, Arcadia); Jo'burg (Map p531; ☎ 403 7372, 403 2036; 6th fl, Braamfontein Centre, 23 Jorissen St)

UK high commission in Pretoria (Map pp540–1; ☎ 012-421 7600; http://ukinsouthafrica.fco.gov.uk; 255 Hill St, Arcadia); Cape Town (Map pp412–13; ☎ 021-405 2400; Southern Life Centre, 8 Riebeeck St, City Bowl); Durban (Map pp486-7; ☎ 031-572 7259; FWJK Court, 86 Armstrong Rd, La Lucia Ridge)

USA embassy in Pretoria (Map pp540–1; ☎ 012-431 4000; http://southafrica.usembassy.gov; 877 Pretorius St, Arcadia); Cape Town (Map pp404–5; ☎ 021-702 7300; 2 Reddam Ave, Westlake); Durban (☎ 031-304 4737; 29th fl, Durban Bay House, 333 Smith St); Jo'burg (☎ 011-644 8000; 1 River St, Killarney)

Zimbabwe high commission in Pretoria (Map pp540–1; ☎ 012-342 5125; zimpret@lantic.net; 798 Merton St, Arcadia); Jo'burg (Map p531; ☎ 011-838 2156; admin@zimbabweconsulate.co.za; 17th fl, 20 Anderson St)

FESTIVALS & EVENTS

South Africa hosts dozens of festivals, and there's always something going on somewhere in the country. For more events, see our destination sections and the websites www.safrica.info/plan_trip/holiday/culture_heritage/festivals.htm and www.festivals.co.za.

January

Kaapse Klopse (Cape Minstrel Carnival) Cape Town's most colourful street party runs for a month from early January, with ribald song and dance parades, costumes, floats and general revelry. It's followed by a grand parade to mark the opening of parliament.

February

Kavadi Festival The major Hindu festival, held twice annually (January/February and April/May) in Durban, in honour of the Hindu god Muruga. It's accompanied by body piercing with skewers as a sign of devotion.

March

Cape Argus Cycle Tour (www.cycletour.co.za) Held in the second week of March, this spin around the Cape Peninsula is the world's largest bicycle race, with more than 30,000 entries.

Absa Klein Karoo National Arts Festival (www.absakknk.co.za) Enjoy all things Afrikaans at this festival that aims to seek unity between Afrikaans speakers of all races; held in Oudtshoorn (Western Cape) in late March/early April.

April

Splashy Fen Music Festival (www.splashyfen.co.za) Rock, pop and jazz with a fringe; held in early April at Splashy Fen Farm, about 20km north of Underberg in the foothills of the southern Drakensberg.

June

National Arts Festival (www.nafest.co.za) Get in touch with South Africa's creative pulse at the country's largest arts festival, held from late June to early July at Grahamstown (Eastern Cape).

November

Afrika Burns (www.afrikaburns.com) A subcultural blowout and a survivalist challenge, 'the Burn' brings art installations and themed camps to the Karoo, between Worcester and Calvinia.

Diwali The Durban Indian community's three-day Festival of Lights.

HOLIDAYS

New Year's Day 1 January
Human Rights Day 21 March
Good Friday March/April

Easter Sunday March/April
Easter Monday March/April
Family Day 17 April
Constitution or Freedom Day 27 April
Workers' Day 1 May
Youth Day 16 June
Women's Day 9 August
Heritage Day 24 September
Day of Reconciliation 16 December
Christmas Day 25 December
Day of Goodwill 26 December

School Holidays

South Africa's major holiday periods are the December–January school holidays and the Easter break. Many shops and businesses close, accommodation in national parks and tourist areas is fully booked and high-season prices are charged. At the beginning and end of these holiday periods, public transport fills up, as do seats on domestic and international flights, and you'll likely encounter long queues at popular border crossings.

The situation is similar during other school holidays, but not as intense. During these times, accommodation prices often increase, but not by as much.

The provinces stagger their school holidays. They are approximately late March to early April (varying, depending when Easter is); late June to mid-July; late September to early October; and early December to mid-January. For exact dates, see www.saschools.co.za.

INTERNET ACCESS

Internet access is widely available in South Africa. Accommodation options often offer access and there are internet cafes in major towns and, sometimes, smaller locations. Costs average R30 to R40 per hour. Many accommodation options, cafes and eateries (including chains such as Ocean Basket) have wi-fi, often for free. Branches of PostNet, found nationwide, normally have a few terminals.

MAPS

Some good maps are Map Studio's *Tourist Map* (1:2,500,000) and the Automobile Association of South Africa (AASA) series of maps covering the country. **Map Studio** (www.mapstudio.co.za) is a good place to look for these, with branches in Cape Town and Jo'burg. CNA bookshops also usually stock a good selection of road atlases.

For hiking done away from established trails, a topographical map is highly recommended. Government maps are available from **Maps Direct** (☎ 012-663 9345; www.mapoffice.co.za; cnr John Vorster St & Lenchen Dr North, Centurion, Jo'burg). Drakensberg maps – essential if you plan on hiking there – are available from Ezemvelo KZN Wildlife (p566).

MONEY

South Africa's currency is the rand (R), which is divided into 100 cents. The coins are one, two, five, 10, 20 and 50 cents, and R1, R2 and R5. The notes are R10, R20, R50, R100 and R200. There have been forgeries of the R200 note and some businesses are reluctant to accept them.

Although the value of the rand has fluctuated wildly in recent years, travelling in South Africa is still less expensive than in Western Europe and North America.

The best currencies to bring are US dollars, euros or British pounds in a mixture of cash and travellers cheques, plus a Visa or MasterCard for withdrawing money from ATMs.

Because South Africa has a reputation for scams, many banks abroad automatically prevent transactions in the country. Particularly if you plan to use a credit card in South Africa, contact your bank before leaving home and inform it of your travel plans.

ATMs

ATMs are widespread, both in the cities and beyond, but stash some cash if visiting rural areas. For safety precautions see p569.

Credit Cards

These are widely accepted, especially MasterCard and Visa, and can also be used at many ATMs. Nedbank is an official Visa agent and Standard Bank is a MasterCard agent; both have branches nationwide.

Moneychangers

Cash is readily exchanged at banks (First National, Nedbank and Standard Bank are usually the best) and foreign-exchange bureaus in all major cities.

Most banks change travellers cheques in major currencies with varying commissions. Nedbank and Absa are associated with American Express, and First National Bank and Nedbank are associated with Visa.

Thomas Cook has travellers cheques in rand, though it works out best in the end to buy US dollar cheques.

The Thomas Cook agent in South Africa is the Rennies Travel chain of travel agencies, and there are American Express offices in major cities. Neither charges a commission for its own travellers cheques, though you'll usually get a higher rate of exchange from a bank. Rennies also changes other travellers cheques without fees.

Keep at least some of your exchange receipts as you'll need these to reconvert leftover rand when you leave.

Taxes & Refunds

South Africa has a value-added tax (VAT) of 14%, but departing foreign visitors can reclaim much of this on goods being taken out of the country. To make a claim, the goods' total value must exceed R250; visit www.taxrefunds.co.za for more information.

Tipping

Wages are low, and tipping is expected; around 10% to 15% is usual in tourist areas.

POST

Post offices are open from 8.30am to 4.30pm Monday to Friday and 8am to noon Saturday. For mailing anything of value consider using a private mail service such as PostNet.

TELEPHONE

South Africa has good telephone facilities. Local calls are inexpensive (about R1 for three minutes), whereas domestic long-distance calls (from about R2 per minute) and international calls (from R7 per minute to Europe) are pricier. Phonecards are widely available. There are also private phone centres where you can pay cash for your call, but at double the rate of public phones. These are recommended for quick local calls, as are the phones you see on tables in the street. International calls are cheaper between 8pm and 8am Monday to Friday, and over the weekend. For reverse-charge calls, dial ☎ 0900.

PHONE CODES

South Africa's country code is ☎ 27. To make an international call from South Africa, dial ☎ 00, followed by the country code, local area code (without the initial zero) and telephone number.

Telephone numbers in South Africa are 10 digits, including the local area code, which must always be dialled. There are also several four-digit nationwide prefixes (for use within South Africa only) followed by six-digit numbers. These prefixes include ☎ 0800 (toll free), ☎ 0860 (charged as a local call), and ☎ 0861 (flat-rate calls).

MOBILE PHONES

The mobile-phone network covers most of the country, and there are GSM and 3G digital networks.

The major mobile networks are **Vodacom** (www.vodacom.co.za), **MTN** (www.mtn.co.za), **Cell C** (www.cellc.co.za) and **Virgin Mobile** (www.virginmobile.co.za). Hiring a mobile phone is relatively inexpensive, but call charges average about R2.50 per minute. A cheaper alternative is to bring your own phone (check ahead that it's compatible) and insert a local SIM card. These cards are widely available in cities and larger towns, and tend to be more expensive in airport shops.

The main codes for mobile phones are ☎ 082 (Vodacom), ☎ 083 (MTN) and ☎ 084 (Cell C); ☎ 07 numbers are also in use as more customers join the networks.

TOURIST INFORMATION

The main government tourism organisation is **South African Tourism** (☎ 011-895 3000, 083 123 6789; www.southafrica.net), which has a helpful website with news of upcoming events and links.

For more details on individual provinces, there are provincial tourism organisations, of varying quality. Additionally, almost every town in the country has a tourist office – often private entities, surviving on commissions (5% is usually built into their hotel rates). Many will only recommend the services of paid-up member organisations, and staff is often badly informed, so asking your accommodation for assistance may prove more useful.

Provincial tourist offices include the following:

Eastern Cape Tourism Board (☎ 043-701 9600; www.ectourism.co.za)

Free State Tourism Board (☎ 051-447 1362; www.dteea.fs.gov.za)

Gauteng Tourism Authority (☎ 011-639 1600; www.gauteng.net)

KwaZulu-Natal Tourism Authority (☎ 031-366 7500; www.kzn.org.za)

Limpopo Tourism Board (☎ 015-290 7300, 0860 730 730; www.golimpopo.com)

Mpumalanga Tourism Authority (☎ 013-759 5300; www.mpumalanga.com)
Northern Cape Tourism Authority (☎ 053-832 2657; www.northerncape.org.za)
North-West Province Parks & Tourism Board (☎ 018-397 1500, 0861-111 866; www.tourism northwest.co.za)
Western Cape Tourism Board (☎ 021-426 5639; www.tourismcapetown.co.za)

TRAVELLERS WITH DISABILITIES

South Africa is one of the best destinations on the continent for disabled travellers, with an ever-expanding network of facilities catering to those who are mobility impaired or blind. **SAN Parks** (☎ 012-426 5000; www.sanparks.org) has a detailed and inspirational overview of accommodation and trail accessibility for the mobility impaired at all its parks.

Another helpful initial contact is the **National Council for Persons with Physical Disabilities in South Africa** (☎ 011-726 8040; www.ncppds a.org.za).

VISAS

Visitors on holiday from most Commonwealth countries (including Australia and the UK), most Western European countries, Japan and the USA don't require visas. Instead, you'll be issued with a free entry permit on arrival, valid for a stay of up to 90 days. Your passport must be valid for at least 30 days after the end of your intended visit.

If you aren't entitled to an entry permit, you'll need to get a visa (R425 or US$47 or €43) before you arrive. These aren't issued at the borders, and must be obtained at a South African embassy or consulate, found in most countries. Allow at least a month for processing; for more information, visit the **Department of Home Affairs** (www.home-aff airs.gov.za).

VISA EXTENSIONS

Applications for extensions to visas or entry permits should be made at the Department of Home Affairs, which has branches in Cape Town, Durban, Jo'burg and Pretoria.

VOLUNTEERING

Volunteer work is possible, especially if you're interested in teaching or wildlife conservation. A good starting point is **Volunteer Abroad** (www.volunteerabroad.com), with extensive listings of opportunities in the country.

Unless you have a UK passport, anyone coming to South Africa to do volunteer work needs to get a work permit. Applications for these should be made through the South African embassy or consulate in your home country; allow at least one month.

TRANSPORT IN SOUTH AFRICA

GETTING THERE & AWAY

Entering South Africa

Once you have an entry permit or visa, entering South Africa is straightforward and hassle-free. Travellers arriving by air are sometimes required to show an onward ticket – preferably an air ticket, though an overland ticket also seems to be acceptable.

If you're coming to South Africa after travelling through the yellow-fever zone in Africa (which includes most of East, West and central Africa) or South America, you must have an international vaccination certificate against yellow fever. No other vaccinations are mandatory, although there are some you should consider (see p769).

Air

AIRPORTS & AIRLINES

The major air hub for South Africa, and for the surrounding region, is Jo'burg's **OR Tambo International Airport** (ORTIA; ☎ 011-921 6911; www.airports.co.za). It has a full range of shops, restaurants, internet access, ATMs, foreign-exchange bureaus, reliable 24-hour luggage storage, and mobile-phone and car-hire outlets.

Cape Town International Airport (CPT; ☎ 021-937 1200; www.airports.co.za) receives many direct flights from Europe, and is becoming an increasingly important gateway. It has a foreign-exchange bureau, and mobile-phone and car-hire outlets.

Durban International Airport (DUR; ☎ 031-451 6666; www.airports.co.za), set to be replaced by **King Shaka International Airport** (☎ 011-921 6262; www.airports.co.za), handles several regional flights; as does **Mpumalanga Kruger International Airport** (MQP; ☎ 013-753 7500; www.kmiairport.co.za) near Nelspruit and Kruger National Park.

National airline **South African Airways** (SAA; airline code SA; ☎ 0861-359 722, 011-978 5313; www .flysaa.com; hub ORTIA) has an excellent route network and safety record. In addition to its international routes, it operates regional flights together with its subsidiaries **SAAirlink** (☎ 011-961 1700; www.saairlink.co.za) and **SA Express** (☎ 011-978 9900; www.flys ax.com).

Some other international carriers flying to/from Jo'burg (except as noted):

Air France (AF; ☎ 0861-340 340; www.airfrance.co.za) Hub: Paris.

Air Mauritius (MK; www.airmauritius.com) Cape Town (☎ 021-934 5506); Jo'burg (☎ 011-262 7100) Hub: SSR Airport, Mauritius. Also serves Cape Town.

British Airways (BA; www.britishairways.com) Cape Town (☎ 021-936 9000); Jo'burg (☎ 011-441 8400) Hub: London. Also serves Cape Town.

Cathay Pacific (CX; ☎ 011-700 8900; www.cathay pacific.com) Hub: Hong Kong Airport.

Egyptair (MS; www.egyptair.com.eg) Cape Town (☎ 021-390 2202); Jo'burg (☎ 011-880 4360) Hub: Cairo.

Emirates Airlines (EK; ☎ 0861-364 728, 011-303 1951; www.emirates.com) Hub: Dubai.

Kenya Airways (KQ; ☎ 011-571 8832, 011-928 8529; www.kenya-airways.com) Hub: Nairobi.

KLM (KL; ☎ 0860-247 747, 011-881 9696; www.klm .com) Hub: Amsterdam. Also serves Cape Town.

LTU International Airways (LT; ☎ 0800-981 393; www.ltu.de) Hub: Düsseldorf. Only serves Cape Town.

Lufthansa (LH; ☎ 0861-842 538; www.lufthansa.com) Hub: Frankfurt. Also serves Cape Town.

Malaysia Airlines (MH; www.malaysiaairlines.com) Cape Town (☎ 021-419 8010); Jo'burg (☎ 011-880 9614) Hub: Kuala Lumpur. Also serves Cape Town.

Qantas (QF; ☎ 011-441 8550; www.qantas.com.au) Hub: Sydney.

Qatar Airways (QR; www.qatarairways.com) Cape Town (☎ 021-425 3663); Jo'burg (☎ 011-523 2928) Hub: Doha. Also serves Cape Town.

Singapore Airlines (SQ; www.singaporeair.com) Cape Town (☎ 021-674 0601); Jo'burg (☎ 011-880 8560) Hub: Singapore. Also serves Cape Town.

Swiss International Airlines (LX; ☎ 0860-040 506; www.swiss.com) Hub: Zurich.

Virgin Atlantic (VS; ☎ 011-340 3400; www.virgin -atlantic.com) Hub: London. Also serves Cape Town.

Bicycle

There are no restrictions on bringing your own bicycle into South Africa. Two helpful sources of information are the **International Bicycle Fund** (☎ in the USA 206-767 0848; www.ibike .org) and **Cycling SA** (http://cms.cy clingsa.com).

Border Crossings

BOTSWANA

There are 18 official South Africa–Botswana border crossings. All are open between 8am and 4pm, and many have longer hours.

Grobler's Bridge (🕑 8am-6pm) Northwest of Polokwane/Pietersburg.

Kopfontein/Tlokweng Gate (🕑 7am-midnight) North of Zeerust; a main border crossing.

McCarthy's Rest (🕑 8am-4.30pm) Near Kgalagadi Transfrontier Park.

Pont Drift (🕑 8am-4pm) Convenient for Mapungubwe National Park (Limpopo) and Tuli Block (Botswana).

Ramatlabama (🕑 6am-8pm) North of Mafikeng; a main border crossing.

Skilpadshek/Pioneer Gate (🕑 6am-10pm) Northwest of Zeerust; a main border crossing.

Some of the more remote crossings are impassable to 2WD vehicles, and may be closed during periods of high water. Otherwise, the crossings are hassle-free.

By Bus

From Jo'burg/Pretoria, **Intercape** (☎ 0861-287 287; www.intercape.co.za) runs daily buses to Gaborone (from R170, 6¾ hours). A less safe and comfortable alternative is one of the minibuses that run throughout the day between Jo'burg and Gaborone (about R200, 6¾ hours) via Mafikeng (North-West Province). These leave from the main bus station in Gabarone, starting at about 6am. In Jo'burg, departures are from Park Station. To do the trip in stages, take a bus from Jo'burg to Mafikeng, from where there are direct minibuses over the border to Lobatse (1½ hours) and Gabarone (2½ hours). There are also direct minibuses between Jo'burg and Palapye (Botswana) via Martin's Drift (eight hours).

LESOTHO

All of Lesotho's borders are with South Africa and are straightforward to cross. The main crossing is at Maseru Bridge, east of Bloemfontein; queues here are often very long exiting Lesotho and, on some weekend evenings, coming into Lesotho.

By Bus

Big Sky Coaches (www.bigskycoaches.co.za) runs daily buses between Bloemfontein and Maseru Bridge (R40, three hours), with express weekend services. Tickets are sold at the Big

Sky booths at Bloemfontein's Central Park, and on the bus at Maseru Bridge.

Via minibus taxi, the quickest connections are from Bloemfontein to Botshabelo (Mtabelo; R35, one hour), and then from there to Maseru (R20, 1½ hours). There are also at least three buses weekly between Jo'burg and Maseru (six to seven hours), and daily minibus taxis between both Jo'burg and Ladybrand (16km from the Maseru Bridge border crossing) and Maseru. All these routes will bring you into Maseru coming from South Africa; leaving Maseru, you'll need to go to the South Africa side of Maseru Bridge.

Other useful connections include a daily minibus taxi between Mokhotlong (Lesotho) and Underberg (South Africa) via Sani Pass; and several minibus taxis daily between Qacha's Nek (Lesotho) and Matatiele (South Africa; about R20, 45 minutes). If you're travelling between Jo'burg and northern Lesotho, take a minibus taxi to Ficksburg, cross the border, and then get a minibus taxi on to Butha-Buthe and points north. There are sometimes direct taxis between Jo'burg and Butha-Buthe via the Caledonspoort border crossing (about R135, five hours).

By Car & Motorcycle

The easiest entry points for car and motorcycle are on the northern and western sides of the country. Most of the entry points to the south and east are unpaved, though most are possible in a 2WD; there is now a good sealed road running westwards from Qacha's Nek. You'll need a 4WD to enter and exit Lesotho via Sani Pass.

MOZAMBIQUE

The South Africa–Mozambique border crossings include the following:

Giriyondo (🕒 8am-4pm Oct-Mar, to 3pm Apr-Sep) Between Kruger National Park's Phalaborwa Gate and Massingir (Mozambique).

Komatipoort/Ressano Garcia (🕒 6am-10pm) East of Nelspruit, with fast-track visa processing and, during holiday periods, 24-hour opening.

Kosi Bay/Ponta d'Ouro (🕒 8am-4pm) On the coast, well north of Durban.

Pafuri (🕒 8am-4pm) In Kruger National Park's north-eastern corner.

By Bus

Several large 'luxury' buses run daily between Jo'burg/Pretoria and Maputo via Nelspruit and Komatipoort (R180 to R300, eight to nine hours), including the following:

Greyhound (☎ 083 915 9000; www.greyhound.co.za)
Intercape (☎ 0861-287 287; www.intercape.co.za)
Translux (☎ 011-774 3333; www.translux.co.za)

Intercape also has a weekly service from Durban to Maputo (R210), via Stranger and Empangeni in KwaZulu-Natal, and Swaziland. It leaves Durban on Sunday, Tuesday and Thursday, returning the following days.

Alternatively, the Baz Bus (see p578) links Jo'burg/Pretoria, Nelspruit and Durban with Mbabane (Swaziland), from where you can get a minibus taxi to Maputo.

Daily minibuses depart from Maputo in the morning for the Namaacha/Lomahasha post on the Swazi border (US$3, 1¾ hours), with some continuing to Manzini (US$5, 3¼ hours).

By Car & Motorcycle

For travel to/from Mozambique via the Kosi Bay border, you'll need your own vehicle (4WD is necessary on the Mozambique side). Alternatively, most places to stay in Ponta d'Ouro (Mozambique) do transfers for about US$20. Hitching between the border and Ponta d'Ouro is easy at weekends and during South African school holidays.

There's a good sealed toll road connecting Jo'burg with Maputo via Ressano Garcia, with tolls on the South African side between Middelburg and Witbank, at Machadodorp and 45km east of Nelspruit.

By Train

Shosholoza Meyl (☎ 0860-008 888, 011-774 4555; www.shosholozameyl.co.za) runs a daily (except Saturday) trans-Karoo tourist-class train linking Jo'burg with Komatipoort via Pretoria and Nelspruit (economy class only, 11 hours). Trains in both directions travel overnight. Once at Komatipoort, you can change to the Mozambican train to Maputo (economy class only, five hours), but it's much quicker to take a minibus (1½ hours). If you take the train the whole way, you'll need to buy the ticket for the Mozambique section at the border.

NAMIBIA

South Africa–Namibia border crossings include those at Nakop/Ariamsvlei (24 hours) west of Upington; at Vioolsdrif/Noordoewer (24 hours) north of Springbok and en route to/from Cape Town; and at Rietfontein/Aroab (8am to 4.30pm) just south of Kgalagadi Transfrontier Park. There's also a border crossing at Alexander Bay/Oranjemund (6am to 10pm) on the coast, but public access is usually not permitted. Namibian visas are not available at any of these border crossings. Nationals of most countries don't require a visa (see p382), but you can pick one up at the high commission in Pretoria (p570) or Namibia Tourism in Cape Town (p381).

By Bus

Intercape (☎ 0861-287 287, 021-380 4400; www.intercape.co.za) runs between Cape Town and Windhoek (from R540, 21 hours) via Springbok on Tuesday, Thursday, Friday and Sunday.

By Train

The **Trans-Namib** (☎ in Namibia 061-298 2657; www.transnamib.com.na/Starline.htm) 'StarLine' train runs twice-weekly between Upington and Keetmanshoop (12½ hours), 12 hours southeast of Windhoek by train. Trains depart from Keetmanshoop at 8.50am; from Upington, trains depart at 5am.

SWAZILAND

There are 11 South Africa–Swaziland border crossings, all of which are hassle-free. Note that small posts close at 4pm. The busiest crossing (and a good place to pick up lifts) is at Oshoek/Ngwenya (open 7am to 10pm) approximately 360km southeast of Pretoria. Some others include the following:

Golela/Lavumisa (🕒 7am-10pm) En route between Durban and Swaziland's Ezulwini Valley.

Josefsdal/Bulembu (🕒 8am-4pm) Between Piggs Peak and Barberton (Mpumalanga); can be tricky in wet weather.

Mahamba (🕒 7am-10pm) The best crossing to use from Piet Retief (Mpumalanga).

Mananga (🕒 7am-6pm) Southwest of Komatipoort (Mpumalanga).

Matsamo/Jeppe's Reef (🕒 7am-8pm) Southwest of Malelane (Mpumalanga) and a possible route to Kruger National Park.

Onverwacht/Salitje (🕒 8am-6pm) North of Pongola (KwaZulu-Natal).

By Bus

The best connections are on the Baz Bus (see p578), which runs from Jo'burg/Pretoria to Mbabane via Nelspruit, and from Swaziland down the KwaZulu-Natal coast to Durban.

Minibus taxis run daily between Jo'burg (Park Station), Mbabane and Manzini (R160, four hours), and between Manzini and Durban (R140, eight hours). For many routes, you'll need to change minibuses at the border. Most long-distance taxis leave early in the morning.

ZIMBABWE

The only border crossing between Zimbabwe and South Africa is at Beitbridge (24 hours) on the Limpopo River. There's lots of smuggling, so searches are thorough and queues often long. The closest South African town to the border is Musina (15km south), where you can change money.

When entering or leaving South Africa, vehicles pay a toll at the border to use the Limpopo Bridge. South Africans need a visa (free) to get into Zimbabwe but can obtain it at the border. Most other nationalities, including Commonwealth and US passport holders, require visas, which are available at the border and payable in US dollars only.

Ignore the touts on the Zimbabwe side trying to 'help' you through Zimbabwe immigration and customs. Despite their insistence, there's no charge for the government forms needed for immigration.

By Bus

Greyhound (☎ 083 915 9000; www.greyhound.co.za) runs buses from Jo'burg/Pretoria to Harare via Limpopo and Bulawayo. On both the northbound and southbound services, passengers can get on but not disembark before the bus crosses the border.

Bus & Minibus Taxi

Numerous buses cross the borders between South Africa and all of its neighbours. These are the most efficient way to travel overland, unless you have your own vehicle. Other than sometimes-lengthy queues, there are usually no hassles. At the border, you'll need to disembark to take care of visa formalities, then reboard your bus and carry on. Visa prices are not included in the ticket price for transborder routes. Many bus lines offer student discounts, upon presentation of a student ID.

It's also possible to travel to/from all of South Africa's neighbours by local minibus taxi. A few routes go direct, though sometimes it's necessary to walk across the border and pick up onward transport on the other side.

Car & Motorcycle

If you're arriving in South Africa via car or motorcycle, you'll need the vehicle's registration papers, liability insurance and your driving licence or international permit. You'll also need a *carnet de passage en douane,* which acts as a temporary waiver of import duty; arrange for this through your local automobile association. South African–registered vehicles don't need a *carnet* to visit South Africa's neighbouring countries.

Border crossings generally don't have petrol stations or repair shops; you'll need to go to the nearest large town.

Tours

Dozens of tour and safari companies organise package tours to South Africa including for various special interests (birdwatching etc). Following is a list of some companies (see also p581):

AUSTRALIA

Adventure World (☎ 02-8913 0755; www.adventureworld.com.au) Offers a wide range of tours, safaris, car hire and hotel packages in South and Southern Africa.

Peregrine Travel (☎ 03-8601 4444; www.peregrine.net.au) Caters to all budgets, from overland truck tours to upscale wildlife safaris, including an eight-day tour of Kruger National Park and Swaziland.

FRANCE

Makila Voyages (☎ 01 42 96 80 00; www.makila.fr) Upper-end tailored tours in South Africa and its northern neighbours, plus safaris.

UK

Exodus Travels (☎ 0845 863 9600; www.exodustravels.co.uk) Organises a variety of tours, including overland trips, and walking and cycling itineraries, covering South Africa, Lesotho and Swaziland.

Guerba (☎ 020-3147 7777; www.guerba.com) Overland tours.

USA

Adventure Centre (☎ 510-654 1879, 800-228 8747; www.adventurecenter.com) Budget to midrange tours and overland trips, including a 20-day South Africa circuit that takes in bits of Swaziland and Lesotho.

Africa Adventure Company (☎ 954-491 8877, 800 882 9453; www.africa-adventure.com) Upper-end wildlife safaris, including the private reserves around Kruger National Park, plus other itineraries in Cape Town and along the Garden Route.

Born Free Safaris (☎ 800 472 3274; www.bornfreesafaris.com) Offers a good range of Cape to Kruger itineraries.

GETTING AROUND

Air

National airline **South African Airways** (SAA; ☎ 0861-359 722, 011-978 5313; www.flysaa.com) is the main domestic carrier, with an extensive network of routes. Its subsidiaries, **SAAirlink** (☎ 011-961 1700; www.saairlink.co.za) and **SA Express** (☎ 011-978 9900; www.flysax.com), also serve domestic routes and share SAA's excellent safety record.

Domestic fares aren't cheap; one way to save significantly is to book online. Other airlines flying domestically:

1time (☎ 0861-345 345; www.1time.aero) No-frills flights linking Jo'burg, Cape Town, Durban, East London, George and Port Elizabeth. Also offers car hire.

Comair (☎ 011-921 0222; www.comair.co.za) Operates British Airways flights in Southern Africa, and has flights linking Cape Town, Durban, Jo'burg and Port Elizabeth.

Kulula.com (☎ 0861-444 144; www.kulula.com) No-frills flights linking Jo'burg, Cape Town, Durban, George and Port Elizabeth. Also offers hotel bookings and car hire.

Mango (☎ 0861-162 646; ww5.flymango.com) No-frills flights linking Jo'burg, Cape Town, Durban, and Bloemfontein. Also offers car hire and hotel bookings.

Bicycle

South Africa offers some rewarding cycling. The Cape Peninsula and the Winelands of the Western Cape are excellent biking areas. The Wild Coast in the Eastern Cape is beautiful and challenging, while the northern lowveld offers wide plains.

When planning, keep in mind that much of the country (except for Western Cape and the west coast) gets most of its rain in summer (late November to March), often in the form of violent thunderstorms. When it isn't raining, summer days can be unpleasantly hot, especially in the steamy lowveld, and distances between major towns are often long.

Cycling SA (http://cms.cyclingsa.com) carries news stories, background information and links. Other things to remember are that it's illegal to cycle on highways, and that roads near urban areas are too busy for comfort.

Mixing cycling with public transport doesn't always work, as most bus lines don't want bicycles in their luggage holds, and minibuses don't carry luggage on the roof. Trains can carry bikes, though.

Bus

Buses in South Africa aren't the deal that they are in many countries. However, together with the less-appealing minibus taxis, they're the main form of public transport, with a reliable and reasonably comfortable network linking all major cities. Note that many long-distance services run through the night; travellers should take care of their valuables and women might feel more comfortable sitting near the front of the bus.

An alternative to the standard bus lines is the **Baz Bus** (☎ 021-439 2323; www.bazbus.com), catering almost exclusively to backpackers and travellers. It offers hop-on, hop-off fares and hostel-to-hostel service between Cape Town and Jo'burg via the northern Drakensberg, Durban and the Garden Route. It also has a loop from Durban via Zululand, Swaziland and Nelspruit (near Kruger National Park) to Jo'burg. Point-to-point fares are more expensive than on the other major lines, but can work out more economically if you take advantage of the hop-on, hop-off feature. It's also worth checking out its travel passes (one/two/three weeks R1300/2300/3100).

The Baz Bus has transfer arrangements with some accommodation options off the main routes for a nominal extra charge. You can book directly with the company, as well as with most hostels. The Baz Bus is a convenient option, and it has a strong presence in South Africa's hostels, but using it consigns you to a backpacker bubble. It's worth giving some thought to whether you want your trip to take that form.

In partnership with Translux, **City to City** (☎ 011-774 3333, 0861-589 282; www.translux.co.za) has taken over the routes that once carried people from the homelands to/from the big cities during the apartheid regime. Services are less expensive than on the other lines, and go to many off-the-beaten-track places, including townships and mining towns. It's not as safe as other companies for night-time travel. Destinations from Jo'burg include Mthatha, Nelspruit, Hazyview, Beitbridge (for Zimbabwe), Piet Retief, and various towns in KwaZulu-Natal. Many services originate at Jo'burg's Park Station transit centre, where there are booking counters and an information desk.

The main long-distance bus operator **Translux** (☎ 011-774 3333, 0861-589 282; www.translux.co.za), has services connecting Cape Town, Knysna, Plettenberg Bay, Durban, Bloemfontein, Port Elizabeth, East London, Mthatha, Nelspruit (en route to Mozambique) and various towns along the Garden Route.

Offering an extensive network, with routes and pricing similar to those for Translux, **Greyhound** (☎ 083-915 9000; www.greyhound.co.za) also has a Jo'burg to Durban route via Zululand and Richards Bay, and offers frequent special deals.

With an extensive network stretching from Cape Town to Victoria Falls (Zimbabwe) and Maputo (Mozambique), **Intercape** (☎ 0861 287 287, 021-380 4400; www.intercape.co.za) prices are somewhat less than Translux and Greyhound. For longer hauls, it's worth paying more for a reclining seat on one of Intercape's Sleepliner buses.

SA Roadlink (☎ 011-333 2223; www.saroadlink.co.za) links Pretoria and Jo'burg with Bloemfontein, Port Elizabeth, East London, Mthatha, Durban and points in between. Prices are very reasonable.

There are no class tiers on any of the bus lines, although major companies generally offer 'luxury' service, with air-con and often video and a toilet. City to City's service is no-frills.

Except for the Baz Bus, which has its own pricing structure, fares are roughly calculated by distance, although short runs are disproportionately expensive. Some approximate one-way fares and durations: Jo'burg to Cape Town (R450, 19 hours); Jo'burg to Durban (R170 to R250, eight hours); and Cape Town to Knysna (R195 to R270, eight hours). Baz Bus one-way fares for the hop-on, hop-off service are: Cape Town to Durban via the Garden Route (R2330); Jo'burg–Swaziland–Durban–Drakensberg–Jo'burg loop (R1450).

Prices rise during school holidays; all lines offer student and senior-citizen discounts, and Intercape has backpacker and ISIC discounts. Inquire about travel passes if you'll be taking several bus journeys, and always check with the bus companies to see if they are running any specials, which can sometimes save you up to 40%.

For the main lines, reservations should be made at least 24 hours in advance, and as far in advance as possible for travel during peak periods. It's sometimes possible to get a seat at the last minute, but don't count on it. You can buy tickets for the major companies at branches of Shoprite/Checkers supermarkets and **Computicket** (☎ 083 915 8000; www.computicket.com), as well as on its website.

Car & Motorcycle

South Africa is ideal for driving, and away from the main bus and train routes, having your own wheels is the best way to get around. If you're in a group, it's also often the most economical. Most major roads are in excellent condition, and off the main routes there are interesting back roads to explore.

The country is crossed by many national routes (eg N1). On some sections a toll is payable, based on distance. There's always plenty of warning that you're about to enter a toll section (marked by a black 'T' in a yellow circle), and there's always an alternative route (marked by a black 'A' in a yellow circle). On alternative routes, signposting is sparse, generally only giving route numbers or directing you to the nearby towns, rather than the next large city. Smaller roads are numbered (eg R44 – shown in this book as Rte 44), and when giving directions most people will refer to these numbers rather than destinations, so it pays to have a good road map.

DRIVING LICENCE

In South Africa, you can use your driving licence from your home country if it is in English (or you have a certified translation) and it carries your photo; otherwise you'll need an international driving permit, obtainable from a motoring organisation in your home country.

FUEL

Petrol costs about R8 per litre for leaded or unleaded. There's no self-service. An attendant will always fill up your tank for you, clean your windows and ask if your oil, water or tyres need checking; if they do check your oil etc, tip them between R2 and R5.

Along main routes in South Africa there are plenty of petrol stations, many open 24 hours.

HIRE

Car hire is relatively inexpensive in South Africa. Most companies have a minimum age requirement of 21 years. All accept major credit cards, and most do not accept debit cards. Rates start below R200 per day, including insurance and 200km free per day (unlimited mileage in some cases); rental of a 4WD starts below R900 per day.

Avis (☎ 0861-113 748, 011-923 3660; www.avis.co.za)
Budget (☎ 0861-016 622, 011-398 0123; www.budget.co.za)
Hertz (☎ 0861-600 136, 021-935 4800; www.hertz.co.za)
Imperial (☎ 0861-131 000, 011-574 1000; www.imperialcarrental.co.za)

Local car-hire companies are usually less expensive, though they tend to come and go. Also check the budget domestic airlines and backpackers hostels; many can arrange good deals.

Abba (☎ 011-917 3037; www.abbacarrental.co.za)
Around About Cars (☎ 0860-422 4022; www.aroundaboutcars.co.za)
First Car Rental (☎ 011-230 9999; www.firstcarrental.co.za)
Tempest (☎ 011-552 3900; www.tempestcarhire.co.za)
Xpress Car & Van Rental (☎ 0861-116 000; www.xpressrental.co.za) Offers *bakkie* (pick-up truck) and van rental in Cape Town, Jo'burg, Durban and Pietermaritzburg.

Hiring a camper van is another option, although one-way hire is not always possible. Some camper-van rentals include camping gear. *Bakkie* campers, which sleep two in the back of a canopied pick-up, are cheaper. Two places to try, both in Jo'burg, are **African Leisure Travel** (☎ 011-475 2902; www.africanleisure.co.za) and **Britz 4x4 Rentals** (☎ 011-396 1860; www.brit z.co.za).

For motorcycle rental, good contacts include **Motozulu** (www.motozu.lu.ms) in Port Shepstone (KwaZulu-Natal), and **LDV Biking** (☎ 083 528 0897; www.ldvbiking.co.za) in Cape Town.

INSURANCE

Insurance for third-party damage, and damage to or loss of your vehicle is highly recommended, though not legally required for private-vehicle owners. The **Automobile Association of South Africa** (AASA; ☎ 011-799 1000, emergencies 083 843 22; www.aasa.co.za) is a good contact and insurance agencies include **Sansure** (☎ 021-914 3488, 0860 786 847; www.sansure.com) in Cape Town.

ROAD HAZARDS

South Africa has a horrific road-accident record, with the annual death toll around 10,000. The N1 between Cape Town and Beaufort West is considered to be the most dangerous stretch of road in the country.

The main hazards are your fellow drivers, with overtaking blind and overtaking with insufficient passing room the major dangers. This is particularly true of minibus taxi drivers, who often operate under pressure on little sleep. Drivers on little-used rural roads often speed and assume that there is no other traffic. There is alcohol breath-testing, but given the high blood-alcohol level permitted (more than 0.05%) drunk drivers remain a danger.

Animals and pedestrians on the roads are another hazard, especially in rural areas such as the Wild Coast. Standard advice is that if you hit an animal in an area in which you're uncertain of your safety, it's best to continue to the nearest police station and report it there. During the rainy season, and especially in higher areas of KwaZulu-Natal, thick fog can slow you to a crawl. In the lowveld, summer hailstorms can damage your car.

Crime

In Jo'burg, and to a lesser extent in the other big cities, carjacking is a problem, though it's more likely if you're driving something flash rather than a standard rental car. Stay alert, keep your taste in cars modest, avoid driving in urban areas at night, keep windows wound up and doors locked. If you're waiting at a red light and notice anything suspicious, it's standard practice to check that the junction is clear, and run the light. If you do get carjacked, don't resist, just hand over the keys immediately. The carjackers are almost always armed, and people have been killed for their cars.

The cheapest hire cars, typically an Opel Corsa or VW Chicco, often don't have central locking, so remember to lock the boot and passenger doors.

ROAD RULES

Driving is on the left-hand side of the road and seatbelts are mandatory for the driver and front-seat passenger.

There are a few local variations on road rules – most significantly the 'four-way stop' (crossroad), which can occur even on major roads. All vehicles are required to stop, with those arriving first the first to go (even if they're on a minor cross street). On freeways, faster drivers will expect you to move into the emergency lane to let them pass, and will probably flash their hazard lights as thanks. At roundabouts, vehicles already in the roundabout, and those approaching it from the right, have the right of way.

If you are parking in the street or a car park in larger towns and cities in South Africa, you will often be approached by a 'car guard'. They are usually otherwise unemployed Africans from across the country's borders, and they will (most usefully) keep an eye on your motor for R2 to R5; they may also offer to wash it for an extra charge.

Hitching

Hitching is never entirely safe in any country. This is especially true in South Africa, particularly in and near urban areas, and it's not a form of travel we recommend. Sometimes in rural areas it may be the only way to get somewhere; do it in pairs and avoid hitching at night.

Local Transport

For getting around within a city or town, the main options are city buses, minibus taxis and regular taxis – either shared or private hire. In a few places you'll have other options, such as Cape Town's Rikkis (a cross between a taxi and a shared taxi) and rickshaws in Durban. Cape Town, Jo'burg and Pretoria have metro commuter trains.

BUS

Cape Town, Jo'burg, Pretoria and several other urban areas have city bus systems. Fares are cheap and routes, which are signboarded, are extensive. However, services usually stop running early in the evening, and there aren't many buses on weekends.

MINIBUS TAXI

Minibus taxis run almost everywhere in South Africa – within cities, to the suburbs and to neighbouring towns. They leave when full and – happily, especially if you've travelled elsewhere in sub-Saharan Africa – 'full' in South Africa isn't as full as in many neighbouring countries. Most accommodate 14 to 16 people, with the slightly larger 'Sprinters' taking about 20.

Minibus taxis have the advantages of an extensive route network and cheap prices. These are outweighed, however, by the fact that driving standards and vehicle conditions are often poor, and there are many accidents. Things have settled down following a spate of gangster-style clashes between various companies competing for business, but minibuses in some areas and on some routes are still considered highly unsafe, and reports of muggings and other incidents remain a regular feature. In other areas, notably central Cape Town, they're a handy and popular way to get around during daylight hours.

Away from train and main bus routes, minibus taxis may be the only choice of public transport. They're also a good way to get insights into local life. If you want to try one, read the newspapers, don't ride at night, seek local advice on lines and areas to avoid before using minibus taxis as transport, and be especially alert in the often-dodgy stations. As most minibus taxis don't carry luggage on the roof, stowing backpacks can be a hassle.

PRIVATE TAXI

Larger cities have a private taxi service. Occasionally, you'll find a taxi stand, but usually it's easiest to telephone for a cab. Prices average about R10 per kilometre.

SHARED TAXI

In some towns (and on some longer routes), the only transport option is a shared taxi, basically a smaller version of the minibus taxi. These are slightly more expensive than minibus taxis, and comparable in safety.

Tours

There are dozens of tours run by local companies, ranging from budget-oriented overland truck tours to exclusive luxury safaris. The best way to get information on budget tours is from the nationwide network of backpacker hostels; many have travellers' bulletin boards, and some are affiliated with tour operators.

Some tour operators to try include the following:

African Routes (☎ 031-464 8513; www.africanroutes.co.za) Offers Southern African tours aimed at the 50-plus age group.

BirdWatch Cape (☎ 072-635 1501; www.birdwatch.co.za) Small, Cape Town–based outfit for twitchers, with tours including a nationwide package.

Bok Bus (☎ 082 320 1979; www.bokbus.com) Five-day, budget-oriented tours along the Garden Route.

Cape Gourmet Adventure Tours (☎ 083 693 1151; http://gourmet.cape-town.info) Mouthwatering tours of Cape Town and the Western Cape.

Eden Routes (☎ 015-263 6473; www.edenroutes.co.za) Limpopo-based operator offering 'specialist ecosafaris' throughout Southern Africa.

Intrepid Bundu (☎ 011-675 0767; www.intrepidbundu.com) Budget-oriented tours ranging from four days to several months, and generally including Kruger National Park.

Signature Tours (☎ 021-975 1061; www.signaturetours.co.za) Tours focused on topics including botany, birding and the environment.

Springbok-Atlas (☎ 021-460 4700; www.springbokatlas.com) Bus tours nationwide.

Thavhani (☎ 015-963 1264; thavhani@gmx.net) Small, Venda-based outfit offering recommended cultural tours of this intriguing region and other northern areas.

Wilderness Safaris (www.wilderness-safaris.com) Upscale, conservation-focused operator offering high-end safaris and special-interest trips.

Wildlife Safaris (☎ 011-791 4238; www.wildlifesaf.co.za) Midrange safaris from Jo'burg to Kruger and Pilanesberg National Parks.

Train

South Africa's **Shosholoza Meyl** (☎ 0860-008 888, 011-774 4555; www.shosholozameyl.co.za, www.premierclasse.co.za) offers regular services connecting major cities, with 'premier-', 'tourist-' and economy-class trains available. Premier class is a luxurious experience, offering a more affordable alternative to the country's premium lines. Cars can be transported for a surcharge.

The other trains are relatively affordable, and unlike on long-distance buses, fares on short sectors are not inflated. Tourist class is recommended – a scenic and safe, albeit sometimes slow, way to travel.

On overnight journeys, tourist-class fares include a sleeping berth (with a small additional charge for bedding hire). Couples are normally given two-berth coupés and single travellers and larger groups are put in four-berth compartments. If you are travelling alone and you want a coupé to yourself, you could buy two tickets. Meals and drinks are available in the dining car, or in your compartment.

Economy class does not have sleeping compartments (with the exception of the Jo'burg–East London service) and is not a comfortable or secure option for overnight travel.

Tickets must be booked at least 24 hours in advance (you can book up to three months in advance). Bookings for anywhere in the country can be done by phone (not as simple as it sounds, as you have to deposit the payment in Shosholoza Meyl's bank account) or at train stations. Timetables can and do change.

For an overview of the South African rails, consult the **Man in Seat 61** (www.seat61.com/SouthAfrica.htm).

ROUTES

Main routes include the following:

Cape Town–Durban Via Kimberley, Bloemfontein, Kroonstad and Ladysmith; 36 hours; tourist and economy class (both once weekly).

Cape Town–East London Via Matjiesfontein, De Aar and Queenstown; 28 hours; economy class (once weekly).

Cape Town–Port Elizabeth Via Oudtshoorn; 24 hours; premier class (once weekly).

Jo'burg–Cape Town Via Kimberley and Matjiesfontein; 27 hours; premier class (twice weekly), tourist (Monday, Wednesday, Friday, Sunday) and economy (daily).

Jo'burg–Durban Via Ladysmith and Pietermaritzburg; 13½ hours; premier class (twice weekly), tourist (once weekly) and economy (daily except Tuesday).

Jo'burg–East London Via Bloemfontein; 20 hours; economy class with sleepers (daily except Saturday).

Jo'burg–Port Elizabeth Via Kroonstad, Bloemfontein and Craddock; 21 hours; tourist class (twice weekly) and economy (daily except Saturday).

Jo'burg/Pretoria–Musina Via Louis Trichardt/Makhado; 17 hours; economy class (daily except Saturday).

Jo'burg/Pretoria–Komatipoort Via Nelspruit; 13 hours; economy class (daily except Saturday); connects to the Komatipoort–Maputo train.

Some sample fares: premier class Durban–Jo'burg R750 to R1100; tourist class Cape Town–Jo'burg R350; economy class Jo'burg–Musina R110.

Luxurious special lines include the famous **Blue Train** (☎ 012-334 8459, 021-449 2672; www.bluetrain.co.za), which runs weekly between Pretoria and Cape Town (one-way per person sharing from R12,485, including meals and drinks); and **Rovos Rail** (☎ 012-315 8242; www.rovos.co.za), which has regular trips including Pretoria–Cape Town, stopping at Kimberley and Matjiesfontein; Pretoria–Durban; and Cape Town–George.

METRO TRAINS

There are metro services in Jo'burg, Cape Town and Pretoria. Most lines aren't recommended for security reasons, although those linking Cape Town with Simon's Town and the Winelands are considered reasonably safe during daylight hours. The **Gautrain** (www.gautrain.co.za) will soon connect Jo'burg and Pretoria via OR Tambo International Airport.

Swaziland

Embedded between Mozambique and South Africa, the kingdom of Swaziland is one of the smallest countries in Africa. What the country lacks in size it makes up for in its rich culture and heritage, and relaxed ambience. With its laid-back, friendly people and relative lack of racial animosity, it's a complete change of pace from its larger neighbours.

Visitors can enjoy rewarding, delightfully low-key wildlife watching, adrenaline-boosting activities, stunning mountain panoramas and lively traditions. Swaziland also boasts superb walking and high-quality handicrafts.

Overseeing the kingdom is King Mswati III, one of three remaining monarchs in Africa. The monarchy has its critics, but combined with the Swazis' distinguished history of resistance to the Boers, the British and the Zulus, it has fostered a strong sense of national pride, and local culture is flourishing. This is exemplified in its national festivals – the Incwala ceremony and the Umhlanga (Reed) dance (see the boxed text, p593).

The excellent road system makes Swaziland easy to get around. Accommodation includes a decent network of hostels, family-friendly hotels, wilderness lodges to upscale retreats. Many travellers make a flying visit on their way to South Africa's Kruger National Park, but it's well worth lingering here if you can.

FAST FACTS

- **Area** 17,364 sq km
- **Capital** Mbabane
- **Country code** ☎ 268
- **Famous for** Monarchy, cultural festivals
- **Languages** Swati, English
- **Money** Lilangeni, plural emalangeni (E)
- **Phrase** *Sawubona/sanibona* (hello)
- **Population** 900,000

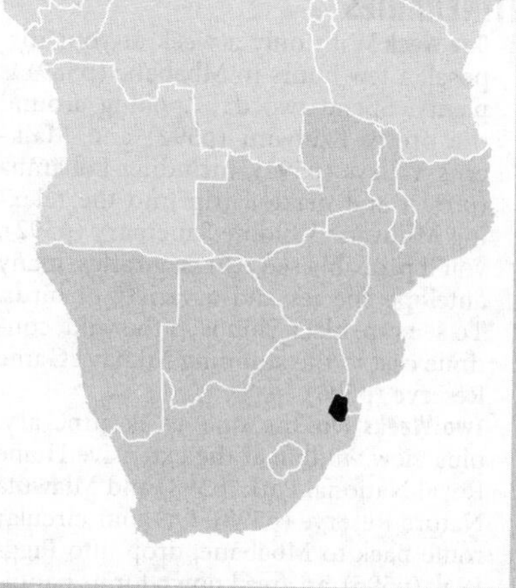

HOW MUCH?

- **Traditional dance/cultural group** E120
- **Internet per hour** E25
- **Coffee** E8-15
- **Batik hanging** E75
- **Basket** E40

LONELY PLANET INDEX

- **1L of petrol** E7 (but fluctuates)
- **1L of bottled water** E7
- **Bottle of beer** E8-15
- **Souvenir T-shirt** E80
- **Barbecued maize** E4

HIGHLIGHTS

- **Mkhaya Game Reserve** (p598) See rare black rhinos in the wild.
- **Ezulwini Valley** (p592) and the **Malkerns Valley** (p594) Browse this attractive area's craft shops and royal heartland.
- **Usutu River** (see the boxed text, p594) Shoot wondrous white-water rapids.
- **Mlilwane Wildlife Sanctuary** (p592) Cycle or meander in the wilderness and relax in its bargain lodges.
- **Off the beaten track** Hike in the superb Malolotja Nature Reserve (p596) and explore the Ngwempisi Gorge (p599), staying in novel huts along the way.

ITINERARIES

- **One Week** With only a week at your disposal, a few hours in Mbabane (p589) is plenty. Spend two days poking around the pretty Ezulwini (p592) and Malkerns Valleys (p594), including Lobamba (p592), and make a trip into the relaxing Mlilwane Wildlife Sanctuary (p592); you'll probably see zebras, giraffes, many antelope species and a variety of birds. To see rare black rhinos in the wild, continue east to the stunning Mkhaya Game Reserve (p598).
- **Two Weeks** Do the one week itinerary, plus view wildlife at the extensive Hlane Royal National Park (p598) and Mlawula Nature Reserve (p598). On your circular route back to Mbabane, drop into Piggs Peak (p596), an area known for its handicrafts, and detour to hike in Malolotja Nature Reserve (p596), an unspoiled wilderness, or visit the fascinating village of Bulembu (p597). You could do this route clockwise, starting in Mbabane and heading north to Malolotja.
- **One month** You can absorb most of Swaziland in this time. Join the previous two itineraries and take extra time for some action: hike in the Ngwempisi Gorge (p599) and shoot the rapids on the Usutu River (p594). If Swaziland is incorporated into your one-month trip through South Africa, it's well worth diverting here for its friendly people, relaxed atmosphere, unique culture, and pretty and accessible wildlife parks and reserves.

CLIMATE & WHEN TO GO

Most rain falls in summer, usually in torrential thunderstorms and mostly in the western mountains. Summers on the lowveld are very hot, with temperatures often over 40°C; in the high country the temperatures are lower and in winter it can get cool. Winter nights on the lowveld are sometimes very cold.

The rains usually begin around early December and last until April. May to August are the coolest months, with frosts in June and July.

HISTORY

The area that is now Swaziland has been inhabited for a long time – in eastern Swaziland archaeologists have discovered human remains dating back 110,000 years – but the Swazi people arrived relatively recently.

During the great Bantu migrations into Southern Africa, one group, the Nguni, moved down the east coast. A clan settled in the area near what is now Maputo in Mozambique, and a dynasty was founded by the Dlamini family. (For detailed information on the Bantu migrations, see p33.)

In the mid-18th century increasing pressure from other Nguni clans forced King Ngwane III to lead his people south to lands by the Pongola River, in what is now southern Swaziland. Today, Swazis consider Ngwane III to have been the first king of Swaziland.

Clan encroachment continued, and the next king, Sobhuza I, also came under pressure from the Zulus. He withdrew to the Ezulwini Valley, which remains the centre of

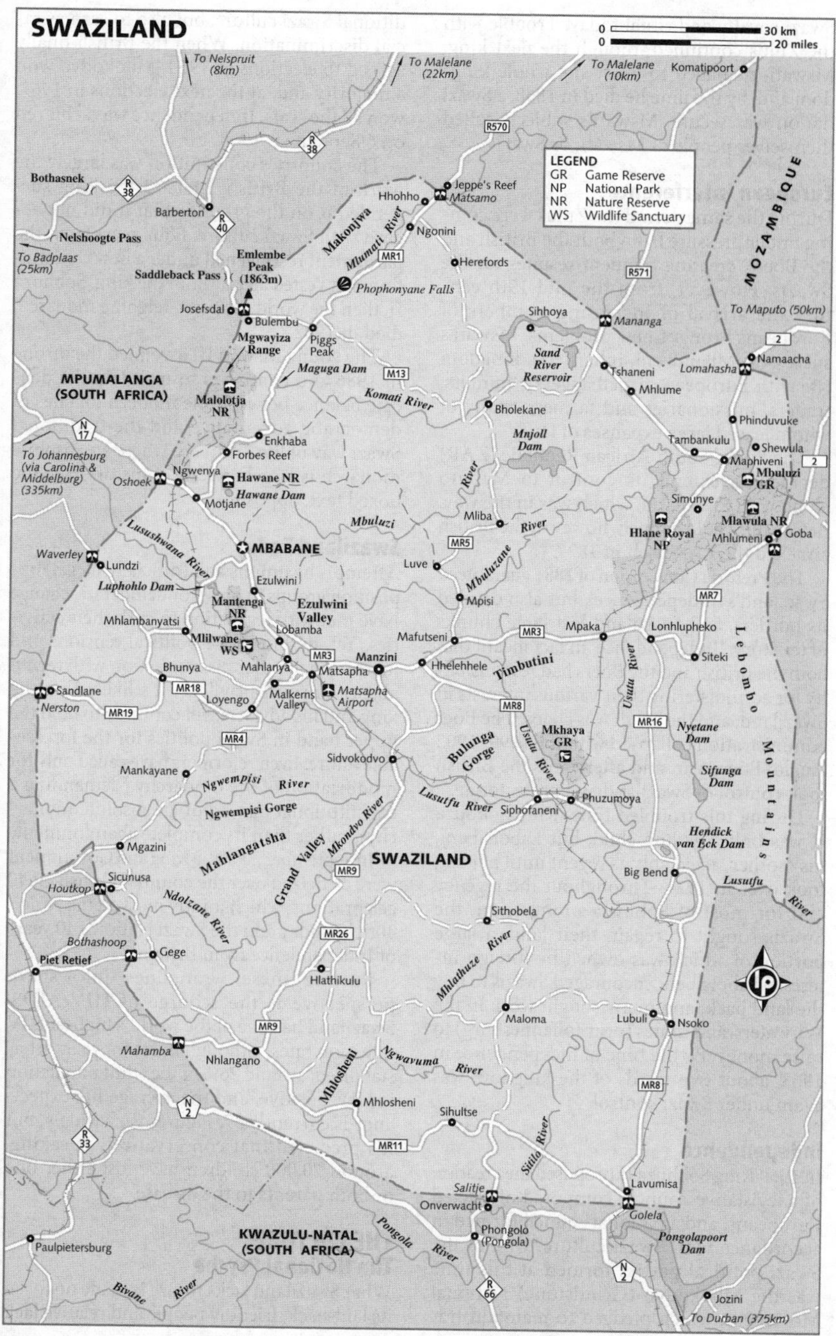
SWAZILAND
0 30 km
0 20 miles
LEGEND
GR Game Reserve
NP National Park
NR Nature Reserve
WS Wildlife Sanctuary
To Nelspruit (8km)
To Malelane (22km)
To Malelane (10km)
Komatipoort
R570
R38
Bothasnek
Barberton
R40
Nelshoogte Pass
To Badplaas (25km)
Emlembe Peak (1863m)
Saddleback Pass
Josefsdal
Bulembu
Mgwayiza Range
Jeppe's Reef
Matsamo
Hhohho
Makonjwa
Mlumati River
Ngonini
MR1
Herefords
Phophonyane Falls
Piggs Peak
Maguga Dam
MR13
Komati River
Sihhoya
Sand River Reservoir
Mananga
R571
MOZAMBIQUE
To Maputo (50km)
2
Namaacha
Lomahasha
Tshaneni
Mhlume
Bholekane
Phinduvuke
Mnjoli Dam
Tambankulu
Shewula
Maphiveni
Mbuluzi GR
MPUMALANGA (SOUTH AFRICA)
Malolotja NR
N17
Enkhaba
Forbes Reef
To Johannesburg (via Carolina & Middelburg) (335km)
Oshoek
Ngwenya
Hawane NR
Hawane Dam
Motjane
Simunye
Mlawula NR
Mliba
Mbuluzi
River
Hlane Royal NP
Mhlumeni
Goba
Lusushwana River
Waverley
Lundzi
MBABANE
MR5
Luve
Mbuluzane
Ezulwini
Luphohlo Dam
Mantenga NR
Ezulwini Valley
Mpisi
MR7
Mhlambanyatsi
Lobamba
Mlilwane WS
MR3
Mafutseni
Mpaka
Lonhlupheko
Siteki
Usutu River
Bhunya
Mahlanya
Manzini
Matsapha
Hhelehhele
Timbutini
Sandlane
Nerston
MR18
Loyengo
Malkerns Valley
Matsapha Airport
MR19
MR8
MR16
Lebombo Mountains
MR4
Nyetane Dam
Mkhaya GR
Bulunga Gorge
Usutu River
Sidvokodvo
Mankayane
Sifunga Dam
Ngwempisi River
Lusutfu River
Siphofaneni
Phuzumoya
Ngwempisi Gorge
Mkondvo River
Hendick van Eck Dam
Mgazini
Mahlangatsha
Grand Valley
SWAZILAND
MR9
Big Bend
Sicunusa
Houtkop
Lusutfu River
Ndolzane River
Sithobela
MR26
Bothashoop
Gege
Piet Retief
Mhlathuze River
Hlathikulu
Maloma
Lubuli
Nsoko
MR9
Mahamba
Nhlangano
Mhlosheni
Ngwavuma River
MR8
Mhlosheni
N2
Sihultse
R33
MR11
Sitilo River
Salitje
Lavumisa
Onverwacht
Golela
KWAZULU-NATAL (SOUTH AFRICA)
Paulpietersburg
Phongolo (Pongola)
Pongola River
Pongolapoort Dam
N2
R66
Bivane River
Jozini
To Durban (375km)

Swazi royalty and ritual today. Trouble with the Zulus continued, though the next king, Mswati, managed to unify the whole kingdom and, by the time he died in 1868, a Swazi nation was secure. Mswati's subjects called themselves people of Mswati, or Swazis.

European Interference

During the same period the Zulus were coming under pressure from both the British and the Boers, creating frequent respites for the Swazis. However, from the mid-19th century the arrival of increasing numbers of Europeans brought new problems. Mswati's successor, Mbandzeni, inherited a kingdom rife with European carpetbaggers – hunters, traders, missionaries and farmers, many of whom leased large expanses of land.

The Boers' South African Republic (ZAR) decided to extend its control to Maputo along with Swaziland, which was in the way. Before this could happen, however, the British annexed the ZAR itself in 1877.

The Pretoria Convention of 1881 guaranteed Swaziland's 'independence', but also defined its borders, and Swaziland lost large chunks of territory. 'Independence' in fact meant that both the British and the Boers had responsibility for administering their various interests in Swaziland, and the result was chaos. The Boer administration collapsed with the 1899–1902 Anglo–Boer War, and afterwards the British took control of Swaziland as a protectorate.

During this troubled time, King Sobhuza II was only a young child, but Labotsibeni, his mother, acted ably as regent until her son took over in 1921. Throughout the regency and for most of Sobhuza's long reign, the Swazis sought to regain their land, a large portion of which was owned by foreign interests. Labotsibeni encouraged Swazis to buy the land back, and many sought work in the Witwatersrand mines (near Johannesburg) to raise money. By the time of independence in 1968, about two-thirds of the kingdom was again under Swazi control.

Independence

In 1960 King Sobhuza II proposed the creation of a legislative council, composed of elected Europeans, and a national council formed in accordance with Swazi culture. One of the Swazi political parties formed at this time was the Mbokodvo (Grindstone) National Movement, which pledged to maintain traditional Swazi culture, but also to eschew racial discrimination. When the British finally agreed to elections in 1964, Mbokodvo won a majority and, at the next elections in 1967, won all the seats. Independence was achieved on 6 September 1968.

The country's constitution was largely the work of the British. In 1973 the king suspended it on the grounds that it did not accord with Swazi culture. Four years later, the parliament reconvened under a new constitution that vested all power in the king. Sobhuza II, then the world's longest-reigning monarch, died in 1982.

The young Mswati III ascended the throne in 1986 and continues to maintain the delicate balance between the modern dictates of democratic governance and the traditional Swazi way of life, in an era where an absolute monarch is largely a relic of history (see the boxed text, opposite).

Swaziland Today

Attempts by unions and (officially illegal) opposition groups to press for democratic change have met with legislation to curb their activities. Yet, despite these political tensions and increasing popular dissatisfaction with recent abuses of royal privilege, it's likely that the king and his advisers will continue to hold the upper hand in Swazi politics for the foreseeable future. Even reformers have called only for modification of the monarchy (demanding a constitutional instead of an absolute monarchy), rather than its complete abandonment.

In September 2008 the King and Government were criticized over the country's lavish 40:40 celebrations, which jointly marked the King's 40th birthday and the Swazi Nation's 40 years of Independence from Britain.

Putting these wranglings into sharp perspective is the scourge of HIV/AIDS: Swaziland has one of the world's highest HIV infection rates, although in recent years it has stabilised; around 26% of the adult population is HIV positive, and the average life expectancy is currently 37. Figures vary widely, but it's predicted that conservatively speaking, around 70,000 children have lost either one or both parents to the disease.

THE CULTURE

The National Psyche

What Swaziland lacks in size is made up for in its laid-back, friendly people and relative lack

MOVERS & SHAKERS: KING MSWATI III

King Mswati III, Africa's last absolute monarch, courts both popularity and controversy. The second of 67 sons, King Mswati III was crowned in 1986 when he was 18, and he has since ruled the country with his mother. He has taken 13 wives, including one fiancée (those who've not borne him a child), and has more than 200 siblings.

His actions – most notably his expensive tastes and opulent lifestyle in the face of his country's extreme poverty and high incidence of HIV/AIDS – have upset critics. His constitution has been strongly criticised for its nonprogressive and authoritarian nature by Swazi critics, foreign governments and human rights groups.

The king has caused royal ripples several times over in choosing his wives. In 2001 he married a 17-year-old, two months after imposing a five-year sex ban on the kingdom's teenage females to fight the spread of HIV/AIDS. He ended the ban a year early. At the 2002 Umhlanga (Reed) festival, again in keeping with tradition, he chose a young woman, 18-year-old Zena Mahlangu, to become his 10th wife. Zena's mother tried to take the king to court, accusing him of abducting and holding Zena against her will.

Reformers, however, must reckon with the fact that the king is a highly revered figurehead; he is the Ngwenyama (Lion), a descendant of the great kings (and queen mothers) who secured the independence of the Swazi nation. Even pro-democracy advocates seek to maintain a constitutional monarch under a democratic system of government.

Meanwhile, for the king, traditional laws and customs reign supreme. He believes in perpetuating customs important to his country, including polygamy. Indeed, a Swazi king's power and the clan links resulting from his marriages might be seen as the source of Swaziland's relative stability, as well as being the foundation of its continued independence.

of racial animosities. The Swazis' distinguished history of resistance to the Boers, the British and the Zulus – along with the monarchy – has fostered an extraordinary sense of Swazi identity and ethnic pride, integral to their being. A nonconfrontational people, they dislike embarrassment of any kind; Swazis are as gracious and good-humoured as they are proud of their small but culturally strong kingdom.

That said, there is widespread dissatisfaction with the lack of progress in their country's current socio-economic climate, as well as the perceived disintegration in family life and morals, as reflected in the devastating effects of HIV/AIDS. Swazi critics and women's rights advocates rally against the current system, which stifles individual autonomy and rights, especially those of women. But the patriotic and deeply religious Swazis tend to dislike outsiders meddling in internal political and social affairs. As the symbolic head of the Swazi family, the king is, in general, very highly regarded and disrespect for him is often interpreted as a lack of respect for the Swazis themselves (see the boxed text, above).

Daily Life

Ancient traditions are vital to and inherent in everyday life – business may be conducted in *emahiya* (traditional Swazi dress, often complemented with a shield and knobkerries) or Western suits – and cultural festivals are followed closely.

As in other parts of Africa, the extended family is integral to a person's life. While polygamy is permitted and exists, it is not always practised. Traditional marriage allows for the husband to take a number of wives, although many Swazis also follow Western marriage conventions, rejecting polygamy but permitting divorce. Marriage arrangements are traditionally initiated by a request to the fathers of the couple by the mothers of the couple.

Many people in rural areas continue to live in the traditional beehive huts, while others, particularly in the cities, live in Western-style houses.

Schooling is not compulsory. The rate of attendance is decreasing due to social circumstances, particularly the effects of the HIV/AIDS epidemic.

Population

The ancestors of modern-day Swazis were part of the general, gradual migration of Bantu-language speakers from central Africa who broke from the main group and settled in Mozambique, finally moving in the mid-18th century into what became known as Swaziland. Today, Swazis still share a close cultural and linguistic heritage with other Southern African peoples including the Zulu and the Ndebele. Almost all people here are Swazi. The rest are Zulu, Tsonga (Shangaan) and European.

The population, which was about 85,000 in 1904, today hovers at around a million people, although the future for many of them looks bleak. Around 26% of Swazi adults are thought to be HIV positive; a reduction in population statistics in the next couple of decades seems certain.

RELIGION

Around 70% of the population is Zionist, a mix of Christianity and traditional indigenous worship, with Roman Catholics, Anglicans and Methodists making up the balance. Muslims, Baha'i and Jewish faiths have small followings also.

ARTS & CRAFTS

Music

Traditional music is integral to Swazi festivals and dancing, most prominently the Incwala and Umhlanga festivals. Music and rhythm also play an important role in other festivals, such as harvest and marriage. Traditional instruments include the calabash, kudu horn, rattle and reed flute.

The country's most prominent jazz musician (formerly lumped under the banner of South African musicians) was Zakes Nkosi, whose career in jazz began in the 1940s.

For more information on music in Southern Africa, see p48.

Architecture

The architecture of Swaziland ranges from the traditional round beehive hut of the rural areas to the more Western-style house in the suburbs and larger towns. The beehive huts are thatched with dry grass and often surrounded by reed fences.

The traditional *umuti* (homestead) is important to the Swazi social unit. In a polygamous homestead, each wife has her own huts, plus a yard surrounded by reed fences for privacy. Larger homesteads have huts for bachelors' quarters and guest housing. The cattle byre, a circular area enclosed by logs and branches, is central to the traditional homestead. This area has an important ritualistic and practical significance, reflecting both wealth and prestige. The hut opposite the cattle byre is occupied by the mother of the headman. Nowadays, while many construct square houses from cement blocks and corrugated iron, they still maintain the layout of the traditional homestead.

Dance

Dance is an integral part of Swazi cultural festivals (see the boxed text, p593).

The *sibhaca* dance is a vigorous, foot-stamping dance performed by teams of males. The energy and physical nature of this rhythmic dance is awesome. As well as being performed at festivals and formal occasions, it is sometimes performed competitively and occasionally done for fun.

Handicrafts

Swaziland's handicrafts include pottery, jewellery, weapons and implements. Woven grasswares such as *liqhaga* (grassware 'bottles') and mats are popular, as are wooden items, ranging from bowls to knobkerries.

ENVIRONMENT

The Land

Swaziland, although tiny, has a wide range of ecological zones, from montane forest in the northwest to savanna scrub in the east.

The western edge of the country is highveld, consisting mainly of short, sharp mountains where there are large plantations of pine and eucalyptus. The mountains dwindle to middleveld into the heavily populated centre of the country. The eastern half is scrubby lowveld, lightly populated, but now home to sugar estates. To the east, the harsh Lebombo Mountains form the border with Mozambique.

Wildlife

ANIMALS

Swaziland has about 121 species of mammals, representing a third of nonmarine mammal species in Southern Africa. These days the larger animals are restricted to the nature reserves and private wildlife reserves dotted around the country. Many species (such as elephants, warthogs, rhinos and lions) have been reintroduced to nature reserves. Mongooses and large-spotted genets are common throughout the country, while hyenas and jackals are found in the reserves.

Leopards are present, but you'd be lucky to see one. Poaching is an ongoing problem in some parks.

The most common of the 19 recorded species of bat is the little free-tailed bat, which can be found roosting in houses in the lowveld and middleveld.

PLANTS

Although small in size, Swaziland is rich in flora and accounts for 14% of the recorded plant life in Southern Africa. The remoteness of parts of the countryside means there are probably species that have not yet been brought to the attention of botanists. Nature reserves help to conserve indigenous plants.

National Parks

Swaziland's nature reserves reflect the country's geographical diversity. Easiest to get to is Mlilwane Wildlife Sanctuary (p592) in the Ezulwini Valley. Hlane Royal National Park (p598) and Mkhaya Game Reserve (p598) are also well worth visiting. These three reserves are privately run as part of the **Big Game Parks** (Map p592; ☎ 528 3943/4; www.bigga me.co.sz).

Mantenga (p592), Hawane, Malolotja (p596) and Mlawula Nature Reserves (p598) used to be under the jurisdiction of the **Swaziland National Trust Commission** (Map p592; ☎ 416 1151, 416 1178; www.sntc.org.sz), based at the National Museum in Lobamba (Ezulwini Valley). However, at the time of research, there was talk of the Swaziland NTC possibly outsourcing the tourism facilities; for booking details, check the status with the **Ezulwini tourist information office** (Map p592; ☎ 416 1834; www.swazi.travel; Mantenga Craft Centre, Ezulwini Valley).

Malolotja (p596) is a rugged highlands reserve with some very good hiking trails. Mlawula (p598) is in harsh lowveld country near the Mozambican border.

Environmental Issues

While the importance of traditional practices and customs provides a strong sense of cultural identity and national cohesiveness, some traditional practices are not kind to the environment. As in Lesotho, the overgrazing of cattle has caused soil erosion. Some items of male traditional attire, such as the *majobo,* which is made from the skin of the grey duiker, have resulted in illegal hunting. The use of and reliance on natural medicinal plants has lead to the loss of certain indigenous plants. Poverty is a major cause of land degradation; land-management issues focused on sustainability are simply not on the agendas of individuals struggling to eke out a living or dealing with the impact of HIV/AIDS.

FOOD & DRINK

Although it's not exactly a gourmet's paradise, you won't eat badly in Swaziland. There's a good range of places to eat in Mbabane and the tourist areas of the Malkerns and Ezulwini Valleys. Portuguese cuisine, including seafood, can be found. In more remote areas, African staples such as stew and *pap* (also known as *mealie meal*) are common.

MBABANE

Swaziland's capital, Mbabane (pronounced mba-*baa*-nay), is pretty nondescript and there isn't that much to see or do here. It's in a pleasant setting in the Dlangeni Hills. These make Mbabane cooler than Manzini, one reason why the British moved their administrative centre here from Manzini in 1902. The adjacent Ezulwini and Malkerns Valleys have plenty of attractions.

ORIENTATION

Mbabane is a little disjointed. The main street is Gwamile St, which runs north–south, but most things are available in Swazi Plaza, off Western Distributor Rd and the Mall on Plaza Mall Dr.

RINGING IN CHANGES – NEW TELEPHONE NUMBERS

At the time of going to print, Swaziland announced changes to its telephone system.

As of April 2010 all mobile/cell numbers in Swaziland will have a prefix of 7. Previously all MTN cell numbers in Swaziland would have started with 6, as in ☎ 602 0261. The number will now be ☎ 7602 0261.

Landline numbers will also be changing – all landline numbers will be prefixed with a 2. The implementation date is yet to be confirmed.

INFORMATION

Emergency

Fire (☎ 404 3333)
Police station (☎ 404 2221) The police emergency number is ☎ 999.
Traumalink 911 (☎ 606 0911) A 24-hour paramedic ambulance service.

Internet Access

There are internet centres at Swazi Post, located upstairs at Swazi Plaza, and in the Mall, near Spar. Internet access starts from E25 per hour.

Medical Services

Mbabane Clinic (☎ 404 2423; St Michael's Rd) For emergencies try this clinic in the southwest corner of town just off the bypass road.
Medi-Sun Clinic (☎ 416 2800; Ezulwini Valley) Behind Gables Shopping Complex, Ezulwini Valley.

Money

Banks with ATMs include First National Bank, Nedbank and Standard Bank; these are located in Swazi Plaza.

Post

Post office (Msunduza St) You can also make international (though not reverse-charge) calls here.

Tourist Information

Tourist information office (☎ 404 2531; www.welcometoswaziland.com; Cooper Centre office, 2 Sozisa Rd; 🕑 8am-4.45pm Mon-Thur, 8am-4pm Fri, 9am-1pm Sat) Free maps and brochures on hotels, restaurants and entertainment. These include the tourist bible *What's Happening in Swaziland* and the smaller *What's on in Swaziland*.

DANGERS & ANNOYANCES

Mbabane is becoming unsafe at night, so don't walk around by yourself away from the main streets. Take precautions in the streets even during the day – muggings are on the increase.

SIGHTS & ACTIVITIES

There's not really much to see in Mbabane. Eight kilometres northeast of Mbabane is **Sibebe Rock** (admission E30), a massive, sheer granite dome hulking over the surrounding countryside; the area is managed by the local community. **Swazi Trails** (☎ 416 2180; www.swazitrails.co.sz; Mantenga Craft Centre) in Ezulwini Valley takes half-day nontechnical climbs up the rock (per person E585, including transport).

The Ezulwini and Malkerns Valleys are where most people go for sightseeing, activities and crafts (see p592).

SLEEPING

Budget

Thokoza Church Centre (☎ 404 6681; Polinjane Rd; s/d with shared bathroom E181/218, s/d E216/253) Fittingly monastic in nature, these small clean rooms might convert you to Mbabane. Inexpensive meals can be arranged in the new dining room and breakfast is included. Turn left at the police station and head up Polinjane Rd for 500m; take a taxi at night (E30 from Swazi Plaza). Breakfast is included.

Veki's Guest House (☎ 404 8485; www.swazilodgings.com/vekis; 233 Gilfillan St; s/d E270/400, apt from E350) This nondescript but friendly place has homely, clean rooms decorated with animal print decor. Rooms have DSTV (cable TV); meals are available on request. Veki has several other options, including cottages and apartments.

Midrange & Top End

Kapola Guest House (☎ 404 0906; s/d incl breakfast E350/650) This comfortable abode's massive porch overlooks greenery. Busy rooms, and simple meals on request (E30 to E65). It's about 5km from Mbabane beside the MR3; watch for the wall painted with flags.

Brackenhill Lodge B&B (☎ 404 2887; www.brackenhillswazi.com; Mountain Drive; s/d E450/660) Located 4.5km north of Mbabane, this attractive place in tranquil gardens has a range of rooms, some more luxurious than others, but all airy and of the 'puffy pillow' variety. Ring for directions.

Foresters Arms (☎ 467 4177; www.forestersarms.co.za; s & d with half board from E480) Penelope Keith (from *To the Manor Born*) would enjoy the cream teas and the cosy, British-style interiors here. Situated 27km southwest of Mbabane in the hills around Mhlambanyatsi.

Mountain Inn (☎ 404 2781; www.mountaininn.sz; s/d incl breakfast from E525/670; ⊠ 💻 🏊) It's not five-star luxury, but this inn has a pleasant and homely ambience, a pool, library, restaurant and panoramas.

EATING

Portofino (The Mall; snacks E21-40; 🕑 8.30-5.30pm Mon-Fri, 8.30am-5pm Sat) A small and relaxed coffee shop serving reasonable coffee.

Indingilizi Gallery & Restaurant (☎ 404 6213; 112 Dzeliwe St; light meals from E30-50; 🕑 8am-5pm Mon-Fri,

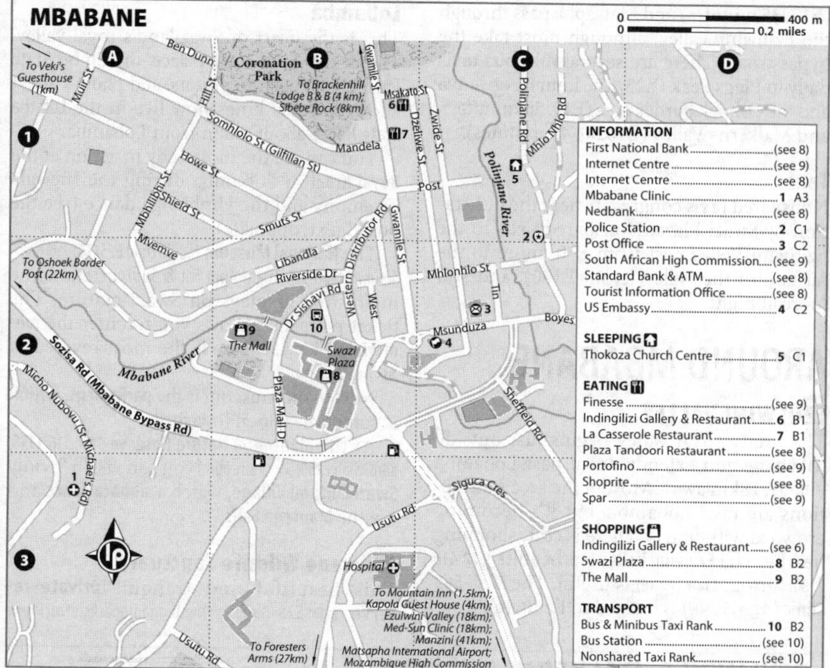

8.30am-1pm Sat) This small outdoor cafe-cum-gallery offers salads, crepes and curries.

Plaza Tandoori Restaurant (☎ 404 7599; Swazi Plaza; mains E35-90; ⌚ lunch & dinner) It's not the size of the Taj Mahal, but it's certainly got the atmosphere. As well as great-value curries, the usual grills and burgers add a touch of the international.

Finesse (☎ 404 5936; The Mall; mains E60-100; ⌚ lunch & dinner Mon-Sat) This French-owned place offers a smart and elegant setting under a covered terrace, and serves a good range of seafood and meat dishes.

La Casserole Restaurant (☎ 405 0778; Gwamile St; mains E65-100; ⌚ lunch & dinner) It has a French name, but this long-standing friendly place serves German and international cuisine, including pizzas. It also offers a few vegetarian dishes, plus a good wine selection.

There's a Shoprite at Swazi Plaza and a Spar at the Mall.

SHOPPING

Swazi Plaza is a large and modern shopping centre with most services and a good range of shops. Nearby, the Mall also has a number of shops and services.

Indingilizi Gallery & Restaurant (☎ 404 6213; 112 Dzeliwe St; ⌚ 8am-5pm Mon-Fri, 8.30am-1pm Sat) Has a range of contemporary art and collectables from Swaziland and elsewhere in Africa. Exhibitions are held regularly.

GETTING THERE & AWAY

Minibus taxis to South Africa (mostly northbound) leave from the taxi rank near Swazi Plaza; otherwise your best bet is to catch one from Manzini.

GETTING AROUND

To/From the Airport

A taxi from Mbabane to Matsapha International Airport costs around E150. Buses and minibuses from Mbabane to Manzini go past the turn-off to the airport, from where it's a long walk to the terminal.

Bus & Minibus Taxi

The main bus and minibus taxi rank is near Swazi Plaza. Vehicles heading towards Manzini

(E13, 35 minutes) and Matsapha pass through the Ezulwini Valley, although most take the bypass road. There are several minibus taxis daily to Piggs Peak (E25, one hour), Ngwenya and the Oshoek border post (E10, 50 minutes), and Malkerns Valley (E10.50, 45 minutes).

Taxi

Nonshared taxis congregate near the bus station by Swazi Plaza. Nonshared taxis to the Ezulwini Valley cost from E70, more to the far end of the valley (from E100), and still more at night.

AROUND MBABANE

EZULWINI VALLEY

The pretty royal valley begins just outside Mbabane and extends down past Lobamba village, 18km away. Most of the area's attractions are near Lobamba, but it's becoming crowded with hotels. There is craft shopping nearby. The **Ezulwini Valley tourist office** (☎ 416 2180; Mantenga Craft Centre) is useful. The **Medi-Sun Clinic** (☎ 416 2800) is located in Ezulwini.

Lobamba

This is the heart of Swaziland's royal valley. The British-built royal palace, the Embo State Palace, isn't open to visitors, and photo's aren't allowed. Swazi kings now live in the **Lozitha State House** about 10km from Lobamba.

You can see the monarchy in action at the **Royal Kraal** in Lobamba during the Incwala ceremony and the Umhlanga dance (see the boxed text, opposite).

The **National Museum** (adult/child E25/15; 🕒 8am-4.30pm Mon-Fri, 10am-4pm Sat & Sun) offers some interesting displays on Swazi culture. The ticket price also allows you to enter the **memorial to King Sobhuza II**, the most revered of Swazi kings.

Next to the museum is the **parliament**, which is sometimes open to visitors.

At the **Mantenga Nature Reserve** (☎ 516 1178; admission E150; 🕒 7am-6pm) you can visit a 'living' **Swazi Cultural Village**, watch a **sibhaca dance** and see the **Mantega Falls**.

Mlilwane Wildlife Sanctuary

This beautiful and tranquil **private reserve** (☎ 528 3943; www.biggameparks.org; www

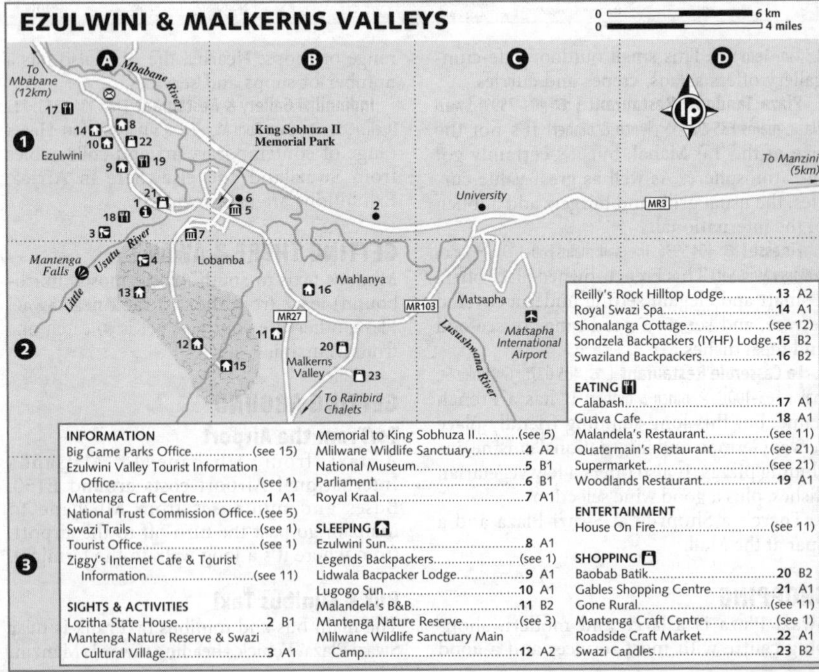

SWAZI CEREMONIES

Incwala

The Incwala (sometimes Ncwala) is the most sacred Swazi ceremony. During this 'first fruits' ceremony the king gives his people permission to eat the first crops of the new year.

Preparation for the Incwala begins some weeks in advance. *Bemanti* (learned men) journey to the Lebombo Mountains to gather plants, other groups of *bemanti* collect water from Swaziland's rivers and some travel to the Indian Ocean (where the Dlamini clan lived long before the Swazi nation came into being) to skim foam from the waves.

On the night of the full moon, young men all over the kingdom begin a long trek to the Royal Kraal at Lobamba. They arrive at dawn and build a *kraal* (hut village) with branches gathered on their journey. Participants sing songs prohibited during the rest of the year, and the *bemanti* arrive with their plants, water and foam.

On the third day a bull is sacrificed. On the fourth day, the king breaks his retreat and dances before his people. He eats a pumpkin, the sign that Swazis can eat the new year's crops. Soon after, the rains are expected to fall.

Umhlanga

Not as sacred as the Incwala, the Umhlanga (Reed) dance serves a similar function in drawing the nation together and reminding the people of their relationship to the king. It is something like a week-long debutante ball for marriageable young Swazi women and a showcase of potential wives for the king.

On the sixth day young women perform the Umhlanga dance and carry their reeds to the queen mother. They repeat the dance the next day. Princesses wear red feathers in their hair.

.mlilwane-wildlife-sanctuary.com; admission E25; ⌚ 6.30am-5.30pm summer, 6am-6pm winter) near Lobamba was Swaziland's first protected area, created in the 1950s by conservationist Ted Reilly. Reilly later opened Mkhaya Game Reserve (p598) and supervised the establishment of Hlane Royal National Park (p598). Mlilwane means 'Little Fire', named after the many fires started by lightning strikes in the region.

While it doesn't have the drama or vastness of some of the South African parks, the reserve is easily accessible and worth a visit. Its terrain is dominated by the precipitous Nyonyane (Little Bird) peak, and there are some fine walks in the area. Animals include zebras, giraffes, warthogs, antelope species, crocodiles, hippos and a variety of birds, including black eagles.

Activities are a must here. There are horse rides (one to three hours E120, fully catered overnight trips E1085), mountain biking (per person per hour E95) and wildlife walks (per person per hour E50).

Sleeping

All accommodation in the sanctuary can be booked (and paid) in advance through **Big Game Parks** (☎ 528 3943/4; www.biggameparks.org). You can make bookings via telephone or email.

BUDGET & MIDRANGE

Sondzela Backpackers (IYHF) Lodge (campsites per person E45, dm E80, s/d with shared bathroom E155/220, rondavel s/d E170/240) This place needs a good touch up here and there (it's looking a bit scruffy around the edges), but its delightful gardens, and a hilltop perch in Mlilwane, provide one of the best backpackers' settings in Southern Africa.

Mlilwane Wildlife Sanctuary Main Camp (campsites per person E60, hut s/d E315/450) This homely camp is set in a scenic wooded location 3.5km from Mlilwane's entry gate, complete with simple thatched huts – including traditional beehive huts.

Mantenga Nature Reserve (☎ 516 1178; mnr@africaonline.co.sz; beehives E80, s/d safari tents incl breakfast E430/585) Adjacent to Milwane, this reserve has safari tents, offering soft 'safari' adventure in stylish canvas comfort. There's a good on-site restaurant.

Shonalanga Cottage (s/d E350/500, per extra person E140) This spacious self-catering cottage is near the main camp, and a good choice for families.

GO WILD!

Wildlife Drives

For wildlife drives, the Big Game Parks reserves organise good-value tours. Mkhaya (p598) offers Land Rover day trips (E475, minimum two people, includes lunch). These trips must be pre-booked through **Big Game Parks** (Map p592; ☎ 528 3943/4; www.biggameparks.org). Set arrival and departure times are 10am and 4pm. Hlane (p598) has a two-hour sunrise/sunset drive (E190, minimum two people); Mlilwane (p592) offers a shorter game drive (E165, minimum two people). Check the website www.biggameparks.org for the latest activities on offer, as these do change.

White-Water Rafting

One of Swaziland's highlights is white-water rafting on the **Usutu River**. This largely sluggish river turns to rapids through the narrow Bulungu Gorge. In sections, you'll encounter Grade IV rapids, which aren't for the faint-hearted, although even first-timers with a sense of adventure should handle the day easily. You may glimpse a 'flat dog' (crocodile) along the more sedate sections.

Swazi Trails (Map p592; ☎/fax 416 2180; www.swazitrails.co.sz; Mantenga Craft Centre, Ezulwini Valley) offers full- and half-day trips (E750/650 per person, including lunch and transport, minimum two people). Trips run from the Ezulwini Valley.

SWAZILAND

Other good budget hostels close to Milwane:

Legends Backpackers Lodge (☎ 416 1870; legends@mailfly.com; campsites per person E45, dm E90, d with shared bathroom E220; 💻)

Lidwala Backpacker Lodge (☎ 550 4951; www.all-out.org; campsites R50, dm & safari tents per person E90, d R220)

TOP END

Reilly's Rock Hilltop Lodge (s/d from E840/1200) This tranquil, colonial-world luxury accommodation within Milwane has views of the valley and Mdzimba Mountains.

The Sun group's hotels (www.suninternational.com), in Ezulwini, offer the most opulent accommodation in the country. There's the **Royal Swazi Spa** (☎ 416 5000; s/d E2355/2480; ❄ 💻 🏊) with golf course and casino; the **Lugogo Sun** (☎ 416 4500; s/d E1480/1590; ❄ 🏊) and the **Ezulwini Sun** (☎ 416 6500; s/d E1640/1745; ❄ 🏊), across the road from the other two.

Eating

Quatermain's (☎ 416 3023; Gables Shopping Centre; mains E50-100; 🕑 lunch & dinner) Has an extensive menu. Arrive hungry.

Woodlands Restaurant (☎ 416 3466; mains E75-143; 🕑 lunch & dinner) Good vegetarian options and international cuisine on a lovely shady verandah.

Calabash (☎ 416 1187; mains E80-130; 🕑 lunch & dinner) Specialises in German and Swiss cuisine.

For light meals, head to **Guava Cafe** (☎ 416 1343; snacks E50-90, light meals from E30; 🕑 9am-5pm Tue-Sat, 10am-5pm Sun).

There is a supermarket located in the Gables Shopping Centre as well as several other good restaurants.

Shopping

The best crafts are to be found at the **Roadside Craft Market** (🕑 dawn - dusk), opposite the Royal Swazi Spa in Ezulwini. Also in Ezulwini, the **Mantenga Craft Centre** (☎ 416 1136; 🕑 8am-5pm) has been recycled into a community of artists, and craft shops with a sustainable focus. The more modern **Gables Shopping Centre** (🕑 8am-5pm Mon-Fri, to 1pm Sat) has a supermarket and also offers internet and necessities, including an ATM.

Getting There & Away

During the day you could get on a Manzini-bound minibus, but make sure the driver knows that you want to alight in Ezulwini Valley, as many aren't keen on stopping.

Nonshared taxis from Mbabane cost E70 to E130, depending on how far down the valley you go.

If you're driving from either Mbabane or Manzini, take the Ezulwini Valley/Lobamba exit off the bypass road to the MR103.

MALKERNS VALLEY

About 7km south of Lobamba on the MR103 is the turn-off to the fertile Malkerns Valley, known for its arts and crafts outlets, and offering a scenic and fun drive.

There's internet access and tourist information at **Ziggy's Internet Cafe & Tourist Information**

(☎ 528 3423; per hr E25; ⌚ 8am-5pm Mon-Fri, 10am-5pm Sat & Sun) at the Malandela's complex.

Sleeping & Eating

Swaziland Backpackers (☎ 528 2038; campsites per person E45, dm E80, d with shared bathroom E200;) This super laid-back place – with dorms, camping, kitchen and other services – has the feel of a giant holiday house. It has well-organised dorms and an airy lounge with bright cushions. It's on the M103, at the junction with the turn-off to Malendela's.

Malandela's B&B (☎ 605 2598, 528 3448; r per person with breakfast E180;) Along the MR27, this place offers stylish, ethnic African rooms, a pool and a sculpture garden.

Rainbird Chalets (☎ 603 7273; s/d E380/660) Three lovely log chalets set in a manicured, rose-filled private garden near the owners' house. All are fully equipped, and have pine floors and smart bathrooms with claw-foot baths. Ring to ask for directions.

Malandela's Restaurant (☎ 528 3115; mains E45-80; ⌚ lunch & dinner Mon-Sun) Part of the Malandela's complex, this is one of the best restaurants in the region.

Entertainment

House on Fire (☎ 528 2001; www.house-on-fire.com) This well-known venue, at the Malandela's complex is a fantastically decorated experimental-performance space – it hosts everything from African theatre to raves. Since 2007, it has hosted the annual Bush Fire Festival (www.bush-fire.com), featuring poetry, theatre and music, among other performances.

Shopping

Gone Rural (☎ 528 3436; www.goneruralswazi.com; ⌚ 8am-5pm Mon-Sat, 9am-5pm Sun) Located in the Malendala's complex, this is the place to go for baskets, mats and traditional clay pots.

Baobab Batik (☎ 528 3242; www.baobab-batik.com; ⌚ 8am-5pm) If you're dye-ing for a hanging there's this place. It's well signed.

Swazi Candles (☎ 528 3219; www.swazicandles.com; ⌚ 8am-5pm) Wax lyrical about the designs here. Also well signed.

MANZINI

Manzini, Swaziland's largest town and the country's industrial centre, was the administrative centre for the squabbling British and Boers from 1890 to 1902. During the Anglo-Boer War a renegade Boer commando burnt it down.

Today Manzini is an active commercial and industrial hub whose small centre is dominated by office blocks and a couple of shopping malls. There is a slight hint of menace – watch out for pickpockets and be careful; crime – including muggings – is more common here than elsewhere in Swaziland.

Manzini's main drawcard is its colourful **market** (cnr Mhlakuvane & Mancishane Sts; ⌚ closed Sun). The upper section is packed with handicrafts. Apart from visiting the market, you can happily move on.

Tours

Kaphunga Homestead Swaziland Cultural Tours (☎ 604 4102; www.swazi live/myxo/html), headed by local Swazi Myxo Mdluli, runs highly recommended village visits and overnight stays (E550 to E720) to Kaphunga, 55km southeast of Manzini.

Sleeping & Eating

Myxo's Backpackers (☎ 604 4102; campsites E45, dm/d with shared bathroom E90/200) This casual backpackers is in an old farm house 5km northeast of Manzini and 1km off the main road, and offers shared rooms and doubles overlooking indigenous forest. Owner Myxo runs village tours (see above).

Tum's George Hotel (☎ 505 8991; www.tgh.sz; cnr Ngwane & du Toit Sts; s/d incl breakfast from E680/890;) Manzini's fanciest hotel attempts an international atmosphere, and caters for the conference crowd. It has a pool bar and stylish restaurants.

Gil Vincente Restaurant (☎ 505 3874; Ngwane St; mains R30-100; ⌚ lunch & dinner Tue-Sun) This is an elegant choice, with smart decor and high-quality Italian and international cuisine. It's in the Makhaya Centre, down from Tum's George Hotel.

Takeaways abound in Bhunu Mall and on Ngwane St.

Getting There & Away

The main bus and minibus taxi rank is at the northern end of Louw St, where you can also find some nonshared taxis. A minibus taxi trip up the Ezulwini Valley to Mbabane costs E15 (35 minutes). A nonshared taxi to Matsapha International Airport costs around E50. Minibus taxis to Mozambique leave from the car park next to KFC up the hill.

See p290 and p576 for more info.

NORTHWESTERN SWAZILAND

Lush hills, plantations and woodlands, streams and waterfalls and plunging ravines are the main features of Swaziland's beautiful north, along with some excellent hiking and accommodation options. Beware the heavy mists that roll in during the summer months – they can limit visibility to almost zero.

NGWENYA

Tiny Ngwenya (Crocodile) is 5km east of the Oshoek border crossing on the road to Mbabane. At **Ngwenya Glass Factory** (☎ 442 4142; 🕑 8am-4.30pm Mon-Fri, 8am-4pm Sat & Sun) recycled glass is used to create African animals and birds as well as vases and tableware. Further up the hill is the newer **Etulu Cultural High Grounds**, with tapestries and basic crafts. Both are within 1km of each other and signposted from the main road.

Also near here is the **Ngwenya iron ore mine** (admission E20; 🕑 8am-4pm), dating from around 40,000 BC and one of the world's oldest known mines.

Hawane Resort (☎ 627 6714; www.hawane.com; dm E115, s/d chalet incl breakfast E550/840;) offers stylish chalets that are a blend of traditional Swazi materials and glass with ethnic African interiors. Backpackers are stabled in a converted barn. It's about 8km up the Piggs Peak road from the junction of the MR1 and MR3, and 1.5km off the main road.

MALOLOTJA NATURE RESERVE

This beautiful middleveld/highveld **reserve** (☎ 442 4241; www.malolotja.com; adult/child E28/14; 🕑 6am-6pm) is a true wilderness area, rugged and for the most part unspoiled. The terrain ranges from mountainous and high-altitude grassland to forest and lower-lying bushveld, all with streams and cut by three rivers, including the Komati River.

It's an excellent walking destination, with around 200km of hiking trails, and an ornithologist's paradise, with over 280 species of birds. Wildflowers and rare plants are added attractions; several are found only in this part of Africa.

Basic brochures outlining hiking trails are available for free at reception; arrange a permit here as well. Hikes range from short trails to a week-long jaunt that extends from Ngwenya in the south to the Mgwayiza Range in the north. For all longer walks, you'll have to bring whatever food you'll need, as well as a camp stove, as fires are not permitted outside the base camp. Wildlife drives can be arranged with advance notice.

Accommodation consists of **camping** (per person at main campsite/on trails E70/50), either at the well-equipped (but infrequently used) main site, with ablutions and braai (barbecue) area, or along the overnight trails (no facilities). Self-catering wooden **cabins** (per person E230, minimum E400, children half-price) sleep a maximum of six people. At the time of research, Hawane Resort (see left) had formed a joint venture project with Swaziland National Trust Commission with plans to upgrade the accommodation within the reserve and construct a restaurant; prices may have increased on those quoted here.

The entrance gate for Malolotja is about 35km northwest of Mbabane, along the Piggs Peak road (MR1); minibus taxis will drop you here.

WORTH THE TRIP

If you have time, it's worth taking a detour to the community-run **Nsangwini Rock Art Shelter** (☎ 637 3767; per person R25). The paintings are under a small, but impressive rock shelter, which is perched over the Komati River and affords lovely views across the mountains. The cave was believed to be that of the Nsangwini Bushmen. Nsangwini is signed from the main Piggs Peak road and the Maguga Dam loop road. Follow a dirt road for 7.5km; parking is available at the small reception hut. A local guide will take you on the slightly steep and rocky walk (15 minutes down, 20 minutes up) and will give a brief explanation.

PIGGS PEAK

This small, gritty town is the centre of Swaziland's logging industry. Tragically, much of the forested area – pine plantations – was destroyed by forest fires in 2007. The town was named after a prospector who found gold here in 1884.

As well as its scenery, including the **Phophonyane Falls** about 8km north of town, this area is known for its handicrafts. Check these out at the Peak Craft Centre just north of Orion Piggs Peak Hotel & Casino, where you'll find **Likhweti Kraft** (☎ 437 3127) and a branch of **Tintsaba Crafts** (☎ 437 1260; www.tintsaba.com), which sells sisal baskets, jewellery, and many other Swazi crafts. There are also numerous craft vendors along the road up from Mbabane.

Sleeping

Jabula Guest House (☎ 437 1052; www.swaziplace.com/jabulaguesthouse; s/d incl breakfast E295/445;) The best B&B in Piggs Peak (Swaziland even), whose delightful owner runs small, neat rooms in a pretty, residential setting. Turn right at the Piggs Peak Clinic sign and follow the signs.

Phophonyane Lodge & Nature Reserve (☎ 437 1319; www.phophonyane.co.sz; safari tent s/d incl breakfast per person from E650/920, cottage s/d incl breakfast from E860/1300;) This stunning hideaway, run by keen conservationists, lies northeast of Piggs Peak on a river in its own nature reserve of lush indigenous forest. There's a network of walking trails around the river and waterfall. Accommodation is in comfortable cottages (with a self-catering option), stylish beehives and luxury safari tents overlooking cascades. Excellent meals are available in the pleasant dining area (mains from E50). Day visitors to the reserve are charged E30/20 per adult/child, lodge residents E20/10. The lodge is about 14km north of Piggs Peak. Follow the signposts off the main road – you will cross a bridge over the waterfall and turn right 500m on.

Getting There & Away

The minibus taxi stand is next to the market at the top end of the main street, with several vehicles daily to Bulembu (E8, 30 minutes) and Mbabane (E20, one hour).

The stretch of dirt road running west from Piggs Peak to Bulembu can be boggy when wet. The road to Barberton (Mpumalanga) in South Africa has been recently paved.

BULEMBU

An interesting detour from Piggs Peak is to wind your way 20km through scenic plantation country to the historic town of Bulembu, built in 1936 for the former Havelock asbestos mine. Following its closure, the 10,000 workers left and by 2003 Bulembu was a ghost town with around 100 residents. Several years ago, the town's new investors started a community tourism project (based on Christian principles) bringing the town back to life. Thousands of deserted corrugated iron houses and many art deco buildings which nestle on a pretty hilly landscape, are being renovated. There's even a former cableway. Stunning hikes include the highest mountain in Swaziland, Emlembe Peak (1863m). Note: asbestos dumps exist around the village.

Accommodation is available in the main **Bulembu Lodge** (☎ 437 3888, 602 4577; www.bulembu.org; per person from E240) in the former general manager's residence or stylish directors' cottages, all renovated. Alternatively, you can choose a spacious and delightfully converted house, known as 'village stays' (E130). Basic meals are served in the lodge's **dining room** (breakfast E35-60, lunch/dinner E40/85).

SWAZILAND

EASTERN SWAZILAND

The hot, northeastern corner of Swaziland is a major sugar-producing area. The arid foothills of the Lebombo Mountains epitomise what most people think of as 'Africa'.

This area's notable parks and reserves are Hlane, Mlawula and Mkhaya. The towns of Tshaneni, Mhlume, Tambankulu and Simunye are the main population centres in the country's northeast.

SITEKI

Heading for Siteki is the fastest route to Mozambique from Manzini, through the Mhlumeni–Goba border. This nice enough, if uneventful, place lies above the surrounding lowveld, with wide views and cooler temperatures.

The town was originally named when Mbandzeni (great-grandfather of the present king) gave his frontier troops permission to marry – Siteki means Marrying Place.

The highly recommended **Mabuda Farm** (☎ 343 4124; www.geocities.com/mabudafarm; campsites E70, dm E95, d incl breakfast E500-550) has a range of delightful choices: self-contained cottage-style rondavels (decorated with colonial relics), newer self-contained four-person chalets, a backpackers' and a camping area. It's on a working farm just outside Siteki.

Minibus taxis from Manzini run twice daily (E26, one hour). There are daily minibus taxis

COMMUNITY STAYS

Several excellent community-owned tourism projects operate in Swaziland. **Shewula Mountain Camp** (☎ 603 1931, 605 1160; www.shewulacamp.com; dm/r E90/260), a camp northeast of Simunye in the Lebombo Mountains, is 36km by dirt road (15km as the crow flies). You can camp or stay in basic rondavels, with shared ablutions and self-catering facilities. Bring fly spray (domesticated animals still roam through the camp; the manure seems to attract flies) and binoculars (for the wonderful views from the camp). Local meals can also be arranged (breakfast/lunch/dinner E35/50/65; must be booked in advance) as can guided cultural walks to nearby villages plus guided nature- and birdwatching walks (per person E30). The newer **Mahamba Gorge Lodge** (☎ 268 617 9880; s/d E250/350; day visitors E10), near Nhlangano, has received good reports for its clean, modern stone chalets and wonderful guided walks (per person E50) through the nearby gorge, where there are nesting eagles. Contact the tourism office in Mbabane (p590) or the **Ezulwini Tourist Information Office** (Map p592; ☎ 416 1834; www.swazi.travel; Mantenga Craft Centre, Ezulwini Valley) for more information.

connecting Siteki with Big Bend (E28, one hour) and Simunye (E15, 30 minutes).

HLANE ROYAL NATIONAL PARK

This **national park** (☎ 528 3943; www.biggameparks.org, www.hlane-national-park.com; admission E25; 🕑 6am-6pm) in the northeast is near the former royal hunting grounds and offers wonderfully low-key wildlife watching (white rhinos, antelope species, elephants and lions). There are guided walking trails (per person E75), two-hour wildlife day drives (per person E145 to E155, minimum two people), a cultural village tour with dance performances (per person E50, minimum four) and mountain-bike rentals (two hours E120). Minibus taxis to Simunye will drop you at the entrance to Hlane (E5; 7km from Simunye).

Ndlovu Camp (campsites per person E40, rondavel s/d from E295/410, 8-person cottages per person E220) is a pleasant and rustic fenced-off camp, with no electricity, a communal area and a restaurant.

our pick **Bhubesi Camp** (cottages E350-460) is the pick of the spots: it overlooks a river about 10km from Ndlovu Camp. Accommodation is in tasteful, stone, four-person, self-catering cottages.

Book for both through the **Big Game Parks office** (Map p592; ☎ 528 3943/4; www.biggameparks.org).

MLAWULA NATURE RESERVE

This tranquil **reserve** (☎ 383 8885; www.mlawula.com; adult/child E25/12; 🕑 6am-6pm), where the lowveld plains meet the Lebombo Mountains, boasts antelope species, hyenas and crocodiles, plus rewarding birdwatching. You can bring your own mountain bike, and walking (from two- to nine-hour hikes) along plateaus, or to caves and a waterfall is a highlight here.

There's tented accommodation at **Sara Camp** (s/d E150/300), and **Siphiso camping ground** (campsites per person E60). **Mapelepele Cottage** (up to 8 people, minimum E500) is self-catering. At the time of research, booking arrangements were changing; you should be able to arrange accommodation at the reserve's reception office, but check this with the **Ezulwini Tourist Information Office** (Map p592; ☎ 416 1834; www.swazi.travel; Mantenga Craft Centre, Ezulwini Valley) or the **National Trust Commission** (Map p592; ☎ 416 1151, 416 1178; www.sntc .org.sz).

MBULUZI GAME RESERVE

The small and privately owned **Mbuluzi Game Reserve** (☎ 383 8861; mbuluzi@swazi.net; adult/child E25/12.50) boasts a range of animals, including giraffes, zebras, hippos, antelope species and wildebeests. There have also been over 300 bird species recorded here.

Accommodation at Mbulzi, in some lovely self-catering **lodges** (5-/8-person lodges E400/E720-1600;), is more luxurious than at neighbouring Mlawula Nature Reserve. Some lodges have spacious verandahs, wooden viewing decks and are set on the Mlawula River. **Campsites** (per person E30) are also available near the Mbuluzi River.

The turn-off for Mbuluzi is the same as for Mlawula; the reserve entrance is about 300m from the turn-off on the left.

MKHAYA GAME RESERVE

This top-notch **private reserve** (☎ 528 3943/4; www.biggameparks.org, www.mkhaya-game-reserve.com), off the Manzini–Big Bend road near the hamlet of Phuzumoya, was established in 1979 to save the pure Nguni breed of cattle from extinction. Its focus expanded to antelopes, elephants, and white and black rhinos. The reserve's name comes from the *mkhaya* (or knobthorn) tree, which abounds here.

You can't visit or stay in the reserve without booking in advance, and even then you can't drive in alone; you'll be met at Phuzumoya at a specified pick-up time, usually 10am or 4pm. While day tours can be arranged, it's ideal to stay for at least one night.

our pick **Stone Camp** (all-inclusive s/d with full board E1650/2700) has a smart, slightly colonial feel; it's well worth the stopover. Accommodation is in rustic and luxurious semi-open stone and thatch cottages (a proper loo with a view). The price includes wildlife drives, walking safaris, park entry and meals; it's excellent value compared with many of the private reserves near Kruger National Park in South Africa.

SIMUNYE

Simunye is a manicured sugar-company town with little of interest for travellers, except as a possible stocking-up point for visiting nearby Hlane Royal National Park, or Mlawula and Mbuluzi Nature Reserves, or a bed if you're caught short.

Tambankulu Country Club B&B (☎ 373 7111; s/d E310/464, guest house s/d E406/677;) has plain but comfortable rooms and a guest house, set in delightful grounds with lush lawns and garden, a swimming pool and a tennis court; it also has a bar and restaurant. The club is north of Simunye; head 6km west of the junction at Maphiveni, and another 3km off the Tshaneni road.

Simunye Country Club (☎ 313 4792; www.visitswazi.com; s/d from E329/624, cottage s/d E448/624;) is a friendly and tranquil spot with small single rooms, modern self-catering cottages and a bar-restaurant. Although it's a club, visitors are welcome and can use the club facilities (swimming pool, golf course, tennis and squash courts).

Several minibus taxis run daily from Manzini to Simunye (one hour), and further north to the junction for Mlawula and Mbuluzi. There's also at least one minibus taxi daily to/from Piggs Peak (2½ hours).

BIG BEND

Picturesque Big Bend is a sleepy sugar town on – not surprisingly – a big bend in the Lusutfu River, and makes a convenient stop en route to/from KwaZulu-Natal in South Africa.

Riverside Hotel (☎ 363 6910; s/d with breakfast E250/350;) Friendly with decent rooms and a good restaurant (mains E40 to E80; open breakfast, lunch and dinner). It's nearly 2km further south past Lismore Lodge on the MR8.

Lebombo Villa B&B (☎ 603 6585; www.swazilive.com; s/d R320/550;) A modern Italianate mansion with 10 highly organised rooms in all shapes and sizes. Call for directions.

LL Restaurant Bar (☎ 363 6080; mains E40-80; lunch & dinner) On the MR8, here you can get reasonable seafood dishes, including calamari and seafood curry.

Minibus taxis go daily to Manzini (E33, one hour) and to the Lavumisa border post (one hour).

SOUTHERN SWAZILAND

In former years, because of its easy access to KwaZulu-Natal, southern Swaziland was frequently visited for its roulette tables, rather than its surroundings. Nowadays many tourists don't gamble on a visit; they think it lacks the north's dramatic scenery. While the entire area is quiet and rural, this is the place to set off on a bike or on foot to discover the 'real' and remote Swaziland, especially around the Ngwempisi Gorge.

NGWEMPISI GORGE

The **Ngwempisi Gorge** (☎ 625 6004), 30km south of the Malkerns Valley, is one of the country's few remaining untouched environments with beautiful forests and the Ngwempisi River. Adventure-seekers will love the Ngwempisi Hiking Trail, a community-run 33km trail in the Ntfungula Hills on the Mankayane–Vlelzizweni road. You can spend two to three days exploring the area and sleep en route in atmospheric huts. It's recommended you take a **local guide** (per day E50, plus per hiker E10).

Horseshoe Estate B&B (☎ 606 1512; per person E150), is near the trail entrance and can also arrange hikes.

SWAZILAND DIRECTORY

ACCOMMODATION

There are few designated campsites in Swaziland, except in many of the national parks and reserves. It's usually possible (and

SWAZILAND

PRACTICALITIES

- The *Times* (www.times.co.sz), a virtual mouthpiece for royalty and a would-be lurid tabloid, is a fascinating read as much for what it doesn't say as what it does.
- The *Swazi Observer* is a daily publication.
- The electricity supply in Swaziland is 220V. Plugs have three large round pins as used in South Africa.
- Swaziland uses the metric system.

safe) to camp in rural areas, but *always* ask permission from local people.

You'll find hostels and budget accommodation in Mbabane, Manzini and Ezulwini Valley. Many of the country's hotels are expensive, but there are some good midrange B&B options available.

Prices for accommodation in this chapter are: budget E300 and below, midrange E300 to E800, top end E800 and above.

ACTIVITIES

Small in size, big on action. Swaziland offers some terrific white-water rafting (in the rainy season), horse riding, mountain biking and birdwatching.

Hikers can enjoy the walking trails in several parks, plus the countless ancient walking tracks. Make sure you are well prepared and seek local advice on conditions.

BOOKS & FILMS

The Kingdom of Swaziland, by D Hugh Gillis, is a history (to independence) of the kingdom seeking to maintain its traditional way of life in the face of an overwhelming European influence.

All the King's Animals: The Return of Endangered Wildlife to Swaziland, by Cristina Kessler and Mswati III, is the story of the conservationist Ted Reilly and the successful reintroduction of endangered wildlife into the kingdom.

The film, *Wah-Wah*, the account of actor Richard E Grant's childhood in Swaziland, is worth seeing.

BUSINESS HOURS

Offices and shops are usually open 8am to 5pm Monday to Friday. Bank hours are 8.30am to 3.30pm Monday to Friday, with some banks also opening 9.30am to 11.00am on Saturday.

CHILDREN

Travelling with little 'uns should be hassle-free in Swaziland. Most accommodation options, especially the more upmarket establishments, cater to young visitors. Many hotels have pools and entertainment facilities. Elsewhere, national parks are good to visit with kids. It's best to bring a baby-rucksack – negotiating a pram anywhere in the country would be tricky. Stock up on baby food before heading to remote areas.

CUSTOMS REGULATIONS

You're permitted to import 400 cigarettes and 50 cigars and 250g of tobacco; one bottle (maximum 750mL) of alcoholic beverage; and 284mL of perfume per person. The import and export of protected animal products such as ivory is not permitted.

DANGERS & ANNOYANCES

Beware of both schistosomiasis (bilharzia) and malaria. (For more information on how to avoid contracting these potentially deadly diseases, see p771.) Malaria is a risk in the northeast near Mozambique; you'll be at highest risk from November to April. In the late 1990s there was a sturdy eradication program around this area to eliminate malaria (controversially, in the form of DDT), but it's best to be cautious.

EMBASSIES & CONSULATES

Mozambique (☎ 404 3700; Princess Dr, Mbabane)
South Africa (Map p591; ☎ 404 4651; The Mall, PO Box 2507, Mbabane)
USA (Map p591; ☎ 404 6441; http://mbabane.us embassy.gov; 7th fl, Central Bank Bldg, Warner Street, Mbabane) Note that hours for visas are limited.

FESTIVALS & EVENTS

Sibhaca dancing competitions are held – ask the Mbabane tourist office for details. You can see performances in the Mantenga Nature Reserve (see p592).

The most important cultural events in Swaziland are held near Lobamba in the Ezulwini Valley: the Incwala ceremony, held sometime between late December and early January, and the Umhlanga (Reed) dance held in August or September (see the boxed text, p593). Photography and sound recording are not permitted at the Incwala, but photography is allowed at the Umhlanga dance.

GAY & LESBIAN TRAVELLERS

Swaziland is more conservative than South Africa and some other African countries. Gay sexual relationships are culturally taboo and officially illegal in Swaziland – imprisonment and fines apply. Open displays of affection are generally frowned upon whatever your gender or orientation.

HOLIDAYS

Public holidays observed in Swaziland:

New Year's Day 1 January
Easter (March/April) Good Friday, Holy Saturday and Easter Monday
King Mswati III's Birthday 19 April
National Flag Day 25 April
King Sobhuza II's Birthday 22 July
Umhlanga (Reed) Dance August/September
Somhlolo Day (Independence) 6 September
Christmas Day 25 December
Boxing Day 26 December
Incwala Ceremony December/January (dates vary each year)

INTERNET ACCESS

Internet facilities are scarce outside Mbabane, Manzini and the Ezulwini and Malkerns Valleys.

INTERNET RESOURCES

Discover Swaziland (www.welometoswaziland.com) A commercial, but most thorough site.
Swaziland National Trust Commission (www.sntc.org.sz) Helpful site with information about Swaziland's cultural heritage.

LANGUAGE

The official languages are Swati and English, and English is the official written language. For some useful words and phrases in Swati, see p784.

MAPS

The main tourist information office hands out a free map of Swaziland, which has city plans for Mbabane and Manzini shown on the reverse. The Swaziland Tourism Authority also has hiking maps of most popular hiking spots including Shewula, Mlawula, Sibebe, Mlilwane, Mantenga, Mahamba, Ngwempisi and Malolotja. Topographical maps (1:50,000) are available from the **Ministry of Public Works** (☎ 404 6267; Mhlambanyatsi Rd, Mbabane), although these maps have not been reprinted for years while the office is digitising new data.

MONEY

The unit of currency is the lilangeni (plural emalangeni – E), which is fixed at a value equal to the South African rand. Rand are accepted everywhere and there's no need to change them. Emalangeni are difficult to change for other currencies outside Swaziland. (For more details on exchange rates, see the Quick Reference page on the inside front cover of this book.)

Only a few ATMs accept international credit or debit cards. The most convenient are those listed at Swazi Plaza, Mbabane, and inside the Royal Swazi Spa's casino, Ezulwini.

NedBank and First National Bank change cash and travellers cheques. Most banks ask to see the receipt of purchase when cashing travellers cheques.

The normal practice for tipping in rural parts of Swaziland is to round up a bill. In smarter tourist establishments, 5% to 10% is usual.

PHOTOGRAPHY & VIDEO

Film and photographic accessories are available in Mbabane and Manzini.

Don't take photos of soldiers, police, airports or government buildings. It is prohibited to photograph or sound record the Incwala ceremony. It goes without saying that you should always ask permission before taking a photo of anyone, particularly in ethnic villages.

POST

Post offices are open from 8am to 4pm weekdays, and until 11am Saturday.

TELEPHONE

See p589 for details of changes to Swaziland's phone network announced at the time this book went to print.

Swaziland has a reasonable telephone network. The international country code is ☎ 268; there are no area codes. International calls are most easily made using MTN phone cards. Dial ☎ 00 for international, then the country code and city code.

Mobile-phone services are MTN and **Vodacom** (www.vodacom.co.za). These do not generally reach mountainous regions.

TOURIST INFORMATION

Swaziland's main **tourist information office** (Map p591; ☎ 404 2531; www.welcometoswaziland.com; Cooper Centre office 2 Sozisa Rd; 8am-4.45pm Mon-Thur, 8am-4pm Fri, 9am-1pm Sat) is in Mbabane. The websites of **Swazi National Trust** (www.sntc.org.sz) and **Big Game Parks** (www.biggameparks.org) offer useful parks information. Privately run by Swazi Trails, the **Ezulwini Tourist Information Office** (Map p592; ☎ 416 1834; www.swazi.travel; Mantenga Craft Centre, Ezulwini Valley) also supplies tourist information.

VISAS

Most people don't need a visa to visit Swaziland. Those who do, need to obtain them in advance from the **Swaziland High Commission** (☎ South Africa 012-344 1910; 715 Government Avenue, Arcadia) in Pretoria. Anyone staying for more than 30 days must apply for an extension of stay. If staying for longer than 60 days you must apply for a temporary residence permit from the **Chief Immigration Officer** (☎ 404 2941; PO Box 372, Mbabane) whose offices are in the Ministry of Home Affairs.

TRANSPORT IN SWAZILAND

GETTING THERE & AWAY

This section covers travel between Swaziland and its neighbours, South Africa and Mozambique. (For information on reaching Swaziland from elsewhere on the African continent and from other continents, see p755.)

Entering Swaziland

Most travellers enter Swaziland overland from South Africa, although it's also possible to fly in from Johannesburg and Mozambique. A passport is required for entering Swaziland and entry is usually hassle-free. No vaccination certificates are required unless you have recently been in a yellow-fever area.

Air

Swaziland Airlink (☎ 518 6155; www.saairlink.co.za) operates out of Matsapha airport, north of Manzini. It flies daily between Swaziland and Johannesburg (M770).

Border Crossings

SOUTH AFRICA

There are 13 South Africa–Swaziland border crossings, including the following:

Golela–Lavumisa (7am-10pm)
Houtkop–Sicunusa (8am-6pm)
Josefsdal–Bulembu (8am-4pm)
Mahamba (7am-10pm)
Matsamo–Jeppe's Reef (7am-8pm)
Oshoek–Ngwenya (7am-10pm)

To/From Durban & Johannesburg

The **Baz Bus** (☎ in South Africa 021-439 2323; www.bazbus.com) runs from Jo'burg/Pretoria to Durban via Mbabane and Malkerns Valley three times a week, and from Swaziland down the KwaZulu-Natal coast to Durban.

Minibus taxis run daily between Jo'burg (Park Station), Mbabane and Manzini (R160, four hours) and between Manzini and Durban (R140, eight hours). For many routes, you'll need to change minibuses at the border. Most long-distance taxis leave early in the morning.

MOZAMBIQUE

Swaziland shares two border crossings with Mozambique: **Lomahasha–Namaacha** (7am-8pm) in the extreme northeast of the country, and **Goba–Mhlumeni** (7am-6pm).

To/From Maputo

Minibuses between Maputo (Mozambique) and Manzini depart daily in the morning via the Namaacha–Lomahasha border crossing (E40, 1½ hours); if entering Swaziland, some continue on to Manzini (E50, 3½ hours). See also p290.

Bicycle

There are no restrictions on bringing your own bicycle into Swaziland.

DEPARTURE TAX

A E50 departure tax is levied at Matsapha airport.

Car & Motorcycle

If you're arriving in Swaziland via car or motorcycle you'll need the vehicle's registration papers, liability insurance and your licence. If carrying any expensive spare parts, such as a gearbox, you'll also need an import waiver, or *carnet de passage en douane*. Border posts generally don't have petrol stations or repair shops.

GETTING AROUND

Bicycle

Mountainous Swaziland is great for mountain biking. The main towns and heavily travelled Ezulwini Valley are not ideal for leisurely meanders. Minor roads are often unsealed. Both Hlane Royal National Park and Mlilwane Wildlife Sanctuary offer mountain-bike rentals and trails.

Bus & Minibus Taxi

There are infrequent (but cheap) domestic buses; most depart and terminate at the main stop in the centre of Mbabane. Minibus taxis leave when full; no reservations necessary. These are plentiful, run almost everywhere and stop often. Sample fares include Mbabane to Manzini (E13, 35 minutes), Big Bend (E13, one hour) and Piggs Peak (E25, one hour).

There are also nonshared taxis in some of the larger towns.

Car & Motorcycle

DRIVING LICENCE

A domestic (with photo ID) or international driving licence is compulsory.

FUEL & SPARE PARTS

Many petrol stations are open 24 hours, and the price of petrol is similar to that of South Africa (see p579). There are Automobile Association (AA) agents in Manzini, Piggs Peak and Mbabane.

HIRE

Hiring a car will allow you to cover much of the country in a couple of days. Note: if you have hired your car in South Africa, ensure that you have the written agreement from the rental company to enter Swaziland. There's a small road tax payable on entry.

Car hire in Swaziland is available from **Avis** (☎ 518 6222; www.avis.co.za) at Matsapha International Airport and **Imperial Europe** (www.imperialcarrental.co.za) at Matsapha (☎ 518 4393) and Engen Auto Plaza, Mbabane (☎ 404 1384). You have to be 23 years old to hire cars from most companies.

INSURANCE

Insurance for third-party damage and damage to or loss of your vehicle is highly recommended.

ROAD CONDITIONS & ROAD HAZARDS

Swaziland has good sealed roads and highways. The main one from east to west is the MR3. There are some rough back roads through the bush. The road northwest of Hlane Royal National Park and Piggs Peak is gravel for most of the way. Beware slippery and boggy conditions when wet. The other main dangers are people and animals on the road, plus the odd kamikaze minibus driver.

ROAD RULES

In Swaziland, vehicles are driven on the left-hand side. Wearing seat belts is compulsory. Always pull over and stop for official motorcades or road stops. The speed limit on highways is 120km/h, on national roads 80km/h and in built-up areas 60km/h.

Hitching

Hitching is easier here than in South Africa, but hitching alone is foolhardy, especially for women. Hitchhikers might wait a long time for a car on back roads, and there's keen competition from locals.

Tours

Swazi Trails (Map p592; ☎ /fax 416 2180; www.swazitrails.co.sz; Mantenga Craft Centre, Ezulwini Valley) Specialises in one-day and half-day tours around the country, including white-water rafting tours, cultural tours, and hiking.

Bundu Bus (☎ in South Africa 011-675 0767; www.bundusafaris.co.za; PO Box 697, Wilgeheuwel, 1735 Gauteng, South Africa) A South African operator that runs a seven-day around South African tour that includes one day in Swaziland.

Victoria Falls

Victoria Falls is the largest, most beautiful and most majestic waterfall on the planet, and is the Seventh Natural Wonder of the World as well as being a Unesco World Heritage Site. A trip to Southern Africa would not be complete without visiting this unforgettable place. But it isn't just the one million litres of water that fall – per second – down a 108m drop along a 1.7km wide strip in the Zambezi Gorge that makes Victoria Falls so awesome; it's the whole natural context in which the falls are located that makes Victoria Falls so special.

Jump into the gorge, get drenched by the spray of the falls, raft along the rapids or cruise gently along the great Zambezi River. Whether it's wildlife that attracts you or the chance to fill your life with wildness, this place is rare and extraordinary and yet easy and unspoilt. Victoria Falls is to be seen, heard, tasted and touched: it is a treat that few other places in the world can offer, a Must See Before You Die spot.

Victoria Falls has a wet and dry season: when the river is higher and the falls fuller it's the Wet and when the river is lower and the falls aren't smothered in spray it's the Dry. The falls are spectacular at any time of year, except if all you want to do is ride those famous rapids, in which case you want the river low, the rocks exposed and the rapids pumping. The weather is never too hot or too cold, and all else on offer – from fine dining to zipping across a border on a high wire – are also there year round. The high seasons are June to August and Christmas, but April, with all the spray, is special too. Although Zimbabwe and Zambia share it, Victoria Falls is a place all of its own, which is why we give it its own chapter.

HIGHLIGHTS

- Gazing in amazement at Victoria Falls from the **Zambian** (p615) or **Zimbabwean** (p620) side (or preferably both)
- Visiting the falls during the full moon and seeing the enigmatic **lunar rainbow** (p615 or p620)
- Drinking a cocktail at the **Royal Livingstone Hotel** (p613) on a deck on the river near the lip of the falls
- Enjoying a spot of high tea at the **Terrace** (p619) at the elegant Victoria Falls Hotel
- Getting your **adrenaline kicks** (p605) with bungee jumping, microlighting, white-water rafting, jet-boating or a Gorge Swing

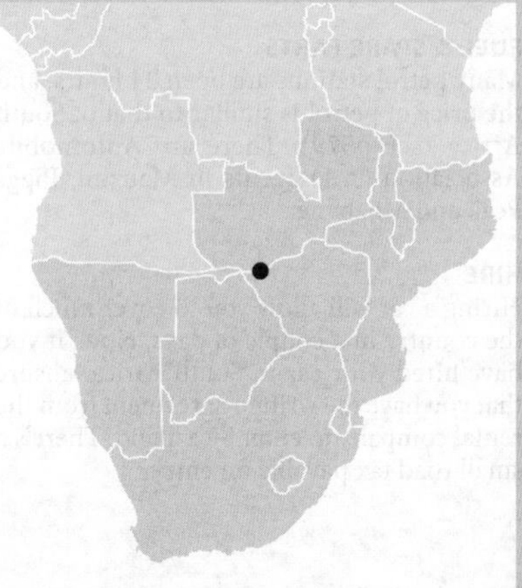

ACTIVITIES: A-Z

Face fear and enjoy the rush: Victoria Falls has got it all! Activities listed in this section can be booked through your accommodation and started from either Livingstone (Zambia) or Victoria Falls (Zimbabwe) for about the same cost. Confirm any extra costs such as park or visa fees, at the time of booking. All operators give package prices too and for around US$125 you can sample all the adrenalin leaps. The operators usually offer photos and videos of your escapades as well (US$35 for videos, US$15 for single shots, US$45 for both). Note that rates given in this section are approximate and subject to change.

Abseiling

Spend the day rappelling down cliffs and swinging across the canyons and gorges the rushing Zambezi cuts through in the scenic Batoka Gorge. Half-/full-day excursions cost US$80/100.

Bird Walk

Check out the amazing birds that inhabit the area around the falls for around US$70.

Botswana/Chobe Day Trip

Located a mere one-hour's drive from Victoria Falls, this day trip includes a breakfast boat cruise, a game drive in Chobe National Park, lunch and transfer back to Victoria Falls by 5pm. Wildlife viewing is excellent: lions, elephants, wild dogs, cheetahs, buffaloes and plenty of antelopes. The price is US$150 per person.

Bungee Jumping

Tackling the third-highest jump in the world (111m) costs single/tandem US$105/$130. There are two main spots, and both jumps are from the same height.

Canoeing & Kayaking

Half-/full-day trips along the Zambezi River cost US$60/75; overnight jaunts cost US$150, and three-night trips start at US$300.

Clay Pigeon Shooting

Morning, lunch and afternoon sessions are available, the latter with dinner, which you eat in a boma with panoramic views over the rolling African bush. Situated only 3km from Victoria Falls, these sessions are of an international standard with instructors and are good for both beginners and the experienced. Costs start at US$55.

Elephant-Back Safaris

Take a journey on the back of an elephant through stunning national parkland or nature reserves. See the boxed text, p607, for information on some issues with wild animal encounters.

Fishing

Tackle the mighty tiger fish of the Zambezi with a half-day trip including tackle, rods, lures and bait, all for around US$90.

Fixed-Wing Flights

Whether you fly in a modern Cessna or a vintage Tiger Moth, you'll have amazing views of the falls, the spray and the river from above. Flights range from US$80 to US$160 depending on the type of craft and the route.

Flying Fox

Zip across the Batoka Gorge for just US$25.

Game Drives & Walks

Take a morning or evening guided safari in a national park, either in a 4WD or by foot. Enjoy the African landscape at its best in the gentle morning or early evening light. Costs are from US$50 per person or game walks US$70. Note that this is for group bookings only.

Golf

Enjoy scenic game drives between rounds on immaculate fairways on both sides of the border, in Zimbabwe at The Elephant Hills Hotel or in Zambia at Livingstone Royal Golf & Country Club. A game of nine holes costs US$10 (equipment hire US$10) and 18 holes costs $US20 (equipment hire US$20). Caddy fees are US$5 extra.

Gorge Slide

This is a lot like the Flying Fox but you whiz down into the Batoka Gorge and back up the other side (single/tandem $35/45) – an adrenalin rush for starters.

Gorge Swing

For those who want to be brave enough to bungee jump but never will be, this is perfect. It's located at the Batoka Gorge.

Jump

Jump feet first, free fall for four seconds but you'll end up the right-way-up, swinging but not upside down. There are tandem options of this too. There are two main spots, one right off the Victoria Falls Bridge, and the other a bit further along the gorge. Costs are US$75.

Helicopters

The 'Flight of the Angels' is a 15-minute joy ride (US$115 excluding park fees) over the falls or 30 minutes (US$260) across the falls and Zambezi National Park.

Hiking

Embark on a hike with guides around the Zambezi National Park (Zimbabwe) or Mosi-oa-Tunya National Park (Zambia). Day hikes cost US$50, while overnight camping is an additional US$10.

Horse-Riding

Tracks go alongside the Zambezi, and you can indulge in a bit of wildlife spotting from horseback. Two-/three-hour rides cost about US$45/60, while half-/full-day rides are about US$85/160.

Hwange Day Trips

Don't miss the park with one of the largest number of elephants in the world. A day trip will cost around US$250.

Interactive Drumming

Spend an evening by a campfire drumming under the southern African sky. A one-hour session followed by a traditional meal costs US$25.

Jet Boats

Go straight into whirlpools! This hair-raising trip costs US$90, and is combined with a cable-car ride down into the Batoka Gorge.

Microlights & Ultralights

These motorised hang-gliders offer fabulous aerial views, and the pilot will take pictures for you with a camera fixed to the wing. Prices are US$104 for 15 minutes over the falls and US$185 for 30 minutes for the falls and Zambezi National Park.

ZAMBEZI RIVER: HIGHS & LOWS

During the rainy season (March to May), the Zambezi's flow can be 10 times higher, while in the dry season (September to December), the volume of water can be as low as 4% of the peak flow.

Night Game Drives

Only available on the Zimbabwean side, these take place in the Zambezi National Park, and cost US$90 for a full night drive.

Quadbiking

Discover the spectacular landscape surrounding Livingstone, Zambia, and the Batoka Gorge, spotting wildlife as you go on all-terrain quad bikes. These ultimate adventure vehicles allow all riders to go at their own pace, under supervision of qualified guides. Trips vary from eco trail riding at Batoka Land to longer range cultural trips in the African Bush. A one-hour spin costs US$60.

Rafting

There are high-water runs through rapids 11 to 18 (or 23), which are relatively mild and can be done between 1 July and 15 August, though in high rainfall years they may begin as early as mid-May. Wilder low-water runs operate from roughly 15 August to late December, taking in the winding 22km from rapids 4 to 18 (or 23) if you put in on the Zimbabwean side, and from Rapids 1 to 18 (or 23) if you put in on the Zambian side. Half-/full-day trips cost about US$110/125, and overnight trips about US$165. Longer jaunts can also be arranged.

Retail Therapy

You'll find markets located in Victoria Falls town and on the Zambian side of the bridge after immigration, near the entrance to the National Park and the falls.

Rhino Walks

These and other nature walks are done on the Zambian side, through the Masi-oa-Tunya National Park. It must be noted that, as with all safaris, although guides do their best, viewing of particular animals cannot be guaranteed. Walks costs $US85 per person, for groups of up to eight. Organised by Bwaato Adventures, you can book online through www.zambiatour

NATIONAL PARK FEES

You can pay your park fees at the national park entrances and national park offices inside the parks.

- US$10 Victoria Falls Entrance – from the Zambian side
- US$20 for overseas residents in Zimbabwe
- US$15 for regional residents in Zimbabwe
- US$20 Victoria Falls Entrance – from the Zimbabwean side

ism.com, but this can also be booked through your hotel or hostel.

River-Boarding

How about lying on a boogie board and careering down the rapids? 'Waterfall surfing', as it's sometimes called, costs from US$135/150 for a half/full day. The best time of year for river-boarding is February to June.

Sitting

Not to be underestimated is the fine art of sitting while at Victoria Falls and soaking up the atmosphere, gazing about you while watching the world go by. You can sit either at a restaurant (Zambezi Waterfront for example; see p611) or bar (Royal Livingstone for preference; see p613) with the river rushing underneath you, or have the falls and bungee jumpers plummeting in front of you (Drop Zone Viewing Platform) on the Zambian side of the Bridge. In Zimbabwe you can make like a local and sit on The Rock, which is near The Big Tree – stunning! And absolutely free.

Steam Train Trips

A variety of steam train tours ranging from the Royal Tea Run to the Victoria Falls Bridge, to an *Out of Africa* Bush Breakfast or sunset steamer (only for prebooked groups, a minimum of 25) cost about US$95.

Traditional Dancing

Great as a spectator sport or you can join in for US$40.

Victoria Falls Tour

The best way to see the falls is on the Zimbabwean side. You enter through the National Park gates (open from 6am to 6pm), show your passport and pay a US$20 fee per person. Hire a raincoat and umbrella just inside those gates if you go in April, or you may as well walk in your swimming suit – you *will* get drenched! The walk is along the top of the gorge on a path, which is signposted with the best vantage points and can sometimes be shared with monkeys and warthogs. The former are cheeky and the latter are shy. Note that you can get to the bridge, but not onto it, from this path.

Wildlife Drives

Head out on a guided safari in Mosi-oa-Tunya Game Park, Zambia, which is a great place to see white rhinos. Wildlife drives here cost around US$50. Or choose a river safari on the Zambezi. River cruises along the Zambezi range from civilised jaunts on the *African Queen* to full-on, all-you-can-drink sunset booze cruises. Prices range from US$30 to US$60. Great for spotting wildlife, though some tourists get just as much enjoyment out of the free drinks!

TRAVEL & ADVENTURE COMPANIES

What's so easy is that 99% of all bookings for activities in the falls are done through the lodge, hotel or backpacking hostel you are staying in. Prices for activities are all basically the same, and arranging it from where you stay means transfers are included.

You can also go directly to tour operators who have activities operators on their books too. Try **Wild Horizons** (☎ 44571; www.wildhorizons.co.zw) with an office in Victoria Falls town,

ANIMAL ENCOUNTERS: SHOULD YOU AVOID THEM?

There are some dodgy operators out there, so do think about what they are offering in terms of the welfare of the animals. For example, what happens to the young lion cubs or elephants when they get older? If elephants are to be used for commercial purposes, there are a few good operations in Africa that are 'using' elephants in the right way, ie by doing walks with elephants rather than riding them. This serves to educate the public about elephants and satisfies the desire for tourists to have close contact with elephants, which is after all an extraordinary privilege.

VISAS

You will need a visa to cross sides from Zim to Zam or vice versa. These are applicable to most nationalities and they are available at the border posts.

- Day visit: US$20 for 24 hours
- Single entry: US$50
- Double/multi-entry: US$80
- Multi-entry: on application

African Horizons (☎ 323432; www.adventure-africa.com) in Livingstone, or **Safari Par Excellence** (☎ in Zambia 326629, 421190, 011205306; www.safpar.net) which all cover activities on either side.

If you want independent advice, visit **Backpackers Bazaar** (Map p618; ☎ 013-45828; bazaar@mweb.co.zw; off Parkway; 8am-5pm Mon-Fri, 8am-4pm Sat & Sun) in the town of Victoria Falls.

ZAMBIA

While Zimbabwe is working hard to rekindle its economy, Zambia is stable; the 73 tribes coexist peacefully and the currency (the kwacha) is strengthening. The recent tourist swing to the Zambian side of Victoria Falls due to Zimbabwe's troubles has initiated a construction boom. Local business owners are riding the tourism wave and are building and renovating for even more expected growth. The Zambezi River waterfront is rapidly being tastefully developed as one of the most exclusive destinations in Southern Africa.

LIVINGSTONE

☎ 0213

The historic town of Livingstone, named after the first European to set eyes on Victoria Falls, sprung to life following the construction of the Victoria Falls Bridge in 1904. During the remainder of the 20th century, Livingstone existed as a quiet provincial capital. However, during the political and economic troubles in Zimbabwe, Livingstone quickly lifted its game and was able to cater for a new wave of tourists. Historic buildings got much-needed facelifts, new construction projects began and plans were hatched for increased transport links.

Today, Livingstone is the preferred base for backpackers visiting Victoria Falls. The town is not much to look at but it is a fun place for backpackers: It's set 11km away from the falls and unless you've gone for the option of staying on the Zambezi riverfront, you are not staying in a natural setting, but an African border town. That said, it has excellent (read: fun, cheap and well-organised) hostels, all with internet access and the full gamut of activities on offer within, plus restaurants and bars in town catering to every type of traveller – from those on a shoestring to those on a once in a lifetime event such as a honeymoon.

History

Although several explorers and artists visited the area following its 'discovery', Victoria Falls were largely ignored by Europeans until the construction of Cecil Rhodes' railway in 1905. During the British colonial era and the early years of Zambian and Zimbabwean independence, the falls emerged as one of the most popular tourist destinations in southern Africa. However, tourist numbers plummeted in the late 1960s in response to the guerrilla warfare in Zimbabwe, and the climate of suspicion aimed at foreigners under the rule of Zambian President Kenneth Kaunda.

During the 1980s, tourism surged once more as travellers started flocking to the region in search of adrenaline highs. The town of Victoria Falls (p616) in Zimbabwe billed itself as a centre for extreme sports, while sleepy Livingstone absorbed some of the tourist overflow. By the end of the 20th century, Victoria Falls was receiving over a quarter of a million visitors each year, and the future (on both sides of the falls) was looking bright.

In a few short years however, the civil unrest resulting from Zimbabwean President Robert Mugabe's controversial land reform program brought tourism in the town of Victoria Falls to a halt. Although foreigners safely remained on the sidelines of the political conflict, hyperinflation of the currency, lack of goods and services and the absence of commodities such as petrol all served as significant deterrents to tourism.

On the Zambian side of the falls however, business is booming. After years of playing second fiddle to the town of Victoria Falls, Livingstone has been reaping the benefits of Zimbabwe's decline. New hotels, restaurants

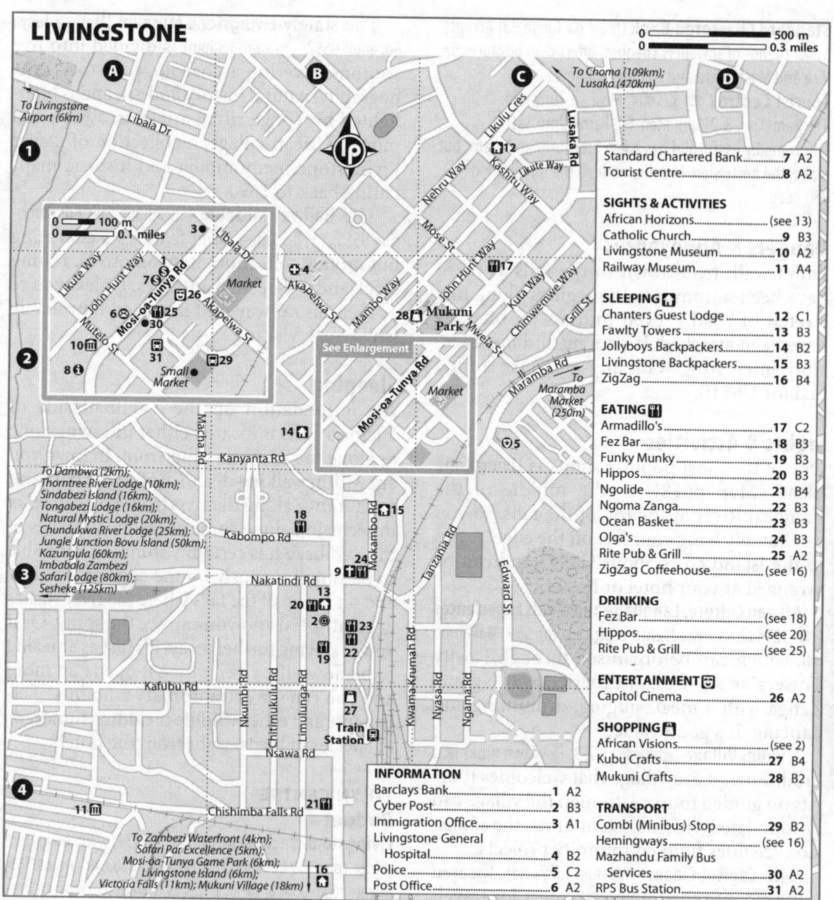

and shopping malls are popping up all over town and along the Zambezi riverfront, while increased flights and bus routes are making it easier for travellers to arrive en masse. While Zimbabwe still has political tensions, the dollarisation and other moves to revitalise the economy will no doubt have their effect here on Livingstone.

Orientation

Livingstone is a small African town that has taken on the role of a backpacking mecca. The town centres itself around one main road, Mosi-oa-Tunya Rd, meaning 'The Smoke That Thunders', which is exactly what the falls look like from Livingstone. The town centre itself is 11km from the entrance to the falls. Several establishments are set right on the Zambezi River, but most of the action is set a bit back from the waterfront.

Information

Barclays Bank (cnr Mosi-oa-Tunya Rd & Akapelwa St) Accepts major brands of travellers cheques, offers cash advances on Visa and MasterCard and changes money.

Cyber Post (216 Mosi-oa-Tunya Rd; per hr US$4) Also offers international phone calls and faxes. All the hostels now have wi-fi or at least internet access.

Livingstone General Hospital (☎ 321475; Akapelwa St)

Police (☎ 320116; Maramba Rd)

Post office (Mosi-oa-Tunya Rd) Has a poste restante and fax service.

Standard Chartered Bank (Mosi-oa-Tunya Rd) Accepts major brands of travellers cheques, offers cash advances on Visa and MasterCard and changes money.

Tourist Centre (☎ 321404; Mosi-oa-Tunya Rd; ⌚ 8am-1pm & 2-5pm Mon-Fri, 8am-12pm Sat) This is mildly useful and has a few brochures and maps, but really, the hostels are heaving with all the information you need.

Dangers & Annoyances

Don't walk from town to the falls as there have been a number of muggings along this stretch of road – even tourists on bicycles have been attacked. It's a long and not a terribly interesting walk anyway. Take a blue taxi for US$10.

Sights & Activities

One of the most popular sights is **Livingstone Island** (Map p618), in the middle of the Zambezi River at the top of the falls, so you can literally hang your feet off the edge. A trip to the island costs about US$45 and can be arranged at your hotel or hostel.

African Culture, Language and Meals Experiences (☎ 323432; www.adventure-africa.com; 559 Makambo Rd), which can be organised through Fawlty Towers, is an African experience at Ngoma Zanga with a meal, singing, drumming and dancing. It's good value.

Mukuni Village (admission US$3; ⌚ dawn-dusk) is a 'traditional' Leva village that welcomes tourists on guided tours. Although the village can be inundated with tourists at times, the admission fee does fund community projects.

The **Capitol Cinema** (Mosi-oa-Tunya Rd), located quite close to the Jollyboys, caters for travellers, and at the time of writing it was showing a James Bond Film Festival. They also screen football matches.

The stately **Livingstone Museum** (Mosi-oa-Tunya Rd; adult US$2; ⌚ 9am-4.30pm) is divided into five sections covering archaeology, history, ethnography, natural history and art, and is highlighted by Tonga ritual artefacts, a life-sized model African village, a collection of David Livingstone memorabilia and historic maps dating back to 1690.

The **Railway Museum** (Chishimba Falls Rd; admission US$5; ⌚ 8.30am-4.30pm) features a charming but motley collection of locomotives, rolling stock and rail-related antiques. Unless you're a ravenous railway buff however, it probably isn't worth visiting.

Sleeping

Accommodation on the Zambian side of Victoria Falls is located either in Livingstone or along the Zambezi waterfront. In town you are within walking distance of all the bars and restaurants; along the riverfront you can relax in seclusion along some gorgeous stretches of the Zambezi. It is certainly stunning to be able to be simultaneously on the edge of the river and on the lip of the falls where the river rushes at great speed and you can see the spray. Or if you're staying further away, it's just as amazing to be down the river where it opens up more and you can see extraordinary amounts of elephants and other wildlife including hundreds of species of birds, right from the hotel.

TOWN CENTRE

Budget

Livingstone Backpackers (☎ 323432; www.adventure-africa.com; 559 Makambo Rd; camping US$3, dm from US$5, private room US$20; 🖳) This is a brand new offering; it's Fawlty Towers Mark II set in a nearby location, only this is bigger, better and cheaper than ever. It has an outdoor bar, nice pool,

VISITING ZAM FROM ZIM (OR VICE VERSA)

From Victoria Falls you can walk, take a taxi, or a complimentary bus service from your hotel to the Zimbabwean immigration post, and then continue 1.3km on foot over the Victoria Falls Bridge. Enjoy the thrilling atmosphere of the bungee jumpers, and their audiences, halfway across the bridge. Just past the bridge is the Zambian border crossing, and 100m beyond it, the entrance to Mosi-oa-Tunya National Park.

Take a blue taxi (US$10) to Livingstone, about 11km away. Mugging is common along this route and it's too far to walk.

Most travel agencies and hotels in Victoria Falls and Livingstone charge about US$25 for minibus transfers between the two towns. If you're crossing into Zambia for the day, advise the Zimbabwean officials before leaving the country so you won't need to buy a new visa when you return later in the day.

Jacuzzi, snazzy open-air living room, climbing wall, pool table, DSTV (a digital satellite TV company) with all the sport channels and self-catering kitchen. In total it offers 78 beds, and is a great deal for both groups or individuals.

Jollyboys Backpackers (☎ 324229; www.backpackzambia.com; 34 Kanyanta Rd; camping per person US$6, dm from US$6, d from US$25;) Located behind the museum, this place won the prize for the best hostel in Zambia in 2008. From the sunken pillow lounge to the pool, cheap restaurant, bar, barbeque, DSTV and lofty observation tower, everything has been carefully designed by the fun-loving owners. At night, management will not let you bring in people who are not staying at the hostel.

Midrange

Fawlty Towers (☎ 323432; www.adventure-africa.com; 216 Mosi-oa-Tunya Rd; s/d half board US$25/45;) This backpacking institution has been renovated into a guest house, full of upmarket touches: free internet and wi-fi, hip bar, shady lawn, a great pool plus a well-organised, on-the-pulse vibe, which comes directly from its owner, Richard Sheppard, a campaigner for bringing back budget travel. There is also a towering thatched bar-restaurant on the premises called Hippos (p613) which is one of the hottest nightspots in town.

ZigZag (☎ 322814; www.zigzagzambia.com; Mosi-oa-Tunya Rd; s/d US$45/70, f US$90; P) This place consists of 12 motel-style rooms, a lovely swimming pool and a small craft shop. Comfortably and peacefully set in a 1.5 acre garden, this very friendly family-run business has all the mod cons such as air-con and wi-fi. Lovely baking really takes the cake here, though. It also has ZigZag Coffee House (p613).

Chanters Guest Lodge (☎ 323412; www.chanters-livingstone.com; Likulu Cres; s/d incl breakfast US$55/65, f incl breakfast US$85; P) This lodge has 10 motel-style rooms in suburban Livingstone, a pool and restaurant and is set in quiet surroundings. This is a good option for families.

ZAMBEZI RIVERFRONT

Prebooking for hotels along the riverfront is necessary.

Budget

Jungle Junction Bovu Island (☎ 323708; www.junglejunction.info; camping per person US$10-15, huts per person $20-30; P) Hippos, hammocks and harmony. Located on a lush island in the middle of the Zambezi River, Jungle Junction attracts travellers who want to do nothing more than lounge beneath the palm trees, or engage in some fishing. Meals are available (from US$7 to US$12).

Midrange

All prices include meals and transfers from Livingstone.

Zambezi Waterfront (☎ 320606; www.safpar.net; camping per person US$10, s/d pre-set tents US$30/20, s/d incl breakfast per person from US$125/110, f US$200; P) Accommodation is varied, and includes luxury tents, standard and riverside chalets as well as executive rooms and family suites. It includes a great open-air beer garden right on the Zambezi River.

Natural Mystic Lodge (☎ 324436; www.naturalmysticlodge.com; s/d from US$85/95; P) The atmosphere at Natural Mystic is significantly less lavish than at some of the more upmarket lodges, though it makes for a peaceful retreat. It's 20km from Livingstone and 30km from the falls. Transfers are usually provided.

Top End

Chundukwa River Lodge (☎ 324452; info@maplanga.co.za; camping per person US$10, huts per person US$125; P) This simple but rustic lodge consists of thatched huts perched directly on the water. Sightings of elephants and hippos from the rooms are commonplace, there is a cooling plunge pool right on the riverbank and yummy home-cooking Zambian style.

Imbabala Zambezi Safari Lodge (☎ in South Africa 27 11 921 0225; per person from US$157) Set on a riverine fringe of the Zambezi River where Zimbabwe, Botswana and Zambia converge, 80km west of Victoria Falls, this lodge offers amazing game viewing and bird watching. It is set in a national parks concession bordering the Chobe Forest Reserve – a park renowned for its massive elephant population.

Thorntree River Lodge (☎ 324480; www.safpar.com/thorntree.htm; chalets per person US$250; P) The Thorntree River Lodge is located within the borders of Mosi-oa-Tunya National Park, and features rustic chalets with panoramic views of elephants frolicking along the Zambezi River. Prices include full board.

Zambezi Sun (Map pp614-5; ☎ 321122; www.sunint.co.za; s/d from US$275/300; P) The closest Zambian hotel to the falls, this huge complex, with restaurants, bars and a casino, is Moroccan-inspired, and designed to simulate

THE MAN, THE MYTH, THE LEGEND

David Livingstone is one of a few European explorers who is still revered by modern-day Africans. His legendary exploits on the continent border the realm of fiction, though his life's mission to end the slave trade was very real (and ultimately very successful).

Born into rural poverty in the south of Scotland on March 19, 1813, Livingstone began working in a local cotton mill at the age of 10, though his first passion was for the classics. After studying Greek, medicine and theology at the University of Glasgow, he worked in London for several years before being ordained as a missionary in 1840. The following year, Livingstone arrived in Bechuanaland (now Botswana) and began travelling inland, looking for converts and seeking to end the slave trade.

As early as 1842, Livingstone had already become the first European to penetrate the northern reaches of the Kalahari. For the next several years, Livingstone explored the African interior with the purpose of opening up trade routes and establishing missions. In 1854, Livingstone discovered a route to the Atlantic coast, and arrived in present-day Luanda. However, his most famous discovery occurred in 1855 when he first set eyes on Victoria Falls during his epic boat journey down the Zambezi River.

Livingstone returned to Britain a national hero, and recounted his travels in the 1857 publication *Missionary Travels and Researches in South Africa*. Livingstone's oft-cited motto was "Christianity, Commerce and Civilization", and he believed that navigating and ultimately controlling the Zambezi was crucial to this agenda.

In 1858, Livingstone returned to Africa as the head of the 'Zambezi Expedition', a government-funded venture that aimed to identify natural resource reserves in the region. Unfortunately for Livingstone, the expedition ended when a previously unexplored section of the Zambezi turned out to be unnavigable. The British press labelled the expedition as a failure, and Livingstone was forced to return home in 1864 after the government recalled the mission.

In 1866, Livingstone returned to Africa, and arrived in Zanzibar with the goal of seeking out the source of the Nile River. Although the British explorer John Hanning Speke arrived on the shores of Lake Victoria in 1858, the scientific community was divided over the legitimacy of his discovery (in actuality, the Nile descends from the mountains of Burundi halfway between Lake Tanganyika and Lake Victoria).

In 1869, Livingstone reached Lake Tanganyika despite failing health, though several of his followers abandoned the expedition en-route. These desertions were headline news in Britain, sparking rumours regarding Livingstone's health and sanity. In response to the growing mystery surrounding Livingstone's whereabouts, the *New York Herald* newspaper arranged a publicity stunt by sending journalist Henry Morton Stanley to find Livingstone.

According to Stanley's published account, the journalist had once asked the paper's manager how much he was allowed to spend on the expedition. The famous reply was simple: "Draw £1000 now, and when you have gone through that, draw another £1000, and when that is spent, draw another £1000, and when you have finished that, draw another £1000, and so on – but find Livingstone!"

After arriving in Zanzibar and setting out with nearly 200 porters, Stanley finally found Livingstone on November 10, 1871 in Ujiji near Lake Tanganyika. Although Livingstone may well have been the only European in the entire region, Stanley famously greeted him with the line 'Dr Livingstone, I presume?'.

Although Stanley urged him to leave the continent, Livingstone was determined to find the source of the Nile. Livingstone penetrated deeper into the continent than any European prior. On May 1, 1873, Livingstone died from malaria and dysentery near Lake Bangweula in present-day Zambia. His body was carried for thousands of kilometres by his attendants, and now lies in the ground at Westminster Abbey in London.

a north African kasbah. It contains a great playground for kids.

Royal Livingstone (Map pp614-5; ☎ 321122; www.sunint.co.za; s/d from US$415/450; P ✣ ✣) Very stylish colonial accommodation with a manicured lawn leading to the river, the hotel has an atmosphere of indulgence and yesteryear glamour, and is absolutely fab for a honeymoon.

Tongabezi Lodge (☎ 323235; www.tongabezi.com; cottages/houses per person US$430/530; P ✣ ✣) Here you'll find sumptuous spacious cottages and open-faced 'houses', with trees as part of the structure and private dining decks. Guests are invited to spend an evening on nearby Sindabezi Island (per person per night US$350), selected by the *Sunday Times* as the best remote place to stay in the world.

Eating & Drinking

Livingstone is home to a number of high-quality tourist-oriented restaurants, including a batch of excellent newcomers.

Royal Livingstone (Map pp614-5; ☎ 321122; www.sunint.co.za; cocktails US$4) Try a refreshing beverage on the extraordinary drinks deck upon the water not far from the lip of the falls.

Funky Munky (216 Mosi-oa-Tunya Rd; snacks & mains US$5) This laid-back bistro is a popular backpackers' hang out and prepares baguettes, salads and pizzas in a comfortable setting.

ZigZag Coffee House (Mosi-oa-Tunya Rd; mains US$5) This place offers an eclectic range of dishes, from tacos to tandoori, and is ideal for a coffee or milk shake.

Olga's (cnr Mosi-oa-Tunya & Nakatindi Rds; mains US$5-10) This new place is a good bet for pizza. It's opposite Fawlty Towers and behind the Catholic church.

Armadillo's (Mosi-oa-Tunya Rd; mains US$5-10) Located in the centre of town, this is a new and homey but nice place, with 'international' dishes cooked by an internationally trained chef: fish as well as local food. It can cater for large groups.

Ngolide (Mosi-oa-Tunya Rd; mains US$5-10) This place is a very popular Indian tandoori restaurant which also sells spicy chicken, so is popular with the locals as well as tourists. The chef is from India and it is good value for money. Groups are welcome and takeaways are available.

Ocean Basket (82 Mosi-oa-Tunya Rd; mains US$5-10) This popular South African restaurant specialises in (not surprisingly) fish. Sure, you're dining in a landlocked country but the quality and selection here is good.

Fez Bar (Kabompo Rd; mains US$6) This Moroccan-inspired bar and lounge serves tasty and eclectic meals throughout the day, though things really get kicking here once the sun goes down.

Hippos (Limulunga Rd; mains US$6) This raucous but newly renovated bar-cum-restaurant at the back of Fawlty Towers is housed underneath a soaring two-storey thatched roof.

Rite Pub & Grill (Mosi-oa-Tunya Rd; mains US$7) This centrally located pub draws in a good mix of travellers and locals, and serves tasty pub grub amid a kitschy Wild West setting.

Ngoma Zanga (Mosi-oa-Tunya Rd; meal US$25) This restaurant allows you to release your inner tourist! It has comparatively expensive but excellent African cuisine, in a typical 'traditional' scenario, from the welcoming routine to the performances while you eat the local fare.

Shopping

African Visions (216 Mosi-oa-Tunya Rd) Near the Livingstone Adventure Centre, this is a charming place selling quality fabrics and crafts from all over Africa.

Kubu Crafts (Mosi-oa-Tunya Rd) This shop offers a vast selection of classy souvenirs. You can admire your purchases while sipping a tea or coffee in the shady tea garden.

Mukuni Crafts (Mosi-oa-Tunya Rd) The craft stalls in the southern corner of this park are a pleasant, and relatively hassle-free place to browse for souvenirs.

Getting There & Away

AIR

Proflight Zambia (☎ 0211-271032; www.proflight-zambia.com) connects Livingstone to destinations throughout Zambia, Botswana and Namibia. **South African Airways** (www.flysaa.com) and **British Airways** (www.britishairways.com) both have daily flights to and from Johannesburg, and the cheapest economy fare starts at around US$450 return.

BICYCLE

Bikes can be ridden to/from Zimbabwe; do be cautious as cyclists have been mugged while riding to/from the Zambian border and Victoria Falls.

BUS & COMBI (MINIBUS)

Domestic

RPS (Mutelo St) has two bus services a day travelling to Lusaka (K65,380 to K84,060),

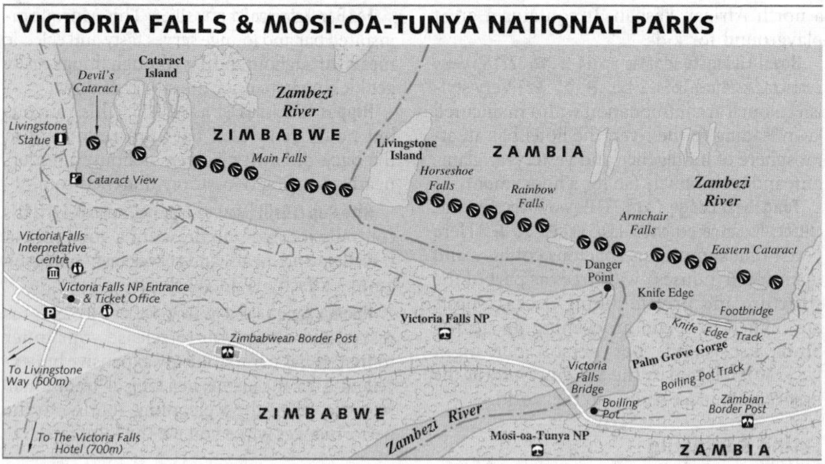

VICTORIA FALLS & MOSI-OA-TUNYA NATIONAL PARKS

seven hours). **CR Carriers** (cnr Mosi-oa-Tunya Rd & Akapelwa St) runs four services a day to Lusaka (K65,380 to K84,060, seven hours). Buses to Sesheke (K32,690, five hours) leave at around 10am from Mingongo bus station next to the Catholic church at Dambwa village, 3km west of the town centre. Direct buses to Mongu (K51,370, nine hours) leave at midnight from Maramba market, though you might feel more comfortable on a morning bus to Sesheke, and then transfer to a Mongu bus (K23,350, four hours).

Combis (minibuses) to the Botswana border at Kazungula (K18,680, one hour) depart from Dambwa, 3km west of the town centre, on Nakatindi Rd.

International

For information about travelling to Botswana, and crossing the Zambia–Botswana border at Kazungula, see p116. For information about travelling to Namibia, and crossing the Zambia–Namibia border at Katima Mulilo, see p383. For information about crossing into Zimbabwe along the Victoria Falls Bridge, see p610.

CAR & MOTORCYCLE

If you're driving a rented car or motorcycle, be advised that the vast majority of companies do not insure their vehicles in Zambia.

HITCHING

With patience, it's fairly easy to hitch from Kazungula, Botswana, and Katima Mulilo, Namibia, to Livingstone. The best place in all three towns to arrange a lift is at any petrol station. See warnings about hitching on p641 and p683.

TRAIN

The *Zambezi Express* leaves Livingstone for Lusaka (US$4/5/7/8 economy/standard/1st class/sleeper, 15 hours), via Choma, on Tuesday, Thursday and Sunday at 7pm. Reservations are available at the **train station** (☎ 320001), which is signed off Mosi-oa-Tunya Rd.

Getting Around

TO/FROM THE AIRPORT

Livingstone Airport is located 6km northwest of town, and is easily accessible by taxi (US$10 each way).

CAR & MOTORCYCLE

If you're planning on renting a car in Zambia, consider using **Hemingways** (☎ 320996, 323097; www.hemingwayszambia.com), based in Livingstone. They have new Toyota Hi-Lux campers, fully kitted.

COMBIS & TAXIS

Combis run regularly along Mosi-oa-Tunya Rd to Victoria Falls and the Zambian border, and cost US$0.50 for 15 minutes. Taxis, which are blue, cost US$10.

MOSI-OA-TUNYA NATIONAL PARK

Zambia's smallest national park is located 11km from Livingstone, and is divided into

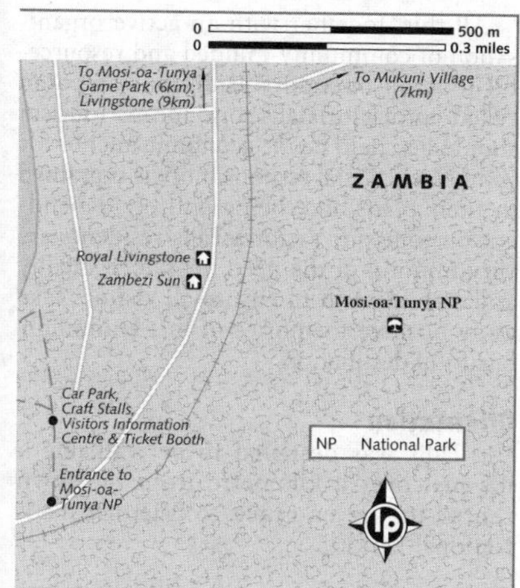

two sections – the Victoria Falls World Heritage National Monument Site and Mosi-oa-Tunya Game Park.

Victoria Falls World Heritage National Monument Site

The entrance to the **park** (admission US$10, 6am-6pm) is located just before the Zambian border post. From the entrance, a path leads to the visitor information centre, which has modest displays on local fauna, geology and culture as well as a healthy number of craft stalls.

From the centre, a network of paths leads through thick vegetation to various viewpoints. You can walk upstream along a path mercifully free of fences – and warning notices (so take care!) – to watch the Zambezi waters glide smoothly through rocks and little islands towards the lip of the falls.

For close-up views of the **Eastern Cataract**, nothing beats the hair-raising (and hair-wetting) walk across the **footbridge**, through swirling clouds of mist, to a sheer buttress called the **Knife Edge**. If the water is low, or the wind is favourable, you'll be treated to a magnificent view of the falls as well as the yawning abyss below. Otherwise, your vision (and your clothes) will be drenched by spray. Then you can walk down a steep track to the banks of the great Zambezi to see the huge whirlpool called the **Boiling Pot**.

Like its counterpart on the Zimbabwean side, the park is open again in the evenings during (and just before and after) a full moon in order to see the amazing **lunar rainbow**. The tickets cost an extra US$10 – hours of operation vary, though you can inquire through your accommodation.

Mosi-oa-Tunya Game Park

Upriver from the falls, and only 3km southwest of Livingstone, is this tiny **wildlife sanctuary** (per person US$10; 6am-6pm), which has a surprising range of animals including rhinos, zebras, giraffes, buffaloes, elephants and antelopes.

Getting There & Away

The Zambian side of the falls is 11km south of Livingstone and along the main road to the border with Zimbabwe. Plenty of minibuses and shared taxis ply the route from the minibus terminal along Senanga Rd in Livingstone. As muggings have been reported, it is best to take a taxi.

ZIMBABWE

Although Zimbabwe was long the preferred base for visiting Victoria Falls, in recent years travellers have been reluctant to cross the border. In all fairness, there were plenty of reasons to be alarmed, especially since the international media held a glaring spotlight on stories of petrol rationing, hyperinflation, rampant land reform and food shortages. At the time of research, the US-based *Foreign Policy* magazine ranked Zimbabwe second (after Somalia) in their top 10 list of failed states.

As a testament to their resilience, however, Zimbabweans always believe this will get better and fortunately tourists and tourist locations are not targets for political violence. So foreign tourists continue to remain safely on the sidelines of the majority of Zimbabwe's ongoing problems.

Despite the threat of nation-state collapse, Zimbabwe has always been on the map for certain groups of intrepid travellers. For the luxury-seeking international jet setters, the generator-fuelled power in the five-star lodges has never flickered, and the imported fine wine has never stopped flowing. For shoestringers looking to bolster their travel resumes with a bit of street cred, travelling around Zim has always had undeniable appeal. But Victoria Falls is good for Granny, adrenaline junkies, nature freaks and everyone in between.

While it is recommended that you monitor the situation closely before visiting Zimbabwe, at the time of research the recent introduction of the US dollar means shortages are not an issue in Vic Falls, and that the town is safe to visit. The farcical Zim dollar is now just being sold as a souvenir, and while dollarisation hasn't helped everyone in the country, food is back in the stores and petrol is back in the pumps. And, although it remains to be seen whether or not newly elected Prime Minister Morgan Tsvangirai can continue to share power with the country's big man, President Robert Mugabe, a coalition government was a fascinating development in Zimbabwean politics.

Walking through the streets of Vic Falls can make you wonder how it looked when it was heaving. Locals eke out a meagre living by tending to the few remaining tourists. As when making plans to visit any African country, remember that situations can change. Zimbabwe is the path less travelled right now, yet it is extraordinary and unforgettable.

VICTORIA FALLS

☎ 013

Unlike Livingstone, the town of Victoria Falls (or simply Vic Falls) was built for tourism. It is right upon the falls with neat, walkable streets lined with hotels, bars, shops and craft markets. These days, however, Vic Falls feels like a resort in off-season. The off-season for this side has been long and tragic, but it's no longer deserved. The Zimbabwean side is a safe, calm and fully functional tourist resort.

Remote in terms of the rest of Zimbabwe, Vic Falls remained largely untouched by the violent troubles elsewhere in the country. And with road access to and from Zambia, Namibia and Botswana, the lodges and smart hotels remained relatively well-stocked even in the hard times. Dollarisation happened in Vic Falls years ahead of the rest of the country, but now the place sells Zim dollars as souvenirs! And yes, there was a Z100 trillion dollar note.

The people of the town are passionate about their home and boy have they got some generous hospitality to offer too. However, it isn't all-paradise here and visitors can expect to be approached by touts.

All this, together with an active organisation of community-minded and resourceful tourism operators leading a campaign called gotovictoriafalls.com, means tourism should be/could be *the* economic anchor for Zimbabwe. Social responsibility is ingrained in their plans and, being entirely dependent on tourism, Victoria Falls residents are very mindful of the need for safety, quality and stability and to ensure all visitors take away positive memories of this stunningly beautiful destination.

Orientation

Vic Falls was designed to be walkable – it's just over a kilometre from the town centre to the entrance to Victoria Falls National Park.

Information

EMERGENCY

Medical Air Rescue Service (MARS; ☎ 44764)
Police (☎ 44206; Livingstone Way)
Victoria Falls Surgery (☎ 43356; West Dr)

INTERNET ACCESS

Telco (☎ 43441; Phumula Centre; per hr US$1; 🕒 8am-6pm) Surprisingly reliable internet access.

MONEY

Barclays Bank (off Livingstone Way)
Standard Chartered Bank (off Livingstone Way)

POST

Post office (off Livingstone Way)

TELEPHONE

Telephone calls can be made at telephone offices and travel agencies upstairs in Soper's Arcade. To dial Livingstone you don't need the country or city code – simply dial ☎ 8, then the local number.

TOURIST INFORMATION

Zimbabwe Tourism Authority (☎ 44376; zta@vicfalls.ztazim.co.zw; 258 Adam Stander Dr; 🕒 8am-4.30pm Mon-Fri) gives away a few brochures and can book accommodation throughout the country.

Dangers & Annoyances

Mugging is not such a problem in Victoria Falls any more, but at dawn and dusk wild animals such as lions, elephants and warthogs do roam the streets away from the town centre, so take taxis at these times. Although it's perfectly safe to walk to and from the falls, it's advisable to stick to the more touristed areas.

Sights & Activities

The **Big Tree**, which is a huge baobab tree with a 20m circumference and historical importance, is on Zambezi Dr heading north from near the entrance to the falls. This was the main trading spot for Zimbabweans and Zambians – the latter canoed across the river before the bridge was built.

Further on from there, take the first broad and clear path leading to the river. It leads to a spot called **The Rock**, a wonderful place to watch the wildly rushing water right at the lip of the falls. Local guides can take you. Ask them also about **The Lookout**, 8km out of town, another local secret, where you really hear the sound of the Smoke That Thunders.

The **Falls Craft Village** (☎ 44309; Adam Stander Dr; ⏲ 8am-5pm) is a touristy mock-up of a traditional Zimbabwean village. Souvenirs start at US$20. It offers the chance to watch craftspeople at work, consult with a *nganga* (fortune teller) and see some remarkable 'pole dancing' (but not the sort you might find in a Western strip joint).

The **Crocodile Ranch and Wildlife Nature Sanctuary** (☎ 40509-11; Parkway; admission incl guided tour US$10; ⏲ 8am-5pm) offers lots of crocs, lions and leopards.

The impressive **Victoria Falls Aquarium** (Livingstone Way; admission US$5; ⏲ 9.30am-5.30pm) is apparently the largest freshwater aquarium in Africa. It's worth a visit for the bright and imaginative displays about the aquatic life in the Zambezi River.

The **Elephant's Walk Museum** (Elephant's Walk Shopping Village, off Adam Stander Dr; admission free; ⏲ 8am-5pm) houses a small but worthwhile private collection detailing the cultural heritage of local ethnic groups.

The **Zambezi Nature Sanctuary** (☎ 44604; Parkway; admission incl guided tour US$5; ⏲ 8am-5pm) offers lots of crocs, as well as lions and leopards. It shows informative videos, and houses a museum, aviary and insect collection. Try to get there for the lion and croc feeding, which takes place around 4pm daily.

Sleeping

There are budget and midrange places in Zimbabwe but on the whole, accommodation in Zimbabwe is expensive.

BUDGET & MIDRANGE

Victoria Falls Backpackers (☎ 42209, www.victoriafallsbackpackers.com; 357 Gibson Rd; camping per person US$4, dm US$8, s/d with shared bathroom US$10/20; P 💻 🏊) Although it's a bit further out than other places, Victoria Falls Backpackers is superbly set up for independent and budget travellers.

Shoestrings Backpackers (☎ 40167; 12 West Dr; camping per person US$6, dm US$9, d US$35; P 🏊) Shoestrings is a popular stop for the overland truck crowd, though the laid-back ambience also draws in a good number of independent travellers.

VICTORIA FALLS

ZIM OR ZAM?

Victoria Falls straddle the border between Zimbabwe and Zambia, and is easily accessible from both countries. However, the big question for most travellers is: do I visit the falls from the town of Victoria Falls, Zimbabwe or from Livingstone, Zambia? The answer is simple: Visit the falls from both sides and, if possible, stay in both towns.

From the Zimbabwean side, you're further from the falls, though the overall views are better. From the Zambian side, you can almost stand on top of the falls, though your perspective is narrowed. Admission is cheaper on the Zambian side, though the Zimbabwean side is less-touristed and much quieter.

The town of Victoria Falls was built for tourists, so it's easily walkable and located right next to the entrance to the Falls. It has a natural African bush beauty.

Livingstone is an attractive town with a relaxed ambience and a proud, historic air. Since the town of Victoria Falls was the main tourist centre for so many years, Livingstone feels more authentic, perhaps because locals earn their livelihood through means other than tourism. Livingstone is bustling with travellers year round, though the town is fairly spread out, and located 11km from the falls.

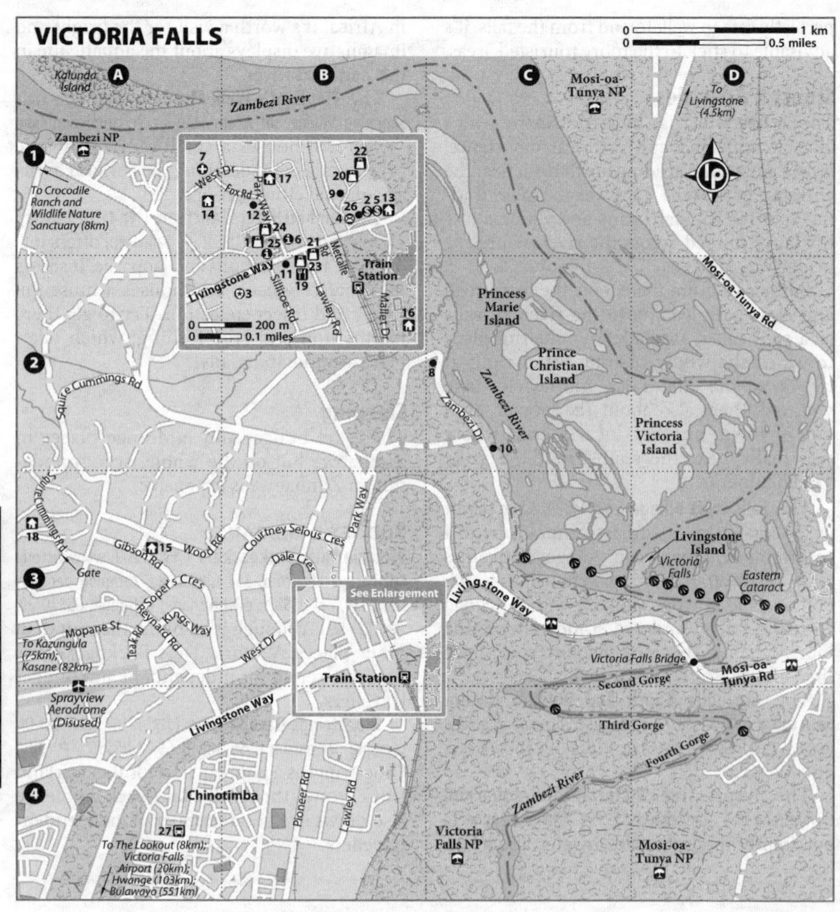

Victoria Falls Restcamp & Lodges (☎ 40509-11; www.vicfallsrestcamp.com; cnr Parkway & West Drs; camping US$10, dm US$11, s/d chalets with shared bathroom US$25/34, fitted dome tents US$60, s/d cottages with bathroom US$67; P) Now run by the same people who do the sumptuous Ilala Lodge Hotel. This institution still has a great pool and the restaurant, In-Da-Belly (see opposite), but is doing well under new management. The rooms are very clean and you can now book all your falls activities here. Everything under one roof.

TOP END

Victoria Falls Safari Lodge (☎ 43201; www.vfsl.com; Squire Cummings Rd; s/d incl breakfast from US$315/395; P) If you were only coming to Victoria Falls on your Africa trip, staying here would give you it all: set in a national park you get the bush experience of a tented camp complete with waterhole where wildlife drink at sunset (as you drink your sundowner or dine on gourmet bush cuisine), on top of your trips to the falls and the river.

Victoria Falls Hotel (☎ 44751; www.victoriafallshotel.com; Mallet Dr; s/d incl breakfast from US$216/232; P) This historic hotel (the oldest in Zimbabwe) oozes elegance and sophistication, and occupies an impossibly scenic location. Looking across manicured lawns to the gorge and bridge, you can't see the falls as such but, they are just there, and you do see the spray. High tea here is an institution.

Ilala Lodge (☎ 44737; www.ilalalodge.com; 411 Livingstone Way; s/d incl breakfast from US$256/320;

INFORMATION
Backpackers Bazaar 1 B1
Barclays Bank 2 B1
Police 3 B2
Post Office 4 B1
Standard Chartered Bank 5 B1
Telco .... (see 24)
Tourist Information Office 6 B1
Victoria Falls Surgery 7 A1

SIGHTS & ACTIVITIES
Adrenalin .... (see 12)
Big Tree 8 C2
Elephant's Walk Museum .... (see 22)
Falls Craft Village 9 B1
Rock 10 C2
Safari Par Excellence .... (see 24)
Victoria Falls Aquarium 11 B2
Wild Horizons 12 B1

SLEEPING
Ilala Lodge 13 B1
Shoestrings Backpackers 14 A1
Victoria Falls Backpackers 15 A3
Victoria Falls Hotel 16 B2
Victoria Falls Restcamp & Lodges 17 B1
Victoria Falls Safari Lodge 18 A3

EATING
Boma .... (see 18)
In-Da-Belly Restaurant .... (see 17)
Mama Africa 19 B2
River Cafe .... (see 24)
Terrace .... (see 16)
Victoria Falls Safari Lodge .... (see 18)

DRINKING
Shoestrings Backpackers .... (see 14)

SHOPPING
Craft Markets 20 B1
Curio Shops .... (see 23)
Curio Shops 21 B1
Elephant's Walk Shopping Village 22 B1
Landela Centre 23 B2
Phumula Centre 24 B1
Soper's Arcade 25 B1

TRANSPORT
Air Zimbabwe 26 B1
Chinotimba Bus Terminal 27 A4

) This hotel is situated just 300m from the main entrance to the mighty Victoria Falls and is a truly magnificent hotel. A colonial relic, it is adorned with mounted rifles, hunting trophies and oil paintings; classically decorated rooms face out towards the manicured lawns and elaborate gardens.

Matetsi Water Lodge (☎ 04 731295; www.andbeyond.com; per person sharing US$435;) Situated 30km from the falls, along the banks of the Zambezi, this shows Zimbabwean finesse in hospitality at its best. Each uber-luxurious bungalow has its own pool yet is set in the wild. There are very good specials throughout the year so contact them for cheaper rates.

Eating

In-Da-Belly Restaurant (☎ 332077; Victoria Falls Restcamp & Lodges; meals US$5-8) The name is a play on Ndebele, one of the two major population tribes in Zimbabwe, and it serves good bistro-style cuisine.

Mama Africa (☎ 41725; meals US$5-8) This perennial tourist haunt behind the Landela Centre specialises in local dishes, steaks and game meats when available.

River Cafe (☎ 42994; Landela Centre) This cafe serves a variety of cafe-style meals. It's a nice spot to hang out and have a meal or drinks. You can shop for curios in the complex too.

Terrace (Victoria Falls Hotel, Mallet Dr; meals US$20) The Terrace at the stately Victoria Falls Hotel overlooks the hotel gardens and the Victoria Falls Bridge, and brims with English colonial ambience. High tea here is a must – just do it.

Boma (☎ 43201; Victoria Falls Safari Lodge, Squire Cummings Rd; meals US$40 buffet) Boma is the place to release your inner tourist without being tacky and enjoy a taste of Africa: do interactive drumming or get your fortune told by a witch doctor.

Drinking

There's unfortunately not much life in Vic Falls after sunset, though the bar at **Shoestrings Backpackers** (☎ 40167; 12 West Dr; drinks from US$3) is the place to go. Here you can meet the local guides off duty, and they can give you local knowledge on places to visit.

Shopping

The **craft market** (Adam Stander Dr) has loads of curios, while the nearby Elephant's Walk Shopping Village complex stocks mainly upmarket crafts. The craftsmen eke out a mea-

FURTHER READING

Want to know a bit more about Victoria Falls? We suggest having a read or a look at:

- *Exploring Victoria Falls* by Prof Lee Berger and Brett Hilton-Barber
- *Mosi-oa-Tunya: Handbook to the Victoria Falls Region* by DW Phillipson
- www.wildzambezi.com
- www.gotovictoriafalls.com
- www.africaalbidatourism.com
- www.africanencounter.com
- www.zctf.mweb.co.zw – Zimbabwe Conservation Task Force
- www.zimbabwe-art.com – Zimbabwe Conservation Art Programme

THE MIGHTY ZAMBEZI RIVER

The Zambezi River emerges from the northwestern tip of Zambia, one of the greatest rivers of Africa. It descends from 1500m above sea level and traverses six countries before its epic 2574km journey ends. The Indian Ocean receives its largest fresh water discharge through this incredible catchment. The Zambezi has a basin of more than 1,570,000 square kms and is the lifeblood of the people that reside on the river. The life it supports – from people to vast populations of animals – is as wild as it is captivating.

gre living by selling to tourists, so it would be good for lots of reasons to go shopping! African items are often made from recycled items and they do look good at home.

The Phumula Centre is a small mall of shops for locals and tourists, supermarkets and small restaurants.

Getting There & Away

AIR

Check out www.flightsite.co.za, where you can search all the airlines including low cost carriers (and car hire companies) for the cheapest flights and book yourself. **South African Airways** (☎ 011-808678; www.flysaa.com) and **British Airways** (www.britishairways.com) fly every day to Johannesburg from around US$320 return. **Air Namibia** (www.airnamibia.com) flies to Windhoek for around US$530 return.

BICYCLE

Bikes can be ridden to/from Zambia, however, bear in mind that cyclists have been mugged while riding to/from the Zambian border and the falls.

BUS & MINIBUS

Minibuses or combis are no longer recommended to travellers as they become so neglected and overused that they break down and are frequently involved in fatal accidents.

For information on travelling to Botswana, and crossing the Zimbabwe–Botswana border at Kazungula, see p732. For information about travelling to Namibia, see p733. For information about crossing into Zambia along the Victoria Falls Bridge, see p610.

CAR & MOTORCYCLE

If you're driving a rented car or motorcycle from Zambia, you'll need a letter from your rental company stating that you are permitted to enter Zimbabwe.

HITCHING

It's fairly easy to hitch between Victoria Falls and Kazungula, Botswana. If you head to the petrol station in both towns you'll have the best chance of a lift; see also p734.

TRAIN

The *Mosi-oa-Tunya* train leaves Victoria Falls daily at 6.30pm for Bulawayo, Zimbabwe (economy/2nd/1st class, US$1/3/4, 12 hours). Make reservations at the **ticket office** (☎ 44391; 7am-12pm & 2-4pm Mon-Fri, 7am-10am Sat & Sun) inside the train station.

Getting Around

TO/FROM THE AIRPORT

Victoria Falls Airport is located 20km southeast of town, and is easily accessible by taxi (US$20 each way).

CAR & MOTORCYCLE

When planning your trip, find out what the situation is with petrol availability, as this is an issue that has cycles all of its own. At the time of writing, petrol was readily available in petrol stations but this may change.

TAXIS

A taxi around town costs about US$10 and slightly more after dark. Taxis don't use meters, so you'll have to bargain. The taxi cabs themselves are all pretty shabby, but they get you from A to B.

VICTORIA FALLS NATIONAL PARK

The entrance to the **national park** (Map pp614-5; admission US$20, 6am-6pm) is located just before the Zimbabwean border post. The admission price must be paid in US dollars. One of the most dramatic spots is the westernmost point known as **Cataract View**. Another track leads to the aptly named **Danger Point**, where a sheer, unfenced 100m drop-off will rattle your nerves. From there, you can follow a side track for a view of the **Victoria Falls Bridge**.

Like its counterpart on the Zimbabwean side, the park is open again in the evenings during (and just before and after) a full moon in order to see the amazing **lunar rainbow**. The tickets cost an extra US$10 – hours of operation vary, though you can inquire through your accommodation.

ZAMBEZI NATIONAL PARK

This **national park** (Map p618; admission US$10; 6am-6.30pm) consists of 40km of Zambezi River frontage and a spread of wildlife-rich mopane forest and savannah. The park is best known for its herds of sable antelopes, but it is also home to lions, giraffes and elephants. The entrance to the park is situated only 5km northwest of the Victoria Falls town centre, and is easily accessible by private vehicle. If you don't have your own wheels (or your petrol is running low), tour operators on both sides of the border offer wildlife drives, guided hikes and fishing expeditions in the park.

Zambia

Zambia, with its dreamy landscapes and astonishing density of wildlife, fits perfectly into a trip to Southern Africa. Its unique appeal is its rough edge: known as the 'real Africa', Zambia is not set up for independent tourism and travel here is challenging – a crumbling infrastructure, little signage and long distances between major towns make it one big adventure. You don't have to get far out of the cosmopolitan capital, Lusaka, to get off the beaten track.

What makes it all worthwhile is the stunning landscapes, made up of unspoiled miombo woodland, floodplains, snaking rivers, countless waterfalls and vast wilderness areas, and the concentration and variety of wildlife. A fact you'll become acutely aware of when you spot your first leopard skulking around its kill, or watch a grunting hippo haul itself onto a grassy bank under a blood red sunset, or admire the fish eagle as it swoops across glassy waters while you canoe the Zambezi River. In fact the endless sound of thousands of lechwe (antelope) hooves clattering and splashing through the marshes of a wetland could well sear itself in your mind.

South Luangwa, one of the best national parks on the continent, and monstrous Kafue National Park, classic African safari territory with an area larger than Switzerland, epitomise the country's riches. And then there's Victoria Falls (see the Victoria Falls chapter), the dazzling waterfall that is truly one of the greatest spectacles on the planet.

There's also the cultural side of Zambia, and witnessing the Kuomboka ceremony, one of Southern Africa's last great festivals, could be the highlight of your trip here. Also, try to get out to a local village – you'll understand why Zambians are so highly regarded for their welcoming hospitality and their irrepressible warmth.

FAST FACTS

- **Area** 752,614 sq km
- **Capital** Lusaka
- **Country code** ☎ 260
- **Famous for** National parks with the Big Five, fishing for tigerfish along the Lower Zambezi and Victoria Falls
- **Languages** English, Bemba, Lozi, Nyanja and Tonga
- **Money** Zambian kwacha
- **Phrases** *Muli shani* (hello; Bemba), *muli bwanji* (hello; Nyanja), *natotela* (thanks; Bemba), *zikomo* (thanks; Nyanja)
- **Population** 12 million

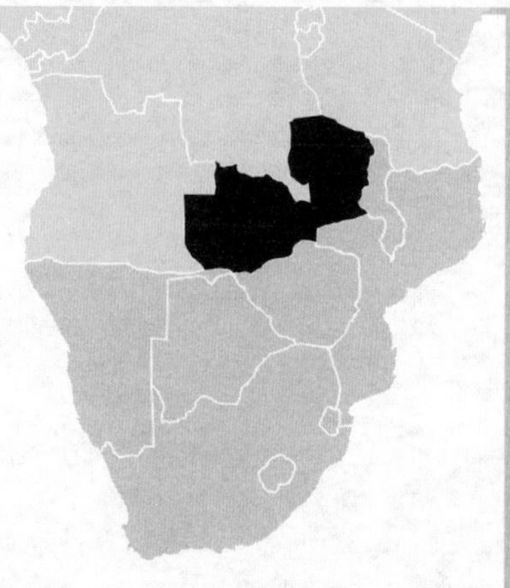

HIGHLIGHTS

- **South Luangwa National Park** (p652) Identify the incredible diversity of winged, hoofed and furred creatures along the stunning landscapes of Zambia's premier park.
- **Lower Zambezi National Park** (p663) Canoe along a stunning wilderness landscape, watching in awe as elephants stroll along the bank and birds of prey soar overhead.
- **Kafue National Park** (p670) Explore vast, classic wildlife country – one of the best places to spot leopards in Africa.
- **Northern Zambia** (p644) Get lost in Zambia's land of adventure, the immense untamed north, with rarely another tourist in sight.
- **Lake Kariba** (p660) Motor out to remote islands on one of Africa's largest artificial lakes.

HOW MUCH?

- **Small woodcarving** US$12
- **Bunch of bananas at roadside** US$1
- **Traditional dance** US$10–20
- **Walking safari** US$45
- **Batik** US$13

LONELY PLANET INDEX

- **1L of petrol/diesel** US$1.30/1
- **1L of bottled water** US$3
- **Bottle of Mosi lager** US$1.50
- **Souvenir T-shirt** US$15
- **Street snack** US$2

ITINERARIES

One consideration is your method of travel; travellers without their own transport cannot reach the remote places that are easily accessible by private vehicle or organised tour. Also, the bizarre shape of Zambia can frustrate your travel plans.

- **One Week** With only one week, hit one of *the* attractions of Southern Africa: Victoria Falls (p604) or South Luangwa National Park (p652).
- **Two Weeks** With two weeks, you'll have time for the great Victoria Falls as well as one or two of the national parks – maybe South Luangwa, Lower Zambezi (p663) or Kafue (p670).
- **Three Weeks** With extra time and money, go to Victoria Falls, South Luangwa National Park, a lodge on the Lower Zambezi, the Copperbelt Province (p642) to see wild chimps, and Kasanka National Park (p645). If you are travelling to or from Tanzania or Malawi, or are able to set aside even more time, explore the Northern Province, including the Bangweulu Wetlands (p646) and the dramatic southern tip of Lake Tanganyika.

CLIMATE & WHEN TO GO

Zambia's altitude creates a temperate climate. There are three distinct seasons: the dry season (mid-April to August), when temperatures drop at night and the landscape is green and lush; the hot season (September to mid-November), which is the best time to see wildlife, as flora is sparse; and the wet season (mid-November to mid-April), which is ideal for birdwatching, though some camps and lodges in the national parks close due to flooded roads. Rainfall is higher in the north of the country.

Refer to the Victoria Falls chapter (p604) for details about the best time to visit there, and see p745 for climate charts.

HISTORY

The precolonial history of the area that became Zambia, along with the rest of Southern Africa, is covered on p32.

The Slave Trade & Early Europeans

The first Europeans to enter what is now Zambia were Portuguese explorers. In the 1790s, several of them travelled from Angola as far as the headwaters of the Zambezi River. Around the same time, another group of Portuguese pushed inland from Mozambique to Lakes Mweru and Bangweulu.

The Portuguese generally followed routes established many centuries earlier by Swahili-Arab slave-traders, who had penetrated the region from their city-states on the east coast of Africa. Often in collaboration with the chiefs of powerful tribes, the slave-traders captured many people from Zambia and took them across Lake Malawi and through Mozambique or Tanzania to be sold in the slave markets of Zanzibar.

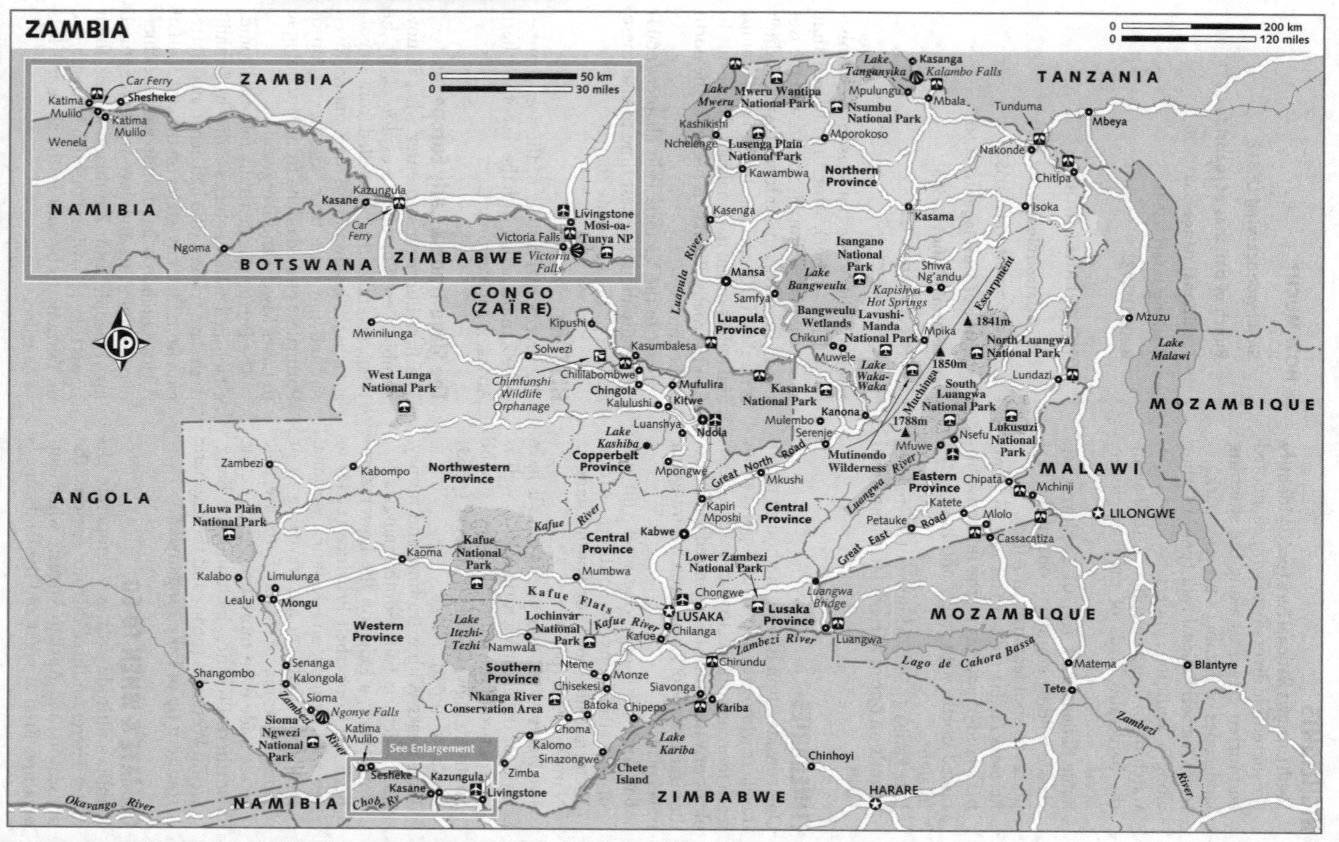
ZAMBIA
0 200 km
0 120 miles
ZAMBIA
Car Ferry
Katima Mulilo
Sesheke
Katima Mulilo
Wenela
0 50 km
0 30 miles
NAMIBIA
Kasane
Kazungula
Car Ferry
Livingstone
Mosi-oa-Tunya NP
Victoria Falls
Victoria Falls
Ngoma
BOTSWANA
ZIMBABWE
CONGO (ZAÏRE)
TANZANIA
MOZAMBIQUE
MALAWI
LILONGWE
MOZAMBIQUE
ANGOLA
NAMIBIA
ZIMBABWE
HARARE
LUSAKA
Lake Tanganyika
Kasanga
Kalambo Falls
Mpulungu
Mbala
Lake Mweru
Mweru Wantipa National Park
Nsumbu National Park
Kashikishi
Nchelenge
Lusenga Plain National Park
Mporokoso
Kawambwa
Northern Province
Tunduma
Mbeya
Nakonde
Chitipa
Isoka
Kasama
Kasenga
Luapula River
Mansa
Isangano National Park
Lake Bangweulu
Samfya
Shiwa Ng'andu
Kapishya Hot Springs
Escarpment
Bangweulu Wetlands
Lavushi-Manda National Park
Mpika
1841m
Chikuni
Muwele
Luapula Province
Mzuzu
Lake Malawi
North Luangwa National Park
1850m
Lake Waka-Waka
Muchinga
South Luangwa National Park
Lundazi
Kasanka National Park
Kanona
Mulembo
Serenje
1788m
Mfuwe
Nsefu
Lukusuzi National Park
Mutinondo Wilderness
Luangwa River
Mwinilunga
Kipushi
Solwezi
Kasumbalesa
West Lunga National Park
Chililabombwe
Chimfunshi Wildlife Orphanage
Chingola
Mufulira
Kalulushi
Kitwe
Luanshya
Ndola
Lake Kashiba
Copperbelt Province
Mpongwe
Great North Road
Mkushi
Eastern Province
Chipata
Mchinji
Zambezi
Kabompo
Northwestern Province
Kapiri Mposhi
Central Province
Katete
Petauke
Mlolo
Cassacatiza
Great East Road
Liuwa Plain National Park
Kafue River
Kafue National Park
Central Province
Kabwe
Lower Zambezi National Park
Kaoma
Mumbwa
Luangwa Bridge
Kalabo
Limulunga
Lealui
Mongu
Kafue Flats
Chongwe
Lusaka Province
Western Province
Lake Itezhi-Tezhi
Lochinvar National Park
Kafue River
Chilanga
Kafue
Namwala
Luangwa
Zambezi River
Lago de Cahora Bassa
Chirundu
Matema
Blantyre
Tete
Senanga
Shangombo
Kalongola
Southern Province
Nteme
Monze
Chisekesi
Siavonga
Nkanga River Conservation Area
Kariba
Sioma
Zambezi River
Ngonye Falls
Sioma Ngwezi National Park
Batoka
Chipepo
Choma
Katima Mulilo
See Enlargement
Kalomo
Lake Kariba
Zambezi River
Chinhoyi
Sinazongwe
Chete Island
Sesheke
Kazungula
Zimba
Kasane
Livingstone
Chobe R
Okavango River

In the 1820s, the effects of the *difaqane* (forced migration in Southern Africa; see p36) rippled through to Zambia. Matabele migrants entered western Zimbabwe and threatened the Makololo, who moved into southern Zambia, displacing the Tonga people and threatening the Lozi people on the upper Zambezi.

The celebrated British explorer David Livingstone travelled up the Zambezi in the early 1850s in search of a route to the interior of Africa and hoped to introduce Christianity and the principles of European civilisation to combat the horrors of the slave trade. In 1855, he reached the awesome waterfall that he coined Victoria Falls.

Livingstone's work and writings inspired missionaries to come to the area north of the Zambezi; close on their heels came explorers, hunters and prospectors searching for whatever riches the country had to offer. The 'new' territory did not escape the notice of entrepreneur Cecil John Rhodes, who was already establishing mines and a vast business empire in South Africa. Rhodes' British South Africa Company (BSAC) laid claim to the area in the early 1890s and was backed by the British Government in 1895 to help combat slavery and prevent further Portuguese expansion in the region.

The Colonial Era

Like many parts of Southern Africa, Zambia's history was largely influenced by the BSAC during the next few decades. Two separate territories were initially created – Northwestern Rhodesia and Northeastern Rhodesia – but these were combined in 1911 to become Northern Rhodesia. In 1907, Livingstone became the capital.

At around the same time, vast deposits of copper were discovered in the area now called the Copperbelt. The indigenous people had mined there for centuries, but now large European-style opencast pits were dug. The main source of labour was Africans, who had to earn money to pay the new 'hut tax'; in any case, most were driven from their land by European settlers.

In 1924 the colony was put under direct British control and in 1935 the capital was moved to Lusaka. To make them less dependent on colonial rule, settlers soon pushed for closer ties with Southern Rhodesia and Nyasaland (Malawi), but various interruptions – including WWII – meant the Federation of Rhodesia and Nyasaland did not come about until 1953.

Nationalist Resistance

Meanwhile, African nationalism was becoming a more dominant force in the region. The United National Independence Party (UNIP) was founded in the late 1950s by Dr Kenneth Kaunda, who spoke out against the federation on the grounds that it promoted the rights of white settlers to the detriment of the indigenous African population.

Through the 1960s, as many other African countries gained independence, Zambian nationalists opposed the colonial forces. This resulted in a massive campaign of civil disobedience and a small but decisive conflict called the Chachacha Rebellion.

The federation was dissolved in 1963 and Northern Rhodesia became independent a year later, and changed its name to Zambia. While the British government had profited enormously from Northern Rhodesia, the colonialists chose to spend a large portion of this wealth on the development of Southern Rhodesia (now Zimbabwe). Zambia still suffers from the effects of this staggering loss of capital and the difference between the development of the two countries during and since colonial times is obvious.

Independence

After gaining independence, Zambia inherited a British-style multiparty political system. Kaunda, as leader of the majority UNIP, became the new republic's first president. The other main party was the African National Congress (ANC), led by Harry Nkumbula. But Kaunda disliked opposition. In one swift move during 1972, he disbanded the Zambian ANC, created the 'second republic', declared UNIP the sole legal party and made himself the only presidential candidate.

Consequently, Kaunda remained in power for the next 27 years. His rule was based upon 'humanism' – his own mix of Marxism and traditional African values. The civil service was increased, and nearly all private businesses (including the copper mines) were nationalised. But corruption and mismanagement, exacerbated by a fall in world copper prices, doomed Zambia to become one of the poorest countries in the world by the end of the 1970s. The economy continued

MOVERS & SHAKERS: KENNETH KAUNDA

Revered as the father of Zambia, Kenneth Kaunda – also known as KK – was instrumental in bringing independence to Zambia in 1964, and served as president until 1991. Born in 1924, in 1949 he served as interpreter and adviser on African affairs to liberal white settler Sir Stewart Gore-Brown, of the legislative council. He then went on to join the anticolonial African National Congress (ANC), of which he became secretary-general in the early 1950s. When members of the ANC started to quarrel over its direction in 1958–59, he started the breakaway Zambia African National Congress, which he used to rally against the British plan for a federation of the three colonies: Nyasaland, Northern Rhodesia and Southern Rhodesia. He managed to dissuade the British from forming the federation and was also jailed, making a martyr of himself and elevating him to hero status among the Zambian people.

After being released in early 1960, KK was elected president of the United National Independence Party (UNIP). He was invited by the British to discuss decolonisation, which began in 1962 and was completed in 1964. After general elections, the UNIP won by a small margin over the ANC, and Kaunda became the first Zambian president.

In the 1970s, KK imposed sanctions on Southern Rhodesia and allowed black guerrillas to use Zambia as a base to attack its southern neighbour to dissuade white rule. In 1976, he assumed emergency powers and was re-elected president in 1978 and 1983 in one-candidate elections. The plummet in copper prices during the 1970s and KK's continued grip on the presidency led to public dissatisfaction, which forced him to legalise multiparty elections in 1990. In 1991, KK stepped down as president.

In 1986, KK's son died of AIDS, and since then Kaunda has become a champion in the nation's fight against the disease. He also has his own political column in the independently owned *Post* newspaper.

to flounder while Zambia's trade routes to the coast through neighbouring countries (eg Zimbabwe and Mozambique) were closed in retaliation for Kaunda's support for several liberation movements in the region.

The 1980s

In the early 1980s two important events occurred that had the potential to significantly improve Zambia's economy: Rhodesia gained independence (and became Zimbabwe), which allowed Kaunda to take his country off a war footing; and the Tazara railway to Dar es Salaam (Tanzania) was completed, giving Zambia unencumbered access to the coast. Yet the economy remained on the brink of collapse: foreign exchange reserves were almost exhausted, serious shortages of food, fuel and other basic commodities were common, and unemployment and crime rates rose sharply.

In 1986, an attempt was made to diversify the economy and improve the country's balance of payments. Zambia received economic aid from the International Monetary Fund (IMF), but the IMF conditions were severe and included cutting basic food subsidies. Subsequent price rises led to country-wide riots in which many people lost their lives. Kaunda was forced to restore subsidies.

Turning Point

The winds of change blowing through Africa during the late 1980s, coupled with Zambia's disastrous domestic situation, meant something had to give. Following another round of violent street protests against increased food prices in 1990, which quickly transformed into a general demand for the return of multiparty politics, Kaunda was forced to accede to public opinion.

He announced a snap referendum in late 1990 but, as protests grew more vocal, he was forced to legalise opposition parties and announce full presidential and parliamentary elections for October 1991. Not surprisingly, UNIP (and Kaunda) were resoundingly defeated by the Movement for Multiparty Democracy (MMD), led by Frederick Chiluba, a former trade union leader. Kaunda admirably stepped down without complaint, which may have saved Zambia from descending into anarchy.

President Chiluba moved quickly to encourage loans and investments from the IMF and World Bank. Exchange controls were liberalised to attract investors, particularly from South Africa, but tough austerity measures were also introduced. Once again, food prices soared. The civil service was rationalised, state industries privatised or simply closed, and thousands of people lost their jobs.

By the mid-1990s, the lack of visible change in Zambia allowed Kaunda to confidently re-enter the political arena. He attracted strong support and soon became the UNIP leader. Leading up to the 1996 elections, the MMD panicked and passed a law forbidding anyone with foreign parents to enter politics (Kaunda's parents were from Malawi). Despite intercessions from Western aid donors and world leaders such as Nelson Mandela – not to mention accusations that Chiluba's parents were from Congo (Zaïre) – the law was not repealed. The UNIP withdrew all its candidates in protest and many voters boycotted the election. Consequently, Chiluba and the MMD easily won, and the result was grudgingly accepted by most Zambians.

In October 1997 a bungled coup attempt allowed Chiluba to announce a state of emergency, and many opposition figures were arrested. Kaunda, who claimed the coup was a set-up, was placed under house arrest until March 1998. This endeared him further to UNIP supporters and MMD opponents.

Zambia in the 21st Century

The political shenanigans continued unabated into the new millennium: in mid-2001, Vice-President Christon Tembo was expelled from parliament by Chiluba, so he formed an opposition party: the Forum for Democratic Development (FDD). Later, Paul Tembo, a former MMD national secretary, joined the FDD, but was assassinated the day before he was due to front a tribunal about alleged MMD corruption.

Chiluba was unable to run for a third presidential term in December 2001 (though he badly wanted to change the constitution so he could). He anointed his former vice-president, Levy Mwanawasa, as his successor, but Mwanawasa only just beat a coalition of opposition parties known as the United Party for National Development (UPND). Again, allegations from international observers about the MMD rigging the results and buying votes fell on deaf ears. To Chiluba's horror, Mwanawasa stripped his predecessor of immunity from prosecution and proceeded to launch an anticorruption drive, which targeted the former president. In August 2009, after a long-running trial, Chiluba was cleared of embezzling US$500,000 by Zambia's High Court. His wife, however was not so lucky, receiving a jail term earlier in the year for receiving stolen funds while her husband was in office. In a separate case, the High Court in Britain ruled Chiluba and four of his aides conspired to rob Zambia of about US$46 million, but it remains to be seen whether this judgement will be enforced within Zambia.

Because Zambia was deemed to be a Heavily Indebted Poor Country, most of its US$7 billion international debt was eliminated in 2005. Though Zambia is still a poor country, its economy experienced strong growth in the early 21st century with GDP growth at around 6%. However, the country is still very dependant on the world prices of its minerals (copper and cobalt). By the global economic slump of 2008/09, and with the price of minerals such as copper falling rapidly, Zambia appeared, once again, to be at the whim of the market. There has been large foreign investment in the mines, though (especially from China).

In 2008 President Mwanawasa died in Paris, where he was seeking treatment for a stroke he suffered earlier in the year. Rupiah Banda narrowly won an election victory and was sworn in as president, although Michael Sata, the main opposition candidate, alleged fraud.

THE CULTURE

The National Psyche

With corruption in government circles on the rise in 2009, Banda is proving to be an unpopular president with the people, who are fed up with politicians enriching themselves and their cronies. What really riled people was Banda making a donation of food aid to Zimbabwe from a country where many of his own people (about 70%) live below the poverty line.

HIV/Aids is, unfortunately, a big topic as Zambia has one of the world's most devastatingly high rates of infection. More than one in every seven adults in Zambia is infected, and the disease has claimed enough lives to lower the average life expectancy at birth to just over 40 years. People are finally starting to get tested, though not in the droves that aid agencies have been hoping for.

A social issue that is seemingly always discussed on the radio is cohabitation rather than marriage. Many Zambians feel that cohabitation will rock the foundations of their traditional values and will, hence, be the beginning of the end of society.

Finally, football (soccer) is always a topic on the minds of Zambians, especially with the impending World Cup about to kick off in South Africa in 2010.

Daily Life

HIV/Aids has had a huge effect on the daily lives of Zambian people. A new population of 'street kids' has emerged, who live in roadside sewers and on middle-of-the-road dividers in urban centres. There are also funeral processions on a daily basis, as the disease continues to claim many young lives.

Life is difficult for many Zambians. Almost 45% of the population live in urban centres; compounds designed for 50,000 now house more than 150,000. Cholera has become a problem in overpopulated Kapiri Mposhi and Lusaka during the wet season. And most unskilled labourers work six to seven days per week, making around US$60 per month, therefore forcing families to live on less than US$1 per day.

In rural Zambia, life has not changed much: subsistence agriculture, village hierarchies and a melange of traditional religions and Christian beliefs are its mainstays.

Population

The population density is about 15 people per square kilometre, making Zambia one of the most thinly populated countries in Africa. The concentration of people in urban centres (mostly Lusaka and the cities of the Copperbelt) is a high percentage for a developing country. This is noticeable as you travel through rural areas; you can go for hours without seeing more than a couple of small villages.

Intermarriage among the 73 officially recognised ethnic groups (tribes) is common, and Zambia is justifiably proud of its almost complete lack of tribal problems. The groups are (in order of size) the Bemba, originally from the Congo (Zaïre) and now settled in northern Zambia, the Copperbelt and Lusaka; the Tonga, who are linked to other groups in Zimbabwe and live in southern Zambia; the Nyanja, a collective term for about 1.5 million people living in eastern Zambia and Lusaka; the Ngoni, descendants of Zulus from South Africa now settled in the east around Chipata; and the Lozi in western Zambia.

Immigration & Emigration

Zambia has an interesting immigration history – both recent and historical – of demographic change. While most descendants of the original white settlers have since moved away, one can still find a fair number of those of English and Eastern European descent, mostly farmers and business types respectively. Indians and Pakistanis have long been a part of the mix, so don't be surprised to hear them proudly call themselves Zambians.

Newcomers to the country are South African businesspeople and Zimbabwean farmers who lost their land thanks to Robert Mugabe. Zimbabwean farmers mostly farm tobacco and flowers.

SPORT

Football (soccer) is by far the country's biggest sport. No matter what the season, it's the talk of the town. Though Lusaka is dotted with soccer stadiums, the two main places to catch a game are Independence Stadium in Matero and the stadiums in the Showgrounds. Other sports played in Lusaka include golf (there are more than a few courses), polo and polocross – a mixture of polo and lacrosse. Polo games can be seen at the Showgrounds at around 11.30am on weekends between May and August.

RELIGION

The majority of Zambians are Christians (75%), though other religions include Muslims and Hindus (24%) and animists (1%). Most Christians follow either Jehovah's Witness, Catholic or Evangelical sects, though beliefs in sorcery are still strong.

Churches have been playing a major role in trying to mitigate the spread of HIV, while also providing a strong support system for those living with HIV/Aids.

ARTS & CRAFTS

Zambia has a thriving contemporary art scene. One of the country's most famous and respected painters is the late Henry Tayali. His works – described by critics as 'crowded social realism' – have inspired many other Zambian painters and enjoyed a popular following among ordinary folk. If you want to know more about the local art scene, it's worth visiting the studio and exhibition centre named after him in Lusaka (see p633).

Other internationally recognised artists include Agnes Yombwe, who works with purely natural materials and uses traditional ceramics and textile designs in her striking sculptures; Shadreck Simukanga, arguably the finest painter working in Zambia; and the country's best-known artist, Stephen Kapata. Prominent sculptors include Eddie Mumba and the prolific Friday Tembo.

Zambian artistry includes skilfully woven baskets from Barotseland (Western Province) and Siavonga; malachite jewellery from the north; and woodcarvings and soapstone sculptures from Mukuni village, near Livingstone. Most of these crafts are sold in markets around the country, along the roadsides of intercity highways and in souvenir shops in touristy areas.

Dance

The most notable traditional dance is the *makishi*, which features male dancers wearing masks of stylised human faces with grass skirts and anklets. It probably originated in the Congo (Zaïre) region and was brought to northwestern Zambia by the Luvale or Luchasi people, before being adopted by other ethnic groups. *Makishi* is now found in many parts of Zambia, mainly at boys' initiation ceremonies. But any local celebration seems to be a good excuse for the men to boogie down.

Music

Each of Zambia's ethnic groups has its own musical traditions. The Lozi are famous for the large drums played during the remarkable Kuomboka ceremony (see the boxed text, p669), while the Bemba are also renowned drummers. Other traditional musical instruments used by most groups include large wooden xylophones, often with gourds underneath the blocks for resonance, and tiny thumb pianos with keys made from flattened metal.

Contemporary Zambian musicians who have achieved some international fame include Larry Maluma, who blends traditional Zambian beats with reggae, and had just released his 9th album, *Tusekelele* (Let's Celebrate), at the time of writing. Other popular musicians who play traditional styles include the Sakala Brothers from the Eastern Province and Mpunda Mutale from the Northern Province. Younger Zambians prefer reggae – both the old-school Jamaican style and the softer version popular in Southern Africa – and contemporary Zambian R&B and hip-hop. K'Millian is a hugely popular Zambian R&B artist. Also well loved is JK who plays a mixture of hip-hop, reggae and traditional Zambian beats. Zambians love Congolese *soukous* (termed rhumba in Zambia), which is blasted at deafening levels at local bars and nightclubs.

Theatre

Once thriving, Lusaka's theatre scene has taken a turn for the worse, though many Zambian writers still produce plays and other works, from slapstick comedy through to hard political comment. From time to time, the Lusaka Playhouse has a show worth seeing (see p640).

ENVIRONMENT

The Land

Landlocked Zambia is one of Africa's most eccentric legacies of colonialism. Shaped like a contorted figure of eight, its borders do not correspond to any tribal or linguistic area. And Zambia is massive, about the size of France, England and the Republic of Ireland combined.

Zambia sits on an undulating plateau, sloping to the south. To the north, the plateau drops steeply to Lake Tanganyika, one of the Rift Valley lakes that Zambia shares with Tanzania, Burundi and Congo (Zaïre).

Zambia's main river is the Zambezi, which flows in the west of the country. It forms the border between Zambia, Namibia, Botswana and Zimbabwe, and flows into the Victoria Falls and Lake Kariba. Other major rivers include the Kafue, which starts in the highlands between Zambia and Congo (Zaïre) and flows into the Zambezi southeast of Lusaka, and the Luangwa, which rises near the Tanzanian border and also flows into the Zambezi.

Wildlife

ANIMALS

Because of Zambia's diverse landscape, plentiful water supplies, and position between Eastern, Southern and Central Africa, the diversity of animal species is huge. The rivers, of course, support large populations of hippos and crocs, and the associated grasslands provide plenty of fodder for herds of zebras, impalas and pukus (antelope common in Zambia, but not elsewhere). Other antelopes found in Zambia include waterbucks and lechwes; in fact, vast herds of rare black lechwe live near Lake Bangweulu, and endemic Kafue lechwes settle in the area around the Kafue River. Kasanka National Park is one of the best places on the continent to see rare water-loving antelopes called sitatungas. Two more endemic species are Thornicroft giraffes and Cookson's wildebeests, both found in South Luangwa National Park.

These antelopes naturally attract predators, so most parks contain lions, leopards, hyenas (which you'll probably see) and cheetahs (which you probably won't). The other two big drawcards – buffalo and elephants – are also found in huge herds in the main national parks.

Bird lovers can go crazy in Zambia, where about 750 species have been recorded. Twitchers used to the 'traditional' Southern African species listed in the *Roberts* and *Newman's* field guides will spend a lot of time identifying unusual species – especially in the north and west. Most notable are the endangered shoebill storks (found in the Bangweulu Wetlands); fish eagles (Zambia's national bird); and endemic Chaplin's barbets (mostly around Monze).

PLANTS

The country's main vegetation zones are miombo woodland, which covers the plateau areas (about 65% of Zambia); mopane woodland in the hotter, lower parts of the country, such as the Zambezi and Luangwa Valleys; and acacia woodland and semi-evergreen forest in the south and west.

National Parks

Zambia boasts 19 national parks and reserves, but after decades of poaching, clearing and general bad management, many are just lines on the map that no longer protect (or even contain) much wildlife. However, four national parks do accommodate healthy stocks of wildlife, and are among the best in Southern Africa: South Luangwa (p652), Lower Zambezi (p663), Kafue (p670) and Mosi-oa-Tunya (p614).

In a scheme unique in Zambia (and unusual in Southern Africa), Kasanka National Park has been leased to a private operator since 1990. This park is now fully funded by donations and tourism, and functions very well. An example of successful cooperation between an ecofriendly organisation, the government and the Zambian park authorities is the ongoing rehabilitation of the previously neglected Liuwa Plain National Park (p670) in the far west of the country, a stunning wildlife area.

Zambia also has 34 vaguely defined game management areas (GMAs). These mainly act as buffer zones around the major national parks, and are mostly used for commercial hunting. All the GMAs and national parks/reserves (except Kasanka) are administered by the semi-autonomous Zambia Wildlife Authority (ZAWA) – see p633 for contact details.

Admission fees to the parks vary, so they're listed in the appropriate sections later in this chapter. Each ticket is valid for 24 hours from the time you enter the park, but if you're staying inside the park at official accommodation this admission fee is valid for seven days. Taking a vehicle inside the park costs between US$15 and US$30 per day, depending on the size and weight. Landing a plane costs US$30 per aircraft, and using a private boat is US$20 a day.

Environmental Issues

Although the population is growing rapidly, it is still relatively sparse, so Zambia doesn't suffer many of the environmental problems encountered by its neighbours. However, around Lusaka, Livingstone and the cities of the Copperbelt, denudation of local vegetation is apparent. And unsustainable deforestation (and associated soil erosion) in the countryside is a pressing environmental problem. Land is regularly cleared for agricultural purposes, local people chop down wood for charcoal fires, and the timber industry clears vast tracts of trees to meet the demand from China for wood. The government has banned the export of raw timber to other countries in the Southern African Development Community (SADC), but illegal logging and timber smuggling continues.

During the 1970s and 1980s, many Zambian parks were effectively abandoned and poaching became a major problem. Then, under pressure from international conservation organisations, the government slowly came to realise that tourism was a major source of foreign currency for the government (and local people) – and that this depended on healthy national parks. Despite successes in some parks, notably South Luangwa, Lower Zambezi and Mosi-oa-Tunya National Parks, poaching and poor management remain major problems. And the detrimental impact of tourism is obvious along the Zambezi River (particularly near Victoria Falls), where lodges continue to be built unabated and dozens of cruise boats shuttle along every day looking for the diminishing wildlife.

See p20 for information on how you can do your part to contribute to responsible travel.

FOOD & DRINK

The national dish is unquestionably *nshima*, a bland but filling porridgelike maize substance. It's eaten with your hands and always accompanied by a *relish*, such as beans or vegetables (in inexpensive eateries), or chicken or fish (in slightly better restaurants). Most cheaper restaurants serve meals without meat, because locals can't afford anything but *nshima*, rice and vegetables anyway. Most other cheap meals are an unimaginative and unhealthy choice of fried eggs, fried sausages, fried chicken and burgers – all laden with chips (French fries).

In the cities and larger towns, many restaurants – especially those in the hotels – offer Western meals such as steak and grilled chicken (and sometimes French and Italian food). Prices start from US$5, depending on the surroundings as much as the food itself, and whether you eat in or take away. Chinese and Indian restaurants are also found in the larger urban spaces. Restaurants in Lusaka, and those operated by many of the lodges and camps in and around national parks, are where you'll find the best food. Dishes are usually variations on Western meals, and sometimes local game meat (kudu is excellent) is available; there are often options for vegetarians, too. At most top-end establishments such as these, main courses start from about US$12.

In better restaurants a 10% service charge is often added (which technically means tipping is not required), as well as the normal 17.5% value-added tax (VAT). All prices in this chapter, and the Zambian section of the Victoria Falls chapter, include all charges and taxes, though most restaurants list prices *without* service charge and VAT.

Markets and stalls on the roadside sell fresh vegetables and fruit, while supermarkets in the cities and larger towns are well stocked.

Tea, coffee, bottled mineral water and soft drinks are widely available and inexpensive; for a refreshing drink on a hot day, try a Malawi or rock shandy. The local beer is good: Mosi is arguably tastier than Castle and the Ndola-brewed Rhino Lager, although Windhoek Draught (from Namibia) is our favourite. Traditional 'opaque' beer made from maize is sold commercially in cardboard cartons, but make sure you shake the carton before drinking.

LUSAKA

☎ 0211/ pop 1.3 million

In this part of the world, all roads lead to Lusaka. Like it or not there's no easy way of bypassing Zambia's capital and largest urban zone, with its mishmash of dusty tree-lined streets, bustling African markets, Soviet-looking high-rise blocks and modern commerce. If that doesn't sound appealing it's because Lusaka does not easily lend itself to superlatives. There are no real attractions, grand monuments to drool over, or historical treasures to unearth. For some, this is an attraction in itself and it's certainly an easy enough place to spend time with a genuine African feel, a cosmopolitan populace, some excellent restaurants and quality accommodation options. It's a good spot to let loose too – the expat bars and the homegrown nightclub scene will see you through to the wee hours.

ORIENTATION

The main street, Cairo Rd, is lined with shops, cafes, supermarkets, travel agencies, banks and bureaux de change. To the north is a major traffic circle and landmark, the North End Roundabout; to the south is the creatively named South End Roundabout. East of Cairo Rd are the wide jacaranda-lined streets of the smarter residential suburbs and the area officially called Embassy Triangle (not surprisingly, home to many embassies and high commissions). West of Cairo Rd are 'compounds' (read 'townships').

See p641 for more information on getting around Lusaka.

Maps
The dusty, government-run **Map Sales office** (maps ZK20,000-30,000; 8.30am-3.30pm Mon-Fri) is beneath the Ministry of Lands & Natural Resources building, southwest of the junction of Independence Ave and Nationalist Rd. Note that while the topographical maps can be very useful, most maps are no newer than 1986, so any road networks are out of date.

Modern commercial maps of Zambia (ZK70,000) and southern Africa are available at bookshops and supermarkets at the **Manda Hill Shopping Centre** (Great East Rd) and **Arcades Shopping Centre** (Great East Rd).

INFORMATION
Bookshops
Book Cellar (☎ 255475; Manda Hill Shopping Centre, Great East Rd; 9am-6pm Mon-Sat, to 2pm Sun) Great selection of regional travel guides, novels and some useful road maps of Zambia.

Emergency
Ambulance (☎ 992)
Police (☎ 991; Church Rd)
Specialty Emergency Services (☎ 273303; www.ses-zambia.com) For evacuations. Has bases in Lusaka, Livingstone and Kitwe but operates throughout the country. Also has ambulances and in-patient care.

Internet Access
Wireless internet is available all over Lusaka now – at many cafes, restaurants and hotels. Look for the 'I Spot' sign.
Computer Lab (☎ 238375; Nkwazi Rd; per min ZK150; 8.30am-4.30pm Mon-Thu, to 11.45am & 2-4.30pm Fri, 8.30am-12.30pm Sat) High speed internet cafe – best in the city centre.
Microlink I Zone (Arcades Shopping Centre, Great East Rd; per min ZK200; 9am-9pm Mon-Sat, 10am-7pm Sun) Reliable, fast internet access, plus wireless facility.

ZAMBIA

Media
The monthly *Lowdown* magazine (ZK5000) is available at bookshops and supermarkets at the **Manda Hill Shopping Centre** (Great East Rd) and **Arcades Shopping Centre** (Great East Rd). It has a calendar of what's happening around town, lists restaurants, has a small classifieds section and advertises lodges around the country.

Medical Services
Care for Business (☎ 256731, 255728; Addis Ababa Dr)
Corpmed (☎ 222612, 226983; Cairo Rd) Behind Barclays Bank. Has doctor on duty 24 hours and is probably the city's best-equipped facility. Also runs its own ambulance service.
Hilltop Hospital (☎ 263407; Plot 148, Kabulonga Rd, Ibex Hill)
Greenwood Pharmacy (☎ 227811; 680 Cairo Rd; 8am-8pm daily)

Money
Along Cairo Rd, Barclays, Indo-Zambian Bank, Stanbic Bank and Standard Chartered Bank have branches with ATMs. These banks also have ATM branches elsewhere in Lusaka, such as on Haile Selassie Ave, and at the **Manda Hill Shopping Centre** (Great East Rd) and **Arcades Shopping Centre** (Great East Rd). Keep in mind that the only debit and credit cards accepted at ATMs are those bearing the Visa logo.

Changing travellers cheques is very difficult in Zambia (see p676) and usually not possible at bureau de change offices. To change cash, try the following, which don't charge commission, and bear in mind that when changing US dollars you often get a better rate for US$50 and US$100 bills:
Fx Foreign Exchange (Cairo Rd; 8am-4pm Mon-Fri, to noon Sat) At least three branches along Cairo Rd.
Stero Bureau de Change (☎ 255765; Manda Hill Shopping Centre, Great East Rd; 9am-6pm Mon-Fri, to 5pm Sat, 10am-2pm Sun)
Zampost Bureau de Change (cnr Cairo & Church Rds; 8am-5pm Mon-Fri, to 12.30pm Sat) Inside the main post office.

Post
Main post office (cnr Cairo & Church Rds; 8am-5pm Mon-Fri, to 12.30pm Sat) Contains Zambia's only reliable poste restante.

Telephone & Fax
A dozen telephone booths (using tokens and phonecards) can be found outside the post office. 'Phone shops' and 'fax bureaux' are dotted along Cairo Rd.
Zamtel (cnr Cairo & Church Rds) International calls and faxes can be made at the telephone office upstairs from the main post office.

Tourist Information
Zambia National Tourist Board (☎ 229087; www.zambiatourism.com; Century House, Cairo Rd; 8am-1pm & 2-5pm Mon-Fri, 9am-noon Sat) The head office has friendly enough staff, but information is limited to Lusaka and its environs. It's located next to the Shoprite supermarket, down a laneway on the southern side; look for the sign.

Zambia Wildlife Authority (ZAWA; ☎ 278524; info@zawa.org.zm; Kafue Rd; 8am-5pm Mon-Fri) In Chilanga, about 16km south of the city centre, facing Munda Wanga. It's a labyrinth of offices with no signage and not really worth visiting as, paradoxically, staff seem more interested in issuing hunting licences than helping foreigners visit national parks. The ZAWA office is accessible on the minibus to Chilanga or Kafue town from the City Bus Station or South End Roundabout.

Travel Agencies

Bimm Travel Agency (☎ 234372; www.bimmtourszambia.com; shop 3, Luangwa House, Cairo Rd; 8am-5.30pm Mon-Fri, to 1pm Sat) Just south of the post office, it's reliable and locally run. It can also arrange car hire.

Bush Buzz (☎ 256992; www.bush-buzz.com; 4169 Nangwenya Rd; 9am-5pm Mon-Fri, to 1pm Sat) This agency is especially popular for trips to Kafue and Lower Zambezi National Parks. It also organises a range of trips to South Luangwa and Livingstone.

KNP Promotions (☎ 266927; www.knp-promotions.com; 13 Chindo Rd Ext; 8am-5pm Mon-Fri, to noon Sat) This agency, located in the Woodlands neighbourhood, acts on behalf of every lodge and camp in and around Kafue National Park.

Steve Blagus Travel (☎ 227739; www.steveblagus.com; 24 Nkwazi Rd; 8am-4pm Mon-Fri, to 11.30am Sat) This is *the* agency for AmEx and a dozen upmarket lodges/camps. Also organises regional and domestic tours.

Voyagers (☎ 253082; www.voyagerszambia.com; Suez Rd) Perhaps the most popular agency in Zambia, it arranges flights, hotel reservations and car hire.

DANGERS & ANNOYANCES

As in most African cities, pickpockets take advantage of crowds, so be alert in the markets and bus stations and along the busy streets immediately west of Cairo Rd. At night, most streets are dark and often empty, so even if you're on a tight budget, take a taxi. It would be foolish to wander the streets after dark, especially in and around Cairo Rd. The corner of Church and Cairo Rds, and around the railway line, are currently hot spots for pickpockets and local thugs. Locals advise 'stand on your foot', which means don't back down if approached and hassled – tell them to get lost, and they usually will. Take this advice with a grain of salt, though, if someone pulls a knife or other weapon (although this is not common).

Lumumba Rd, parallel to and just west of Cairo Rd, has a bad reputation for robbery, especially from cars at a standstill in traffic jams, and especially from foreigners. Keep your windows up and doors locked if driving down this road.

Zambian markets are organised chaos – some more organised than others. For any market, watch your belongings and be aware of pickpockets. Don't flash a mobile (cell) phone around and don't carry a bag. Take only the cash you need in your pockets. Soweto market in particular is notorious for robbery and pickpockets (if in a car, wind windows up and lock doors), and there is a township nearby with a very bad reputation, so be careful around here.

SIGHTS & ACTIVITIES

The downstairs galleries in the **National Museum** (Nasser Rd; adult/child US$2/1; 9am-4.30pm), a big square box of a building with plenty of natural light, offer a snapshot of Zambia, both past and present. Highlights are the displays of contemporary Zambian paintings and sculpture. Upstairs are exhibits of cultural, ethnographical and archaeological interest; don't miss the display about witchcraft and initiation ceremonies. Access the museum off Independence Ave.

Check out **Henry Tayali Visual Arts Centre** (☎ 254440; Showgrounds; admission free; 9am-5pm Mon-Fri, 10am-4pm Sat & Sun) if you're in a buying mood for local contemporary art. It's a small collection but well worth a look. There are scenes of everyday Zambian rural life as well as abstract pieces. You can pick up an oil painting for between ZK1,000,000 and ZK2,000,000. Ask about the **studio** nearby where you can see these working artists sharing workspaces and learning from each other.

The **Town Centre Market** (Chachacha Rd; 7am-7pm) is chaotic and, frankly, malodorous, but fascinating. Zambians get their bargains here, whether it's fruit or veg, new or second-hand hardware, tapes or clothes. The market is pretty relaxed and probably a good first venture for visitors unfamiliar with African markets.

The **Lusaka City Market** (Lumumba Rd; 7am-5pm) is large and lively, but not as atmospheric (or smelly) as the Town Centre Market. The nearby **Soweto Market** (New City Market; Los Angeles Rd; 7am-7pm) is the largest market in Lusaka (and Zambia). This is one place where you are most likely to be relieved of your valuables – so be careful (see left). The sheer scale of the market and the amount of goods on offer and people buzzing around can be overwhelming – consider a visit on a Sunday when things are quieter and it's easier to move about. Note that

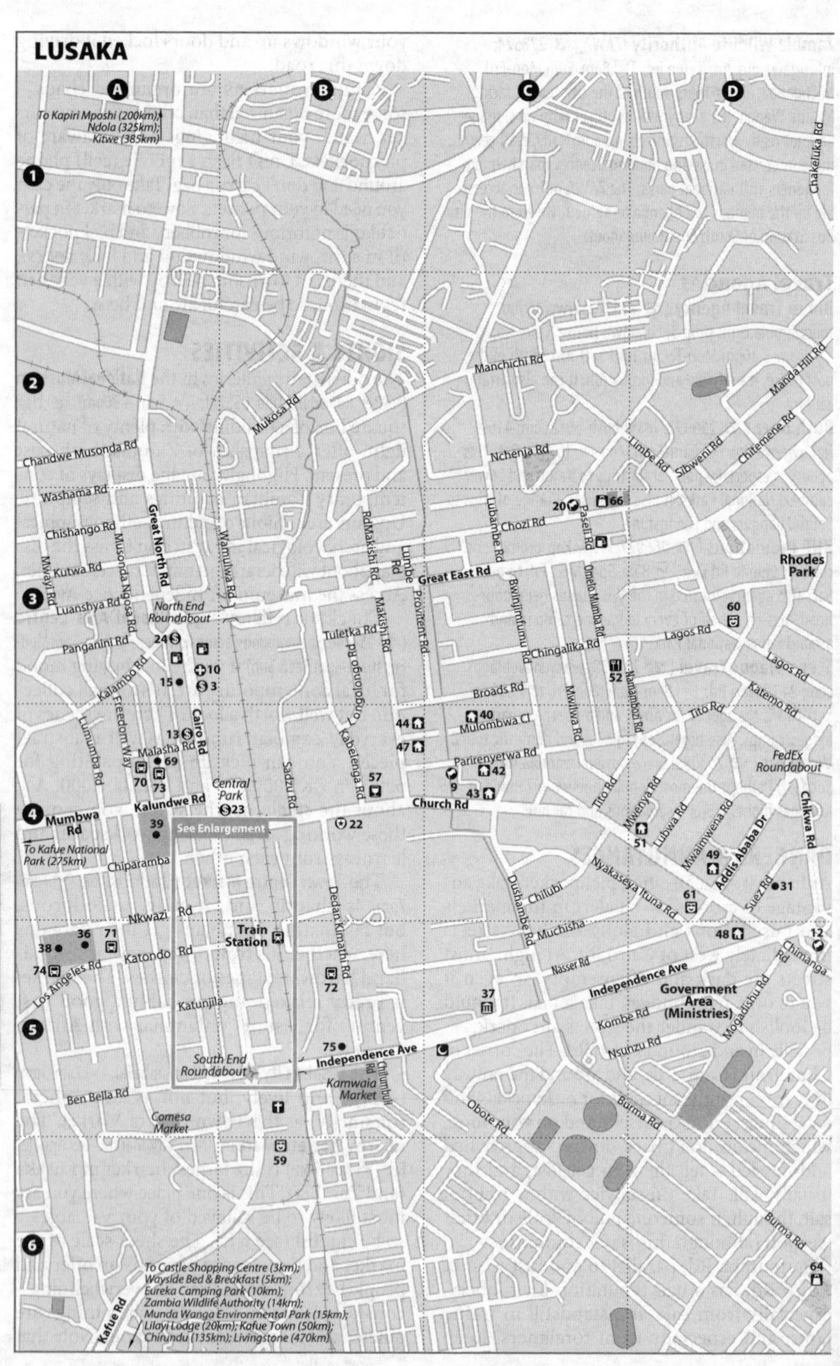

LUSAKA
To Kapiri Mposhi (200km); Ndola (325km); Kitwe (385km)
Manchichi Rd
Manda Hill Rd
Chakeluka Rd
Mukosa Rd
Chitemene Rd
Sibweni Rd
Limbe Rd
Nchenja Rd
Chandwe Musonda Rd
Washama Rd
Chishango Rd
Kutwa Rd
Luanshya Rd
Panganini Rd
Great North Rd
Musonda Ngosa Rd
Mwayi Rd
Wamulwa Rd
Chozi Rd
Paseli Rd
Lubambe Rd
Makishi Rd
Lumbe Rd
Great East Rd
Rhodes Park
North End Roundabout
Tuletka Rd
Provitent Rd
Bwinjimfumu Rd
Omelo Mumba Rd
Lagos Rd
Chingalika Rd
Kalambo Rd
Freedom Way
Cairo Rd
Longolongo Rd
Broads Rd
Mwilwa Rd
Namambozi Rd
Katemo Rd
Tito Rd
Lumumba Rd
Malasha Rd
Mulombwa Cl
Kabelenga Rd
Sadzu Rd
Parirenyetwa Rd
FedEx Roundabout
Central Park
Kalundwe Rd
Church Rd
Mwenya Rd
Lubwa Rd
Mwaimwena Rd
Addis Ababa Dr
Chikwa Rd
Mumbwa Rd
See Enlargement
To Kafue National Park (275km)
Chiparamba
Dedan Kimathi Rd
Dushambe Rd
Chilubi
Nyakaseya Ituna Rd
Suez Rd
Nkwazi Rd
Train Station
Muchisha
Chimanga Rd
Katondo Rd
Los Angeles Rd
Katunjila
Nasser Rd
Independence Ave
Government Area (Ministries)
Kombe Rd
Mogadishu Rd
Nsunzu Rd
South End Roundabout
Chilumbulu Rd
Kamwala Market
Ben Bella Rd
Comesa Market
Obote Rd
Burma Rd
Kafue Rd
To Castle Shopping Centre (3km); Wayside Bed & Breakfast (5km); Eureka Camping Park (10km); Zambia Wildlife Authority (14km); Munda Wanga Environmental Park (15km); Lilayi Lodge (20km); Kafue Town (50km); Chirundu (135km); Livingstone (470km)
ZAMBIA

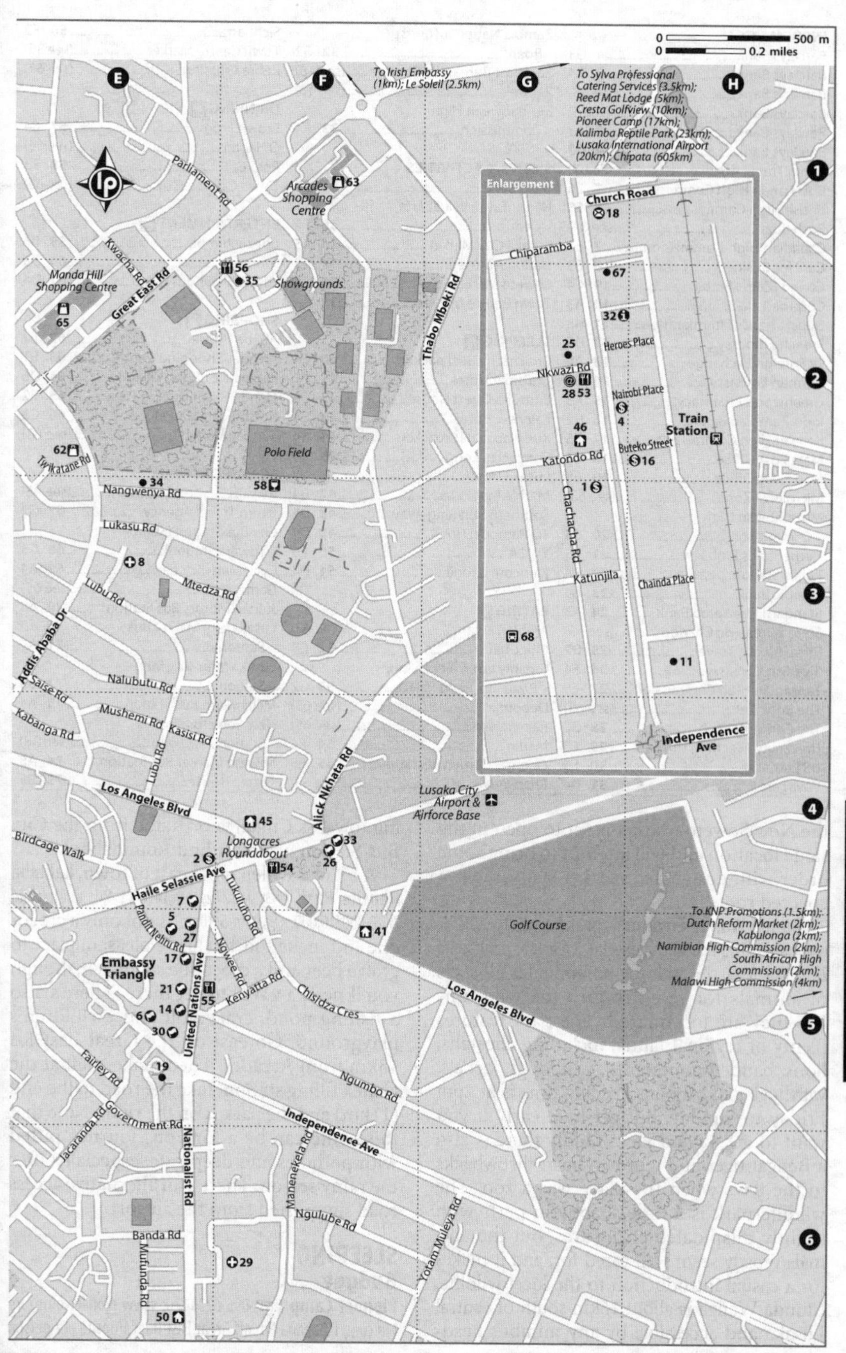
0 500 m
0 0.2 miles
To Irish Embassy (1km); Le Soleil (2.5km)
To Sylva Professional Catering Services (3.5km); Reed Mat Lodge (5km); Cresta Golfview (10km); Pioneer Camp (17km); Kalimba Reptile Park (23km); Lusaka International Airport (20km); Chipata (605km)
Enlargement
Church Road
Chiparamba
Heroes Place
Nkwazi Rd
Nairobi Place
Train Station
Buteko Street
Katondo Rd
Chachacha Rd
Katunjila
Chainda Place
Independence Ave
Parliament Rd
Arcades Shopping Centre
Kwacha Rd
Great East Rd
Manda Hill Shopping Centre
Showgrounds
Thabo Mbeki Rd
Polo Field
Twikatane Rd
Nangwenya Rd
Lukasu Rd
Mtedza Rd
Lubu Rd
Addis Ababa Dr
Nalubutu Rd
Saise Rd
Mushemi Rd
Kasisi Rd
Kabanga Rd
Lubu Rd
Alick Nkhata Rd
Los Angeles Blvd
Lusaka City Airport & Airforce Base
Birdcage Walk
Longacres Roundabout
Haile Selassie Ave
Tukuluho Rd
Pandit Nehru Rd
Ngwee Rd
Embassy Triangle
United Nations Ave
Kenyatta Rd
Chisidza Cres
Los Angeles Blvd
Golf Course
To KNP Promotions (1.5km); Dutch Reform Market (2km); Kabulonga (2km); Namibian High Commission (2km); South African High Commission (2km); Malawi High Commission (4km)
Fairley Rd
Ngumbo Rd
Government Rd
Jacaranda Rd
Nationalist Rd
Independence Ave
Manenekela Rd
Ngulube Rd
Yotam Muleya Rd
Banda Rd
Mufunda Rd
ZAMBIA

INFORMATION
Barclays Bank 1 G3
Barclays Bank 2 E4
Barclays Bank (see 63)
Barclays Bank (see 5)
Barclays Bank 3 A3
Barclays Bank 4 G2
Bimm Travel Agency (see 67)
Botswanan High Commission 5 E5
British High Commission 6 E5
Bush Buzz (see 34)
Canadian High Commission 7 E4
Care for Business 8 E3
Congo (Zaïre) Embassy 9 C4
Corpmed 10 A3
Department of Immigration 11 H3
French Embassy 12 D5
Fx Foreign Exchange 13 A4
German Embassy 14 E5
Greenwood Pharmacy 15 A3
Indo-Zambian Bank 16 H2
Kenyan High Commission 17 E5
Main Post Office 18 G1
Map Sales Office 19 E5
Microlink I Zone (see 63)
Mozambican High Commission 20 C3
Netherlands Embassy 21 E5
Police Station 22 B4
Stanbic Bank 23 B4
Standard Chartered Bank 24 A3
Stero Bureau de Change (see 65)
Steve Blagus Travel 25 G2
Swedish Embassy 26 F4
Tanzanian High Commission 27 E5
The Book Cellar (see 65)
The Computer Lab 28 G2
University Teaching Hospital 29 F6
US Embassy 30 E5
Voyagers 31 D4
Zambia National Tourist Board 32 G2
Zampost Bureau de Change (see 18)
Zamtel (see 18)
Zimbabwean High Commission 33 F4

SIGHTS & ACTIVITIES
Bush Buzz 34 E3
Henry Tayali Visual Arts Centre 35 F2
Lusaka City Market 36 A5
National Museum 37 C5
Soweto Market 38 A5
Town Centre Market 39 A4

SLEEPING
Chachacha Backpackers 40 C4
Chrismar Hotel 41 F5
Endesha Guest House 42 C4
Fairview Hotel 43 C4
Kuomboka Backpackers 44 B4
Longacres Lodge 45 F4
Lusaka Hotel 46 G2
Marble Inn 47 B4
Southern Sun Ridgeway 48 D5
Taj Pamodzi Hotel 49 D4
YWCA 50 E6
Zamcom Lodge 51 D4

EATING
Arabian Nights (see 63)
Chit Chat 52 C3
Creamy Inn, Chicken Inn, Pizza Inn, Food Palace 53 G2
Debonairs (see 65)
Kilimanjaro (see 65)
Marlin 54 F4
Oriental Garden Restaurant 55 E5
Rhapsody's (see 63)
Sichuan 56 F2
Town Centre Market (see 39)
Zebra Crossing (see 62)

DRINKING
Brown Frog 57 B4
O'Hagans (see 65)
Polo Grill 58 F3
Times Cafe (see 63)

ENTERTAINMENT
Chez-Ntemba 59 B6
Johnny's 60 D3
Lusaka Playhouse 61 D4

SHOPPING
Ababa House 62 E2
Arcades Shopping Centre 63 F1
Kabwata Cultural Village 64 D6
Manda Hill Shopping Centre 65 E2
Northmead Market 66 C3
Sunday Market (see 63)

TRANSPORT
Avis (see 48)
Bimm Travel Agency 67 G2
City Bus Station (Kulima Towers Station) 68 G3
CycleMart 69 A4
Game (see 65)
Juldan Motors Bus Station 70 A4
Lusaka City Market Bus Station 71 A5
Lusaka Inter-City Bus Station 72 B5
Millennium Bus Station 73 A4
New Soweto Minibus Station (see 38)
Soweto Market Bus Station 74 A5
Tazara House 75 B5

the New Soweto Market is set to open in the same location and will attempt to bring some order with designated market stalls under a covered roof.

Munda Wanga Environmental Park (☎ 278456; www.mundawanga.com; Kafue Rd, Chilanga; adult/child ZK20,000/10,000; 8am-5pm) rehabilitates all sorts of animals for re-entry into the wild, unless they are too injured. The park features plenty of regional fauna, including cheetahs, lions, banded mongooses, wild dogs, jackals, warthogs and baboons; feeding time is at 2pm Friday to Sunday, but get here early if you want to get a good view. Oddly there is also a Bengal tiger and a brown bear, throwbacks to the days when the place was a zoo. The wildlife park is a little shabby in parts with slightly dilapidated enclosures, but the animals mostly seem well cared for, and it makes for a casual introduction to the local wildlife. Munda Wanga is about 16km south of central Lusaka and accessible by any minibus heading towards Chilanga or Kafue from the City Bus Station or South End Roundabout.

A bit of a schlep northeast of town, **Kalimba Reptile Park** (☎ 213272; off District Rd; adult/child ZK20,000/10,000; 9am-5.30pm) is not only a crocodile and snake zoo, but also a pleasant place to grab a beer and a crocodile sandwich, though you'll need a 4WD to get there. There's also a fishing pond, crazy golf and a children's playground. Go east on the Great East Rd 13km from Arcades. Then make a left at the Caltex filling station, take the road to the end (11km) and the park is on the right. Note that this route can be a tortuous journey pitted with potholes and deep ruts, especially after the rainy season. There's an alternative access road signposted from the airport.

SLEEPING
Budget

Pioneer Camp (☎ 096 6731420; www.pioneercampzambia.com; Palabana Rd, off Great East Rd; campsite per person

ZK25,000, s/d chalets with shared bathroom US$45/60, s/d/tr 2-room chalets US$55/70/90, d luxury chalet US$120) A marvellous, isolated 25-acre camp, surrounded by bird-rich woodland, this makes a great alternative to staying in central Lusaka. Its seclusion and tranquillity make it very popular, and to save you self-catering there's a bar and restaurant. It's signposted 5km south of Great East Rd and 17km east of the Manda Hill Shopping Centre.

Chachacha Backpackers (☎ 222257; www.chachachasafaris.com; 161 Mulombwa Cl; campsite per person ZK27,500, dm ZK66,000, s, d, tw with shared bathroom ZK137,500;) When there are so few hostels around it's unsurprising that this place is popular with young backpackers. It's a fairly relaxed hostel and a good spot for meeting independent travellers. Dorms have four to six beds and decent mattresses while rooms are simple, clean and bare. The courtyard, pool and bar are inviting, and other facilities include a restaurant (serving basic meals), a tub for doing laundry, a communal, dilapidated kitchen and baggage store. Airport transfer available.

Eureka Camping Park (☎ 272351; eureka@zamnet.zm; campsite per person ZK28,000, chalets ZK275,000-358,000;) The campsite here is grassy and shaded by big trees and the security is good, while the swimming pool and bar (which sells snacks) are nice touches. It's about 12km south of the city centre. Minibuses from the City Bus Station and South End Roundabout go past the gate.

Kuomboka Backpackers (☎ 222450; kvkirkley@zamtel.zm; Makanta Close; dm ZK45,000, d with shared bathroom ZK125,000) A labyrinthine place, accommodation here is around one big main building; there are three dorms, each with 10 beds and low ceilings, which feel a bit cramped, especially when the place gets crowded. Plain but serviceable rooms come with clean, shared bathroom. Staff are laid-back. Recommended by readers. Airport transfer available.

YWCA (☎ 252726; Nationalist Rd; tw with shared bathroom/cooking facilities ZK150,000/180,000) The Y offers budget accommodation with a local feel for men and women. It's a tatty ol' place, the premises are quite dingy and the rooms need fixing up, but staff do try to keep it clean.

Midrange

All rooms in the places listed below contain a private bathroom, fan and TV, and all rates include breakfast.

Endesha Guest House (☎ 225780, 095-5550532; Parirenyetwa Rd; r without/with bathroom ZK180,000/220,000) A cosy pension (guest house) with eight rooms, this place is set in an unattractive concrete compound and the rooms are sparse but it's pretty good value, especially for the excellent location. The 'standard' rooms have unattached but private bathrooms, while the more expensive rooms have a private bathroom inside. All rooms have TV and fridge and mosquito nets draped over the beds.

Reed Mat Lodge (☎ 293426; reedmatlodge@yahoo.com; 5th St, Chudleigh; s/d ZK200,000/275,000, chalet ZK375,000;) In a big garden plot, the rooms here are jazzed up with African patterned fabrics, prints and textiles, which gives them a great feel, particularly in the rondavel-style chalets. Overall the place is a bit crowded but very clean and the African stylistic touches and strong cultural ethic really differentiate this place. There's also a gym here with simple equipment (ZK15,000 per day). Children are welcome.

Marble Inn (☎ 230617; marbleinn.lusaka@gmail.com; Makanta Cl; r ZK200,000) This place is a motel-style arrangement, which is unusual for Lusaka. Each room is big, airy and scrupulously clean with huge tiled showers. There's not much in the way of decor, but for the space and cleanliness this is a good Lusaka deal. It may be noisy from the backpackers next door, so keep this in mind when choosing your room. The entrance is the gate to the right of Kuomboka Backpackers.

Crystal Garden Lodge (☎ 290044; crystalgarden2020@yahoo.com; Kabompo Cl, Kalundu; s/d ZK225,000/250,000;) This place feels a bit like it's been put out to pasture – past its best – but it's good value, in a quiet part of town and has helpful staff. There are 10 rooms in a white, weathered building; the compound contains several other buildings around a small pool and a garden, and these are rented out to local students. Rooms are clean but old and a bit frail, with dark wood furniture and fridges; some have bath, others a shower. Meals are available at its restaurant, but don't just wander in – advance notice is required.

Zamcom Lodge (☎ 251811, 097 8953019; doreen@zamcom.ac.zm; Church Rd; d ZK250,000-300,000;) The spick-and-span rooms in this motel-style complex are devoid of charm, but simple and good value for what you get and the lodge is in a great location. It's mainly used for conferences and wedding receptions. Room 20 is the best double.

Longacres Lodge (☎ 254847; Los Angeles Blvd; s/d ZK250,000/300,000, ste ZK350,000;) This absolute warren of a place with its institutional feel and low-slung ceilings is a revamped government hostel with functional rooms. It's very spread out with lots of paved courtyard, but not many trees. Though friendly and spotless, it's not the most interesting place to stay. Rooms are pretty good though, with the bedroom separate from the small living areas that contain comfy chairs and TV. A suite buys you a bigger bed and slightly more space.

Lusaka Hotel (☎ 229049; www.lusakahotel.com; cnr Cairo & Katondo Rds; s/d from ZK295,000/315,000, d with air-con ZK365,000;) Given the central location of Lusaka Hotel on the maddening Cairo Rd, it has a surprisingly serene entry. The longest-standing hotel in Lusaka has a rather dark and sombre feel to it inside, and hallways are somewhat institutional too, but the rooms are a good size, all with bathroom; the more expensive ones come with kingsize beds and armchairs. It would suit business travellers, although anyone can take advantage of the excellent central location.

our pick **Fairview Hotel** (☎ 222604; www.fairview.co.zm; Church Rd; s/d ZK312,000/339,000;) The Fairview is an old-style hotel with dated rooms that could really do with sprucing up (and a few repairs). It's a very friendly, convivial place to stay, though, and there's a regimental routine to cleaning the rooms and changing the beds. Ask for a room facing away from the casino, which gets noisy, even during the week. The suites are the best deal, more like small flats with separate bedroom, living room with couches, balcony and fridge. The terrace bar is perfect on a warm evening and a nightly barbecue is also held here.

our pick **Wayside Bed & Breakfast** (☎ 273439, 272736; www.wayside-guesthouse.com; 39 Makeni Rd, Makeni; s US$80-90, d US$100-120;) This upmarket guest house is one of the best in Lusaka with only a handful of snug rooms with private bathroom. It used to be a farm and today the sizeable grounds are devoted to the owners' love of gardening, and really are magnificent; a place where you can wander well away from other guests. There's also an impressively (or disconcertingly) high level of security.

Top End

All rooms in the hotels listed here have a bathroom, air-con and TV, and all rates include breakfast.

Lilayi Lodge (☎ 279024; www.lilayi.com; s/d from US$105/120, incl all meals & activities about US$235/280;) This is one of Lusaka's finest options. The bungalows in this private wildlife reserve are very comfortable, and the gardens and pool are lovely. It offers horse riding and the chance to learn to play polo. The lodge is about 8km off Kafue Rd and about 12km south of the city centre.

Chrismar Hotel (☎ 323141; www.chrismarhotels.com; Los Angeles Blvd; r US$120-150;) This contemporary offering doesn't present much in the way of individuality, but its features and comfort level stand as a bridge between the midrange and top end markets in Lusaka. Standard rooms are in the old part of the hotel, while suites are in a newer wing and have African-style prints and wall hangings. It's simple, modern and good value, especially if you're looking for an oasis, away from Lusaka's perpetually busy streets.

Southern Sun Ridgeway (☎ 251666; res@southernsun.co.zm; cnr Church Rd & Independence Ave; s/d US$180/200;) The expected muted tones in the foyer decor here give way to an outdoor sitting area around a fishpond with resident baby crocs. Rooms are what you'd expect with a high level of comfort. The newly renovated wing is the plushest with the best furniture. Try to nab room 315, 317, 319 or 321 for the best views in the house.

Taj Pamodzi Hotel (☎ 254455; pamodzi.lusaka@tajhotels.com; Church Rd; s/d from US$300/325;) Decked out in shades of cream and brown, with fountains and plenty of greenery at the entry, this is by far the fanciest of the slick hotels in Lusaka. It's a large multistorey complex with surprisingly personal touches, and an impressive level of service. Rooms have balconies and those near the top floor have striking views. Call for discounted room prices.

EATING

Restaurants

Sylva Professional Catering Services (☎ 290344; University of Zambia, Great East Rd; mains ZK10,000; lunch, dinner) This is a unique place to sample quality Zambian food. It's a simple dining hall at the university, a couple of kilometres on from Arcades Shopping Centre. You'll find dishes like goat or chicken (and *nshima* of course), but it's the local vegetable dishes that are particularly recommended by locals.

Oriental Garden Restaurant (☎ 252163; United Nations Ave; mains ZK25,000-40,000; lunch, dinner;)

This place surely serves some of the best Indian food to be found in the country. The spices are a sophisticated and subtle blend, while the marinades are spicy and very tasty: all evidence of a superior chef who maintains an extensive menu. Good veggie options are on the menu, such as an excellent masala kofta. It's located opposite the Netherlands embassy.

our pick **Rhapsody's** (☎ 256705/6; www.rhapsodys.co.za; shop 41, Arcades Shopping Centre, Great East Rd; mains ZK30,000-70,000; ⏰ from 11.30am daily; V) This is one of the best places to eat in Lusaka. It has huge eating areas, inside and outside, and the international-style menu does everything from steaks to Thai chicken, salads and even nasi goreng! Try the chicken espetada, a delicious Portuguese-inspired chicken dish whose presentation will have you playing hangman in minutes – tip: go easy on the jalapeno.

Sichuan (☎ 253842; Showgrounds, off Nangwenya Rd; mains ZK35,000-50,000; ⏰ 11am-2.30pm & 6pm-10.30pm Mon-Sat, dinner Sun; V) The best Chinese restaurant in Lusaka is bizarrely situated at the back of a warehouse at the Showgrounds. Wood-panelled ceilings and lots of Chinese decoration contribute to the ambience. The usual suspects are on the menu and are well prepared in record time from the kitchen – don't miss the crocodile offerings.

Marlin (☎ 252206; Longacres Roundabout, Los Angeles Blvd; mains ZK50,000-70,000; ⏰ lunch & dinner Mon-Sat) Housed in the colonial-era Lusaka Club, this perennial, wood-panelled favourite is the best steakhouse in Zambia. While it does serve gargantuan portions of every cut of meat under the sun, most guests come for the aged fillet with mushroom or pepper sauce. It has an old-style easy-going dining ambience. Reservations are strongly recommended.

Arabian Nights (☎ 257085; shop 37, Arcades Shopping Centre, Great East Rd; mains ZK70,000-95,000; ⏰ lunch, dinner Mon-Sat) With a fairly authentic exotic Middle Eastern feel, complete with hookah pipes and brass artefacts, it's nice to be transported beyond African borders for a couple of hours of fine dining. This refined place attempts a head-spinning variety, although quality Pakistani dishes are the mainstay. Try the Kenyan coriander lamb, Parmesan meatballs or Pakistani barbecue.

Cafes

Zebra Crossing (Ababa House, cnr Addis Ababa Dr & Twikatane Rd; breakfast & light meals ZK25,000-30,000; ⏰ 9am-5pm Mon-Sat) At this small boutique (see p640) you can eat at shaded tables overlooking a garden surrounded by woodcarvings and African artwork. Chow down on carrot and marmalade muffins, wraps and sandwiches. A children's playground makes it popular with families and it's a very pleasant stop for fuel after a browse through the nearby shop and gallery.

Kilimanjaro (☎ 255830; Manda Hill Shopping Centre, Great East Rd; mains ZK25,000-50,000; ⏰ breakfast, lunch; 💻 📶 V) The drab entryway here belies the eclectic, cluttered interior chock-a-block full of African curios, textiles and artworks, and souvenirs all for sale. There's an impressive range of breakfasts and bakery items, even muesli. Sandwiches, rolls, salads, pastas and burgers, with scores of different combos, feature for lunch.

our pick **Chit Chat** (☎ 097 7774481; 5A Omelo Mumba Rd; mains ZK30,000-50,000; ⏰ noon-3pm Mon, 8.30am-midnight Tue-Sat; 📶) A popular place for lunch and dinner in a relaxed, open-air atmosphere, Chit Chat has an eclectic menu featuring burgers, tortilla wraps, salads, pastas, kebabs, Mexican and a variety of breakfasts served on colourful African tablecloths. There's even playground equipment and a grassed area for kids. Sunday hours vary.

Quick Eats

For local meals, the food stalls at the **Town Centre Market** (Chachacha Rd) serve cheap local food, but the scavenging dogs roaming the increasing piles of garbage around the market may affect your appetite. In any case ,they are not for the squeamish. Sausages and steaks are grilled before your eyes, and served with a generous portion of veg and *nshima* for ZK10,000 or less. Cleaner food stalls are at the **Lusaka Inter-City Bus Station** (Dedan Kimathi Rd). Alternatively, jump on a minibus to one of the two modern shopping centres, **Manda Hill** (Great East Rd) and **Arcades** (Great East Rd), where you'll find a range of Western-style fast-food outlets such as **Debonairs** (Manda Hill Shopping Centre; pizzas ZK30,000-45,000; ⏰ lunch & dinner Sun-Thu, 24hr Fri & Sat). If you're desperate and on Cairo Rd, pop into Creamy Inn, Chicken Inn, Pizza Inn or Food Palace – all offering fast-food meals for around ZK30,000.

DRINKING & ENTERTAINMENT

our pick **Polo Grill** (2374 Nangwenya Rd; ⏰ 8am-midnight) A large, open-air bar under an enormous thatched roof overlooking a huge, well-kept polo field (where you can occasionally catch a live match), it's all rather incongruous for Lusaka, but an exceedingly pleasant place to knock back a few Mosi's.

Times Cafe (Arcades Shopping Centre; until late nightly) For a drink in trendy, semi-industrial decor with a clubby feel, try this place which also shows English Premier league football matches. Better to come here with friends; it's not much of a solo drinker's haunt.

O'Hagans (255555; shop 42, Manda Hill Shopping Centre) This South African chain pub is ideal if you like fake Irish pubs and a more Western drinking experience. It's very popular with South Africans and Brits. There are decent beers and a great outdoor terrace, even if it does overlook a car park.

Johnny's (252197; 9 Lagos Rd; 7pm-late Fri & Sat;) An extremely popular nightclub with a ramshackle feel, Johnny's is the only disco in Zambia with an indoor pool, into which the occasional drunken dancer jumps. Weekend nights are the big occasions.

Brown Frog (Kabelenga Rd; 11am-11pm) Popular with NGO workers who come to dance at weekends, this British-style pub is a bit of an institution. Propping yourself at the bar is a good opportunity to meet Zambians, or go for a booth if you're after seclusion.

Chez-Ntemba (Kafue Rd; admission ZK20,000; until late Wed, Fri & Sat) This traditional nightclub in the downtown area usually blasts out loud rhumba and the folk in here shake their booty until the wee hours on weekend nights. It's a good place to party and is in a convenient downtown location.

Lusaka Playhouse (cnr Church & Nasser Rds; tickets ZK20,000-50,000) From time to time, local performers put on a good show. Check signs outside to see what's playing.

SHOPPING

Northmead Market (Chozi Rd; 9am-5pm) The best place for kitschy souvenirs. Local traders here will appreciate your business. The choice is limited, but the carvings, fabrics and pottery on offer are reasonably priced.

Kabwata Cultural Village (Burma Rd; 9am-5pm) You'll find a scruffy collection of thatched huts and stalls at this place southeast of the city centre, near some decrepit white apartment blocks. Prices are cheap, however, because you can buy directly from the workers who live here. The specialities are carvings, baskets, masks, drums, jewellery and fabrics.

Ababa House (cnr Addis Ababa Dr & Twikatane Rd; 9am-5pm Mon-Sat) This place is a smart boutique full of imaginative creations from Zambian and Zimbabwean artists, furniture-makers and weavers. If you're a chocoholic you'll be in heaven, as there's also a shop selling handmade Belgian chocolates.

Sunday market (Arcades Shopping Centre; 10am-6pm Sun) This weekly market features Lusaka's best range of artisanal goodies, especially wooden carvings, curios made from malachite, and African prints. Sellers from other markets such as Northmead and Kabwata also come here to display their wares. Note that while the range is extensive this market is also the priciest, so be prepared to bargain hard.

For the rest of Lusaka's markets, see p633.

GETTING THERE & AWAY

Air

For details about international and domestic flights to/from Lusaka, see p679 and p681.

Bus & Minibus

To avoid some inevitable confusion and frustration, take a taxi to whichever station your bus/minibus leaves from.

DOMESTIC

Buses and minibuses leave from in front of the massive and chaotic **Lusaka City Market Bus Station** (Lumumba Rd) for nearby towns such as Kafue (ZK10,000, 10 to 15 daily), Chirundu (ZK30,000, five to seven daily), Siavonga (ZK45,000, three to five daily) and Luangwe Bridge (ZK50,000, one or two a day) and most destinations are signposted.

Public transport to nearby towns, especially minibuses, also leaves from the **Soweto Market Bus Station** (Los Angeles Rd), but here *nothing* is signposted, so you're better off avoiding it if possible. Note though that the New Soweto Market, set to be built on the same site, will also incorporate a new bus station in front of it, so buses/minibuses should start to leave from there and (fingers crossed) the signposting might be improved.

To add to the confusion, minibuses to places not far south of Lusaka also leave from the **City Bus Station** (off Chachacha Rd), also called the Kulima Towers Station. So it's possible to get to Kafue town, Chirundu and Siavonga from here too. And minibuses heading to the north (eg to the Manda Hill Shopping Centre) depart from the **Millennium Bus Station** (Malasha Rd).

All long-distance public buses (and most private ones) use the **Lusaka Inter-City Bus Station** (Dedan Kimathi Rd), where there is a left-luggage office and inquiries counter. A range of buses from different companies usually cover the destinations listed here (all leaving from this bus station unless otherwise stated) – we've quoted the highest prices because they represent the best companies, with the most comfortable buses (two-storey with reclining seats).

From this terminal, buses go to destinations in the Copperbelt such as Ndola (ZK65,000, four hours, five daily) and Kitwe (ZK70,000, five hours, five daily). Kapiri Mposhi (ZK50,000, 2½ hours, five daily) is also reached along this route. Tracking northeast, Germins and Jordan are the best companies making a beeline for Kasama (ZK130,000, 14 hours, four daily) and Mpulungu (ZK150,000, 18 hours, four daily). Heading southwest, there are plenty of buses to Livingstone (ZK100,000, seven hours, at least seven daily), but we'd recommend travelling with Mazahandu Family Bus or Bookers Express. Both these bus companies travel on to Kazungula (for Botswana; ZK105,000, four daily), and Sesheke (for Namibia; ZK115,000, four daily). Travelling east, many companies operate services to Chipata (for South Luangwe or Malawi; ZK115,000, eight hours, eight daily); all operate from Lusaka Inter-City Bus Station except one service, which leaves from Juldan Motors on Freedom Way. Heading west, 10 buses a day go through Kafue National Park and on to Mongu (ZK115,000, seven hours).

Another option worth considering is the post bus, which is normally less crowded and carries mail (and passengers) to Chipata (ZK80,000; 7am Tuesday, Saturday), Ndola (ZK40,000; 7.30am Monday to Saturday) and Kasama (ZK85,000; 6.30am Monday, Wednesday, Friday) from just behind the **main post office** (cnr Cairo & Church Rds). Tickets are available in advance at the post bus counter inside the post office.

INTERNATIONAL

All buses mentioned here (unless stated otherwise) leave from the **Lusaka Inter-City Bus Station** (Dedan Kimathi Rd).

To Botswana, Zambia–Botswana has buses to Gaborone (ZK180,000, 22 hours, three weekly), via Kasane and Francistown.

For South Africa, City to City has buses leaving every day for Johannesburg (ZK300,000, 26 hours, one daily). Trans Africa, however, is far more comfortable with services to Jo'burg (ZK360,000) three times a week. All buses between Lusaka and Jo'burg travel via Harare, Masvingo and Pretoria.

To Zimbabwe, take any bus going to South Africa – or a Pioneer, Zupco or First Class bus directly to Harare (ZK70,000, nine hours, one daily each).

For Malawi there's no direct service to Blantyre, but there are three services a week to Lilongwe (ZK150,000, 12 hours), where you can change buses.

Zambia–Tanzania and Takwa Bus Services both make the run to Dar es Salaam (ZK250,000, 27 hours, six weekly), but services can be a bit haphazard (and the train is a lot more fun).

Hitching

Although we don't recommend hitching, many locals do it. There are several recognised places to wait for lifts: for eastern Zambia, including Chipata, wait just beyond the airport turn-off; for places to the south, go to the Chirundu–Livingstone junction 10km past Kafue town; and to the north, try at the junction north of Kapiri Mposhi.

Train

The *Zambezi Express* travelling to Livingstone (economy class ZK40,000, 14 hours) via Choma, leaves Lusaka at 11.50pm on Monday and Friday; it no longer has 1st or sleeper class. Tickets are available from the reservations office inside the **train station** (btwn Cairo & Dedan Kimathi Rds). Get there early and be prepared for hustle and bustle. Slow, 'ordinary' trains to Ndola (standard class ZK25,000, 12 hours), via Kapiri Mposhi (ZK17,000, eight hours), depart Tuesday and Saturday at 1.20pm.

For information about the Tazara train between Kapiri Mposhi and Dar es Salaam (Tanzania), see p681.

GETTING AROUND

To/From the Airport

The international airport is about 20km northeast of the city centre. Taxis to and from the airport to central Lusaka cost ZK120,000 (although many drivers will charge ZK150,000). There's no airport bus, but the upmarket hotels send courtesy minibuses to meet international flights, so you may be able to arrange a ride into town with the minibus driver (for a negotiable fee).

Bus & Minibus

Local minibuses run along Lusaka's main roads, but there are no route numbers or destination signs, so the system is difficult to work out. See p640 for explanations about the confusing array of bus and minibus stations.

Otherwise, it is possible to flag down a minibus along a route. For instance, from the South End Roundabout, the 'Kabulonga' minibus goes along Independence Ave to Longacres Roundabout and then heads back towards the city along Los Angeles Blvd and Church Rd; the 'Chakunkula' or 'Chelston' minibus shuttles down Kafue Rd to Kafue town; and the 'Chilanga' minibus heads to Chilanga, via Kafue Rd. The standard fare is ZK2000 to ZK3000.

Car & Motorcycle

Several international car-rental companies have counters at the airport, including **Avis** (Airport ☎ 271303; Lusaka ☎ 251652; Southern Sun Ridgeway, cnr Church Rd & Independence Ave) – which also has an office in the city – and **Imperial** (☎ 271221).

Bimm Travel Agency (☎ 234372; www.bimm.co.zm; Luangwa House, Cairo Rd) offers the cheapest hire-car rates. Vehicles cost from US$45 per day and US$0.30 per kilometre, plus US$10 per day for insurance, but the company inexplicably charges extra for keeping the car outside of Lusaka overnight.

If you want a car and driver to help get you around Lusaka, you're better off hiring a taxi for the day. One of the official blue taxis should charge around ZK300,000 to ZK350,000 for a day, unofficial taxis are cheaper.

Taxi

Official taxis can be identified by the numbers painted on the doors and their colour – light blue – but hundreds of unofficial taxis also cruise the streets (you'll hear them beep their horn as they go past you on the street, looking for business). Official taxis can be hailed along the street or found at ranks near the main hotels and markets. Fares are negotiable, but, as a guide, ZK30,000 will get you between Cairo Rd and Manda Hill Shopping Centre during the day. If you're unsure, official taxis should carry a pricelist for journeys around the city – ask to have a look.

Hundreds of unofficial taxis also cruise the streets (you'll hear them beep their horn as they go past you on the street, looking for business). Some unofficial taxis are really decrepit vehicles (we had the overwhelming smell of petroleum in the back seat of one we caught) so have a good look before jumping in one. Generally they'll be ZK5000 to ZK10,000 cheaper for a single journey within the city.

THE COPPERBELT

The Copperbelt Province is the industrial heartland of Zambia and the main population centre outside of Lusaka. The region is rarely visited by tourists, but unique attractions, such as the largest chimpanzee sanctuary in the world, make it well worth the trip. It's also the only place in the country (outside of Lusaka) where you can see the urban side of Zambia, and Ndola in particular makes that a very pleasant experience.

The world copper market slumped during the 1970s, so vast opencast mines cut back production, thereby creating high unemployment in the area. The cost of copper and cobalt went through the roof in the early part of this century; however the global economic crisis of 2008/09 saw demand, and therefore prices, plummet once again.

KAPIRI MPOSHI

☎ 0215

This dismal town, about 200km north of Lusaka, is at the southern end of the Tazara railway from Dar es Salaam (Tanzania) and at the fork in the roads to Lusaka, the Copperbelt and the Northern Province. If you get stuck at Kapiri Mposhi, head for one of the resthouses along the main road, such as **Eros Lodge** (Main Rd; s/tw/d ZK50,000/70,000/90,000). Only the doubles have a private bathroom, and it's well worth spending the extra kwacha to get one – No 5 is probably the best.

If you're coming from Tanzania, there's a passport check before you can get out of the station, then from outside the station there's a mad rush for buses to Lusaka and elsewhere. Thieves and pickpockets thrive in the crowds and confusion, so take great care.

Buses and minibuses from Lusaka (see p640) leave regularly and are a quicker and more convenient option than the local train from the capital. Note that the daily Lusaka–Kitwe service (Lusaka; ZK17,000, twice weekly) stops at Kapiri Mposhi, which is 2km from New Kapiri Mposhi station (the official name of the Tazara station). Refer to p681 for details about the trains from Kapiri Mposhi to Dar es Salaam.

NDOLA

☎ 0212 / pop 500,000

Ndola, the capital of the Copperbelt Province, is a peaceful, prosperous little city that provides relief from the pace, pollution and chaos of its larger cousin, Lusaka. There are lots of shady trees on the streets and no real traffic congestion, making it very pleasant to wander around. While you're in town, drop into the **Copperbelt Museum** (☎ 617450; Buteko Ave; adult/child ZK15,000/10,000; 9am-4.30pm), showcasing the local industry.

OK, so there's nothing 'new' about it, but the **New Ambassador Hotel** (☎ 097-7773909/374396; President Ave; s/tw/d K100/130/210;) is the best value in town. Try to get a light and airy room on the 3rd floor; some of these have great views. Ask for a room with private bathroom; the shared bathrooms make some terrifying screeching noises.

The grandiose **New Savoy Hotel** (☎ 611097; savoy@zamnet.zm; Buteko Ave; s/d incl breakfast ZK425,000/475,000, exec d/ste all incl breakfast ZK505,000/545,000;) in the centre of town is holding up standards well. Old-fashioned yes, but not without charm and plenty of smiles from helpful staff. The standard rooms are fine, but exec rooms buy you a lot more space for not a lot more kwacha. It practically faces the museum and is 600m north of the public bus station.

The wood-fired pizzas at **Michelangelo** (☎ 620325; 126 Broadway; mains ZK38,000-60,000; 7am-3pm & 7pm-10pm Mon-Fri, 8am-2pm & 7pm-10pm Sat) are excellent. The restaurant is cheerful and gaudy with a mock italianate interior and is crammed full of Mediterranean furnishings and themes. Takeaway is available on Sundays.

Ndola is about 325km north of Lusaka. Every day, **Proflight Zambia** (☎ 0211-271032; www.proflight-zambia.com) flies between Lusaka and Ndola (US$60 one-way), while **South African Airlink** (☎ 0211-254350; www.saairlink.co.za) has daily flights to Johannesburg for around US$280.

See p640 for information about buses and trains between Lusaka and Ndola. From the **public bus station** (cnr Broadway & Maina Soko Rd), three blocks south of Buteko Ave, minibuses and buses run every few minutes to Kitwe (bus; ZK14,000, ¾ hour). The **train station** (☎ 617641; off President Ave Nth) is 700m north of the museum.

Avis (☎ 620741) and **Voyagers/Imperial Car Rental** (☎ 620604) both have offices at the airport.

KITWE

☎ 0212 / pop 700,000

Zambia's second-largest city and the centre of the country's mining industry, Kitwe feels far more urban than quiet Ndola. It's larger and rougher around the edges, with an African feel and an air that can be slightly intimidating. The main reason to stop here is the excellent selection of accommodation and eating places.

Dazi Lodge (☎ 095-5460487; Palmo Ave; r ZK180,000-260,000;) has a wonderful kitschy air about it. Some rooms have private bathrooms. others come with shared facilities. and all are spick and span. Note that rooms overlooking the swimming pool can be noisy from the adjacent bar.

For its Scottish theme and central location, consider splashing out at the **Hotel Edinburgh** (☎ 222188; cnr Independence & Obote Avenues; s/d ZK340,000/440,000, business d ZK475, suites ZK500-750;), whose presidential suite comes with two bathrooms! Failing that, try to get a room on or close to the 5th floor – they have terrific views and heaps of light from large windows.

Mukwa Lodge (☎ 224266; www.mukalodge.co.zm; 26 Mpezeni Ave; s/d incl breakfast ZK500,000/600,000;) has gorgeous rooms with stone floors that are beautifully furnished – the bathrooms are as good as you'll find in Zambia. Even mosquito nets are moulded into the design of the place. Its well-laid out restaurant, the **Courtyard Cafe** (mains ZK55,000-75,000), is a soothing dining sensation, especially with the sound of trickling water in the courtyard garden. Service can be a bit hit and miss, but the food is on the money. There are Western-style steak, chicken, fish and shellfish dishes. The Lisbon-style prawns in particular are delicious.

Kitwe is about 60km northwest of Ndola. See p640 for details about buses and trains to Kitwe from Lusaka. Frequent local minibuses and buses run to Ndola (ZK14,000, ¾ hour) and Chingola (ZK13,500, ½ hour).

Voyagers (☎ 617062; Enos Chomba Ave) is very helpful and can sort out car hire and other travel arrangements.

CHINGOLA

☎ 0212

Chingola is basically a huge mine with a settlement wrapped around it. The reason to come here is because it's the closest town to Chimfunshi (see below) and has a decent range of accommodation. Traditional bed and breakfast is served up at homely **Hibiscus Guest House** (☎ 313635; 33 Katutwa Rd; r per person incl breakfast ZK250,000), or try **Mica's** (☎ 097 7188782; 5th St; r incl continental breakfast ZK200,000) where rooms are neat as a pin and come with TV, fan and mosquito net. Chingola is 50km northwest of Kitwe. The **bus station** (13th St) is in the centre of town. There are frequent buses and minibuses to Kitwe (ZK13,500, ½ hour).

CHIMFUNSHI WILDLIFE ORPHANAGE

On a farm in a beautiful location deep in the African bush, approximately 70km northwest of Chingola, is this magnificent **chimpanzee sanctuary** (chimfunshiwildlife@iwayafrica.com; day visit project area adult/child ZK50,000/25,000, orphanage ZK25,000/10,000; 9am-3pm daily). It's home to nearly 100 adult and young chimps that have been confiscated from poachers and traders in neighbouring Congo and other parts of Africa; it's the largest of its kind in the world. This is not a natural wildlife experience, but it's still a unique and fascinating opportunity to observe the chimps as they feed, play and socialise. It could well be one of the highlights of your trip to Zambia.

Visitors to the sanctuary provide much-needed income – your entry fees go directly into helping it remain financially viable. *Please*, though, do not come though if you're sick; the chimps can easily die of a simple disease like the flu. A very special way to experience this place would be to do a chimpanzee bush walk (US$100) with some of the younger chimps. Ask about volunteering opportunities too.

You can visit on a day trip or stay overnight at the **campsite** (per person US$10, coal for fires extra) or in the **self-catering cottage** (per person sharing US$25, whole cottage US$200) at the education centre, which has 10 beds, self-catering facilities and bed linen. Note that at the time of writing accommodation was about to undergo a serious overhaul.

By car, take the Solwezi Rd for about 43km northwest from Chingola, then turn right at the signposted junction and follow it for 18km to the orphanage, it's then a further 12km to the project area. Note that this road is in bad condition, particularly after the wet season. However, a new road that has been built and is currently being graded, is much better and shorter (it's about 20km off the main road straight to the project area), and is 55km from Chingola and well signposted.

NORTHERN ZAMBIA

People with a spirit of adventure and who love wild open spaces will have a blast in Zambia's untamed north. Northern Zambia starts once you've passed the 'Pedicle' – the thin slice of Congo (Zaïre) territory that juts sharply into Zambia, almost splitting it in two. From here onwards the Great North Road shoots its way straight up to Tanzania, passing national parks, vast wilderness areas and waterfalls along the way. Topping the list of highlights: Kasanka National Park, where you can camp by the side of a river and listen to the sound of hippos without another soul in sight, or watch sitatungas splashing in the swamps at dawn from high up in a mahogany tree; Mutinondo Wilderness, a vast area of whaleback hills, rivers and valleys so still and untouched you feel almost transported to a prehistoric era; and startling Shiwa Ng'andu, a grand English mansion buried deep in the Zambian bush. And hidden on the rocks and in caves of this vast, beautiful landscape are thousands of ancient rock paintings, some of the most important in southern Africa.

SERENJE

☎ 0215

Serenje is a pretty nondescript town. The only reason for travellers to pass through is as a convenient refuelling stop (both petrol and food wise) on the way to more exciting destinations. There are two main hubs in the town: the turn-off at the junction, which has a petrol station, a couple of shops and a few basic restaurants, and the town centre, 3km north of the Great North Road, which has a bank, a market, bus station and a couple of places to stay.

Sleeping

Mapontela Inn (☎ 382026; r US$65) This charming guest house is hidden from the heat of the street behind a green and brick facade. Opening out onto the courtyard are a number of bright homely rooms with fan and spotless bathrooms. It's the best place to stay in town.

Siga-Siga Resthouse (☎ 82362; d with shared bathroom ZK50,000) This is a useful option if you're travelling by public transport as it's right by the junction with the Great North Road. Rooms here are pretty basic and share acceptable bathrooms.

Getting There & Away

All buses between Lusaka (ZK60,000, five hours) and Kasama (ZK90,000, four to five hours) pass through Serenje. The Tazara train also stops at the Serenje train station, 3km north of the town centre.

KASANKA NATIONAL PARK

One of Zambia's least-known wilderness areas and a real highlight of a visit to this part of the country is the privately managed **Kasanka National Park** (www.kasanka.com; admission US$10; 6am-6pm). At only 390 sq km, it's pretty small compared with most African parks, doesn't have many facilities and sees very few visitors, and this is what makes it special. Kasanka is perhaps most famous for its swampland – it's here that you'll see the park's shy and retiring star, the sitatunga, a semi-aquatic antelope distinguished by its long splayed hooves and oily coat. During the months of November and December this park is home to five million migratory fruit bats – the biggest such gathering anywhere in the world – which can blanket the sky for several minutes at dusk. A trip to Kasanka isn't complete without viewing the park from the heights of the **Fibwe Hide**, a 15-minute drive from Wasa Lodge. It's not for those with a fear of heights, though. You climb 20m up an old mahogany tree via a rickety wooden ladder, and lo and behold there's a platform where you can sit and watch the swamps below.

Sleeping

Wasa Lodge (873 76 2067957; www.kasanka.com; self-catering chalets per person US$50, full board incl all activities per person US$360) doubles up as the park headquarters. Accommodation consists of thatch bungalows in two different sizes. The real advantage of a stay here is the setting. The lodge overlooks Lake Wasa and you can look out over the swamp and spot hippos and puku and sometimes even sitatungas.

Conservation Centre (campsite per person US$10, room per person US$30) Just inside the park is a small conservation centre with a campsite as well as basic twin rooms in thatch chalets. There's a shared bathroom for every pair of rooms. School groups often book these out, but if they're empty then visitors are most welcome to stay. It's convenient but lacks the atmosphere or the views of the other places inside the park.

There are three basic campsites in Kasanka, where you'll be kept company by the noise of animals, the stars and little else. The **Pontoon Campsite** (campsite per person US$10) and the **Kabwe Campsite** (campsite per person US$10) both look out over the Kasanka River, and the **Fibwe Campsite** (campsite per person US$10) is a short walk from the Fibwe Hide. All are around 10km to 12km from the main Wasa Lodge and all come equipped with long drop toilets and bucket showers.

Getting There & Away

From Lusaka, take a bus in the direction of Mansa, or take any bus from Lusaka to Serenje and change onto a minibus for Mansa. After turning off the Great North Road, ask the driver to drop you at Kasanka National Park (near Mulembo village), not at Kasanka village, which is much further away. The journey should cost you about ZK100,000 from Lusaka or ZK30,000 from Serenje. From the gate to Wasa Lodge is 12km; you can radio Wasa Lodge for a lift.

If you have your own vehicle, continue north along the Great North Road from Serenje for 36km, then turn left onto the road towards Mansa. It's then 55km on a good road to the Kasanka entrance gate – clearly signposted on your left.

AROUND KASANKA

Drivers with 4WD and high clearance may like to take the 'back route' from Kasanka direct to the Great North Road, which winds past several attractions.

History buffs can go in search of the **David Livingstone Memorial** – a simple stone memorial topped with a cross – which honours the famous explorer, who died here in 1873 whilst searching for the source of the Nile. The local villagers buried Livingstone's heart under a mupundu tree before his body was sent home to the mother country; the memorial marks that spot, though the tree is no longer there. To get here, pass the Kasanka National Park gate and continue 11km to the Livingstone Memorial turn-off, which will be on your right. Take the first left, from where it's another 25km to the memorial.

This route also winds past beautiful little **Lake Waka-Waka**, with glassy, croc-free waters (though always check the situation locally before jumping in) encircled by miombo woodland. Accommodation is in the form of a small community **campsite** (campsite per person US$5) with basic bucket showers, barbecues and long-drop toilets. Local villages will collect clean water for you and prepare fires. To get here, pass the Kasanka gates and take the turn-off to the Livingstone Memorial, but this time continue straight on for 35km, leaving the Livingstone Memorial road on your left.

In between Kasanka National Park and the Bangweulu Wetlands (see below) is the **Nakapalayo Tourism Project** (contact via Kasanka Trust; per person campsite incl village tour & entertainment US$20, hut incl village tour & entertainment per person with/without meals US$60/40), a community initiative that allows tourists to experience life in a real Zambian village. Visitors can camp, or stay in specially made huts with double beds and nets. Activities revolve around village life and include learning how to pound cassava, meeting local healers, and bush walks where you're taught about traditional uses for plants and trees. Meals are local fare, eaten with the villagers. Day visits are also available for US$20 per person. To get here, continue just past Lake Waka Waka, where the road will fork. Take the left-hand fork and continue on for 35km to Chiundaponde, where you'll find the project.

BANGWEULU WETLANDS

Some 50km to the north of Kasanka are the Bangweulu Wetlands – a watery wilderness of lake, seasonally flooded grasslands, swamp, and unspoiled miombo woodland. This rarely visited part of Zambia is the only place in Africa where you'll see major numbers of black lechwes (antelopes with long, curved antlers). There are estimated to be some 100,000 here – few places in the world contain such large antelope herds – and the endless sound of thousands of lechwe hooves clattering and splashing through the marshes could be one of your strongest memories of Zambia. The best time to visit the area to see the lechwe herds is June to July; September to November is great for general birdwatching.

Sleeping

Shoebill Island Camp (www.kasanka.com; self-catering chalets with shared bathroom per person US$50, chalets incl meals, transfers from the nearest airstrip & several activities per person US$360) This camp sits in the heart of the wetlands, splendidly positioned on a tiny permanent island with only birds, hippos, lechwes and the occasional passing fishermen for company. Bookings are essential, especially if you want meals and need to be taken to the camp by boat.

Getting There & Away

The only ways into the wetlands are by private vehicle and chartered plane. Dirt roads lead here from Kasanka via Lake Waka-Waka and the Nakapalayo Tourism Project (see left). The Chikuni ranger post and Nsobe Camp are 65km on from Nakapalayo, and from here it's another 10km to Shoebill Camp in the dry; in the wet, you'll have to travel this last stretch by boat. You will definitely need a fully equipped 4WD to attempt this trip as the going is tough. Set off from Kasanka in the early morning in order to reach Bangweulu before it gets dark. The folk at Kasanka can provide you with a detailed information sheet about getting to the wetlands.

SAMFYA

Perched on the western shore of Lake Bangweulu, about 10km east of the main road between Mansa and Serenje, is Samfya, a small and dusty trading centre with little going for it except for its excellent location. Just outside town is a long strip of blinding white beach bathed by startling blue waters. Don't jump in here, though, unless you fancy being a crocodile's dinner.

Samfya Sun & Sand Resort (s/d ZK90,000/110,000), just a short walk from the Samfya Beach Hotel, has basic thatch huts on the beach, a restaurant and campsite.

Samfya Beach Hotel (campsite per person ZK40,000, s/d ZK120,000) has a pretty good location, though the rooms are poky, with basic bathrooms, and the food isn't much cop. If you have a tent you'll probably be better off camping. To get here take the first turning on the left as you enter the town from about 2km north of the town centre.

Samfya is regularly served by minibuses from Serenje (ZK60,000, four to five hours). Buses from Lusaka (ZK95,000, nine to 10 hours) may drop you into town or at the junction 10km away, from where local pick-ups shuttle passengers to and fro.

MUTINONDO WILDERNESS

This is perhaps the most stunning place in Northern Zambia. A beautiful 10,000-hectare wilderness littered with whaleback hills or inselbergs (isolated ranges and hills; literally 'island mountains') – huge, sweeping hulks of stone in varying shades of black, purple, green and brown. The landscape here feels unspoiled and somehow ancient. Scramble to the top of one of those great granite beasts (and they do look like they could be giant animals who've been asleep for so long they've sunk back into the earth) and you can easily imagine a time when Stone Age hunters wandered the valleys, woodlands and rivers below.

Activities

Other than hiking and taking in the views, you can canoe and swim in the river, ride horses and, during the mushroom-friendly rainy season, go in search of the largest edible mushroom in the world! The area also contains rock paintings and Iron Age workings.

Sleeping

our pick **Mayense Camp** (www.mutinondozambia.com; s/d per person incl meals & activities from ZK420,000/350,000. It's tough to design accommodation that fits in with the splendour of this setting, but the folk here have managed it. Built into the hillside is a handful of individually designed chalets which, while not fancy, are beautiful in their simplicity and blend in seamlessly with their natural environment. They are far enough apart from each other to give a real sense of privacy and all have outstanding views. The majority are open to the elements so it feels as if you're sleeping out in the middle of the wild. There is also a fantastic **campsite** (campsite per person ZK40,000, s/d tent with bedding ZK150,000/180,000) here.

The friendly and energetic owners are keen to protect the environment and use a number of alternative sources of energy at the camps, such as solar panels, a wind generator and sun stoves. The food here uses as much locally sourced produce as possible and campers can arrange to have meals at the main Mayense Camp.

Getting There & Away

The turn-off to Mutinondo is 164km past Serenje heading north on the Great North Rd. It's signposted to the right, Mutinondo is 25km down a 2WD-friendly track.

Road transfers for a maximum of five people can be arranged from Mpika (US$100) or Lusaka (US$500). If you'd like to charter a plane there's also an airstrip.

SHIWA NG'ANDU

Deep in the Northern Zambian wilderness sits **Shiwa Ng'andu** (www.shiwangandu.com), a grand country estate and labour of love of eccentric British aristocrat Sir Stewart Gore-Brown. The estate's crowning glory is **Shiwa Ng'andu Manor House**, a glorious brick mansion. Driving up to the house through farm buildings, settlements and workers houses it almost feels like an old feudal domain. Today Gore-Brown's grandchildren live on and manage the estate, which is a working farm.

Shiwa House (tours US$20; 9-11am Mon-Sat, 10-11am Sun) itself is the main draw here and visitors can go on guided tours. The house is full of old family heirlooms, photographs and stories, and standing out on the perfectly manicured lawns in front of it you could almost forget that you're in Southern Africa and imagine instead that you're at a 1920s garden party on an English summer's day.

Kapishya Hot Springs is 20km west of Shiwa House, but still on the Shiwa Ng'andu estate. The setting is marvellous – a blue-green steaming lagoon of hot water, surrounded by palms. If staying at Kapishya Lodge (below), then you can use the springs for free; the cost for day visitors is US$5. From the lodge, **walking**, **fishing** and **canoeing** trips are also offered.

Sleeping

Kapishya Lodge (☎ 0211-229261; www.shiwasafaris.com; per person campsite US$10, self-catering chalets US$90, full board US$130) This is a beautiful spot. The chalets are light and spacious, with wide wooden decks complete with inbuilt fireplaces and views down over the river and the gardens. Bring your own food for the staff to prepare, or meals (and very good ones at that) can be provided with enough notice.

Shiwa House (bookings through Kapishya Lodge; full board from US$350) This old place is suitably attired for a grand old English manor, with fireplaces, four-poster beds, oil paintings and big old roll-top baths. There's also a glorious guest sitting room looking out onto the front lawn, which is even more atmospheric at night when lit by candles and a crackling fire. The hosts (the grandchildren of Sir Stewart Gore-Brown) are happy to chat and to give you personal tours of the house. If you're staying here you could even browse the Gore-Brown archives – a fascinating collection of Sir Stewart's journals and letters, as well as old photographs.

STEWART GORE-BROWN

Shiwa Ng'andu was the brainchild of Stewart Gore-Brown, an eccentric Englishman who first came to Northern Rhodesia in 1914 when working for the Anglo–Belgian border commission. He decided to look for somewhere to settle in the area, came across the lake of Shiwa Ng'andu (the 'Lake of the Royal Crocodiles' in the local language) and negotiated with the local chief to buy the land surrounding it. He then went back home, but returned to Africa after the end of WWI to build his little piece of England in Africa. What was built was an English-style manor, made entirely from materials found locally, or transported on foot by porters from the nearest town of Ndola – an eye-watering 110km and three weeks' walk away. The mansion sprang up on a hill overlooking the lake, complete with manicured lawns and servants clad in white gloves and pillbox hats. Around the manor grew an estate, which included workers' houses, schools and a post office.

Gore-Brown became a well-known figure in Northern Rhodesia and in England. He was knighted by George VI and served as an adviser to Kenneth Kaunda, Zambia's first president. When he died in 1967 he was, unusually for a foreigner, given a full state funeral. He is buried on the hill overlooking the lake at Shiwa.

Getting There and Away

To reach Shiwa House, head along the highway by bus (or car) from Mpika for about 90km towards Chisoso. Look for the signpost to the west, from where a 13km dirt road leads to the house. Kapishya Hot Springs and the Lodge are a further 20km along this track. You can also get to Shiwa from the Mpika–Kasama road – this time look for the signpost pointing east and it's then 30km down the dirt track to Kapishya. There is no public transport along this last section, but vehicle transfers are available from the Great North Road turn-off for US$40 per vehicle (maximum four people). Transfers can also be arranged from Mpika (US$300 per vehicle) and from Kasama (US$400 per vehicle).

KASAMA

☎ 0214

Kasama is the capital of the Northern Province and the cultural centre of the Bemba people, and with its wide leafy streets and handsome old tin-roofed colonial houses, it is the most appealing of the northern towns.

Thorn Tree Guesthouse (☎ 221615, 096 951149; www.thorntreesafaris.com; 612 Zambia Rd; rooms per person from US$30) is family run, homely and very popular – you should definitely book before turning up. As you reach Kasama from Lusaka, turn left at the first crossroads, keep right at the forks and continue past the Heritage Centre for 1km.

Also recommended are **JB Hotel** (☎ 221452, 0977 844149; Golf Rd; s/d without bathroom 50,000/55,000, 120,000/140,000), a good-quality, friendly hotel right in the heart of town near the bus station, and the **Kalambo Guest House** (☎ 222221; Luwingu Rd; s/d from ZK50,000/60,000), where the welcome is warm and the rooms are spotless.

Buses and minibuses leave for Lusaka daily. CV Transport departs at 3.30pm daily for Lusaka (ZK120,000, 10 hours), via Serenje (ZK90,000, four hours). Northbound buses go to Mbala (ZK40,000, two hours) and Mpulungu (ZK50,000, three hours). The Tazara train station is 6km south of the town centre.

MBALA

This sleepy town sits on the periphery of the Great Rift Valley, from where the road drops over 1000m down to Lake Tanganyika. It was once a colonial centre called Abercorn, and today the only reason to visit is the local museum, or as a way station en route to Kalambo Falls. **Moto Moto Museum** (admission US$3; 9am-4.45pm daily), about 3km from the town centre, is a huge and fascinating collection of artefacts based on the cultural life of the Bemba people. Items on display here include old Bemba drums, traditional musical instruments, and an array of smoking paraphernalia. Particularly noteworthy is an exhibition detailing how young Bemba women were traditionally initiated into adulthood. It includes a life-size, walk-in example of an initiation hut.

Makungo Guest House (self-contained s/d ZK40,000/45,000) is the best place to stay in town. Rooms are clean and good value and are centred on a courtyard that also doubles up as a minibus garage. The guest house is about 100m off the main road; take the turning opposite the fuel station. Note that this is a different place to the Makungo Rest House, which is located on the main street and is not recommended.

KALAMBO FALLS

About 40km northwest of Mbala on a good sealed road, and along the border between Zambia and Tanzania, is the 221m-high **Kalambo Falls** (adult/child US$3/2, per car US$3, campsite US$10). Twice as high (but nowhere near as expansive) as Victoria Falls, Kalambo is the second-highest single-drop waterfall in Africa (after Tugela Falls in South Africa). From spectacular viewpoints near the top of the falls, you can see the Kalambo River plummeting off a steep V-shaped cliff cut into the Rift Valley escarpment and into a deep valley, which then winds down towards Lake Tanganyika. There is a campsite here, with stunning views out over the rift valley. Facilities are basic (there's only a long-drop toilet), but there is a caretaker.

The best way for travellers without a car to get here is from Mpulungu (see below). A thrice-weekly taxi boat serves villages along the lakeshore east of Mpulungu, but it moves quite slowly and makes plenty of stops so just getting to the base of the falls can take all day – you don't want to risk arriving in the dark as it's two to three hours' walk uphill to the viewpoint (and the campsite). It's also possible to hire a private boat from Mpulungu harbour, which will cost around ZK300,000 a day including fuel. Ask around at the market near the lake in Mpulungu.

Another alternative would be to stay in one of the lakeshore lodges near the falls, from where you could hike to the falls or visit on an organised boat trip. Charity at Nkupi Lodge in Mpulungu can also help you out with boats to the falls.

MPULUNGU

☎ 0214

Resting at the foot of mighty Lake Tangyanika, Mpulungu is a crossroads between Eastern, Central and Southern Africa. As Zambia's only international port, it's the terminal for the ferry across the lake to Tanzania. Although it's always very hot, don't be tempted to swim in the lake in this area because there are a few crocs.

Sleeping

Nkupi Lodge (☎ 455166; campsite per person ZK40,000, rondavels from ZK80,000) By far the best place for independent travellers, this shady campsite and lodge is a short walk out of town and has plenty of soft, grassy earth for erecting tents as well as a number of rondavels, including a huge self-contained number with fresh stone floors and a large comfy bed.

New Harbour Inn (☎ 0978-571331; r from ZK80,000) A simple, friendly place just a short walk from the centre of town, this small inn has rooms in little cottages in the grounds. They are large and clean with separate sitting areas, large fans, DSTV and huge tiger-face rugs. It's a friendly place and there is a small restaurant too.

Getting There & Away

Most buses and minibuses tie in with the Lake Tanganyika ferry. To/from Lusaka, Juldan Motors depart at noon daily (ZK130,000, 13 hours), travelling via Kasama (ZK50,000, three hours) and Mbala (ZK10000, one hour). Minibuses also depart from near the BP petrol station in Mpulungu heading for Mbala (ZK15,000, 50 minutes). The drive can be a bit bumpy as the road between Mbala and Mpulungu is very potholed.

NSUMBU (SUMBU) NATIONAL PARK

Hugging the southern shores of Lake Tanganyika, little-visited **Nsumbu** (admission US$10; 6am-6pm) is a beautiful 2020 sq km of hilly grassland and escarpment, interrupted by rivers and wetlands. Like other remote parks in Zambia, Nsumbu was virtually abandoned in the 1980s and 1990s and poaching seriously affected wildlife stocks here. Conditions have improved over the past decade, though. Poaching has come under control, and animal numbers have increased, in part thanks to a buffer zone created by

GETTING TO TANZANIA

The MV *Liemba*, a hulking ex-German warship, leaves from Mpulungu harbour every Friday, arriving in Kigoma, Tanzania on Sunday. Fares for 1st, 2nd and economy class are US$60, US$45 and US$35 respectively. Visas can be issued on the ferry and cost US$50 single entry.

two Game Management Areas that adjoin the park.

Herds of elephants and buffalo are seen here once again, often coming to the lake to drink. There are also plenty of antelopes, including roan and sable antelopes, waterbucks and sitatunga. All of these animals attract predators, and these days lions and hyenas can often be heard at night. In the lake itself are hippos as well as some of the largest crocodiles in Africa. For anglers, Lake Tanganyika offers top-class sport: Nile perch, tigerfish and *nkupi* (yellow belly) are plentiful, while golden perch and giant tigerfish all exist in the waters.

Sleeping

Ndole Bay Lodge (☎ 0966-780196, 0212-711150; www.ndolebaylodge.com; per person campsite US$10, chalets with full board from US$100;) Set back from a pretty beach just outside Nsumbu National Park, this lodge has several spacious thatch chalets, most with private bathroom, dotted around the grounds. There is also a campsite right under the trees on the sandy beach and a large communal area right by the beach with plenty of comfy chairs and hammocks – perfect for a day of lazing. All kinds of activities are on offer here.

Nkamba Bay Lodge (www.nkambabaylodge.com;) This exclusive private lodge is currently the only accommodation operating within Nsumbu National Park itself. It's set in a gorgeous, pristine cove, and has nine luxurious but understated chalets, decorated with African prints and art. Game drives, birdwatchinging and fishing are the main activities here, but you could also go on canoe trips or walks in the surrounding rainforest.

Getting There & Away

Each lodge will arrange transfers for guests from the airstrip at Kasaba Bay, or across the lake from Mpulungu. Hardy overlanders can drive, but come from the southwest, where the roads are in better condition. There are good roads up to Mporokoso, followed by a rough dirt road to Nsumbu, for which you'll need a 4WD. Many maps will show a road going directly from Mbala to Nsumbu National Park, but you cannot safely access the park by this route at present. Some of the roads in the north were being upgraded at the time of research, though, so check with the lodges for up-to-date information.

EASTERN ZAMBIA

This part of the country contains one of Zambia's finest attractions – South Luangwa National Park, often considered one of the greatest parks in Africa for the density and variety of its game and for the beauty of the landscape. Sitting further north is wild North Luangwa, more difficult to access than its southern cousin and far less developed but also notable for its density of game.

The Eastern Zambia chapter covers the Great East Road – and sections around it – extending east of Lusaka to the border with Malawi, some 600km. There are several buses a day up to Chipata and through to Malawi and frequent flights between Lusaka and South Luangwa National Park.

LUANGWA BRIDGE

The Great East Road crosses the Luangwa River on a large suspension bridge about halfway between Lusaka and Chipata. It's unusual to see such a construction in Zambia, and there's a permanent security checkpoint manned by the army. The nearby settlement of Luangwa Bridge is near the eastern end of the Lower Zambezi National Park, and far from the South and North Luangwa National Parks. It serves as an ideal place to break up a journey.

Luangwa Bridge Camp (☎ 097 7197456; www.bridgecampzambia.com; Feira Rd; per person campsite ZK40,000, chalets ZK85,000-205,000;) is on the western side of the river, about 3km south of the main road. This place does make a convenient stop between Lusaka and Chipata, the food is very good and the stone chalets are simple and comfortable. However, the pricing system for the accommodation is confusing and it's overpriced (especially when the single supplement kicks in). Shared ablution blocks are clean, there's also a book exchange and, best of all, a great upstairs deck with views over the muddy river.

Get off any bus between Lusaka and Chipata at the place called 'Luangwa station', from where it's a 3km walk to the camp.

KATETE

☎ 0216

About 90km from Chipata and 500km from Lusaka, Katete is a small town just south of

CULTURAL EXPERIENCES AROUND KATETE

Tikondane Community Centre can organise a unique Zambian experience – watching traditional dances in the nearby village of Kachipu. This is an authentic opportunity to see African culture up close; there's nothing 'put on' or 'staged' about these events.

There's a women's initiation dance, undertaken before they are married, called Chinamwali; men are not usually allowed into these events, but white men are considered 'honorary women'. The other traditional dance held in the village, most frequently in the months leading up to August, is the Ghost Dance. Elaborate masks are worn, as are grass costumes; mythological creatures may be present and huge drumbeats are employed to assist the stomping of men from the village. It's not to be missed. When it's running, the Ghost dance usually takes place on a Saturday.

You'll need to give Tikondane a few days' notice if you'd like to attend, and the cost is ZK80,000 per trip (not per person) to Chinamwali and ZK120,000 per trip (not per person) to the Ghost Dance. Transport is by oxcart (ZK35,000 one-way) and a guide (ZK25,000) is available, as is dinner (ZK25,000).

the Great East Road. On the main road, 4km west of Katete, is **Tikondane Community Centre**, a grassroots initiative that works with local villages. Among its many activities, it focuses on adult and child education, agricultural initiatives, and trains home-based carers for Aids victims. Tikondane also accepts volunteers to work at its centre and on its projects (see www.tikondane.org for details). If you're interested in having a look at what this place offers, or just wanting a break from the road, consider staying at its **Guest House** (Tiko Lodge; ☎ 252122; Great East Road; s without bathroom ZK60,000, d ZK90,000, tr ZK105,000). The simple rooms here come with bed, and small chair and table. They are cool inside and monastic in size and feel. It's simple digs but very good value for the price. An internet cafe and further guest accommodation is planned.

CHIPATA

☎ 0216

Chipata is a large busy town – it's the primary urban space in this district – yet despite its size, it has a rural feel. There are some decent and affordable accommodation options making it a very useful stop between Zambia and Malawi (30km from the border), as well as a launching pad into South Luangwa National Park. If you're stuck for transport into the park, make enquiries with the owner of Dean's Hill, who may be able to arrange something. There are petrol stations and banks with ATMs along the main road.

Sleeping

our pick **Dean's Hill View Lodge** (☎ 221673; deanmitch@zamtel.zm; campsite ZK25,000, dm or tw per person ZK50,000) This lodge is a great little place run by an affable British chap. It features upstairs dorms, twin rooms and camping, a nice big sloping garden, spacious and spotless shared ablutions and grand views over Chipata and the hills. Coming from Lusaka, take the first right after the welcome arch, just before the Total petrol station.

Mama Rula (☎ 097 790226; mamarula@iwayafrica.com; campsite US$8, full board per person US$75; 💻 🍴) There's a huge grassy garden campsite here with a large bar that's very popular with the overland crowd. Next door is the bed and breakfast, which has some lovely, cosy rooms; each one is themed a little differently. It's a great place to stay, 4km out of Chipata along the Mfuwe Rd to South Luangwa.

Katuta Lodge (☎ 221210; katutalodge@iwayafrica.com; campsite per person ZK50,000, r ZK100,000-250,000; 🍴) This sprawling place is the closest accommodation in Chipata for the run to Mfuwe, for those headed into the park. There's a big range of spacious rooms, and although (as usual) the bathrooms aren't all that great, there are varying degrees of luxury (such as cane couches, fridges, satellite TV).

Ndanji Lodge (☎ 097 6656460; r with/without bathroom ZK120,000/100,000) If you prefer a guest-house vibe, then this friendly, locally run place makes an excellent choice. Rooms are reasonably basic, but have a homely feel, reflecting the rest of the house. Meals are available, although self-catering is also possible.

Getting There & Away

There are currently five different bus companies in Lusaka offering services to Chipata, so buses are frequent – refer to p640 for

CROSSING THE ZAMBIA–MALAWI BORDER

The Zambian border post is around 30km from Chipata (on the Malawian side, the town of Mchinji is closer to the Malawian border post). At both border posts you'll need to get your passport stamped and at the Malawian border post you'll need to fill in an entry card (exit card if you're leaving). There are plenty of moneychangers hanging around, however FX Bureau de Change in Chipata is the best place to change money, before you cross the border. Note that visas into Malawi are free for most nationalities.

By Car

At the Zambian border post, enter the immigration-customs building (park your car before the gate), complete the vehicle ledger at the customs window, and request a Temporary Export Permit (TEP). Complete this (note that you'll need lots of detail about your car, such as engine number, chassis number, vehicle weight etc, which your rental company should have provided) and take your copy with you. Then ask the customs officer where to purchase insurance (sometimes called COMESA) for Malawi. This is *very* important! You should not enter Mchinji (in Malawi) without insurance, as the police prey on unsuspecting tourists. You have the options of buying the insurance at the Zambian border post (ZK55,000 for one month, valid for one country), or just after you've gone through the formalities on the Malawian side (MK5,500). Try to buy it on the Zambian side as it's much cheaper and the office in Malawi is sometimes closed.

Go back to your car and drive through the gate to the nearby Malawian immigration-customs building (just up the road). Here, go to the customs window and request and complete a Temporary Import Permit (TIP), after of course filling in the obligatory ledger for vehicles. After receiving your copy of the TIP, move to the cashier's window and pay MK1200 for the TIP. Proceed through the gate and, if you have your Malawian insurance, on into Malawi. If not, stop 100m up the road at Prime Insurance Company (on the right) – this is your last opportunity to purchase insurance. In the town of Mchinji, up the road, there will be a police checkpoint for sure, and if you don't have your insurance they'll slap you with a big fine.

By Public Transport

From Chipata regular minibuses and shared taxis go to the Malawi border crossing (ZK20,000). Once you've passed through Zambian customs, it's a few minutes' walk to the Malawian entry post. From the border post you can catch a shared taxi to nearby Mchinji (MK300) before getting a minibus or bus all the way to Lilongwe.

details. See p657 for details about travelling between Chipata and South Luangwa National Park.

SOUTH LUANGWA NATIONAL PARK

☎ 0216

For scenery, variety and density of animals, accessibility and choice of accommodation, **South Luangwa** (admission US$25, Zambian-/non-Zambian vehicle ZK15,300/US$15; 🕒 6am-6pm) is the best park in Zambia and one of the most majestic in Africa. In fact when the best parks in Africa are being considered, experts often have South Luangwa in their top handful for the continent. Impalas, pukus, waterbucks, giraffes and buffalo wander on the wide-open plains; leopards, of which there are many in the park, hunt in the dense woodlands; herds of elephants wade through the marshes; and hippos munch serenely on nile cabbage in the Luangwa River. The bird life is also tremendous: about 400 species have been recorded – large birds such as snake eagles, bateleurs and ground hornbills are normally easy to spot.

The quality of the park is reflected in the quality of its guides – the best in Zambia. The local professional guide association sets standards, and anyone who shows you around this park should have passed a set of tough examinations.

The focal point is Mfuwe, a village with shops, as well as a petrol station and market. Around 1.8km further along is **Mfuwe Gate**, the main entrance to the park, where a bridge crosses the Luangwa River and several cheaper lodges and 'camps' (a confusing term often used to describe expensive lodges) and campsites are set up. This part of the park can get quite busy with vehicles in the high season, but only because it's the best wildlife-viewing area. But in Zambia everything is relative: compared to the rush-hour/rally-style safaris in South Africa's Kruger National Park, for example, it's positively peaceful around Mfuwe. (Note that lots of wild animals in this area makes walking around at night *very* dangerous.)

Away from Mfuwe, in the northern and southern parts of the park, the camps and lodges enjoy a quieter and more exclusive atmosphere. The animals may be less used to vehicles and slightly harder to find, but there are fewer visitors in these areas and watching the wildlife here is immensely rewarding.

Although South Luangwa is hard to visit on the cheap, there are more options for the budget-conscious here than at most other parks in Zambia.

Most of the park is inaccessible between November and April (especially February and March), so many lodges close at this time.

SOUTH LUANGWA NATIONAL PARK

SLEEPING
- Cobra Resthouse.........1 B3
- Croc Valley.................2 B3
- Flatdogs Camp............3 B3
- Kaingo Camp...............4 B3
- Kapani Lodge..............5 A3
- Kawaza Village............6 B4
- Marula Lodge..........(see 11)
- Mushroom Lodge & Presidential House..7 B2
- Nkwali.........................8 A3
- Puku Ridge Camp.......9 A4
- Thornicroft...............10 B3
- Track & Trail River Camp.......................11 B3
- Wildlife Camp............12 A3

EATING
- Cobra Resthouse.......(see 1)

SHOPPING
- Tribal Textiles...........13 B4

TRANSPORT
- Petrol Station............14 B3

Flora & Fauna

Vegetation ranges from open grassy plains to the strips of woodland along the river bank, dominated by large trees including ebony, mahogany, leadwood and winterthorn, sometimes growing in beautiful groves. As you move away from the river onto higher ground, the woodland gets more dense and finding animals takes more patience.

Not that you'll ever be disappointed by Luangwa's wildlife. The park is famous for its herds of buffalo, which are particularly large and dramatic when they congregate in the dry season and march en masse to the river to drink. Elephant numbers are also very healthy, even though ivory poaching in the 1980s had a dramatic effect on the population. Elephants are not at all skittish, as they are very used to human activity and game vehicles, especially around Mfuwe. Hippos are found in abundance in the Luangwa River and their grunting breaks the evening serenity as they haul themselves onto the grassy banks to forage for the night. This park is also a great place to see lions and leopards (especially on night drives), and local specialities include Cookson's wildebeest (an unusual light-coloured subspecies) and the endemic Thornicroft's giraffe, distinguished from other giraffes by a dark neck pattern.

There's a stunning variety of 'plains game'; the numerous antelope species include bushbucks, waterbucks, kuduw, impalaw and pukuw. Roan antelopes, hartebeests and reedbucks are all here, but encountered less often.

The bird life in South Luangwa is also tremendous. As small lagoons dry out, fish writhe in the shallows and birds mass together as 'fishing parties'. Pelicans and yellow-billed storks stuff themselves silly, and become so heavy they can't fly. Herons, spoonbills and marabou storks join the fun, while grasses and seeds around lagoons attract a moving coloured carpet of queleas and Lilian's lovebirds. Other ornithological highlights are the stately crowned cranes and the unfeasibly colourful carmine bee-eaters, whose migration here every August is one of the world's great wildlife spectacles.

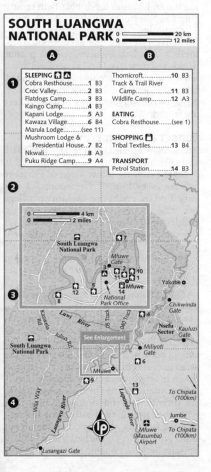

SOUTH LUANGWA CONSERVATION SOCIETY

This society, partly funded by lodges in and around the park, supports and works closely with the Zambian Wildlife Authority (ZAWA) by pursuing ways to conserve local wildlife and resources. Specifically, it spearheads antipoaching and antisnaring initiatives and also trains and supports ZAWA scouts. The South Luangwa Conservation Society does much work for both conservation and education in the area and acts as an umbrella organisation for local projects. If you're interested in learning more about the society's work, go to www.slcs-zambia.org. You may be able to visit while you're in South Luangwa – ask at Flatdogs Camp (right).

Activities

Unlike other parks in Zambia, boat trips are not available in South Luangwa, but all lodges/camps run excellent day or night **wildlife drives** (called 'game drives' in Zambia) and some have **walking safaris** (June to November). These activities are included in the rates charged by the upmarket places, while the cheaper lodges/camps can organise things with little notice. A three-hour morning or evening wildlife drive normally costs around US$40 to US$45, and the evening drive in particular offers the chance to spot an elusive leopard and shy nocturnal creatures such as a genet or a serval. You also have to pay park fees on top of this, but only once every 24 hours, so you can have an evening drive on one day and a morning drive on the next. A walking safari (US$45) is perhaps the best way of all to experience the park, offering the chance to break out of the confines of the vehicle and experience the African bush first hand with an expert guide.

ZAMBIA

Sleeping

Most lodges/camps in South Luangwa are along the banks of the river or at an oxbow lagoon. Several lodges/camps also have smaller 'bush camps' deep in the park, where they operate walks or drives away from the busier areas. Despite the rustic title, most 'bush camps' are very comfortable, with large tents, private bathrooms and excellent food. Joining a walking safari for a few days from one bush camp to the next is a popular and wonderful way to really experience the sights, sounds and smells of the bush.

Several budget places are located just outside the park boundary, so you don't pay admission fees until you actually enter the park. Note that some lodges/camps open only in the high season (April to November by their definition), but those in and around Mfuwe are open all year. Places that open in the low (or 'green') season offer substantial discounts – often up to 40%. However, at this time of year, the grass is high, walking safaris are for the most part unavailable and many tracks are impassable, so while it's cheaper you mightn't actually see that much wildlife.

The rates listed here are per person during the high season for double/twin rooms; single supplements usually cost 30% more. The camping rates are also per person. All-inclusive rates include accommodation, meals, snacks, laundry, activities such as game drives, and park fees. Local alcohol and house wine, and transfers are also usually included, but you should double check when booking. None of the lodges/camps described here are fenced.

BUDGET & MIDRANGE

All places mentioned here are outside the park and open all year.

Cobra Resthouse (Mfuwe village; s/d with shared bathroom ZK30,000/40,000) The rooms of this very budget resthouse in Mfuwe village are rather hopefully named after animals. Inside, pretty dismal concrete boxes are for the extremely budget conscious only, or if you're on a crack-of-dawn minibus early in the morning. At least try and get a room with a working fan. Melas are available from ZK16,000.

our pick **Flatdogs Camp** (☎ 246038; www.flatdogscamp.com; campsite US$7.50, safari tent US$35-40, self-catering chalets US$50; 💻 🍴) This large camp has a wide choice of affordable accommodation, great facilities and is very popular, so you should book well ahead in high season. The safari tents are our favourites, perched right on the river's edge with outside tables and chairs for enjoying the view. The chalets, which sleep six, are enormous and surprisingly luxurious, with large, mosaic-tiled bathrooms and self-catering facilities – very good for families or small groups. No 4 is the best with a brilliant upstairs deck overlooking the river.

Croc Valley (☎ 246074; crocvalleycamp@iwayafrica.com; campsite US$7.50, dorm US$25, chalets US$50;) Set under a tangle of trees on a large grassy area, with backpacker rooms that are surprisingly good value and very comfortable, this place is probably the best deal for budget travellers. (If you're on the bone-crunching minibus from Chipata, try asking the driver to take you straight here instead of dropping in Mfuwe village.) The chalets have a designer look, with sunken bathrooms, and safari tents sitting under thatched roofs are also a good option. There's a bar-restaurant and plenty of hammocks and shaded chill-out spots.

Wildlife Camp (☎ 246026; www.wildlifecamp-zambia.com; campsite US$10, safari tents US$40; chalets US$60;) If you want a classic safari-camp atmosphere without breaking the bank, this place is ideal. A spacious, secluded spot, about 5km southwest of Mfuwe village, its chalets sleep up to three people, but they don't have great views. The safari tents and spacious campsite are much better situated, with their own bar and pool, and perfect sundowner views. The camp operates in association with the Wildlife & Environmental Conservation Society of Zambia, so you know that part of your money is going directly into conservation and development projects.

Marula Lodge (☎ 246073, 097 6676757; www.marulaluangwa.com; r per person US$40, full board US$155;) Marula has new owners who are making extensive refits to their elderly chalets. The refurbishments were taking place when we dropped by, so it's early days, but the signs are good. The range of accommodation is limited to chalets, but they are a good size, have private bathrooms, and are very comfortable – the only downside is that the tin roofs will heat them up in summer.

Kawaza Village (www.kawazavillage.co.uk; full board US$70, day visits US$25) This enterprise is run by the local Kunda people and gives tourists the opportunity to visit a rural Zambian village while helping the local community. The village has four rondavel huts (each sleeps two) reserved for visitors and there are open-air reed showers and long-drop toilets. Visitors are encouraged to take part in all aspects of village life. Many visitors describe a visit here as the highlight of their trip to South Luangwa. Transfers can be arranged from Flatdogs Camp.

TOP END

South of Mfuwe Gate

our pick Track & Trail River Camp (☎ 246020; www.trackandtrailrivercamp.com; full board chalet/safari tent US$190/170;) This place is a great choice – in extensive grounds, with many riverside nooks to park yourself (including hammocks and a fantastic pool area) and observe the wildlife on the opposite bank. There are four luxurious chalets sleeping up to four, each with a top-stairs deck overlooking the river. Camping is also available (US$12.50). The grounds are just lovely, with a bridge walk over a former home to crocs (when this was a croc farm) shaded by a giant African fig. It's located about 400m east of Mfuwe Gate.

NORMAN CARR & SOUTH LUANGWA

The history of South Luangwa National Park is inextricably linked with the story of Norman Carr, a leading wildlife figure whose influence and contribution to conservation has been felt throughout Africa.

In 1939, one year after the North and South Luangwa Game Reserves were created, to protect and control wildlife populations, Carr became a ranger there. With the full backing of the area's traditional leader, Carr created Chief Nsefu's Private Game Reserve in 1950 and opened it to the public (until this time reserves had been for animals only). All visitor fees were paid directly to the chief, thus benefiting the wildlife and the local community.

Carr was years ahead of his time in other fields too: he built Nsefu Camp, the first tourist camp in Zambia, and developed walking safaris. In the following decades, other game reserves were created, more tourists came to Luangwa parks and more camps were built along the river.

In 1972 Nsefu and several game reserves were combined to form the South Luangwa National Park, but poaching of elephants and rhinos soon became an increasing problem. So in 1980 Carr and several others formed the Save the Rhino Trust, which helped the government parks department to deter poachers.

In 1986 Carr opened yet another camp, Kapani Lodge, and continued operating safaris from this base. He retired from 'active service' in the early 1990s, and died in 1997, aged 84.

Thornicroft (☎ 265 01-757120; www.landlake.net; full board & game drives US$250;) This new camp is operated by Land & Lake Safaris, which are based in neighbouring Malawi. There are 10 stone and wood chalets all with verandahs overlooking the Luangwa River. The decor is earthy and the chalets are quite stylish inside with mod cons and newish fittings. It's located along the river to the east of Track & Trail River Camp, not far from the confluence of the Luangwa and Lupande Rivers.

Kapani Lodge (☎ 246015; www.normancarrsafaris.com; all-incl ste US$550; all year) The most famous of the top-end lodges is this classic Luangwa camp built by Norman Carr in Lupande Game Management Area (GMA). The 10 thatched cottages and large circular houses all have private verandahs, set among neat lawns and colourful gardens overlooking a beautiful green lagoon frequented by birds and weed-munching hippos. Accommodation is among the most comfortable and roomy of the smaller camps in and around South Luangwa. The lodge runs highly rated walking safaris, usually to and between four smaller rustic bushcamps, ideal for experiencing the African bush. It's located about 4km southwest of Mfuwe Gate.

Nkwali (☎ 246090; www.robinpopesafaris.net; all-incl cottages US$550; all year;) A long-standing classic Luangwa lodge, run by Robin Pope Safaris, Nkwali has just six small cottages, each sleeping two people, with delightful open-air bathrooms. They're all very comfortable, but with no unnecessary frills, which gives a feel of the bush – rustic, but also quite classy. It is located in the Lupande GMA, overlooking the park, incorporating acacia and ebony woods, making it a favourite spot for elephants and giraffes. Walking safaris are conducted throughout the year.

Puku Ridge Camp (☎ 27-11-438 4650 in South Africa; www.sanctuarylodges.com; all-incl safari tents US$600;) The voluminous safari tents here, of which there are only six, are a travel agent's dream – they have massive mahogany beds, separate seating areas, sunken corner baths, indoor and outdoor showers (complete with puku-skull towel rails) and expansive balconies. The views are incredible – the plains stretch on for miles and there's so much wildlife on display that you hardly need to go on a safari drive.

North of Mfuwe Gate

North of the main gate are several other top-end options; each is inside the park.

Mushroom Lodge & Presidential House (☎ 246117; www.mushroomlodge.com; all-incl chalets US$425;) This historic lodge was built at the whim of former president Kaunda about 40 years ago. Reddish chalets with thatched roofs are very comfortable and, as with the rest of the place, overlook Mfuwe Lagoon. Children are well catered for here with a babysitting service and meals and games available especially for them.

Kaingo Camp (☎ 245190; www.kaingo.com; all-incl cottages US$650; mid-May–Oct) Run by the highly respected safari guide Derek Shenton, Kaingo, in the northern part of the park, is relaxed, understated and exclusive with five delightful cottages surrounded by bush overlooking the Luangwa River. The honeymoon suite has a huge skylight – ideal for bedtime stargazing – and a private section of river bank, complete with hammocks and outside bathtub. A highlight is the camp's three hides, popular with photographers; from them, you can view elephants, hippos, and carmine bee-eaters.

Eating

All the lodges/camps and campsites provide meals – from simple snacks, to haute cuisine at the top-end places. Flatdogs Camp probably has the best food of the 'drop in' lodge restaurants. There are also a couple of basic eateries in Mfuwe village.

Cobra Resthouse (Mfuwe village; meals ZK16,000) It claims to have the best food in Mfuwe (maybe true); Cobra is a basic restaurant serving *nshima*-based meals for the budget-conscious and those looking to escape the sanitised nature of the lodges.

Shopping

Most of the lodges/camps have souvenir shops selling the usual array of carvings. Other locally made mementoes include ceramics and elephant-dung paper (mostly made in Malawi, however).

Tribal Textiles (☎ 245137; www.tribaltextiles.co.zm; 7am-4.30pm daily) Along the road between Mfuwe village and the airport is a large enterprise that employs a team of local artists to produce, among other things, bags, wall hangings, bed linens and sarongs, much of which is sold abroad. Tribal Textiles have some striking original designs and it's quite a refined place for a shop. Short (free) tours around the factory are good fun. Local craftspeople outside in the car park sell animal carvings, jewellery and even the odd carved wooden mask. It's a relaxed place to have a browse with no hassle, but the range is limited.

Getting There & Away

AIR

Most people reach South Luangwa by air. Mfuwe (Masumba) airport is about 20km southeast of Mfuwe Gate and served by chartered flights from Lusaka and, occasionally, from Lilongwe (Malawi). **Proflight** (☎ 0211-271032; www.proflight-zambia.com) offers regular flights between Lusaka and Mfuwe every day for US$250 one-way (during high season there are two to three flights a day). There are also regular daily flights to/from Livingstone for US$230. Most lodges will meet clients who have made reservations.

MINIBUS & PRIVATE VEHICLES

Minibuses between Chipata and Mfuwe village leave when *really* full one or two times a day. Fares are squarely priced for foreigners (about US$8). From Mfuwe village, it's easy to walk (about 1km) to Flatdogs and Croc Valley, or hitch to the Wildlife Camp – but, to repeat, do *not* walk at night. Alternatively, offer some extra kwacha to the minibus driver to take you to one of these three campsites or to Mfuwe Gate.

It may also be possible to arrange a private shared lift in Chipata for about US$25 – ask at Dean's Hill (p651).

If you're in a group, consider chartering your own minibus from Chipata for a negotiable US$70 to US$80 one-way.

CAR

To get to Mfuwe Gate and the surrounding camps from Chipata you definitely need a 4WD high-clearance vehicle. In the dry season the dirt road is usually poor and the drive takes about three hours. In the wet season, however, the drive can take all day – or be impassable – so seek advice before setting off.

In places the road was in a pretty bad way when we came through. Be patient and alert, especially as people and animals frequently wander over it. From Chipata take the turn-off to the left, just before you cross under the welcome arch into town (this is also the road to Mama Rula's). The tar soon runs out, and after you travel 70km on a fairly decent gravel road you'll come to a Zambian Wildlife Authority (ZAWA) checkpoint where you can turn left and follow the ZAWA sign to South Luangwa National Park (and some lodges such as Flatdogs are signed as well); or go straight ahead on a single track road, which runs back into the main road some 18km on. The advantage of taking the track straight ahead is avoiding some of the worst parts of the main road. However you should check locally before you do this (Dean's Hill in Chipata is a good place to ask; see p651) as conditions of both tracks do vary each year. After you are back on the main road, travel about 20km to another ZAWA sign, which directs you left (this road takes you to the airport – a much better route than going straight to Mfuwe, as the road is in really bad condition here). At the airport a right-hand turn (just before you enter the airport) will take you onto a sealed road from where it's a straight drive (around 25km) into Mfuwe village and onto Mfuwe Gate and into the national park. This route information may become redundant if the planned upgrade to the Chipata–Mfuwe road actually takes place. It's been rumoured for years now – fingers crossed...

NORTH LUANGWA NATIONAL PARK

This **park** (admission US$20, vehicle US$15; 🕑 6am-6pm) is large, wild and spectacular, but nowhere *near* as developed or set up for tourism as its southern counterpart. The big draw of North Luangwa is its walking safaris, where you can get up close to the wildlife in a truly remote wilderness.

It's important to note that most of the southern part of the park has been set aside as a wilderness area. There are not many roads and only three smallish camps, which mainly run walking safaris. The only way to access this part of the park is to arrange your stay with one of these operators. However, to the north is a zone which allows wider self-drive access with one main track and several smaller tracks running off it. Note though that you'll need to have a fully equipped 4WD vehicle to attempt this.

Natangwe Community Camp Site (natwangw@yahoo.com; campsite US$10) is run by the Mukungule Community and is set in woodland by the northern park entrance gate. The campsites are very pleasant, with recently upgraded hot showers and flush toilets. There are also barbecue spots (you need to be fully self-sufficient) and you can sometimes arrange to visit one of the villages in the area.

Buffalo Camp (☎ 0211-229261; www.shiwasafaris.com; per person self-catering chalets US$100, all-incl chalets US$300, game drive/walk US$30/15; Jun-Oct) in the south of the park, is a quiet, secluded place run by knowledgeable and helpful staff. It's good value and the chalets have been rebuilt here in recent times in traditional style, with thatched roofs overlooking the river. Book ahead for the 'self-catering rates', because these are normally only available when there's a paucity of big-spending guests on the all-inclusive package (full board plus activities). Transfers for those without vehicles are usually possible from Kapishya Lodge (see p647) or Mpika (maximum four people).

Mwaleshi Camp (☎ 061-240561; www.remoteafrica.com; all-incl chalets per person US$520) is a relaxed and luxurious bush-camp. Accommodation is in four simple chalets made from reeds and thatch with open-roofed bathrooms. Walking is the main activity, and that's a fortunate thing once you've tasted the excellent food. Spotted hyenas are commonly seen in this area as are buffalo and of course lions. The spectacular Mwaleshi Falls is another highlight. Most guests on organised tours fly in and out on chartered planes.

If you are coming into the park independently, remember that you need to be well set up with a fully equipped 4WD, and your accommodation must be prebooked – unless you're staying at a campsite (even then, be prepared to be fully self-sufficient). Also, get advice regarding the state of the road into the park and make sure you've got maps that cover the area (and also have GPS); these should be supplemented by a map of the park, usually available at Mano Gate and detailing where you're allowed to drive.

SOUTHERN ZAMBIA

This region is a real highlight of Zambia with some wonderful natural attractions. There are national parks, with the Lower Zambezi in particular highly regarded for both its wildlife (especially elephants) and its scenic landscape. The area is also home to the remote Lochinvar National Park, a World Heritage Wetland site with pristine wetlands well worth a visit. Then there's the massive Lake Kariba, with Siavonga's sandy beaches and Chinkanka Island (smack in the middle of the lake) providing fascinating views of the night sky and a glimpse of the 60 elephants that make their way between the islands.

This section covers the following areas in relation to Lusaka: southwest down to Livingstone, south to Lake Kariba, and southeast to incorporate the Lower Zambezi National Park. See the Victoria Falls chap-

DRIVING IN SOUTHERN ZAMBIA

The Lusaka–Livingstone road: from Lusaka to Mazabuka this road is poor in parts – narrow and with heavy traffic, so drive carefully. The Munali Hills (not far from the turn-off to Chirundu) give lovely vistas north and south. From Monze heading south, the road is generally in good shape (although narrow in parts) until the south side of Zimba, approximately 50km outside of Livingstone, where a new road is being put through – there's a diversion in rough gravel, and then there's a very poor section of potholed (but sealed) road to negotiate before the last short leg to Livingstone: allow for extra time (perhaps an extra hour) when planning the last stretch of this drive.

Kafue town down to Siavonga on Lake Kariba: from the Livingstone turn-off, for a few kilometres down this road, the condition of the sealed road is shocking with plenty of potholes to look out for. But then there's an excellent 34km section navigating through the worst of the twists and turns and bends of this hilly country. Before this new road it was a nightmare run, with trucks broken down everywhere and accidents a frequent occurrence. However, the road is already showing signs of wear and poor craftsmanship; hopefully it will hold up for a few years yet. From the turn-off to Siavonga, you're on pretty good sealed road all the way (last 60km or so), but it's narrow with livestock frequently about, so be alert. Rewarding views of the lake come into view over the last 20km or so and are well worth a picture from the side of the road.

If you're continuing down to Chirundu, about 20km from the Siavonga turn-off, watch out for the potholes – some are axle-breakers.

ter (p604) for detailed information about Livingstone, the Zambezi waterfront and the magnificent falls.

MONZE

☎ 0213

Monze is a small town with a nearby campsite that makes one of the best places to break a journey between Lusaka and Livingstone. It's also a great base from which to make a foray into nearby Lochinvar National Park.

Located 11km north of Monze on an old farm, our pick **Moorings Campsite** (☎ 250049; www.mooringscampsite.com; campsite ZK30,000, chalets s/d ZK180,000/260,000) is perhaps the most beautifully landscaped campsite in Zambia. It's a lovely secluded spot with plenty of grass and there are open-walled thatched huts spotted around the campsite with a light for reading and a braai next to them for cooking. At sunset this is a particularly beautiful place, with nothing but the sound of birdsong in the African bush.

Proceeds are used to support an on-site clinic and the Malambo Women's Centre, a women's textile collective with offshoots of basketry and papier mâché run by Tonga women from the farm and nearby villages. The collective is walking distance from the campsite, and for sale is a colourful myriad of bedspreads, wall hangings, quilts and other knitted and sewn arts. The textiles capture scenes of Zambian life, often incorporating oral culture by representing traditional folk tales. The Centre's stated goals are economic growth, individual skills training, community development and cultural preservation; purchasing one of their products is a great way to support the local community.

LOCHINVAR NATIONAL PARK

This small, 410 sq km **park** (admission US$10, vehicle US$15; 6am-6pm), northwest of Monze, consists of grassland, low wooded hills, and the seasonally flooded Chunga Lagoon – all part of a huge World Heritage Wetland Site called the Kafue Flats. You may see buffalo, wildebeests, zebras, kudu and some of the 30,000 Kafue lechwes residing in the park. Bushbucks, oribis, hippos, jackals, reedbucks and common waterbucks are also found here. Lochinvar is also a haven for bird life, with more than 400 species recorded.

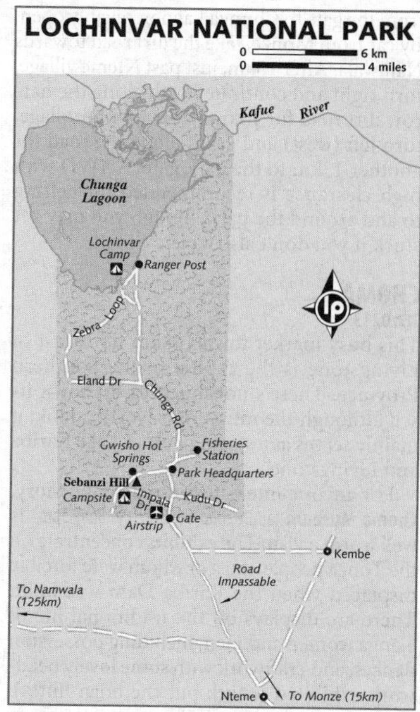

Gwisho Hot Springs, near the southern edge of the park, is the site of a Stone Age settlement, today surrounded by palms and lush vegetation with steaming water far too hot to swim in.

Lochinvar was virtually abandoned in the 1980s. By late 2001, a tour operator, Star of Africa, had started to redevelop the park. It also built the superb Lechwe Plains Tented Camp, under a clump of acacia trees along the shores of the Chunga Lagoon. The camp, now called **Lochinvar Camp**, was taken over by **Sanctuary Lodges & Camps** (www.sanctuarylodges.com); it's currently closed until 2010. When reopened it should offer the usual game drives along with mokoro (canoe) trips and walking safaris. Cultural trips visiting nearby fishing villages should also be available.

Otherwise, provided you bring all your own gear, you should be able to camp – ask the scouts at the gate for the latest on viable campsites within the park. Remember that facilities will be basic, and don't forget to bring your own food.

The network of tracks around the park is still mostly overgrown, with only the track from the gate to Chunga Lagoon reliably open. By car from Monze, take the dirt road towards Namwala. After 15km, just past Nteme village, turn right and continue north along the narrow dirt road for 13km. Near Kembe village, turn left (west) and grind along the road for another 13km to the park gate. A 4WD with high clearance is recommended for getting to and around the park, though you may get stuck if you don't also have a winch.

CHOMA

☎ 0213

This busy market town 188km northeast of Livingstone is the capital of the Southern Province. There's not much to the town itself although the museum is worth a look; it mainly serves as a staging post to Lake Kariba and Livingstone.

For anyone interested in regional history, **Choma Museum** (adult/child US$2/1; 8am-5pm) is well worth a visit. The exhibits concentrate on the Tonga people, most of whom were forcibly displaced when the Kariba Dam was built. There are displays on the traditional life of Tonga women and men, including possession dances, and craftwork with some lovely beadwork exhibited (check out the horn flutes). The museum is about 1.5km east of the town centre along the road to Lusaka.

'New' is probably an exaggeration at the basic **New Choma Hotel** (☎ 097 9311997; Main Rd; r ZK85,000-130,000), with its range of rooms that are all pretty similar. It's worth paying a bit more than the basic rate to get extra space as well as a fan and a less decrepit bathroom.

our pick **Leon's Lodge** (☎ 097 8666008, 095 5799756; r ZK180,000-200,000, chalet ZK250,000-350,000) was being refurbished at the time of writing and the results look terrific. Rooms are huge, spotlessly clean, and come with DSTV, fridge and bathroom – they're a real bargain. Chalets have traditional thatched roofs and are a step up in luxury. It's very central to town and quiet as it's off the main drag.

All daily buses and trains between Livingstone and Lusaka stop at Choma. To Luska, buses cost ZK65,000, to Livingstone its ZK50,000, and there are many departures every day.

NKANGA RIVER CONSERVATION AREA

This rudimentary **conservation area** (admission ZK30,000) covers a few local farms and is a tourism venture aimed squarely at birdwatchers, but welcoming everyone. It protects many different varieties of antelope too including eland, sable, wildebeest and kudu. It's an excellent area for birdwatching with in excess of 400 species recorded, including the Zambia (Chaplin's) barbet, Zambia's only endemic species.

Bruce-Miller Farms (☎ 0213-225592, 097 7863873; nansaibm@zamtel.zm; campsite ZK30,000, d incl full board ZK300,000) has a tranquil campsite set on the banks of the Nkanga River, surrounded by bird life, and bushbucks are commonly seen. Otters and marsh mongooses are common here, too, but shy. The campsite facilities are basic, with flush toilets, cold showers, fireplaces and an open dining-cooking area. Make sure you bring your own food and utensils. Three double rooms at the farmhouse – an old, classic colonial house boasting a beautiful garden – are also available. Kids are welcome. Game drives are available or pick up a guide and head off in your own wheels. Fishing for bream and barbel, canoeing and bird walks are all on offer from the farmhouse.

The comfortable **Masuku Lodge** (☎ 0213-225225; www.masukulodgezambia.com; d incl breakfast US$85, full board US$105) has spacious rondavels with luxury fittings in an attractive, remote area. There are beautiful shaded grounds with plenty of grass and this makes a nice place to spoil yourself; it's all very civilised. You'll probably be greeted by a horde of friendly, motley pooches on arrival.

The turn-off to Nkanga River is about 3km north of Choma, and then it's about 20km on a decent gravel road to Masuku Lodge and another 5km to Bruce-Miller Farms. It's not a bad idea to call or email for exact directions as a new sealed road may be up and running by the time you read this.

LAKE KARIBA

Beyond Victoria Falls, the Zambezi River flows through the Batoka Gorge then enters the waters of Lake Kariba. Formed behind the massive Kariba Dam, this is one of the largest artificial lakes in Africa. The lake is enormous and spectacular with the silhouettes of jagged Zimbabwean peaks far across its shimmering waters. The Zambian side of Lake Kariba is not *nearly* as developed or as popular as the southern and eastern shores in Zimbabwe. Refer to p704 for information about this huge artificial lake.

THE PLIGHT OF THE TONGA

The Zambezi Valley between Victoria Falls and the Kariba Gorge is the homeland of the Tonga people – known as the Tonka or Batonka in Zimbabwe, and the Valley Tonga in Zambia, to distinguish them from their Plateau Tonga cousins who live on the high ground further north.

Unlike many Bantu peoples of Southern Africa, the Tonga did not have a tradition of powerful chiefdoms, but instead established a more decentralised and less warlike society. In precolonial days they were frequent targets for slave hunters, or raids from more aggressive tribes. The Makololo, a Zulu offshoot who migrated to the Zambezi Valley in the 1830s, subjugated the Tonga before moving upstream to lord it over the Lozi for 40 years.

Towards the end of the 19th century, the Lozi overthrew the Makololo, and continued oppression of the Tonga. Through the colonial period the Tonga remained largely ignored and among the least developed of Zambia's tribes.

In the 1950s the Tonga received the toughest blow of all when the creation of Lake Kariba put a big slice of their territory underwater. A huge and expensive project called Operation Noah rescued rhinos, lions and other species trapped on islands by the rising waters, and brought them to the mainland – mostly on the Zimbabwean side of the lake. At the same time, the Tonga were virtually forgotten, with their land submerged and nowhere else to go.

Some groups were allocated new land, but it was 'spare' precisely because it was no good for farming. Many people were forced to move on, and look for work in the cities. Those who resisted the longest were simply rounded up, loaded into trucks and relocated with nothing (or very little) in the way of compensation. Eventually, a total of about 60,000 Tonga were displaced from their ancestral lands – an issue that remains unresolved today.

Foreign embassies in Zambia warn of land mines (left over from the Rhodesian civil war) in the Sinazongwe area on the shores of Lake Kariba. Avoid hiking off the beaten track in this area.

Chikanka Island

This beautiful private island (actually an archipelago of three islands since a rise in water levels), 8km from Sinazongwe, is privately owned and is mostly wooded. There are impalas, kudu, zebras and bushbucks with elephants dropping in occasionally too. **Chikanka Island Camp** (☎ 097 9493980; reservations@lakeview-zambia.com; full board per person US$100) on one of the islands here has A-frame chalets built in their own private space and looking out towards Zimbabwe, providing great early-morning views. Transfers by boat can be arranged (US$100 for up to 10 people) from Lake View (right).

Sinazongwe

☎ 0213

Near the southwestern end of Lake Kariba, Sinazongwe is a small Zambian town used by *kapenta* (sardine) fisherman as an outpost. If Zambian tourism to the lake does pick up, this town is well placed to become a major hub on the lakeshore; however, at the moment things are a touch quiet.

A kilometre from town and easy to find is **Lake View** (☎ 097 9493980; reservations@lakeview-zambia.com; s/d ZK200,000/300,000) where simple chalets with ceiling fan have a secluded terrace overlooking the lake. There's also a small beach area and a braai. Meals are ZK40,000 and you can hire a boat for ZK300,000 per hour. This would make a good spot to do the washing and chill out for a few days.

A lot further away, but with an excellent array of accommodation options, is **Kariba Bush Club** (☎ 097 9493980; www.siansowa.com; campsite per person US$10, dm US$15, d US$40, 6-/10-bed guest house US$250/200;), a beautifully landscaped site. Traditional buildings have dorm accommodation as well as a double, twin and family room with shared bathrooms; and there are two very comfortable guest houses for groups with DSTV, brilliant locations and gobsmacking views. Activities include walking safaris on their private islands. To get to the Club, about 2km before Maamba take the dirt road to the left and follow the signs.

Ask in Choma for minibuses that can take you to Sinazongwe. By car head to Batoka on the main Lusaka–Livingstone road, just north of Choma. From here take the turn-off to Maamba. After about 50km look for the turn-off to Sinazongwe, the town is a short distance down this dirt road.

ZAMBIA

Siavonga

☎ 0211

Siavonga, the main town and resort along the Zambian side of Lake Kariba, has an enviable location – among hills and verdant greenery, just a few kilometres from the massive Kariba Dam. Views of the lake pop up from many vantage points. Although set up primarily for the conference and business market, Siavonga is popular with urban Zambians (especially those from Lusaka) who tear down here towing their sleek boats. The accommodation is spread out, so you're better off with your own wheels. It's a good place to kick back and relieve some hard days on the road. The tiny **Zanaco Bank** (Government Rd) has an ATM that theoretically accepts Visa cards and changes US dollars after 10am. There's also a **post office** (Government Rd) nearby.

ACTIVITIES

A visit to the dam wall is a must while you're here – most lodges organise boat trips, otherwise you can take your own wheels (make sure you get a stamped pass to the dam wall at Zambian immigration).

The lodges organise activities in and around the lake and Eagles Rest has the greatest variety of options. It organises the following (all should be booked in advance, especially the canoe safari and village tour): a **canoe** (ZK60,000, three hours) on the lake; a **sunset cruise** (ZK60,000 per person, two hours) on the lake for a minimum of eight people – if fewer than eight people it's ZK480,000 to have the boat to yourselves; and a **boat trip and village tour** (ZK265,000 per person, minimum eight people; ZK580,000 per person, minimum two people) that includes a lake cruise to Village Point, visiting a small lodge that focuses on ecotourism, lunch, a village tour where you visit a working village and get to see traditional life, and finally a lake cruise back to Eagles for sunset. There are also one-day to four-night **canoe safaris** on the Zambezi where you'll canoe through the gorgeous Zambezi Gorge.

Leisure Bay Lodge (☎/fax 511136, 097-7755531) also rents out **canoes** (ZK30,000 per person per hour) and Lake Safari Lodge organises **boat trips** on the lake – banana boat ZK290,000 per hour, suncruiser ZK400,000 per hour, and a fast boat ZK340,000 per hour.

Lake Kariba Inns organises lots of different **boat trips** on the lake, ranging from a trip to the dam wall, which costs ZK135,000 to ZK530,000 depending on the size of the boat, to a longer-distance motor around to Lottery Bay (ZK1,540,000).

SLEEPING & EATING

our pick **Eagles Rest** (☎ 511168; www.eaglesrestresort.com; campsite per person ZK40,000, with tent supplied ZK90,000, chalets ZK200,000;) With the only campsite around town, this place is directed squarely at tourists. It's the best value in Siavonga with large, spacious chalets that boast stone floors, a double and single bed and great decking outside with patio furniture overlooking the lake. The food here is excellent too as the restaurant is a branch of Lusaka's Chit Chat (p639), which ensures quality meals are available.

Hill Top Lodge (☎ 097 7404115; r ZK150,000) Come up here for the views, not the luxury. Basic rooms have newly tiled floors, TV, hot water, private bathrooms and sparse furnishings. It's superfriendly and there's a simple bar with pool table and million-dollar views across the lake. It's a very rough but short road with a massive, craterlike pothole to negotiate up to the lodge.

Lake Safari Lodge (☎ 511148; www.lake-safari.com; s/d incl breakfast from ZK195,000/255,000;) Slightly upscale and nicely situated on the shore, with accommodation options enjoying an elevated position over the lake and

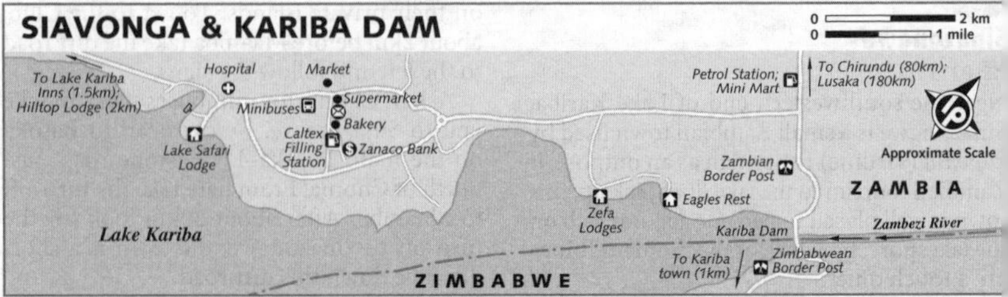

providing wonderful views. Basic rondavels pull off a cute look quite successfully (mind your head).

Zefa Lodges (☎ 511480; r ZK250,000-400,000;) The rooms at this guest house are of a high standard. Spotlessly clean and with plenty of space, rooms 1 to 6 are probably the best, and the Exec and VIP are huge – try negotiating a rate on one of these. It's on the road down to Eagles Rest and everything is negotiable when it's quiet.

Lake Kariba Inns (☎ 511290/249; www.karibainns.com; s/d from ZK305,000/420,000;) This fine establishment is good value for the added bit of Zambian luxury that guests receive. Executive rooms have a bit more space, can be set up for kids and have a verandah, some with views over the lake. The restaurant is a grandiose affair, ablaze with African carvings and decoration. There's a sense of space up here and a certain refinement, not to mention some good freebies, such as use of the gym, sauna and pedal boats.

GETTING THERE & AWAY

Minibuses from Lusaka (ZK45,000, three hours, three to five daily) leave when bursting to capacity for Siavonga and the nearby border. Alternatively, get a bus towards Chirundu and get dropped off at the Siavonga turn-off, from where a local pick-up costs ZK15,000 for the rest of the way. From the makeshift bus stop in Siavonga, you can easily walk to Lake Safari Lodge. There are no taxis in Siavonga, but your hotel may be able to arrange a private car to the border; otherwise, take the Lusaka minibus, which detours to the border.

CHIRUNDU

☎ 0211

This border town is on the main road between Lusaka and Harare. The only reason to stay here is if you're going on to Zimbabwe or planning to explore the Lower Zambezi National Park. The town isn't up to much – there are a few shops and bars, as well as a bank (Barclays with ATM) and a number of moneychangers, but that's about it. What's more, the roads are permanently clogged with snaking queues of heavy-duty trucks, all heading for, or coming from, the border.

There is no petrol station in town. Gwabi Lodge has a couple of fuel pumps but there is a limited supply, so it's safer to stock up in Lusaka or Kafue.

Sleeping

Gwabi Lodge (Map p664; ☎ 515078; www.gwabiriverlodge.com; campsite per person US$5, s/d chalets incl breakfast US$60/100;) This renovated lodge is spacious with a large grassy and well-equipped campsite, and solid chalets with stone floors. Take advantage of the decking in front of the à la carte restaurant with its lovely elevated outlook over the river, to observe birds and wallowing hippos along the riverfront. The lodge is located 12km from Chirundu towards the Lower Zambezi National Park.

Zambezi Breezers (Map p664; ☎ 097 9279468; campsite ZK40,000, s/d tented chalets incl breakfast ZK300,000/500,000, block rooms ZK150,000;) This friendly lodge has some great accommodation options including a huge grassed area for camping alongside the riverbank. There are also six tented chalets with simple clean setups and great decks overlooking the water. It's 6km from Chirundu along the same road as Gwabi River Lodge.

Nyambadwe Motel (s/d ZK65,000/70,000, standard tw ZK120,000, exec ZK150,000) Right on the border in Chirundu, this motel is noisy and unappealing, but certainly convenient. Standards are pretty ordinary, but would do at a pinch.

Getting There & Away

Minibuses leave regularly for Chirundu from Lusaka (ZK30,000, 3½ hours, five to seven daily). To reach Siavonga (on Lake Kariba) from Chirundu, catch a minibus towards Lusaka, get off at the obvious turn-off to Siavonga and wait for something else to come along. See p681 for more on getting to Zimbabwe from Chirundu.

LOWER ZAMBEZI NATIONAL PARK

Zambia's newest **national park** (admission US$25, vehicle US$15; 6am-6pm) covers 4092 sq km along the northwestern bank of the Zambezi River. This is now one of the country's premier parks, with a beautiful flood plain alongside the river, dotted with acacias and other large trees, and flanked by a steep escarpment on the northern side, covered with thick miombo woodland. Several smaller rivers flow through the park, and there are also some pans and swamp areas. On the opposite bank, in Zimbabwe, is Mana Pools National Park, and together the parks form one of Africa's finest wildlife areas.

The elephant population has made a strong comeback from poaching. Other mammals

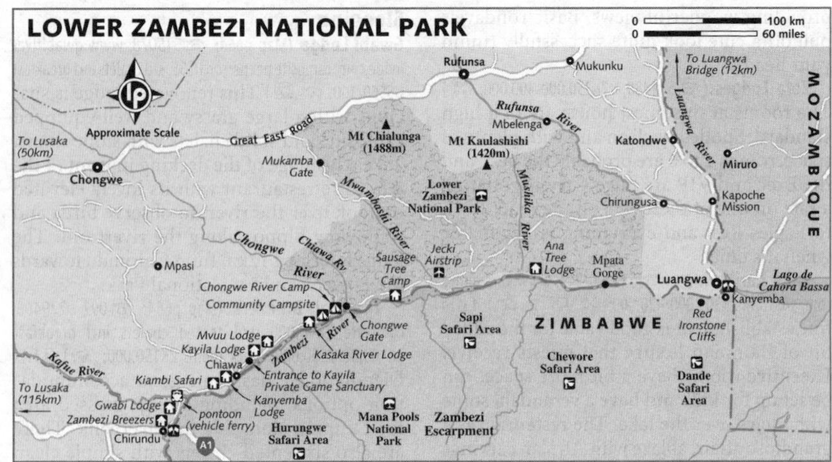

species include pukus, impalas, zebras, buffalo, bushbucks, lions and cheetahs, and more than 400 bird species have been recorded, including the unusual African skimmer and narina trogon. Seeing elephants swim across the river, or hundreds of colourful bee-eaters nesting in the steep sandy banks, could be the highlight of your trip. The best time to visit is May to December.

The main entrance is at **Chongwe Gate** along the southwestern boundary. There are gates along the northern and eastern boundaries for hardy travellers.

Activities

The best wildlife viewing is on the flood plain and along the river itself, so **boat rides** are a major feature of all camps and lodges; doing a boat trip down the river (about US$30) is certainly a rewarding activity and it won't be long before you're lulled into the majesty of the Zambezi.

Alternatively, one of the best ways to see the Lower Zambezi is in a **canoe**. Drifting silently past the river bank you can get surprisingly close to birds and animals without disturbing them. Nothing beats getting eye-to-eye with a drinking buffalo, or watching dainty bushbucks tiptoe towards the river's edge. Excitement comes as you negotiate a herd of grunting hippos or hear a sudden 'plop' as a croc you hadn't even noticed slips into the water nearby.

Most of the camps and lodges have canoes so you can go out with a river guide for a few hours. Longer **canoe safaris** are even more enjoyable, with stops at seasonal camps along the river or makeshift camps on midstream islands; ask what is available at your lodge.

Sleeping

The rates listed here are per person during the high season (April to November) staying in twins/doubles unless mentioned otherwise; single supplements are usually 30% extra. (The rates for camping are also per person.) Also, add on transfers if you haven't got your own wheels. None of the lodges described in this section are fenced and all offer wildlife-viewing activities by boat or by safari vehicle.

Community Campsite (campsite US$5) A basic place a few kilometres before Chongwe Gate – don't expect any frills here. It's mainly set up for travellers with their own vehicles. Run by local people, the modest profits are put back into the community.

our pick Kiambi Safari (☎ 097 7186106; www.kiambi.co.za; campsite US$17, full board from US$126;) This well-run operation at the confluence of the Zambezi and Kafue Rivers has a smattering of different, affordable accommodation options. Tented chalets here are a soothing airy option – elevated and very comfy. The air-con chalets are a luxurious option, good if the humidity is getting a bit much. Campers maybe get the best deal of all with a separate bar (with pool table) and upstairs viewing platform, perfect at sunset with a cold drink from below. And don't worry if you've forgotten a tent, Kiambi will provide one with bedding for an extra US$7. If you're not on a full-board deal, note that meals are set choice, but prices are comparatively reasonable – US$23 for dinner.

Mvuu Lodge (☎ 27-12-660 5369 in South Africa; www.mvuulodge.com; campsite US$20, safari tents d & tw US$160) Mvuu has comfortable tented rooms overlooking the Zambezi River, with balconies and sandy outdoor fireplaces that are lit outside your tent every night. There's a superb deck overlooking the river that makes a perfect spot for a sundowner, with grunting hippos below. The campsite is a mix of grass and hard dirt areas but there are private ablution facilities. Relatively new owners are still feeling their way here, but the signs are good. Note the rate above is for the safari tent and is not per person, making it a good deal. Full-board deals in a safari tent run from about US$210 per person.

Kanyemba Lodge (☎ 097 7755720; www.kanyemba.com; full board around US$330;) This lodge has phenomenal river views and proximity to big wildlife, as well as authentic, homemade Italian food and a cappuccino machine that's ready to roll 24 hours a day. The chalets are an excellent option if you're after a slice of luxury but don't want to burn too big a hole in the hip pocket. The well-developed verdant garden puts plenty of shrubbery between you and your neighbouring chalet, meaning privacy is valued here. The lodge has an enviable, elevated spot above the river – the island you can see offshore is owned by the lodge and it also runs the luxury Kanyemba Island Bush Camp there. You're sure to see more wildlife than in many of the big parks. If you don't have your own wheels, take a bus to Chirundu and someone will collect you there.

Kasaka River Lodge (☎ in Lusaka 0211-256202; www.kasakariverlodge.com; all-incl tented chalets US$500; Apr-Nov) Kasaka caters especially well for families, with specifically designed safaris for kids. Tented chalets on stone platforms are very luxurious and there's even a honeymoon suite with Ottoman-style bed and open-air bath. The hippo pod is good for families and has its own viewing deck, while the luxury acacia suite caters for four in two separate chalets done in a Bedouinstyle and linked by a central boma. Cultural visits to a local community and local schools are a good way to break up the wildlife viewing.

Ana Tree Lodge (☎ 0211-250730; www.anatreelodge.com; all-incl tented chalets US$575; Apr-Nov) On the Mushika River near an airstrip this lodge offers a good way into the park and, as such, is quieter and feels more isolated. It has a spread of tented chalets on concrete pads that are a bit dated inside but still very comfortable. Ana Tree is popular with anglers and especially noted for its nearby catches of tigerfish – rods for beginners are available at the camp. Note that neither drinks purchased at the bar nor fishing permits are included in the tariff.

Sausage Tree Camp (☎ 0211-845204 in Lusaka; www.sausagetreecamp.com; all-incl tents US$895; May–mid-Nov;) Overlooking the Zambezi, deep inside the national park, Sausage Tree is exclusive and slightly unconventional. Traditional safari decor is rejected in favour of cool and elegant Bedouin-style tents completely rebuilt in 2008, each in a private clearing, with minimalist furniture, cream fabrics and vast open-air bathrooms that continue the North African theme. Each tent has a discreet *muchinda* (butler), while other features are the library tent with couches and cushions, and the airy dining tent with a Paris-trained chef.

Also recommended:

Kayila Lodge (bookings through Safaris Par Excellence, ☎ 0213-320606; www.safpar.com; full board US$180;) The chalets here have mosquito-screen walls so you have a fantastic feeling of space all around you – at night it's as if you're sleeping under the stars.

Chongwe River Camp (☎ 0211-286 808; www.chongwe.com; all-incl tented chalets US$650; Apr-Nov;) Enviable position with plenty of game around the camp, but without the park fees. There are tented chalets with twin beds, shaded verandahs and open-air bathrooms well spaced along the edge of the river. Chongwe also has other options in the area.

Getting There & Away

There's no public transport to Chongwe Gate, nor anything to the eastern and northern boundaries, and hitching is very difficult. Most people visit the park on an organised tour, and/or stay at a lodge that offers wildlife drives and boat rides as part of the deal.

If you have your own vehicle (you'll need a high-clearance 4WD), head down to Chirundu. As you enter the town, you are looking for a left-hand turn to Gwabi Lodge (not far from Gwabi Lodge in the GMA is a pontoon which you'll need to take to cross a river; it costs ZK40,000 for a Zambian-registered vehicle, or US$20 for a non-Zambian-registered vehicle, foot passengers free) and from there onto the Chongwe Gate into the Lower Zambezi (all the same route). The turn-off can be tricky to spot as there are often trucks parked in front of it, and it's an unmarked track. It's basically at the bottom of the hill before the green-roofed police station. There are also tracks via the north for those heading to the eastern side of the park, but these are far less used: there's an approach road accessed from the great Eastern Road, 100km east of Lusaka that will take you to Mukanga Gate; and there's a track from Leopards Hill in Lusaka. Seek local advice before attempting either of these routes.

For budget travellers, ask at Chachacha Backpackers (p637) in Lusaka or Jollyboys (p611) in Livingstone for deals on budget safaris into the Lower Zambezi.

Getting Around

Remember that you'll need a well-equipped 4WD to access and get around the park. You must drive slowly in the GMA area and the park itself – watch especially for elephants alongside the roadside at all times! There are several loops inside the park for wildlife viewing, but these change from year to year, especially after the rainy season, so pick up a guide at any of the gates.

WESTERN ZAMBIA

Western Zambia is at the bottom of some travellers' itineraries and at the top of others'. If you're after easy access, lots of other tourists and well-known attractions, look

DRIVING TO CHONGWE GATE IN THE LOWER ZAMBEZI NATIONAL PARK

The often-bad condition of the road makes driving from Chirundu to Chongwe Gate an adventure in itself, and hopefully the following will help you find your way – it would have helped us as we got lost plenty of times!

The road from the pontoon (vehicle ferry) up to Chiawa village is mostly excellent graded gravel road. The track from Chiawa village to the Gate, however, is in very poor condition – and generally worse just after the rainy season (ie April/May). Check with locals before you set off and make sure you have a high-clearance 4WD. When you reach the entrance to Kayila Private Game Sanctuary the track is in better shape, apart from a few steep dry-riverbed crossings. However, be aware that finding your way from here to the Chongwe Gate is difficult as there are unmarked turn-offs and T-junctions with no signage. Also the route can change slightly from year to year depending on the condition of the track. Try to bring the best maps you can get your hands on, as well as a compass. Ask for directions and advice along the way – especially at lodges, as they are using the track into the park all the time and should have up-to-date information. Be aware that it's a long and potentially frustrating drive to the Gate; leave plenty of time. Your last hurdle into the park is crossing the Chongwe River. There are three crossings – again ask which is the best to use (ie where the river is at its lowest) and have a look at where the vehicle tracks head (ie what crossing the wildlife drives are using). Across the river is Chongwe Gate into the park.

To help you keep on track, the following are distances between major points and most of the lodges:

Destination	Distance (km)
Chirundu to:	
Zambezi Breezers	5.7
Gwabi Lodge	9.1
Pontoon (vehicle ferry)	11.6
Kiambi Safaris	21.4
Chiawa Village (Bad Road) turn-off	37.1
Kayila Private Game Sanctuary	55.4
Kayila Lodge	58.3
Mvuu Lodge	63.7
Kasaka River Lodge	74.3
Community Campsite	79.9
Chongwe river crossing (Chongwe Gate)	83.4

CROSSING THE BORDER INTO BOTSWANA

Coming from Livingstone, it's about 60km west to Kazungula, the Zambian border town: across the river, a short pontoon ride away, is Botswana. There are one or two buses (ZK20,000, 35 minutes) daily from Livingstone, departing from Nakatindi Rd in the morning. The Zambian side of the border is disorder and frankly, at times, chaos. There are huge lines of trucks on the road leading up to the border and then a mess of trucks near the pontoon.

Heaps of guys at the Zambian border post will hassle you to change money; and you will need pula if you're bringing a car across the border into Botswana. Give these guys a wide berth, though, and change your money at the Stero Bureau de Change (a clearly visible shack on your left as you approach the border – it should be open, even if these guys tell you otherwise). Keep in mind that you need around 200 pula, and whatever sum you require for a visa (if you need one). Note that US dollars and other currencies are not accepted at the Botswana border post.

If driving, park your car just before you go through the border gate and go to change money. Then walk through the gate and around to the back of the building immediately on your left. Go inside and get your passport stamped. If you have a vehicle, fill out a temporary export permit (TEP), as well as filling in the register with details of your vehicle. This costs nothing – make sure you get a copy of the TEP form (after it's stamped). Then proceed down to the departure point for the pontoon. Walk into the pontoon company building and pay K30,000/40,000 for an ordinary/large vehicle, or US$20 for a non-Zambian registered vehicle. (Foot passengers pay ZK4000.) Then proceed back to your vehicle, and drive through to the pontoon departure point and wait to be directed onto the pontoon.

Only one truck and a couple of cars fit onto this decrepit river-crossing platform and the deck is pretty beaten-up, with splintered bits of wood everywhere, so be careful when driving on.

At the border post in Botswana, it's a huge contrast; orderly with no hassle. Proceed to the immigration-customs building up the road from the pontoon, a short drive or walk away. Fill in an entry card, get your passport stamped (or a visa if you require one), and then fill in a Temporary Import Permit for your vehicle if you're driving, and get that stamped. Go to the payment window and pay for the permit (120 pula), insurance (50 pula) and road duty (20 pula). This is all very straightforward, and the immigration-customs staff are helpful.

Lastly, if you're in a vehicle drive through a puddle of water and get out of the car to stamp your feet on a mat – it's a foot-and-mouth disease control measure. The town of Kasane is only 12km west and is the jumping-off point for excursions into Chobe National Park.

elsewhere; but if you're after a truly wild Africa experience, then you're heading in the right direction. Kafue National Park is the biggest single park in Africa, and is magnificent, with all the big mammals, marvellous birdwatching and a thousand different landscapes. Other highlights include the chance to experience even more remote wilderness areas such as Liuwa Plains National Park; thundering waterfalls and tremendous views of floodplains; an exploration of Barotseland, site of the colourful Kuomboka, Zambia's best-known traditional ceremony; and easy access to two of Southern Africa's best – Botswana and Namibia.

SESHEKE

☎ 0211

Sesheke, 200km upstream from Livingstone (virtually opposite the Namibian town of Katima Mulilo), consists of two towns on either side of the Zambezi River linked by a new bridge. The major part of town is on the eastern side of the river, before you cross the bridge. There's not much to actually see or do here, it's really just a transit point between Zambia and Namibia. The smaller section of town, on the western side of the river, is centred on the Zambian border post, with the Namibian border a few hundred metres down the road (see p668).

Friendly **our pick** **Brenda's Best & Baobab Bar** (☎ 097 9011917; campsite per person ZK30,000, chalet ZK150,000-250,000) is the best place to stay in Sesheke. It offers homely and airy chalets with thatched roofs and a relaxing but basic campsite with a popular bar built around a massive baobab. A restaurant should be open by the time you read this. The entrance to

CROSSING THE BORDER INTO NAMIBIA

If you have a vehicle, drive straight through Sesheke and over the bridge that spans the Zambezi river. Curve right after the bridge and the immigration-customs building is the last building on your left. Go in and get your passport stamped at immigration. Customs is out the back of this building – it's an unmarked door; ask at the immigration desk for directions. This is where you fill in a Temporary Export Permit (TEP) for your vehicle. Before you leave the Zambian side, ensure that you have enough Namibian dollars or SA rand to pay for your visa (if you require one) and for the Cross Border Charge Permit for your car/4WD (180 Namibian dollars), motorcycle (110 Namibian dollars). For help to change money – ask in the immigration-customs building.

Cross the border and Namibian formalities at Wenela border post are just up the road. Here, go into the immigration/customs building, fill in an arrival card and get your passport stamped. If you have a vehicle, complete a Cross Border Charge Permit and you'll be given a certificate to take with you confirming it has been paid. Don't forget to walk over the mat for foot-and-mouth disease control, just outside of immigration. You may also need to stop at the military checkpoint on your way out to fill in a register with details of your vehicle. The Namibian town of Katima Mulilo is then only a few kilometres away.

Brenda's is 200m beyond the western side of the church on the main street, down an unmarked road towards the river.

Small buses link Sesheke with Natakindi Rd in Livingstone (ZK45,000, two hours, two or three daily), usually in the morning, and minibuses also make the run. Occasional minibuses also link Sesheke with Katima Mulilo.

SIOMA & NGONYE FALLS

☎ 0217

The village of Sioma is about 60km southeast of Kalongola. It has a large mission, a row of shops, and that's about it. The only reason to come here is **Ngonye Falls** (Sioma Falls; admission free; ⏰ 24hr) – a 1km-wide chain of waterfalls, rapids and rocky islands cutting across the Zambezi River. It's beautiful and very impressive and would be a major attraction if it weren't so difficult to reach; imagine something almost as majestic as the Victoria Falls, but with almost no other person in sight.

If you can, stop at the National Parks & Wildlife Service office near the falls, which can advise on the best way to visit the falls and point out a local campsite (US$10). You should be able to engage an official guide here.

The falls are less than 1km east of the main road, about 10km south of Sioma. For drivers, access is not difficult from Sesheke, but far more problematic from Senanga (see right). Otherwise, hitch a ride and ask to be dropped by the turn-off (look for the 'Wildlife Department' sign).

SENANGA

☎ 0217

If you're coming from Lusaka, Senanga has a real 'end of the line' feel – the sealed road ends, and the dusty dirt road that continues south is quiet and rarely travelled – although the main street can be surprisingly lively, especially in the evening, and the views of the Zambezi are beautiful. It is the best place to break up a journey between Mongu and Ngonye Falls or Sesheke.

The best accommodation option is **Senanga Safaris** (☎ 230156; campsite per person ZK30,000, d incl breakfast US$60). It offers comfortable rondavels with splendid views over the Zambezi plains – spoilt only by the giant satellite TV dish in the garden. The bar sells cold beer and the restaurant serves expensive meals.

Minibuses and pick-ups run between Senanga and Mongu (US$4.50, two to three hours) several times a day. About 30km south of Senanga (and accessible by minibus), a pontoon carries passengers (free) and vehicles (US$20/30 for 2WD/4WD) across the Zambezi to the tiny settlement of Kalongola (on the west bank of the river), from where the sandy road continues south towards Sesheke and Namibia. Often the ferry doesn't operate between February and June and the road between Senanga and Kalongola is flooded and impassable, so passengers take a small boat, but car drivers may have to charter a larger, different pontoon. Kalongola is marked as Sitoti on some maps, but this is a separate village about 5km south of Kalongola.

MONGU

☎ 0217

The largest town in Barotseland, and the capital of the Western Province, is on high ground overlooking the flat and seemingly endless Liuwa Plain. This is a low-key town, less hectic than other Zambian towns, but still with plenty of activity on the streets. It's quite strung out with no real centre, and the highlight is the outlook over the floodplains – the town has an enviable position, making for spectacular views. From a harbour on the southwestern outskirts of town, an 8km canal runs westwards to meet a tributary of the Zambezi. The river port is a fascinating settlement of reed and thatch buildings, where local fishermen sell their catch, and it's a good spot for people watching as longboats glide down the river transporting people and goods to nearby villages.

Sleeping

Lyambai Hotel (☎ 221138; Lusaka Rd; r ZK80,000-100,000) Yes, the Lyambai has seen better days – much better. It's ragged around the edges, not to mention in the middle. However, this beaten-up place does have character, shade, sublime views over the floodplain and friendly staff. We like it! It's 1.2km west of the public bus station and past the post office.

Crossroad Guesthouse (☎ 221649; Lusaka Rd; r ZK100,000;) This place has a bar at the front of the building with rooms out the back that are a good distance from the road outside. Although it doesn't look much from the outside, the rooms, which have private bathrooms, are actually pretty good, kept very clean and would do nicely for a night or two.

Getting There & Away

The public bus station is on the southeastern edge of town, behind the Catholic church. Several companies offer buses between Lusaka and Mongu (ZK115,000, eight hours).

A daily bus operates between Livingstone and Mongu (ZK120,000, 10 hours) via Sesheke, Kalongola and Senanga, but you're advised to break up this horror journey in Senanga. Better still, go to Lusaka from Livingstone and take the bus along the sealed road from Lusaka.

Minibuses and pick-ups leave for Senanga (US$4.50, three hours) on a fill-up-and-go basis from near the Caltex filling station in Mongu, from where minibuses head to Sesheke.

AROUND MONGU

Limulunga

The village of Limulunga is 15km north of Mongu. Here you can see the palace of the

KUOMBOKA CEREMONY

The Kuomboka (literally, 'to move to dry ground') is probably one of the last great Southern African ceremonies. It is celebrated by the Lozi people of western Zambia, and marks the ceremonial journey of the *litunga* (the Lozi king) from his dry-season palace at Lealui, near Mongu, to his wet-season palace on higher ground at Limulunga. It usually takes place in late March or early April, and sometimes ties in with Easter. The dates are not fixed, however; they're dependent on the rains. In fact the Kuomboka does not happen every year: in 1994, 1995 and 1996 the floods were not extensive enough to require the *litunga* to leave Lealui.

The palace at Limulunga was built in 1933 by Litunga Yeta III. Although the Kuomboka was already a long-standing tradition, it was Yeta III who first made the move from Lealui to Limulunga a major ceremony.

Central to the ceremony is the royal barge – the *nalikwanda,* a huge wooden canoe, painted with black-and-white stripes, that carries the *litunga*. It is considered a great honour to be one of the hundred or so paddlers on the *nalikwanda,* and each paddler wears a head-dress of a scarlet beret with a piece of a lion's mane and a knee-length skirt of animal skins. Drums also play a leading role in the ceremony. The most important are the three royal war drums, *kanaona, munanga* and *mundili,* each more than 1m wide and said to be at least 170 years old.

The journey from Lealui to Limulanga takes about six hours. The *litunga* begins the day in traditional dress, but during the journey changes into the full uniform of a British admiral, complete with all regalia including an ostrich-plume hat. The uniform was presented to the *litunga* in 1902 by the British King Edward VII, in recognition of the treaties signed between the Lozi and Queen Victoria.

litunga (the Lozi king; see p669), though you can't go inside and photos aren't allowed. Of more interest is the **Nayuma Museum** (admission ZK5,000; 8am-5pm daily), with its colony of bats in the roof and exhibits about the Lozi, *litunga* and Kuomboka, including a large model of the *nalikwanda* boat used in the ceremony. There are also some fascinating shots of royal pageantry, Zambian-style. Minibuses run between Mongu and Limulunga throughout the day.

Lealui

The village of Lealui, on the flood plain 15km northwest of Mongu, is the site of the *litunga's* main palace; he lives here for most of the year (July to March), when the waters are low. The palace is a large single-storey Lozi house, built with traditional materials (wood, reeds, mud and thatch) and meticulously maintained. Around the palace are smaller houses for the wives and family of the *litunga*; a tall reed fence surrounds the whole compound. Avoid visiting at weekends, when the *kotu* (court) is closed, because you need permission from the king's *indunas* (advisors) to get a close look at the palace and even to take photos.

Public longboats between Mongu harbour and Lealui (US$2, one hour) leave once or twice a day. Alternatively, charter a boat to Lealui for about ZK500,000 return, which could take six people: the price includes fuel and is usually negotiable. There are many more options for boats around the time of the Kuomboka ceremony, when it's possible to get a ride for around ZK70,000 per person if you ask around. Make enquiries at the shed on the left as you enter the harbour. Buses do the trip in the late months of the dry season.

LIUWA PLAIN NATIONAL PARK

About 100km northwest of Mongu, **Liuwa Plain National Park** (☎ 097 7158733; liuwa@africanparks.co.zm; per person per day US$40, campsite per person per night US$10, scout per day US$10; Jun-Nov) is 3600 sq km of true African wilderness on the Angolan border. A remote and rarely visited wild grassland area, it's where vast numbers of wildebeests and other grazing species such as lechwes, zebras, tsessebes and buffalo gather at the beginning of the wet season. Although their gathering is often called a migration, it's more of a meander, but the wall-to-wall herds are nonetheless spectacular. Roan antelopes, wild dogs, cheetahs and, in particularly high numbers, hyenas can be found in the park.

Although it became a national park in 1972, for years the park was in decline with no government funds to rehabilitate it until an organisation called **African Parks** (www.african-parks.org) signed a lease agreement in 2004; it now manages the welfare and facilities of the park.

Access to Liuwa Plain National Park is restricted to the most part of the dry season, and even then you should seek information about the state of the roads from Mongu through to the park before attempting the run. November is actually the best time to go for the wildlife, just after the rains start (the later the better), but make sure you leave before the flood waters rise, or you'll be stuck for months.

Getting here independently, via the park headquarters at Kalabo, is restricted to well-equipped and completely self-contained vehicles and is a real expedition – hence the small visitor numbers (only 25 vehicles are allowed in at any one time; and a GPS is advisable). Despite a network of tracks, the park is serious 4WD territory – a lot of the tracks are very sandy, wet or both, and it's easy to get yourself into trouble here. Taking a scout with you is highly recommended and also financially assists the national park; this can be organised at the park headquarters.

There are three campsites in the park, Kwale, Lyangu and Katoyana, open to independent travellers, and run by the local community in partnership with African Parks. Remember that you must be totally self-sufficient, including bringing all your food for yourself and for your guide.

Alternatively, you can see Liuwa on an organised safari – one company that offers quality safaris is **Robin Pope Safaris** (www.robinpopesafaris.net); a trip out to Liuwa Plains will cost about US$2500 for four nights.

KAFUE NATIONAL PARK

This stunning **park** (per person US$15, per vehicle US$15; 6am-6pm) is about 200km west of Lusaka and is a real highlight of Zambia. Covering more than 22,500 sq km (nearly the size of Belgium), it's the largest park in the country and one of the biggest in the world. This is the only major park in Zambia that's easily accessible by car, with a handful of camps just off the highway.

Kafue is classic wildlife country. In the northern sector, the Kafue River and its main

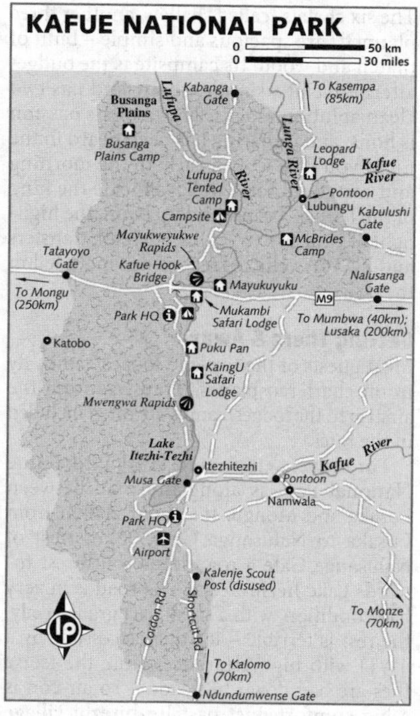

tributaries – the Lufupa and Lunga – are great for boat rides to see hippos in great grunting profusion, as well as crocodiles. Away from the rivers, open miombo woodlands and dambos (grassy, swampy areas) allow you to more easily spot animals, especially the common antelope species such as waterbuck, puku and impala, and the graceful kudu and sable. This area is also one of the best places in Zambia (even Africa) to see leopards – regularly spotted on night drives.

To the far north is Kafue's top highlight, the Busanga Plains, a vast tract of Serengeti-style grassland, covered by huge herds of near-endemic red lechwes and more solitary grazers such as roan antelopes and oribis. (Note that this area is accessible only between late July and November.) Attracted by rich pickings, lions and hyenas are plentiful.

The main road between Lusaka and Mongu runs though the park, dividing it into northern and southern sectors. (You don't pay park fees if you're in transit.) There's an incredible amount of animals to be seen just from the main road – wildlife watching doesn't get much easier than this! There are several gates, but three main ones: **Nalusanga Gate** along the eastern boundary, for the northern sector; **Musa Gate** for the southern sector; and **Tateyoyo Gate**, for either sector if you're coming from the west. Rangers are also stationed at the two park headquarters: at Chunga Camp and another 8km south of Musa Gate.

Sleeping

We list a selection of the numerous campsites and lodges/camps offered in and around the park. Several lodges/camps are just outside the park boundaries, which means that you don't have to pay admission fees until you actually visit the park. The inexplicable 'bed levy' (US$10) charged to tourists is usually included in the rates charged by the upmarket lodges, but elsewhere the levy is added to your accommodation bill (unless you're just camping). Rates here are per person per night based on two people sharing.

SOUTHERN SECTOR

our pick Mukambi Safari Lodge (☎ www.mukambi.com; contact for rates) This very accessible lodge along the northeastern bank of the Kafue River is a great place to stay and very easy to reach from Lusaka. There are chalets set along the river's edge that are extremely comfortable and simply but elegantly furnished, including sink-in-and-smile beds. Close by in its own private setting is the bush camp (available as full board or self-catering). The food is outstanding, especially dinner; your three-courses will rarely disappoint. Mukambi also runs Busanga Plains Camp in a wetland area in the north of the park. It's a luxury, tented camp on huge floodplains with islands of palms and plenty of animals to be seen including lions.

Puku Pan (☎ 0211-266927; www.pukupan.com; campsite US$10, chalets incl full board & 1 activity US$195; ⏲ all year) A beautifully situated, low-key spot with eight cottages plus verandahs overlooking the hippo- and croc-filled river. There's also a campsite here with hot showers and clean facilities. It's Zambian managed and is a straightforward, comfortable, but no-frills place.

Mayukuyuku (www.kafuecamps.com; campsite US$12, tent US$60, full board US$150) A rustic bush camp, small and personal, Mayukuyuku is set in a gorgeous spot on the river. It has a campsite and three safari tents with a fourth planned and is a great option for backpackers and budget travellers. The camp does pick-ups (US$30

ZAMBIA

per vehicle) from the nearby Hook Bridge on the main highway (jump off from any Lusaka–Mongu bus or minibus). If you don't have your own camping gear, don't worry – you can even rent tents here (US$15/25 for a small/large tent). Mayukuyuku is accessible by 2WD and is only 5km off the main road on decent gravel.

KaingU Safari Lodge (☎ 0211-256992; www.kaingu-lodge.com; campsite US$25, full board & 2 activities US$355; 🕑 all year) Set on an absolutely beautiful stretch of the Kafue River, about 10km south of Puku Pan in the GMA; the waterway just outside your tent here is definitely the highlight of a stay. The Meru-style tents raised on rosewood platforms with stone bathrooms overlook the river and have large decks to enjoy the view. They are tastefully furnished and thoughtfully set up, including their incorporation into the surrounding landscape. There are also two campsites, each with its own ablution and braai facilities.

NORTHERN SECTOR

Lufupa Tented Camp (www.wilderness-safaris.com; campsite US$10, all-incl tents US$450; 🕑 May-Jan;) At the confluence of the Lufupa and Kafue Rivers this large camp is the epicentre of the northern part of the park. Accommodation is in Meru-style tents with private bathroom, each with decks overlooking the water. Although help is at hand, this is not the kind of place where you'll be waited on hand and foot, despite the tariff.

Leopard Lodge (☎ in South Africa 027-82 416 5894; www.leopard-lodge.com; campsite US$12.50, all-incl chalets US$260; 🕑 all year) It's a small, family-run camp in an enviable location, about 4km from one of Zambia's best hot springs. In 2007 the camp underwent a wide-ranging refurbishment and the five brick chalets with thatched roofs are very comfortable with cotton linen and ceiling fans. There's a newly built bar and restaurant on site, although private lunches and dinners in the bush are the way to go, and a picnic on a river island is a highlight.

our pick **McBrides Camp** (www.mcbridescamp.com; campsite incl park entry fees US$45, all-incl chalets US$370) This is one of the best places to stay in Kafue. It's designed to give visitors maximum exposure to the bush – cleverly built around wildlife paths, the camp has lots of open space around it and animals such as lions, elephants and hippos all wander through – so a few nights here is about as genuine as it gets. The six chalets (called shallets, another three planned) are spacious and simple – built of thatch and wood. Its campsite is the budget alternative; it's simple, shady and has two clean ablution blocks. The owner's passion is lions, and if roaring has been heard in the night you'll be woken early in the morning and carted off for a walk to locate the king of the felines. It may end up being the highlight of your trip to Africa. Alcohol, transfers and ZAWA vehicle fees are not included in the tariff.

Getting There & Away

Most guests of the top-end lodges/camps fly in on chartered planes. Transfers from the airstrip to the lodges/camps are often included in the rates.

For drivers, the main road into Kafue National Park is along the road between Lusaka and Mongu. It's about 200km from Lusaka to Nalusanga Gate; 30km west of Nalusanga Gate a road leads southwest towards Lake Itezhi-Tezhi. The road is in very bad condition, with a small part graded only; the rest is terrible – it's only accessible by a 4WD with high clearance. Note the tsetse flies are bad down here, too – so air-con is a big comfort. Just past Itezhitezhi village is Musa Gate, from where the road crosses Lake Itezhi-Tezhi to New Kalala Camp and Musungwa Lodge.

For Mukambi Safari Lodge, continue west along the main road from Lusaka until about 10km before Kafue Hook Bridge (or 82km from Nalusanga Gate) and look for the signposted turn-off to the south. On the western side of the bridge, a main track leads into the northern sector of the park, and a dirt road leads southeast to Puku Pan.

Note that there are rumours that Kafue will become more easily accessible from Livingstone with the road between Livingstone and Itezhi-Tezhi Lake set to be sealed.

There's no public transport in the park, but you could get off the bus between Lusaka and Mongu and reach Mukambi Safari Lodge on foot (but due to the wild-animal population, don't attempt this walk after dark), or get off at the Kafue Hook Bridge and Mayukuyuku will pick you up. Alternatively, take the slow daily bus, or one of the more regular minibuses, from Lusaka to Itezhitezhi village (US$12, six hours).

From the village bus stop wait around for a lift (because of the number of wild animals it may not be safe to hike).

ZAMBIA DIRECTORY

ACCOMMODATION

Prices for all accommodation listed in this book are for the high season – ie April/May to October/November – and are based on the 'international rates'. Often, lodges offer residents rates that are much lower than these – sometimes as little as half the rate paid by international visitors.

Accommodation has been listed in budget order, from cheapest to most expensive. The parameters for dividing accommodation into categories by price is as follows: budget is up to ZK150,000, midrange between ZK150,000 and ZK350,000, and top end upwards of ZK350,000. This is a guide only, however, and lodges and camps in and around national parks are considerably more expensive due to their remote locations and, in some cases, their exclusive nature. It's also worth noting that prices for rooms with private bathrooms (called self-contained rooms in Zambia) are about 40% higher than rooms without, and that all accommodation in Lusaka is about 50% higher than anywhere else in Zambia. Most midrange and top-end hotels include either a continental or cooked breakfast in their rates.

Budget

Most cities and larger towns have campsites where you can pitch your tent, but most are way out in the suburbs. Camping is also possible at privately run campsites at the national parks, though most are located just outside the park boundaries to avoid admission fees (until you actually want to visit the park). No campsites are run by the national wildlife authority. Many lodges around national parks will accept independent campers – this can be a great deal as you have access to the lodge's facilities while paying a pittance for accommodation.

The (*very*) few youth hostels around Zambia are not part of any international organisation, so hostel cards are useless. But hostels in Lusaka and the major tourist areas are well set up with swimming pools, bars, restaurants and travel agencies offering organised tours.

Some of the cheapest hotels in the cities are actually brothels. The better budget hotels charge by the room, so two, three or even four people travelling together can get some real (if crowded) bargains. Single travellers may find some prices steep, though negotiation is always possible.

Midrange to Top End

Most accommodation in Zambia falls into these categories. All national parks are dotted with expensive privately operated lodges and 'camps' (a confusing term often used to describe expensive lodges). They offer the same

PRACTICALITIES

- The *Daily Times* and *Daily Mail* are dull, government-controlled rags. The independent *Post* (www.postzambia.com), featuring a column by Kenneth Kaunda, continually needles the government. Published in the UK but printed in South Africa, the *Weekly Telegraph*, the *Guardian Weekly* and the *Economist* are available in Lusaka and Livingstone.
- The monthly *Lowdown* magazine (www.lowdown.co.zm; ZK5000), aimed at well-off residents in Lusaka, has useful information for visitors, such as restaurant reviews and lists of upcoming events in the capital, as well as handy adverts for package deals for lodges around Zambia.
- Both of the Zambian National Broadcasting Corporation (ZNBC) radio stations can be heard nationwide; they play Western and African music, as well as news and chat shows in English. ZNBC also runs the solitary government-controlled TV station every evening, but anyone who can afford it subscribes to South African satellite TV. *BBC World Service* can be heard in Lusaka (88.2FM) and Kitwe (89.1FM); *Radio France Internationale* (RFI) can also be heard in Lusaka.
- Televisions use the PAL system.
- Electricity supply is 220V to 240V/50Hz and plugs are of the British three-prong variety.
- The metric system is used in Zambia.

sort of luxury and exclusivity as other lodges and camps in Southern Africa – all upwards of US$150 per person per night (twin share). Rates usually include all meals, drinks, park fees and activities, such as wildlife drives, but not transfers by road, air and/or boat. Lodges/camps should be booked in advance, either direct or through an agent in Lusaka or abroad. Some lodges/camps close around November to April; those that do stay open are likely to offer discounts of up to 50%.

Lusaka and other large towns have a good number of midrange hotels, lodges and guest houses, while real top-end hotels are less common (although easily found in Lusaka and Livingstone). Facilities and standards in midrange places can vary a great deal, and they are often set up for the conference trade rather than travellers.

ACTIVITIES

Companies in Livingstone (and Victoria Falls town in Zimbabwe) offer a bewildering array of activities (see p605), such as white-water rafting in the gorge below the falls or river-boarding and canoeing on the quieter waters above the falls. Those with plenty of nerve and money can try bungee jumping or abseiling, or take a ride in a microlight or helicopter. The less adventurous may want to try hiking or horse riding.

Canoeing is also a great way to explore the Zambezi River and can be arranged in Siavonga (p662). Fishing along the Zambezi, and at several lakes in northern Zambia, is also popular; the tigerfish are almost inedible, but provide a tough contest for anglers. Fishing and boating are also possible on Lakes Kariba, Bangweulu and Tanganyika.

Most national parks, including Kasanka, Kafue, Lower Zambezi and South Luangwa, have activities for visitors, with wildlife drives and walks being the main focus of these places, and the main drawcard for visitors to Zambia.

Many tour companies in Livingstone offer short wildlife drives in Mosi-oa-Tunya National Park (p614) near Victoria Falls, while companies in Lusaka and Livingstone can also arrange longer wildlife safaris to more remote national parks. In some parks (eg Kafue and South Luangwa), you can turn up and arrange wildlife drives or walking safaris on the spot.

BUSINESS HOURS

Government offices are open from 8am or 9am to 4pm or 5pm Monday to Friday, with an hour for lunch sometime between noon and 2pm. Shops keep the same hours, but also open on Saturday. Supermarkets are normally open from 8am to 8pm Monday to Friday, 8am to 6pm Saturday and 9am to 1pm Sunday (although some are open 8am to 10pm daily at the big shopping centres in Lusaka). Banks operate weekdays from 8am to 2.30pm (or 3.30pm), and from 8am to 11am (or 12pm) on Saturday. Post offices open from 8am or 9am to 4pm or 4.30pm weekdays. Restaurants are normally open for lunch between 11.30am and 2.30pm and dinner between 6pm and 10.30pm, though bar-restaurants in Lusaka are often open until 11pm on Friday and Saturday. Reviews in this chapter generally won't list business hours unless they deviate from these standard hours.

CHILDREN

While most people do not travel with children in Zambia, lodges such as Mushroom Lodge & Presidential House (p656) in South Luangwa National Park, and Kasaka River Lodge (p665) in the Lower Zambezi National Park, will specifically accommodate them with activities and facilities set up for kids, and perhaps even offer lower rates for them.

In Lusaka many upmarket cafes and restaurants, such as Chit Chat (p639) and Kilimanjaro (p639), have play areas for kids, either outside on the grass with swings, slides etc, or inside with soft play areas and toys.

See also Lonely Planet's *Travel with Children* by Cathy Lanigan.

CUSTOMS REGULATIONS

There are no restrictions on the amount of foreign currency tourists can bring in or take out of Zambia. Import or export of Zambian kwacha, however, is technically forbidden, but if you bring in/out a small amount (say, US$25 worth), it's unlikely to be a problem.

DANGERS & ANNOYANCES

Generally, Zambia is very safe, though in the cities and tourist areas there is always a chance of being targeted by muggers or con artists. In Zambia, thieves are known as *kabwalalas*.

For as long as the seemingly endless civil strife continues in Congo (Zaïre), avoid any areas along the Zambia–Congo (Zaïre) bor der. Foreign embassies in Zambia warn of land mines (left over from the Rhodesian civil war) in the Sinazongwe area on the shores of Lake Kariba. Avoid hiking off the beaten track in this area.

The possession, use and trade of recreational drugs is illegal in Zambia and penalties are harsh: in 1999, two New Zealand travellers received six months in jail with hard labour after being caught with a relatively small amount.

It's also worth noting that some travellers with an Asian background have reported annoying glares and racial slurs from Zambians.

Visitors hiring a car and travelling independently should take sensible precautions, such as carrying a mobile phone, getting the best maps they can find and letting someone know where they intend travelling (and for those getting more off the beaten track a satellite phone and GPS may be advisable).

See p633 for specific information about keeping safe in Lusaka.

DISCOUNT CARDS

Hostel cards and senior cards are generally useless in Zambia, though student or youth cards may be useful for buying tickets on major international airlines and the Tazara railway between Zambia and Tanzania.

EMBASSIES & CONSULATES

The following countries have embassies or high commissions in Lusaka (area code ☎ 0211). The British high commission looks after the interests of Aussies and Kiwis because the nearest diplomatic missions for Australia and New Zealand are in Harare. Most consulates are open from 8.30am to 5pm Monday to Thursday and from 8.30am to 12.30pm Friday, though visas are usually only dealt with in the mornings.

Botswana (☎ 250555; fax 253895; 5201 Pandit Nehru Rd)
Canada (☎ 250833; fax 254176; 5119 United Nations Ave)
Congo (Zaïre; ☎ 235679, 213343; fax 229045; 1124 Parirenyetwa Rd)
France (☎ 251322; fax 254475; 74 Independence Ave, Cathedral Hill)
Germany (☎ 250644; 5209 United Nations Ave)
Ireland (☎ 291298; 6663 Katima Mulilo Rd)
Kenya (☎ 250722; 5207 United Nations Ave)
Malawi (☎ 265764; fax 260225; 31 Bishops Rd, Kabulonga)
Mozambique (☎ 220333; fax 220345; 9592 Kacha Rd, off Paseli Rd, Northmead)
Namibia (☎ 260407/8; fax 263858; 30B Mutende Rd, Woodlands)
Netherlands (☎ 253819; fax 253733; 5208 United Nations Ave)
South Africa (☎ 260999; 26D Cheetah Rd, Kabulonga)
Sweden (☎ 251711; fax 254049; Haile Selassie Ave)
Tanzania (☎ 227698; fax 254861; 5200 United Nations Ave)
UK (☎ 423200; http://ukinzambia.fco.gov.uk/en; 5210 Independence Ave)
USA (☎ 250955; http://zambia.usembassy.gov; cnr Independence & United Nations Aves)
Zimbabwe (☎ 254006; fax 254046; 11058 Haile Selassie Ave)

FESTIVALS & EVENTS

One remarkable festival to look out for is **Ukusefya pa Ng'wena**, practised by the Bemba people of northern Zambia. This program of music, drama and dance, which is held near Kasama over four days in August, commemorates the victory of the Bemba over the marauding Ngoni in the 1830s.

N'cwala is a Ngoni festival held near Chipata in eastern Zambia on 24 February. At this time, food, dance and music are all enjoyed by participants, who celebrate the end of the rainy season and pray for a successful harvest.

Refer to the boxed text for details about the remarkable **Kuomboka Ceremony** (p669).

Information about these and other festivals can be found on the official Zambian tourism website: www.zambiat ourism.com.

FOOD

Eating listings are in order of price, starting with the cheapest first. Generally a budget meal in Zambia is under ZK20,000, midrange is between ZK20,000 and ZK50,000, while a top-end feed is upwards of ZK50,000. Remember that this is a guide only and prices will be considerably more in many lodges and camps in national parks. Also note that we've used a V symbol to denote places that serve vegetarian dishes.

For more information on food and drink in Zambia, see p631.

HOLIDAYS

During the following public holidays, most businesses and government offices are closed:

New Year's Day 1 January
Youth Day Second Monday in March

Easter March/April
Labour/Workers' Day 1 May
Africa (Freedom) Day 25 May
Heroes' Day First Monday in July
Unity Day First Tuesday in July
Farmers' Day First Monday in August
Independence Day 24 October
Christmas Day 25 December
Boxing Day 26 December

INTERNET ACCESS

Zamnet is the country's largest internet service provider. Internet centres are in Lusaka (p632), Livingstone (p608), and the bigger towns such as Mongu and Ndola, and are spreading rapidly. Access at internet centres is cheap – about ZK150 to ZK200 per minute – but connections can be horribly slow, depending on equipment and, importantly, the provider used. Wireless is becoming more common, particularly as most accommodation places outside of the national parks are set up for business folk and conferences. If you travel with a laptop that has wireless connectivity you'll be surprised at how useful it can be, even in remote towns.

INTERNET RESOURCES

Your first 'cyber-stop' should be the outstanding website run by the **Zambia National Tourist Board** (www.zambiatourism.com). See also p23. Other websites worth checking out include the following:

Zambia Online (www.zambia.co.zm) This lively site has webzines, news summaries and links to many other sites.
Zambiz (www.zambiz.co.zm) Ideal for all business, including booking lodges and tours.
Zamnet (www.zamnet.zm) Provides links to all major national newspapers and several other useful sites.

LANGUAGE

Of the 70 languages and dialects spoken in Zambia, seven are recognised by the government as official 'special languages'. These include Bemba (mainly spoken in the north); Tonga (in the south); Nyanja (in the east), which is similar to Chichewa, spoken in Malawi; and Lozi (in the west).

As the official national language, English is widely spoken across Zambia. The Language chapter (p775) contains some useful words and phrases in Chichewa and Lozi.

MAPS

The *Zambia Road Map* (ZK70,000) by German publisher Ilona Hupe Verlag is currently the best available map for touring around Zambia – it shows petrol stations and important wildlife areas. Also easy to find is Globetrotter's *Zambia & Victoria Falls* map, which includes regional and national park insets, and *Street Guide Lusaka & Livingstone* (ZK35,000), which is a book-form collection of blow-ups of the two cities. All are available at bookshops in Lusaka.

See if you can get your hands on the South African Boraro map of *Inside Zambia*, available from www.discovering-africa.com – it has some detailed insets of the national parks, such as Lower Zambezi. For coverage of more remote regions, detailed survey maps (ZK20,000 to ZK30,000) of various scales, but none published later than 1986, are sometimes available from the government-run Map Sales office in Lusaka (p632).

MONEY

Zambia's unit of currency is the kwacha (k), sometimes listed as 'ZMK' (Zambian kwacha) or 'kw'. In this book it is noted as ZK to distinguish it from Malawian kwacha. Bank notes come in denominations of ZK50,000, ZK20,000, ZK10,000, ZK5000, ZK1000, ZK500, ZK100, ZK50 and ZK20 notes, the last of which are extremely rare and virtually worthless. One hundred ngwee equals one kwacha, so, not surprisingly, ngwee coins have become souvenirs.

Inflation is high in Zambia (around 14%) and some prices in this chapter are quoted in kwacha and others in US dollars (US$), as different businesses base their rates on the different currencies.

Most tourist-oriented places in Zambia quote prices in US dollars, but you must by law pay in kwacha – except for international airfares, top-end hotels and lodges/camps, visas and most organised tours. In reality however, US dollars are commonly (and gratefully) accepted by most hotels, budget campsites, tour operators and national park scouts.

See also the inside front cover for exchange rates and p19 for information on costs while you're in Zambia.

Cash & ATMs

In the cities and larger towns you can obtain cash (kwacha and sometimes US dollars) over the counter at Barclays, Stanbic and Standard Chartered banks with a Visa card. But it can take most of the day and you may be slugged a fee of about US$10. Larger branches of these banks have ATMs that accept Visa, but only kwacha can be withdrawn. Although ATMs have had a patchy record, malfunctioning on occasion, they are usually OK to use. ATM cards bearing the MasterCard mark are fairly useless.

Credit Cards

Some shops, restaurants and better hotels and lodges/camps accept major credit cards, though Visa is the most readily recognised. A surcharge of 4% to 7% may be added to your bill if you pay with a credit card, so you're probably better off using it to draw cash and paying with that.

Moneychangers

The best currencies to take to Zambia (in order of preference) are US dollars, UK pounds and South African rands. Euros have yet to take off and the currencies of most neighbouring countries are worthless in Zambia, except at the relevant borders. The exception is Botswana pula, which can also be exchanged in Lusaka.

In the cities and larger towns, you can change cash at branches of Barclays Bank, Stanbic and Standard Chartered Bank. In smaller towns, try the Zambia National Commercial Bank. Theoretically these banks also change travellers cheques, however they are generally loathe to do so. Infuriatingly and inexplicably they usually require you to have your original purchase sales receipt in order to change (defeating the purpose of travellers cheques) and even then they will only recognise some kinds of sales receipt!

Foreign-exchange offices – almost always called bureaux de change – are easy to find in all cities and larger towns. Their rates for cash and travellers cheques (rarely accepted) are around 5% better than the banks' rates; the service is also faster and there are no additional fees.

You might get a few kwacha more by changing money on the street, but it's illegal and there is a chance that you'll be ripped off, robbed or set up for some sort of scam. However, moneychangers at the borders are more or less legitimate, but may take (slight) advantage of your ignorance about the current exchange rates.

Tipping

While most restaurants add a 10% service charge, rarely does it actually get into the pockets of waitstaff. Therefore, you may choose to tip the waitstaff directly.

Travellers Cheques

It's worth avoiding travellers cheques for several reasons: they are not accepted at most bureaux de change; banks are loathe to change them (see left); and they attract high charges and lower exchange rates (5% to 8% lower than for cash). Commission rates vary, so it's always worth shopping around. The standard commission charged by Barclays and Standard Chartered banks is about 1%, but often with a minimum of US$15. If you look likely to be charged a ridiculous commission, try negotiating for a lower commission.

You can pay for some items (such as tours, activities, hotels and lodges) directly with travellers cheques, but a few hotels and tour operators have a nasty habit of adding a surcharge (up to US$20) for doing this.

Barclays, AmEx, Thomas Cook and Visa are by far the most accepted brands.

PHOTOGRAPHY & VIDEO

In Lusaka and Livingstone it costs ZK10,000/12,000 for a roll of 24-/36-exposure print film, while a roll of 36 exposure slide film is about ZK30,000 (without processing). Developing and printing 24-/36-exposure print film costs about ZK25,000/35,000, but developing slide film is almost impossible. It costs ZK10,000 to burn a CD of your digital photos, and around ZK1500 to ZK3000 per digital image to develop. Bring everything you need for video cameras.

Zambian officials do not like foreigners photographing any public buildings, bridges, dams, airports or anything else that could be considered strategic. If in doubt, ask; better still, save your camera for the national parks.

POST

Normal letters (under 20g) cost ZK2700 to send to Europe and ZK3300 to the USA, Canada, Australia and New Zealand, while postcards are a flat-rate ZK1650. Sending international letters from Lusaka is surprisingly efficient (three or four days for delivery to Europe), but from elsewhere in the country it's less reliable and much slower. Parcels up to 1kg to Europe cost ZK55,500 by airmail and ZK60,600 to the USA, Canada, Australia and New Zealand. The cost is about half this for surface mail.

Poste-restante service is available at the main post office in Lusaka (p632) for a negligible fee.

TELEPHONE

Almost all telecommunication services are provided by the government monopoly, Zamtel. Public phones operated by Zamtel use tokens, which are available from post offices (ZK500) and from local boys (ZK1000) hanging around phone booths. These tokens last three minutes, but are only good for calls within Zambia. Phone booths operated by Zamtel use phone cards (ZK5000, ZK10,000, ZK20,000 and ZK50,000), available from post offices and grocery shops; these phone cards can be used for international calls. But it's often easier to find a 'phone shop' or 'fax bureau', from where all international calls cost about ZK12,000 per minute.

International services are generally good, but reverse-charge (collect) calls are not possible. The international access code for dialling outside of Zambia is ☎ 00, followed by the relevant country code. To call Zambia from another country, the country code is ☎ 260, but drop the initial zero of the area code.

Mobile Phones

MTN, Celtel and Zain (best coverage) all offer mobile (cell) phone networks. It's almost impossible to rent mobile phones in Zambia, though if you own a GSM phone, you can buy a SIM card for around ZK8000 without a problem. In Lusaka the best place to buy a cheap mobile phone is around Kalima Towers (corner Chachacha and Katunjila Rds); a basic Zain model is about ZK80,000 to ZK100,000

Scratch cards come in denominations of ZK1000, ZK2000, ZK5000, ZK10,000, ZK20,000, ZK50,000 and ZK100,000. Numbers starting with ☎ 095, ☎ 096, ☎ 097 and ☎ 099 are mobile phone numbers.

Mobile phone reception is getting better all the time; generally it's very good in urban areas and surprisingly good in some rural parts of the country, with reception now possible in South Luangwa National Park!

Phone Codes

Every landline in Zambia uses the area code system; you only have to dial it if you are calling outside of your area code. Remember to drop the zero if you are dialling from outside of Zambia.

TOURIST INFORMATION

The regional tourist offices in Lusaka and Livingstone are worth visiting for specific inquiries, but provide limited information about Zambia in general. Refer to the relevant sections for contact details.

The **Zambia National Tourist Board** (ZNTB; www.zambiatourism.com; UK ☎ 020-7589 6655; zntb@aol.com; 2 Palace Gate, Kensington, London W8 5NG; South Africa ☎ 012-326 1847; zahpta@mweb.co.za; 570 Ziervogel St, Hatfield, Pretoria) is worth contacting for some guidance with your planning. The official website is outstanding, and provides links to dozens of lodges, hotels and tour agencies.

The **Tourism Council of Zambia** (tcz@zamnet.zm) is an umbrella group of private companies throughout the country involved in the promotion of tourism.

VISAS

All foreigners visiting Zambia need visas, but for most nationalities tourist visas are available at major borders, airports and ports. However, it's important to note that you should have a Zambian visa *before* arrival if travelling by train or boat from Tanzania.

Citizens of South Africa and Zimbabwe can obtain visas for free. For all other nationalities, costs of tourist visas have been standardised, with most nationalities paying US$50 for single entry (up to one month), US$80 for double entry (up to one month), and US$160 for multiple entry (up to three months). Note that only a single- or double-entry visa is available from Lusaka airport. Make sure you request how long you want, as you may not automatically be given the maximum time for any type of visa.

Payment can be made in US dollars, and sometimes UK pounds, although other currencies such as euros, South African rand, Botswana pula and Namibian dollars, may be accepted at borders – but don't count on it.

Tourist and business visas can also be obtained from Zambian diplomatic missions abroad, and application forms can be downloaded from the websites run by the **Zambian high commission** (www.zhcl.org.uk in UK; www.zambiaembassy.org in USA).

If you come to Zambia from Zimbabwe on a free-visa transfer from Victoria Falls, make sure you keep all your paperwork; you may be asked later why there is no indication on your passport that you have paid for a Zambian visa and then be forced to buy one.

VISAS FOR ONWARD TRAVEL

If you're travelling to neighbouring countries, here's some information about getting that all-important visa (see p675 for contact details). It's always best to visit any embassy or high commission in Lusaka between 9am and noon from Monday to Friday. You will probably need two passport-sized photos.

Your chances of obtaining a visa for Congo (Zaïre) or Angola are extremely remote in Lusaka, so get it before you arrive in Zambia.

- **Botswana High Commission** (for visa applications 8am-12.30pm & 2-3.30pm Mon, Tue, Wed) Visa ZK358,000; ready in 7 days; bring two passport photos.
- **Malawian High Commission** (8.30am-noon Mon-Thu, 8.30am-11am Fri) Transit visa US$70, single US$100, multiple for 6/12 months US$220/300; takes three days to process; bring one passport photo, photocopy front of passport.
- **Namibian High Commission** (10am-3pm Mon-Fri) Visa US$50; takes two days to issue; bring two passport photos, photocopy front of passport.
- **Tanzanian High Commission** (Mon-Fri) Visa US$50 (no kwacha); apply by 8am, processed by 2pm the same day; bring two passport photos.

Visa Extensions

Extensions for all types of tourist visas are possible at any Department of Immigration office in any main town in Zambia, though you're likely to be more successful in Lusaka (Memaco House, Cairo Rd) and Livingstone (Mosi-oa-Tunya Rd). Normally, a month extension can cost up to US$100 (depending on your nationality).

If the paperwork seems overwhelming, and the fees exorbitant, simply cross into Zimbabwe, Mozambique, Namibia, Botswana or Malawi (the easiest options) and pay for a new visa when you return to Zambia.

TRANSPORT IN ZAMBIA

GETTING THERE & AWAY

Information about travelling to Southern Africa, including Zambia, from elsewhere in the continent, and from some Western countries, is included in the Transport in Southern Africa chapter (p755).

Entering Zambia

See opposite for full information on visa requirements for entering Zambia.

A yellow-fever certificate is not required before entering Zambia, but it *is* often requested by Zambian immigration officials if you have come from a country with yellow fever. And it is certainly required if you're travelling from Zambia to South Africa (and, possibly, Zimbabwe). For all sorts of reasons, it pays to get a jab before you come to Southern Africa and carry a certificate to prove it.

Air

Zambia's main international airport is in Lusaka, though some international airlines fly to the airports at Livingstone (for Victoria Falls), Mfuwe (for South Luangwa National Park) and Ndola. Until 2009, the major domestic and international carrier was Zambian Airways, but it suspended operations early that year, citing high fuel costs – although its high debt was probably the real reason. Zambia remains well connected with Southern Africa, though. **Zambezi Airlines** (www.flyzambezi.com) flies to regional destinations such as Johannesburg in South Africa (from Lusaka and Ndola) and to Dar es Salaam in Tanzania; while **South African Airways** (code SA; ☎ 0211-254350; www.flysaa.com) is the major regional airline, flying regularly to Lusaka from its hub in Jo'burg, from where there are onward regional and international connections.

In addition, **Air Malawi** (code QM; ☎ in Zambia 0211-228120; www.airmalawi.com) connects Lusaka with Lilongwe three times a week, and with Blantyre twice a week; while **Air Zimbabwe** (code UM; ☎ 0211-221750; www.airzimbabwe.com) also flies to Lusaka from Harare on the way to Nairobi. There is also an increasing number of flights to Livingstone for Victoria Falls: both South African Airways and **British Airways** (code BA; ☎ 0211-254444; www.britishairways.com) fly there from Jo'burg.

DEPARTURE TAX

The departure tax for all international flights is US$20. This tax is *sometimes* included in the price of your airline ticket, but if not must be paid at the airport (in US dollars only).

Airlines providing links with East Africa include the following: **Ethiopian Airlines** (code ET; ☎ 0211-236402/3; www.flyethiopian.com), which flies to/from Lusaka daily from its base in Addis Ababa; and **Kenya Airways/KLM** (code KQ; ☎ 0211-228886; www.kenya-airways.com), which provides direct flights (as well as stopovers in either Harare or Lilongwe) on its way to Nairobi.

Border Crossings

Zambia shares borders with eight countries, so there's a huge number of crossing points. All are open daily from 6am to 6pm, though the border closes at 8pm at Victoria Falls and at 7pm at Chirundu. The following borders issue visas to foreigners on arrival:

Botswana Zambia and Botswana share what is probably the world's shortest international boundary: 750m across the Zambezi River at Kazungula. The pontoon across the Zambezi is 65km west of Livingstone and 11km south of the main road between Livingstone and Sesheke. You can buy the Botswana visa at the border, when you get off the ferry there.

Congo (Zaïre) The main border is between Chililabombwe (Zambia) and Kasumbalesa (Congo). Visas are issued to tourists in Lusaka, but can be difficult to obtain.

Malawi Most foreigners use the border at Mchinji, 30km southeast of Chipata, because it's along the road between Lusaka and Lilongwe.

Mozambique The main border is situated between Mlolo (Zambia) and Cassacatiza (Mozambique), but most travellers choose to reach Mozambique by going through Malawi.

Namibia The only border is at Sesheke (Zambia), on the northern and southern bank of the Zambezi, while the Namibian border is at Wenela near Katima Mulilo.

Tanzania The main border by road, and the only crossing by train, is between Nakonde (Zambia) and Tunduma (Tanzania).

Zimbabwe There are three easy crossings: at Chirundu, along the road between Lusaka and Harare; between Siavonga (Zambia) and Kariba (Zimbabwe), about 50km upstream from Chirundu; and between Livingstone (Zambia) and Victoria Falls town (Zimbabwe).

BOTSWANA

See p667 for detailed information about crossing the border into Botswana from Zambia with your own vehicle or via public transport.

A quicker and more comfortable (but more expensive) way to reach Botswana from Zambia is to cross from Livingstone to Victoria Falls (in Zimbabwe), from where shuttle buses head to Kasane – refer to the Victoria Falls chapter (p604) for details. Buses to Gaborone, via Kasane and Francistown, leave several days a week from Lusaka (see p641).

MALAWI

See p652 for detailed information about crossing the border into Malawi via the main border crossing near Chipata on the Lusaka–Lilongwe road.

Further north is another border crossing at Nakonde. Going either way on public transport is very difficult – you really need your own wheels. Coming from Malawi into Zambia, the Malawi border crossing is at Chitipa, which is a 60km drive along a very bad road from Karonga (which takes about four hours). There are some *matola* (pickups) and minibuses that go along that route (about MK500), but they are very infrequent. The Malawi border crossing is five kilometres out of Chipata. Then it's another 80km (three- to four-hour drive) to the Zambia immigration post at Nakonde. The only way to get past this bit without a car is to hitch on a truck, but vehicles are infrequent on this road. At Nakonde you can get a bus to Mpika for around ZK100,000.

MOZAMBIQUE

There is no public transport between Zambia and Mozambique and the only common border leads to a remote part of Mozambique. The main crossing is at Luangwa, just to the east of the Lower Zambezi National Park and about 100km south of the Great East Road. There's another crossing south of Katete on the Great East Road, about 80km southwest of Chipata.

Most travellers choose to visit Mozambique from Lilongwe in Malawi.

NAMIBIA

See p668 for detailed information about crossing the border into Namibia from Zambia with your own vehicle or via public transport. Alternatively, cross from Livingstone to Victoria Falls (in Zimbabwe) and catch a shuttle bus to Windhoek.

See p640 and p667 for information about buses to Sesheke, the Zambian border town, from Lusaka and Livingstone respectively.

On the Namibian side, it's a 5km walk to Katima Mulilo, from where minibuses depart for other parts of the country.

SOUTH AFRICA

There is no border between Zambia and South Africa, however, several buses travel daily between Jo'burg and Lusaka (see p640 for details), travelling via Harare and Masvingo in Zimbabwe. But make sure you have a Zimbabwean visa (if you need one before arrival) and a yellow-fever certificate for entering South Africa (and, possibly, Zimbabwe).

TANZANIA

Although travelling by bus to the border is quicker, the train is a better, more comfortable alternative.

See p640 for details about buses from Lusaka to Dar es Salaam. Alternatively, walk across the border from Nakonde, and take a minibus from Tunduma to Mbeya in Tanzania.

The Tazara railway company usually runs two international trains per week in each direction between Kapiri Mposhi (207km north of Lusaka) and Dar es Salaam. The 'express train' leaves Kapiri Mposhi at 5.15pm on Tuesday, while the 'ordinary train' leaves Kapiri Mposhi at 5.15pm on Friday. The journey time for both trains is 48 hours and the fares on the express train for 1st/2nd/3rd class are ZK237,000/198,000/145,000 respectively (1st and 2nd class are sleeping compartments) and ZK187,000/151,000/125,000 on the ordinary train. A discount of 50% is possible with a student card.

Tickets are available on the spot at the New Kapiri Mposhi (Tazara) train station in Kapiri Mposhi and up to three days in advance from **Tazara House** (Map pp634-5; ☎ 0211-222280; Independence Ave, Lusaka). If there are no more seats left at the Lusaka office, don't despair because we've heard from travellers who were able to buy tickets at Kapiri Mposhi, and upgraded from one class to another while on board.

It's prudent to get a Tanzanian visa in Lusaka (or elsewhere), see p679, before you board the train; at least, contact the Tanzanian high commission in Lusaka about getting a Tanzanian visa on the train or at the border. You can change money on the train, but take care because these guys can be sharks.

ZIMBABWE

Plenty of buses travel every day between Lusaka and Harare, via Chirundu – see p640 for details. If you're travelling from Siavonga, take a minibus or charter a car to the border, and walk (or take a shared taxi) across the impressive Kariba Dam to Kariba, from where buses leave daily to Harare. Most travellers cross at Livingstone – see p613 for details.

GETTING AROUND

Air

The main domestic airports are at Lusaka, Livingstone, Ndola, Kitwe, Mfuwe, Kasama and Kasaba Bay, though dozens of minor airstrips cater for chartered planes.

AIRLINES IN ZAMBIA

There are plenty of charter services in Zambia, but only one airline offers scheduled flights. **Proflight Zambia** (www.proflight-zambia.com) has filled the domestic gap since Zambian Airways went out of business and is flying regularly (up to two or three times daily) from Lusaka to Mfuwe (for South Luangwa National Park), Lower Zambezi, Livingstone (for Victoria Falls) and Ndola.

Charter-flight companies cater for guests staying at upmarket lodges/camps in national parks. Charter flights only leave with a minimum number of prebooked passengers and fares are always high, but it's sometimes worth looking around for a last-minute flight. Check for special deals advertised in

DOMESTIC DEPARTURE TAX

The departure tax for domestic flights is US$8. It is *not* included in the price of airline tickets bought in or outside of Zambia, and must be paid at the airport in US dollars.

Lowdown magazine, available at bookshops in Lusaka.

Bicycle

If you plan on cycling around Zambia, do realise that Zambian drivers tend not to give you any room, even if there is no vehicle in the oncoming lane. Save being hit by a car, it is safe to cycle Zambia. Mountain biking is rapidly becoming popular in and around Lusaka. The two best places to purchase mountain bikes are in Lusaka: **CycleMart** (Map pp634-5; ☎ 222062; cnr Chachacha & Malasha Rds; 🕑 8am-5pm Mon-Fri, to 1pm Sat) and **Game** (Map pp634-5; Manda Hill Shopping Centre, Great East Road). Road cyclists will have to bring their own bikes and gear.

Bus & Minibus

Distances are long, buses are often slow and many roads are badly potholed, so travelling around Zambia by bus and minibus can exhaust even the hardiest of travellers, even if they *do* like a good butt massage.

All main routes are served by ordinary public buses, which either run on a fill-up-and-go basis or have fixed departures (these are called 'time buses'). 'Express buses' are faster – often terrifyingly so – and stop less, but cost about 15% more. In addition, several private companies run comfortable European-style express buses along the major routes, eg between Lusaka and Livingstone, Lusaka and Chipata, and Lusaka and the Copperbelt region. These fares cost about 25% more than the ordinary bus fares and are well worth the extra kwacha. Tickets for these buses can often be bought the day before. See p640 for more on express buses zipping around the country.

Many routes are also served by minibuses, which only leave when full – so full that you might lose all feeling in one butt cheek. Their fares can be more or less the same as ordinary buses. In remote areas the only public transport is often a truck or pick-up.

Car & Motorcycle

BRING YOUR OWN VEHICLE

If you're driving into Zambia via a rented or privately owned car or motorcycle, you will need a carnet; if you don't have one, a free Customs Importation Permit will be issued to you at major borders instead. You'll also be charged a carbon tax if it's a non-Zambian registered vehicle; which just means a bit more paperwork and about ZK200,000 at the border depending on the size of your car.

While it is certainly possible to get around Zambia by car or motorbike, many sealed roads are in bad condition and the dirt roads can range from shocking to impassable, particularly after the rains. If you haven't driven in Africa before, this is not the best place to start. We strongly recommend that you hire a 4WD if driving anywhere outside Lusaka, and certainly if you're heading to any of the national parks or other wilderness areas. Wearing a seat belt in the front seat is compulsory.

DRIVING LICENCE

Foreign licences are fine as long as they are in English, and it doesn't hurt to carry an international driver's licence (also in English).

FUEL & SPARE PARTS

Diesel costs around ZK5500 per litre and petrol ZK6500. Shortages do occur from time to time. Distances between towns with filling stations are great and fuel is not always available, so fill the tank at every opportunity.

It is advisable to carry at least one spare wheel, as well as a filled jerry can, though petrol is far more volatile than diesel. For spare parts, the easiest (and cheapest) to find are those of Toyota and Nissan.

HIRE

Cars can be hired from international and Zambian-owned companies in Lusaka, Livingstone, Kitwe and Ndola, but renting is expensive, so consider hiring a car in a neighbouring country and taking it across to Zambia. Avis, Europcar, and Voyagers/Imperial are at Lusaka airport.

Voyagers/Imperial Car Rental (www.voyagerszambia.com/imperialrates.htm) charges from US$43 per day for the smallest vehicle, plus US$0.32 per kilometre (less per day for longer rental periods). Add to this insurance (from US$26 per day), VAT (17.5%) and petrol. Other companies, such as **4x4 Hire Africa** (www.4x4hireafrica.com), rent old-school Land Rover vehicles, unequipped or fully decked out with everything you would need for a trip to the bush, with prices for an unequipped vehicle starting at about US$120 per day. The best thing about this company is that vehicles come with unlimited kilome

ZAMBIA

tres and you can take them across borders, making it easy to nip over to Malawi, Chobe National Park in Botswana or the Caprivi Strip in Namibia.

Most companies insist that drivers are at least 23 years old and have held a licence for at least five years.

INSURANCE

Compulsory third-party insurance for Zambia is available at major borders (or the nearest large towns) and costs about US$12 per month. However, it is strongly advised to carry insurance from your own country on top of your Zambian policy.

ROAD CONDITIONS

While many main stretches of sealed road are OK, be aware that sections of minor roads and even highways (such as west to Mongu or south to Livingstone) can be in a pretty bad way, with gaping potholes, ridges, dips and very narrow sections that drop steeply off the side into loose gravel. Be wary and alert at all times. Gravel roads vary a lot from pretty good to pretty terrible. Road conditions are probably at their worst soon after the end of the wet season (April, May, June) when many dirt and gravel roads have been washed away or seriously damaged – this is especially the case in and around national parks. Seriously consider travelling by 4WD if using a private vehicle – it's compulsory if you're visiting national parks.

ROAD RULES

Speed limits in and around cities are enforced, though on the open road buses and Land Cruisers fly at speeds of 140kph to 160kph. Beware of vehicles in front of you that signal; if they signal right, it could mean that they are turning, or that there is another vehicle in the oncoming lane. If the vehicle signals left, they are turning or the oncoming lane is clear and you can pass. Or else, it's possible that their signal lights are simply broken.

If you break down, you must place orange triangles about 6m in front of and behind the vehicle.

Hitching

Despite the general warning (see p765), hitching is a common way to get around Zambia. Some drivers, particularly expats, may offer you free lifts, but you should expect to pay for rides with local drivers (normally about the same as the bus fare, depending on the comfort of the vehicle). In such cases, agree on a price beforehand.

Local Transport

The minibuses that zip around main roads in all cities and larger towns are quick and plentiful. For more comfort, however, taxis are also very good value. They have no meters, so rates are negotiable.

Tours

Tours and safaris around Zambia invariably focus on the national parks. Since many of these parks are hard to visit without a vehicle, joining a tour might be your only option anyway. Budget-priced operators run scheduled trips, or arrange things on the spot (with enough passengers), and can often be booked through a hostel. Upmarket companies prefer to take bookings in advance, directly or through an agent in Zambia (see p633), South Africa or your home country.

For companies running tours around Zambia as part of wider trips around Southern Africa, see p760. Most Zambian tour operators are based in Lusaka or Livingstone. Several companies in Lilongwe (Malawi) may also offer tours to South Luangwa National Park.

Train

The Tazara trains between Kapiri Mposhi and Dar es Salaam in Tanzania (see p681) can also be used for travel to/from northern Zambia. While the Lusaka–Kitwe service does stop at Kapiri Mposhi, the Lusaka–Kitwe and Tazara trains are not timed to connect with each other, and the domestic and international train station are 2km apart.

Zambia's only other railway services are the 'ordinary trains' between Lusaka and Kitwe, via Kapiri Mposhi and Ndola, and the 'express trains' between Lusaka and Livingstone. Refer to the relevant sections for schedules and costs.

Domestic trains are unreliable and slow, so buses are always better. Conditions on domestic trains generally range from slightly dilapidated to ready-for-scrap. Most compartments have no lights or locks, so take a torch and something to secure the door at night.

Tickets for all classes on domestic trains (but not the Tazara service) can be bought up to 30 days in advance.

CLASSES

On the 'express train' between Lusaka and Livingstone, a 'sleeper' is a compartment for two people; 1st class is a sleeper for four; 2nd (or 'standard') class is a sleeper for six; and 'economy' (or 3rd) class is a seat only. On the 'ordinary train' between Lusaka and Kitwe, 'standard' class is also just a seat. Sometimes the domestic services will only have economy or standard class available – just a seat.

Zimbabwe

Zimbabwe continues to dip in and out of international headlines, often creating an unclear but daunting vibe for prospective visitors. In 2008 the economy finally collapsed and there was a cholera outbreak that killed around 4000 people. But in February 2009 many Zimbabweans dared to dream (again) when Robert Mugabe's 29-year-old regime formed a unity government with the opposition. Today, the cholera has abated, the economy has dollarised and, at least in the urban areas, things are easier.

There remain, of course, plenty of reasons for the world's media to focus on Zimbabwe. However, tourists will experience something worlds apart from outside perceptions. From the absolute wilderness of Mana Pools National Park to the serene capital, Zimbabwe remains the one of Southern Africa's most beautiful and – right now – untouristed countries.

Having been forced to sacrifice so many things, Zimbabweans are resilient and down-to-earth. They have a community spirit that could teach the world a lesson, together with an extraordinary ability to make something stunning out of nothing: music, art, craft and luxury tented camps in the wilderness. With so few visiting the country, those who do can expect royal treatment. They need you.

Zimbabwe is no longer as dirt cheap as it once was, but it's not expensive either and, best of all, its record-breaking inflation stories are consigned to history. Whether you arrange everything through a tour operator or figure it out for yourself, a country of charm, beauty and intrigue awaits. Oh, and Zimbabwe's got one of the world's best climates…even the worst politicking can't destroy that.

FAST FACTS

- **Area** 390,580 sq km (slightly larger than Germany)
- **Capital** Harare
- **Country code** ☎ 263
- **Famous for** Victoria Falls, Mana Pools, Hwange National Park, Zambezi River canoe safaris, Robert Mugabe
- **Languages** English, Shona, Ndebele
- **Money** The US dollar is now used legally throughout Zimbabwe
- **Phrases** *Siyabonga kakulu* (thank you; Ndebele); *tatenda* (thank you; Shona)
- **Population** 13 million (officially, though up to three million Zimbabweans are thought to have emigrated since 2001)

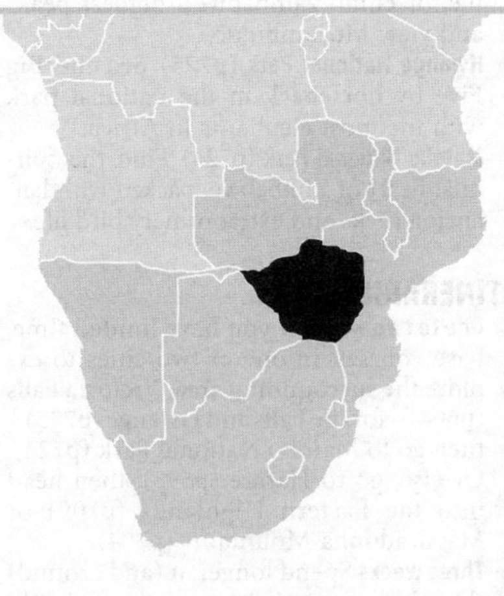

HOW MUCH?

- Wooden carving US$1-100
- Soapstone sculpture US$2-200
- Steak US$7
- Sunscreen US$7
- Safari US$50-350

LONELY PLANET INDEX

- 1L of petrol US$1.20
- 1L of bottled water US$0.80
- Bottle of beer US$3
- Souvenir T-shirt US$20
- Plate of chips US$1

HIGHLIGHTS

- **Lake Kariba and Matusadona National Park** (p706) See wildlife close up as you safari on boats and the Big Five drink, swim and live in the same water as you.
- **Mana Pools** (p707) Visit Africa's only national park (with lions) that allows unguided walking safaris, then canoe the Zambezi past hippos and crocs.
- **Harare** (p695) Shop for crafts and don't miss the incredible HIFA – Harare's International Festival of the Arts – in the last week of April.
- **Eastern Highlands** (p709) Fish, golf, gamble, or climb Zimbabwe's highest peaks and view Mozambique.
- **Hwange National Park** (p725) See the Big Five by horseback in the national park with the most elephants in Africa.
- **Matobo National Park** (p724) Find the spiritual heart of Zimbabwe, packed with balancing rocks and extraordinary bird life.

ITINERARIES

- **One to two weeks** If you have limited time, base yourself in one of two cities to explore the surrounding area: Victoria Falls (p604) – for the Falls and Hwange (p725) – then go to Matobo National Park (p724). Or else, go to Harare (p695), then head into the Eastern Highlands (p709) or Mavuradonha Mountains (p704).
- **Three weeks** Spend longer at (and around) the places mentioned above, and add in either Nyanga (p713), Lake Kariba (p704) or Mana Pools National Park (p707). Alternatively, try a semicircular route: Victoria Falls (p604), Hwange National Park (p725), Bulawayo (p721), Gweru (p717), Masvingo (p718), Mutare (p709), the Eastern Highlands (p709), Harare (p695), Kariba (p704) and Mana Pools National Park (p707).
- **One month** One excellent route: fly Johannesburg to Victoria Falls (see p604), spend a few days there, then be driven to Hwange National Park (p725) for a stunning safari far from the madding crowds. Then fly to Harare (p695) and take a road trip to the Bvumba Mountains (p711) overlooking Mozambique. Another option: land in Harare, take a charter flight to Lake Kariba (p706) or Mana Pools (p707) on the banks of the Zambezi, safari, fish, then fly back to Harare and drive south for three hours to Masvingo (p718) and the Great Zimbabwe (p718) ruins.

CLIMATE & WHEN TO GO

Zimbabwe enjoys a wonderfully temperate climate all year round. The cool, dry months (April to October) have warm, sunny days and cold, clear nights. The low-lying areas of the south and the Zambezi Valley to the north and west enjoy warm temperatures all year.

The 'rainy season' lasts around three months, sometime between November and April. Afternoon electrical rainstorms are dramatic, and stunning to watch if you are safely indoors – Zimbabwe has the second-

SHOULD YOU GO?

If your only doubts about holidaying to Zimbabwe concern your dollars going to government cronies, then pack away your worries and get out your passport. Yes, the government has a stake in some hotels and the national airline, but other than that there are thousands of talented sculptors, guides, small businesses, waiters and artists who are all on the breadline because tourism has all but dried up in Zimbabwe. They need you in Zimbabwe, both for your business and your tips, but also so that the country and its people continue to get an outsider's perspective. There could be nothing worse for everyday Zimbabweans than a boycott from tourists.

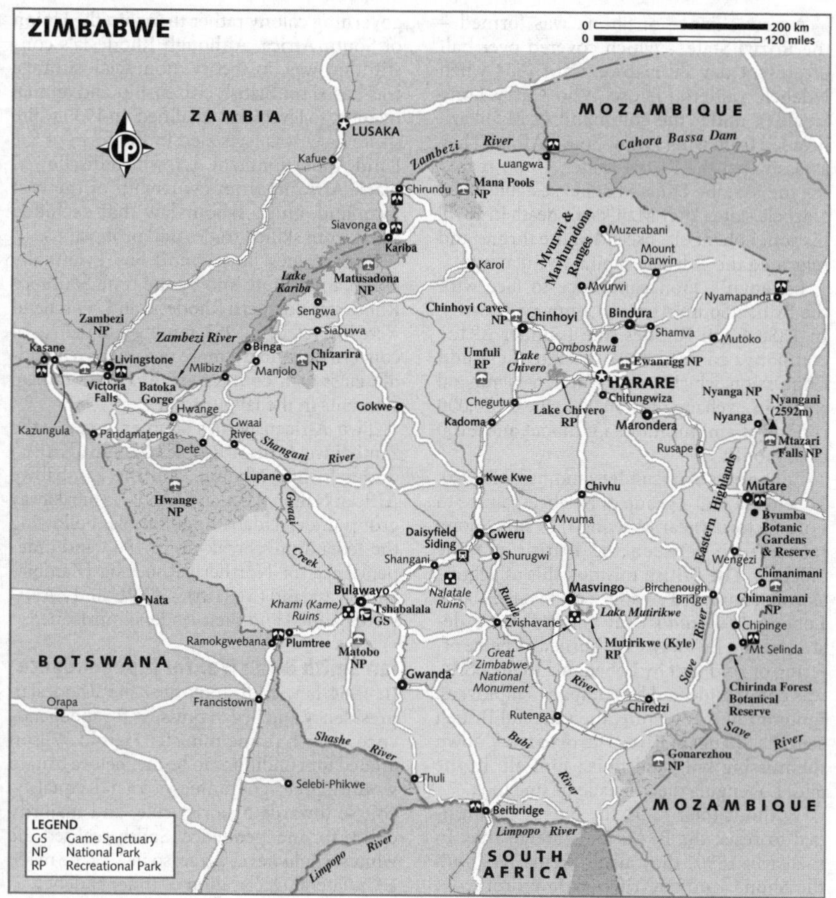

highest incidence of lightning strikes in the world, so be careful.

Winter, consisting of several dry months, is the best time for wildlife viewing because animals tend to congregate at the diminishing water holes. It is also the best time for white-water rafting at Vic Falls. At the end of winter, September/October, enormous herds of elephants are commonly seen. This can also be the best time for canoeing the Zambezi, while April and Christmas are the most popular times for houseboats.

HISTORY

For the precolonial history of the area that became Zimbabwe, along with the rest of Southern Africa, see p32.

The Shona Kingdoms & the Portuguese

In the 11th century, the city of Great Zimbabwe was wealthy and powerful from trading gold and ivory for glass, porcelain and cloth from Asia with Swahili traders. However, by the 15th century, its influence was in decline because of overpopulation, overgrazing, political fragmentation and uprisings.

During this twilight period, Shona dynasties fractured into autonomous states. In the 16th century Portuguese traders arrived in search of riches and golden cities in the vast empire of Mwene Mutapa (or 'Monomatapa' to the Europeans). They hoped to find King Solomon's mines and the mysterious land of Ophir.

A new alliance of Shona was formed – the Rozwi State – which covered over half of present-day Zimbabwe, until 1834 when Ndebele raiders (Those Who Carry Long Shields), under the command of Mzilikazi, invaded from what is now South Africa. They assassinated the Rozwi leader. Upon reaching the Matobo Hills, Mzilikazi established a Ndebele state. After Mzilikazi's death in 1870, his son, Lobengula, ascended the throne and relocated the Ndebele capital to Bulawayo.

Lobengula soon came face to face with the British South African Company (BSAC). In 1888 Cecil Rhodes, the founder of the company, coerced him to sign the Rudd Concession, which granted foreigners mineral rights in exchange for 10,000 rifles, 100,000 rounds of ammunition, a gunboat and £100 each month.

But a series of misunderstandings followed. Lobengula sent a group of Ndebele raiders to Fort Victoria (near Masvingo) to stop Shona interference between the British and the Ndebele. The British mistook this as aggression and launched an attack on Matabeleland. Lobengula's *kraals* (hut villages) were destroyed and Bulawayo was burned. A peace offering of gold sent by Lobengula to the BSAC was commandeered by company employees. Ignorant of this gesture, the vengeful British sent the Shangani River Patrol to track down the missing king and finish him off. In the end, Lobengula died in exile of smallpox.

Without their king, the Ndebele continued to resist the BSAC and foreign rule. In the early 1890s they allied themselves with the Shona, and guerrilla warfare broke out against the BSAC in the Matobo Hills. When Rhodes suggested a negotiated settlement, the Ndebele, with their depleted numbers, couldn't refuse.

Meanwhile, finding little gold, the colonists appropriated farmlands on the Mashonaland Plateau. By 1895 the new country was being called Rhodesia, after its heavy-handed founder, and a white legislature was set up. European immigration began in earnest: by 1904 there were some 12,000 settlers in the country, and seven years later the figure had doubled.

Beginnings of Nationalism

Conflicts between blacks and whites came into sharp focus after the 1922 referendum in which the whites chose to become a self-governing colony rather than join the Union of South Africa. Although Rhodesia's constitution was, in theory, nonracial, suffrage was based on British citizenship and annual income, so few blacks qualified. In 1930 white supremacy was legislated in the form of the Land Apportionment Act, which disallowed black Africans from ownership of the best farmland, and a labour law that excluded them from skilled trades and professions.

Poor wages and conditions eventually led to a rebellion, and by the time Southern Rhodesia, Northern Rhodesia and Nyasaland were federated, in 1953, mining and industrial concerns favoured a more racially mixed middle class as a counterweight to the radical elements in the labour force.

Two African parties soon emerged – the Zimbabwe African People's Union (ZAPU) under Joshua Nkomo, and the Zimbabwe African National Union (ZANU), a breakaway group under Ndabaningi Sithole. Following the federation's break-up in 1963 and independence for Northern Rhodesia (Zambia) and Nyasaland (Malawi) – ZAPU and ZANU were banned and their leaders imprisoned.

Ian Smith & the War for Independence

In 1964 Ian Smith took over the Rhodesian presidency and began pressing for independence. British prime minister Harold Wilson argued for conditions to be met before Britain would agree: guarantee of racial equality, course towards majority rule, and majority desire for independence. Smith realised the whites would never agree, so in 1965 he made a Unilateral Declaration of Independence.

Britain responded by declaring Smith's action illegal and imposed economic sanctions, which were also adopted by the UN in 1968 (in fact, sanctions were ignored by most Western countries and even by some British companies). Meanwhile, ZANU and ZAPU opted for guerrilla warfare. Their raids struck deeper into the country with increasing ferocity, and whites, most of whom had been born in Africa and knew no other home, abandoned their properties.

On 11 December 1974, South Africa's John Vorster and Zambia's Kenneth Kaunda persuaded Smith to call a ceasefire and release high-ranking nationalists – including Robert Mugabe – and to begin peace negotiations. The talks, however, broke down; ZANU split and Mugabe fled to Mozambique. The following year, ZANU chairman Herbert Chitepo was assassinated in Lusaka by Rhodesian intelligence.

The nationalist groups fragmented and reformed. ZANU and ZAPU created an alliance known as the Patriotic Front (PF), and their military arms – Zipra and Zanla – combined to form the Zimbabwe People's Army.

Smith, facing wholesale white emigration and a collapsing economy, was forced to try an 'internal settlement': Sithole, and the leader of the African National Congress (ANC), Abel Muzorewa, joined a so-called 'transitional government' in which whites were guaranteed 28 out of the 100 parliamentary seats; veto over all legislation for 10 years; guarantee of their property and pension rights; and control of the armed forces, police, judiciary and civil service. And an amnesty was declared for PF guerrillas.

The effort was a dismal failure. Indeed, the only result was an escalation of the war. To salvage the settlement, Smith entered into secret negotiations with Nkomo, offering to ditch both Sithole and Muzorewa, but Nkomo proved to be intransigent. Finally, Smith was forced to call a general, nonracial election and hand over leadership to Muzorewa, but on much the same conditions as the 'internal settlement'.

Independence

On 10 September 1979, delegations met at Lancaster House, London, to draw up a constitution favourable to both the PF of Nkomo and Mugabe, and the Zimbabwean Rhodesian government of Muzorewa and Smith. Mugabe, who wanted ultimate power, initially refused to make any concessions, but after 14 weeks the Lancaster House Agreement was reached. It guaranteed whites (then 3% of the population) 20 of the 100 parliamentary seats.

In the carefully monitored election of 4 March 1980, Mugabe prevailed by a wide margin and Zimbabwe and its majority-rule government joined the ranks of Africa's independent nations.

Soon after, the economy soared, wages increased, and basic social programs – notably education and health care – were initiated. However, the initial euphoria, unity and optimism quickly faded: a resurgence of rivalry between ZANU (run mostly by Shona people) and ZAPU (mostly by Ndebele) escalated into armed conflict, and the ZAPU leader, Nkomo, was accused of plotting against the government. Guerrilla activity resumed in ZAPU areas of Matabeleland, and Mugabe deployed the North Korean–trained Fifth Brigade in early 1983 to quell the disturbances. Villagers were gunned down and prominent members of ZAPU were eliminated in order to root out 'dissidents'. The result was massacres in which tens of thousands of civilians, sometimes entire villages, were slaughtered. A world that was eager to revere Mr Mugabe closed its eyes. The eyes of Zimbabweans were forced shut.

Nkomo, meanwhile, fled to England until Mugabe (realising the strife threatened to erupt into civil war) publicly relented and guaranteed his safe return. Talks resulted in a ZAPU and ZANU confederation (called ZANU-PF) and amnesty for the dissidents, thereby masterfully sweeping the matter – but not the underlying discontent – under the rug. Zimbabwe's one-party state had begun. Mugabe had his dream. Zimbabweans' nightmare was just beginning.

Life as the Opposition

In 1999 thousands attended a Zimbabwe Congress of Trade Unions (ZCTU) rally to launch the Movement for Democratic Change (MDC). Morgan Tsvangirai, the secretary general, stated he would lead a social democratic party fighting for workers' interests. The arrival of the MDC brought waves of new hope and real opportunity for the end of Mugabe's era.

In 2000, Mugabe's chief propaganda architect, Jonathan Moyo, led the president's campaign for a new constitution. Three months later – and despite the full weight of state media and Treasury – the president's constitution was given the thumbs down by the people. It was Mugabe's first defeat and it notified him of MDC's very real strength at the ballot box. A parliamentary election was due later that year. Ironically, the MDC's greatest success would soon lead to a nasty defeat.

Mugabe responded to the threat of defeat with waves of violence, voter intimidation, and a chaotic and destructive land-reform program. Despite this, and the election being damned by the US and EU as 'neither free nor fair', the MDC lost by a mere four seats. Two years later Mugabe's rule was under even greater threat during the country's presidential elections. Again, an election marred by violence and intimidation, backed by a new set of repressive laws, with no independent monitors and huge numbers of voters turned away, was stolen by Mugabe.

The next parliamentary election – in 2005 – was not so close. Mugabe and his security and propaganda networks had had five years since 2000 to readjust the playing field. Newspapers were closed (bombed in one case); the state dominated print, radio and TV; voters were bought with food (and threatened with no food); the leader of the opposition, Morgan Tsvangirai, went through two treason trials; and up to one million ghost voters were created on the role. Mugabe won the elections.

Mugabe's toughest ever electoral challenges came in 2008 in the presidential and parliamentary elections. Although the MDC led by Morgan Tsvangirai had been able to campaign in rural areas that were closed to it in previous elections, the 2008 election was again seen as deeply flawed, with areas where the number of votes cast exceeded the number of enrolled voters. Following election day, with growing signs that Mugabe had lost, Mugabe's men took more than a month to 'count' votes. When they were finally announced, Tsvangirai won 47.9% against Mugabe's 43.2%. With neither man having attained 50%, a second round of voting was needed, before which Mugabe's ruling ZANU-PF unleashed waves of brutal violence across the countryside. MDC supporters who had shown their allegiance to the party before the first round of voting were now easily identified. Scores – perhaps hundreds – were killed, many more tortured, and thousands fled. In an attempt to stop some of the violence against his supporters, Tsvangirai withdrew from the second round a week before it was scheduled to take place. The second round went ahead anyway, and led to yet another victory for Mugabe.

But while South Africa under then-president Thabo Mbeki continued to fail Zimbabweans and support Mugabe, pressure from other areas was growing. The economy had officially collapsed, Mugabe could not pay his army or civil service, and then came the cholera.

In February 2009, Morgan Tsvangirai signed a coalition deal with Zanu-PF, a mutual promise to restore the rule of law and to 'ensure security of tenure to all land holders'. Nonetheless, the violence and evictions continued. At the time of writing, MDC was in government with Mugabe's party, but largely impotent. The ever-pervading Zimbabwean optimism that things would 'come right' still existed, despite no actual basis for it. But with the 'dollarisation' of the economy, life in the urban areas had become easier. The supermarkets were full of local and imported food, albeit with prices similar to those in the West. Life in rural areas remains extremely arduous.

Mass protests – even rumoured coups – were continually 'planned' against the government, but this young population, who has grown up in a culture of fear and repression, would rather try and feed their families than fight the well-armed state.

THE CULTURE

The National Psyche

No matter what their race, Zimbabweans have a stoicism reminiscent of bygone eras. In Zimbabwe, the Southern African expres-

THE PARADOX THAT IS ZIMBABWE

Zimbabwe is a funny place: so perfect in terms of climate and natural beauty. The winter is dry and gentle, with dwarfing blue skies and odd, scant clouds. In October, just before summer, the country heaves with blooming jacaranda trees. The economic breakdown caused all development – and even maintenance by municipal councils – to stop; now grass grows as tall as trees wherever there aren't buildings, giving parts of the capital, Harare, the look of being reclaimed by the lowveld.

The standard of living for residents has fallen dramatically over the last 10 years, and Zimbabwe in the time of Mugabe and cholera saw thousands die, millions suffer acutely and others struggle day to day with weeks of no electricity or functioning telephone networks.

Every African country has its own set of challenges, and this is true for Zimbabwe, including for the thousands of desperate – yet optimistic – and incredibly talented sculptors, guides, small businesses, waiters and artists who live on the breadline. So, although it is no longer dirt cheap, the traveller these days will find it safe and easy in a country oft and aptly called a wonderland.

MONEY MATTERS – THE SWITCH TO AMERICAN DOLLARS

For those who are jaded by Zimbabwean hyperinflation stories and, given that anything written on the matter is dated as soon as it is written, here is one final word on the matter: from the end of 2007 to the end of 2008, the real rate of inflation in Zimbabwe was seven sextillion per cent. Then the economy finally collapsed. The country has now switched from Zimbabwean dollars to US dollars. At first costs quadrupled in real terms because Zimbabwean retailers, used to hyperinflation, knew only how to jack their prices right up, but they soon realised they could stabilise prices.

The use of US dollars was a crime until the end of 2008, so it was a feeble face-saving effort when the government claimed the only reason for finally allowing US dollars was to accustom the population to dealing with the said currency in time for the 2010 World Cup, when an influx of tourists is expected. Officially, the country is a 'multicurrency' economy where sterling, pula, rand and US dollars are accepted. The bottom line is good and bad news for the traveller to Zimbabwe. No longer will you have to change money, but it does mean that Zimbabwe has gone from being one of the best-value-for-money African countries to visit to one where prices are similar to those at home.

sion to 'make a plan' can be defined as: 'If it's broke, fix it. If you can't fix it, live with it, or, change your life' (overnight if need be). This kind of mental strength and generosity, combined with a deep love of Zimbabwe, are the keys to their survival.

Daily Life

Unfortunately, Zimbabwe's great gains made since independence – life expectancy, education, health – have all been reversed since 1998 (due to gross mismanagement, corruption, and HIV/AIDS).

Certainly, many Zimbabweans experience major difficulties in their day-to-day lives. For the masses, basics such as water and electricity are hardly available. There was a cholera outbreak at the end of 2008 to which the government was unable to respond as the health sector had collapsed. The general hospitals in Harare were effectively closed (as there was no medicine and no staff) and even private clinics with money (Zim dollars) were unable to import necessary supplies or to adequately maintain equipment.

Dollarisation – at the beginning of 2009 – solved many problems for those with access to cash (see the boxed text, above). So at the time of writing, things were looking up. Diaspora funding has always buoyed the economy, which avoided collapse for years longer than it should have. It is estimated that 60% of Zimbabweans have someone from the diaspora sending them money. Those who do not – and are in rural areas – remain dangerously below the poverty line.

Somehow, despite the immense hardship for everyday Zimbabweans, crime still remains relatively low.

Population

About 65% of the population lives in rural areas, while around 40% of the population is under 18 years old. The average life expectancy is about 40 years.

Most Zimbabweans are of Bantu origin; 9.8 million belong to various Shona groups and about 2.3 million are Ndebele. The remainder are divided between the Tonga (or Batonga) people of the upper Kariba area, the Shangaan (or Hlengwe) of the lowveld, and the Venda of the far south. Europeans (18,000), Asians (10,000), and mixed Europeans and Africans (25,000) are scattered around the country.

SPORT

For a long time Zimbabwe punched well above its weight in sport, due largely to good administration and an ideal climate for getting outdoors. The team did well in its number-one passion, football (soccer), constantly upset heavyweights in cricket, produced some cracking tennis players, and won Olympic gold.

However, Zimbabwe's sporting teams have followed the same trajectory as the country's economy.

Zimbabwe had a rare sporting reason to smile when their darling swim star, Kirsty Coventry, won gold at the 2004 Olympics, and then backed it up with a gold and three silver at Beijing in 2008. She was then described by the head of Zimbabwe's

Olympic Committee, Paul Chingoka, as 'our national treasure'.

RELIGION

The majority of Zimbabweans are Christian, although traditional spiritual beliefs and customs are still practised, especially in rural areas, where merciless economic times have led to an increase in faith (and fraud).

Noticing this drive towards religion, more and more government ministers are tying themselves to the church. Most worryingly, perhaps, senior church leaders are tying themselves to government. For years concerned church leaders have tried to meet President Mugabe (a Jesuit-educated Catholic). In mid-2006 the president finally agreed. In a country with the lowest life expectancy for women, the highest rises in child mortality, and the world's fastest-falling economy, it was a God-given opportunity for church leaders to discuss the suffering of Zimbabweans.

Somehow, though, the church leaders lost their nerve. At the end of the meeting the head of the delegation and president of the Zimbabwe Council of Churches told national TV cameras that, 'we know we have a government that we must support, interact with and draw attention to concerns. Those of us who have different ideas about this country must know we have a government who listens.'

ARTS & CRAFTS

Zimbabwe's festivals, fairs and streetside stalls, live music and poetry, dance, art and sculpture are great expressions of Zimbabwe and a wonderful way for visitors to meet the locals and learn about their lives. Most Zimbabweans are creative in some way: whether they bead, embroider, weave, sculpt or carve.

For information on music in Southern Africa, see p48.

ZIMBABWEAN SCULPTURES

The word 'Zimbabwe' means 'great stone house', so it is fitting that stone sculpture – also referred to as Shona sculpture – is the art form that most represents the people of Zimbabwe. The exuberance of the work, the vast varieties of stone, and the great skill and imagination of the sculptors has led to many major, critically acclaimed exhibitions worldwide over the years. Zimbabwean stone sculptures are a truly contemporary force that works successfully with its ancient cultural heritage. The art is direct, powerfully human and often extremely beautiful.

Literature

Easy to find before you travel and most contemporary, *Mukiwa* (A White Boy in Africa) and its sequel, *When a Crocodile Eats the Sun*, by Peter Godwin, are engrossing memoirs detailing the life of a small boy who witnesses the death of his neighbour by guerrillas, the beginning of the end of white rule in Africa and, eventually, life as an adult journalist in the beginning of the economic and political downward spiral. Likewise, *Don't Let's Go to the Dogs Tonight – An African Childhood*, by Alexandra Fuller, is about nature and loss, and the unbreakable bond some people have with Africa, the continent that comes to define, shape, scare and heal them.

Since independence, Zimbabwean literature has focused on the struggle to build a new society. *Harvest of Thorns*, by Shimmer Chinodya, on the Second War for Independence, won the 1992 Commonwealth Prize for Literature. Another internationally renowned writer, Chenjerai Hove, wrote the war-inspired *Bones*, the tragic *Shadows* and the humorous *Shebeen Tales*.

ENVIRONMENT

The Land

Landlocked Zimbabwe is roughly three times the size of England. It lies within both tropics and consists of middleveld and highveld plateaus; 900m to 1700m above sea level. A low ridge, running northeast to southwest across the country, marks the divide between the Zambezi and Limpopo–Save River systems.

The northwest is characterised by bushveld dotted with rocky hills. The hot, dry lowveld of southern Zimbabwe slopes gradually towards the Limpopo River.

The mountainous region is the east, straddling the border with Mozambique. Zimbabwe's highest peak, Nyangani, rises to 2592m.

There are few countries better placed than Zimbabwe from which to view and study the stars: because Zimbabwe lies in low latitudes, 97% of the celestial sphere of the stars is available for observation. Also, away from the urban areas there is virtually no industrial or light pollution; for much of the year the skies are clear of cloud, the twilight is brief and the night is long.

Wildlife

ANIMALS

The Big Five and most of the animals highlighted in the Wildlife guide (p145) are found in Zimbabwe. The number of elephants is almost at plague proportions, with Hwange having the most out of any park in the world.

Zimbabwe's rivers, dams and lakes are home to 117 species of fish, including the powerful tigerfish, prized by anglers. Its common name comes from the lateral stripes along the body and its large sharp protruding teeth – it is also related to the piranha.

The largest lizards are the leguans (water monitors), docile creatures that are often over

HOW CLOSE UP SHOULD YOU GET? *Rhett Butler*

The issues of elephant riding and walking with lions, and elephant numbers and culling, are some of the most controversial in the wildlife field. For example, my partner of over 25 years in the tourist industry is against any form of elephant culling, while I have always been in favour. Take Hwange for example. There were no permanent water holes there until National Parks started pumping water. Before this, for thousands of years, elephants would have been wet-season visitors to the area, and would have had to leave the area during harsh, dry seasons. Today, due to permanent pumped water holes, the elephants are resident and have bred up to huge numbers, and they inflict massive damage on vegetation, especially around water holes. This is the case in many other areas of the northwest of the country, and in neighbouring Botswana it is even worse, with the beautiful Chobe riverine forest that I knew in my youth reduced to sandy waste with a couple of woolly caper bushes. The diversity of mammals, birds, insects and virtually every other form of life is impoverished. Mammals such as the bushbuck and birds such as Livingstone's Lourie are now rare along the Chobe River. However, my partner will argue that elephants process seeds through their digestive tracts and help spread such species, that the huge amount of dung that the elephants produce enrich the soil and attract insects, that nothing stays the same and that woodland becoming grassland is not a bad thing, that elephants are special and intelligent and more important than the smaller species. Pro-culling lobbies can argue that Stone Age man was a predator on elephants, and thus culling is natural, and also that as we have created wildlife reserves, unless we manage the numbers of species, they will increase unnaturally, as they are unable to migrate. And of course many people have economic interests at stake; local villagers will want to protect their crops and will want the benefit of meat from the culling; tour operators will want lots of elephants as this brings in the tourists; animal protection societies that rely on supporters who are against any killing of animals will be against any form of culling. And nowadays, with the increasing poaching of many species, many people argue that elephant numbers will be reduced by poaching, and thus culling is not appropriate. So when it comes to elephant numbers and culling, you can get a thousand different opinions by speaking to a thousand different people. But if you are asking my opinion, the number of elephants in Zimbabwe should be reduced from the current 70 000 or so to about 30 000.

Moving on to the subject of walking with the lions and elephant riding, I have always been against the domestication of wild animals; it often involves cruelty and sometimes ends in tragedy, with people getting hurt and animals being destroyed for just following their instincts. I am sure that operators do not especially go out of their way to harm any of their animals. Any cruelty to the animals is a form of training – after all adult humans used to beat their young (and still do in Zimbabwe) to instil discipline, so one could argue that a little bit of beating when it comes to training animals could also be justified. The irony is that the majority of your readers would probably support walking with the lions and riding elephants as most visitors from first-world countries think of animals more in the form of pets and livestock, and thus the idea of being close to lions and elephants is appealing; on the other hand when it comes to important conservation issues such as elephant culling they would probably be against it on emotional grounds. In fact, just the wrong way around in my opinion!

Rhett Butler is a conservation expert for Southern Africa

2m long. Other reptiles include geckos, chameleons and legless snake lizards.

There are hundreds of bird species found all over the country, including vultures, storks and herons, and Matobo National Park is home to one-third of the world's eagle species.

PLANTS

The ubiquitous msasa tree is the mascot for Zimbabwe, but in the town centres a multitude of jacarandas and fire trees bloom between September and November, creating a riot of purple mixed with red. All year round, bougainvillea twists over bushes and huge mature trees. Gardens host succulent tropical flowers and palms, and, thanks to the English and their love of gardens, ubiquitous roses and stunning gardens remain one of the happiest colonial legacies.

The Zimbabwean highveld is dominated by *miombo* woodland of which the msasa tree is the most immediately recognisable species. *Miombo* is particularly beautiful in the spring (August to October), when its leaves flush reds and greens. Perhaps the most charismatic lowveld species is the baobab, instantly recognisable from its enormous bulbous trunk and frequently leafless branches. The baobab is one of Africa's most useful and valued trees, providing food and medicine to both humans and animals across the continent.

In among these are towering cactus (euphorbias), aloes and wildflowers.

National Parks

Most of Zimbabwe's national parks are – or contain – Unesco World Heritage Sites. With the current paucity of tourists, you will have the parks and reserves to yourself – or feel as though you do. Close to 20% of Zimbabwe's surface area is protected, or semiprotected, in national parks, privately protected game parks, nature conservancies and recreational parks.

Each of Zimbabwe's national parks has its own special attraction. Hwange National Park (p725) is well known for its abundant wildlife (100 species of animals and 400 species of birds) and for being one of the few great elephant sanctuaries left in Africa – herds of up to 100 can be seen. Matobo National Park (p724) has a bizarre and stunning landscape of round, balancing boulders and has long been considered the centre of spiritual power in Zimbabwe. It is also one of the best places in Zimbabwe to see black rhinos up close. Chimanimani National Park (p715) has lush, top-of-the-world mountain scenery; and Mana Pools National Park (p707) and its Zambezi riverside environment is about walking with the animals – or gently paddling right past them in a canoe.

VISITING PARKS & RESERVES

Zimbabwe's national parks are desperately struggling for revenue. As a result, the parks face constant problems – such as artificially pumped water holes often going dry – and the park-run facilities range from basic to shabby. The main source of revenue for national parks comes through hunters (see p65 for more on hunting). Due to its lack of funds, National Parks & Wildlife Zimbabwe (NPWZ) put some of its camps out for private tender; you can enquire and book these lodges – and NPWZ-run campsites – through the **NPWZ central reservations office** (Map p696; ☎ 706077; fax 726089; national-parks@gta.gov.zw; cnr Borrowdale Rd & Sandringham Dr, Harare; 🕑 8am-4pm Mon-Fri). Alternatively, you can book accommodation through tour operators.

Park entry fees range from US$5 to US$20 per day. Never enter without paying the fee (which constitutes a permit), as national parks are zealously guarded against poaching.

There are different rates for vehicles – none are free – and an average entry fee for a four-seater vehicle is US$5, but exact rates would have to be confirmed when booking. Go to www.zimparks.com for the latest figures.

Environmental Issues

Zimbabwe is dry for at least nine months of the year and many areas suffer from long-term drought. And, as with most environmental issues, each issue negatively impacts on others: soil erodes and food chains break down. On top of this, the Land Grab was not only about agricultural land, but private game parks and conservation areas as well. Poaching, hunting and the destruction of the land has caused serious stress on flora, fauna and the land. Lakes and rivers have also been overfished. This then impacts on those whose lives depend on a properly functioning environment.

To learn more about Zimbabwe's ecological problems, contact **Wildlife & Environment Zimbabwe** (www.zimwild.org) or **Conservation Task Force** (www.zctf.mweb.co.zw), or email marufu@forestry.co.zw for information on forestry issues.

Anyone interested in helping out physically can volunteer for the **Mana Pools Game Count**, which is held over the weekend of the first full moon in September; see p708 for details.

FOOD & DRINK

Food

If you are eating in Victoria Falls, you can have a five-star fine-dining experience of ostrich, warthog, crocodile tail and various members of the antelope family. Otherwise, cafes and restaurants in all the big towns serve Western dishes. The staple for locals is *sadza*, a white maize meal made into either porridge or something resembling mashed potato. The locals are crazy about it, and eat it with tomato-based relishes, meat and/or gravy.

Zimbabwe, once one of the world's great beef producers, still has good beef widely available. Popular fish include trout from rivers or dams in the Eastern Highlands, and bream, or the whitebait-like dried *kapenta*, another staple, both plentiful in Lake Kariba.

The cities and bigger towns offer a variety of restaurants. In Harare they are mostly in converted houses with beautiful gardens. All tourist hotels serve European and vegetarian dishes. Generally the restaurants are good, and a meal will cost US$5 to US$30.

Drinks

NON-ALCOHOLIC DRINKS

The tap water in Zimbabwe is not safe to drink, but bottled mineral water, fruit juices and soft drinks are widely available.

Tea and coffee are grown in the Eastern Highlands. Cafes and restaurants in the cities serve espresso coffee from either local or imported beans, while some establishments, especially away from the main cities, serve instant coffee or chicory. If you are a connoisseur, check when ordering. Nyanga tea is also good and available throughout Zimbabwe.

ALCOHOLIC DRINKS

The religious majority aren't big drinkers, but *chibuku* (also known as scuds), sold in large brown plastic containers, are popular with men. It's a kind of beer made from fermented yeast and sold in bottle shops (sometimes grandly called 'cocktail bars') and township beer halls.

The beer you will more commonly see is lager, which is always served cold. The domestically brewed lagers – Zambezi and Bohlinger's – are really good.

Although the climate isn't suited to grape growing, Zimbabwe does have a small wine industry, particularly east and southeast of Harare. The best safaris include South African and Australian wines in the price and an unlimited supply of spirits (after all, evenings on safari are nothing without gin-and-tonics).

HARARE

☎ 04 / pop 2 million

More attractive than most other Southern African capitals, Harare has enough to do and see to keep visitors satisfied for a day or two. It is a safe, calm and laid-back city. Its best attractions tend to be natural, though the live music and shopping for craft and homewares is excellent. The town centre has high-rise office buildings ranging from cool to wacky, while the downtown fringe is busy and mad, comprising a huge bus station on one side and bargain Asian-goods shopping on the other.

ORIENTATION

The city is compact, comprising small blocks in a grid system, and easy to get around on foot. Shopping in and around Robert Mugabe St is hectic, with Indian fabric shops, cheap shoes and clothes shops and outlets for spare car parts. First St, right in the centre and heading south from where it forms a T-intersection with Kwame Nkrumah Ave, retains a small part of the buzz it had 10 years ago: there are internet cafes, fast-food joints, local eateries, craft and souvenir shops, bookshops selling local books, and then preachers, buskers and other street performers. Note though, that this area, like most areas with shops, closes for the weekend at 12.30pm on Saturdays.

Maps

Your hotel, travel agent or tour operator will be able to give you a map. Car-hire places will also provide maps, and you may find a compact *Central Harare* map at a petrol station, if you are lucky.

INFORMATION

Bookshops

There were no longer any good bookshops at the time of writing, but you could buy secondhand books at Avondale markets.

HARARE

0 — 4 km
0 — 2 miles

INFORMATION
Africa Albida Tourism....................1 D3
Arundel Spar Cafe....................(see 24)
Australian High Commission....................2 C3
Botswana High Commission....................3 B4
Experience Africa Safaris....................(see 24)
Malawian High Commission....................4 B4
Namibian High Commission....................5 C3
National Parks & Wildlife Zimbabwe Central Reservations Office....................6 B4
South African High Commission....................7 B4
Trauma Centre....................8 B4
UK Embassy....................9 B3

SIGHTS & ACTIVITIES
Epworth Balancing Rocks....................10 D6
Mukuvisi Woodlands Environmental Centre....................11 C5
National Archives of Zimbabwe....................12 C4
National Botanic Gardens....................13 B4

SLEEPING
Amanzi Lodges....................14 D3
Small World Backpackers Lodge....................15 B4
York Lodge....................16 C5

EATING
Amanzi....................17 C4
Bottom Drawer....................18 B4
Cocoa Tree....................(see 32)
DV8....................19 C4
Italian Bakery....................(see 25)
Jaipur....................20 B5
Shalagashe....................(see 28)
Shamwari....................21 B4
Shop Café....................(see 28)
Sopranos....................22 B4
Victoria 22....................23 C4

ENTERTAINMENT
7 Arts....................(see 25)
Elite 100....................(see 25)
Ster-Kinekor Cinema....................(see 33)
Vistarama....................(see 25)

SHOPPING
Arundel Village....................24 B4
Avondale Markets....................(see 25)
Avondale Shopping Centre....................25 B4
Chisipite Shopping Centre....................26 D4
Crystal Passions....................27 D3
Doon Estate....................28 D5
Flea Markets....................(see 32)
Glenara Avenue Shopping Centre....................29 C4
Kumusha....................30 C5
Newlands Shopping Centre....................31 C4
Sam Levy's Village....................32 C3
Westgate Shopping Centre....................33 A4

TRANSPORT
Kukura Kurerwa Office....................(see 34)
Mbare Musika Bus Terminal....................34 B5
Pioneer Bus Office....................(see 34)

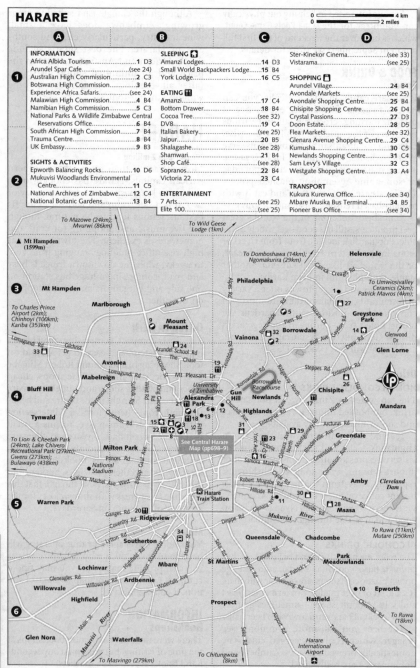

See Central Harare Map (pp698–9)

Avondale Bookshop (off Map pp698-9; King George Rd) Sells newspapers, magazines and a few locally written books; opposite Avondale Shopping Centre.

Emergency

Medical Air Rescue Service (MARS; ☎ 727540)
Police station (Map pp698-9; ☎ 733033; cnr Inez Tce & Kenneth Kaunda Ave)

Internet Access

The town centre, radiating out from First St, has many internet centres, which also offer phone and fax services. A few with reliable power are listed. All charge around US$2 per hour. There is also wireless internet access at several cafes around the northern suburbs, including Italian Bakery (p700), 40 Cork Road (p701), **CeeCees** (Celebration Centre, Swan Rd, Borrowdale; 🕑 7am-10pm) and **Arundel Spar Cafe** (Map p696; Arundel Village, Quorn Ave, Mt Pleasant; 🕑 24 hr).
One Stop Internet Cafe (Map pp698-9; 60 Speke Ave)
Quick N Easy Internet Shop (Map pp698-9; ☎ 799224/5; Linquenda House, cnr First St & Nelson Mandela Ave)
Telco Internet (Map pp698-9; ☎ 751263; Shop 22, Ximex Mall, cnr Angwa St & Jason Moyo Ave)

Internet Resources

African Encounter (www.africanencounter.com) A good travel agent who can help with information on getting around Harare and Zimbabwe: bus timetables, hiring cars and international and domestic flights.
Getaway Magazine (www.getaway.co.za) About holidaying in Southern Africa.
Twin Arts (www.twinarts.co.zw) Reliable source of up-to-date information and what's on in Zimbabwe, particularly in arts, music and dance. The site also covers festivals, shopping, hiking and other activities, with links to NGOs, civic organisations and news links relevant to Zimbabwe.
ZWNews (ironhorse@zwnews.net; email with 'subscribe' as subject) A free online subscription for daily news coverage about Zimbabwe from around the world.

Media

Zimbabwe's media is heavily controlled. The state runs the radio stations and the lone TV station, which broadcasts national news, international news and music programs in English, Shona and Ndebele. The state also owns the only daily newspaper, the *Herald*.

A touch of balance comes through Friday's *Independent* (a very good read) and *The Zimbabwean* (which is produced by expat Zimbabweans living in London).

Medical Services

Night pharmacies are listed in the *Herald*, but Shamrock Pharmacy, opposite Avondale Shopping Centre, is open 8am to 8pm every day.
Avenues Clinic (Map pp698-9; ☎ 251180-99; cnr Mazowe St & Baines Ave) Recommended by expats.
Trauma Centre (Map p696; ☎ 700666/815; Lanark Rd, Belgravia) Also recommended by expats.

Post

Main post office (Map pp698-9; Inez Tce; 🕑 8am-4pm Mon-Fri, to 11.30am Sat) Stamp sales and poste-restante facilities are in the arcade, while the parcel office is downstairs.

Telephone

Telephone booths are long gone, so take a phone with international roaming (it's impossible to buy SIM cards in Zimbabwe) or use internet/telephone centres – around First St in town – or your hotel.

Tourist Information

Department of Immigration Control (Map pp698-9; ☎ 791913; 1st fl, Linquenda House, cnr Nelson Mandela Ave & First St) To extend your visa, contact this office.
Harare Publicity Association (☎ 752577-9, 781810, 775622; hhem@africaonline.co.zwcnr; cnr Jason Moyo Ave & Sam Nujoma St)
National Parks & Wildlife Zimbabwe central reservations office (Map p696; ☎ 706077; fax 726089; national-parks@gta.gov.zw; cnr Borrowdale Rd & Sandringham Dr; 🕑 8am-4pm Mon-Fri) Information and accommodation bookings relating to Zimbabwe's national parks and reserves are available here. Sandringham Dr forms the northern border of the National Botanic Gardens.
Zimbabwe Tourism Authority (Map pp698-9; ☎ 758730; www.zimbabwetourism.co.zw; 55 Samora Machel Ave; 🕑 8am-4.30pm Mon-Fri) Has general tourism information.

Travel Agencies

African Encounter (Map pp698-9; www.africanencounter.com) Does backpacking and overland bookings for more than two people.
Experience Africa Safaris (Map p696; ☎ 301494/369185/369136, 11603613; belinda@xafricasafaris.com; Shop 37, Arundel Village, Quorn Ave, Mt Pleasant) The best travel agent in town.
Premier Travel & Tours (Map pp698-9; ☎ 704781-6, 0912-306481, 011-605244; info@premier.co.zw; 24 Cleveland Ave, Milton Park) Has a mailing list you can join with news and updates.

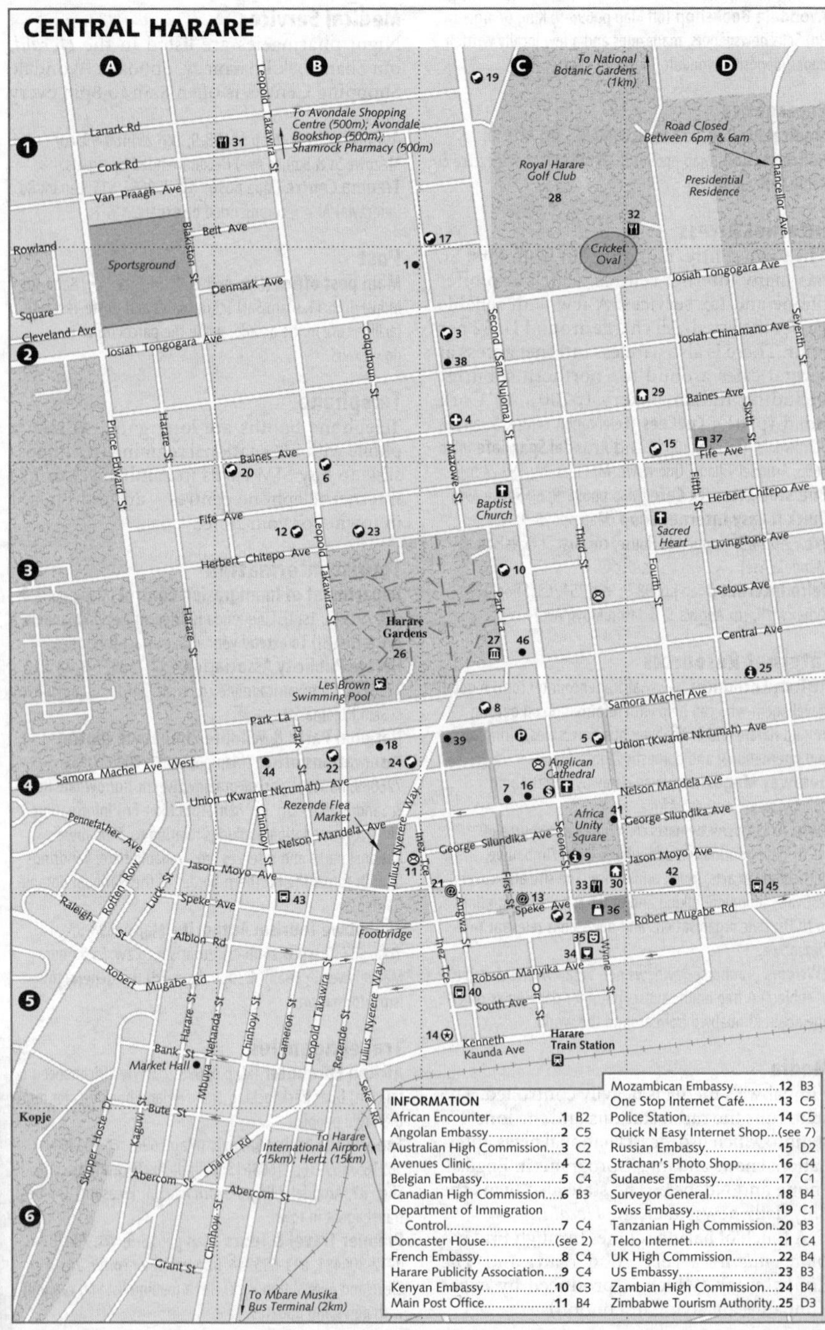
CENTRAL HARARE
A
B
C
D
1
2
3
4
5
6
To National Botanic Gardens (1km)
To Avondale Shopping Centre (500m); Avondale Bookshop (500m); Shamrock Pharmacy (500m)
Road Closed Between 6pm & 6am
Lanark Rd
Cork Rd
Van Praagh Ave
Beit Ave
Rowland Square
Sportsground
Blakiston St
Denmark Ave
Cleveland Ave
Josiah Tongogara Ave
Leopold Takawira St
Colquhoun St
Royal Harare Golf Club
Cricket Oval
Presidential Residence
Chancellor Ave
Josiah Chinamano Ave
Seventh St
Second (Sam Nujoma) St
Baines Ave
Sixth St
Fife Ave
Fifth St
Herbert Chitepo Ave
Prince Edward St
Harare St
Mazowe St
Baptist Church
Sacred Heart
Livingstone Ave
Third St
Fourth St
Selous Ave
Central Ave
Park La
Harare Gardens
Les Brown Swimming Pool
Samora Machel Ave
Union (Kwame Nkrumah) Ave
Samora Machel Ave West
Park St
Anglican Cathedral
Nelson Mandela Ave
George Silundika Ave
Africa Unity Square
Jason Moyo Ave
Rezende Flea Market
Pennefather Ave
Rotten Row
Luck St
Chinhoyi St
Julius Nyerere Way
Inez Tce
Speke Ave
Raleigh St
Footbridge
Albion Rd
Angwa St
First St
Robert Mugabe Rd
Wynne St
Robson Manyika Ave
South Ave
Orr St
Mbuya Nehanda St
Cameron St
Rezende St
Kenneth Kaunda Ave
Harare Train Station
Bank St
Market Hall
Bute St
Kopje
Skipper Hoste Dr
Kaguvi St
Charter Rd
Seke Rd
To Harare International Airport (15km); Hertz (15km)
Abercorn St
Grant St
To Mbare Musika Bus Terminal (2km)
INFORMATION
African Encounter....1 B2
Angolan Embassy....2 C5
Australian High Commission....3 C2
Avenues Clinic....4 C2
Belgian Embassy....5 C4
Canadian High Commission....6 B3
Department of Immigration Control....7 C4
Doncaster House....(see 2)
French Embassy....8 C4
Harare Publicity Association....9 C4
Kenyan Embassy....10 C3
Main Post Office....11 B4
Mozambican Embassy....12 B3
One Stop Internet Café....13 C5
Police Station....14 C5
Quick N Easy Internet Shop....(see 7)
Russian Embassy....15 D2
Strachan's Photo Shop....16 C4
Sudanese Embassy....17 C1
Surveyor General....18 B4
Swiss Embassy....19 C1
Tanzanian High Commission....20 B3
Telco Internet....21 C4
UK High Commission....22 B4
US Embassy....23 B3
Zambian High Commission....24 B4
Zimbabwe Tourism Authority....25 D3

Tour Operators

Africa Albida Tourism (Map p696; ☎ 4885200; www.africaalbidatourism.com; Greystone Park Shopping Center, Gaydon Rd)

Natureways (Map p696; ☎ 744133/42916907; www.natureways.com; 8 Kirkwood Rd, Alexandra Park)

Varden Safaris (Map p696 ☎ 4861766; www.vardensafaris.com) Offers horseriding safaris.

DANGERS & ANNOYANCES

Bag snatching, pickpocketing and carjacking are on the rise, as are robberies at bars and nightclubs. When you're in a car, take precautions by always keeping your windows up and keeping your bags, including handbags, in the boot or, if not possible, safely wedged under your feet.

None of the internal political hostilities are directed at visitors, though this should not tempt you to openly espouse your political views (particularly if they are critical of President Mugabe – this is a crime). Nonetheless, despite the way Zimbabwe is featured in the foreign press, the country is safe for the visitor and the locals, for the most part, very gentle and welcoming.

SIGHTS

National Gallery of Zimbabwe

This **collection** (Map pp698-9; ☎ 704666; cnr Julius Nyerere Way & Park Lane; admission US$1; ⏲ 9am-5pm) is in the southeast corner of Harare Gardens. It has a mix of contemporary Zimbabwean and African art, including paintings (you can usually purchase paintings), stone sculptures, masks and carvings. The attached shop is excellent for sculptures, crafts and books on Zimbabwean art. There's also a nice cafe for cake and filtered coffee or tea and an internet cafe adjoining it.

Harare Gardens

This is the city's largest **park** (Map pp698-9; admission free). Look for the islandlike stand of rainforest with its miniature Victoria Falls and Zambezi Gorge. No cycling is allowed.

National Archives of Zimbabwe

Founded in 1935, this **building** (Map p696; Ruth Taylor Rd; admission US$1; ⏲ 8.30am-4pm Mon-Fri, 8am-noon Sat), off Borrowdale Rd, is the repository for the history of Rhodesia and modern Zimbabwe: artefacts, photos, accounts of early explorers and settlers, and a display about the Second Chimurenga (Civil War).

National Botanic Gardens

In a city of extraordinary gardens, the 58-hectare **botanical gardens** (Map p696; Fifth St; admission US$5; ⌚ dawn-dusk) have suffered some neglect. Most Zimbabwean species are represented, as well as specimens from Southern Africa. It has an outdoor cafe.

Mukuvisi Woodlands Environmental Centre

Just 7km east of the city centre is this **environmental centre** (Map p696; ☎ 747152; Glenara Ave; admission US$1; ⌚ 8am-5pm). Most of the 265 hectares are is natural msasa parkland, ideal for picnics, walking, horse riding and birdwatching. There are a few enclosures with animals and the remaining area is a wildlife park where antelopes, zebras, giraffes and warthogs roam free. Watch them from the viewing platform.

ACTIVITIES

Between November and May, **Zimsculpt** (Map pp698-9; ☎ 0912-907758; www.zimsculpt.com; info@zimsculpt.com; costs on demand) offers personal meet-the-sculptor tours, where you'll learn about the latest cutting-edge sculptures being produced in Zimbabwe, meet the artists and their families and watch them work. You can even buy directly from the artists.

The most famous of the seven golf courses around Harare is the internationally acclaimed **Royal Harare Golf Club** (Map pp698-9; ☎ 702920; Fifth St; ⌚ 6am-6pm). Guests are welcome for a temporary membership fee of US$12.

FESTIVALS & EVENTS

Harare International Festival of Arts (HIFA; ☎ 300119; www.hifa.co.zw) is *the* annual event, held in the last week of April. It could stand proudly alongside any international arts festival. Embassies and corporate sponsors bring out international acts to produce a crammed timetable alongside Zimbabwean artists. Performances include opera, classical music, jazz, soul, funk, theatre and dance. Workshops and craft markets feature alongside the action during the day and at night you can eat, dance and party. If you're in the region don't miss it.

SLEEPING

Small World Backpackers Lodge (Map p696; ☎ 335341; mail@backpackerslodge.com; 25 Ridge Rd; dmUS$11, d & f US$35-70) An old faithful that's still in good form, with clean rooms, a pool, pool table, internet access, bar and a tree-top drinking deck with a leafy outlook. It's within walking distance of Avondale Shopping Centre.

Bronte (Map pp698-9; ☎ 700691/796631; 132 Baines Ave; s/d US$97/122) Located on the eastern edge of town within a pretty and peaceful walled garden, Bronte has plain rooms but is walking distance from town. There are reports of sleaziness here, but it's not directed at travellers.

In so many ways private lodges, from $100 per night are better for most visitors, cosier and all with stunning African decor. The following are tried and tested:

Manor (☎ 332193/4, 0912-604263; chelmsfordmanor@zol.co.zw; 8 Chelmsford Rd, Avondale; s/d with half-board US$100/120) This new boutique lodge is set on a beautiful estate. All eight rooms have bathrooms and air-con. There's a pool and a three-course dinner is available for US$35.

York Lodge (Map p696; ☎ 746622; 1 York Ave, Newlands; s/d US$130/170) This is a lovely safari-style lodge set in the suburbs and run by a very nice couple.

Amanzi Lodges (Map p696; ☎ 480880, 0913-275786; www.amanzi.co.zw; 1 Masasa Lane, Kambanji; s/d $185/280) Sister of the hip and chic restaurant, gorgeous African decor and a stunning garden. There are 12 luxury lodges, each beautifully styled. It's peaceful and welcoming and offers intimate, five-star service.

Meikles (Map pp698-9; ☎ 795655; www.meikles.com; cnr Jason Moyo Ave & Third St; r US$240;) This is the fanciest hotel in town, sister of the Victoria Falls Hotel. It has fine dining, a smart bar, a gym, pool, bar and beautician on the rooftop, and a couple of shops in the foyer.

EATING

Cafes

Most cafes serve espresso coffee for US$1, cakes and snacks from US$4, and light meals from US$7. Cafes are generally open from 9am to 5pm Monday to Thursday, with some open later on Friday and Saturday. Many are closed on Sunday.

Italian Bakery (Map p696; ☎ 339732; ground fl, Avondale Shopping Centre, King George Rd; ⌚ 7.30am-11pm) The views are of the car park but the decor is old-world Italian as the owners are Italian Ethiopian. This means the coffee is good and the meals – rolls, wraps and pastas – tasty.

Sopranos (Map p696; ☎ 333833; Argyle Rd, Avondale; ⌚ 8am-8pm) Named after the long-running American TV series, Sopranos caters for the whole family, with an indoor climbing gym for kids, and steak, fish and vegetarian meals.

40 Cork Road (Map pp698-9; ☎ 253585; 40 Cork Rd, Belgravia) Like many businesses in Harare, this is a house-turned-restaurant with a huge garden. It also has an art gallery and an interiors and plant shop. It has some of the best coffee and cakes in Harare.

Cocoa Tree (Map p696; ☎ 870848) In Village Walk, next to Sam Levy's Village in Borrowdale (on the TM supermarket side), Cocoa Tree sells fantastic cakes and biscuits, and is great for brunch, lunch or coffee and cake. It's one of the few places open for Sunday breakfast, and a good spot to grab a coffee before or after visiting the market (every Sunday behind the shops).

Bottom Drawer (Map p696; ☎ 745679; 12 Maasdorp Rd, Belgravia) Grab a coffee or a yummy brunch before shopping for classic interiors items. Great for shoppers but also for kids – lots of cute garden toys, a trampoline, a wendy house, birds and bunnies and chickens running freely. Off Second Street Extension.

Shop Cafe (Map p696; ☎ 446684; Doon Estate; 1 Harrow Rd, Msasa; 9am-3pm Mon-Sat) Harare's only fully vegetarian cafe is perfect for brunch and lunch. It serves some of the tastiest food in Zimbabwe and will put you in the mood for browsing in the attached shop for hand-printed textiles, hand-painted ceramics and cane and teak furniture.

Shalagashe (Map p696; ☎ 447019, Doon Estate) A winner for hearty steak or chicken pies, curry, fish, chicken or sandwiches. Sit-down or takeaway, this is great home-style cooking.

Restaurants

Restaurants are open for lunch or dinner but most are closed on Sundays.

Keg & Maiden (Map pp698-9; ☎ 700037; Harare Sports Club; mains US$15) Tuck into bangers and mash or steak and chips in a cheerful pub atmosphere. You can also order a veg meal. Check out the magnificent international cricket ground (sadly, minus cricketers).

DV8 (Map p696; ☎ 745202; Groombridge shops, cnr the Chase & Teviotdale Rd; mains US$15) The steaks here are the best in Zimbabwe.

Amanzi (Map p696; ☎ 497768, 0912-336224; restaurant@amanzi.co.zw; 158 Enterprise Rd, Highlands; dinner per person US$25) Set in a stunning colonial house with African decor and an even more amazing garden, Amanzi has delicious international food and a great vibe. You can also buy a painting from a local artist on the way out. A must.

Victoria 22 (Map p696; ☎ 776429; 22 Victoria Rd, Newlands; dinner US$40) Yet another restaurant in a colonial house, this is a favourite among well-heeled locals. It is pretty formal (by Harare standards), with choices within a set menu of four delicious courses.

Willowmead (☎ 776429; cnr Rolf Valley Rd & Willowmead Lane, Borrowdale; lunch US$10) For breakfast, lunch, coffee, tea and cakes; Willowmead adjoins a lovely fresh fruit and vegetable market, both only open till late afternoon.

Olympia (Map pp698-9; Miekles Arcade; sadza & meat meals US$1) A kiosk with a couple of tables, selling the local staple meal of *sadza* with 'relish' or meat, and soft drinks. It's clean and a pretty safe bet. It's neighbours with Afrik Batik, a good souvenir/craft shop, selling skins, sculptures and so on. It's located behind the Miekles Hotel.

The following are open on Sundays:

Jaipur (Map p696; ☎ 740919; Sunrise Sports Club, Hurtsview Rd, Ridgeview; meals per person US$10) Delicious Indian food – including vegetarian thalis – upstairs overlooking a cricket ground where Harare's Indian community plays cricket.

Wild Geese Lodge (☎ 860466; 2 Buckland Lane, off Alpes Rd) Try this place for a yummy Sunday roast. Twenty minutes' drive north from the town centre, it has views across the grassy highveld to wildlife. It also offers accommodation in nine private thatched suites.

Shamwari (Map p696; ☎ 776429; cnr Churchill Rd & Second St; dinner US$10) This place does breakfast and lunch, with tables mainly in the garden and a leather handbag and interiors shop attached.

ENTERTAINMENT

For information about upcoming events check the listings in the weekly Standardplus supplement (Thursdays) in the *Standard* and the entertainment page of the Friday and Saturday *Herald*, or online at www.twinarts.co.zw.

Bars & Nightclubs

You can enjoy good music performances at bars and cafes around the capital where well-known local musicians play regularly. Never walk to or from any of these (or any other) late-night spots after dark; take a taxi.

Jazz 105 (Map pp698-9; ☎ 722516; cnr Second St & Robson Manyika Ave) A local haunt with live Afro jazz on Sunday and Wednesday evenings.

Book Cafe (Map pp698-9; upstairs, Fife Avenue Shopping Centre, The Avenues) is no longer a bookshop, just a place for live music, food and drinks and the **Mannenburg Jazz Club** (Map pp698-9; ☎ 730902), right next door, has live performances every night except Sunday. There are always notices and signs around town about events.

Cinemas

Cinemas offering recent films and cheap and comfortable seats ($3) include the **Ster-Kinekor Cinema complex** (Map pp698-9; Robert Mugabe Rd), opposite the Eastgate Centre and also at Westgate shopping centre (Map p696), and the **Elite 100**, **Vistarama** and **7 Arts cinemas**, all at the Avondale Shopping Centre (Map p696). The **Goethe-Institut** (☎ 796836; 51 Lawson Ave, Milton Park), run by the German Society, often has events such as documentary screenings and feature films.

SHOPPING

Shopping centres around Harare include the **Eastgate Centre** and **Fife Avenue Shopping Centre** in the centre (Map pp698–9); and **Arundel Village**, **Chisipite**, **Glenara Avenue**, **Newlands**, **Sam Levy's Village** and **Westgate** further out (Map p696). But the best shopping is at **Avondale markets** (Map p696), situated on top of the old car park at **Avondale Shopping Centre**; go here for carvings, beaded jewellery and other crafts. Also try the Sunday **flea markets** (Map p696) at Sam Levy's Village, behind the shops – though there are fewer crafts here.

Doon Estate (Map p696; 1 Harrow Rd, Msasa) Has a number of shops, including Art Mart, which is stocked with the work of dozens of local artisans and craftspeople. Veldemeers (more commonly known as The Belgian chocolate shop) is also here, and has to be experienced to be believed. Its novelty chocolates make great presents.

Kumusha (Map p696; ☎ 446944; 2 Coronation St, Msasa) Sublime, handmade Zimbabwean furniture and household goods for interiors and exteriors. A must to check out.

Umwinsivalley Ceramics (☎ 883959) Along the Umwinsidale Rd, this is a workshop, gallery and shop specialising in hand-painted china and set on the top of a hill. You can watch the artists at work but the view over the valley alone is worth the trip.

Patrick Mavros (☎ 860131; www.patrickmavros.com) Follow the signpost to the studio and gallery at the end of Haslemere Lane, 1km off the Umwinsidale Rd. A visit is a must for its spectacular setting atop a hill, overlooking a picture-perfect valley complete with wildlife. This place sells designer silverware from jewellery to tableware and whimsical items. Mavros' signature style in his jewellery is the ndoro shell, the original currency of Zimbabwe. He also has a shop in Knightsbridge, London, though this one is cheaper!

Crystal Passions (Map p696; ☎ 882466; www.ourcrystalpassion.com; 24 Newbold Rd, Greystone Park) Extraordinary, designer, hand-cut and polished Zimbabwean stones and crystal jewellery for fashion and healing. You can have something designed specifically for you or buy off the rack. Open Wednesday afternoon and Saturday morning or by appointment only.

Dendera Gallery (Speke St) This gallery has the best of Zimbabwean and African craft: masks, baskets, textiles, wooden carvings and paintings. Between First and Second Sts.

GETTING THERE & AWAY

Air

For details about international flights to and from Harare, see p732.

Air Zimbabwe (Map pp698-9; ☎ 253752; Eastgate Centre) operates flights to/from Bulawayo (one way/return US$140/250, 45 minutes) and Victoria Falls (one way/return US$230/375). The following airlines also have offices in Harare: **Air Botswana** (Map pp698-9; ☎ 793195/228/229; Travel Plaza); **Air Namibia** (Map pp698-9; ☎ 732094/5; Travel Plaza); **South African Airways** (Map pp698-9; ☎ 794511/2/6/47/83; SCC House); **Air Tanzania** (Map pp698-9; ☎ 752537/8 Tanzanian High Commission); **Air Malawi** (Map pp698-9; ☎ 752563).

Air France, British Airways, Cathay Pacific, KLM and Lufthansa can all be contacted by calling ☎ 703880.

Bus

Bus companies include the following:

Blue Arrow (Map pp698-9; ☎ 729514; barrow@africaonline.co.zw; Chester House, Speke Ave)
Greyhound (Map pp698-9; ☎ 720801; Road Port Terminal)
Kukura Kurerwa (Map p696; ☎ 669973/6; Mbare Musika Bus Terminal)
Pioneer Bus (Map p696; ☎ 795863/790531; Mbare Musika Bus Terminal)
Zupco (Map pp698-9; ☎ 704933; Road Port Terminal)

City Link Express is a new company that departs Harare for Bulawayo daily at 7.30am and arrives in Bulawayo at 1pm. The return service departs Bulawayo at 2pm and arrives in Harare at 7.30pm. For more details you can contact **African Encounter Travel** (reservations@africanencounter.org).

Train

The train station (Map pp698–9) is near the corner of Kenneth Kaunda Ave and Second St. In theory, trains go to Mutare (9.30pm, US$6, 8½ hours) and Bulawayo (9pm, sleeper US$10, nine hours), and from Bulawayo on to Victoria Falls (8pm, sleeper US$11). Check with travel agents if you want to go by train for the latest information.

GETTING AROUND

To/From the Airport

All international and domestic airlines use Harare International Airport, 15km southeast of the city centre. Charter flights and other light aircraft operate out of Charles Price airport, 2km northwest of Harare. Book charter flights through tour operators and they will provide transfers.

TAXIS

Airport taxis cost US$30 to town, the inner suburbs or 30km in any direction. Official services include **Rixi Taxi** (☎ 753080/1/2), **AA Taxi** (☎ 704222) and **Al Taxi** (☎ 706996/8, 703334).

Car

Car-rental companies in Harare include **Avis** (Map p696; ☎ 796409/10; Third St) and **Europcar** (Map pp698-9; 750622/4; carhire@europcar.co.zw; 19 Samora Machel Ave).

FUEL

At the time of writing fuel was freely available, at a cost of around US$1 to US$1.20 per litre for petrol, and US$0.85 per litre for diesel. Contact tour operators such as **African Encounter** (www.africanencounter.com) to check current prices and availability.

AROUND HARARE

Most places listed in this section can be visited on day trips from the capital, but don't travel the roads in and out of Harare after dusk – they become too dangerous with bad potholes and eroding edges, little to no lighting, bad drivers and people walking on the streets.

BALLY VAUGHAN SANCTUARY

Meet the 'family' of rescued African animals at **Bally Vaughan** (☎ 0912-592944/264160, 11-601131; www.ballyvaughan.co.zw; Shamva Rd; admission US$3; 🕑 9am-5pm Tues-Sun) in the Enterprise Valley, 60km from Harare. It's an extraordinary orphanage/refuge – run on donations. Help feed predators, monkeys and serval cats and meet the biggest lions in Africa, all in lush surrounds. There's a restaurant and bar, and there is also a volunteer program. It's a 30-minute drive from Harare. Take the Enterprise Road, turn left into Shamva Rd then look out for the Mermaids Pool turn-off – the sanctuary is just beyond that.

LION & CHEETAH PARK

This **park** (admission per adult/vehicle US$15/3; 🕑 8am-5pm) sits on a private estate, 24km west of Harare and just off the road to Bulawayo. There are no cheetahs, but there are certainly lots of lions. There's an enclosure for a kind of 'self-drive safari', though it's only about one hectare in size. The Kiosk, which is in fact a zoo, has baboons, crocodiles, hyenas and Tommy, the 300-year-old tortoise who walks around freely, as well as a kiosk with food and craft souvenirs. There's also a large self-drive safari area where you can see warthogs and zebras. It's safe for a picnic, but all sadly very run down.

EPWORTH BALANCING ROCKS

They can be found in many places in Zimbabwe, but these are probably the most famous **balancing rocks** (admission with guided tour US$4; 🕑 6am-6pm), located 13km southeast of Harare, off Chiremba Rd.

ROCK ART

Domboshawa Caves (☎ 790044; admission US$4; 🕑 6am-6pm) – whose name means 'Red Rock' in Shona – 30km northeast of Harare, are known for their prehistoric rock paintings. A well-marked 15-minute walk takes you across a rock range with stunning 360-degree views to the caves where the paintings are.

Ngomakurira (☎ 790044; admission US$2; 🕑 6am-6pm) offers even more spectacular rock paintings (especially photogenic in the afternoon). Both sites make a half-day trip from Harare. For Domboshawa, drive (or take a taxi) 20 minutes north along Borrowdale Rd to Domboshawa village, watch carefully for the turn-off, or ask the locals, and then it's 1km in from the main road. For Ngomakurira, follow the same directions until the Domboshawa turn-off, but go 15km further to Ngomakurira village (45km north of Harare). The entrance is 2km in from the main road.

IMIRE SAFARI RANCH

Located 105km east of Harare, **Imire Safari Ranch** (☎ 0912-522201/243072, 022-2094; www.imiresafariranch.com; adults US$12) was built on a farm where indigenous wildlife – including black rhinos and elephants – were once hunted to clear land for farming, and now contributes enormously to the conservation of Zimbabwean wildlife. It is renowned for breeding and releasing black rhinos into Matusadona National Park and for providing orphan elephants a home. It's good value for money and great for kids too, with guaranteed animal spotting and feeding, and even – after years of research into the best handling and teaching methods – riding elephants at the dam. There is a student volunteer program. Travel 70km on the Mutare road; 3km before Marondera you will see an Imire signpost – turn right here. Drive for 2.5km, turn left at the Imire sign, drive for 40km. Go 800m past the Imire butchery, and at the Sable Lodge turn off, turn left and go 1km to the lodge.

LAKE CHIVERO RECREATIONAL PARK

This 5500-hectare park is 32km southwest of Harare. It spreads around the 57-sq-km **Lake Chivero**; you can take a picnic and do a day trip from Harare or spend the weekend. Rhinos, ostriches, zebras and giraffes may be seen. You can fish, barbecue or do a self-drive safari, but you can't hire boats and must avoid swimming: crocs and bilharzia bugs lurk.

On the northern shore, the Admiral's Cabin (right) offers horse riding, braais (barbecues) and you can ask about boat/canoe hire. Within its grounds there is the **Kuimba Shiri Bird Sanctuary** (admission US$7; 🕒 10am-5pm Mon-Wed & Fri, 9am-5pm Sat & Sun), boasting more than 450 types of birds, apparently the largest variety of indigenous species in Africa.

Sleeping & Eating

National Parks Accommodation (lodges with 2/4/5 beds US$2/3/4, chalets with 1/4/5 beds US$1/2/3; 🅿) Guests at this place on the northern shore of the lake can use the swimming pool – if it has water in it – and braai pits. The views are stunning.

Admiral's Cabin (☎ 062-2309; birdpark@mango.zw; campsites per person US$3, chalets incl breakfast per person US$12) Offers clean accommodation right near the lake, with attached bar and restaurant.

NORTHERN ZIMBABWE

The major attractions in this part of the country are the Matusadona National Park on the eastern section of Lake Kariba, the islands and Mana Pools National Park. The Mavuradonha Mountains and Chinhoyi Caves National Park are also both fascinating.

MAVURADONHA MOUNTAINS

☎ 091

This area, little known to visitors, is pristine wilderness, a rugged blend of grey granite with the red serpentine soils of Zimbabwe's Great Dyke Complex. It's the escarpment of the Zambezi Valley, where deep valleys bisect towering rock faces and grass-covered mountains. Once home to nomadic San Bushmen and people of the Mutapa state, it is now home to species such as elephants, buffaloes, sables, kudus and zebras.

It is idyllic for horseback safaris and/or staying in rustic accommodation and eating fresh bush cuisine; arrange a visit through **Varden Safaris** (☎ 861766; www.vardensafaris.com; all-inclusive horseback safaris US$250). Sustainable wildlife conservation, minimal environmental impact and local community involvement are key to preserving these unique habitats. Varden Safaris are part of the Muzarabani Rural District Council Campfire Project, which means villagers benefit from tourism to discourage poaching. Varden will provide transfers from Harare. There is also 'equine volunteer' work available (US$40 per day), which means working with horses in the African bush.

KARIBA

☎ 061 / pop 15,000

The small lakeside town of Kariba is spread out along the steep lakeshore. From Lake Dr, the road that, unsurprisingly, runs alongside the lake, another road winds up through the tree-covered hills to Kariba Heights. There are lovely lake views and elephants often come through town. You can get information from

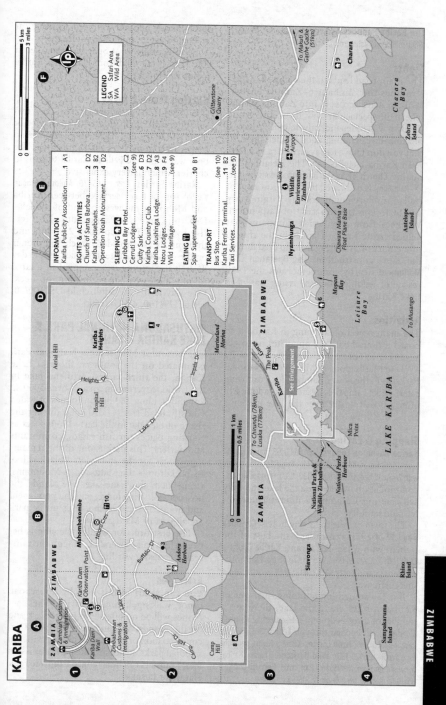

KARIBA

INFORMATION
Kariba Publicity Association..........1 A1

SIGHTS & ACTIVITIES
Church of Santa Barbara..........2 D2
Kariba Houseboats..........3 B2
Operation Noah Monument..........4 D2

SLEEPING
Caribbea Bay Hotel..........5 C2
Cerruti Lodges..........(see 9)
Cutty Sark..........6 D3
Kariba Country Club..........7 D2
Kariba Kushinga Lodge..........8 A3
Nzou Lodges..........9 F4
Wild Heritage..........(see 9)

EATING
Spar Supermarket..........10 B1

TRANSPORT
Bus Stop..........(see 10)
Kariba Ferries Terminal..........11 B2
Taxi Services..........(see 5)

the **Kariba Publicity Association** (Lake Dr; ☎ 2277, 2498; mabhena@yahoo.com).

Sights

The main road leads to the **dam wall**, which straddles the Zimbabwe–Zambia border. Walk or drive across it, into Zambia, or just take in the spectacular view. If you are visiting the dam wall independently, tell the Zambian or Zimbabwean immigration officials there, so that you don't have to pay any extra visa fees.

In Kariba Heights (or 'The Heights') the quaint **Church of Santa Barbara** (admission free; 8am-6pm) is dedicated to the patron saint of Italian military engineers, the Virgin Mary and St Joseph (patron saint of carpenters). Workers from the Italian company that helped create Kariba Dam built the church in memory of 21 colleagues who died during the dam's construction. The **Operation Noah Monument** nearby commemorates the 1959 rescue of wildlife from the rising waters of Lake Kariba.

Activities

The main object of stopping in Kariba is to board a houseboat (see opposite) or to get a transfer to one of the islands by boat or by 4WD to Matusadona or Mana Pools National Parks, or to the Lower Zambezi for a canoeing safari. Most campsites in the Matusadona will offer a boat transfer over the lake if clients arrive in Kariba town.

Sleeping & Eating

Kariba Kushinga Lodges (☎ 3041/2/3; natureways@iwayafrica.com; Stand 780, Camp Hill; campsites US$5, chalets with 2/4/6/12 beds US$40/60/70/120) Comfortable accommodation overlooking the lake and fully self-catering. Camping facilities include toilets and laundry.

The town has the following hotels: **Caribbea Bay** (☎ 2452-7) is central and the best of the bunch, with a fair restaurant; **Kariba Country Club** (☎ 2283/2339) is value for money, but nothing fancy; and **Cutty Sark** (☎ 2321/2) is quite nice in a rustic way.

But for something stunning, just out of Kariba, further along the lake, there are a number of three-bedroom, self-catering houses ('lodges'), all booked through **Trish** (☎ 3127/2225; baobab@zol.co.zw): **Nzou Lodges** (Charara, Kariba; per night for 6 people US$120-180), **Wild Heritage** (Charara, Kariba; per night for 6 people US$160-200) and **Cerruti Lodges** (Charara, Kariba; per person US$35-55). They are all lovely places, but you will need a private car or boat to get around once you're there.

Food is available at Spar Supermarket in Kariba or bring food from Harare, as Kariba is not well stocked.

Getting There & Away

CATS (☎ 04-332141/2; info@centralair.co.zw) does reasonably priced flight charters from Kariba or Harare to Mana and back. Air Zimbabwe no longer flies from Vic Falls to this area. The only way from Vic Falls to Kariba town is to charter, which is very expensive.

Kariba Ferries (☎ 04-65476; Andora Harbour, Kariba) runs a ferry service between Kariba and Mlibizi at the western end of the lake. Departure time is at 9am at both places (arrive by 8am). The trip takes 22 hours and three meals are provided: lunch and dinner on the day of departure, breakfast on the day of arrival. Sleeping is communal in a large saloon, and, weather permitting, on deck. One-way tariffs are adult/child US$100/50, sedan US$100, 4WD $160.

MATUSADONA NATIONAL PARK & LAKE KARIBA ISLANDS

The beautiful Matusadona National Park is situated on the southern shore of Lake Kariba, the third-largest artificial lake in the world, covering an area of over 5000 sq km and holding 180 billion tonnes of water. Ghostly dead trees – drowned during the rising of the lake in the early 1960s – act as roosting places for fish eagles, cormorants and darters. This park is one of the remaining refuges for the endangered black rhino. Its backdrop is the Matusadona Mountains, rising 600m above the lake. The islands, the occasional floating lodge, and the permanent and nonpermanent bush camps in the park are all part of Matusadona.

The best time for wildlife viewing is between July and November, though the rainy season is also rewarding.

Activities

You can safari in this area by houseboat, canoe, walking, hiking or driving. These activities will be on offer both in the park and on the islands, and are included in the accommodation price, but rates for activities in national parks do not include park admission fees. Transfers can be arranged from Vic Falls, Harare or Lusaka.

HOUSEBOATS

Houseboats are an amazing way to do a safari in the park because not only do you feel as though you have the lake to yourselves, but you get to observe animals, particularly elephants, at close range. The main two top houseboat companies in Zimbabwe to book through are **Rhino Rendezvous** (☎ 04-745644/745642; rhinoren@mweb.co.zw) and **Marineland Harbour** (☎ 061-2237; bookings@marinland.co.zw).

WILDLIFE DRIVES

Wildlife drives around the Matusadona National Park are offered by lodges or camps on the islands, or camps in the park.

Sleeping

The following places are best booked through Harare-based travel agents before you travel to Zimbabwe, or through a travel agent in Harare, such as **Experience Africa Safaris** (☎ 04-301494/369185; belinda@xafricasafaris.com; Shop 37, Arundel Village, Quorn Avenue, Mt Pleasant).

Musango (www.musangosafricamp.com; per person per night $US260-300) is the most popular (permanent) 'tented' camp in Lake Kariba because of its location, good guiding and abundant wildlife, given its proximity to Matusadona National Park. It is a very small island, close to the shoreline, and joins up to the mainland when lake levels are low. It is not very child-friendly, though, with electric fences surrounding the camp and a lack of activities.

Spurwing Island (www.spurwing.co.zw) is a good lodge for kids as it has a pool, is safely fenced and has babysitters. It's about 45 minutes by boat from Kariba town.

Rhino Island Safari Camp (☎ 04-753901-5, 0912-205000; rhino.safari.camp@mail.com) is also wonderful – very remote and very wild. But, again, not a place to take children. It's basic and there are many lions in the area. It is on a peninsula at Elephant Point, just before the Tashinga Basin.

Tiger Bay is quite far down the Ume River and set on its banks (near Bumi Hills).

Gache Gache (bernie@chapungusafaris.co.zw; per person per night $US95-110) is on the shoreline in the mouth of the Gache Gache River, in the Sanyati West area. It's in a beautiful setting with the best fishing but not much wildlife.

Bumi Hills Safari Lodge (http://xafricasafaris.com; per person per night around $US200) is newly renovated and sits on the shoreline over at Bumi, up in the hills, overlooking the lake. There are 20 lodges, all with balconies and views of the lake. It has its own airstrip – guests are picked up in an open-air safari truck – and boat transfers are also available from Kariba.

Classic Africa Safaris (www.classicafricasafaris.com; per person for 3 nights around US$1775) offers high-end luxury, owner-operated tented camps, designed around your ideas and set up for each booking.

Maronga Tented Camp (http://xafricasafaris.com; per person per night around US$350), set at the bottom of the mountain range along the Maronga River is a newly renovated permanent camp sleeping 12. Track black rhinos on foot or try boating, fishing, canoeing and game drives.

There is also a National Parks campsite at Tashinga.

Getting There & Away

You can fly from Vic Falls to the Matusadona via a new scheduled flight operated by **Bumi Hills Safari Lodge** (http://xafricasafaris.com) – you don't have to stay there to book it. You will land at Bumi Hills airstrip where your tour operator will collect you.

MANA POOLS NATIONAL PARK

This magnificent 2200-sq-km **national park** (admission US$15; ⏰ 6am-6pm) is a Unesco World Heritage Site, and its magic stems from its remoteness and pervading sense of the wild and natural. This is one park in Zimbabwe where you're guaranteed to see plenty of hippos, crocs, zebras, antelopes and elephants, and almost guaranteed to see lions, and perhaps some painted dogs.

The defining difference to Mana is that none of it is fenced in, so there can be elephants strolling by while you have your breakfast. This is what sets Mana Pools apart from just about any other safari park in the world. You're also allowed to walk around without a guide, as you can see for miles around. But be aware, this is about personal responsibility: wild animals are incredibly dangerous – and fast.

Fishing and canoeing on the Zambezi provide some breathtaking (read: heart in mouth) experiences. Also for the brave at heart: book a side trip to the famous Chitake Springs; these isolated springs have prearranged camping only, and are known for the number of lions that live and roam around there.

Anyone interested in helping out physically can volunteer for the **Mana Pools Game**

Count which is held over the weekend of the first full moon in September. Admission to the park is free for the weekend only, but you have to pay all your own expenses and bring all supplies with you – there are no shops in Mana. In brief, you count animals during the day and enjoy a braai and 'much merriment' at night. For more information or to sign up, contact Jane and Kelvin Hein on bushpig@mango.zw.

Sleeping

There are three main options for visitors to Mana. The first is to book a tented camp – this is the Africa you dream of. Options range from basic to luxurious, but at the very least you can expect a pre-erected walk-in tent with comfortable camp beds and a camp cook to provide three full meals per day. For classic tented-camp safaris, the best known are Natureways Safaris with guides James Varden or Craig Van Zyl; for more information see right.

Kanga Bush Camp (belinda@xafricasafaris.com; per person per night US$400) is a very private, permanent-but-seasonal camp, sleeping 12. It is built around a water hole, the only permanent water source in its area, so it heaves with wildlife. **Ruckomechi** and **Vundu** (www.safarizuri.com/zimbabwe; per person per night US$350) are also permanent-but-seasonal camps in Mana, ie only open in the dry season (roughly March to October). Talk to a travel agent, or directly to a tour operator, about the different options, and they'll be able to match the right camp to your tastes and needs.

A second option is the newly renovated, top-end **Chikwenya Safari Lodge** (www.safarizuri.com/zimbabwe; per person per night US$350), comprising nine extraordinary rooms nestled secretly into the bush, made of tented walls beneath thatch, and huge gauze windows to take in massive views. The setting looks across the Sapi River mouth to acacia floodplains, the Zambezi River and Chikwenya Island, with the Zambian escarpment as an awesome backdrop. Sleep to the honking of hippos.

The third option is to book a self-catering lodge through **National Parks & Wildlife Zimbabwe** (Map p696; ☎ 706077; fax 726089; national-parks@gta.gov.zw; cnr Borrowdale Rd & Sandringham Dr, Harare; 8am-4pm Mon-Fri). National Parks lodges have the prime locations in terms of views and animal spotting. The lodges are basic and the experience is similar to camping in a lot of ways, with the chief difference being comfortable chairs and beds, and solid walls between you and the lions. Bookings for these lodges open three months in advance. September/October is the most popular time to visit – you'd need to get to the National Parks office at 3am to queue on the morning of 1 June or 1 July to book for those months.

Getting There & Away

Private vehicles cannot access Mana Pools National Park during the wet season (November to April), mainly because the dirt roads to and within the park become corrugated in most areas, but there is no service available for assisting cars and trucks that get caught in mud or flooding.

Charter flights can be arranged through **Experience Africa Safaris** (☎ 04-301494/369185; belinda@xafricasafaris.com; Shop 37, Arundel Village, Quorn Ave, Mt Pleasant).

MIDDLE ZAMBEZI CANOE SAFARIS

Adventurous residents and visitors describe canoe trips down this awesome wilderness route as one of the best things they've ever done. Several companies run canoe trips between Kariba and Kanyemba (on the river junction with Zimbabwe, Zambia and Mozambique).

The trip is normally done in stages: Kariba to Chirundu (three days), Chirundu to Mana Pools National Park (three to four days) and Mana Pools to Kanyemba (four to five days). Any combination is possible, but if you can do only one stage the Chirundu to Mana Pools segment offers the best scenery and diversity of wildlife. July to October are the peak months for wildlife viewing. Some readers have even complained about too *much* wildlife at times, because thirsty hippos and frisky elephants can be dangerous obstacles.

Most canoe safaris run from April/May to October/November, but some operate year-round. November, during the dry season, is the best time for game viewing on the lower Zambezi. After that, in the wet season, vehicles cannot access Mana, so they are not able to do 'back-up service', which is what the higher-end camps get. Natureways (p699), however, is the one company that does operate all year round as they do all levels of camps.

Since Zimbabwe limits the number of operators allowed on each of the three segments (and restricts their days of operation), some companies run from the less-regulated Zambian side of the river. Zimbabwe's regulations stipulate that, to become a guide, one has to have done at least 1000 hours training on the river under a full guide; there are no such regulations in Zambia. Zambia also allows motor boats on their side, which is very disturbing for hippos, and generators, which are very disturbing for Zimbabwean operators and guests.

Finally, two points to remember. Firstly, the currents along this part of the Zambezi are deceptively strong. Secondly, all canoeists must stay within the territorial waters and remain close to the bank of the country they started in. Operators from Zambia are not permitted to cross the invisible border along the Zambezi into Zimbabwe (or vice versa), despite what they may claim. Please encourage your operator to observe good environmental practices.

Canoe Safari Operators

Some tour operators for canoe safaris include transport to and from Kariba or Harare and visas (if required) so check because these things can be a 'movable feast' in Zimbabwe. Natureways may include transfers for trips that start and end in Kariba. Rates include transport from the booking office, guides, canoes, food and tented accommodation, but do not include admission fees to Mana Pools National Park. The high season is about July to October.

For classic tented-camp safaris to hiking or canoe trails, try **Natureways Safaris** (Map p696; ☎ 04-744133/2916907; www.natureways.com; 4 Mount Rd, Avondale, Harare). Natureways can also organise cheaper 'participating' canoe trips, where all your kit goes with you in the canoe (tents, cooking, equipment, clothes) and you have a canoe guide. On the more expensive 'shoreline canoe trails', with tented camps and 'back-up' service, guests pay more to have a fully licensed guide to do safari walks inland and a team to go ahead and set up camp down river each night – guests are generally flown in for these. Charter flight costs are extra and vary depending on the originating point – they average US$1500 per plane.

Goliath Safaris (goliath@africaonline.co.zw) is more expensive and exclusive but very popular as the owner-guide, Stretch Ferreira, is an iconic character and great guide. **Classic Africa Safaris** (www.classicafricasafaris.com; per person for 3 nights around US$1775) is exclusive and a bit pricey, but offers really special owner-guide safaris.

CHINHOYI CAVES NATIONAL PARK

This small but worthwhile 'roadside' **national park** (admission US$12; 🕒 6am-6pm) is 115km northwest of Harare. It's riddled with limestone and dolomite caves and sinkholes, which have been used for storage and refuge by traditional people for nearly 1500 years. The focus is **Sleeping Pool** or Chirorodzira (Pool of the Fallen), so named because locals were cast into the formidable hole by the invading Ngoni tribes in the early 19th century. The pool maintains a constant temperature of 22°C.

From **Dark Cave** (the rear entrance to Chirorodzira), the views through the sombre shadows to the sunlit waters far below are magical: the clear water admits light so perfectly that the water line disappears and the pool takes on the appearance of a smoky blue underworld.

Caves Motel (☎ 067-22340; fax 067-22113; s/d incl breakfast US$25/31; 🅿) is at the park entrance. Has a restaurant, pool and petrol supplies.

EASTERN HIGHLANDS

Few travellers to Zimbabwe expect to find anything like the Eastern Highlands, but once they discover them they can't get enough. The narrow strip of mountain country that makes up Manicaland isn't the Africa that normally crops up in armchair travellers' fantasies. It's a land of mountains, national parks, pine forests, botanical gardens, rivers, dams and secluded getaways.

MUTARE

☎ 020 / pop 200,000

Mutare is set in a pretty valley surrounded by hills. Zimbabwe's third-largest city, it has a relaxed rural-town atmosphere. Its real value, though, is its proximity to either Mozambique or the Bvumba region and Nyanga National Park.

Information

Internet Cyber Cafe (☎ 67939; 67 Fourth St; per hr US$2.20)

Manicaland Publicity Bureau (☎ 64711; fax 67728; cnr Herbert Chitepo St & Robert Mugabe Rd; 🕒 8.30am-12.45pm & 2-4pm Mon-Fri) Offers a book exchange and

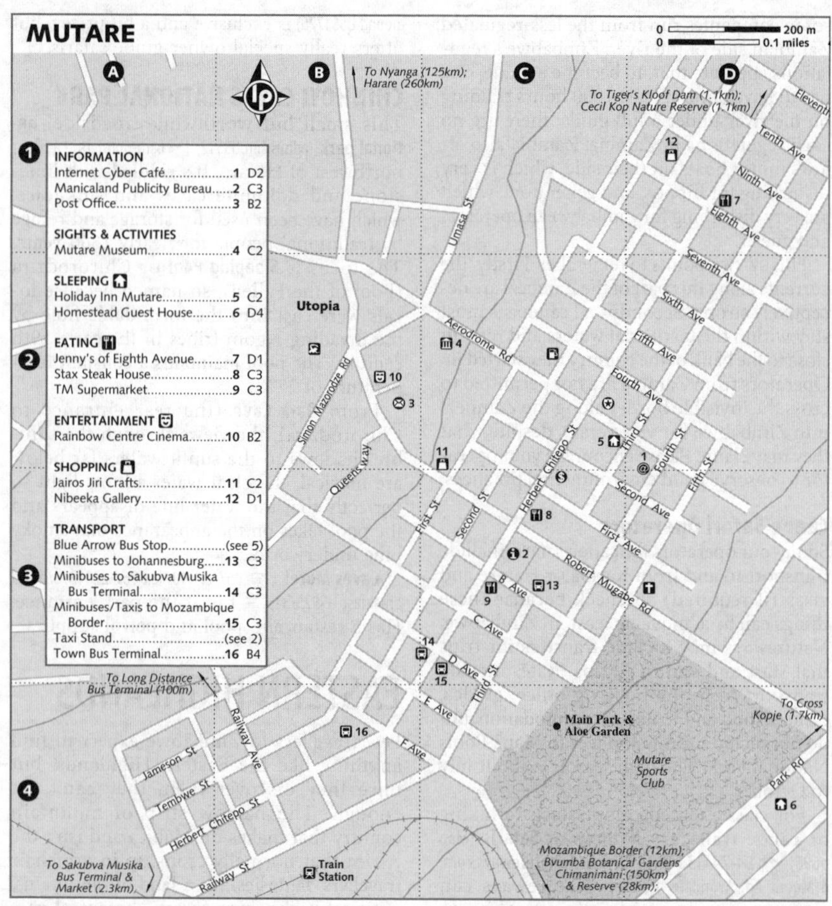

informal luggage-storage facility as well as accommodation, activities and transport information.

Post office (Robert Mugabe Rd) Four blocks west of the publicity bureau.

Sights

The **Mutare Museum** (☎ 63630; Aerodrome Rd; admission US$10; 🕓 9am-5pm) is close to the centre and has interesting exhibits on geology, history, anthropology, technology, zoology and the arts.

The 1700-hectare **Cecil Kop Nature Reserve** (☎ 61537; admission US$3; 🕓 dawn-dusk) wraps around the northern side of Mutare and abuts the Mozambican border. Part of the park that can be reached without a vehicle is **Tiger's Kloof Dam**. Try to visit Tiger's Kloof at feeding time (about 4pm) when rhinos, antelopes, giraffes and zebras congregate at the dam.

Sleeping & Eating

Most travellers stop only briefly in Mutare on their way up to or down from the Eastern Highlands.

Homestead Guest House (☎ 65870; 52 Park Rd; s/d US$20/35; 🏊) This renovated late-19th-century home is set in a pretty garden with a pool. It has clean and comfortable rooms.

Holiday Inn Mutare (☎ 64431; reservations@him.zimsun.co.zw; cnr 3rd St & Aerodrome Rd; r US$130) Typical of Holiday Inns. Not flash, but clean and provides good service.

Stax Steak House (☎ 62653; First Mutual Arcade, Herbert Chitepo St; dinner US$25) As well as succulent steaks, this restaurant serves veggie burgers, salads and desserts.

Jenny's of Eighth Avenue (☎ 67764; cnr Eighth Ave & Herbert Chitepo St; mains around US$8) You can pop into this craft-shop cafe for a coffee or lunch.

Self-caterers can stock up at the **TM Supermarket** (cnr Herbert Chitepo St & B Ave) or visit the fruit and vegetable market at the Sakubva Musika Bus Terminal.

Entertainment

Rainbow Centre Cinema (Robert Mugabe Rd) Shows Hollywood flicks.

Shopping

Jairos Jiri Crafts (41 First St) Offers a number of cheap souvenirs, such as batiks, carvings, wall hangings and T-shirts, with the added bonus that all profits go to charity.

Nibeeka Gallery (Green Coucal Cafe, 111 Second St) This is more avant-garde, with hand-painted textiles and other crafts.

Getting There & Away

There are buses, both 'local' and express, that leave daily for Mutare from Mbare Musika and Road Port Terminal, but the safest, quickest and most convenient way to get there is to hire a car from Harare (Avis or Eurocar).

BVUMBA MOUNTAINS

☎ 020

Just 28km southeast of Mutare, the Bvumba (pronounced Vumba) Mountains are characterised by cool, forested highlands and deep, dense valleys. In the language of the Manyika Shona people, Bvumba means 'drizzle' and you'll probably see why. With its meadows, apple orchards, country gardens and teahouses, the area seems akin to the British countryside. If you're going to be staying for more than a few days, pick up *Bvumba: Magic in the Mist* by David Martin from bookshops around First St in Harare.

Sights

BUNGA FOREST BOTANICAL RESERVE

This sprawling 1558-hectare **reserve** (admission free) is a rare pocket of forest that has not been (and cannot be) chopped down or burnt off. There are no facilities, but the 39 hectares that straddle the main road to the botanical gardens do feature some ill-defined and overgrown hiking tracks, with plenty of butterflies, chameleons and birds to keep you company.

BVUMBA BOTANICAL GARDENS & RESERVE

These **gardens** (admission US$14; 7am-5pm) are divided into a landscaped botanical garden (159 hectares), with specimens from around the world and wide lawns, and a wild **botanical reserve** (42 hectares), crisscrossed with footpaths through natural bush. Wildlife includes samango monkeys (unique to the Eastern Highlands), as well as elands, duikers, bushbucks and sables.

Activities

Even if you can't tell a putter from a wedge, don't miss out on a round of **golf** at the Leopard Rock Hotel (below), with its superb grounds and breathtaking vistas. The European PGA ranked it the second-toughest course in the world. There is a dress code: shirts with collar.

Twitchers can do a two-hour bird-life walk with **Seldomseen Farm** (☎ 68482). Keep your eyes peeled for a buff-spotted fluff tail or stripe-cheeked bulbul.

Sleeping & Eating

Ndundu Lodge (☎ 63777; www.ndundu.com; Bvumba Rd; campsites or dm per person US$5, s/d US$20/28) This delightful thatched cottage, 10 minutes' walk from Bvumba Botanical Reserve, has a library, an impressive CD collection, a well-stocked bar and a restaurant offering veg and meat dishes. The enthusiastic owners have mapped out great walking and bike trails (for free) through the Bvumba.

Genaina Lodge (☎ 68177; s/d US$100/140, cottages US$200) Located 24km along Bvumba Rd from Mutare. Has tiny private, thatched cottages with a sometimes-open gallery of African artefacts. Serves breakfast and lunch.

Leopard Rock Hotel (☎ 60192; s/d US$150/200) Once a favourite of English royalty and one of Zimbabwe's grand old dames, it's at the end of the Bvumba Rd. Although it reeks of glory from another era, it is still fancy and luxurious with stunning views across to Mozambique.

Inn on the Vumba (☎ 67449; s/d US$100/140;) At the start of Bvumba Rd, 5km from Mutare. Has five cottages and two family rooms. Great for kids, with a swimming pool and playground.

Tony's Coffee House (Bvumba Rd; coffees from US$1, cakes from US$3; 10am-5pm Wed-Mon) Going to this legendary little thatched-roof cafe is an experience you'll always remember. The entertaining host will give you a lowdown

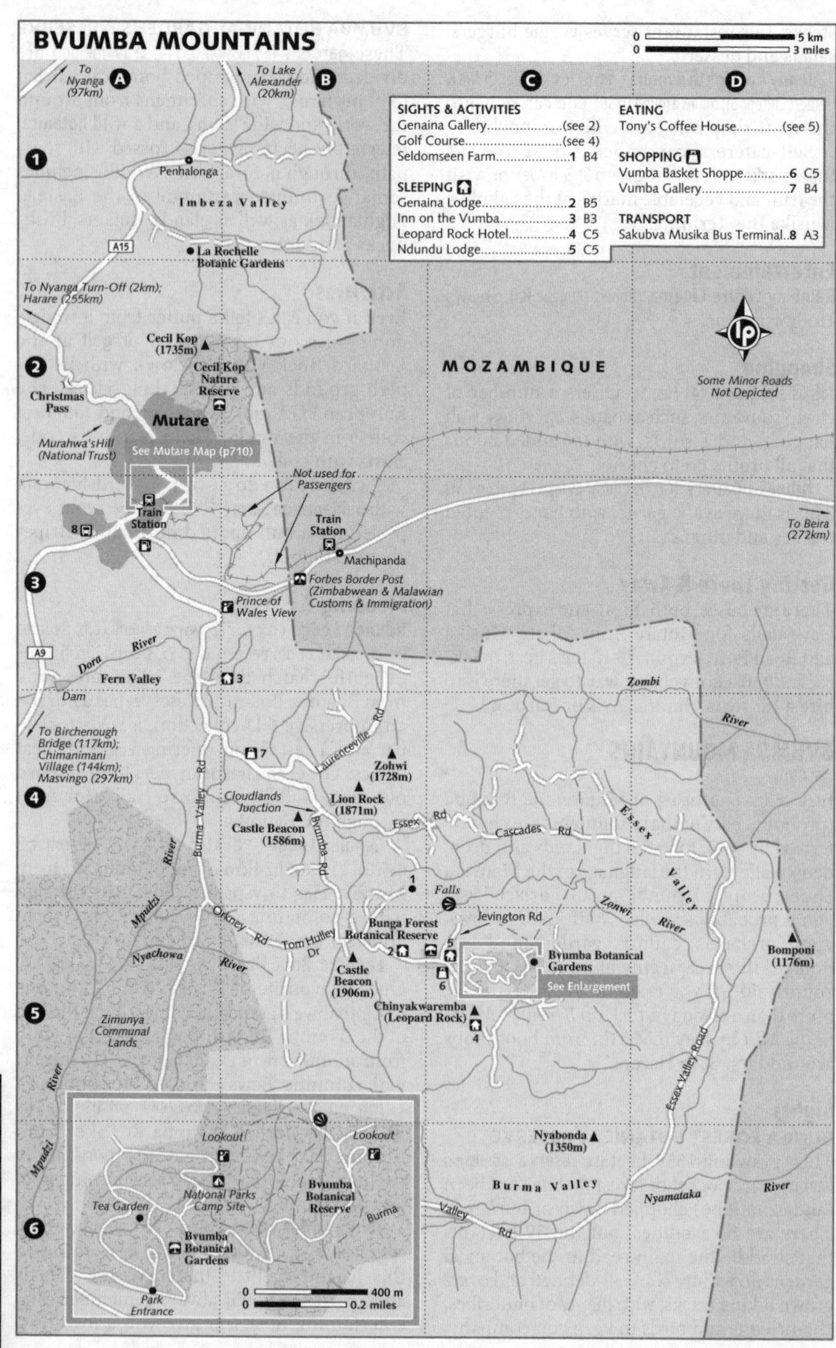

BVUMBA MOUNTAINS
0 5 km
0 3 miles
SIGHTS & ACTIVITIES
Genaina Gallery....................(see 2)
Golf Course............................(see 4)
Seldomseen Farm.........................1 B4
SLEEPING
Genaina Lodge..............................2 B5
Inn on the Vumba..........................3 B3
Leopard Rock Hotel........................4 C5
Ndundu Lodge................................5 C5
EATING
Tony's Coffee House............(see 5)
SHOPPING
Vumba Basket Shoppe..............6 C5
Vumba Gallery..........................7 B4
TRANSPORT
Sakubva Musika Bus Terminal..8 A3
To Nyanga (97km)
To Lake Alexander (20km)
Penhalonga
Imbeza Valley
A15
La Rochelle Botanic Gardens
To Nyanga Turn-Off (2km); Harare (255km)
Cecil Kop (1735m)
Cecil Kop Nature Reserve
Christmas Pass
Mutare
Murahwa'sHill (National Trust)
See Mutare Map (p710)
MOZAMBIQUE
Some Minor Roads Not Depicted
Not used for Passengers
Train Station
Train Station
Machipanda
To Beira (272km)
Forbes Border Post (Zimbabwean & Malawian Customs & Immigration)
Prince of Wales View
A9
Dora River
Fern Valley
Dam
To Birchenough Bridge (117km); Chimanimani Village (144km); Masvingo (297km)
Laurenceville Rd
Zohwi (1728m)
Lion Rock (1871m)
Cloudlands Junction
Castle Beacon (1586m)
Burma Valley Rd
Bvumba Rd
Essex Rd
Cascades Rd
Essex Valley
Zombi River
Mpudzi River
Falls
Jevington Rd
Zonwi River
Orkney Rd
Tom Hulley Dr
Bunga Forest Botanical Reserve
Castle Beacon (1906m)
Bvumba Botanical Gardens
See Enlargement
Nyachowa River
Chinyakwaremba (Leopard Rock)
Bomponi (1176m)
Zimunya Communal Lands
Essex Valley Road
Nyabonda (1350m)
Burma Valley
Valley Rd
Nyamataka River
Lookout
Lookout
National Parks Camp Site
Tea Garden
Bvumba Botanical Reserve
Burma
Bvumba Botanical Gardens
Park Entrance
0 400 m
0 0.2 miles

on the area while he watches you devour his delectable but sinful cakes, coffees, teas and hot chocolates. You won't need to eat for the rest of the day.

Shopping

Along Bvumba Rd you'll see women sitting underneath embroidered tablecloths, aprons and hankies, all strung up and swaying in the breeze. You'll literally make their day if you buy from them.

Vumba Basket Shoppe (Hivu Nursery, Tea Garden & Lodge, Bvumba Rd) Sells cheap basketware, as well as the famous Bvumba cheese.

Vumba Gallery (Bvumba Rd) This massive gallery houses an extensive range of cheap T-shirts, baskets and pottery.

Genaina Gallery (Bvumba Rd) Sells more expensive, high-quality crafts from Zimbabwe and the region.

NYANGA NATIONAL PARK

☎ 029

The 47,000-hectare **Nyanga National Park** (admission US$10; 6am-6pm) is a geographically and scenically distinct enclave in the Eastern Highlands. Cecil Rhodes fell in love with the area, so he simply bought it for his own residence. Near Nyanga (Rhodes) Dam, he built a luxurious homestead for himself and created an English-style garden with imported European hardwoods. It is now the Rhodes Hotel.

Close to the old hotel is the **main gate** (☎ 8274) to Nyanga National Park. The **Nyanga Publicity Association** (☎ 8435; 8am-1pm & 2-4pm Tue-Fri, 9-11am Sat) is housed in the Nyanga village library, halfway between the village centre and the appropriately named Village Inn.

Sights & Activities

The **Rhodes Hotel**, with its tropical verandah and well-kept gardens overlooking the Nyanga Dam, was once the home of Cecil Rhodes. It's worth a visit for a meal or drink or to admire the gardens.

The **Nyanga Historical Exhibition** (Rhodes Museum; admission US$4; 9am-1pm & 2.30pm-5.30pm Thu-Tue) is housed in the old man's former stables in the grounds of what is now the Rhodes Hotel.

World's View (admission US$4; permanently open) is perched atop the Troutbeck Massif on a precipice above Troutbeck. This National Trust site affords broad views of northern Zimbabwe. It's 11km up a winding, steep road from Troutbeck – follow the signposts.

The flat-topped and myth-shrouded **Nyangani** (2592m) is Zimbabwe's highest mountain. From the car park 14km east of Nyanga Dam, the climb to the summit takes two to three hours. Note that the weather can change abruptly, and when the mists drop the view becomes irrelevant.

Sleeping & Eating

The main **park lodges** (☎ 04-495 980, 0913-235 112) are at Rhodes Dam, which is about 50m from the main gate as you enter the park. There are other lodges near Udu Dam – keep on the road to Nyanga for about 1km past the sign to the main park gate; the lodges are on the left, but you have to go to main office anyway to book in for them.

There are also lodges at Mare Dam, with a lovely setting overlooking the dam; go past the main office at Rhodes on the Mare River road, and follow the signs to Mare Dam, about 10kms from main gate.

Many hotels listed here are popular with expats in Mutare and business conferences from Harare, so it can be worth booking ahead.

Troutbeck Inn (☎ 8305; zimsuncro@zimsun.co.zw; s/d US$140/156) A very English-style inn with a lake, lovely views, roaring fires and hearty English food, including high tea. Good for families, with play equipment for kids.

Inn on Rupurara (☎ 3021/4; rupurara@innsofzimbabwe.co.zw; s/d with full board US$110/140) A beautifully appointed hotel of African-style bungalows with verandahs. Ask for views overlooking the valley to Rupurara Mountain (or Bald Man's Head), not the 'water views', as the water is more like a pond.

Montclair Hotel & Casino (☎ 2441; fax 2447; s/d incl breakfast US$16/20;) Once a three-star place but now very run down. The rooms are large and if the fires in the foyer are roaring it is a nice touch.

Getting There & Away

There are buses from Harare to Rusape, which is located along the Mutare road. At the time of writing Rusape was a politically contentious area, and travelling by bus is not recommended. It's best to hire a car and self-drive or enquire when booking your hotel as to whether transfers are currently available.

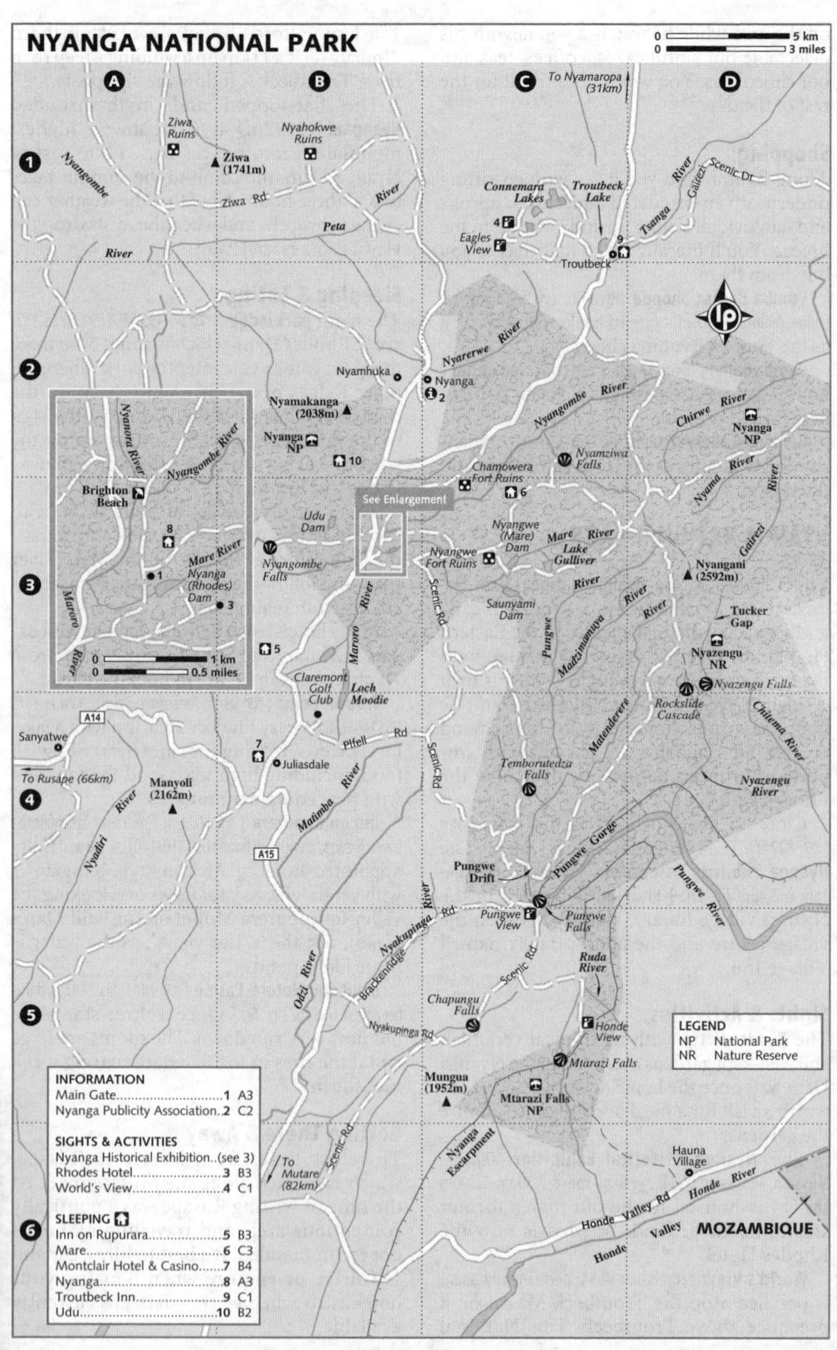

NYANGA NATIONAL PARK
0 5 km
0 3 miles
A
B
C
D
1
2
3
4
5
6
To Nyamaropa (31km)
Ziwa Ruins
Ziwa (1741m)
Nyahokwe Ruins
Nyangombe
River
Ziwa Rd
Peta
River
Connemara Lakes
Troutbeck Lake
4
Eagles View
9
Troutbeck
Tsanga
River
Gairezi
Scenic Dr
Nyamhuka
Nyanga
2
Nyarerwe River
Nyamakanga (2038m)
Nyanga NP
10
Nyangombe River
Chirwe River
Nyanga NP
Nyamziwa Falls
Chamowera Fort Ruins
6
Nyama River
River
See Enlargement
Udu Dam
Nyangombe Falls
Nyangwe (Mare) Dam
Mare River
Lake Gulliver
Nyangwe Fort Ruins
Gairezi
Nyangani (2592m)
Scenic Rd
Saunyami Dam
River
River
River
Tucker Gap
Nyazengu NR
Maroro River
Pungwe
Matzimamuya
Nyazengu Falls
Rockslide Cascade
5
Claremont Golf Club
Loch Moodie
Matendere
Chitema River
Nyazengu River
A14
Sanyatwe
To Rusape (66km)
7
Juliasdale
Pfell Rd
Scenic Rd
Temborutedza Falls
Manyoli (2162m)
River
Nyadiri
Matimba River
A15
Pungwe Gorge
Pungwe Drift
Pungwe River
Pungwe View
Pungwe Falls
Nyakupinga Rd
River
Odzi River
Brackenridge
Scenic Rd
Ruda River
Chapungu Falls
Nyakupinga Rd
Honde View
Mtarazi Falls
Mungua (1952m)
Mtarazi Falls NP
Nyanga Escarpment
Scenic Rd
To Mutare (82km)
Hauna Village
Honde Valley Rd
Honde River
Valley
Honde
MOZAMBIQUE
LEGEND
NP National Park
NR Nature Reserve
Nyanora River
Nyangombe River
Brighton Beach
8
1
Mare River
Nyanga (Rhodes) Dam
3
Maroro River
0 1 km
0 0.5 miles
INFORMATION
Main Gate....1 A3
Nyanga Publicity Association..2 C2
SIGHTS & ACTIVITIES
Nyanga Historical Exhibition..(see 3)
Rhodes Hotel....3 B3
World's View....4 C1
SLEEPING
Inn on Rupurara....5 B3
Mare....6 C3
Montclair Hotel & Casino....7 B4
Nyanga....8 A3
Troutbeck Inn....9 C1
Udu....10 B2

CHIMANIMANI

☎ 026

Chimanimani village, 150km south of Mutare, is enclosed by green hills on three sides, and opens on the fourth side to the dramatic wall of the Chimanimani Mountains. Even if you're not going to Chimanimani National Park, the tiny village is certainly worth visiting for its serenity and scenery.

There are information notice boards at the Chimanimani Hotel, Blue Moon Bar and Msasa Cafe. There's a post office on the street past the village green. Be careful about muggings while walking in remote areas.

Sights & Activities

You can walk (not drive, the road is shocking) around **Nyamzure**, also known as Pork Pie Hill (because of the shape). The well-defined path (5km uphill) to the summit starts near the church and offers spectacular views all around, though there's not much wildlife left due to poaching. The same path continues for another 2km to the entrance of the **Pork Pie Eland Sanctuary** (admission US$6; dawn-dusk).

There are guides available in the village for mountain hikers but local guy Doug, whom you can find by asking at the Kweza Lodge, is the most knowledgeable person around.

For information on hiking in the national park, see right.

Sleeping, Eating & Drinking

Unfortunately, most of the lodges and hotels that were located on farms have been taken over by war veterans and therefore have ceased to exist.

Chimanimani Hotel (☎ 2511; s/d with full board US$75/100;) In the village, this place is very nice, surrounded by pleasant gardens, a pool and a casino – which is still open. Ask for a room with mountain views.

Kweza Lodge (☎ 3351, 3030, 0912-101283; d US$10) Located opposite the Frog & Fern, this place is clean and cosy with incredibly friendly and helpful managers. Offers horse riding.

Frog & Fern (☎ 2294; d US$15) It's very hard to contact this hotel but it's worth it for its three pretty stone lodges, or the Round House for six. It's very comfortable, with great views of the mountains. It is located 1.2km west of the village.

Msasa Cafe (mains around US$10; 8am-5pm Mon-Sat) This place is the best spot in the village for eating out. It offers a wide variety of meals and snacks, from local *sadza* and stew to delicious Mexican tortillas. Do warn the owner, Daphne, in advance, however, if you want dinner.

For a cheap drink, and a long chat with some locals, head to Blue Moon Bar.

Getting There & Away

Buses run from Mutare's bus terminal to Chimanimani, but are not recommended. Self-driving or a charter flight are your best options.

CHIMANIMANI NATIONAL PARK

Chimanimani National Park is a hiker's paradise. The northern end of the park, called **Corner**, is still very wild and unspoiled, but the road there is not good.

To go hiking in **Chimanimani National Park** (admission US$10; 6am-6pm), 19km from Chimanimani village, you must sign in and pay park fees at Mutekeswane Base Camp. The road ends here and the park is then only accessible on foot.

From base camp, Bailey's Folly is the shortest and most popular route to the mountain

MOVERS & SHAKERS: OLIVER MTUKUDZI

Oliver Mtukudzi's music is so ubiquitous in Zimbabwe and the man himself so accomplished and so loved that he is seen across generations as a father figure. His lyrics are largely socially driven and are an inspiring force in a country where most of the people have been silenced. He is candid about AIDS, honest about politics and savvy about mixing it all with essential doses of hope.

A prolific musician with more than 30 albums to his name, the composer of three movie soundtracks and a contributor to Mahube, Southern Africa's super-group, Oliver Mtukudzi has made the most of his 54 years. His music is described as soul and R&B, a mix of his homeland and South African townships. He is known as 'Tuku', and across Southern Africa people will talk of Tuku tunes and the sounds that are like a balm for so many Southern African souls.

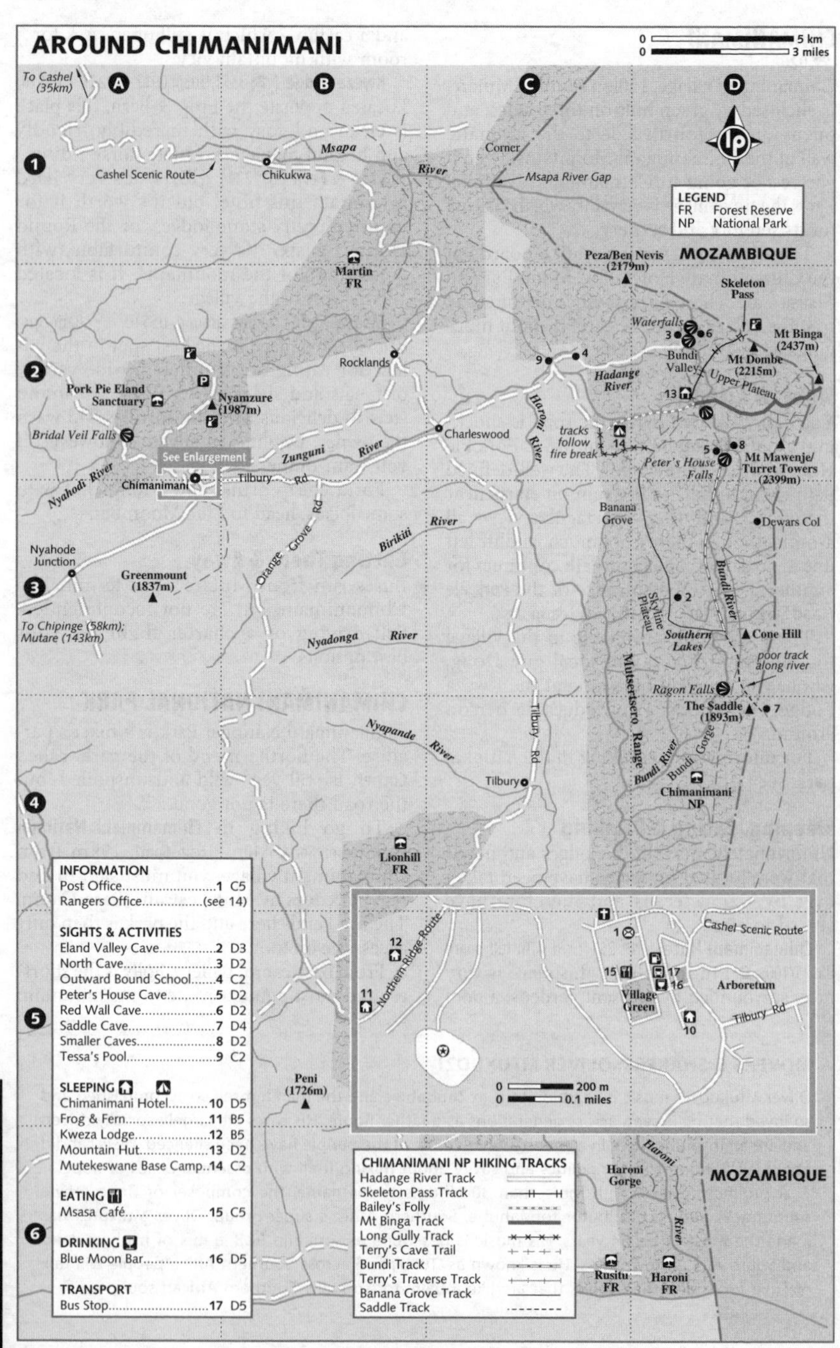

INFORMATION
Post Office 1 C5
Rangers Office (see 14)

SIGHTS & ACTIVITIES
Eland Valley Cave 2 D3
North Cave 3 D2
Outward Bound School 4 C2
Peter's House Cave 5 D2
Red Wall Cave 6 D2
Saddle Cave 7 D4
Smaller Caves 8 D2
Tessa's Pool 9 C2

SLEEPING
Chimanimani Hotel 10 D5
Frog & Fern 11 B5
Kweza Lodge 12 B5
Mountain Hut 13 D2
Mutekeswane Base Camp 14 C2

EATING
Msasa Café 15 C5

DRINKING
Blue Moon Bar 16 D5

TRANSPORT
Bus Stop 17 D5

CHIMANIMANI NP HIKING TRACKS
Hadange River Track
Skeleton Pass Track
Bailey's Folly
Mt Binga Track
Long Gully Track
Terry's Cave Trail
Bundi Track
Terry's Traverse Track
Banana Grove Track
Saddle Track

hut (around three hours). Another option is the gentler Banana Grove Track. From the mountain hut, it's an easy 40-minute walk to **Skeleton Pass**, a former guerrilla route between Zimbabwe and Mozambique. Go in the late afternoon for an unsurpassed view into Wizard Valley in Mozambique.

The highest point in the Chimanimani Range is the 2437m-high **Mt Binga** on the Mozambican border, a stiff three-hour climb from the hut. Carry plenty of water. The last stream for a fill-up is less than halfway between the hut and the summit.

Hadange River Track is a good but challenging exit route that emerges near the **Outward Bound School** (☎ 0912-918032; outwardboundzim@stargaze.co.za) and **Tessa's Pool**, a lovely swimming hole and a great place to cool off. If you exit this way, you'll need to walk back along the road to sign out at base camp. The Bundi Valley is riddled with **caves** and rock overhangs, which make ideal (free) camp sites. The most accessible caves lie near the valley's northern end. **North Cave**, a 30-minute walk north of the mountain hut, overlooks a waterfall and opens onto views of the highest peaks. Above the waterfall is a pool, ideal for a teeth-chattering dip if you need some refreshment. **Red Wall Cave** lies 10 minutes further on.

Sleeping & Eating

At Chimanimani National Park you can either camp at **Mutekeswane Base Camp** (campsites per person US$2), which is at the park entrance, or stay in the **mountain hut** (per person US$5), which is a long and steep half-day walk from the base camp. This hut is a bit grubby but has running water.

THE MIDLANDS & SOUTHEASTERN ZIMBABWE

Geographically, the Midlands are known as the highveld, while the warmer, lower-lying southeast is the lowveld. At the transition of the regions is Masvingo. Nearby are Lake Mutirikwe and Great Zimbabwe. The lowveld's finest attraction is the beautiful, often-ignored Gonarezhou National Park.

KWE KWE

☎ 055 / pop 75,000

Kwe Kwe is a worthy place to break up the journey between Harare and Bulawayo, though you're unlikely to spend the night there.

The worthwhile **National Mining Museum** (First Ave; admission incl guided tour US$2; 9am-5pm) provides a good introduction to commercial gold-mining in Zimbabwe, past and present.

GWERU

☎ 054 / pop 128,000

Zimbabwe's fourth-largest city isn't a travellers' destination, though many pass through at some stage.

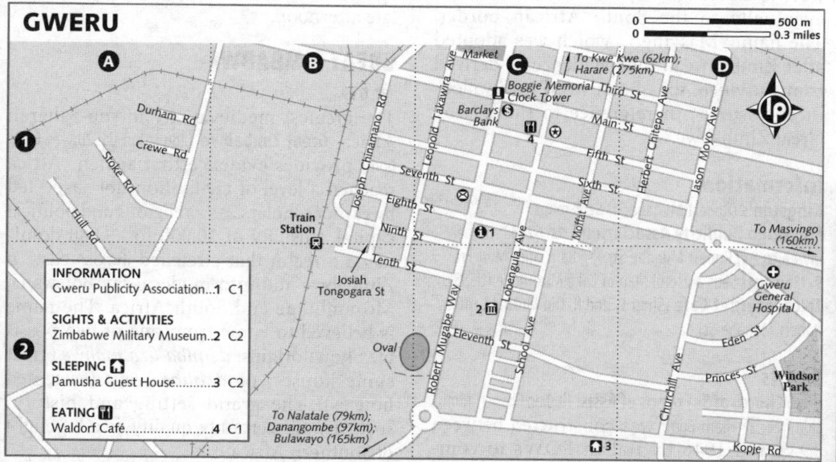

ZIMBABWE

The **Zimbabwe Military Museum** (Midlands Museum; Lobengula Ave; admission US$2; 9am-5pm) houses a collection of weapons, costumes and medals, as well as tanks, planes and other big toys.

Pamusha Guest House (23535; 73 Kopje Rd; s/d with shared bathroom US$18/22, s/d US$28/50) offers the best value in town. It's quaint and friendly, some rooms contain massive, new bathrooms and all rooms come with breakfast.

The **Waldorf Cafe** (54 Fifth St; meals under US$1) serves African fare, and has a good bakery inside.

AROUND GWERU

Nalatale (also spelt Nalatela or Nalatele) rates among the best of Zimbabwe's 150 walled ruins. This simple structure on a remote granite hilltop enjoys a commanding view across the hills, plains and *kopjes* (little hills). The main feature, a decorated wall, exhibits all the primary decorative wall patterns found in Zimbabwe: chevron, chequer, cord, herringbone and ironstone.

The ruins are well signposted. From Gweru, turn south off the Bulawayo road at Daisyfield Siding and follow the gravel road approximately 27km to the signposted left turn-off. The site is 1km uphill from the parking area.

MASVINGO

039 / pop 51,000

Masvingo is a classic grid-patterned country town. It is a crossroads town from where people head slightly inland for the ruins, or west to Bulawayo or, much further south, eventually to the South African border. The name 'Masvingo', which was adopted after Zimbabwean independence, is derived from *rusvingo*, the Shona word for 'walled-in enclosures', in reference to the nearby Great Zimbabwe.

Information

Kingston's (Robert Mugabe St) Sells maps.

Masvingo Publicity Association (62643; mgpa@mweb.co.zw; Robert Mugabe St; 8am-5pm Mon-Fri, 9-11am Sat) Sells a useful map of Lake Mutirikwe (US$3).

Telco Internet Cafe (Shop 5, 2nd fl, Old Mutual Centre, Robert Mugabe St)

Sights

The **Church of St Francis of Assisi** (Italian Chapel; admission free; 8am-6pm) was constructed between 1942 and 1946 by Italian POWs to commemorate 71 of their compatriots who died in Zimbabwe during WWII. Drive 4km east towards Mutare from the caravan park, take the left turn at the signpost and then turn immediately left again. Just in front of the military barracks, turn left yet again.

The small **Shagashe Game Park** (admission US$8; dawn-dusk) lies 5km north of Masvingo along the road to Harare.

Sleeping

Backpackers Rest (63960; Josiah Tongogara Ave; dm US$20, s/d with breakfast & shared bathroom from US$36/48) Offers dark, musty and noisy rooms, but it is convenient and friendly. The hostel is upstairs and easy to miss; the entrance is along Robertson St.

Flame Lilly (s/d incl breakfast US$40/60) Set within a large garden, this place is secure and friendly and right in the centre of town.

Chevron Hotel (63581; chevron@icon.co.zw; 2 Robert Mugabe St; s/d incl breakfast US$60/90;) Don't expect your usual 'Chevron', but this is convenient, and most rooms have a TV and overlook the pool and garden.

Getting There & Away

Note that the Masvingo road, which goes from the southernmost point of Zimbabwe, Beitbridge – the border with South Africa – to Harare, and then north to Zambia and Malawi, is used by importing/exporting cargo trucks 24/7 and is in shocking disrepair. Do not catch a bus along this road, do not hitch. Arrange transport through a travel agent, or, if you self-drive, do not drive after late afternoon.

GREAT ZIMBABWE

039

The greatest medieval city in sub-Saharan Africa, **Great Zimbabwe** (admission US$20; 6am-6pm) provides evidence that ancient Africa reached a level of civilisation not suspected by earlier scholars. As a religious and political capital, this city of 10,000 to 20,000 dominated a realm that stretched across eastern Zimbabwe and into modern-day Botswana, Mozambique and South Africa. The name is believed to come from one of two possible Shona origins: *dzimba dza mabwe* (great stone houses) or *dzimba woye* (esteemed houses). The grand setting and history-soaked walls certainly qualify as a highlight of Southern Africa.

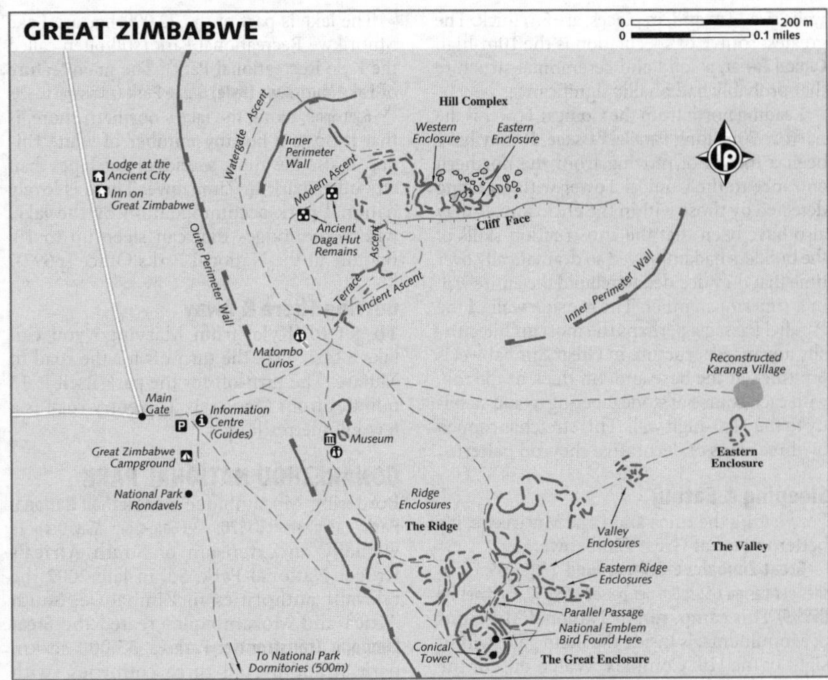

If you need more information about the site than we can provide here, try to find one of the latest *Great Zimbabwe* booklets (US$6) at the main gate or *A Trail Guide to the Great Zimbabwe National Monument* from bookshops around Zimbabwe. Alternatively, arrange a two-hour guided tour (about US$12 per person) at the **main gate** (☎ 7055) or the Information Centre at the start of the walking trails.

Inside the complex, Matombo Curios offers a huge selection of souvenirs and cold drinks.

History

Great Zimbabwe was first occupied in the 11th century. The settlers probably comprised several scattered groups that recognised the safety of numbers. Construction of the Hill Complex commenced in the 13th century, while the remainder was built over the next 100 years.

Fuelled by the Swahili gold trade, the city grew into a powerful religious and political capital, and became the heart of Rozwi culture. Royal herds increased and coffers overflowed. But eventually Great Zimbabwe probably became a victim of its own success: by the 15th century the growing human and bovine population, and their associated environmental impacts, had depleted local resources, necessitating emigration to more productive lands. Great Zimbabwe declined rapidly and when the Portuguese arrived in the 16th century the city was virtually deserted.

Sights

The site is divided into several major ruins. Probably the first of the Great Zimbabwe structures to be completed, the **Hill Complex** (once known as the Acropolis) was a series of royal and ritual enclosures. Its most salient feature is the Western Enclosure, where the Ancient Ascent and Terrace Ascent converge.

The **Valley** is a series of 13th-century walls and *daga* (traditional round house) platforms. The area yielded metal tools and the soapstone birds that became the national symbol of Zimbabwe.

The **Great Enclosure**, thought to have served as a royal compound, is the structure most identified with Great Zimbabwe. Nearly 100m wide and 255m in circumference, it's the largest ancient structure in sub-Saharan Africa. The mortarless walls rise 11m and, in places, are 5m thick. The greatest source of speculation is the 10m-high **Conical Tower**, a solid and ceremonial structure that probably had phallic significance.

Leading north from the Conical Tower is the narrow 70m-long **Parallel Passage**. It may have been a means of moving from the northern entrance to the Conical Tower without being detected by those within the enclosure. It may also have been that the construction skills of the builders had improved so dramatically over time that they decided to rebuild the entire wall in a superior manner. The outside wall of the Parallel Passage, perhaps the most architecturally advanced structure in Great Zimbabwe, is 6m thick at the base and 4m thick at the top, with each course of stone tapering to add stability to the 11m-high wall. This stretch is capped by three rings of decorative chevron patterns.

Sleeping & Eating

For visiting the ruins and Lake Mutirikwe, it's better to stay at Great Zimbabwe.

Great Zimbabwe Campground (☎ 7055; campsites per person US$3, dm per person US$1.50, rondavel s/d US$5/9) This camp, run by National Museums & Monuments, is inside the main gate, within sight of the Hill Complex. Watch out for the thieving baboons and monkeys.

National Park Accommodation (campsites per person US$8, dm US$25, rondavels with shared bathroom per person US$40) Strung out along a trail that heads south of the main gate. The rondavels are small, but cheap, while the campsite offers little shade or security. The dormitory building is fenced off, but isolated – about 1km from the main gate. These places are not run by National Parks & Wildlife Zimbabwe, so book at the main gate.

Lodge at the Ancient City (☎ 7205; per person incl breakfast US$145) Beautifully designed individual African lodges set among re-created 'ruins' to blend beautifully with the landscape and the concept of the place.

Inn on Great Zimbabwe (☎ 64879; iogz@innsofzimbabwe.co.zw; B&B US$180) This tranquil place on a wooded hill above Lake Mutirikwe, 6km east of Great Zimbabwe, is good value. The decor is dated, but it is comfortable.

LAKE MUTIRIKWE (KYLE) RECREATIONAL PARK

☎ 039

In 1961 a 305m-wide wall was built across Mutirikwe River to create Lake Mutirikwe, Zimbabwe's second-largest dam (90 sq km).

The lake is part of the 22,000-hectare Lake Mutirikwe Recreational Park (still often called the Kyle Recreational Park). The main feature of **Lake Mutirikwe (Kyle) Game Park** (admission US$20; 🕑 6am-6pm), along the lake's northern shore, is that it hosts a healthy number of white rhinos. It also has more species of antelopes than any other park in Zimbabwe. There is lovely national park accommodation by the lake, with some lodges that can sleep up to 10. Enquire at the National Parks Office (p697).

Getting There & Away

To get to 'Kyle' from Masvingo you can take a taxi. Take the turn-off for the road to Mutare. The turn-off for the park itself is 15 minutes from Masvingo. The entry road is a few kilometres long.

GONAREZHOU NATIONAL PARK

Bordering Mozambique, **Gonarezhou National Park** (admission US$20; 🕑 6am-6pm May-Oct) is virtually an extension of South Africa's Kruger National Park. So, in late 2002 the relevant authorities in Zimbabwe, South Africa and Mozambique created the **Great Limpopo Transfrontier Park**, a 35,000-sq-km park straddling all three countries (with no boundaries). This prototype park was deemed successful enough that another will be created in the west of Zimbabwe, taking in Botswana and Zambia.

Although some roads in the park are passable to 2WD vehicles, most are rough and require a 4WD, especially in the south. From November to April, there's no access to the national park camps at Chipinda Pools, Mbalauta and Swimuwini.

Sleeping

The costs of camping range from US$20 to US$50 per person, while chalets at Swimuwini cost about US$70. Book at National Parks & Wildlife Zimbabwe in Harare (p697) or Bulawayo (opposite).

Pamushana (☎ 04-369136; www.singita.com; head office, PO Box MP845, Mt Pleasant, Harare; bungalows all-inclusive US$800) Zimbabwe's uberluxurious lodge (Michael Douglas and Catherine Zeta-Jones are two past guests) is situated on its own private concession called Malilangwe. Separate bungalows are set among the trees and perched upon a cliff. Some overlook a hippo-laden lake. Each has a private sundeck, infinity pool and outdoor rock shower.

There's also delicious food and a yoga room. It is nonprofit and dedicated to protecting and saving endangered species of wildlife.

Getting There & Away

Pamushana has its own airstrip and can organise charter flights and transfers for guests staying at the hotel. Self-driving is the other way to go.

WESTERN ZIMBABWE

With three of the country's major attractions, Victoria Falls (see p604), Hwange National Park and Matobo National Park, western Zimbabwe is an excellent place to spend the majority of your time in Zimbabwe.

BULAWAYO

☎ 09 / pop 1 million

With its wide streets and colonial buildings, Zimbabwe's pretty second city was originally called Gu-Bulawayo (Killing Place), which probably came about because of the executions undertaken on Thabas Indunas (Hill of Chiefs) under Mzilikazi. Bulawayo is also a base for trips to nearby attractions, such as the Khami Ruins and Matobo National Park. It's also an ideal staging point for trips to Hwange National Park, on the way to Victoria Falls.

Information

BOOKSHOPS

Kingston's (Map p723; 91 Jason Moyo St) Kingston's bookshop sells maps, novels and a few international magazines.

EMERGENCY

Main police station (Map p723; ☎ 72516; cnr Leopold Takawira Ave & Fife St) For emergencies contact this office or the smaller office in Central Park.

Medical Air Rescue Service (MARS; Map p723; ☎ 60351; 42 Robert Mugabe Way) For ambulance services.

MEDICAL SERVICES

Bulawayo Central Hospital (Map p722; ☎ 72111) The best-equipped and most accessible public hospital; near the Ascot Racecourse, off St Lukes Ave.

Galen House Emergency Medical Clinic (Map p723; ☎ 540051; cnr Josiah Tongogara St & Ninth Ave) This privately run clinic is better than the central hospital.

POST

Main post office (Map p723; ☎ 62535; cnr Eighth Ave & Main St; ⌚ 8am-5pm Mon-Fri, to 11am Sat)

TOURIST INFORMATION

Bulawayo Publicity Association (Map p723; ☎ 60867; www.arachnid.co.zw/bulawayo; ⌚ 8.30am-4.45pm Mon-Fri, to noon Sat) In the City Hall car park, off Leopold Takawira Ave; has information on accommodation, transport, tours, activities and events in Bulawayo. It sells the detailed *Bulawayo Mobil Street Atlas* and distributes *Bulawayo This Month,* which lists upcoming events and useful addresses.

National Parks & Wildlife Zimbabwe (Map p723; ☎ 63646; cnr Herbert Chitepo St & Tenth Ave; ⌚ 8am-4pm Mon-Fri) Takes accommodation bookings for Matobo National Park.

Wildlife & Environment Zimbabwe (Map p723; ☎ 77309; 105 Fife St) Aims to encourage Zimbabweans to take an active interest in their wildlife heritage, and has therefore developed nature reserves and camps throughout the country.

TOUR OPERATORS

Bulawayo-based tour operators (for Matobo and surrounds) include the following:

Adventure Travel (☎ 66775)

Black Rhino (☎ 246448)

Driving You Wild (☎ 64868/9)

Eco Logical Africa (☎ 61189, 69559, 888790, 0912-239729, in South Africa 082-8284514; www.ecologicalafrica.com) Has 28 years of professional wilderness guiding plus charter flights.

Southern Comfort (☎ 281340)

Touch the Wild (☎ 888968/889088)

UTC (☎ 61402/74701)

Dangers & Annoyances

Bulawayo is more laid-back than Harare, but massive increases in unemployment and general desperation mean it's not nearly as safe as it once was. Avoid walking alone anywhere at night.

Sights

Set in a beautiful 100-year-old colonial building, the **National Art Gallery** (Map p723; ☎ 70721; Douslin House, cnr Main St & Leopold Takawira Ave; admission US$2; ⌚ 9am-5pm Tue-Sun) has temporary and permanent exhibitions of contemporary Zimbabwean sculpture and paintings. There's also a souvenir shop, a cafe and studios where you can see artists at work.

Sleeping

Packer's Rest (Map p723; ☎ 251111; packers@mweb.co.zw; 1 Oak Ave, Suburbs; campsites per person US$5, dm per person US$5, s/d US$20/25; 💻) Convenient to the city, this welcoming hostel offers phone and internet access. Enter off Twelfth Ave.

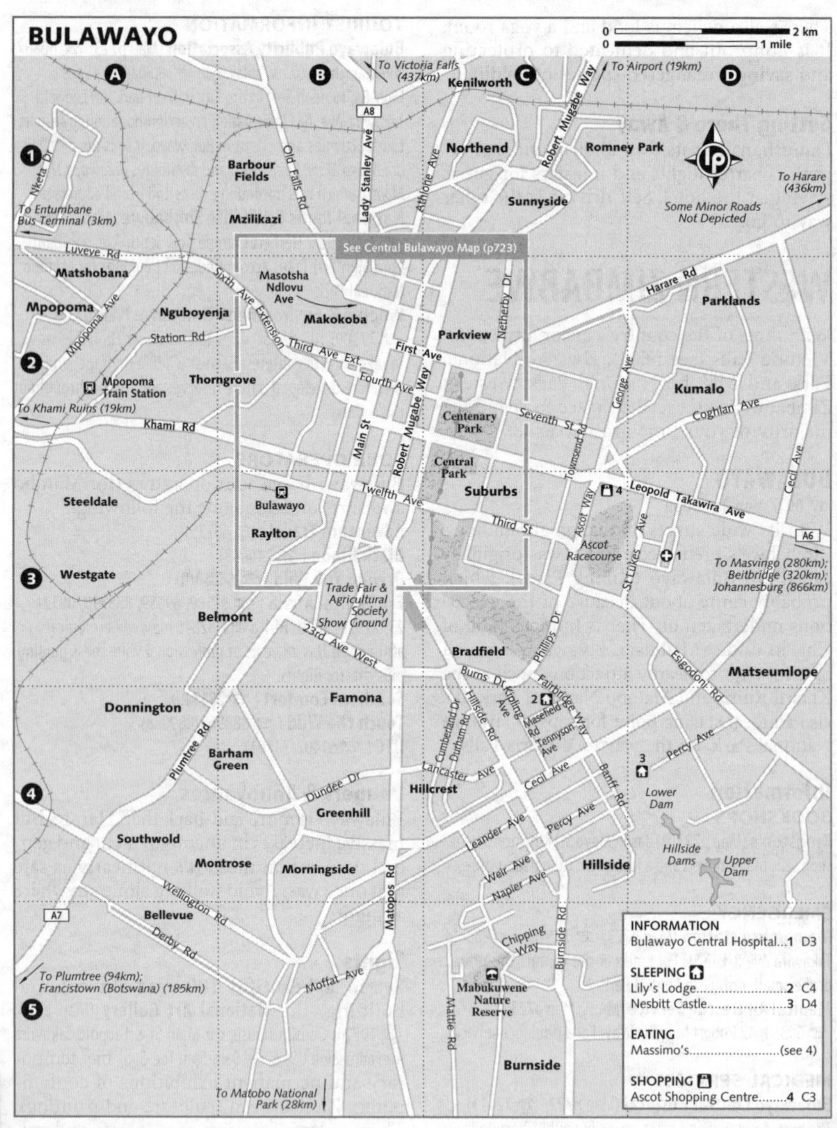

Lily's Lodge (☎ 245356; nyararai@excite.com; 3 Masefield Rd, Malindela; r US$30) This large house is popular with locals. Lily organises traditional evenings with food and dancing for guests.

Nesbitt Castle (Map p722; ☎ 282726/735/736; www.nesbittcastle.co.zw; Percy Ave, Hillside; s/d US$120/190) Built by an eccentric Englishman as his house, this place is quite surreal in its decor, each of the eight guestrooms being totally different – a great place for a decadent and romantic interlude. The food is good too.

Eating

Cafe Baku (Map p723; ☎ 883809; Bulawayo Centre, Main St; snacks from US$3; to late) This small, trendy cafe serves coffee, cakes and sandwiches.

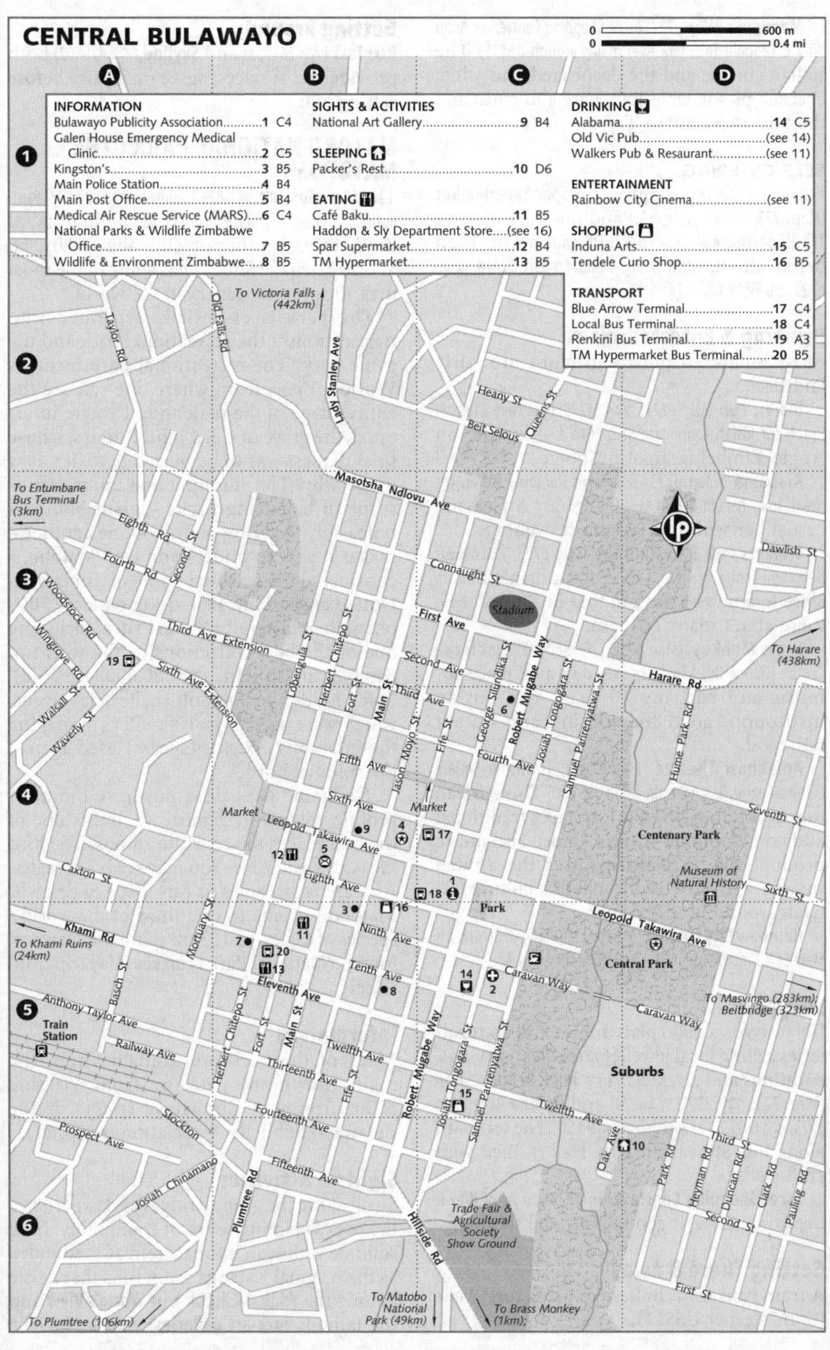
CENTRAL BULAWAYO
0 600 m
0 0.4 mi
INFORMATION
Bulawayo Publicity Association....1 C4
Galen House Emergency Medical Clinic....2 C5
Kingston's....3 B5
Main Police Station....4 B4
Main Post Office....5 B4
Medical Air Rescue Service (MARS)....6 C4
National Parks & Wildlife Zimbabwe Office....7 B5
Wildlife & Environment Zimbabwe....8 B5
SIGHTS & ACTIVITIES
National Art Gallery....9 B4
SLEEPING
Packer's Rest....10 D6
EATING
Café Baku....11 B5
Haddon & Sly Department Store....(see 16)
Spar Supermarket....12 B4
TM Hypermarket....13 B5
DRINKING
Alabama....14 C5
Old Vic Pub....(see 14)
Walkers Pub & Resaurant....(see 11)
ENTERTAINMENT
Rainbow City Cinema....(see 11)
SHOPPING
Induna Arts....15 C5
Tendele Curio Shop....16 B5
TRANSPORT
Blue Arrow Terminal....17 C4
Local Bus Terminal....18 C4
Renkini Bus Terminal....19 A3
TM Hypermarket Bus Terminal....20 B5
To Victoria Falls (442km)
To Entumbane Bus Terminal (3km)
To Harare (438km)
To Khami Ruins (24km)
To Masvingo (283km); Beitbridge (323km)
To Plumtree (106km)
To Matobo National Park (49km)
To Brass Monkey (1km);
Taylor Rd
Old Falls Rd
Lady Stanley Ave
Heany St
Beit Selous
Queens St
Masotsha Ndlovu Ave
Eighth Rd
Fourth Rd
Second St
Connaught St
Stadium
First Ave
Woodstock Rd
Wingrove Rd
Walsall St
Waverly St
Third Ave Extension
Sixth Ave Extension
Lobengula St
Herbert Chitepo St
Fort St
Main St
Second Ave
Third Ave
Jason Moyo St
Fife St
George Silundika St
Robert Mugabe Way
Josiah Tongogara St
Samuel Parirenyatwa St
Harare Rd
Hume Park Rd
Dawlish St
Fourth Ave
Fifth Ave
Sixth Ave
Market
Leopold Takawira Ave
Seventh St
Centenary Park
Museum of Natural History
Sixth St
Caxton St
Eighth Ave
Park
Ninth Ave
Khami Rd
Mortuary St
Tenth Ave
Caravan Way
Central Park
Eleventh Ave
Basch St
Anthony Taylor Ave
Train Station
Railway Ave
Twelfth Ave
Thirteenth Ave
Suburbs
Fourteenth Ave
Stockton
Prospect Ave
Twelfth Ave
Oak Ave
Third St
Park Rd
Heyman Rd
Duncan Rd
Clark Rd
Pauling Rd
Second St
Fifteenth Ave
Josiah Chinamano
Plumtree Rd
Hillside Rd
Trade Fair & Agricultural Society Show Ground
First St

Massimo's (Map p722; Ascot Shopping Centre, cnr Ascot Way & Leopold Takawira Ave; mains around US$15) The Italian cuisine and the decor (red-and-white checked plastic tablecloths) are authentic, and the host is eccentric. Try the pasta.

SELF-CATERING

For self-catering supplies, try **Spar Supermarket** (Map p723; Herbert Chitepo St) and the truly massive **TM Hypermarket** (Map p723; Eleventh Ave) or, even better, the **Haddon & Sly Department Store** (Map p723; cnr Eight Ave & Fife St).

Drinking & Entertainment

Most Bulawayo pubs and clubs are fairly laid-back.

Old Vic Pub (Map p723; ☎ 881273; Bulawayo Rainbow Hotel, cnr Josiah Tongogara St & 10th Ave) Exudes an Anglo-Zimbabwean atmosphere.

Alabama (Map p723; Bulawayo Rainbow Hotel, cnr Josiah Tongogara St & 10th Ave; 🕑 Wed-Sun) A pleasant, casual bar with live jazz most evenings.

Walkers Pub & Restaurant (Map p723; ☎ 69527; Bulawayo Centre, Main St) Good for a drink and as close to a pub as you can find in Zimbabwe – there aren't many of them.

Brass Monkey (Map p722; ☎ 880495; Zonk'Izizwe Centre, Hillside Rd) Had its heyday as a place for music and partying 10 years ago, but an institution, good for a drink and decent pub food.

Amakhosi Theatre (☎ 62652; Township Square Cultural Centre, Basch St; admission US$1.50) This African theatre, off the Old Falls Rd, stages traditional and contemporary theatre, dance and music productions. It also organises the annual Inxusa Festival, a traditional folk culture festival, around June and July.

Rainbow City Cinema (Map p723; Bulawayo Centre, cnr Main St & Ninth Ave) Still shows a few flicks.

Shopping

Bulawayo is a good place for art and craft galleries selling local jewellery, textiles, carvings, paintings and artefacts. Try **Tendele Curio Shop** (Map p723; ☎ 52391; 90 Fife St) and **Induna Arts** (Map p723; ☎ 69179; 121 Josiah Tongogara St). The footpath along Fife St near the City Hall is lined with craft stalls.

Ascot Shopping Centre (Map p722; cnr Ascot Way & Leopold Takawira Ave) is good for general shopping.

Getting There & Away

A train runs from Bulawayo to Victoria Falls (8pm, sleeper US$11).

Getting Around

Rixi Taxi (☎ 261933) and **Skyline** (☎ 470502) both provide taxi services; agree on a price before setting out.

MATOBO NATIONAL PARK ('THE MATOPOS')

The **Matopos** (☎ 083-8258; admission US$23; 🕑 6am-6pm) is one of the unsung highlights of Zimbabwe. Another of Zimbabwe's Unesco World Heritage Sites, it has some of the most majestic granite scenery in the world.

The park is essentially separated into two sections – the recreational park and the game park. The recreational park includes World's View, from where one can see the entire scope of the park and, if you're interested, the grave of Cecil John Rhodes, whose final request was to be buried here. It's easy to see why. The stunning and unique landscape of balancing rocks – giant boulders unfeasibly teetering on top of one another – makes it easy to understand why Matobo is considered the spiritual home of Zimbabwe. Dotted around the 425-sq-km park are 3000 officially registered rock-art sites, including one of the best collections in the world of San paintings (many over 20,000 years old). Some hidden niches still shelter clay ovens, which were used as iron smelters in making the infamous *assegais* (spears) used against the colonial hordes.

The game park does not have the most prolific wildlife in Zimbabwe, but is one of the best places to see white rhinos. The bird life is also extensive. You may see black eagles, African hawk eagles or rare Cape eagle owls; Matobo is home to one-third of the world's species of eagles. Just 33km south of Bulawayo, Matobo National Park is an easy day trip from the city.

Information

Maps of the park are available from the main (northern) gate; or from Wildlife & Environment Zimbabwe (p721) or the Bulawayo Publicity Association (see p721).

Sights & Activities

Stroll along the granite ridges and experience the overwhelming sense of tranquillity. Find solitude within an intimate retreat as secluded as the original Kalanga grain bins that nestle among the rocks. Check out **World's View** and the famous **rock-art galleries**, visit a Ndebele village, go horse riding in the Matobo Game Park or on an organised walk.

The busiest part of Matobo is **Maleme Dam**, with its campsite, general store, horse stables, rangers' offices and picnic sites. The area west and northwest of Maleme Dam is home to antelopes, baboons, hyraxes and zebras.

The **Northern Wild Area** offers glorious views down the Mjelele Valley to the Mjelele Dam.

Cecil Rhodes' Grave is atop the mountain he called World's View, which the Ndebele people knew as Malindidzimu (Dwelling Place of Benevolent Spirits). A display at the bottom of the hill outlines highlights of Rhodes' remarkable life and career. The **Shangani River Memorial**, just downhill from Rhodes' Grave, was erected in 1904 to the memory of Allan Wilson and 33 soldiers of his Shangani River Patrol; the entire troop was wiped out by General Mtjaan and his 30,000 Ndebele warriors.

Masiye Camp (☎ 880834; www.masiye.com) offers the following activities, at US$5 each, to raise money for orphans: zipline, abseiling, Burma Bridge (all high rope activities), canoeing and team-building activities.

Tour Operators

Safari operators and lodges offer walking and driving excursions to Matobo National Park and Whovi Game Park (day trip/overnight from US$50/90). For safari operators into Matobo and surrounds, see p721.

Sleeping & Eating

Matobo National Park (loydmasine@yahoo.com; campsites per person US$11, chalet/lodge tw US$74/112; executive r US$326) There are several campsites in the park, and there are chalets and lodges at Maleme Dam. You must book in advance at the parks office in Bulawayo (p721). Vehicle use is US$10.

Matobo Hills Lodge (☎ 881273; reservations@byorainbow.co.zw) Built on a granite outcrop are these stunning, luxury hilltop lodges, with 34 beds and sweeping panoramic views over the exquisite surroundings.

Big Cave Camp (☎ 245051; res@prideofplaces.co.za) The seven thatched A-frame cottages are actually built into the rocks, and have private bathrooms and balconies.

Masiye Camp (☎ 880834; www.masiye.com; tw chalets with shower & toilet per person US$15; 5-person self-catering cottages US$75, honeymoon suite US$35) is run by the Salvation Army to raise money for life-skills training camps for orphans. Available upon request, for those who would also like a genuine Ndebele cultural experience, is the opportunity of staying in a hut in the local village; hot water for bathing plus traditional meals can be offered by arrangement.

Granite Ridge (☎ 60867/72969; cozim@coz.co.zw; per person incl breakfast US$35 or full board US$55) Twelve cottages with twin or double rooms, each with its own kitchenette. There's also a garden and swimming pool.

Camp Amalinda (☎ 243954, 11-438162; www.campamalinda.com; per person US$255) Tucked away into an old bushman's shelter – read caves – in the Matobo Hills. Features a chess room in the tree tops. There are 10 thatched chalets carved into huge granite boulders, including a honeymoon suite.

Getting There & Away

The Matopos are just 33km from Bulawayo and can even be done as a day trip. If you don't have transfers prearranged by your accommodation, take a taxi and expect to pay $US40.

HWANGE NATIONAL PARK

Hwange (admission per day US$15; ⏲ about 6am-6pm) is the largest (14,651 sq km) and most wildlife-packed park in Zimbabwe.

Hwange ('Wang-ee'; sometimes still pronounced 'Wankie') is home to some 400 species of birds and 107 types of animals, including one of the largest populations (30,000) of elephants in the world. The best time for wildlife viewing is July to October, when animals congregate around the 60 water holes or 'pans' (most of which are artificially filled by noisy, petrol-powered pumps). But when the rains come and the rivers are flowing, successful viewing requires more diligence, because the animals spread out across the park, seeking a bit of trunk and antler room. Most visitors will only see a fraction of this park, though wildlife viewing is good throughout.

Access is possible in any sturdy vehicle between May and October, but seek advice if driving a 2WD during the wet season. And always consult a ranger (at any of the three camps) about road conditions before heading off too far into the park, regardless of what sort of vehicle you're driving.

Maps and information about the park are available at the rangers' offices at the Hwange Main Camp, Sinamatella Camp and Robins Camp. Robins Camp is 60km west of

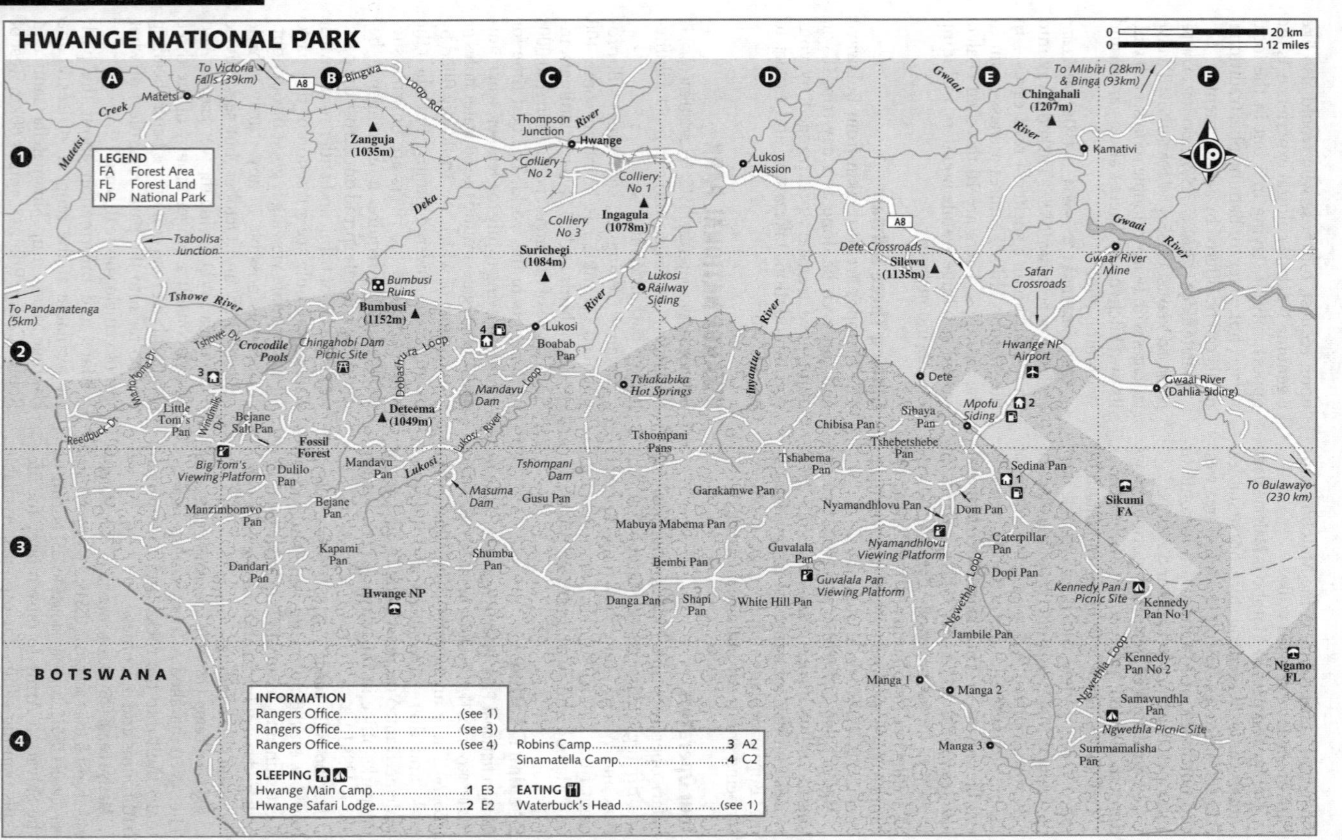
HWANGE NATIONAL PARK
0 20 km
0 12 miles
LEGEND
FA Forest Area
FL Forest Land
NP National Park
INFORMATION
Rangers Office (see 1)
Rangers Office (see 3)
Rangers Office (see 4)
Robins Camp 3 A2
Sinamatella Camp 4 C2
SLEEPING
Hwange Main Camp 1 E3
Hwange Safari Lodge 2 E2
EATING
Waterbuck's Head (see 1)
To Victoria Falls (39km)
To Pandamatenga (5km)
To Mlibizi (28km) & Binga (93km)
To Bulawayo (230 km)
Matetsi
Matetsi Creek
Tsabolisa Junction
Bingwa
Loop Rd
A8
Zanguja (1035m)
Deka
Thompson Junction
River
Hwange
Colliery No 1
Colliery No 2
Colliery No 3
Ingagula (1078m)
Surichegi (1084m)
Lukosi Mission
Lukosi Railway Siding
Lukosi
Boabab Pan
Mandavu Loop
Mandavu Dam
Mandavu Pan
Lukosi River
Dobashura Loop
Deteema (1049m)
Bumbusi Ruins
Bumbusi (1152m)
Chingahobi Dam Picnic Site
Crocodile Pools
Tshowe River
Tshowe Dr
Mahohoma Dr
Reedbuck Dr
Windmills Dr
Little Tom's Pan
Bejane Salt Pan
Big Tom's Viewing Platform
Fossil Forest
Dulilo Pan
Bejane Pan
Manzimbomvo Pan
Kapami Pan
Dandari Pan
Hwange NP
Masuma Dam
Gusu Pan
Shumba Pan
Tshompani Dam
Tshompani Pans
Tshakabika Hot Springs
Inyantue River
Mabuya Mabema Pan
Bembi Pan
Danga Pan
Shapi Pan
White Hill Pan
Garakamwe Pan
Guvalala Pan
Guvalala Pan Viewing Platform
Tshabema Pan
Chibisa Pan
Tshebetshebe Pan
Sibaya Pan
Dete Crossroads
Silewu (1135m)
Dete
Mpofu Siding
Hwange NP Airport
Safari Crossroads
Gwaai River
Gwaai River Mine
Gwaai River (Dahlia Siding)
Chingahali (1207m)
Kamativi
Nyamandhlovu Pan
Nyamandhlovu Viewing Platform
Dom Pan
Sedina Pan
Caterpillar Pan
Dopi Pan
Sikumi FA
Ngwethla Loop
Jambile Pan
Manga 1
Manga 2
Manga 3
Kennedy Pan I Picnic Site
Kennedy Pan No 1
Kennedy Pan No 2
Samavundhla Pan
Ngwethla Picnic Site
Summamalisha Pan
Ngamo FL
BOTSWANA

Sinamatella, and park regulations stipulate that you must leave Robins by 3pm to reach Sinamatella (and vice versa). Robins is 150km west of Hwange Main Camp, so to get there you must depart Robins by noon (and vice versa). Similarly, Sinamatella is 125km northwest of Hwange Main Camp, so you must leave Sinamatella by 2pm (and vice versa).

Hwange Main Camp

The main **camp** (☎ 371; fax 378; 🕑 office 7am-6pm) is at the major park entrance. It offers most services, including a rangers' office, grocery shop (open 7am to 7pm), souvenir shop, petrol station and restaurant.

Most visitors make a few loops starting near the main camp. One highlight is the **Nyamandhlovu Pan**, featuring the high-rise **Nyamandhlovu Viewing Platform** overlooking a popular water hole. On the way from the main camp, check to see if there's any wildlife hanging around **Dom Pan**. South of the main camp is **Ngwethla Loop**, accessible to any vehicle. It passes the magnificent **Kennedy Pans**, popular with elephants, though the greatest variety of wildlife can be found at the **Ngwethla Picnic Site**.

Hwange Main Camp is accessible in three ways: along two sealed roads from the highway between Bulawayo and Victoria Falls; via Dete; and via the airport and Hwange Safari Lodge.

Robins Camp

This **camp** (☎ 3503; office 🕑 7am-6pm), at the park's western boundary, has a sparsely stocked shop and restaurant-bar. The best wildlife viewing spots nearby are **Big Tom's Viewing Platform** and **Little Tom's Pan**.

Sinamatella Camp

The best of the three main camps is **Sinamatella** (☎ 2775; 🕑 office 7am-6pm). It sits atop a 55m mesa with a commanding and truly stunning 50km panorama over the open plains. By day, you'll see buffaloes and antelopes in the grassy patch below the camp, but it's at night that Sinamatella really comes alive: expect to be haunted by the roaring of lions and the disconcerting howling of hyenas at the foot of the hill, along with a host of unidentified screeches, thumps and bumps. At any time, vicious little honey badgers skitter around the restaurant looking for hand-outs and even invade the chalets if given half a chance – keep the doors closed! The camp has a basic restaurant and bar with mediocre food, but with views like that you'll barely notice. Check in advance to confirm that the restaurant is operating.

Activities

If you stay at Hwange Main Camp, you can book **guided safaris in vehicles** through either individual operators that hang around outside the main office, or through the nearby Hwange Safari Lodge. At Sinamatella and Robins camps the only options available are guided walks with the national parks rangers – so for excursions further afield you just drive yourself.

Newly introduced to rave reviews are the **horse-riding safaris** with luxury tent accommodation, run by the private company Varden Safaris (below). Two-hour **walking safaris** (per person US$45) to Sedina Pan with armed National Parks guards can be organised at Hwange Main Camp, and to Mandavu Dam from Sinamatella Camp. These walks must be booked in advance at Hwange Main Camp. Children under 12 are not permitted on walks. Other walks can be organised through your lodge/operator and are included in your cost.

Sleeping & Eating

Miombo Lodge, another of African Encounter's lodges, offers budget accommodation and provides a perfect base for wildlife drives into Hwange National Park. Their campsite too is fully equipped, and welcomes independent travellers, overlanders and groups. Right on the border of Hwange National Park, 300km from Bulawayo and 180km from Victoria Falls, it can be a perfect stopover, or even a side trip from Victoria Falls by charter flight.

Hwange Safari Lodge (☎ 750; fax 337; s/d incl meals & activities US$180/220; 🅿) On a massive private estate within the Sikumi Forest Area, this looks more like a motel than a lodge, though all rooms overlook a popular water hole. Amenities include a restaurant-bar (open to nonguests) and swimming pool. Tours and activities are also available to the public.

Hide Safari Camp (☎ 04-498835; www.thehide.com; head office Triton Centre, 176 Enterprise Rd, Chisipite, Harare; per person all-inclusive US$275) One of the best safari camps in the country. Named after the hiding points built to view elephants close-up, the Hide has good guides, lovely accommodation and excellent food.

Varden Safaris (☎ 04-861765; www.riding-in-hwange.com; per person all-inclusive US$325) Offering horse-riding safaris in Hwange for experienced riders only. Explore winding animal trails, canter beneath the acacia canopies and across open vleis, or swim in a muddy pan as the elephants do. A combination of luxury tented camps, mobile tented camps, fine cuisine, top professional guides and friendly staff will make this a most memorable African experience.

Ivory Lodge (☎ 09-243954/011-215904; www.ivorysafarilodge.com; per person US$255) This place offers six luxurious treehouse-style suites set in a teak forest. You'll see loads of elephants here, sometimes in herds of 100, drifting around the stilted platforms.

Waterbuck's Head (meals US$10) A charming bar-restaurant right outside the main gate and rangers' office at Hwange main camp.

Getting There & Away

Hwange National Park is between Bulawayo and Victoria Falls (at a distance of 300km and 180km respectively), best for self-driving or private road transfer – most lodges do provide transfers from Vic Falls, or you can charter a flight from Victoria Falls. Private vehicles are needed to access the park.

ZIMBABWE DIRECTORY

ACCOMMODATION

Zimbabwe's tourism industry has almost collapsed in terms of backpackers and DIY travellers, but top-end and regional travellers have kept coming, so accommodation remains some of the best in the region. Victoria Falls has five-star food, accommodation, service and access to well-organised activities. Elsewhere, while some lodges and hotels have closed, just as many are being built or renovated. Those that remain often offer stunning locations, good amenities and friendly service. Surviving the collapse of the tourism sector clearly means they have something worthwhile to offer.

Typical Zimbabwean accommodation is in 'lodges', meaning individual bungalows built in close harmony with nature: thatched roofs, natural flooring, teak furniture, large windows, verandahs and stunning views. There are also tented camps, which range from fairly basic to luxurious. (Note that a 'tented camp' never means you have to pitch your own tent – at the very least there are pre-erected walk-in tents with comfortable camp beds, and a camp cook to provide three full meals per day, usually at a table set on a riverbank.)

Breakfast is usually included in the price in lodges and hotels, and in all package deals for camps.

National Park Accommodation

Zimbabwe's national park accommodation provides the chance to stay in the best locations in Zimbabwe, indeed some of the best places in Africa. The **National Parks & Wildlife Zimbabwe reservations office** Harare (Map p696;

PRACTICALITIES

- The government's relentless campaign to control all media – initially by force – has resulted in much self-censorship and bland press (though for the visitor on a short stay, newspapers and TV can be quite entertaining).
- The only surviving dailies (the *Herald* and the *Standard*) are both state-run. Friday's *Independent* and *The Zimbabwean,* which is produced out of London, offer the week's only dose of propaganda-free political reporting.
- Oddly enough, the latest issues of *Vanity Fair* and *The Economist* can be found at some service stations for a fraction of the US-dollar cover price.
- The government controls all TV and radio, though most hotels and many lodges have great DSTV satellite TV. Zimbabwe boasts the best coverage of world sport in Southern Africa.
- Zimbabwe uses the metric system.
- Zimbabwe's electricity is generated at 220V, in theory, but it can seem much weaker. You will substantially notice the difference when generators are used. Use circuit breakers for important electrical items. Wall sockets provide for both three round prongs used in South Africa and three square prongs as used in England.

(☎ 04-706077; fax 04-726089; national-parks@gta.gov.zw; cnr Borrowdale Rd & Sandringham Dr; ⏰ 8am-4pm Mon-Fri); Bulawayo (Map p723; ☎ 63646; cnr Herbert Chitepo St & Tenth Ave; ⏰ 8am-4pm Mon-Fri) is very efficient or you can book through travel agents. Due to a lack of funds, many lodges and camps are now being privately managed, and they are doing better than before.

Fees vary from park to park and over time; expect to pay at least US$20 per person per day on top of the costs of your accommodation and vehicle rates. The cost of accommodation can still sometimes be as little as US$3 per person per night, however.

ACTIVITIES

Victoria Falls is the epicentre of activities in Southern Africa. The adventurous can get their adrenalin pumping with white-water rafting, helicopter rides, gorge swings and bungee jumping. There and elsewhere, it's all about natural features in Zimbabwe: river cruises, walks along the falls, classic driving safaris, hiking in the cool Eastern Highlands, horse riding and wildlife viewing in national parks, canoeing safaris on the Zambezi River, houseboating on Lake Kariba, and fishing or golfing almost anywhere.

BOOKS

This section covers books specific to Zimbabwe. For details on books about the Southern Africa region, see p22.

Guidebooks & Coffee-Table Books

Journey from the Depths of Zimbabwe: The Stone Sculptures by Vivienne Prince is a stunning book that captures the ever-important sculpture work of Zimbabwean artists. Buy online from www.zimsculpt.com or at the National Gallery of Zimbabwe in Harare.

Great Zimbabwe Described & Explained, by Peter Garlake, attempts to sort out the history, purpose and architecture of the ancient ruins at Great Zimbabwe. Also by Peter Garlake is *The Painted Caves – An Introduction to the Prehistoric Art of Zimbabwe*, a detailed guide uncovering major prehistoric rock-art sites in Zimbabwe.

The Painted Hills – Rock Art of the Matopos, by Nick Walker explores the revealing and interesting rock art of the Matopos.

Beneath a Zimbabwe Sun by Beverley Whyte has some lovely photos, though others are dated. The hardback and paperback versions are available throughout Zimbabwe.

History & Politics

Where We Have Hope, by Andrew Meldrum, is a good overview of post-independence Zimbabwe, up to 2003. It's not beautifully written, but Meldrum has some good insights.

Mugabe, by Colin Simpson and David Smith, is a biography of the Zimbabwean president tracing his controversial rise to power.

The Struggle for Zimbabwe, by David Martin and Phyllis Johnson, is a popular history of the Second Chimurenga, the tragic war that led to independence.

The Great Betrayal, by Ian Smith, is the autobiography of colonial Rhodesia's most controversial leader, chronicling a tumultuous, emotion-charged period in Zimbabwean history.

BUSINESS HOURS

Shops and restaurants are generally open from 8am to 1pm and 2pm to 5pm Monday to Friday, and 8am to noon on Saturday. Very little (including restaurants) is open on Sunday.

CHILDREN

Zimbabwe is a great place to travel with kids. Travellers should organise their tours through travel agents who can tailor trips and accommodation to suit all needs and wants. Some safari operations won't take children, but travel agents will know not only those who do, but those who cater best for them too. Most lodges these days will accept children, though others have an age limit for safety reasons.

CUSTOMS REGULATIONS

Visitors may import a maximum of US$350 in items not for trade, excluding personal effects. Travellers over 18 years of age can also import up to 3L of alcohol, including 1L of spirits.

DANGERS & ANNOYANCES

Zimbabwe is nowhere near as dangerous as foreign media makes out, but crime is on the rise. Carjacking and smash and grabs are the current dangers. Although the number of incidents and degree of violence are a far cry from that in Johannesburg and others, it is a reality. Drivers should take the following precautions: avoid stopping at traffic lights at night, lock all doors, lock all valuables in the boot and keep windows up.

EMBASSIES & CONSULATES

The following embassies and high commissions are based in Harare.

Angola (Map pp698-9; ☎ 04-790070; www.projectvisa.com; Doncaster House; 26 Speke Ave)
Australia (Map p696; ☎ 04-852471/870566; www.zimbabwe.embassy.gov.au; 1 Green Close, Borrowdale)
Belgium (Map pp698-9; ☎ 04-700112/700943; www.diplomatie.be/harare; 5th fl, Tanganyika House, 23 Third St/Union Ave)
Botswana (Map p696; ☎ 04-794645/7/8; www.embassiesabroad.com/embassies-of/Botswana; 22 Phillips Ave)
Canada (Map pp698-9; ☎ 04-252181/2/3/4/5; www.harare.gc.ca; 45 Baines Ave)
France (Map pp698-9; ☎ 04-703216; www.ambafrance-zw.org; First Bank Bldg, 74-76 Samora Machel Ave, Greendale)
Kenya (Map pp698-9 ☎ 04-704820/833/937; kenhicom@africaonline.co.zw; 95 Park Lane)
Malawi (Map p696; ☎ 04-798584; emba@embamoc.org.zw; 42-44 Harare St, Alexandra Park)
Mozambique (Map pp698-9; ☎ 04-253871; 152 Herbert Chitepo Ave)
Namibia (Map p696; ☎ 04-885841; 69 Borrowdale Rd)
Norway (☎ 04-252426; www.norway.org.zw; 5 Lanark Rd, cnr Sam Nujoma St, Belgravia)
Russia (Map pp698-9; ☎ 04-701957/8; russemb@africaonline.co.zw; 70 Fife Ave)
South Africa (Map p696; ☎ 04-753147/8/9; dhacon@mweb.co.zw; 7 Elcombe Ave)
Sudan (Map pp698-9; ☎ 04-700111; www.sudaniharare.org.zw; 4 Pascoe Ave, Belgravia)
Switzerland (Map pp698-9; ☎ 04-703997/8; 9 Lanark Rd; Belgravia)
Tanzania (Map pp698-9; ☎ 04-721870; tanrep@icon.co.zw; Ujamaa House, 23 Baines Ave)
UK (Map p696; ☎ 04-772990; www.britishembassy.gov.uk/zimb, cnr Norfolk Rd & Second St Extension)
USA (Map pp698-9; ☎ 04-250593/4; www.usembassy.state.gov/zimbabwe; Arax House, 172 Herbert Chitepo Ave)
Zambia (Map pp698-9; ☎ 04-773777; zambians@africaonline.com; 6th fl, Zambia House, 48 Union Ave)

For any embassies or websites not listed here, go to www.embassiesabroad.com/embassies-in/Zimbabwe to find addresses and contact details.

FESTIVALS & EVENTS

Harare International Festival of Arts (HIFA; ☎ 300119; www.hifa.co.zw) Held annually in the last week of April.
Chimanimani Arts Festival Happens in May, on Africa Day weekend, and features Zimbabwe's top musicians
Bulawayo Music Festival Mid-June.
Mana Game Count Held the first full moon in September at Mana Pools National Park.

GAY & LESBIAN TRAVELLERS

Homosexual activities for men are illegal and officially punishable by up to five years in jail (though penalties are invariably not nearly as severe), yet lesbianism is not illegal.

Contact **Gays & Lesbians of Zimbabwe** (☎ 741736/740614; www.galz.co.zw; 35 Colenbrander Rd, Milton Park, Harare) for information about gay and lesbian clubs and meeting places in Zimbabwe.

HOLIDAYS

During the following public holidays, most government offices and other businesses are closed.

New Year's Day 1 January
Independence Day 18 April
Workers' Day 1 May
Africa Day 25 May
Heroes' Day 11 August
Defence Forces' Day 12 August
National Unity Day 22 December
Christmas Day 25 December
Boxing Day 26 December

INTERNET ACCESS

There are internet centres in all the main cities and towns. Internet access is around US$2 per hour.

Wi-fi access is pretty prevalent these days; you can find it in backpacker hostels, cafes in Harare and the occasional Spar supermarket. If there isn't wi-fi, there are internet cafes popping up everywhere in the main towns, including places like the National Gallery of Zimbabwe.

LANGUAGE

The official language of Zimbabwe is English. It's used in government, legal and business proceedings, but is the first language for only about 2% of the population. Most Zimbabweans speak Shona (mainly in the north and east) or Ndebele (in the centre and west). Another dialect, Chilapalapa, is a pidgin version of Ndebele, English, Shona and Afrikaans, and isn't overly laden with niceties, so most people prefer you sticking to English.

See p781 and p782 for phrases in Ndebele and Shona.

LEGAL ISSUES

There are several things to keep in mind if you're travelling to Zimbabwe while

ZIMBABWE

THE MORE THINGS CHANGE...

Zimbabwe works in waves or cycles, so what was true last year may not be true this year, though it may recur the following year. At times it is the land of milk and honey, then there's no food in the shops, then the shops are stacked again. There's fuel, there's no fuel; there's cash around, there's no cash around. And somehow, fittingly, it is also a place where a lot goes on but nothing really happens. Due to the political and economic upheavals over the last 30 years, the country has flatlined in terms of development. A return traveller could never complain that the place was *so much less developed the last time they came*! The exception to this would be the advent of wi-fi, which is readily available: at supermarket cafes, hotels, galleries...

Robert Mugabe is still in power. It is illegal to criticise the government (best to avoid talking about the government at all, though it's always nail-bitingly fascinating to see how much artists get away with it at the Harare International Festival of the Arts); it is illegal to take photographs in the cities and main towns without permission; illegal to drink on the streets or in public parks and it is illegal to be gay. Drink driving, on the other hand, seems to be OK – so watch out for other drivers.

MAPS

Hotels are the best place to find any decent 'tourist maps'. More detailed maps of the cities and national parks are available from the **Surveyor General** (Map pp698-9; Samora Machel Ave, Harare).

MONEY

Since 'dollarisation', Zimbabwe is now very easy to go to again, but it's nowhere near as cheap as it once was. Several years ago a main at a good restaurant cost the equivalent of US$3 to US$5; now the same meal would cost the equivalent of US$5 to $15, as these days everything is imported.

Early in 2009, Zimbabwe became a 'multicurrency' economy, meaning they were officially accepting sterling, rand, pula and the American dollar. The reality at the time of writing was that the US dollar and, to a lesser extent, the rand, were the ones being accepted: prices were quoted in dollars and rand were accepted at a rate of 10:1. See the boxed text, p691, for information about Zimbabwe's currency. The only time you might see these dollars is at souvenir stalls in Vic Falls! Keep in mind that the currency situation is a sore point for the government for many reasons and that it could all change back again at any time.

Also note carefully: change for cash is a big problem, so have plenty of small notes.

ATMs

At the time of writing, ATMs were not being used because of the 'multicurrency' situation.

Credit Cards

Credit cards were being accepted in top hotels and some restaurants and shops, with the costs being quoted in US dollars.

Tipping

Some restaurants automatically add a 10% service charge to the bill; if so, no tip is required. Otherwise any tip is hugely appreciated.

Travellers Cheques

Don't take travellers cheques to Zimbabwe. Use a credit card or cash.

PHOTOGRAPHY & VIDEO

You can take your digital camera or flash card in to **Strachan's Photo Shop** (Map pp698-9; 66 Nelson Mandela Ave) in Harare to download or print your images.

POST

Sending letters and postcards by surface mail to Europe and the UK costs US$0.80, and US$1.10 to the rest of the world.

TELEPHONE

Telephone booths are long gone. You can make international calls from your hotel or lodge. It is impossible to buy a SIM card in Zimbabwe. It's best to put mobile phones on international roaming.

If calling from overseas, the country code for Zimbabwe is ☎263, but drop the initial zero for area codes. The international access code from within Zimbabwe is ☎00.

TOURIST INFORMATION

The **Zimbabwe Tourism Authority** (Map pp698-9; ☎ 758730; www.zimbabwetourism.co.zw; 55 Samora Machel Ave, Harare; 8am-4.30pm Mon-Fri) has general tourist info. There are Publicity Associations in Harare, Bulawayo, Victoria Falls, Kariba, Masvingo and Nyanga. Some are very efficient, helpful and have useful information and advice, but others have little more to offer than a smile.

VISAS

With a few exceptions, visas are required by nationals of all countries. They can be obtained at your point of entry. Single-/double-entry visas cost US$30/45 (and can be issued upon arrival) and multiple-entry visas (valid for six months) cost US$55, but are only issued at Zimbabwean diplomatic missions. British citizens pay US$55/70 for single/double entry.

For visa extensions, contact the **Department of Immigration Control** (Map pp698-9; ☎ 791913; 1st fl, Linquenda House, cnr Nelson Mandela Ave & First St, Harare).

Vaccination for yellow fever is not required for entry to Zimbabwe unless you have recently been to an infected area. However, for all sorts of reasons, get a jab before you come to Southern Africa and carry a certificate to prove it.

Visas for Onward Travel

Harare is one of the best places in Southern Africa to pick up visas for regional countries (see p697). Requirements constantly change, but nearly all require a fee (US dollars) and two passport-sized photos.

Visas for Zambia, Namibia, Malawi and Botswana are easy to obtain on arrival in those countries for most visitors, so no need to obtain them in advance. In theory South Africa is easy too, though such are the queues at Harare's South African Embassy each day that it's best to get one in advance.

TRANSPORT IN ZIMBABWE

GETTING THERE & AWAY

For information about travelling to Southern Africa from elsewhere in the continent, and from overseas, see p755.

Air

Some international flights arrive in Harare, and there are also direct flights between Victoria Falls and Johannesburg. International flights link Zimbabwe to Johannesburg (one way/return US$227/339, 1½ hours), Gaborone (US$572/906, 1½ hours), Windhoek (US$716/962, 2½ hours), Maputo (US$468/767, 1½ hours), Lilongwe (US$999/1112, one hour), Lusaka (US$729/956 50 minutes), Dar es Salaam (US$1154/1888, 2½ hours) and Nairobi (US$1070/1274, 3½ hours).

Airlines with services to/from Zimbabwe:

Air Botswana (Map pp698-9; ☎ 04-793795/228/229)
Air Malawi (Map pp698-9 ☎ 04-752563)
Air Namibia (Map pp698-9; ☎ 04-732094/5)
Air Tanzania (Map pp698-9 ☎ 04-752537/8)
Air Zimbabwe (Map pp698-9; ☎ 04-253751/2; Eastgate Centre, Harare)
South African Airways (Map pp698-9; ☎ 04-794511/2/6/47/83)

Border Crossings

Most of Zimbabwe's border posts are open from 6am to 6pm with the exception of Beitbridge (to South Africa, open 24 hours) and Victoria Falls (to Zambia, open 6am to 10pm). Its other border posts are Plumtree and Kazungula (Botswana); Kariba and Chirundu (Zambia); and Mutare and Nyamapanda (Mozambique).

BOTSWANA

Zupco ($15) and PCJ Coaches ($60) run from Harare to Francistown. Zupco departs 6.30am Tuesday, Thursday and Friday; PCJ departs every day at 6pm.

MALAWI

The most direct route between Malawi and Zimbabwe is via Mozambique's Tete Corridor. You'll need a transit visa for Mozambique if travelling through Mozambique to Malawi.

Zupco runs from Harare to Blantyre (US$35) every day from 6.30am.

MOZAMBIQUE

You can go to Beira via Mutare. Take a minibus from Mutare to the border, then catch another bus on the Mozambique side. You can get to Malawi from Nyamapanda by minibus. Minibuses run infrequently between Nyamapanda and Tete (Mozambique) and

PUBLIC TRANSPORT WARNING

The information in this section can change for any reason and, at the time of writing, buses and trains in Zimbabwe were becoming increasingly dangerous due to a lack of repairs. If you want to travel in Zimbabwe, which is otherwise a very safe and gentle place, it's best to overland it; self-drive in a hire car or book lodges through travel agents and have them organise road or air transfers for you.

more frequently between Tete and Zóbuè on the border with Malawi.

NAMIBIA

There's no direct overland connection between Zimbabwe and Namibia. The most straightforward route is to take the Botswana bus and then connect from Botswana.

SOUTH AFRICA

The following companies have services to Johannesburg (around US$70).

Blue Arrow (Map pp698-9; ☎ 04-729514; barrow@africaonline.co.zw; Chester House, Speke Ave, Harare)
Kukura Kurerwa (Map p696; ☎ 04-669973/6; Mbare Musika Bus Terminal, Harare)
Pioneer Bus (Map p696; ☎ 04-795863/790531; Mbare Musika Bus Terminal, Harare)
Greyhound (Map pp698-9; ☎ 04-720801; Road Port Terminal, Harare)

Departure times are subject to change without notice. It's best to call ahead.

Trains are once again running between Zimbabwe and South Africa. Rovos Rail operates its train from Pretoria to Victoria Falls travelling through Zimbabwe via Bulawayo. This trip is a three-day, two-night journey each way.

ZAMBIA

Zupco (Map pp698-9; ☎ 04-704933; Road Port Terminal, Harare) has buses departing for Lusaka (via Chirundu) at 6.30am every day (US$25).

GETTING AROUND

Air

Air Zimbabwe (Map pp698-9; ☎ 04-253751; Eastgate Centre, Harare) has one flight per day between Harare and Bulawayo (one way/return US$140/250) and Harare and Victoria Falls (one way/return US$230/375). There's a domestic departure tax of US$5. Air Zimbabwe no longer flies to Hwange or Kariba, but agents can organise charter flights.

All charters differ in price and the fees need to always be reconfirmed. As a guide, a charter from Lusaka to Mana Pools is US$935, from Kariba to Mana Pools is US$390, from Harare to Mana Pools is US$1250 and Victoria Falls to Mana Pools is US$2395. These are all quoted for one way.

Boat

Kariba Ferries (Map p705; ☎ 04-65476; Andora Harbour, Kariba) occasionally runs a ferry service between Kariba at the eastern end of the lake and Mlibizi at the western end. The ferry departs when there is sufficient demand.

Bus

The express or 'luxury' buses operate according to published timetables. They mainly leave from Road Port Terminal (Map pp698–9) in town, which is where international services leave from, or designated pick-up points at hotels such as Holiday Inn/Rainbow Towers. Destinations are both within Zimbabwe (to major towns such as Bulawayo, Mutare, Gweru) and throughout Southern Africa.

However, check carefully, as most bus companies have *both* local ('chicken buses' for locals) and luxury coaches. So Pioneer, Zupco and Kukura Kurerwa have both luxury and chicken buses.

Car & Motorcyle

DRIVING LICENCE

All foreigners can use their driving licence from their home country for up to 90 days in Zimbabwe as long as it's written in English. However, given the growing possibility of police trying to elicit bribes, it's best to ensure you also have an international driving licence.

FUEL

The cost of petrol ranges from US$1 to $1.10/litre.

HIRE

The minimum driving age required by rental companies varies, but is usually between 23 and 25 years. The maximum age is normally about 65 years.

It's important to note that most collision damage waiver (CDW) insurance policies do not cover 2WD vehicles travelling on rough roads in national parks, especially in Mana Pools National Park.

ROAD HAZARDS

Zimbabwe has some awful drivers and rarely any functioning streetlights, so many residents make a rule of not driving outside the major towns after dark. At the time of writing, the roads were badly decaying, with eroding edges and potholes everywhere. In cities speeding drink drivers tend to ignore red lights, so you should slow right down at every 'robot', even if it's green, then proceed with caution.

Hitching

Hitching is not recommended for travellers for issues of safety, yet is an official means of transportation for the masses in Zimbabwe. Private operators in 'bakkies' (pick-up trucks) charge the same as buses, usually about 50 cents or one to three dollars for longer trips.

Local Transport

Taxis are safe and can be booked through your hotel. Most are metered, charging between $1 and $2.50 for 1km at the time of writing. Harare taxis travel within a 40km radius of the city. Most reliable taxis are booked through the hotel front desk. Always take a taxi at night. There are taxi stands on the corner of First St and Nelson Mandela Ave; on Samora Machel Ave near First St; on Union Ave between Angwa St and Julius Nyerere Way; and in front of large hotels. Other large towns, such as Bulawayo, Masvingo and Victoria Falls, also have taxis.

Travel Agents & Tour Operators

Travel agents are invaluable for trips: for booking flights, rental cars and safaris, and for local knowledge. You can get on mailing lists while in the planning stages and/or get travel agents to organise tailor-made safaris around the region, taking in the best locations. Trips can include safari lodges, tented camps, walking, canoeing and horse-riding safaris. Zimbabwe is so diverse and it is easy to get around – you can do it all in one holiday (see p697).

Train

Train timetables are unreliable and trains are not recommended as safe or pleasant for tourists, yet some backpackers have given positive feedback on their experiences. Consider it another moveable feast, with no absolutes.

Connecting Harare, Bulawayo, Mutare and Victoria Falls, all major services travel at night. Sleeping compartments with bedding are available, which is fortunate as the trains are very slow. The good news is that train travel is very cheap and that parts of the trip, especially through Hwange National Park at dawn, are stunning. First and second class sleep four and six people respectively, and there are also separate women's and men's compartments. Third class is seating only, and is crowded and noisy. The tracks and trains are in desperate need of servicing and parts, and serious accidents continue to occur. Check with travel agents first regarding the current safety of long-distance train travel.

Southern Africa Directory

CONTENTS

This chapter describes general aspects of travel, including activities, accommodation and common facilities in the Southern African region. There is also a separate Directory in each country chapter, which provides more detailed information.

ACCOMMODATION

Accommodation in Southern Africa encompasses a wide variety of definitions, from a patch of turf to pitch a tent on to opulent lodges that defy any star rating. Options in this book are listed in order of price. Although prices vary immensely from country to country, budget travellers can generally get a night's sleep for under US$50, or even under US$40 in South Africa, Mozambique, Malawi, Swaziland and Lesotho. Midrange options cost from US$50 to US$100 (although this can be up to US$150 in parts of the region, such as Mozambique). Top-end options charge from around US$100 (although it varies immensely; in Zambia for example, a top-end lodge in a national park starts at US$500). Check individual Directories for the budget breakdown used in that chapter.

B&Bs & Guest Houses

B&Bs and guest houses are interchangeable terms in much of Southern Africa. They range from a simple room in someone's house to well-established B&Bs with five-star ratings and deluxe accommodation. B&Bs and guest houses are most prevalent in South Africa, where the standards are high and features such as antique furniture, private verandahs, florid gardens and a pool are common. Indeed some of the finest accommodation on the continent is found in B&Bs along the Garden Route. Breakfast is usually included and almost always involves gut-busting quantities of eggs, bacon, toast and other cooked goodies.

Camping

Camping is also popular, especially in national parks, in coastal and lakeshore areas, and in more expensive destinations, such as Botswana. Some camping grounds are quite basic, while others have a range of facilities, including hot showers and security fences. Wild (free) camping (ie not at an official site) is another option, but security can be a problem and wild animals are always a concern, so choose your tent site with care.

In the national parks and wildlife reserves, there's a wide choice of accommodation, ranging from simple camping grounds to cabins, chalets, bungalows and luxurious camps and lodges. It's important to note that 'camp' doesn't necessarily denote a campsite

BOOK ACCOMMODATION ONLINE

For more accommodation reviews and recommendations by Lonely Planet authors, check out the online booking service at www.lonelyplanet.com. You'll find the true, insider low-down on the best places to stay. Reviews are thorough and independent. Best of all, you can book online.

PRACTICALITIES

- News magazines that cover the continent include *Africa Today, Business Africa* and the best, BBC's *Focus on Africa*. All are available from newsagents in South Africa and bookshops in capital cities elsewhere. *Getaway to Africa* magazine covers travel in Southern Africa, with articles ranging from epic 4WD trips to active and not-so-active tours all over the region.
- The beautiful, glossy *Africa Geographic*, published bimonthly, should be considered an essential subscription for every Africa buff. Birdwatchers will also want to read the excellent bimonthly *Africa Birds & Birding*. For subscriptions to these magazines contact **Africa Geographic** (☎ 27-21-762 2180; www.africa-geographic.com).
- All the countries covered in this book use the metric system. To convert between metric and imperial units, refer to the conversion chart on the inside front cover of this book.
- Electricity in Southern Africa is generated at 220V to 240V AC. Most plugs have three prongs (or pins), either round or rectangular ('square') in section. In South Africa, round-pin plugs are used. Outside South Africa, British-style square three-pin plugs are common. A voltage adaptor is needed for US appliances.

(although it may). A camp is usually a well-appointed upmarket option run by a private company. Accommodation is usually in tents or chalets made from natural materials. The contact number for these places will be at their office in a larger town, and are for bookings and inquiries only, not for direct contact with the lodge or camp.

In upmarket lodges and camps, the rates will typically include accommodation plus full board, activities (wildlife drives, boat trips etc) and perhaps even house wine and beer. It may also include laundry and transfers by air or 4WD (although these are usually extra).

Hostels

Many towns and cities on the main tourist trail have at least one hostel, and in some places, such as South Africa's Garden Route and increasingly Mozambique and Namibia, you'll have a wide choice. The hostels generally mirror small hostels anywhere else in the world and offer camping space, dorms and a few private doubles. Many also have a TV room, swimming pool, bar, restaurant, and email and phone service, as well as a travel desk where you can book tours and safaris. Several of the smarter places accept credit cards.

Another budget option, albeit dwindling but still available in Malawi and Zambia, are resthouses run by local governments or district councils. These are peppered throughout the region, and many date from colonial times. Some are very cheap and less than appealing; others are well kept and good value. In resthouses and other cheap hotels, the definition of single and double rooms is not always consistent. It may be determined by the number of beds rather than the number of people. Therefore it is not unusual for two people to share a single room (which may have a large bed), paying either the single rate or something just a bit higher. If you want to save money, it's always worth asking.

Hotels

In towns and cities, top-end hotels offer clean, air-conditioned rooms with private bathrooms, while midrange hotels typically offer fans instead of air-con. At the budget end, rooms aren't always clean (and may be downright filthy), and bathrooms are usually shared and may well be in an appalling state. Often, your only source of air will be a hole in the window. Many cheap hotels double as brothels, so if this is your budget level don't be surprised if there's a lot of coming and going during the night. Some countries, including Malawi and Botswana, offer little in the way of hotels between budget and top end.

Many hotels offer self-catering facilities, which may mean anything from a fridge and a hotplate in the corner to a full kitchen in every unit. In some cases, guests will have to supply their own cooking implements – and perhaps even water and firewood.

Throughout the region you'll probably encounter hotels and lodges that charge in tiers. That is, overseas visitors are charged international rates (full price), visitors from other

Southern African countries pay a regional rate (say around 30% less) and locals get resident rates (often less than half the full rate). Most places also give discounts in the low season. In this book, where possible we've quoted the international high-season rates, including the value-added tax (VAT), which ranges from 10% to 30%. If you intend staying at mostly top-end hotels and lodges, it's worth scanning the internet beforehand as you may discover some heavily discounted rates.

ACTIVITIES

Southern Africa's climate and landscape make the region ideal for numerous outdoor activities – from peaceful and relaxing to energetic and downright terrifying. The following list is not exhaustive, but provides some tantalising food for thought. For finer detail check the Directory of each country chapter.

Adrenaline Activities

Southern Africa is something of a gathering place for adrenaline nuts, and a range of weird and wonderful activities keep them happily crazed. The top spots for extreme sports are Victoria Falls and Livingstone, where white-water rafting in the Zambezi and bungee jumping off the Victoria Falls bridge are hourly occurrences. The highest bungee jump in the world (allegedly) can be found in South Africa at Bloukrans River Bridge (p462), but if you're only half-nuts you can try any number of smaller ones.

Swakopmund is the adventure capital of Namibia, and sandboarding, skydiving and quad biking through the dunes are popular pastimes arranged by hostels and hotels. In Malawi waterfall abseils and rope swings around Manchewe Falls (p176) near Livingstonia are all the rage.

Finances and infrastructure make South Africa the easiest destination to scare yourself silly. A growing craze is kloofing, a mix of climbing, hiking, swimming and jumping, which is commonly known elsewhere as canyoning. Hot spots include Cape Town and the Drakensberg Escarpment in Mpumalanga. See p566 for more information.

South Africa is also one of the world's top destinations for paragliding, particularly at Cape Town's Table Mountain. Although the flying is good year-round, the strongest thermals are from November to April. See p565 for more information.

There is excellent and challenging climbing on the close-to-sheer faces of the KwaZulu-Natal Drakensberg (see p567) in South Africa. Climbing Namibia's Spitzkoppe (p336) is not for beginners and requires technical expertise and proper equipment, though plenty of locals and travellers tackle the summit each year.

Canoeing, Kayaking & White-Water Rafting

The Zambezi River lures white-water rafters from around the globe to tackle its angry churn, and there are plenty of operators in Zimbabwe (see p616) and Livingstone, Zambia (see p608). Canoeing is a less treacherous way to appreciate the river's flora and fauna and equally easy to organise.

In South Africa canoeing and white-water rafting are popular pursuits on the Blyde and Sabie Rivers, both in Mpumalanga province. Other watery avenues include the waterways around Wilderness National Park in the Western Cape; the Orange River, particularly through Augrabies Falls National Park; and the Tugela. See p566 for more information. There's also some serene canoeing at the iSimangaliso Wetland Park (p499). In Swaziland, the classic rafting destination is the Great Usutu River (see the boxed text, p594).

Gorongosa National Park (p253) and Niassa Reserve (p271) in Mozambique both offer canoeing opportunities in wonderful wilderness areas.

Rafting is highly rain-dependent, and the best months usually fall between December/January to April.

Sea kayaking is popular in sporadic locations along the coast, but it's best experienced on Lake Malawi. There are outfits in Nkhata Bay (p182) that can oblige. Alternatively in Mozambique you can try a live-aboard dhow safari (p282), in custom-built traditional wooden dhows.

Diving & Snorkelling

The best diving and snorkelling in the region is along the coast of Mozambique, particularly the Bazaruto Archipelago (p249) and Vilankulo (p247), Ponta D'Ouro (p237), Tofo (p243), Pemba (p273), Nacala (p268) and Inhaca Island (p236). Quality equipment, instruction and certification are readily available at most of these locations. But the country's least explored but arguably finest diving is the

RESPONSIBLE DIVING

Please consider the following tips when diving and help preserve the ecology and beauty of reefs:

- Never use anchors on the reef, and take care not to ground boats on coral.
- Avoid touching or standing on living marine organisms or dragging equipment across the reef. Polyps can be damaged by even the gentlest contact. If you must hold on to the reef, touch only exposed rock or dead coral.
- Be conscious of your fins. Even without contact, the surge from fin strokes near the reef can damage delicate organisms. Take care not to kick up clouds of sand, which can smother organisms.
- Practise and maintain proper buoyancy control. Major damage can be done by divers descending too quickly and colliding with the reef.
- Take great care in underwater caves. Spend as little time within them as possible as your air bubbles may be caught within the roof and thereby leave organisms high and dry. Take turns to inspect the interior of a small cave.
- Resist the temptation to collect or buy corals or shells or to loot marine archaeological sites (mainly shipwrecks).
- Ensure that you take home all your rubbish and any litter you may find as well. Plastics in particular are a serious threat to marine life.
- Do not feed fish.
- Minimise your disturbance of marine animals. *Never* ride on the back of turtles.

Quirimbas Archipelago; see p277 for more information. March to June and November are generally the best months for diving in Mozambique, and February (due to heavy rains) is the worst.

In South Africa the Cape Peninsula offers superb wreck diving and giant kelp forests. The east coast is home to good coral formations and there is excellent warm-water diving on the KwaZulu-Natal north coast, particularly around Sodwana Bay (p500). The best visibility here occurs from May to September.

For a freshwater flutter, Lake Malawi offers some of the best snorkelling and diving in the world. There are good outfits in Nkhata Bay (p182) and Cape Maclear (p190).

Fishing

Southern Africa's wild and varied coastline and wealth of rivers and lakes make for profitable fishing expeditions. Cape Maclear is a good launching pad for fishing trips along Lake Malawi (see p189), and you can also fish for trout on the Zomba Plateau and at Nyika National Park (p177).

In Zambia the tigerfish of the Lower Zambezi River give a good fight, but not as good as the vundu, a catfish weighing upwards of 45kg. Most lodges along the river's banks include fishing in the rates.

In South Africa anglers fish for introduced trout in many of the country's parks and reserves; there are some particularly good highland streams in the Drakensberg.

Lesotho is an insider's tip among trout anglers. The season runs from September to May (same in South Africa), and there is a small licence fee, a size limit and a bag limit of 12 fish. The nearest fishing area to Maseru is the Makhaleng River. Other places to fish are the Malibamat'so River near Oxbow; the Mokhotlong River in the northeast; and the Thaba-Tseka main dam. See p140 for more information.

Mozambique's coast is legendary among anglers, particularly in the south between Ponta d'Ouro and Inhassoro, and in the far north around Pemba. Saltwater fly-fishing is also becoming increasingly popular. Inland, the most popular fishing areas are Barragem de Cahora Bassa near Tete, and Barragem de Chicamba Real near Chimoio. Species you are likely to encounter include marlin, kingfish, tuna, sailfish and more. Marlin season is from October/November to February/March. Tag and release is encouraged at many resorts. Officially, no more than 6kg of any one type of catch from sports and deep-sea fishing can be taken out of the country. See p283 for more information.

Football (Soccer)

Football is Africa's most popular participation and spectator sport. If you want to play, the universities and municipal stadiums are the best places to find a good-quality game, but nearly every town in Africa has pitches where informal matches are played most evenings (in coastal areas, the beach works equally well). Foreigners are usually warmly welcomed, and joining in a game is one of the best ways to meet the locals. Bring along your own ball (which could be deflated for travelling), and you'll be the hit of the day.

Otherwise, the ball used may be more suitable for tennis, or it may be half-deflated or just a round bundle of rags, and each goal a couple of sticks, not necessarily opposite each other. You may have to deal with puddles, ditches and the odd goat or donkey wandering across the pitch, but the game itself is taken very seriously, and play is fast and furious, with the ball played low.

Hiking

Across Southern Africa there are many excellent opportunities for hiking, and this is one of the most popular activities in the region.

Namibia's Fish River Canyon (p375) is one of Africa's most spectacular hikes, but proper gear, food, water and experience are musts. In Malawi you can trek the scenic peaks of Mt Mulanje (p205), the Zomba Plateau (p196) and the Nyika Plateau (see the boxed text, p179).

Mozambique boasts beautiful vantage points to trek to but little infrastructure so you'll likely be on your own. The country's best mountain climb is up Mt Namúli (see the boxed text, p260), which is relatively accessible and needs no special equipment. Mt Gorongosa (p253) is also good and equally straightforward. The Chimanimani Mountains are beautiful for hiking, but lack any infrastructure other than a handful of basic campsites. Other areas for hikes include Penha Longa (see Manica, p255), west of Chimoio, and the verdant hills around Gurúè (p259). Elsewhere, a combination of minimal infrastructure, the risk of land mines, and vast expanses of trackless bush make hiking and trekking the domain of adventurers, well equipped with compasses or a good GPS (global positioning system), camping equipment and provisions.

South Africa's undulating topography offers superb hiking opportunities. The best time to embark on any trek is between March and October, outside the heat and wet of summer. Among the best walks are: the Hoerikwaggo hiking trails of Table Mountain National Park (see p410), the five-day Whale Route in De Hoop Nature Reserve (p437) and the celebrated Otter Trail (p462), a five-day journey along the Garden Route that needs to be booked months in advance. Some other notable hikes include the Tsitsikamma Trail (p462), which runs parallel to the Otter Trail, KwaZulu-Natal's Giant's Cup Trail (p508) – up to five days in the southern Drakensberg – and Mpumalanga's Blyde River Canyon Hiking Trail (p522). See the relevant sections and the South Africa Directory (p566) for more information.

TRAILS

Most hiking trails in Southern Africa are established and maintained by national park authorities, conservation bodies and private landowners. In South Africa, Namibia and sometimes in other countries you must pay a fee to use the trail, which covers the use of campsites or accommodation (ranging from simple shelters to comfortable cabins) along the route. These trails are sometimes called overnight hikes; routes that take more than one day. Typically, you can do the route in only one direction (some are traverses while others are circular), and to preserve the condition of the trail, only a limited number of people are allowed to hike on any one day. In fragile areas, departures are permitted only once or twice per week, and even day and time of departure is sometimes stipulated. You must complete the trail in the set number of days and may not link two days together (except perhaps the last two) or stay extra nights at any campsite or hut, so they never become overcrowded.

Some trails have their own regulations. For example, few hikes allow fires (hikers need to carry camping stoves), and most are limited to parties of no fewer than three and no more than 10 people. For some of Namibia's

RESPONSIBLE HIKING

To help preserve the ecology and beauty of Southern Africa, consider the following tips when hiking.

Rubbish

- Carry out *all* your rubbish. Don't overlook easily forgotten items, such as silver paper, orange peel, cigarette butts and plastic wrappers. Empty packaging should be stored in a dedicated rubbish bag. Make an effort to carry out rubbish left by others.
- Never bury your rubbish: digging disturbs soil and ground cover and encourages erosion. Buried rubbish will likely be dug up by animals, who may be injured or poisoned by it. It may also take years to decompose.
- Minimise waste by taking minimal packaging and no more food than you will need. Take reusable containers or stuff sacks.
- Sanitary napkins, tampons, condoms and toilet paper should be carried out despite the inconvenience. They burn and decompose poorly.

Human Waste Disposal

- Contamination of water sources by human faeces can lead to the transmission of all sorts of nasties. Where there is a toilet, please use it. Where there is none, bury your waste. Dig a small hole 15cm deep and at least 100m from any watercourse. Cover the waste with soil and a rock. In snow, dig down to the soil.

Washing

- Don't use detergents or toothpaste in or near watercourses, even if they are biodegradable.
- For personal washing, use biodegradable soap and a water container (or even a lightweight, portable basin) at least 50m away from the watercourse. Disperse the waste water widely to allow the soil to filter it fully.
- Wash cooking utensils 50m from watercourses using a scourer, sand or snow instead of detergent.

Erosion

- Hillsides and mountain slopes, especially at high altitudes, are prone to erosion. Stick to existing trails and avoid short cuts.

tougher routes, participants must provide a doctor's certificate of health.

In South Africa and Namibia, popular multiday hiking trails typically require a reservation through the national parks office or other relevant authority. Only the popular classics such as the Otter Trail and Fish River Canyon are likely to be fully booked out. In South Africa, you can sometimes find a slot when someone else has cancelled (this is no longer allowed in Namibia unless it's privately arranged).

Once space has been confirmed, you are issued with a permit. This is sent by post if you have a local address, or is held ready for collection at the national park headquarters. You can pay in advance with a credit card, or on arrival. Included in the price may be an information sheet or map of the route. You must turn up at the start of the trail on the arranged date and report to the 'officer-in-charge'. You'll also have to fill in a register (with details of the number of people in your party, experience, equipment, colour of backpacks), to be used in case of an emergency. Although this sounds like an incredibly complicated way to just take a walk, travellers who have completed the popular routes – especially in South Africa – recommend the hikes highly.

Because of the bureaucracy surrounding the national parks' routes in Namibia, a growing number of private landholders have established their own long-distance routes, and

- If a well-used trail passes through a mud patch, walk through the mud so as not to increase the size of the patch.
- Avoid removing the plant life that keeps topsoils in place.

Fires & Low-Impact Cooking

- Don't depend on open fires for cooking. The cutting of wood for fires in popular hiking areas can cause rapid deforestation. Cook on a light-weight kerosene, alcohol or Shellite (white gas) stove, and avoid those powered by disposable butane gas canisters.
- If you are trekking with a guide and porters, supply stoves for the whole team. In alpine areas, ensure that all members are outfitted with enough clothing so that fires are not a necessity for warmth.
- If you patronise local accommodation, select those places that do not use wood fires to heat water or cook food.
- Fires may be acceptable below the treeline in areas that get very few visitors. If you light a fire, use an existing fireplace. Don't surround fires with rocks. Use only dead, fallen wood. Remember the adage 'the bigger the fool, the bigger the fire'. Use minimal wood, just what you need for cooking. In huts, leave wood for the next person.
- Ensure that you fully extinguish a fire after use. Spread the embers and flood them with water.

Wildlife Conservation

- For information on hunting in Southern Africa, see the boxed text, p65.
- Don't buy items made from endangered species.
- Don't attempt to exterminate animals in huts. In wild places, they are likely to be protected native animals.
- Discourage the presence of wildlife by not leaving food scraps behind you. Place gear out of reach and tie packs to rafters or trees.
- Do not feed the wildlife as this can lead to animals becoming dependent on handouts, to unbalanced populations and to diseases.

Camping

- Always seek permission to camp from landowners.

many are just as rewarding as the well-known ones, but tend to cost a bit more.

One last point – in South Africa and Namibia the Afrikaans word *wandelpad* seems to refer to any kind of trail. Therefore, it's best to check the English translation, just to make sure your planned day-walk doesn't turn into a week's expedition.

Horse Riding

One of Malawi's greatest treats is a bout of horse riding in Nyika National Park (p177). Exploring the park on horseback is an excellent way to get up close and personal with the diversity of antelopes on the plateau; note though at the time of publication a new operator (Wilderness Safaris; www.wilderness-safaris.com) was taking over, so check if horse riding is still available.

In South Africa it's easy to find rides ranging from several hours to several days, and for all experience levels. Particularly good areas include the iSimangaliso Wetland Park (p499) and Limpopo's Waterberg range (p562). Riding is also offered in several national parks.

Lesotho is horse-riding utopia, with ample possibilities to navigate the mountainous terrain by horseback. The best places to organise rides are through Malealea Lodge (p138), where the rides are operated by locals, with the profits being ploughed back into the local community, and Semonkong Lodge (p137), which has a similar arrangement. You can

DESERT HIKING

While desert areas of Southern Africa – especially parts of Namibia, Botswana and South Africa – offer a host of hiking opportunities, the conditions are quite different from those to which most visitors are accustomed. Tramping through this lonely countryside is a wonderful experience, but hiking isn't recommended during the heat of the summer months, when temperatures can exceed 40°C. In national parks, summer hiking is officially forbidden, and most hiking trails are closed from November or December to April or May.

In the desert heat, hikers should carry 4L of water per person per day (an excellent way to carry water is in 2L plastic Coke bottles, which are available all over the region). The most effective way to conserve water isn't necessarily to drink sparingly. Before setting off in the morning (assuming that water is available at your overnight stop), flood your body's cells with water. That is, drink more water than you feel you can possibly hold! After a few hours, when you grow thirsty, do the same again from the supply you're carrying. Believe it or not, with this method you'll actually use less water and feel less thirsty than if you drink sparingly all day long.

Another major concern is the desert sun, which can be brutal. Wear light-coloured and lightweight clothing, use a good sunscreen (at least UV Protection Factor 30) and never set off without a hat that shelters your neck and face from the direct sun.

If the heat is a major problem, it's best to rise before the sun and hike until the heat becomes oppressive. You may then want to rest through the heat of midday and begin again after about 3pm. (Note, however, that summer thunderstorms often brew up at around this time and may continue into the night.) During warmer months, it may also be worthwhile timing your hike with the full moon, which will allow you to hike at night.

Because many trails follow canyons and riverbeds, it's important to keep a watch on the weather. Rainy periods can render normally dry kloofs and streambeds impassable, and rivers with large catchment areas can quickly become raging torrents of muddy water, boulders and downed trees. Never camp in canyons or dry riverbeds, and always keep to higher ground whenever there's a risk of flash-flooding.

ride for as many days as you like. Highlights include traditional Basotho villages and the jaw-dropping scenery.

Mountain Biking

It goes without saying that a region so rich in hiking opportunities will have equally rewarding mountain-biking possibilities. Outside South Africa and the main tourist areas in the region, it's relatively difficult to hire bikes, so you'll need to bring your own. For information on bringing your own bike to Southern Africa, see p758.

You can also hire local-style sit-up-and-beg steel roadsters. These are good for getting around towns (especially flat ones) or exploring rural areas at a leisurely pace.

South Africa is littered with excellent biking trails, but among the best are in the De Hoop Nature Reserve (p437), with overnight and day trails, and Citrusdal (p452), with a network of trails. Then there's Cape Town (see p415), which is something of an unofficial national hub. Nearby in Swaziland there are trails in the Mlilwane Wildlife Sanctuary (p592).

A series of dirt and gravel roads and a massive network of single-track trails in the hills south and east of Lusaka in Zambia provide hundreds of miles of mountain biking for those who want to get some exercise while exploring Zambia's rural villages. Many of the trails link together to form loops ranging from pleasant two-hour excursions to epic seven-hour circuits that wander through the rugged terrain at the edge of the Zambezi Escarpment.

Surfing

Any surfer worth their wax is familiar with the legendary waves at J-Bay, better known to nonconverts as Jeffrey's Bay (p462). Situated on the Garden Route, the town's choppy surf lures experts and amateurs from around the globe. South Africa also offers a myriad of less-celebrated alternatives, particularly along the Eastern Cape coast from Port Alfred northwards. The best time of the year for surfing the southern and eastern coasts is autumn and early winter (from about April to July).

Although undeveloped for surfers, Namibia's Skeleton Coast (p344) is famous for rough waves and unspoilt beaches. This stretch is only for the seriously experienced and brave, though; savage rips, icy water temperatures and the odd Great White add new dimensions of difficulty to the task at hand.

Mozambique's best waves are at Ponta d'Ouro (p237) in the far south of the country and (for skilled surfers) at Tofinho (p244) – Mozambique's unofficial surfing capital, just south of Tofo. Boards can be rented at both places.

Wildlife Watching

Wildlife and birdwatching are two of the main activities that lure travellers to Southern Africa. Details on the region's fascinating wildlife are provided in the Environment chapter (p56), while visual aid is found in the colour Wildlife Guide (p145). The obvious place to spot the region's furred, feathered and scaled delights is in one of the numerous national parks – see p61 for more information. Individual country chapters also provide specifics about the best spots. For direction on organising wildlife safaris, see Tours in the Transport sections of each country.

In most places in Southern Africa, large animals are confined to national parks (or similar conservation areas), and the only way to see them is by vehicle – this is both by law and by default, as there's rarely any public transport. If you don't have a vehicle (motorcycles and bicycles don't count), your only option is to join an organised safari.

The term 'safari' (which means 'we go' in Swahili) may perhaps conjure up the image of a single-file procession of adventurers and porters stalking through the bush behind a large elephant gun, but modern usage is broader and may extend to bushwalking, river rafting, horse riding, canoeing, playing golf or just warming a seat on a train or vehicle. That said, most safaris involve wildlife viewing, which is most often done from a vehicle with open sides, large windows, or a pop-up roof to allow clear views and photographic opportunities. A driver (who doubles as guide) comes with the vehicle.

The range of wildlife-viewing safaris available in Southern Africa is enormous. They can last from a day to a month, and participants may camp outside and cook over an open fire or stay in luxury lodges and be served gourmet meals. You could charter a safari customised for your group's interests or join an already established group or prescheduled safari. You could spend a frantic day ticking species off a list or spend hours by a single water hole watching the comings and goings.

And of course, there's also a range of prices available. The best value will be participation safaris, in which clients muck in to pack and unpack the vehicle, put up their own tents, and help with cooking and washing up. These are typically good value, and are almost always highly rewarding, especially when you get off the beaten track. At the other end of the spectrum, you can pay up to US$500 per person per day and enjoy all the comforts of home, with a camp staff to take care of all the chores.

Lots of overseas agencies (see p760) cobble together programs using local operators, but these are typically quite expensive. Packages are generally more economical when organised on site (the exception is for safaris involving upmarket lodges, which are often block-booked by overseas agents who can get deals that are lower than rack rates). Locally, the best places to organise safaris are Cape Town, Windhoek, Harare, and the tourist towns of Livingstone and Vic Falls.

If you're on a real shoestring budget and can't afford even the cheapest of safaris, you'll probably be frustrated by the rules and regulations that appear to be designed specifically to keep you out of the parks. There is no public transport, and hitching is forbidden. Even in parks where walking is permitted, you usually have to start from the park headquarters, which is accessible only by vehicle. Hitching is prohibited *inside* the parks, but hours spent waving your thumb at the entrance gate may result in a lift that takes you where you want to go. Plan on long waits and have plenty of food and water.

BOOKS

This section lists publications covering most of Southern Africa; see also p22. Books on individual countries are listed in the relevant country chapters. Note that many books have different publishers in different countries, and that a hardcover rarity in one country may be a readily available paperback in another, so we haven't included publishers in this list (unless relevant). In any case, bookshops, libraries and online booksellers allow you to search by title or author.

FIELD GUIDES

Southern Africa's incredible floral and faunal diversity has inspired a large number of field guides for visitors and wildlife enthusiasts. In the UK, an excellent source for wildlife and nature titles is **Subbuteo Natural History Books Ltd** (☎ 0870-0109 700; www.wildlifebooks.com). International mail orders are welcome. In Australia, check out **Andrew Isles Natural History Books** (☎ 03-9510 5750; www.andrew isles.com).

Field Guide to the Snakes and Other Reptiles of Southern Africa by Bill Branch is the one to consult if you want to know what it is that's slithering underfoot – and whether or not it's dangerous.

South African Frogs by Neville Passmore and Vincent Carruthers has all the answers for frogophiles. It concentrates on South Africa, but includes most species found north of the border.

The Field Guide to the Butterflies of Southern Africa by Igor Migdoll isn't totally comprehensive, but you probably won't encounter a butterfly that isn't included in this guide.

Complete Guide to Freshwater Fishes of Southern Africa by Paul Skelton is a favourite with anglers.

Medicinal Plants of South Africa provides background information on regional medicinal plants; it's available from **Briza Publications** (☎ 12-329 3896; www.briza.co.za) in South Africa.

GENERAL

Raymond Bonner's *At the Hand of Man* discusses conservation issues and the destruction of African wildlife, holding that conservation will work only if African people see real benefits themselves.

Zambezi: Journey of a River by Michael Main is a very readable combination of history, geography, geology, anthropology, careful observation, humour, rumour and myth, following the Zambezi River through Zambia, Angola, Zimbabwe and Mozambique, with side-tracks into Malawi.

Although a personalised selection of observations on wildlife and humans, *Kakuli* by Norman Carr also raises deeper issues and suggests some practical solutions to current conservation problems. The author spent a lifetime working with animals and people in the South Luangwa National Park.

Challenging the effectiveness of aid in Africa, Zambian-born Dambisa Moyo explodes the myths in *Dead Aid*, arguing that aid is actually a major cause of poverty.

GUIDEBOOKS

If you're looking for more in-depth guidebook coverage, Lonely Planet also publishes *South Africa, Lesotho & Swaziland; Botswana & Namibia; Zambia & Malawi* and *Mozambique* guides. If you're travelling the entire continent, you may want to check out *Africa on a Shoestring*. Lonely Planet also publishes guidebooks to a number of other African countries, as well as *Trekking in East Africa*, which includes routes in Malawi.

Another guidebook is *Hiking Trails of Southern Africa* by Willie and Sandra Olivier, which covers major backpacking routes in South Africa and Namibia. If walking is your game, the *Complete Guide to Hiking Trails in Southern Africa* by Jaynee Levy describes more than 350 trails in South Africa (plus another 50 or so in Namibia, Botswana, Swaziland, Lesotho, Zimbabwe and Malawi), from short nature strolls to major expeditions in wild areas.

Pan-continental motorcyclists should grip the *Adventure Motorbiking Handbook* by Chris Scott. It contains lots of information on riding through Africa.

The *Illustrated Guide to Southern Africa* (Readers Digest) and *Secret Southern Africa* (AA of South Africa) are large-format books full of photos, maps and touring descriptions. Both books are recommended for motoring around the region.

HISTORY & POLITICS

Africa by Phyllis Martin and Patrick O'Meara is the nearest you'll get to a pocket library, with scholarly but accessible essays on a wide range of subjects including history, religion, colonialism, sociology, art, popular culture, law, literature, politics, economics and the development crisis.

Africa: Dispatches from a Fragile Continent by Blaine Harden provides provocative and pessimistic reading on several topics, such as the failure of African political leadership. In any case, the author maintains that African values endure and will eventually save the day.

Chris Munion's *Banana Sunday – Datelines from Africa* contains humorous accounts of this journalist's coverage of various African wars.

Blood on the Tracks by Miles Bredin chronicles an essentially hopeless journey between Angola and Mozambique. It's a tale of war, bureaucracy, corruption and inefficiency that neatly outlines the problems faced by modern Africa.

BUSINESS HOURS

Standard opening hours vary slightly from region to region; specifics can be found in the Directory of each country. However, in general you can expect banks to open their doors on weekdays between 8am and 9am, and to close between 3pm and 3.30pm. On Saturday banks close sometime between 11am and 1pm. Shops generally open from 8am or 9am until 5pm, and supermarkets in bigger cities tend to stay open a little longer – usually until at least 8pm or so. In some countries, such as Mozambique, shops often close for an hour over lunch. Cafes open as early as 7.30am and close around 5pm, often daily; however, some are closed on Sunday or Monday. Restaurants serve lunch from 11am until about 3pm and dinner from 6pm to around 10pm.

CHILDREN

Southern Africa presents few problems specific to children, and while health concerns are always an issue, food and lodging are mostly quite familiar and manageable. What's more, foreigners with children are usually treated with great kindness, and a widespread local affection for the younger set opens up all sorts of social interaction for travelling families.

In South Africa, away from the coast, many resorts, hotels and national park lodges and camping grounds have a wide range of facilities for children. Many families hire campervans in South Africa to tour the region. There are fewer child-oriented facilities in the other countries, but here the attractions usually provide entertainment enough: large wild animals in the national parks are a major draw, and even bored teenagers have been known to enjoy Vic Falls and its adrenaline activities. Namibia also lends itself to family travel by campervan, and the attractions – such as the wildlife of Etosha National Park, or the world's biggest sandbox at Sossusvlei – are entertainment in themselves. Lake Malawi has plenty of child-friendly lodges and the highland areas of Malawi such as Viphya Plateau, and Zomba Plateau are also good for families.

In tourist hotels and lodges, family rooms and chalets are normally available for only slightly more than doubles. Otherwise, it's normally easy to arrange more beds in a standard adult double for a minimal extra charge. On public transport children are expected to pay for their seats unless they spend the entire journey on their parents' laps.

In Southern Africa, compared with some other parts of the world, there are few nasty diseases to worry about, and good (if expensive) medical services are almost always within reach; see p769 for more information on health. On the downside, distances between sites of interest can be long, especially on public transport, so parents may well need to invent creative games or provide some supplementary entertainment. Children will normally enjoy having their own small backpacks to carry favourite toys or teddies, books, crayons and paper.

Outside cities and major towns in South Africa, do not plan on finding pasteurised milk, formula, or disposable nappies. They may be available sporadically (especially in Mozambique), but this is the exception rather than the rule. Breastfeeding in public is fairly common for locals, but in rural areas it's likely to attract significant unwanted attention for visitors.

For more advice and anecdotes, see Lonely Planet's *Travel with Children*. Also see the Directory in country chapters for more specific information.

CLIMATE CHARTS

In Southern Africa, summer runs from about November to March/April, while winter is from May to July/August. By March and April, temperatures and rainfall drop and by May, the much drier winter season begins (snow may even fall on the highlands of South Africa and Lesotho). Through June and July the weather remains dry: warm on the coast but with a huge temperature range in the interior – from 20°C in the day to below freezing at night.

From August, temperatures begin to rise and by October, most of the region is hot, and the first rains are arriving in the northernmost regions.

In the Western Cape, which is the only part of Southern Africa to experience a Mediterranean (that is, winter rainfall) climate, the pattern is different. Here, summers

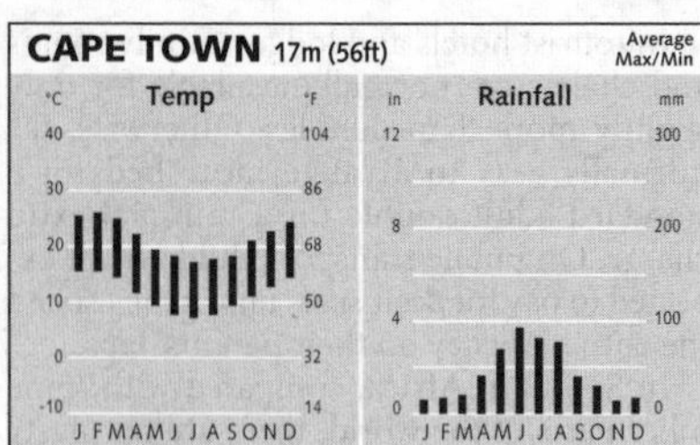
CAPE TOWN 17m (56ft)
Average Max/Min
Temp
Rainfall
°C °F in mm
J F M A M J J A S O N D

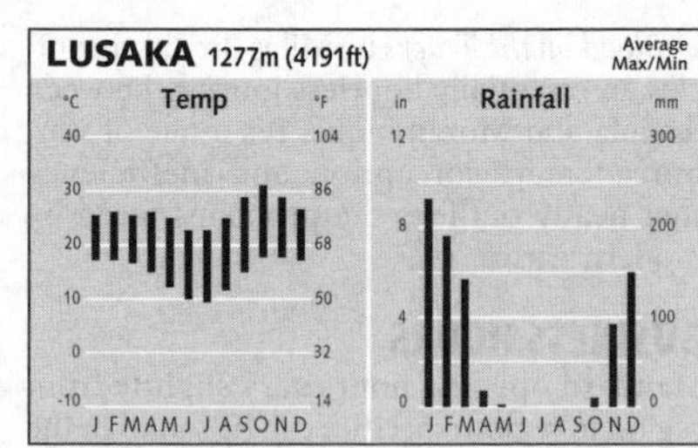
LUSAKA 1277m (4191ft)
Average Max/Min
Temp
Rainfall
°C °F in mm
J F M A M J J A S O N D

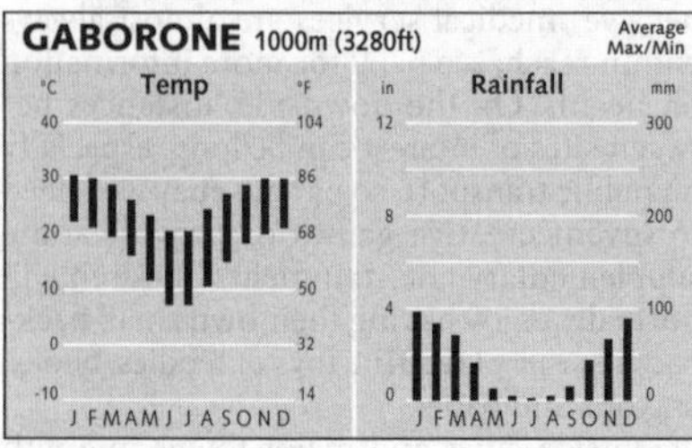
GABORONE 1000m (3280ft)
Average Max/Min
Temp
Rainfall
°C °F in mm
J F M A M J J A S O N D

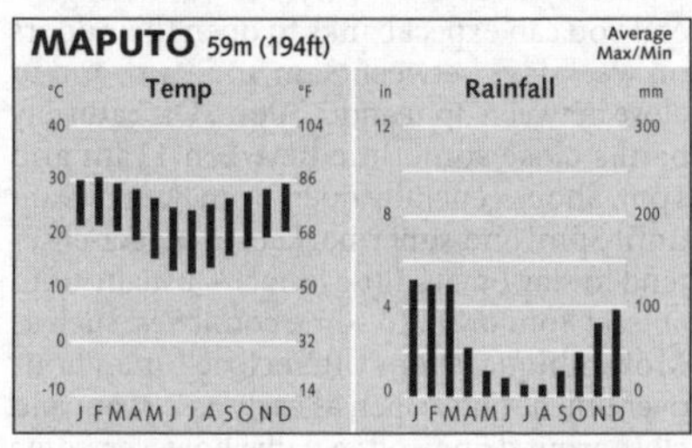
MAPUTO 59m (194ft)
Average Max/Min
Temp
Rainfall
°C °F in mm
J F M A M J J A S O N D

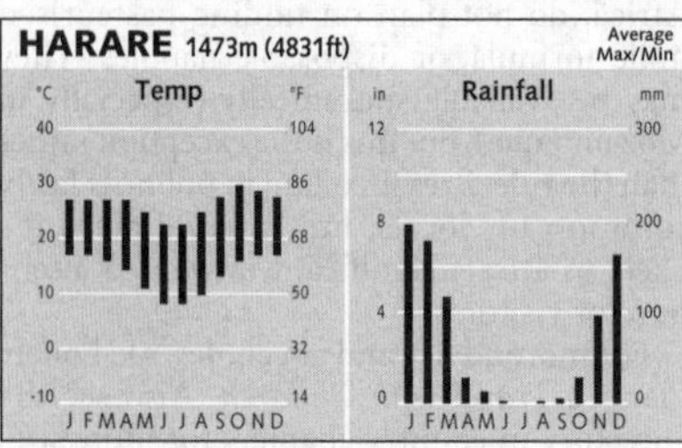
HARARE 1473m (4831ft)
Average Max/Min
Temp
Rainfall
°C °F in mm
J F M A M J J A S O N D

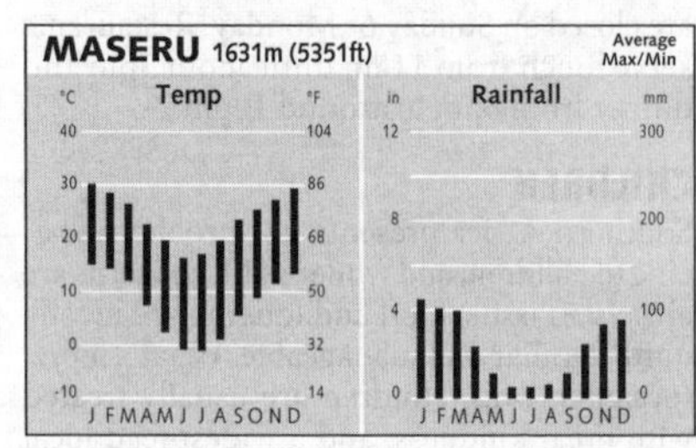
MASERU 1631m (5351ft)
Average Max/Min
Temp
Rainfall
°C °F in mm
J F M A M J J A S O N D

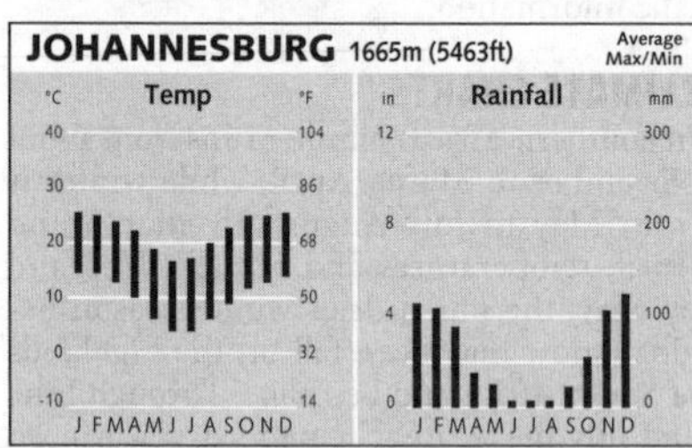
JOHANNESBURG 1665m (5463ft)
Average Max/Min
Temp
Rainfall
°C °F in mm
J F M A M J J A S O N D

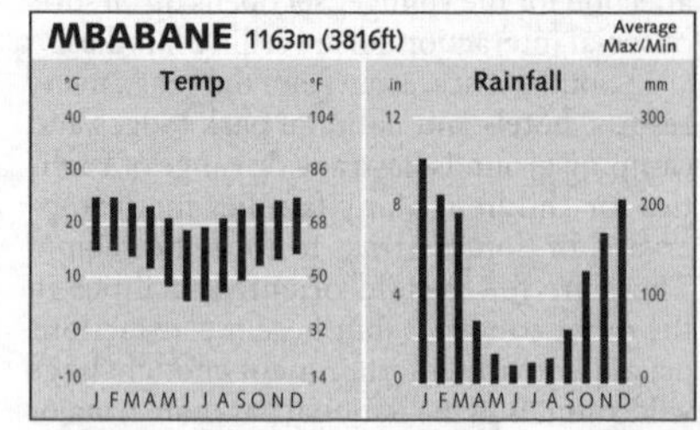
MBABANE 1163m (3816ft)
Average Max/Min
Temp
Rainfall
°C °F in mm
J F M A M J J A S O N D

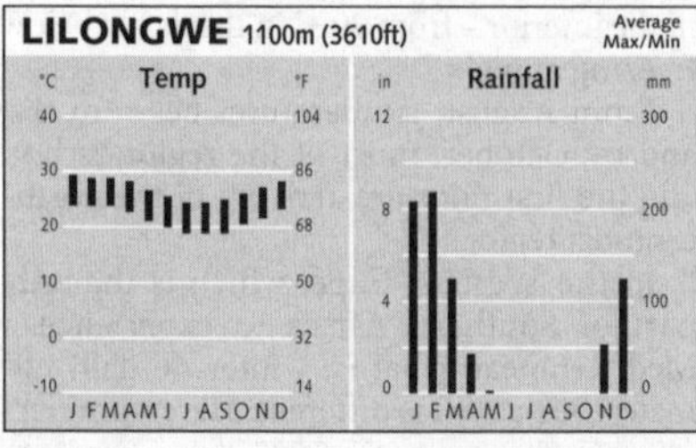
LILONGWE 1100m (3610ft)
Average Max/Min
Temp
Rainfall
°C °F in mm
J F M A M J J A S O N D

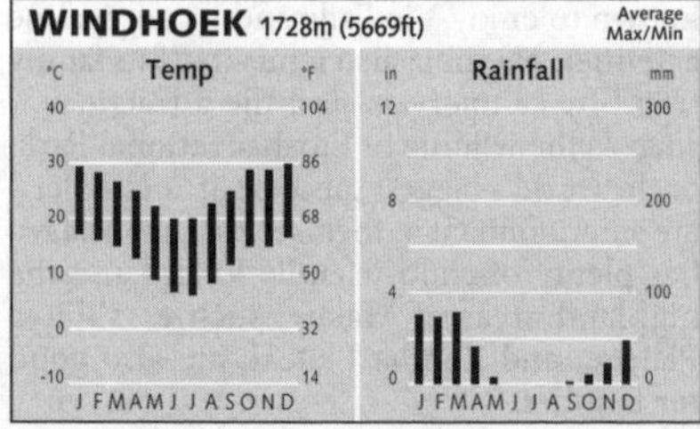
WINDHOEK 1728m (5669ft)
Average Max/Min
Temp
Rainfall
°C °F in mm
J F M A M J J A S O N D

are warm and sunny, while winter brings typically changeable and often rainy weather.

COURSES

Courses offered in Southern Africa generally focus on activities. South Africa is one of the world's top destinations for paragliding, and there are ample opportunities for beginners to learn the ropes. The **South African Hang Gliding & Paragliding Association** (☎ 012-668 1219; www.sahpa.co.za) can provide names of operators, and there are numerous schools offering courses for beginners.

For education of a far less active nature you can ensconce yourself in an atmospheric B&B in South Africa's Winelands and enrol in a wine-tasting course. Useful contacts include **Cape Wine Academy** (☎ 021-889 8844; www.capewineacademy.co.za), which is based in Stellenbosch and runs courses in both Stellenbosch and Cape Town.

Scuba diving is also extremely popular throughout the region, and Southern Africa is one of the cheapest places in the world to learn. See the Diving & Snorkelling section (p737) for the best spots to dive in the region; there is usually a good choice of schools littered around the main sites. Schools in Malawi generally win first prize for best value, with the longevity and reputation to match.

CUSTOMS REGULATIONS

See this section in the Directory under the individual country chapters for customs information, which varies from country to country in the region.

DANGERS & ANNOYANCES

It is very important not to make sweeping statements about personal safety in Southern Africa. While some areas are undeniably risky, most places are completely safe. Essentially, violent robbery is much more prevalent in cities and towns than in rural or wilderness areas. But even towns can differ; there's more of a danger in those frequented by foreigners than in places off the usual tourist track. Details are provided in the Dangers & Annoyances section of individual country Directories.

The main annoyances you'll come across in Southern Africa are the various hustlers, touts, con artists and scam merchants who recognise tourists as easy prey. Although these characters aren't always dangerous, they can part you from your valuables. Awareness, vigilance and suitable precautions are advisable, and should help you deal with them.

Popular scams include young people carrying sign-up sheets, requesting sponsorship for their school, sports team, youth club, grandmother's liver transplant or other apparently worthwhile causes. The sheets will invariably include the names of 'generous' foreigners who have donated US$100 or more. These are almost invariably a scam; ignore them and politely take your leave. Another scam to look out for is people selling bogus bus tickets in and around bus stations. Always purchase your tickets from official sources, even if that's a hole in the wall with a penned sign above it.

In the major cities of Zimbabwe, South Africa and Mozambique it's advisable to keep your wits about you when using an ATM. There are dozens of scams that involve stealing your cash, your card or your personal identification number (PIN) – usually all three. The ATM scam you're most likely to encounter involves the thief tampering with the machine so your card becomes jammed. By the time you realise this you've entered your PIN. The thief will have seen this, and when you go inside to report that your card has been swallowed, he will take the card and leave your account significantly lighter.

Safety Tips

Some simple precautions will hopefully ensure that you have a trouble-free journey. Travellers who exercise due caution rarely have problems. The precautions suggested in this section are particularly relevant to Johannesburg and parts of Cape Town, but it's worth reading them if you're travelling in other main urban centres as well.

- Be discreet with your belongings when on the street. Consider leaving your daypack and camera in your hotel room if the room is safe.
- Don't wear jewellery or watches, however inexpensive they may be. Use a separate wallet for day-to-day purchases, and keep the bulk of your cash out of sight, preferably hidden in a pouch under loose-fitting clothing.
- Walk confidently, but not aggressively. Never look like you're lost (even if you are!). Don't obviously refer to this guidebook. Tear out the pages you need, or duck into a shop to have a look at the map to get your bearings.

- At night get off the streets and take a taxi – a couple of dollars for the fare could save you a lot of pain and trouble.
- Don't fall into the trap of thinking all robbers are on the street. Although most hotels are reputable, some travellers have left money in a safe, only to find that less reputable staff members with a spare key have helped themselves. Often this trick involves taking just a few notes, in the hope that you won't notice. To avoid this, store any valuables in a safe inside a pouch with a lockable zip, or in an envelope you can seal.

EMBASSIES & CONSULATES

Embassies of most travellers' home countries (UK, USA etc) in Southern Africa are listed in the individual country chapters. Embassies are most plentiful in South Africa, where whole suburbs of Pretoria are a Who's Who of global representation (see p569). Where home countries have no embassy, often a consul is appointed, who is not a full-time diplomat but has certain diplomatic responsibilities. Australia, Canada and New Zealand have few embassies in Southern Africa, but there is limited emergency assistance available from the British High Commission.

See p573 for important information regarding visas.

It's important to realise what your own embassy can and can't do to help you if you get into trouble. Generally speaking, it won't be much help if whatever trouble you're in is remotely your own fault. Remember that you are bound by the laws of the country you are in. In genuine emergencies you might get some assistance, but only if other channels have been exhausted. If you have all your money and documents stolen, your embassy might assist with getting a new passport, but that's about it.

GAY & LESBIAN TRAVELLERS

All the countries covered in this book are conservative in their attitudes towards gay men and lesbians, and homosexuality is rarely discussed in public. In traditional African societies, gay sexual relationships are a cultural taboo. In 2001, President Sam Nujoma of Namibia famously said:

> In Namibia we don't allow lesbianism or homosexuality… We will combat this with vigour… Police are ordered to arrest you and deport you and imprison you… Those who are practising homosexuality in Namibia are destroying the nation. Homosexuals must be condemned and rejected in our society.

While this may seem both alarming and deluded, observers see it – along with Zimbabwean president Robert Mugabe's vociferous diatribes against homosexuals – as just a way of deflecting attention from greater governmental problems.

Officially, homosexual activity is illegal in all the countries in this book, except South Africa and Lesotho. Lesbian activities are ignored in some countries because officials aren't really aware of them.

This said, homosexual activity – especially among younger men – does occur. South Africa's constitution is one of the few in the world that explicitly prohibits discrimination on the grounds of sexual orientation, and there are active gay and lesbian communities and scenes in Cape Town, Jo'burg, Pretoria and Durban. Cape Town is without doubt the focal point, and the most openly gay city on the continent. The monthly **Exit** (www.exit.co.za) is South Africa's longest-running gay newspaper. The glossy monthly *OUTright* is for gay males; *Womyn* is its lesbian equivalent. Both are available at CNA and other chain bookstores nationwide. The Gauteng-based magazine *Rush* is also worth looking out for; it's often available at gay venues. There's also a gay and lesbian link on the South Africa tourism website (www.southafrica.net). An excellent website providing accurate and updated information on legalities and cultural issues is www.mask.org.za.

In most places within Southern Africa, open displays of affection are generally frowned upon, whatever your orientation. Please be sensitive to local sensibilities.

INSURANCE

As a rule all travellers need a travel insurance policy, which will provide some sense of security in the case of a medical emergency or the loss or theft of money or belongings. Travel health insurance policies can usually be extended to include baggage, flight departure insurance and a range of other options. See p769 for greater detail about what you should look for in a good travel health insurance plan, and see p764 for information regarding car insurance.

Claims on your travel insurance must be accompanied by proof of the value of any items lost or stolen (purchase receipts are the best, so if you buy a new camera for your trip, for example, hang onto the receipt). In the case of medical claims, you'll need detailed medical reports and receipts. If you're claiming on a trip cancelled by circumstances beyond your control (illness, airline bankruptcy, industrial action etc), you'll have to produce all flight tickets purchased, tour agency receipts and itinerary, and proof of whatever glitch caused your trip to be cancelled.

INTERNET ACCESS

Most capital cities (and some large towns) in the region have at least one internet cafe, and many hotels and backpackers hostels also offer these services. Speed, reliability and hourly rates vary greatly (between about US$1 and US$4). South Africa and Zimbabwe in particular offer plenty of opportunities to get wired. Wireless access is becoming more common everywhere, making a small laptop a handy addition in your luggage. Rural areas in all countries are essentially devoid of internet access, although some small towns may have an internet centre and lodges and camps in and around national parks increasingly have wireless services. For more information see p23.

MAPS

The Automobile Association (AA) of South Africa produces a useful map of South Africa (as well as numerous South African area maps), plus others covering Botswana and Namibia. The maps are available from any AA shop in South Africa.

MONEY

Details on specific currencies and places to exchange money are given in the individual country chapters. All prices quoted in this book are in local currency (if it's considered relatively stable) and US dollars.

Note that Zimbabwe has now taken the US dollar as its official currency. See p691 for more information.

In all countries it's wise to rely on a variety of methods to fund your trip. Local currency, US dollars, travellers cheques and a credit card will cover all bases.

ATMs

ATMs are readily available throughout South Africa and in cities and main urban centres in the rest of the region. If you're planning to travel for lengthy periods of time in rural areas, however, plan ahead as ATMs are still a foreign concept. There are a few ATM scams to be aware of, operating particularly in South Africa and Zimbabwe. See p747 for more information.

Black Market

In some parts of the world, artificially fixed exchange rates in the bank mean you can get more local money for your hard currency by changing on the so-called black market. Not only is this illegal, it's also potentially dangerous. In most of the region, currency deregulation has eliminated the black market. If someone approaches you anywhere in the region offering substantially more than the bank rate, they almost certainly have a well-formulated plan for separating you from your money.

Cash

Most travellers carry a mix of cash and travellers cheques, although cash is more convenient. The best currencies to bring are US dollars or British pounds, preferably in a mixture. The South African rand is also widely recognised throughout the region, but it's not worth changing your currency into rand before converting it to kwacha, pula or whatever.

It's always wise to have at least an emergency US$20 note tucked somewhere safe in case you find yourself suddenly devoid of all other possessions. Due to counterfeiting, few places accept US$100 notes unless they have a light machine to check validity.

Credit Cards

Most credit and debit cards can be used in ATMs, which are found all over South Africa, Malawi, Botswana and Namibia. In other countries, they're found only in capital cities and larger towns, and may not be reliable.

Credit cards work for purchases all over South Africa, Namibia and Botswana, and in tourist establishments in other countries. You can also use credit cards to draw cash advances (but even in South Africa this can take several hours).

Whatever card you choose to use, it isn't wise to rely totally on plastic, as computer or telephone breakdowns can leave you stranded. Always have some cash or travellers cheques as backup.

Moneychangers

Throughout the region, you can exchange currency at banks and foreign exchange bureaus, which are normally found near borders, in larger cities and in tourist areas. You can also change money at some shops and hotels (which almost always give very poor rates).

The easiest currencies to exchange are US dollars, euros or British pounds. At border crossings where there is no bank, unofficial moneychangers are usually tolerated by the authorities. It's always important to be alert, though, as these guys can pull all sorts of stunts with poor exchange rates, folded notes and clipped newspaper sandwiched between legitimate notes.

Tipping

When it comes to tipping, every country is different. Generally, it isn't necessary in small local establishments, midrange restaurants, backpackers lodges, hotels or fast-food places, but in any upmarket restaurant that doesn't automatically include a service charge (which isn't obligatory if the service has been poor), it may be appropriate. There is a grey area between midrange and upmarket restaurants, because tipping is rarely expected from locals but may be expected of foreigners. On the other hand, wealthier Africans may sometimes tip even at smaller restaurants, not because it's expected, but as a show of status.

At safari lodges and on tours, everyone is expected to leave a blanket tip to be divided among the staff. Safari guides are typically tipped separately.

Taxi drivers aren't normally tipped, but may expect about 10% from well-heeled travellers; in larger cities, even backpackers may be expected to fork over a bit extra.

If you're driving – especially in cities – you are expected to tip parking guards, who'll watch your car while you're away (in a few cases, this is a protection racket, but they're mostly legitimate). However, there's no need to tip the guys who wave you into the parking space you were going to take anyway.

Travellers Cheques

It's wise to purchase a range of travellers cheque denominations so you don't have to exchange US$100 in a country where you need only half that. When exchanging travellers cheques, many places want to check your purchase receipts (the ones the travellers cheque company told you to always keep separate), but carry them with you only when you want to change money. Just be sure to have photocopies of them, along with the international numbers to call in case of loss or theft. Be aware that it's increasingly difficult to change travellers cheques in Zambia and Malawi; some banks don't recognise modern purchase receipts (or perhaps don't want to), although US dollars cash in the same institutions is welcomed with open arms.

PHOTOGRAPHY & VIDEO

In South Africa, film (slide and print), cameras and accessories are readily available in large towns, and processing, including slide processing, is generally of a high standard. In Namibia, you'll find slide film in Windhoek and Swakopmund, but in other countries, availability of any sort of film is restricted to cities and tourist centres, and prices are higher. The best advice is to carry a supply of film and any special requirements from home.

The sunlight in Africa is intense, so most people find Fujichrome Velvia 50, Kodachrome 64 or any 100ISO (ASA) film perfectly adequate, with a 200ISO film suitable for long-lens or evening shots. Useful photographic accessories might include a small flash, a cable or remote shutter release, filters and a cleaning kit. Also, remember to take spare camera batteries.

Some African airports may have old X-ray machines, so it's always wise to request a hand check of your film and camera equipment. Even newer film-safe models can affect high-speed film (1000ISO and higher), especially if it passes through several checks during your trip (the effects are cumulative). Travellers coming from the US should carry all film and camera equipment in their hand luggage, as antiterrorism X-ray machines for checked baggage are not film safe.

In all countries, be careful about taking photos of soldiers, police, airports, defence installations and government buildings. It goes without saying that you should always ask permission before taking a photo of anyone, but particularly so if you're in a village.

Blank video tapes are available in capital cities and large towns, but the qualities and formats vary, and African tapes won't work on North American machines. You can recharge batteries in hotels and lodges as you go, but you'll need a charger, plug adaptors and applicable transformers for the countries you're visiting. For more information, check out Lonely Planet's *Travel Photography*.

Transfer of digital images to CD is becoming increasingly common in Southern African cities, particularly in internet cafes and at photography shops.

Wildlife Photography

To score some excellent wildlife photos, a good lightweight 35mm SLR automatic camera with a lens between 210mm and 300mm – and a modicum of skill – should do the trick. Video cameras with a zoom facility may be able to get closer and digital cameras will perform all sorts of magic. If your subject is nothing but a speck in the distance, resist wasting film but keep the camera ready. An early start is advisable because most wildlife is active during the cooler hours. When photographing animals, take light readings on the subject and not the brilliant African background or your shots will be underexposed. The best times to take photos on sunny days are the first two hours after sunrise and the last two before sunset, both of which take advantage of the low sun's colour-enhancing rays. Filters (eg ultraviolet, polarising or skylight) can also produce good results; ask for advice in a good camera shop.

SOLO TRAVELLERS

Solo travel in Southern Africa, whether you're male or female, is straightforward. While you may be a minor curiosity in rural areas, especially solo women travellers, it's likely that in most places nobody will even bat an eye. Times when you'd likely want to find a group to join would be for a safari (to cut costs), on hiking trails (many in South Africa have a three-person minimum for safety reasons) and at night. Solo women should always exercise extreme caution at night and avoid isolating situations. If you're hitting the pubs and bars in a major city it's much wiser and safer to go with a group. For more safety tips for women, see p753.

TELEPHONE

South Africa in general, and major cities elsewhere in the region, has good telephone facilities. Although local calls are relatively inexpensive, long-distance calls and international calls can be pricey. Aside from public phones, there are also private phone centres where you can pay cash for your call, but at double the rate of public phones. International dialling codes for the countries in this book are given in the inside front cover. For information on areas codes within countries, see each chapter's Directory.

Mobile Phones

In Southern Africa, mobile phones are very popular, due in no small part to the often dismal state of national landline service providers. Reception varies from country to country; see the Directory of individual countries for more information. Airports in some countries often have a counter where you can rent a mobile phone for the duration of your stay.

TIME

In the southern summer, Southern Africa is two hours ahead of UTC (Universal Time Coordinate, formerly called GMT, or Greenwich Mean Time). The only Southern African country with daylight-saving time is Namibia, which turns its clocks forward one hour in September, and back one hour in April.

In the southern winter, however, the region is on the same time as British Summer Time (daylight-saving time).

TOILETS

There are two main types of toilet in Africa: the Western style, with a toilet bowl and seat; and the African style, which is a squat toilet with a hole in the floor. Standards of both types vary tremendously, from pristine to nauseating.

In rural areas, long-drop squat toilets are built over a deep hole in the ground, where waste matter decomposes naturally as long as people avoid depositing rubbish (including tampons or sanitary pads, which should be disposed of separately).

There's also a bizarre hybrid, in which an unplumbed Western toilet is perched over a long-drop hole. As you can imagine, the lack of running water can turn these into an unspeakable horror.

TOURIST INFORMATION

All countries in Southern Africa have national tourist boards, but their efficiency and benefit range from excellent to little more than a friendly smile. South Africa's tourist information centres are prolific and fabulous. Usually staffed by devoted locals, they are a great source of microscopic information for travellers. In Zimbabwe, Mozambique, Malawi and Zambia the tourist boards' websites are useful for preplanning, but the offices themselves don't provide very much enlightenment. See Tourist Information in the Directory of individual country chapters for more information.

TRAVELLERS WITH DISABILITIES

People with mobility limitations will not have an easy time in Southern Africa. Even though there are more disabled people per head of population here than in the West, facilities are few. South Africa stands out from its neighbours by the weight of disabled organisations it boasts; see above. In South Africa and the capitals of some other countries, some official buildings have ramps and lifts, but these are probably not the sort of places you want to visit!

For the imaginative, Zambezi raft trips, mokoro (dugout canoe) trips in the Okavango Delta (where at least one mobility-disabled person works as a *mokoro* poler), wildlife drives and cruises, lie-down sandboarding in the Namib Dunes (if you can reach the top on a quad bike), and other activities won't be inaccessible. In almost all cases, safari companies – including budget operators – are happy to accommodate travellers with special needs, so it never hurts to ask!

In South Africa, the South African National Parks' website (www.sanparks.org) has a detailed and inspirational overview of accommodation and trail accessibility for the mobility impaired at all its parks, including Kruger.

Most wheelchair users find travel easier with an able-bodied companion, and happily, travel in Southern Africa does offer a few advantages compared with other parts of the developing world: footpaths and public areas are often surfaced with tar or concrete, rather than with sand, mud or gravel; many buildings (including safari lodges and national park cabins) are single storey, and assistance is usually available on domestic and regional flights. Car hire is easy in South Africa, Namibia and Botswana and, with permission, vehicles can be taken to neighbouring countries.

Organisations

In the US, **Mobility International** (☎ 541-343 1284; www.miusa.org; 132 E Broadway, suite 343, Eugene OR 97401) advises disabled travellers on mobility issues. It primarily runs educational exchange programs, and some include African travel. Also in the US, assistance and advice are available from the **Society for Accessible Travel & Hospitality** (☎ 212-447-7284; www.sath.org; 347 Fifth Ave, suite 605, New York NY 10016).

In the UK, a useful contact is the **Royal Association for Disability & Rehabilitation** (☎ 020-7250 3222; www.radar.org.uk; 12 City Forum, 250 City Rd, London EC1V 8AF).

Access-Able Travel Source (www.access-able.com) is a US-based site providing information on disabled-friendly tours and hotels in South Africa.

VISAS

Visa requirements change according to your nationality. More details about who needs what are given in the individual country chapters and on Lonely Planet's website (www.lonelyplanet.com), which also has links to other visa sites.

In general, travellers from North America, Commonwealth countries and most of Western Europe don't require visas for much of the region. To visit Mozambique, however, almost everyone needs a visa, either purchased at most points of entry (except when coming from Tanzania – arrange in advance) or preissued from a Mozambican embassy or consulate. The other exceptions are Zimbabwe and Zambia, where just about everyone requires a visa, but these can be purchased at most points of entry.

If you're from Asia, Africa, Eastern Europe or Latin America, you should check with the local embassies of the countries you intend to visit, as some may accept only visas issued in your home country. This may also apply to travellers of Asian descent (even those with a Western passport), who may require visas even though their black or white compatriots don't. Note also that some visas have limited validity – that is, in some cases you're required to enter the country in question within a specified time period.

Please note that at some time in the future (perhaps by the time you read this?) visa conditions may have changed. In 2006, the Southern Africa Development Community (SADC) announced a univisa system, to be theoretically introduced when all countries are up to speed on the technical and security arrangements required to implement such a system. Basically it will enable tourists to obtain a single visa for all countries within Southern Africa. Bureaucratic progress tends to move slowly in this part of the world though, so don't hold your breath.

Other Documents

Depending on which countries you're visiting, you may need the following: a vaccination certificate to show you have had all the right jabs (see p769); a driver's licence, and perhaps an International Driving Permit (for the rare occasions when it may be required to hire a vehicle, or for insurance purposes if you're buying a vehicle); as well as a youth hostel card and a student or youth identity card (such as ISIC), which may be good for accessing discounts on flights, long-distance buses and visits to sites of interest (especially museums).

VOLUNTEERING

Unemployment in Southern Africa is high and finding work is difficult. Volunteer work is a more likely possibility, especially if you are interested in teaching or wildlife conservation. A good initial contact is the organisation **Volunteer Abroad** (www.volunteerabroad.com), which has extensive listings of volunteer opportunities in the region.

The following agencies are also useful for long-term paid or volunteer work:

Australian Volunteers International (☎ 03-9279 1788; www.australianvolunteers.com) Places qualified Australian residents on one- to two-year contracts.

Earthwatch (www.earthwatch.org) Places paying volunteers in short-term environmental projects around the globe.

UN Volunteers (☎ 228-815 2000; www.unv.org; Postfach 260 111 D-53153 Bonn, Germany) Places volunteers with qualifications and experience in a range of fields.

Volunteer Service Abroad (☎ 04 472 5759; www.vsa.org.nz) Organises professional contracts for New Zealanders.

Voluntary Service Overseas (VSO) Canada (☎ 1-888-434 2876; www.vsocanada.org); Netherlands (☎ 030 23 20 600; www.vso.nl); UK (☎ 020-8780 7500; www.vso.org.uk) Places qualified and experienced volunteers for up to two years.

There are also some excellent local, grassroots opportunities for travellers wanting to volunteer – see the country chapters for details.

WOMEN TRAVELLERS

Generally speaking, women travellers in Southern Africa will not encounter serious gender-related problems. In fact, compared with North Africa and the Middle East (especially Morocco, Egypt and Turkey), South America and many Western countries, the region is relatively safe and unthreatening for women travellers.

Southern Africa is one of the few places in the developing world where women can meet and communicate with local men – of any race – without automatically being misconstrued. That's not to say that sexual harassment against travellers never happens, but local white women (mostly South Africans, Namibians, Zambians and Zimbabweans) have done much to refute the idea that women of European descent are willing to hop into bed with the first taker.

That said, it's still rare to find local women travelling alone for no apparent purpose, and lone foreign women seen to be idly wandering around the country may be viewed as something of a curiosity, especially in remote areas. Aside from this, attitudes towards foreign women travelling alone tend to be fairly liberal. Although you'll still get questions about what you are doing, and where your husband and children are, reactions are usually matter-of-fact. It is often reported that in some countries (such as Mozambique) solo women are shown much kindness and sisterly treatment from local women that they may not otherwise receive.

When it comes to evening entertainment, both black and white societies in Southern Africa are very much conservative, traditional and male-dominated. Therefore, women travellers may face a few glass walls and ceilings. Many bars are male only (by law of the establishment, or by law of tradition), and even where women are 'allowed', cultural conventions often dictate that women don't enter without a male companion. If you ignore these conventions, be aware that accepting a drink from a local man is usually construed as a come-on (much as it would be in many other parts of the world). However distasteful that may seem to liberated Westerners, trying to buck the system may lead to an uncomfortable situation – or worse. The best maxim is, 'An ounce of prevention is worth a pound of cure'. Prevention in the form of commonsense precautions is well worth heeding: don't wander around alone anywhere at night, and during the daytime, avoid anywhere that's isolated, including streets, beaches and parks. To avoid attracting unwanted attention, it's best to solicit and follow local female advice on which places are acceptable. Additionally, many budget hotels double as brothels, and are best avoided if you're travelling solo. See the Accommodation section of country Directories for more specific information.

It may be difficult to connect with some local women – especially older women, who may have received very little education and therefore speak little English. Similarly, women with young children are normally expected to stay home and attend to domestic duties, which leave them little time to socialise with outsiders. On the other hand, in recent years an increasing number of girls have been permitted to stay in school while boys are sent away to work. Although there is a wide gap between male and female literacy rates, female literacy is becoming more prevalent all over the region and, as a result, many of the employees in government offices – including tourist offices – are educated, young to middle-aged women. In rural areas, most of the teachers and healthcare workers are women.

For women who do meet someone they like, or who wish to sample local hospitality, never forget that in Africa, HIV/AIDS presents a threat that's unimaginable in the West. Throughout the region, local sex workers are almost always infected, and men may see a foreign woman as a safe alternative. Don't be naive, don't do anything stupid and, at the very least, always use a condom.

There's also a very high level of sexual assault and other violence against women in South Africa specifically, the majority of which occurs in townships and rural areas.

While the countries in this region are considerably safer than some other parts of the world, hitching is not recommended and hitching alone is foolish. If you decide to thumb it, you should refuse a lift if the driver is drunk (a sadly common condition) or the car is chock-a-block with men (eg a military vehicle). Use common sense and things should go well.

Tampons and sanitary napkins are sold in pharmacies and supermarkets in major towns, although tampons are rare in Mozambique. They may also be available from shops at hotels and upmarket safari lodges.

Female travellers may like to contact the global organisation called **Women Welcome Women World Wide** (☎ /fax 01494-465441; www.womenwelcomewomen.org.uk; 88 Easton St, High Wycombe, Bucks HP11 1LT, UK), which fosters international friendship by enabling women of different countries to visit one another.

Transport in Southern Africa

CONTENTS

GETTING THERE & AWAY

This section describes access possibilities to Southern Africa from other parts of the world. Regional access is described in the Getting Around section (p761). Details on travel between and around individual countries are provided in their respective chapters.

Flights, tours and train tickets can be booked online at www.lonelyplanet.c om/travel_services.

ENTRY REQUIREMENTS

Visitors require a valid passport to enter every country covered in this book. To accommodate visas and border stamps, you'll need at least one or two empty pages per country you intend to visit, especially if your itinerary calls for multiple border crossings. If your passport is close to full, get a new one or pick up an insert – but apply for it well in advance. If your passport is due to expire, replace it before you leave home, as some officials won't admit you unless your passport is valid at least three (or even six) months beyond the end of your stay.

THINGS CHANGE

The information in this chapter is particularly vulnerable to change. Check directly with the airline or a travel agent to make sure you understand how a fare (and ticket you may buy) works and be aware of the security requirements for international travel. Shop carefully. The details given in this chapter should be regarded as pointers and are not a substitute for your own careful, up-to-date research.

For information on visas, see p752.

AIR

Most flights into Southern Africa arrive at Jo'burg (South Africa) and this is usually the cheapest access point for the region. Although not the most salubrious city to kick-start your travels, it is the heart of the new South Africa and change – be it good or bad – is in your face. The airport itself is in between Jo'burg and Pretoria, so it's easy enough to catch a bus in the other direction and stay in a more relaxing city.

Airports & Airlines

AIRPORTS

You can fly to any major city in Southern Africa from anywhere in the world, but some routes are more popular (and therefore usually cheaper) than others.

From Europe most flights go through London, from where you can fly into most major Southern African cities; most other European capitals also fly to the region, but the main continental hubs are Amsterdam and Frankfurt. From America, Atlanta and New York have direct flights to Jo'burg. From Australia, Sydney and Perth are hubs for flights to Jo'burg, and there are also direct flights from Singapore, Hong Kong and Kuala Lumpur (Malaysia) in Asia. From Africa there are good links between major cities such as Nairobi (Kenya) and Jo'burg: other easy links include Dar es Salaam (Tanzania) and Lilongwe (Malawi), and Addis Ababa (Ethiopia) and Lilongwe, or Lusaka (Zambia).

The major air hub for Southern Africa is **OTR Tambo International Airport** (formerly Johannesburg

CLIMATE CHANGE & TRAVEL

Climate change is a serious threat to the ecosystems that humans rely upon, and air travel is the fastest-growing contributor to the problem. Lonely Planet regards travel, overall, as a global benefit, but believes we all have a responsibility to limit our personal impact on global warming.

Flying & Climate Change

Pretty much every form of motor travel generates carbon dioxide (the main cause of human-induced climate change) but planes are far and away the worst offenders, not just because of the sheer distances they allow us to travel, but because they release greenhouse gases high into the atmosphere. The statistics are frightening: two people taking a return flight between Europe and the US will contribute as much to climate change as an average household's gas and electricity consumption over a whole year.

Carbon Offset Schemes

Climatecare.org and other websites use 'carbon calculators' that allow jetsetters to offset the greenhouse gases they are responsible for with contributions to energy-saving projects and other climate-friendly initiatives in the developing world – including projects in India, Honduras, Kazakhstan and Uganda.

Lonely Planet, together with Rough Guides and other concerned partners in the travel industry, supports the carbon offset scheme run by climatecare.org. Lonely Planet offsets all of its staff and author travel.

For more information check out our website: lonelyplanet.com.

International; code JIA or JNB; ☎ 011-921 6262; www.worldairportguides.com/johannesburg-jnb) which is undergoing a major upgrade ahead of the 2010 World Cup. It is now a world-class airport with a full range of shops, restaurants, internet access, ATMs, foreign-exchange bureaus, and mobile-phone and car-rental outlets. Other useful airports for visitors are Cape Town, Windhoek (Namibia), Lusaka and Lilongwe. Gaborone (Botswana) is a pricey access point.

The town of Victoria Falls is best accessed via Harare or Johannesburg, however Livingstone (p608, Zambia) has become a more popular access point for Victoria Falls (p616) in the last few years since the troubles in Zimbabwe.

Remember that your access point need not necessarily be the nearest point to your intended destination. For example, it's often cheaper to fly into South Africa, from where you can take a short hop to Harare, Windhoek or Lusaka for less than the price of a direct flight. On the other hand, bargain deals to Namibia, Zimbabwe or Zambia may be cheaper than a direct flight to South Africa. Advance research will greatly improve your chances of finding an economical airfare, so start looking early.

AIRLINES

Most major European airlines serve Southern Africa, including British Airways, KLM-Royal Dutch Airlines, Lufthansa Airlines, Swiss, Air France, Virgin and TAP Air Portugal. Additionally, Emirates, Kenya Airways, South African Airways and Air Namibia fly between Europe and the region, and unlikely sounding carriers such as Ethiopian Airlines often offer good-value services between Europe and many parts of Africa.

Although several airlines fly between the USA (Atlanta) and Southern Africa, many prospective visitors find it less convenient, but considerably cheaper, to fly via Europe. From Australia, Qantas has regular services from Sydney and Perth to Johannesburg. Note that there has been a reduction in the number of airlines servicing Zimbabwe.

See the Transport sections in individual country chapters for the list of the main airlines flying to and from that country.

Tickets

When buying your air ticket, you may want to check out 'open-jaw' deals – ie flying into one country and out of another. Sometimes though, even if you want to do a linear trip (starting in Cape Town and finishing in Lusaka, for example), it may be easier and cheaper to get a standard return (eg in and out of Cape Town) and a one-way regional flight (Lusaka to Cape Town) at the end of your trip.

Note that fares quoted in this book for international flights are full-fare economy. Always ask about seasonal and advance purchase discounts, and other special rates, and always check the airline websites for online deals. Some useful online ticket sellers:

www.cheaptickets.com
www.flightcentre.com
www.lowestfare.com
www.onetravel.com
www.priceline.com
www.travel.yahoo.com
www.travelocity.com

Jo'burg and Cape Town are the most popular Southern African stops on a Round the World (RTW) itinerary, and this usually means flying into one city and out of the other. Travel agents can also put together 'alternative' RTW tickets, which are more expensive, but more flexible, than standard RTW itineraries.

Africa

Many travellers on trans-Africa trips fly some sections, either because time is short or simply because the routes are virtually impassable.

The overland route between East Africa and Southern Africa is extremely popular, but it's also easy to find a flight between Nairobi and cities in the region such as Jo'burg or Lusaka. Alternatively, it's a short hop between Dar es Salaam and Lilongwe, which avoids a gruelling overland stretch. Coming from Cairo (Egypt) or Ethiopia, most flights to Southern Africa go via Nairobi.

If you're travelling from West Africa, you have to fly as the overland route is blocked by turmoil in Democratic Republic of Congo (Zaïre). Travellers also tend to avoid Nigeria and Congo-Brazzaville. Options include flying from Accra (Ghana) or Dakar (Senegal) to Jo'burg. Flying from Abidjan (Côte d'Ivoire) to Jo'burg is also possible but less popular.

Australia & New Zealand

Airlines flying from Australia to Southern Africa include Qantas and South African Airways (SAA). There are direct flights from Sydney and Perth on Qantas, and from Perth on SAA, to Jo'burg (flying time about 14 hours from Sydney, 10½ hours from Perth). If flying between New Zealand and Southern Africa you must go via Australia. One of the best places to start looking for cheap deals is the ads in major weekend newspapers.

Two well-known agencies for cheap fares in Australia:

Flight Centre (☎ 131 600; www.flightcentre.com.au) This agency has offices throughout Australia.

STA Travel (☎ 1300 733 035; www.statravel.com.au) Offices are in all major cities and on many university campuses.

These agencies are also represented in New Zealand:

Flight Centre (☎ 0800 243 544; www.flightcentre.co.nz) This agency has many branches throughout the country.

STA Travel (☎ 0508-782 872; www.statravel.co.nz) STA Travel has a main office in Auckland, and other offices in Hamilton, Palmerston North, Wellington, Christchurch and Dunedin.

In addition, the following agencies specialise in Africa travel:

Africa Travel Company (☎ 02-9264 7661; level 1, 69 Liverpool St, Sydney 2000, NSW)

African Wildlife Safaris (☎ 1300 363 302, 03-9249 3777; www.africanwildlifesafaris.com.au) Cobbles together custom tours to Namibia and the entire region. The focus is on wildlife safaris.

Continental Europe

You can fly to Southern Africa from any European capital, but the main hubs are Amsterdam and Frankfurt, and to a lesser extent Zurich and Lisbon (for Maputo, Mozambique). The most popular routes are generally the cheapest, which means that Jo'burg or Cape Town will normally be destinations of choice. Specialist travel agencies advertise in newspapers and travel magazines, so check there for advertisements before ringing around.

There are bucket shops by the dozen in cities such as Paris, Amsterdam, Brussels and Frankfurt. Many travel agents in Europe have ties with STA Travel, where you'll find cheap tickets. STA Travel and other discount outlets in major transport hubs include the following:

Airfair (☎ 0900-7717 717; www.airfair.nl) Netherlands.

Alternativ Tours (☎ 030 21 23 41 90; www.alternativ-tours.de) Germany.

Anyway (☎ 0892 302 301; www.anyway.fr) France.

Barcelo Viajes (☎ 902 200 400; www.barceloviajes.com) Spain.

CTS Viaggi (☎ 06 462 0431; www.cts.it) Italy; specialising in student and youth travel.

STA Travel Germany (☎ 069 743 032 92; www.statravel.de); Switzerland ☎ 0900-450 402; www.statravel.ch)

UK & Ireland

Numerous airlines fly between Britain and Southern Africa, and you'll occasionally find excellent rates. The least expensive point of arrival will probably be Jo'burg, although an increasing number of flights arrive in Cape Town, which is a safer introduction to Africa.

London is normally the best place to buy a ticket, but specialist agencies elsewhere in the UK can provide comparable value. Also check the ads in the travel pages of the weekend broadsheet newspapers, in *Time Out*, the *Evening Standard*, in the free online magazine **TNT** (www.tntmagazine.com) and in the free *SA Times*, which is aimed at South Africans in the UK.

Some companies listed under Tours (p761) also sell flights, and some of the agents listed here also sell tours and safaris:

Africa Travel Centre (☎ 0845-450 1520; www.africatravel.co.uk)
North-South Travel (☎ 01245-608291; www.northsouthtravel.co.uk) Profits at this experienced agency support development projects overseas.
Quest Travel (☎ 0871-423 0135; www.questtravel.com)
STA Travel (☎ 0871-230 0040; www.statravel.co.uk) STA Travel has branches in London, Manchester, Bristol and most large university towns.
Trailfinders (☎ 0845-0585 858; www.trailfinders.co.uk) This popular company has several offices in London, as well as Manchester, Bristol and several other cities.
Travel Bag (☎ 0871-703 4698; www.travelbag.co.uk)
Travel Mood (☎ 0800-0111 945; www.travelmood.com)

USA & Canada

SAA flies direct from New York to Jo'burg (17½ hours), while Delta flies direct from Atlanta (15 hours) and this is generally one of the least expensive routings. To reach one of the other capitals, such as Lusaka, Lilongwe or Maputo, you can get a connection from Jo'burg. It may be cheaper to fly on an economy hop from the USA to London (on British Airways or Virgin Atlantic) or Amsterdam (on KLM), and then buy a discount ticket from there to Southern Africa. Canadians also will probably find the best deals travelling via Atlanta or London.

North Americans won't get the great deals that are available in London, but discount agencies to watch out for include the following:

Air Brokers (☎ 800-883 3273, 415-836 8718; www.airbrokers.com) A consolidator that can come up with good rates on complicated itineraries.
High Adventure Travel/Airtreks (☎ 877-247 8735; www.airtreks.com) Specialises in round-the-world travel including Southern Africa stops.
Premier Tours & Travel (☎ 800-545 1910; www.premiertours.com)
Spector Travel (☎ 617 351 0111; www.spectortravel.com) Combines tours with discounted airfares.
STA Travel (☎ 800 781 4040; www.statravel.com) This organisation, which isn't limited to students, has offices all over the USA.
Travel Cuts (☎ 866-246 9762; www.travelcuts.com) The Canadian student travel association.

LAND

However you travel (by car, bike or public transport), if you're planning to reach Southern Africa overland, your first decision should be which of the main routes through Africa you want to take.

Bicycle

Cycling is a cheap, convenient, healthy, environmentally sound and, above all, fun way to travel. It can also be addictive. It's quite straightforward to take your bike onto a plane and use the bike to get around on the ground. For air travel, you can dismantle the bike and box it up. Bike boxes are available at airports and most bike shops. If you're willing to risk damage to your bike, it's also possible to deflate the tyres, remove the pedals and turn the handlebars sideways, then just wheel the bike up to the check-in desk (if your bike doesn't hold up to baggage handlers, it probably won't survive Africa!). Some airlines don't charge to carry a bike, and don't even include it in the weight allowance. Others charge an extra handling fee of around US$50.

Outside South Africa, you'll have difficulty buying hi-tech European or American spares, so bring anything essential along with you, and know how to make your own repairs. Plan for frequent punctures, and take lots of spare inner tubes. Because automobile tyres are constantly being repaired, patches and glue are available almost everywhere. However, it may be worth carrying a spare tyre, in case of a really devastating blow-out. For more on cycling, see p762.

Border Crossings

For information on specific border crossings between countries in Southern Africa, see the Transport section in country chapters.

The most frequented routes into Southern Africa are from Tanzania into Malawi at Songwe (see p213 for details) and from Tanzania into Zambia at Nakonde (see p681).

The crossing points from Tanzania into Mozambique provide an excellent introduction to the region, but they are off the beaten track and for intrepid travellers only. From Tanzania, the main border post is at Kilambo (Namiranga or Namoto on the Mozambique side). For more, see p290. Further west, it's also possible to cross now at Negomano, where the new Unity Bridge is under construction. The bridge isn't yet finished (although it should be within the lifetime of this book), but meanwhile there is sometimes – depending on river levels – a temporary pontoon bridge that vehicles can use, and canoes for nondriving travellers. Continuing westwards, there is a new bridge open south of Songea (crossing over to Segundo Congresso in Mozambique) that also has an immigration post, and which makes a handy albeit adventurous entry to the Lake Niassa and Lichinga areas (see p290). Back on the coast, there are Mozambique border and customs officials at Palma and Moçimboa da Praia for those arriving in the country from Tanzania by dhow.

Other countries bordering the Southern African region include Angola and the troubled Congo (Zaïre). From Congo, the main border crossing is at Chilabombwe into Zambia. Due to safety issues, though, few travellers use this option.

The situation has improved in Angola with the end of the 27-year war in 2002. Some travellers are crossing in from Namibia, and things have apparently stabilised, though you need to arrange your visa in advance before entering. From Angola, the main border crossings into Namibia are at Ruacana, Oshikango and Rundu. A few intrepid travellers are also crossing the border between Angola and Zambia, but this is a very remote crossing and you should research this in advance.

Car & Motorcycle

Driving from Europe to Southern Africa is a major undertaking. The main points to emphasise include the incredibly long distances, the appalling nature of most roads and the constant challenge of dealing with police and/or border officials. Overland drivers will have to be mechanically competent and carry a good collection of spares. You'll also need vehicle registration papers, liability insurance, a driver's licence and International Driving Permit, as well as a *carnet de passage*, effectively a passport for the vehicle and temporary waiver of import duty, designed to prevent car-import rackets. Your local automobile association can provide details.

Your home liability insurance won't be valid in many countries, and some require international drivers to purchase expensive (and effectively useless) insurance when crossing borders. In most cases, this is just a racket, and no matter what you spend on local insurance, you'll effectively be travelling uninsured.

You might want to check the website www.sahara-overland.com for information about crossing the Sahara.

East Africa

From Nairobi, the most popular route runs via Mombasa (Kenya) or Arusha (Tanzania) to Dar es Salaam (Tanzania). From here, drivers follow the Great North Rd, and those without wheels take the Tanzania–Zambia railway (Tazara; p681); both lead to Kapiri Mposhi (Zambia), which is within easy reach of Lusaka, Livingstone and Victoria Falls. Alternatively, get off at Mbeya (in southern Tanzania) and enter northern Malawi at Songwe (p213). Another option from Dar es Salaam takes you across the country to Kigoma on Lake Tanganyika, then by steamer to Mpulungu (Zambia), from where you can continue overland to Lusaka and beyond.

Other possibilities from Nairobi include travelling through Uganda, Rwanda and Burundi (although this country has stabilised with the last remaining rebel group disarmed in early 2009, banditry was still a problem so travel through Burundi is not currently recommended), catching the Lake Tanganyika steamer from Bujumbura (Burundi; if it's running), and connecting with the previously outlined route at Mpulungu (Zambia). When the troubles have ended, this route will be a rewarding option.

North & West Africa

The threat of terrorism and kidnappings makes travel to Algeria dangerous, particularly in rural areas, and most trans-Sahara travellers still use the Morocco and Mauritania route into Senegal and the rest of West Africa. Due to unrest, the route from Algeria into Mali and Niger is still not recommended. Once through West Africa, your route to Southern Africa will next be blocked by more unrest in Congo (Zaïre). This means a flight – probably from Accra (Ghana) or Lagos (Nigeria) to Nairobi (Kenya), from where you can follow the route outlined under East Africa.

Northeast Africa

The Nile Route through northeast Africa starts in Egypt, and goes into Sudan (either via Lake Nasser or via the Red Sea from Suez or Hurghada); note, however, that these days travel through Sudan is not advised, especially southern Sudan, including the region bordering Uganda, anywhere around the border with Eritrea, and definitely not in the Darfur region in the west of the country, which has ongoing civil unrest. Most people fly from Cairo (Egypt) or Khartoum (Sudan) to Kampala (Uganda) or Nairobi, where again you can follow the route outlined under East Africa.

SEA

For most people, reaching Southern Africa by sea is not a viable option. The days of working your passage on commercial boats have vanished, although a few travellers do manage to hitch rides on private yachts along the east coast of Africa from Mombasa (Kenya) to Mozambique or South Africa.

Alternatively, several cargo-shipping companies sail between Europe and South Africa, with comfortable cabins for public passengers. The voyage between London and Cape Town takes about 16 days. Contact **Strand Voyages** (☎ 020-7921 4340; www.strandtravel.co.uk) for details.

TOURS

Overlanding

Although overlanding across Africa from Europe or the Middle East has become quite difficult due to the various 'roadblocks' imposed by unrest, some overland tour operators still take up the challenge. Some begin in Morocco and head down through Mauritania, Mali, Niger and onward as far as possible. Others take the easier option and begin in Kenya. While these trips are popular, they're designed mainly for inexperienced travellers who feel uncomfortable striking out on their own or for those who prefer guaranteed social interaction to the uncertainties of the road. If you have the slightest inclination towards independence or would feel confined travelling with the same group of 25 or so people for most of the trip (although quite a few normally drop out along the way), think twice before booking an overland trip.

Around Southern Africa

When deciding upon your preferred method of travel, the same thing about overland tours can very much be applied to tours around Southern Africa. If you feel inexperienced, are unsure of travelling by yourself or just a sucker for constant company, then tours can be a very good option. However, many find the experience quite suffocating and restrictive. Our advice, to hedge your bets, is to take a shorter tour and see how you like it – this gives you the option of either taking another tour or striking out on your own with the benefit of having visited some of the places you may like to spend more time in.

Literally hundreds of tour and safari companies now organise package tours to Southern Africa, but it always pays to shop around for details and deals. Especially in Europe, it's becoming increasingly popular to look for late bookings, which may be advertised in travel sections of weekend newspapers, or even at special late-bookings counters in some international airports. If you prefer a more independent approach, you can prebook flights and hotels for the first few nights, then join tours locally (see p766).

One of the best places to begin looking for reputable agencies is weekend newspapers or travel magazines, such as *Wanderlust* in the UK and *Outside* or *National Geographic Adventure* in the US. It's also useful to attend travel fairs or ask around discount travel agencies.

Speciality magazines for flower, birdwatching, wildlife-viewing, railway and other buffs may also include advertising for tours focusing on their own areas of interest.

Following is a list of possibilities:

AUSTRALIA

Adventure World (☎ 02-8913 0755; www.adventureworld.com.au) Organises tours, safaris, car hire and hotel packages all over Southern Africa.

African Wildlife Safaris (☎ 03-9249 3777, 1300 363 302; www.africanwildlifesafaris.com.au) Designs customised wildlife safaris around Southern Africa.

Peregrine Travel (☎ 1300 791 485, 03-8601 4444; www.peregrineadventures.com) This Africa specialist cobbles together all types of adventures, for all budgets.

FRANCE

Makila Voyages (☎ 01-42 96 80 00; www.makila.fr) This upmarket company organises tours and safaris all over East and Southern Africa.

UK

Explore Worldwide Ltd (☎ 0845 013 1539; www.exploreworldwide.com) Organises group tours through South Africa, Zambia, Botswana and Namibia, focusing on adventure and wildlife safaris.

In the Saddle (☎ 01299-272 997; www.inthesaddle.com) Appeals specifically to horse aficionados, including a range of adventurous horse-riding routes.

Naturetrek (☎ 01962-733051; www.naturetrek.co.uk) This company's aim is to get you to where the animals are. It offers specialised wildlife-viewing itineraries.

Temple World (☎ 020-8940 4114; www.templeworld.co.uk) This sophisticated and recommended company organises middle- to upper-range tours to the best of the region.

USA

Adventure Center (☎ 510-654 1879, 800 228 8747; www.adventurecenter.com) A travel specialist that organises budget to midrange tours and is the US agent for several overland operators, including Guerba, Dragoman and Karibu.

Africa Adventure Company (☎ 800 882 9453, 954-491 8877; www.africa-adventure.com) These top safari specialists can organise any sort of Southern Africa itinerary.

Born Free Safaris (☎ 800 472 3274; www.bornfreesafaris.com) Safaris, trekking cultural tours and flights.

Bushtracks (☎ 800 995 8689; www.bushtracks.com) Private luxury air safari operator cobbling together a variety of unforgettable experiences.

Mountain Travel Sobek (☎ 888-831 7526; www.mtsobek.com) Offers package trips to Botswana and throughout Southern Africa including Zambia and Malawi.

Premier Tours & Travel (☎ 800 545 1910; www.premiertours.com) Premier sells discount tickets and organises inexpensive participation camping safaris all over Southern Africa.

Voyagers (☎ 800 633 4734; www.voyagers.com) Specialises in photographic and wildlife-viewing safaris.

Wilderness Travel (☎ 800 368 2794, 510-558 2488; www.wildernesstravel.com) Offers guided group tours with an emphasis on down-to-earth touring, including hikes and other hands-on pursuits.

GETTING AROUND

This section briefly outlines the various ways of travelling around Southern Africa. For specifics, see the Getting Around section in each of the individual country chapters.

AIR

Distances are great in Africa, and if time is short, regional flights can considerably widen your options. For example, after touring South Africa for a while you could fly from Cape Town to Victoria Falls and then tour Zimbabwe or southern Zambia. Alternatively, fly to Lilongwe, which is a good staging point for trips around Malawi or eastern Zambia, or to Windhoek, which opens up all the wonders of Namibia.

Even within a country, tight schedules can be accommodated with short hops by air. Both domestic and regional flights are usually operated by both state airlines and private carriers, and except in Botswana and Zambia, the competition generally keeps prices down to reasonable levels.

Sometimes the only practical way into remote parks and reserves is by air, and charter flights provide easy access to national-park or remote-lodge airstrips. Although these are normally for travellers on less restrictive budgets, access to the best of the Okavango Delta is possible only by charter flight.

Airlines in Southern Africa

The following list includes regional airlines with domestic and intra–Southern Africa routes. For information on airline safety records see the Transport section in the individual country chapters.

Airlink (☎ 27-11-978 1111; www.saairlink.co.za) Flights throughout the region, connecting South Africa with most other countries including Swaziland.

Air Botswana (☎ 267-390 5500; www.airbotswana.co.bw)

Air Malawi (☎ 265-1-620811; www.airmalawi.com) Connects Lusaka to Lilongwe.

Air Namibia (☎ 264-61-299 6000; www.airnamibia.com.na)

Air Zimbabwe (www.airzimbabwe.com)

British Airways Comair (☎ 27-11-921 0111; www.comair.co.za)

Linhas Aereas de Moçambique (☎ 258-1-426001; www.lam.co.mz/english)

Pelican Air (☎ 011 973 3649; www.pelicanair.co.za) Useful service between Jo'burg and Vilankulo/Bazaruto Archipelago, some flights via Nelspruit.

Proflight Zambia (www.proflight-zambia.com) Regular flights around Zambia and between Zambia and Jo'burg.

South African Airways (☎ 27-11-978 5313, 0861-359722; www.flysaa.com) An excellent airline with many reliable routes around the region and beyond.

South African Express (☎ 27-11-978 9905; www.flysax.com)

Air Passes

The Star Alliance African Airpass allows flexible travel around sub-Saharan Africa including all the countries in this book except Swaziland and Lesotho. It covers 30 airports in 23 different countries, and you can buy between three and 10 coupons (each coupon representing a single trip, ie Jo'burg to Windhoek). The Airpass allows for substantial savings, and flights are operated by South African Airways and EgyptAir – see www.staralliance.com for more.

BICYCLE

On a bicycle, travellers will often be on an equal footing with locals, and will have plenty of opportunities to meet and visit people in small towns and villages along the way. Pointers on bringing a bike on the plane are found on p758.

For getting around, traditional touring bikes will cope with most sealed roads (and some good dirt roads) with little trouble, but narrow tyres are normally unsuitable and to get off the main routes, you'll need a mountain bike with fat tyres. On sandy roads, however, even balloon tyres won't help, and you'll wind up pushing the bike.

A cyclist's greatest cause for alarm will be motorists. Cyclists are usually regarded as second-class road users, so make sure you know what's coming up behind you and always be prepared to make an evasive swerve onto the verges. For this purpose, a rear-view mirror (handlebar or helmet mounted) will prove invaluable.

Other factors to consider are the heat, the long distances and finding places to stay. Aim to travel in cool, dry periods, and carry at least 4L of drinking water. If you get tired, or simply want to cut out the boring bits, bikes can easily be carried on buses or trucks – although you'll need to pay an extra luggage fee, and be prepared for some rough handling as your beloved machine is loaded onto a roof rack.

A good source of information may be your national cycling organisation. In Britain, the **Cyclists' Touring Club** (☎ 0844 736 8450; www.ctc.org.uk) provides cycling advice and also organises group cycling tours. In the USA, the **International Bicycle Fund** (☎ /fax 206-767 0848; www.ibike.org) organises socially conscious tours and provides information.

If you don't have a bike but fancy a few days' cycling, you'll normally be able to hire a bike locally, especially in tourist areas. Otherwise, local people in villages and towns are often willing to rent their bikes for the day. Ask at your hotel or track down a bicycle repair shop (every town market has one).

BOAT

Boat types and services in the region vary greatly from large ferries and cargo ships to traditional dhows plying the coastline of Mozambique and *mokoros* (dugout canoes) skimming along the Okavango Delta.

Based in South Africa, **Tall Ships** (www.tallships.co.za) has cargo ships between Durban and various Mozambican ports that sometimes take passengers; and **Starlight Lines** (www.starlight.co.za) is a good contact for connections to Mozambique, Madagascar and Mauritius.

The **Ilala Ferry** (☎ 01-587311; ilala@malawi.net) chugs passengers and cargo up and down Lake Malawi. Stops include Monkey Bay, Nkhotakota, Nkhata Bay and Likoma Island in Malawi (see p214); and Metangula on the Mozambique side of the lake (see p288).

There is a ferry crossing between Zambia and Botswana (see p116), departing from Kazungula, Botswana, which takes vehicles.

BUS

Long-distance buses operate regularly between most Southern African countries. Keep in mind that prices quoted in this book are for single fares, unless indicated otherwise. Most routes are covered by fairly basic, cheap and often slow services; major links include between Francistown (Botswana) and Bulawayo (Zimbabwe), Gaborone (Botswana) and Johannesburg (Jo'burg; South Africa), Harare (Zimbabwe) and Jo'burg, Lilongwe (Malawi) and Lusaka (Zambia), Blantyre (Malawi) and Harare. From Cape Town and Jo'burg, larger and more comfortable buses run to many destinations in the region including Maseru (Lesotho), Mbabane (Swaziland), Maputo (Mozambique) and Windhoek (Namibia).

The following are major bus companies operating throughout the region. They are generally safe and reliable, and standard facilities usually include air-con, video, sound system, reclining seats and an on-board toilet:

Greyhound (☎ 083 915 9000; www.greyhound.co.za) Jo'burg, Cape Town, Harare, Bulawayo and Maputo.

Intercape Mainliner (☎ 0861 287 287, 021-380 4400; www.intercape.co.za) Extensive services with destinations including Jo'burg, Cape Town, Maputo, Windhoek, Victoria Falls and Gaborone.

AN ALTERNATIVE TO THE BUS – OVERLAND TRUCKS

Lots of companies run overland camping tours in trucks converted to carry passengers. Sometimes the trucks finish a tour, then run straight back to base to start the next one. Often, drivers are happy to carry 'transit' passengers on their way back to base. This is not a tour, as such, but can be a comfortable way of transiting between Vic Falls and Jo'burg, or Harare and Nairobi (Kenya), for around US$25 per day, plus foodkitty contributions. Those looking for rides should check around truck stops in well-known tourist areas, such as Cape Town, Jo'burg, Harare, Victoria Falls, Windhoek or Lilongwe or visit backpackers' hostels (where these companies invariably leave stacks of brochures).

Panthera Azul (☎ 011-618 8811, Maputo 021-302 077; panthera@tvcabo.co.mz) Jo'burg, Durban, Nelspruit, Maputo.
Translux (☎ 011-774 3333; www.translux.co.za) Jo'burg, Pretoria, Maputo, Blantyre, Lusaka.

For bus travellers, border crossings can be tedious while customs officials search through huge amounts of luggage. Minibus services may be more efficient, as fewer passengers will mean less time at the border.

There are also several international bus services especially designed for backpackers and other tourists. These companies normally use comfortable 16-seat buses and have helpful drivers, on-board music and pick-ups/drop-offs at main tourist centres and backpackers' hostels. Among these is the **Baz Bus** (☎ 021-439 2323; www.bazbus.com), which links Cape Town, Jo'burg, Pretoria and Durban with Manzini (Swaziland), from where you can get a minibus taxi to Maputo (Mozambique).

For more information on bus travel between countries, see the Getting There & Away sections under Transport in the individual country chapters, or seek out the latest information at backpackers' hostels and budget travel agents throughout Southern Africa.

Buying Tickets

In general it's always better to buy tickets in advance, over the phone, or by dropping into an office in person (you can also book online with some companies), although sometimes it may not be necessary. Contact the bus operator before your trip to see if advance purchase is advised. Sample fares include approximately US$30 for Jo'burg to Gaborone, and US$80 for Cape Town to Windhoek; both one-way. See the destinations in individual country chapters for detailed fare information.

CAR & MOTORCYCLE

Information on bringing your own wheels to Southern Africa is found on p759. More information on getting around, and other matters related to car and motorcycle travel, is provided under the Getting Around heading in the Transport section of individual country chapters.

Fuel & Spare Parts

Fuel and spare parts are available across the region, although both have recently been scarce in Zimbabwe. If you're driving in remote areas, such as Zambia, careful planning is required to ensure you have enough fuel until you reach the next petrol station.

Hire

Car rental isn't cheap, but can be a very convenient way to travel, especially if you're short of time or want to visit national parks and other out-of-the-way places. Costs can be mitigated by mustering a group to share the rental and petrol, and will open up all sorts of opportunities. In all the countries covered by this book, to hire a vehicle you must be at least 21 years old (in some cases as old as 25).

A list of local car-rental firms is included in the Getting Around sections of country chapters. Firms are usually accessible via email, and it pays to book before you leave home. If you're visiting more than one country, check whether you're able to cross borders with a rental vehicle. This is usually allowed by South African companies, which will let you take vehicles into Namibia, Botswana, Lesotho and Swaziland, as well as Zimbabwe (but not Mozambique), with payment of an additional cross-border fee (usually around US$100).

Companies advertising the lowest daily rates will typically also require payment of a per-kilometre fee, so if you're doing a lot of driving, you'd do better to pay extra for an unlimited mileage deal. Also, check on the fees for other items such as tax, damage and insurance, all of which can add considerably to the final bill.

TO GO OR NOT TO GO?

A dangerous traffic quirk in Southern Africa concerns the use and significance of indicator lights. When a car comes up behind a slow vehicle, wanting to overtake, the driver of the slower vehicle will often flash one indicator to let the other driver know whether or not it's safe to overtake. Logically, the left indicator would mean 'go' (that is, it may potentially be turning left, and the way is clear) and the right would mean 'don't go' (it may potentially be turning right, indicating that the way is not clear). Unfortunately, quite a few confused drivers get this backwards, creating a potentially disastrous situation for a trusting driver in the vehicle behind. The moral is, ignore the well-intentioned signals and never overtake unless you can see that the road ahead is completely clear.

Generally, South Africa is the cheapest place to hire a car (from US$30 per day), although Namibia and Botswana are also pretty good (around US$40 to US$50 per day) and Malawi isn't too bad. Zimbabwe is ridiculously expensive and in Zambia and Mozambique you're looking at a minimum of US$100 per day to take a 2WD out of the city.

In South Africa and Namibia you can hire campervans (RVs) that accommodate two to six people. With additional payment, these come with as much equipment as you may need for demanding safaris. In most countries, you can also opt for a 4WD vehicle, which will typically cost from around US$150 per day (from about US$100 in South Africa), with unlimited mileage. A 4WD is almost mandatory in Zambia anywhere outside of Lusaka, and recommended in other countries (with the exception of South Africa) if you intend visiting parks or going into rural areas.

Insurance

When hiring a car always check the insurance provisions and any excess that you may be liable to pay in the event of an accident. It's also worth checking if the insurance covers driving into other Southern African countries (depending on where you intend going) and driving on dirt roads for 2WDs. If you need insurance for your own car, see information about the AA on opposite.

Purchase

An increasing number of travellers opt to buy a car, tour the region, then sell it at the end of their trip. Although you need a relatively large amount of money up front, you can expect to get at least some of it back, and travelling this way can work out a lot cheaper than car rental – especially if costs are split among several people.

For visitors, South Africa is the best place to buy a car (other countries place restrictions on foreign ownership, have stiff tax laws, or simply don't have the choice of vehicles). Also, South African-registered vehicles don't need a *carnet de passage* to visit any of the countries covered by this book. Travelling through Botswana, Lesotho, Namibia and Swaziland is easy, while for Malawi, Mozambique, Zimbabwe and Zambia you'll easily get temporary import permits at the border.

It's usually cheaper to buy privately, but for tourists it is often more convenient to go to a dealer. The weekly **Cape Ads** (www.capeads.com) is the best place to look for a private sale. Also try **Auto Trader** (www.autotrader.co.za), which advertises thousands of cars around the country.

Although prices tend to be cheaper in Jo'burg, most people do their buying in Cape Town – a much nicer place to spend the week or two that it will likely take for the process. Cape Town's main congregation of used-car dealers is on Voortrekker Rd between Maitland and Belleville metro train stations.

Some dealers might agree to a buy-back arrangement – if you don't trash the car, you can reasonably expect to get a decent percentage of your purchase price back after a three-month trip, but you need to check all aspects of the contract to be sure this deal will stick.

A recommended contact in Cape Town is **Graham Duncan Smith** (☎ 021-797 3048), who's a Land Rover expert and has helped people buy a 4WD in the past; he charges a R150 consultation fee and R200 per hour for engineering work.

No matter who you buy from, make sure that the car details correspond accurately with the ownership (registration) papers, that there is a current licence disc on the windscreen and that the vehicle has been checked by the **police clearance department**

(☎ Cape Town 021-467 8000). Check the owner's name against their identity document, and check the car's engine and chassis numbers. Consider getting the car tested – in Cape Town, try **Same Garage** (☎ 021-434 1058; 309 Main Rd, Sea Point). A full test can cost up to R500; less detailed tests are around R220.

Cheap cars will often be sold without a roadworthy certificate. This certificate is required when you register the change-of-ownership form (RLV) and pay tax for a licence disc. A roadworthy used to be difficult to obtain, but some private garages are now allowed to issue them (a few hundred rand), and some will overlook minor faults.

For something decent, plan on spending at least R25,000. For a 4WD, Series 1, 2 and 3 Land Rovers will cost from R15,000 to R40,000, depending on the condition.

To register your car, present yourself along with your passport and a photocopy, the registration certificate (in the seller's name), a roadworthy certificate, proof of purchase, a valid licence and your money at the **Cape Town Motor Vehicle Registration Authority** (☎ 0860 103 089) in the Civic Centre on the foreshore in Cape Town. Call ahead to check how much cash you'll need; it shouldn't be more than a few hundred rand. Plus if the licence has expired, you will have to pay a penalty. Blank change-of-ownership forms are also available at the authority.

Insurance against theft or damage is highly recommended, though not legally required for private-vehicle owners. It can be difficult to arrange by the month. The **Automobile Association of South Africa** (AASA; ☎ 011-799 1000, emergencies 083 843 22; www.aasa.co.za) is a good contact, and may be willing to negotiate payment for a year's worth of insurance with a pro-rata refund when you sell the car. Insurance agencies include **Sansure** (☎ 021-914 3488, 0860 786 847; www.sansure.com) in Cape Town.

Road Conditions

The good news is that most main roads in Southern Africa are in fair to excellent condition, and are passable for even small compact cars. In Malawi, Zambia and Mozambique, however, you may be slowed down considerably by sealed roads that haven't seen any maintenance for many years and are plagued with bone-crunching and tyre-bursting potholes. On lesser roads, standards vary considerably, from relatively smooth highways to dirt tracks (see the boxed text, p766).

Road Hazards

Whatever vehicle you drive, prepare to deal with some of the world's worst, fastest and most arrogant and aggressive drivers.

Tree branches on the road are the local version of warning triangles, and usually indicate a broken-down vehicle ahead. If you come up behind someone on a bicycle, hoot the horn as a warning and offer a friendly wave as you pass. This isn't considered offensive, and the cyclist will appreciate the heads-up.

On rural highways, always be on the lookout for children playing, people selling goods, seeds drying or animals wandering around on the loose. Livestock is always a concern, and hitting even a small animal can cause vehicle damage, while hitting something large – like a cow or a kudu – can be fatal (for both the driver and the animal). If you see kids with red flags on the road, it means they're leading a herd of cows. Slow down, even if you can't see any cows (especially if you can't see any cows).

These things become much harder to deal with in the dark. Additionally, many vehicles have faulty lights – or none at all – so avoid driving at night if at all possible.

Road Rules

In all the countries covered in this book, traffic officially drives on the left – but that may not always be obvious, so be especially prepared on blind corners and hills.

HITCHING

Hitching is a way of life in Southern Africa, and visitors may well have the opportunity to join the throng of locals looking for lifts. While this is a good way to get around places without public transport (or even with public transport), there is a protocol involved. As a visitor, you're likely to take precedence over locals (especially with white drivers), but if other people are hitching, it's still polite to stand further along the road so they'll have the first crack (that is, unless there's a designated hitching spot where everyone waits).

Another option is to wait around petrol stations and try to arrange lifts from drivers who may be going your way. If you do get a lift, be sure to determine what sort of payment is expected before you climb aboard. In most cases, plan on paying just a bit less than the equivalent bus fare.

As in any other part of the world, hitching is never entirely safe, and we therefore don't

BUSH DRIVING

While Southern Africa has a good network of sealed roads, driving on unsealed roads requires special techniques and appropriate vehicle preparation.

- For rough road conditions, you'll need a robust, high-clearance vehicle, but you'll have to engage the 4WD only when driving in sand or mud, or over boulder-sized rocks.
- In especially rocky conditions, have someone get out and direct the driver over the route of least resistance.
- At river crossings, always check the water depth and bottom conditions before starting across. It will be obvious that sand, stones and gravel are preferable to mud and muck!
- Make sure your vehicle is in good running order before you start. Carry tools, spares and equipment, including towrope, torch, shovel, fan belts, vehicle fluids, spark plugs, wire, jump leads, fuses, hoses, a good jack and a wooden plank to act as a base in sand. A second spare tyre is highly advised, and even a third if you've got room. You could also carry tyre levers, a tyre pump, spare tubes and repair kit, but mending punctures in the bush is much harder than the manuals imply, and should be avoided if possible. And of course you'll need the expertise to handle and install all this stuff…
- Wrap tools and heavy objects in blankets or padding. Pack supplies likely to be pitched around in strong plastic or metal containers, and strap everything down tightly on the roof or in the back. Keep breakable items in the cab. Once you're on unsealed roads, dust permeates everything – so tightly wrap food, clothing and camera equipment in strong dustproof containers.
- When calculating fuel requirements, estimate your intended distance and then double it to allow for getting lost and emergencies. For serious off-roading, remember to allow for petrol consumption up to four times higher than in normal conditions – especially on sandy tracks.
- Carry at least 5L of water per person per day in indestructible container to allow for delays and breakdowns. Extra petrol should be carried in strong, leak-proof jerry cans.
- Take the best maps you can find, plus a GPS or compass that you know how to use. Take readings periodically to make sure you're still travelling in the right direction. To get an accurate compass reading, stand at least 3m from the vehicle.

recommend it. Travellers who hitch should understand that they are taking a small but potentially serious risk.

LOCAL TRANSPORT

Within individual countries, public bus services range from basic to luxurious. In addition to the typically spluttering big buses, many countries also have minibuses, which are faster, run more frequently and perhaps are even more dangerous due to their speed. Note that minibuses or combis in Zimbabwe are no longer recommended to travellers – they get so neglected and overused that they break down and constantly have lethal accidents. See the individual country chapters for more details.

In Southern Africa, there's a notable lack of long-distance shared service taxis (such as the seven-seat Peugeots that are so popular in other parts of Africa). Some travellers occasionally get a group together and hire a city taxi for a long trip, but this is rare.

In rural areas, the frequency of bus services drops dramatically. In such cases, public transport may be limited to the back of a pick-up truck (ute). Everyone pays a fare to the driver, which is normally comparable to the bus fare for a similar distance. This can be great fun – however uncomfortable – and it's often your only option.

TOURS

Travellers are faced with a boggling array of organised tour options in Southern Africa, and the only problem will be making your selection. In addition to the very convenient hop-on, hop-off bus services in South Africa, there are plenty of budget tours and safaris

Bush Tracks

Bush tracks rarely make an appearance on maps, and their ever-changing routes can utterly confound drivers. Some bush tracks will provide access to remote cattle posts or small villages and then disappear, often to re-emerge somewhere else. Some tracks never re-emerge, leaving you stranded.

- Take care driving through high grass – seeds can block radiators and cause overheating. Dry grass next to the exhaust pipe can also catch fire. Stop regularly and remove plant material from the grille or exhaust.

Sand

In sandy conditions you may be following a faint track – often just the wheel marks of previous vehicles – or driving across completely bare wilderness. Either way, driving is easier if the air is cool (usually mornings), as the sand is more compact at these times.

- Tyre pressure should be low – around half that required for normal road conditions. To prevent bogging or stalling, move as quickly as possible and keep the revs up, but avoid sudden acceleration. Shift down a gear before you reach deep sandy patches, not when you're in them.
- Allow the vehicle to wander along the path of least resistance when negotiating a straight course through rutted sand. Anticipate corners and turn the wheel slightly earlier than you would on a solid surface – this will allow the vehicle to slide smoothly around.

Pans

Many of the rules for bush-track or sand driving apply here, but some extra points are worth making.

- First, never drive on a pan unless you know exactly what you're doing. If you do venture onto a pan, stick to the edges until you're sure it's dry.
- Even if the pan *seems* dry, it can still be wet underneath – vehicles can break through the crust and become irretrievably bogged. Foul-smelling salt can mean the pan is wet and potentially dangerous. If in doubt, follow the tracks of other drivers (unless, of course, you see bits of vehicle poking above the surface).
- If you do get bogged and have a winch, anchor the spare wheel or the jack – anything to which the winch may be attached – by digging a hole and planting it firmly in the muck. Hopefully you'll be able to anchor it better than the pan has anchored the vehicle.

available to take you to the regional highlights. You'll have the most options in Cape Town, Jo'burg, Victoria Falls, Livingstone, Maun, Windhoek and other places frequented by tourists. As with all tours, the range of options is enormous: they can last from two days to three weeks and can involve camping and mucking-in to luxury shuttles between five-star lodges. Vehicles may be private aircraft, Kombi vans, no-frills safari trucks or comfortable buses with air-con and chilled wine in the fridge.

For countries with a choice of locally based tour companies, a selection is listed under Tours in the Getting Around sections of those country chapters, with further choices also under some specific destinations. Some countries may have only a limited selection of operators, which are often attached to local travel agencies or budget hotels. For details, see specific destinations in the individual country chapters.

Local operators that arrange tours around Southern Africa include the following:

Barefoot Safaris (☎ 265-01-707346; www.barefoot-safaris.com) Small group safaris, self-drive, hiking and sailing; covers Zambia, Malawi, Botswana, Mozambique and Namibia.

Dana Tours (☎ 258-21-497 483; www.danatours.net) Combined Mozambique–South Africa–Swaziland itineraries. Offices in Maputo and Nelspruit.

Kiboko Safaris (☎ 265-01-751226; www.kiboko-safaris.com) Excellent budget camping and lodge safaris in Malawi and South Luangwa, Zambia; also luxury safaris in Malawi and Mozambique.

Makomo Safaris (☎ www.makomo.com) Combinations for adventurous types that include Malawi, Mozambique and eastern Zambia.

Oceans, Islands, Safaris (☎ 021-701 9014; www.oceanislandsafari.com) This company and its sister company Wildlife Adventures – both Cape Town–based – are good for upscale South Africa–Mozambique–Quirimbas Archipelago itineraries. It also offers tours in most other countries in the region.

Wayfarer Adventures (☎ /fax 021-715 0875; www.allworld-vacation.com/wayfarer-adventures) Wilderness adventure travel throughout Southern Africa, including Land Rover tours around Namibia.

Wilderness Safaris (☎ 011-807 1800; www.wilderness-safaris.com) This organisation offers a range of tours in all Southern African countries. In addition to the standard luxury lodge-based tours in remote areas, it offers fly-in safaris and activity-based trips. It also actively supports conservation and community projects.

TRAIN

Rail travel around Southern Africa focuses on the South African network and its offshoots into Botswana, Mozambique, Namibia, Swaziland, Zimbabwe and Zambia. For example for train service between Mozambique and South Africa, the only current route is Maputo–Komatipoort, where you need to disembark at the border and change trains. Trains on the Mozambique side, however, are very bad and slow. It's much better to travel via train on the South Africa side, and then bus or chapa for the Mozambique stretch (Ressano Garcia to Maputo).

Currently the only cross-border train services are the Tazara line between Zambia and Tanzania (see p681) and the **Trans-Namib** (☎ Namibia 061-298 2175; www.transnamib.com.na) 'StarLine' between Windhoek and Upington (25 hours).

Travelling by train within the various countries is still a decent option – and it's almost always fun – but can be a slow way to go. For details, see under Train in the Getting Around sections of individual country chapters.

Health

CONTENTS

As long as you stay up to date with your vaccinations and take basic preventive measures, you're unlikely to succumb to most of the health hazards covered in this chapter. While countries in Southern Africa have an impressive selection of tropical diseases on offer, it's more likely you'll get a bout of diarrhoea or a cold than a more exotic malady. The main exception to this is malaria, which is a widespread risk in Southern Africa, and precautions should be taken.

BEFORE YOU GO

A little predeparture planning will save you trouble later. Get a check-up from your dentist and your doctor if you have any regular medication or chronic illness, eg high blood pressure or asthma. You should also organise spare contact lenses and glasses (and take your prescription with you); get a first-aid and medical kit together; and arrange necessary vaccinations.

Travellers can register with the **International Association for Medical Advice to Travellers** (IAMAT; www.iamat.org), which provides directories of certified doctors. If you'll be spending much time in remote areas, consider doing a first-aid course (contact the Red Cross or St John's Ambulance), or attending a remote medicine first-aid course, such as that offered by **Wilderness Medical Training** (WMT; www.wildernessmedicaltraining.co.uk).

If you are bringing medications with you, carry them in their original containers, clearly labelled. A signed and dated letter from your physician describing all medical conditions and medications, including generic names, is also a good idea. If carrying syringes or needles, be sure to have a physician's letter documenting their medical necessity.

INSURANCE

Find out in advance whether your insurance plan will make payments directly to providers, or will reimburse you later for overseas health expenditures. In most countries in Southern Africa, doctors expect payment upfront in cash. It's vital to ensure that your travel insurance will cover any emergency transport required to get you to a hospital in a major city, or all the way home, by air and with a medical attendant if necessary. Not all insurance covers this, so check the contract carefully. If you need medical assistance, your insurance company might be able to help locate the nearest hospital or clinic, or you can ask at your hotel. In an emergency, contact your embassy or consulate.

RECOMMENDED VACCINATIONS

The **World Health Organization** (WHO; www.who.int/en) recommends that all travellers be covered for diphtheria, tetanus, measles, mumps, rubella and polio, as well as for hepatitis B, regardless of their destination. The consequences of these diseases can be severe, and outbreaks do occur.

According to the **Centers for Disease Control & Prevention** (www.cdc.gov), the following vaccinations may be recommended for travel in Southern African countries: hepatitis A, hepatitis B, rabies and typhoid, and boosters for tetanus, diphtheria and measles. Yellow fever is not a risk in the region, but the certificate is an entry requirement if you're travelling from an infected region (see p773). Consult your medical practitioner for the most up-to-date information.

MEDICAL CHECKLIST

It's a very good idea to carry a medical and first-aid kit with you, to help yourself in the case of minor illness or injury. Following is a list of items to consider packing.

- antibiotics (prescription only), eg ciprofloxacin (Ciproxin) or norfloxacin (Utinor)
- antidiarrhoeal drugs (eg loperamide)
- acetaminophen (paracetamol) or aspirin
- anti-inflammatory drugs (eg ibuprofen)
- antihistamines (for hay fever and allergic reactions)
- antibacterial ointment (eg Bactroban) for cuts and abrasions (prescription only)
- antimalaria pills, if you'll be in malarial areas
- bandages, gauze
- scissors, safety pins, tweezers, pocket knife
- DEET-containing insect repellent for the skin
- permethrin-containing insect spray for clothing, tents, and bed nets
- sun block
- oral rehydration salts
- iodine tablets (for water purification)
- sterile needles, syringes and fluids if travelling to remote areas

INTERNET RESOURCES

There is a wealth of travel health advice on the internet. The Lonely Planet website at www.lonelyplanet.com is a good place to start. The World Health Organization (WHO) publishes the helpful *International Travel and Health,* available free at www.who.int/ith. Other useful websites include **MD Travel Health** (www.mdtravelhealth.com) and **Fit for Travel** (www.fitfortravel.scot.nhs.uk).

Some official government travel health websites:

Australia www.smartraveller.gov.au/tips/travelwell.html
Canada www.hc-sc.gc.ca/index_e.html
UK www.dh.gov.uk/PolicyAndGuidance/HealthAdviceForTravellers/fs/en
USA www.cdc.gov/travel

FURTHER READING

- *A Comprehensive Guide to Wilderness and Travel Medicine* (1998) Eric A Weiss
- *Healthy Travel* (1999) Jane Wilson-Howarth
- *Healthy Travel Africa* (2000) Isabelle Young
- *How to Stay Healthy Abroad* (2002) Richard Dawood
- *Travel in Health* (1994) Graham Fry
- *Travel with Children* (2004) Cathy Lanigan

IN TRANSIT

DEEP VEIN THROMBOSIS

Prolonged immobility during flights can cause deep vein thrombosis (DVT) – the formation of blood clots in the legs. The longer the flight, the greater the risk. Although most blood clots are reabsorbed uneventfully, some might break off and travel through the blood vessels to the lungs, where they could cause life-threatening complications.

The chief symptom is swelling or pain of the foot, ankle or calf, usually but not always on just one side. When a blood clot travels to the lungs, it may cause chest pain and breathing difficulty. Travellers with any of these symptoms should immediately seek medical attention. To prevent DVT, walk about the cabin, perform isometric compressions of the leg muscles (ie contract the leg muscles while sitting), drink plenty of fluids and avoid alcohol.

JET LAG

If you're crossing more than five time zones you could suffer jet lag, resulting in insomnia, fatigue, malaise or nausea. To avoid jet lag try drinking plenty of fluids (nonalcoholic) and eating light meals. Upon arrival, get exposure to natural sunlight and readjust your schedule (for meals, sleep etc) as soon as possible.

IN SOUTHERN AFRICA

AVAILABILITY & COST OF HEALTH CARE

Good-quality health care is available in the urban areas of many countries in Southern Africa, and private hospitals are generally of a good standard. Public hospitals by contrast are often underfunded and overcrowded; in off-the-beaten-track areas, reliable medical facilities are rare.

Prescriptions are required in most countries in Southern Africa. Drugs for chronic diseases should be brought from home. In many countries there is a high risk of contracting HIV from infected blood transfusions. The **BloodCare Foundation** (www.bloodcare.org.uk) is a useful source of safe, screened blood, which can be transported to any part of the world within 24 hours.

INFECTIOUS DISEASES

Following are some of the diseases that are found in Southern Africa, though with a few basic preventive measures, it's unlikely that you'll succumb to any of these.

Cholera

Cholera is caused by a bacteria, and spread via contaminated drinking water. In South Africa, the risk to travellers is very low; you're likely to encounter it only in eastern rural areas, where you should avoid tap water and unpeeled or uncooked fruits and vegetables. The main symptom is profuse watery diarrhoea, which causes debilitation if fluids are not replaced quickly. An oral cholera vaccine is available in the USA, but it is not particularly effective. Most cases of cholera can be avoided by close attention to drinking water and by avoiding potentially contaminated food. Treatment is by fluid replacement (orally or via a drip), but sometimes antibiotics are needed. Self-treatment is not advised.

Dengue Fever (Break-Bone Fever)

Dengue fever, spread through the bite of mosquitos, causes a feverish illness with headache and muscle pains similar to those experienced with a bad, prolonged attack of influenza. There might be a rash. Mosquito bites should be avoided whenever possible. Self-treatment: paracetamol and rest.

Filariasis

Filariasis is caused by tiny worms migrating in the lymphatic system, and is spread by the bite from an infected mosquito. Symptoms include localised itching and swelling of the legs and/or genitalia. Treatment is available. Self-treatment: none.

Hepatitis A

Hepatitis A is spread through contaminated food (particularly shellfish) and water. It causes jaundice and, although it is rarely fatal, it can cause prolonged lethargy and delayed recovery. If you've had hepatitis A, you shouldn't drink alcohol for up to six months afterwards, but once you've recovered, there won't be any long-term problems. The first symptoms include dark urine and a yellow colour to the whites of the eyes. Sometimes a fever and abdominal pain might be present. Hepatitis A vaccine (Avaxim, VAQTA, Havrix) is given as an injection: a single dose will give protection for up to a year, and a booster after a year gives 10-year protection. Hepatitis A and typhoid vaccines can also be given as a single-dose vaccine, hepatyrix or viatim. Self-treatment: none.

Hepatitis B

Hepatitis B is spread through infected blood, contaminated needles and sexual intercourse. It can also be spread from an infected mother to the baby during childbirth. It affects the liver, causing jaundice and occasionally liver failure. Most people recover completely, but some people might be chronic carriers of the virus, which could lead eventually to cirrhosis or liver cancer. Those visiting high-risk areas for long periods or those with increased social or occupational risk should be immunised. Many countries now routinely give hepatitis B as part of the childhood vaccination program. It is given singly or can be given at the same time as hepatitis A (hepatyrix).

A course will give protection for at least five years. It can be given over four weeks or six months. Self-treatment: none.

HIV

HIV, the virus that causes AIDS, is an enormous problem across Southern Africa, with a devastating impact on local health systems and community structures. The virus is spread through infected blood and blood products, by sexual intercourse with an infected partner, and from an infected mother to her baby during childbirth and breastfeeding. It can be spread through 'blood to blood' contacts, such as with contaminated instruments during medical, dental, acupuncture and other body-piercing procedures, and through sharing used intravenous needles. At present there is no cure; medication that might keep the disease under control is available, but these drugs are too expensive, or unavailable, for the overwhelming majority of those living in Southern Africa. If you think you might have been infected with HIV, a blood test is necessary; a three-month gap after exposure and before testing is required to allow antibodies to appear in the blood. Self-treatment: none.

Malaria

Malaria is a widespread risk in Southern Africa. Apart from road accidents, it is

ANTIMALARIAL A TO D

- A – Awareness of the risk. No medication is totally effective, but protection of up to 95% is achievable with most drugs, as long as other measures have been taken.
- B – Bites, to be avoided at all costs. Sleep in a screened room, use a mosquito spray or coils, sleep under a permethrin-impregnated net at night. Cover up at night with long trousers and long sleeves, preferably with permethrin-treated clothing. Apply appropriate repellent to all areas of exposed skin in the evenings.
- C – Chemical prevention (ie antimalarial drugs) is usually needed in malarial areas. Expert advice is needed as resistance patterns can change, and new drugs are in development. Not all antimalarial drugs are suitable for everyone. Most antimalarial drugs need to be started at least a week before and continued for four weeks after the last possible exposure to malaria.
- D – Diagnosis. If you have a fever or flulike illness within a year of travel to a malarial area, malaria is a possibility, and immediate medical attention is necessary.

probably the only major health risk that you face travelling in this area, and precautions should be taken. The disease is caused by a parasite in the bloodstream spread via the bite of the female anopheles mosquito. There are several types of malaria; falciparum malaria is the most dangerous type and the predominant form in South Africa. Infection rates vary with season and climate, so check out the situation before departure. Several different drugs are used to prevent malaria, and new ones are in the pipeline. Up-to-date advice from a travel health clinic is essential as some medication is more suitable for some travellers than others (eg people with epilepsy should avoid mefloquine, and doxycycline should not be taken by pregnant women or children aged under 12).

The early stages of malaria include headaches, fevers, generalised aches and pains, and malaise, which could be mistaken for flu. Other symptoms can include abdominal pain, diarrhoea and a cough. Anyone who develops a fever in a malarial area should assume malarial infection until a blood test proves negative, even if you have been taking antimalarial medication. If not treated, the next stage could develop within 24 hours, particularly if falciparum malaria is the parasite: jaundice, then reduced consciousness and coma (also known as cerebral malaria) followed by death. Treatment in hospital is essential, and the death rate might still be as high as 10% even in the best intensive-care facilities.

Many travellers think that malaria is a mild illness, and that taking antimalarial drugs causes more illness through side effects than actually getting malaria. This is unfortunately not true. If you decide against antimalarial drugs, you must understand the risks, and be obsessive about avoiding mosquito bites. Use nets and insect repellent, and report any fever or flulike symptoms to a doctor as soon as possible. Some people advocate homeopathic preparations against malaria, such as Demal200, but as yet there is no conclusive evidence that this is effective, and many homeopaths do not recommend their use.

Malaria in pregnancy frequently results in miscarriage or premature labour, and the risks to both mother and foetus during pregnancy are considerable. Travel throughout the region when pregnant should be carefully considered. Adults who have survived childhood malaria have developed immunity and usually only develop mild cases of malaria; most Western travellers have no immunity at all. Immunity wanes after 18 months of nonexposure, so even if you have had malaria in the past and used to live in a malaria-prone area, you might no longer be immune.

Rabies

Rabies is spread by receiving bites or licks from an infected animal on broken skin. Few human cases are reported in Southern Africa, with the risks highest in rural areas. It is always fatal once the clinical symptoms start (which might be up to several months after an infected bite), so postbite vaccination should be given as soon as possible. Postbite vaccination (whether or not you've been vaccinated before the bite) prevents the virus from spreading to the central nervous system. Animal handlers should be vaccinated, as should those travelling to remote areas where a reliable source of postbite vaccine is not available within 24 hours. Three preventive injections are needed over a month. If you have not been vaccinated you'll need a course of five injections starting 24 hours or as soon as possible after the injury. If you have been vaccinated, you'll need fewer postbite injections, and have more time to seek medical help. Self-treatment: none.

Schistosomiasis (Bilharzia)

This disease is a risk when swimming in freshwater lakes and slow-running rivers – always seek local advice before venturing in. It's spread by flukes (minute worms) that are carried by a species of freshwater snail, which then sheds them into slow-moving or still water. The parasites penetrate human skin during swimming and then migrate to the bladder or bowel. They are excreted via stool or urine and could contaminate fresh water, where the cycle starts again. Swimming in suspect freshwater lakes or slow-running rivers should be avoided. Symptoms range from none to transient fever and rash, and advanced cases might have blood in the stool or in the urine. A blood test can detect antibodies if you might have been exposed, and treatment is readily available. If not treated, the infection can cause kidney failure or permanent bowel damage. It's not possible for you to infect others. Self-treatment: none.

Tuberculosis

Tuberculosis (TB) is spread through close respiratory contact and occasionally through infected milk or milk products. BCG vaccination is recommended if you'll be mixing closely with the local population, especially on long-term stays, although it gives only moderate protection against the disease. TB can be asymptomatic, being picked up only on a routine chest X-ray. Alternatively, it can cause a cough, weight loss or fever, sometimes occurring months or even years after exposure. Self-treatment: none.

Typhoid

This is spread through food or water contaminated by infected human faeces. The first symptom is usually a fever or a pink rash on the abdomen. Sometimes septicaemia (blood poisoning) can occur. A typhoid vaccine (typhim Vi, typherix) will give protection for three years. In some countries, the oral vaccine Vivotif is also available. Antibiotics are usually given as treatment, and death is rare unless septicaemia occurs. Self-treatment: none.

Yellow Fever

Although not a problem within Southern Africa, you'll need to carry a certificate of vaccination if you'll be arriving from an infected country. For a list of infected countries see the websites of **WHO** (www.who.int/wer/) or the **Centers for Disease Control & Prevention** (www.cdc.gov/trav el/blusheet.htm).

TRAVELLERS' DIARRHOEA

This is a common travel-related illness, sometimes simply due to dietary changes. It's possible that you'll succumb, especially if you're spending a lot of time in rural areas or eating at inexpensive local food stalls. To avoid diarrhoea, eat only fresh fruits or vegetables that have been cooked or peeled, and be wary of dairy products that might contain unpasteurised milk. Although freshly cooked food can often be a safe option, plates or serving utensils might be dirty, so be selective when eating food from street vendors (make sure that cooked food is piping hot all the way through). If you develop diarrhoea, be sure to drink plenty of fluids, preferably an oral rehydration solution containing lots of water and some salt and sugar. A few loose stools don't require treatment but, if you start having more than four or five stools a day, you should start taking an antibiotic (usually a quinoline drug, such as ciprofloxacin or norfloxacin) and an antidiarrhoeal agent (such as loperamide) if you're not within easy reach of a toilet. If diarrhoea is bloody, persists for more than 72 hours or is accompanied by fever, shaking chills or severe abdominal pain, you should seek medical attention.

Amoebic Dysentery

Contracted by eating contaminated food and water, amoebic dysentery causes blood and mucus in the faeces. It can be relatively mild and tends to come on gradually, but seek medical advice if you think you have the illness as it won't clear up without treatment (which is with specific antibiotics).

Giardiasis

This, like amoebic dysentery, is also caused by ingesting contaminated food or water. The illness usually appears a week or more after you have been exposed to the offending parasite. Giardiasis might cause only a short-lived bout of typical travellers' diarrhoea, but it can also cause persistent diarrhoea. Ideally, seek medical advice if you suspect you have giardiasis, but if you are in a remote area you could start a course of antibiotics.

ENVIRONMENTAL HAZARDS

Heat Exhaustion

This condition occurs following heavy sweating and excessive fluid loss with inadequate replacement of fluids and salt, and is primarily a risk in hot climates when taking unaccustomed exercise before full acclimatisation. Symptoms include headache, dizziness and tiredness. Dehydration is already happening by the time you feel thirsty – aim to drink sufficient water to produce pale, diluted urine. Self-treatment: fluid replacement with water and/or fruit juice, and cooling by cold water and fans. The treatment of the salt-loss component consists of consuming salty fluids as in soup, and adding a little more table salt to foods than usual.

Heatstroke

Heat exhaustion is a precursor to the much more serious condition of heatstroke. In this case there is damage to the sweating mechanism, with an excessive rise in body temperature, irrational and hyperactive behaviour, and eventually loss of consciousness and death. Rapid cooling by spraying the body with water and fanning is ideal. Emergency fluid and electrolyte replacement is usually also required by intravenous drip.

Insect Bites & Stings

Mosquitoes might not always carry malaria or dengue fever, but they (and other insects) can cause irritation and infected bites. To avoid these, take the same precautions as you would for avoiding malaria (see p771). Bee and wasp stings cause real problems only to those who have a severe allergy to the stings (anaphylaxis), in which case, carry an adrenaline (epinephrine) injection.

Scorpions are found in arid areas. They can cause a painful bite that is sometimes life-threatening. If bitten by a scorpion, take a painkiller. Medical treatment should be sought if collapse occurs.

Ticks are always a risk away from urban areas. If you get bitten, press down around the tick's head with tweezers, grab the head and gently pull upwards. Avoid pulling the rear of the body as this may squeeze the tick's gut contents through the attached mouth parts into the skin, increasing the risk of infection and disease. Smearing chemicals on the tick will not make it let go and is not recommended.

Snakebites

Basically, avoid getting bitten! Don't walk barefoot, or stick your hand into holes or cracks. However, 50% of those bitten by venomous snakes are not actually injected with poison (envenomed). If bitten by a snake, do not panic. Immobilise the bitten limb with a splint (such as a stick) and apply a bandage over the site with firm pressure, similar to bandaging a sprain. Do not apply a tourniquet, or cut or suck the bite. Get medical help as soon as possible.

Water

In most areas of Southern Africa you should stick to bottled water rather than drinking water from the tap, and purify stream water before drinking it.

Language

CONTENTS

Due to colonial influences, English is an official language in every Southern African country except Mozambique (where it's Portuguese). English-speaking visitors should have few communication problems.

Afrikaans is also widely used throughout the region and is the first language of millions of people of diverse ethnic backgrounds.

In Mozambique and parts of northern Namibia along the Angola border, Portuguese is the European language of choice.

In parts of Namibia, German is also widely spoken, but is the first language of only about 2% of Namibians.

AFRIKAANS

Afrikaans is often used between members of different groups (eg Xhosa and Zulu, Herero and Namaa) who may not speak another common language. It's also used as a lingua franca in both South Africa and Namibia.

Pronunciation

a	as the 'u' in 'pup'
aai	as the 'y' sound in 'why'
ae	as 'ah'
e	when word stress falls on **e**, it's as in 'net'; when unstressed, it's as the 'a' in 'ago'
ee	as in 'deer'
ei	as the 'ay' in 'play'
i	when word stress falls on **i**, it's as in 'hit'; when unstressed, it's as the 'a' in 'ago'
o	as the 'o' in 'fort', but very short
oe	as the 'u' in 'put'
oë	as the 'oe' in 'doer'
ooi/oei	as the 'ooey' in 'phooey'
r	a rolled 'r' sound
tj	as the 'ch' in 'chunk'
u	as the 'e' in 'angel' with lips pouted

Greetings & Conversation

Hello.	*Hallo.*
Good morning.	*Goeiemôre.*
Good afternoon.	*Goeiemiddag.*
Good evening.	*Goeienaand.*
Good night.	*Goeienag.*
Please.	*Asseblief.*
Thank you (very much).	*(Baie) Dankie.*
How are you?	*Hoe gaan dit?*
Good, thank you.	*Goed dankie.*
Pardon.	*Ekskuus.*
Yes.	*Ja.*
No.	*Nee.*
What?	*Wat?*
How?	*Hoe?*
How many/much?	*Hoeveel?*
Where?	*Waar?*
from …	*van …*

Do you speak English?
Praat U Engels?

Do you speak Afrikaans?
Praat U Afrikaans?

I only understand a little Afrikaans.
Ek verstaan net 'n bietjie Afrikaans.

Where are you from?
Waarvandaan kom U?

son/boy	*seun*
daughter/girl	*dogter*
wife	*vrou*
husband	*eggenoot*
mother	*ma*
father	*pa*
sister	*suster*
brother	*broer*

EMERGENCIES – AFRIKAANS

Help!	*Help!*
Call a doctor!	*Roep 'n doktor!*
Call the police!	*Roep die polisie!*
I'm lost.	*Ek is veloorer.*

nice/good/pleasant	*lekker*
bad	*sleg*
cheap	*goedkoop*
expensive	*duur*

Shopping & Services

art gallery	*kunsgalery*
bank	*bank*
church	*kerk*
city	*stad*
city centre	*middestad*
emergency	*nood*
exit	*uitgang*
information	*inligting*
inquiries	*navrae*
office	*kantoor*
pharmacy/ chemist	*apteek*
police	*polisie*
police station	*polisiestasie*
post office	*poskantoor*
rooms	*kamers*
tourist bureau	*toeristeburo*
town	*dorp*

Transport

avenue	*laan*
car	*kar*
freeway	*vrymaak*
highway	*snelweg*
road	*pad, weg*
station	*stasie*
street	*straat*
track	*spoor*
traffic light	*verkeerslig*
utility/ pick-up	*bakkie*

arrival	*aankoms*
departure	*vertrek*
one-way ticket	*enkel kaartjie*
return ticket	*retoer kaartjie*

to	*na*
from	*van*
left	*links*
right	*regs*
at the corner	*op die hoek*

In the Country

bay	*baai*
beach	*strand*
caravan park	*woonwapark*
field/plain	*veld*
ford	*drif*
game reserve	*wildtuin*
hiking trail	*wandelpad*
lake	*meer*
marsh	*vlei*
mountain	*berg*
river	*rivier*

Time & Days

When?	*Wanneer?*
am/pm	*vm/nm*
soon	*nou-nou*
today	*vandag*
tomorrow	*môre*
yesterday	*gister*
daily/weekly	*daagliks/weekblad*
public holiday	*openbare vakansiedag*

Monday	*Maandag (Ma)*
Tuesday	*Dinsdag (Di)*
Wednesday	*Woensdag (Wo)*
Thursday	*Donderdag (Do)*
Friday	*Vrydag (Vr)*
Saturday	*Saterdag (Sa)*
Sunday	*Sondag (So)*

Numbers

1	*een*
2	*twee*
3	*drie*
4	*vier*
5	*vyf*
6	*ses*
7	*sewe*
8	*ag*
9	*nege*
10	*tien*
11	*elf*
12	*twaalf*
13	*dertien*
14	*veertien*
15	*vyftien*
16	*sestien*
17	*sewentien*
18	*agtien*
19	*negentien*
20	*twintig*
21	*een en twintig*
30	*dertig*
40	*veertig*

50	*vyftig*
60	*sestig*
70	*sewentig*
80	*tagtig*
90	*negentig*
100	*honderd*
1000	*duisend*

PORTUGUESE

Portuguese pronunciation takes some learning. Pronunciation guides have been included with the words and phrases below, however, which will make things easier for the uninitiated.

Portuguese uses masculine and feminine word endings, usually '-o' and '-a' respectively – to say 'thank you', a man will say *obrigado;* a woman, *obrigada.* Masculine and feminine are noted in this guide by the abbreviations 'm' and 'f' respectively. For more information about Portuguese, check out Lonely Planet's *Portuguese Phrasebook.*

Conversation & Essentials

Hello./Good day.	*Bom dia.*	bong *dee*·a
Hi.	*Olá./Chao.*	o·*la*/chow
Goodbye.	*Adeus./Chao.*	a·*dyoos*/chow
See you later.	*Até logo.*	a·*te lo*·goo
How are you?	*Como está?*	*ko*·moo shta
Fine, and you?	*Tudo bem, e tu?*	*too*·doo beng e too
Yes.	*Sim.*	seeng
No.	*Não.*	nowng
Please.	*Faz favor.*	fash fa·*vorr*
Thank you (very much).	*(Muito) Obrigado/a.* (m/f)	(*mweeng*·too) o·bree·*ga*·doo/da
You're welcome.	*De nada.*	de *na*·da
Excuse me.	*Desculpe.*	des·*koolp*

(before asking a question/making a request)

What's your name?
Como se chama? — *ko*·moo se *sha*·ma

My name is ...
Chamo-me ... — *sha*·moo·me ...

Where are you from?
De onde é? — de *ong*·de e

I'm from ...
Sou (da/do/de) ... — so (da/do/de) ...

Do you speak English?
Fala inglês? — *fa*·la eeng·*glesh*

I (don't) understand.
(Não) entendo. — (nowng) eng·*teng*·doo

Could you please write it down?
Pode por favor escrever num papel? — *po*·de porr fa·*vorr* es·kre·*verr* noom pa·*pel*

EMERGENCIES – PORTUGUESE

Help!
Socorro! — soo·*ko*·rroo

I'm lost.
Estou perdido/a. (m/f) — shto perr·*dee*·doo/da

Where are the toilets?
Onde ficam os lavabos? — *ong*·de *fee*·kam oos la·*va*·boos

Go away!
Vai-te embora! — *vai*·te eng·*bo*·ra

Call ...!	*Chame ...!*	sham ...
a doctor	*um médico*	oong *me*·dee·koo
the police	*a polícia*	a poo·lee·*see*·a

I'm looking for a ...	*Procuro ...*	proo·*koo*·roo ...
camping ground	*um parque de campismo*	oong park de kang·*peezh*·moo
cheap hotel	*uma pensão*	*oo*·ma pen·*sowng*
hotel	*um hotel*	oong oo·*tel*

I'd like a ... room.	*Queria um quarto de ...*	*kree*·a oong *kwarr*·too de ...
double	*casal*	ka·*zal*
single	*individual*	ing·dee·vee·*dwal*
twin	*duplo*	*doo*·ploo

Where is ...?	*Onde fica ...?*	*ong*·de *fee*·ka ...
a bank	*um banco*	oong *ban*·koo
the market	*o mercado*	oo merr·*ka*·doo
a pharmacy/ chemist	*uma farmácia*	*oo*·ma far·*ma*·sya
the police station	*o posto de polícia*	oo *pos*·too·de poo·*lee*·see·a
the post office	*o correio*	oo koo·*ray*·oo
the toilet (Men/ Women)	*a casa de banho (Senhores/ Senhoras)*	a *kaa*·za de *ba*·nyoo (se·*nyo*·resh/ se·*nyo*·rash)

Can I pay by...?	*Posso pagar com ...?*	*po*·soo pa·*garr* kom ...
credit card	*cartão de crédito*	karr·*towng* de *kre*·dee·too
travellers cheque	*cheque de viagem*	*she*·ke de vee·*oo*·zheng

How much is it?
Quanto é? — *kwang*·too e

Where is ...?
Onde fica ...? — ongd *fee*·ka ...

How far is it?
Qual a distância daqui? — kwal a dees·*tan*·see·a da·*kee*

LANGUAGE

TUMBUKA & YAO IN MALAWI

After Chewa, the two other principal indigenous languages of Malawi are Tumbuka (in the north) and Yao (in the south). Nearly all Tumbuka and Yao people also speak Chewa, and many speak English as well. Nevertheless, a few simple words in Tumbuka and Yao will be most welcome.

English	Tumbuka	Yao
Hello.	*Yewo.*	*Quamboni.*
How are you?	*Muliwuli?*	*Iliwuli?*
Fine.	*Nilimakola.*	*Ndiri chenene.*
And you?	*Manyi imwa?*	*Qualinimye?*
Goodbye.	*Pawemi.*	*Siagara gani ngwaula.*
Thank you (very much).	*Yewo (chomene).*	*Asante (sana).*
What's your name?	*Zinolinu ndimwenjani?*	*Mwe linachi?*
My name is ...	*Zinalane ndine ...*	*Une linaliangu ...*
Where are you from?	*Mukukhalankhu?*	*Ncutama qua?*
I'm from ...	*Nkhula khu ...*	*Gutama ku ...*

Can you show me (on the map)?
Pode mostrar-me (no mapa)? pod moos·*trarrm* (noo *ma*·pa)

straight ahead
em frente eng frengt

to the left/right
à esquerda/à direita a *skerr*·da/a dee·*ray*·ta

Which ... goes to (Maputo)?	*Qual é o ... que vai para (Maputo)?*	kwal e oo ... ke vai *pa*·ra (ma·*poo*·to)
bus	*autocarro/ machibombo*	ow·too·*kaa*·rroo/ ma·shee·*bom*·bo
(ferry) boat	*barco (de travessia)*	*barr*·koo (de tra·*ve*·sya)
converted passenger truck	*chapa/ chapa-cem*	*sha*·pa/ sha·pa·*seng*
train	*comboio*	kom·*boy*·oo

Is this the (bus) to ...?
Este (chapa) vai para ...? esht (*sha*·pa) vai *pa*·ra ...?

What time does it leave?
Que horas sai? ke *o*·ras sai

What time does it get to ...?
Que horas chega a ...? ke *o*·ras *she*·ga a ...

A ticket to ...
Um bilhete para ... oong bee·*lyet pa*·ra ...

When?	*Quando?*	*kwang*·doo
now	*agora*	a·*go*·ra
today	*hoje*	ozh
tomorrow	*amanhã*	a·ma·*nyang*

0	*zero*	*ze*·roo
1	*um/uma* (m/f)	oong/*oo*·ma
2	*dois/duas* (m/f)	doys/dwash
3	*três*	tresh
4	*quatro*	*kwa*·troo
5	*cinco*	*seeng*·koo
6	*seis*	saysh
7	*sete*	set
8	*oito*	*oy*·too
9	*nove*	nov
10	*dez*	desh
1000	*mil*	meel

BANTU & KHOISAN LANGUAGES

As a first language, most Southern Africans speak either a Bantu language or a Khoisan language. Due to common roots, a number of Bantu varieties in the region, including Zulu and Ndebele, as well as Sotho and Tswana, are mutually intelligible.

Many native Khoisan speakers also speak at least one Bantu and one European language, usually Afrikaans.

CHEWA (CHICHEWA)

Chewa, a Bantu language, is the national language of Malawi and is also a very close relative of Nyanja, spoken in Zambia – the two are mutually intelligible. It is a complex language: word prefixes and suffixes change according to context, so one single word cannot always be given for its English equivalent. The most common forms are given here, but do remember that although these words and phrases may not be 'proper' Chichewa, you'll be understood. Most Malawians and Zam-

REMOTE HIMBA

The Himba living in remote areas speak a slightly different dialect. Again, people will greatly appreciate your efforts.

Hello./Good day.	*Moro.*
Good evening.	*Huenda.*
Goodbye.	*Kara/Karee nawa.* (to one/many)
How are you?	*Muwepe nduka?/Kora?*
Fine, thanks.	*Nawa.*
	Ami mbiri nawa. (polite)
Yes.	*Eee.*
No.	*Kako.*
Where is the ...?	*... iripi?*

How much do you want for this?
Imbi mokosisa vingapi?
Do you know the road to ...?
Motjiua ondjira ndjijenda ...?

bians will be pleased to hear even a few words of their language spoken by a foreigner.

Conversation & Essentials

Bambo, literally meaning 'father', is a polite way to address any Malawian man. The female equivalent is *amai* or *mai. Mazungu* means 'white person', but isn't derogatory.

Hello.	*Moni.*
Hello, anybody in?	*Odi.* (when knocking on door or calling at gate)
Come in./Welcome.	*Lowani.*
Goodbye. (if leaving)	*Tsala bwino.* (lit: 'stay well')
Goodbye. (if staying)	*Pitani bwino.* (lit: 'go well')
Good night.	*Gonani bwino.*
Please.	*Chonde.*
Thank you./Excuse me.	*Zikomo.*
Thank you very much.	*Zikomo kwambile/kwambiri.*
Yes.	*Inde.*
No.	*Iyayi.*
How are you?	*Muli bwanji?*
I'm fine.	*Ndili bwino.*
And you?	*Kaya-iwe?* (to one person)
	Kaya inu? (to several people)
Good./Fine./OK.	*Chabwino.*

Numbers

Chichewa speakers talking together will normally use English for numbers and prices. Similarly, time is nearly always expressed in English.

1	*chimonzi*
2	*ziwili*
3	*zitatu*
4	*zinayi*
5	*zitsano*

DAMARA/NAMA

The Damara and Nama peoples' traditional lands take in most of Namibia's wildest desert regions. Their languages belong to the Khoisan group and, like other Khoisan varieties, they feature several of the tricky 'click' sounds (see How to Click, p782).

Conversation & Essentials

Good Morning.	*!Gai//oas.*
How are you?	*Matisa?*
Thank you.	*Eio.*
Pardon.	*Mati.*
Yes.	*Ii.*
Goodbye. (if leaving)	*!Gaise hare.*
Goodbye. (if staying)	*!Gure.*
Do you speak English?	*Engelsa !goa idu ra?*
What's your name?	*Mati du/onha?*
My name is ...	*Ti/ons ge a ...*
I'm from ...	*Tita ge a ...*
How much is this?	*Ne xu e matigo marie ni gan?*
Where is the ...?	*Maha ... ha?*

Numbers

1	*/gui*
2	*/gam*
3	*!nona*
4	*haga*
5	*goro*
6	*!nani*
7	*hu*
8	*//khaisa*
9	*khoese*
10	*disi*

HERERO/HIMBA

Herero and Himba, both Bantu languages, are quite similar, and will be especially useful when travelling around Kaokoland and remote areas of north central Namibia, where Afrikaans remains the lingua franca and few people speak English. Most people, however, are delighted when foreign visitors attempt to communicate in Herero/Himba.

NAMING RITES

The actual title of several Southern African languages can cause confusion for visitors. For example, the language of the Basotho people (from Lesotho) is Sesotho. Usually, the prefixes ('se', 'chi', 'isi', 'otji' etc) simply mean 'language', but they're only used when actually speaking that language. To say 'I can speak isiZulu' is like saying 'I can speak Français'. When speaking English, the prefixes are usually omitted. However, some languages, such as Chewa/Chichewa, may retain the prefix regardless of the language you're speaking.

Following are the the current official English designations for the predominant languages of Southern Africa, with their indigenous titles in brackets: Chewa/Chichewa, Herero/Himba (Otjiherero/Otjihimba), Ndebele (Sindebele), Northern Sotho (Sepedi), Owambo (Otjiwambo), Southern Sotho (Sesotho), Swati (siSwati), Tsonga (Xitsonga), Tswana (Setswana), Venda (Tshivenda), Xhosa (isiXhosa), Zulu (isiZulu).

Conversation & Essentials

Hello.	*Tjike.*
Good morning, sir.	*Wa penduka, mutengua.*
Good afternoon, madam.	*Wa uhara, serekaze.*
Good evening.	*Wa tokerua.*
Good night.	*Ongurova ombua.*
Please.	*Arikana.*
Thank you.	*Okuhepa.*
How are you?	*Kora?*
Fine.	*Naua.*
Well, thank you.	*Mbiri naua, okuhepa.*
Pardon.	*Makuvi.*
Yes.	*Ii.*
No.	*Kako.*
Where are you from?	*Ove ua za pi?*

Do you speak ...?	*U hungira ...?*
English	*Otjingirisa*
Herero/Himba	*Otjihimba*
Owambo	*Otjiwambo*

daughters	*ovanatje ovakazona*
sons	*ovanatje ovazandu*
wife	*omukazendu ngua kupua*
husband	*omurumendu ngua kupa*
mother	*mama*
father	*tate*
younger sister/brother	*omuangu*
older sister/brother	*erumbi*

caravan park	*omasuviro uo zo karavana*
game reserve	*orumbo ro vipuka*
(long/short) hiking trail	*okaira ko makaendero uo pehi (okare/okasupi)*
river (channel)	*omuramba*
road	*ondjiira*
rooms	*omatuuo*

Numbers

1	*iimue*
2	*imbari*
3	*indatu*
4	*iine*
5	*indano*
6	*hamboumue*
7	*hambomabari*
8	*hambondatu*
9	*imuvyu*
10	*omurongo*

!KUNG SAN

The clicks of the Khoisan languages in Namibia and Botswana are among the world's most difficult sounds for outsiders to learn (see How to Click, p782). Perhaps the most useful dialect is that of the !Kung people, who are concentrated in eastern Bushmanland in Namibia and around northwestern Botswana.

To simplify matters, in the phrase list that follows, all clicks are represented by **!k**, as locals will usually forgive you for ignoring the clicks and using a 'k' sound instead.

Hello.	*!Kao.*
Good Morning.	*Tuwa.*
Goodbye, go well.	*!King se !kau.*
What's your name?	*!Kang ya tsedia/tsidia?* (to a man/woman)
How are you?	*!Ka tseya/tsiya?* (to a man/woman)
My name is ...	*!Kang ya tse/tsi ...* (man/woman speaking)
Thank you.	*!Ka.*
Thank you very much.	*!Kin!ka.*

LOZI

Lozi, a Bantu language, is spoken throughout much of western Zambia and in the Caprivi region of Namibia.

LANGUAGE

THE 'OTHER' NDEBELE

The Ndebele language of South Africa is spoken in the country's northeastern region. It shares many linguistic features with Northern Sotho but, contrary to what the name suggests, is not mutually intelligible with the Ndebele language spoken in Zimbabwe. Here are a few phrases that may prove useful:

Hello.	*Lotsha.*
Goodbye.	*Khamaba kuhle./Sala kuhle.*
Yes.	*I-ye.*
No.	*Awa.*
Please.	*Ngibawa.*
Thank you.	*Ngiyathokaza.*

What's your name?
Ungubani ibizo lakho?
My name is ...
Ibizo lami ngu ...
I come from ...
Ngibuya e ...

Conversation & Essentials

When greeting a close friend, use *Lumela, mwana* or *Lumela, wena.*

Hello.	*Eeni, sha./Lumela.*
Good morning.	*U zuhile.*
Good afternoon/evening.	*Ki manzibuana.*
Good night.	*Ki busihu.*
Goodbye.	*Siala foo./Siala hande.*
Come in./Welcome.	*Kena.*
How are you?	*U cwang'./W'a pila./W'a zuha?*
I'm fine.	*N'i teng'./N'a pila./N'a zuha.*
And you?	*Wen'a bo?/Wena u cwang'?*
Please.	*Sha.* (only used with people of higher social standing)
Thank you.	*N'itumezi.*
Excuse me.	*Ni swalele.* (informal) *Mu ni swalele.* (polite)
Thank you very much.	*N'i tumezi hahulu.*
Good./Fine.	*Ki hande.*
OK.	*Ku lukile.*
Yes.	*Ee.*
No.	*Awa.*
Do you speak English?	*Wa bulela sikuwa?*
How much?	*Ki bukai?*

Numbers

1	*il'ingw'i*
2	*z'e peli or bubeli*
3	*z'e t'alu or bulalu*
4	*z'e ne or bune*
5	*z'e keta-lizoho*
6	*z'e keta-lizoho ka ka li kang'wi*
7	*supile*
10	*lishumi*
20	*mashumi a mabeli likiti*

NDEBELE

The language of Zimbabwe's Ndebele people is spoken primarily in Matabeleland in the western and southwestern parts of the country. It's a Bantu language related to Zulu and is not mutually intelligible with Shona.

The Ndebele of Zimbabwe and that of South Africa (also known as Southern Ndebele) are quite distinct languages. See the boxed text The 'Other' Ndebele, left, for some useful phrases in the South African variety.

Conversation & Essentials

Hello. (on meeting)	*Sawubona./Salibonani.*
Hello. (as reply)	*Yebo.*
Welcome.	*Siyalemukela.*
Good morning.	*Livukenjani.*
Good afternoon.	*Litshonile.*
Good evening.	*Litshone njani.*
How are you?	*Linjani?/Kunjani?*
I'm well.	*Sikona.*
Goodbye. (if staying)	*Lisale kuhle.*
Goodbye. (if leaving)	*Uhambe kuhle.*
Yes.	*Yebo.*
No.	*Hayi.*
Please.	*Uxolo.*
Thank you.	*Siyabonga kakulu.*
What's your name?	*Ibizo lakho ngubani?*
My name is ...	*Elami igama ngingu ...*
I'm from ...	*Ngivela e ...*
sir/madam	*umnimzana/inkosikazi*
How much?	*Yimalini?*
Where is the (station)?	*Singapi (isiteshi)?*

Numbers

1	*okukodwa*
2	*okubili*
3	*okutathu*
4	*okune*
5	*okuyisihlanu*

HOW TO CLICK

Khoisan languages (as well as several Bantu languages, including Xhosa and Ndebele) are characterised by 'click' elements, which can make them difficult for learners to pronounce.

The clicks are made by a sucking motion with the tongue against different parts of the mouth to produce different sounds. Words that include an exclamation point (!) should be rendered by drawing the tongue down from the roof of the mouth, making a hollow tone like that when pulling a cork from a bottle. The click made by quickly drawing the tongue away from the front teeth (represented by */*) is like the tutting sound (tsk!) in English used to indicate disapproval. The sideways click sound, like the sound made when encouraging a horse, is represented here by *//*.

If the lingual gymnastics prove too much, just render all the clicks as a 'k' sound.

6	*okuyisithupha*
7	*okuyisikhombisa*
8	*okuyisitshiyangalo mbila*
9	*okuyisitshiyangalo lunye*
10	*okuli tshumi*

NORTHERN SOTHO (SEPEDI)

Northern Sotho is a Bantu language spoken in South Africa's northeastern provinces.

Hello.	*Thobela.*
Goodbye.	*Sala gabotse.*
Yes.	*Ee.*
No.	*Aowa.*
Please.	*Ke kgopela.*
Thank you.	*Ke ya leboga.*
What's your name?	*Ke mang lebitso la gago?*
My name is ...	*Lebitso laka ke ...*
I come from ...	*Ke bowa kwa ...*

OWAMBO (OSHIWAMBO)

A Bantu language, Owambo – and specifically the Kwanyama dialect – is the first tongue of more Namibians than any other language, and is the choice of the ruling Swapo party. As a result, it's spoken as a second or third language by many non-Owambo Namibians of both Bantu and Khoisan origin.

Conversation & Essentials

Good morning.	*Wa lalapo.*
Good evening.	*Wa tokelwapo.*
How are you?	*Owu li po ngiini?*
I'm fine.	*Ondi li nawa.*
Thank you.	*Tangi.*
Please.	*Ombili.*
Yes.	*Eeno.*
No.	*Aawe.*
Maybe.	*Andiya manga.*
Excuse me.	*Ombili manga.*
I'm sorry.	*Onde shi panda.*
I don't know.	*Ombili mwaa sho.*
I'm lost.	*Ombili, onda puka.*
Do you speak English?	*Oho popi Oshiingilisa?*
How much is this?	*Ingapi tashi kotha?*
Can you please help me?	*Eto vuluwu pukulule ndje?*
beer	*ombiila*
soft drink/soda pop	*pumbwa okanar-nunate*
wine	*owaina*

Where is the ...?	*Openi pu na ...?*
bank	*ombaanga*
hospital	*oshipangelo*
pharmacy	*oaputeka*
police station	*opolisi*
post office	*opoosa*
telephone	*ngodhi*
toilet	*kandjugo*

Numbers

1	*yimwe*
2	*mbali*
3	*ndatu*
4	*ne*
5	*ntano*
6	*hamano*
7	*heyali*
8	*hetatu*
9	*omugoyi*
10	*omulongo*

SHONA

Shona, a Bantu language, is spoken almost universally in the central and eastern parts of Zimbabwe. The 'high' dialect, used in broadcasts and other media, is Zezuru, which is indigenous to the Harare area.

Although most urban Zimbabweans have at least a little knowledge of English, many rural dwellers' English vocabulary is limited, so it helps to know a few words and phrases in Shona or Ndebele (see p781). Even those Zimbabweans who speak English well will be pleasantly surprised to hear a foreigner attempt a few words in the indigenous languages.

Where two translations are given for the same word or expression in the following section, the first is used when speaking to one person; the second, to more than one.

Pronunciation

Shona, like Ndebele, was first written down by phonetic English-based transliteration, so most letters are pronounced as they would be in English. Differences of note:

dya pronounced 'jga', as near to one syllable as possible
tya as 'chka', said quickly
sv say 's' with your tongue near the roof of the mouth
zv like the 'sv' sound in 'is very'
m/n before consonants at the start of a word, they're pronounced as a light 'm' or 'n' humming sound

Conversation & Essentials

Hello.	*Mhoro./Mhoroi.*
Hello. (as reply)	*Ahoi.*
Welcome.	*Titambire.*
How are you?	*Makadii?/Makadi-ni?*
I'm well.	*Ndiripo.*
Good morning.	*Mangwanani.*
Good afternoon.	*Masikati.*
Good evening.	*Manheru.*
Goodbye. (if staying)	*Chisarai zvakanaka.*
Goodbye. (if leaving)	*Fambai zvakanaka.*
Please.	*Ndapota.*
Thank you.	*Ndatenda./Masvita.*
Yes.	*Ehe.*
No.	*Aiw.*
What's your name?	*Unonzi ani zita rako?*
My name is ...	*Ndini ...*
I'm from ...	*Ndinobva ku ...*
How much?	*I marii?*

Numbers

1	*potsi*
2	*piri*
3	*tatu*
4	*ina*
5	*shanu*
6	*tanhatu*
7	*nomwe*
8	*tsere*
9	*pfumbamwe*
10	*gumi*

SOUTHERN SOTHO (SESOTHO)

Southern Sotho, a Bantu language, is one of two official languages in Lesotho (English being the other). It is also spoken by the Basotho people in the Free State, North West and Gauteng provinces in South Africa. It's useful to know some words and phrases if you're planning to visit Lesotho, especially if you want to trek in remote areas.

Hello.	*Dumela.*
Greetings father.	*Lumela ntate.*
Peace father.	*Khotso ntate.*
Greetings mother.	*Lumela 'me.*
Peace mother.	*Khotso 'me.*
Greetings brother.	*Lumela abuti.*
Peace brother.	*Khotso abuti.*
Greetings sister.	*Lumela ausi.*
Peace sister.	*Khotso ausi.*

There are three commonly used ways of saying 'How are you?' (followed by suitable responses):

How are you?	*O kae?* (sg)
	Le kae? (pl)
How do you live?	*O phela joang?* (sg)
	Le phela joang? (pl)
How did you get up?	*O tsohele joang?* (sg)
	Le tsohele joang? (pl)
I'm here.	*Ke teng.* (sg)
	Re teng. (pl)
I live well.	*Ke phela hantle.* (sg)
	Re phela hantle. (pl)
I got up well.	*Ke tsohile hantle.* (sg)
	Re tsohile hantle. (pl)

These questions and answers are quite interchangeable. Someone could ask you *O phela joang?* and you could answer *Ke teng.*

When trekking, people always ask *Lea kae?* (Where are you going?) and *O tsoa kae?* or the plural *Le tsoa kae?* (Where have you come from?). When parting, use the following expressions:

Stay well.	*Sala hantle.* (sg)
	Salang hantle. (pl)
Go well.	*Tsamaea hantle.* (sg)
	Tsamaeang hantle. (pl)

'Thank you' is *kea leboha*, pronounced 'ke·ya le·bo·wa'. The herd boys often ask for *chelete* (money) or *lipompong* (sweets), pronounced 'dee·pom·pong'. If you want to say 'I don't have any', the answer is *ha dio*, pronounced 'ha dee·o'.

SWATI (SISWATI)

Swati is one of two official languages in Swaziland (the other is English). A Bantu language, it's very similar to Zulu, and the two languages are mutually intelligible.

Yebo is often said as a casual greeting. It's the custom to greet everyone you meet. Often you will be asked *U ya phi?* (Where are you going?).

Hello.	*Sawubona.* (to one person)
Hello.	*Sanibona.* (to more than one person)
How are you?	*Kunjani?*
I'm fine.	*Kulungile.*
Goodbye. (if leaving)	*Sala kahle.* (lit: 'stay well')
Goodbye. (if staying)	*Hamba kahle.* (lit: 'go well')
Please.	*Ngicela.*
I thank you.	*Ngiyabonga.*
We thank you.	*Siyabonga.*
Yes.	*Yebo.* (also an all-purpose greeting)
No.	*Cha.*
Sorry.	*Lucolo.*
What's your name?	*Ngubani libito lakho?*
My name is …	*Libitolami ngingu …*
I'm from …	*Ngingewekubuya e …*
How much?	*Malini?*

TSONGA (XITSONGA)

Tsonga, a Bantu language, is spoken in South Africa (north of Hluhluwe in KwaZulu-Natal) and in parts of Mozambique.

Hello.	*Avusheni.* (morning) *Inhelekani.* (afternoon) *Riperile.* (evening)
Goodbye.	*Salani kahle.*
Yes.	*Hi swona.*
No.	*A hi swona.*
Please.	*Nakombela.*
Thank you.	*I nkomu.*
What's your name?	*U mani vito ra wena?*
My name is …	*Vito ra mina i …*
I come from …	*Ndzihuma e …*

TSWANA (SETSWANA)

Tswana, a Bantu language, is widely spoken throughout Botswana and in some parts of South Africa (in the eastern areas of Northern Cape, in North West and in western Free State). There are clear similarities in vocabulary between Tswana and the two Sotho languages, and the speakers of each can generally understand one another.

The letter **g** is pronounced as the 'ch' in Scottich 'loch'; **th** is pronounced as a slightly aspirated 't', ie with a puff of air.

The greetings *dumela mma* or *dumela rra* are considered compliments and Batswana people appreciate their liberal usage. When greeting a group, say *dumelang*. Another useful phrase, which is normally placed at the end of a sentence or conversation is *go siame*, meaning the equivalent of 'all right, no problem'.

Conversation & Essentials

Hello.	*Dumela mma.* (to a woman) *Dumela rra.* (to a man) *Dumelang.* (to a group)
Hello!	*Ko ko!* (on arrival at a gate or house)
Goodbye.	*Tsamaya sentle.* (to one leaving) *Sala sentle.* (to one staying)
Yes.	*Ee.*
No.	*Nnyaa.*
Please.	*Tsweetswee.*
Thank you.	*Kea leboga.*
Excuse me./Sorry.	*Intshwarele.*
Pardon me.	*Ke kopa tsela.*
OK./No problem.	*Go siame.*
How are you?	*A o tsogile?* (in the morning) *O tlhotse jang?* (in the afternoon/evening)
Come on in!	*Tsena!*
Do you speak English?	*A o bua Sekgoa?*
Does anyone here speak English?	*A go na le o o bua Sekgoa?*
I understand.	*Ke a tlhaloganya.*
I don't understand.	*Ga ke tlhaloganye.*
How much is it?	*Ke bokae?*

Where is a/the …?	*E ko kae …?*
I'm looking for a/the …	*Ke batla …*
bank	*ntlo ya polokelo*
camping ground	*lefelo la go robala mo tenteng*
guesthouse	*matlo a baeng*
hotel	*hotele*
market	*mmaraka*
post office	*poso*
public toilet	*matlwana a boitiketso*
tourist office	*ntlo ya bajanala*

Numbers

0	*lefela*
1	*bongwe*
2	*bobedi*
3	*borara*
4	*bone*
5	*botlhano*
6	*borataro*
7	*bosupa*
8	*boroba bobedi*
9	*boroba bongwe*
10	*lesome*

VENDA (TSHIVENDA)

Venda, a Bantu language, is spoken in the northeastern region of South Africa's Limpopo province.

Hello.	*Ndi matseloni.* (morning) *Ndi masiari.* (afternoon) *Ndi madekwana.* (evening)
Goodbye.	*Kha vha sale zwavhudi.*
Yes.	*Ndi zwone.*
No.	*A si zwone.*
Please.	*Ndikho u humbela.*
Thank you.	*Ndo livhuwa.*
What's your name?	*Zina lavho ndi nnyi?*
My name is …	*Zina langa ndi …*
I come from …	*Ndi bva …*

XHOSA (ISIXHOSA)

Xhosa is the language of the people of the same name. A Bantu language, it's the dominant indigenous variety in Eastern Cape in South Africa, although you'll meet Xhosa speakers all throughout the region. *Bawo* is a term of respect used when addressing an older man.

Hello.	*Molo.*
Goodbye.	*Sala kakuhle.*
Goodnight.	*Rhonanai.*
Please.	*Nceda.*
Thank you.	*Enkosi.*
Are you well?	*Uphilile na namhlanje?*
Yes, I'm well.	*Ewe, ndiphilile kanye.*
Yes.	*Ewe.*
No.	*Hayi.*

Do you speak English?	*Uyakwazi ukuthetha siNgesi?*
Where are you from?	*Uvela phi na okanye ngaphi na?*
I'm from …	*Ndivela …*
I'm lost.	*Ndilahlekile.*
Is this the road to …?	*Yindlela eya … yini le?*
How much is it?	*Idla ntoni na?*

ZULU (ISIZULU)

Zulu, a Bantu language, is spoken in South Africa by the people of the same name. As with several other Nguni languages, Zulu uses a variety of clicks (see How to Click, p782). To ask a question, add *na* to the end of a sentence.

Hello.	*Sawubona.*
Goodbye.	*Sala kahle.*
Please.	*Jabulisa.*
Thank you.	*Ngiyabonga.*
Yes.	*Yebo.*
No.	*Cha.*

Where does this road go?
Iqondaphi lendlela na?
Which is the road to …?
Iphi indlela yokuya ku …?

Is it far?	*Kukude yini?*
left	*ekhohlo*
right	*ekumene*
food	*ukudla*
water	*amanzi*

LANGUAGE

Glossary

Although English is widely spoken in most Southern African countries, native speakers from Australasia, North America and the UK will notice that many words have developed different meanings locally. There are also many unusual terms that have been borrowed from Afrikaans, Portuguese or indigenous languages. This glossary includes some of these particular 'Afro-English' words, as well as some other general terms and abbreviations that may not be understood.

In African English, repetition for emphasis is common: something that burnt you would be 'hot hot'; fields after the rains are 'green green'; a crowded minibus with no more room is 'full full', and so on.

For useful words and phrases in local languages, see p775.

4WD – four-wheel drive; locally called 4x4

apartheid – literally, the state of being apart; a political system in which peoples were officially segregated according to their race
asimilados – Mozambican term for Africans who assimilated to European ways
assegais – spears; used against the colonialists in Zimbabwe

baixa – commercial area in Mozambique
bakkie – pronounced 'bucky'; utility or pick-up truck
barchan dunes – migrating crescent-shaped sand dunes
Basarwa – Batswana name for the San people
Batswana – citizens of Botswana
bemanti – Swazi learned men
biltong – a chewy dried meat that can be anything from beef to kudu or ostrich
bobotie – traditional Malay dish; delicately flavoured curry with a topping of beaten egg baked to a crust, served with stewed fruits and chutney
Boer – farmer in Afrikaans; a historic name for the Afrikaner people
boerewors – sausage of varying quality made by Afrikaner farmers
bogobe – sorghum porridge, a staple in Botswana
bojalwa – an inexpensive sorghum beer drunk in Botswana that is also brewed commercially
boma – in Zambia, Malawi and some other countries, this is a local word for 'town'; in East Africa the same word means 'fortified stockade'; in Zimbabwe, Botswana, Namibia and much of South Africa, it's normally just a sunken campfire circle; it may be derived from the colonial term BOMA (British Overseas Military Administration), applied to any government building, such as offices or forts
boomslang – dangerous 2m-long tree snake
braai – a barbecue; a Southern African institution, particularly among whites
braawors – barbecue sausages
brötchen – little bread rolls available in Namibia
bushveld – flat, grassy plain covered in thorn scrub

camarões – Mozambican term for prawns
camião – truck in Mozambique
campeamento principal – Mozambican term for main entrance
capulanas – colourful sarongs worn by Mozambican women around their waist
capuzinio – mission in Mozambique
casal – room with a double bed, for married couples, in Mozambique
cascata – Mozambican term for waterfall
chapa – word for converted passenger truck or minivan in Mozambique or Malawi
chibuku – local style mass-produced beer, stored in tanks and served in buckets, or available in takeaway cartons (mostly in Zimbabwe and Malawi) and plastic bottles known as *scuds;* it's good for a quick euphoria and a debilitating *babalass* (hangover)
chili bites – spicy *biltong,* seasoned with *piri piri*
chiperone – damp misty weather that affects southern Malawi
Comrade – a Marxist title used mainly by the media, referring to black Zimbabweans, especially government officials; also Cde
Concession – a communal land area governmentally designated for use by a given commercial entity for a set amount of time – usually five years; a popular concept in both Namibia and Botswana
coupé – two-person compartment on a train
cuca shops – small shops in northern Namibia; named after the Angolan beer once sold in them

daga hut – a traditional African round house consisting of a wooden frame, mud and straw walls, and thatched roof (mainly in Zimbabwe)
dagga – pronounced da-kha; Southern African term for marijuana
dambo – area of grass, reeds or swamp alongside a river course

dassies – herbivorous gopherlike mammals of two species: *Procavia capensis,* also called the rock hyrax, and *Dendrohyrax arborea* or tree hyrax; they're in fact not rodents, but are thought to be the closest living relatives of the elephant
dhow – Arabic sailing vessel that dates from ancient times
difaqane – forced migration by several Southern African tribes in the face of Zulu aggression; also known as *mfeqane*
donga – steep-sided gully caused by soil erosion
dorp – a small country settlement in South Africa
drankwinkel – literally 'drink shop'; a Namibian or South African off-licence or bottle shop
drift – a river ford; most are normally dry
dumpi – a 375ml bottle of beer
duplo – term for a room with twin beds used in Mozambique
dwalas – bald, knoblike domes of smooth rock

eh – (rhymes with 'hay') all-purpose ending to sentences, even very short ones such as 'Thanks, eh?'
eumbo – immaculate Owambo *kraal;* much like a small village enclosed within a pale fence
euphorbia – several species of cactuslike succulents; most are poisonous to humans

fly camp – temporary camp set up in the bush away from the main camp
fynbos – literally 'fine bush', primarily proteas, heaths and ericas

galabiyya – men's full-length robe
gap it – make a quick exit; often refers to emigration from troubled African countries
garni – a hotel in Namibia that lacks a full dining room, but does offer a simple breakfast
gemütlichkeit – a distinctly German appreciation of comfort and hospitality

half-bus – Malawian term for a bus with about 30 seats – to distinguish it from big buses or minibuses
heks – entrance gates, farm gates
high season – in most of Southern Africa, this refers to the dry season, from late June to late September; in South Africa's Cape regions, it refers to the dry season, from late November to early April
highveld – high-altitude grassland
Homelands – formerly self-governing black states (Transkei, Ciskei, Bophuthatswana, Venda etc), which were part of the apartheid regime's plan for a separate black and white South Africa

Incwala – most sacred Swazi ceremony in which the king gives permission to his people to eat the first crops of the new year
inselberg – isolated ranges and hills; literally 'island mountains'
Izzit? – rhetorical question that most closely translates as 'Really?' and is used without regard to gender, person or number of subjects; therefore, it could mean 'Is it?', 'Are you?', 'Is he?', 'Are they?', 'Is she?', 'Are we?' etc; also 'How izzit?' for 'How's it going?'

joala – sorghum beer in Lesotho
Jugendstil – German art-nouveau architecture prevalent in Namibia, especially in Swakopmund and parts of Windhoek and Lüderitz
just now – refers to some time in the future but implies a certain degree of imminence; it could be half an hour from now or two days from now

kalindula – rumba-inspired music of Zambia
kampango – catfish in Malawi
kapenta – an anchovylike fish *(Limnothrissa mioda)* caught in Lake Kariba and favoured by Zimbabweans
karakul – variety of Central Asian sheep, which produce high-grade wool and pelts; raised in Namibia and parts of Botswana
kerk – church in Afrikaans
kgadi – alcoholic drink found in Botswana; a brew of brown sugar and berries or fungus
kgosi – chief in Botswana (Setswana language)
kgotla – village meeting place (Botswana)
Khoisan – language grouping taking in all Southern African indigenous languages, including San and Khoikhoi (Nama), as well as the language of the Damara (a Bantu people who speak a Khoikhoi dialect)
kizomba – musical style popular in Namibia
kloof – a ravine or small valley
kloofing – canyoning into and out of kloofs
kokerboom – quiver tree; grows mainly in southern Namibia and the Northern Cape province
konditorei – German pastry shops; found in larger Namibian towns
kopje – pronounced 'koppie'; a small hill or rocky outcrop on an otherwise flat plain
kotu – king's court in Zambia
kraal – Afrikaans version of the Portuguese word *curral;* an enclosure for livestock, a fortified village of mud huts, or an Owambo homestead
kwacha – currency in Malawi and Zambia
kwasa kwasa – Congo-style rhumba music

laager – wagon circle
lagosta – crayfish in Mozambique
lapa – large, thatched common area; used for socialising
lekolulo – a flutelike instrument played by herd boys in Lesotho
liqhaga – grassware 'bottles'
litunga – king in Zambia

location – alternative Namibian and South African word for township, usually affiliated with a rural town
lowveld – see bushveld
lupembe – wind instrument made from animal horn

mabele – sorghum, a traditional Batswana meal
machibombo – large bus in Mozambique
madila – thickened sour milk drunk in Botswana
mageu – a light and non-intoxicating drink made from *mielies*, drunk in Botswana
mahango – millet; a staple of the Owambo diet and used for brewing a favourite alcoholic beverage
majika – traditional rhythmic sound
makalani – a type of palm tree that grows in the Kalahari region; also *mokolane*
makhosi – Zulu chiefs
makishi – a dance performed in Zambia featuring male dancers wearing masks of stylised human faces, grass skirts and anklets
makwaela – a dance characterised by a cappella singing and sophisticated foot percussion performed in southern Mozambique
malva – apricot pudding of Dutch origin
mapiko – masked dance of the Makonde people
marimba – African xylophone, made from strips of resonant wood with various-sized gourds for sound boxes
marrabenta – typical Mozambican music, inspired by traditional *majika* rhythms
mataku – watermelon wine
matola – Malawian term for pick-up or van carrying passengers
mbanje – cannabis in Zimbabwe
mbira – thumb piano; it consists of five to 24 narrow iron keys mounted in rows on a wooden sound board
mbongi – holders and performers of a Xhosa group's oral history; a cross between a bard and a court jester
mealie pap – maize porridge, which is a dietary staple throughout the region; also called *mielie pap*
mfeqane – see *difaqane*
mielie pap – see *mealie pap*
mielies – cobs of maize
miombo – dry, open woodland, also called *Brachystegia* woodland; it's composed mainly of mopane and acacia *bushveld*
mojito – Cuban cocktail made of mint, rum, lime juice, sugar and soda
mokolane – see *makalani*
mokoro – dugout canoe used in the Okavango Delta and other riverine areas; the *mokoro* is propelled by a well-balanced poler who stands in the stern
mopane – hardwood tree native to Southern Africa (also called ironwood), highly resistant to drought
mopane worms – the caterpillar of the moth *Gonimbrasiabelina,* eaten as a local delicacy throughout the region
morama – underground tuber with pods that have edible beans, source of water
mpasa – lake salmon in Malawi
msasa – small, shrubby tree with compound leaves and small, fragrant flowers
mujejeje – rocks that resonate when struck
multa – a fine in Mozambique
musika – a Zimbabwean market outside the town centre; also called *renkini* in Ndebele
muti – traditional medicine

nalikwanda – huge wooden canoe, painted with black and white stripes, that carries the *litunga*
Nama – popular name for Namibians of Khoikhoi, Topnaar or Baster heritage
não faz mal – 'no problem' in Portuguese; useful in both Mozambique and Angola
!nara – type of melon that grows in desert areas; a dietary staple of the Topnaar people
nartjie – pronounced 'narkie'; South African tangerine
ncheni – lake tiger fish in Malawi
Ngwenyama – the Lion; term given to the king of Swaziland
n!oresi – traditional San lands; literally, 'lands where one's heart is'
now now – definitely not now, but sometime sooner than 'just now'
nshima – filling maize porridgelike substance eaten in Zambia
nxum – the San people's 'life force'
nyama – meat or meat gravy

oke – term for bloke or guy, mainly heard in South Africa
ondjongo – dance performed by Himba cattle owners to demonstrate the care and ownership of their animals
oshana – normally dry river channel in northern Namibia and northwestern Botswana
oshikundu – tasty alcoholic beverage made from *mahango;* popular in traditional areas of northern Namibia
otjipirangi (for men) and **outjina** (for women) – Herero dance in which a plank is strapped to one foot in order to deliver a hollow, rhythmic percussion

pan – dry flat area of grassland or salt, often a seasonal lake-bed
pap en wors – maize porridge and sausage
participation safari – an inexpensive safari in which clients pitch their own tents, pack the vehicle and share cooking duties
pensão – inexpensive hotel in Mozambique
peri-peri – see *piri-piri*
pint – small bottle of beer or can of oil (or similar), usually around 300mL to 375mL (not necessarily equal to a British or US pint)

piri-piri – very hot pepper sauce of Portuguese Angolan origin; the basis for the chicken concoction of Nando's chain; also known as *peri-peri*
plus–minus – meaning 'about'; this scientific/mathematical term has entered common parlance – eg 'the bus will come in plus–minus 10 minutes'
pondo – 'pound', occasionally used in Botswana to refer to two *pula*
potjie – pronounced *poy*-kee; a three-legged pot used to make stew over an open fire. The word also refers to the stew itself, as well as a gathering in which a *potjie* forms the main dish
potjiekos – meat and vegetable stew cooked in a *potjie*
praça – town square in Mozambique
praia – beach in Mozambique
pula – the Botswanan currency; means 'rain' in Setswana
pungwe – all-night drinking and music party in Zimbabwe

relish – sauce of meat, vegetables, beans etc eaten with boiled corn meal (*nshima, sadza, mealie pap* etc)
renkini – Ndebele version of *musika*
rijsttafel – rice with side dishes; Dutch interpretation of Indonesian *makan besar*
Rikki – small, open van; cross between a taxi and a shared taxi
robot – no, not R2D2 – it's just a traffic light
rondavel – round, African-style hut
rooibos – literally 'red bush' in Afrikaans; herbal tea that reputedly has therapeutic qualities
rusvingo – Shona word for walled-in enclosures

sadza – maize-meal porridge
San – language-based name for indigenous people formerly known as Bushmen
sandveld – dry, sandy belt
sangoma – witch doctor; herbalist
scud – plastic drink bottle
seif dunes – prominent linear sand dunes, as found in the central Namib Desert
setolo-tolo – a Lesotho stringed instrument played with the mouth
shame! – half-hearted expression of commiseration
shebeen – an unlicensed township drinking establishment (which may also include a brothel)
sibhaca – type of Swazi dance
Sperrgebiet – forbidden area; alluvial diamond region of southwestern Namibia
Strandlopers – literally 'beach walkers'; term used to describe the ancient inhabitants of the Namib region, who may have been ancestors of the San or Nama peoples; occasionally also refers to the brown desert hyena
sua – salt as in Sua Pan, Botswana
sungwa – a type of perch in Malawi
swaartgevaar – Afrikaans for the 'black threat'

tambo – fermented millet and sugar drink, popular in rural areas of Namibia
thomo – a stringed instrument played by women in Lesotho
timbila – a form of xylophone played by Chope musicians
township – indigenous suburb, typically a high-density black residential area
Trekboers – nomadic pastoralists descended from the Dutch
trouk – jail (Afrikaans)
tsama – bitter desert melon historically eaten by the San people; it's also eaten by livestock
tsotsi – hoodlum, thief
tufo – traditional dance style from Ilha de Moçambique
tuk-tuk – Asian-style motorised three-wheel vehicle

uitlanders – pronounced 'ait-landers'; foreigners
Umhlanga – reed dance; sacred Swazi ceremony
umuzi – 'beehive' huts
upshwa – maize- or cassava-based staple in Mozambique
Uri – desert-adapted vehicle produced in Namibia

veld – pronounced 'felt'; open grassland, normally in plateau regions
vlei – pronounced 'flay'; any low, open landscape, sometimes marshy
volkstaal – people's language
Volkstaat – people's state
Voortrekkers – fore-trekkers, pioneers
vundu – Malawian catfish

wag 'n bietjie – pronounced 'vak-n-bee-kee'; literally 'wait a bit'; Afrikaans name for the buffalo thorn acacia
walende – a drink distilled from the *makalani* palm that tastes like vodka
wandelpad – short hiking trail
waterblommetjie bredie – water-flower stew; meat served with the flower of the Cape pondweed
welwitschia – bizarre cone-bearing shrub *(Welwitschia mirabilis)* native to the northern Namib plains

xima – maize- or cassava-based staple in Mozambique, usually served with a sauce of beans, vegetables or fish

The Authors

ALAN MURPHY

Coordinating Author, Zambia

Alan remembers falling under Southern Africa's spell after bouncing around in the rear of a *bakkie* from Jo'burg airport in 1999. Since then he's been back four times for Lonely Planet, including this trip to Zambia, during which the logistical challenges of getting around hit home when he was told: 'go down the track and then take a right at the turn-off where the sign has fallen down…' Whether watching elephants cross a river, tracking lions, glimpsing elusive wild dogs or chuckling at the clownish behaviour of baboons, he finds wildlife watching exhilarating. This trip was one big adventure, made even more enjoyable by a 4WD named Bessie and a travelling companion named Smitzy.

KATE ARMSTRONG

Lesotho, Swaziland

Kate was bitten by the African bug when she lived and worked in Mozambique and has returned to Southern Africa frequently. For this edition she coaxed her 2WD wheels for hundreds of kilometres over Lesotho's remote mountainous passes (and learnt more about catalytic converters than she ever intended) and danced her way through Swaziland. Kate is continually humbled by the generosity of the local Swazi and Basotho people. When Kate's not eating, hiking and talking her way around parts of Africa, Europe and South America, her itchy feet are grounded in Sydney where she is a freelance writer.

JAMES BAINBRIDGE

South Africa

A fan of all things African, James was lucky enough to research South Africa twice in the space of six months for Lonely Planet. He explored Limpopo while coordinating *South Africa, Lesotho & Swaziland*, then returned for a pre-2010 World Cup poke-around, arriving just in time to watch President Zuma's inauguration. The London-based journalist's writing about Africa has appeared in publications including the *Guardian*, *Songlines* world-music magazine, and LP's *Africa* and *West Africa* guides. His favourite South African journeys are the drive along the Zimbabwean border to Mapungubwe National Park and the train from Jo'burg to Cape Town.

LONELY PLANET AUTHORS

Why is our travel information the best in the world? It's simple: our authors are passionate, dedicated travellers. They don't take freebies in exchange for positive coverage so you can be sure the advice you're given is impartial. They travel widely to all the popular spots, and off the beaten track. They don't research using just the internet or phone. They discover new places not included in any other guidebook. They personally visit thousands of hotels, restaurants, palaces, trails, galleries, temples and more. They speak with dozens of locals every day to make sure you get the kind of insider knowledge only a local could tell you. They take pride in getting all the details right, and in telling it how it is. Think you can do it? Find out how at **lonelyplanet.com**.

MATTHEW D FIRESTONE

Botswana, Namibia

Matt is a trained biological anthropologist and epidemiologist who is particularly interested in the health and nutrition of indigenous populations. His first visit to Botswana and Namibia in 2001 brought him deep into the Kalahari, where he performed a field study on the traditional diet of the San. Unfortunately, Matt's promising academic career was postponed due to a severe case of wanderlust, though he has relentlessly travelled to more than 50 different countries in search of a cure. Matt is hoping that this book will help ease the pain of other individuals bitten by the travel bug, though he fears that there is a growing epidemic on the horizon.

MARY FITZPATRICK

Mozambique

Mary is from the USA, where she spent her early years in Washington, DC – dreaming, more often than not, of how to get across an ocean or two to more exotic locales. After finishing graduate studies, she set off for several years in Europe. Her fascination with languages and cultures soon led her further south to Africa, where she has spent the past 15 years living and working all around the continent, including almost four years in Mozambique. She has authored and coauthored numerous other guidebooks on various destinations in Africa and heads off to Mozambique's beaches at every opportunity.

NANA LUCKHAM

Malawi

Born in Tanzania to a Ghanaian mother and an English father, Nana started life criss-crossing Africa by plane and bumping along the roughest of roads. She first made it to Southern Africa in 1994 when she spent six months living in Zimbabwe. After several years as an editor and a UN press officer she got into travel writing full-time, and has hauled her backpack all over Africa researching guidebooks to destinations such as Algeria, Kenya, South Africa and Benin. She was thrilled to return to Malawi (the scene of her very first Lonely Planet assignment) for this book.

NICOLA SIMMONDS

Victoria Falls, Zimbabwe

Nicola Simmonds has worked in and backpacked around Indonesia, India, Sri Lanka, Europe, Japan, and Central and South America. Having then lived in Angola and Zimbabwe for seven years (with her husband and, eventually, three kids), mastering water shortages, African bureaucracy and out-of-control economies, covering Zimbabwe post-'dollarisation' was nothing but joy. She has just spent a year in Sri Lanka and is currently figuring out where to go next...

CONTRIBUTING AUTHORS

David Lukas wrote the Wildlife & Habitat chapter. David teaches and writes about the natural world from his home on the edge of Yosemite National Park. He has contributed Environment and Wildlife chapters for more than 25 Lonely Planet guides, including *Tanzania, East Africa, South Africa, Botswana & Namibia* and *Ethiopia & Eritrea.*

Jane Cornwell wrote the Music in Southern Africa chapter. Jane is a London-based, Australian-born writer, broadcaster and journalist with a long-time interest in African music. She is world music critic for the London *Evening Standard,* a contributing editor on the world-music magazine *Songlines,* a writer for Peter Gabriel's Real World Records and for newspapers including the *Times,* the *Telegraph,* the *Guardian* and the *Australian.*

Behind the Scenes

THIS BOOK

This 5th edition of Southern Africa was coordinated by Alan Murphy, who also wrote the Zambia chapter. Matthew D Firestone updated Botswana and Namibia; Kate Armstrong updated Lesotho and Swaziland; Nana Luckham updated Malawi; Mary Fitzpatrick updated Mozambique; James Bainbridge updated South Africa; and Nicola Simmonds updated Zimbabwe and Victoria Falls. David Lukas wrote the Wildlife & Habitat chapter and Jane Cornwell wrote the Music in Southern Africa chapter. The 4th edition was also coordinated by Alan Murphy, with contributions from Kate Armstrong, Matthew D Firestone, Mary Fitzpatrick, Michael Grosberg, Nana Luckham, Andy Lebold and Harrier Martin. This guidebook was commissioned in Lonely Planet's Melbourne office, and produced by the following:

Commissioning Editors Holly Alexander, Stefanie Di Trocchio, Will Gourlay, Shawn Low
Coordinating Editors Louisa Syme, Kate Whitfield
Coordinating Cartographer Andrew Smith
Coordinating Layout Designer Wibowo Rusli
Managing Editor Brigitte Ellemor
Managing Cartographers Alison Lyall, Adrian Persoglia
Managing Layout Designer Laura Jane
Assisting Editors Judith Bamber, Jackey Coyle, Helen Yeates, Adrienne Costanzo, Kate Evans
Assisting Cartographers Ildiko Bogdanovits, Eve Kelly, Ross Butler, Jolyon Philcox
Assisting Layout Designer Nicholas Colicchia
Cover Naomi Parker, lonelyplanetimages.com
Internal Image Research Jane Hart, lonelyplanet images.com
Project Manager Chris Girdler
Language Content Robyn Loughnane

Thanks to Shahara Ahmed, Lucy Birchley, Rebecca Chau, Melanie Dankel, Sally Darmody, Ryan Evans, Emma Gilmour, Evan Jones, Indra Kilfoyle, Lisa Knights, Martine Power, Kirsten Rawlings, Lyahna Spencer, Angela Tinson, Glenn van der Knijff, Jeanette Wall

THANKS

ALAN MURPHY

Firstly I'd like to thank Smitzy, my travelling companion – his curiosity, incisive observations on the road and help with research were invaluable. It was a special treat to travel together. Thanks mate. Francis, a reliable taxi driver in Lusaka, helped with research, especially public transport information. Thanks to the many lodge owners in and around national parks who provided me with loads of useful information. Thanks also to Elke at Tikondane for taking me into a local village and helping me understand some of the challenges faced by

THE LONELY PLANET STORY

Fresh from an epic journey across Europe, Asia and Australia in 1972, Tony and Maureen Wheeler sat at their kitchen table stapling together notes. The first Lonely Planet guidebook, *Across Asia on the Cheap,* was born.

Travellers snapped up the guides. Inspired by their success, the Wheelers began publishing books to Southeast Asia, India and beyond. Demand was prodigious, and the Wheelers expanded the business rapidly to keep up. Over the years, Lonely Planet extended its coverage to every country and into the virtual world via lonelyplanet.com and the Thorn Tree message board.

As Lonely Planet became a globally loved brand, Tony and Maureen received several offers for the company. But it wasn't until 2007 that they found a partner whom they trusted to remain true to the company's principles of travelling widely, treading lightly and giving sustainably. In October of that year, BBC Worldwide acquired a 75% share in the company, pledging to uphold Lonely Planet's commitment to independent travel, trustworthy advice and editorial independence.

Today, Lonely Planet has offices in Melbourne, London and Oakland, with over 500 staff members and 300 authors. Tony and Maureen are still actively involved with Lonely Planet. They're travelling more often than ever, and they're devoting their spare time to charitable projects. And the company is still driven by the philosophy of *Across Asia on the Cheap*: 'All you've got to do is decide to go and the hardest part is over. So go!'

SEND US YOUR FEEDBACK

We love to hear from travellers – your comments keep us on our toes and help make our books better. Our well-travelled team reads every word on what you loved or loathed about this book. Although we cannot reply individually to postal submissions, we always guarantee that your feedback goes straight to the appropriate authors, in time for the next edition. Each person who sends us information is thanked in the next edition and the most useful submissions are rewarded with a free book.

To send us your updates – and find out about Lonely Planet events, newsletters and travel news – visit our award-winning website: **lonelyplanet.com/contact**.

Note: we may edit, reproduce and incorporate your comments in Lonely Planet products such as guidebooks, websites and digital products, so let us know if you don't want your comments reproduced or your name acknowledged. For a copy of our privacy policy visit lonelyplanet.com/privacy.

Zambians. Thanks to my co-authors – their help with the front and back chapters was invaluable and their comprehensive research has ensured this edition is a beaut. Lastly, thanks to the Zambian people we met who were warm, friendly and unfailingly helpful – except for the policemen who gave Smitzy two traffic infringements in two days ('no mate you can't drive through Stop signs in Zambia…').

KATE ARMSTRONG

Many thanks to all the travellers who helped me along the way, especially the Australian Volunteers and Peace Corps. In Swaziland, thanks to Darron Raw, Mike Richardson and Benita; in Lesotho a massive thanks to Darren Elder, plus Di Jones and Stephen Gill. Thank you once again to Rose, Camilla and Carlos for their kindness, and Peter Bendheim and Jenny Govender of Durban Tourism.

JAMES BAINBRIDGE

Many thanks to the helpful folk at the accommodation I crashed at – notably in Cape Town, Durban, Jo'burg and Soweto. Cheers also to Evelien Klokman for helping to set things up in Kruger for myself and the three French musketeers; to Julian and Nina for nights out in Jo'burg; to Eric in Port Edward for all your anecdotes; to Sam, Eva, Carmen and everyone I 'chillaxed' with on the Wild Coast; to Prudence for dinner and getting lost with me on Lion's Head; to Leigh-Robin for showing me Camps Bay, even if it was 3am; to Isabel at Clarke's Bookshop for the literary advice; and to Chanelle (AKA DJ Charm) at Cape Town Tourism for your encyclopaedic knowledge of the Mother City's club scene. Finally, another shout out to everyone who helped me in Limpopo in 2008.

MATTHEW D FIRESTONE

To my wonderfully supportive parents, thank you so much for always sticking by my side, through both the highs and the lows. To Kim and Aki, thank you both for finally taking the trip out to Namibia and experiencing the country that I love so much. To my editor Stef, thank you for all the guidance and support you've shown me throughout this project. And to Alan, thank you for coordinating another strong and solid edition of *Southern Africa*.

NANA LUCKHAM

At Lonely Planet my thanks go to Tashi Wheeler, Will Gourlay, Stefanie Di Trocchio and my co-author Alan Murphy. In London, thanks as ever to Patrick Smith for his predeparture advice and contacts. Thanks also to Gilbert at Njaya Lodge in Nkhata Bay, Patrick Jere at Mwabvi Wildlife Reserve, Ackson Kasonde for driving me around Southern Malawi, and to Patrick and Jona from Budget Safari for their kindness, good humour and company in northern Malawi and Zambia.

NICOLA SIMMONDS

There are four people I want to keep thanking: James Elder, my husband, for covering for me while I was gone, and always; Justine Smith for donning her backpack and joining me on the road – and off the Falls!; the world's best travel agent: Belinda at Experience Africa Safaris in Harare; and finally, Richard Sheppard of Fawlty Towers, Livingstone, Zambia, who's on a passionate crusade to bring back budget travel so more and more people will come to Africa for 'the experience of their lifetime' – his words.

OUR READERS

Many thanks to the travellers who used the last edition and wrote to us with helpful hints, useful advice and interesting anecdotes:

Richard Aberson, David Abraham, Anita Appel, Thalia Arzoglou, Ethan Baron, Colette Bastin, Caroline Beukes, Magda Biernat, Ian

Webster, Paul Bouwman, Martin And Anita Bucx And Hartholt, Carol Bullen, Helaine Cadman, Denis Crampton, Chris Cummins, Lisa Desroches, Jack Egerton, Henning Ericson, Marti Fine, Carolin Gatzke, Mieko Gethin, Mieko Gethin, Calie Geyser, Hermann Hafele, Catherine Keating, Louise Hooley, James Howson, Kenneth Hugh, Petra Janssens, Ian Kingsley, Paul Koekemoer, Sarah Mccombe, Ian Mccombe, Francis Monck-Mason, Keren Moshes Laden, Debra Munjunga, Blair Nelson, Shaun O'Driscoll, Nikita Otto, George Perkins, Jennifer Phillips, Karin Ravenshorst, Anton Rijsdijk, Maurice Sadlier, Brett Saunders, Valeska Schaudy, Francesco Sebaste, Akbar Sharfi, Sean Smith, Lauren Smith, Emanuela Tasinato, Kelly Thompson, Sophie Turner, B L Underwood, Thijs Van Aubel, Kevin Whalley, Linda Wotherspoon, Darren Zimmermann, Sam Zozo

ACKNOWLEDGMENTS

Many thanks to the following for the use of their content:

Globe on title page ©Mountain High Maps 1993 Digital Wisdom, Inc.

Index

ABBREVIATIONS

B	Botswana
GP	Game Park
GR	Game Reserve
L	Lesotho
Mal	Malawi
Moz	Mozambique
NP	National Park
NR	Nature Reserve
S	Swaziland
SA	South Africa
Zam	Zambia
Zim	Zimbabwe

000 Map pages
000 Photograph pages

C

INDEX

INDEX

INDEX

INDEX

000 Map pages
000 Photograph pages

INDEX

000 Map pages
000 Photograph pages

INDEX

GreenDex

It seems like everyone's going green these days, but how can you know which businesses are actually ecofriendly, and which are simply jumping on the eco/sustainable bandwagon? Many lodges and camps in and around national parks, for example, claim to be involved in conservation activities – and many are, supporting important practices such as antipoaching measures.

The following tours, attractions and accommodation choices have all been selected by Lonely Planet authors because they demonstrate an active sustainable-tourism policy. Many are involved in conservation or environmental activism, some are owned and operated by locals, and some are genuine cultural experiences that promote, maintain and preserve local identity and culture.

We want to keep developing our sustainable-tourism content. If you think we've omitted someone who should be listed here or if you disagree with our choices, email us at www.lonelyplanet.com/feedback and set us straight for next time. For more information about sustainable tourism and Lonely Planet, see www.lonelyplanet.com/responsibletravel.

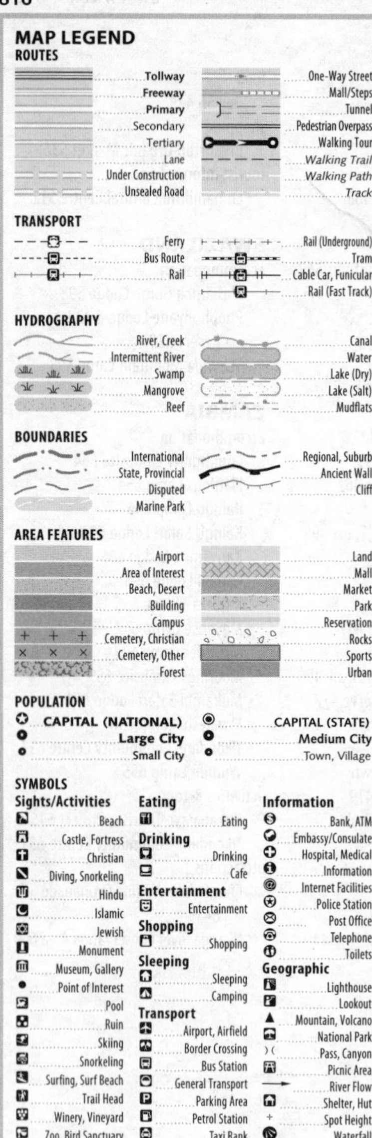

Although the authors and Lonely Planet have taken all reasonable care in preparing this book, we make no warranty about the accuracy or completeness of its content and, to the maximum extent permitted, disclaim all liability arising from its use.

LONELY PLANET OFFICES

Australia (Head Office)
Locked Bag 1, Footscray, Victoria 3011
☎ 03 8379 8000, fax 03 8379 8111
talk2us@lonelyplanet.com.au

USA
150 Linden St, Oakland, CA 94607
☎ 510 250 6400, toll free 800 275 8555
fax 510 893 8572
info@lonelyplanet.com

UK
Media Centre, 201 Wood Lane,
London W12 7TQ
☎ 020 8433 1333, fax 020 8702 0112
go@lonelyplanet.co.uk

Published by Lonely Planet
ABN 36 005 607 983

Cover photograph: Meerkat family on the lookout at the edge of its burrow, Thomas Dressler/Ardea.com. Many of the images in this guide are available for licensing from Lonely Planet Images: lonelyplanetimages.com.

10 9 8 7 6 5 4 3

Printed in China